Heidi Hansen

# BUSINESS

# BUSINESS

**O.C. FERRELL**
Memphis State University

**GEOFFREY HIRT**
DePaul University

**HOUGHTON MIFFLIN COMPANY**    Boston
Dallas  Geneva, Illinois  Princeton, New Jersey  Palo Alto

Cover image: Planar Forms Abstract by Clayton Price/The Image Bank

(continued after Index)

Printed in the U.S.A.

Library of Congress Catalog Card Number: 88-81330

ISBN: 0-395-47277-6

BCDEFGHIJ-VH-9543210-89

To Gwyneth M. Vaughn, for her commitment and dedication to this project.

# Contents

▶ *Chapter* 3   Ethics and Social
Responsibility   69

## ▶ *Chapter* 4   Forms of Business Organization   105

▶ *Chapter* 5   Small Business and Franchising   139

# *Part* II  Management   173

▶ *Chapter* 6   Management Principles   175

► *Chapter* 7    The Role of Organizations    209

## ▶ *Chapter* 8    Human Relations    241

## ▶ *Chapter* 9    Human Resources Management    271

▶ *Chapter* 10   Labor Unions and Labor Management   309

## ▶ *Chapter* 11   Production and Operations Management   341

# *Part* III Marketing   379

▶ *Chapter* 12    Marketing Principles   381

▶ *Chapter* 13    Product and Price   413

## ▶ *Chapter* 14    Distribution    449

## ▶ *Chapter* 15  Promotion  481

# *Part* IV Financial Management  515

## ▶ *Chapter* 16  Money and the Financial System  517

► *Chapter* 17   Accounting and Financial Statements   551

## ► *Chapter* 18   Short-Term Finance: Working Capital Management   585

## ► *Chapter* 19   Long-Term Finance: Stocks, Bonds, and Securities Markets   615

▶ *Chapter* 20   Risk Management and Insurance   649

# Part V  Special Topics

▶ *Chapter* 21  Computers and Information Systems  685

▶ *Chapter* 22  International Business  715

# Preface

The business world today is more challenging and competitive than ever before. One in every four students is making business their choice of major area of study. Every major industry faces international competition to produce high quality goods and services. Technological developments in computers and information systems, and the changing relations between labor and management make it critical to keep abreast of the latest developments in business.

## Real World

*Business* helps students master the knowledge that will give them a competitive edge in the business world. *Business* gives students insight about the risks and challenges in making business decisions and about the rewards available to those who succeed. *Business* fosters a sense of excitement about business activities and uses real-world examples of entrepreneurs and companies to enable students to learn first-hand about success in the business world.

Ideas related to creative thinking in business need to be used and implemented in daily decisions. The Business Experiences, Business Encounters, and the cases in the text, as well as examples and exercises in each chapter, focus on implementation. By reading these examples, students can sharpen their thinking and test their judgment. The content, examples, and cases in *Business* provide up-to-date coverage of business. Everything in the text was written, revised, or updated only months before the book went to press.

## Integrated

Students need a systematic overview of business to provide an integrated view of all business functions. *Business* has a unique model that appears at the beginning of each part. This model is a visual framework for organizing the text. It provides students with a map of what is in each part of the book and relates parts of the book to other material in the text.

The Careers Appendix is a special feature in *Business*. It is a useful tool for career evaluation; students can get an overview of opportunities for careers in management, marketing, and finance. The appendix has information on position titles, job descriptions, educational requirements, and salary ranges.

# Organization

*Business* is organized into five major parts. Part I includes the dimensions of the contemporary business world and the American economy. Part II deals with the major business functions of management. Part III focuses on marketing. Part IV focuses on financial management. Part V covers support areas and special topics in the field of business.

*Business* provides numerous features to facilitate student learning:

▶ learning objectives at the beginning of each chapter inform the student about what should be achieved by reading the chapter
▶ a Business Experience at the beginning of each chapter provides a business situation that relates to issues discussed in the chapter
▶ real world examples about familiar organizations, products, and events illustrate and explain concepts and issues
▶ three Business Encounters in each chapter focus on recognizable firms, so the student can benefit from observing the successes and failures of other individuals and organizations
▶ two concise, challenging cases at the end of each chapter test the students' judgment and decision making skills
▶ a glossary, name index, and subject index aid in finding definitions and topics
▶ other learning devices include questions for review and discussion and exercises

# Support Material

There are several materials useful to the student:

**Study Guide.** Each chapter includes a chapter summary, space to respond to learning objectives, list of terms to understand, twenty true/false questions, fifteen multiple-choice questions, matching questions, a cross word puzzle, a real-world case, and a computerized self-test (floppy disk is included).

**MicroStudy Plus.** An interactive, computerized version of the printed Study Guide. A continuous scoring system automatically updates and tallies student scores. A unique feedback feature to the multiple-choice option provides an immediate screen response as to why an answer is right or wrong. Text page references accompany the rejoinder for the correct response.

**Projects Manuals.** *Investing in Business*, 2/e; *Opening a Business*, 2/e; *Careers in Business*, 2/e. Each project has its own set of objectives and is independent of the other projects. These projects offer students an opportunity to apply basic business principles discussed in the textbook to real-world situations and to make decisions comparable to those in the business world.

***Business Careers.*** This book by Robert H. Luke describes, in an informal way, the characteristics of careers in the fields of marketing, management, accounting, entrepreneurship, and finance.

***Entrepreneur: A Simulation, 2/e.*** Provides student players with simulated real-world experience involving the takeover and continuing operation of a retail store. Ongoing decisions include areas of pricing, advertising, quality control, cash flow, market research, and inventory management.

A complete list of instructional material is described in the front of the Instructor's Manual.

The pedagogical elements in *Business* make it ideal as a reference book. Students will find that the Glossary, Careers Appendix, and extensive coverage of business issues, make this text a valuable addition to their personal libraries.

We want *Business* to be the highest quality teaching package possible for instructors and students. We are interested in your reaction to our text and invite your comments, questions, or criticism. We remain flexible and are willing to improve our materials to enhance teaching and learning of business. Your suggestions will be sincerely appreciated.

O. C. Ferrell

Geoffrey A. Hirt

# ► Acknowledgments

Many people have assisted us in our writing of *Business*. Their contributions have strengthened the entire project and we are thankful for their helpful comments, recommendations, and support. We extend special appreciation to the following persons:

Constantine G. Petrides
Borough of Manhattan Community College

Frederik Williams
North Texas State University

Nicholas Siropolis
Cuyahoga Community College

Jeffrey L. Seglin
Seglin Associates

Marsha Rule
Orozco, Rule, Locke, & Quinn, P.C.

James Hoffman
Borough of Manhattan Community College

Joe Farinella
DePaul University

Scott Saunders
Texas A&M University

Donna Legg
American Airlines

Joyce Dompke
DePaul University

Rebecca Hurtz
State Farm Insurance Co.

John Bajkowski
American Association of Individual Investors

Linda Nafziger
MZD Advertising

Nick Sarantakes
Austin Community College

M. Lou Cisneros
Austin Community College

John McDonough
Menlo College

Jay Todes
North Lake College

Wayne Taylor
Trinity Valley Community College

Suzanne Bradford
Angelina College

Thomas Lloyd
Westmoreland County Community College

Richard Lewis
East Texas Baptist College

Martin St. John
Westmoreland County Community College

Jerry E. Wheat
Indiana University—Southeast

Joseph Hrebenak
Community College of Allegheny County—Allegheny Campus

Nicky Buenger
Texas A&M University

Gareth Gardiner
Linfield College

Jon Bibb
Millikin University

# BUSINESS

GOVERNMENT AND LEGAL FORCES • ECONOMY • ETHICS AND SOCIAL RESPONSIBILITY • GOVERNMENT AND LEGAL FORCES • ECONOMY • ETHICS AND SOCIAL RESPONSIBILITY • GOVERNMENT AND LEGAL FORCES • ECONOMY • ETHICS AND SOCIAL RESPONSIBILITY • GOVERNMENT AND LEGAL FORCES • ECONOMY AND SOCIAL RESPONSIBILITY • GOVERNMENT FORCES • ECONOMY AND SOCIAL GOVERNMENT FORCES • AND SOCIAL GOVERNMENT FORCES • AND SOCIAL GOVERNMENT FORCES • ECONOMY AND SOCIAL RESPONSIBILITY GOVERNMENT AND LEGAL FORCES • ECONOMY AND SOCIAL RESPONSIBILITY GOVERNMENT AND LEGAL FORCES • ECONOMY • ETHICS AND SOCIAL RESPONSIBILITY • GOVERNMENT AND LEGAL FORCES • ECONOMY • ETHICS AND SOCIAL RESPONSIBILITY • GOVERNMENT AND LEGAL FORCES • ECONOMY • ETHICS AND SOCIAL RESPONSIBILITY •

Finance

Owner

Employee    Customer

Management              Marketing

# Part I

# CONTEMPORARY BUSINESS

- ▶ Introduction to the Business World
- ▶ The American Economy
- ▶ Ethics and Social Responsibility
- ▶ Forms of Business Organization
- ▶ Small Business and Franchising

## Outline

# Chapter 1

# Introduction to the Business World

## Objectives

After reading this chapter, you will be able to:

▶ Understand how studying business can help you in your day-to-day activities.

▶ Describe the basic activities and functions performed in a business.

▶ Identify current trends in the business world.

# Business Experience

In 1977, 20-year-old Debbi Fields was studying English and history at a community college, wondering what to do with her life. She did not want to work a traditional nine-to-five job, and she was willing to take some risks to avoid doing so. Since she was in her teens, she had been making soft, chewy chocolate-chip cookies and had always received rave reviews for them; so she decided to go into business for herself, making chocolate-chip cookies. Her family and friends thought she was crazy.

She borrowed $50,000 and bought used ovens and mixers to make the money stretch as far as possible. After looking around, she decided to open shop in an international food arcade near Stanford University in Palo Alto, California.

The first morning her shop was open for business, no one bought any of her cookies. Worried, she took a freshly baked sheet of cookies out to the sidewalk and gave away samples. Her sampling attracted customers, and by the end of the first day, she had sales of $50.

Today, there are five hundred Mrs. Fields' Cookies stores in thirty-seven states. The company, based in Park City, Utah, earned $16 million on sales of $87 million in 1986. Debbi and her husband Randy Fields own and maintain tight control over each store and their forty-five hundred employees. They do not franchise the stores because they do not want to give up control and jeopardize the quality of the product.

Mrs. Fields' Cookies has been successful for several reasons. Debbi Fields constantly sets goals for herself. She sets hourly sales goals to motivate herself and her employees and to keep tabs on the company's progress. She pays unyielding attention to detail, particularly to maintaining quality. When she opened her first store, she established the policy that all her cookies would have a maximum shelf life of two hours. Cookies not sold after two hours were given to charity. The policy is now in effect at all five hundred stores. Mrs. Fields treats her employees as well as she treats her customers. She believes that it is un-realistic to expect an employee who is treated poorly to go out to the counter and provide a potential cookie buyer with a pleasant experience.

Debbi Fields had a vision of a product that she thought would make people feel good. She decided to take a chance on that idea, and the risk paid off.

---

These facts are from Tom Richman, "Mrs. Fields' Secret Ingredient," *Inc.* 9 (October 1987): 65–67, 70, 72; "She's One Smart Cookie," *The Miami Herald,* November 21, 1986, p. 1B; "The Golden Age of Goo," *Esquire* 102 (December 1984): 324–30; and "All the Chips Fall into Place for Mrs. Fields," *Advertising Age,* April 2, 1984, p. 20.

# Introduction

Success in business often starts with a vision. Jeno F. Paulucci had such a vision when he successfully developed Chun King Corp. (canned and frozen Chinese food) and Jeno's, Inc. (frozen pizza and frozen foods). Paulucci started canning bean sprouts and chop suey nearly fifty years ago; that small business grew and became Chun King. In 1966 he sold Chun King to R. J. Reynolds for $63 million. Paulucci started Jeno's in 1967 and sold it to Pillsbury in 1981. Paulucci is now developing a nationwide Chinese-food home-delivery service. He hopes to operate one thousand China Kwik stores by 1991.[1]

To achieve success like that of Chun King and Jeno's, an individual needs knowledge as well as vision. Making money in business requires, among other things, down-to-earth learning from experience and the practical vision that experience brings. It also requires good judgment, something you develop as you acquire knowledge and experience.

To be successful in business, you need to develop three basic human resources: knowledge, experience, and good business judgment. This book can help you gain knowledge and it provides examples of insightful experiences. However, a good business sense, the crucial ingredient, is not something you can learn from a textbook. It is an outgrowth of knowledge and experience. All kinds of life experiences—with family and friends, as an employee, as a student, as a parent, in sports and art, as a consumer—are valuable. Your challenge is to use them and the knowledge you gain from them to make good business judgments.

Someone with an M.B.A. (Master of Business Administration) degree from Harvard Business School and a $50,000 inheritance from a rich aunt will not succeed in business without good judgment. A person with no college degree at all and $2,000 in savings may end up wealthy because of good business judgment. Steven Jobs started Apple Computers with a few thousand dollars and developed the first mass-market personal computer. So great was his success that IBM and other large corporations were obliged to create new products to compete with Apple.

"A good business sense," "shrewdness," "savvy," "being ahead of your time," and "having a good head on your shoulders" are all expressions that connote good judgment. Whatever you call it, the challenge in business is to demonstrate good judgment. It is not a simple thing to translate experience into business sense. If it were, almost everyone would be successful in business. To make the translation, the first thing you need is knowledge of the basics of business. This book provides an overview of them. Figure 1-1 is a representation of the contemporary business world as discussed in this text. Owners, employees, and customers directly derive benefits from the operation of a business. Management (including production), marketing, and finance are major functions in any business. Social responsibility, ethics, legal forces, government, and the economy affect the successful operation of businesses. Numerous support areas such as information systems, computers, and legal services are of importance to the business world and are covered in this book.

**Life experiences help students understand the business world.** The women's rowing team of the Massachusetts Institute of Technology won its early morning workout. In a team situation, members learn to work and take risks together.

A businessperson needs management skills to develop the marketing and financial operations that provide goods and services to satisfy the needs of customers. A businessperson must know how to structure an organization. A businessperson must be socially responsible and abide by laws and government regulations. A businessperson must be able to adapt quickly to economic and social changes.

As you increase your knowledge of the business world, you will have the opportunity not only to plan your career in business but also to become a better informed and more productive member of society. In general, business is all the activities of people who, for a profit, manage, market, and finance the goods and services that satisfy the needs of society. The rest of this chapter will help you develop your understanding of business and of its impact on our daily lives.

## ▶ The Business World Around You

Business owners, employees, and customers are the three main parties that determine the success of a business. In large corporations, the ownership and management of the business may be separate. The president of General Motors does not own General Motors. He is an employee who is responsible for managing all the other employees in such a way that the stockholders, who are the real owners, receive a return on their investments. The stockholders expect General Motors to be profitable and to pay dividends on the money they have invested in the company.

**Figure 1-1**
Overview of the Business World

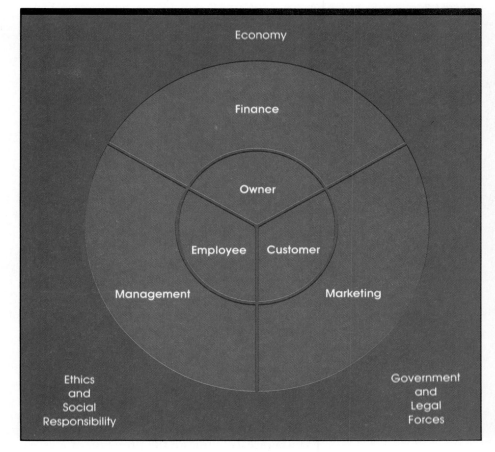

GM employees include not only managers, but also union members who operate the assembly lines and bargain with management to determine their wages and benefits. The employees of General Motors expect to receive adequate compensation for their efforts, to work in a safe environment, and to have management acknowledge their accomplishments and their right to join the United Auto Workers union.

If you drive a Chevrolet, Pontiac, Buick, Oldsmobile, or Cadillac, you are a General Motors customer, and your expectations about your relationship with General Motors are quite different from those of the company's employees and owners. You expect to obtain a quality product requiring minimal service, a vehicle that is safe, reliable, and a good value. You may care about the style and general image of the car relative to the cars offered by GM's competitors.

Many exchanges and a large measure of mutual understanding are needed for the business system to function. All participants in the system must work to create an environment of trust through fair and ethical behavior. The relationship among owners, employees, and customers is illustrated in Figure 1-2. Each party to a business exchange gives up something of value in order

**Figure 1-2**

Relationship among the Business, Employees, and Customers

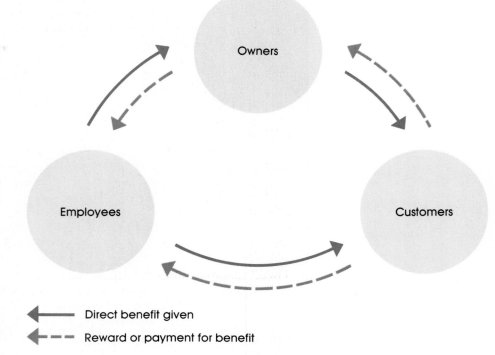

Owners

Employees

Customers

→ Direct benefit given

→ - - - Reward or payment for benefit

to receive something of value from the other parties. The solid-line arrows in Figure 1-2 indicate the provision of a service, good, or idea. The broken-line arrows indicate an obligation for payment or the return of a benefit to the first party in exchange for the service, good, or idea. Owners are willing to risk money and other resources in order to reap a financial reward. Employees exchange their personal skills and abilities for a salary or wage that allows them to sustain their personal lives. Customers exchange money and other financial resources in order to obtain products that they need and want. By purchasing products, customers directly support employees and owners. In theory, all parties in the world of business should benefit and obtain what they want out of life.

This simplified overview of business is more readily apparent in the world of small business, where the owner often takes on more than one role. Consider a woman who makes quilts in her home for sale to others. This part-time activity is a small-business operation. The woman has to purchase supplies such as quilting materials and thread and a frame on which to sew the quilt together. She provides the labor to patch together pieces of fabric into an attractive pattern and hand-stitches the patterned fabric, the batting material (the lining inside), and the bottom fabric layer together on the frame to make a quilt. She uses her understanding of the market to price her quilt and to find customers willing to pay a fair price. She is both owner and employee as she serves customers. Even though her business is small, it is subject to legal and regulatory requirements. For example, if the woman is selling quilts to the general public, she must obtain a retail-sales-tax license and collect sales tax on her sales to customers.

Domino's Pizza began as a small business. Tom Monaghan and his brother opened the first store in 1960 in Ypsilanti, Michigan. Because sales were slow, they decided to make delivery their primary focus. After Monaghan bought his brother's half of the store (with a Volkswagen), he became involved in every aspect of the business—from baking the pizzas to marketing them to Detroit residents, from hiring and firing employees to arranging financing. Although Monaghan started out with only one store and a few employees, his delivery idea was so successful that today Domino's Pizza is the world's largest delivery-only company with more than four thousand stores and thousands of employees. With $2 billion in sales, it is the second largest pizza chain in the United States.[2] Like Domino's Pizza, many businesses start off small, with the owners responsible for most business activities. As they grow larger, however, managers and employees are needed to make the business function.

These examples illustrate that business relies on many people to work toward common goals. A business can be as simple as one person making a product and selling it to friends or as complex as Procter & Gamble, which in a recent year had sales of $17 billion on hundreds of products sold worldwide.[3] In most cases, general business principles apply to the operation of both small and large businesses, from the quilt maker to Procter & Gamble. Therefore, the concepts and ideas discussed in this book will help you develop knowledge that will assist you not only as an employee, but also as a customer.

The impact of business on your everyday life is great, and some knowledge of business will only improve the quality of your personal business decisions. Decisions about how to earn a living, how to manage your money, and how to organize your time will benefit from your knowledge of basic business principles.

## ▶ The Everyday Importance of Business

The world of business is all around you. The purchases you make on a daily basis involve you interacting with business. You observe and interact with employees in many different organizations, often without really thinking about the roles played by any one person within the organization. Your professors, for example, have responsibilities to you (the customers) as well as to the college or university where they are employed to teach.

When you walk through a department store such as Sears, you can observe employees engaged in many activities necessary to run a business. You may see clerks assisting shoppers with their purchases, buyers merchandising the store's clothing and other goods, and managers issuing instructions to various employees. Any time that you have worked full- or part-time, you gained experience and observed business first hand. For example, if you worked in

**Money management occurs at all levels.** In business, at home, and in school you are well aware of the responsibilities and detail required in managing money. Money must be carefully divided to cover college expenses, transportation expenses, food, and clothing.

a Dole cannery, you received a paycheck from the owners (Castle and Cooke) in exchange for your labor to turn fresh pineapples into a canned slices, tidbits, and chunks. In any employment situation you also have an opportunity to see how people feel about their work environment and their supervisors. You might notice how the company used various management techniques to motivate you and your coworkers to achieve company goals.

You must also manage your personal finances, no matter how small or large they may be. You must make decisions such as whether to open a checking or savings account and how much cash to carry around with you. Other decisions relate to obtaining credit cards and paying bills such as rent, electricity, cable, and insurance. You have to budget your money so that you can pay all outstanding obligations, for instance, a car loan or a student loan that financed your college education.

## Buying a Car

When you buy a car, you are making a personal business decision. You are trying to identify a vehicle that will provide you transportation and personal satisfaction at a price you can afford. To do this, you consider your needs, your desires, and your options and you evaluate costs, just as a business does.

You rule out a bicycle, motorcycle, or public transportation because these do not meet your needs. You recognize, however, that you are interested in more than just transportation. You want the excitement and personal adventure that results from driving and owning your own car. You decide, therefore, that what you really want is a sporty, two-seat roadster that has exhilarating acceleration. Diamond-Star (a joint venture between Chrysler and Mitsubishi) has no doubt gone through a similar process in deciding what type of car to manufacture at its Normal, Illinois, plant. Perhaps Diamond-Star ruled out making station wagons and luxury cars because they are too costly to produce or do not suit the capabilities of the company's plants and workers. In addition, large cars may be a highly competitive market. Your goal is to buy a car that gives the adventure you want at a price you can afford. Diamond-Star's goal is to make a profit by providing cars that meet the needs of customers like you.

Next, you determine what you can afford. You look at your income, and you estimate how large a monthly car payment you can handle while you are also paying for insurance, gas, and maintenance for the car, as well as for food, clothing, and shelter for yourself. You decide you do not have the financial resources to buy a sporty new roadster. Diamond-Star made a similar sort of evaluation. The company has looked at its potential income from car sales and has estimated its expenses—for steel, engines, tires, and other materials, plant upkeep, pay for employees. On the basis of its financial resources, the company has decided it can afford to manufacture only two-hundred forty thousand cars for the 1989 model year.[4] Coming to that decision, the car manufacturer considered not only financial resources but also human resources—the number of workers available in the Normal, Illinois, area. Diamond-Star has also taken into account its material resources, such as plant equipment and inventory, as well as advanced technology such as robotics and computer-aided manufacturing processes.

When you shop around from dealer to dealer for a sporty car, you are performing a standard business practice of comparison shopping. Diamond-Star does the same thing with suppliers in order to get the best deal on component parts such as the tires it needs to build cars. When you consult magazines such as *Consumer Reports*, *Road & Track*, and *Motor Trend* or talk to a knowledgeable friend, you are using information resources. In your case, acquiring information is an informal matter. For a business, it is a formal matter because of the amount of information needed and the importance of information in making business decisions. A business, therefore, sets up and uses a management information system.

You finally decide you want a two-seater Mitsubishi roadster with a removable hardtop powered by a two-liter, sixteen-valve, turbocharged, intercooled four-cylinder engine with four-wheel drive. Unfortunately, this model costs $20,000—far more than you can afford. However, Diamond-Star had someone with your budget in mind when it developed its basic sports hatchback coupe. The coupe seats four, has a 1.8 liter engine, and has a chassis similar to the Mitsubishi roadster you wanted. Best of all, the Diamond-Star coupe costs around $10,000. Thus, you decide that the coupe is affordable, an excellent value, sporty with good acceleration, and therefore, it is the car you will buy.

Diamond-Star distributes cars to Chrysler-Plymouth and Mitsubishi dealers in different regions of the country. Because it has different models and engines, varied names, and retail prices ranging from $10,000 to $20,000, Diamond-Star appeals to many different customers in the sport-car market.

As you can see, a personal business decision such as buying a car requires the same initial step that a business takes—setting a goal that makes financial sense. In buying a car, you also take the next steps of running a business—managing financial, material, human, and informational resources. And, if you sell your old car, you do the same basic marketing that the car maker selling you your new car does. You set a price and place an ad in the newspaper the same way a business plans its product, prices, distribution, and promotion—and for the same reason, to create an exchange.

As you read through this book, you will be adding more information to these basic steps and others, helping you develop business knowledge and skills.

## Managing Money

Managing money is something everyone has to do. No matter how much money you have, you have to decide how to spend it. Learning how to manage your finances is directly related to an understanding of how a business manages its finances.

Ideally, you decide how much money to save, and you spend the rest. (Sometimes, however, you spend first and find that there is nothing left to save.) When there is money left to save, you must decide how to invest it. You also have to determine when you will need the money—next week, next summer for vacation, or forty years from now for retirement.

Businesses have to make the same decisions. They have to determine when they will need money—next week for payroll, by April 15 to pay income taxes, or years from now when retirement benefits must be paid out. Businesses have to take care of these needs and others, and they use money management strategies that consider needs, economic conditions, and degrees of risk.

For most individuals, there is no single way to protect finances from all threats. A traditional bank certificate of deposit, for example, can guarantee against loss of principle (the amount you initially invested), up to $100,000, but will not protect you against losing your purchasing power if inflation increases while the money is invested. Many other investment choices are available—U.S. Treasury securities, money market mutual funds, corporate securities such as common stocks and bonds, and real estate (these are defined and discussed in Chapters 16 through 19). The same investment choices that are available to businesses, pension funds, and financial institutions are available to individuals. What you learn about business financial management in this book is applicable to the management of your personal finances.

## Finding a Job

Many of you have had some experience in finding a job. Sometimes the first job is the first step toward gaining experience that will result in a career.

Most people are looking for a rewarding career that will provide personal satisfaction and the opportunity to be self-sufficient.

Deciding exactly which career will be most rewarding is often difficult. This book will help you in making a career decision. As you learn about the activities that go on in businesses, as well as facts about jobs, the economy, and other business-related subjects, you will be in a good position to make a sound career choice.

Reading and studying about career opportunities is essential to developing your career. Establishing your own file (perhaps on a floppy disk on a home computer) about job opportunities, job requirements, and facts about various jobs will give you a head start. Here are some general areas that you could use as headings in your file:

▶ Financial services (banking, credit)
▶ Production (supervision and management)
▶ Marketing
▶ Management
▶ Accounting
▶ Computers (applications, information management)
▶ Investments
▶ Personnel management
▶ Small business
▶ Advertising
▶ International business
▶ Nonbusiness areas (government and nonprofit organizations)
▶ Retailing
▶ Affirmative action manager
▶ Public relations
▶ Strategic planning

Consider how you might find a part-time job while you go to school. First, you need to decide what you are most capable of doing; then you need to find a business that needs your skills. You must find a business that can provide you with enough income to meet your financial needs, and one where you can work hours that do not conflict with your studies. Finally, you need to communicate your desire for a job and your assets and skills to businesses that are looking for someone with your abilities. Many college students work in the evening at McDonald's, 7-Eleven, or Sears to earn spending money or to finance their education. In fact, many Americans got their first job at McDonald's[5] while working their way through college.

## Understanding International Business

Another aspect of the business world that you probably know about from personal experience is the growing importance of international business. If you read the newspapers or watch television, you gain a lot of information about how American businesses meet the challenge of foreign competitors such as the Japanese, Canadians, and Europeans.

**Work experience.** Working in areas of interest or areas related to your career choice before graduating can be helpful. For example, if you are studying communication and broadcasting with the hopes of becoming a radio D.J. or TV personality it would be beneficial to work as a disc jockey as this student at Fordham University does.

Many of the products that you use every day were made outside the United States. Perhaps you drive your Volkswagen (made in West Germany) to a nearby park, play basketball with an AMF Voit basketball (made in China), and wear your Reebok basketball shoes (made in South Korea by a British company). Perhaps you go walking in a Ralph Lauren polo shirt (made in Malaysia) while eating a Dole banana (grown in Honduras). Perhaps you go home and listen to the latest recording by the Rolling Stones or U2 (from England and Ireland, respectively) on a compact disc (made in Japan) on your Yamaha compact-disc player (made in Japan). Business Encounter 1-1 is the story of a Swedish auto maker, Saab.

The loss of manufacturing leadership in areas such as consumer electronics, automobiles, and steel has become so serious that the American trade deficit—the difference between the value of American products exported to other nations and the value of other nations' products imported into the United States—reached $61 billion in 1983, went over $100 billion in 1984, and reached approximately $171 billion in 1987. Economic growth in South Korea and Japan is nearly twice as great as the growth rate in the United States.

American businesspeople must learn how to compete with foreign companies to obtain a greater share of world markets and decrease the trade deficit. Chapter 22 focuses on the world of international business.

**Soft drinks in Japan.** The presence of international businesses is more noticeable in some industries than others. In this photo of vending machines in Japan, consumers are readily aware of their domestic soft drinks as differentiated from the U.S. imports, Coke and Pepsi.

# ▶ Inside the Business World

Now that you've had an opportunity to discover that you know more about business than you thought you did, take a closer look at Figure 1-1. That overview is a simplification, but it does identify the participants in business, the major functions and activities that businesses perform, as well as some of the elements from the environment that affect the performance, functions, and decisions of participants. The diagram gives you an overview of the topics covered in this book. Keep in mind that specialized areas like forms of organization, small business, international business, and computers are also covered in this book.

## Business Encounter 1-1
### *A Saab Story*

Saab (Svenska Aeroplan Aktiebolaget) was formed in Sweden in 1937 to manufacture military aircraft. After World War II ended, orders for warplanes declined and the company needed another product to manufacture. Because of similarities in design and construction between airplanes and automobiles, the company decided to make cars. Its first efforts resulted in an odd-looking prototype, the Saab 92, which was presented to the automotive press on June 10, 1947.

Because the designers of the Saab 92 were aircraft engineers, not automotive engineers, they had no predispositions toward any one automobile design. Not surprisingly, they applied aerodynamic principles to the designing of the car (they subjected a scale model to wind-tunnel testing). The prototype Saab 92 looked like no other automobile in the world, and when the press first viewed it, they were pointedly skeptical. The engineers had borrowed parts for the prototype from a wrecked German DKW auto because automobile parts were scarce in the last days of the war. They had given the Saab 92 a tiny two-stroke, 25-horsepower engine.

The first full year of production of the Saab 92 was 1950, and the 1,246 cars produced (all green) were sold quickly. Saab stopped production of the 92 in 1956, but its basic aerodynamic shape remained visible in Saab models for the next thirty years. In 1969, Saab was renamed Saab-Scania after merging with Scania-Vabis, a truck manufacturer. Now, trucks and buses account for 52 percent of the company's world sales; cars make up 34 percent and airplanes the rest.

In the 1970s, Saab's sales declined because the design and performance of its cars did not meet the needs of car buyers. In 1977, the company researched its automobiles and automobile buyers in general and decided to make cars for consumers who wanted a high-quality luxury car and had the money to buy one. Saab told its engineers to experiment until they designed a car for that group of consumers.

The result of the experimentation was the Saab 900, the first turbo-charged automobile. The engineers gave the car a new, sleek look. The 900 came with lots of standard features and safety equipment to enhance its high-quality, high-value image (Saabs were the first to have seat belts and other safety gear). These features appealed to a growing segment of American car buyers. Today, a typical Saab owner is between 30 and 40 years old, college-educated, and earns between $50,000 and $80,000 a year.

Saab-Scania never expected the 900, and later the 9000, to be the huge successes they turned out to be. Although Saab is still a tiny company relative to giants like General Motors, its cars do well in car showrooms. Saab has learned that it pays to be different, to have a product that stands out. Nevertheless, the company has also learned that it must manufacture a product that meets the needs of consumers, or at least a certain group of consumers. Because of Saab's small size, the company has an advantage in adapting to the changing needs of car buyers around the world.

These facts are from Henry Rasmussen, "The Original Saab Story," *Motor Trend* 39 (November 1987): 105–09, 149; Bernie Whalen, "Tiny Saab Drives Up Profits with Market Niche Strategy Repositioning," *Marketing News,* March 16, 1984, pp. 14–16; and Louis Richman, "Saab-Scania Kicks into High Gear," *Fortune,* November 26, 1984, pp. 105–06.

## Owners

Notice that the owners of the business are at the top of the inner circle because most businesses start with the vision of an individual or a group of people who decide to pool their resources to provide some good or service. Chapter 4 describes forms of business ownership ranging from the simple (the sole proprietorship) to the complex (the corporation). In all cases, owners have to put up resources—money or credit—to start the business. You or your parents may have bought some shares of stock in a corporation such as

**Small businesses are started every day, but few succeed.** One success is John Shorb, who founded his company Landscape Projects, Inc., when he was thirteen years old. Shorb's lawn mowing and landscaping business was operated out of his parents' home in Rockville, MD. Today he operates a $400,000 business out of his own warehouse and employs ten people.

IBM or Johnson & Johnson, and therefore are a stockholder and owner of the company.

## Finance

Owners and finance are in the same segment of Figure 1-1 because—although management and marketing have to deal with financial considerations—it is the primary responsibility of the owners to provide financial resources for the operation of the business. Moreover, the owners have the most to lose if the business makes no profits or fails.

Financial management is all the activities concerned with obtaining money and using it effectively. Owners sometimes have to borrow money to get started or attract additional owners who become partners or stockholders. Owners often need money, and small businesses especially rely on bank loans for funding.

Financial managers need short-term financing for periods of less than one year and long-term financing for periods longer than a year. Short-term loans help a business smooth the flow of cash into and out of the organization. They may be used to pay taxes, purchase inventory, or extend credit to customers to spur the growth of sales. Long-term financing is usually used to finance the purchase of new equipment, land, or buildings, or to acquire new businesses. Methods of financing are discussed in Chapters 18 and 19.

The amount of money needed by a large corporation such as Chrysler is amazing. When Chrysler faced bankruptcy in 1979, it borrowed $1.5 billion from the U.S. government. One reason the federal government agreed to lend Chrysler the money was to avoid throwing tens of thousands of automobile workers out of work. The government was also concerned that the U.S. pension fund insurance program might not be able to meet the pension liabilities of a bankrupt Chrysler. The loans turned out to be a good deal for everyone. The workers kept their jobs. Chrysler modernized its plants and equipment, designed and sold new cars, and paid off the loans early.

## Employees

Employees are vital to an organization's success. Employees are responsible for the work that goes on within the organization. Managers (either owner-managers or employees who are managers) are responsible for maintaining the business so that it can accomplish its tasks. Managers' main goal is to achieve some stated or implied objective by organizing, directing, planning, and controlling the activities of their subordinates. Techniques for managing employees are discussed in Chapters 8 and 9.

It was as an employee that you probably first learned something about the world of business. Working at Burger King or Kroger's or a part-time job in a factory provides valuable insights on the real world of work.

Labor-management relations are important issues. A few years ago, the players' union of the National Football League went on strike, and management had to hire replacement players. In 1988, when members of the Writers' Guild went on strike, the television networks had to show reruns because there were no new scripts. Labor-management relations are explored in Chapter 10.

All businesses must manage their relationships with their employees and try to motivate and reward them for working to achieve company objectives. Of course, it is impossible to motivate employees unless the managers understand their personal needs and desires and provide incentives and support to help them reach their personal goals. Figure 1-2 shows the relationship among the business, employees, and customers.

## Management

Notice that in Figure 1-1 management and employees are in the same segment of the circle. Managers coordinate human resources to achieve organizational objectives. They organize people to work efficiently and motivate them to achieve company goals. Management is also concerned with acquiring, developing, and using people effectively in a business. Chapter 6 examines the role of management in detail.

In terms of Figure 1-1, an employee could be in management, finance, or marketing. Management and employees are in the same area because managers use management principles to guide and direct employees throughout the organization. Leadership is an important aspect of management. The top manager of a company, the chief executive officer (CEO), is responsible not only for directing employees but also for managing financial and physical resources. Business Encounter 1-2 profiles Roberto Goizueta, the CEO of Coca-Cola.

Production, which is associated with engineering, manufacturing, and technology, is a major function within many organizations. Because the individuals who are ultimately responsible for guiding and directing employees involved in the production process are managers, in this book production is discussed within the context of management, in Chapter 11.

# Business Encounter 1-2
## Profile: Roberto C. Goizueta of the Coca-Cola Company

One factor in business success is strong leadership—leadership willing to take risks to get ahead. The Coca-Cola Company has one of the strongest leaders in American business today in Roberto C. Goizueta (pronounced Goy-SWET-ah). When he became chief executive officer of the company in 1981, Coke's share of the U.S. soft-drink market had been declining steadily. By streamlining the company and taking some big risks, Goizueta has reversed that decline and propelled the company into its most profitable years ever.

Goizueta, the son of a Cuban sugar plantation owner, obtained a degree in chemical engineering from Yale University in 1953. The following year he went to work in Coca-Cola's research laboratories in his hometown, Havana, Cuba. When Fidel Castro came to power in Cuba and took over Coke's facilities there, Goizueta and his family fled to the Bahamas, where he oversaw Coca-Cola's local research facilities. In 1964, the company moved him to Atlanta, and he slowly advanced through the executive ranks and became chief executive in March 1981.

In July 1982, violating the company's long-standing prohibition against using the Coke trademark on anything but Coke, Goizueta introduced diet Coke to an increasingly calorie-conscious marketplace. Although some company insiders viewed the action as heresy, diet Coke proved to be a raging success; today it is the leading diet soft drink and third best-selling soft drink. Goizueta followed diet Coke's success with caffeine-free versions of diet Coke, Coca-Cola, and Tab. Despite these successes, some thought Goizueta had gone too far when he risked the company's trademark in a decision to change the formula of the company's 99-year-old flagship brand.

In April 1985, the company replaced the flagship Coke with a reformulated, sweeter Coke to compete head on with its major competitor, Pepsi. The new Coke quickly generated much controversy and confusion. Marketing analysts claimed Goizueta had committed the blunder of the decade. Admitting that tampering with the popular brand had been a mistake, he returned the original Coca-Cola to the market in July, under the name Coca-Cola classic. The entire Coca-Cola family of soft drinks sells 40 percent of all American soft drinks. Pepsi sells 31 percent.

Goizueta also diversified the company, taking it outside of its traditional soft-drink markets. In 1982, Coke purchased Columbia Pictures and launched Tri-Star Pictures later that year with CBS and HBO. The company also purchased Merv Griffin Enterprises and Embassy/Tandem Productions, which owns the money-making TV show Wheel of Fortune. The company also bought out several of its independent bottlers, increasing its control over the distribution end of the business.

Goizueta has more plans for making the Coca-Cola Company more profitable, including strengthening its food operations. The company hopes to make Coke number one around the world. Although that is not an easy goal to meet, with Roberto Goizueta in the driver's seat the century-old company will continue to be highly profitable.

These facts are from Susan Caminiti, "He Put the Kick Back into Coke," Fortune, October 26, 1987, pp. 46–56; Nancy Giges, "Adman of the Year: Coca-Cola's Roberto Goizueta Engineers Startling Comeback," Advertising Age, December 29, 1986, pp. 1, 26–27; and Scott Scredon and Marc Frons, "Coke's Man on the Spot," Business Week, July 29, 1985, pp. 56–61.

# Customers

Every time you buy a compact disc, order a pizza, or hire someone to type a term paper, you are a customer. The major role of any company is to satisfy its customers. A business must first find out what customers want and need. With this information, the business can create satisfying products that customers will want to buy. The business then must get these products into customers' hands. The process does not end there: The business must continue to alter, adapt, and develop products to keep pace with customers' changing desires and preferences.

In attempting to satisfy customers, businesses must consider not only short-run, immediate needs but also broad, long-term desires. Trying to satisfy customers' current needs while ignoring their long-term desires will produce strong dissatisfaction. For example, people want efficient, low-cost energy to power their homes and automobiles, yet most react adversely to energy producers that pollute the air and water, kill wildlife, or cause disease and birth defects because consumers do not desire these long-term effects.

To meet short- and long-term needs and desires, a business must coordinate all its activities. Production, finance, accounting, personnel, and marketing departments must work together to ensure customers' satisfaction.

# Marketing

Marketing and customers are in the same segment of Figure 1-1 because the focus of all marketing activities is customer satisfaction. Marketing involves activities designed to provide goods and services that satisfy customers. These activities are discussed in detail in Chapters 12 through 15. All types of organizations perform marketing activities to provide for exchanges among individuals, groups, and organizations.

Universities, colleges, and students engage in exchanges. To receive knowledge, entertainment, room, board, and a degree, students give up time, money, effort, perhaps services in the form of labor, and opportunities to do other things. In return, the institution provides instruction, food, medical services, entertainment, recreation, and the use of land and facilities.

Marketers gather information and conduct marketing research to find out what customers want. Sony, for example, conducted research that discovered that consumers would buy a small portable radio/tape player that could be attached to the body with earphones. The Sony Walkman was introduced and record sales were achieved. Marketers plan and develop products to satisfy customers' needs and wants. Marketers make decisions about the price of products and where to make their products available. Making products available through wholesalers, retailers, or direct marketing (mail order, radio, TV) relates to distribution. The area of marketing that you are probably most familiar with is promotion. Advertising, personal selling, sales promotion (coupons, games, sweepstakes, and special incentives to buy), and publicity are promotional activities that communicate to consumers the benefits and advantages of a product. Business Encounter 1-3 explains how Coca-Cola used Max Headroom to communicate the benefits of its reformulated Coca-Cola to consumers.

# Business Encounter 1-3

## M-M-Max Headroom

Many companies use a person or symbol to help consumers identify with their product. Probably the best-known company spokesthing of the 1980s was the computer-generated character Max Headroom, who pushed the reformulated version of Coca-Cola in the Coca-Cola Company's "C-C-Catch the Wave" advertising campaign. Max appeared as the head "c-c-cokologist" in futuristic commercials for the company, exhorting young cokologists not to utter the dreaded "P-word" (Pepsi). The computer-generated persona delighted small children and adults alike with his stuttering wit.

Peter Wagg and Chrysalis Visual Programming applied lots of makeup to actor Matt Frewer and altered Frewer's voice with a computer to create the stuttering, computer-like Max Headroom. Max's first role was host of a music-video show in London. He proved to be such a hit that HBO ran a movie about Max that was later expanded for the American TV series, *Max Headroom*. According to the TV series, Max started out as Network 23 investigative reporter Edison Carter. Carter discovered that his network was using compressed TV commercials to keep viewers from changing channels. Network 23 executives tried to prevent Carter form exposing the story; their efforts culminated in a motorcycle chase through a parking garage where Edison Carter crashed. The last tning Carter saw before he died was a sign reading "Maximum Headroom 2.3m." Network 23 tried to cover up the accident by recreating Carter on a computer, but they wound up with M-M-Max Headroom—and a great new TV series.

The Coca-Cola Company saw Max Headroom's potential immediately. Max was funny, colorful, bold, and (because he is computer-generated), perfect. These are characteristics that Coca-Cola wanted consumers to associate with its reformulated Coke. Max appealed to a generation of consumers who were far more experienced with computers than any generation before them. He championed the good on his TV show and helped his friends fight injustice and wrongdoing. A persona like Max gives consumers a good feeling, and Coca-Cola hoped a little bit of that would rub off on Coke's image. Max Headroom gave young viewers a hero, and Coca-Cola is probably glad it got him before Pepsi (Oops, "You said the "P-word"!) did.

Research by Video Storyboard Tests, Inc., found that more consumers remembered Max Headroom commercials than any other commercials. He reminded consumers to drink "new" Coca-Cola every time they saw him on a billboard or T-shirt or on his TV series. Despite Max Headroom's success, ABC-TV canceled the TV series late in 1987 and Coca-Cola dropped Max Headroom and the "C-C-Catch the Wave" campaign soon after.

However, sales of "new" Coke had been falling steadily since its introduction in 1985. When first introduced, the reformulated Coke had a 15 percent share of the soft-drink market. That dropped to 2.3 percent in 1986, and by the end of 1987 "new" Coke was tied for tenth place with a mere 1.7 percent of the market. Coca-Cola did not want to admit that "new" Coke was a failure, so Max Headroom got another chance in 1988. Coca-Cola reintroduced Max Headroom as a mock presidential candidate in the 1988 election year with the campaign slogan "New Coke. New Issues. Think About It." Coca-Cola budgeted $35 million to push its mock candidate and "new" Coke on television. The company had high hopes and expected Max Headroom to boost sales of "new" Coke once again.

Every company needs someone or something to help consumers identify with its products, and Max Headroom kept Coca-Cola on the minds of consumers. Nevertheless, Max is a timely, fashionable character, and though he may salvage "new" Coke for the Coca-Cola Company, like all fad characters, Max will eventually fade away.

These facts are from Jeffry Scott, "Coca-Cola to Stick with 'New Coke' as Brand Flounders in No. 10 Spot," *Adweek's Marketing Week*, February 22, 1988, p. 2; "The 100 Leading National Advertisers," *Advertising Age*, September 24, 1987, p. 75; Scott Ticer, "Max Headroom Speaks the Dreaded 'P-Word,'" *Business Week*, March 16, 1987, pp. 40–41; " 'Ultimate Talking Head' C-C-Catches Fancy of Youth," *Marketing News*, September 26, 1986, pp. 1, 19; Lenore Skenazy, "Taking Mythology to the Max," *Advertising Age*, September 15, 1986, p. 64; and *Max Headroom*, the ABC-TV series, 1986 and 1987 seasons.

# The Economy

Environmental forces are beyond the outer ring in Figure 1-1 because many of these forces cannot be controlled by business. Businesses operate within an economic system but as individuals, each business has little impact on the economic environment. Collectively, however, business behavior, consumer behavior, and government economic policies on taxing, spending, and interest rates can affect the economic environment. Other factors affecting the economic environment are employment, gross national product, inflation, international trade, and productivity. These topics are discussed in Chapter 2.

One of the most important variables affecting business is interest rates. When the Federal Reserve Board raises interest rates, borrowing becomes more expensive, and both businesses and consumers borrow less. When interest rates rise, consumers stop borrowing for durable goods such as cars and appliances and for other expensive goods and services. Because interest expense for consumer purchases is no longer fully deductible for income tax purposes, interest rates have become an important factor in the purchase of new automobiles, and most automobile companies use low-interest rates to promote their cars.

The economy also affects the customer and the employee. When more people are employed and the economy is growing, consumer spending helps maintain growth. Because the employees of one company are the consumers of other companies' products, high rates of employment mean that consumers have more money to spend.

One area of growing concern in the American economy is the ability of the United States to compete with the rest of the world. One way the United States can be competitive is to make sure that American productivity increases as fast as productivity in the rest of the world. Increased productivity keeps costs and prices down and helps keep jobs in the United States.

# Government and Legal Forces

Businesses must abide by the laws, regulations, and legal requirements of society. Congress passes legislation to protect consumer and business interests, and the federal government creates and operates regulatory agencies to ensure that business abides by the law. There are laws that affect pricing, advertising, personal selling, distribution, product development, product warranty, and repair policies. Other laws regulate competition between businesses, the hiring and firing of employees, and international trade. These laws protect consumers, employees, and business owners from unfair, harmful, and deceptive activities. For example, the Wheeler-Lea Act of 1938 protects consumers by prohibiting false or misleading advertising of foods, drugs, and cosmetics. The Federal Trade Commission enforces this law as part of its mission to prevent unfair methods of competition between businesses. Chapter 23 takes a look at the legal environment of business.

The government sometimes plays the role of consumer. Government agencies purchase a wide variety of goods and services to carry out their

**The government is a major purchaser of goods and services.** Rockwell International is shown assembling the nation's fifth Space Shuttle Orbiter. Intense teamwork and attention to detail is required to meet the government's and Rockwell's standards.

responsibilities—everything from space shuttles to telephones, from guns to food for military kitchens. Businesses should not overlook the power that the government wields as a regulator, producer, and consumer.

## Ethics and Social Responsibility

Ethics and social responsibility are important concerns in making decisions in all aspects of our life. As Figure 1-1 illustrates, ethics and social responsibility affect business as does the economy and government and legal forces. According to Jody Powell, former White House press secretary, "[There is] a growing degree of cynicism and sophistication in our society—a sense that all things are relative and that nothing is absolutely right or wrong."[6] One of the biggest problems found in résumés, according to a survey of personnel experts, is distortions and lies; 36 percent of the experts thought that this was a major problem.[7] A *U.S. News*–CNN poll found that 72 percent of Americans in a national study admitted that they sometimes tell a falsehood, not just a "white lie." The government and the business world are reeling as a result of insider-trading scandals on Wall Street and officials who openly admit that they have violated the trust of their supervisors and the public. Even religious leaders have misused funds or engaged in highly questionable personal moral behavior. All this underscores the importance of ethics and social responsibility in business.

Executives at Beech-Nut made a decision in the early 1980s to ignore warnings by employees that the company was selling adulterated apple-juice products. Although product labels said "100 percent fruit juice," employees charged that the products were a blend of synthetic ingredients. In November 1987, Beech-Nut pleaded guilty to 215 violations of food and drug laws.[8] A socially responsible business recognizes that its decisions affect society, not just the profitability of the organization.

Consumers can vote for socially responsible firms by not buying products from businesses that pollute the air or water, engage in unfair employment practices, or fail to consider customer safety. To be socially responsible often means incurring added costs, but most businesses view social responsibility as a natural part of doing business. Ethics and social responsibility are discussed further in Chapter 3.

# ▶ Trends in the Business World

Several major trends affecting the world of business are described in this book. The growth of small business, the increasing numbers of minorities and women in business, the use of computers to manage the flow of information, and the increasing importance of international trade—all are having a major impact.

The subject of Chapter 5 is small business and franchising. The characteristics of an entrepreneur are described, and definitions of small business are given. Why certain fields attract small business and why small businesses succeed and fail are also examined.

The role of women and minorities in business is discussed in Chapter 9, the management of human resources, in addition to examples provided throughout the text. There are over 26 million blacks, 20 million Hispanics, and about 5 million Asians living in the United States today. More than half of all mothers are now in the labor force, and an estimated six million preschool children spend all or part of their day in a nursery school or day-care center. The number of women starting small businesses and moving up into middle management in large corporations has increased rapidly. However, only two women head any of the *Business Week* Top 1000 corporations, and no blacks currently head a Top 1000 corporation.[9]

Minorities and women face special problems in the business world. The biggest concern is that they have an equal opportunity for employment and advancement. In 1968, a government report found that unemployment among blacks was twice as high as among whites. According to Bureau of Labor Statistics, the situation is the same twenty years later. Moreover, blacks' median income has remained at 58 percent of whites' median income during the same twenty-year period.[10] Businesses need to develop programs that ensure equality in hiring and compensation. They also need to give special consideration to minorities and women when they develop products and services because the needs and desires of those groups have not always been met.

**The diversity of computer use has grown over the past several years.** At the Frye Regional Medical Center, a new computerized cardiac catheterization lab helps cardiologists diagnose heart disease and determine the amount of damage caused by heart attacks.

In Chapter 21, how the various components of a computer system help process information within the business firm is described. The different types of computers used by businesses and the computer's role in the management of information are discussed. The functions of a management information system and the role of statistics in a management information system are described.

Chapter 22 examines the importance of foreign trade in the global economy and the factors that have created a global marketplace. Economic considerations in world trade including the influence of the U.S. balance of trade and balance of payments on U.S. economic stability are discussed. Marketing, management, and financial considerations involved in international business are examined.

## ▶ The Organization of This Book

To be successful in business, you need knowledge, experience, and good judgment. The topics covered in this book provide some of the knowledge you need to understand the world of business. The Business Experience at the beginning of each chapter, business encounters, examples within each chapter, and cases at the end of each chapter describe experiences to help

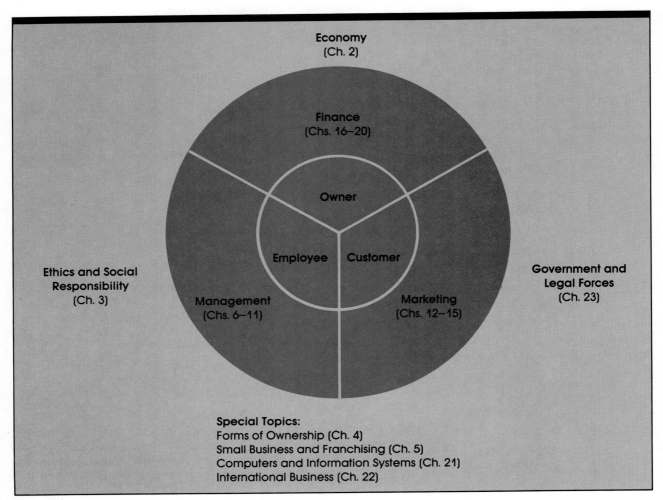

Economy
(Ch. 2)

Finance
(Chs. 16–20)

Owner

Employee   Customer

Ethics and Social
Responsibility
(Ch. 3)

Management
(Chs. 6–11)

Marketing
(Chs. 12–15)

Government and
Legal Forces
(Ch. 23)

Special Topics:
Forms of Ownership (Ch. 4)
Small Business and Franchising (Ch. 5)
Computers and Information Systems (Ch. 21)
International Business (Ch. 22)

**Figure 1-3**
The Organization of This Book

you develop good business judgment. Remember, however, that good judgment is based on knowledge and experience plus personal insight and understanding. Therefore, you need more courses in business along with some practical experience in the business world to help you develop that special insight necessary to put your personal stamp on knowledge as you apply it. The challenge in business is in the area of judgment, and judgment does not develop from memorizing an introductory business textbook. If you are observant in your daily experiences as an employee, as a student, and as a consumer, you will improve your ability to make good business judgments.

Figure 1-3 is an overview of how the chapters in this book are linked together and how the chapters relate to the participants, the functions, and the environmental variables found in the business world. The topics presented in the chapters that follow are those that will give you the best opportunity to begin the process of understanding the world of business.

# Notes

1. Pete Engardio, "Jeno Paulucci: When Chop Suey and Pizza Aren't Enough," *Business Week*, February 29, 1988, pp. 80, 81.
2. Fact Sheets provided by Domino's Pizza, Ann Arbor, Michigan, 1988.
3. Procter & Gamble Company 1987 Annual Report.
4. Jonathan Thompson, "Mitsubishi X2S Roadster" *Road and Track*, 39 (April 1988): 48.
5. John F. Love, " 'Behind the Arches' Author Love Chronicles McDonald's Claims to Fame," *Advertising Age*, December 8, 1986, p. 41, from John F. Love, *McDonald's: Behind the Arches* (New York: Bantam Books, 1986).
6. Merrill McCoughlin, with Jeffry L. Sheler and Gordon Witkin, "A Nation of Liars," *U.S. News and World Report*, February 23, 1987, p. 54.
7. Burke Marketing Research for Robert Hall, Inc., as reported in *USA Today*, October 2, 1987, p. B-1.
8. Chris Welles, "What Led Beech-Nut down the Road to Disgrace," *Business Week*, February 22, 1988, pp. 124–28.
9. "The Corporate Elite," *Business Week*, October 23, 1987, pp. 1–350.
10. Alex Kotlowitz, "Racial Gulf: Blacks' Hopes, Raised by '68 Kerner Report, Are Mainly Unfulfilled," *The Wall Street Journal*, February 26, 1988, p. 1.

# Summary and Review

▶ The world of business affects your everyday activities, from purchasing a hamburger to writing a check, from working in a grocery store to signing up for this business course. You participate in a variety of exchanges every day in the role of owner, employee, or customer. Your participation in these exchanges is affected by the economy, by the government and laws, and by ethical and social responsibility issues. You are deeply involved in business, even though you may not have realized it.

▶ Businesses and individuals have similar needs and perform similar functions. Both make decisions about how to manage money, about what and how to buy and sell and to whom. Both are interested in survival. Both must obey laws and conform to social customs.

▶ The main characters in business are owners, employees, and customers, who engage in management, finance, and marketing and are affected by the economy, government and legal forces, and a sense of ethics and social responsibility.

▶ Current trends in business include the increasing importance of international trade, the growing use of computers to process information, and increased participation in business by minorities and women. It is important to accommodate trends like these to satisfy the consumer as well as to increase profits.

# Topics for Review and Discussion

1. What do you need to be successful in business?
2. What are the basic activities in business?
3. Who are the main characters in business?
4. How does buying a car relate to the decisions made by a business?
5. Compare the role of the owner of a small business (the quilt maker, for instance) to that of the owners of a large corporation (The Coca-Cola Company or Domino's Pizza, for example). How are their roles similar? How are they different?

# Exercises

1. Discuss ways that studying business can help you make better business decisions in your personal life.
2. Relate the world of business to other courses you have taken, such as science, English, math, and others.

## Case 1-1
### *Rother's Bookstores*

Dennis Rother and his two brothers incorporated in 1976 as Triro, Inc., and opened Rother's Bookstore in College Station, Texas. Rother's sells textbooks and related college materials, along with Texas A&M T-shirts, hats, and other items to Texas A&M University students—the Aggies. Dennis Rother had gained experience selling books at another college bookstore while he was a business management student at Texas A&M. He had managed that bookstore four years before he and his brothers decided to open their own. When the Rothers opened their store, four other bookstores were already serving A&M students. The first few years were rough, but the Rothers knew that being in business for themselves required dedication, hard work, and long hours to achieve success.

Although Texas A&M is now served by more college bookstores (nine) than any other university in the nation, Rother's business continues to increase. The Rothers now have two bookstores in College Station and three in Austin, Texas, home of the Aggies' archrival, the University of Texas Longhorns. Rother's individualizes each of the stores according to its location and tailors the merchandise to meet customers' needs and preferences. The store located closest to Texas A&M caters mainly to the Texas A&M Corps of Cadets and the tourist market (mostly parents, "old Ags," and future Aggies) by carrying a lot of traditional Texas Aggie paraphernalia. The other College Station store, located several miles from the A&M campus, caters more to off-campus students, sororities, fraternities, and nearby Blinn Community College. The first Rother's in Austin opened in 1978 at the University of Texas Law School to serve law students. The Rothers opened the second Austin store on the Guadeloupe Street "drag" across from the University of Texas in 1984. This was the first off-campus bookstore to serve the Longhorns. The Rothers opened a third store in an Austin shopping mall in 1986; it depends largely on the sale of Texas Longhorn paraphernalia. All five stores have experienced a steady growth in sales, and the bookstore market in Austin is thriving because of UT's large student base—forty-five thousand.

Although the Rothers are happy with the success of their stores, they are cautious about opening additional stores. They believe that steady, controlled growth is the key to continued success, and they carefully examine the needs of each store to plan for its growth. The brothers also believe in offering up-to-date products and services. Rother's tries to offer the newest merchandise at competitive prices. The brothers keep their stores innovative by sending representatives to universities throughout the country to look for new ideas and merchandise. They believe that carrying the latest merchandise keeps customers coming back. However, they also know that friendly service and word-of-mouth advertising contribute to customer loyalty.

Rother's expanded each of its existing stores internally by branching into silk-screening and mail-order operations. The silk-screening business arose from Rother's philosophy of offering the latest merchandise. The brothers anticipated a demand for silk-screening services because so many Aggie and Longhorn organizations wanted their own group T-shirts. The silk-screening equipment enabled Rother's to sell Cotton Bowl victory T-shirts within half an hour after the Texas A&M Aggies had won the 1988 Cotton Bowl.

Rother's mail-order business evolved as a way to increase sales without increasing overhead costs. It came about because out-of-town customers often phoned and requested things that they had not purchased while they were in town. The Rothers recognized that the mail-order market was virtually untapped, and they believe that their mail-order business will continue to grow if their stores cater to the tourist trade in both College Station and Austin.

Another factor leading to the success of Rother's Bookstores is the policy of promoting from within. The manager of the first Austin store had been an employee in College Station. Rother's hires good people with management capabilities and lets them work their way up through the company. However, the brothers do not hire people with experience in managing bookstores, because they don't want to retrain people to do things the Rother's way.

The Rothers' bookstores have been successful because of the brothers' dedication to hard work, their philosophy of offering the latest merchandise at competitive prices, and their goal of slow, steady growth. The future should be profitable for Rother's as it steadily expands into other markets.

------

These facts are adapted from Darla-Jean Weatherford, "Rother Brothers Are Booked into a Growth Path," *The Courier* 1 (September 1987): 1, 5, 9, 10, 12.

**Questions**

1. How do the concepts of knowledge, experience, and judgment relate to the success at Rother's bookstores?
2. Why have Rother's bookstores been successful in managing their growth?
3. Discuss the role of marketing management and finance in Rother's bookstores' success.

---

## Case 1-2
### *Levi Strauss and the 501 Blue Jeans*

During the California Gold Rush, a young entrepreneur introduced one of the longest-lived products in American history. Levi Strauss had intended to sell dry goods to prospectors and settlers in the 1850s. Upon his arrival in California, however, an old prospector told him, "Should'a brought pants. Pants don't wear worth a hoot up in the diggins. Can't get a pair strong enough to last." Strauss had a tailor turn his tent canvas into the first pairs of jeans, and so begins the story of Levi's 501 blue jeans, now worn by people of every social class in the United States and abroad.

The first Levi's were made of brown canvas and had one back pocket and no belt loops. When Strauss ran out of tent canvas, he made jeans out of French cotton (called *serge de nîmes*, later shortened to *denim*) and dyed them blue. The blue jeans had a button fly and shrank to fit the wearer after several washings. Word quickly spread among the miners that Levi's were quality pants, and Levi Strauss opened a shop in San Francisco to make them. The company added copper rivets to reinforce the pockets after miners complained that heavy gold nuggets ripped out the pockets. Strauss made other, minor alterations over the years in direct response to the needs of cowboys, students, and other wearers of Levi's. The jeans were assigned the lot number 501, which has stayed with them over the years.

In 1873, Strauss added the trademark pattern on the back pockets of his jeans, shaped roughly like the wings of a seagull in flight. The pattern, called a "double arcuate," has been used longer than any other American clothing trademark. Later, Strauss added to the rear waistband of the 501s a leather guarantee patch showing two horses trying to pull apart a pair of copper-riveted pants, another classic trademark.

The popularity of 501s spread with the opening of dude ranches in the 1930s, and they were soon available nationwide. During World War II, the government declared the making of Levi's "an essential industry," and only people involved in the defense effort were allowed to purchase them. In the 1950s, the jeans became the uniform of American teenagers as they copied James Dean and Marlon Brando. Thus, Levis 501s have been worn by just about everyone from cowboys to soldiers, from hippies to yuppies. Webster's dictionary defines the word *Levi's*, and a pair of Levi's is on display in the Smithsonian Institution in Washington, D.C. According to *Fortune* magazine, Levi's 501 blue jeans are one of one hundred products that the United States makes better than any other nation in the world. Although Levi Strauss & Co. now makes all kinds of clothing for men, women, and children, and no longer sells dry goods, the company's 501 button-fly jeans are still its best-selling product after more than 135 years.

In 1971, Levi Strauss & Co. went public—that is, management sold shares of the company to investors. The money obtained from sales of Levi stock helped to pay for the expansion of the company. Levi Strauss expanded its product lines and increased its sales efforts overseas. Despite the company's success on the public market, relatives of Levi Strauss's nephews wanted to regain control of their ancestor's company, and in 1985 the company bought back all its stock. Levi Strauss & Co. is currently a private company owned by the Haas and Koshland families, relatives of the founder.

In 1984, sales of basic blue jeans fell for all producers. To reverse that decline, Levi Strauss & Co. introduced an innovative advertising campaign, the largest campaign for a single product in the history of the clothing industry. The key message of the campaign was that Levi's 501 jeans give the wearer a uniquely personal fit and that only Levi's 501 jeans shrink to fit the wearer's body. These spots featured real people, not actors, doing real, everyday things, against a background of original blues (of course) music. The ads halted the decline in sales of Levi's; in fact, the "Blues" campaign netted a 50 percent increase in the sales of 501s. Many have attributed the revival of consumer interest in back-to-basic jeans to the Levi Strauss "Blues" advertisements. The ads were also successful artistically. They won several awards, including a Clio (an award for excellence in advertising) and an award from the National Blues Foundation. One ad was recognized for its portrayal of a handicapped man.

Levi Strauss & Co. continues to be a major force in the clothing industry because it applies the same high standards to its jeans that Levi Strauss set in the 1850s. The company is responsive to the needs of consumers who buy and wear the jeans and is willing to make changes and introduce new products to fulfill the needs of those consumers. A highly successful, creative advertising campaign and careful management also help to keep the company running smoothly.

---

These facts are from "100 USA Products That Are World's Best," *USA Today*, March 10, 1988, p. 7B; "Everyone Knows His First Name," Levi Strauss & Co. "Evolution of an American Classic: Levi's 501 Jeans," Levi Strauss & Co. press release, July 1986; "Man at His Best," *Esquire* 106 (September 1986): 37; fact sheets on the 1985 and 1986 advertising campaigns, provided by Levi Strauss & Co. Marketing Department, San Francisco, Calif., 1986; "Big Ad Campaign Comes Up Winners," *Patterns* 2 (January 1985): 1; and "A Business Success, An Artistic Triumph," *Patterns* 2 (January 1985): 3.

### Questions

1. Why has Levi Strauss survived as a successful business for 135 years?
2. Levi's 501 blue jeans are one of the top 100 products that the United States makes better than any country. Explain why this is true.
3. How can Levi's be even more successful in the 1990s?

## Outline

# Chapter 2

# The American Economy

## Objectives

After reading this chapter, you will be able to:

▶ Understand what an economic system is and what it does.

▶ Compare different economic systems, and describe how they operate in the global economy.

▶ Discuss the concepts of supply and demand.

▶ Understand how the American economic system developed.

▶ Explain the role of the entrepreneur as the driving force behind innovation and productivity in the American economy.

▶ Define the concepts of gross national product, inflation, expansion, contraction, recession, and depression.

▶ Explain the role of government in the American economy.

▶ Discuss current issues facing the American economy.

# Business Experience

When a baseball player has a very good season, competing baseball teams want to put him under contract. Because the baseball player is in demand, the price for his services rises. This has not always been the case, however.

Until the early 1970s baseball players were committed to a team for the duration of their careers unless the team decided to release or trade them. Team owners decided how much to pay without regard for the players' value to the team. Owners did not "bid up" the prices of valuable players, such as Hank Aaron and Brooks Robinson, who could help a particular ball team win a World Series championship. Superstars were worth much more than they were paid. When a player's contract expired, he signed a new contract with his old team without having the opportunity to determine the value of his skills to any of the other major-league ball clubs. Options were limited for a dissatisfied player. He could leave baseball altogether or try his luck in the Japanese leagues.

In the 1970s the system was challenged by a St. Louis Cardinal named Curt Flood. Flood filed suit charging that the system used by major-league team owners was unfair and unconstitutional because the players were not allowed to compete. The United States Supreme Court agreed with Flood and paved the way for the system known as free agency. Now, when the contracts of players like Rick Suttcliffe or Don Mattingly expire, teams compete for their services. The team that wants them the most offers them the highest-priced contract.

In 1987, superstar free agents Tim Raines, André Dawson, and others were not offered the high salaries that had been offered to free agents the summer before. Team owners said that the high salaries paid to free agents in the past had increased the owners' cost, lowered profits, and forced the owners to raise ticket prices. The increase in ticket prices, coupled with poor team win-loss records, had caused game attendance to drop in some cities, reducing the profits of some teams.

Somebody has to pay the ball player, and ultimately that somebody is the baseball fan. The team owners pass high salary costs on to the fans in the form of higher ticket prices. Fans who think that the players' performances do not justify their hefty salaries and the more expensive tickets stop going to the games. In the American economy, the prices offered to baseball players will eventually be brought into line with what the fans think the players are worth, because in the American economy the fan—the consumer—determines prices.

---

These facts are from Gary Karch, DePaul University, Chicago, IL.

# Introduction

**Economics**

The study of how resources are distributed for the production of goods and services within a social system

**Economics** is the study of how resources are distributed for the production of goods and services within a social system. Several economic systems operating in the world today determine how wealth is distributed in a society. This chapter introduces you to economics and to the American economy. It discusses economic variables such as economic growth, unemployment, and inflation, and other terms you may be familiar with from television and newspapers.

# Nature of Economic Systems

**Economic system**

Determines how a society distributes its resources to produce goods and services that satisfy the needs of its people

An **economic system** determines how a society distributes its resources to produce goods and services that satisfy the needs of its people. Several economic systems exist to deal with an unlimited demand for goods and services in a world with a limited supply of resources. The resources used to produce goods and services are sometimes called factors of production. Natural resources are resources not made by people, such as land, forests, minerals, and water; they are in limited supply. Human resources are all the physical and mental abilities that people use to produce goods and services. Financial resources, or capital, are the money used to pay for the natural and human resources needed to make goods and provide services. (The term *physical capital* refers to manufactured items such as machinery, tools, equipment, and buildings used in the production of goods and services.)

Although different economic systems handle the distribution of resources in different ways, all economic systems must answer three questions:

1. What goods and services and how much of each will satisfy the needs of the consumer?
2. How will the goods and services be produced? Who will produce them, and with what resources?
3. How are the goods and services to be distributed to the consumer?

The demand for goods and services may be determined by a central government planning agency or by consumers as they make purchases. In the 1980s, for example, Americans who wanted high-quality sound systems began to purchase compact disc players. When manufacturers realized that American consumers wanted CD players, they began to make more of them. Eventually the price of CD players began to fall as competition among manufacturers increased.

Competition generally determines who will produce a product and which factors of production will be used to make a product, although in some economies a government planning agency may answer this question. Producers

**Producing the best product at the lowest cost.** Farmers such as John Scarrone must carefully monitor production costs to stay in business.

try to use the least expensive resources to make a product according to quality standards. If the cost of a resource, such as electrical energy, goes up, manufacturers try to substitute a cheaper resource, such as gas-generated energy.

Goods and services can be distributed equally, on the basis of need, or on the basis of a person's contribution to the economy. In the United States, people earn a salary or wage based on how much they contribute to the economy. They can spend their income on whatever goods and services they need and want. However, the goods have to be available when and where consumers can purchase them, and consumers must allocate their income to cover all the goods and services they want to have. People may have to postpone some purchases until they are affordable. Some items, such as food, however, have top priority in most people's spending patterns.

## ▶ Types of Economic Systems

This chapter discusses four economic systems—communism, socialism, capitalism, and mixed economies (Table 2-1).

### Communism

**Communism**

A society in which the government owns all the nation's resources

Karl Marx (1818–83) first described **communism** as a society in which the people, without regard to class, own all the nation's resources. Marx believed

**Table. 2-1 Comparison of Communism, Socialism, and Capitalism**

|  | Communism | Socialism | Capitalism |
|---|---|---|---|
| Business ownership | Most businesses are owned and operated by the government. | The government owns and operates major industries; individuals own small businesses. | Individuals own and operate all businesses. |
| Competition | None. The government owns and operates everything. | Restricted in major industries; encouraged in small business. | Encouraged by market forces and government regulations. |
| Profits | Excess income goes to the government. | Profits earned by small businesses may be reinvested in the business; profits from government-owned industries go to the government. | Individuals are free to keep profits and use them as they wish. |
| Product availability and price | Consumers have a limited choice of goods and services; prices are usually high. | Consumers have some choice of goods and services; prices are determined by supply and demand. | Consumers have a wide choice of goods and services; prices are determined by supply and demand. |
| Employment options | Little choice in choosing a career; most people work for government-owned industries or farms. | Some choice of careers; many people work in government jobs. | Unlimited choice of careers. |

*Handwritten notes:*

Incentives
• negatives do not work well
• materialistic are much better

demand = willingness and ability

• more govt. control
• authoritarian

• more freedom
• more market than control
• stock exchange
• democracy

that members of the working class would revolt against the capitalists who exploited them. In his ideal economy, everyone would contribute according to ability and receive benefits according to need. However, no ideal communist economy exists today that satisfies Marx's ideal.

In a communist economy such as in the Soviet Union or North Vietnam, the government owns and operates all business. Central government planning answers the three economic questions. It determines what goods and services will satisfy citizens' needs, how the goods and services will be produced, and how they will be distributed. People in a communist society have no choice of jobs; they work where the government tells them to, in government-owned and operated factories and farms, and they buy the goods and services the government provides.

Communists claim that their economic system is more efficient than other economic systems and that they distribute their society's wealth equally. There is little labor unrest in communist countries. These nations, however, have a low standard of living, and the government spends its profits not on the goods and services desired by consumers but on defense. There are often

**Private enterprise in Moscow.** In communist economies, the government owns and operates most businesses. The government determines how most products will be made available and people generally have limited choice in jobs. Shown here is a unique example of private enterprise in Moscow.

critical shortages of important consumer goods—food, toilet paper, shoes—and prices for those goods are quite high. In spite of the communist ideal, in the Soviet Union and in other communist nations there is a definite professional class that is much better off than the rest of the people.

In some nations, **free-market communism**, a modified form of communism, has developed. It grew out of the ideas of Yugoslavian Communist party leader Marshal Tito (1891–1980), who believed that compromise is necessary in pure communism. In Yugoslavia, factory-worker committees help decide how factory profits should be spent. In China, the government is permitting some private enterprise and entrepreneurship as an incentive for individuals to work hard and produce more. In the Soviet Union, Mikhail Gorbachev, general secretary of the Communist party, has started to change the way business is conducted with his policy of *perestroika*, economic reform. Business Encounter 2-1 describes Gorbachev's efforts in detail.

Free-market communism motivates people by allowing workers to share in the profits of a business, either through better wages or through profit-sharing agreements with management. Moreover, it encourages people to be innovative and exchange ideas instead of simply doing things the way they have always been done.

**Free-market communism**

A modified form of communism

# Business Encounter 2-1

## *Shades of Capitalism in the Soviet Union*

Although no pure form of communism exists anywhere except in Karl Marx's *Communist Manifesto*, the economy of the Soviet Union has been presented to students as an example of a communist economy for nearly seventy years. However, Mikhail S. Gorbachev, Russian leader since 1985, wants to make his country more productive and competitive, particularly against the United States. Under *perestroika*, Gorbachev is permitting and even advocating some private enterprise to lead his country toward that goal.

Gorbachev wants the Soviet Union to rely more on the market forces of supply and demand to determine what products are to be available and at what price. To this end, managers of forty-eight thousand enterprises were given broad authority to make many of their own business decisions in 1988. For the first time, they can make their own financing decisions and even negotiate prices with their suppliers and customers. Economists say this market pricing will help improve the efficiency of Soviet business. For the first time, managers are also able to lay off workers who are unnecessary or unproductive (although the word "unemployment" is taboo in Soviet society), and no limits are set on workers' earnings. Along with the authority to make decisions, however, comes accountability for profits and losses; Gorbachev has threatened to close unprofitable enterprises.

Small businesses are thriving under Gorbachev's new, limited capitalism. Families and groups are permitted to own and operate a variety of enterprises, including restaurants and auto repair garages. Other groups are allowed to farm private plots of land and to sell the produce at prices determined by supply and demand.

Gorbachev has tried to streamline the role government plays in the Soviet economy. The State Planning Committee, which once issued compulsory production orders to the entire economy, now issues mere guidelines. The eighty ministries that regulated the daily activities of businesses and enterprises may be reduced to twenty, and other bureaucratic payrolls may also be slashed. Obviously, there will be resistance to these actions, particularly among the bureaucrats of ministries and employees of unprofitable businesses who will lose their jobs.

The Soviets are also revamping their banking system. Currently, everyone is required to maintain an account in Gosbank. Gosbank acts primarily as a bureaucratic agent and financial policeman, but it does offer short-term credits at very low interest rates. The Stroybank finances capital investments. The Soviets want to change the bureaucratic, policing role of the banks and make them partners with state enterprises. Specialized banks will be created to meet the needs of farmers, the consumer industry, and individuals who are taking advantage of the legalization of limited capitalism. These banks will set up credit agreements with Soviet businesses that spell out their mutual commitments. They will have the authority to decide what projects to finance and whether prospective borrowers are creditworthy. Such authority is new to Soviet bankers, but it complements Gorbachev's policy of giving managers authority to decide how best to run their own enterprises.

Even Soviet economists agree that free enterprise is necessary to create a strong market for Soviet goods and services, despite the resulting possibility of unemployment. They are beginning to realize that profit is not a dirty word, that profit is, in fact, a measure of how well an enterprise is working. The Soviet Union is turning to capitalism to solve some of its economic woes and to motivate its people to become more concerned about their business enterprises.

These facts are from Peter Galuszka and Bill Javetski, with John Pearson and Rose Brady, "Reforming the Soviet Economy," *Business Week*, December 7, 1987, pp. 76–88; Bill Javetski and John Pearson, with Peter Galuszka, "Gorbachev's Das Kapitalism," *Business Week*, July 13, 1987, pp. 30–31; Mark D'Anastasio, "Soviets Set Out to Transform Banking, Making It Active Participant in Reform," *The Wall Street Journal*, September 4, 1987, p. 4; and Nikolay Shmelyov, "Toward a Soviet Market Economy," excerpts from *Novy Mir* (June 1987), as published in *The Wall Street Journal*, August 26, 1987, p. 24.

In most communist nations there is a thriving, illegal economy called the black market. From the black market, people obtain goods that the government cannot or will not provide—aspirin, blue jeans, shoes, books, records, the Bible. Americans traveling in the Soviet Union have been offered as much as $100 for the blue jeans they are wearing.

# Socialism

**Socialism**

An economic system in which the government owns and operates basic industries but individuals are allowed to own small businesses

Many nations, including Sweden and India, have a socialist economic system. **Socialism** is an economic system in which the government owns and operates basic industries—postal service, telephone, utilities, transportation, banking, and some manufacturing—but individuals are allowed to own small businesses. Citizens are dependent on the government for many goods and services. The government determines what basic goods and services it will produce, how they will be produced, and how they will be distributed. Individuals and small businesses provide other goods and services based on consumer demand and the availability of resources.

Most socialist nations are democratic and recognize basic individual freedoms. Citizens have some voice, but the government usually does what it feels is best for the nation. People are free to go into the occupation of their choice, but they often work in government-operated factories. Socialists believe that socialism permits a higher standard of living than other economic systems, but the difference applies primarily to the nation, not to individuals. Socialist economies profess egalitarianism—equal distribution of income and social services. They believe their economies are more stable than those of other nations. Although this may be true, taxes and unemployment are generally higher in socialist countries.

Socialism is becoming increasingly unpopular. Socialists have lost recent elections in Jamaica and Denmark, and Britain is selling much of its nationally owned industry to the public to create a more capitalistic system.

# Capitalism

**Capitalism**

An economic system in which individuals own and operate the majority of businesses that provide goods and services

**Capitalism**, or private enterprise, is an economic system in which individuals own and operate the majority of businesses that provide goods and services. Competition and consumer demand determine which goods and services are produced, how they are produced, and how they are distributed.

There are two forms of capitalism: pure capitalism and modified capitalism. In pure capitalism, also called a free-market system, all economic decisions are made without government intervention. This economic system was first described by Adam Smith in *The Wealth of Nations* (1776). Smith, often called the father of capitalism, believed that the "invisible hand of competition" would best regulate the economy. Competition would determine what goods and services people need. Competition would force producers to offer the best products at the most reasonable price, and those who failed to do so would not be able to stay in business. Smith's system is also called laissez-faire ("to leave alone") capitalism because the government does not interfere.

**New enterprises.** In a socialist economy, the government owns and operates basic industries while individuals are allowed to own small businesses. This vegetable market in India is an example of private enterprise.

Modified capitalism operates much like pure capitalism, but the government intervenes and regulates business to a certain extent. One of the ways in which the American government regulates business is through antitrust laws. Laws such as the Sherman Antitrust Act (1890) prevent one business from monopolizing a market for a product or service.

*The Rights of Capitalism.* A number of basic individual and business rights must exist in order for capitalism to work.

1. *Private property*: Individuals have the right to own property and to pass this property on to their heirs. This right motivates people to work hard and save to buy property.
2. *Profits*: Individuals and businesses have the right to earn profits and to use the profits as they wish.
3. *Business decisions*: Individuals and businesses have the right to make decisions that determine the way the business operates.
4. *Choice*: Individuals have the right to decide what career to pursue, where to live, what goods and services to purchase, and more. Businesses can decide where to locate, what goods and services to produce, what resources to use in the production process, and so on.

**Competition**

The rivalry among businesses to gain sales

**Pure competition**

When there are many small businesses selling one standardized product

**Supply**

The quantity of goods or services that businesses are willing to sell at different prices at a specific time

**Demand**

The quantity of products and services that consumers are willing to buy at different prices at a specific time

**Equilibrium price**

The price where the quantity of products that businesses are willing to supply equals the quantity of products that consumers are willing to buy at a specific point in time

*Competition.* **Competition** is the rivalry among businesses to convince consumers to buy goods or services. It is a vital element in capitalism. It promotes efficiency among businesses and lowers prices for goods and services. It improves the quality of the goods and services that are available.

Within the private-enterprise system, there are four types of competitive environment: pure competition, monopolistic competition, oligopoly, and monopoly. **Pure competition** exists when there are many small businesses selling one standardized product. Agricultural commodities such as wheat and corn are sold in a pure-competition environment in the United States. No one business sells enough of the product to influence the product's price. Producers cannot differentiate their products, so prices are determined by the forces of supply and demand.

**Supply** is the quantity of goods or services that businesses are willing to sell at different prices at a specific time. In general, sellers are willing to sell more of a product at higher prices. For example, a business that sells Michael Jackson T-shirts may be willing to sell eight T-shirts at $8 each, ten T-shirts at $10 each, and twelve T-shirts at $12 each. The relationship between those prices and the quantities of T-shirts the business is willing to supply at those prices can be shown graphically with a supply curve (Figure 2-1).

**Demand** is the quantity of products and services that consumers are willing to buy at different prices at a specific time. Consumers will usually buy more of an item as its price falls. Consumers may be willing to buy twelve Michael Jackson T-shirts at $8 each, ten at $10 each, but only eight at $12 each. The relationship between the prices and the quantities consumers are willing to buy at those prices can also be shown graphically, with a demand curve (Figure 2-1).

The supply and demand curves intersect at the point where supply and demand are equal—at the price where the quantity of products that businesses are willing to supply equals the quantity of products that consumers are willing to buy at a specific point in time. This is the **equilibrium price**.

The T-shirt business is willing to supply ten T-shirts at $10, and consumers are willing to buy ten T-shirts at $10. Therefore, $10 is the equilibrium price for T-shirts at that point in time (Figure 2-1), and most businesses will price their T-shirts at $10. A business that prices its T-shirts above $10 will not sell enough shirts to earn a profit; a business that prices its T-shirts below $10 accepts a lower profit per T-shirt than could be made at the equilibrium price.

If the cost of making T-shirts goes up, the business will probably not be willing to offer as many T-shirts at the old price. Changing the price would alter the supply curve, and a new equilibrium price would result. This is an ongoing process. Prices for various goods and services vary according to the quantity businesses are willing to sell and the quantity consumers are willing to buy.

Critics of supply and demand say that the system does not distribute resources equally. The forces of supply and demand prevent sellers who have to sell at higher prices (because their costs are high) and buyers who cannot afford to buy goods at the equilibrium price from participating in the market. In other words, according to critics, the wealthy can afford to buy more than

**Figure 2-1**

Equilibrium Price of T-shirts

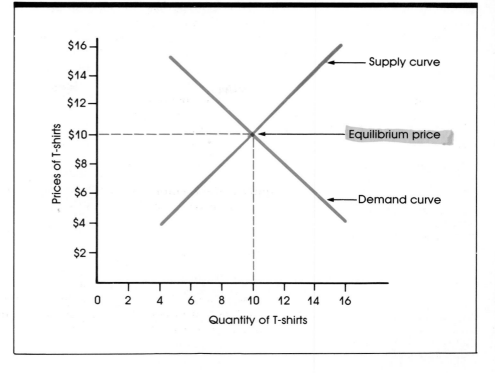

*they need, but the poor are unable to buy enough of what they need to survive.*

**Monopolistic competition**

When there are fewer businesses than in a pure-competition system and businesses focus on creating differences between their products

*most advertising!!*

**Monopolistic competition** exists when there are fewer businesses than in a pure-competition system and the differences between the goods sold by these businesses are small. Aspirin, soft drinks, and vacuum cleaners are examples of such goods. These products differ slightly in packaging, warranty, name, and other characteristics, but all meet the same consumer need.

In monopolistic competition, producers exercise some power over the price they charge because they can promote different features of their product. Consumers value some features more than others and are usually willing to pay higher prices for a product with the features they want. For example, Advil, a nonprescription pain reliever, contains ibuprofen instead of aspirin. Consumers who cannot take aspirin or who believe ibuprofen is a more effective pain reliever do not mind paying a little extra for the ibuprofen in Advil.

**Oligopoly**

When very few businesses sell a product

*OPECK - oil*

*don't advertise*

An **oligopoly** exists when very few businesses sell a product. The product they sell can be similar (as in the case of aluminum and steel) or different (as in the case of automobiles and airline services). In an oligopoly, individual businesses have control over a product's price because each supplies a large portion of the products sold in the marketplace. Nevertheless, the prices charged by different producers stay fairly close because a price cut or increase by one producer will trigger a price cut or increase by the other producers.

In the 1980s many airlines engaged in price wars. When one cut its fares to boost sales, others had to cut their fares to remain competitive.

Oligopolies exist when it is expensive for new firms to enter the marketplace. Not just anyone can acquire enough financial capital to build an automobile production facility. Business Encounter 2-2 describes the efforts of Chevrolet to hold on to its number-one position in the American auto market in the 1980s.

# Business Encounter 2-2

## *Chevy Competes to Be Number One in the American Marketplace*

Private enterprise encourages competition among businesses. Because businesses are constantly developing and improving products to stay ahead of their competitors, consumers ultimately get better products at lower prices. The American automobile marketplace illustrates this process, and competition between Ford Motor Company and the Chevrolet Division of General Motors is at an all-time high.

In 1987, for the first time in more than thirty years, Ford sold more cars and light-duty trucks than did General Motors' Chevrolet Division. In fact, Ford sold about 180,000 more vehicles than Chevy did in the 1987 model year, which ended on September 30, 1987. In the previous model year, Chevy had outsold Ford by more than 300,000 units. Because the Chevrolet Division sells about 50 percent of all GM's cars and trucks and also sells GM's lowest-priced vehicles, Chevrolet was upset about losing its number-one spot to Ford. General Motors had been the top auto maker for many years, so the market-share loss sent the company scrambling to recover its number-one position.

Chevy's defeat reflected trends in the auto industry. Ford was riding a crest of popularity while GM was struggling. Ford had four of the five top-selling vehicles in the industry while Chevrolet had only one. Ford's popular Escort was the best-selling small car for the sixth consecutive year. In addition, Ford sold more trucks than any other U.S. competitor. At about the same time, Ford was earning a reputation as the trendsetter in automotive design. Ford product quality and owner loyalty increased, adding to Chevy's difficulties.

Chevy planned several actions and strategies to regain its lost market share. It tried to eliminate confusion resulting from similarities among its products by reducing the number of brand names and models offered. It reduced the number of truck models from 288 to 219. It also eliminated the Chevette. Chevrolet officials believed these streamlining efforts would give consumers a real choice between automobiles.

Nevertheless, the Chevrolet Division faced other, internal problems. Several important Chevrolet models overlapped with cars offered by other GM divisions, especially Pontiac. In addition, Chevrolet's recovery was hindered by the carryover of models from previous years, while Ford and Chrysler were introducing new models.

In 1988, Chevy introduced the new Corsica and Beretta cars and redesigned its full-size pickup trucks. However, increases in sales for the new models were achieved at the expense of sales for some of Chevy's earlier models. Truck sales remained low because Chevy did not immediately eliminate its less-expensive, old-style trucks.

Ford and Chevy are likely to continue their battle to be the number-one auto maker. Chevrolet says it does not intend to be second for long. It is redesigning its products to improve quality and offer consumers a clearer choice. On the other hand, Ford has vowed not to relinquish the top spot. The demand and buying habits of consumers will decide the winner, although in a free-enterprise system the ultimate winners are the consumers themselves and the prizes are better products.

These facts are from Melinda Grenier Guiles, "Chevrolet Faces Rough Ride in Bid to Regain Sales Lead from Ford," *The Wall Street Journal*, October 6, 1987, p. 33; Ford Motor Company 1986 Annual Report; and General Motors Corporation 1986 Annual Report.

**In our capitalistic society very few monopolies exist.** Those that do are regulated by the government and are allowed to exist as a monopoly for the good of consumers. A utility company such as Con Edison competes alone because the start-up costs are high and new competitors could probably not compete for sales and survive against existing companies.

**Monopoly** *one "person" controls*

When there is only one producer of a product in a given market

*don't need to advertise*

A **monopoly** exists when there is only one producer of a product in a given market. Utility companies that supply electricity, natural gas, and water are monopolies. The government allows these monopolies because the cost of creating the product or service is so great that new producers would not be able to compete for sales and still survive. Government-granted monopolies are subject to government-regulated prices.

Some monopolies exist because of technological developments that are protected by patent laws. Patent laws grant the developer of new technology a period of time (usually seventeen years) during which no other producer can use the same technology without the agreement of the original developer. This moratorium allows the developer to recover research, development, and production expenses and to earn a reasonable profit. Examples of this type of monopoly are the dry-copier process developed by Xerox and the self-developing photographic technology created by Polaroid. Both companies existed for years without competition and could charge premium prices because no alternative products existed to compete with their products. Through continuous development, Polaroid maintains market dominance. Xerox's patents have expired, however, and many imitators have forced market prices to decline.

# Mixed Economies

**Mixed economy**

Has elements from more than one economic system

No country practices a pure form of communism, socialism, or capitalism. Most nations, including the United States, operate as **mixed economies**. A mixed economy has elements from more than one economic system. In socialist Sweden, most businesses are owned and operated by private individuals. In capitalist United States, the federal government owns and operates the postal service and the Tennessee Valley Authority, an electric utility. In socialist Great Britain, the government owns most of the communications services and regulates many major industries, but allows individuals to operate the industry. In communist Hungary, many capitalist ideas have been implemented, including private ownership of some small businesses.

# ▶ The American Economy

The United States is a mixed economy based on capitalism. In the United States, answers to the three economic questions are determined by competition and the forces of supply and demand, although the federal government does intervene in economic decisions to a certain extent. In order to understand the current state of the American economy, it is helpful to examine its history and the role of the entrepreneur.

## History of the American Economy

*The Early Economy.* The thirteen British colonies that became the United States were primarily an agricultural society. The land was fertile, and the weather good for farming. People were self-sufficient and produced everything they needed at home, including food, clothing, and furniture. Abundant natural resources fostered the development of industries such as fishing, shipping, and fur trading. A few manufactured goods and money for the colonies' infant industries came from England.

As the nation expanded slowly toward the Pacific, people found natural resources such as coal, copper, and iron ore and used them to produce goods such as horseshoes, farm implements, and kitchen utensils. Families who produced surplus goods sold or traded them for things they could not produce themselves, such as fine furniture and window glass. Some farm families also spent spare time turning raw materials into clothes and household goods. Because these goods were produced at home, this system was called the domestic system. (Today such home-based production is known as cottage industry.)

*The Industrial Revolution.* The nineteenth century and the Industrial Revolution saw the development of new technology and factories. A factory brought together all the resources needed to make a product—materials, machines, and workers. Work in the factories became specialized as workers focused on one or two tasks. As work became more efficient, productivity increased, making more goods available at lower prices.

The railroad brought major changes. Farmers could send their surplus crops and goods all over the nation for barter or for sale. Factories began to spring up along the railways to manufacture farm equipment and a variety of other goods to be shipped by rail.

Samuel Slater set up the first American textile factory after he had memorized the plans for an English factory and had emigrated to the United States. Eli Whitney revolutionized the cotton industry with his cotton gin. Francis Cabot Lowell's factory organized all the steps of manufacturing cotton cloth for maximum efficiency and productivity. John Deere's farm equipment greatly increased farm production and reduced the number of farmers required to feed the young nation. Farm workers began to move to the cities to find jobs in the factories and a higher standard of living. Henry Ford developed the assembly-line system to produce automobiles. Workers focused on one part of an automobile and then pushed it down the assembly line to the next stage. When the product came off the assembly line, it was a finished automobile. Ford's assembly line could manufacture many automobiles efficiently, and the price of his cars was only $200, making them affordable to many Americans. Trucks, too, began hauling goods quickly and cheaply as a new mode of transportation.

***The Manufacturing Economy.*** Industrialization brought increased prosperity, and the United States gradually developed a manufacturing economy—one devoted to manufacturing goods and services rather than producing agricultural commodities. The assembly line was used in more industries, increasing the goods available to the consumer. Businesses became more concerned with the needs of the consumer; and buying on credit, marketing, and advertising were born. Expensive goods such as cars and appliances could be purchased on a time-payment plan. Companies conducted marketing research to find out what consumers needed and wanted. Advertising made consumers aware of differences in products and prices.

Because these developments occurred in a private-enterprise system, consumers determined what goods and services were produced. They did this by purchasing the products they liked at prices they were willing to pay. The United States prospered, and American citizens had one of the highest standards of living in the world.

***The Service Economy.*** Americans had more money and more time with the increased standard of living. They began to pay others to perform services that made their lives easier. The economy gradually changed to a service economy—one devoted to the production of services that make life easier for busy consumers. Service industries grew rapidly—banking, medicine, utilities, child care, leisure-related industries, education.

**Entrepreneur**

A person who risks his or her wealth, time, and effort to develop for profit an innovative product or way of doing something

# The Role of the Entrepreneur

An **entrepreneur** is a person who risks his or her wealth, time, and effort to develop for profit an innovative product or way of doing something. In

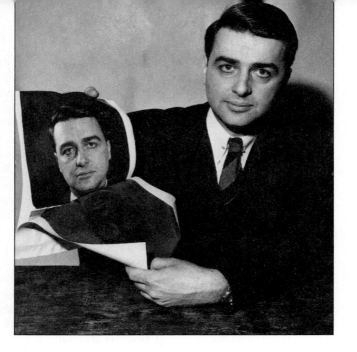

**Entrepreneurs have shaped our way of life.** Henry Ford brought us the automobile and mass production orientation; Ray Kroc brought us the milk shake machine and ultimately billions of hamburgers through McDonald's. Edwin H. Land, shown here, founded the Polaroid Corp. and brought us instant photographs.

venture capitalists ~ give money to entrepreneurs for them to get a product rolling

the past, entrepreneurs were often inventors who brought all the factors of production together to produce a new product. Thomas Edison, whose inventions include the record player and light bulb, fits this definition. Entrepreneurs have been associated with such uniquely American concepts as Mrs. Fields' Cookies, Levi's 501 blue jeans, TCBY Yogurt franchises, Dr Pepper, and Dell Computers.

*Early American Entrepreneurs.* The first entrepreneurs to take financial risks in order to turn a profit distributed raw materials to farm families and paid them to turn the materials into finished products such as furniture and household goods. As the Industrial Revolution fueled the growth of American business, entrepreneurs took bigger risks to achieve their goals. John D. Rockefeller built Standard Oil out of the new oil industry. Andrew Carnegie invested in railroads and founded the United States Steel Corporation. Andrew Mellon built the Aluminum Company of America and Gulf Oil. J. P. Morgan started financial institutions to fund the business activities of other entrepreneurs.

*Modern American Entrepreneurs.* Entrepreneurs are constantly changing American business practices with innovative management techniques and new technology. Edwin Land developed the Land camera, which eventually evolved into Polaroid instant photography. Steven Jobs and Steve Wozniak developed a small personal computer in their garage. Their company, Apple Computers, became quite successful and turned them both into millionaires. Bill Gates followed suit with Microsoft, a software producer of disk operating systems used in the personal computer. Ross Perot built Electronic Data Systems into a dynamic computer service company; he

**Current American entrepreneurs.** Liz Claiborne, (shown in the middle with two of her employees) specializes in women's apparel that is fashionable, functional, and affordable. Her idea was to provide "dress for success" clothes to women before it was popular to do so.

eventually sold it and a great deal of stock to General Motors for more than $700 million. Business Encounter 2-3 looks closer at the entrepreneurs of today.

# ▶ The Role of Government in the American Economy

The American economic system is best described as modified capitalism because the federal government regulates business and protects individuals. Laws such as the Sherman Antitrust Act (1890) prevent a company from

# Business Encounter 2-3

## *The New Entrepreneurs*

People have always thought of entrepreneurs as pioneers, innovators, astute businesspeople, who take risks and pursue opportunities in the marketplace. In 1985, U.S. entrepreneurs started almost 1.5 million business ventures, compared to just ninety thousand in 1950. In the past few years, rapid changes in technology have made it possible for entrepreneurs to enter new fields in manufacturing and service industries. Life in the United States is faster paced and more urban than ever before. These developments, coupled with new technology, presented entrepreneurs with new opportunities, and people like Tom Monaghan (Domino's Pizza), Jeno F. Paulucci (Chun King Corp. and Jeno's, Inc.), and Michael Dell (Dell Computers) recognized those opportunities and seized them.

The new entrepreneur is also different from those in the past. *She* is typically under 40, independent and imaginative, and a college graduate. In fact, women start three times as many entrepreneurial ventures as men. She may have attended one of the nation's top business schools. She has a great deal of know-how, acquired from business school, from working in a corporation for a few years, or from a lifetime of reading and studying. Today's entrepreneur has a good knowledge of sophisticated business techniques but may also believe in the humanistic values of the 1960s.

Entrepreneurs today are stifled in the corporate environment and often start their own companies to find excitement, success, values closer to their own, and, of course, money. The prevalent attitude among them is that they can be successful without working for a large corporation. Money is the prime motivator for a new entrepreneur. Money is fashionable again, and people who start successful businesses are highly respected by their peers. Entrepreneurs are realizing that there are opportunities to make a lot of money in the business world.

Although there is a new-found respect for entrepreneurship in the United States, it still has risks. Currently, two out of three new businesses fail. About half of those that fail do so in the first five years. In spite of the risks, many entrepreneurs who fail try again with the backing of venture capitalists (partners or investors who provide money in return for part ownership of the business). If the business succeeds, the venture capitalist usually receives a high rate of return from the original investment.

No one knows how long the current Age of the Entrepreneur will last. In the past, wars, depressions, and changes in the tax laws influenced the rise and fall of entrepreneurship. These factors are still important, but as long as money is king, entrepreneurship will continue to be popular.

---

These facts are from Tom Richman, "The Hottest Entrepreneur in America," *Inc.* 9 (February 1987): 50–56; Leslie Wayne, "A Pioneer Spirit Sweeps Business," *The New York Times*, March 25, 1984; pp. 3–1, 3–12, 3–13; and Donald L. Sexton, "The Entrepreneur: Social Misfit, Mythical Creature, or Radiology Department Director," *Administrative Radiology* 6 (October 1987): 19–21.

---

monopolizing a market. Laws such as the Occupational Safety and Health Act (1970) set health and safety standards. The government protects businesses by providing copyrights and patents for creative and innovative work. These prohibit others from profiting from someone else's creativity and allow profits to go to the original creator. There are also laws that prevent unfair or deceptive trade practices.

Laws protect individuals from false advertising and from dangerous products. The government provides support to individuals by offering food stamps, aid to families with dependent children, and unemployment compensation. It authorizes and subsidizes small-business loans. Although the government seldom offers direct support to businesses, it did provide

**The government is a consumer.** The government spends billions of dollars on defense products purchased from the private sector. Government purchases such as this submarine made by Honeywell can substantially influence profits of defense contractors.

substantial loan guarantees to Chrysler Corporation in the 1970s to prevent it from going bankrupt and bailed out Lockheed Aircraft, a major defense contractor.

## Gross National Product

Government agencies such as the U.S. Department of Commerce measure the value of goods and services produced in the United States and the overall performance of the American economy. One way the government measures the state of the economy is by calculating the **gross national product (GNP)**—the sum of all goods and services produced in the United States during a year. (Other countries also measure their GNP.) The 1987 GNP of the United States was $4.487 trillion. The number itself does not provide much information, but the fact that the GNP rose 6 percent from the year before shows that the economy grew in 1987. Economists compare changes in the annual GNP to determine the progress and impact of economic policies.

The United States economy consists of three basic sectors: households, government, and business. Our trading partners from the rest of the world also contribute to our domestic economy. Figure 2-2 depicts the basic flow of

**Figure 2-2**

Flow of Funds Through the
Economy

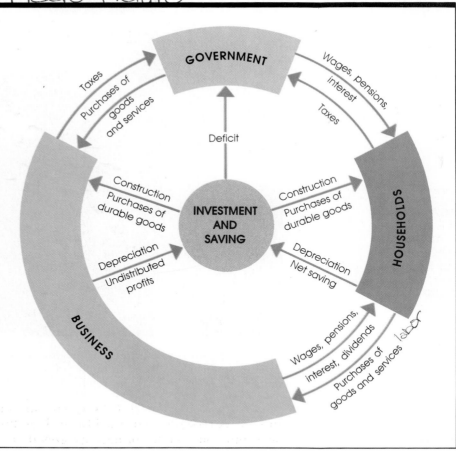

*Macro Picture)*

*Rule of 72*
*÷ into by the*
*inflation rate,*
*income worth*
*that much*
*less each 2*
*yrs.*

funds through the three-sector economy. Notice that at the center of the flow of funds is savings and investment. (Chapter 16 examines how savings and investment are allocated by the financial system.) Examples of the basic flows of funds are presented, with the direction of the flows indicated by the arrows. While you may not understand each flow, it is important that you understand that the three sectors of the economy interact to create GNP.

GNP measurement is complicated by **inflation**, a continuing rise in prices. The **real gross national product** measures economic output in so-called constant dollars—that is, dollars with constant buying power, not dollars whose buying power has decreased because of inflation. In other words, real GNP reflects changes in output without including inflation in the measurement. In 1987, the real GNP (based on 1982 constant dollars) was $3,820.3 billion, up 2.9 percent from 1986. Figure 2-3 shows GNP growth from 1977 to 1987, based on the value of the dollar in 1982. Alan Greenspan, chairman of the Federal Reserve Board, predicted that the 1988 GNP would rise

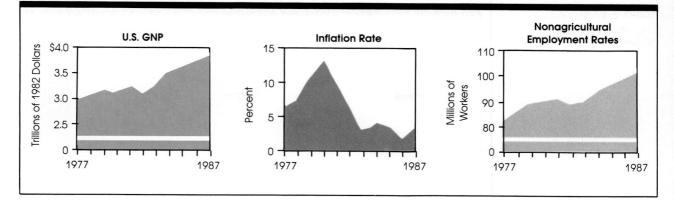

**Figure 2-3**

U.S. GNP, Inflation Rate, and Nonagricultural Employment Rates, 1977–1987
Source: U.S. Bureau of Economic Analysis and U.S. Bureau of Labor Statistics

approximately 4.0 percent as a five-year period of expansion slows.[1]

The amount of GNP generated by each sector of the economy is measured by the U.S. Bureau of Economic Analysis. Figure 2-4 shows the contribution of each sector.

Real GNP shows whether the physical output of the economy is expanding or contracting. Economic expansion occurs when people spend more money. Their purchases stimulate the production of goods and services, and the nation's standard of living rises because more people are employed. Economic contraction occurs when spending decreases. Businesses cut back on production and lay off workers, and the economy as a whole slows down. Contractions of the economy lead to **recession**—a decline in production, employment, and income. A recession is defined by the U.S. Bureau of Economic Research as six continuous months of negative growth in real GNP.

**Recession**

Six continuous months of negative growth in real GNP

The American economy expands and contracts in response to changes in consumer and government spending. The economy is influenced by several variables, including trade laws, U.S. government expenditures for defense and for domestic programs, and consumers' willingness to save and spend. Although fluctuations in the economy are inevitable and to a certain extent predictable, their effects—inflation and unemployment—disrupt American lives. Figure 2-5 shows the annual percentage change in consumer prices.

# Government Intervention in Economic Cycles

**Employment Act of 1946**

Gave the government the right to take certain actions to minimize the disruptive effects of economic fluctuations and reduce unemployment

The **Employment Act of 1946** gave the government the right to take certain actions to minimize the disruptive effects of economic fluctuations and reduce unemployment, the condition in which a percentage of the population wants to work but is unable to find jobs. The federal government uses monetary and fiscal policy to stabilize economic activity.

Monetary policy is the management of the U.S. money supply and interest rates. The Federal Reserve Board (Fed), an independent government agency, is responsible for the management of monetary policy. The Fed exerts a

**Figure 2-4**

Gross National Product by Sector

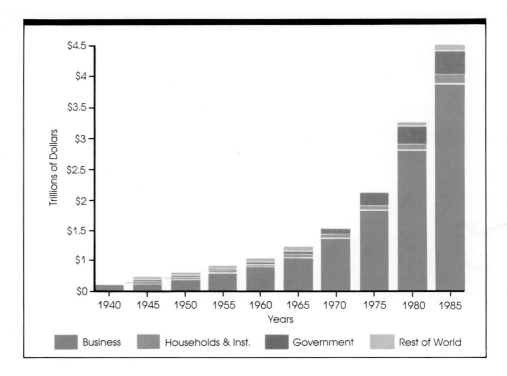

major influence on interest rates charged by lenders; in other words, it is a major force in determining how much money costs.

When unemployment levels get too high, the Federal Reserve Board loosens the money supply and stimulates the economy by lowering interest rates. Lower interest rates encourage consumers and businesses to borrow money to buy goods and services. When people increase their purchases of goods and services, businesses boost production and hire workers to meet the increased demand. The overall effect is a rise in employment.

When inflation is too high, the Federal Reserve Board tightens the money supply and restricts the economy by raising interest rates. Consumers and businesses then spend less money because the cost of borrowing money is more than they want to pay. Because they do not want to borrow money at high costs, businesses cut back production and lay off workers. The economy slows, and the effect of inflation eases.

In the 1970s, the federal government followed this policy in an effort to reduce double-digit inflation. The Federal Reserve Board raised interest rates to make it more expensive for Americans to use credit. With credit more expensive, most Americans reduced their level of spending. The federal government hoped that reduced spending would force producers to cut prices in order to attract reluctant consumers. In that way, inflation would decline. However, actions taken by the government do not always have the expected results. Inflation was over 13 percent in 1979 and did not fall to

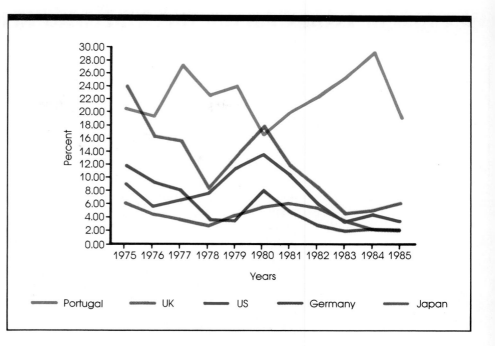

acceptable levels until 1982, after the government used fiscal policy to help in the fight against inflation.

Fiscal policy involves changing the levels of government spending and government income (taxes). It is determined by the budget created by Congress and the President. The impact of the government's fiscal policy on the economy is more long term than is its monetary policy. Both fiscal and monetary policy help to maintain stable prices, foster economic growth in GNP, create high levels of employment, and balance trade with America's international trading partners.

Despite the government's tightening of the money supply in the late 1970s, inflation increased and the economy stagnated. Economists coined the term **stagflation** to describe the situation—high levels of unemployment combined with high rates of inflation. Figure 2-3 charts inflation and unemployment levels from 1977 through 1987.

The federal government introduced a new fiscal policy, **supply-side economics**, to ease stagflation. Supply-side economists advocate reducing taxes and balancing the federal budget. Politicians thought that tax reductions would encourage businesses to invest in production and consumers to spend. The increase in production would reduce unemployment, boost the economy, and raise federal tax revenues in the long run. The tax reduction, combined with a cut in federal spending, was supposed to reduce inflation. As Figure 2-3 shows, inflation levels began to fall and employment rose by the mid-1980s but both were still unsatisfactory to many Americans. As of 1988, the government was unsuccessful in significantly cutting its expenses.

**Stagflation**

The situation of high levels of unemployment combined with high rates of inflation

**Supply-side economics**

A policy that advocates reducing taxes and balancing the federal budget

# ► Current Issues Facing the American Economy

Major issues facing the American economy include unemployment, productivity, the federal deficit, and the trade deficit.

## Unemployment

In 1982, the peak unemployment rate was 10 percent. By early 1988 this unemployment rate had declined to 5.6 percent. This was a significant improvement but still an unacceptably high rate. Many of the unemployed live in poverty, and some are homeless. Technological advances have enabled many American businesses to improve productivity—but at the expense of many jobs. Robots and computers have replaced many American workers. American businesses and the government try to provide some of these displaced workers with training and education so that they can find new jobs in an economy becoming more oriented to skilled workers and services. New training programs attempt to improve worker skills so that they can become more productive in today's economy.

## Productivity

Productivity is the total output of goods and services in a given period of time divided by the number of hours worked. A high level of productivity reduces the costs of production and lets the producer lower the selling price of goods in the marketplace. Foreign producers in Japan and South Korea, are more productive than their American counterparts, largely because of participative management techniques and newer industrial facilities.

Productivity may be increased by plant modernization and innovative management techniques (various participative management techniques are discussed in Chapter 8). If these steps can make the United States more competitive in international markets, increased output may mean more jobs in the long run because of the growth of U.S. exports.

## The Federal Deficit

**Federal deficit**

The difference between government revenue (taxes) and government expenditures

**National debt**

The total amount of money the federal government has borrowed

The **federal deficit** is the difference between government revenue (taxes) and government expenditures. Throughout the 1980s the federal government spent far more than it took in from taxes. The government is obligated to spend money for social programs such as Social Security; and it is also obligated to protect Americans, so it must spend money for national defense. Because Americans do not want their taxes increased, it is difficult for the federal government to bring in more revenue. Like consumers and businesses, when the government needs money, it borrows from the public, financial institutions, and from Federal Reserve Banks. Because of increased spending by the government in the last decade, the **national debt**—the amount of money the federal government owes lenders—grew to 2.3 trillion dollars in 1987.[2]

**Imports up, exports down.**   Recently U.S. imports of foreign products have exceeded the export of domestic products. This occurrence causes a trade deficit between the U.S. and foreign countries. Shown here are Japanese cars arriving on Baltimore shipping docks.

In order to decrease the federal deficit and the national debt, Americans must decide what programs are most important. Many advocate cutting the defense budget drastically; others fear doing so would leave the nation vulnerable to nuclear attack. Many believe the solution is to cut social programs such as Social Security and welfare. Social programs such as subsidized low-income housing have been reduced to save federal money.

There is no easy way to bring federal spending in line with federal income. The Tax Reform Act of 1986 reduced the amount of taxes Americans pay but closed many loopholes in the tax laws in order to increase federal revenues. Improving the American standard of living, through increased productivity, may also swell tax revenues. Nevertheless, politicians must decide how to cut federal spending to reduce the rising national debt to a manageable level.

## The Trade Deficit

**Trade deficit**

The difference between the value of American products exported to other nations and the value of foreign products imported into the United States

The **trade deficit** is the difference between the value of American products exported to other nations and the value of foreign products imported into the United States. In recent years, Americans have bought far more foreign goods and services, particularly Japanese goods, than foreigners have bought

American goods and services. The trade deficit has been climbing steadily throughout the 1980s; in 1987, it reached $171 billion.[3]

American companies have been doing their best to compete, and American economic policy has emphasized making American goods more price-competitive in world markets. Nevertheless, Americans are still buying foreign goods, taking sales and profits away from American producers. Because of declining sales of American goods, many American producers had to cut back on production or close down and lay off workers.

Because the American dollar is the international currency, the exchange rate between the dollar and other currencies such as the Japanese yen and German deutsche mark influence the relative value of goods traded between countries. One cause of the trade deficit was the increase in the value of the American dollar during the late 1970s and early 1980s relative to the value of foreign currencies. This increase made foreign goods much cheaper, despite the cost of importing them to the United States. Moreover, the United States no longer has technological superiority. South Korea and Taiwan not only have access to U.S. technology but also have a cost advantage because their labor costs are lower. The lack of new plant technology and high labor costs have made some U.S. manufacturers, particularly in the automobile industry and the computer and semiconductor industries, less competitive than foreign producers.

At the close of the 1980s, the situation began to look better for the United States. The value of the dollar dropped 50 percent between 1985 and 1988,

**Figure 2-6**

U.S. Imports and Exports with Major Trading Partners

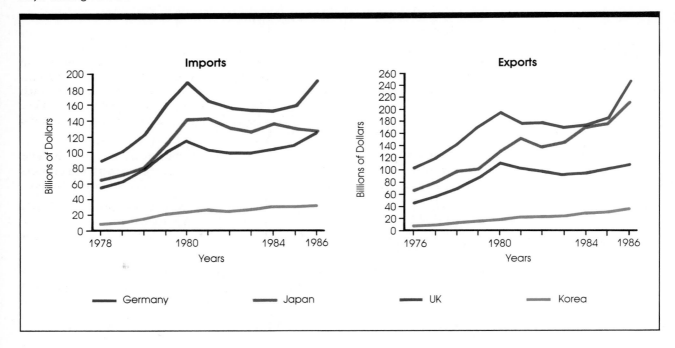

making American goods more competitive abroad. As a result, exports rose 19 percent in 1987, and imports rose only 5 percent as Americans recognized that they needed to buy American goods. If this trend continues, some economists predict that the foreign trade deficit may fall back to $50 billion by the mid-1990s.[4] This may be the first step toward a more balanced trade picture between the United States and its major trading partners.

Figure 2-6 indicates the imports and exports between the United States and some of its major trading partners.

# Notes

1. Daniel Horgan, "Greenspan: Slow Growth, No Recession," *USA Today*, February 24, 1988, p. 1B.
2. Paul Magnusson, with Mike McNamee, Steven J. Dryden, and Vicky Cahan, "Reaganomics: The Good, the Bad, and the Ugly," *Business Week*, February 1, 1988, p. 59.
3. William J. Holstein, with Steven J. Dryden, Gail Schares, Ted Holden, and Jonathan B. Levine, "Made in the U.S.A.," *Business Week*, February 29, 1988, p. 60.
4. Ibid.

# Summary and Review

▶ An economic system determines how a society distributes its resources to produce goods and services that satisfy the needs of its people. An economic system must answer three questions: (1) What goods and services and how much of each will satisfy the needs of the people? (2) How will the goods and services be produced; who will produce them, and with what resources? (3) How are the goods and services to be distributed to the people?

▶ Communism is an economic system in which the government owns and operates all business. Government planning determines what goods and services will be produced, how they will be produced, and how they will be distributed.

▶ Socialism is an economic system in which the government owns and operates all major industries, but individuals own small businesses. Government planning determines the answers to the three economic questions, but the forces of supply and demand are also important.

▶ Capitalism is an economic system in which individuals own and operate all business. The forces of supply and demand determine the answers to the three economic questions.

▶ Mixed economies contain elements from more than one economic system.

▶ Supply is the quantity of products that businesses are willing to make available at different prices at a specific time. Demand is the quantity of products that consumers are willing to buy at different prices at a specific time. The equilibrium price is the point where supply equals demand.

▶ Entrepreneurs risk their time, wealth, and efforts to develop an innovative good or service in order to make a profit. Entrepreneurs are important because they take risks to develop new ideas.

▶ Gross national product is the sum of all goods and services produced in a nation during a year. Inflation is a continuing rise in prices. Expansion occurs when people spend more money and their purchases stimulate the economy. Contraction occurs when spending decreases and the economy slows down. A recession is a decline in production, employment, and income.

▶ The federal government intervenes in economic cycles to minimize the disruptive effects of economic fluctuations and reduce unemployment. It uses monetary policy—the management of the U.S. money supply—and fiscal policy—changing the levels of government spending and revenue—to stabilize economic activity.

▶ Issues facing the American economy today are rising employment, increasing productivity, and reducing the federal deficit and the trade deficit.

# Key Terms and Concepts

economics
economic system
communism
free-market communism
socialism
capitalism
competition
supply
demand
equilibrium price
pure competition
monopolistic competition
oligopoly

monopoly
mixed economy
entrepreneur
gross national product (GNP)
inflation
real gross national product
recession
Employment Act of 1946
stagflation
supply-side economics
federal deficit
national debt
trade deficit

# Checking Your Understanding

This chapter introduced you to the subject of the American economy. To test and reinforce your understanding, fill in the blanks below.

1. _competition_ is the rivalry among businesses to convince consumers to buy their products or services.

2. The physical and mental abilities that people use to produce goods and services are known as _human resources_

3. In a _socialist_ economic system, the government owns all basic industries while individuals own small businesses.

4. In a _capitalist_ economic system, individuals own a majority of the businesses providing goods and services.

5. A business operates under a _monopoly_ when there is no competition for its goods or services.

6. Decisions about what goods and services will be produced, how they will be produced, and how they will be allocated are made by an _economic system_

7. _demand_ is the quantity of goods and services consumers are willing to buy at different prices at a specific point in time.

8. A continuing rise in price levels is called _inflation_

9. In a _communist_ economic system, the government owns everything and most people work in government-operated businesses.

10. _supply_ is the quantity of goods and services sellers are willing to offer at different prices at a specific point in time.

11. The difference between the government's revenue and its expenditures is known as the _federal deficit_

# Topics for Review and Discussion

1. Compare and contrast the four major economic systems.

2. Explain, using examples, why there is no pure form of any economic system.

3. Describe the rights of capitalism.

4. Differentiate among the four forms of competition. Give examples of each.

5. Discuss Adam Smith's concept of capitalism. Compare it to the U.S. economy today.

6. Describe how the United States developed from an agriculturally based economy to become one of the leading world powers.

7. How and why does the American government participate in the economy?

8. What are the basic factors of production? Give examples of each.

9. Discuss the role of an entrepreneur in the U.S. economy.

10. Describe how the Employment Act of 1946 guides economic policy.

11. How do monetary policy and fiscal policy differ?

12. Explain the difference between gross national product and real gross national product. Why is it important to understand the difference between them?

13. Discuss the current economic problems facing the United States.

# Exercises

1. Find a company that could be considered a modern success story. Research the company's history, and write a short paper describing the entrepreneurial nature of the firm's founders and what made the business successful.

2. Go to *Business Week, Fortune, Barron's,* the *Federal Reserve Bulletin,* or some other publication and find the latest GNP and real GNP figures.

3. Find an article on the current state of international competition and the U.S. economy. Provide the class with an update on U.S. progress in solving its competitive problems.

## Case 2-1
### *Procter & Gamble Grows with the American Economy*

If any one company mirrors the growth of the American economy, it is Procter & Gamble, which has been doing business for nearly three-fourths of the history of the United States. Because of its emphasis on quality products, research and development, extensive advertising, and loyalty to its employees, the company was able to celebrate its 150th anniversary in 1987 with sales of $17 billion.

Candlemaker William Procter and soapmaker James Gamble joined forces in Cincinnati in 1837 because they each used wood ash and animal fat to make their respective products. Gamble ran the production end of the business; Procter ran the administrative end. They were honest businessmen at a time when many businesses were taking advantage of consumers. Gamble once wrote, "When you cannot make pure goods and full weight, go to something else that is honest, even if it is breaking stone." That integrity, combined with careful planning and innovation, set the tone for the future of Procter & Gamble.

Expansion of the railroad and other transportation improvements enabled Procter and Gamble to expand their business beyond Cincinnati. Before the Civil War, the company hoarded the raw materials needed to make its products. When the war began, Procter & Gamble was the only company with enough raw materials on hand to supply candles and soap to the Union army. After the war, shortages of some raw materials meant substitutes had to be found, so Procter & Gamble engaged in research and development to find substitutes to continue production of its products.

As the young country grew, new technology led to changes in the market for consumer goods. The invention of the light bulb led to the decline of Procter & Gamble's candle business, but indoor plumbing increased the demand for its soaps. The company's research led to the introduction of a white soap in 1878. Ivory soap was a first in many ways. Yellow or brown soaps sold in unwrapped chunks often damaged both skin and clothing.

Ivory, however, was a gentle soap that came in uniformly sized, neatly wrapped cakes, with the company's name on the wrapper. Procter & Gamble advertised Ivory directly to housewives—an unheard-of practice at that time. The company advertised the soap with the slogans "It floats," and "99 and 44/100% pure." The company also used testimonials by customers to sell the product, along with premium offers and promotions. Ivory became a huge success.

The growing company was a pioneer in employee relations. William Cooper Procter, grandson of the founder, worked his way through the company from the bottom, acquiring special insight into the employees' feelings about their employer. It was this insight that led P&G to give employees Saturday afternoons off, with pay (in 1885). William Cooper Procter instituted the first profit-sharing plan in an American company (1887), giving productive workers a percentage of the company's profits. The profit-sharing plan continued even after the company incorporated in 1890. P&G was the first to offer a comprehensive sickness/disability/retirement insurance package (1915) and one of the first to switch to an eight-hour day, five-day work week (by 1933).

Procter & Gamble worked steadily to improve its soaps and develop new products such as White Naptha and later Chipso and Oxydol, laundry detergents developed for the newly invented washing machine. Research led to the use of glycerin and cottonseed oil in place of animal fat in soap. New technology enabled researchers to turn liquid cottonseed oil into solids, and P&G quickly applied this hydrogenation process to the development of Crisco, an all-vegetable shortening for use in cooking. P&G applied its marketing expertise to promote the new product, which virtually changed the way America cooked.

Procter & Gamble was one of the first corporations to eliminate the middleman from its distribution process. In the early 1900s, P&G began to deal directly with store owners and retailers, to ensure that consumers would get fair prices at every store. Wholesalers (the middlemen) were angry that Procter & Gamble would not deal with them and boycotted the company's products, but in the end P&G won. The company built its first international factory in 1915. By then, the company was earning annual profits exceeding $1 million.

The innovative company naturally took advantage of the tremendous advertising potential of radio. The first shows sponsored by Crisco were broadcast in 1923. P&G sponsored daytime serials for its many soap products; the serials soon became known as "soaps." The company also sponsored the "soaps" when they moved to television in the 1940s. It now spends more than $450 million on network-television advertising.

Procter & Gamble continued its research to find new products to meet the changing needs of the American consumer. Tide laundry detergent answered housewives' need for a detergent that would clean clothes made from synthetic materials. Tide was soon outselling the company's own Oxydol detergent. P&G followed Tide's success with Cheer, Dash, Bold 3, Era, and Liquid Tide to meet the changing needs and wants of consumers.

The company expanded into shampoos with products like Prell and Drene and developed the Lilt home permanent. Procter & Gamble entered the toothpaste market with Gleem in 1953. Researchers discovered a combination of ingredients to make an anti-tooth-decay toothpaste in the 1950s, and P&G used those ingredients to develop Crest soon after. P&G accomplished another first when the American Dental Association put its stamp of approval on Crest, the first product endorsed by the ADA. P&G made the most of that endorsement, and Crest quickly became the best-selling toothpaste in America. P&G continued to improve Crest over the years and introduced the Tartar Control version in 1985.

The list of successful Procter & Gamble products seems endless. The company currently sells eighty-two brands in the United States and more than one hundred overseas. Today, P&G concentrates its research in the health field and hopes to introduce a low-calorie, cholesterol-free fat substitute that it calls Olestra. The new product could once again revolutionize the American diet. Such innovation has always characterized the 150-year-old company in its search for excellence. Procter & Gamble prides itself on being a producer of the highest-quality products, and it continues to spend millions of dollars on improving those products and introducing new ones to meet the needs of a rapidly changing society.

---

These facts are from Laurie Freeman, "The House That Ivory Built," *Advertising Age*, August 20, 1987, pp. 4–14, 162–200; *Procter & Gamble: Celebrating 150 Years of Excellence*, Procter & Gamble, 1987; 1987 Procter & Gamble Annual Report; "People & Products," Procter & Gamble, 1980; R. Craig Endicott, "Where Those Ad Dollars Go," *Advertising Age*, August 20, 1987, p. 134; and Zachary Schiller, "Procter & Gamble Goes on a Health Kick," *Business Week*, June 29, 1987, pp. 90–92.

### Questions

1. Compare the development of Procter & Gamble in the early years with today's new entrepreneurs. Is it more difficult to start a new business today?
2. How did the expansion and development of the American economy help Procter & Gamble grow?
3. What has Procter & Gamble contributed to the American economy?

## Case 2-2
### *America's Excellent Companies*

Although American business acquired a reputation for low-quality goods and poor service in the 1970s and 1980s, there are excellent American companies that pride themselves on high quality goods and services, excellent customer and employee relations, as well as high profits. Who are these companies? According to *In Search of Excellence* (Tom Peters and Robert Waterman), *Fortune* magazine, and other business journals, some of America's excellent companies include Merck, Rubbermaid, Dow Jones, Procter & Gamble, Liz

Claiborne, 3M, Phillip Morris, J.P. Morgan, RJR Nabisco, Wal-Mart, IBM, Digital Equipment Corp., L.L. Bean, American Express, McDonald's, Johnson & Johnson, and Hewlett-Packard. This is *not* to say that other American companies are not excellent, but rather that these are the businesses that are lauded year after year for high standards in quality and service; excellent relations with customers, suppliers, and employees; innovation; financial soundness and value as an investment; and high profits.

What makes these companies excellent? They take extraordinary efforts to hire the right people, to train and to motivate them and then they give those people the authority to do their jobs well. They ask their customers to rate the quality of their service so that they can continue to improve it. They invest in technology to support customer service and they keep enough supplies on hand to meet customer and employee needs. Many involve customers in the product development process to ensure that products do what customers need them to do.

According to *In Search of Excellence,* America's excellent companies are guided by eight principles:

1. A bias for action—when something needs to be done, these companies do it and then get on with business. They do not produce thousands of pages of analyses on the nature of the problem and its development, they simply solve the problem. When a problem surfaces, such as declining sales or an increase in bad debts, the company works on the problem until it is resolved.

2. Close relationships with customers—these companies recognize that customers are their sole reason for existence and treat them well. They find out what consumers need and want, and they make the product or service that answers those needs and wants. The excellent companies offer a high degree of service. IBM, for example, trains its employees to stay close to customers with regular sales calls and follow-up visits. It also measures customer satisfaction monthly to see how good a job it is doing.

3. Autonomy and entrepreneurship for employees—excellent companies break down into small groups and encourage these groups to be independent, creative, and competitive. These groups are often motivated by a volunteer champion who fires up group members and insulates them from corporate pressures. Procter & Gamble is organized by brands and competition between Procter & Gamble brands is intense. At Hewlett-Packard and 3M, groups are given autonomy to create and develop new ideas.

4. Productivity through people—these companies know that their success comes from their employees. They recognize that employees are people with needs, wants, and valuable ideas and therefore treat them with trust, respect, and dignity. Most importantly, these companies tell their employees what is going on in the company. IBM, Hewlett-Packard, Wal-Mart, McDonald's and the other excellent companies regularly ask employees to contribute their ideas for improving production, sales, and all other aspects of the business. But they don't stop there: They also implement the employees' suggestions.

5. Hands-on, value-driven management—excellent companies clearly state what they stand for and what business they are in. They are guided by a set of carefully chosen values, such as being the best or having the best quality,

that are shared by everyone in the organization. These values are communicated through stories and legends, like the ones American Express tells about its emphasis on helping customers no matter what the cost.

6. Sticking to businesses they know—excellent companies stick with businesses they understand and stay away from ones they don't. 3M, for example, although it makes a huge variety of products, makes only products that use a basic coating and bonding technology. Procter & Gamble sticks to basic household products and John Deere makes only farm equipment.

7. Simple, lean organizations—these companies have the simplest organization possible, allowing them to respond quickly to changes in the market, while companies that have complicated organizations must wait for information to move up through the chain of command and then wait for a decision to move down the chain of command. Moreover, the excellent companies push authority down into the lowest ranks of the company.

8. Loose-tight organizations—excellent companies are rigidly controlled by their values and their focus on customers, yet they allow autonomy, entrepreneurship, creativity, and competition. The tightness ensures that the company does things right, but the looseness allows the company to grow and move quickly.

Most companies do some of these things described by Peters and Waterman; only excellent companies do all of them. What really stands out most about the excellent companies, however, is that they focus on people: customers and employees, not products, reports and memos, or equipment. And what is most amazing about the excellent companies' efforts, which often cost a great deal of money, is that they are among the most profitable companies in the nation because customers not only like them, but they also buy their products and services.

---

These facts are from Ellen Schultz, "America's Most Admired Corporations," *Fortune,* January 18, 1988, pp. 32–52; Bro Uttal, "Companies That Serve You Best," *Fortune,* December 7, 1987, pp. 98–116; H. John Steinbreder, "Products of the Year," *Fortune,* December 7, 1987, pp. 120–125; George Russell, with Meg Grant and William Szonski, "Where the Customer Is Still King," *Time,* February 2, 1987, pp. 56–60; Stephen Koepp, with Jay Branegan, Lawrence Malkin, and Edwin M. Reingold, "Pul-leeze! Will Somebody Help Me?" *Time,* February 2, 1987, pp. 46–55; Thomas Peters and Robert Waterman, *In Search of Excellence* (New York: Warner Books, 1982).

### Questions

1. Why do you think that L. L. Bean and McDonald's are two of America's excellent companies?
2. Why is close contact with customers and autonomy for employees so important? How are these ideas related?
3. Why are the excellent companies in this case the most profitable companies?

# Answers to Checking Your Understanding

1. competition
2. human resources
3. socialist
4. capitalist
5. monopoly
6. economic system

7. demand
8. inflation
9. communist
10. supply
11. federal deficit

## Outline

# Chapter 3

# Ethics and Social Responsibility

## Objectives

After reading this chapter, you will be able to:

▶ Define ethics and understand ethical issues in business.

▶ Understand the impact of different moral philosophies on decision making in business.

▶ Understand how businesses can change the organizational environment to promote ethical behavior by employees.

▶ Define social responsibility and trace the evolution of the concept.

▶ Discuss four business approaches to social responsibility.

▶ Explain the effect of social audits on a company's social responsibility agenda.

# Business Experience

In addition to its famous chocolates, the Swiss-based Nestlé S.A. also makes an infant formula to substitute for a mother's milk. Nestlé sells most of this formula in Third World countries because of the rising birthrates there. The formula comes in a powdered form and must be mixed with water before it is bottle-fed to an infant. The problems Nestlé faced as a result of marketing this formula taught them and many other companies some valuable lessons about public opinion, ethics, and social responsibility.

In the 1970s, several health and consumer groups accused Nestlé and other companies that market infant formulas of contributing to the high rate of infant deaths in Third World nations. Nestlé was singled out because it held the largest share of the infant formula market in those countries. Critics questioned Nestlé's marketing of the formula in Third World countries where many consumers had poor sanitation and little or no health care, and were largely illiterate. As a result, mothers often mixed the formula with contaminated water, put it in unsterile containers, or diluted it to make it last longer. Each of these practices contributed to the high rate of infant mortality.

Nestlé was criticized for aggressively promoting their infant formula in Third World countries. Radio, billboards, vans with loudspeakers, and direct customer contact were all used to promote the product. Nestlé directed its promotional efforts to physicians and other health care personnel in addition to consumers. Perhaps the most controversial charge involved Nestlé's use of so-called milk nurses—nurses, nutritionists, and midwives employed by Nestlé to visit mothers and give out free samples of the formula. Critics charged that the milk nurses were actually saleswomen. In addition, critics said this practice took advantage of the naivete of Third World consumers easily influenced by someone wearing a nurse's uniform. Finally, critics charged that Nestlé's advertising encouraged mothers to stop breast-feeding by portraying it as primitive and inconvenient.

Public emotions continued to heat up, and in 1977 consumer groups began boycotting all Nestlé products, not just the formula. Other groups joined the boycott, which spread to nine countries by 1982.

Finally, Nestlé worked with the World Health Organization, UNICEF, and various consumer groups to establish the WHO Code of Marketing of Breastmilk Substitutes and in 1984 agreed to support the code. Nestlé agreed to halt several marketing practices, including advertising the formula to the general public, using milk nurses, and distributing free samples (except under special circumstances). The company revised the wording on labels and educational materials to clearly state the dangers of using infant formulas incorrectly, and assert that breast-feeding is always preferable to the use of a formula. Most groups ended their boycott because of Nestlé's work on and support of the code.

Nestlé estimated the boycott cost the company nearly $40 million in lost revenue. The loss was probably far greater than this, because the sales of all Nestlé products, not just the formula, were affected. It may take Nestlé many years to recover from the loss in public faith, and the company will have to monitor its activities more carefully. Nestlé learned the hard way that society expects business to act in an ethical and socially responsible manner.

These facts are from "Nestlé's Infant Formula: The Consequences of Spurning the Public Image," in *Marketing Mistakes*, 3rd ed., ed. Robert F. Hartley (Columbus, Ohio: Grid Publishing Co., 1986): 47–61; "The Dilemma of Third World Nutrition: Nestlé and the Role of Infant Formula," a report prepared for Nestlé S.A. by Maggie McComas, Geoffrey Fookes, and George Taucher, Nestlé S.A., 1983; "Nestlé and the Role of Infant Formula in Developing Countries: The Resolution of a Conflict," a series of reports, articles, and press releases provided by Nestlé Coordination Center for Nutrition, Inc., 1984; and the 1983 Nestlé Annual Report.

# Introduction

Highly publicized instances of questionable conduct ranging from insider trading scandals on Wall Street to mismanagement of funds by religious organizations underscore the importance of ethics and social responsibility in business. Business has come under scrutiny because of recent exposed episodes of deception, corruption, and illegality.

This chapter is an overview of the role of ethics and social responsibility in business decision making. Ethical beliefs provide a standard against which the decisions and behavior of individuals and organizations can be evaluated. One aim of this chapter is to provide some understanding of how ethical decisions are made. Closely related to the subject of business ethics is the concept of social responsibility in business—the obligation of business to anticipate how its decisions will affect society as a whole and the impact on various individuals and groups within society, not just on owners and stockholders. Socially responsible businesses consider issues that extend far beyond financial returns. Individuals in all groups, not just the owners, employees, and customers, are affected by businesses' sense of ethics and social responsibility.

# ▶ Business Ethics Defined

**Ethics**

The study of morals and moral choices

A high ethical standard requires organizations and individuals to aspire to succeed in accordance with sound moral philosophies—that is, to ground their behavior on principles of fairness, justice and trust.[1] **Ethics** is the study of morals and moral choices. It focuses on standards, rules, and codes of conduct that govern the behavior of individuals and groups. In simplest terms, business ethics are moral principles that define right and wrong behavior in the world of business. What constitutes right and wrong behavior in business is determined by the public, interest groups, and business organizations, as well as an individual's personal morals and values.

Ethical considerations influence all business decisions. Although people in business often act in their economic self-interest, ethical business relationships are grounded on fairness, justice, and trust. Buyers should be able to trust sellers; lenders should be able to trust borrowers. Ethical violations destroy trust and make the continuation of business exchanges difficult, if not impossible.[2]

A national survey found that most senior business executives believe that people are occasionally unethical in their business dealings (Figure 3-1). Heavily publicized cases involving well-known organizations only strengthen the perception that ethical standards in business need to be raised. Eastern Airlines, for example, was fined $9.5 million for 78,372 safety violations.[3] The 1987 football season at Southern Methodist University was cancelled because of violations that occurred while the university was already on probabion for paying players. When customers whose Bic lighters had

**Figure 3-1**

A Question of Ethics.
Source: McFeeley Wackerle
Jett, Public Relations, 1987, Chicago IL

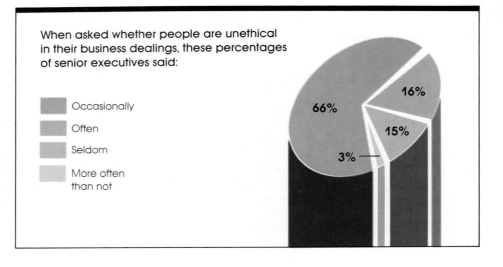

When asked whether people are unethical in their business dealings, these percentages of senior executives said:

- Occasionally
- Often
- Seldom
- More often than not

66%  16%  15%  3%

exploded because of a condition known as after-burn sued the Bic Corporation, the company admitted it had been aware of the problem but had marketed the lighters anyway.[4] In Texas, some companies are selling plastic "Caco-Calo" and "Diet-Pipsi" labels to disguise beer cans to permit drivers to evade open-container laws that prohibit drinking while driving in Texas.[5] The labels are not illegal, but their manufacture and sale do raise ethical questions because the labels allow people to flout the law and drive under the influence of alcohol (not to mention the possibility of trademark infringements against Coca-Cola and PepsiCo).

Such examples support the notion that most business decisions can be characterized as right or wrong, ethical or unethical. In the case of Eastern, safety and proper maintenance inspections might have required the airline to increase fares, yet passengers would probably rather pay higher fares than fly on unsafe airplanes. Performing the safety inspections when necessary and as required by law would have been the most ethical course of action.

# ▶ Ethical Issues

## Conflict of Interest

**Bribes**

Personal payments, gifts, or special favors granted improperly to influence the outcome of a decision.

A conflict of interest exists when an individual is in the position of having to decide whether to advance the interests of the business or to operate in his or her own personal interests. In an ethical environment, employees scrupulously separate their private financial interests from their business dealings. They do not accept **bribes**—personal payments, gifts, or special favors granted improperly, to influence the outcome of a decision.

**Protecting the environment is expensive but necessary.**   These trees in Mt. Mitchell, North Carolina have been destroyed by acid rain. While businesses have begun to respond by spending billions of dollars on anti-pollution devices, it will cost billions more to fit all power plants with pollution-control devices.

## Fairness and Honesty

At a minimum, businesspersons are expected to follow all applicable laws and regulations. But beyond obeying the law, they are expected not to knowingly harm customers, clients, and competitors through deception, misrepresentation, or coercion. For example, in the advertising business, it has become a fairly common practice to "bury" certain expenses in charging a client. An advertising agency might charge client meals back to the client by adding their cost to production bills. The clients would probably agree that this is not fair or honest behavior.

## Communications

False and misleading advertising or promotion, as well as deceptive personal-selling tactics, can cause a business to collapse and angers consumers. Communications about the safety of products and about business activities such as pollution control is another important issue. The U.S. Surgeon General currently requires cigarette manufacturers to clearly indicate on cigarette packaging that smoking cigarettes is harmful to the smoker's health. Many consumers would like to see similar warnings on alcoholic beverages as well. In an ethical environment, every aspect of the product, from pricing to promotion to the product itself must be handled in an honest and forthright manner.

Lying may be a significant problem in the United States. A national poll revealed that people believe they are lied to not only by politicians and car mechanics but also by their spouses, doctors, and best friends, among others (Figure 3-2).

# Relationships Within a Business

**Plagiarism**

Taking someone else's work and presenting it as one's own without mentioning the source

Ethical issues within a business have to do with maintaining confidentiality, meeting obligations and responsibilities, and avoiding undue pressure that may force others to behave unethically. **Plagiarism**—taking someone else's work and presenting it as one's own without mentioning the source—is another problem.

People can always find opportunities to maximize their personal welfare in a way that hurts others or the organization. One way to evaluate whether a specific behavior is acceptable is to ask other individuals in the business if they approve of it. Another way is to see whether the company has a specific policy on the activity. An activity approved of by most individuals in the organization and customary in the industry is likely to be ethical. A rule of thumb for identifying an ethical decision is that the decision will withstand open discussion and survive untarnished. Openness does not eliminate ethical problems, but it does promote both trust and learning in the organization.[6]

Managers should set an example and provide leadership in solving ethical problems. They must carefully introduce employees to any situation that is different from normal and that poses an ethical dilemma. Managers should determine who will be affected and give employees an opportunity to adapt or to change through ethically acceptable behavior.

**Figure 3-2**

Beliefs About the Truthfulness of Others. Research of 1,006 adults from February 6–9, 1987. There is a four-point margin of error. Some figures may not add up because some respondents did not respond.
Source: *U.S. News & World Report,* February 23, 1987.

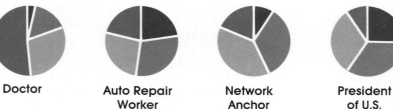

# ▶ Understanding Ethical Decision Making

Ethical issues arise out of everyday business decisions. An individual's personal beliefs and the moral atmosphere of the organization in which one works significantly affect the behavior one exhibits. Moral philosophies, organizational relationships, and opportunity influence behavior, as does the organizational environment (Figure 3-3).

## The Role of Moral Philosophies in Decision Making

**Moral Philosophy**

A set of principles setting forth what is believed to be the right way to behave

Something that is moral conforms to a standard of acceptability. A philosophy is a study of the general principles of a subject, such as morality. In essence, then, a **moral philosophy** is a set of principles setting forth what is believed to be the right way to behave. Individuals learn these principles through socialization by family members, social groups, and formal education.

**Utilitarian philosophy**

Seeking the greatest satisfaction for the largest number of individuals

Moral philosophies can be broken down into two categories: utilitarian and humanistic. Believers in the **utilitarian philosophy** seek the greatest satisfaction for the largest number of individuals, or, as Mr. Spock said in *The Wrath of Khan* (*Star Trek II*), "The needs of the many outweigh the needs of the few . . . or the one." The utilitarian philosophy is illustrated by actions

**Figure 3-3**

Factors Influencing Behavior

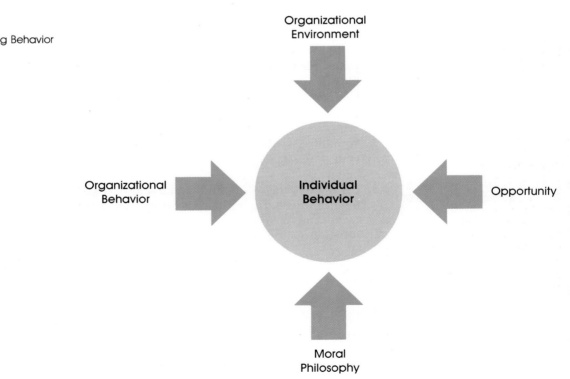

taken by the Johns-Manville Corporation. Many years ago, top executives of the company decided to conceal from their employees the fact that asbestos, the firm's principle product, causes disease and death. When the matter came to light, a California court said the company had hidden the danger rather than find a safe way to deal with it. Johns-Manville's justification was that the public benefits provided by asbestos outweighed the health consequences to a few employees. The company found that paying workers' compensation claims was less costly than making working conditions safe for employees.[7] Of course, presenting the health issue to the employees would have been the most ethical way to deal with the problem.

**Humanistic philosophy**

Focuses on human rights and values and asserts the dignity and worth of the individual

Believers in the **humanistic philosophy** focus on human rights and values and assert the dignity and worth of the individual. A business grounded in the humanistic viewpoint believes it has a moral obligation to safeguard workers' health and safety and makes these decisions to support individual rights without regard for the cost. A company's decision to avoid discrimination in hiring is based on humanistic principles of equality.

Because moral philosophies provide standards that help people make decisions, managers want to know how employees acquire their beliefs. Managers also want to know how these beliefs may be altered to ensure that ethical behavior is congruent with management's goals. Lawrence Kohlberg's model for cognitive moral development sheds some light on how individual ethical decision making occurs within a business organization.

Within an organization individuals react to the same situation differently because they are at different stages of moral development. In Kohlberg's model there are three broad stages of moral development:

**Preconventional stage**

The individual is concerned with his or her immediate interests and external rewards and punishments

1. **Preconventional stage:** The individual, like a young child, is concerned with his or her immediate interests and with external rewards and punishments. Inside traders on Wall Street are interested only in immediate payoffs.

**Conventional stage**

The individual believes that right is that which society or a significant reference group defines as proper

2. **Conventional stage:** The individual believes right is that which society or a significant reference group defines as good behavior. When you visit someone's home for the first time, you probably don't put your feet on your host's coffee table, not because you fear punishment but because your parents taught you that putting your feet on the furniture is improper behavior.

**Principled stage**

The individual sees beyond norms, law, or authority to determine what is right or ethical

3. **Principled stage:** The individual sees beyond norms, law, or authority to determine what is right or ethical. People who follow the Golden Rule, for example, treat others as they want to be treated themselves. This humanistic approach is the highest level of moral development:[8]

As individuals pass through these stages, their awareness of and concern about ethical behavior increases.

# Organizational Dimensions of Ethical Behavior

Individual decisions about how to react to daily issues are fundamentally ethical decisions. Managers are successful to the extent that they achieve the company's objectives. If the pressure to produce a result, such as increasing profits, is especially great on subordinates, the pressure to perform is also especially great. Whether an employee responds in an ethical or unethical fashion depends in part on the moral climate of the organization.

Individuals learn values, attitudes, and norms from members of various groups with which they are associated. Each group may have its own norms, values, and attitudes. A person often learns ethical or unethical behavior while interacting with friends or colleagues in social groups. The more an individual is exposed to ethical behavior, the greater is the likelihood that the individual's behavior will be ethical. Conversely, the greater the exposure to unethical behavior, the greater the likelihood that the individual will behave unethically. Employees' perception of the ethics of their peers (the people they work with on an equal basis) and of top management is often a stronger predictor of behavior than what employees believe to be right or wrong.[9] An employee who sees a coworker inflate an expense account is likely to do the same even though he or she believes this action to be unethical.

The authority of an employee's superiors also has an impact on behavior. Powerful superiors can affect an employee's day-to-day activities and directly influence behavior by putting into practice the company's standard of ethics.

## How Opportunity Influences Ethical Behavior

Opportunity is a set of conditions that limit unfavorable behavior or reward favorable behavior. The rewards may be internal or external. Internal rewards are feelings of goodness and worth, like the feeling you get when you do something nice for a neighbor without expecting anything in return. External rewards are tangible. An individual receives an external reward in exchange for a service, idea, or product. The external reward could be a raise at work.

An individual who is rewarded (internally or externally) or is not punished for unethical behavior is likely to repeat the behavior. A person who receives no reward, or is punished for behaving unethically probably will not repeat the action. The greater the reward and the less the punishment for unethical behavior, the greater is the likelihood that unethical behavior will reoccur. Opportunity to engage in unethical behavior has been found to be a better indicator of unethical behavior than personal beliefs or the beliefs of peers.[10]

Continental Illinois Bank (CIB) got into financial trouble because of unethical lending practices and nearly went out of business. Investigators learned that a bank officer who had taken a kickback by borrowing money for himself while securing loans for CIB had merely been reprimanded by his superiors.[11] This weak punishment sent a message to other bank employees that such actions would be tolerated in the interest of increasing profits, and it may have encouraged unethical behavior by other officers, contributing to CIB's legal and financial problems.

**Codes of ethics**

Statements of ethics-related corporate policy

Professional **codes of ethics** and statements of ethics-related corporate policy help limit the opportunity factor. These codes represent the company's expectations of its employees. The enforcement of such codes and policies through the use of rewards and punishments increases the acceptance of ethical standards by employees. Figure 3-4 is a summary of the code of ethics adopted by the American Marketing Association.

**Figure 3-4**

American Marketing Association's Code of Ethics. Source: American Marketing Association

**Code of Ethics**
**AMERICAN MARKETING ASSOCIATION**

**CODE OF ETHICS**

Members of the American Marketing Association (AMA) are committed to ethical professional conduct. They have joined together in subscribing to this Code of Ethics embracing the following topics:

**Responsibilities of the Marketer**

Marketers must accept responsibility for the consequences of their activities and make every effort to ensure that their decisions, recommendations, and actions function to identify, serve, and satisfy all relevant publics: customers, organizations and society.

Marketers' professional conduct must be guided by:
1. The basic rule of professional ethics: not knowingly to do harm;
2. The adherence to all applicable laws and regulations;
3. The accurate representation of their education, training and experience; and
4. The active support, practice and promotion of this Code of Ethics.

**Honesty and Fairness**

Marketers shall uphold and advance the integrity, honor, and dignity of the marketing profession by:
1. Being honest in serving consumers, clients, employees, suppliers, distributors and the public;
2. Not knowingly participating in conflict of interest without prior notice to all parties involved; and
3. Establishing equitable fee schedules including the payment or receipt of usual, customary and/or legal compensation for marketing exchanges.

**Rights and Duties of Parties in the Marketing Exchange Process**

Participants in the marketing exchange process should be able to expect that:
1. Products and services offered are safe and fit for their intended uses;
2. Communications about offered products and services are not deceptive;
3. All parties intend to discharge their obligations, financial and otherwise, in good faith; and
4. Appropriate internal methods exist for equitable adjustment and/or redress of grievances concerning purchases.

It is understood that the above would include, *but is not limited to,* the following responsibilities of the marketer:

**In the area of product development and management,**
- disclosure of all substantial risks associated with product or service usage;

- identification of any product component substitution that might materially change the product or impact on the buyer's purchase decision;
- identification of extra-cost added features.

**In the area of promotions,**
- avoidance of false and misleading advertising;
- rejection of high pressure manipulations, or misleading sales tactics;
- avoidance of sales promotions that use deception or manipulation.

**In the area of distribution,**
- not manipulating the availability of a product for purpose of exploitation;
- not using coercion in the marketing channel;
- not exerting undue influence over the resellers choice to handle a product.

**In the area of pricing,**
- not engaging in price fixing;
- not practicing predatory pricing;
- disclosing the full price associated with any purchase.

**In the area of marketing research,**
- prohibiting selling or fund raising under the guise of conducting research;
- maintaining research integrity by avoiding misrepresentation and omission of pertinent research data;
- treating outside clients and suppliers fairly.

**Organizational Relationships**

Marketers should be aware of how their behavior may influence or impact on the behavior of others in organizational relationships. They should not demand, encourage or apply coercion to obtain unethical behavior in their relationships with others, such as employees, suppliers or customers.
1. Apply confidentiality and anonymity in professional relationships with regard to privileged information;
2. Meet their obligations and responsibilities in contracts and mutual agreements in a timely manner;
3. Avoid taking the work of others, in whole, or in part, and represent this work as their own or directly benefit from it without compensation or consent of the originator or owner;
4. Avoid manipulation to take advantage of situations to maximize personal welfare in a way that unfairly deprives or damages the organization or others.

Any AMA members found to be in violation of any provision of this Code of Ethics may have his or her Association membership suspended or revoked.

# Top Management and Codes of Ethics Can Improve Behavior

There is evidence that businesses are beginning to set standards and establish ethical principles to be implemented within the organizations. One reason businesses have been slow to consider ethical principles in their decision making is the lack of understanding of how managers develop their moral philosophies. Robert Lomon, chairman of E. F. Hutton (now owned by Shearson Lehman Hutton) once said, "I never thought ethics was something that could be formally taught. I thought ethics was something you learned growing up at home, in school and in church."[12] In fact, Lomon learned the hard way that ethics is something that top management must be concerned about on a daily basis. In 1985 his company pleaded guilty to two thousand counts of fraud as a result of check overdrafts. Some executives thought they were doing E. F. Hutton a favor by increasing profits through the overdraft scheme.[13]

Businesses establish codes of ethics and corporate policies on ethics to foster ethical decision making by reducing the opportunity for unethical activity. Enforcement of corporate policies is a common way of dealing with ethical problems. A survey by the Center for Business Ethics at Bentley College indicated that 80 percent of the *Fortune* Top 1000 industrial and service companies are incorporating ethical values and concerns into their daily operations. Of those companies, 93 percent have written codes of ethics to govern the actions of their employees.[14] Business codes of ethics, however, stress some things, such as conflicts of interest and accurate recordkeeping, and are more likely to put less emphasis on such issues as product safety and product quality. Table 3-1 summarizes the findings of a study of 202 corporate codes of conduct. Topics listed in the lefthand column were included in at least 75 percent of the codes; those listed in the righthand column were not present in at least 75 percent of the codes.

The establishment of corporate policies and codes of ethics helps employees understand what is expected of them. Understanding how individuals choose their standards of ethics, and what prompts a person to engage in unethical behavior may reverse the current trend toward unethical activity in business.

People learn ethical behavior from interacting with individuals in social, business, and other groups. Thus, businesses should examine their structure to see how policies, rewards and punishments affect ethical behavior. Without uniform policies and standards, employees have difficulty determining what is acceptable behavior in the company. Without company-wide standards for behavior, employees generally base ethical decisions on their observations of peers and management.

To encourage ethical behavior, top management needs to eliminate opportunities for unethical behavior and formalize rules and operating procedures. Codes of ethics are formal statements of what the company expects of its employees. Within the organization, they tend to eliminate opportunity because employees know what is expected of them and what the punishment will be if they engage in unethical behavior. Allied-Signal, Inc., has taken steps to enforce its corporate policies on ethics, as Business Encounter 3-1 illustrates.

If a company is to maintain ethical behavior, its policies, rules, and standards must be worked into its control system. Reducing unethical behavior is a business goal no different from increasing profits. The business sets a goal—achieving greater ethical behavior among company employees—and measures the outcome. If the number of employees making ethical decisions on a regular basis is not increasing, the company needs to determine why and take corrective action through stronger enforcement of current standards and policies or by strengthening the standards and policies themselves. Ethical behavior occurs only when a plan is developed and successfully implemented.

# ▶ Social Responsibility

Surveys conducted by Roper, Gallup, Harris, and Opinion Research indicate that the public's opinion of business is at the lowest point ever.[15] Americans are unhappy with business because of unethical behavior, and because business

**Table 3.1  What business codes of ethical conduct stress.**
Source: M. Cash Mathews, "Codes of Ethics: Organizational Behavior and Misbehavior," in *Research in Corporate Social Performance and Policy,* ed. by William C. Frederick (Greenwich, CT: JAI Press Inc., 1987): 107–130.

| Included | Frequency | Not Included | Frequency |
|---|---|---|---|
| Relations with U.S. government | 86.6% | Personal character matters | 93.6% |
| Customer/supplier relations | 86.1 | Product safety | 91.0 |
| Political Contributions | 84.7 | Environmental affairs | 87.1 |
| Conflicts of interest | 75.3 | Product quality | 78.7 |
| Honest books or records | 75.3 | Civic and community affairs | 75.2 |

has failed to take responsibility for activities that have led to pollution, dangerous products, false information, and inequality in the work force. They feel that business should not only make a profit but should consider the social implications of its activities.

**Social responsibility** is the obligation a business assumes to maximize its positive impact and minimize its negative impact on society. Most companies today consider the implementation of socially responsible actions a cost of doing business. It may be cheap and easy to dump waste chemicals into a river, but the long-term costs of doing so may far exceed the short-term savings.

In general, a business has two main responsibilities. The first is to obey the law. The second is to earn profits to continue operations, pay employees, and provide a return to owners and stockholders. Management and owners must keep these two factors in mind when they address social responsibility issues.

**Social responsibility**

The obligation a business assumes to maximize its positive impact and minimize its negative impact on society

# The Nature of Social Responsibility

Consumers actually vote for products and companies when they make a purchase. If a product is priced fairly, satisfies their needs and has no negative side effects, they will probably buy it more than once. But if the product fails or has negative side effects, they will probably select another product and may become so angry at the manufacturer that they never purchase another of their products. Consumers can vote against firms that pollute the environment or engage in unfair employment practices by not buying their products. Declining sales send a quick message to the business that it is not satisfying the consumer; most businesses will want to know why so they can resolve the problem.

A business whose sole objective is to maximize profitability is not likely to act out of a sense of social responsibility, although its activity will probably be legal. A business that says it is concerned about society as well as about maintaining profitability is likely to invest voluntarily in socially responsible activities. For example, the former president of Pizza Hut, Orr Gunther, implemented a program called "Book-it." This program rewarded children with a free personal-pan pizza for reading a certain number of books. Such a business may win the trust and respect of its customers and of society in general by implementing such a program and in the long run increase profits.

# Business Encounter 3-1
## *Ethics At Allied-Signal, Inc.*

As a result of the increasing awareness of ethics in the 1980s, many businesses want to make sure their employees know how to handle ethical dilemmas. Allied-Signal Inc., was concerned about how its employees would deal with such dilemmas and has taken steps to provide them with guidelines for handling questionable situations. The company holds seminars to illustrate to employees the kinds of situations they may find themselves in when doing business. Ethics is also addressed in the company's executive development programs at the firm, which manufactures a variety of aerospace, automotive, and engineered materials products. In addition, some six thousand managers, and employees working in sensitive areas were asked to agree in writing to Allied-Signal's "Proper Business Practices," which cover everything from conflicts of interest to questionable or improper payments.

In 1987, the company took a close look at its policies to find ways to improve their effectiveness. It has issued an ethical behavior guideline manual for *all* Allied-Signal employees. The manual points out that employees are responsible for bringing violations of ethical policy to the attention of their managers, who, in turn, are responsible for taking whatever action is necessary.

The company does more than just write manuals and policies on ethical behavior, however. It also punishes employees who do not behave in accordance with Allied-Signal's ethical guidelines. An employee is caught stealing, for example, is fired, and the company cooperates with law enforcement officers to prosecute the guilty employee. A manager who worked with representatives of foreign customers was caught accepting a bribe from a foreign government. He was fired and Allied-Signal took action to prevent similar incidents. A clerk who was caught embezzling lost her job and was prosecuted.

Why is Allied-Signal so concerned about ethics? The company realizes that unethical conduct is a constant problem, especially in large, competitive, international organizations. Because the company values its reputation, it established policies for conduct, and it enforced them. Moreover, Allied-Signal is a U.S. government defense contractor and must abide by the rules and regulations imposed on it by the federal government. The company also wants to be sure new employees who join the firm when a new contract is awarded understand the code of conduct. One of the company's goals is that all employees "behave honestly for honesty's sake."

Allied-Signal's code of ethics spells out employees' obligations and encourages employees to report violations of the code. Allied-Signal takes its ethical responsibilities seriously and expects its employees to do so too.

---

These facts are from "Best Behavior," *OMNIA* (the quarterly magazine of Allied-Signal, Inc.), (Winter 1986): 16–17.

## Groups That Evaluate Social Responsibility

Many groups examine business practices and evaluate them on the basis of different sets of criteria:

▶ Owners, investors, and management examine business practices and base their evaluation on profitability, cost and rate of return.
▶ Customers base their evaluation of business practices on long- and short-term satisfaction.
▶ Employees are concerned with hiring procedures, on-the-job safety, fair compensation and opportunities for advancement.
▶ Local, state, and national government and regulatory systems use both existing and potential laws to monitor business practices.

**Maintaining a social conscience.**   Ronald McDonald, New York Governor Mario Cuomo, and Ed Rense, president of McDonald's U.S.A., cut the ribbon for the 100th Ronald McDonald House. By committing its resources to the Ronald McDonald House program, McDonald's gives back something to the communities in which it does business.

▶ Special-interest groups are concerned about the impact of business practices on public health, workers' safety, and pollution.
▶ Competitors are concerned about how business practices affect freedom and fairness in the marketplace.

Because these groups are able to speak out, their words and actions can have a strong impact upon the future of a business. A socially responsible business evaluates feedback received from all these public and private groups.

# ▶ Evolution of the Social Responsibility Concept

The social responsibility area has developed primarily over the past seventy years. Social responsibility, though, did not become a major concern to businesses and society as a whole until the 1950s and 1960s. The following text reviews the three eras in the development of social responsibility concepts:

the Industrial Revolution which caused an early recognition of the concept; the 1920s to 1950s which saw the preliminary enforcement and acceptance of social responsibility; and the 1950s to the present, the consumer era, which has been an era of increased responsibility taken by businesses without government's enforcement of such actions.

## The Industrial Revolution Causes Recognition of Social Responsibility

During the last half of the nineteenth century, the Industrial Revolution was a major force in business development. Electricity, rail transportation, the assembly line, and mass production improved the efficiency of manufacturing. As a result of new production techniques and the expansion of the railroads, products flooded into the marketplace, and consumer demand for manufactured goods rose. Working conditions reflected the ideas of scientific management; jobs became highly specialized, and pay was based on output. The standard work week often exceeded 60 hours, and employee benefits such as workers' compensation, sick pay, and paid vacations did not exist.

At this stage, businesses were largely responsible for defining how they would interact with society. The idea that business had a social responsibility was unheard of. Most businesses chose not to invest in pollution control, employee benefits, good working conditions, and safe products because the expenditures would increase costs and put products at a competitive disadvantage. Therefore, the rule for consumers was *caveat emptor*—let the buyer beware, which meant the consumer assumed all risks associated with using a product. Although consumers could take legal action against business because of unscrupulous activity or defective products, such action was expensive and the chances of winning slim. There were no government agencies to police businesses and hold them accountable for their actions. In addition, consumers were so anxious for the new products being manufactured that they did not want government intervention. However, as more and more competitors entered the marketplace, competition grew fierce and abuses continued until it seemed inevitable that the government would have to intervene to protect consumers and workers.

## Early Developments in Social Responsibility

Government regulation in the early 1900s was minimal. Nevertheless, most consumers believed that competition and general market activity would correct the abuses of the marketplace. With so many competitors and products in the marketplace, more than efficient production was needed to persuade customers to buy a product. From 1920 to 1950, businesses used aggressive sales methods to expand their profits. They believed that the best ways to inform consumers about products were personal selling and advertising. The Model T faced its first competition when Oldsmobile entered the marketplace, so Ford introduced more car models.

As the marketplace became increasingly competitive, however, the Congress passed laws to reduce the monopolistic tendencies of big business and forced

**A school uses the newspaper to good advantage.** In 1981 *The Chicago Tribune* adopted the Eugene Field School in Chicago through the city's Adopt-A-School program. Here a teacher uses the Tribune's food section to teach her students about nutrition. The *Tribune* has a Newspapers in Education program, which encourages students and teachers to use newspapers for information about topics ranging from geography and science to history and government.

companies to provide social services to individuals. Businesses gradually developed a sense of social responsibility when they realized that sales and efficient production alone would not increase profits. Businesses began to realize the need to develop identities on which to build their growing product lines.

## Social Responsibility Today

By the early 1950s, some businesspeople saw that efficient production and extensive promotion did not guarantee that consumers would buy their products. Finding that the key to increasing sales is to produce things that people want and need, businesses planned products to meet customers' needs. At the same time, employees were demanding better working conditions, and management and owners listened to them. Customers provided input about what products they wanted, and for the first time there was a public outcry for product safety and reliability.

# ► Social Responsibility Issues

Although social responsibility may seem an abstract ideal, managers consider it on a daily basis as they deal with real issues. A business must monitor changes and needs in society in order to behave in a socially responsible way.

Society expresses what it does not want in several ways. Lawmakers and regulatory groups attempt to prohibit and control undesired business practices. A wide variety of laws and guidelines relate to product safety, warranties, packaging, labeling, advertising, personal selling, and pricing, not to mention competitive and environmental issues. In addition to legal and regulatory forces, special-interest groups pressure business to achieve desired performance standards or to change certain ongoing activities.

To be successful, a business must determine what customers, employees, government regulators, and competitors, as well as society in general, want or expect in terms of social responsibility. Business must consider social responsibility issues such as consumerism, employment practices, and the environment. Social responsibility is a dynamic area because issues and desires of those affected by businesses activities are changing constantly.

## Consumerism

**Consumerism**

The activities undertaken by independent individuals, groups, and organizations to protect their rights as consumers

The activities undertaken by independent individuals, groups, and organizations to protect their rights as consumers are known as **consumerism**. Many of the desires of those involved in the consumer movement have a foundation in John F. Kennedy's consumer bill of rights, which highlighted four areas: the right to safety, the right to be informed, the right to choose, and the right to be heard. These four rights are the basis of much of the consumer legislation passed over the last three decades.

***The Right to Safety.*** To ensure product safety, business must not knowingly sell anything that could result in personal injury or harm to consumers. Defective or dangerous products erode public confidence in the ability of business to serve society. An automobile manufacturer, for example, was indicted on criminal charges for recklessly causing the death of three teenagers who died in the crash of a compact car. The jury in the case said that the manufacturer had been aware that the car's fuel tank was unsafe but had done nothing to solve the problem. Although that verdict was controversial—because the manufacturer had not actually caused the accident—it does illustrate that some members of society want businesses to assume an active role in providing safe products. Although the final ruling was in favor of the manufacturer, automobiles today may be safer because consumer groups protested so loudly about that unsafe automobile.

The right to safety means that a product must be safe for its intended use, must include thorough and explicit directions for use, and must have been properly tested to ensure reliability and quality. Federal regulatory agencies like the Food and Drug Administration and Consumer Product Safety Commission monitor safety issues in the manufacture and sale of products.

### The Right to Be Informed.

The right to be informed gives consumers the freedom to review complete information about a product before they buy. This means that detailed information about ingredients and instructions for use are to be printed on labels and packages. The right to be informed also applies to services. The true cost of borrowing money and repayment terms, for example, must be clearly stated in a contract.

Encouraged by aggressive consumer lobbying against smoking in public areas, forty-two states have imposed restrictions on lighting up in public areas. In recent years, more than sixty bills have been introduced in Congress to limit smokers' freedom. Non-smokers have become informed about the dangers of smoking and are pushing hard to enforce what they consider to be their right to clean air. In 1988, Northwest Airlines took advantage of the increasing interest in non-smokers rights and introduced smokeless flights on all Northwest planes. The Federal Aviation Administration has banned smoking on all flights that are less than two hours.

### The Right to Choose.

The right to choose ensures that consumers have access to a variety of products and services at competitive prices. The assurance of both satisfactory quality and service at a fair price is also a part of the consumer's right to choose. The right to choose means that competition is free to flourish. No company becomes so dominant that it limits consumers' opportunities to find new, improved products that provide better value.

There is some concern today that the increasing number of mergers among major companies are limiting the consumer's right to choose. Because of mergers in the airline industry, for example, travelers have fewer alternatives and may pay higher prices and receive poorer quality service than they would if competition were greater.

### The Right to Be Heard.

The right to be heard assures consumers that their interests will receive full and sympathetic consideration when the government formulates policy. It also assures the fair treatment of consumers who voice their complaints about a purchased product. Consumer concerns have been heard at the top levels of government because of the efforts of consumer advocates, such as Ralph Nader, who take it upon themselves to inform lawmakers about issues and problems important to consumers. In addition, many trade groups have been organized to process grievances so that consumers can appeal beyond a company if they are unable to resolve a problem with the manufacturer or provider of a service. Most businesses realize that one highly dissatisfied, vocal customer can have a widespread, negative impact on its image or reputation. Therefore, most businesses try very hard to reduce consumers' dissatisfaction and resolve their complaints.

## Employment Practices

Employees want to work in a safe environment; they want to know what is going on within their company; and they want employers to listen to their grievances. They also want to be paid adequately for their work, in the form of wages and benefits, and they want employers to treat them fairly.

***Safety and Management Issues.*** Congress has passed several laws regulating safety in the work place, and many of these laws are enforced by the Occupational Safety and Health Administration (OSHA). Labor unions have also made significant contributions to achieving safety in the work place and improving wages and benefits. Employers are beginning to realize the importance of obtaining input from even the lowest-level employees to help the company reach its objectives. Many corporations, such as General Motors and Procter & Gamble, are turning to participative management to get employees involved and make them care about the company's success.

***Equality Issues.*** Even though laws like the Civil Rights Act of 1964 require business to provide equal opportunities for employment regardless of sex, age, race, religion, or nationality, inequalities still exist. Women, blacks, Hispanics, and handicapped people typically earn less than white men, even when they have the same education and experience. The problem of inequality was dramatically illustrated in a profile of the CEOs of the *Business Week* Top

**IBM supports affirmative action.** IBM is helping more minority students become engineers. IBM supports the efforts of the National Action Council for Minorities in Engineering which provides scholarship funds, high school programs, and career guidance for prospective engineers.

Is this the only chance he'll have to be an engineer?

No one can say for sure. But the fact is, only 3 percent of today's engineering graduates are Black, and even fewer are Hispanic or American Indian.

One organization seeking to correct that imbalance is the National Action Council for Minorities in Engineering (NACME). Through scholarship funds, high school programs and career guidance, NACME encourages and supports minority students who want to become engineers.

Last year, NACME provided scholarship funding to nearly 4,000 students in 145 engineering schools nationwide.

IBM, along with other corporations, supports NACME in its efforts.

Through these efforts, more minority students are studying engineering. Which means more dreams of building bridges are becoming reality.

© Copyright IBM Corporation 1988. LEGO® is a registered trademark of INTERLEGO, A.G.

IBM

1000: no blacks were on the list of leaders of America's leading companies, and only two women were listed.[16] Women and minorities have traditionally been denied opportunities for experience in organizations that would enable them to assume leadership roles in corporate America.

Many businesses have instituted affirmative action programs to reduce these inequalities. Such programs try to improve employment opportunities for women and minorities. Affirmative action, however, has been accused of reverse discrimination because the programs sometimes force a company to consider only minorities or women in its hiring program, instead of concentrating on hiring the person who is best qualified. In an ideal world a business would always hire the person who is best qualified, without regard to race or sex; but because women and members of minority groups often lack qualifications for a position because of discrimination against them, affirmative action programs give them preferential treatment.

***Training the Hard-Core Unemployed.*** Social responsibility in employment practices sometimes requires a company to provide extra training to qualify people for employment. Some people who want to work do not have skills or have a history of chronic unemployment that keeps them from getting even low-level jobs. These people have traditionally depended on government welfare programs for survival. Organizations like the National Alliance of Businessmen fund programs to train the hard-core unemployed so that they can find jobs and support themselves. In addition to fostering self-support, such training opportunities enhance self-esteem, and help people become productive members of society.

# Environmental Issues

Consumers want not only a multitude of products that improve the quality of life but also a healthy environment so that they can maintain a high standard of living over their lifetimes. Responsible businesses and the government have made significant efforts to reduce various forms of **pollution** and conserve natural resources. Key environmental concerns about pollution relate to the contamination of water, air, and land.

**Pollution**

Contamination of water, air, and land through the actions of business, governments, individuals, and other groups

***Water Pollution.*** Water pollution results from the dumping of toxic chemicals and raw sewage into rivers and the burial of industrial waste in the ground where it filters into underground water supplies. Fertilizers and insecticides used in farming also drain into water supplies with each rainfall. A few years ago the governor's mansion in Baton Rouge, Louisiana posted a no-fishing sign because the governor's lake contained PCB, a dangerous organic chemical that causes cancer. In areas like Louisiana, where tons of waste containing harmful metals and toxic chemicals are produced daily, water pollution problems are severe. In October of 1984, *The Wall Street Journal* reported that "In some swamps, groves of cypress [trees] stand dead because of water pollution."[17]

When a pollution problem occurs, the best action is a quick solution that eliminates the problem so consumers and the press will not be able to dwell on the negative aspects of the incident. For example, when Union Carbide found that a pesticide it marketed under the name Temik had contaminated

**Regulation is essential to prevent pollution.**   Dumping raw sewage into rivers and waterways causes water pollution. When companies bury industrial waste where it can work its way into underground water supplies, the result can be disastrous.

thousands of household wells on Long Island, the company agreed to pay for the installation and maintenance of water filtration systems for the homes affected by the contamination.[18] The toxic-substance problem most widely reported by states is the contamination of water by heavy metals like lead, along with toxic chemicals, including pesticides. The public is demanding that water supplies be clean and healthful to reduce the potential danger from these chemicals.

*Air Pollution.*   Carbon monoxide and hydrocarbons emitted by motor vehicles pollute the air. Another major cause of air pollution is smoke and other pollutants emitted by manufacturing facilities. Air pollution can be controlled by pollution-control devices like the catalytic converters used in automobiles. Over the past few years private industry has spent more than $50 billion on emission-control devices and other anti-pollution devices. Manufacturers of aerosol products have made a conscious effort to put as many of their products in non-aerosol or some other type containers to voluntarily minimize the negative effects of aerosol on the ozone layer of the atmosphere. (See Business Encounter 3-2.)

# Business Encounter 3-2

## Du Pont Stops Making Environmentally Harmful Products

Scientists have long contended that chlorofluorocarbons (CFCs) are destroying the ozone layer in the upper atmosphere, which shields Earth from the sun's harmful ultraviolet rays. Chlorofluorocarbons are inert substances used in refrigeration and foam packaging. They were used as propellants in aerosol containers but Congress banned that usage in the 1970s when researchers first learned that CFCs were destroying the ozone. On March 15, 1988 the results of an international study on the ozone problem reported that the ozone layer over the Northern Hemisphere was being rapidly and seriously depleted. Scientists had already discovered a hole in the ozone over Antarctica the year before. Du Pont & Co., which holds 25 percent of the CFC market with its product Freon, realized that the company had to take socially responsible action to protect the environment.

Until the 1988 report was released, Du Pont had contended that CFCs are not as deadly as scientists say they are and the company would not stop production of Freon, which accounts for about $600 million in Du Pont sales. However, when the international study results were announced, the company recognized that it had an obligation to act in a socially responsible manner and therefore announced that it would phase out production of CFCs as soon as it had substitutes ready for the market. The company expects to reduce production 95 percent by the year 2003. Du Pont has been spending $10 million a year trying to develop a substitute for CFCs and has two already in production.

Du Pont is also asking other nations and companies that produce CFCs to abide by a 1987 treaty that calls for at least a 50 percent reduction in the production of CFCs by the year 1999. Scientists, however, say the treaty is not enough and is too late to stop the problem of the deteriorating ozone. They believe that the deterioration of the ozone layer will result in an increase in skin cancer, damaged crops, and harm to marine life.

The second largest producers of CFCs, Allied-Signal, Inc. and Pennwalt Corp., also called for an end to production to CFCs but neither company halted production of the chemical. Allied-Signal is developing its own substitutes for CFCs and Pennwalt says it expects to phase out production of CFCs as soon as it is practical.

Environmental groups praised Du Pont's decision to stop making the harmful chemical as an example of corporate social responsibility. These groups hope that the company's action will encourage other companies to stop producing CFCs. Although Du Pont stands to lose millions of dollars in sales by discontinuing production of Freon, the company realized that it had an obligation to stop making the product because of the damage it has done, and is yet to do, to the environment.

---

These facts are from Mary Lu Carnevale, "Du Pont Plans to Phase Out CFC Output," *The Wall Street Journal*, March 25, 1988, p. 2, 4; "Ozone: Du Pont Does Good," *U.S. News & World Report*, April 4, 1988, p. 13; Tim Smart, with Joseph Weber, "An Ozone Hole over Capitol Hill," *Business Week*, April 4, 1988, p. 35.

***Land Pollution.*** Pollution of the land is taking a toll all over the United States. Land pollution results from the dumping of industrial waste, strip mining, forest fires, and poor forest conservation. Land pollution is tied directly to water pollution because many of the chemicals and toxic wastes that are dumped on the land eventually work their way into the water supply. The Environmental Protection Agency can sue companies that are guilty of dumping chemicals at specific waste sites. Congress has created a superfund to finance the cleanup of hazardous waste sites across the nation, but hazardous waste sites are still a major source of land pollution.

**Eliminating a health and safety hazard in New Jersey.** A clean-up firm decontaminated more than 160 tanks and 1500 drums of material when they cleaned up the former site of a chemical manufacturer. Combustion Engineering provided groundwater sampling and analysis, project management, site cleanup, and land restoration to this land so it could meet state environmental regulations.

# ▶ Social Responsibility Strategies

There are four basic social responsibility strategies: reaction, defense, accommodation, and proaction. These strategies are ways of dealing with social responsibility systematically.

## Reaction Strategy

A business following the **reaction strategy** allows a condition or potential problem to go unresolved until the public finds out about it. The situation may be known to management (as was one auto maker's problems with gas-tank combustibility) or it may be unknown (as was the sudden acceleration of the Audi 5000 with no direct action from the driver). In either case, the business denies responsibility, but tries to resolve the problem, deal with its consequences, and continue doing business as usual to minimize the negative impact.

## Defense Strategy

A business using the **defense strategy** tries to minimize or avoid additional obligations. Commonly used tactics include legal maneuvering and seeking the support of trade unions that embrace the company's way of doing business and support the industry. Businesses often lobby to avoid government action or regulation. For example, Advo, a direct-mail firm, lobbied against an increase in bulk postal rates because it knew it would have to pass these increases on to its clients, advertisers, and advertising agencies. Advo realized that significant increases in postal rates could put the company at a competitive disadvantage with print media, such as newspaper inserts, that do not use the U.S. Postal Service.

## Accommodation Strategy

**Accommodation strategy**

When a business assumes responsibility for its actions

A business using the **accommodation strategy** assumes responsibility for its actions. A business might adopt the accommodation strategy when special-interest groups are encouraging a particular action or when the business perceives that if it doesn't react Congress will pass a law to ensure compliance.

For example, McDonald's developed a nutrition-oriented advertising campaign to soothe dietitians and nutritionists who were urging legal action in several states to require that accurate nutritional information be provided on each fast-food product. McDonald's campaign, however, instead of soothing groups, stirred them up. The groups claim that McDonald's portrayal of its food as healthful is inaccurate. A McDLT, fries, and shake contain 1,283 calories, approximately 60 percent of the entire recommended daily calorie intake for an adult woman. In addition, that meal contains 15 teaspoons of fat, 10 teaspoons of sugar, no fiber, and approximately 70 percent of the daily allowance of salt. Dietitians and nutritionists have petitioned the U.S. Food and Drug Administration in the hope that the government will require product nutritional labeling to alert consumers to the high levels of fat, sodium, and sugar and low levels of starch and fiber.[19]

McDonald's chose to take an accommodation strategy to curtail the lobbying. The company should have adopted the proactive strategy.

## Proactive Strategy

**Proactive strategy**

A business assumes responsibility for its actions and responds to accusations made against it, but takes socially responsible action without outside pressure or the threat of government intervention

A business that uses the **proactive strategy** assumes responsibility for its actions and responds to accusations made against it, but in addition the business will take socially responsible action without outside pressure or the threat of government intervention.

The proactive strategy requires management, of its own free will, to support an action or cause. Business Encounter 3-3 illustrates Johnson & Johnson's use of a proactive strategy to deal with several deaths caused by cyanide-laced Tylenol capsules.

# ▶ Self-Regulation and Social Responsibility

Many businesses recognize that social responsibility is necessary for survival. In the absence of government regulation and in an attempt to prevent government intervention, some businesses try self-regulation, often by industry trade associations. Even though self-regulatory programs are not a

## Business Encounter 3-3
### Social Responsibility and the Tylenol Deaths

In 1961 McNeil Labs (a subsidiary of Johnson & Johnson) introduced Tylenol as an aspirin substitute. Tylenol proved to be highly profitable, and by 1982 it was the number-one pain reliever, with 35 percent of the market. Then disaster struck. In September 1982, several deaths in Chicago were linked to Extra-Strength Tylenol capsules that had been laced with cyanide. Again, in 1986, cyanide-laced Tylenol capsules were blamed for the death of a New York woman. In both cases, Johnson & Johnson took immediate, responsible action to ensure the safety of American consumers, without a government request or order to do so.

After the first deaths, Johnson & Johnson voluntarily recalled Tylenol products from retailers and consumers at a cost of $100 million. Soon after, the federal government required that all over-the-counter medicines be sold in tamper-resistant packages. But that wasn't enough for McNeil Labs: Tylenol was repackaged with glued end flaps, a plastic neck seal, an inner foil seal, and a new label warning consumers, "Do not use if safety seals are broken." The government required only one of the three preventive measures, but Johnson & Johnson did not want to take any chances. The company worked hard to get the newly packaged product to consumers quickly.

Tylenol's new, safer packaging helped restore consumer trust. To further rebuild consumer confidence in Tylenol, Johnson & Johnson implemented a promotional program encouraging consumers to "Continue to Trust Tylenol." Newspaper advertisements offered consumers a $2.50 coupon to replace products they might have thrown out. Consumers could also call a toll-free number to receive a coupon. Within six months, Tylenol's market share rose to 27 percent; within one year, it nearly recaptured its previous market share.

When the second tampering incident occurred in 1986, Johnson & Johnson again acted quickly and responsibly. In addition to the recall and replacement of Tylenol capsules, which cost $130 million this time, Johnson & Johnson stopped producing all its over-the-counter medicines in the form of capsules, although capsules accounted for 30 percent of Tylenol sales. The company asked consumers to buy caplets—oval-shaped tablets developed as an alternative to capsules after the 1982 incident. The company believed that consumers could more easily spot any tampering with the caplets. Johnson & Johnson also offered $100,000 for information leading to the arrest of anyone involved with the tampering.

Johnson & Johnson takes its consumer responsibility very seriously. The company's actions in the Tylenol-death incidents were quick, well-publicized, and socially responsible. Johnson & Johnson made every effort to show sensitivity and concern—not just in words, but in actions.

These facts are from "The 100 Leading National Advertisers," *Advertising Age*, September 24, 1987, pp. 120–121; "Tylenol Firm Abandoning All Capsules," *Houston Post*, February 18, 1986, p. 1; "Johnson & Johnson Reincarnates a Brand," *Sales and Marketing Management*, January 16, 1984, p. 63; Rebecca Famin, "Diary of an Amazing Comeback," *Marketing & Media Decisions* (Spring 1983): 129–134; "The Rise—and Fall?" *Advertising Age*, October 11, 1982, p. 78; Thomas Moore, "The Fight to Save Tylenol," *Fortune*, November 29, 1982, pp. 44–49; and the 1983 Johnson & Johnson Annual Report, p. 26.

direct outgrowth of laws, many come about to avoid legal action or proposed legislation. Numerous programs have been created to stop or slow the development of laws and government regulatory groups that would monitor and evaluate business practices. Many of these programs focus on ethical and social issues.

Self-regulation has many advantages over laws and government guidelines. These programs are usually less expensive to establish and implement than government-mandated programs, and their goals and expectations are more realistic and operational. Perhaps the most important benefit to business is that industry self-regulation reduces the need to expand the government bureaucracy. Businesses tend to embrace the principle known as laissez faire—the belief that the best government is the least government.

An example of the use of self-regulation to ward off government intervention can be found in the real-estate appraisal industry, where fraudulent and inaccurate appraisals have resulted in the failure of some lending institutions. Congress is considering legislation that would require practitioners in the industry to meet educational and competency standards to be determined by a private foundation. Groups such as the FSLIC would supervise and evaluate the quality of appraisals made for federal projects.[20] To reduce the complexity of the legislation, it is hoped that the industry will achieve significant improvements through voluntary self-regulation before the law is enacted.

Self-regulatory programs designed and implemented by business do have some limitations. When a trade association creates a set of industry guidelines, companies that do not belong to the association are not required to follow the guidelines. Many self-regulatory programs lack the resources and the authority to enforce the guidelines. Finally, guidelines in self-regulatory programs are often less strict than those established by government agencies.

## The Better Business Bureau

**Better Business Bureau**

A self regulatory agency supported by local businesses

Perhaps the best-known nongovernment regulatory organization is the **Better Business Bureau,** a local regulatory agency supported by local businesses. Today more than 140 bureaus help settle problems between consumers and specific business firms. They also act to preserve good business practices in a community, although they usually do not have strong enforcement tools. When a business continues to violate what the Better Business Bureau believes to be good business practices, the Bureau warns consumers through local newspapers.

## National Advertising Review Board

**National Advertising Review Board**

A self-regulatory unit created by the Council of Better Business Bureaus, a national organization, and three advertising trade organizations

The Council of Better Business Bureaus, a national organization, and three advertising trade organizations have created a self-regulatory unit called the **National Advertising Review Board** (NARB). In addition to screening national advertisements for honesty, the NARB processes complaints about deceptive advertising. For example, the NARB recently said that Brown & Williamson Tobacco Corporation cannot call the five bonus cigarettes in a pack of Richland 25's "free," because the five extra cigarettes are part of the company's marketing campaign for Richland 25's.[21]

The National Advertising Division of the Council of the Better Business Bureaus serves as the investigative arm of the NARB, although the NARB has no official enforcement powers. However, if a business refuses to comply with its decisions, the NARB publicizes the questionable practice and files a complaint with the Federal Trade Commission.

# Social Audits

**Social audit**

The systematic examination of the objectives, strategies, organization, and performance of the social responsibility function

A measure of corporate performance is needed for a business to meet the demands of diverse sectors of society. The business must make decisions in terms of goal statements that identify the group or organization to be served. The **social audit** is the systematic examination of the objectives, strategies, organization, and performance of the social responsibility function. It is the intelligence system management uses to gather information needed to determine whether a strategy is working. In the social audit, management evaluates a company's long- and short-term contributions to social responsibility. The social audit can also assist management in improving the company's social responsibility efforts by evaluating the effectiveness of current programs and recommending social responsibility activities for the future.[22]

The social audit aids in business evaluation by:

1. Describing current activities, and relating results to sales, costs, prices, profits, and other sources of performance feedback such as consumers and public reaction
2. Gathering information about customers' needs and interests, competitive activity, and environmental and legal developments that may affect social responsibility activities within the business
3. Exploring opportunities and alternatives for improving the social responsibility stance of the business
4. Providing a data base to be used in evaluating the company's organizational goals and social responsibility objectives

Management should conduct a social responsibility audit on a regular basis—perhaps annually—to develop a good benchmark of where the company has been and where it is going.

Conducting the audit is fundamentally a five-step process:

1. Identifying ongoing and new programs that support socially responsible actions and programs
2. Determining the resources and the cost of resources that are required to support the programs and the benefits that have been achieved to date
3. Identifying organizational objectives and making certain that social responsibility activities support those objectives
4. Defining the reasons for undertaking particular social responsibility programs or supporting certain causes
5. Evaluating the success of each social responsibility program undertaken and identifying benchmark goals for future involvement.

The concept of auditing implies an official examination of social responsibility activities. However, these audits are designed to occur informally. Most of the problems that arise in the audit can be attributed to the fact that there are few standards for evaluating social responsibility; primarily because social responsibility issues tend to rest in grey areas such as religion, politics, and philosophy.

# Notes

**1.** Donald P. Robin and R. Eric Reidenbach, "Social Responsibility, Ethics, and Marketing Strategy: Closing the Gap Between Concept and Application," *Journal of Marketing* 51 (January 1987): 45.

**2.** Vernon R. Loucks, Jr., "A CEO Looks at Ethics," *Business Horizons* 30 (March–April 1987): 4.

**3.** Mike Sheridan, "Eastern Agrees to Pay $9.5 Million Fine," *The Houston Chronicle,* February 11, 1987, p. 3-1.

**4.** "20/20," broadcast by ABC-TV, October 2, 1987.

**5.** "Some New Soft Drinks in Texas Have Awfully Big Heads on Them," *The Wall Street Journal,* October 14, 1987, p. 33.

**6.** Sir Adrian Cadbury, "Ethical Managers Make Their Own Rules," *Harvard Business Review* 65 (September–October 1987): 72.

**7.** Saul W. Gellerman, "Why Good Managers Make Bad Ethical Choices," *Harvard Business Review* 64 (July–August 1986): 86.

**8.** Lawrence Kohlberg, *The Meaning and Measurement of Moral Development* (Worcester, Mass.: Clark University Press, 1981).

**9.** O. C. Ferrell and Larry Gresham, "A Contingency Framework for Ethical Decision Making in Marketing," *Journal of Marketing* 49 (Summer 1985): 87–96.

**10.** Ibid.

**11.** Gellerman, p. 87.

**12.** Joel Dressang, "Companies Get Serious About Ethics," *USA Today,* December 21, 1986, pp. 1B, 2B.

**13.** Daniel B. Moskowitz, "Where Business Goes to Stock Up on Ethics," *Business Week,* October 14, 1985, pp. 63–66.

**14.** Center for Business Ethics at Bentley College, "Are Corporations Institutionalizing Ethics?" *Journal of Business Ethics* 5 (1986): 85.

**15.** Nicholas J. Mauro, "Ethics Should Inform Decision Making and Balance Profits," *Nation's Restaurant News,* February 23, 1987, p. F8.

**16.** "The Corporate Elite: Chief Executives of the *Business Week* Top 1000," *Business Week,* October 23, 1987, pp. 99–337.

**17.** Thomas Petzinger, Jr., and George Getschow, "In Louisiana, Pollution and Cancer Are Rife in the Petroleum Area," *The Wall Street Journal,* October 23, 1984, p. 1.

**18.** Kevin McCray, "Tapping the Water Market," *American Demographics* 9 (January 1987): 61.

**19.** "McD Ads Draw Protests from Nutritional Experts," *Nation's Restaurant News,* June 22, 1987, p. 26.

**20.** William Celis, III, "Embattled Appraisal Industry Faces Stiffening of Standards," *The Wall Street Journal,* July 29, 1987, p. 17.

**21.** Ronald Alsop, "Advertisers Get Reprimanded for Saying 'Free' Too Easily," *The Wall Street Journal,* March 26, 1987, p. 33.

**22.** Abe Schuchman, "The Marketing Audit: Its Nature, Purposes and Problems," in *Analyzing and Improving Marketing Performance,* Report 32 (New York: American Management Association, 1959), pp. 16–17.

# Summary and Review

▶ Ethics is the study of morals and moral choices. Business ethics are moral principles that define right or wrong behavior. Ethical business relationships are based on fairness, justice, and trust.

▶ Moral philosophies affect business because they help individuals decide how to behave in particular situations, including situations that may present an ethical dilemma.

▶ Formal codes of ethics can improve the organizational environment. Formal codes and policies reduce the incidence of unethical behavior by informing employees what is expected of them and providing punishments for those who fail to comply.

▶ Social responsibility is the obligation of an organization to consider how its activities affect society. Socially responsible businesses try to minimize the negative effects and maximize the positive effects of their activities.

▶ A business's acceptance of social responsibility may increase expenditures for pollution controls, more equitable hiring practices, and contributions to charitable organizations; however, such a business may increase long-term profits because of public goodwill generated by these activities.

▶ Social audits increase social responsibility in an organization by evaluating the effectiveness of current social responsibility programs, determining whether they meet the organization's objectives, and whether they should be continued or improved.

# Key Terms and Concepts

ethics
bribe
plagiarism
moral philosophy
utilitarian philosophy
humanistic philosophy
preconventional stage of moral
   development
conventional stage of moral
   development
principled stage of moral
   development

code of ethics
social responsibility
consumerism
pollution
reaction strategy
defense strategy
accommodation strategy
proactive strategy
Better Business Bureau
National Advertising Review Board
social audit

# Checking Your Understanding

This chapter introduced you to ethics and social responsibility. To test and reinforce your understanding, fill in the blanks below.

1. _Bus. ethics_ are moral principles defining right and wrong behavior in the business environment.
2. Believers of the _utilitarian philosophy_ seek the greatest satisfaction for the largest number of individuals.
3. _humanistic phil._ focus on human rights and values.
4. A person at the _conven. stage_ believes that what is right is what society defines as good behavior.
5. A person at the _principle stage_ looks beyond laws and mores to determine what is right or ethical.
6. _Code of ethics_ establish what is acceptable and ethical behavior in a particular organization.
7. _Social respons._ is the obligation of business to maximize its positive impact on society and minimize its negative impact.
8. _Consumerism_ is the activities undertaken by individuals and organizations to protect their rights to safety, to be informed, to choose, and to be heard.
9. A business following the _reaction strategy_ does nothing about a problem until the public finds out about it.
10. A business following the _Proactive strat._ assumes full responsibility for its actions and acts without the threat of outside interference.
11. _Self regulation_ is the effort by business to police itself so that government interference is unnecessary.
12. A _social audit_ is the systematic evaluation of a businesses' social responsibility efforts.

# Topics for Review and Discussion

1. Discuss some recent examples of a business engaging in unethical practices. Are these practices issues of conflict of interest, fairness and honesty, communications, or relationships within a business? Why do you think the business chose to behave unethically? What action should the business have taken?
2. Discuss the role of a code of ethics in reducing unethical behavior in business.
3. Compare and contrast the four approaches to social responsibility in business. Discuss situations where each might be used and why.

# Exercises

1. Find some examples of socially responsible businesses in newspapers or business journals. Explain why you believe their actions are socially responsible. Why do you think the company chose to act as it did? Do you believe their actions were undertaken for long term or short term objectives?

**2.** Discuss with your class some possible methods of increasing ethical standards in business. Do you think that business should regulate its own activities or should the federal government establish and enforce ethical standards. How do you think businesspeople feel?

## Case 3-1
### *Insider Trading on Wall Street Creates Ethical Issues*

There has been a tremendous amount of growth in the financial services provided by Wall Street brokerage and security firms in recent years. Nevertheless, growth is not the only reason Wall Street is in the news these days. The news media have reported scandal after scandal involving unethical, and often illegal, activities on Wall Street. Many of the scandals have involved insider trading, where someone with "inside" knowledge of events in a particular corporation invests in that company's stock before other investors have legitimate access to the information. The Securities Exchange Act of 1934 made insider trading illegal, punishable by fines and jail.

The biggest insider trading scandal on Wall Street to date surfaced when Dennis B. Levine, a merger specialist at the investment banking firm of Drexel Burnham Lambert, Inc., admitted that he stole confidential information and gave it to stock speculator Ivan Boesky. Levine notified Boesky in advance of merger and takeover announcements—based on information obtained from Drexel Burnham Lambert clients. Levine and Boesky struck a deal: Levine provided the valuable insider information to Boesky in exchange for up to 5% of the profits Boesky earned from that information. Boesky purchased stock in companies that were targets for mergers or acquisition by other companies on the assumption that the stock would increase in value when the public learned about the merger. For example, Boesky purchased shares in Carnation, a leading cat food and other consumer products marketer, based on inside information that Nestle was going to purchase Carnation. When the news became public, Boesky's shares in Carnation increased in value for more than a $28-million profit. In many cases, Levine and Boesky's activities were not only unethical but also illegal.

Ivan F. Boesky paid a $100-million Securities and Exchange Commission (SEC) penalty, the biggest ever for insider trading. Ivan Boesky was fairly-well respected as a stock speculator; he had been invited to speak at leading business schools and has published a book stating that his takeover attempts were a public service.

Possibly no industry has had its ethical standards questioned more than the securities and investment banking industry in the 1980s. Herbert A. Allen, Jr., President of Allen S. Company, Inc. states that investment bankers routinely trade confidential information. "A major disquieting factor is the loss of confidentiality, well short of illegality. Important clients often find out inside information about other important clients." Such activity obviously undermines public confidence in the Wall Street financial community.

When the Levine/Boesky insider-trading scandal emerged over two years ago, the press indicated that many more inside traders might be caught. In reality, many inside traders in the Boesky scandal probably remain uncaught. It has also been suggested that the SEC contributed to opportunity for insider trading when it allowed Boesky to reduce his partnerships' liabilities by $1.3 million through the sale of stocks or other securities before the government publicly announced the crimes in 1986 (because Boesky cooperated and led authorities to others involved in the scandal)—perhaps the ultimate piece of inside information. This special treatment saved Boesky an additional $100 million in fines. Congress wondered why, if New York Stock Exchange computers flagged 47 suspicious trades by Boesky between 1983 and 1986—many before merger announcements—why Boesky was not caught before Levine disclosed his activities late in 1986. Apparently there is still much opportunity for insider trading in the securities industry.

Insider-trading scandals have strained relationships between investment bankers (who finance mergers and acquisitions) and their clients (firms that want mergers or acquisitions). There is a new atmosphere of caution and mistrust. Before the Levine/Boesky affair, many deals were sealed with the traditional handshake or over the telephone. Now, clients are worried that their own bankers will sell information on their companies to the highest bidder. This doubt and suspicion has led some clients to demand confidentiality and high standards, often in writing.

There is a positive side to the unethical activities and scandals on Wall Street. Most stock brokers, investment bankers and other members of the financial community in general are ethical and are above the type of behavior conducted by Boesky and Levine. Their abuses will not destroy the securities industry, any more than a few bank failures will destroy the banking system. There are several proposals pending in Congress that deal with takeovers and insider trading. In the future there will probably be tougher penalties and more safeguards placed on activities to combat abuses in the financial community.

William A. Schreyer, Chairman and Chief Executive Officer of Merrill Lynch and Co. offers some suggestions to improve ethical behavior on Wall Street. First, fairness could be improved by preventing people with access to market-sensitive information from profiting at the expense of others; second, whatever remedies Congress develops, it should take steps to ensure that the markets continue to function swiftly and effectively; third, rules should be simple and easy to understand so that the cure does not become worse than the disease; and fourth, society in general needs to accept a higher ethical standard of doing business.

Both the financial industry and specific firms are developing codes of ethics and policies that forbid questionable insider information exchanges. Wall Street's creativity, combined with new technology, means that the industry evolves faster than regulators can oversee these changes. While tougher penalties and expanded enforcement may be one solution, ultimately it is the investment banking firms that must restore public confidence. Success depends on clear, fair rules, rigorously applied and enforced.

These facts are from William A. Schreyer, "Ethics and Wall Street," *American Way,* September 1, 1987; Ford S. Worthy, "Wall Street's Spreading Scandal," *Fortune,* December 22, 1986, p. 27; Joel Dressang, "Companies Get Serious About Ethics," *USA Today,* December, 1986, p. 1-2B; James B. Stewart, "Insider-Trading Plot Unraveled as Profits Lured Copycat Buyers," *Wall Street Journal,* July 15, 1987, p. 1; Myron Magnet, "The Decline and Fall of Business Ethics," *Fortune,* December 8, 1986, pp. 65–72; and John Byrne, "Corporate Clients Feel Seduced and Abandoned," *Business Week,* March 2, 1987, p. 34.

### Questions

1. Why is insider trading unethical?
2. Who suffers financially because of insider trading and what other negative effects arise from this unethical activity?
3. Explain why some critics complained that the Securities Exchange Commission actually contributed to insider trading?
4. What can Wall Street firms and the government do to eliminate insider trading abuses?

## Case 3-2
## *Social Responsibility at American Express*

American Express is one corporation that has infused public and social responsibility into its corporate values. This sense of responsibility is apparent in many of the company's business practices and in its consumer education programs. Throughout its history, American Express has combined its concern for profit with a concern for the health and welfare of society. While some critics say the company's tradition of social responsibility is a way of getting publicity, American Express knows that it's simply good business sense to try to improve the quality of life in communities where it does business.

In 1978, the company's Board of Directors established a Public Responsibility Committee. This committee guides managers in developing and monitoring corporate practices and policies that deal with public concerns and the company's own daily business practices. According to Vernon E. Jordan, Jr., chairman of the committee, American Express takes its corporate responsibility very seriously. As a result, social responsibility is management's responsibility.

American Express shows its concern for society in many ways. One of the company's concerns is meeting the needs of the handicapped. To this end, the company established a corporate-wide task force in 1981 to review business practices towards the handicapped. The task force recommended several actions to assist disabled people, including finding them jobs, marketing to them, and helping them gain access to business and public offices. As a result, Shearson Lehman (a division of American Express) became a founding member of Project Access to Computer Training (PACT) which trains qualified physically-handicapped candidates for jobs in computer-related professions.

American Express has hired several of PACT's graduates for computer-programming positions. In addition, the Merchandise Services Operations Center installed toll-free telephone lines for use by deaf and hearing-impaired customers to allow them to shop from home. Moreover, American Express now designs all of its buildings to be accessible to the handicapped.

American Express also established various programs to help young people entering the business world, and provide those already in the work force with the support they need to succeed. To support cultural development, American Express contributes to a wide base of performing-arts institutions, international traveling exhibitions, and preservation projects. The company has also started the Fund for New American Plays (in conjunction with the Kennedy Center for the Performing Arts) which helps nonprofit professional theaters perform high-quality plays.

One of the major ways that American Express shows its social responsibility is through its charity activities. The company believes that charity activities should bring about needed changes in society, so it invests a great deal of financial resources and employee time towards its efforts. American Express's philanthropic programs concentrate on community service, education, employment and training, cultural diversity, and national heritage.

The company provides many grants and encourages employees to work for community service organizations. The company has also committed itself to doubling its corporate contributions to the United Way by 1991.

American Express uses cause-related marketing for worthy situations or events. In cause-related marketing, American Express donates a specified amount of money to a particular cause or organization whenever an American Express card holder makes a purchase on their card. TRS (American Express Travel Related Services, Inc.) has used cause-related marketing in an attempt to incorporate philanthropy in the marketing of travel-related services and products. As a result, TRS has increased its profits, increased its support of nonprofit groups, and increased overall goodwill for American Express.

Finally, American Express encourages its employees to donate to worthy charitable causes through its employee gift-matching program. The company matches the donations made by its employees to nonprofit educational institutions and cultural organizations. Those employees donated one-and-a-half million dollars to various organizations in 1986. The company also matches donations made by employees who serve as directors of nonprofit organizations.

American Express's sense of social responsibility is evident in many things it does. While the company has no doubt increased its goodwill through its efforts, it has also managed to increase its profits at the same time. Thus, American Express has proved that a concern for society and a concern for profits can go hand in hand.

---

These facts are from "American Express Public Responsibility, A Report of Recent Activities," American Express Company, 1987; Philanthropy at American Express," American Express Company, 1987; American Express Company 1986 Annual Report.

**Questions**

1. How does American Express benefit from such an extensive social responsibility program?
2. What type of social responsibility strategy does American Express use?
3. Do American Express's social responsibility activities pressure other financial service companies to act similarly?

# Answers to Checking Your Understanding

1. Business ethics
2. utilitarian philosophy
3. Humanistic philosophies
4. conventional stage
5. principled stage
6. Code of ethics
7. Social responsibility
8. Consumerism
9. reaction strategy
10. proactive strategy
11. Self-regulation
12. social audit

## **Outline**

# Chapter 4

# Forms of Business Organization

## Objectives

After reading this chapter, you will be able to:

▶ Explain how sole proprietorships, partnerships, and corporations differ.

▶ Compare the advantages and disadvantages of sole proprietorships, partnerships, and corporations.

▶ Understand how the form of organization affects taxes, the distribution of profits, the ownership and control of a business, and the liabilities of business owners.

▶ Explain how a corporation's board of directors, management, and stockholders relate to one another.

▶ Describe the activities of cooperatives and holding companies.

# Business Experience

After Georgena Terry received her education in business and engineering, she worked for a variety of large corporations, including PPG Industries and Xerox. She did not stay with any of those companies for long, she says, because the work bored her. She finally realized the problem was not the work. The problem was that she did not like working for other people. She wanted to be in control, so she quit her job and started building women's bicycles.

Her first bicycles were the result of experiments to find the most comfortable frame for her own five-foot-two, 98-pound body. With the help of a blowtorch, she shortened the frame on a store-bought, designed-for-a-man bicycle until she produced a frame that provided a comfortable position. Some of her friends tried the bike, loved it, and asked her to shorten their bicycle frames too. Two years later, Georgena Terry was still shortening bicycle frames. She liked working for herself and in 1985 decided to organize Terry Precision Bicycles for Women, Inc.

Terry Precision Bicycles have a shorter top tube and a smaller front wheel than other manufacturers' bikes. The rest of a Terry Precision Bicycle is made from standard components bought off the shelf. The only thing Georgena Terry actually does to her bikes is shorten the frame to provide a more comfortable ride for women.

In the early 1980s, most bicycle manufacturers did not take women's bicycling seriously, so Terry's bikes seemed destined for success. She took some of them to the New England Area Rally in 1985 to show them off. She sold three at the rally and took orders for four more. Women raved because the bikes are comfortable to ride and are designed by a woman. Terry Precision Bicycles for Women, in its first year of operation, sold twenty bikes. In 1986, the company sold thirteen hundred, in 1987, five thousand. The first Terry Precision Bicycles sold for around $1,000 each. Terry now makes models that sell for as little as $319 and as much as $1,600.

When prospective customers first started calling about Terry Precision Bicycles, Georgena Terry always asked them the name of their local bicycle shop. After making a sale, she would call and congratulate the shop for selling a Terry bike. The shop owner would inevitably ask for two or three Terry bikes. Using this unusual marketing approach, Terry quickly established a network of loyal dealers willing to sell Terry Precision Bicycles. Georgena Terry is a favorite with dealers because she always delivers what she promises, on time. She hired a public relations agency, and Terry Precision Bicycles suddenly attracted the attention of the bicycling press. The attention boosted sales.

Terry Precision Bicycles for Women cost $600,000 to organize. Half of the money came from bank loans and half from private investors. Terry Precision Bicycles have been a hit with women, and other bicycle manufacturers are taking women's bicycling seriously these days. Six companies now market bicycles designed just for women, but Terry Precision Bicycles for Women is still holding its own.

As the market grows, however, companies like Huffy and Schwinn will want a piece of the action. Other companies will certainly try to bring the quality of their bikes in line with that of Terry Precision Bicycles. Georgena Terry now must decide where she is going with her small bicycle company. She may have to raise money to expand into a larger company or she may choose to keep the company small. As the sole owner the choice is hers.

---

These facts are from Paul B. Brown, "Spokeswoman: Georgena Terry, Erstwhile Financial Analyst, Stockbroker, Student, and Engineer, Has Finally Found a Home: Making Bikes That Really Are Built for Women," *Inc.* (June 1987): 31, 32.

# Introduction

The legal form of ownership taken by business is not often of great concern to customers. When you eat at a restaurant, you probably don't care whether the restaurant is owned by one person (a sole proprietorship), has two or more owners who share the business (a partnership), or is an entity owned by stockholders (a corporation). All you want is good food. When you buy a foreign car, you probably don't care if the foreign company that made it has a different set of laws from U.S. laws governing its form of organization. You are buying the car because it is well made, fits your price range, or appeals to your sense of style.

A sole proprietorship is a business that is owned and operated by one person. Most sole proprietorships are small businesses employing fewer than fifty people. A partnership is a business that is controlled by two or more people. Partnerships are usually larger than proprietorships but smaller than corporations. A corporation is a legal entity that is allowed to make contracts just as a person is. Corporations may be owned by a few people or by many people. They may be small like Crown Resources (a silver-mining company) or large like General Motors. Most people associate large companies like General Electric, IBM, Eastman Kodak, and McDonald's with the corporate form of business.

Those firms *are* all organized as corporations, but were they always corporations? Most of them started out small, either as a sole proprietorship or as a partnership. Henry Ford did not start with a corporation, but the Ford Motor Company is now one of the largest corporations in the world. Most businesses start out small. As a business grows, however, it needs money for expansion. To obtain money, a business can either borrow or find people who are willing to invest in the business. A corporation allows an unlimited number of investors to buy a share of the business. A corporation can raise capital from anyone who has money to invest. Corporations have the potential to tap sources of capital that are unavailable to sole proprietorships or partnerships. Even so, not all businesses are corporations, and for some businesses the corporate form of organization is a disadvantage.

This chapter examines three forms of business ownership—sole proprietorship, partnership, and corporation—and weighs the advantages and disadvantages of each.

# ▶ Sole Proprietorships

**Sole proprietorship**

A business owned and operated by one individual

**Sole proprietorships,** businesses owned and operated by one individual, are a very popular form of business organization. The majority of all American businesses take this form of organization. Common examples include most restaurants, barber shops, flower shops, and independent grocery stores. Sole

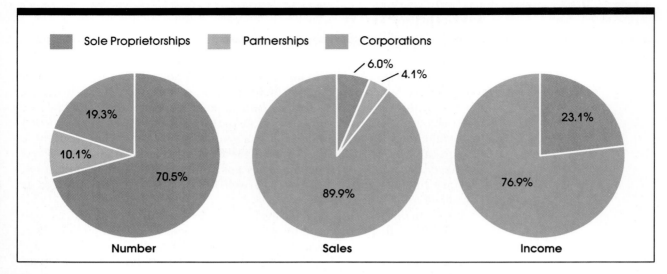

**Figure 4-1**

Comparison of Sole Proprietorships, Partnerships, and Corporations, 1985

proprietorships are typically small businesses. There are approximately 11.7 million of them in the U.S. (70 percent of all businesses), but they account for only 6 percent of total business sales and 23 percent of total income. Figure 4-1 compares the number, sales, and income of sole proprietorships, partnerships, and corporations.

## Advantages of Sole Proprietorships

Because a sole proprietorship is owned by one person, its management structure is simple, and the owner/manager can make decisions quickly. Sole proprietorships offer those and other advantages.

***Ease and Cost of Formation.*** Forming a proprietorship is easy and inexpensive. In some states creating a sole proprietorship requires only an announcement in the local newspaper. Some proprietorships such as barber shops also require state and local licenses and permits because of the nature of the business or occupation. The cost of these permits may run from $25 to $100. No lawyer need be hired to create the enterprise, and the owner can take care of the required paperwork.

***Secrecy.*** Sole proprietorships make possible the greatest degree of secrecy. The proprietor, unlike the owners of a partnership, does not have to discuss operating plans with anyone. Trade secrets may be easily kept out of the hands of competitors. Financial reports need not be publicly disclosed, as do the financial reports of publicly owned corporations.

***Distribution and Use of Profits.*** All profits from a sole proprietorship belong to the owner. Profits do not have to be shared with anyone. The owner decides how to use the profits—for expansion, for salary increases, for a trip to Paris.

*[handwritten margin notes:]*
*tax – individual*
*formation – easy*
*dissolution – death*
*capital – difficult*
*Management = can be chaos*
*1 man band problem*

**One-man show.** Sole proprietorships, businesses owned by one individual, represent 70% of all U.S. businesses. A sole proprietor, such as this shop owner, has a simple management structure and the ability to make quick decisions.

***Control of the Business.*** The proprietor has direct control over how the business is run and can make decisions on the spot without the approval of anyone else. This control allows the owner to respond quickly to competitive business conditions or to changes in the economy.

***Government Regulation.*** Sole proprietorships have the most freedom from government regulation. Many government regulations—both state and federal—are applicable only to businesses that have a set number of employees, and securities laws apply to publicly owned corporations.

***Taxation.*** Profits from the business are considered personal income to the sole proprietor and are taxed at individual tax rates. The owner pays one income tax. Owners of corporations, in contrast, are taxed twice: The company pays a corporate income tax, and the owners pay another income tax on the dividend payments they receive from the corporation.

Another tax benefit is that a sole proprietor is allowed to establish a tax-exempt retirement account or a tax-exempt profit-sharing account. Such accounts are exempt from current income tax, but retirement payments are taxed when they are received. An additional point is that under the tax reform law enacted in 1986, individual tax rates are lower than corporate tax rates for large companies.

***Closing the Business.*** A sole proprietorship can be dissolved easily. No approval of co-owners or partners is required. The only legal condition is that all loans must be paid off.

# Disadvantages of Sole Proprietorships

What may be seen as an advantage by one person may turn out to be a disadvantage to another. The goals and talents of the individual owner are the deciding factors. For profitable businesses run by capable owners, many of the following factors do not cause a problem. Proprietors starting out with little management experience and little money are likely to encounter many of the disadvantages.

***Unlimited Liability.*** The sole proprietor has unlimited liability in meeting the debts of the business. If the business cannot pay its creditors, the owner might have to use personal, nonbusiness holdings such as a car or a house to pay off the debts. In Texas and other states, however, houses and homesteads cannot be taken by creditors even if the proprietor declares bankruptcy. The more wealth an individual has, the greater is the disadvantage of unlimited liability.

***Limited Sources of Funds.*** A sole proprietor can borrow money from a bank, friends, family, and the Small Business Administration or can provide funds himself or herself. Relatively few sources of money are available to the business. The credit standing of a sole proprietorship reflects the owner's personal financial condition. Often the only way a sole proprietor can borrow for business purposes is to use a car, a house, real estate, financial securities or other personal assets to guarantee the loan. If the business fails, the owner may lose his or her personal assets as well as the business. Publicly owned corporations, in contrast, can not only obtain money from commercial banks but can sell stocks and bonds to the public. Publicly owned companies can search for financing nationwide. If a public company goes out of business, the owners do not lose personal assets.

***The Generalist.*** The owner of a proprietorship must be able to perform many functions. The proprietor's skills must reach into diverse fields such as management, marketing, finance, accounting, bookkeeping, and personnel. Although the owner can rely on specialized professionals to provide advice, he or she must make the final decision in each of these areas.

***Existence of the Business.*** The life expectancy of a sole proprietorship is directly related to that of the owner and his or her ability to work. The serious illness of the owner could cause bankruptcy if competent help cannot be found.

It is difficult to arrange for the sale of a proprietorship and at the same time assure customers that the business will meet their needs as it did in the past. For example, how does one sell a dental practice? A dentist's major asset is patients. If the dentist dies suddenly, the equipment can be sold but the patients cannot. A dentist who wants to retire could take in a younger partner and sell the practice to the partner over time. The advantage to the partnership is that not all the patients are likely to look for a new dentist.

***Qualified Employees.*** It is usually difficult for a small sole proprietorship to match the wages and benefits offered by a large competing corporation because the proprietorship's level of profits may not be as high. In addition, there is little room for advancement within a sole proprietorship. Thus a sole proprietor may have difficulty attracting and retaining qualified employees.

***Taxation.*** Under the tax reform law enacted in 1986, single individuals pay a higher marginal tax rate than do small corporations on income between $17,850 and $75,000. Married proprietors filing jointly pay a higher tax rate than do corporations on income between $29,750 and $75,000. Table 4-1 contrasts tax rates for individuals, married proprietors, and corporations. Whether the tax issue is an advantage or disadvantage depends on the proprietor's income. The tax effect often determines whether a sole proprietor incorporates his or her business. One point to keep in mind when looking at Table 4-1 is that a proprietor who incorporates receives a salary taxable at individual rates. The remaining corporate income after taxes can be reinvested into the corporation. Any dividends paid to the owners by the corporation are taxed a second time at the owners' individual tax rate. This double taxation of cash dividends to the owners make the total tax on corporate income higher than it may appear, if one looks only at the tax tables.

## ▶ Partnerships

*[handwritten notes: tax – partners / formation – Easy (-) / dissolusion – if not in agreement; death of a partner / capital – easier than a proprietorship]*

Most states have a partnership law based on the Uniform Partnership Act, which is a model law governing partnerships. It allows partners with offices in several states to operate under similar partnership laws. The Uniform Partnership Act defines a **partnership** as "an association of two or more persons who carry on as co-owners of a business for profit." There are three basic types of partnership: general partnership, limited partnership, and joint venture.

*[handwritten note: Management – easier]*

## Types of Partnership

A **general partnership** involves a complete sharing in the management of a business. In a general partnership, each partner has unlimited liability for the debts of the business. Professionals such as lawyers, accountants, and architects often join together in general partnerships.

A **limited partnership** has at least one general partner, who assumes unlimited liability, and at least one limited partner, whose liability is limited to his or her investment in the business. Limited partnerships exist for risky investment projects where the chance of loss is great. The general partners accept the risk of loss; the limited partners' losses are limited to their initial investment. Limited partners are barred from participating in the manage-

**Partnership**

An association of two or more persons who carry on as co-owners of a business for profit

**General partnership**

A complete sharing in the management of a business

**Limited partnership**

Has at least one general partner and at least one limited partner

| Taxable Income Brackets, 1988 and After | | | | | |
|---|---|---|---|---|---|
| | Filing Status | | | | |
| Marginal Tax Rate | Corporation | Married, Joint Return | Head of Household | Single | Married, Separate Return |
| 15% | First $50,000 | First $29,750 | First $23,900 | First $17,850 | First $14,875 |
| 25% | $50,001 to $75,000 | — | — | — | — |
| 28% | | Over $29,750 | Over $23,900 | Over $17,850 | Over $14,875 |
| 33% | | Over $71,900 | Over $61,650 | Over $43,150 | Over $35,950 |
| 34% | Over $75,000 | — | — | — | — |
| 38% | | Over $149,250 | Over $123,790 | Over $89,560 | Over $113,300 |

| Average Tax Rate on Taxable Income of $175,000 for Single Proprietor vs. Corporation | | | | |
|---|---|---|---|---|
| Filing Status | Tax | Total Tax on Income | Taxable Income | Average Tax Rate |
| Corporation | | | | |
| First $50,000 | $ 7,500.00 | $ 7,500.00 | $ 50,000 | 15.00% |
| Next $25,000 | $ 6,250.00 | $13,750.00 | $ 75,000 | 18.33% |
| Next $100,000 | $34,000.00 | $47,750.00 | $175,000 | 27.29% |
| Single Proprietor | | | | |
| First $17,850 | $ 2,677.50 | $ 2,677.50 | $ 17,050 | 15.00% |
| Next $25,300 | $ 7,084.00 | $ 9,761.50 | $ 43,150 | 22.62% |
| Next $46,410 | $15,315.30 | $25,076.80 | $ 89,560 | 28.00% |
| Next $85,440 | $23,923.00 | $49,000.00 | $175,000 | 28.00% |
| Married, Joint Return | | | | |
| First $29,750 | $ 4,462.50 | $ 4,462.50 | $ 29,750 | 15.00% |
| Next $42,150 | $11,802.00 | $16,264.50 | $ 71,900 | 22.62% |
| Next $77,350 | $25,525.00 | $41,790.00 | $149,256 | 28.00% |
| Next $25,750 | $ 7,210.00 | $49,000.00 | $175,000 | 28.00% |

Table 4-1 Tax Rates Based on the Tax Reform Act of 1986

ment of the business but share in the profits in accordance with the terms of the partnership agreement. Usually the general partner receives a larger share of the profits after the limited partners have received their initial investment back. Popular examples of limited partnerships involve oil-drilling partnerships and real-estate partnerships.

**Joint venture**

A partnership established for a specific project or for a limited time

A **joint venture** is a partnership established for a specific project or for a limited time. In recent years, joint ventures between American and foreign corporations have become increasingly common. Chrysler and Mitsubishi, Ford and Mazda, and General Motors and Nissan have all formed joint ventures to manufacture cars in the United States.

## Articles of Partnership

Articles of partnership are legal documents that set forth the basic agreement between the partners. Most states require articles of partnership, but even if they are not required, it makes good sense for partners to draw them up. The following issues are usually covered:

1. Statement of money or assets that each partner has contributed to the partnership (called partnership capital)
2. Statement of each partner's individual management role or duty
3. Statement of how the profits and losses of the partnership will be divided between the partners
4. Provisions that describe how a partner may leave the partnership and any other restrictions that might apply to the agreement

# Advantages of Partnerships

Not every partnership has each of the following advantages. Law firms, accounting firms, and investment firms with several hundred partners have partnership agreements that are quite complicated in comparison to the partnership agreement between two or three people owning a corner store. The advantages must be compared to those offered by other forms of business organization.

*Ease of Organization.* Starting a partnership requires little more than drawing up articles of partnership. No legal charters have to be granted, but the name of the business should be registered with the state.

*Credit Rating.* When a business has several partners, the partnership can rely on a combination of talents and on pooled financial resources. Partnerships tend to be larger than sole proprietorships and therefore have greater earning power and better credit ratings. Because many limited partnerships have been formed for tax purposes rather than for economic profits, the combined income of all U.S. partnerships is negative, and that is why Figure 4-1 shows zero income for partnerships. Nevertheless, the professional partnerships of many lawyers, accountants, and investment banking firms make quite large profits. Goldman Sachs, a large New York investment banking partnership, earns several hundred million dollars in an average year.

*Specialization.* Partnerships can provide diverse skills because partners are able to specialize in their areas of expertise. This makes it possible for the business to be run by a management team of specialists instead of by a generalist sole proprietor. For service-oriented partnerships in such fields as law, financial planning, and accounting, this diversity may attract customers because clients may think that the service offered by a diverse team is of higher quality than that provided by one person.

*Decision Making.* Small partnerships can react more quickly to changes in the business environment than can large partnerships and corporations. Relatively fast reactions are possible because the partners are involved in day-to-day operations and can make decisions quickly after consultation. Large partnerships having hundreds of partners in many states are not common. In those that do exist, decision making is likely to be slow.

**Successful partnership.** Partnerships are voluntary arrangements to achieve a common objective. Partners are allowed to act on each other's behalf. Many advertising agencies are the result of partnerships. This agency's billings are $13 million annually.

*Regulatory Controls.* Like a sole proprietorship, a partnership has fewer regulatory controls affecting its activities than does a public corporation. A partnership does not have to file public financial statements with the Securities and Exchange Commission or send out quarterly financial statements to several hundred thousand owners, as do corporations such as Eastman Kodak and Ford.

*Distribution of Profits.* Partners invest in the business, and profits earned by the business are distributed to the partners in the proportions specified in the articles of partnership. In a corporation, the board of directors decides what percent of the profits to pay the owners each year.

## Disadvantages of Partnerships

Partnerships have many advantages compared to sole proprietorships and corporations, but they also have some disadvantages. Limited partners have no voice in the management of the partnership. Limited partners may bear most of the risk of the business while the general partner reaps a larger share of the benefits. In joint ventures, such as Chrysler-Mitsubishi, there may be a clash of organizational cultures or a change in the goals and objectives of one partner but not the other. This can cause friction, forcing an end to the partnership or giving rise to a joint venture that fails to satisfy both parties. Major disadvantages of partnerships include the following.

*Unlimited Liability.* In general partnerships, the general partners have unlimited liability for the debts incurred by the business. This can be a distinct disadvantage to one partner if his or her personal financial resources are much greater than those of the other partners. A potential partner should check to make sure that all partners have comparable resources to help the business in time of trouble. This disadvantage is eliminated for limited partners, who can lose only their initial investment.

*Business Responsibility.* All partners are responsible for the business actions of all other partners. Partners may have the ability to enter the partnership into a contract without approval of the other partners. A bad decision by one partner may put the other partners' personal resources in jeopardy. Personal problems such as a divorce can eliminate a significant portion of one partner's financial resources and weaken the financial structure of the whole partnership.

*Life of the Partnership.* A partnership is terminated when a partner dies or withdraws. In a two-person partnership, if one partner withdraws, the liabilities would be paid off and the assets divided between the partners. The partner who wishes to continue in the business would be at a serious disadvantage. The business could be disrupted; financing would be reduced; and management skills might be lost with the departing partner. The remaining partner would have to find another partner or reorganize the business as a sole proprietorship. In very large partnerships such as those found in law firms and investment banks, the continuation of the partnership may be provided for in the articles of partnership. The provision may simply state the terms for a new partnership agreement among the remaining partners. In such cases, the disadvantage to the other partners is minimal.

*Selling a Partnership Interest.* Selling a partnership interest creates the same effect as the death or withdrawal of a partner. It is difficult to place a value on a partner's share of the partnership. No public value is placed on the partnership as there is on publicly owned corporations. What is a law firm worth? What is the local hardware store worth? Coming up with a fair value that all partners can agree to is not easy. Selling a partnership interest is easier if a clause in the articles of partnership specifies the method of valuation for the partnership. Even if a clause does set forth the procedure for selling one partner's interest, the old partnership must still be dissolved and a new partnership created. In contrast, in the corporate form of business, the departure of owners may have little effect on the financial resources of the business, and the loss of managers does not cause long-term changes in the structure of the organization.

*Handwritten note in margin:* Limited partner - just invested in business, you're not liable for anything except for your investment.

***Sharing of Profits.*** Partners must share the profits with each other in the manner dictated by the articles of partnership. The biggest disadvantage is that the division of the profits may not reflect the work each partner put into the business. For example, in a two-person partnership where profits are shared fifty-fifty, one partner may work sixty hours a week and the other may work forty hours. Each partner might be making an equal contribution, or the one working forty hours might be making a bigger contribution because his or her skills are very specialized and would be expensive if purchased in the labor market. In this case, a fifty-fifty profit-sharing agreement may cause tension between the partners, and unhappy partners can have a negative effect on the profitability of the business. Students working on a joint case study often experience this disadvantage. One student often feels that he or she did most of the work and that the other students in the group got grades based on his or her efforts.

***Limited Sources of Funds.*** The sources of funds available to a partnership are limited because no public value is placed on the business. Potential partners do not know what one partnership share is worth. Because partnership shares cannot be bought and sold easily in public markets, potential owners may not want to tie up their money in assets not readily sold on short notice. Accumulating enough funds to operate a national business, especially a business requiring intensive investments in plant and equipment, can be difficult. Partnerships may also have to pay higher interest rates on borrowed money than large corporations do because partnerships may be considered greater risks. A type of partnership that eliminates some of these disadvantages is the subject of Business Encounter 4-1.

## Taxation of Partnerships

Partnerships are quasi-taxable organizations. This means that partnerships do not pay taxes when submitting the partnership tax return to the Internal Revenue Service. The tax return provides information about the profitability of the organization and the distribution of profits among the partners. Partners must report their share of profits on their individual tax returns at the income tax rate for individuals.

## ▶ Corporations

**Corporation**

A separate legal entity created by the state

A **corporation** is a separate legal entity, or body, created by the state. Its assets and liabilities are distinct from those of the owners of the corporation. As a legal entity, a corporation has many of the rights, duties, and powers of a person. These rights and powers include receiving, owning, and transferring property. Corporations can enter into contracts with individuals or with other legal entities. They can sue and be sued in court. Incorporated businesses (unlike partnerships) must pay taxes on their income, but the corporation's owners pay taxes only if profits are distributed to them as

## Business Encounter 4-1
### *Master Limited Partnerships*

A master limited partnership (MLP) is a limited partnership with partnership interests, called units, traded on a recognized stock exchange. The first MLP was established in 1981. MLPs are subject to state laws that require limited partnerships to have a large number of limited partners and a high asset value. Most MLPs have been in the oil and real-estate industries; but because of the unique advantages offered by MLPs, more and more businesses have been reorganizing into MLPs—including the Boston Celtics basketball team in 1987.

A MLP offers many of the advantages of a corporation but eliminates the double taxation of corporate earnings. MLPs do not pay corporate income taxes because they send their earnings directly to unit holders, who are the limited partners. The unit holders then pay taxes on this income based on individual tax rates. The highest average tax rate for individuals is currently 28 percent; for corporations, it is 34 percent. Because the corporate tax rate is greater than the personal tax rate, limited partners receive larger after-tax cash flows than do the shareholders of a traditional corporation.

MLPs offer other corporate advantages: unlimited life, limited liability, transferable ownership. However, an MLP reduces its owners' control over management in matters not mentioned in the partnership agreement. MLPs are not well suited for firms with low corporate tax rates and high earnings-retention rates. Furthermore, an MLP increases administrative costs because it requires much more detailed recordkeeping, since each partner must be tracked individually for tax purposes.

MLPs are advantageous to investors because they are classified as passive income generators. As defined by the tax code, passive income is earnings from a business in which the investor is not a direct participant. Thus, earnings from MLPs can be used to balance out passive losses, thereby reducing an investor's tax bill.

Since MLPs are traded on stock exchanges, they are extremely liquid—that is, an investor can easily convert his or her partnership shares into cash. In addition, an investor can purchase a unit of an MLP with only 50 percent of the cost up front, borrowing the rest. This factor contributes to the high yields offered by MLPs.

Although MLPs have been popular with both corporations and investors since their inception, several issues that may change the MLPs' image have surfaced. Congress wants to tax MLPs as corporations. The Internal Revenue Service is considering changing its classification of MLP payouts from passive income to portfolio income; the reclassification would increase the tax liability of unit holders. Moreover, many investors are realizing that some MLPs are merely "shell" corporations that exist for the sole purpose of paying out huge sums of money to their large unitholders. These developments could reduce the popularity of MLPs or even eliminate their use as a form of organization.

---

These facts are from Donald R. Katz, "Are MLP's Worth a Shot?" *Esquire* 108 (September 1987): 79–80; William H. Lurz, "Why the Door May Be Closing on Master Limited Partnerships," *Professional Builder* (August 1987): 20–21; Ellyn E. Spragins, "A New Financing Tool Is in Trouble Already," *Business Week*, No. 3005, June 29, 1987, p. 84; Jack Egan, "The Master Limited Loophole," *U.S. News & World Report*, March 30, 1987, p. 63; and J. Markham Collins and Roger P. Bey, "The Master Limited Partnership: An Alternative to the Corporation," *Financial Management*, 15 (Winter 1986): 5–7, 12–13.

dividends. The owners of the corporation own shares (called common stock) of the corporation. These shares can be bought, sold, given as gifts, or inherited.

## Creation of a Corporation

A corporation is created under the laws of the state in which it incorporates. The individuals creating the corporation are known as incorporators. Each

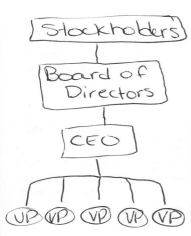

state sets forth a specific procedure, sometimes called chartering the corporation, for incorporation. Most states require a minimum of three incorporators. Another requirement is that the company's name cannot be similar to the name of another business. In most states, the company name must end in "company," "corporation," "incorporated," or "limited" to show that the owners have limited liability. (In this text, the word *company* means an organization engaged in a commercial enterprise and can refer to a sole proprietorship, a partnership, or a corporation.)

The incorporators must complete and file articles of incorporation with the appropriate state office (often the secretary of state).

The articles of incorporation contain basic information about the business. The following ten items are found in the Model Business Corporation Act, issued by the American Bar Association, which is followed by most states:

1. Name and address of the corporation
2. Objectives of corporation
3. Classes of stock (common, preferred, voting, nonvoting) and the number of shares for each class of stock to be issued
4. Expected life of the corporation (corporations are usually created to last in perpetuity)
5. Financial capital required at the time of incorporation
6. Provisions for transferring shares of stock between owners
7. Provisions for the regulation of internal corporate affairs
8. Address of the business office registered with the state of incorporation
9. Names and addresses of the initial board of directors
10. Names and addresses of the incorporators

**Corporate charter**

Issued to the company by the state in which the business incorporates

Based upon the information in the articles of incorporation, a **corporate charter** is issued to the company by the state in which the business incorporates. After a charter is secured, an organizational meeting is held by the owners at which the corporate bylaws are adopted and the board of directors is elected. The bylaws might set up standing committees of the board of directors and describe the rules and procedures for their operation. If the corporation does business in the state in which it is chartered, it is known as a domestic corporation. In other states where the corporation does business, it is known as a foreign corporation.

# Board of Directors

**Board of directors**

Elected by the stockholders to oversee the general operation of the corporation

The **board of directors,** elected by the stockholders to oversee the general operation of the corporation, sets the long-range objectives of the corporation. It is the board's responsibility to ensure that the objectives are achieved on schedule. Board members are legally liable for the mismanagement of the firm or for any misappropriation of funds. Many companies provide insurance for board members to cover any liabilities that arise because of their mistakes. An important duty of the board of directors is to elect corporate officers, such as the chairman of the board and the president, who are responsible to the directors for the management and daily operations of the firm.

Directors can be employees of the company (inside directors) or people unaffiliated with the company (outside directors). Inside directors are usually the officers responsible for running the company. Outside directors are often top executives from other companies, lawyers, bankers, even professors. They are not part of management and are not involved in the day-to-day operations of the firm. One of the chief responsibilities of outside directors is to hold the corporate officers responsible for meeting the goals and objectives of the firm. Because the board of directors consists of both the officers and the outside directors, the outside directors must maintain objectivity in their appraisal of management's performance. Most boards have outside directors because it is assumed that inside directors are likely to have a narrow and biased view of the company's progress.

# Ownership of Corporations

**Private corporation**

Has only a few shareholders, closely involved in managing the business

A corporation may be privately owned or publicly owned. A **private corporation** may be owned by one person or by a group of people, often a family. These people own all the shares of the corporation, and no shares are sold to the public. A private corporation generally has only a few shareholders, and they are closely involved in managing the business. Many corporations are quite large, yet remain private.

A private corporation that needs an infusion of money to take advantage of expansion opportunities may have to obtain financing through the public sale of its stock. Privately owned firms are occasionally forced to "go public" with stock offerings when a major owner dies and the heirs have enormous estate taxes to pay. The tax payment becomes possible only with the proceeds of the sale of stock. This happened to the brewer Adolph Coors, Inc. When Adolph Coors died, his business had to go public. His family sold shares of stock to the public to pay the estate taxes. Privately owned corporations are not required to publicly disclose financial information, but they must pay taxes.

**Public corporation**

Issues certificates of ownership that may be traded on stock exchanges

A **public corporation** issues certificates of ownership, called **common stock,** that may be traded on stock exchanges such as the New York Stock Exchange. Anyone can buy and sell shares of common stock. Owners of stock are referred to as shareholders or stockholders.

**Common stock**

Certificates of ownership in corporations

General Electric, Sears, K-mart, and Exxon are some of the biggest public corporations in the world; each has annual sales of over $10 billion. There are thousands of smaller public corporations in the United States, with sales under $10 million. The stock of these companies is often traded in the over-the-counter market (discussed in Chapter 19).

**Preferred stock**

Usually has no vote in the election of the board of directors but does get preference in the distribution of the company's earnings

Corporations may also issue preferred stock to investors. **Preferred stock** usually has no vote in the election of the board of directors but does get preference in the distribution of the company's earnings. Preferred stockholders receive a fixed dividend before common stockholders receive any dividends on their shares. The fixed dividend is set by the board of directors when the preferred stock is sold and usually stays the same over the life of the preferred stock. In contrast, common stock dividends can go up and down with the profitability of the business. Table 4-2 lists the thirty large public corporations known as the Dow Jones Industrials. The market price

Now when you rent from Avis Inc., you can deal directly with the owners.*

Recently we, the employees of Avis, Inc., bought the company.
Sure, that's good news for us. But it's even better news for you.
Because we know our success depends on your satisfaction. And we intend to be very successful.

We'll do it by giving you low SuperValue Rates for business and leisure, and fast services like Roving Rapid Return. It's the new Avis Carside Computer℠ that speeds you on your way with a printed receipt in just seconds.‡

So the next time you need a car, stop by any Avis corporate rent a car location and shake hands with a new owner.
For information or reservations, call 1-800-331-1212. Or call your travel consultant. It'll be the beginning of a great friendship.

Come meet the new owners of Avis, Inc., at corporate locations.

AVIS
We're trying harder than ever.℠

**Meet the owners.**   Privately held corporations do not offer their stock to the general public. Avis, which at one time was a publicly traded company, is now owned entirely by its employees. Avis promotes new stronger service, commitment to success, and that you deal with the owners when you call to make a reservation.

of these corporations make up a well-known index (the Dow Jones Industrial Average) that measures stock-market performance. These are often termed "blue-chip" stocks, after the most valuable chip in a poker game. Table 4-3 lists the largest companies operating in Europe. One surprise is that Japanese companies are on the European list of large industrial companies.

In large public corporations such as IBM, the owners (shareholders) are often far removed from the management of the company. In small public corporations, the managers are often the founders and the major shareholders. Publicly owned corporations must disclose financial information to the public under specific laws known as securities laws.

## Rights of Common Stockholders

Common stockholders—owners of common stock—are accorded certain rights by the corporate charter. These rights vary slightly from state to state,

**Table 4-2  Dow Jones Industrial Companies**

| | |
|---|---|
| Allied-Signal | International Paper |
| Aluminum Co. of America | McDonald's |
| American Express | Merck |
| American Telephone | Minnesota Mining (3M) |
| Bethlehem Steel | Navistar International |
| Boeing | Phillip Morris |
| Chevron | Primerica |
| Coca-Cola | Procter & Gamble |
| Du Pont | Sears |
| Eastman Kodak | Texaco |
| Exxon | USX |
| General Electric | Union Carbide |
| General Motors | United Technologies |
| Goodyear Tire & Rubber | Westinghouse |
| IBM | Woolworth |

but in general the articles of incorporation spell out voting rights, rights to receive profits, and rights to maintain an original ownership position.

*Voting.* Common stockholders are the voting owners of a corporation. They own shares of common stock and are usually entitled to one vote per share. During the annual stockholders' meeting, the common stockholders elect a board of directors by majority voting or by cumulative voting. The majority voting system allows stockholders owning over 50 percent of the common stock to elect all the directors. The cumulative voting system allows stockholders owning less than 50 percent of the total shares to elect a minority of the directors.

Cumulative voting gives stockholders one vote per share of stock owned multiplied by the number of directors being elected. If ten directors are to

**Table 4-3  The Largest Industrial Corporations in Europe, Ranked by Sales, 1987**

Source: *Fortune*, August 3, 1987, p. 215. © 1987 Time Inc. All rights reserved. Reprinted by permission.

| Company | Country | Sales (000s) |
|---|---|---|
| 1. Royal Dutch Shell Group | Netherlands/ Great Britain | 64,843,217 |
| 2. British Petroleum | Britain | 39,855,564 |
| 3. IRI | Italy | 31,561,709 |
| 4. Toyota Motor | Japan | 31,553,827 |
| 5. Daimler-Benz | West Germany | 30,168,550 |
| 6. Matsushita Electric Industrial | Japan | 26,459,539 |
| 7. Unilever | Netherlands/ Great Britain | 25,141,672 |
| 8. Volkswagen | West Germany | 24,317,154 |
| 9. Hitachi | Japan | 22,668,085 |
| 10. ENI | Italy | 22,549,921 |

be elected by cumulative voting, each share would have ten votes. Under this system, the ten directors with the most votes win. Cumulative voting gives minority owners a chance to elect someone to the board of directors. Assume that seven directors are to be elected. Under cumulative voting, a stockholder who owns 100 shares has 700 votes (7 directors × 100 shares). The stockholder can give all 700 votes to one director or divide the votes in any fashion. If all minority owners maximize their votes, they are sometimes able to elect one or more directors. How many they actually elect depends on the total percentage of shares they control. Formulas to implement cumulative voting may be found in many books on corporate finance or law.

Common stockholders may vote by proxy. A **proxy** is a written authorization by which stockholders assign their voting priviledge to another individual, who then votes for his or her choice at the annual stockholders' meeting. It is a normal practice for management to request proxy statements from shareholders who are not planning to attend the annual meeting. Most owners do not attend annual meetings of the very large companies, such as General Electric or Boeing, unless they live in the city where the meeting is held. If a majority of shareholders stay home but sign proxies mailed by management, they allow management to maintain its position within the corporation.

When shareholders become dissatisfied with management, many submit proxies to a dissident stockholder group. The dissident group may represent a large percentage of the ownership shares, but the majority voting may prevent them from controlling enough shares to elect their own board of directors. If the dissidents receive proxies from enough other dissatisfied shareholders, they can control the election of directors and replace management with their own management team. This strategy is expensive to implement, and the odds of winning against entrenched management are usually slim.

***Distribution of Profits.*** Common stockholders are entitled to the corporate profits. As owners, the stockholders receive profits after all expenses, including interest expense on debt and taxes, have been paid. In effect, stockholders are entitled to all profits that are left after all other obligations have been paid. Stockholders receive profits from the business in the form of dividend payments, which represent a percentage of profits.

For example, if a corporation earns $100 million after expenses and taxes, and the board of directors decides to pay the owners $40 million in dividends, the stockholders receive 40 percent of the profits in cash dividends. Not all aftertax profits are paid to the stockholders in dividends. In this example, $60 million of profits was retained by the board of directors to purchase corporate assets for expansion and to replace worn-out equipment. The board of directors determines on a quarterly basis what dividends will be paid to stockholders.

***Preemptive Rights.*** In most states, when the directors decide to sell new shares of common stock in the marketplace, common stockholders have the first right, known as a preemptive right, to purchase shares of the stock from the corporation. A preemptive right is often included in the articles of incorporation. This provision safeguards stockholders' ownership position in

**Serious business for stockholders.** Shareholders, the owners of stock in a corporation, have voting rights in the corporation. Common stockholders elect a board of directors during the annual stockholders' meeting. If stockholders do not wish to attend the meeting, they can vote by proxy or allow another individual to cast their vote.

the company by letting them purchase shares to maintain their original positions.

Even though a state may require preemptive rights for *new* corporations, many *older* corporations have amended their articles of incorporation through proxy votes to eliminate preemptive rights. Many shareholders, failing to understand the benefits of preemptive rights, have foolishly signed proxies allowing management to eliminate preemptive rights. Preemptive rights are especially important to small companies. A significant percentage of ownership may be lost in the absence of preemptive rights. For corporations like General Motors, no one shareholder owns a large enough percentage of the shares for preemptive rights to make any difference.

## Rights of Preferred Stockholders

Preferred stockholders who own preferred stock are a special class of owners. They generally do not have voting rights, but they do have a claim to profits before common stockholders do. Consequently, dividends cannot be paid to the common stockholders unless the preferred stockholders have already been paid. Dividend payments on preferred stock are usually a fixed percentage of the initial issuing price. For example, if preferred stock was originally priced at $100 per share and the dividend rate is stated at 7½ percent, the dividend payment will be $7.50 per share per year.

Most preferred stock carries a cumulative claim to dividends. This means that if preferred-stock dividends are not paid in one year because of losses, the dividends accumulate to the next year. Such dividends unpaid from previous years must also be paid to preferred stockholders before common stockholders can receive their dividends.

## Advantages of Corporations

Because a corporation is a separate legal entity, it has some very specific advantages over the partnership and sole proprietorship. The biggest advantage may be the limited liability of the owners. Business Encounter 4-2 explains the steps involved in incorporating.

*Limited Liability.* The liability or potential loss of stockholders is limited to the amount of their original investment. Creditors can sue a corporation for not paying its debts, forcing the corporation to declare bankruptcy. Creditors, however, cannot make the stockholders pay the corporation's debts out of their personal assets. Occasionally, the owners of a private corporation may pledge personal assets to secure a loan for the corporation; this would be most unusual for a public corporation.

*Transfer of Ownership.* Stockholders can transfer shares of stock to others without causing the termination of the corporation, and they can do this without the prior approval of other shareholders. Shares of common stock in a public corporation can be bought or sold relatively inexpensively. Using a discount stockbroker, an investor can buy or sell 100 shares of stock at a maximum cost of $45. This $45 cost would be approximately a 1 percent sales commission on a $4,500 purchase or sale. The transfer of ownership (unless it is a majority position) does not affect the daily or long-term operations of the corporation.

*Perpetual Life.* A corporation is usually chartered in perpetuity unless its articles of incorporation stipulate otherwise. The existence of the corporation is unaffected by the death or withdrawal of its stockholders. The corporation survives until the owners sell it or liquidate its assets. In some cases, bankruptcy ends a corporation's life. Figure 4-2 shows the number of bankruptcies in the United States from 1978 to 1987. Bankruptcies occur when companies are unable to compete and earn profits. Eventually uncompetitive businesses cannot pay their bills and must close or seek protection from creditors in bankruptcy court while the business tries to reorganize.

*External Sources of Capital.* Capital (long-term funds) can be raised more easily by a public corporation than by a partnership or a sole proprietorship because its stock and bonds (debt securities) are bought and sold in public markets such as the New York Stock Exchange. The price of ownership is known, and when the company wants to raise new funds, it can sell new shares or bonds to the public and attract funds from anywhere in the United

## Business Encounter 4-2
### Why and How to Incorporate Your Business

You can incorporate a business, whether you are a professional (perhaps a doctor or an accountant) or run a small business (maybe a part-time lawn-care service to finance your college education). In some states (Delaware is one), you can incorporate as a one-person operation, where you act as president, secretary, treasurer, and employee. Other states require that there be at least three officers in a corporation.

Incorporating your small business is a good idea for several reasons. After incorporation, you are no longer personally liable for your company's debts. Transferring ownership is easier, as is raising money, and your corporation can survive after your death. As a corporation, you may find it easier to obtain discounts from suppliers. Even if you are the only employee, you are eligible for worker's compensation benefits as an employee of your company. And finally, incorporating your business may reduce your total tax bite, even though corporate income is taxed twice. You are not taxed twice on the same money (you pay taxes on your salary, and the corporation pays taxes on everything else), and your total tax bill could decline by as much as 50 percent because of the difference between corporate and personal tax rates.

Although incorporating sounds like a complex process, for a small company it is largely a matter of time and paperwork. The first step is to apply for an Employer Identification Number (sort of like a Social Security Number for your corporation) in the name of your prospective corporation. The next, and most important, step is to apply for a Corporate Charter, called a certificate of incorporation in some states. This part of the incorporation process varies according to individual state laws, so you must check with the secretary of the state in which you plan to incorporate

to determine the correct procedure. You may have to pay a filing or application fee. In New York, the fee is $110. The state will probably ask you to specify what fiscal year your company will follow. The most obvious choice is January 1 to December 31, but many corporations elect to go from July 1 to June 30. The state will probably also ask what kind of stock and how many shares the company will issue. (You can be the sole owner of all the stock.) The issued stock may be designated to have a par value or to have no-par value. The no-par value option is usually cheaper and easier to set up, but the difference between the two is mostly an accounting difference and not that significant.

The next step in the process involves ordering a set of corporate records and a corporate seal. The corporate records include stock certificates, a stock ledger transfer, and places for you to attach your certificate of incorporation, your corporate seal, and related materials. The corporate seal is used to stamp important documents. Finally, after you have received your corporate seal and Employer Identification Number, you may open bank accounts in your corporation's name.

The process would be more complex for a huge company like Exxon, but most companies start small. Despite the paperwork, incorporation may be advantageous for your small business. If you decide it is, check with the secretary of your state for more information, current laws, and the exact procedure for incorporation.

These facts are from Judith H. McQuown, *INC. Yourself* (New York: Warner Books, 1984); Ted Nicholas, *How to Form Your Own Corporation Without a Lawyer for Under $50.00* (Wilmington, Del.: Enterprise Publishing, 1981); and Ted Nicholas, *Cash: How to Get It into and out of Your Corporation* (Wilmington, Del.: Enterprise Publishing, 1980).

States and from foreign investors. The larger a corporation becomes, the more sources of financing are available to it.

***Expansion Potential.*** Because large public corporations can find long-term financing readily, they can easily expand into national and international markets. Because a corporation is a legal entity, it can enter into contracts without as much difficulty as a partnership.

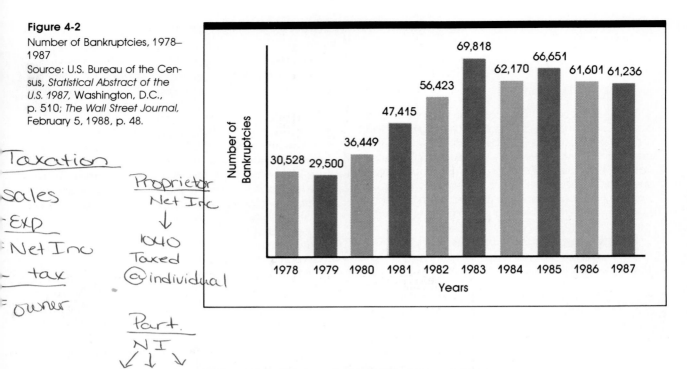

*Handwritten margin notes:*

Taxation

Sales
-Exp
=Net Inc
- tax
= owner

Proprietor
Net Inc
↓
1040
Taxed
@ individual

Part.
NI
↓ ↓ ↓
1040's
taxed
@ partners

corporations
NI
-CORP tax
(NI @ tax)
↓ stockholders
Dividends
↓
Stockholders
Inc. Tax

Securities and Exchange Commission

Government regulatory agency

# Disadvantages of Corporations

Corporations have some distinct disadvantages resulting from tax laws and government regulation.

***Double Taxation.*** The corporation is treated as a legal entity and must pay taxes on its taxable income. When aftertax corporate profits are paid out in dividends to the stockholders, the dividends are taxed a second time as part of the individual owner's income. This process creates double taxation for the stockholders of dividend-paying corporations. Double taxation does not occur with the other forms of business organization.

***Forming a Corporation.*** The formation of a corporation can be costly. A charter must be obtained, and this usually requires the services of an attorney and payment of legal fees. Filing fees ranging from $25 to $150 must be paid to the state that awards the corporate charter, and certain states require that an annual fee be paid to maintain the charter.

***Disclosure of Information.*** Information must be made available to the owners. This is usually done by means of an annual report to shareholders. The annual report contains financial information about the firm's profits, sales, plant and equipment, and debts. It also contains descriptions of the company's operations, products, and plans. Public corporations must also file reports with a government regulatory agency called the **Securities and Exchange Commission (SEC).** The larger the firm, the more data the SEC requires. Because all reports filed with the SEC are available to the public, competitors have access to them.

The cost of the annual report and the SEC documents is great. A typical annual report may cost between $2.50 and $3.50 a copy to produce, not including the wages of the people involved collecting the information. If a corporation has 500,000 stockholders, as many large companies do, the cost can exceed $1 million.

***Employee-Owner Separation.*** Many employees are not stockholders of the company they work for. This separation of owners and employees may cause employees to feel that their work benefits only the owners. Non-owner employees do not always see how they fit into the corporate picture and do not understand the importance of profits to the health of the organization. If management is a part owner but other employees are not, management-labor relations takes on a different, sometimes difficult, aspect from those in partnerships and sole proprietorships.

## Subsidiary Corporations

**Subsidiary corporation**

A corporation that has the majority of its stock owned by another corporation

A **subsidiary corporation** is a corporation that has the majority of its stock owned by another corporation known as the parent company. The subsidiary company has its own corporate structure with a president and other senior officers. Usually the officers of a subsidiary are selected by the officers of the parent company with the approval of the parent company's board of directors. Chevron Corporation is a large international oil company with over fifty subsidiaries and affiliates. Its annual report states that about forty-five subsidiaries are 100 percent owned by Chevron and ten are partially owned by Chevron. Table 4-4 presents a partial listing of Chevron's subsidiaries.

## Holding Companies

**Holding company**

A corporation that has control over one or more other corporations through ownership of its common stock

A **holding company** is a corporation that has control over one or more other corporations through ownership of its common stock. The other corporations remain separate entities, legally responsible for their own operation. They have stockholders besides the holding company and are not wholly owned subsidiary companies.

Ownership of more than 50 percent of a corporation's common stock guarantees that the holding company can control the affairs of that corporation. A holding company may own less than a 50 percent interest in a company, yet still have voting control. This can occur because the other stockholders are unorganized and have such small minority interests that they lack collective power.

The holding company was popular in the early 1900s and is still in use. Typically, utilities formed holding companies so that they could buy companies outside of the government-regulated utility industry. In the 1970s and 1980s, the most popular form of holding company was in the commercial banking industry. Banking has been regulated by the states and the federal government. For example, Illinois denied banks from having branches (more than one main facility) and did not allow banks from other states to own banks within Illinois. By forming holding companies, banks were able to buy other banks within the state and create a banking network similar to branch banking.

Table 4-4 Chevron
Corporation Subsidiaries

| Company | Principal Business | Area of Operation |
|---|---|---|
| Chevron U.S.A., Inc. | Exploration, producing, transportation, refining, marketing | United States |
| American Gilsonite Co. | Producing and marketing gilsonite | Colorado and Utah |
| Chandeleur Pipe Line Co. | Gas transportation | Louisiana and Mississippi |
| Chevron Capital U.S.A., Inc. | Financing | California |
| Chevron Chemical Company | Agricultural and industrial chemicals | United States |
| Chevron Canada Limited | Exploration, producing, refining, marketing | Western Canada |
| Chevron do Brasil Ltda. | Lubricating oil, additives, and asphalt | Brazil |
| California Asiatic Oil Co. | Exploration, producing | Eastern Hemisphere |

The main advantage of the holding company is that it allows control of 100 percent of a corporation's assets without 100 percent investment. In addition, there is the advantage that the holding company is not responsible for the debt of the other corporation because they are two separate firms with separate stockholders.

Taxation is a major disadvantage for a holding company. The holding company (Firm A) receives dividends from the companies it owns (Firm X, Firm Y, and Firm Z). The dividends provide income but give rise to triple taxation: Firms X, Y, and Z pay taxes on their incomes, and the holding company pays on the dividends. If the holding company pays out dividends to its shareholders, a *third* tax on the same income or profit will be paid by them. Another disadvantage is administrative problems. With multiple managements, boards of directors, dividend policies, and reporting systems, expenses are high and the opportunities for problems are substantial.

# ► Cooperatives

**Cooperative**

An organization composed of individuals or small businesses that have banded together to reap the benefits of belonging to a larger organization

A **cooperative (co-op)** is an organization composed of individuals or small businesses that have banded together to reap the benefits of belonging to a larger organization. A co-op is set up not to make money as an entity but so that its members can become more profitable or save money. Co-ops are generally expected to operate without profit or to create only enough profit to maintain the co-op organization.

A co-op can purchase supplies in large quantities and pass the savings on to its members. It can also help distribute the products of its members more efficiently than each member could on an individual basis. A cooperative can advertise its members' products and thus generate demand.

**Cranberry growers cooperate.** A cooperative allows individuals to act together to receive the benefits common to a large organization—allowing greater cost savings and profitability for members. Farmers, such as this cranberry grower, are among the best-known members of cooperatives.

Many cooperatives exist in small farming communities. The co-op stores and markets grain; orders large quantities of fertilizer, seed, and other supplies at discounted prices; and reduces costs and increases efficiency with good management.

Consumer co-ops allow members to purchase products at reduced prices through large-quantity discounts. Warehouse buying clubs give consumers bulk-rate discounts with their membership. Financial co-ops (credit unions) reduce the cost of financial services to members. Credit unions acquire funds from members' deposits and allow members to borrow from the existing pool of money. Because credit unions are not profit-oriented businesses, the average 1 or 2 percent profit margin can be eliminated, and credit unions can pay a higher interest rate on deposits and charge a lower interest rate on loans than can competing banks and other financial institutions. Large credit unions offer many of the same services as large commercial banks.

## Business Encounter 4-3

*Ford Motor Company*

Not all family-owned businesses are successful right from the beginning. Henry Ford is one of those examples of "if at first you don't succeed, try, try again." Even when Henry Ford showed talent with mechanical things as a young man, few people would have predicted that his company would be one of the leading manufacturers in the world, with subsidiaries from Canada to Brazil and from France to Taiwan.

Henry Ford resigned from the Edison Illuminating Company in 1899 to organize the Detroit Automobile Company. Within two years the company went bankrupt and then was reorganized into the Henry Ford Company. After conflicts with his business partners over his ideas, Henry Ford quit the Henry Ford Company in 1902 to pursue his dream. The company dropped his name from the title of the business and Henry Ford became quite successful at building and racing cars. This enabled him to form a new company on June 16, 1903 called the Ford Motor Company. He owned 25.5 percent of the original stock. The firm had only $100,000 of organizational capital, of which $28,000 was paid in cash. In 1906 Ford increased his ownership to 51 percent and by 1919 Ford Motor Company was entirely owned by members of the Ford family.

The Model T entered the market in 1908 priced at $825 to $850 depending upon the model selected and in 1909 over 10,000 Model Ts were sold. By 1914 over 250,000 cars had been sold and a total of 15 million Model Ts were sold over its lifetime. As a contrast, during the 1987 model year Ford Motor Company sold over 6 million cars, trucks, and tractors worldwide, with 3.67 million coming from U.S. sales. In the early 1900s Ford Motor Company was the leader in the industry but by the 1920s it was facing stiff competition from General Motors Corporation, and by 1940 its market share was only 20 percent of the U.S.

market. Edsel Ford died in 1943 and Henry Ford in 1947. His grandson Henry Ford II took over as president of the company in 1945 at the age of 28 and is credited with saving Ford Motor Company from collapse. Ford struggled throughout the 50s, 60s, and 70s behind General Motors. When Henry Ford II died in 1987 Ford was on the upswing and posted record earnings in 1986 and 1987. Even though sales were not greater than General Motors', earnings exceeded GM's for two years in a row.

After eighty-five years in business, the Ford family still has effective control over the Ford Motor Company. The company did sell shares of common stock to the public, which are traded on the New York Stock Exchange. However, Henry Ford created two different classes of common stock—one for the family and one for the public. The Ford family common stock is called class B common stock and maintains 40 percent of the voting power versus 60 percent for the public. This relationship holds, even though there are 38.6 million class B shares and 472.4 million common shares. Common stock has one vote and class B stock has votes in proportion to the common stock so that total votes amount to 40 percent of the total.

Because public ownership is so widespread, the Ford family maintains effective control of the company and has three members of the Ford family on the company's board of directors. This is just an example of how many company founders try to keep control of their companies in family hands even after they die.

*Automotive News*, October 5, 1987, 520 pp. 1, 74–77; *Automotive News, The Year in Review Extra*, 1987; Standard NYSE Stock Reports, Vol. 55/No. 45, Sec. 7, March 7, 1988, Standard and Poor's Corporation; Moody's Industrial Manual, Vol. 1, A-I. 1987; Value Line Investment Survey, Edition 1, March 25, 1988, p. 104.

# Summary and Review

▶ A sole proprietorship is a business owned and managed by one person. Sole proprietorships account for the majority of business organizations today. The major advantages of a sole proprietorship are the following: (1) They are easy and inexpensive to form. (2) They provide a high level of secrecy. (3) All profits belong to the owner. (4) The owner has direct control over the business. (5) Government regulation is minimal. (6) Taxes are paid only once. (7) The business can be closed easily.

▶ The disadvantages of a sole proprietorship are the following: (1) The owner must use his or her own assets to support borrowing. (2) Sources of external funds are difficult to find. (3) The owner must be a jack-of-all-trades. (4) The survival of the business is tied to the life of the owner and his or her ability to work. (5) Qualified employees are hard to find. (6) Wealthy owners pay a higher tax than they would under the corporate form of business.

▶ A partnership is a business formed by several individuals. Partnerships take three forms: general partnerships, limited partnerships, and joint ventures. Partnerships offer the following advantages: (1) They are easy to organize. (2) Higher credit ratings can exist because the partners may have more combined wealth. (3) Partners can specialize. (4) Partnerships can make quick decisions compared to larger businesses. (5) Government regulations are few. (6) Profits are paid directly to the owners.

▶ Partnerships have several disadvantages: (1) General partners have unlimited liability to pay the debts of the partnership. (2) Partners are responsible for each other's decisions. (3) The death or termination of one partner requires a new partnership agreement to be drawn up. (4) It is difficult to sell a partnership interest at a fair price. (5) The distribution of profits may not reflect the amount of work done by each partner. (6) Large partnerships cannot find external sources of funds as easily as large corporations.

▶ A corporation is a business treated as a single legal entity. Corporations are chartered by a state through articles of incorporation. They have a board of directors made up of corporate officers or people from outside the company. Corporations can be private or public. They are owned by stockholders. Common stockholders have the right to elect the board of directors. Two voting systems are followed: cumulative and majority. Some companies have preferred stockholders, who do not have a vote but get preferential dividend treatment over common stockholders.

▶ Several advantages belong to the corporate form of business: (1) The owners are not responsible for the debts of the firm and have limited liability. (2) Ownership interests can be easily transferred. (3) Corporations usually have a perpetual life. (4) External capital is more easily raised than in other forms of business. (5) Expansion into new businesses is simpler because of the ability of the company to enter into contracts. This expansion can take place through the ownership of subsidiary companies.

▶ Corporations are not without disadvantages: (1) The company gets taxed on its income, and owners pay a second tax on any profits received as dividends. (2) Forming a corporation can be expensive. (3) Much information must be made available to the public and to government agencies. (4) Owners and managers are not always the same and can have different goals.

▶ Holding companies result from one company owning two or more other companies and operating them as separate entities with their own management and ownership structure. A holding company may own less than 50 percent of another company yet still control its operations.

▶ A cooperative exists to benefit a group of small businesses. Farmers band together in order to receive preferential treatment in buying and selling goods in large quantities.

# Key Terms and Concepts

sole proprietorship
partnership
general partnership
limited partnership
joint venture
corporation
corporate charter
board of directors
private corporation
public corporation
common stock

preferred stock
majority voting system
cumulative voting system
proxy
preemptive right
Securities and Exchange Commission
  (SEC)
subsidiary corporation
holding company
cooperative (co-op)

# Checking Your Understanding

This chapter introduced you to the subject of forms of business ownership. To test and reinforce your understanding, fill in the blanks below.

1. An individual who creates a corporation is an _incorperator_

2. A _joint_ venture is a form of partnership established to accomplish a specific task or to operate for a limited time.

3. A sole _proprietorship_ is a business owned by one individual.

4. A document in which common stockholders assign their votes to another individual is called a _proxy_

5. _Preferred_ stock is a special class of stock that generally does not carry voting rights.

6. A corporation is a legal _entity_ with all the rights, duties, and power of a person.

7. _Public_ corporations offer stock for sale to the public.

8. Common _stock_ represents shares of ownership in a corporation.

→ 9. _Cumulative_ voting enables stockholders owning less than 50 percent of the total shares to elect a minority of the directors.

10. Stockholders receive corporate profits in the form of _dividends_

11. A _general_ partner assumes unlimited liability.

12. Common stockholders have limited _liability_

13. The form of organization that is considered a separate legal entity is called a _corporation_

14. An organization composed of individuals or small businesses banded together to benefit from belonging to a larger organization is called a _coop_.

→ 15. _Inside_ directors are also employed in the day-to-day operation of the corporation.

16. The name for a corporation that owns a subsidiary corporation is a _parent_ company.

17. _Common_ stockholders receive the residual profits and are entitled to vote.

18. The abbreviation for the government regulatory agency that collects and inspects financial data of public corporations is _SEC_.

# Topics for Review and Discussion

1. Compare the tax features of corporations, partnerships, and sole proprietorships.
2. What are five advantages of a sole proprietorship?
3. Why are most sole proprietorships small businesses?
4. What is the difference between a subsidiary company and a holding company?
5. List the three different types of partnerships, and describe each one.
6. Compare the liability position of partnerships, sole proprietorships, and corporate shareholders.
7. Which form of business organization has the least government regulation? Which has the most?
8. What are five of the ten items usually found in the Model Business Corporation Act?
9. The most common examples of cooperatives are farm co-ops and consumer co-ops. Explain the reasons for this and the benefits that result for members of cooperatives.
10. Why would secrecy in operating a business be important to an owner?
11. What are the four provisions of the articles of partnership?
12. Which form of business requires the most specialization of skills? Which requires the least? Why?
13. How are profits distributed in sole proprietorships, partnerships, and corporations?
14. Explain the legal benefits of being organized as a corporation.
15. Describe the board of directors for a company, and explain how board members are chosen.
16. What is the difference between an outside director and an inside director? Why do corporations have both kinds of directors?
17. A corporation can be public or private. What are the differences between these two forms of companies?
18. Stockholders have the right to vote. For what can they vote?
19. Explain the two different methods of voting used by common stockholders.
20. Describe the features of preferred stock.
21. Define preemptive right, and explain its purpose.

# Exercises

1. Select a publicly owned corporation, and bring to class a list of its subsidiaries. This data should be available in a corporate annual report, *Standard and Poor's Corporate Records*, or *Moody Corporate Manuals*. Ask your librarian for help if these sources are unavailable. Use a company on the list of Dow Jones Industrial Companies in Table 4-2, or select some other company.
2. Select one of the companies from the list of Dow Jones Industrials companies in Table 4-2 and make a list of its outside directors. Information of this nature can be found in several places in your library: the company's annual report, list of corporate directors, and various financial sources. If possible, include each director's title and the name of the company that employs him or her on a full-time basis.

# Case 4-1
## *Al Dente Pasta*

In 1981, Monique Deschaine began to make gourmet pasta by hand in a friend's restaurant after it had closed for the night. Today her small business, Al Dente, Inc., is a thriving corporation with annual sales over $200,000. Al Dente pasta located in Whitmore Lake, Michigan, has achieved a national reputation thanks to write-ups in national magazines such as *Atlantic Monthly* and *The Gourmet Retailer*. Deschaine's pasta was even featured in a recipe at the Waldorf Astoria Hotel in New York.

Monique Deschaine started her pasta business as a sole proprietor, making all the pasta herself, about 7 pounds at a time, on one small machine. She made the pasta at night, laying it out to dry on the restaurant tables. She had to rush to finish and clean up before the restaurant opened for business in the morning. She promoted her pasta by demonstrating recipes in stores. Her hard work paid off, and today she leaves the pasta making to four full-time employees in her own shop. However, she still supervises the pasta-making technique. With a state-of-the-art pasta machine, Al Dente can now press 100 pounds of linguine and spaghetti at a time, although the product is still hand-rolled and hand-sheeted. Each day, the company makes about 500 pounds of pasta, which is distributed in Chicago, Detroit, and on both coasts.

Deschaine insists on using the freshest ingredients: 100 percent semolina flour moistened with hand-cracked eggs fresh from a nearby farm. Ingredients for different flavored pastas—egg, tomato, spinach, herb-flavored, spicy sesame, blue corn, walnut, three-pepper, and wild mushroom—are mixed right into the dough. Deschaine uses no salt, preservatives, or artificial additives. She refuses to compromise on quality: "Making perfect pasta is a painstaking, step-by-step process. We pride ourselves on doing each step well, so that Al Dente pasta looks, cooks, and tastes right." The term *al dente* literally means "to the tooth" and refers to perfectly made and cooked pasta.

In 1982, Deschaine incorporated her growing small business into Al Dente, Inc., a private corporation. She owns 60 percent of the company; her husband owns the other 40 percent. Deschaine decided to incorporate to reduce her liability, to boost the company's credibility, and to legally separate her business from other family businesses, such as her husband's windsurfing retail store.

The success Al Dente now enjoys did not come easily. Deschaine had to put in long hours to establish her business. She attributes much of her business success to her family, most of whom work at Al Dente. Her sister Nanette runs the pasta machine. Her husband Dennis helps out whenever he can get away from his windsurfing shop—which happens to be next door—and her infant son supervises from his walker.

Deschaine advises those who want to own their own small business to be prepared to work long and hard. She points out that new business owners should not expect to earn a lot of money or have a lot of time off at first. She also recommends that anyone interested in starting a business not hesitate to ask for help from friends and family. They can offer support, advice, labor, and financing. Most importantly, she stresses sound financial management to ensure the success of the business—whether it be a sole proprietorship or a corporation. "Spend wisely," she advises.

---

These facts are from Karen Grassmuck, "Pasta Point of No Return," *Ann Arbor News*, January 17, 1988; Al Dente press releases, 1987 and 1988; and a telephone interview with Monique Deschaine, March 21, 1988.

**Questions**

1. Discuss the advantages and disadvantages of Monique Deschaine's decision to incorporate Al Dente, Inc.
2. Al Dente, Inc. is a private corporation. Did incorporation make it easier for Deschaine to obtain financing than when she was a sole proprietor?
3. What are some of the advantages that Deschaine might have maintained if she had remained a sole proprietor?

---

## Case 4-2
### *Merck & Co.*

Merck & Co., headquartered in Rahway, New Jersey, is one of the most successful pharmaceutical corporations. The company traces its origins to a seventeenth-century German apothecary. In the 1980s, the company introduced several new drugs, the most promising of which is Mevacor, an anticholesterol drug. In 1987, sales increased by 23 percent over the previous year's level to $5.1 billion, and profits increased by 34 percent to $906 million.

Merck's success has not gone unnoticed by the business community. In fact, the company was named "America's Most Admired Corporation" three years in a row by *Fortune* magazine. Merck's success has also been noticed by investors. Merck has had a market value of about $28 billion, making it number nine in market value among U.S. corporations (ahead of companies like Amoco, Wal-Mart Stores, and Dow Chemical). In March 1988, the company's stock traded at $160 per share. Because of its public corporate structure and high market valuation, Merck has access to a tremendous amount of money, which it puts into researching and developing new drugs.

Merck has blended scientific initiative with business skill to become the world's number-one maker of prescription drugs. More than 90 percent of the company's revenues come from drugs. It is also one of the least diversified pharmaceutical firms. It sold its consumer products business in the 1970s, and it recently undertook a substantial restructuring that involved the closing of subsidiaries in six countries.

Merck's current chairman, Roy Vagelos, was appointed by the company's board of directors in 1985. Vagelos is one of the few chief executives in the pharmaceutical business with an M.D. Under his leadership, Merck actively pursues talented young scientists. Many are attracted by the chance to work at Merck's lavishly equipped facilities in an atmosphere that resembles that of a college campus. Merck gives its research scientists extraordinary freedom to decide on which projects to work. In addition, promising employees are often rapidly promoted at Merck, increasing employee motivation.

Merck's research structure is informal and is divided into twelve therapeutic divisions, ranging from antibiotics to cardiovascular drugs. Each one has a leader whose job is to provide new ideas and keep workers excited about the possibility of a new drug discovery. The research process is unusual because no project team has its own budget or a grant of authority. Instead, team members from each discipline must commit their own scientific resources to a project. This helps to foster teamwork and unity of purpose among researchers.

A large part of Merck's success is the result of the large sums of money that it spends on research and development. In 1987, Merck spent 11 percent of its revenues on research and development, more than any rival drug company. These efforts have been extremely rewarding. Merck had an unprecedented thirteen different drugs with sales of more than $100 million in 1987. In addition, the company had another fifty drugs in the works.

Researching and developing prescription drugs is an expensive and time-consuming process. Mevacor, for example, has been in development since 1956, when Merck researchers first isolated mevalonic acid, one of the links in the formation of cholesterol. That discovery and others ultimately led to scientists' understanding of the cholesterol-formation process. In 1978, Merck scientists identified a substance that inhibits the enzyme that forms mevalonic acid, essentially blocking the formation of cholesterol. In 1985 and 1986, Merck spent as much as 25 percent of its research and development budget getting Mevacor into the final development and test stages.

Like all corporations, Merck has to deal with government regulations. Most of these regulations come from the Food and Drug Administration (FDA). Pharmaceutical companies such as Merck must submit a patent application for a new drug to the FDA, which may take two or three years to act on it. Although drug patents can last up to twenty-two years, FDA testing after the filing can take several years, often giving competitors time to develop their own versions of the drug. Another full year often passes before the drug is publicly reviewed by an FDA advisory panel. Through years of experience, Merck has learned to maintain a close relationship with the FDA by constantly informing it of the status of and progress made on new drugs. As a result, Merck won FDA approval for Mevacor after only nine months of review, instead of the usual thirty months.

Although Merck has achieved the reputation of being "America's Most Admired Corporation," Chairman Vagelos knows that Merck must constantly produce new products in order to remain competitive in the ever-changing pharmaceutical industry. Thus, Vagelos is constantly pushing his researchers to come up with the next generation of wonder drugs. According to Vagelos, "You'll die if you sit on your laurels."

---

These facts are from Gordon Bock, with Raji Samghabadi, "Merck's Medicine Man," *Time*, February 22, 1988, pp. 44–45; Jane H. Cutaia, "A Healthy Payoff from Nonstop Research," *Business Week*, January 11, 1988, p. 119; John A. Byrne, "The Miracle

Company," *Business Week,* October 19, 1987, pp. 84–90; Stuart Gannes, "Merck Has Made Biotech Work," *Fortune,* January 19, 1987, pp. 58–64; and Daniel Horgan, "IBM's Market Value Is Tops," *USA Today,* March 29, 1988, p. 1B.

**Questions**

1. How has Merck benefited from being a public corporation?
2. Merck is one of the thirty large public corporations known as the Dow Jones Industrials. Why did Merck become one of these "blue chip" companies?
3. What are the rights of Merck common stockholders?

# Answers to Checking Your Understanding

1. incorporator
2. joint
3. proprietorship
4. proxy
5. Preferred
6. entity
7. Public
8. stock
9. Cumulative
10. dividends
11. general
12. liability
13. corporation
14. cooperative
15. Inside
16. parent
17. Common
18. SEC

## Outline

# Chapter 5

# Small Business and Franchising

## Objectives

After reading this chapter, you will be able to:

▶ Define small business, and explain why there is more than one definition of this term.

▶ Discuss why certain fields attract small business.

▶ Analyze why small businesses succeed and fall.

▶ Describe the services offered by the Small Business Administration.

▶ List the advantages and disadvantages of franchising.

▶ Describe the protections offered by law to franchisees.

# Business Experience

After Peter Salisbury graduated from Northeastern University, he took a job in the mail room of Ropes & Gray, a prestigious Boston law firm. He was soon running the mail room and continued to do so for five-and-a-half years. It was there that he learned the ropes of the shipping business and heard constant complaints about mail-room mix-ups, the high price of Federal Express' overnight delivery service, and bad accounting.

Salisbury knew that if he could get twenty-five or thirty clients, he could ship enough overnight packages to earn a volume discount from Federal Express and other overnight shippers. In December 1983, with $5,000, Salisbury formed Mercury Business Services with his brother-in-law Robert Hodgkins and their wives, Wendy Salisbury and Brenda Hodgkins.

Mercury quickly found thirty-five regular clients (ten of whom shipped nightly) and had little trouble getting a volume discount from Federal Express. Mercury passed some of the savings on to its customers and also provided services such as package pickup, filling out airbills, tracing lost packages, and invoicing the day after a package was sent. Salisbury figures these services save up to ten work-hours a day for Mercury's clients.

By invoicing clients the day after a package is sent, Mercury enables third-party billers (such as law firms, accountants, and public relations firms) to turn right around and bill their clients for Federal Express expenses. According to Salisbury, the big problem law firms have with Federal Express is that it takes from 2.5 to 4 weeks for bills to come in. If a law firm has finished its work with a client, it's not good form to bill the client belatedly. "That's not the way you stay prestigious," says Salisbury.

Bob Hodgkins is proud that Mercury can decrease a client's overnight shipping costs by at least $2 per package, with savings ranging up to 25 percent. Salisbury figures Mercury can save Ropes & Gray, his former employer and current client, around $50,000 a year from cuts in overtime, excess package costs, and accounting.

Salisbury recognized a need in the marketplace, and with a small initial investment and the time and effort of the other Mercury founders he was able to establish a company that caters to the needs of downtown Boston professional companies. Because Mercury was not developing a product from scratch but was adding value to an already existing business, Mercury's start-up costs were relatively low.

Succeeding as a small business operator is no easy task, particularly in the services industry. In 1987, sixty-one thousand businesses failed in the United States, a decrease of .6 percent from 1986. But services topped the failure list at 24,029—almost 40 percent. To guard against failure, Mercury Business Services does more than provide good service. Rather than rely solely on Federal Express or lawyer clients, it uses other shippers and serves other clients. Mercury uses the overnight shipping service that gives the best breaks on prices and gets the packages to the correct destinations at the desired time. Recent shipments have ranged from legal briefs to lobsters to Boston Celtic Larry Bird's basketball shoes.

Salisbury's initial $5,000 investment really paid off. In its first full year of operation, Mercury Business Services billed clients just over $160,000. By 1987, that figure had increased more than tenfold to $1.8 million in annual sales.

"It's getting to the point where we feel we're going to be the biggest volume Federal Express user in town," beams Salisbury.

---

These facts are from Jeffrey L. Seglin, *America's New Breed of Entrepreneurs* (Washington, D.C.: Acropolis Books, 1986), pp. 36–39.

# Introduction

Small businesses are the heart of the U.S. economic and social system because of the opportunities they offer and because they express the freedom that Americans have to make their own destinies. The risks are indeed great— but the opportunities for success, both financial and psychological, are greater.

The characteristics of the successful small business owner are rewarded not just in the world of small business, but in other areas as well. Creativity, innovation, and willingness to take risks also characterize the most successful managers in large businesses and government.

But starting and running a successful small business is no easy task. Franchising has successfully become an avenue that many prospective small business owners take to go into business for themselves. By doing so, they hope to avoid many of the pitfalls that small business owners can find themselves facing. This chapter examines the world of small business and how franchising has increasingly become an avenue of entry into small business ownership.

# ▶ Nature of Small Business

In the last decade small businesses generated more than half of all new jobs in the United States.[1] Clearly, small business is crucial to the country's economy. Nevertheless, defining small business is no easy task. Mercury Business Services, with less than $2 million in annual sales, falls easily into the small-business category. But when does a small business become a big business?

Smallness is relative. Ben & Jerry's Homemade, a manufacturer of premium ice cream in Waterbury, Vermont, has sales of $19.7 million a year.[2] That's small in comparison to Nabisco, which has annual sales of more than $16 billion.[3] But Ben & Jerry's is certainly not small in comparison to a neighborhood ice cream shop or a mom-and-pop convenience store.

Even bankers, when asked to define small business in terms of sales, could not reach a consensus. Their responses ranged from "under $5 million in annual sales" (62.5 percent) and "under $10 million" (21.7 percent) all the way up to "under $25 million" (3.3 percent) and "under $50 million (1.7 percent)."[4]

**Small business** may be defined as any business that is independently owned and operated, is not dominant in its field, and does not employ more than five hundred people. This definition parallels the definition used by the president of the United States in his report to Congress on the state of small business[5] and by the **Small Business Administration (SBA)**, an independent agency of the federal government that offers managerial and financial assistance to small businesses. Table 5-1 shows additional standards that the SBA uses to determine which businesses can receive its help.

**Small business**

Any business that is independently owned and operated, is not dominant in its field, and does not employ more than five hundred people

**Small Business Administration (SBA)**

An independent agency of the federal government that offers managerial and financial assistance to small businesses

| Type of Business | Size of Business |
|---|---|
| Manufacturers | Employing fewer than |
| Petroleum refining | 1,500 people |
| Electronic computers | 1,000 |
| Macaroni and spaghetti | 500 |
| Wholesalers | Employing fewer than |
| Sporting goods | 500 people |
| Furniture | 500 |
| Paints and varnishes | 500 |
| Retailers | Earning sales of less than |
| Grocery stores | $13.5 million a year |
| Automobile agencies | 11.5 |
| Restaurants | 10.0 |
| Services | Earning sales of less than |
| Computer—related services | $12.5 million a year |
| Accounting services | 4.0 |
| Television repair | 3.5 |

There is, in fact, no generally accepted definition of small business. Some commentators argue that franchised operations, such as Subway Sandwiches & Salads (a 982-outlet fast-food restaurant), are not small businesses because the granter of the franchises (in this case Doctor's Associates, Inc.) sets management standards for individual store owners.[6] By this reasoning, the store owner is not truly independent. Figure 5-1 shows the relative proportion of small businesses by industry.

A firm developing and marketing highly specialized medical equipment might dominate its particular segment of the market. To be considered a small business, however, it could not dominate the medical equipment industry as a whole. Thus the word *field* in the definition above should be understood in a broad sense.

Some people even consider defining a small business as one with five hundred employees or less problematic because a business that paid five hundred employees only $120 a week would have to earn $3.12 million a year just to meet its payroll. A White House conference defined a small business as one with four hundred or fewer employees.

The Committee on Economic Development suggested that any business meeting more than two of the following criteria should be considered a small business:

▶ Independent management owns the business
▶ A small number of individuals are responsible for capital contributions
▶ A local orientation to the firm's business
▶ A small market share compared to the industry as a whole[7]

Studies have shown that the general public uses a very restrictive definition. The average person uses the term *small business* to refer to an owner-

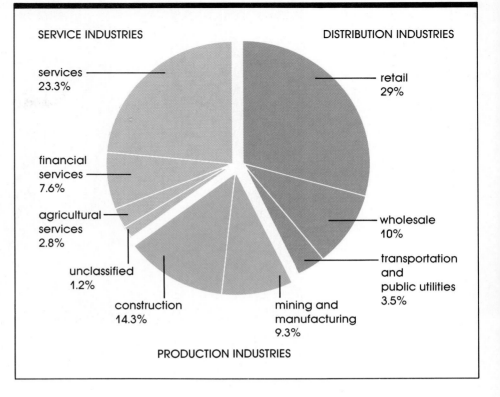

SERVICE INDUSTRIES

DISTRIBUTION INDUSTRIES

services 23.3%

retail 29%

financial services 7.6%

agricultural services 2.8%

unclassified 1.2%

construction 14.3%

mining and manufacturing 9.3%

wholesale 10%

transportation and public utilities 3.5%

PRODUCTION INDUSTRIES

managed business that employs a handful of people—not more than twenty or twenty-five.

No matter how small business is defined, one fact is clear: Small businesses are critical to the soundness of the American economy. In terms of numbers, small businesses dominate the U.S. economy. As Table 5.2 indicates, businesses employing twenty or fewer people account for 91.3 percent of all businesses, and 99.8 percent of all businesses employ less than five hundred people.

Successful firms are built on innovation, which takes many forms. Joanna Doniger started her company, One Night Stand, after making a dress and renting it to a friend. She came up with the idea of renting evening and

**Table 5-2 Number of Companies by Employment Size**
Source: U.S. Department of Commerce, Bureau of the Census, *1982 Enterprise Statistics,* (Washington, D.C.: GPO, October 1986), Table 3.

| Employees per Firm | Number of Firms | Percentage of All Firms |
|---|---|---|
| 500 plus | 7,030 | 0.2 |
| Less than 500 | 4,249,213 | 99.8 |
| Less than 100 | 4,206,745 | 98.8 |
| Less than 20 | 3,886,375 | 91.3 |

**Creativity and innovation cannot be taught.** Linda Mason, co-founder and president of Bright Horizons day care centers, has learned this from experience. Mason and her husband, Roger Brown, employ fifty "faculty" and a full time educational specialist. They try to maximize employee output and satisfaction in this low-paid, high-burnout career.

formal wear to women who did not want to buy a dress they would wear only once. Doniger applied the rental tuxedo concept to formal evening wear for women and opened a shop in New York with $100,000 of her own money and $300,000 from other investors. Today, she has two shops in London in addition to her original store in New York, and she rents dresses made by designers such as Scaasi and Oscar de la Renta to about 150 women a week. The dresses rent for $75 on up; they might have retailed for $500 to $5,000.[8]

With the energy, creativity, and innovative abilities of small-business owners have come jobs for other people. One study found that firms with fewer than twenty employees created about 82 percent of the new jobs in the United States between 1981 and 1985.[9] Table 5-3 compares the contributions of businesses of various sizes to the 2 million jobs created in 1985. Not surprisingly, companies with fewer than one hundred employees led the way.

Retailing, services, and high technology are attractive to entrepreneurs because these fields tend to be easy to enter and require low initial financing. It is also easier to pick a market niche in these fields than in others, and new firms suffer less from heavy competition, at least in the early stages, than do established firms.

| Table 5-3 Which Companies Create the Most Jobs? | Size of Company | Percentage of New Jobs Created in 1985 |
|---|---|---|
| | 1 to 99 employees | 52.7 |
| | 100 to 999 employees | 29.0 |
| | 1,000 or more employees | 18.3 |

## Retailing

A retailer acquires goods from producers or wholesalers and sells them to consumers. Main streets and shopping strips are lined with independent record stores, sporting-goods shops, dress boutiques, drugstores, groceries, and hardware stores. Retailing particularly attracts prospective small-business owners because gaining experience and exposure in this field is so easy. Retailers always need sales help, and all but the smallest need other types of employees, such as buyers and window-dressers.

From a financial perspective, it is relatively easy to open a store. A retailer entering a new business venture does not have to make the heavy investment in equipment and distribution systems that a manufacturing business would require. All that the new retailer needs is a lease on store space, a minimal amount of merchandise, and enough capital to sustain the business through the always difficult start-up period.

Consider Al Felly, who had run up such a bill with a local florist in Madison, Wisconsin, than when he returned from World War II he was forced to work for the florist to pay off his debt while he studied for his undergraduate degree at the University of Wisconsin. In 1949, he decided to open his own small flower shop. Today, Felly has six stores and sells $2.5 million worth of flowers. His are the largest per capita sales in a metropolitan area in the United States.

## Services

The term *service* describes work that is done for others and that does not involve the production of goods. Real-estate and insurance and personnel agencies, barbershops, banks, computer repair shops, copy centers, and accounting firms are all service businesses. Services also attract individuals—such as beauticians, morticians, and jewelers—whose skills are not usually needed by large firms. Many service providers are also retailers because they provide their services to ultimate consumers.

One of the best-known examples of a small service business that burgeoned into a large business is H & R Block, Inc., the tax preparation company. The business began when Henry W. Bloch, a decorated navigator, returned from World War II. With $5,000 borrowed from an aunt, he started United Business Services with his younger brother Richard. The firm provided bookkeeping, management advice, and income tax preparation for small businesses. By 1954, the bulk of the business was tax preparation, so in 1955 the brothers dissolved United Business Services and formed H & R Block, Inc. The company prepares more than 10 million tax returns and is valued at more than $500 million.[10]

## High Technology

High technology is a broad term for the new and innovative businesses that depend heavily on advanced scientific and engineering knowledge. People who have been able to develop innovations or identify new niches in the fields of computers, biotechnology, genetic engineering, robotics, and a dozen other markets have become today's high-tech giants. Many of them, however, started out working in garages, basements, or kitchens.

Bill Gates, founder of Microsoft, began writing computer software when he was in the seventh grade. By the time he was a senior in high school, he was writing programs for TRW. Now in his thirties, Gates is one of America's richest people.

Hardware may take more money to develop than software, but there are also many success stories in computer hardware. Apple Computers, for instance, began in a garage. The Apple prototype was financed by the proceeds Steven Wozniak received from selling his Hewlett-Packard calculator and Steven Jobs got from selling his van.[11]

# ▶ Owning a Small Business

A small-business owner or entrepreneur does not always have to be skilled in the area of a new business venture. Many small-business owners with no background in engineering or high technology apply the latest in high technology to make their businesses succeed. J. Paul Costello, one of the principals of Costello, Erdlen & Co., a human resources consulting firm in Massachusetts, had been using a file card system to trace résumés for the prospective employees of his client companies. One Saturday in 1981, when he was playing with his son's Apple computer, Costello hit on the idea for a software package that would perform the same function as his card system. Today, the ResTrac software system sells for more than $8,000 a unit and in 1985 did around $2 million in sales.[12]

Bud Brimberg started ProCreations in 1975 to publish commemorative posters. In early 1985 he began marketing Plan-A-Flex Home Designer kits— kits that allow buyers to create floor plans for every room in their home. The floor plans are quarter-inch scale and consist of a plastic grid on which electrostatic vinyl pieces of furniture and fixtures can be placed. By 1987, Brimberg had sold more than a hundred thousand Plan-A-Flex kits retailing for $24.95 each.[13]

It would be difficult to call Costello or Brimberg typical of all small-business owners or entrepreneurs, simply because there are no typical entrepreneurs or small-business owners. The two do share at least one particular characteristic with many small-business people: They both began their own businesses

**SBA to the rescue.** When making decisions about whether to pursue a small business venture, there are several support sources which may be contacted for free information and guidance. When Lisa Ruffolo and Susan Smith were considering starting a computer instruction manual business, they sought free pamphlets and advice from the Small Business Administration and the University of Wisconsin.

because they wanted to call their own shots. Independence is one of the great rewards of small-business ownership.

A small-business owner takes risks. If the potential rewards—whether financial or psychological—were not enormous, no one would start a small business. A million or so people each year balance the risks and rewards of small-business ownership and decide to take the plunge. Society rewards innovation and risk taking, if the small business owner can persist.

## Rewards of Small-Business Ownership

The desire to be your own boss is certainly a major reason for going into business for yourself. In 1988 alone, experts were suggesting that Americans would start a total of 1.3 million new business enterprises, consisting of seven hundred thousand new corporations, one hundred thousand new partnerships, and five hundred thousand new sole proprietorships. In 1950, by comparison, there were only ninety thousand new partnerships.[14]

Many people strike out on their own because they believe they will do better for themselves than they could do by remaining with their current employer or by changing jobs. They may feel that they are stuck on the corporate ladder, that no business would take them seriously enough to fund their ideas, or that they simply do not want to work for someone else.

Sometimes the people who venture forth to start their own small business are people who simply cannot work for someone else. More often, they just want the freedom to choose whom they work with, the flexibility to pick

**New and improved.** Being able to take an existing product, improve it, and market it through unique channels is one way a small business may ensure success. Cushman Fruit Company in West Palm Beach, Florida, did that by crossing the best Florida grapefruit with the best tangelos. The result is the Cushman HoneyBell, the mainstay of their retail and mail-order business.

where and when to work, and the option of working in a family setting. The development of the so-called electronic cottage, filled with computer, copying, telephone, and video equipment, has permitted many people to work at home. Only a few years ago, most of them would have needed the support that an office provides.

Historically, immigrants to the United States found that starting their own business was the best way to enter the American mainstream. This pattern continues today among Hispanics, blacks, Asians, and women. For instance, according to the U.S. Census Bureau, the number of woman-owned businesses rose 329 percent, from 700,000 to 3 million, between 1979 and 1984.[15] By 1982, 1.8 percent of the minority population owned business, compared to 6.4 percent business ownership in the overall population. Asians were most likely to own businesses, followed by Hispanics and blacks.[16] Business Encounter 5-1 describes Bing Steel, the number-twelve business on the *Black Enterprise* Top 100 list in 1986.

## Risks of Small-Business Ownership

The idea of running a small business is so enticing that it's no wonder many people dream of it. Unfortunately, however, of every ten businesses formed, 50 percent will stay around for five years, 38 percent for ten years, and only 31 percent for 15 or more years. The financial risks of running a small business are very high, although some businesses are considerably less risky than others. Businesses most likely to survive are veterinary services, funeral services, dentists' offices, commercial savings banks, hotels and motels, campgrounds and trailer parks, physicians' offices, barbershops, bowling and billiards establishments, and cash grain crops.[17] Table 5-4 identifies the fastest-growing and slowest-growing businesses.

Even if a business keeps going, the odds are not great that it will turn out to be another Esprit de Corp, which grew from a tiny San Francisco dressmaking operation fifteen years ago to a trend-setting fashion apparel manufacturing giant with $1 billion in sales by 1988. A small business is more

# Business Encounter 5-1

## Profile: Dave Bing of Bing Steel

Dave Bing has combined the skills of athlete, scholar, and businessman to produce a successful business. His company, Bing Steel, was named National Minority Small Business of the Year in 1984 and ranked twelfth on the *Black Enterprise* Top 100 businesses of 1986, with sales of more than $48 million.

Dave Bing was a basketball star in his home town of Washington, D.C., and went on to become one of Syracuse University's finest players. He started out as a history major at Syracuse but switched to economics in his junior year and graduated with a degree in marketing and economics in 1966. He earned All-American honors at Syracuse while averaging 24.8 points per game. He was picked up by the Detroit Pistons in the first round and was named National Basketball Association Rookie of the Year in 1967. He later played with the Washington Bullets and then the Boston Celtics. Bing's star-studded NBA career lasted eleven more years and included such honors as leading the league in scoring in 1968 and being named most valuable player of the All-Star game in 1976.

Bing pursued his interest in business in the off-season during his basketball career. He worked seven years for the National Bank of Detroit, where he learned about money, financing, and the banking industry. He also worked in various management training programs at Chrysler Corporation for two years. At one time, Bing thought he wanted to open his own Chrysler dealership when he retired from professional basketball. Instead, he went to work at Paragon Steel Company in Detroit (now bankrupt) in a two-year training program. At Paragon, Bing learned the steel business

from the bottom up. Before long, he decided he wanted to start his own steel company.

Bing founded Bing Steel, Inc., in 1980 with $80,000 of his own savings and a $250,000 line of credit obtained through his banking contacts. Bing Steel is a steel service company—that is, it does not make steel but instead buys the metal from other mills and fabricates it into parts according to customers' specifications. When the firm first opened, it had only a few contracts. The company had four employees and lost $90,000 in its first six months. In late 1980, Bing Steel got a big break by landing a contract to provide steel to a General Motors plant in Detroit. With this contract in hand, the company was able to secure business from other large companies. Today Bing Steel operates two plants and has more than seventy employees. It primarily serves the automobile and construction industries and is the largest minority-owned steel service center in the nation.

Dave Bing has successfully made the transition from star basketball player to star businessman. He was recently named National Minority Small Business Person of the Year. Bing is active in community and charity affairs and takes his position as role model quite seriously. He has plans to expand Bing Steel and expects sales of over $70 million in 1988. In the next few years, Bing hopes that Bing Steel will become the number-one minority company in the country.

These facts are from a fact sheet provided by Bing Steel, 1988; Andrena Crockett, "Dave Bing: A Business Superstar," *Washington Living* (April 1987): 13–15; and Lloyd Gite, "Scoring with Steel," *Black Enterprise* 15 (January 1985): 63–66.

**Table 5-4 Fastest-growing and Slowest-growing Small Businesses**
Source: *The State of Small Business: A Report of the President*, (Washington, D.C.: GPO, 1987), p. 13.

| Industry | Increase in Employment from December 1985 to December 1986 |
|---|---|
| Fastest-growing business | |
| Amusement and recreation services | 12.2% |
| Masonry, stonework, and plastering | 11.8 |
| Credit reporting and collection | 11.6 |
| Outpatient health care | 10.9 |
| Millwork and plywood | 10.5 |
| Medical and dental laboratories | 10.1 |
| Highway and street construction | 9.8 |
| Management and public relations | 8.3 |
| Painting, paper hanging, and decorating | 7.4 |
| Carpentry and flooring | 7.2 |
| Slowest-growing business | |
| Oil and gas field services | −34.8 |
| Oil and gas extraction | −15.5 |
| Fabricated structural steel | − 5.5 |
| Nonstore retailing | − 5.0 |
| Special industry machinery | − 4.9 |
| Leather and leather products | − 4.7 |
| Combined real estate and insurance | − 4.2 |

likely to provide a living for its owner, but not much more. There are always worries about new equipment, expanding inventory, rent increases, competition, or changing market demand.

Even Esprit found its stunning growth stalled when competitors beat it to the marketplace with the more conservative look that customers were demanding. By the spring of 1988, company founders Doug and Susie Tompkins were facing a decrease in sales, had laid off seven hundred of the company's twenty-two hundred employees in the United States, and had started a cost-cutting campaign at headquarters. By bringing in outside professionals and addressing the desires of consumers, Esprit hoped to turn around its sagging sales figures and get back on the growth track it had experienced since its inception.[18]

In addition to facing financial and psychological stresses, small-business owners tend to be victims of physical stress. The small-business person is often the owner, manager, sales force, shipping and receiving clerk, bookkeeper, and custodian. Sixteen-hour days quickly become standard, and vacations are rarely possible. Many creative persons succeed or fail not because of their business concepts but rather because of difficulties in managing their business. Figure 5-2 shows the average age for entrepreneurs.

## Keys to Success

Despite their failure rate, small businesses have some advantages over their larger competitors.

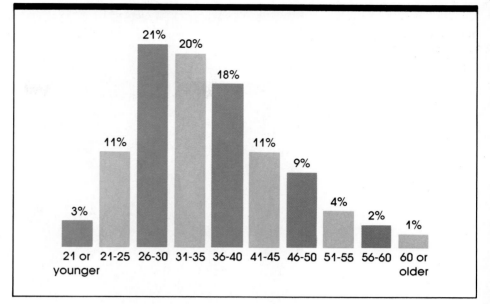

*Flexibility.* With small size comes the flexibility to adapt to changing market demands. Small businesses usually have only one layer of management—the owners. Decisions therefore can be made and carried out quickly. In larger firms, decisions about even routine matters can take weeks because they must pass through two or more levels of management before action is authorized.

Some companies have recognized this problem and have taken steps to stay in touch with day-to-day operations. Henry Quadracci, for example, founder of Quad/Graphics, one of the most successful printing companies in the United States, decided that his office should be located between the visitors' waiting area and his washroom so that he could keep in touch with whoever happened to be in the waiting room.[19]

*Focus.* Small firms can focus their efforts on a few key customers or on a precisely defined market niche. Many large corporations must compete in the mass market or for large market segments. Firms like Near East Food Products, Inc., the leading seller of packaged rice pilaf in the United States, identified a niche, captured a market, then gradually expanded its lines and customer base. Near East originally offered only rice pilaf mix; today it offers a complete line of rice and side dishes, including couscous, Spanish rice, long grain and wild rice, tabouli, sesame tahini, falafel, wheat pilaf, and chicken-flavored rice.[20]

*Reputation.* Small firms, because of their capacity to focus on narrow niches, can develop enviable reputations for quality and service. A good example is Four Seasons Cycling, a year-round bicycle touring company based

**Flexibility is a key to success.** When Sam Holt's original partner left the business, he brought in a new partner, Homer Watts. Since then Zack's Famous Frozen Yogurt stores have gone from one stand to over 125 stands, with a goal of 1,000 stands by 1991.

in Williamsburg, Virginia. It offers "sunshine insurance," a 25 percent discount on your next Four Seasons Cycling tour if one or more days of a weekend tour are rained out or if three or more days of a week or longer tour are rained out. Another example of a small business with a formidable reputation is W. Atlee Burpee & Co., the country's premier bulb and seed cataloger. Burpee has an unqualified returns policy (complete satisfaction or your money back) that demonstrates a strong commitment to customer satisfaction. Business Encounter 5-2, Marketplace Casseroles, is an example of a small business where the owners capitalized on their reputations for good food.

## Paths to Failure

Small businesses fail for dozens of reasons. A poor business concept—such as offering air-conditioner repair services above the Arctic Circle—will produce disaster nearly every time. Expanding a hobby into a business may work if a genuine market niche exists, but all too often people start such a business without identifying a real need for the goods or services. Over-optimism is a great trap. Other notable causes of small-business failure include disproportionate burdens imposed by government regulation, insufficient reserves to withstand slow sales, and vulnerability to competition from larger

# Business Encounter 5-2
## *Market Place Casseroles*

Two Texas women are taking advantage of the trend of more women working outside the home and smaller households where both spouses work but have no children (DINKS—double income, no kids). Virginia and Barbara Gaskamp had developed a reputation in Brenham, Texas for preparing delicious, nutritious meals and they incorporated into Market Place Casseroles to sell their homemade, family-sized, frozen casseroles out of Brenham. In 1987, Market Place Casseroles had sales of $185,000 and they expected to double that in 1988.

Barbara and Virginia Gaskamp (they are married to cousins) realized that women working outside the home often do not have the time to prepare nutritious meals for their families. Instead, they often purchase single-serving frozen dinners that go directly from freezer to microwave or oven in just minutes. The Gaskamps recognized that working women would be willing to purchase family-sized, easy-to-prepare nutritious meals if they were a good value. Market Place Casseroles accordingly come in one- or two-pound sizes, are packaged in an aluminum tray, and are priced competitively with other frozen dinner products. The casseroles have been successful thus far because they are home cooked with high-quality ingredients and are promoted on that basis.

Market Place Casseroles actually grew out of the Gaskamp's Brenham catering business. They catered a church fellowship dinner and people raved about their chicken spaghetti. People kept asking the Gaskamps to make more of the casserole so they did. They were soon making large batches of chicken spaghetti, freezing them, and selling them. They added more recipes—King Ranch-styled chicken, tamale bake, and beef enchilada casserole, to name a few. They added a freezer and finally, had to move to a larger building to meet state inspection standards. They incorporated into a master limited partnership in 1986, selling 25 percent of the company's stock, but the Gaskamps still retain control and a majority ownership.

At first the Gaskamps sold Market Place Casseroles out of a small retail shop in Brenham, but they soon began distributing the casseroles to a few Houston grocery stores, and gradually expanded to Austin, College Station, and surrounding east-central Texas. They do not want to expand their distribution area too quickly because they want to maintain the quality on which they have built their reputation.

The Gaskamps say their business takes lots of time and energy, but they do not mind because they enjoy it. They believe they have an excellent product that satisfies the needs of many working women. They plan to carefully control the quality of their product and their company's growth to ensure that Market Place Casseroles has a very profitable future.

---

These facts are from a telephone interview with Barbara Gaskamp of Market Place Casseroles, March 16, 1988; telephone interview with Virginia Gaskamp, March 21, 1988; Mike George, "Market Place Casseroles," KBTX 10:00 News, March 11, 1988; a Texas A&M marketing study on Market Place Casseroles prepared by Gerhard Baumann, Jill Hubred, Alan Blankley, and Chris Smith, Texas A&M, 1987.

companies. Two major paths to failure among small businesses deserve a close look: an inability to cope with growth and a lack of capital to continue the business.

***Inability to Cope with Growth.*** Sometimes, the very factors that are advantages turn into serious disadvantages when the time comes for a small business to grow. Growth often requires the owner to give up a certain amount of direct authority, and it is often hard for someone who has called all the shots to give up control. Similarly, growth requires specialized

**Fitness for the whole family.** Although failure is common in small business, the key to success is often tied directly to the strength of the market niche pursued. Phil and Mary Baechler developed a unique stroller that allows runners to run while wheeling the baby along. The tripod-shaped stroller brought sales of $250,000 on 1,600 units in 1986.

management skills in areas such as credit analysis or promotion—skills that the founder may lack or not have time to apply.

The tendency of a small company to focus narrowly on a few customers or on a single market niche can lead to disaster if customers suffer a business downturn. During the auto industry's long recession in the 1970s and 1980s, the major automakers saw their pool of suppliers shrink drastically. To maintain a healthy supply system, the automakers now generally do not buy more than 40 percent of their requirements for a particular part from any single source.

Poorly managed growth probably affects a company's reputation more than anything else, at least initially. Products that do not arrive on time or goods that are poorly made can quickly destroy a company's reputation.

**Undercapitalization**

The lack of funds to operate a business normally

***Undercapitalization.*** The shortest path to failure in business is **undercapitalization**—the lack of funds to operate a business normally. Fifty percent of small businesses close within five years, most often because they are undercapitalized. Too many entrepreneurs think that all they need is enough money to get the doors open. They believe that the business can survive on cash generated from sales after getting started. But almost all businesses suffer from seasonal variations in sales, which make cash tight, and few businesses make money from the start.

A key element of business success is a **business plan**—a meticulous statement of the rationale for the business and a step-by-step explanation of how it will achieve its goals. The plan must set forth a strategy for acquiring sufficient financing to keep the business going.

# ▶ Financial Resources Available to Small-Business Owners

Someone wishing to start even a small retail store will probably need at least $50,000 to rent space, add necessary equipment and furnishings, buy initial inventory, and use as **working capital**—the money necessary to fund the regular operations of the business. Ideally, the small-business owner puts up a significant percentage of the necessary capital. Few new business owners have the entire amount, however. They must therefore look to other sources for additional financing. Figure 5-3 shows sources of capital for entrepreneurs.

## The Owner's Personal Resources

The most important source of funds for any new business is the owner. Most people have more wealth than they realize. One form of wealth is **equity.** Equity represents an ownership position in assets and does not include

**Figure 5-3**

Sources of Capital for Entrepreneurs

Source: Adapted from "Small Business in America," © 1981, National Federation of Independent Business Research and Education Foundation.

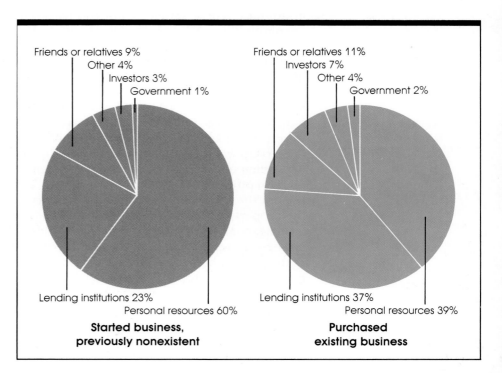

Friends or relatives 9%
Other 4%
Investors 3%
Government 1%

Friends or relatives 11%
Investors 7%
Other 4%
Government 2%

Lending institutions 23%
Personal resources 60%
**Started business, previously nonexistent**

Lending institutions 37%
Personal resources 39%
**Purchased existing business**

assets financed through borrowing. Many owners' personal resources are represented by equity in a home or accumulated value in a life-insurance policy or in a savings account. If the owner has assets that could be used in the business, those assets become part of his or her equity in the firm. A computer, a typewriter, desks, and the like are common examples. The owner can also provide working capital for the business by reinvesting profits into the business or simply by not drawing a full salary.

## Family and Friends

People starting small-business ventures often look to family and friends as sources for loans of long-term funds, or **capital**. Often this capital takes the form of assets such as a computer or automobile that are exchanged for an ownership interest in a business. Family and friends often find it difficult to turn down a small-business owner in need of cash. If the business goes bad, however, the emotional losses for all concerned may greatly exceed the money involved. Anyone lending a friend or family money for a venture should state the agreement clearly in writing.

Despite potential disadvantages, loans from family members are appealing to small-business owners. Usually, they can structure a favorable repayment schedule, and sometimes they can negotiate an interest rate below current bank rates.

## Financial Institutions

Inevitably, businesses must at some time borrow from a financial institution. Typically, small-business owners start shopping for financing in their local institutions. These sources know the market in which the entrepreneur is operating. When CB Sports of Bennington, Vermont, decided to go into the business of manufacturing ski apparel, its founder, C. B. Vaughan, put together a business plan and $5,000 of his own money and sought start-up financing of $50,000 from a small bank in Manchester, Vermont. The bank not only made that loan but each year increased the amount to meet CB Sports' needs. That is the kind of service that entrepreneurs look for from local institutions. By 1984, CB Sports was borrowing $15 million from a variety of banks and was doing $31.5 million in sales.[21]

Start-up ventures sometimes borrow up to 75 percent of their needs, depending on a bank's evaluation of the venture's likelihood of success and of the entrepreneur's ability to repay the loan. The institution will often require the entrepreneur to give it a **security interest,** a financial interest in the property or fixtures of the business that secures the payment of a debt or obligation. The property securing the debt is called **collateral.** The small-business owner may have to offer some personal property as collateral, such as the owner's home. In this case the security is called a **mortgage,** a security interest in real property. If the small-business fails to repay the loan, the lending institution may eventually claim and sell the collateral to recover its loss.

Financial institutions can also grant a small business a **line of credit,** an agreement by which a financial institution promises to lend a business a

### Capital
Long-term funds provided to finance the purchase of assets

### Security interest
A financial interest in property or fixtures that secures the payment of a debt or obligation

### Collateral
The property securing a debt

### Mortgage
A security interest in real property

### Line of credit
An agreement by which a financial institution promises to lend a business a predetermined sum on demand

predetermined sum on demand. A line of credit permits an entrepreneur to take quick advantage of opportunities that require a bank loan.

## Other Sources of Funding

Some community groups sponsor revolving loan funds to encourage the development of particular types of businesses. State and local agencies may guarantee loans, especially to minority businesspeople or for development in certain areas. The Small Business Administration has four financial assistance programs:

- ▶ *Direct loans,* which are usually made only to businesses that do not qualify for loans from financial institutions
- ▶ *Guaranteed loans,* which ensure that a direct loan made by an institution to a qualified small business will be repaid
- ▶ *Participation loans,* a combination of guaranteed loans and direct loans in which the SBA guarantees an institution's loan for part of the firm's needs and makes up the balance in a direct loan
- ▶ *Minority Enterprise Small Business Investment Companies (MESBICs),* which are financing companies partially funded by the SBA that make loans to minority-run businesses

Many small-business owners try to combine funds from a variety of sources to finance their business ventures. Leeann Chin of Minneapolis, Minnesota, began her first restaurant with $125,000 borrowed from friends, $15,000 of her own savings, and $165,000 from a Small Business Administration loan. Her second and third restaurants were financed with $100,000 from a bank, $100,000 from the cash flow of the first restaurant, and the rest from developers. Chin never hesitated to scour the market for all sources of funds and to ask for what she needed to run her restaurants successfully.

# ▶ Sources of Management Help for Small-Business Owners

Because of the key role that small business plays in the economy and society of the United States, efforts are made by various organizations to improve the small-business owner's ability to compete.

## Entrepreneurial Training Programs

Creativity and innovation are difficult to teach. What *is* being taught, in seminars and college classrooms from Harvard to the University of Washington, are marketing, management, and financing principles—skills that are crucial to a venture's success. Knowledge, experience, and judgment are necessary for success in a new business. While knowledge can be communicated and some experiences can be simulated in the classroom, good judgment must be developed by the entrepreneur.

## The Small Business Administration

When most people think of government help for small businesses, they think of the Small Business Administration (SBA). The SBA offers many types of management assistance to small businesses, including counseling for firms in difficulty, consulting on improving operations, training for owner/managers and their employees.

The SBA funds Small-Business Development Centers (SBDCs). These are business clinics, usually located on college campuses, that provide counseling at no charge and training at only a nominal charge. SBDCs are often the SBA's principal means of providing direct management assistance. In 1987, universities in thirty-one states were taking part in the SBDC program.

**Service Corps of Retired Executives (SCORE)**

A volunteer agency funded by the SBA to provide advice for small firms

**Active Corps of Executives (ACE)**

A volunteer agency funded by the SBA to provide advice for small firms

The **Service Corps of Retired Executives (SCORE)** and the **Active Corps of Executives (ACE)** are volunteer agencies funded by the SBA to provide advice for small firms. Both are staffed by experienced managers whose talents and experience the small firms could not ordinarily afford. Together, SCORE and ACE have about twelve thousand counselors working out of 350 chapters throughout the country. In 1987 alone, they counseled more than 120,000 business owners about their problems and opportunities.

The SBA has organized Small Business Institutes (SBIs) on almost five hundred university and college campuses in the United States. Seniors and graduate students and faculty at each SBI provide on-site management counseling. In 1987, 510 colleges and universities took part in the program, counseling more than ten thousand entrepreneurs.

## ▶ Nature of Franchising

**Franchise**

A license to sell another's products or to use another's name in business, or both

**Franchiser**

The company that sells the franchise

**Franchisee**

The purchaser of the franchise

A license to sell another's products or to use another's name in business, or both, is a **franchise.** The company that sells the franchise is the **franchiser.** The purchaser of the franchise is the **franchisee.** The franchisee acquires the rights to a name, logo, certain methods of operation, national advertising, products, and other elements associated with the franchiser's business. Dunkin' Donuts and Jiffy Lube are franchisers with well-known logos and national visibility. Figure 5-4 shows the growth in franchise units and sales.

Generally, the franchisee pays a flat fee to the franchiser for the franchise. Depending on the quality of the franchise, the initial fee and start-up costs can range from $1,000 to more than $800,000. In addition, the franchisee pays the franchiser a monthly or annual fee based on a percentage of sales or profits. Franchisees of Novus Windshield Repair pay the franchiser between $600 and $2,900 for a franchise fee, spend $1,400 to $6,700 in start-up costs, and pay an annual royalty fee of 6 percent. On the other end of the spectrum, franchisees of Wendy's Old Fashioned Hamburgers pay a franchise fee of

**New help for old business.**   Although there are several sources of information for small-business owners provided at no charge, some businesses want more specialized information. The owner of this antique store employed a professional consultant to assist in improving sales in this specialty market.

$30,000, spend from $196,000 to $876,000 in start-up costs, and pay an annual royalty of 4 percent.[22]

Franchises have been growing at a fast pace. By 1987, sales of goods and services at more than 498,000 franchise outlets were expected to reach more than $591 billion—around 6 percent higher than in 1986 and 77 percent above the sales level at the start of the 1980s. Minority-owned franchises grew 13 percent from 1984 to 1985, but minorities account for only a small percentage of the total ownership of franchises.[23] By 1988, women owned 11 percent of all franchise outlets, and male-female partnerships accounted for ownership of another 20 percent.[24]

Not only is franchising a good way for a new business owner to enter the market, but more and more existing business owners see it as a way to expand their business and increase their cash flow without having to invest a lot of their own capital. Merle Harmon's Fan Fair, a Midwestern chain of sporting-apparel shops, expanded from ten family-owned stores in 1986 to more than eighty stores by franchising.[25]

**Figure 5-4**

The Growth in Franchise Units and Sales

Source: U.S. Bureau of the Census, *Statistical Abstract of the United States, 1987,* 107th edition (Washington, D.C.: U.S. Government Printing Office, 1986), p. 742.

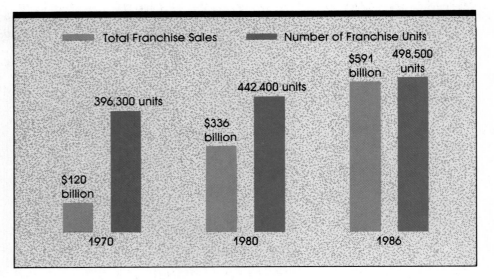

Although as many as four hundred new franchisers entered the market in 1986, franchising is not risk-free. In 1986, 78 franchises (5,667 outlets representing $574 million) failed, and another 105 (5,082 outlets representing $2.3 billion in sales) closed their doors.[26]

# ▶ Advantages of Franchising

## Advertising and Promotion

Most franchisers provide advertising and promotion for their entire system. Franchisers typically charge an advertising fee pegged to a percentage of the franchisee's sales. Wendy's, for example, charges a 4 percent fee for advertising. The promotion might include nationally recognized logos like Wendy's freckle-faced girl or McDonald's golden arches. Many franchisers are not national, however, and their marketing help may be quite limited.

## Management Assistance and Training

Many prospective small-business owners choose to operate a franchised operation in the hopes that they can avoid the pitfalls of starting a completely new business. For instance, many expect to receive management assistance from the franchisee.

Some franchisers offer their franchisees extensive management assistance and training. The older and more successful the franchiser, the better this

## Business Encounter 5-3

### A Successful McDonald's Franchiser

Phil Springer owns and operates five McDonald's restaurants in the Bryan/College Station area of Texas. He takes the business of being a McDonald's franchise owner seriously. Because McDonald's is often in the spotlight, consumers usually remember and criticize McDonald's franchises that are not up to par, yet they may ignore the good ones.

Springer overcame several obstacles on his way to becoming a McDonald's franchise owner. Before he was even granted an interview with McDonald's to discuss obtaining the franchise, Springer had to work fifty hours as a regular McDonald's crew person. Later, he had to attend various training schools, work many hours in various stores, and finally wait several months for assignment to a store. In addition, he had to put up a substantial sum of cash and obtain a large loan from the McDonald's Corporation.

McDonald's commitment to quality was one factor that Springer felt was especially important in his decision to become a franchiser. As a result, he takes extra effort to make sure that his customers get a quality product. Springer is a member of McDonald's Quality Assurance Committee for his region. In this role, Springer assists other McDonald's owners with quality control efforts. He toured plants where the company produces some of its prepackaged ingredients and saw further evidence of McDonald's demands for quality.

Springer's efforts to maintain his franchises at McDonald's strict quality levels have benefited him in several ways. First of all, Springer feels that McDonald's understands what business is all about and has a good attitude toward business. In addition, McDonald's monitors and recognizes the progress and efforts of individual owners. A franchiser who is doing a good job can usually count on McDonald's help if he or she wants to expand. If the company plans to expand within the area of a successful franchiser, it offers the franchiser the first opportunity to purchase the new franchise. McDonald's exercises total control over its growth and expansion but recognizes that its success is due to the efforts of individual owner/operators.

Because Phil Springer's franchises are all in a college town, he often hires students who have worked in McDonald's in their hometowns. This practice has been successful for Springer, but there is one drawback. Not all the student workers were trained by the same set of stringent McDonald's guidelines that Springer's stores use. Springer therefore developed a written set of policies for his franchises to use.

Springer's business know-how and successful franchises have not gone unnoticed. In 1984, McDonald's gave him the Ronald Award, which recognizes outstanding operators in each of the corporation's regional divisions. In addition, in 1987, the Bryan/College Station Chamber of Commerce named Springer its Small Business Person of the Year.

These facts are from Darla-Jean Weatherford, "It's Mac Tonight for Phil Springer's Crews," *The Courier* (October 1987): 1, 7, 8, 9; Stephen McDaniel and Ron Blatchly, unpublished document on McDonald's franchise requirements, Texas A&M University, 1987; and John F. Love, "Behind the Arches," *Advertising Age*, December 8, 1986, p. 41.

help is likely to be. Some firms like McDonald's, Dunkin' Donuts, and Mister Donut even have training centers for their franchisees.

Some franchisers require especially stiff management experience of their franchisees. Domino's Pizza requires that a franchisee must first become a manager at an existing franchise. Since most managers work for a year as a delivery person or pizza maker, the prospective franchisee also has to fill those roles en route to owning a Domino's Pizza franchise. Existing franchisees will sponsor prospective franchisees by hiring them. After the prospective

**Fantastic franchising.** Successful concepts over the years have often been franchised to receive extensive distribution quickly. Lonear Heard is a successful McDonald's franchisee in Compton, California. Heard owns seven McDonald's franchises, with the average franchise doing $1,396,000 in gross sales.

franchisee leaves to set up a new franchise outlet, the sponsor gets a percentage of the former employee's profits for three years.[27]

Some people question whether a franchisee really maintains enough independence to be considered a small business. They argue that the franchisee has a tendency to become overly dependent on the franchiser for guidance on management decisions. The franchisee's success or failure also depends to a large extent on that of the franchiser. This dependence can be a distinct disadvantage if the franchiser runs into problems.

## Central Purchasing and Product Consistency

Many franchisers provide the supplies that franchisees need to do business. The hamburger chains usually sell beef patties to their franchise stores. The advantages to the individual franchisees are assured supplies and uniform quality throughout the system, a major factor in customer decisions. The disadvantage of centralized purchasing may be prices that are higher than they would be in the open market.

# ▶ Disadvantages of Franchising

Some franchisers do not offer central purchasing or do not carefully monitor the quality of what franchisees buy. Product inconsistency in such systems can badly hurt franchisees' quality control and reputation.

The sometimes stiff fees and capital requirements associated with franchises can be either an advantage or a disadvantage to the franchisee. If properly administered, the fees and capital requirements of franchising assure the financial integrity of the franchiser and the system. Some franchisers, like Tubby's Sub Shops, look for franchisees who will finance no more than 50 percent of their total investment, which in this case would be half of approximately $375,000.[28] Such capital requirements are probably the major reason that only 5 percent of start-up franchised outlets fail.

If a system is not well run or its marketing is not effective, the franchise fees become a burden. Some franchisees have forced franchisers to reduce fees and increase and improve promotion when national advertising campaigns prove unsuccessful.

# ▶ Legal Protections for Franchisees

The earliest major franchisers were the automobile manufacturers and oil companies. Their retail dealers were, and still are, franchisees. Franchisees in both industries are protected by federal laws from the arbitrary termination of their franchises. Other types of franchisees may not be protected.

The principal legal protections for franchisees are contained in Federal Trade Commission (FTC) regulations. These stipulations require the franchiser to supply a prospective franchisee with a disclosure statement at least ten days before the franchisee signs a franchise agreement. This document includes information such as

- ▶ The names, addresses, and telephone numbers of other purchasers
- ▶ A fully audited financial statement of the seller
- ▶ The background and experience of the key executives
- ▶ The cost required to start and maintain the business
- ▶ The responsibilities of franchiser and franchisee[29]

The FTC also recommends that prospective franchise buyers read its consumer bulletin on franchises—"Advice for Persons Who Are Considering an Investment in a Franchise Business" (Consumer Bulletin No. 4, Federal Trade Commission, 6th Street and Pennsylvania Avenue, N.W., Washington, D.C. 20580).

The best protection, however, is an aggressive investigation of the franchiser and its competitors, the opportunities and risks in the particular franchise area, the terms of the franchise agreement, and all the other factors that go into a business plan.

# Notes

1. *The State of Small Business: A Report of the President* (Washington, D.C., GPO, 1987), p. xvi.
2. "The *Inc.* 100," *Inc.* (May 1987): 52.
3. "LNA-Media Spending by 100 Leading Advertisers," *Advertising Age*, September 4, 1986, p. 14.
4. Deborah Colletti, Marjolijn van der Velde, and Jeffrey L. Seglin, *Small Business Banking: A Guide to Marketing and Profits* (Rolling Meadows, Ill.: Bank Administration Institute, 1987), p. 2.
5. *The State of Small Business*, p. 16.
6. "The Franchiser 100," *Venture* (November 1987): 42–44.
7. Committee on Economic Development, *Meeting the Special Problems of Small Business* (New York: Committee on Economic Development, 1974), p. 14.
8. Sheryl Jean, "Dresses Perfect for a One-Night Stand," *Venture* (April 1988): 11.
9. David L. Birch, *Job Creation in America* (New York: Free Press, 1987), p. 14.
10. A. David Silver, *Entrepreneurial Megabucks* (New York: Wiley, 1985), p. 146–49.
11. Greg Williams and Rob Moore, "The Apple Story," *Byte* (December 1984): 67–71.
12. Jeffrey L. Seglin, *America's New Breed of Entrepreneurs* (Washington, D.C.: Acropolis Books, 1986), p. 39.
13. Deborah Grace Winer, "The Hernia Prevention Kit," *Venture* (June 1987): 9.
14. David L. Birch, "The Truth About Start-Ups," *Inc.* (January 1988): 14.
15. "The *Savvy* 60," *Savvy* (April 1985): 50, 51–52.
16. *The State of Small Business*, pp. 224–25.
17. Birch, p. 14, 18.
18. Peter Waldman, "Flagging Spirit: Esprit's Fortunes Sag as Couple at the Helm Battle over Its Image," *The Wall Street Journal*, March 16, 1988, pp. 1, 17.
19. Robert H. Waterman, Jr., *The Renewal Factor* (New York: Bantam Books, 1987), p. 141.
20. Seglin, pp. 23–29.
21. Jeffrey L. Seglin, "Growing by Their Bootstraps," *Venture* (July 1985): 48–52.
22. "The Franchiser 100," pp. 42–47.
23. Andrew Kostecka, *Franchising in the Economy: 1985–1987* (Washington, D.C.: U.S. Department of Commerce, January 1987), pp. 1, 10.
24. Lynn Asinof, "Business Bulletin," *The Wall Street Journal*, March 24, 1988, p. 1.
25. Kenneth Stoffels, "Merle Harmon's Plans Major Expansion," *The Business Journal* (Milwaukee), March 24, 1986, p. 1; Jeffrey L. Seglin, *Marketing Financial Advisory Services* (Englewood Cliffs, N.J.: Prentice-Hall, 1988), pp. 31–41.
26. Kostecka, p. 12.
27. Gail Ignacio, "How Domino's Dominates," *Venture* (February 1988): 21.
28. A. Spector, "5 Franchisers Discuss Growth," *Independent Restaurants* (October 1985): 42, 45.
29. C. R. Stigelman, *Franchise Index/Profile* (Washington, D.C.: Small Business Administration, 1986), pp. 43–45.

# Summary and Review

▶ A small business is a business that is independently owned and operated, is not dominant in its field, and does not employ more than five hundred people. Smallness, however, is relative, and because different industries make different demands in terms of start-up costs and number of employees, no single definition of small business satisfies everyone.

▶ Retailing, services, and high technology are the fields most attractive to small businesses. They tend to be fairly easy to enter, require less initial financing than other types of businesses, and allow firms to serve a small segment of the market.

▶ Small businesses have some advantages over their larger competitors: flexibility, the ability to focus their efforts on a few key customers or on a precisely defined market niche, and the chance to develop a reputation for quality and service.

▶ Small businesses fail for many reasons: the inability to cope with growth, undercapitalization, a poor business concept, failure to identify a real need for the goods or services being offered, disproportionate burdens imposed by government regulation, insufficient reserves to withstand slow sales, and vulnerability to competition from larger companies.

▶ The Small Business Administration offers counseling, consulting, and training services. Small Business Development Centers (SBDCs) provide low-cost or free counseling and training. The Service Core of Retired Executives (SCORE) and Active Core of Executives (ACE) provide assistance to individual businesses. The SBA also offers financial assistance to businesses that cannot obtain funding from other sources.

▶ Advantages of franchising include the availability of a proven product and marketing plan; having the benefit of the franchiser's advertising and promotion program, management assistance, and training; and the economies of central purchasing and control.

▶ Disadvantages of franchising include stiff financial requirements, which may prevent potential franchisees from entering the business (this restriction may also be viewed as an advantage because it helps prospective franchisees avoid undercapitalization), lack of independence and control, and dependence on the reputation of other franchisees and on the performance of the franchiser.

▶ By law, investors in franchises have a right to receive a disclosure statement prepared by the franchiser and delivered at least ten business days before the individual makes a commitment to purchase a franchise. Franchisers must provide a written explanation of all earnings claims. Franchisees have a right to obtain any promised refund as long as they meet all the conditions for obtaining it.

# Key Terms and Concepts

| | |
|---|---|
| small business | undercapitalization |
| Small Business Administration (SBA) | business plan |

working capital
equity
capital
security interest
collateral
mortgage
line of credit

Service Corps of Retired Executives
   (SCORE)
Active Corps of Executives (ACE)
franchise
franchiser
franchisee

# Checking Your Understanding

This chapter introduced you to the subjects of small business and franchising. To test and reinforce your understanding, fill in the blanks below.

**1.** A license to sell another's products or to use another's name in business, or both, is a _____.

**2.** The _____ _____ _____ is an independent agency of the federal government that offers both managerial and financial assistance to small businesses.

**3.** A firm that acquires goods from a manufacturer or wholesaler and then turns around and sells these goods to a consumer is a _____.

**4.** When a business lacks sufficient funds to operate a business normally, it is suffering from _____.

**5.** When a prospective small-business owner sets out to start a business, one of the first things she or he does is to write a meticulous step-by-step statement of the rationale for a business and how it will achieve its goals. This statement is called a _____ _____.

**6.** The small-business owner's own resources, family and friends, financial institutions, and vendors are all potential sources of _____ for the small business.

**7.** A _____ _____ is any business that is independently owned and operated, is not dominant in its field, and does not employ more than five hundred people.

**8.** Most people have more wealth than they realize. One form it often takes is _____, ownership interest in a home or accumulated value in a life-insurance policy or in a savings account.

**9.** The property securing a debt is called _____.

**10.** The term _____ describes work that is done for others that does not involve the production of goods.

**11.** The _____ _____ _____ _____ _____ and _____ _____ _____ _____ are volunteer agencies funded by the Small Business Administration to provide advice for small firms. Both are staffed by experienced managers whose talents and experience the small firms could not ordinarily afford.

# Topics for Review and Discussion

1. What are the risks and benefits of buying a franchise?
2. Describe the franchising relationship.
3. What are the principal reasons for the high failure rate among small businesses?
4. Describe the potential advantages that small businesses have over their large competitors.
5. Compare and contrast the various definitions of small business.
6. What types of financing do small entrepreneurs typically use? What are the pros and cons of each?
7. List the types of management assistance that the Small Business Administration offers.
8. What types of financial assistance does the Small Business Administration provide?
9. Which fields tend to attract small businesses most? Why? Explain.
10. What are the potential advantages of owning a small firm? What are the disadvantages?

# Exercises

1. Using Figure 5-3, explore whether there are franchisable businesses in your community. Ask two or three business owners the fifteen questions and score the results. Discuss your findings.
2. Assume you are planning to open a small convenience food store in your community. One option is to seek a franchise. A second option is to open your own store and purchase the merchandise from a wholesale food distributor. What are the advantages and disadvantages of each option?
3. Make a list of five ideas for a small business. Discuss the risks and potential rewards of each. Focus on start-up costs, rates of failure, and competition. How would franchising these businesses help or hurt your potential for success?
4. Make a list of twenty small-business firms that opened approximately two years ago. Then place a checkmark beside the name of each business that is no longer open. In your opinion, why did these firms close?

## Case 5-1
### *American Business Cards, Inc.*

Mark and Janice Zimmer wanted to start their own business. After extensive research into possible entrepreneurial opportunities, they became convinced that a thermographic printing firm specializing in business cards, letterheads, and envelopes could be very successful. The Zimmers decided to specialize in thermographic printing after carefully considering its potential, recent growth rate, future projections and its cost relative to other specialized printing processes. Thus, they incorporated into American Business Cards, Inc. (ABC).

At the time the Zimmers incorporated their business, thermography was a relatively new process with few competitors at the local level. Three national firms dominated the market. The thermography printing process, often referred to as "poor-man's engraving," involves dropping powder onto wet ink on the paper just as it leaves the press. The powder is baked to a hard, enamel-like finish as the paper passes under heating elements above a conveyor belt. The result is a raised-letter effect that, if properly produced, provides a very professional image.

After deciding what business they wanted to pursue, the Zimmers had to decide where to do business. They analyzed potential markets and identified three with the potential for success; (1) the metropolitan area of Chicago; (2) central Illinois, which includes five metropolitan areas; (3) the metropolitan area of St. Louis, which is smaller and less geographically diverse than Chicago. They eliminated metropolitan Chicago because of extensive competition. This left a choice between a large, rapidly growing regional market with four cities of 100,000 population and one of about 250,000, all within approximately 60 to 90 miles of each other, and the medium-sized metropolitan area of St. Louis. Although there was less competition in the regional market, the Zimmers selected St. Louis. A large number of Fortune 500 corporations had their headquarters in this city. There were few thermographers, particularly those specializing in the quick turnaround of business cards, letterheads, and envelopes. However, thermographic franchises such as Business Cards Tomorrow were beginning to enter the specialty printing market.

When the Zimmers were starting out, most thermographic products were sold through direct-mail catalogs. Mark Zimmer believed that personal service would make a big difference in the thermography printing market if the products met high standards of quality, quick turnaround time, and reasonable prices.

Zimmer believed he would be successful in this new endeavor because of his ability to define the customers' needs and provide adequate solutions to their problems. He knew that his strength was his marketing expertise and his ability to deal with people. His research indicated a need for high-quality, service-oriented specialty printing. No major competitor at the national or local level seemed to be meeting that need. Zimmer also knew that his lack of technical experience in the printing industry could be damaging, so he contracted with an outside firm to produce the product for ABC.

In April 1982, American Business Cards opened its doors for business in St. Louis. Zimmer's next major decision was to decide which segment of the population (target market) he should attempt to attract. A careful analysis of the market for high-quality, service-oriented specialty printing suggested that several groups could be potential customers of the products of American Business Cards. These potential customers could be divided into two major categories—wholesalers and end users. The wholesale markets consisted of brokers and other printers. Many of the printers in the area sold the same kinds of products as ABC, but they did not have the capability of producing thermography. Therefore most (85 to 90 percent) of them had been buying thermographic products from the major national catalog suppliers. The end-user markets consisted of the government, major corporate headquarters and regional offices, medium-sized local corporations, professionals (doctors, lawyers, accountants), and all other businesses and individuals.

ABC ultimately decided to focus on the printers because of already existing business. The Zimmers found that printers were willing to try ABC because of its competitive price and quick turnaround. ABC beat the traditional turnaround time by a week and established a pick-up-and-deliver service to increase its share of printing sales in St. Louis. ABC also found business in the corporate markets, both large and regional, but did not have as much luck with the professional group. Nevertheless, ABC has proved to be quite successful.

---

This case is contributed by Professor Jon F. Bibb, Department of Marketing, Millikin University, Decatur, Illinois, 1987.

### Questions

1. Do you think that Zimmer would have been as successful if he had purchased a thermographic franchise rather than starting his own independent business? Why?
2. From the facts in this case, what is the secret of ABC's success?
3. What market should ABC focus on in the future—wholesalers or end users? Defend your answer.

## Case 5-2
## *The Hard Rock Cafe*

Isaac Tigrett and Peter Morton opened the first Hard Rock Cafe in London in 1971. The Hard Rock Cafe was radically different from other London restaurants because it specialized in American food and offered high-quality, moderately priced food and beverages. It was different too because of its basic theme—rock 'n' roll. The restaurant quickly became popular with trendy Londoners and tourists and became known as "the place to be." Celebrities like Jack Nicholson and Dustin Hoffman frequented the Hard Rock, adding to its popularity.

The success of the original Hard Rock Cafe convinced the owners to open other Hard Rock cafes in various places around the world. Today there are Hard Rock cafes in New York, Tokyo, Reykjavik, and Houston, among other places. The cafes always have long lines of tourists, celebrities, and trend setters waiting to sample the music, the food, and the drinks.

One reason customers keep coming back to the Hard Rock cafes is the owners' focus on quality. Although the Hard Rock cafes serve a limited menu, each item sold is subject to strict quality standards. Cooks prepare hamburgers, barbecue, ribs, sandwiches, salads, and desserts according to special Hard Rock Cafe recipes. Customers receive large portions of food for their money. The owners strongly believe that the food must be good to attract repeat customers. Each Hard Rock Cafe offers full bar service as well.

Although all Hard Rock cafes use the rock-'n'-roll theme, no two are exactly alike in size or appearance. The atmosphere of each Hard Rock is very important because the owners want the customers to "eat" atmosphere as well as food. The New York cafe has the back end of a 1960 Cadillac suspended over the front entrance. The interior decor of the Hard Rock includes celebrity and rock memorabilia along with various odds and ends that help create an informal atmosphere. Various Hard Rock cafes are now home to such items as Elvis Presley's jumpsuit, guitars played by Jimi Hendrix, Eric Clapton, George Harrison, and Pete Townsend, a drum played by Ringo Starr, and Jerry Lee Lewis' shoes.

All the restaurants play very loud rock 'n' roll over expensive sound systems. The loud music encourages customers to eat fast and leave. Because most of the Hard Rocks have only about two hundred seats, there must be a high turnover rate to generate profits. Each Hard Rock Cafe also sells T-shirts, jackets, watches, and hats with the Hard Rock Cafe logo. This merchandise, accounting for 43 percent of total sales, is a major source of promotion; the cafes do not use any formal advertising.

The Hard Rock cafes became so successful that Tigrett bought out Morton in 1983 and took the company public by offering 25 percent of its stock on the London over-the-counter market. The two former partners reached an agreement on franchising the name and the cafes. In the United States, Tigrett got rights to the Hard Rock Cafe east of the Mississippi River, and Morton got rights west of the Mississippi. Both have the right to franchise in the international market.

Franchising a unique concept like the Hard Rock Cafe has proved to be difficult. The Hard Rock currently limits its locations to major metropolitan areas. Because going to a Hard Rock Cafe is a trendy experience, some analysts question the feasibility of opening up more than one franchise in a given area. Also, some wonder whether a Hard Rock can be successful outside of major metropolitan areas.

Between 1985 and 1987, Hard Rock cafes expanded rapidly. Tigrett's half of the company went public on the American Stock Exchange. Tigrett also took on Yul Brynner and Dan Aykroyd as partners for some of his restaurants, and the association with those two celebrities added to the appeal of the restaurants. Some feel that rapid expansion has been at the expense of exclusivity. Only time will tell whether Hard Rock cafes will benefit or suffer from the increased franchising efforts. For now, the lines outside Hard Rock cafes in Dallas, New York, and other major cities are blocks long as people come to participate in the Hard Rock experience.

---

These facts are from Jeffrey A. Trachtenberg, "Ballad of a Mad Cafe," *Forbes*, November 19, 1984, pp. 288–94; "Hard Rock Cafe PLC," *Fortune*, December 7, 1987, p. 150; and Drexel Burnham Lambert, *Hard Rock Cafe Prospectus*, April 1987.

**Questions**

1. Why do you think the first Hard Rock Cafe became successful?
2. Was franchising the Hard Rock name and cafe a good business decision? Why?
3. Some people believe that the Hard Rock Cafe has been expanded at the expense of exclusivity. Explain why you agree or disagree with this statement.

# Answers to Checking Your Understanding

1. franchise
2. Small Business Administration
3. retailer
4. undercapitalization
5. business plan
6. capital
7. small business
8. equity
9. collateral
10. service
11. Service Corps of Retired Executives (SCORE), Active Corps of Executives (ACE)

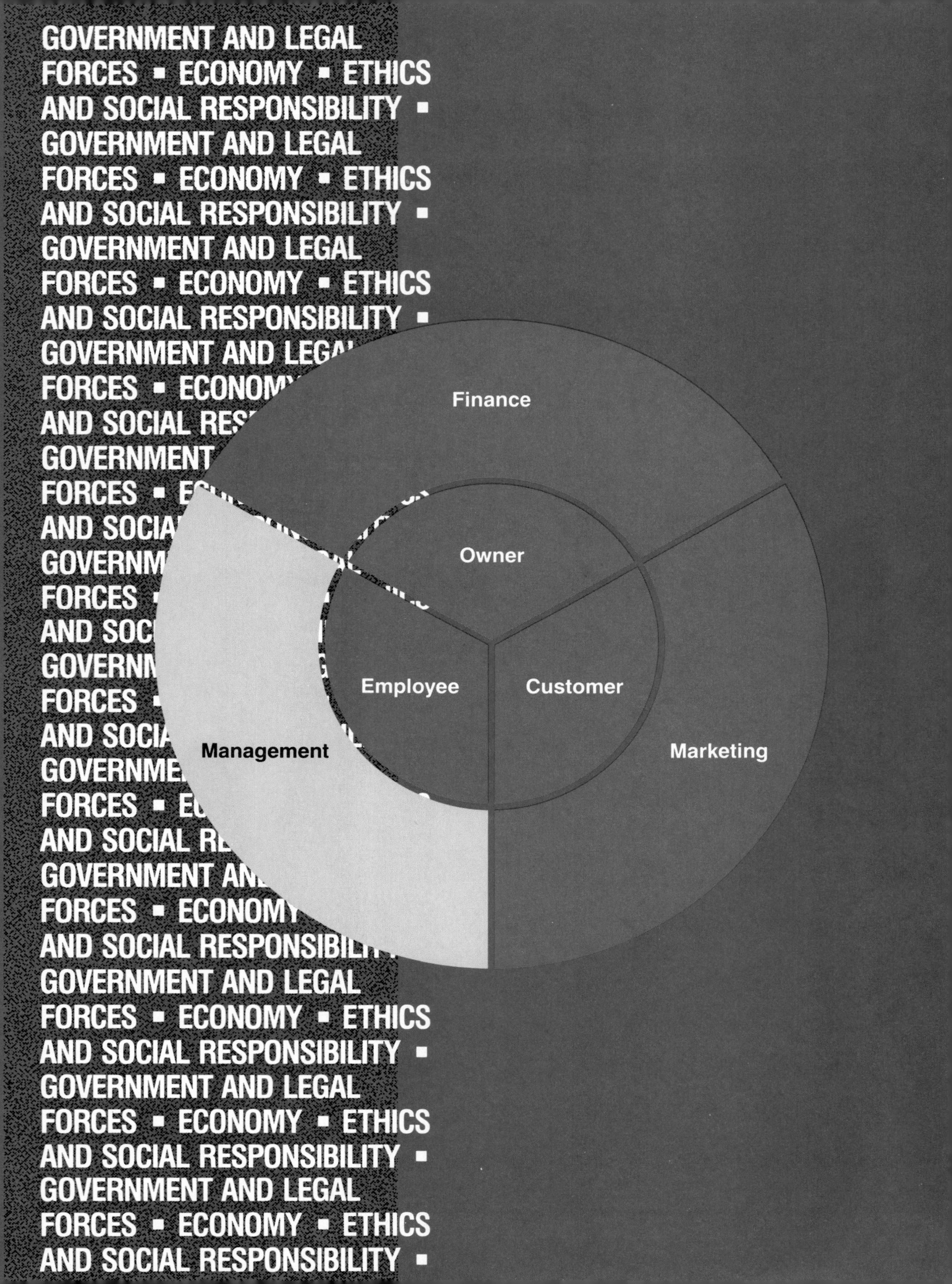

GOVERNMENT AND LEGAL
FORCES ▪ ECONOMY ▪ ETHICS
AND SOCIAL RESPONSIBILITY ▪
Finance
Owner
Employee
Customer
Management
Marketing

*Part* II
# MANAGEMENT

## Outline

# Management Principles

## Objectives

After reading this chapter, you will be able to:

▶ Define management and understand its role in the achievement of organizational objectives.

▶ Identify three levels of management and explain how the focuses of managers at each level differ.

▶ Identify the major functions of management.

▶ Identify specialized areas of management and discuss the responsibilities of managers in each area.

▶ Describe the skills managers need in order to be successful.

▶ Describe three styles of leadership.

▶ Discuss the systematic approach to decision making used by many businesses.

# Business Experience

For the third year in a row, Wes Creel's Houston-based graphic-design firm had just made the INC. 500 list of the fastest-growing private companies. Rapid growth, however, was proving to be a mixed blessing, creating problems for Creel Morrell Inc., and for Creel himself. The company had over forty employees designing signs for shopping malls, designing and printing annual reports, and doing other graphic-design work. Orders were coming in faster than they could be processed; the company was drowning in its own success. The faster the company grew, the more difficulty Creel had in coordinating, organizing, and controlling the workflow. Some employees joked that the firm's initials, CMI, stood for "crisis management inc."

One problem Creel faced was coordinating the big jobs (such as annual reports) with little jobs (such as business cards). Creel made all the decisions, important and trivial. He chose the soft drinks that were stocked in the company vending machine and authorized payment of even the smallest bills. When his health began to deteriorate (he gained weight from eating too much between crises), he saw that something drastic had to be done.

Creel hired Robert M. Donnelly, a former corporate planner for Exxon and IBM, to advise him on how to deal with his management problems. The first step was to identify the problems: (1) Because Creel Morrell Inc. rarely turned down a job, Creel often hired people for specific projects but did not adequately train them to meet the company's needs. (2) Employees were burned out by the huge workload and too exhausted to work efficiently. (3) The company was chronically short-handed because of the combination of rapid growth and high employee turnover.

Donnelly met with the employees and managers of the firm to find out what was not working. He asked them to list the strengths and weaknesses of the company and to suggest solutions to the problems. Donnelly helped Creel to see what Creel Morrell Inc. was good at and what it was not good at. He helped Creel and his managers identify objectives and strategies to achieve those objectives.

One positive result was the development of an intern program. Interns were brought in to work on small projects such as business cards, freeing the senior designers to work on the major projects. The program provided a pool of workers who would already be trained if CMI decided to hire them on a full-time basis.

Creel Morrell Inc. expected its profits to reach nearly 15 percent on $6 million in sales in 1987 and had definite plans for future growth. The company, as well as Wes Creel, was recovering from the lack of focus and planning. There was still room for improvement though as one customer noted after receiving his complimentary 1987 CMI datebook in the mail—on January 23. But problems aside, with careful planning and directing by management the company should succeed.

---

These facts are from Paul B. Brown, "Stop the Treadmill, I Want to Get Off," *INC.* 9 (May 1987): 92–98.

# Introduction

Management is the process of coordinating people, materials, machinery, equipment, and money to achieve an organization's objectives. Managers are responsible for planning, organizing, staffing, directing, and controlling the work that goes on in an organization. In short, the aim of management is to maintain an organization so that it can accomplish its tasks.

This chapter provides an overview of management. It surveys the various levels and functions of management and examines different areas of management in business. The skills managers need for success and the steps that lead to effective decision making are also discussed.

# ▶ Nature of Management

**Management**

The process of coordinating human, physical, and financial resources to achieve an organization's objectives

**Organization**

Any group of individuals who work together for the achievement of some stated or implied objective

**Management** is the process of coordinating human, physical, and financial resources to achieve an organization's objectives. Management is universal. It takes place not only in business settings but also in hospitals, schools, the military, labor unions, government, religious groups—in any situation calling for the coordination of resources.

An **organization** is any group of individuals who work together for the achievement of some stated or implied objective. A business organization may be a large automobile manufacturer, a grocery store, or an accounting firm. Both the auto maker and the grocery store sell tangible products (automobiles and food); the accounting firm sells intangible products (financial services). Services, tangible goods, or a combination of the two are referred to as products. Regardless of the products they sell, all three types of business consist of a group of individuals who work together to achieve an objective. The objective of most business organizations is to increase profits, percentage of market share, or sales volume; to gain customers; or to minimize costs.

Likewise in nonprofit organizations, such as schools, political parties, and charities, people work together to achieve objectives. The objectives of such organizations may be to transmit knowledge, solve national problems, or find shelter for the homeless.

Management and managers may be found wherever people are working together to achieve some common objective.

Every organization, in the pursuit of its objectives, must acquire resources and coordinate the use of these resources to turn out a final product or service. The resources that organizations coordinate are employees (human resources), materials and machinery (physical resources), and money (financial resources).

**Human resources**

People who are ready, willing, and able to use their skills and knowledge to advance organizational objectives

**Human resources** are people (employees) who are ready, willing, and able to use their skills and knowledge to advance organizational objectives. **Physical**

**resources** are the raw materials, supplies, machinery, and equipment used by the organization. **Financial resources** (often referrred to as capital) are the organization's supply of money and other valuable assets, such as buildings and inventory. Financial resources are necessary for the acquisition of human and physical resources.

Human and physical resources are useless by themselves. Employees must use their labor, skills, and knowledge to transform physical resources into finished products both tangible and intangible. The sale or use of products generates new financial resources. Consequently, organizations must have adequate resources of all types, and managers must carefully coordinate the use of these resources if they are to achieve the organization's objectives.

The manager of a local movie theater, for example, must make decisions about seating, projectors, sound equipment, screens, concession stands, and ticket booths. All this equipment must be in proper working condition. The manager must also make decisions about materials. There must be films to show, popcorn and candy to sell, and so on. Simply having the materials and equipment on hand is not enough, however. In order to transform the physical resources into final products, the manager must also have human resources—employees to sell the tickets, to run the concession stand, to run the projector, and to maintain the facilities. Finally, the manager needs adequate financial resources. Without them, none of the activities just mentioned will be possible. The primary source of funding is the money generated from sales of tickets and snacks.

In any organization, managers must carefully coordinate the use of human, physical, and financial resources. Such coordination requires numerous, interrelated decisions.

# ► Levels of Management

In general, there are three levels of management—top management, middle management, and first-line, or supervisory management. These levels form a pyramid (Figure 6-1). At the top of the pyramid is top management. Chrysler Corporation Chairman Lee Iacocca is at the top level of the management pyramid in his organization. Below top management is a larger number of middle managers. The manager of one of Chrysler's manufacturing plants is at the middle level of the management pyramid. The base of the pyramid is made up of an even larger number of first-line managers. At Chrysler, an assembly-line supervisor is a first-line manager. Very small organizations may have only one manager, who assumes the responsibilities of managers at all three levels. Large businesses have many managers at each level to coordinate the use of the organization's resources.

## Top Management

In business, the president and other top executives, such as the chief executive officer (CEO) and executive vice president, who have overall

**David T. Kearns, Xerox Chairman and CEO, and Barry Rand, President of Xerox's U.S. Marketing Group.** These men occupy top management positions and contribute to the planning and controlling of the company.

**Top management**

The president and other top executives who have overall responsibility for the organization

responsibility for the organization are known as **top management.** In government and education, top management refers to a governor, a mayor, a chancellor of a university, or a county superintendent of education. Top-level managers spend most of their time on strategic decisions, decisions that focus on an overall scheme or key idea for using the organization's resources to take advantage of opportunities. They decide whether to add products, acquire companies, sell unprofitable business segments, and move into foreign markets. Given the importance and range of top management's decisions, top managers generally have many years of varied experience.

## Middle Management

**Middle management**

Plant managers, division managers, and department managers

In business, plant managers, division managers, and department managers make up the level of **middle management.** Examples of middle managers in education and government are the department chairperson in a university and the head of a state public health department. The responsibility of middle managers is more narrowly focused than that of top managers. Rather than making strategic decisions about the whole organization, middle managers are responsible for the development of operating plans for their particular area and for the development of plans that will implement the general guidelines established by top management. Middle managers are involved in the specific operations of the organization.

**Figure 6-1**

Levels of Management

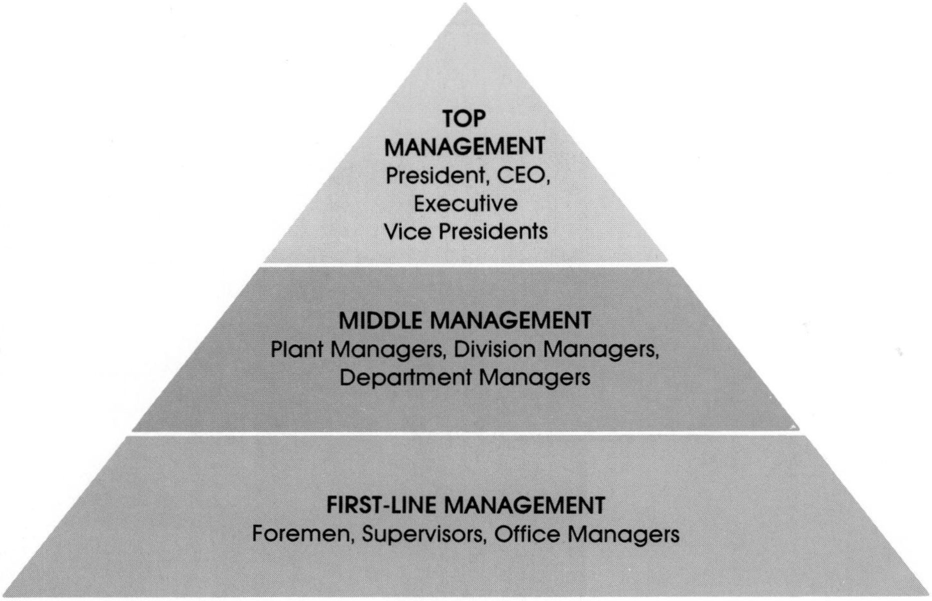

## First-Line Management

**First-line management**

Managers who supervise workers

Managers who supervise workers are known as **first-line management.** Due to their contact with workers, first-line managers are involved in the day-to-day operations of the organization. They are responsible for implementing the plans established by middle management. Common titles for supervisory managers are foreman, supervisor, and office manager.

Most people get their first managerial experience as first-line managers. First-line management entails coordinating the work of subordinates so that the plans and objectives set by middle managers can be achieved. In order to coordinate the efforts of subordinates, first-line managers need good human relations, or people, skills. They need to be able to communicate goals and expectations. They have to understand their employees' needs so that they can motivate their employees to perform. First-line managers must also provide leadership that is appropriate for the situation.

## ▶ Functions of Management

In order to coordinate the use of resources to achieve organizational objectives, managers engage in a series of activities: planning, organizing, staffing, directing, and controlling. Although each function is described separately, the five functions are interrelated, and managers sometimes perform two or more of them at the same time.

**First line manager.** Donna Cassese of Scott Paper Company, directs the activities of her employees in the Northeast woodlands of Maine.

# Planning

**Planning** is the process of selecting a course of action to achieve organizational objectives. It involves forecasting events and determining the best course of action from a set of options or choices. The plan itself specifies what should be done, by whom, where, when, and how. Planning is the first function of management; it lays the groundwork for the other functions. The plans developed by management should lead to the achievement of the objectives set by the organization.

*Objectives.* Objectives, the ends or results desired by the organization, derive from the organization's **mission.** In essence, the organization's mission is the broad task the organization wants to achieve. IBM, for example, has stated that it is in the business of helping businesspeople make decisions and that it is not just in the computer business. A photo lab might say that its mission is to provide customers with memories.

Objectives may be quite elaborate or very simple. Common objectives include profit, competitive advantage, efficiency, and growth. Organizations with profit as a goal want to have money and assets left over after paying off business expenses. Competition is the rivalry between organizations for sales and customers. Objectives regarding competitive advantage are generally stated in terms of percentage of sales increase and market share. Efficiency objectives involve making the best use of the organization's resources. Due to the variety of resources involved, efficiency objectives are quite varied. An example of an efficiency issue would be the minimization of production of defective products which would either be scrapped or sold at a discount. Growth objectives relate to the organization's ability to adapt and to get new products to the marketplace in a timely fashion. Other organizational objectives include service, social, and community goals. When objectives are written down and carefully defined, they serve as guidelines for the organization. Objectives provide direction for all managerial decisions. Additionally, objectives establish criteria by which performance can be evaluated.

*Plans.* There are two general types of plans—strategic plans and tactical plans—for meeting objectives. **Strategic plans** are the long-range plans developed by top-level managers. These plans are used to assess opportunities and determine the use of resources. Strategic plans include plans to add products, to purchase companies, to sell unprofitable segments of the business, to issue stock, and to move into international markets. Strategic plans must take into account the capabilities and resources of the organization, the changing environment, and organizational goals. Management Encounter 6-1 describes a company whose strategic plans went awry because they failed to take into account the organization's resources and capabilities. The broad, strategic plans developed by top management are refined by middle management and implemented by first-line management.

**Strategic plans**

The long-range plans developed by top-level managers, used to assess opportunities and determine the use of resources

**Magic with style.** To bring the dream to reality and open Euro Disneyland's Magic Kingdom in 1992, long-term strategy planning is required.

**Tactical plans**

Short-range plans that enable the organization to make quick changes when situations unforeseen by the strategic plan arise

**Tactical plans** are short-range plans that enable the organization to make quick changes when situations unforeseen by the strategic plan arise (perhaps a new competitor enters the market or a potentially profitable new product is developed). Because tactical plans permit the organization to react to changes in the environment while continuing to focus on the overall strategy of the organization, management must periodically review and update them.

A retailing organization with a five-year strategic plan to invest $2.7 billion in 750 new retail stores may develop five tactical plans (each covering one year) specifying how much to spend to set up each new store, where to locate each new store, and when to open each new store. Tactical plans are designed to execute the overall strategic plan. Because of their short-term nature, they are easy to adjust or abandon if changes in the environment or the company's performance so warrant.

# Organizing

**Organizing**

The structuring of resources and activities to accomplish objectives in an efficient and effective manner

Rarely are individuals in an organization able to achieve common goals without some form of structure. **Organizing** is the structuring of resources and activities to accomplish objectives in an efficient and effective manner (the organizing function is discussed in detail in Chapter 7). Structure is the arrangement of positions within the organization or the pattern of interdependent relationships.

Managers carry out their organizing function by reviewing strategic and tactical plans and determining what is necessary to implement the plans; then, they divide the work into small units and assign it to specific individuals or groups. By assigning specific tasks to individuals or groups, managers put into action the organization's plans.

For work to be done efficiently, individual jobs must be grouped into meaningful arrangements. Jobs may be grouped according to area (accounting, finance, production, marketing, personnel), product line, customer group, or geographic location. The idea is to group jobs in the best way to achieve organizational objectives.

Organizing also requires managers to establish lines of authority and accountability. An employee who has been delegated the authority to do a job is then held accountable for the successful completion of the job.

# Staffing

**Staffing**

Hiring people to carry out the work of the organization

**Recruiting**

The process of attracting qualified applicants for a job

Once managers have determined what work is to be done, they must ensure that the organization has the staff necessary to do the work. Employees must be available in appropriate quantity and with appropriate skills. In order to acquire these human resources, management must perform the staffing function (staffing is discussed in detail in Chapter 9). Hiring people to carry out the work of the organization is known as **staffing.** There are two steps to staffing: recruitment and selection.

**Recruiting** is the process of attracting applicants qualified for a job. By writing a description of the job and listing the necessary qualifications (skills, education, experience, and abilities) managers can readily spot applications from people who are clearly not qualified. Managers like to have a group of applicants from which to choose the best candidates. If the applicant pool is too small, managers may be forced to choose between hiring unqualified people or leaving the position unfilled.

**Selection,** the process of choosing the best candidate, is done by gathering information about applicants and basing decisions on this information. Sources of information for staffing decisions are employment applications, interviews, testing, and reference checks.

**Selection**

The process of choosing the best candidate

# Directing

Once the needed employees have been hired, management must provide guidance. The directing function is performed by all managers. However, directing is of primary importance to first-line managers because they are the ones who must deal on a daily basis with the employees operating the organization. **Directing** is motivating and leading employees to achieve organizational objectives.

*Motivating.* **Motivating** is giving employees reasons or incentives, such as the promise of a raise, or to work to achieve organizational objectives. Motivation is an inducement or motive for action; it accounts for why people behave as they do. Motivation is an inner state of need or desire that directs behavior toward satisfaction. When an individual recognizes or feels a need, he or she is motivated to take action to satisfy it. Most workers, for example, want more than money from their jobs: They need to know that their

**Directing**

Motivating and leading employees to achieve organizational objectives

**Motivating**

Giving employees reasons or incentives to work to achieve organizational objectives

**Managers provide direction to employees.** This airline reservation manager guides and motivates her employees on a daily basis.

employer values their ideas and input. Smart managers, therefore, ask workers to contribute ideas for reducing costs, making equipment more efficient, or even developing new products. This participation makes the worker feel important, and the company gets the benefit of new ideas. Managers who understand the needs and desires of workers can motivate their employees to work hard and productively. (The motivation of employees is discussed in detail in Chapter 8.)

## Controlling  *must be planned*

**Controlling** The process of evaluating and correcting activities to keep the organization on course

*Budget – biggest control function*

**Controlling** is the process of evaluating and correcting activities to keep the organization on course. There are five steps to the control process:

1. Measuring the performance of the organization
2. Comparing present performance with standards or objectives
3. Identifying deviations from the standards
4. Investigating the causes of deviations
5. Taking corrective action when necessary

Controlling and planning are very closely linked. The planning function establishes goals and therefore standards for performance. By monitoring performance and comparing it to standards, managers can determine whether performance is above standard, below standard, or on target. When performance is substandard, management must determine why and take appropriate corrective action. Texas Instruments noticed that one of its chips manufactured in Japan had a high defect rate—17,500 per million chips. One of the company's quality teams identified the cause of the defects and took corrective action, saving Texas Instruments $64,000 a year.[1] The control process helps managers assess the success of their plans. When plans have not been successful, the control process facilitates revision of the plans.

## Importance of Management Functions

Managers at all three levels perform all five management functions to varying degrees (Figure 6-2). Top managers, concerned with developing strategic plans, perform all five functions but spend the most time planning. Middle managers, concerned with developing tactical plans, also undertake all five functions but in most cases spend more time organizing than other managers. First-line managers, charged with implementing the plans of middle managers and supervising operating employees, likewise perform all five functions but devote most of their time to directing and controlling.

## ▶ Evaluating Managerial Performance

Performance is a measure of how well a task or action is carried out. It has two interrelated components: effectiveness and efficiency. Effectiveness is the

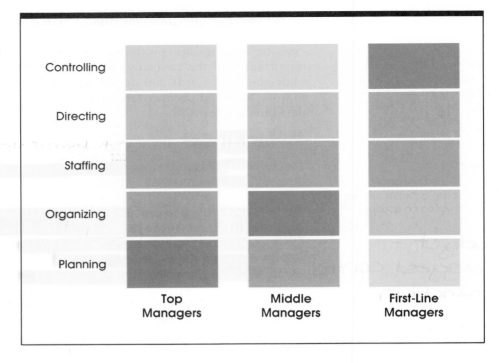

extent to which organizational objectives are achieved. Efficiency is the amount of resources used to achieve organizational goals. An effective manager produces the desired results; an efficient manager conserves resources.

When New Coke was launched in 1985, it was neither effective nor efficient in competing with Pepsi. But Coke's president, Roberto C. Goizueta, was both effective and efficient in bringing back Coke Classic to compete with Pepsi. Two Cokes turned out to be better than one. Coca-Cola increased its market share, (percentage of the market) and the cost of bringing back Coke Classic was minimized.[2]

Managers should strive to be both effective and efficient. One way for an organization to maximize performance is to be sure that each manager knows to whom he or she is accountable and the extent of that accountability.

# ▶ Areas of Management

At each level of management, there are managers who specialize in particular areas. There are, for example, financial managers, production and operations managers, personnel managers, marketing managers, and administrative managers.

# Financial Management

**Financial managers**

Managers who deal primarily with the organization's financial resources

*maximize Profits*

*make owners Rich*

**Financial managers** deal primarily with the organization's financial resources. They are concerned with obtaining the money needed for successful operation of the organization and with using that money in accordance with organizational goals. Financial managers are typically involved in the following types of activities.

1. Projecting income and expenditures over a specified period
2. Determining short-term and long-term financing needs

## Management Encounter 6-1
### AM International Tries to Make a Comeback

In the 1970s under the leadership of Roy Ash, AM International established strategic plans to enter high-tech electronics markets in an effort to boost the company's profitability. The company moved away from its traditional duplicating, phototypesetting, and graphics business because of intense competition and low profits. AM International made several major acquisitions of high-tech companies that made everything from facsimile machines to office automation equipment. The company's long-term strategic plans, however, failed to tie the new companies' products in with the company's old operations. Customers and employees alike became confused about what business AM International was actually in.

The company began to lose money rapidly, suffering a $245 million loss in 1981. CEO Ash left the same year. From 1978 to 1982, AM International went through four chief executives. The company's Bruning division had seven presidents in seven years, and forty men occupied six vice-president positions in four years. Employees joked about putting turnstiles on the corporate doors. Ash's successor sold off many of the new acquisitions, but the company continued to do poorly and he quit the next year. The next CEO, Joe Freeman, filed Chapter 11 bankruptcy proceedings to buy the company time to reorganize while he figured out how to make it profitable again.

In 1984, Merle H. Banta assumed the CEO position and AM International's problems. Banta helped restore relations with some of the company's creditors and brought the company out of bankruptcy in September 1984. He refocused the company on what it knew best: duplicating machines and graphics supplies. He

restructured the company and cut costs, eliminating two thousand mostly administrative jobs. Banta won the employees' support for the turnaround by tying the top managers' bonuses to the achievement of their individual goals. Signs with AM's stock price were prominently posted to remind the ten thousand employees—who own more than 10 percent of the company—how much was at stake in the turnaround.

In 1986, AM International purchased Harris Graphics Corporation, which makes offset presses for printing magazines and advertisements, a complement to AM International's traditional businesses. The company was careful to blend Harris's operations in with operations of the company's other divisions and products. The acquisition of Harris doubled the company's sales to $1.2 billion in 1987.

Banta's hard work has begun to show results. AM International's strategic plans now focus on traditional products and the application of high technology to those products instead of the acquisiton of companies in markets in which the company has no experience. Banta says, "We don't want to die on the cutting edge of technology again." Banta returned the company to profitability with earnings of $51 million in 1987.

---

These facts are from the 1987 AM International Annual Report; William P. Sommers, Joseph Nemec, Jr., and John M. Harris, "Repositioning with Technology: Making It Work," *Journal of Business Strategy* 7 (Winter 1987): 16–27; George Garneau, "AMI Streamlines Harris Graphics," *Editor & Publisher*, August 30, 1986, p. 36; John N. Frank, "AM International: Profits Are In, High Tech's Out," *Business Week*, July 7, 1986, pp. 77–78; and Ellyn E. Spragins, "Cleaning Up the Mess at AM International," *Business Week*, December 3, 1984, pp. 165–66.

3. Identifying sources of financing
4. Selecting the most appropriate sources of financing
5. Identifying and selecting appropriate ways to invest available financial resources
6. Monitoring the income and disbursement of financial resources
7. Protecting the financial resources of the organization

All organizations must have adequate financial resources in order to acquire the physical and human resources that are necessary to create products and services. Consequently, financial resource management is of the utmost importance. Many corporate presidents have risen through the ranks of financial management, especially in finance-related businesses such as insurance, banking, and securities.

# Production and Operations Management

**Production and operations managers** are concerned with the actual transformation of the firm's resources into goods and services ready for the marketplace. Production managers coordinate the production of tangible products; operations managers coordinate the production of services. Production and operations managers are typically involved in the following types of activities:

**Sharing wisdom and work.** A manager at Bayer has an opportunity to share his knowledge with a younger electrician while they work together.

1. Planning the capacity of production facilities
2. Planning the degree of automation in the production process
3. Planning the design of production facilities
4. Planning output to reflect demand
5. Purchasing raw materials and supplies
6. Inventory control
7. Scheduling
8. Quality control

Because no organization can exist without the production of products (either tangible or intangible), production and operations managers are vital to an organization's success. As a result, manufacturing companies, such as Caterpillar Tractor, often have presidents with a background in production; and oil companies, such as Texaco and Exxon, usually have presidents with backgrounds in engineering and production.

# Personnel Management

**Personnel managers** deal with employees in a formalized manner. Personnel managers are typically involved in the following activities:

1. Planning human resource requirements
2. Developing systems for recruiting, selecting, and hiring employees
3. Developing and implementing employee benefits programs
4. Developing and maintaining training programs
5. Developing and maintaining performance appraisal programs
6. Dealing with government regulations concerning employment practices

Personnel managers play a support role and rarely move up to become company presidents.

# Marketing Management

**Marketing managers** are responsible for planning, pricing, promoting products and making them available to customers. Within the realm of marketing there are several areas of specialization—distribution, sales, marketing research, retailing, advertising, promotion, and product management. Marketing is very important to an organization. Accordingly, a number of corporate presidents have received their training in marketing. Among them are Lee Iacocca, president of Chrysler Corporation, who gained valuable experience in marketing during his early years with Ford Motor Company (See Management Encounter 6-2).

# Administrative Management

**Administrative managers** are not specialists; rather they manage an entire business or a major segment of a business, such as the Cadillac Division of General Motors. Such managers coordinate the activities of specialized

## Management Encounter 6-2

*Profile: Lee Iacocca*

Lee Iacocca is one of the most widely recognized managers in the United States today. He is highly praised as a good manager and marketer, and is credited with saving Chrysler Corporation from bankruptcy. What makes the man so capable? Good management skills.

Iacocca honed his marketing skills at the Ford Motor Company in the 1960s and early 1970s. In the 1960s he saw that American's taste in automobiles was moving toward small, sporty models. After extensive market research, Iacocca came up with an idea for a new model that he hoped would make Ford the number-one maker of domestic automobiles. The car—the Mustang—would be small, sporty, and inexpensive. It could be souped up for performance or jazzed up for luxury with a number of options. Iacocca used promotion and publicity to tell America about the Mustang, and Americans bought the Mustang in such large numbers that it became one of Ford's best selling models.

When Iacocca took over the ailing Chrysler Corporation in 1979 he did not forget what he learned at Ford. Restructuring Chrysler was a monumental task, but he persisted until he got the company moving in the direction he wanted. Iacocca has often said that the most important ingredients for a successful business are people, product, and profits, and that is the recipe he used to save Chrysler.

Iacocca had to make long-range strategic plans for Chrysler and figure out how to make the plans work so that the company would again be profitable. He reorganized the internal structure of the company, consolidating some operations and eliminating jobs and departments that did not fit into his long-term plans. He brought in new people to carry out his plans—many from Ford Motor Company. He instituted a quarterly review system to direct employees' activities. All managers meet with their superiors every three months to discuss objectives, plans, and priorities, and to assess how well they have achieved their goals and plans. That system keeps employees throughout the organization aware of the company's long-and short-term objectives and motivates employees to be productive and to supply ideas. Iacocca maintains control of the company by constantly monitoring and comparing performance to the standards set in his strategic plans.

Lee Iacocca has all the skills needed by managers, but is especially strong in the areas of leadership and human relations. These skills enable him to communicate with his employees and with outsiders, such as government officials and potential customers, who are important to the future of Chrysler. He has maintained a strong sense of direction to keep his company on course, and he has been awarded with new profits from the company that everyone thought would die.

---

These facts are from Lee Iacocca, with William Novak, *Iacocca: An Autobiography* (New York: Bantam Books, 1985).

managers; consequently, administrative managers are often called general managers. This does not mean that administrative managers do not have expertise in any particular area. Many top executives have risen through the ranks of financial management, production and operations management, or marketing management; but most top managers are actually administrative managers, utilizing skills in all areas of management. Roxanne Decyk is an administrative manager (senior vice president for administration) at Navistar International Corporation. Decyk, who started out as a corporate secretary, now plays a major role in all decisions, from labor relations to strategic planning.[3]

# ▶ Skills Needed by Managers

In order to be successful, managers must demonstrate certain types of skills—leadership, technical expertise, conceptual skills, human relations skills, and inferential skills.

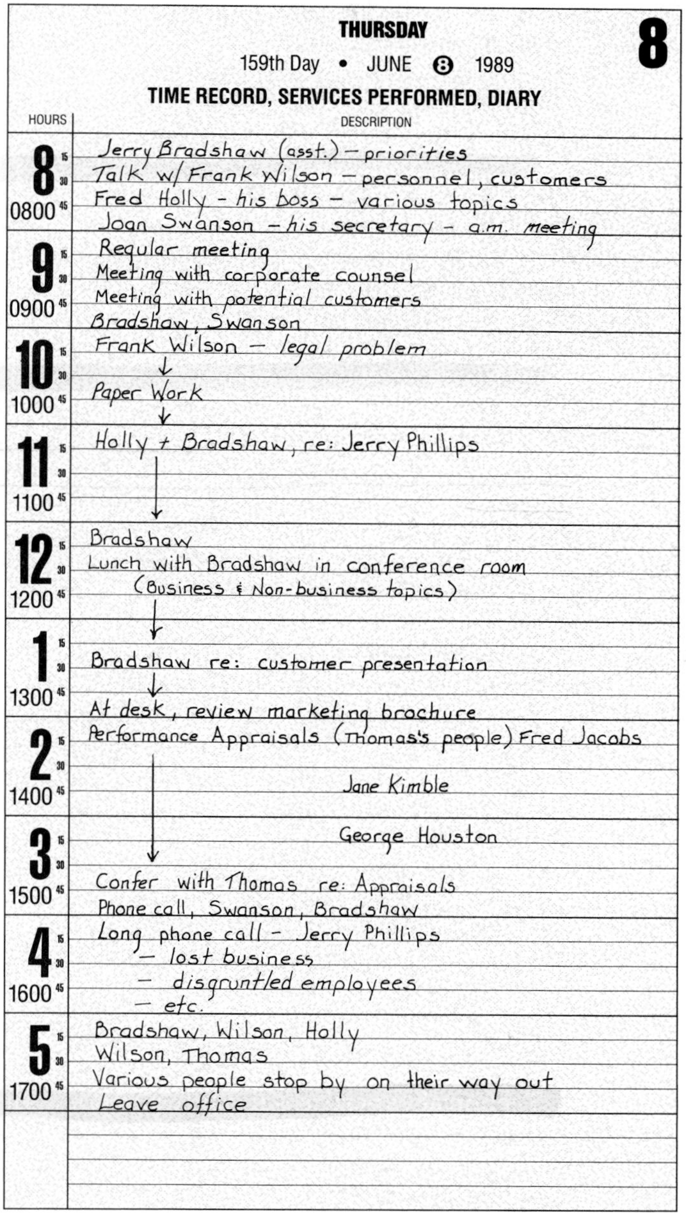

**Figure 6-3**

A day in the life of a manager Adapted from John P. Kotter, "What Effective Managers Really Do," *Harvard Business Review* 60 (November-December 1982): 156–58.

---

**THURSDAY**

159th Day • JUNE 8 1989 — **8**

**TIME RECORD, SERVICES PERFORMED, DIARY**

| HOURS | DESCRIPTION |
|---|---|
| **8** 0800 | Jerry Bradshaw (asst.) — priorities |
| | Talk w/ Frank Wilson — personnel, customers |
| | Fred Holly — his boss — various topics |
| | Joan Swanson — his secretary — a.m. meeting |
| **9** 0900 | Regular meeting |
| | Meeting with corporate counsel |
| | Meeting with potential customers |
| | Bradshaw, Swanson |
| **10** 1000 | Frank Wilson — legal problem |
| | Paper Work |
| **11** 1100 | Holly + Bradshaw, re: Jerry Phillips |
| **12** 1200 | Bradshaw |
| | Lunch with Bradshaw in conference room |
| | (Business & Non-business topics) |
| **1** 1300 | Bradshaw re: customer presentation |
| | At desk, review marketing brochure |
| **2** 1400 | Performance Appraisals (Thomas's people) Fred Jacobs |
| | Jane Kimble |
| **3** 1500 | George Houston |
| | Confer with Thomas re: Appraisals |
| | Phone call, Swanson, Bradshaw |
| **4** 1600 | Long phone call — Jerry Phillips |
| | — lost business |
| | — disgruntled employees |
| | — etc. |
| **5** 1700 | Bradshaw, Wilson, Holly |
| | Wilson, Thomas |
| | Various people stop by on their way out |
| | Leave office |

# Leadership

**Leadership**

The ability to influence employees to work toward achieving organizational goals

**Leadership** is the ability to influence employees to work toward the achievement of organizational goals. Three basic styles of leadership are autocratic, democratic and free rein. No particular style of leadership is best in all situations.

**Autocratic leaders**

People who make all the decisions and then tell employees what must be done and how to do it

**Autocratic leaders** make all the decisions and then tell employees what must be done and how to do it. These leaders generally use their authority and economic rewards as incentives to get employees to comply with their decisions. An advantage of autocratic leadership is that it allows managers to make decisions quickly because they do not have to consider input from a lot of people. Its major disadvantage is its disregard for the ideas of employees. However, the autocratic style can be very effective when employees are unskilled, untrained, or unmotivated.

**Democratic leaders**

People who allow their employees to get involved in decisions

**Democratic leaders** allow their employees to get involved in decisions. The manager presents a decision situation to subordinates and encourages them to express opinions and contribute ideas. The manager then considers the employees' points of view and makes the decision. Employees who have been involved in decision making generally require less supervision than those not similarly involved. Democratic leadership does slow the decision-making process, however.

**Free-rein leaders**

People who let their employees work without much interference

**Free-rein leaders** let their employees work without much interference. The manager sets performance standards and allows subordinates to find their own ways to meet them. For this style to be effective, employees must know what the standards are, and they must be motivated to attain the standards. The free-rein style of leadership can be a powerful motivator because it shows a great deal of trust and confidence in the employee.

The effectiveness of the autocratic, democratic, and free-rein styles depends on several factors. One consideration is the type of employees. An autocratic style of leadership is generally needed to motivate unskilled, unmotivated employees; highly skilled, trained, and motivated employees may respond better to democratic or free-rein leaders.

Two other considerations are the abilities of the manager and the situation itself. If a special task force must be set up to solve a quality control problem, a normally democratic manager may give free rein to the task force. Many managers, however, are unable to use more than one style of leadership. Some are unable to allow their subordinates even to participate in decision making, let alone make any decisions. When the situation requires quick decisions, an autocratic style of leadership may be best. The leadership style that is "best" depends on specific circumstances. Able leadership permitted Lee Iacocca to lead Chrysler from near bankruptcy to a profitable status.

# Technical Expertise

**Technical expertise**

The specialized knowledge needed to perform a job

**Technical expertise** is the specialized knowledge needed to perform a job. Managers need technical knowledge and skills related to their area of management. Accounting managers need to be able to perform accounting jobs, and production managers need to be able to perform production jobs.

**What is a manager?** Pat Riley, coach of the Los Angeles Lakers, manages the team by providing strong leadership and guidance, to win back-to-back world championships.

Although the manager may not actually perform a job, the manager needs technical expertise in order to train employees, answer questions, and provide guidance. Technical skills are most needed by first-line managers and least critical to top-level managers.

Today, most organizations rely on computers to perform routine data processing to simplify complex calculations, to organize and maintain vast amounts of information, and to help managers make sound decisions. Technical expertise, however, pertains not only to computers but to any specialized training or knowledge. For example, Ellen Monahan, now vice president for planning at RJR Nabisco, learned many valuable technical skills early in her career, as a research assistant.[4]

## Conceptual Skills

**Conceptual skills** The ability to think in abstract terms; the ability to see how parts fit together to form the whole

**Conceptual skills** involve the ability to think in abstract terms, the ability to see how parts fit together to form the whole. Conceptual skills also involve the ability to think creatively. Creative thinking is behind the development of many innovative products and ideas, including fiber optics and compact disks. Recent scientific research has revealed that people can learn to think creatively. As a result, IBM, AT&T, GE, and other top U.S. firms are hiring creative consultants to teach their managers how to think creatively. Managers at all levels and in all areas need conceptual skills, but none more so than top-level managers.

## Human Relations Skills

**Human relations skills** are the ability to deal with people, both inside and outside the organization. Getting along with people is an important skill for all managers. Those who can relate to others, understand the needs of others, and show a true appreciation for others are generally more successful than managers who lack human relations skills. People skills are especially important in hospitals, airline companies, banks, and other organizations that provide services.

## Inferential Skills

**Inferential skills** are the ability to identify relevant issues and recognize the degree of their importance, understand the relationships between issues, and perceive the underlying causes of a situation. When managers have identified the important factors and causes of a situation, they can take appropriate action. The ability to think logically is needed by all managers but is probably most important to the success of top-level managers. Steve Jobs, the founder of Apple Computer, Inc., displayed well-honed inferential skills in recognizing the need for personal computers and then producing an inexpensive product to meet that need.

## ▶ Where Do Managers Come From?

*[handwritten note: Don't put yourself in a position that will make you responsible for a wrong doing.]*

*[handwritten note: Responsibility vs. Authority — Personally take all the responsibility for wrong doings. NO COP-OUTS / If they don't give you authority you are not responsible for it.]*

Good managers are not born; they are made. An organization acquires managers in three ways: promoting employees within the organization, hiring employees from other (similar) organizations, and hiring employees out of schools and universities.

Promoting people within the organization into management positions can be an excellent idea. It tends to increase motivation by showing employees that those who work hard and are competent can advance in the company. Internal promotion also provides managers who are already familiar with the company's goals and problems. Procter & Gamble is one company that prefers to promote managers from within.[5] This practice provides managers who are familiar with the company's products and policies, and it builds company loyalty. Promoting from within, however, can lead to problems. It may limit innovation. The new manager may continue the practices and policies of previous managers. Thus it is vital for companies, even companies committed to promotion from within, to hire outside people from time to time to bring new ideas into the organization.

Finding managers with the skills, knowledge, and experience required to run an organization or department is sometimes difficult. Specialized executive employment agencies, sometimes called headhunters, recruitment managers or executive search firms often provide the needed skills to locate viable candidates from other companies. Even though outside people can bring fresh ideas to a company, hiring them may cause resentment among existing employees.

Schools and universities provide a large pool of potential managers. Entry-level applicants can be screened for their potential to develop into managers. People with specialized management skills, like those with an M.B.A. (Master of Business Administration) degree are especially good candidates. Some companies offer special training programs for potential managers just getting out of school. Foley's (owned by May's department stores) and J. C. Penney's department stores offer such programs.

# ▶ Decision Making

**Decision making**

The process of making logical choices among options

**Decision making** is the process of making logical choices among options. Decision making is important in all management functions at all levels of management, whether the decisions are strategic or tactical. A systematic approach using the following steps usually leads to more effective decision making:

1. Recognizing and defining the decision situation
2. Developing options
3. Analyzing options
4. Selecting the best option
5. Implementing the decision
6. Monitoring the consequences

The Ralston Purina Company followed this decision-making process in devising a marketing strategy for its Puppy Chow in the 1970s.[6] Research had indicated that 20 percent of all dogs are under one year of age and that puppies have different nutritional needs than adult dogs. Ralston Purina created a marketing strategy to achieve quick entry into the dog-food market.

## Recognizing and Defining the Decision Situation

The first step in decision making is recognizing and defining the situation. A decision situation may be positive or negative. An example of a negative situation is huge losses on a particular product and the need to take action. An example of a positive situation is the existence of excess cash and the need to select one out of several good investment opportunities. Ralston Purina recognized the opportunity to market a new puppy food and had to decide how to position the new product in the minds of dog owners. The decision situation faced by Ralston Purina was positive.

Situations calling for small-scale decisions often occur without warning. Situations requiring large-scale decisions, however, generally occur after some warning signals. Effective managers pay attention to such signals. Declining profits, small-scale losses in previous years, inventory build-up, and retailers' unwillingness to stock a product are signals that may warn of huge losses

**A challenging future.** Careful and innovative planning has encouraged Robert L. Crandall, President and CEO of AMR Corp. and American Airlines, to anticipate a successful future for his corporation.

before they occur. If management pays attention to these signals, the negativity of a decision situation can be lessened.

Once the decision situation has been recognized, management must define it. Huge losses reveal a problem: a failing product. One manager might define the situation as a product quality problem; another might define it as a change in consumer preference. These two definitions of the situation may lead to vastly different solutions to the problem. The first manager, for example, may seek new sources of raw materials that are of better quality. The second manager may believe that the product's life cycle has run out and decide to kill the product. This example emphasizes the importance of carefully defining the problem rather than jumping to conclusions.

## Developing Options

Once the decision situation has been recognized and defined, management must develop a list of possible courses of action. The best lists include both standard courses of action and creative ones; the list should not be limited to routine or standard options. While exploring creative options, management should remember that there are certain unavoidable limitations—namely, legal restrictions, moral and ethical norms, authority constraints, technological constraints, and economic limitations.

Managers at Ralston Purina developed three potential marketing strategies for introducing Puppy Chow: (1) a special-needs strategy emphasizing that puppies have special nutritional requirements; (2) an extended-use strategy emphasizing that puppies need special food until they are one year old; (3) a brand-name strategy emphasizing the reputable Purina name.

As a general rule, more time and expertise are devoted to the development stage of decision making when the decision is of major importance. When the decision is of lesser importance, less time and expertise will be spent on this stage.

# Analyzing Options

**Feasibility**

The practicality of an option

After developing a list of possible courses of action, management should analyze the feasibility, appropriateness, and consequences of each option. **Feasibility** is the practicality of an option. An option may be deemed infeasible because of a lack of financial resources to implement it, legal restrictions, or lack of information and inability to acquire the information necessary to implement the option.

When assessing appropriateness, management should consider whether the option adequately addresses the decision situation. When analyzing the consequences of an option, management should consider both the consequences on the situation at hand and the consequences on other parts of the organization. For example, when considering a price cut in order to boost sales volume, management must consider the consequences of the action on the organization's cash flow and consumers' reactions to price change.

In the case of Ralston Purina, two options seemed viable. The special-needs strategy would create a need for the product in the minds of puppy owners. The extended-use strategy would enlarge the potential market for the product. The brand-name strategy was weakest because at that time Puppy Chow faced no real competition.

## Selecting the Best Option

When all courses of action have been analyzed and more than one remains as an option, management must select the best one. Selection is often a subjective procedure because many situations do not lend themselves to mathematical analysis. Ralston Purina chose the first option—the special-needs strategy—to introduce Puppy Chow to the market. This strategy allowed the company to explain to consumers that puppies' nutritional needs are different from dogs' and that Purina Puppy Chow would meet those needs. It is not always necessary to select only one option and to reject all others; it may be possible to select and use several options. At different times in the life cycle of Puppy Chow, Ralston Purina used both the special-needs and the extend-use strategies.

## Implementing the Decision

In order to deal with the decision situation at hand, the selected option or options must be put into action. Ralston Purina implemented its special-needs strategy in television advertisements that compared the special nutritional requirements of puppies to those of human babies. Implementation can be fairly simple or very complex, depending on the nature of the decision. Effective implementation requires planning. When the decision involves actions such as abandoning a product, closing a plant, or purchasing a new business, management must carefully plan the implementation.

For example, when a product is dropped, management must decide how to handle distributors and customers and what to do with the idle production facility. Additionally, management should anticipate resistance from people within the organization (people tend to resist change because they fear the unknown). Finally, management should be ready to deal with unexpected consequences. No matter how well planned implementation is, unforeseen problems will arise. Management must be ready to address these situations when they occur.

## Monitoring the Consequences

When managers have implemented the decision, they must monitor its consequences: They must determine whether the decision accomplished the desired result. Without proper monitoring, the results and consequences of decisions may not be known quickly enough to make efficient changes.

If the desired result is achieved, management can reasonably assume that a good decision was made. If the desired result is not achieved, further analysis is warranted. Was the decision simply wrong, or did the situation change? Should some other option be implemented?

At Ralston Purina, Puppy Chow achieved an acceptable percentage of total dog-food sales in its first year in the marketplace. However, research indicated that the product was not selling well to one segment of its market: puppies six months to one year in age. Management decided to implement the extended-use strategy to make dog owners aware that puppies needed the nutrition of Puppy Chow until at least the age of one year. The change in strategy greatly increased the sales of Puppy Chow. If another major pet food manufacturer introduces a puppy-food product that poses a threat to Purina Puppy Chow, management is likely to change strategy again, resorting to the brand-name strategy to maintain its share of the puppy-food market.

If the desired result is not achieved, management may discover that the decision situation was incorrectly defined from the beginning. That finding would require management to start the decision-making process over again. Finally, management may determine that the decision was good even though the desired results have not yet shown up or in spite of flawed implementation. In the latter case, management would not change the decision but would change the way in which the decision is implemented.

Management Encounter 6-3 describes how Toshiba went through the decision-making process when it faced negative publicity resulting from the sale of sensitive technology.

# ▶ The Reality of Management

Management is not a cut and dried process. There is no mathematical formula for managing an organization. Management is a widely varying process for achieving organizational goals. Although managers plan, organize, staff, direct, and control, management expert John P. Kotter says these functions can usually be boiled down into two basic activities:

1. Figuring out what to do despite uncertainty, great diversity, and an enormous amount of potentially relevant information

## Management Encounter 6-3
### Toshiba Management Pays For Mistake

Early in the 1980s, Toshiba sold militarily sensitive technology to the Soviet Union. Unfortunately for Toshiba and its partner, Norwegian-based Kongsberg Vaapenfabrikk, the sale violated the rules of COCOM, a NATO organization charged with coordinating trade with communist countries. COCOM rules prohibit the trade of technology that may be used in military equipment. Officials in the United States and NATO were appalled, and wanted Toshiba to pay for its action. Toshiba was concerned about what action the U.S. government might take and about its loss in public faith.

The problem faced by management at Toshiba was how to redeem itself in America. Management had to find a course of action that would assure the United States that such a lapse would not occur again. Toshiba publicly apologized to the American people in full-page newspaper ads and detailed the actions it would take to prevent a recurrence of trade violations. The top two executives of the company resigned, the highest form of apology in the Japanese business world. Management instituted strict measures and safeguards to prevent other trade violations. It fired the key people involved in the Soviet deal and

cooperated fully with an American investigation into the incident. Finally, management developed a compliance program in cooperation with the governments of the United States and Japan.

The management of Toshiba faced a negative decision situation as a result of the illegal trading activities and followed certain steps in trying to resolve the matter. Management identified the problem—the illegal sale, which resulted in the loss of American confidence and could result in lost revenues if Congress banned the import of Toshiba's products. Management considered many solutions before deciding on a course of action—apologizing publicly and toughening controls.

Toshiba will be monitoring the consequences of these decisions for a long time to come. If the American people are not appeased, Toshiba will have to begin the decision-making process again, or lose profits and business.

These facts are from Susan F. Rasky, "Toshiba Devises a Plan to Calm Americans," *The New York Times*, July 6, 1987, pp. 19, 24; "Toshiba: Hard Pounding," *The Economist*, July 11, 1987, p. 64; Steven J. Dryden, Larry Armstrong and Jonathan Kapstein, "Congress Wants Toshiba's Blood," *Business Week*, July 6, 1987, p. 80; Toshiba apology in *The Wall Street Journal*, July 20, 1987, p. 7.

**2.** Getting things done through a large and diverse set of people despite having little direct control over most of them[7]

Managers spend as much as 75 percent of their time working with others—not only with subordinates but with bosses, people outside of their hierarchy at work, and people outside of the organization itself. In these interactions they discuss anything and everything remotely connected with their business.

Managers spend a lot of time establishing and updating an agenda of goals and plans for carrying out their responsibilities. An **agenda** contains both specific and vague items, covering short-term goals and long-term objectives. An agenda helps the manager figure out what must be done and how to get it done to meet the objectives set by the organization. Managers also spend a lot of time networking—building relationships and sharing information with colleagues who can help them achieve the items on their agendas. Managers spend much of their time communicating with a variety of people

**Agenda**

Contains both specific and vague items, covering short-term goals and long-term objectives

**Meeting a need.** Attention to design, detail, and individual customer's needs are reasons for her success, according to Ellen Woliner, owner of a New York-based graphic design and production company.

and participating in activities that on the surface do not seem to have much to do with the goals of their organization. Nevertheless, these activities are crucial to getting the job done. Networks are not limited to immediate subordinates and bosses; they include other people in the company as well as customers, suppliers, and golf partners. These contacts provide managers with information and advice on diverse topics. Managers ask, persuade, and even intimidate members of their network to get information and to get things done. Networking helps managers carry out their responsibilities.

## Notes

**1.** Richard Alm, "Employee Teams Lead TI's Quest for Quality," *Dallas Morning News,* July 28, 1987, p. 7A.

**2.** Scott Screndon and Marc Frons, "Coke's Man on the Spot," *Business Week,* July 29, 1985, pp. 56–61.

**3.** Laurie Baum, "Corporate Women," *Business Week,* June 22, 1987, p. 72.

**4.** Ibid., p. 74.

**5.** Phil Moss, "What It's Like to Work for Procter & Gamble," *Business Week's Guide to Careers* 5 (March–April 1987): 18.

**6.** David J. Luck and O. C. Ferrell, "Ralston Purina Company," in *Marketing Strategy and Plans* (Englewood Cliffs, N.J.: Prentice-Hall, 1985), pp. 442–44.

**7.** John P. Kotter, "What Effective General Managers Really Do," *Harvard Business Review* 60 (November–December 1982): 160.

# Summary and Review

▶ Management is the process of coordinating human, physical, and financial resources to achieve the objectives of the organization. Managers are concerned with maintaining the organization so that it can accomplish its tasks.

▶ There are three levels of management. Top management (president, CEO, executive vice presidents) is responsible for the whole organization. Middle management (division managers, plant managers, department managers) develops plans for specific operating areas and carries out the general guidelines set by top management. First-line, or supervisory management (foreman, supervisor, office manager) supervises the workers and day-to-day operations. The focus of managers at each level is different: Top management is primarily concerned with strategic planning. Middle management is engaged in operational planning and implementation. First-line management is primarily concerned with directing workers' daily performance on the job.

▶ Management functions include planning (selecting a course of action that will lead to the achievement of organizational objectives); organizing (structuring resources and activities to accomplish objectives); staffing (recruiting and selectinjg employees); directing (providing leadership and motivation); and controlling (evaluating and correcting activities to keep the organization in line with its objectives). These five functions are aimed at converting resources into finished products that will be successful in the marketplace.

▶ To be successful, managers need leadership skills, technical expertise, conceptual skills, human relations skills, inferential skills. There are three styles of leadership: autocratic, democratic, and free rein.

▶ The decision-making process involves making logical choices among carefully studied options. A systematic approach to decision making follows these steps: recognizing and defining the situation, developing options, analyzing options, selecting the best option, implementing the decision, and monitoring the consequences.

# Key Terms and Concepts

| | |
|---|---|
| management | organizing |
| organization | staffing |
| human resources | recruiting |
| physical resources | selection |
| financial resources | directing |
| top management | motivating |
| middle management | autocratic leaders |
| first-line management | democratic leaders |
| planning | free-rein leaders |
| mission | controlling |
| strategic plans | financial managers |
| tactical plans | production and operations managers |

personnel managers
marketing managers
administrative managers
leadership
technical expertise
conceptual skills

human relations skills
inferential skills
decision making
feasibility
agenda

# Checking Your Understanding

This chapter introduced you to the subject of management. To test and reinforce your understanding, fill in the blanks below.

1. An organization's _mission_ is the broad task the organization wants to achieve.
2. The process of attracting qualified applicants for a job is called _recruiting_.
3. _Technical_ skills are needed to perform a specialized job.
4. _Management_ is the process of coordinating human, physical, and financial resources to achieve organizational objectives.
5. The structuring of resources and activities to accomplish objectives is called _organizing_.
6. _Tactical_ plans enable the organization to react quickly when unforeseen situations arise.
7. _Strategic_ plans are long-range plans developed by top-level managers.
8. _Autocratic_ leaders make all decisions and then tell employees to carry them out.
9. _Leadership_ is the ability to influence employees to work toward the achievement of organizational goals.
10. _First line_ managers direct workers involved primarily with the firm's day-to-day operations.
11. The _marketing_ manager is responsible for planning, pricing, and promoting products and services and making them available to the customers.

# Topics for Review and Discussion

1. What is the purpose of management, and why is management so important?
2. Identify the three levels of management. Contrast the focus of managers at each level.
3. Name the five functions of management, and briefly describe each function.
4. What skills do managers need? Give examples of how managers use these skills to do their jobs.
5. Identify the different areas of management, and explain the role of each in achieving organizational goals.
6. Name the three styles of leadership. Describe situations in which each style would be appropriate.
7. Explain why the American Heart Association might need management, even though its goal is not profit.

**8.** Why must an organization have financial resources before it can utilize human and physical resources?

**9.** Explain the steps in the decision-making process.

# Exercises

**1.** Give examples of the activities that each of the following managers might be involved in if he or she worked for the Coca-Cola Company:

▶ Financial manager
▶ Production and operations manager
▶ Personnel manager
▶ Marketing manager
▶ Administrative manager
▶ Foreman

**2.** Do the same for the managers of Citibank.

**3.** You are a manager of a firm that manufactures conventional ovens. Over the past several years, sales of many of your products have declined; and this year your losses may be quite large. Using the steps of the decision-making process, briefly describe how you arrive at a decision to correct the situation.

## Case 6-1
## *Crisis Management at Ashland Oil, Inc.*

Early Sunday morning, January 3, 1988, management at Kentucky-based Ashland Oil learned it had a crisis on its hands. The day before, workers near Pittsburgh, Pennsylvania, had been filling a storage tank owned by Ashland when the tank ruptured, spilling millions of gallons of diesel fuel. One million gallons of the fuel flowed over a dike and into the Monongahela and Ohio rivers—the primary sources of drinking water for many cities. The oil spill not only killed fish and wildlife as it moved downstream but also threatened the water supplies of half-a-million residents.

Ashland's crisis-management team went to the scene of the spill to find out what had happened and to direct cleanup operations. Ashland's management needed to know all the facts so that it could explore options and resolve the situation. Ashland's CEO John Hall did not want to make a public appearance until he could honestly reassure the public and company employees that the company was doing everything that could be done.

On January 4, things began to fall apart for Ashland Oil. The crisis-management team reported that although workers had immediately tried to contain the spill, much of the oil had got past them. Cities along the rivers were shutting down their water-intake systems to prevent contamination, and many homes would be without water for several days. Businesses and schools in Pittsburgh and its suburbs were closing to conserve water until the oil passed by. Moreover, reporters had discovered that the ruptured tank was forty years old and had been moved from another site and reassembled without a written permit. The reassembled tank had not been subjected to Ashland's normal testing procedures, although the testing it had undergone met federal regulations. (Ashland normally filled oil-storage tanks completely with water to check for leaks and pressure problems.)

Ignoring the advice of Ashland's attorneys, Mr. Hall decided to fly to Pittsburgh and issue a formal apology to the people affected by the spill. Hall admitted to reporters that there were discrepancies in the testing procedure on the tank and accepted full responsibility for the spill. "If we made mistakes, we have to stand up and admit them," he said. Hall further promised the public and local officials that Ashland would pay for cleaning up the spill.

Many companies are unprepared to handle a crisis like the one faced by Ashland Oil. In a study by Western Union Corporation, only half of the two hundred companies surveyed had a crisis-management team. Such teams try to imagine worst-case scenarios—the most difficult crises that could occur. Some stage mock disasters to give employees practice in coping. When a real emergency does occur, a company that has a crisis-management team is better able to handle the problem than a company that does not have one. Of course, a crisis-management team and simulated disasters are no guarantee that a company will face a disaster with flying colors. Nevertheless, establishing a crisis-management team at least ensures that in an emergency employees will know where to call to relay and obtain information. The team can also serve as a liaison between the company, the press, and the public, freeing other managers to deal with the problem itself.

Ashland Oil's crisis-management team was experienced in handling oil spills. Many believe Ashland Oil and John Hall handled the disaster well. When the oil spill threatened or disrupted the water supply of millions of people, however, the situation indeed became a disaster.

Like the environmental effects of the spill on the Monogahela and the Ohio and their shores, the oil spill will haunt Ashland Oil for many years to come as people file suit against the company for damages. By January 8, three class-action lawsuits had been filed, and Ashland's attorneys were getting ready to handle many more resulting from the disruption to commerce and the pollution of drinking water. Experts have estimated the cleanup costs to be at least $25 million, which Ashland and its insurance company will pay. The cost to Ashland from lawsuits and loss of reputation will be much higher.

These facts are from Clare Ansberry, "Oil Spill in the Midwest Provides Case Study in Crisis Management," *The Wall Street Journal*, January 8, 1988, p. 15; Rick Wartzman, "Ashland Says Its Tank May Have Lacked Filling Clearance Prior to Diesel Spillage," *The Wall Street Journal*, January 6, 1988, p. 6; "Ashland Is Sued over the Collapse of Its Fuel Tank," *The Wall Street Journal*, January 8, 1988, p. 6; Denise Kalette and Rae Tyson, "Oil Spill Is 'Nightmare Come True,'" *USA Today*, January 6, 1988, pp. 1, 2A; "After the Spill: The Struggle to Cope," *USA Today*, January 6, 1988, p. 5A; and Nancy Jeffrey, "Preparing for the Worst: Firms Set Up Plans to Help Deal with Corporate Crises," *The Wall Street Journal*, December 7, 1987, p. 23.

**Questions**

1. How effective was top management "managing" this crisis?
2. What type of leadership skills were used in dealing with the crisis?
3. How can future crisis management be avoided through strategic planning? What tactical actions were necessary in this case?

---

## Case 6-2
### *Sigma Marketing Concepts*

Sigma Marketing Concepts publishes creatively designed promotional calendars. The company sells calendars directly to businesses for use in their own promotions. From 1985 to 1987, Sigma experienced a growth in sales volume of approximately 200 percent. To continue growing in an orderly fashion, Sigma reviewed its past performance and recent organizational changes, developed long-range strategic plans, and made some changes in its approaches to decision making.

President Don Sapit, a mechanical engineer with an M.B.A., started Sigma Press, Inc., as a small commerical printer in Ottawa, Illinois, in 1972. The company worked hard to establish a reputation for creative and high-quality printing within its service area. Management knew, however, that success in the printing industry requires specialization. Sigma's management noticed that the demand for customized desk-pad calendars was increasing and thought that producing these calendars might provide an opportunity for specialization and expansion. After defining and investigating the situation, management wrote a three-year strategic plan.

The strategic plan focused on exploiting the opportunities presented by the desk-pad calendar by improving the product and promoting it. To meet the needs of individual customers, Sigma customized desk-pad calendars with unusual designs, advertising messages, and creative photographic techniques. Sigma advertised the product in sales and marketing-oriented publications. The ads generated a lot of inquiries but did not increase sales. Promoting the calendars through direct mail, primarily to manufacturers, did produce results.

Sales of Sigma's desk-pad calendars increased 40 percent per year between 1976 and 1980. The increasing demand soon exceeded the company's production capacity. In 1979 and 1980, Sigma made major financial commitments to add a new, large, high-speed, two-color press and to purchase, redesign, and rebuild a specialized collating machine to further automate the assembly process. Management developed and implemented new marketing ideas to complement the state-of-the-art machinery. Improved direct-mail techniques allowed the identification of prospective customers by Standard Industrial Code (SIC) number and sales volume. A toll-free phone line was installed to encourage direct response by interested parties. The company generally responded to inquiries with a sample calendar containing advertising ideas related to the respondent's line of business and followed up with a personal phone call within eight to ten days.

Calendar sales continued to improve, representing 40 percent of total sales and approximately 75 percent of net profit by 1983. Reorder rates were usually in the 90 percent range. In spite of the success, Sapit recognized that the market for his product was declining and that competition was increasing in the commercial segment, particularly in Sigma's area. After analyzing the situation, Sigma's management decided to sell the commericial portion of its business and become an exclusive producer of custom-designed calendar products. The company found a buyer for the plant, equipment, and goodwill of the commercial portion of the business. Sigma and the buyer signed a long-term contract under which the buyer agreed to produce all Sigma calendars, using the same plant and staff that had handled production over the past twenty years.

The sale freed Sigma from the daily problems of production and plant management and allowed the company to commit all its resources and efforts to creating, producing, and selling new calendar products. Sapit had long wanted to move the business to the Sun Belt because of the better weather and, more important, because of the better business climate. In May 1985, the corporate offices were moved to Jacksonville, Florida. At the same time, Sapit's son Mike, who has a degree in graphic arts from Illinois State University, joined the business.

One of the first decisions the new organization made was to revise its potential customer base to include blue-chip, service-oriented companies. To appeal to these companies, Sigma expanded its product line to include wall planners, pocket planners, and diaries. Each of these products was designed to allow Sigma to maintain its differential advantage of offering advertising flexibility and creativity.

The company also developed a more aggressive marketing program. New, sophisticated techniques were used to select and contact prospective customers. Prospects were chosen by their sales volume, and advertising budget. After prospects were selected, direct-mail and telemarketing efforts were effectively integrated. Sigma first contacted key marketing executives by phone, then sent prospective customers sample calendars and appropriate literature. Within a week or ten days after mailing the package, Sigma followed up with a phone call to determine interest, answer questions, and encourage orders.

Although results from the new marketing efforts are not yet conclusive, they appear to be positive. Sigma now includes such prime accounts as Federal Express, Nabisco Brands, Fidelity Investments, and Brach Candies among its satisfied customers.

Sigma Marketing Concepts continues to monitor and evaluate its internal and external environments. The company has installed a new computer system to coordinate and analyze operations. It has also doubled the number of employees since the move to Jacksonville and recently completed construction of a new office building, which will allow years of comfort and growth.

---

These fact were provided by Donald Sapit, Renee Mudd, and Warren Eldridge, Sigma Marketing Concepts, Jacksonville, Fla., 1988.

**Questions**

1. What are some of the strategic decisions made by Sigma over the past ten years?
2. Since Sigma is a small business, what type of leadership style do you think would work best?
3. What challenges will management face in maintaining continued growth at Sigma? Which management function may be most important for continued success? Why?

# Answers to Checking Your Understanding

1. mission
2. recruiting
3. technical
4. management
5. organizing
6. tactical

7. strategic
8. autocratic
9. leadership
10. first-line
11. marketing

## Outline

# Chapter 7

# The Role of Organizations

## Objectives

After reading this chapter, you will be able to:

▶ Understand what organizational structures are and what forms they take.

▶ Understand how organizational structures evolve and how they are created.

▶ Differentiate between formal and informal organizations and their importance.

▶ Understand the effects of the external environment on organizations.

# Business Experience

When General Bill Creech took over the Air Force's Tactical Air Command (TAC) in 1978, he realized he had a possible national security disaster on his hands. At any one time, half of TAC's fighter planes were not battle ready, and 220 planes were called "hangar queens" because they had been grounded at least three weeks for lack of parts. When General Creech studied the problem, he realized that the best solution would be a new organizational structure for TAC.

In the 1970s, the Air Force was highly centralized and authority was concentrated at the upper levels. To accomplish anything, low-level employees had to go through their superiors and fill out reams of paperwork. Simple repairs took days or even weeks. Because the maintenance crews were not held accountable for the condition of the planes they worked on, maintenance was lackluster at best. Poor maintenance resulted in low-quality training missions as pilots flew planes with no radar or with faulty navigation systems.

General Creech began to decentralize TAC, delegating responsibility and authority to the lowest ranks of the command. He created maintenance teams and assigned each team to a squadron; team members were given responsibility for the maintenance of all planes in their squadron. Creech then moved the maintenance teams down to the flight line to facilitate repairs. Creech's goal was to instill in the members of each squadron and maintenance team a personal interest and pride in the success of the squadron, and he achieved his goal. The results were phenomenal. The squadrons developed very strong identities, and were suddenly competing with each other to look the best, fly the best, and be the safest. Creech's first effort at decentralization showed the lowest-level employees that they were important to the main mission of the Tactical Air Command—fighting and flying.

Creech gave squadron commanders goals for the squadrons' training missions but gave the commanders free rein to design and schedule the missions. Creech made the commanders responsible for the quantity and quality of their missions.

General Creech went to work on the mountains of paperwork that were slowing the repair process because the highest authorities had to approve all requisitions. He moved spare parts from the warehouse down to the flight line, where they were accessible to the maintenance crews. Microcomputers were used to list available parts and to tell the supply department what parts to order. As a result of decentralization, maintenance crews can get hold of most parts in less than fifteen minutes. Creech also ordered that everything at all TAC bases receive a fresh coat of paint, from fighters to buildings. He hoped that improving the appearance of each base would further strengthen the workers' pride in their organization and improve their productivity.

When General Creech retired from the Air Force in 1984, the Tactical Air Command was a different organization. The crash rate had dropped to one crash for every fifty thousand hours flown, and 85 percent of the F-15s were battle ready at any one time. After decentralization, the men of TAC were far more satisfied with their work and thus more productive. Creech had accomplished all this not with additional money, planes, or men but by delegating responsibility, authority, and accountability all the way down to the lowest-level workers, encouraging their initiative and giving them a sense of pride and control.

These facts are from Jay Finegan, "Four-Star Management," *INC.* 9 (January 1987): 42–51.

# Introduction

An **organization** is any group of people working together to achieve an objective. For a business, the objective could be an increase in market share, sales targets, new customers, cost minimization, or higher profit. For nonprofit organizations, the objective could be to solve community problems, to convince people to accept religion, to get a candidate elected, or to win America's Cup. Rarely is a group of individuals able to achieve common objectives without some form of structure. Whether the structure is explicitly defined or only implied, it is necessary for an organization to function properly. Getting people to work together efficiently and coordinating the skills of diverse individuals require careful planning. Developing appropriate organizational structures is a major challenge for business managers.

# ▶ Nature of Organizations

The best way to begin to understand how organizations develop is to consider the evolution of a new business such as a clothing store. At first, the business is a one-person operation in which the owner does everything—purchases, prices, and displays the merchandise; keeps the books; and assists customers. As the business grows, the owner needs help and hires a salesperson and a bookkeeper. As the business continues to grow, the owner hires additional salespeople. Because the business is doing well, the owner must be away from the store frequently, meeting with accountants and advertising agencies and going to fashion shows and conventions. Thus the owner must designate someone to supervise the sales personnel. When branch stores are opened, still more sales help is needed, along with new store managers and supervisors. The various stages of growth are shown in Figure 7-1.

Organizing

Structuring human, physical, and financial resources to achieve objectives in an effective and efficient manner

Growth requires **organizing**—the structuring of human, physical, and financial resources to achieve objectives in an effective and efficient manner. Growth necessitates the hiring of additional people who have specialized skills. With more people and greater specialization, the organization needs a formal structure in order to function efficiently.

Structure

The arrangement or relationship of positions within an organization

**Structure** is the arrangement or relationship of positions within an organization; it is a pattern of interdependent relationships. The structure of an organization comes into being when managers arrange employees into an interdependent pattern of work relationships so that organizational objectives may be achieved. A department store, for example, needs salespersons, merchandise buyers, credit managers, maintenance people, display designers, and department managers, in addition to the store manager. All the people occupying these positions must work together to achieve their objectives.

*designated relationships among all the resources of management system*

*Formal —
outlined*

*Informal —
develop because
of the existance
of the organization*

# ▶ Creating Organizational Structure

Whether the organization is Mobil Oil, the Muscular Dystrophy Foundation, or the convenience store on the corner, the structuring of the organization requires planning and forethought. Managers involved in creating an organizational structure must consider six factors: specialization, departmentalization, delegation of authority, span of management, hierarchy of objectives, and degree of centralization.

## Specialization

**Specialization**

A division of labor that involves dividing work into small, specialized tasks and assigning employees to do a single task

**Specialization**, or division of labor, involves dividing work into small, specialized tasks and assigning employees to do a single task.

To achieve work specialization, management must identify all the activities that must be done in order for the organization to function. These broad activities must then be broken down into small, specific tasks that can be handled by individual employees. When management has made this breakdown, individuals capable of performing the specified duties can be hired. A small business such as the local college bookstore may require only a few specialized employees. A large corporation like USX (formerly U.S. Steel) needs thousands of specialized employees. The process of specialization and division of labor is illustrated in Table 7-1.

The rationale for specialization is efficiency. People can perform more efficiently if they master just one task rather than all tasks. In *Wealth of Nations*, published in 1776, Adam Smith discussed the division of labor, using

*Efficient = best product, lowest cost*

*5 steps of Organizing Process*

*1. Reflect on plans & objectives*

*2. Establish major tasks*

*3. Divide major tasks into sub-tasks*

*4. Allocate resources & directives for a subtasks*

*5. Evaluate the results of implemented organizing strategy*

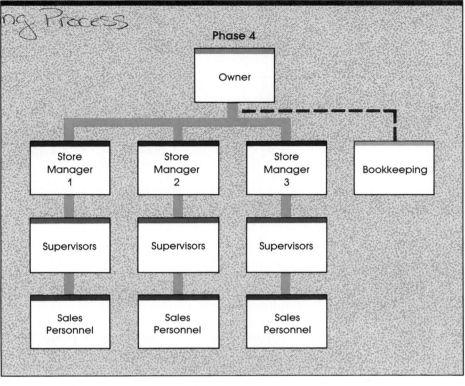

**Phase 4**

Owner

Store Manager 1 — Store Manager 2 — Store Manager 3 — Bookkeeping

Supervisors — Supervisors — Supervisors

Sales Personnel — Sales Personnel — Sales Personnel

as his example of specialization the manufacture of a pin. Individual workers could produce twenty pins a day when each employee worked alone. Thus ten employees working independently of each other would produce 200 pins a day. However, when one man drew the wire, and another straightened it, and a third cut it, and a fourth ground the point, productivity increased substantially. As a result of specialization, ten men were able to produce 48,000 pins per day.[1] The benefits of specialization also led to the development of the automobile assembly line by Henry Ford.

Efficiency is not the only impetus for specialization. Specialization may also occur when the activities that must be performed within an organization are too numerous for one person to handle. Recall the example of the clothing store. When the business was new, the owner could do everything; but when the business grew, the owner needed help.

Specialization minimizes the time lost that occurs when workers must perform more than one task by shifting from one job to another. Adam Smith's discussion of specialization in the pin factory illustrates this point. At first, workers were performing a set of related tasks. They had to draw the wire, then cut the wire, then straighten the wire, then grind the point. When each task was assigned to separate workers, employees could concentrate on one aspect of production and did not lose time shifting from one job to the next. The division of labor also makes possible the use of specialized

**Table 7-1  Job specialization and division of labor**

| Job | Specific Task | Employee's Function |
|---|---|---|
| Automobile assembly | Employee 1: Attach doors<br>Employee 2: Attach trunk<br>Employee 3: Attach hood | Install specific components |
| Automobile quality control | Employee 4: Check paint for imperfections<br>Employee 5: Check for leaks<br>Employee 6: Check for workmanship flaws in car interior | Maintain high-quality production |

equipment, which can perform tasks rapidly and increase productivity. Finally, specialization simplifies the training of employees.

Specialization, if carried too far, can have negative consequences. Workers may become bored and dissatisfied with their jobs, and the result of their unhappiness is poor quality work and high employee turnover. Although some degree of specialization is necessary for efficiency, because of differences in skills, abilities, and interests, all people are not equally suited for all jobs. The negative consequences of too much specialization and strategies for coping with them are discussed in detail in Chapter 8.

# Departmentalization

**Departmentalization**

Grouping jobs into working units that are usually called departments but may also be called units, groups, or divisions

**Departmentalization** is the grouping of jobs into working units that are usually called departments but may also be called units, groups, or divisions. Departments are commonly organized by function, product, territory, or customer (Figure 7-2). Most organizations use two or more departmentalization schemes to facilitate the achievement of organizational objectives. For example, most advertising agencies have creative, media, accounting, and account service departments (or organization by function).

**Functional departmentalization**

Grouping jobs according to business function

*Functional Departmentalization.* **Functional departmentalization** is the grouping of jobs according to business function. Every organization has three essential functions: production or operations, marketing, and finance. Other major areas of activity are purchasing, personnel, and research and development. Each department is managed by someone who is an expert in the work done by the department—an engineer supervises the production department; a financial executive supervises the finance department. Each department manager needs only the skills that apply to the function of the department. A weakness of functional departmentalization is that because it tends to emphasize departmental units rather than the organization as a whole, decision making that involves more than one department may be slow.

**Product departmentalization**

Grouping jobs around the products of the firm

*Product Departmentalization.* **Product departmentalization** is the grouping of jobs around the products of the firm. General Motors, for example, is organized by product groups. These product groups include

**In-house services.**  Seeking skilled personnel for a new in-house publishing system at Moody's Investor Services requires the specific skills of both these managers. The senior vice president and publisher (left) relies on the resources of the vice president, director-human resources to help her find qualified people for her department.

GMC Trucks, Chevrolet, Pontiac, Oldsmobile, Buick, and Cadillac. The functional activities—production, finance, marketing, and others—are located within each product division. This arrangement allows the coordination of all activities that are related to a product or product group and simplifies decision making. The major disadvantage of product departmentalization is the duplication of specialized functions. In addition, emphasis is on product rather than on the overall objectives of the organization. Management Encounter 7-1 describes how the Pontiac division of GM is trying to differentiate itself from other GM divisions.

**Territorial**
**departmentalization**

Grouping jobs by geographic location

*Territorial Departmentalization.*  **Territorial departmentalization** is the grouping of jobs by geographic location. National sales organizations and international organizations may use this approach because of vast differences between territories. In such cases, the territory may be a continent, individual countries, or regions within a single country. Territorial departmentalization is not restricted to large areas. Many police departments use units called

**Figure 7-2 A and B**

Departmentalization

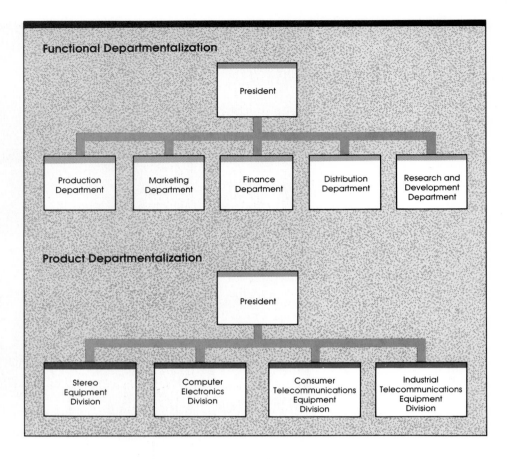

Functional Departmentalization

President

Production Department | Marketing Department | Finance Department | Distribution Department | Research and Development Department

Product Departmentalization

President

Stereo Equipment Division | Computer Electronics Division | Consumer Telecommunications Equipment Division | Industrial Telecommunications Equipment Division

precincts, which may be as small as several city blocks. Territorial departmentalization enables organizations to respond to the unique requirements of each geographic area. A disadvantage of grouping by location is that a large administrative staff and control system are required to coordinate operations.

*Customer Departmentalization.* **Customer departmentalization** is the grouping of jobs around the needs of various types of customers. Banks, for example, usually have separate departments for commercial banking activities and for consumer or retail banking activities. This arrangement allows the bank to respond easily to the unique requirements of each group. Some manufacturing firms are organized into industrial and commercial customer departments. Customer departmentalization, like territorial departmentalization, does not focus on the organization as a whole and therefore requires a large administrative staff to coordinate the operations of the various groups.

# Delegation of Authority

**Delegation of authority** is the assigning of tasks to employees and at the same time giving the employees the power to make the commitments, use

---

**Customer departmentalization**

Grouping jobs around the needs of various types of customers

**Delegation of authority**

Assigning tasks to employees and at the same time giving the employees the power to make the commitments, use the resources, and take the actions that are necessary to accomplish the tasks

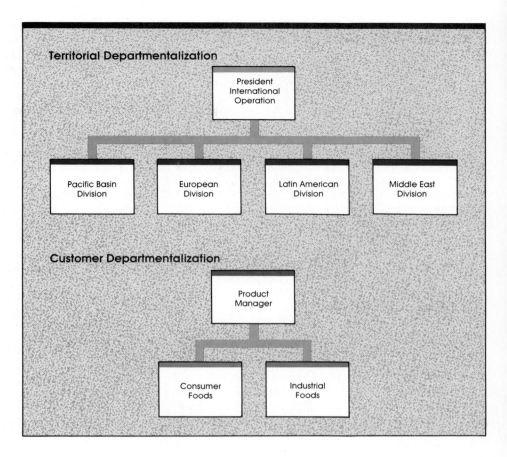

**Territorial Departmentalization**

- President International Operation
  - Pacific Basin Division
  - European Division
  - Latin American Division
  - Middle East Division

**Customer Departmentalization**

- Product Manager
  - Consumer Foods
  - Industrial Foods

*Can not Delegate responsibility But you can assign it.*

*CEO is always responsible!*

the resources, and take the actions that are necessary to accomplish the tasks. As an organization grows, it becomes increasingly difficult for one manager or owner to do everything, and there is a need for specialization and division of labor. Delegation frees the manager to attend to the matters that he or she is specially qualified to deal with. When Apple Computer got too big for Steven Jobs to manage, he delegated manufacturing and marketing jobs to others so that he could focus on major decisions associated with Apple's growth. Delegation lays a **responsibility**, or obligation, on the employee to carry out the assigned task satisfactorily and makes the employee accountable for the proper execution of the work.

The director of marketing at Adolph Coors Co. assigns an employee to find out how well a marketing campaign is doing. To carry out the assignment, the employee needs access to research materials, and the marketing director gives the employee authority to make certain decisions and to obtain information on sales, profits, and so on. Without the authority to carry out the assigned task, the employee would have to get the marketing director's approval for every decision and for every request for materials.

The marketing director who gave the employee responsibility for the job and delegated the authority to carry out the job holds the employee accountable

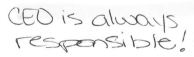

**Responsibility**

The obligation of the employee to carry out the assigned task satisfactorily

## Management Encounter 7-1

### *Pontiac Sets Itself Apart from Other GM Divisions*

In the 1980s General Motors' sales dropped, and for the first time in many decades, Ford's profits were greater than GM's. GM's biggest problem was that cars from all five of its divisions—Buick, Cadillac, Chevrolet, Oldsmobile, and Pontiac—looked alike. Each division handled its own design, production, and marketing, but the company encouraged similarities in design to reduce costs. The Pontiac 6000, Chevrolet Celebrity, Oldsmobile Cutlass Ciera, and Buick Century, for example, all used an "A" chassis. Consumers were confused by the similarities between models, and sales for a particular GM model were often achieved at the expense of other GM models.

The Pontiac Division perhaps suffered most from the company's downturn. Pontiac had been a trend setter during the performance-car era of the 1960s, and the division had set many sales records. During the 1970s and early 1980s, however, Pontiac's sales declined sharply because consumers preferred fuel-efficient cars, and some industry analysts believed that GM might merge Pontiac with the Chevrolet Division.

In the late 1980s, the Pontiac Division took steps to differentiate itself from the other GM divisions. Pontiac wanted to develop a clear image as a producer of performance sports cars. Its decision to return to a performance image was a reversion to the 1960s, when John DeLorean and other young leaders had controlled the division. Pontiac adopted a bold advertising slogan—"We Build Excitement"—to appeal to performance-oriented car buyers. It started offering "option packaging" on special versions of some models. These models came with a specific group of options, with almost no variations. They proved to be immensely popular with car buyers. As luck would have it, Pontiac's sporty performance theme was also timely: It came at a time when gas prices were decreasing and consumers were less concerned with fuel efficiency.

Pontiac's differentiation tactics were not new. It borrowed heavily from the styling features of European sedans and the option packaging of Japanese cars. At the time, the division marketed only one unique car—the Fiero (due to a downturn in sales of two-seater cars, this model was dropped in 1988). However, Pontiac set several of its cars apart from comparable models in other GM divisions with distinctive styling and mechanical features. The Pontiac Grand Am, although built on the same chassis as the Oldsmobile Calais and the Buick Somerset, featured wraparound taillights and wide side-panel molding to differentiate it from the other two models. All Pontiac models had tighter suspension and steering, giving them excellent performance and road handling.

Pontiac's new success from its distinct performance image was not ignored by industry analysts. They believed that other GM divisions should follow Pontiac's lead and try to create their own division identity. This individuality will help GM avoid interdivision competition for sales.

These facts are from Jacob M. Schlesinger, "GM's Recent Progress Hasn't Rescued Its Poor Sales," *The Wall Street Journal*, December 1, 1987, p. 2; William J. Hampton and James R. Norman, "General Motors: What Went Wrong?" *Business Week*, March 16, 1987, pp. 102–10; and Paul Ingrassia, "Pontiac Revives 'Sporty' Image, Setting a Marketing Example for Other GM Units," *The Wall Street Journal*, August 15, 1986, p. 15.

**Accountability**

Employees are answerable to a superior for the outcome of a project

for the quality and timeliness of the work. Subordinates who accept an assignment and the authority to carry it out also accept the principle of **accountability**—that they are answerable to a superior for the outcome of the project. If the marketing report prepared by the Coors employee is inaccurate or arrives on the desk of the marketing director after its scheduled due date, the employee must accept the responsibility or blame. If the report is a model of research skill or is completed ahead of schedule, the employee must accept the credit. Similarly, managers are accountable for the work of their subordinates. The marketing director at Coors, for example, is accountable to his or her superior for all reports prepared by the marketing research staff.

To further illustrate the delegation of authority, consider this example: The president of a firm delegates responsibility for all marketing activities to the vice president of marketing. The vice president accepts this responsibility and has the authority to obtain all relevant information, to make certain decisions, and to delegate any or all activities to his subordinates. The vice president, in turn, delegates all advertising activities to the advertising manager, all sales activities to the sales manager, all product development activities to the product development manager. These managers then delegate specific jobs to their subordinates.

The process of delegation establishes a pattern of relationships and accountability between superior and subordinates. The president has authority over and is accountable for the work of the vice president of marketing. The vice president of marketing has authority over and is accountable for the work of the advertising, sales, and product development managers. The act of delegating responsibility and authority to a subordinate does not relieve the superior of accountability for the delegated job or jobs. Even though the vice president of marketing delegates work to subordinates, he or she is still ultimately accountable to the president for all marketing activities.

## Span of Management *#of people who ~~~~ you directly report*

**Span of management**

The number of subordinates who report to a particular manager

*depends on job!*

**Span of management** refers to the number of subordinates who report to a particular manager. How far should the span of a manager's authority extend? How many subordinates should report to a manager? There is no simple answer. There is general agreement, however, that top managers should not directly supervise more than four to eight people but that lower-level managers who supervise routine tasks are capable of managing a much larger number of subordinates.

**Wide span of management**

A manager directly supervises a very large number of employees

**Narrow span of management**

A manager directly supervises only a few subordinates

*Know these*

***Wide vs. Narrow Span of Management.*** Given the inability of researchers to identify the optimal span of management, researchers and managers have turned their attention to a more general question: Should the span of management be wide or narrow? A **wide span of management** exists when a manager directly supervises a very large number of employees. A **narrow span of management** exists when a manager directly supervises only a few subordinates. Both wide and narrow spans of management are illustrated in Figure 7-3.

To answer the question of whether a span of management should be wide or narrow, managers must take the following circumstances into consideration:

1. The physical distance between superiors and subordinates
2. The responsibilities of managers other than supervision
3. The degree of interaction required between superiors and subordinates
4. The frequency of problems
5. The competence of subordinates
6. The existence of specific operating procedures

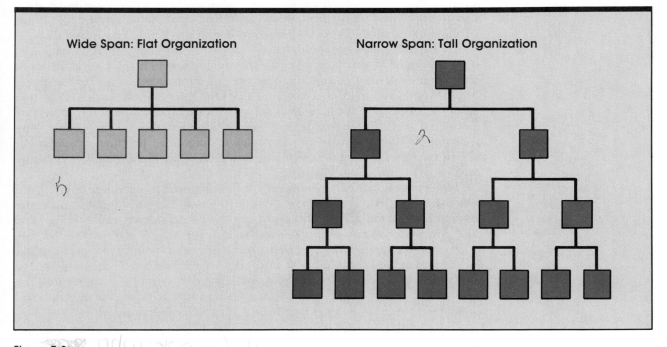

**Figure 7-3**

Span of management: wide span and narrow span

A wide span of management is appropriate when superiors and subordinates are located in close proximity to one another, the manager has few responsibilities other than supervision, the level of interaction between superiors and subordinates is low, few problems arise, subordinates are highly competent, and a set of specific operating procedures governs the activities of managers and their subordinates.

A narrow span of management is appropriate when superiors and subordinates are not in close proximity, the manager has many responsibilities in addition to the supervision of subordinates, the interaction between superiors and subordinates is frequent, and problems are common. The existence of a narrow span does not necessarily imply either a lack of competent employees or a lack of operating procedures; rather it implies that employees require the guidance of their supervisors and that operating procedures are general.

**Organizational layers**

The levels of management in an organization

***Organizational Layers.*** **Organizational layers** are the levels of management in an organization. An organization that has many layers of managers is considered tall. An organization that has few layers of managers is considered flat.

In tall organizations, the span of management is generally narrow (Figure 7-3). Because each manager supervises only a few subordinates, numerous layers of management are necessary to carry out the operations of the business. Because there are more managers in tall organizations than in flat organizations, administrative costs are usually higher. Communication is slower because information must pass through many layers.

**Top management provides swift solutions.** In a flat organization with a wide span of management, managers can quickly gather to communicate and make problem-solving decisions.

In flat organizations, the span of management is generally wide (Figure 7-3). Because managers supervise a large number of employees, fewer management layers are needed to conduct the organization's activities. Managers in flat organizations typically perform more administrative duties than managers in tall organizations because there are fewer managers. They also spend more time supervising and working with subordinates. Many corporations, including Avon, AT&T, and Ford Motor Company, are flattening their organizational structure to reduce costs and to speed the flow of information.

## Hierarchy of Objectives

A **hierarchy of objectives** is an ordering of objectives so that the achievement of all low-level objectives results in the achievement of higher organizational objectives. Overall profit objectives at Procter & Gamble, for example, may be broken down by major product divisions. Divisional objectives may

**Hierarchy of objectives**

Ordering objectives so that the achievement of all low-level objectives results in the achievement of higher organizational objectives

**Figure 7-4**

Hierarchy of Organizational Objectives

be further broken down by region and function. The process of breaking down objectives may continue until individual employees have specific objectives. See Figure 7-4.

Departmentalization can result in an emphasis on functions, territories, products, or customers. As a result, it is essential that management establish a hierarchy of objectives. The process of ordering objectives allows all employees of the organization to know what management expects them to do in order to meet overall objectives. The achievement of each individual objective should contribute positively to overall organizational objectives. It is relatively easy for managers in small organizations to establish a hierarchy of objectives because they have only a few levels of objectives to consider. In large corporations, establishing the hierarchy can be a difficult task.

# Degree of Centralization

When managers develop an organizational structure, they must consider the amount of authority that they are willing to disperse throughout the organization. In some organizations, managers may attempt to restrict authority to the upper levels; in others, managers may attempt to disperse authority throughout the organization and down to the lower levels. The degree to which authority is delegated throughout an organization determines the extent of centralization.

***Centralization.*** A centralized organization is one in which top-level managers delegate very little authority to the lower levels of the organization; authority is concentrated at the top. Although decision-making authority in centralized organizations rests with top levels of management, a vast amount of responsibility for carrying out daily and routine procedures is delegated to even the lowest levels of the organization. The U.S. Army is a prime example of a centralized organization.

Organizations tend to be centralized when the decisions to be made are risky and when low-level managers are not highly skilled in decision making. Over-centralization can cause serious problems for an organization. The Business Experience that opens this chapter describes the difficulties centralization brought to the Tactical Air Command, where for a time workers had to requisition high-ranking supervisors to obtain simple tools to repair planes. On the other hand, some highly centralized organizations, such as K mart and Toys "Я" Us, have been very successful.

***Decentralization.*** A decentralized organization is one in which decision-making authority is delegated as far down the chain of command as possible. Decentralization is characteristic of organizations that operate in complex and unpredictable environments. Retail chain stores may decentralize so that store managers can deal with local markets. Lower-level managers who interact with the external environment on a routine basis often develop a good understanding of it and thus are able to react quickly to changes. The delegation of decision-making authority to lower-level managers may increase the organization's productivity. Decentralization requires that lower-level managers have strong decision-making skills. Some of the largest and most successful companies are decentralized. Both GE and Sears have been quite successful with a decentralized structure. Management Encounter 7-2 describes IBM's efforts to decentralize its organization.

# ► Forms of Organizational Structure

The process of delegation establishes a pattern of authority and accountability within the organization that is often called bureaucracy. In theory, bureaucracies are designed to deal with a large number of people in a fair and equitable manner. However, the difference between theory and practice is

## Management Encounter 7-2
### *IBM Decentralizes*

Concerned about three years of slow sales, a declining reputation for service among its customers, few new products, and much corporate fat, International Business Machines (IBM) began a major reorganization effort in January 1988. Chairman John Akers faced the daunting task of cutting costs and reducing bureaucratic levels of management while maintaining IBM's long-held policy of not laying off any employees.

The company's primary goal in reorganizing was to improve products and service to customers. To that end, IBM combined several divisions to improve efficiency and reduce costs. Personal computers and typewriters were merged into one division because their markets had converged in the last few years. IBM also combined its successful mainframe computer business with its less profitable mid-range computer business. These efforts were designed to move IBM closer to its customers. Akers decentralized the company by pushing decision making down to general managers in six major product and marketing divisions. He hoped that decentralizing would eliminate the bureaucracy that had slowed new-product development. The managers of the six divisions are now responsible for developing products that meet the needs of the customers in their particular markets.

To avoid employee layoffs during the reorganization, IBM asked fifteen thousand employees to retire early and allowed another 24,600 jobs to go unfilled when employees left the company. The company eliminated overtime and temporary positions. Most of these jobs were in areas that IBM wanted to eliminate to reduce the number of management levels. IBM retrained thousands of other employees to fill new positions and promoted or moved twenty-one thousand employees to comparable positions.

Decentralization may not solve IBM's problems. Decentralization results in expensive duplication of marketing, finance, and other functions because divisions handle each of these tasks independently. Decentralization may also lead to problems when divisions compete to sell products to the same customers. However, decentralization will free John Akers to deal with IBM's major problems instead of with corporate bottlenecks and disputes between company divisions. It will reduce costs associated with having a tall organization and speed up decision making and new-product development time.

IBM has long been the leader in the computer market, and its products have a reputation for quality and reliability. The company's reorganization will allow it to improve its products and introduce new ones in order to be responsive to customers' needs.

These facts are from Larry Reibstein, "IBM's Plan to Decentralize May Set a Trend—But Imitation Has a Price," *The Wall Street Journal*, February 19, 1988, p. 17; Geoff Lewis, with Anne R. Field, John J. Keller, and John W. Verity, "Big Changes at Big Blue," *Business Week*, February 15, 1988, pp. 92–98; Aaron Bernstein, "How IBM Cut 16,200 Employees—Without an Ax," *Business Week*, February 15, 1988, p. 98; and Michael W. Miller and Paul B. Carroll, "IBM Unveils a Sweeping Restructuring in Bid to Decentralize Decision-Making," *The Wall Street Journal*, January 29, 1988, p. 3.

great. Most bureaucracies are highly centralized and have a narrow span of management. Departmentalization tends to be functional, and the delegation of authority is usually precise and very formal.

Bureaucracies tend to grow at an alarming rate. C. Northcote Parkinson, a British historian-philosopher, developed his own "law" to explain their rapid growth rate: "Work expands so as to fill the time available for its completion."[2] He meant that the number of employees in a bureaucracy increases over a period of time regardless of the amount of work to be done. Thus, contemporary bureaucracies tend to be large, rather slow-moving, inefficient organizations. They are also rather rigid and inflexible and have trouble coping with change and unexpected events. Management Encounter 7-3 discusses Jack Welch's efforts to reduce the bureaucracy at GE.

Because today's business environment is dynamic, bureaucratic structures are inappropriate, and alternate structures have been devised: line structure, functional structure, line-and-staff structure, matrix structure, and committees.

# Line Structure

**Line structure**

Direct lines of authority that extend from the top executive to employees at the lowest level of the organization

**Line structure** is based on direct lines of authority that extend from the top executive to employees at the lowest level of the organization (Figure 7-5). Decision making is the responsibility of each manager. An advantage

**Figure 7-5**

Line Structure

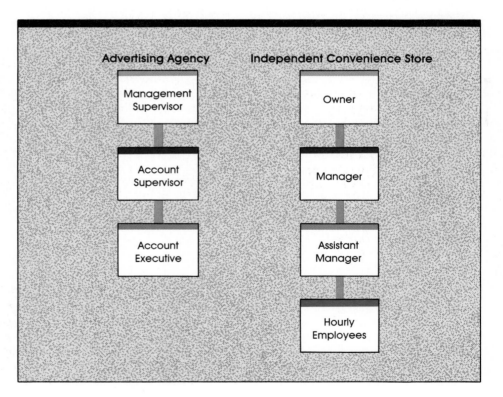

# Management Encounter 7-3
## *Profile: Jack Welch of GE*

GE, once known as General Electric Corporation, has often served as a model for corporate organization. The third-largest American company has frequently set trends in organizational change, from organizing into profit centers in the 1950s to the hiring of strategic planners in the 1970s. In the 1980s, GE is again at the forefront of an organizational trend, this one to turn the company into a streamlined, highly-profitable, competitive machine. Company chairman John Francis "Jack" Welch is behind the streamlining of GE, and he has made both friends and enemies in his quest to cut bureaucratic fat out of the company.

Jack Welch was the only child of Grace and John Francis Welch, a train conductor on the Boston & Maine. Welch's parents were strongly supportive of their son, and they worked hard so that he could go to college. He majored in chemical engineering at the University of Massachusetts at Amherst, and in 1960, obtained his doctorate in chemical engineering from the University of Illinois. Soon after, he accepted an offer from GE to work its plastics division in Pittsfield, Mass. Welch exhibited a surprising flair for marketing there: he even asked customers to come in and help design products so that the products would meet their needs. At age 35, Welch was heading the plastics division, at 37, he was a corporate vice president. In 1981, at age 45, he assumed the position of Chairman and Chief Executive Officer of General Electric.

As Chairman, Welch set ambitious goals for his company. He wanted GE to be number one or two in all of its businesses. He drew three circles to represent manufacturing, service and technology on a sheet of paper. He got rid of several hundred businesses that did not fit into those circles, and acquired others that did, including Kidder, Peabody (an investment bank) and RCA, which also owned NBC. He reduced the corporate staff from 1700 to just over 1000 to eliminate several layers of management. Flattening the organization eliminated bottlenecks in communications and permitted GE to be much faster in decision making.

Welch is sometimes called "Neutron Jack," after the neutron bomb which kills people but leaves buildings intact because he was responsible for laying off one in four GE workers. Union workers are angry about the layoffs, and many employees are insecure about their futures with GE. However, under the new GE, employees have more responsibilities and are encouraged to offer their input. Welch likes to give challenges to employees in addition to taking on challenges for himself. He once held a shouting match with a subordinate in front of other managers. Welch then thanked the man for standing up to him. Welch refers to this as "constructive conflict," but it has many managers and employees on edge.

Although Jack Welch has aroused controversy at GE, the company is much healthier since he took over. GE's earnings are up 48 percent from 1980, and employee productivity is up as well. The company is definitely more efficient at earning profits than it was when Welch assumed the chairmanship, and it has lots of room to grow.

---

These facts are from Russell Mitchell with Judith H. Dobrzynski, "Jack Welch: How Good a Manager?" *Business Week*, December 14, 1987, pp. 92–103; Jack Egan, "What Makes Giant GE Keep on Growing?" *US News & World Report*, November 23, 1987, pp. 48–9; Marilyn A. Harris, with Zachary Schiller, Russell Mitchell, and Christopher Power, "Can Jack Welch Reinvent GE?" *Business Week*, June 30, 1986, pp. 62–7.

---

of such a structure is the clear chain of command, which gives managers the ability to make decisions quickly. A mid-level manager facing a decision must consult only one person, the immediate supervisor, not several people. A weakness of this structure is that it requires managers to possess a wide range of knowledge. Managers have responsibility for a variety of activities and must be knowledgeable about them all. Line structures are most common in small businesses such as a Pizza Hut franchise or a law firm.

**Figure 7-6**
Functional Structure

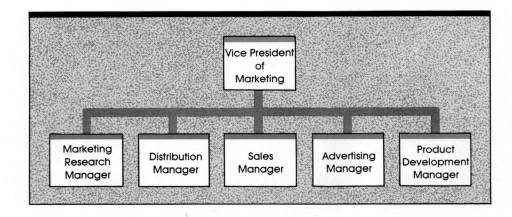

## Functional Structure

**Functional structure**

Divides general managing duties into functional areas and a separate supervisor manages each functional task

A **functional structure** divides general managing duties into functional areas, and a separate supervisor manages each functional task (Figure 7-6). The functional structure overcomes the main problem of line management—namely, the lack of specialization among managers. Functional supervisors are able to specialize in a specific area and provide expert advice to operating employees. Functional structures have one major drawback: Lower-level employees must report to each of the specialized functional supervisors, and conflicts may arise between the orders given by the various functional managers. When such problems result, determining who is at fault is very difficult. Strict functional structures are not common in modern business organizations.

## Line-and-Staff Structure

**Line-and-staff structure**

An attempt to combine the strengths of the line structure and functional structure

The **line-and-staff structure** is an attempt to combine the strengths of the line structure and the functional structure (Figure 7-7). There is a line relationship between superiors and subordinates, and specialized managers, called staff managers, are available to assist line managers. Line departments are directly involved in the operation of the business. Staff departments provide advice and support to line departments on specialized matters, such as finances, engineering, and the law. Staff managers do not have direct authority over line managers or over the line manager's subordinates, but they do have direct authority over subordinates in their own departments. Staff managers exist in most organizations regardless of structure. Many organizations engage a legal adviser to assist managers with legal matters pertaining to their departments. Ford Motor Company has a lawyer to advise on labor relations; other companies have lawyers to audit their hiring practices.

**Figure 7-7**

Line and Staff Structure

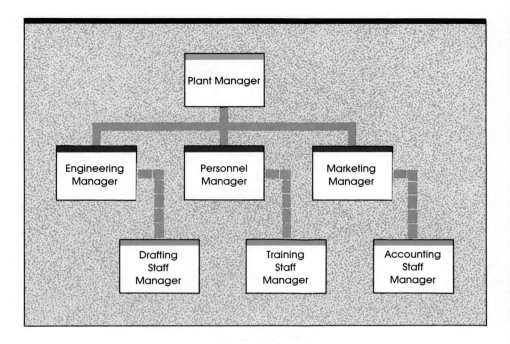

## Matrix Structure

A **matrix structure,** also called a project management structure, involves setting up teams from different departments, thereby creating two or more intersecting lines of authority (Figure 7-8). Matrix structures are usually temporary. Specialists typically go back to their functional department after a project is finished. The project-based departments are superimposed on the more traditional, function-based departments. Teams are developed by bringing together specialists from a variety of areas to work together on a single project. In a matrix structure, employees are responsible to two managers—functional managers and project managers. The advantage of a matrix structure is that it enables the organization to respond quickly to changes in the environment by giving special attention to specific projects or problems. NASA and Procter & Gamble have used the matrix structure.

## Committees

Often an individual manager cannot complete a specific task, so the authority and responsibility for the task are assigned to a group of individuals—a committee. If Polaroid, for example, is trying to decide whether to develop a new product, it might form a committee of managers from several different departments, including research, production, and finance, to help make the decision.

There are different types of committees. An ad hoc committee is generally set up for a specific, short-term purpose, such as deciding whether to develop

**Figure 7-8**

Matrix Structure

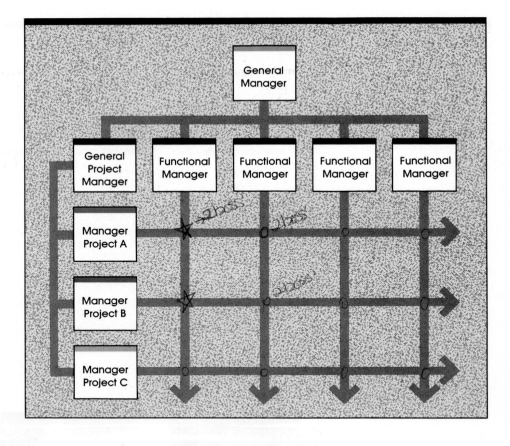

a new product. When its work is completed, an ad hoc committee is usually disbanded. A standing committee is a relatively permanent committee that performs a specific, recurring task, like reviewing departmental budgets, hiring practices, or promotion policies. A task force is a committee established to deal with a major problem or pending decision. For example, if a product line is losing money, a task force might be set up to determine how to salvage the product or whether to abandon it. The Japanese utilize small task forces that they call quality circles to work on the resolution of problems. Many American firms, including the Campbell's Soup Company and Texas Instruments, have adopted quality circles for their own use.

The main advantage of committees is that they allow more information and skills to be brought to bear on a problem than could generally be marshaled by an individual working alone. The main disadvantage of committees is that they typically take longer than individuals to reach a decision. Committee decisions are generally more conservative than those made by individuals and may be based on unnecessary compromise, not on identification of the best alternative. The comment that "a camel is a horse designed by a committee" often applies to committee decisions.

# ► Formalization of Organizations

**Formal organization**

The relationships, channels of communication, and patterns of responsibility and authority that are clearly defined within an organization

**Formal organization** relates to the relationships, channels of communication, and patterns of responsibility and authority that are clearly defined within an organization. Managers describe the formal structure in organization charts, organization manuals, and policy manuals.

An organizational chart is a diagram that shows the authority and responsibility relationships in an organization. An organization chart shows organizational structure, lines of authority, staff relationships, permanent committee arrangements, and lines of communication. Downward communication conveys orders, requests for information, and explanations of decisions. Upward communication conveys status reports, policy questions, and complaints. Horizontal communication conveys information about procedures and methods.

Organizational structure is also formalized through organization manuals and policy manuals. An **organizational manual** gives written descriptions of authority relationships, details the functions of major organizational units, and describes job procedures. A **policy manual** describes personnel activities and company policies.

**Organizational manual**

A written description of authority relationships which details the functions of major organizational units and describes job procedures

**Policy manual**

Describes personnel activities and company policies

Organizational charts, organizational manuals, and policy manuals describe the structure and relationships within an organization at a point in time. As the organization changes and evolves, they must be updated; otherwise, employees will not be able to understand the complex workings of the organization, and the organization may fail to operate at maximum efficiency.

**Horizontal communication.** The exchange of information in an insurance firm allows these employees to learn more about several kinds of insurance.

# ► Informal Organizations

**Informal organization**

The personal and social relationships that evolve in the work environment

The **informal organization** is the personal and social relationships that evolve in the work environment. The informal organization results from the spontaneous and natural relationships that develop as work tasks are performed. Although the organization chart does not reveal informal social relationships, their impact on the climate of the organization can be great: They serve as channels of communication, and they influence work behavior.

Examples of the informal organization are groups of employees who go bowling together or who go to lunch together. The activities of these groups are essentially unrelated to the work of the organization. Other informal groups may evolve with the purpose of forming a union or getting a manager fired. In these situations, the activities clearly are related to the organization. Informal groups may establish work standards that group members are expected to follow. Informal groups may generate disagreement and conflict, or they may enhance morale and job satisfaction.

## Informal Leaders

**Informal leaders**

Individuals who have no formal authority over others yet can influence the behavior of others

**Informal leaders** are individuals who have no formal authority over others yet can influence the behavior of others. Informal leaders influence behavior because they are respected and because others look to them for leadership. Managers should identify informal leaders and gain their support.

**Informal organization is productive.**   It may not always be obvious, but informal meetings and social relationships are important to the work environment because they encourage communication and can influence behavior.

# Grapevine

**Grapevine**

An informal channel of communication, separate from management's formal, official communication channels

The **grapevine** is an informal channel of communication, separate from management's formal, official communication channels. It was an important source of information long before Marvin Gaye recorded "I Heard It Through the Grapevine." Communication along the grapevine does not necessarily follow the communication lines shown on the organization chart. Informal communication flows up, down, diagonally, and horizontally through the organization. Information passed along the grapevine may relate to the job or organization, or it may be gossip and rumors unrelated to either.

The grapevine can act as an early warning system for employees. If employees hear through the grapevine that their company may be sold, they have a little time before the official announcement to think about what they will do. However, the information passed along the grapevine is not always accurate. Employees have left companies because of rumors, only to learn that the rumor was false.

Everyone loves to gossip, and managers need to be aware that grapevines exist in every organization. Managers who understand how the grapevine works can use it to their advantage, feeding it facts to squelch rumors and incorrect information.

# ► Impact of Environment on Organizations

The major objectives of business organizations are to survive, grow, and make a profit. In order to achieve these objectives, the organization must conserve its resources by minimizing duplication of effort and maximizing efficiency and effectiveness. Resources can be conserved by placing a manager in charge of some specific resource and making that person accountable for its utilization or by establising rules and procedures for the utilization of the resource.

Organizations attempt to achieve objectives by making goods and services available to consumers. Organizations must interact with their customers. In order to make goods and services available, firms must first acquire the necessary materials; thus, they must interact with suppliers. Honda of America, in order to assemble its products, must obtain steel, plastic, and other materials from various suppliers. In addition to dealing with suppliers and customers, business firms must interact with other organizations in the external environment (Figure 7-9). These others include government agencies, labor unions, financial institutions, and distributors. Organizations in the external environment may have a substantial impact on how a firm conducts business and consequently on the organization of the firm. Consider, for example, the impact of labor unions. Strikes by the United Auto Workers stopped work at General Motors in the 1980s sending the company scrambling for inventory. Conversely, concessions by the United Auto Workers in 1980 permitted Chrysler to lay off many of its workers temporarily, and the money saved by Chrysler helped keep the company out of bankruptcy.

**Figure 7-9**

The External Environment of
Business

*all the impacts on an organization*

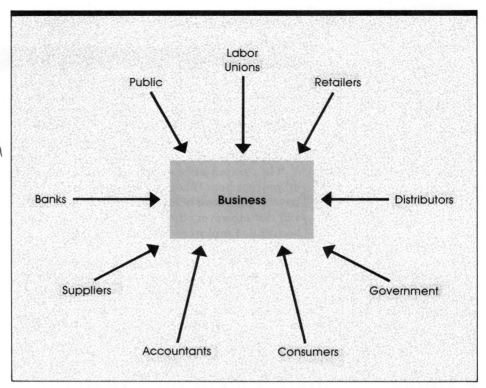

Many employees of an organization rarely come into contact with anyone outside the organization during their workday. Others, who might be called organizational buffers, have varying amounts of contact with outsiders. Buffers range from the president of Chrysler to the person who initially answers the telephone, and they include people like salesmen, repair people, receptionists, and the personnel director. It is important to realize that buffer individuals *are* the organization for many of the people with whom they come into contact. If they are poorly trained or rude, they can harm the organization. If they are knowledgeable and polite, they can advance the organization's objectives. An important function performed by buffers is information gathering. Because they are in contact with the outside world, they can make the organization aware of problems and opportunities in the external environment.

The influence of the external environment on organizational structure is substantial. Businesses may choose to organize by territory because of differences in external environments based on varying geographic locations. Similarly, businesses may choose to organize by product and customer because of the different environments that surround both. In addition, the nature of the environment may affect the degree of centralization in an organization. When the environment is complex or volatile, organizations tend to decentralize so that they can react quickly to new developments.

**Organizational buffers.** The employees who meet the public represent the company and can harm or enhance the company's image.

**You don't have to be seen to make an impact.** These sports announcers serve as an informational link between the radio audience and a baseball game between the Angels and the Yankees. Left to right are: Joe Torre, Bob Starr, Jim Kaat, Billy Martin, Phil Rizzuto, and Bill White.

# Notes

**1.** Adam Smith, *Wealth of Nations* (New York: Modern Library, 1937; originally published in 1776).

**2.** C. Northcote Parkinson, *Parkinson's Law and Other Studies in Administration* (Boston: Houghton Mifflin, 1957).

# Summary and Review

▶ An organization is a group of individuals who work together to achieve a common goal. Structure is the arrangement or relationship of positions within an organization. Organizational structure may exist in these forms: line structure, functional structure, line-and-staff structure, and matrix structure.

▶ Organizations evolve to accommodate growth. Growth requires people with specialized skills. Creating organizational structures requires consideration of specialization, departmentalization, delegation of authority, span of management, hierarchy of objectives, and degree of centralization.

▶ Formal organization relates to the relationships, channels of communication, and patterns of responsibility that are clearly defined within an organization. The formal organization is presented in organizational charts and manuals. Informal organization is the spontaneous, natural, personal, and social relationships that evolve in the work place. The activities of informal groups do not necessarily pertain to work.

▶ The external environment may determine the structure the organization chooses. The environment may also determine the degree of centralization in an organization.

# Key Terms and Concepts

organization
organizing
structure
specialization
departmentalization
functional departmentalization
product departmentalization
territorial departmentalization
customer departmentalization
delegation of authority
responsibility
accountability
span of management
wide span of management

narrow span of management
organizational layers
hierarchy of objectives
line structure
functional structure
line-and-staff structure
matrix structure
task force
formal organization
organization manual
policy manual
informal organization
informal leaders
grapevine

# Checking Your Understanding

This chapter introduced you to the subject of organizational structure. To test and reinforce your understanding, fill in the blanks below.

1. The _formal organization_ is the relationships, channels of communication and patterns of responsibility and authority that are clearly defined within an organization.

2. The _span_ of management is the number of subordinates a manager directly supervises.

3. _Responsibility_ is an employee's obligation to carry out assigned jobs.

4. Geographic location is the basis for _territorial_ departmentalization.

5. _Delegation of Authority_ enables subordinates to use resources and take action.

6. The degree to which authority has been delegated throughout an organization determines the extent of _centralization_.

7. The personal and social relationships developed in the work environment make up the _informal organization_.

8. In _matrix_ structure, teams from different departments are set up, and the result is two or more intersecting lines of authority.

9. The _grapevine_ is an informal communication system.

10. According to the principle of _accountability_, employees are answerable to a superior for the outcome of their assigned activities.

11. _Product_ departmentalization is the grouping of jobs around the products of the firm.

12. The arrangement or relationship of positions within an organization is called _structure_.

# Topics for Review and Discussion

1. Explain why job specialization might be important to an organization.

2. Identify four types of departmentalization, and name a company that has used each type.

3. Define span of management. Why do some organizations have narrow spans and others wide spans?

4. Discuss the different forms of organizational structure. What are the primary advantages and disadvantages of each form?

5. Why must organization charts and manuals be updated regularly?

# Exercises

1. Why does job specialization increase productivity in the automobile industry? What might happen if the industry were not specialized?

2. Explain, using a specific example (perhaps your own future business), how an organizational structure might evolve. How would you handle the issues of specialization, delegation of authority, and centralization? Which structure would you use? Explain your answers.

# Case 7-1
## *Borden's Organizational Structure*

Borden, Inc., is a New York-based corporation that markets a broad range of products—consumer products, chemicals, grocery items, snacks, and dairy products. In the 1980s, the company expanded heavily in consumer products and foods and divested unrelated businesses such as women's apparel and fertilizer. It is now the world's largest dairy company, the number-one pasta seller, and the second largest seller of snack food. Borden has organized itself into six product divisions that it wants to develop and expand: dairy products, snacks, pasta, niche grocery products, nonfood consumer products, and chemicals.

The company's strategy is to buy small regional companies in order to obtain economies of scale in manufacturing and flexibility in marketing. As Borden expands geographically, it centralizes production in the most efficient plants to lower costs and increase profit margins. Since 1980, Borden has acquired forty businesses, adding more than $2 billion to annual sales and giving the company an increased national presence.

Borden's dairy products division is one of the most profitable in the industry. The company maintains profitability by charging high prices—up to a dollar a gallon more for milk than supermarket brands. Borden can get away with charging higher prices because it constantly reinforces its brand name through extensive advertising. Moreover, the company maintains a high level of quality and service standards in its dairy products through a program called the "Borden Difference." Borden acquired several regional dairy companies in the 1980s, increasing its geographic reach. In 1986, the company bought Beatrice's dairy operations for $315 million and renamed the operations Meadow Gold Dairies. With Meadow Gold, Borden distributes dairy products in thirty-eight states as well as internationally. The company introduced several new products in the dairy division, such as Hi-Calcium milk and Eagle brand ice cream, which have been favorably received by consumers.

Borden's snack division is battling Frito-Lay for the number-one market position. Sales of Borden's Wise brand snacks are approaching those of Frito-Lay for some comparable items. The company bought several regional snack producers in an effort to expand its product line. Borden helped these regional companies increase sales by plugging holes in their product lines with other Borden products. In addition, the regional producers create new products and borrow products from one another, further broadening their product lines and Borden's total snack distribution.

Borden's pasta division has grown tremendously in the past few years as a result of the acquisition of several regional pasta makers, including Gioia in Buffalo and Anthony's in Los Angeles. These acquisitions gave Borden the ability to sell its own Creamette brand along with the regional pastas through local sales distribution networks. This strategy enabled Borden to expand national distribution of the Creamette brand to thirty-three states.

Creamette is the only pasta brand to have such widespread distribution in the United States.

Borden markets several niche grocery products such as RealLemon lemon juice, Cracker Jack snacks, Cremora coffee creamer, and Bama brands. Each of these is number one or two nationally or in its region, and the company plans to expand them. The company purchased several more businesses for this division including Doxsee Food Corporation (clam products) and Fisher Cheese (substitute cheese). These purchases expanded the division's product line, which already included grocery products such as NoneSuch mincemeat and Snow's clam products.

Borden's nonfood consumer product line includes things such as Elmer's glues, Krylar paints, car-care products, and wall coverings. These products are targeted to the do-it-yourself market. The company again broadened its distribution network for some of its fastest-growing nonfood. consumer products by acquiring companies in similar lines of business.

The chemical specialties division of Borden concentrates on specialty industrial chemicals such as resins and polyvinyl chloride films. The company expanded its share of this market with the purchase of the Acme Resin Corporation, a foundry resin producer. Borden also sold off its commodity chemicals business so that it could concentrate on specialty chemicals.

Borden's strategy of organizing along product lines has proven to be very profitable. Its revenues from 1987 were nearly $6.5 billion, 30 percent higher than the year before. Earnings increased more than 20 percent during the same period. Moreover, Chairman Romeo Ventres has said Borden is willing to make more acquisitions, as long as it sticks with businesses in the six main product divisions. The company that gave the world Elsie the Cow is on its way to becoming one of the most profitable conglomerates in the United States.

---

These facts are from Bill Saporito, "How Borden Milks Packaged Goods," *Fortune,* December 21, 1987, pp. 139–44; "Borden, Inc., Acquires 8 Businesses for Total of About $55 Million," *The Wall Street Journal,* November 11, 1987, p. 41; Judann Dagnoli, "Borden Pumps Up Consumer Products; Though Not Wild About Wyler's," *Advertising Age,* November 10, 1986, pp. 4, 103; and the 1986 Borden Annual Report.

**Questions**

1. Borden is organized around six main product divisions. Should future acquisitions be related to the six divisions? Why?
2. Since 1980 Borden has acquired forty new companies. How could this impact on the organizational structure?
3. As it acquires new companies, should Borden centralize production? Why?

# Case 7-2
## *The Reorganization of AT&T*

Since AT&T (American Telephone & Telegraph) and the Bell telephone systems were divided up in 1984 as a result of an antitrust suit, the restructured company has found it difficult to earn a profit. Before the breakup, the company was one of the most profitable and best-managed corporations in the United States. After the breakup, although management tried to cut costs, expenses remained too high. AT&T's computer business was losing nearly $1 billion a year, and hundreds of employees had to be laid off. To add insult to injury, an FCC ruling limited profits from AT&T's long-distance phone service, the company's biggest profit maker. The company needed a drastic overhaul if it was to regain the profitability and status it had enjoyed before the breakup.

In 1986, AT&T's management began implementing a broad, long-range reorganization plan. The plan was designed to protect and improve the company's long-distance service and phone equipment business, make its computer business profitable, and increase the percentage of revenues obtained from operations. In addition, the plan required AT&T managers to decide how costs should be cut, what businesses the firm should focus on, and whether to continue to design all new products. The company wanted to change from being a cost-driven utility to being an efficient, profit-driven corporation.

The reorganization plan called for top executives in major lines to come up with plans for improving operations. Cost reductions were the first priority. The company thinned its ranks by eliminating twenty-seven thousand jobs, many from the ranks of management. In addition, the executives closed half of AT&T's retail phone stores. The company reduced its expenses for research and development and shifted research and development efforts away from signal transmission methods such as coaxial cable and satellite to newer transmission methods.

By 1987, AT&T had cut losses by 70 percent in its computer division. New products were introduced on tighter schedules than in the past, and the division stopped trying to develop all its own components. In addition, AT&T improved its computer ordering and distribution networks, improving relations with retailers by avoiding lengthy delays.

AT&T also thoroughly revised its accounting and financial systems. Before, different AT&T businesses had used different accounting techniques, inventory management, and billing systems. Under the reorganization plan, AT&T implemented uniform systems that it hopes will allow it to manage more efficiently. These changes fit into the company's overall plans to make AT&T a slim and responsive organization. The company also believed that cultural differences within the organization would disappear once all its units were using the same accounting and data-processing systems.

The price of AT&T's reorganization has been enormous. Approximately $9 billion had been spent by 1988. The company planned to spend about $15 billion more to improve its phone networks by 1995. Management hopes that by making most of its networks digital, it will enjoy an advantage over its current competitors.

Despite the large costs involved in the reorganization, AT&T has reaped some benefits as a result of restructuring. Net income in 1987 was 50 percent higher than in 1986, well above the forecasted amount. Overall, company costs have been cut by $1 billion a year. In addition, AT&T's stock was one of the most resilient of the blue-chip stocks when the stock market crashed in October 1987. AT&T's stock lost only about 14 percent of its value; other blue-chip stocks lost as much as 24 percent of their value. Moreover, even after the market crash, the company's stock traded higher than it had in the first part of 1987.

Despite all the progress it has made, AT&T is still not the organization that it hopes to be. It has yet to make its computer business profitable. In addition, it has not reached its goal of breaking into foreign phone-equipment markets. Since 1986, however, the company has come a long way. Its long-distance business is stronger than ever, and profits from the company's $10 billion consumer products division are up. It finally appears that AT&T is on the comeback trail and once again will be one of the country's most prosperous and profitable businesses.

---

These facts are from John J. Keller, with Geoff Lewis, Todd Mason, Russell Mitchell, and Thane Peterson, "AT&T: The Making of a Comeback," *Business Week,* January 18, 1988, pp. 56–62; Janet Guyon, "AT&T Sees Glimmerings of Turnaround," *The Wall Street Journal,* November 12, 1987, pp. 2, 18; and Gretchen Morgenson and Michael Sivy, "Telephone Reaches Out," *Money* 15 (January 1986): 13.

### Questions

1. What organizational problems developed in 1984 when AT&T reorganized?
2. AT&T eliminated 27,000 jobs, many from the ranks of management. What impact did this have on decision making?
3. How did the reorganization create new opportunities for AT&T?

# Answers to Checking Your Understanding

1. formal organization
2. span
3. responsibility
4. territorial
5. delegation of authority
6. centralization
7. informal organization
8. matrix
9. grapevine
10. accountability
11. product
12. structure

## Outline

# Chapter 8

# Human Relations

## Objectives

After reading this chapter, you will be able to:

▶ Understand human relations and why the study of human relations is important.

▶ Understand Maslow's hierarchy of needs and why managers should attempt to satisfy the personal needs of their employees.

▶ Explain several theories that have been applied to human relations.

▶ Describe some of the strategies that managers use to motivate employees.

# Business Experience

When Jack Stack took over the nearly bankrupt Springfield Remanufacturing Center Corporation (SRC) in 1979, his introduction to his new employees was not encouraging. He met a room full of blank faces—people who seemed not to care whether the company survived or not. SRC was losing $2 million dollars a year and was plagued with high rates of absenteeism, employee turnover, and accidents. Stack had six months to determine whether the company's owner, International Harvester (now known as Navistar), should scrap SRC. He realized that the only way to save the company was to stimulate the employees' interest in its survival.

SRC employees pressed for unionization because they thought a union would be able to get them the tools and parts that SRC always seemed to lack. Stack and the other managers got down on their knees on the plant floor and begged the employees to give them a chance. Seeing that SRC finally had management that seemed to care, the employees gave them a chance and dropped the idea of union involvement.

Jack Stack then created what he refers to as the "Game," which he designed to get the employees interested in the plant and to raise productivity. He set simple goals for product quality, safety, cleanliness of work spaces, and production. When the employees achieved 100,000 hours with no recordable accidents, Stack closed the plant for a day, and everyone celebrated with a beer bash. By setting measurable performance goals and offering rewards when the goals were reached, Stack found a way to get the employees to care about the fate of the company. When Stack had departments compete with each other for a trophy, production increased dramatically. After only four months, International Harvester decided not to abandon the company; after only nine months, SRC recorded a profit.

Stack improved the Game by offering all employees a full range of business courses—accounting, plant audit, purchasing, and so on—which helped them understand SRC's production reports and financial statements. Stack's goal was to get the employees to understand the huge amount of data required to monitor an organization's performance. He wanted his employees to be able to gauge the effects of their own activities on the plant and set their own performance standards to improve the company.

In 1983, because of hard economic times, International Harvester reduced its capital commitment to SRC, so Stack and twelve other employees bought SRC and ran it themselves. At that point, it became even more important for the employees to understand what the company was doing. Stack continued the training and business courses to get the employees involved in the company. They were given constant reminders of how they were doing. An electronic message board that runs continuous production reports was installed in the cafeteria. Employees who exceeded their production quotas were given bonuses under a plan known as "Stop the Praise—Give Us a Raise." Employees also received bonuses for ideas that improved the company's operations. The employees were motivated to make SRC succeed because they understood not only the physical aspects of their own jobs but also how the company was doing and what needed to be done for success. When the company did well, so did they. Stack's Game, his good relations with his employees, and their involvement in the organization made SRC a very competitive small company with a bright future.

---

These facts are from Lucien Rhodes with Patricia Amend, "The Turnaround," *INC.*, 8 (August 1986): 42–48.

# Introduction

Because employees have the ability to influence the achievement of organizational objectives, most chief executive officers agree that employees are the organization's most valuable resource. In order for organizational objectives to be achieved, employees must perform their jobs efficiently and effectively. Consequently, managers are interested in how to motivate their workers to be more productive.

This chapter examines employees' needs and motivation, management's views of workers, and several strategies for motivating employees. Managers who understand the needs of their employees are able to help them reach high levels of productivity and thus contribute to the achievement of organizational goals.

## ▶ Nature of Human Relations

*to make the firm more profitable*

**Human relations**

The study of the behavior of individuals and groups in organizational settings

**Motivation**

An inner state that directs behavior toward goals

**Goal**

The satisfaction of some need

**Need**

The difference between a desired state and an actual state

**Human relations** is the study of the behavior of individuals and groups in organizational settings; it is concerned with what motivates employees to perform on the job. **Motivation** is an inner state that directs behavior toward goals. A **goal** is the satisfaction of some need, and a **need** is the difference between a desired state and an actual state.

Motivation explains why people behave as they do. An individual who recognizes or feels a need is motivated to take action to satisfy the need and achieve a goal. This motivation model is depicted in Figure 8-1. Consider a person who is cold. Because of the difference between the actual temperature and the desired temperature, the person feels a need. To satisfy the need and achieve the goal of being warm, the person may adjust the thermostat, put on a sweater, reach for a blanket, start a fire, or hug a friend. Human relations is concerned with the needs of employees, their goals and how they try to achieve them, and the impact of these needs and goals on job performance.

One aspect of human relations is morale—an employee's attitude toward his or her job, employer, and colleagues. Low morale may be the cause of high rates of absenteeism and turnover. Conversely, good morale leads to high levels of productivity and employee loyalty. Respect, involvement, appreciation, adequate compensation, promotion, and a pleasant work environment are all morale boosters.

## ▶ Early Studies of Employee Motivation

During the twentieth century, there have been a number of studies to find ways to motivate workers to increase productivity. From these studies have

**Figure 8-1**

The Motivation Process

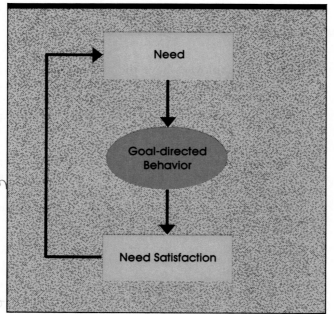

come theories that have been applied to workers with varying degrees of success. A discussion of scientific management and the Hawthorne studies provides a background for understanding the present state of human relations.

## Scientific Management

The birth of the study of human relations can be traced to time and motion studies conducted by Frederick W. Taylor and Frank and Lillian Gilbreth at the turn of this century. In these studies, they analyzed how employees perform specific work tasks in an effort to improve the employee's efficiency. Their efforts to improve the efficiency of employees led to the application of scientific principles to management.

Taylor thought that managers should break down each job into its component tasks, determine the best way to perform each task, and specify the output to be achieved by a worker performing the task. Taylor also suggested that managers link a worker's pay directly to his or her output. He developed the piece-rate system: Employees were paid a certain amount for each unit they produced; those who exceeded their quota were paid a higher rate per unit for all the units they produced.

Taylor and most early twentieth-century managers generally felt that money and job security were the primary motivators of employees. They assumed that satisfactory pay and job security would motivate employees to work hard. Later studies showed that other factors are also important in motivating workers.

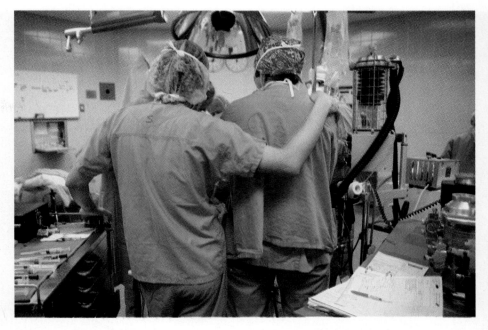

**Critical environment.** It is necessary for this operating room staff to interact efficiently so they can perform the difficult procedures required of them.

## Hawthorne Studies

Taylor's work was continued in a series of studies conducted from 1924 to 1932 by Elton Mayo and a team of researchers from Harvard University. The studies, held at the Hawthorne Works Plant of the Western Electric Company, are known as the Hawthorne studies. Mayo's goal was to determine what physical conditions in the work place, such as light and noise levels would stimulate employees to be most productive. The researchers asked a group of workers to participate in the study and measured their productivity under various physical conditions.

What the researchers discovered was quite unexpected and very puzzling: Productivity increased regardless of the physical conditions. This phenomenon has been labeled the Hawthorne effect. When questioned about their behavior, the employees expressed satisfaction because their coworkers in the experiments were friendly and, more importantly, because their supervisors had asked for their help and cooperation instead of trying to motivate them out of fear. The researchers concluded that social and psychological factors could significantly affect productivity and morale.

The Hawthorne experiments and the results obtained from them marked the beginning of a concern for human relations in the work place. The Hawthorne studies revealed that human factors do influence workers' behavior, and that managers who understand the needs, beliefs, and expectations of people have the greatest success in motivating their workers.

**Attention to detail has excellent results.** These Steinway craftsmen work in small, skilled groups to do the hand-crafting necessary to bend the rim around this Steinway grand piano.

# ▶ Maslow's Hierarchy of Needs

**Maslow's Hierarchy**

The order in which people strive to satisfy their needs

**Physiological needs**

The essentials for living—water, food, shelter, and clothing

Psychologist Abraham Maslow theorized in *Motivation and Personality* that human beings have five basic needs: physiological, security, social, esteem, and self-actualization. He arranged these needs in a hierarchy of importance[1] (Figure 8-2). **Maslow's hierarchy** shows the order in which people strive to satisfy their needs.

**Physiological needs,** the first needs to be satisfied, are the essentials for living—water, food, shelter, and clothing. Here is a basic example of the strength of physiological needs. When a baby is hungry, it cries and cries until it is given food. A hungry baby cannot be distracted by a toy because

**Figure 8-2**

Maslow's Hierarchy of Needs
Source: Adapted from Abraham H. Maslow, "A Theory of Human Motivation," *Psychological Review* 50 (1943): 370–96.

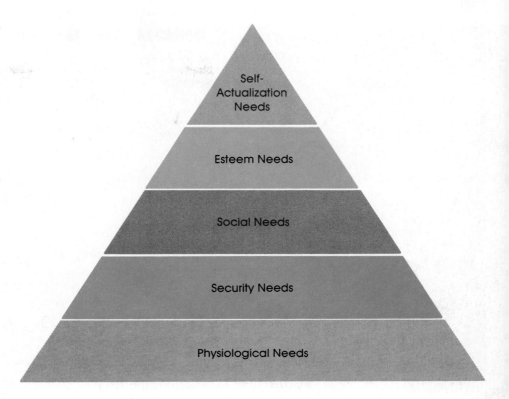

its only concern is satisfying its hunger. According to Maslow, human beings devote all their efforts to satisfying physiological needs until they are met. Only when these needs are met can people focus their attention on satisfying the next level of needs—security.

**Security needs** relate to protecting oneself from physical and economic harm. Actions that may be taken to achieve security include the installation of dead-bolt locks and smoke alarms in the home and the purchase of insurance with income protection in case a person becomes unable to work. A person might also invest money in real estate or gold to stockpile funds against the possibility of economic hardship. Once security needs have been satisfied, people may strive for social goals.

**Social needs** are the need for love, companionship, and friendship—the desire for acceptance by others. To fulfill social needs, a person may try many things: making friends with a neighbor, joining a church group, volunteering at a hospital, throwing a party. Once their social needs have been satisfied, people attempt to satisfy their need for esteem.

**Esteem needs** relate to respect—both self-respect and respect from others. One aspect of esteem needs is competition—the need to feel that one can do something better than anyone else. Competition often motivates people to increase their productivity. A department store contest that promises that anyone in the department with the highest sales will be treated to dinner

**Security needs**

The need to protect oneself from physical and economic harm

**Social needs**

The need for love, companionship, and friendship; the desire for acceptance by others

**Esteem needs**

The need for self-respect and respect from others

**Marriott catering.** Catering for an airline is a continous process that requires food preparation, quality improvement, and product evaluation.

by the store manager may inspire all the sales people. Esteem needs are not as easily satisfied as the needs at lower levels in Maslow's hierarchy, because they do not always provide tangible evidence of success. However, these needs can be realized through rewards and increased involvement in organizational activities. Until esteem needs are met, people focus their attention on achieving respect. When they feel they have achieved some measure of respect, self-actualization becomes the major goal of life.

**Self-actualization needs,** at the top of Maslow's hierarchy, is being the best one can be. Self-actualization involves maximizing one's potential. A self-actualized person feels that she or he is living life to its fullest in every way. For Stephen King, self-actualization might mean being called the best writer in the world; for Bette Midler, it might mean winning an Oscar.

In summary, Maslow's theory groups all human needs into five general categories that are arranged in hierarchical form. Needs at the bottom of the hierarchy must be satisfied before higher-level needs may be met. Thus, people who are hungry and have no home are not concerned with obtaining respect from their colleagues. Only when physiological, security, and social needs have been more or less satisfied do people seek esteem. Maslow's theory suggests that if a low-level need such as security is suddenly reactivated, the individual will try to satisfy that need rather than higher-level needs. For

**Self-actualization needs**

Maximizing one's potential

**Competition can be a motivator.** Recognition in the form of an Oscar satisfies the need for esteem and self-actualization.

example, many automobile workers laid off by General Motors in the 1980s probably shifted their focus from high-level esteem needs to the need for security. Managers should learn from Maslow's hierarchy that employees will be motivated to contribute to organizational goals only if they are able first to satisfy their physiological, security, and social needs through their work.

# ▶ Theories That Explain Employees' Motivation

## Herzberg's Motivational and Maintenance Factors

In the 1950s psychologist Frederick Herzberg proposed a theory of motivation that focuses on the job and on the environment where work is done. Herzberg studied various job factors and their relation to employee motivation and concluded that job factors can be categorized as maintenance

| Table 8.1 Herzberg's Maintenance and Motivational Factors | Maintenance Factors | Motivational Factors |
|---|---|---|
| | Company policy | Achievement |
| | Supervision | Recognition |
| | Working conditions | Work itself |
| | Relationships with peers, supervisors, and subordinates | Responsibility |
| | Salary | Advancement |
| | Security | Personal Growth |

**Maintenance factors**

Relate to the work setting, not to the content of the work

don't care ☹
or
dissatisfy ☹

**Motivational factors**

Relate to the content of the work

don't care ☹
or
positive ☺

factors and motivational factors (Table 8-1). **Maintenance factors** relate to the work setting, not to the content of the work. Maintenance factors include adequate wages, comfortable working conditions, fair company policies, and job security. These factors do not necessarily motivate employees to excel, but the absence of these factors may be a potential source of dissatisfaction. Without such factors, employees may become dissatisfied and leave the organization.

In a 1985 Harris poll, 63 percent of the respondents felt that a good salary is one of the most important job factors, even more important than job security and the chance to use one's mind and abilities.[2] Salary and security, two of the maintenance factors identified by Herzberg, make it possible for employees to satisfy the physiological and security needs identified by Maslow. However, the presence of maintenance factors is unlikely to motivate employees to work harder.

**Motivational factors** relate to the content of the work. Motivational factors include achievement, recognition, the work itself, involvement, responsibility, and advancement. They promote higher levels of performance.

Herzberg's motivational factors and Maslow's esteem and self-actualization needs are similar. Workers' low-level needs (physiological and security) have already been satisfied by minimum-wage laws and occupational-safety standards set by various government agencies and are therefore not motivators. Consequently, in order to improve productivity, management should focus on satisfying workers' higher-level needs (motivational factors). That is what Jack Stack did at Springfield Remanufacturing Center (see the Business Experience at the beginning of this chapter). Stack encouraged his employees to become involved in the company and rewarded them for increased productivity.

Danbury Plumbing Supply in Danbury, Connecticut, has learned to use motivational factors to encourage employees to reduce costs. Management posts a chart showing the company's sales and expenses every month and puts 15 percent of its profits into a bonus pool. Bonuses are distributed to the employees on the basis of their seniority and salary level. The bonuses and the increased involvement in company activities motivates employees to close doors and turn out lights (reducing expenses) and to increase sales (increasing profits). This involvement ultimately fattens the bonuses.[3] Thus, the higher-level goals in Maslow's hierarchy and the motivational factors

**Double reward.** The bonus awarded for his money saving suggestion is evidence of the company's appreciation of this employee's contribution. The company will benefit by saving money in the future, and the employee's need for recognition is satisfied.

identified by Herzberg are important factors in motivating employees to work harder. Management Encounter 8-1 profiles two pioneers of human relations who understood the importance of motivational factors.

## McGregor's Theory X and Theory Y

In *The Human Side of Enterprise,* Douglas McGregor related Maslow's ideas about personal needs to management. McGregor contrasted two views of management—the traditional view, which he named **Theory X,** and a humanistic view, which he named **Theory Y.**

Theory X managers assume that workers generally dislike work and must be forced to do their jobs. They believe that the following statements are true of workers:

1. The average human being naturally dislikes work and will avoid it when possible.
2. Most workers must be coerced, controlled, directed, or threatened with punishment to get them to work toward the achievement of organizational objectives.
3. The average worker prefers to be directed and to avoid responsibility, has relatively little ambition, and wants security.[4]

Managers who subscribe to the Theory X view maintain tight control over workers, provide almost constant supervision, try to motivate through fear, and make decisions in an autocratic fashion, eliciting little or no input from

**Theory X**

A theory that assumes that workers generally dislike work and must be forced to do their jobs

**Theory Y**

A theory that assumes that workers like to work and that under proper conditions employees will seek out responsibility

## Management Encounter 8-1

### *Pioneers in Human Relations: Schwab and Rockefeller*

At the turn of the century, few managers were concerned about their employees' needs or morale. Most cared only that employees produced. Two managers who did attribute their success to highly motivated employees were viewed as "captains of industry": John D. Rockefeller, who built Standard Oil, and Charles Schwab, who ran Bethlehem Steel in the early 1900s.

Charles Schwab, who took the helm of Bethlehem Steel in 1904, realized that he could not buy imagination, loyalty, and productivity from his employees. He set up a system of incentives to motivate his men. He told them, "Do so much and you get so much; do more and you get more—that is the essence of the system." Schwab paid the highest salaries in the steel industry to obtain creativity and loyalty from his employees. He astounded the steel industry by taking fifteen men out of the steel mill and making them partners in the business. Many managers were critical of Schwab's policies, but his ideas worked. Bethlehem Steel's sales increased from $10 million when Schwab assumed control to $230 million in 1916. During the same period, the value of the company's stock increased from $20 to $600 per share.

John D. Rockefeller also motivated his employees to work harder, primarily through example. Rockefeller frequently joined his men at work, even loading wagons in the oil fields. He won the respect of his workers because they knew he understood the oil business from the bottom up. Rockefeller also offered high salaries, generous bonuses, and praise for a job well done. He tried not to chastise workers; but when criticism was needed, he tempered it with praise for what had been done right. Rockefeller recognized and encouraged ideas from his subordinates. He even permitted managers to take time off with pay, but few ever stayed off the job long. Standard Oil's workers were loyal, and the company was rarely plagued by the labor unrest that characterized many other companies of the era. Rockefeller's ideas, though radical for his time, allowed him to recruit and keep the best minds in the oil business. His emphasis on good relations with his employees and his respect for them built Standard Oil into one of the biggest companies in the early twentieth century.

Charles Schwab and John D. Rockefeller managed their employees with common sense. Both men recognized that employees who can fulfill their needs are most likely to be happy and productive in the long run. Both understood that motivating workers requires respect for and faith in the employees and rewards, whether financial or verbal. Schwab and Rockefeller were well rewarded for their understanding and caring with extremely profitable companies.

These facts are from Burt Folsom, *Administrative Radiology* 6 (November 1987): 80–82.

---

their subordinates. The Theory X style of management focuses on physiological and security needs and virtually ignores the higher needs discussed by Maslow.

Upton Sinclair presented a grim illustration of the Theory X style of management in *The Jungle,* his novel about factory life in Chicago early in the twentieth century. The main characters are immigrants who work in slaughter houses. The bosses' only interest is achieving productivity goals while holding costs down. To increase productivity, the factory managers intimidate and bully and threaten the workers with dismissal. The jobs barely fulfill physiological and security needs, and the managers' assumption that the workers dislike the work is correct.

The Theory X view of management does not take into account people's needs for companionship, esteem, and personal growth. Theory Y, the contrasting view of management, does. Theory Y managers assume that workers like to work and that under proper conditions employees will seek out responsibility in an attempt to satisfy their social, esteem, and self-actualization needs. McGregor describes the assumptions behind Theory Y in the following way:

1. The expenditure of physical and mental effort in work is as natural as play or rest.
2. People will exercise self-direction and self-control to achieve objectives to which they are committed.
3. People will commit to objectives when they realize that the achievement of those goals will bring them personal reward.
4. The average person will accept and seek responsibility.
5. Imagination, ingenuity, and creativity can help solve organization problems but most organizations do not make adequate use of these characteristics in their employees.
6. Organizations today do not make full use of workers' intellectual potential.[5]

Obviously, managers subscribing to the Theory Y philosophy have a management style very different from managers subscribing to the Theory X philosophy (the major assumptions of Theory X and Theory Y are listed in Table 8-2). Theory Y managers maintain less control and supervision, do not use fear as the primary motivator, and are more democratic in decision making, allowing subordinates to help make decisions. Theory Y managers address the high-level needs in Maslow's hierarchy as well as physiological and security needs. Management Encounter 8-2 suggests methods for dealing with different types of managers.

Today, Theory Y enjoys widespread support and may have displaced Theory X. Since the 1970s, another management philosophy has been gaining recognition, and many companies have adopted it—Theory Z.

# Theory Z

**Theory Z**

A management philosophy that stresses employee participation in all aspects of company decision making

**Theory Z** is a management philosophy expounded in William Ouchi's book *Theory Z—How American Business Can Meet the Japanese Challenge.* Theory Z stresses employee participation in all aspects of company decision making. Theory Z includes many elements associated with the Japanese approach to management, such as trust and intimacy, but Japanese ideas have been adapted for use in the United States. Table 8-3 is a comparison of the typical American management style, the Japanese management style, and Theory Z (the modified Japanese management style).

The traditional American management style is formal and impersonal: Work relationships are relatively brief; specialization is common; decision making is done by individuals; responsibility is placed on individuals; control is explicit; and managers focus on work-related aspects of their employees' lives. In contrast, Theory Z is less formal and more personal: Work relationships are long term; there is less specialization; there is more group decision making; control is more informal; and managers focus on the worker's whole life. In short, in a Theory Z organization, managers and workers share

**Table 8.2  Assumptions of Theory X and Theory Y**

Source: Douglas McGregor, *The Human Side of Enterprise* (New York: McGraw-Hill, Inc. 1960): 33-4, 47-8.

### Theory X

▶ The average human being has an inherent dislike of work and will avoid it if he or she can.

▶ Because of this human characteristic of dislike of work, most people must be coerced, controlled, directed, or threatened with punishment to get them to put forth adequate effort toward the achievement of organizational objectives.

▶ The average human being prefers to be directed, wishes to avoid responsibility, has little ambition, wants security above all.

### Theory Y

▶ The expenditure of physical and mental effort in work is as natural as play or rest.

▶ External control and the threat of punishment are not the only means for bringing about effort toward organizational objectives. People will exercise self-direction and self-control in the service of objectives to which they are committed.

▶ Commitment to objectives is a function of the rewards associated with their achievement.

▶ The average human being learns, under proper conditions, not only to accept but to seek responsibility.

▶ The capacity to exercise a relatively high degree of imagination, ingenuity, and creativity in the solution of organizational problems is widely, not narrowly, distributed in the population.

▶ Under the conditions of modern industrial life, the intellectual potential of the average human being are only partially utilized.

responsibilities; the management style is participative; and employment is long term and often lifelong. In a Theory Y organization, managers focus on assumptions about the nature of the worker. The two theories can be seen as complementary.

## Variations on Theory Z

General Motors is making serious efforts to improve the quality of its products through the use of modified participative management. When General Motors joined with Toyota to build the new Chevrolet Nova in Fremont, California, the NUMMI (New United Motor Mfg. Inc.) plant became an experiment in participative management for the automobile industry. The plant was less automated than many of GM's other domestic plants. In accordance with Japanese practices, workers were organized into teams. Team members defined their own jobs. They were given control over and responsibility for the quality of their work. They were also given the power to stop the assembly line to handle problems. The results of their participation were impressive: Production costs for the Nova decreased by 21 percent, and the quality of the cars was better than the quality of vehicles produced in GM's highly automated plants.[6] Other companies that have utilized the team concept are Westinghouse, IBM, and Procter & Gamble.

Another way in which the Japanese managers involve workers in decision making is through quality circles, which are groups of workers who meet regularly to discuss ways to improve their work. Quality circles are small,

|  | American | Japanese | Theory Z |
|---|---|---|---|
| Duration of employment | Relatively short term; workers subject to layoffs when business slows | Lifelong; no layoffs. | Long term; layoffs rare. |
| Rate of promotion | Rapid | Slow | Slow |
| Amount of specialization | Considerable; worker develops expertise in one area only | Minimal; worker develops expertise in the whole organization | Moderate; workers learn all aspects of the organization |
| Decision making | Individual | Input from all concerned parties is considered | By consensus; emphasis on quality |
| Responsibility | Assigned to the individual | Shared by the group | Assigned to the individual |
| Control | Explicit and formal | Less explicit and less formal | Informal but with explicit performance measures |
| Concern for workers | Focus is on work only | Focus extends to worker's whole life | Concerned with worker's life and family |

usually having five to eight members who discuss ways to reduce waste, eliminate problems, and improve quality, communication, and work satisfaction. Companies that have begun to use quality circles to increase efficiency and productivity include Texas Instruments in Japan and Campbell's Soup Company in the United States.

The Koreans have also made use of the Japanese style of management and have modified it for use in their American plants. They minimize distinctions between management and workers and emphasize egalitarianism. The president of Samsung International wears a company uniform and eats in the employees' cafeteria. The Koreans also stress teamwork and the idea of the corporation as a pseudo-family. They involve workers in decision making because they believe that the people who know the plant best should take part in the decision-making process.[7]

# Equity Theory

**Equity theory**

How much people are willing to contribute to an organization depends on their assessment of the fairness, or equity of the rewards they will receive in exchange

According to **equity theory,** how much people are willing to contribute to an organization depends on their assessment of the fairness, or equity, of the rewards they will receive in exchange. In an equitable situation, the rewards an individual receives are proportional to the contribution that person makes to the organization. In practice, equity is a subjective notion. Each worker regularly develops a personal input-output ratio and takes stock of his or her contribution (inputs) to the organization in time, effort, skills, and experience

## Management Encounter 8-2
### How to Manage Your Boss

Most people believe that managing is a top-to-bottom process—that management flows downward from the boss to the worker. Management, however, can be a two-way street. Managing your boss is as important as your boss' management of you. Skillfully managing your boss will help you establish a positive working relationship. If you don't manage your boss effectively, you may not be sufficiently productive on the job, and you may lose your job.

Gather information about your boss' leadership style, priorities and goals, and evaluation criteria. This information will help you meet your boss' needs quickly. Coworkers are usually the best source of this information. They can also tell you what attitude the boss expects you to have and what she or he requires of you. You can often determine your boss' style and priorities by observing her or his behavior. Of course, the best way to find out what your boss' priorities are is to ask.

Effective communication will help you manage your boss by strengthening your relationship and eliminating potential conflicts. Be a team player. Avoid public criticism of your boss and of decisions she or he has made. Never try to upstage your boss, even if you believe she or he is less competent than you.

Bosses can be classified into one of four types according to managerial style: (1) the Type A boss, who is impatient and a workaholic boss; (2) the "country-club" boss, who wants everyone to be happy but often procrastinates; (3) the laissez-faire or non-interfering boss, who assumes that the corporate structure will ensure that things get done; and (4) the rarely found ideal boss, who combines the best traits of the first three types. The approach that you take toward managing your boss depends on the classification that fits your boss. If she or he is a Type A, you should negotiate priorities and focus on quality. Country-club bosses need to be nudged into providing feedback, but they offer opportunity for self-starters. With a laissez-faire boss, you can run things the way you think best, but you should try to learn from your mistakes. If you have the ideal boss, count your blessings and learn as much as you can from her or him.

No matter what type of boss you have, build your relationship slowly to get comfortable working with her or him. Take the time to determine the best way to deal with your boss. Keep in mind that managing does not mean being an apple polisher; it means working with your boss to obtain the best results for you, your boss, and the company. Be aware that everything you learn about managing the relationship between you and your boss will help you manage relationships with your peers and subordinates.

These facts are from Marilyn Moats Kennedy, "How to Manage Your New Boss," *Business Week Careers* 5 (March–April 1987): 93–95; Kevin Money, "4 Ways to Work Better with a Boss," *USA Today*, June 22, 1987, p. 58; and "What Type Is Your Boss? Look at Traits," *USA Today*, June 22, 1987, p. 58.

and assesses the rewards (outputs) offered by the organization in pay, benefits, recognition, and promotions. The worker compares his or her ratio to the input-output ratio of some other person—a "comparison other," who may be a coworker, a friend working in another organization, or an "average" of several people working in the organization. If the two ratios are close, the individual will feel that he or she is being treated equitably.

Consider a woman who has a high school education and is earning $13,000 a year. When she compares her input-output ratio to that of a coworker who has a college degree and makes $19,000, she will probably feel that she is being paid fairly. However, if she perceives that her personal input-output ratio is lower, she will probably feel that she is being treated unfairly and will be motivated to seek change. If she learns that a coworker who earns

**Happy children, satisfied parents.** Many companies have realized the importance of offering quality daycare to their employees. It is a benefit that increases morale and employee contribution to the company.

$19,000 has only a high school diploma, she may believe she is being cheated by the organization. To achieve equity, the woman could try to increase her outputs by asking for a raise or promotion. She could also try to have the inputs of the "comparison other" increased or the outputs of the "comparison other" decreased. Failing to achieve equity, the woman may decide to leave the organization.

Because almost all the issues involved in equity theory are subjective, they can cause problems for managers. Managers should try to avoid equity problems by ensuring that rewards are distributed on the basis of performance and that all employees clearly understand the basis for their pay and benefits. Inequity may be one source of stress in the workplace. Management Encounter 8-3 offers some suggestions for dealing with work-related stress.

## Expectancy Theory

**Expectancy theory**

A theory that proposed that motivation depends not only on how much a person wants something but on the person's perception of how likely he or she is to get it

Psychologist Victor Vroom described **expectancy theory** which states that motivation depends not only on how much a person wants something but on

## Management Encounter 8-3

*Identifying and Dealing with Job Stress*

Job-related stress is a problem for individual workers and for the organization as a whole. Experts can pinpoint some of the causes of job-related stress, but they do not agree about what stress is or about what can be done about it.

According to one definition, stress is a physical or emotional demand that temporarily causes a person to be in a state of disequilibrium or distress. The severity of this distress can range from feelings of fear, anger, and frustration to full-blown job burnout. Common physical manifestations of stress include headaches, nausea, and insomnia; prolonged stress may lead to chronic illness, heart disease, and drug or alcohol abuse. Job-related effects of stress are declines in productivity and increases in absenteeism, medical expenses, worker's compensation claims.

Although job stress is unavoidable, workers need to realize that it can be controlled. There are many popular methods for managing or eliminating stress, but the main goal of all them is to relieve excessive responses to stressful situations. It is also important for individuals to learn to minimize stress and to manage the stress that they cannot eliminate or minimize.

The first step in dealing with stress is to identify what is causing it—trying to do too much alone, a negative environment, disorganization, some other factor. The second step is to try to eliminate stress by understanding the factors that intensify it. If it is not possible to eliminate the causes of stress, the next step is to lessen the severity of stressful events by mentally preparing for them. The final step is to try to minimize the amount of stress that is self-generated: Scaring oneself about an impending event only increases the stress surrounding the event.

Common approaches to stress management include exercise, instruction in meditation or muscle-relaxation techniques, behavior modification, and time management. Some businesses are hiring stress-management consultants to help employees handle stress. It is also important to realize that not all stress is negative. The right type and quantity of stress may be helpful. This so-called positive stress can motivate people to make that extra effort necessary to get a job done. Positive stress can challenge people and induce them to make good use of their skills.

Reducing job-related stress often requires a basic shift in management technique and life style. Nevertheless, identifying, defining, and accepting stressful factors can help an individual deal with stress and become more productive and satisfied.

These facts are from Bob Curran, "It's a Matter of Stress," *Supervision* (October 1986): 13; Leonard Kramish, "Stress Management for Managers," *Infosystems* (August 1986): 50, 53; "Coping with Stress at Work," *The New York Times*, May 26, 1987, p. D2; and Joshua Hyatt, "All Stressed-Up and Nowhere to Go," *Inc.* 9 (January 1987): 74–79.

the person's perception of how likely he or she is to get it. A person who wants something and has reason to think he or she will actually get it will be strongly motivated. For example, you really want a car. You have just received a large raise, and you are motivated to purchase a car. However, if you do not believe you can get what you want, you may not be motivated to get it, even though you really want it.

Expectancy theory is complex because it suggests that every action a person takes leads to a number of different outcomes, some that are desirable and some that are not desirable. The entire set of outcomes of any given act and the person's subjective evaluation of each outcome determine motivation. Expectancy theory suggests that managers should show employees that they can achieve the outcomes they desire.

# ▶ Behavior Modification

**Behavior modification**

Involves changing behavior and encouraging appropriate actions by relating the consequences of behavior to the behavior itself

**Behavior modification** involves changing behavior and encouraging appropriate actions by relating the consequences of behavior to the behavior itself. The concept of behavior modification was developed by psychologist B. F. Skinner, who showed that there are two types of consequences that can modify behavior—reward and punishment. Skinner found that behavior that is positively reinforced, or rewarded, will tend to be repeated, while behavior that is punished will tend to be eliminated. In the long run, however, the two strategies may not be equally effective. Punishing unacceptable behavior may provide quick results but may lead to undesirable long-term side effects. In the long run, rewarding appropriate behavior will generally be a more effective way to modify behavior. The manager at Springfield Remanufacturing Center praised employees and awarded trophies to departments that exceeded their production goals. Avon sales representatives who exceed their sales goals receive praise from their supervisors and become eligible for cruises and gifts.

Managers who wish to motivate employees to behave appropriately should carefully consider the long-term effects of punishment and reward before selecting a policy. In a firm having problems with employees' taking long lunches, managers could reward employees when they follow the rules or punish employees who take long lunches. Although the punishment system may yield quick results, it could produce unwanted, long-term side effects such as employee dissatisfaction and increased turnover. Rewarding appropriate behavior may not yield results quickly, but it is not likely to lead to negative side effects.

One company manager has found an alternative to punishment that motivates employees to admit to their mistakes and provides a lesson to the rest of the employees. Steve Ettridge, chief executive officer, at Temps & Co. in Washington, D.C., offers $250 to any employee who admits to a mistake. Ettridge figures that if an employee confesses to a two-thousand-dollar error in judgment in front of twenty other employees, the error becomes a hundred-dollar tuition payment for those twenty people. Ettridge himself won the $250 when he ran out of gas driving an important prospect to the airport.[8] This motivational technique can increase productivity because the employees know that most of their mistakes will be used as a learning experience and not as grounds for dismissal.

# ▶ Job Design

Herzberg identified the job itself as a motivational factor. Managers have several strategies that they can use to structure jobs and thereby promote employee motivation. The strategies are job rotation, job enlargement, job enrichment, flextime, and management by objectives (Table 8-4).

**Table 8.4  Job Design Strategies**

| | |
|---|---|
| Job Rotation | Employees are exposed to a variety of tasks as they move from one job to another. |
| Job Enlargement | Employees learn new tasks in their present job. |
| Job Enrichment | Employees are given more control and authority in their present job along with additional tasks. |
| Flextime | Employees work a standard number of hours per week, but are permitted to set their own start and finish times as long as they are at their position during a specified core period. |
| Management by Objectives | Employees are involved in their own goal-setting process; they set their own objectives, are evaluated, and are given rewards based on their achievement of their objectives. |

# Job Rotation

**Job rotation** is a process that allows employees to move from one job to another in an effort to relieve the boredom that is often associated with job specialization, which breaks work down into small, discrete tasks. Management turned to specialization in hopes of increasing productivity, but there is a negative side effect to this type of job design: Employees become bored and dissatisfied with their jobs, and productivity declines. Job rotation cuts down on the boredom because it enables workers to undertake a variety of tasks and gives them the opportunity to learn new skills.[9] An employee spends a specified amount of time performing one job and then moves on to other, different jobs. The worker eventually returns to the initial job and begins the cycle again. Companies that have experimented with job rotation include Bethlehem Steel and Ford Motor Company.

Job rotation is a good idea, but it has one major shortcoming. Because employees may eventually become bored with all the jobs in the cycle, job rotation does not totally eliminate the problem of boredom. Job rotation is extremely useful, however, in situations where an individual is being trained for a position that requires an understanding of various units in an organization. Many executive training programs require trainees to spend time learning a variety of specialized jobs. Most grocery store managers are required to spend a specified amount of time working in each department of the store before they actually assume a management position.

# Job Enlargement

**Job enlargement** involves adding tasks to a job instead of treating each task as a separate job. Like job rotation, job enlargement was developed to overcome the boredom associated with specialization. The rationale behind this strategy is that jobs are more satisfying as the number of tasks performed by an individual increases. Job enlargement strategies have been more successful in increasing job satisfaction than have job rotation strategies. IBM and Maytag have used job enlargement to motivate employees.

**Job rotation**

A process that allows employees to move from one job to another in an effort to relieve the boredom that is often associated with job specialization

**Job enlargement**

Adding tasks to a job instead of treating each task as a separate job.

**A successful management philosophy.** This assembly group at Tektronix® cross-trained on all jobs, combined their skills and talents, and have not had a single product failure for six consecutive months—a record for Tektronix.

## Job Enrichment

**Job enrichment**

Involves incorporating motivational factors into a job situation

**Job enrichment** involves incorporating motivational factors, such as opportunity for achievement, recognition, responsibility, and advancement, into a job situation. Job enrichment gives workers not only more tasks within the job but more control and authority over the job. Job enrichment programs enhance a worker's feeling of responsibility and provide opportunities for growth and advancement when the worker is able to take on the more challenging tasks. AT&T and General Foods use job enrichment to improve the quality of work life for their employees. The potential benefits of job enrichment are great, but it requires careful planning and execution.

## Flextime and Other Scheduling Strategies

**Flextime**

A system of working that allows employees to choose their starting and ending times as long as they are at work during a specified core period

Most American workers work a traditional 40-hour work week consisting of five 8-hour days with fixed starting and ending times. Facing problems of poor motivation and high absenteeism, many managers are turning to flextime as a possible solution. **Flextime** is a system of working that allows employees to choose their starting and ending times as long as they are at work during a specified core period (Figure 8-3).

Flextime does not reduce the total number of hours that employees work; however, it does give employees flexibility in selecting the hours they work.

**Figure 8-3**

Flextime, showing core and
flexible hours

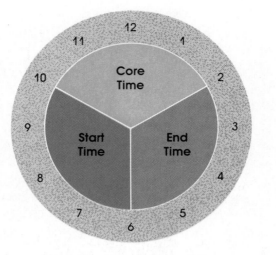

Employees are free to schedule their work around core times in which all
employees must be present. A firm may specify that employees must be present
from 10:00 A.M. to 3:00 P.M. One employee decides to come in at 7:00 A.M.
and leave at the end of the core time. Another employee, a mother who lives
in the suburbs, decides to come in at 9:00 A.M. in order to have time to drop
off her children at a day-care center and commute by public transportation
to her job. Texas Instruments and Apple Computer use flextime.

Because flextime programs are so new, it is difficult to evaluate their
effectiveness. Preliminary results, however, indicate that they increase job
satisfaction. Greater job satisfaction, in turn, leads to increases in productivity.

Two scheduling strategies that are related to flextime are the compressed
work week and job sharing. The **compressed work week** is a four-day (or
shorter) period in which an employee works forty hours. Under such a plan,
employees generally work ten hours per day and have a three-day weekend.
The compressed work week reduces an organization's operating expenses
because its actual hours of operation are reduced.

**Job sharing** occurs when two people do one job. One person may work
from 8:00 A.M. to 12:30 P.M.; the second person comes in at 12:30 P.M. and
work until 5:00 P.M. Job sharing gives both people the opportunity to work
and time to fulfill other obligations, such as parenting. With job sharing, the
company has the benefit of the skills of two people for one job, often at a
lower total cost for salaries than one person working eight hours a day would
be paid.

An extension of job sharing is **work sharing**, a job-saving move in which
a company faced by hard financial times shortens the work week of all the
employees by a few hours. During slow sales times, grocery stores frequently
use work sharing to avoid laying off any employees. When employees
understand why their hours are being reduced, this strategy can keep a
company in business through hard times without layoffs.

**Compressed work week**

A four-day (or shorter) period in
which an employee works forty
hours

**Job sharing**

When two people do one job

**Work sharing**

A job-saving move in which a
company faced by hard financial times shortens the work
week of all employees by a
few hours

**Unconventional commuting.** Not all commuters get caught in rush hour traffic. These employees commute by helicopter to offshore jobs where the shifts are 14 days on and 14 days off.

## Management by Objectives

Management by objectives (MBO) is a process in which a manager and a subordinate conferring together set and agree to goals for the subordinate to achieve. MBO has three basic parts (Figure 8-4):

1. Individuals within an organization negotiate a set of objectives to be achieved within a specified period of time—three months, six months, twelve months.
2. Periodically, the manager conducts performance reviews to determine how well the subordinate is progressing toward the achievement of the goals.
3. At the end of the specified period of time, the subordinate is rewarded on the basis of how close he or she came to achieving goals.

The rationale behind MBO is that employees who are involved in the goal-setting process will be highly motivated to perform. One major advantage of an MBO program is that it constantly emphasizes what must be done in order to achieve organizational objectives. One major disadvantage of such a program is that it is time consuming and expensive. For MBO to succeed,

**Figure 8-4**

Steps in Management by Objectives

Individuals negotiate or are assigned a set of objectives to achieve within a specified period of time.

Individuals are evaluated periodically to see how they are doing.

Individuals are rewarded on the basis of how close they come to achieving their stated goals.

objectives must be carefully defined and realistic. Furthermore, managers must be sure that individual objectives are congruent with the broad goals of the organization.

Chrysler Corporation uses a three-month system of MBO called the quarterly review system. Every three months managers outline to their supervisors their goals for the next three months. They also have to explain how they intend to accomplish their goals. The Chrysler's system works because it lets managers feel as though they are their own boss, motivates employees from within, and unearths new ideas.[10]

# Notes

**1.** Abraham Maslow, *Motivation and Personality* (New York: Harper & Row, 1954).

**2.** Beth Brophy, "Are You Making What You're Worth?," *Business Week*, June 23, 1986, p. 60.

**3.** "Cost Control: Getting Employees to Care," *INC.* 9 (July 1987): 76.

**4.** Douglas McGregor, *The Human Side of Enterprise* (New York: McGraw-Hill, 1960), pp. 33–4.

**5.** Ibid, pp. 47–8.

**6.** William J. Hampton, "Why Image Counts: A Tale of Two Industries," *Business Week*, June 8, 1987, p. 139.

**7.** Laurie Baum, "Korea's Newest Export: Management Style," *Business Week*, January 19, 1987, p. 66.

**8.** "Motivation: Turning Mistakes into Lessons," *INC.* 9 (June 1987): 136.

**9.** William B. Werther, Jr., and Keith Davis, *Personnel Management and Human Resources* (New York: McGraw-Hill, 1985), p. 603.

**10.** Lee Iacocca, with William Novak, *Iacocca: An Autobiography* (New York: Bantam Books, 1984), pp. 50–53.

# Summary and Review

▶ Human relations is the field of study that deals with the behavior of individuals and groups in organizational settings. Its focus is what motivates employees to perform on the job.

▶ Psychologist Abraham Maslow defined five basic needs of all people and arranged these needs in the order in which they must be satisfied. The needs in Maslow's hierarchy are physiological, security, social, esteem, and self-actualization. Physiological needs are at the bottom of the hierarchy; the need for self-actualization is at the top.

▶ Psychologist Frederick Herzberg distinguished between maintenance factors and motivational factors. Maintenance factors relate to the work environment; they include adequate wages and comfortable working conditions. They must be present for employees to remain in a job. Motivational factors relate to the work itself. They include recognition, responsibility, and advancement. They encourage employees to be productive.

▶ Douglas McGregor contrasted two views of management: Theory X (traditional) suggests workers dislike work. Theory Y (humanistic) suggests that workers not only like work but will seek out responsibility to satisfy their higher-order needs.

▶ Theory Z says that employees should be involved in all aspects of company decision making.

▶ Strategies for motivating workers include behavior modification and job design. Managers can structure jobs by means of job rotation, job enlargement, job enrichment, flextime and management by objectives.

## Key Terms and Concepts

human relations
motivation
goal
need
Maslow's hierarchy
physiological needs
security needs
social needs
esteem needs
self-actualization
maintenance factors
motivational factors
Theory X

Theory Y
Theory Z
equity theory
expectancy theory
behavior modification
job rotation
job enlargement
job enrichment
flextime
compressed work week
job sharing
work sharing

## Checking Your Understanding

This chapter introduced you to the subject of human relations in the work place. To test and reinforce your understanding, fill in the blanks below.

1. An internal state that directs behavior toward goals is motivation
2. flextime programs allow employees to set the times they work.
3. Quality circles are small groups of workers who meet regularly to discuss ways to improve their work.

**4.** The study of the behavior of individuals and groups in organizational settings is _human relations_

**5.** _Theory Y_ assumes that workers like to work and will seek out responsibility to satisfy their high-level needs.

**6.** _Maslow's hierarchy_ arranges the needs of humans in order of their importance.

**7.** The difference between a desired state and an actual state is a _need_.

**8.** _MBO_ involves employees in the goal-setting process to motivate them to work harder.

**9.** _Self actualization_ is the highest level in Maslow's hierarchy.

**10.** _Maintenance_ factors must be present for an employee to remain at a job according to Herzberg.

# Topics for Review and Discussion

**1.** Why do managers need to understand the needs of their employees?

**2.** What was the goal of the Hawthorne studies? What was the outcome of those studies?

**3.** Describe the motivation process.

**4.** Explain Maslow's hierarchy of needs. Why is it important?

**5.** Distinguish between Theory X, Theory Y, and Theory Z.

**6.** What is Theory Z? What is the relationship between it and Theory Y?

**7.** Identify and describe the five job design strategies.

# Exercises

**1.** Consider a person who is hungry: How would he or she be motivated and what actions would that person take? Use the motivation process to explain.

**2.** Where could you see Theory X being applied in business? Theory Y?

**3.** How might you, as a manager, make use of Maslow's hierarchy of needs to motivate your employees.

**4.** Describe the scenarios in which you would use reward and punishment to modify behavior.

## Case 8-1

# *Human Relations at Hewlett-Packard*

Hewlett-Packard Co. (HP) began in 1939 as a shirt-sleeves partnership between two Stanford University students, William Hewlett and David Packard. In the early years of HP, the company's mainstay was electronics. The company became increasingly involved with computers, which by the mid-1980s were its principal business. In the 1940s, Hewlett-Packard became known for "the HP way"—the unique manner in which it dealt with employees. William

Hewlett and David Packard had realized very early that their company needed to make a commitment to its employees if it were to grow and prosper. They also realized the need to hire innovative people. As a result, they structured HP to give employees the freedom to work toward overall corporate objectives in ways they felt best for their areas of responsibility.

HP believes that the achievements of an organization are the results of the combined efforts of each individual employee. As a result, the company tries to make sure that it has innovative people at all levels and has taken several steps to ensure that HP employees work in an environment and have incentives that foster creativity. Every employee is treated with consideration and respect. An informal work setting (everyone is on a first-name basis, and there are no time clocks) helps to build employee enthusiasm and morale. The company tries to select enthusiastic people for important managerial positions in the hope that the enthusiasm will be contagious. The management style at HP includes "management by wandering around" so that managers keep in touch with what employees are doing and can encourage them to offer ideas.

The informality at HP extends into its organizational structure. Communication between different groups is encouraged. Although HP's fifty-four small divisions were reorganized into three major business divisions and a marketing and sales division in 1984, informal meetings and cooperation among divisions are still the norm. In addition, top managers encourage employees to think of the company as one big family in which all members are striving together to reach corporate objectives.

HP's policy of no layoffs was severely tested during the 1970 recession. No one was laid off; instead, all employees, including William Hewlett and David Packard, took a 10 percent pay cut and worked 10 percent fewer hours. During the slump in computer sales of the early 1980s, HP again did not lay off any of its more than eighty thousand employees.

Changes in the computer market have made some changes at HP necessary. The switch from numerous autonomous divisions to four distinct divisions was done largely out of a need to control costs. The company recognized that it needed to transform its ten thousand individual products into complete systems. Some employees believed that HP's autonomous-division structure had slowed the development of new products. Despite the new centralized structure, the spirit of cooperation among divisions survives. A new procedure at HP is phase review. A committee reviews a project's feasibility and progress at set phases. Phase review is similar to the informal process used in the past, but it allows for speedier and better decision making.

Recent organizational changes have not tarnished the company's reputation as a "people company." Instead, "the HP way" is alive and well and no doubt will continue to contribute to the success of Hewlett-Packard.

---

These facts are from Jonathan B. Levine, "Mild-Mannered Hewlett-Packard Is Making like Superman," *Business Week,* March 7, 1988, pp. 110–11, 114; Susan Kerr, with Jeff Moad, "New Mind-Set Brings Growing Pains at HP," *Datamation,* July 15, 1987, pp. 20, 23; Eric Nee, "William Hewlett: The Long Shadow of a Director Emeritus," *Electronic News,* March 2, 1987, p. 4; and Thomas J. Peters and Robert H. Waterman, Jr., *In Search of Excellence* (New York: Warner Books, 1982), pp. 122–23, 175–78, 214–15, 288–89.

### Questions

1. Why is Hewlett-Packard called a "people company"?
2. What methods or theories does Hewlett-Packard use to motivate employees?
3. What problems could develop if all companies maintained the same level of informality as Hewlett-Packard?

## Case 8-2
### *Chaparral Steel*

In 1975, Texas Industries, Inc., and Co-Steel International of Canada formed Chaparral Steel Co. in Midlothian, Texas. Texas Industries (TXI) eventually bought Co-Steel International's half of the small steel company and is now the sole owner. Chaparral has doubled in size since 1975 and has an annual capacity of more than 1.2 million tons of steel. The company now produces more steel than any other mill built in the United States in the past thirty years. Even more amazing, Chaparral managed to become a steel exporter when most major U.S. steel producers were facing fierce, low-cost foreign competition. The company is more efficient than its competitors, requiring only 1.6 worker-hours per ton of steel production; the industry average is 1.95 worker-hours. To achieve such amazing numbers, the company practices several management techniques that are unique in the U.S. steel industry.

Chaparral is a lean, flexible organization with few barriers between the plant floor and management. The plant is receptive to change, unlike virtually every other steel company. Chaparral has an open management structure that allows cross-training—moving employees from job to job, broadening their understanding of the mill's production processes.

A nonunion work force also sets Chaparral apart from other steel producers. TXI management believes that it can better represent the needs and interests of its employees than can an outside interest. The company hires most of its employees from nonindustrial areas. Chaparral tries to hire young college graduates who want to learn the steel business. The company pays for additional schooling and training for some of its employees. The educational expense pays off because the employees usually stay with Chaparral, giving the company the benefit of their increased expertise and productivity.

Another interesting approach used by Chaparral is to make every employee a member of the sales department. Management took this step because it believes that every employee should understand customers' needs. In return, management offers employees benefits such as stock options and gives managers direct involvement in the production process.

Chaparral's sabbatical plan for front-line managers also sets it apart from its competitors. The purpose of this program is to prevent burnout and to generate renewed excitement in work. Employees on sabbatical are given special projects to work on, such as researching a new technology or visiting other steel mills and customers. While a manager is on sabbatical, another employee acts as substitute foreman and other workers are shifted around. This cycling of employees increases motivation and productivity.

Chaparral does not have a research and development department or a laboratory. Instead, management views the whole plant as one big laboratory; new ideas are tried out right on the production floor. The production employees are responsible for keeping production processes on the leading edge of technology. They visit other companies and customers to find new ideas and technology that might help their own jobs or Chaparral as a whole. The company also works with universities to generate new ideas.

Only two people work in Chaparral's personnel department. They are responsible for initial screenings and for a few clerical duties. Chaparral's plant supervisors do all their own hiring and training. And, because there are no quality inspectors, the supervisors and their employees are responsible for the quality of the product.

Chaparral Steel has used innovative management and personnel practices to make a name for itself in an industry traditionally dominated by large steel companies such as USX and Bethlehem Steel. Chaparral management understands that its human resources are just as important to the steel-making process as its physical resources. The company understands that employees have needs and desires in addition to money and tries to fulfill those needs. As a result, labor costs at Chaparral are only 10 percent of sales (average labor costs for the whole industry are around 40 percent). Chaparral's understanding of human relations has allowed it to do something not even the big steel companies have done—grow and prosper despite troubled times in the U.S. steel industry.

---

These facts are from George Melloan, "Making Money Making Steel in Texas," *The Wall Street Journal,* January 26, 1988, p. 29; Lisa M. Keefe, "Forward's March," *Forbes,* April 20, 1987, pp. 104–05; and Alan M. Kantrow, "Wide-Open Management at Chaparral Steel," *Harvard Business Review,* (May–June 1986): 96–97, 99–102.

**Questions**

1. Describe Chapparal's management style in motivating employees.
2. What impact does the elimination of communication barriers have on product quality and productivity?
3. Why don't the big steel companies adapt Chaparral's human relations policies?

# Answers to Checking Your Understanding

1. motivation
2. flextime
3. quality circles
4. human relations
5. Theory Y
6. Maslow's hierarchy
7. need
8. management by objectives
9. self-actualization
10. maintenance

## Outline

# Chapter 9

# Human Resources Management

## Objectives

After reading this chapter, you will be able to:

▶ Name the functions of human resources managers.

▶ Describe the process of recruiting and selecting human resources for a company.

▶ Discuss the laws governing the recruiting, selecting, and managing of human resources.

▶ Identify the various ways a worker may be compensated and motivated.

▶ Explain the importance of evaluating workers and describe how performance appraisals are carried out.

# *Business Experience*

Au Bon Pain is a Boston-based chain of food stores that specialize in croissants, fancy sandwiches, and coffees. At one time the chain had a reputation for terrible service, yet the store managers were taking no action to solve the problem. The president of Au Bon Pain admitted that he would not want to be a manager in one of his own stores because the problems and stress simply were not worth the salaries managers were paid.

President Ron Shaich did not realize how desperate things had become until he made an unannounced visit to one of the stores. Shaich watched as an Au Bon Pain clerk first told a customer that he had no croissants to make a sandwich and then, when the customer asked for a sandwich made with bread, told the customer that bread was sold in whole loaves only. Shaich was appalled: Customers were being turned away so that clerks could avoid slicing a loaf of bread—despite Shaich's goal of providing good food and prompt service. The operating standards developed by top management ensured only that managers would not think for themselves. The store managers were mindlessly following the policies and procedures manual and not using common sense.

Although Au Bon Pain was expanding and earning profits, morale was low, and the turnover for hourly employees was 40 percent in 1985 despite the payment of premium wages. With turnover high, store managers frequently had to cook and run counters instead of manage. They were constantly going to Shaich with their problems, and the company was in a state of chaos.

In October 1985, Shaich and his partner Len Schlesinger happened to meet some of the executives of the Golden Corral Corporation. Golden Corral, which owned a number of steak houses, had found a novel way to deal with the problems of running a chain operation: They gave the unit managers a piece of the action. In addition to receiving a modest salary, a Golden Corral manager owned from 20 to 30 percent of his or her store. Shaich and Schlesinger were desperate enough to try anything. They decided to tie each store manager's earnings to the controllable profits of his or her store—that is, profits less rent and depreciation. Store managers would control labor and expenses. Managers who took care of their employees and watched their expenses could make their stores more efficient and profitable. Au Bon Pain tested the idea on two stores. Shaich and Schlesinger explained to the managers of the test stores that Au Bon Pain was essentially leasing the stores to them and would split the profits of the stores fifty-fifty with them, in addition to paying them their salaries.

The two test stores seemed to change almost overnight. One manager began working longer hours, looking for ways to cut costs and increase sales. He redesigned his store to seat more people and raised his employees' wages. The other manager worked on making sure there were enough employees on hand during peak operating hours. Most importantly, both managers were solving problems they had once dumped on Shaich.

The numbers at the test stores were impressive too. Employee turnover dropped drastically, and both stores beat their profit targets by huge margins. One manager exceeded his controllable profit goal by $45,000. The stores were clean, and customers were treated as Shaich had intended when Au Bon Pain first began operations. Au Bon Pain refined the compensation program and applied it to more stores in the chain.

Shaich and Schlesinger are thrilled about the new compensation plan. It motivates the managers to take care of their stores and to sell to their capacity. They put as many hours into the company as they want, but most put in far more than they are expected to. The company is growing rapidly and has plans for expansion, and Ron Shaich even says it has become a place where he would like to work.

---

These facts are from Bruce G. Posner, "May the Force Be with You," *INC*. 9 (July 1987): 70–75.

# Introduction

The human resources of a firm are vital to its success. **Human resources** are all the people who work in an organization. Human resources management is concerned with maximizing the satisfaction of employees, improving their efficiency, and ensuring that within the organization there are enough employees with the appropriate skills to meet organizational objectives. This chapter focuses on management's efforts to optimize the level and quality of human resources.

## ▶ Nature of Human Resources Management

Employees must work both efficiently and effectively in order for an organization to meet its objectives. It is also important that management hire employees who are qualified to perform the required duties and hire employees in sufficient numbers. Unqualified employees will not be able to perform efficiently and effectively; qualified employees will be unable to achieve organizational objectives if there are not enough of them to do the work. Thus, managing the quantity (through hiring and firing) and quality (through training, compensating, and so on) of human resources is an important managerial function.

The area of human resources management has increased in importance over the last few decades, partly because managers have developed a better understanding of human relations through the work of Maslow, Herzberg, and others. Moreover, the nature of the human resources themselves is changing. Employees today are concerned not only about the amount of money a job offers; they are also concerned with job satisfaction, personal performance and the future. Effective human resources managers are aware of these changes and use them to increase the efficiency and productivity of their employees. Every manager in an organization is practicing some of the functions of human resources management at all times.

In order to find and keep an appropriate number of qualified employees, human resources managers engage in several activities, such as planning and forecasting, recruitment and selection, training and development, and compensation.

## ▶ Planning

### Analyzing Employment Needs

**Planning** is analyzing an organization's present and future employment situation and developing a strategy to meet an organization's human resource

**Planning**

Analyzing an organization's present and future employment situation and developing a strategy to meet an organization's human resource needs

needs. The human resources manager or department charged with this task begins by studying the overall objectives of the organization. After determining how many employees and what skills are needed to meet organizational objectives, management determines how many employees are currently employed by the organization then forecasts are developed to determine how many more employees the organization needs to hire and what qualifications they must have. This function also involves forecasting the supply of people in the work force who will have the necessary qualifications to meet the organization's needs. Moreover, management should consider the status of current personnel when planning human resource needs. The human resources manager then develops a strategy for satisfying the organization's human resource needs. If Montgomery Ward, for example, plans to open a new store, it will need to hire an additional store manager, an assistant manager, various department managers, sales personnel, and so on. Management should also consider the status of current personnel when forecasting needs. An examination of employee records may indicate that two current Montgomery Ward managers are planning to retire within the next year. Therefore, the human resource managers would anticipate the need for three store managers, one assistant manager, and so on. This employment analysis establishes the general personnel requirements of the organization. Next, managers analyze the jobs within the organization in order to match the human resources to the available jobs.

# Job Analysis

**Job analysis**

The determination, through observation and study, of pertinent information about a job

**Job analysis** is the determination, through observation and study, of pertinent information about a job—the specific tasks that make up the job; the skills, knowledge, and abilities that are necessary to perform the job; and the environment in which the job is performed. Managers use the information obtained through a job analysis in three ways: to develop a job description, to develop job specifications, and to perform job evaluations.

**Job description**

A formal, written description of a specific job

A **job description** is a formal, written description of a specific job. It typically includes the following: job title, tasks to be performed (for instance, welding), relationship with other jobs, physical and mental skills required (such as lifting heavy boxes or calculating data), duties, responsibilities, and working conditions.

**Job specification**

A written description of the qualifications necessary for a specific job

A **job specification** is a written description of the qualifications necessary for a specific job. Qualifications generally include education (some jobs require a college degree), experience, personal characteristics (newspaper ads frequently request outgoing, hard-working persons), and physical characteristics.

**Job evaluation**

A systematic procedure to determine the relative worth of various jobs

A **job evaluation** is a systematic procedure to determine the relative worth of various jobs. The goal of a job evaluation is to determine which jobs should pay more than other jobs. Obviously, the chief executive officer of Coca-Cola will earn much more than a security guard at a Coca-Cola bottling plant. A job evaluation considers the responsibilities, skills, efforts, and working conditions associated with the job. Evaluations also take into account the going rate for a particular job in the geographic area where the job is performed, as well as in the industry as a whole.

Once management has forecast human resource needs and compared these needs with existing human resources, it should have a general idea about the hiring needs of the organization. With the aid of job analyses (including job descriptions, job specifications, and job evaluations), management is in a position to recruit and select employees who are qualified to fill specific job openings.

# ▶ Recruiting

**Recruiting**

The formation of a pool of qualified applicants from which management will select employees

**Recruiting** is the formation of a pool of qualified applicants from which management will select employees. There are two sources from which to develop this pool of applicants—internal and external sources.

## Internal Sources

**Internal sources**

The organization's current employees

**Internal sources** of applicants are the organization's current employees. Many firms have a policy of giving first consideration to their own employees. The personnel department may review personnel records to identify employees meeting the job specifications, or it may place an announcement (which includes a job description and job specifications) on the bulletin board or in the company newsletter. The cost of hiring current employees to fill job openings is inexpensive when compared to the cost of hiring from external sources, and it is good for employee morale.

## External Sources

**External sources**

Those sources outside of the firm

**External sources** are outside of the firm. They include newspaper advertisements, professional journals, employment agencies, colleges, vocational schools, recommendations from current employees, and unsolicited applications. Using these sources of applicants is generally more expensive than hiring from within, yet it may be necessary if there are no current employees who meet the job specifications or there are better-qualified people outside of the organization.

External sources for recruiting production workers are different from sources for recruiting managers. Most entry-level skilled and unskilled labor positions are filled through advertisements in newspapers or on the radio, employee referrals, or referrals from job placement services such as the U.S. Training and Employment Service. Prospective employees usually apply directly to the employer at the job site. Generally, the labor market for these types of jobs is no more than thirty miles from the job site.

Recruiting for entry-level managerial and professional positions is usually carried out on college and university campuses. Companies send recruiters to campuses all over the nation, armed with brochures, annual reports, and job descriptions to generate student interest in the company. Job seekers may also consult specific newspapers, most notably *The Wall Street Journal's*

**Mutual admiration.**
Walgreens and New Orleans' Xavier University have a long, successful relationship. Walgreens has recruited pharmacists from the university for thirty years.

*Employment Weekly,* that run classified advertisements for all levels of management and professional positions. For managerial or professional positions above the entry level, most firms depend on employment agencies or executive search firms, sometimes called *headhunters,* which specialize in luring qualified people away from other companies. Management Encounter 9-1 explains how headhunters operate.

## ▶ Selection

**Selection**

A series of steps through which the best applicants are offered jobs

**Selection** is a series of steps through which the best applicants are offered jobs; the steps are reviewing the application, testing, interviewing, and checking references (Figure 9-1). Job descriptions and job specifications play an important role in the selection process.

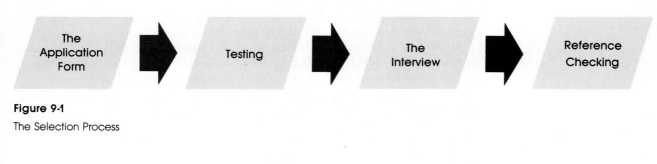

**Figure 9-1**
The Selection Process

## Management Encounter 9-1
### *Executive Headhunters*

Headhunters—or executive search consultants, as they prefer to be called—recruit middle- and top-level managers for client organizations. Their clients are generally corporations, professional firms, and nonprofit organizations that need to fill executive positions. The organization with a position to fill pays the headhunter's fees and expenses.

Businesses use headhunters because of the speed and skill with which they can locate qualified applicants for a particular position. The use of headhunters may be the most cost-efficient way to fill executive positions. Newspaper and magazine ads simply do not attract the most qualified candidates because suitable candidates may already be employed and not actively looking for another job. The headhunter's job is to identify these candidates and get them interested in working for the client company. Headhunters save a company time and money by interviewing candidates to screen out those who are unacceptable.

Headhunters are compensated on either a contingency or a retainer basis. Contingency searchers are paid only when they have filled a position; retainer searchers are paid regardless of whether they find an acceptable candidate. In general, businesses looking for a top-level executive pay a headhunter on a retainer basis, and those looking for middle-level manager pay on a contingency basis. In either case, the headhunter's fee is usually the same—from 20 to 30 percent of the recruited executive's first-year salary.

Businesses that use headhunters typically follow the same steps. As soon as a position in the company opens, the company calls a headhunter. A business may use several headhunters if compensation is on a contingency basis. The firm spells out in detail the specific job requirements and type of candidate it wants for the position. During the search, the headhunter and client communicate constantly to ensure that only qualified candidates are considered.

The working relationship between the searcher and the client is strengthened when each knows exactly what the other expects. The client should not expect an endless search that ultimately produces the perfect candidate. Conversely, the headhunter should not expect to match the firm's qualifications and expectations quickly and easily. The firm and headhunter may have to compromise to fill a position.

Only 50 to 60 percent of executive searches result in the hiring of a candidate who meets all qualifications. Nevertheless, organizations still use headhunters. It is estimated that there are ten thousand headhunters in the United States who generate about $2 billion per year filling executive positions. These figures suggest that headhunters will be around for years to come.

These facts are from Thomas J. Hutton, "Recruitment: Increasing the Odds for Successful Searches," *Personnel Journal* 66 (September 1987): 140, 142, 144; Kenneth E. Richardson, "Comparing Executive Search Firms and Executive Employment Agencies," *Bottomline* 4 (July 1987): 27, 31–32; Beverly Gary Kempton, "The Executive Woman's Guide to Headhunters," *Working Woman* 12 (April 1987): 110–12; and Mitchell L. Berger, "Secrets of an Executive Recruiter," *CPA Journal* 57 (February 1987): 104–05.

## The Application

In the first stage of the selection process, the job seeker usually fills out an application form and perhaps has a brief interview. The application form asks for the applicant's name, address, telephone number, education, and previous work experience (Figure 9-2). In addition to identifying obvious qualifications, the application can provide subtle clues about whether a person would be appropriate for a particular job. For instance, an applicant who gives unusually creative answers may be perfect for a position at an advertising agency; a person who turns in a sloppy, hurriedly scrawled application would not be appropriate for a technical job requiring precise adjustments. Some

**Figure 9-2**

An Application Form

## Employment Application

Form 14650 - N

**3M Staffing and Employee Resources**
Building 224-1W-02, 3M Center
St. Paul, Minnesota 55144-1000

**3M**

Please complete this Application as completely as possible to help us learn about your abilities, experiences, and interests. We will use this information, comparing it with our needs, to make a decision as quickly as possible.

**Personal Data** *(Print or Type)*

**E 120205**

| | Name | Last | First | MI | Social Security Number |
|---|---|---|---|---|---|

**Present Address**

Street Address

City, State and Zip

Home Telephone (Include Area Code)
( )

Work Telephone (Include Area Code)
( )

**Permanent Address**

*Leave blank if same as above*

Street Address

City, State and Zip

Perm. Address Telephone (Include Area Code)
( )

Date of Application

**Job Interest**

Position applied for

Date available for work ▶

Career Interests

Salary desired

Type of position applied for
☐ Regular  ☐ Part-time  ☐ Temporary  ☐ Intern  ☐ Co-op  ☐ Summer  ☐

**Authorization To Work**

It is unlawful for 3M to hire individuals that are not authorized to work in the United States. Accordingly, 3M hires only citizens or aliens that are authorized to work in the United States. If you receive an offer from 3M and you accept the offer, before you will be placed on the payroll, all new employees will be required to document that they are a U.S. Citizen or an alien that is authorized to work in the United States.

If you are one of the following please check this box ☐
- A citizen or a national of the United States.
- An alien lawfully admitted for permanent residence.
- An alien authorized by the Immigration and Naturalization Service to work **indefinately** in the United States.

If you are hired by 3M, one of the following documents must be reviewed before you can begin employment; a U.S. Passport, a Certificate of U.S. Citizenship, a Certificate of Naturalization or an unexpired foreign passport with an attached Employment Authorization.

If you do not have one of the above documents, then you will need to present two documents; one of the following; a State driver's license with a photograph, an I.D. card with a photograph, or information including name, sex, date of birth, height, weight and color of eyes
**AND**
one of the following; an original Social Security Number Card, a birth certificate issued by a State, County or Municipal authority bearing a seal or an unexpired INS Employment Authorization.

**Education History**

| Schools Attended (Last School First) | | Attendance Dates Mo./Yr. | | Grad. Y or N | Degree Type | Major/Minor | Grade Point |
|---|---|---|---|---|---|---|---|
| | | From | To | | | | |
| Name of School | (City, State) | - | | | | | |
| | | - | | | | | |
| High School | | - | | | | | |

Faculty person who knows you best (name, telephone)

**Additional Education Information**

(If additional space needed, attach separate pages)

Academic honors, scholarships, fellowships, memberships in professional and honorary societies and any other extracurricular activities.

Post graduate research, title and description

Publications/Patents Issued

**Employment Record**

*List most current or recent employer first, include periods of unemployment, include U.S. Military Service (show rank/rate at discharge, but not type of discharge). Include previous 3M experience (summer/part time jobs and Cooperative Education assignments and any volunteer experience which relates to the position you are applying for).*

| Employer (company name) | Immediate supervisor's name | Your job title |
|---|---|---|
| Street address | Employment dates (mo. and yr.) From    To | Salary Begin    End |
| City, state, zip code | Reason for leaving | |
| Company's Product or Service | Summarize your job duties | |

| Employer (company name) | Immediate supervisor's name | Your job title |
|---|---|---|
| Street address | Employment dates (mo. and yr.) From    To | Salary Begin    End |
| City, state, zip code | Reason for leaving | |
| Company's Product or Service | Summarize your job duties | |

| | | | | | | |
|---|---|---|---|---|---|---|
| **General Information and Job Requirements** | Are you willing to ▶ | Work shifts ☐ Yes ☐ No | Work overtime ☐ Yes ☐ No | Work a schedule other than M/F ☐ Yes ☐ No | Work a rotation work schedule ☐ Yes ☐ No | |

<table>
<tr><td rowspan="6">General<br>Information<br>and Job<br>Requirements</td><td rowspan="2">Are you willing to ▶</td><td colspan="2">Work shifts<br>☐ Yes ☐ No</td><td>Work overtime<br>☐ Yes ☐ No</td><td>Work a schedule other than M/F<br>☐ Yes ☐ No</td><td colspan="2">Work a rotation work schedule<br>☐ Yes ☐ No</td></tr>
<tr><td colspan="2">Travel    To<br>☐ Yes ____ % ☐ No</td><td colspan="2">Geographic preference</td><td>Are you willing to work elsewhere?<br>☐ No ☐ Yes</td><td>If yes, where?</td></tr>
<tr><td colspan="3">Do you have any physical condition which might limit you in above position ☐ No ☐ Yes ▶</td><td colspan="2">Explain</td><td colspan="2">Are you a U.S. veteran<br>☐ Yes ☐ No</td></tr>
<tr><td colspan="7">If you wish to indicate that you were referred to 3M by any of the following, please check appropriate box and specify.</td></tr>
<tr><td colspan="2">☐ Employment advertisement<br>   (Name of publication)</td><td colspan="2">☐ Employment agency<br>   (Name of agency)</td><td colspan="2">☐ 3M Employee<br>   (Name)</td><td>☐ Other</td></tr>
<tr><td>Are you under 18?<br>☐ Yes ☐ No</td><td>Have you ever</td><td>☐ been employed by<br>☐ previously applied to</td><td colspan="2">3M or any<br>3M subsidiary</td><td colspan="2">If so, please check appropriate box and specify location<br>date</td></tr>
<tr><td rowspan="3">Employee<br>Agreements</td><td colspan="4">Have you ever signed an Agreement relating to inventions or to confidential know-how, etc. with a previous employer?</td><td>☐ Yes</td><td>☐ No</td></tr>
<tr><td colspan="6">If yes to above, please state company with whom Agreement was signed.</td></tr>
<tr><td colspan="6">If available, please include a copy of this Agreement(s) with this application. It will expedite consideration of your employment. 3M must see any such agreements prior to final consideration of your employment.</td></tr>
<tr><td rowspan="2">Reference<br>Approval</td><td colspan="3">Do you have any objections to our contacting your present employer to verify the above?<br>☐ NO, you may contact any time</td><td colspan="3">☐ DO NOT contact now, you may contact at a later date, e.g.:<br>after acceptance of offer, or a specific date, if appropriate</td></tr>
<tr><td>Name</td><td>Phone/Address</td><td colspan="2">Name</td><td colspan="2">Phone/Address      Contact date</td></tr>
<tr><td>Technical<br>Applicants<br>Only</td><td colspan="6">Please list technical hobbies or special interests</td></tr>
<tr><td>Sales<br>Applicants</td><td colspan="2">Do you have a valid drivers license?<br>☐ Yes ☐ No</td><td>If yes, drivers license number</td><td>Expiration date</td><td>State</td><td>Has it been revoked or suspended?<br>☐ Yes ☐ No</td></tr>
<tr><td rowspan="2">Clerical<br>Applicants<br>Only</td><td>WHAT IS YOUR PRESENT SPEED PER MINUTE</td><td>Typewriter</td><td>Shorthand</td><td>Speedwriting</td><td>CAN YOU OPERATE ▶</td><td>Dictating Equipment<br>☐ Yes ☐ No</td></tr>
<tr><td colspan="6">Other office equipment you can operate (word processor, personal computer, etc.)     Keypunch ☐ Yes ☐ No</td></tr>
<tr><td rowspan="4">Skilled<br>Trade<br>Applicants<br>Only</td><td colspan="6">In what skilled trade areas do you have talent</td></tr>
<tr><td colspan="2">Have you completed an apprenticeship in a skilled craft<br>☐ Yes ☐ No</td><td>IF YES ▶</td><td colspan="2">What craft</td><td>Where did you complete it</td></tr>
<tr><td>Was it state endorsed<br>☐ Yes ☐ No</td><td>Date completed</td><td colspan="2">How long have you been a journeyman</td><td>Do you carry a state license for your craft<br>☐ Yes ☐ No</td><td>If yes, type</td></tr>
<tr><td colspan="6">List all machines and equipment you have operated</td></tr>
<tr><td>Relatives<br>At 3M</td><td colspan="6">List any relatives now working at 3M (3M does not employ relatives of company executives.)</td></tr>
</table>

Have you been convicted of a crime in the last 5 years?
☐ Yes ☐ No

If yes, please briefly describe the circumstances of your conviction, indicating date, nature, and place of the offense and disposition of the case. Your answer is looked upon as only one of the factors considered in the employment decision and is evaluated in terms of the nature, severity, and date of the offense.

*I acknowledge and agree to the following:*

1. *I have received a copy of the 3M Drug and Alcohol policy. (Copy enclosed).*

2. *I understand that a pre-placement physical examination, which includes a drug and alcohol test (it is recommended that you do not consume alcohol 8 hours prior to taking this exam), is required as a part of the employment process and agree to submit to the same as a condition of employment with 3M.*

3. *I understand that if I receive an offer of employment from 3M, that offer will be conditioned on receipt by 3M of acceptable results from a pre-employment drug and alcohol test, whether or not so stated in the offer. I agree that I will not take any action in anticipation of employment by 3M, such as leaving my current job or moving my current residence, unless I have received an offer of employment from 3M and I have been informed by 3M that results of my pre-placement medical examination, which includes a drug and alcohol test, were acceptable to 3M, and I have been informed by 3M that any and all other conditions which may have been placed upon the offer of employment have been satisfied.*

**Signature ▶**          Date

3M affirms the right of every person to participate in all aspects of employment without regard to race, color, religion, sex, national origin, age or Vietnam Era Veterans. 3M will provide appropriate opportunity to all persons without regard to mental or physical handicap and disabled veterans.

At 3M, we use job-related criteria in recruiting, hiring, training, and promoting employees in all job classifications. Employee growth and development is a shared responsibility of each employee and the company.

We appreciate your interest in a career at 3M.

job seekers, particularly those aspiring to fill management or professional positions, submit résumés to companies where they would like to work. A résumé is a summary of the person's qualifications and background. The goal of this stage of the selection process is to get acquainted with the applicants and to eliminate those who are obviously wrong for the job.

## Testing

The second stage of the selection process usually involves testing the applicants. Aptitude, IQ, or personality tests may be used to assess an applicant's potential for a certain kind of work. Ability tests are used to determine whether the applicant has the skills that are necessary for the job. For example, applicants for a secretarial position at Smith Barney, an investment firm, would be given a typing test to assess speed and accuracy. Physical examinations may be used to determine whether an applicant has any physical problems that would prevent her or him from performing the

**Job simulation testing proves efficient.** Tests are a way for companies to determine an applicants ability to do a specific job. These applicants at a Toyota plant in Kentucky must assemble a circuit board, then run the business of making them.

job. Applicants for jobs that require security clearance (such as with the FBI or with defense contractors such as General Dynamics) might be required to take a polygraph test. Like the application form and the initial interview, testing serves to eliminate those who do not meet the job specifications.

## The Interview

Applicants who have not been eliminated in the first two stages are interviewed. The interview allows management to obtain in-depth information about previous experience and skills, reasons for changing jobs, attitudes toward the job, communication skills, and an idea of whether the person would fit in with the company. Furthermore, the interviewer can answer the applicant's questions about the requirements for the job, compensation, working conditions, company policies, and so on. A potential employee's questions may be just as revealing as her or his answers. The interview can also help the manager determine the best placement for an applicant based on the applicant's likes and abilities.

## Reference Checking

An applicant's references should be checked prior to final hiring. The reference check usually involves verifying educational background and previous work experience. Managers charged with hiring should be aware that many organizations will confirm only that a person is a former employee and will not release details about the quality of the employee's work.

# ▶ Orientation

**Orientation**

A new employee's introduction to the organization

Once the best applicants have been selected and offered positions and have accepted their offers, they must be introduced to the organization. **Orientation** generally includes a tour of the building; introductions to supervisors, coworkers, and subordinates; and distribution of employee manuals describing the organization's policy on vacations, absenteeism, lunch breaks, company benefits, and so on. Orientation also involves socializing the individual into the ways or culture of the new company. Many larger companies are now able to show videotapes of procedures, facilities and key personnel in the organization to help speed the adjustment process.

# ▶ Legal Considerations

Legal constraints and regulations are present in almost every phase of the recruitment and selection process, and violation of these regulations can result in lawsuits and fines. Therefore, managers should be aware of these restrictions in order to avoid legal problems. Table 9-1 summarizes the human resources laws with which managers should be familiar.

**Table 9.1 Legislation Regulating the Hiring and Compensating of Human Resources**

- **Title VII of the Civil Rights Act (1964)**
  Creates the Equal Employment Opportunity Commission and mandates affirmative action programs. Outlaws employment practices that discriminate on the basis of sex, race, color, or national origin.
- **Age Discrimination in Employment Act (1967)**
  Outlaws employment practices that discriminate on the basis of age, particularly mandatory retirement before age 70.
- **Equal Pay Act (1963)**
  Requires that men and women who do equal work be paid equally.
- **Fair Labor Standards Act (1938)**
  Sets minimum wages and overtime rates (for any time over 40 hours per week).

**Equal Employment Opportunity Commission (EEOC)**

A federal agency created by the Civil Rights Act of 1964 to enforce Title VII

Title VII of the Civil Rights Act of 1964 bans discrimination in employment. The **Equal Employment Opportunity Commission (EEOC)** is a federal agency created by the Civil Rights Act of 1964 to enforce Title VII, which applies to all levels of government, educational institutions, labor unions, employment agencies, and all private companies employing more than fifteen people. EEOC is charged with increasing job opportunities for women and minorities and with eliminating job discrimination based on race, religion, color, sex, or national origin.

**Discarding a stereotype.** For many years it was difficult for disabled people to find jobs where they could use their skills and talents. Equal employment opportunity legislation is changing that situation and encouraging employers to hire qualified disabled people.

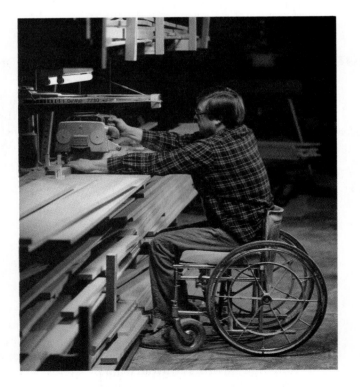

**New opportunities for women and minorities.** Affirmative action programs have made it possible for women and minorities to have careers in fields that were traditionally male dominated. This woman is refueling a plane; she also is an airplane signaler.

**Affirmative action programs**

Programs designed to increase job opportunities for women and minorities

As a result of Title VII, employers must not impose sex distinctions in job specifications, job descriptions, and newspaper advertisements. It is not unusual to see the letters EOE in newspaper ads for employment. The letters stand for Equal Opportunity Employer and indicate that the ad was placed by a company that follows EEOC guidelines. EEOC helps employers set up **affirmative action programs**, which are designed to increase job opportunities for women and minorities through analysis of the present pool of human resources, identification of areas where women and minorities are under-represented, and establishment of specific hiring and promotion goals along with target dates for meeting those goals.

The Civil Rights Act of 1964 also outlaws the use of discriminatory tests for applicants. Aptitude tests and other indirect tests must be validated; in other words, employers must be able to demonstrate that scores on such tests are related to job performance, so that no one race has an advantage in taking the tests.

**Age Discrimination in Employment Act**

Outlaws discrimination based on age

The **Age Discrimination in Employment Act**, passed in 1967 and amended in 1978, specifically outlaws discrimination based on age. It is concerned primarily with banning hiring practices that discriminate against people between the ages of 49 and 69. This act also outlaws policies that require employees to retire before the age of 70. Management Encounter 9-2 describes the age discrimination issue in greater detail.

# Management Encounter 9-2

## *Age Discrimination in the Work Place*

Discrimination on the basis of age is a pressing problem in business today. Age discrimination is the fastest-growing discrimination complaint in the work place. In 1986, almost twenty-seven thousand age-discrimination complaints were filed with federal and state agencies—more than twice the number filed in 1980. Although many age-discrimination cases never reach court (only about one in five do), the rapid increase in the number of complaints has many businesspeople worried.

Most age-discrimination cases originate in right-to-work states (states that prohibit unions from making union membership a requirement for obtaining a job) outside of the Northeast. The typical person who files suit is a white male manager in his fifties who lost his job because of corporate restructuring. These people believe a lawsuit is their only option because they are not protected by union rules and cannot claim racial or sexual discrimination.

Although other countries had had laws preventing discrimination on the basis of age for several years, not until 1967 did Congress pass the Age Discrimination in Employment Act. This act prohibits employers from using age as a basis for hiring or firing people between the ages of 40 and 65. In 1987, the law was amended to include most private and government employees up to age 70 and to eliminate mandatory retirement for workers over age 70 in many industries. In addition, employers are forbidden to discriminate against any individual over age 40 in terms of pay, benefits, or continued employment.

Employers are concerned that the changes in the law will reduce their power to determine the composition of their work forces. Some are afraid to terminate any older worker for fear of a lawsuit.

The Age Discrimination in Employment Act and its amendments should not be interpreted to mean that older workers cannot be fired for unproductivity. Businesses should keep in mind, however, that decisions to hire and fire must be based on ability, not on age. Employers need to evaluate individual employees' ability to carry out job duties, not rely on arbitrary age limits.

Some companies are taking steps to protect themselves from potential age-discrimination lawsuits. Some are offering employees over age 55 who have at least ten years of seniority lucrative early-retirement packages. Such packages help employers plan for the future, and they provide incentives for older workers to retire. Other companies are taking more drastic measures, such as asking retiring employees to sign notarized releases waiving all age-discrimination claims.

Many lawyers believe that the current rash of age-discrimination suits is nothing compared to what is going to happen by the year 2010, when workers over age 40 who are protected by age-discrimination laws will make up half of the work force. Others believe that older people with medical handicaps will be increasingly inclined to file suit. It is likely that companies will need to examine their personnel practices continuously, and make changes on an ongoing basis to avoid age discrimination.

These facts are from Sydney P. Freedberg, "Forced Exits? Companies Confront Wave of Age-Discrimination Suits," *The Wall Street Journal*, October 13, 1987, p. 33; Paul Thorne, with David West and Ron Owen, "The Case for Salvaging the 'Throwaway' Executive," *International Management* (May 1987): 49–50; Stephen J. Cabot, "Living with the New Amendments to the Age Discrimination in Employment Act," *Personnel Administrator* 32 (January 1987): 53–54.

Other regulations affecting human resources management include the Equal Pay Act passed in 1963, which mandates that men and women who do equal work must receive the same wage. Wage differences are acceptable only if they are attributed to seniority, performance, and qualifications. The Fair Labor Standards Act, passed in 1938, sets minimum wages and overtime rates. It has been amended many times to raise the minimum wage in relation to the current cost of living. Table 9-2 shows the minimum wages that have

| Year | Minimum Wage | Average Manufacturing Wage | Minimum Wage as a Percentage of Average Manufacturing Wage |
|------|------|------|------|
| 1938 | $0.25 | $0.62 | 40.3% |
| 1939 | 0.30 | 0.63 | 47.6 |
| 1945 | 0.40 | 1.02 | 39.2 |
| 1950 | 0.75 | 1.44 | 52.1 |
| 1956 | 1.00 | 1.95 | 51.3 |
| 1961 | 1.15 | 2.32 | 49.6 |
| 1963 | 1.25 | 2.46 | 50.8 |
| 1967 | 1.40 | 2.82 | 49.6 |
| 1968 | 1.60 | 3.01 | 53.2 |
| 1974 | 2.00 | 4.42 | 45.2 |
| 1975 | 2.10 | 4.83 | 43.5 |
| 1976 | 2.30 | 5.22 | 44.1 |
| 1978 | 2.65 | 6.17 | 43.0 |
| 1979 | 2.90 | 6.70 | 43.3 |
| 1980 | 3.10 | 7.27 | 42.6 |
| 1981 | 3.35 | 7.99 | 41.9 |
| 1987 | 3.35 | 9.81 | 34.2 |

been set over the years and compares them to average manufacturing wages. Most fast-food chains like Wendy's and Burger King pay their workers the minimum wage to keep costs down. The minimum wage was set at $3.35 an hour in 1981.

# ▶ Discrimination in the Work Place

Although the Equal Pay Act of 1963 and the Civil Rights Act of 1964 prohibit discrimination in hiring and compensating workers, inequities still exist in the work place. More and more women are entering the work force (21 million since 1964[1]), yet they are still underrepresented and underpaid relative to men. Figures 9-3, 9-4, and 9-5 illustrate the situation. The situation for minority races, particularly black and Hispanic women, is even worse.

According to a 1987 report on hourly wages issued by the U.S. Census Bureau, women earn 68 cents for every $1 earned by men. (That is the smallest the wage gap has ever been. In 1985, the gap was 65 cents per $1; in 1970, 59 cents per $1). In 1986, women managers earned an average of

**Figure 9-3**

The Wage Gap

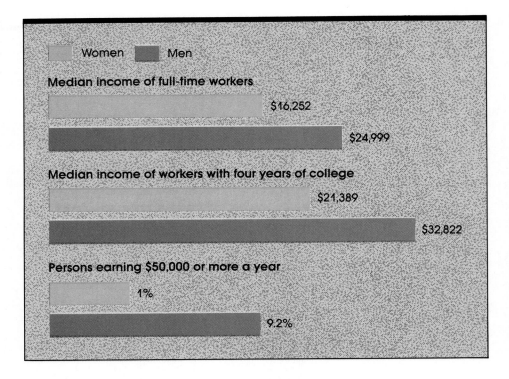

Women    Men

Median income of full-time workers

$16,252

$24,999

Median income of workers with four years of college

$21,389

$32,822

Persons earning $50,000 or more a year

1%

9.2%

$20,000, while their male counterparts earned an average of $31,000.[2] A brief survey of the leading business journals will confirm the relative absence of women, blacks, Hispanics, and Asians from the ranks of corporate America. Women tend to be concentrated in low-paying clerical, sales, and teaching jobs, and in general they do not have as much formal education as do men. The U.S. Census Bureau reported that 57 percent of college-educated American men hold degrees in business, law, medicine, science, and engineering and that 28 percent of college-educated American women hold those degrees. This disparity may account for much of the discrepancy in wages. The situation is even worse for minorities.

**Comparable worth**

The idea that a woman's and a man's pay should be equal when their jobs require equal levels of education, training, skills, responsibility, and effort

One proposed solution to these inequalities has generated much controversy. **Comparable worth** is the idea that a woman's and a man's pay should be equal when their jobs require equal levels of education, training, skills, responsibility, and effort. Establishing comparable worth is not an easy task; it depends on subjective comparisons of jobs and evaluating which jobs performed primarily by men are comparable to jobs performed primarily by women. For example, the skills of a secretary for PepsiCo might be compared to those of a driver for Allied Van Lines.

Proponents say comparable worth will reduce inequities in the system. Opponents argue that it is impossible to decide what is "comparable," and employers say that the very idea of comparable worth is an infringement of their right to use their own pay strategies.[3]

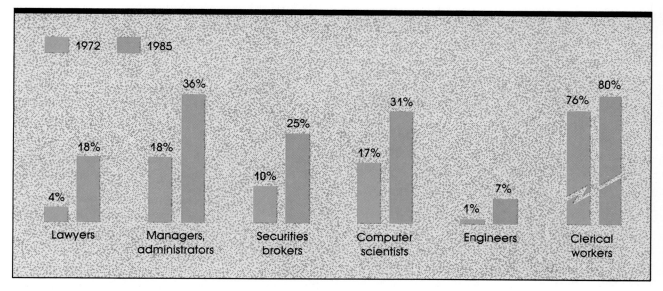

**Figure 9-4**

Percentage of Jobs Held by Women. Source: U.S. Department of Labor.

**Figure 9-5**

Percentage of Women of Childbearing Age Staying in the Workforce. Source: U.S. Department of Labor.

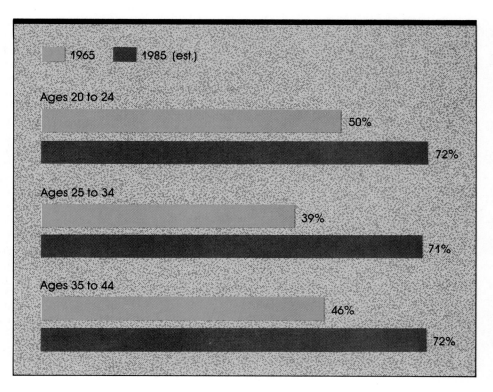

Managers must be aware of these issues and the laws about discrimination when they are considering someone for employment and are determining how much to pay. The laws do not force employers to hire someone just because the applicant is female, black, older; the laws do forbid employers to discriminate against candidates just because they are female, black, or older. Management Encounter 9-3 discusses John Smale of Procter & Gamble and his efforts to hire women at P&G.

# Management Encounter 9-3
## Profile: John Smale of Procter & Gamble

Procter & Gamble (P&G) is one of the largest companies in the United States. With thirteen thousand employed at the company's Cincinnati headquarters, human resources management is no easy task. Nonetheless, Chairman and CEO John Smale knows it is a vital task if the company is to continue introducing successful products like Crest toothpaste and Ivory soap. Procter & Gamble has always been a pioneer in human resources management, and John Smale is continuing the tradition.

John G. Smale was born in Ontario, Canada, in 1927. After earning a business degree from Miami University of Ohio, he went to work for Vick Chemical Company (later Richardson-Vicks, now owned by P&G). He became an entrepreneur in a nose-drop venture for a brief time, but that venture failed. He answered a Procter & Gamble ad in 1952 and has worked for P&G ever since. Smale helped develop Crest toothpaste in the 1950s and steadily progressed through the corporate ranks at P&G. He became company president in 1974 and CEO in 1981. In 1986, he added chairman of the board to his list of accomplishments.

Procter & Gamble, because of its tremendous record of success, is very demanding of its employees. Employees are expected to think up successful new-product ideas, to test those ideas extensively to ensure quality and safety, and to push those ideas aggressively into the market to the consumer. P&G also expects undivided loyalty and expects employees to play by the rules set forth by Procter & Gamble's founders in the 1800s.

In exchange, Procter & Gamble offers its employees many things. Early in its history, the company pioneered traditions like a shorter work week and a profit-sharing plan for employees. In the 1980s, Smale makes sure that the company holds on to its employees by providing some of the best benefits offered by any American company. P&G gives its employees lots of responsibility and rewards them when they come through. It pays well and promotes only from within. It still offers a profit-sharing plan, life and health insurance, and a variety of other benefits. These policies instill strong feelings of loyalty in Procter & Gamble employees. They work hard because they know their efforts will be rewarded and acknowledged. They know that they can rise in the organization just as John Smale did.

Smale is concerned about hiring and keeping women at Procter & Gamble. The company offers a liberal maternity and paternity leave and has provided funding for two day-care centers nearby so that Procter & Gamble mothers and fathers can be near their children. Procter & Gamble extended these policies to cover employees who adopt children. Procter & Gamble understands the problems faced by dual-career couples and tries to help the spouses of new P&G employees find jobs in Cincinnati.

Although managing thirteen thousand employees can tax any manager, Procter & Gamble under the leadership of John Smale is making an effort not only to hire the best employees but to keep them happy. John Smale understands that his employees are the secret ingredient in Procter & Gamble's successful products.

These facts are from Dale Keiger, "John G. Smale: Chairman & CEO, The Procter & Gamble Company," *Sky* 16 (November 1987): 52–59; Julie Franz, "Making the Grade," *Advertising Age*, August 20, 1987, pp. 54–60; and Cecelia Reed, "Leaders of Distinction," *Advertising Age*, August 20, 1987, p. 52.

# ▶ Training and Development

**Training**

Teaching employees at the production level how to do their jobs

**Development**

Teaching managers and professionals how to perform their jobs

The training and development of employees are important aspects of human resources management. **Training** is teaching employees at the production level how to do their jobs, such as teaching cooks at Domino's Pizza how to make pizza. **Development** is teaching managers and professionals how to perform their jobs. For example, even a newly hired chemist who has a doctorate in chemistry must be instructed in the procedures to be followed at Union Carbide after accepting employment there. Development is also used to improve the skills of employees in their present positions and to prepare current employees for increased responsibility and job promotions.

Two types of training programs are common in business today—on-the-job training and classroom training.

## On-the-Job Training

**On-the-job training**

Workers learn by actually performing the tasks of the job

**On-the-job training** allows workers to learn by actually performing the tasks of the job. New employees work under the guidance of an experienced employee who can offer advice and suggestions for performing the job efficiently and effectively. This type of training is often used for operational

**Providing support and leadership.** New employees need the advice and guidance that on-the-job training provides. This claims handler at ITT's Hartford Insurance Group headquarters is getting the benefit of his manager's knowledge.

and production jobs, such as a busboy at Red Lobster or a bottle labeler at Anheuser-Busch.

Some industries use an on-the-job-training method known as apprenticeships. In this system, trainees accompany experienced workers on the job, learning skills and procedures. The apprentice gradually takes on more and more of the tasks until he or she achieves an acceptable level of skill. Electricians often use the apprentice system.

## Classroom Training

**Classroom training** consists of lectures, conferences, videotapes, case studies, and other techniques used in a classroom to teach employees about the job and its requirements. This type of training is often used with complex jobs that require high levels of skill. A store manager for Macy's and an engineer for TRW would receive classroom training. This method lets employees learn the necessary skills without the pressures of the actual job environment.

Sometimes a company realizes that its employees lack skills that are not vital to their jobs but would make them more productive in the long run. Instead of incurring the expense of replacing the employees, the company may elect to offer them specialized training. When Ford Motor Company wanted to institute a job enrichment program, they discovered that many of the assembly-line workers did not have the necessary reading and math skills

**Training and development.**   These bank employees are participating in an intensive two-week training program to develop their skills and learn new techniques in investment banking.

to understand the new program. Ford decided to sponsor basic reading, writing, and math courses for employees who wanted to take them. These training programs enrich the personal lives of the workers, and enhance value of the employees to the company and improve their productivity.[4]

## Assessment Centers

**Assessment centers** are used to identify employees who have managerial potential and to provide them with specialized training. ("Center" is a misnomer because in most companies the assessment center is a program, rather than a specific place). Prospective managers participate in intensive exercises to gauge their management potential. One example is the so-called in-basket simulation, where a managerial candidate is asked to role-play and react to specific scenarios, such as handling a complaint letter from a customer. Trained evaluators carefully observe the candidate's responses. Westinghouse used assessment centers to identify workers who could be promoted to positions of increased responsibility. Assessment centers were first used in World War II by the Office of Strategic Services, the forerunner of the CIA, to select potential spies.

# ▶ Performance Appraisal

**Performance appraisal** is identifying an employee's strengths and weaknesses on the job. It is one of the most difficult tasks for managers. However, performance appraisal is vitally important and has three main objectives:

1. It provides employees with feedback on how they are doing and what they need to do to improve their performance.
2. It provides a basis for determining how to distribute rewards.
3. It provides the organization with information about the quality of its selection, training, and development activities.

There are two basic types of appraisal: objective and subjective. Whether the technique used is objective or subjective, it is vital for the manager to discuss the results with the employee, so that the employee knows how well he or she is doing the job. The results of a performance appraisal become useful only if they are communicated, in a tactful manner, to the employee and are presented as a tool to allow the employee to grow and improve in his or her position and beyond.

## Objective Assessments

An objective assessment is quantifiable. An employee at Texas Instruments might be judged by how many circuit boards he typically produces in one day or by how many of his boards have defects. A Century 21 real estate agent might be judged by the number of houses she has shown or the number of sales she has closed. An organization can also use tests as an objective method of assessment. Whatever method they use, managers must take into account the work environment when they appraise performance objectively.

## Subjective Assessments

When jobs do not lend themselves to objective appraisal, the manager must relate the employee's performance to some other standard. One of the most popular tools used in subjective assessment is the rating scale. A rating scale lists various performance factors on which the manager rates the employee.

# ▶ Promotions, Transfers, and Separations

In the past, employees considered themselves loyal to one company and stayed with the company for most or all of their working life. Today's employees, however, are more likely to change jobs several times as they search for better opportunities. At the same time, many businesses have cut back their work force as they restructure to become more responsive to market concerns. Even so-called "lifetime" employees wonder if their jobs are secure in this time of corporate restructuring. These changes in the work place have resulted in uncertainty for both employers and employees.[5]

Most organizations in the United States experience considerable, costly employee turnover as employees leave for one reason or another. Turnover occurs because of promotions, transfers, and separations.

## Promotions

**Promotion**

An advancement, or vertical movement, within an organization to a position with increased authority, responsibility, and salary

A **promotion** is an advancement, or vertical movement, within an organization to a position with increased authority, responsibility, and salary. In some companies and most labor unions, seniority—the length of time a person has been with the company or at a particular job classification—is the key issue in determining who should be promoted. Most managers base promotions on seniority only when they have candidates with equal qualifications: Managers prefer to base promotions on merit. Eastman Kodak uses merit-based promotions to enhance employees' motivation. Managers, however, should remember the Peter Principle: In any hierarchy, people tend to rise to their level of incompetence. This means that good performance at one job is no guarantee of good performance at another. An employee may be a superior worker on assembly line yet not have the human relations skills to be a good foreman. If this employee is promoted, the organization would lose a good line worker and get an inferior foreman. In such a case, the worker's rewards should be in some form other than promotion.

## Transfers

**Transfer**

A horizontal move from one job to another within a company

A **transfer** is a horizontal move from one job to another within a company; the transferred employee essentially remains at the same wage and job level.

Transfers allow workers to obtain new skills or to find a new position within an organization when their old position has been eliminated because of automation, decreased sales, or some other factor. When Texas Instruments closed its manufacturing plant in College Station, Texas, it tried to transfer as many employees as possible to comparable positions at other Texas Instruments facilities.

## Separations

**Separation**

The departure of the employee from the organization

A **separation** is the departure of the employee from the organization. Separations occur because of resignation, discharge, layoff, and retirement. Resignation is giving up one's job voluntarily. Employees might resign because they find a better job elsewhere or want to go into business for themselves. A discharge is a separation initiated by the employer. Employees may be discharged for poor performance, violation of work rules, absenteeism, and so on. Discharged employees have been fired; employees who have resigned have quit.

A layoff is a suspension of employment due to slow business conditions, the elimination of specific jobs, and/or the closing of work facilities. Layoffs are sometimes temporary; employees may be brought back when business conditions improve. If the layoff is permanent, the employer often helps the individual find another job. When Chrysler Corporation faced bankruptcy in the early 1980s, it closed several of its plants and laid off many workers in an effort to cut costs. However, when Chrysler began to recover, many of the laid-off employees were rehired.

Retirement is separation because of age or after a specified number of years of service. Most workers retire when they reach age 70 and live off a pension provided by their former employer, their savings, or both. Some employees, particularly those in the military, are eligible to retire and receive pensions after twenty years of employment. Many retirees, even after thirty years of service, are still in their fifties and have many more years of productive employment ahead of them. They may put those years to use in self-employment or by working for another organization, while continuing to receive pension income.

A well-organized human resources department strives to minimize losses due to separations and transfers because recruiting and training new employees is very expensive. Employee disciplinary procedures should be carefully explained to all employees and should be set forth in employee handbooks. A high turnover rate in an organization may signal problems with the selection or training process or with the compensation program.

# ▶ Financial Compensation

Designing a fair financial compensation plan for employees is an important task because wages and salaries represent a substantial portion of an organization's expenses. Table 9-3 is a sampling of wages and salaries for a variety of American jobs. Wages and salaries that are too high may result in the

**Table 9.3 Financial Compensation for Various Jobs in the United States, 1986**

Source: *U.S. News & World Reports*, June 23, 1986, pp. 62–63.

Note: The compensation figures here provide recent information on specific jobs unless otherwise noted. They are only samples of what particular jobs in particular locales have paid. Other people holding similar jobs may be compensated differently.

This list may not reveal how much money your colleagues at work get on payday, but it does show amounts received by people in a variety of jobs—from sail seamstress in New England to scriptwriter for "Hill Street Blues." Risking life and limb isn't always reflected in the check. Consider the window washer, 110 stories up, who gets $25,043.

Aerobics instructor ............. per hour, $10
*Nautilus Fitness Factory, Falls Church, Va.*

Aerospace executive
  R. Anderson.................... $3,636,000
*CEO, Rockwell International Corp.*

Air-traffic controller................... $44,430
*O'Hare Airport; 2 years' experience*

Airline captain..................... $125,000
*Pan American Airways 747; 15 years' experience*

Architect of the Capitol ............. $73,600
*Washington, D.C.*

Associate professor of biology ...... $37,000
*Southern Methodist University, Dallas*

Attorney.............................. $25,000
*Public defender's office, New Orleans*

Attorney............................. $150,000
*Partner, 50-member firm, Kansas City, Mo.*

Auto executive Lee Iacocca ... $11,426,000
*CEO, Chrysler Corp.*

Auto-carrier driver.................... $42,000
*Hauls new cars to dealers; Detroit-based*

Ballet dancer ....................... $22,100
*American Ballet Theatre, New York City; starting salary*

Bank executive P. T. Buchanan... $2,533,000
*President, First Boston Corp., New York City*

Bartender ........................... $20,000
*Sloppy Joe's Bar, Key West; including tips*

Basketball player Patrick Ewing .... $750,000
*Center, New York Knicks; base salary*

Bicycle assembler ................... $11,513
*Columbia Mfg. Co., Westfield, Mass.*

Blackjack dealer .................... $29,120
*Trump Casino Hotel, Atlantic City*

Bond trader........................ $150,000
*Major Wall Street firm; plus bonuses*

Boot maker.......................... $12,480
*Tony Lama Boots, El Paso*

Bowling professional Mike Aulby...$201,200
*Professional player of the year 1985*

Brokerage executive D. P. Tully.. $1,301,000
*President, Merrill Lynch & Co.*

Bus driver............................ $25,000
*Greyhound; 10 years' experience*

Cable-car operator................. $29,198
*San Francisco*

Cashier.............................. $6,968
*Zayre Department Store, Macon, Ga.; starting salary*

Chairman, Joint Chiefs of Staff ...... $68,699

Chauffeur ........................... $22,500
*For First Lady Nancy Reagan*

Cheerleader .............. No compensation
*Washington Redskinnettes*

Chemist ............................. $36,000
*Fortune 500 chemical company; Ph.D. degree*

City manager........................ $70,000
*Wichita Falls, Tex.*

Claims adjuster ..................... $29,000
*State Farm Insurance; 5 years' experience*

Coal miner.......................... $32,800
*Fairmont, W.Va.*

Cowboy.............................. $7,200
*Medium-sized ranch, Texas*

Cruise-missile assembler............ $18,770
*San Diego*

Deli clerk........................... $15,000
*Carnegie Delicatessen Restaurant, New York City*

Dentist.............................. $58,590
*Private practice, Illinois; average income*

Drama instructor .................... $44,720
*The American Academy of Dramatic Arts, New York City*

Electrocardiogram technician....... $12,854
*St. Joseph Medical Center, Wichita; 5 years' experience*

Energy executive................... $365,000
*Chief financial officer, Ashland Oil*

Engineer............................. $35,013
*Tennessee Valley Authority; 5 years' experience*

Executive secretary ................. $27,000
*American Motors Corp., Southfield, Mich.*

FBI special agent in charge........ $68,700
*Detroit*

Ferryboat captain .................. $34,052
*New York City*

Film, tape editor .................... $30,000
*CNN, Atlanta*

Financial executive
  Victor Posner................. $12,739,000
*CEO, DWG Corp., Miami*

Firefighter .......................... $26,700
*Wilmington, Del.; 5 years' experience*

Fisherman on scalloper............. $30,000
*New Bedford, Mass.*

Flight attendant.....................$30,500
USAir; 5 years' experience

Football player James Lofton ......$835,000
Wide receiver, Green Bay Packers; not including bonuses

Gardener ...........................$36,000
Beverly Hills; self-employed

Geologist............................$45,000
Major oil firm; M.A. degree, 5 years' experience

Golf professional Nancy Lopez.....$416,472
Winner of 1985 ladies' professional tour

Gravedigger.........................$30,360
San Francisco

Hair stylist Robin Weir ...............$80,000
Many of his Washington, D.C. clients are national political stars

Horse trainer........per horse, per day, $40
Lexington, Ky.

Interpreter...........................$47,972
United Nations, New York City

Investigator..........................$50,354
Nuclear Regulatory Commission

Janitor................................$9,797
Westin Hotel, Atlanta; night shift

Letter carrier........................$24,421
Columbia, S.C.

Librarian.............................$19,008
Chicago Public Library

Lighthouse keeper ..................$13,428
Goat Island Lighthouse, Me.

Loan officer.........................$29,100
Rainier National Bank, Seattle

Longshoreman......................$35,360
New York City

Luggage maker on assembly line ..$16,744
Samsonite Corp. Denver

Lumberjack .........................$32,000
Self-employed, Idaho

Magazine senior editor.............$51,041
Consumer Reports magazine, New York City

Map artist...........................$31,200
National Geographic, Washington, D.C.

Math teacher .......................$17,984
St. John's Prep School, Astoria, N.Y.; M.A. degree and 5 years' experience

Meatcutter..........................$15,288
Esskay Co., Baltimore

Mechanic...........................$31,472
United Airlines; 3 years' experience

Media executive Thomas Murphy ...$625,000
CEO, Cap Cities/ABC

Medical examiner, chief ...........$90,000
Directs staff of 200; New York City

Merger-and-acquisition adviser $1,000,000
Major Wall Street firm

Messenger ..........................$11,000
RCA, Princeton, N.J.

Midwife .............................$23,000
Maternity Center Associates Chartered, Bethesda, Md.; full time, starting salary

Model Linda Spierings...... per day, $3,500
Vogue cover model

Model Christie Brinkley.....per day, $50,000
Typical guarantee

Movie-camera grip........per week, $1,960
Production assistant for Eddie Murphy's new movie, "Golden Child," Los Angeles

Naval officer.........................$34,176
Lieutenant, U.S. Navy; married, 8 years' service; includes living allowance

Newspaper-press operator .........$29,000
The Press, Atlantic City

Night watchman....................$14,000
Metropolitan Museum of Art, New York City

Nurse ...............................$26,885
R.N., Red Cross Blood Donor Center, Detroit

Oil executive
    T. Boone Pickens, Jr..............$8,431,000
CEO, Mesa Petroleum

Opera singer...... per performance, $8,000
Metropolitan Opera; top fee

Operations-facility manager .......$30,000
Nissan auto dealership, Cerritos, Calif.

Personnel director....................$250,000
Large nationwide retailer, Chicago

Pest exterminator....................$25,000
Washington, D.C.

Photographer .............. per day, $2,500
For work on Saks Fifth Avenue national fashion catalog

Physical therapist, nursing home ....$15,000
St. Petersburg, Fla.; starting salary

Playmate of the Month .........fee, $15,000
Playboy magazine

Plastic surgeon.....................$830,000
Beverly Hills

Police officer........................$22,801
Pittsburgh; 1 year's experience

Prison superintendent ...............$56,094
Attica Prison, N.Y.; starting salary

Quality-control manager ............$42,600
Adolph Coors Co., Golden, Colo.

Reporter.............................$66,435
Washington Post; senior position, national staff

Reporter.............................$77,587
National Enquirer; senior position

Reservation clerk....................$12,000
Delta Air Lines; starting salary

Ride operator.....3 summer months, $1,632
Six Flags Over Georgia, Atlanta

Robot repairer .....................$32,677
General Motors, Baltimore

Sail seamstress......................$10,400
East Greenwich, R.I.

Sanitation worker ...................$13,624
Louisville; starting salary

Science teacher.....................$21,320
High school, Sioux Falls, S.D.; M.A. degree and 12 years' experience

Scriptwriter .........................$250,000
"Hill Street Blues"

Secretary............................$15,000
Unemployment office, Youngstown, Ohio; 3 years' experience

Set designer................per play, $1,750
Off-Broadway shows, New York, N.Y.

Sheriff's deputy ......................$24,480
Amarillo, Tex.

Snow-machine operator............$13,000
Vail, Colo.; starting salary

Social worker .......................$16,840
Cuyahoga County, Ohio

Supreme Court Justice............ $104,100
Associate Justice Sandra Day O'Connor

Supreme Court law clerk ...........$31,619
Assistant to Justice O'Connor

Surgeon .............................$67,940
National Institutes of Health; top salary

Telephone lineman .................$32,189
Chicago

Telephone operator ................$21,690
Jackson, Miss.; 6 years' experience

TV actress Cybill Shepherd
    per episode ......................$35,000
"Moonlighting" series

TV news writer.......................$41,190
CBS Evening News, New York City; minimum salary

Theater projectionist ................$23,920
Orson Welles Cinema, Cambridge, Mass.

Ticket host/hostess..................$18,103
Disneyland; 3 years' experience

Toll-booth collector .................$16,581
Pennsylvania Turnpike; 3 years' experience

Union official Jackie Presser........$534,143
President, Teamsters Union; includes expense allowance

Union official Cesar Chavez......... $4,679
President, United Farm Workers

U.S. senator.........................$75,100
Washington, D.C.

Window cleaner ....................$25,043
World Trade Center, New York City

organization's products being priced too high making them uncompetitive in the market. Furthermore, financial compensation can have an impact on employees' morale. When Au Bon Pain restructured the compensation system for store managers, their motivation and profits increased (see the Business Experience at the beginning of this chapter). Remember that compensation is one of the maintenance factors identified by Herzberg. Without adequate pay, employees are likely to become dissatisfied, their work may suffer, and ultimately they may leave the organization.

Designing a fair financial compensation plan is a difficult task because it involves evaluating the relative worth of all jobs within the organization while allowing for individual efforts. Compensation for a specific job is typically determined through a **wage/salary survey**, which is an overview of job evaluations, rates paid by competitors, the cost of living, government legislation, and the organization's ability to pay. Compensation for individuals within a specific job category depends on the compensation for that job and the individual's productivity. Therefore, two employees with identical jobs may not receive exactly the same pay because of individual differences in performance.

Financial compensation falls into two general categories—wages and salaries. **Wages** are financial rewards based on the number of hours the employee works or the level of output achieved. Wages based on the number of hours worked are called time wages. A cook at Denny's, for example, might earn $5 per hour. Time wages are appropriate when employees are continually interrupted and when quality is more important than quantity. Assembly-line workers, clerks, and maintenance personnel are commonly paid on a time-wage basis. The advantage of time wages is the ease of computation. The disadvantage is that time wages provide no incentive to increase productivity. In fact, time wages may encourage employees to do less than a full day's work.

To overcome the disadvantage of time wages, many companies pay on an incentive system, using piece wages or commissions. Piece wages are based on the level of output achieved. Piece wages may be appropriate when the work is standardized and when the output of each employee can be accurately measured. A major advantage of piece wages is that employees are encouraged to supervise their own activities and to increase output. Skilled craftworkers are often paid on a piece-wage basis.

The other incentive system, **commission**, is the payment to the employee of a fixed amount or a percentage of the employee's sales. A car salesman at a Mazda dealership, for example, might receive a specified percentage of the price of each car he sells. This method motivates employees to sell as much as they can. Some companies combine payment based on commission with time wages or salaries.

A **salary** is a financial reward calculated on a weekly, monthly, or annual basis. A personnel manager at Ford Motors might earn $150,000 per year, for example. This compensation method is associated with white-collar workers such as office personnel, executives, and professional employees. Although a salary provides a stable stream of income, salaried workers may be required to work overtime without additional financial compensation.

In addition to the basic wages or salaries paid to employees, management

**Wage/salary survey**

An overview of job evaluations, rates paid by competitors, the cost of living, government legislation, and the organization's ability to pay

**Wages**

Financial rewards based on the number of hours the employee works or the level of output achieved.

**Commission**

The payment to the employee of a fixed amount or a percentage of the employee's sales

**Salary**

A financial reward calculated on a weekly, monthly, or annual basis

**Bonuses**

An addition to regular compensation for exceptional performance

**Profit sharing**

Distributing a percentage of company profits to the employees whose work helped to generate those profits

may wish to offer compensation for exceptional performance as an incentive to increase productivity further. **Bonuses** are an addition to regular compensation for exceptional performance. Many workers receive a bonus at Christmas as a "thank you" for good work and an incentive to continue working hard.

**Profit sharing** involves distributing a percentage of company profits to the employees whose work helped to generate those profits. Some profit-sharing plans involve distributing shares of company stock to employees. Usually referred to as ESOPs—employee stock ownership plans, they have been gaining popularity in recent years. Phillips Petroleum Company and Winn Dixie (a chain of grocery stores) use ESOPs. One reason for the popularity of profit sharing is the sense of partnership that it creates between the organization and employees. Profit sharing can also motivate employees to work hard, because increased productivity and sales mean the profits or the stock dividends will increase.

# ▶ Benefits

**Benefits**

Nonwage and nonsalary forms of compensation

**Benefits**, also known as fringe benefits, are nonwage and nonsalary forms of compensation provided to employees. (Table 9-4 is a listing of various types of financial compensation and benefits.) Examples of employee benefits

**A non-traditional benefit.** Gannett is a trend setter in the area of employee benefits. Many of its employees have taken advantage of its adoption assistance program to create or enlarge their families. The employees feel that Gannett has done them a great service.

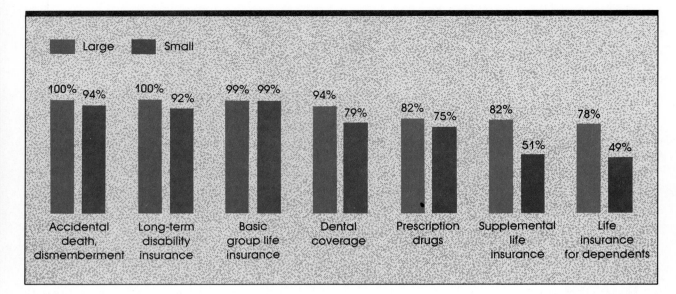

**Figure 9-6**

Percentage of Large and Small Companies Offering Various Employee Benefits. Source: *U.S. News & World Reports*, September 21, 1987, p. 80.

include pension plans, health insurance, life insurance, sick-leave pay, vacation pay, credit unions, health programs, and child care. All companies do not offer all these benefits. Figure 9-6 shows the benefits usually offered by large and small companies. Such benefits increase employee security and, to a certain extent, morale and motivation.

Companies try to provide the benefits they believe their employees want. In response to problems of drug and alcohol abuse by employees, some companies have added drug rehabilitation programs to their list of benefits. Some companies, using flexible benefit programs (often called cafeteria-style benefits programs), allow employees to choose the benefits they would like, up to a specified amount. Over the last two decades, the list of fringe benefits has grown dramatically, and new benefits are being added every year.

Some benefits are required by law. All workers are entitled to Social Security payments upon retirement. Although these payments are not directly provided by businesses, all employers must contribute a percentage of their employees' earnings (around 7 percent each) to the Social Security Fund, which pays benefits to those who have already retired. Employees also contribute to Social Security by having a portion of their income withheld from their pay check. Workers who are injured on the job are entitled to worker's compensation, a program set up in each state, requiring employers to reimburse injured employees for medical expenses and time lost at work. Another state program, unemployment compensation, provides some money for a set period of time to workers who have lost their jobs and who are actively looking for work. Employers are required to contribute to these programs based on a percentage of their employees' earnings.

Employers are not required to provide pensions to retiring employees. However, those that do elect to provide a pension plan must abide by the

| Financial Compensation | Benefits |
|---|---|
| Wages<br>   Time wages<br>   Piece wages<br>Commissions<br>Salaries<br>Bonuses<br>Employee stock ownership plans | Retirement plans<br>Health insurance<br>Life insurance<br>Paid vacation<br>Paid sick leave<br>Credit union services<br>Health programs<br>Child-care services<br>Drug rehabilitation programs |

**Table 9.4  Forms of Financial Compensation and Benefits**

**Employee Retirement Income Security Act (ERISA)**

An act which specifies when and how employees are entitled to receive pensions

**Employee Retirement Income Security Act (ERISA)**, enacted in 1974, which specifies when and how employees are entitled to receive pensions, if they are offered. Pension funds may be insured by the Pension Benefit Guarantee Corporation. ERISA was created to halt abuses of private pension plans, which often denied benefits to workers who thought they were entitled to them.

**Cutting costs by exercising.**   Welders at this Texas plant are a valuable resource to the company. Their efforts to reduce the number of on-the-job accidents are supported by a company-sponsored exercise program.

# ► Industrial Safety

One final aspect of personnel management is the health and safety of an organization's employees. The Occupational Safety and Health Act of 1970 mandates that employers provide safe and healthy working conditions for all workers. The **Occupational Safety and Health Administration (OSHA)** is responsible for enforcing this act. Employers are required to inspect work facilities and remove all hazards. They must also promote job safety and inform employees of their rights and responsibilities. OSHA can make surprise inspections to determine if companies are complying with OSHA regulations. While performing a useful service, OSHA has been criticized by some organizations for excessive paperwork and petty regulations that businesses claim have little impact on health or safety. Recently, OSHA has taken steps to cut back on the paperwork and ease some regulations.

# Notes

1. Martin F. Payson, "Wooing the Pink-Collar Work Force," *Personnel Journal* 63 (January 1984): 50.
2. Beth Brophy, "Are You Making What You're Worth?" *U.S. News and World Reports*, June 23, 1986, p. 61.
3. Bob Arnold, "Why Can't a Woman's Pay Be More Like a Man's?" *Business Week*, January 28, 1985, p. 83.
4. Irwin Ross, "Corporations Take Aim at Illiteracy," *Fortune*, September 26, 1986, pp. 48–54.
5. Don Oldenburg, "Loyalty vs. the Ladder," *The Ann Arbor News*, January 27, 1988, pp. D1-2.

# Summary and Review

► In order to acquire and maintain qualified human resources, management must carry out these functions: planning and forecasting, recruitment and selection, training and development, and compensation.

► In order to acquire human resources, management must recruit applicants from both internal and external sources. The applicants fill out an application form and attend a brief interview. Those who seem acceptable may then undergo testing, and their references will be checked. A follow-up interview is conducted with the remaining applicants. The person or persons who best meet the needs of the company are then offered jobs.

► Managers must be aware of the law in all areas of human resources management. Title VII of the Civil Rights Act (1964) created the Equal Employment

Opportunity Commission to ensure that discrimination is eliminated in the work place. This law also outlaws tests that discriminate against minorities. The Age Discrimination in Employment Act (1967) makes it illegal to discriminate against older persons in the hiring process. The Equal Pay Act (1963) requires that women and men be paid equally for equal work. The Fair Labor Standards Act (1938) sets minimum wages and work times for most jobs. The Occupational Safety and Health Administration Act (1970) created the Occupational Safety and Health Administration to ensure that workers have safe and healthy working conditions.

▶ Wages are financial compensation based on the number of hours worked (time wages) or the number of units produced (piece wages). Commissions are a fixed amount or a percentage of a sale paid as compensation. Salaries are compensation calculated on a weekly, monthly, or annual basis, regardless of the number of hours worked or the number of items produced. Bonuses and profit sharing are types of financial incentives. Benefits are nonwage and nonsalary forms of compensation, such as vacation, insurance, and sick leave.

# Key Terms and Concepts

human resources
planning
job analysis
job description
job specification
job evaluation
recruiting
internal sources
external sources
selection
orientation
Equal Employment Opportunity
    Commission (EEOC)
affirmative action programs
Age Discrimination in Employment
    Act
comparable worth
training
development

on-the-job training
classroom training
assessment centers
performance appraisal
promotion
transfer
separation
wage/salary survey
wages
commission
salary
bonuses
profit sharing
benefits
Employee Retirement Income
    Security Act (ERISA)
Occupational Safety and Health
    Administration (OSHA)

# Checking Your Understanding

This chapter introduced you to the subject of human resources management. To test and reinforce your understanding, fill in the blanks below.

1. _____ is analyzing the current employment situation, forecasting future employment needs, and developing a strategy to met those needs.

2. _____ is forming a pool of qualified applicants from which human resources can be chosen.

3. _____ are compensation based on the number of hours worked or the number of units produced.

4. _____ is the process of introducing new employees to an organization.

5. _____ _____ programs seek to increase job opportunities for women and minorities.

6. _____ _____ _____ is concerned with motivating employees, improving their efficiency, and ensuring that there are sufficient numbers of employees to meet organizational goals.

7. _____ is the process of teaching employees the proper way to perform their job; it is also used to get employees ready to move up in the organization.

8. Job _____ is the determination of information about a specific job, including the skills and knowledge needed to perform it and the environment in which it will be performed.

9. A _____ is an upward movement within a company to a position of increased authority, responsibility and salary.

10. _____ are types of nonwage compensation, such as insurance, vacation and child care.

# Topics for Review and Discussion

1. What activities are involved in acquiring and maintaining the appropriate level of qualified human resources?

2. Which part of the job analysis plays an important role in the selection process? Name the stages of the selection process.

3. What are the two types of training programs common in business today? Relate training programs to kinds of jobs.

4. How are the various types of jobs within an organization compensated?

5. How do federal laws affect the selection process?

6. Relate wages, salaries, bonuses, and benefits to Herzberg's distinction between maintenance and motivation factors.

# Exercises

1. You are a marketing manager at a small bakery. Develop a job description and a job specification for one of your employees.
2. How might a company's recruitment process be affected by the economy?
3. Why, even though there are laws prohibiting discrimination, do women and minorities still generally earn less than white men? Discuss ways to reduce the inequities in the system.
4. Explain how you would go about recruiting and selecting a marketing manager and a bottle distributor if you were a human resource manager for Dr. Pepper.

## Case 9-1
### *Domino's Pizza Employees Deliver*

Home delivery is an important service in the 1980s, and Domino's Pizza is using it to challenge the dominance of hamburger franchises in today's fast-food market. In 1987, Domino's annual sales totaled over $2 billion. The company is growing rapidly, from five hundred stores in 1981 to three thousand in 1987. In 1986, the company opened almost two new stores a day! With such rapid growth, effective training of employees is vital to maintaining the company's quality image. The company's dedication to service helps it deliver pizzas, but Domino's real success comes from the fact that it hires only the best employees and trains them well.

Human resources management at Domino's is a little different than at other growing companies. Domino's managers see themselves as a resource for the workers; their job is to make sure their subordinates succeed. One of the company's seriously taken mottoes is "If you don't make it, bake it, or take it, then you're support for those who do." The company also firmly believes that training is the responsibility of everyone in the organization. To advance in the company, each employee must train someone to take over the responsibilities of his or her present position.

Individual franchise owners or managers train hourly employees right in the store. There are five hourly positions at the store level: order taker, pizza maker, oven tender, router, and driver. Most managers cross-train their crews to fill more than one position in case someone fails to show up for work and to have hands where they're needed during sudden rushes. On-the-job training is supplemented by MTV-style training videos on how to make pizzas, how to deliver pizza safely, security, and customer service. Most of the hourly employees are between 18 and 21 years old, so the music-video approach gets their attention. The videos move fast and are filled with humor and music in addition to information about how to make and deliver pizzas.

Domino's hangs colorful posters with helpful tips over employees' work stations. For instance, near the ovens hang posters showing a perfect pizza and a pizza with several common pizza-making flaws (bubbles, bald spots, and so on) to remind pizza makers what a properly made pizza looks like. Other posters offer driving tips and show a pizza in various stages of preparation.

Managers of Domino's Pizza stores undergo a complex training program before they take over a store. Six courses teach managers-to-be the basics of management, pizza-dough management, people management, cost management, sales building, and training of hourly employees. Most of the managers' training, however, is on-the-job training at various stores. Trainees are given more and more responsibility as they move through four successive levels. They are evaluated after each level according to specifically defined behavior standards (such as consistently offering a friendly greeting to customers). The standards get tougher at each level. At level 1, a trainee must make up and sauce two trays of large and small pizzas in less than twelve minutes; at level 4, a trainee must complete the task (known as Two Tray Time) in less than seven minutes.

Domino's rewards its employees well. After one year, successful store managers can apply to become franchise owners. In fact, only Domino's managers can obtain a Domino's franchise, because they know the company far better than someone who comes from outside. The company also offers from $20 to $1,000 for employee suggestions that the company uses. The company thus gets the benefit of constructive ideas and encourages employees to be independent and innovative.

The company sponsors an annual Two Tray Time competition as well as a Domino's Pizza Distribution Olympics for its distribution subsidiary. These contests encourage employees to try to be the fastest and best pizza makers and ultimately increase the quality of service on a store level. They also generate good-natured competition within each store and between stores.

Domino's advertises its "30 minutes or it's free" policy in some areas and in other areas, $3 off the price if delivered late, so everyone, from hourly workers on up, must make and deliver pizzas quickly. Order takers are expected to answer the phone within three rings and take an entire order in forty-five seconds. Pizza makers have one minute to make up a pizza and get it into the oven. With those requirements, employees have to know what they are doing and get it right the first time. Quality training with a dash of fun and competition helps workers reach those goals.

---

These facts are from Dale Feuer, "Training for Fast Times," *Training* 24 (July 1987): 25–30; "A Gold Medal Boost to Morale at Domino's Pizza," *Personnel Journal* 66 (August 1987): 23, 25; John Hillkirk, "Domino's Service No Game," *USA Today*, July 21, 1987, p. 78; Raymond Serafin, "Domino's Getting a Noid," *Advertising Age*, September 22, 1986, p. 127; and Kevin T. Higgins, "Home Delivery Is Helping Pizza to Battle Burgers," *Marketing News*, August 1, 1986, pp. 1, 6.

**Questions**

1. How does Domino's attitude toward human resources differ from other growing companies?
2. Comment on Domino's philosophy that "If you don't make it, bake it, or take it, then you are support for those who do."
3. How is human resources management geared for the average 18 to 21 year old employee?

## Case 9-2
## *Toyota Selects Employees for New Plant in Kentucky*

In 1986, Toyota Motors began building an $800 million plant in Georgetown, Kentucky. The company hoped the plant would be turning out two hundred thousand cars a year by the early 1990s. Locating an automobile production facility in Kentucky presented Toyota with a unique human resources problem—where to find three thousand qualified workers with industrial experience in a predominantly rural area. Toyota's solution was to implement a selection process consisting of written tests, work-place simulations, and an in-depth interview.

Toyota took such painstaking efforts because it wanted to hire only workers who would be comfortable with the Toyota philosophy, which emphasizes teamwork, corporate loyalty, and job versatility. The company could afford to be choosy because more than forty thousand people applied for twenty-seven hundred production jobs and three hundred office jobs. Toyota gave preference in hiring to residents of Kentucky, because the state desperately needed the jobs.

Toyota's hiring practices departed radically from the practices traditionally used by American automakers. In the past, an applicant who knew someone who worked in the plant, or who had some manufacturing experience, was seriously considered for employment. Toyota, however, required all applicants to take a series of tests, regardless of the positions for which they were applying.

The initial testing covered reading and math, manual dexterity, and technical knowledge. Subjective tests covering human relations skills and tests covering literary and technical knowledge were given. Applicants were asked to rank features of an automobile according to how well buyers would accept them. Other tests had questions on manufacturing and making repairs, but not repairs on cars, because Toyota was more interested in attitude than in experience. Applicants applying for even the lowest-paying jobs had to go through at least fourteen hours of testing.

Applicants next underwent work-place simulations developed for Toyota by an outside consultant. The simulations exposed applicants to a variety of hypothetical situations. They included mock production lines, where applicants were instructed to assemble tubes on circuit boards to show whether they could do tedious work at a fast pace yet remain alert. Such simulations are typically used by American businesses to identify workers with managerial potential. Toyota, however, administered the simulations to both blue- and white-collar applicants.

Only one in twenty advanced to the interview stage. The interviews were conducted by a panel of representatives from various Toyota departments. Employees who came across well in the interview were given a physical examination and a drug test.

Some United Auto Workers officials believed that one goal of Toyota's hiring procedure was to identify and weed out applicants who might be interested in organizing a union. Toyota was not receptive to UAW efforts to organize at Georgetown. Before the plant was built, Toyota had been involved in a national union protest after the Japanese construction manager for the plant said he wanted to use nonunion contractors. Toyota nevertheless insisted throughout the construction of the plant that it was not anti-union.

Toyota's hiring practices at Georgetown came under fire from minority groups after the prime minister of Japan made a derogatory remark about the intelligence of American minorities. However, Toyota hired minorities in proportion to the percentage of minority applications received, although a substantially lower number was hired for managerial positions. State officials met regularly with Toyota during the selection process and concluded that all applicants were being given a fair opportunity.

Toyota was successful in hiring workers only from Kentucky, with the exception of a small number of skilled craftworkers. Thus far, the company seems happy with its American workers. Its extensive selection process enabled it to choose people who are well suited for the job and who fit into Toyota's family of workers. Toyota's efforts are likely to help open the door for other foreign companies that want to build manufacturing plants in the United States.

---

These facts are from Richard Koenig, "Toyota Takes Pains, and Time, Filling Jobs at Its Kentucky Plant," *The Wall Street Journal*, December 1, 1987, pp. 1, 29; Eugene Carlson, "What's a Toyota Plant Worth to Kentucky? Possibly Plenty," *The Wall Street Journal*, June 9, 1987, p. 31; and Joel Dreyfuss, "Toyota Takes Off the Gloves," *Fortune*, December 22, 1986, pp. 77–84.

## Questions

1. What are the long run implications for Toyota's use of testing to hire its employees? Discuss the advantages and disadvantages.
2. What problems could develop if Toyota fails to consider the rights and needs of American minorities?
3. What advantages did Toyota have over American companies in developing its human resources?

# Answers to Checking Your Understanding

1. planning
2. recruiting
3. wages
4. orientation
5. affirmative action
6. human resources management
7. training
8. analysis
9. promotion
10. benefits

# Outline

# Chapter 10

# Labor Unions and Labor Management

## Objectives

After reading this chapter, you will be able to:

▶ Describe the functions and identify two types of labor unions.

▶ Discuss the history of unionization and union-related legislation in the United States.

▶ Describe collective bargaining, contract negotiations, dispute resolution, and labor and management tactics.

▶ Speculate about the future of organized labor.

# Business Experience

On September 21, 1987, players in the National Football League went on strike—that is, they refused to play scheduled football games for the team owners—for the second time in six years. The main issue of the strike was free agency. The players' union, the NFLPA, demanded that any player with more than four years of experience, regardless of salary, be able to choose the team that he wanted to play for. The team owners, however, wanted compensation whenever they lost a free agent. According to Gene Upshaw, then executive director of the NFLPA, free agency meant more to the players than money: "It's not about money, it's about dignity and freedom. It's about who you work for."

Salary was not an issue because the players had won salary increases in a strike in 1982. Between 1982 and 1987, the average NFL player's salary nearly tripled. Other, less important issues of the 1987 strike dealt with pension size and roster size. Nevertheless, according to the management council representing NFL team owners, free agency was the only issue not resolved before the players' strike deadline.

The owners were in favor of liberalizing the free-agent system, but because of the large increase in players' salaries, they were against the changes proposed by the NFLPA. Team owners wanted to fight the issue through labor negotiations instead of through the courts because they were afraid of having to pay damages if they lost an antitrust lawsuit.

When the strike began, most players were in favor of it. As the weeks dragged on, however, more players began to question the issues behind the strike. Some players crossed picket lines and returned to the football field, joining the non-union "scab" players signed by the owners to play games during the strike. With player salaries at an all-time high, the players were unhappy about the NFLPA's focus on the stalemate issue of free agency. In addition, some players worried that a long strike could also reduce their income from endorsements.

Negotiations between the NFLPA and owners stalled, but it was obvious the owners were winning. The owners were not in a hurry to settle the strike: Some of the "scab" teams were earning higher profits than the NFL teams because the "scab" players received lower salaries. The players' union position began to weaken, and the owners increased some of their demands.

On October 15, 1987, the players abandoned the strike. They returned to work without a written contract spelling out the conditions for work for both the players and the owners. Most players were glad that the strike was over, but they did not like the way the owners treated them during the strike. The players believed the owners were out to break the union. According to Gene Upshaw, "The owners have refused to deal fairly with the players and have abused their monopoly powers to the extreme detriment of the players." As a result of these actions, the NFLPA filed an antitrust suit against the National Football League in a federal court, accusing the league and the owners of conspiring to limit competition for players' services.

---

These facts are from Dave Goldberg, "Strike! Players Walk for Freedom to Pick Where They Work," *The Bryan–College Station Eagle*, September 22, 1987, pp. 1B, 3B; Hal Lancaster and Peter W. Barnes, "Delay of Game: Big Stakes in NFL Strike," *The Wall Street Journal*, September 23, 1987, pp. 33, 45; Alex Kotlowitz, "Broken Play: Labor Experts Fault Football Players' Strike Strategy," *The Wall Street Journal*, October 14, 1987, p. 33; Robert Johnson, "Team Owners Discover the Strike Brings a Big Benefit: An Improved Bottom Line," *The Wall Street Journal*, October 14, 1987, p. 33; Dave Goldberg, "Back to Work for the Union," *The Bryan–College Station Eagle*, October 16, 1987, pp. 1C, 3C; Larry Weisman, "Players End NFL Strike," *USA Today*, October 16, 1987, pp. 1, 2C.

# Introduction

The labor force consists of all the individuals who wish to work—including those who are actually working and those who want to work but are unable to find employment. The current civilian labor force in the United States numbers approximately 105 million people, of whom more than 20 million are members of labor unions. Because of this large membership and the legal rights granted unions by the federal government, organized labor exercises considerable power in its dealings with management, and thus labor relations and labor management are important issues for managers.

## ▶ Rationale For Labor Unions

**Labor union**

A group of workers who have joined together to deal with employers

A **labor union** is a group of workers who have joined together to deal with employers and to achieve objectives such as better pay, better (fewer) hours, and better working conditions. Employees who are dissatisfied with their working conditions or compensation have to negotiate with management to bring about change. However, dealing with management on an individual basis is not always effective, so employees may organize themselves into labor unions. Unionized employees are backed by the power of a large group that can hire specialists to represent the entire union in its dealings with management. The United Auto Workers, for example, have tremendous power in their negotiations with Ford Motor Company, General Motors, and Chrysler Corporation. The Teamsters, the Screen Actors Guild, the United Steel Workers, and other unions are similarly powerful.

## ▶ Types of Unions

There are two types of labor unions: craft unions and industrial unions. Craft unions represent workers, such as painters, carpenters, and electricians, in a specific craft or trade, regardless of industry. Industrial unions represent workers in a specific industry, and membership is open to all workers in that industry without regard to skill or trade. The United Auto Workers and the United Mine Workers are industrial unions. Management Encounter 10-1 describes union efforts to organize the health care industry.

## ▶ History of Labor Unions in America

The Industrial Revolution brought far-reaching changes to the American work place in the nineteenth and early twentieth centuries. Large factories

## Management Encounter 10-1

### *Unionization of the Health Care Industry*

Hospitals and other health care facilities have become a hotbed for union-organizing activities in the past few years. Between 1980 and 1985, union membership among the 6.9 million doctors, nurses, medical technicians, and others involved in the health care industry increased from 14 percent to 20 percent. During the same period, union membership in all other industries declined from 23 percent to 18 percent of the work force. In a sense, health care workers are the new hope of the troubled American labor movement.

In the past, unions worked hard to recruit members in the service industry (including health care workers) but lacked the issues needed for success. Today, many unions have shifted their focus from issues that mainly concern factory workers to issues that are important to health care and other service workers.

Health care workers are interested in organizing into unions because of economic factors such as deregulation, increased competition among health care facilities, and especially fears about job security. The trend in the 1980s of mergers and restructuring among health care facilities resulted in the closing of many financially weak institutions and the loss of thousands of jobs.

In order to meet the needs of health care workers, some unions have hired staff specialists who are trained to deal with professionals like nurses and dietitians. These specialists are often college graduates who understand the jargon used by health care professionals as well as the issues that professionals feel are important.

Even doctors are becoming interested in joining unions. Doctors, along with other health care workers, are feeling the effects of cost-cutting measures implemented by many hospital administrators. These measures often reduce the number of patients that doctors see and limit doctors' salaries. Thus, doctors are beginning to view unions as a means of increasing their bargaining power with management.

Hospitals and other health care facilities are not happy about the unionization of health care workers. In fact, union leaders have accused many hospitals and other health care facilities of delaying organization efforts in an attempt to decrease workers' interest. Most administrators believe that unions contribute to the rising cost of health care and hinder scheduling efforts. They believe that unions lead to understaffing and overstaffing problems (because union employees say that specific tasks are "not their job" or because employees from different unions claim responsibility for specific tasks), causing problems with the quality of patient care.

Despite administrators' objections, the unionization of the health care industry is likely to continue. Unions are pleased with the prospects of growth in this sector. As one labor expert put it, "Health care is for unions what the auto industry was in the 1930s."

These facts are from Kevin Kelly and Hazel Bradford, "Labor May Have Found an Rx for Growth," *Business Week*, February 22, 1988, pp. 162, 164, 166; David Burda, "Unions, Hospitals Make Final Pitches on Bargaining Unit Ruling," *Modern Healthcare*, November 6, 1987, p. 118; and Brian McCormick, "Union Activity on the Rise, New AHA Report States," *Hospitals*, December 5, 1986.

and specialized workers replaced traditional small shops and jack-of-all-trades' workers. Specialization and division of labor were the key to industrial growth.

Technological progress and improved living standards were positive results of those changes; long working hours and unsafe working conditions were negative results. At the end of the nineteenth century, the typical work week was sixty hours, and in some industries workers labored as many as eighty-four hours a week. Specialization resulted in boring and tedious work, and the compensation was poor—so poor that many women and children were forced to enter the labor market in order for their families to survive. In 1910, approximately 2 million teenagers and children (some as young as 4

**Pride in America.** The International Ladies Garment Workers Union (ILGWU) members celebrated their founding by wearing period costumes in a New York City parade. Unions offer opportunities for socializing as well as for protesting.

years old) were working for $1 or $2 a week in the clothing and glass industries. Safety standards were virtually nonexistent; injury and death were common. Job security was unheard of: Workers had jobs when the factories prospered but were laid off during economic downturns. There were no unemployment compensation programs to support workers who had lost their jobs; they were totally dependent on the factories for their livelihood.

Workers became dissatisfied with their jobs and wanted some drastic changes in the way employers treated them. Realizing that individual efforts would not bring about the changes that were so badly needed, employees banded together to force management to improve working conditions and raise their wages to a level at which they could survive.

## Early Unionization Efforts

The real impact of organized labor was not felt until the late nineteenth century. Nevertheless, there were several early attempts by employees to join forces to improve conditions. These first unions, or associations, were loosely knit local groups and were generally short-lived. Their primary function was to provide support to members and their families in the event of serious illness, death, or debt. Other early unions sought to bring job-related problems to management's attention, in addition to providing support for members and their families. In 1786, printers in Philadelphia organized and established the first minimum wage in the United States—$1 a day. A century later, streetcar conductors in New York City organized to reduce their workday to twelve hours. However, these and other early organizing efforts accomplished little.

# Knights of Labor

**Knights of Labor**

The first national labor union

The **Knights of Labor**, founded in 1869, was the first national labor union. It began as a secret society for Philadelphia garment workers. Despite opposition from employers, membership grew to more than seven hundred thousand by 1886. Like the earlier unions, the Knights of Labor ran into problems. Some members wanted the federal government to manage all the factories. Other members opposed such socialistic tendencies and wanted to work for improvements in compensation, hours, and working conditions. In 1886, the Knights of Labor were publicly condemned when a bomb exploded at a rally in Chicago's Haymarket Square and killed several people. The rally was organized to call attention to the Knights' demands for a shorter work week. Although the Knights of Labor were not accused of setting the bomb, they quickly lost favor with the public as a result of it. The internal conflict and the Haymarket incident led to the dissolution of the Knights of Labor later that year.

# American Federation of Labor

**American Federation of Labor (AFL)**

Formed by the merger of one faction of the Knights of Labor with a group of unaffiliated craft unions

Samuel Gompers formed the **American Federation of Labor (AFL)** in 1886 by merging one faction of the Knights of Labor (the group favoring private ownership of factories) with a group of unaffiliated craft unions. The AFL focused on improving wages, hours, and working conditions instead of trying to change the economic system, as some of the Knights of Labor had wanted to do. Gompers believed that negotiation between labor and management could lead to improved working conditions. By 1902 membership in the AFL reached 1 million, and by 1920 75 percent of all union members belonged to the AFL. Growth slowed in the 1920s because there were few skilled craftworkers left to organize.

# Congress of Industrial Organizations

**Congress of Industrial Organizations (CIO)**

A national labor union which focused on the affiliation of individual industrial unions

Several AFL unions organized workers in specific industries, regardless of the craft involved. These efforts were extremely successful in the communications, mining, newspaper, steel, rubber, and automobile industries. In 1937, these industrial unions left the AFL and formed the **Congress of Industrial Organizations (CIO)**. The CIO, like the AFL, was a national labor union. The CIO, however, focused on the affiliation of individual industrial unions. In the ten years after its establishment, the CIO grew in power and came to rival the AFL.

# AFL-CIO

**AFL-CIO**

A federation of craft and industrial unions

In 1955 the AFL and the CIO joined together to form the **AFL-CIO**, which is a federation of unions—both craft and industrial. Although this federation does not negotiate with management, it does serve its member unions in several ways:

1. The AFL-CIO speaks for the entire American labor movement before Congress and other branches of government.

**A show of solidarity.** Representatives from various unions march together to show their support for labor's right to organize.

2. The AFL-CIO represents American labor in world affairs through participation in the International Labor Organization (a United Nations agency) and through contact with other labor organizations throughout the free world.
3. The AFL-CIO helps to organize workers all over the country.
4. The AFL-CIO helps coordinate activities such as community services, political action, and voter registration.

The AFL-CIO represents approximately 54 percent of all unions. Nearly 70 percent of all individual union members are affiliated through their unions with the AFL-CIO. Affiliated unions represent all kinds of workers—from movie stars to postal workers, from bricklayers to newspaper reporters. Table 10-1 lists the largest labor unions affiliated with the AFL-CIO. Management Encounter 10-2 profiles Richard Trumka, UMW leader, who wants to integrate the miners' union with the AFL-CIO.

## ▶ Labor-Management Legislation

The development of labor unions gave power to workers, but it generated problems as well. Throughout the history of unionization, management and unions have resorted to various tactics to accomplish their goals; the results have sometimes been violent. At first the government protected the labor unions with legislation to limit the activities of management. However, as the

**Table 10-1 AFL-CIO Labor Unions with 100,000 or More Members, 1985**

Source: American Federation of Labor and Congress of Industrial Organizations, Washington, D.C., "Report of the AFL-CIO Executive Council," in U.S. Bureau of the Census, *Statistical Abstract of the United States, 1987*, Washington, D.C., 1987, p. 408.

* Data for Teamsters Union is not available in this source. The Teamsters rejoined the AFL-CIO in 1987.

| Union | Members × 1,000 | Union | Members × 1,000 |
|---|---|---|---|
| Teamsters* | 2,000 | Plumbers and Pipefitters | 226 |
| State, County, Municipal | | Garment Workers | 210 |
| Employees | 997 | Government Employees | 199 |
| Food and Commercial | 989 | Electrical and Technical | |
| Automobile Workers | 974 | Workers | 198 |
| Electrical Workers | 791 | Letter Carriers | 186 |
| Service Employees | 688 | Fire Fighters | 142 |
| Carpenters | 609 | Printing and Graphic Workers | 141 |
| Steel Workers | 572 | Iron Workers | 140 |
| Communications Workers | 524 | Painters | 133 |
| Machinists | 520 | Bakery, Confectionery, and | |
| Teachers | 470 | Tobacco Workers | 115 |
| Laborers | 383 | Boilermakers | 110 |
| Operating Engineers | 330 | Oil, Chemical Workers | 108 |
| Hotel and Restaurant Workers | 327 | Retail, Wholesale Employees | 106 |
| Postal Workers | 232 | Rubber Workers | 106 |
| Paperworkers | 232 | Railway Clerks | 102 |
| Clothing and Textile Workers | 228 | | |

unions grew more powerful, the government passed legislation to limit their power. An examination of labor legislation reflects the attitudes of management and government toward the labor movement. Managers are well advised to understand this legislation because these laws affect their relations with organized labor.

# Norris-LaGuardia Act

**Injunction**

A court order that prohibits employees from participating in union activities

Prior to the Norris-LaGuardia Act, employers frequently sought an **injunction** (court order) to prevent employees from participating in union activities. Injunctions could prohibit a strike (walkout by employees), picketing (patrolling the entrances of a plant to alert the public that union members are on strike), or participating in a union membership drive. Further, as a condition of employment, employers could require workers to agree to a yellow-dog contract (a contract prohibiting membership in a union). Any employee who broke the contract could be fired and blacklisted by the employer. The blacklist was a list of workers to be barred from employment because of their union activities. Employers circulated the blacklist among themselves and refused to hire the workers named on it.

**Norris-LaGuardia Act**

An act which outlawed yellow-dog contracts and blacklists and made it more difficult for management to obtain injunctions

In 1932 Congress passed the **Norris-LaGuardia Act,** which outlawed yellow-dog contracts and blacklists and made it more difficult for management to obtain injunctions. The Norris-LaGuardia Act was the first act of Congress clearly aimed at protecting the rights of unions.

# Wagner Act

Prior to the Wagner Act, also known as the National Labor Relations Act, union activities were often viewed (usually by management) as monopolistic and therefore illegal under the Sherman Antitrust Act. In 1935 Congress

## Management Encounter 10-2

### Profile: Richard Trumka of the UMW

At age 32, Richard Trumka became one of the youngest leaders of a major union in the United States when he was elected president of the United Mine Workers (UMW) in 1982. In 1987, unopposed, he was re-elected to another five-year-term. Trumka is probably the most popular leader with UMW members since John L. Lewis, who led the union for forty years.

Richard Trumka grew up in western Pennsylvania and worked for seven years in the coal mines there. His father and grandfather were miners. As a boy, Trumka asked his grandfather how he could help miners. His grandfather told him to become a union lawyer and defend his fellow miners. Trumka proceeded to do just that. He earned a degree in accounting from Penn State and a law degree from Villanova University.

Trumka is one of the rising young stars of the labor movement. His irrepressible ego and articulate public speaking skills have made him a successful union negotiator. Some union watchers believe that Trumka has the potential to become one of the best labor leaders in many years.

Trumka's personality and style have helped him make major changes in the UMW. He centralized power by eliminating the union's bargaining council, which reviewed contracts on a regional basis before members voted on them. Contracts are now sent directly to members after Trumka has reviewed them. Union officials believe this move helped restore order to the negotiating process. Trumka also strengthened the union's financial position and hired new, educated staff members who have improved service to members in areas such as health, safety, and grievances.

Trumka has attracted attention outside of the UMW. An outspoken critic of apartheid, in 1986 he initiated a boycott against Shell Oil, which owns coal mines in the United States, for doing business in South Africa. Trumka also spends time lobbying Congress on trade, imports, and health and safety issues. His efforts have increased the UMW's political power.

Trumka has moved to integrate the UMW into the rest of the labor movement. In 1987, he tried to merge the UMW with the Oil, Chemical, and Atomic Workers (OCAW). The merger fell through, but Trumka has not given up the idea because a merger with the OCAW would mean AFL-CIO membership for the United Mine Workers. He regularly speaks at AFL-CIO rallies and has even addressed an AFL-CIO convention. Some observers believe that Trumka may get a shot at the presidency of the AFL-CIO in a few years, even though the UMW is not part of the AFL-CIO. Regardless of what happens, Trumka's efforts with the UMW have endeared him to union members and have transformed a formerly weak union into a powerful labor organization.

These facts are from Rick Wartzman, "UMW Chief's Merger Plan Falls Through," *The Wall Street Journal*, February 25, 1988, p. 27; Hazel Bradford and Michael Schroeder, "Today, the Mine Workers—Tomorrow, the AFL-CIO," *Business Week*, February 15, 1988, pp. 65–66; and Rick Wartzman, "As UMW Leader Trumka Is Sworn In, Chance of New Pact by Christmas Fades," *The Wall Street Journal*, December 23, 1987, p. 23.

---

**Wagner Act**

Recognized employees' right to negotiate with employers

**National Labor Relations Board (NLRB)**

A board that supervises union elections and polices management policies regarding unions

passed the **Wagner Act,** which recognized employees' right to negotiate with employers and thus legalized collective bargaining. This act required employers to bargain with their employees' elected representatives, if a majority of the employees decided to be represented by a union. The act prohibited management from interfering in union activities: Employers could no longer fire workers for joining a union; they could not refuse employment to those who supported union causes; they could not threaten to close the organization if workers elected to join a union; and they could not interfere with union administration. Finally, the Wagner Act set up the **National Labor Relations Board (NLRB)** to supervise union elections and police management policies regarding unions.

# Taft-Hartley Act

Prior to the Taft-Hartley Act, public attention was focused on the rights of unions. The unions had grown very powerful with the passage of legislation in their favor, and they learned quickly how to use the power given to them by Congress. Strikes (sometimes violent) in the steel, coal, and shipping industries paralyzed the nation and alarmed the public. Fighting broke out between unions competing for jurisdiction over groups of workers and resulted in more strikes and violence. In 1947 Congress passed the **Taft-Hartley Act,** which was designed to balance the power between unions and management. The Taft-Hartley Act focused on the rights of management and regulated certain labor practices: closed and union shops, featherbedding, secondary boycotts, and strikes without notice.

A **closed shop** was a factory or other business establishment in which management could hire only union members. Workers had to join the union before being hired and had to remain members of the union in order to continue working. The unions argued that closed shops were necessary for three reasons:

1. If all employees were union members, management would have to recognize the union.
2. One hundred percent union membership gave unions unquestionable power in the areas of wages and working conditions.
3. All employees benefited from union contracts; therefore, all employees should support the union.

Management cited three reasons for outlawing closed shops:

1. Forcing workers to join a union as a condition of employment violates a fundamental principle of freedom.
2. Limiting employment to union members may prevent management from hiring the best-qualified individuals.
3. Guaranteed membership might induce union leaders to become irresponsible and dishonest with their members.

The Taft-Hartley Act supported the management view and declared closed shops illegal.

A **union shop** is a factory or other business establishment in which management may hire any qualified employee, but after a specified period of time, the employee must join the union. The Taft-Hartley Act did not outlaw union shops; however, it did allow individual states to outlaw them. Laws banning union shops are called **right-to-work laws** because they ensure that all employees have the right to work without being forced to join a union. Figure 10-1 shows the states that now have such laws.

Not affected by the Taft-Hartley Act is the **agency shop,** a factory or other business establishment in which all qualified workers may be hired and union membership is not required. Nonmembers, however, are required to pay the union a fee that is equivalent to union dues. The rationale for this arrangement

**Taft-Hartley Act**

An act designed to balance the power between unions and management

**Closed shop**

A factory or other business establishment in which management could hire only union members

**Union shop**

A factory or other business establishment in which management may hire any qualified employee, but after a specified period of time, the employee must join the union

**Right-to-work-laws**

Laws that ensure that all employees have the right to work without being forced to join a union

**Agency shop**

A factory or other business establishment in which union membership is not required

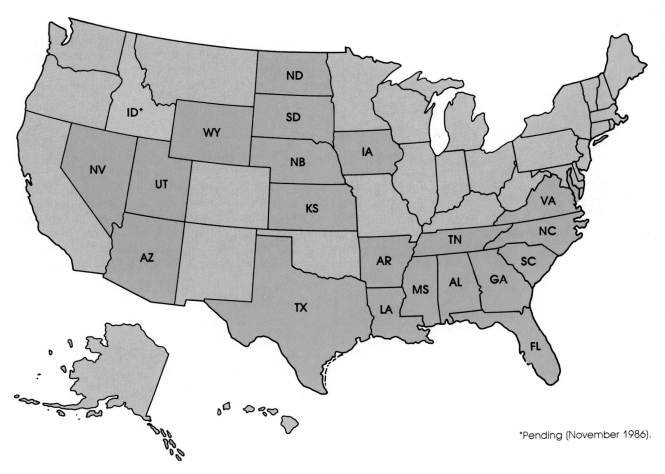

*Pending (November 1986).

**Figure 10-1**

States with Right-to-Work Laws

is that because all employees benefit from union negotiations, all employees should support the union financially.

As a result of the Taft-Hartley Act, unions could no longer refuse to negotiate with management, and they could not strike without first giving sixty days' notice. The act also prohibited **featherbedding**—the practice of requiring an employer to hire unnecessary workers or assign unnecessary work. Also outlawed were **secondary boycotts**—boycotts or work stoppages by union members against their employer in order to force their employer to stop dealing with other firms that are involved in labor disputes. For instance, if the United Steel Workers went on strike against USX and other steel manufacturers, the United Auto Workers might show their support for the Steel Workers by striking Ford or General Motors to force the auto maker to stop buying steel from the companies involved in the dispute with the Steel Workers.

There are many other provisions in the Taft-Hartley Act. Management can sue unions for breach of contract. Employers can engage in anti-union

**Featherbedding**

The practice of requiring an employee to hire unnecessary workers or assign unnecessary work

**Secondary boycotts**

Boycotts or work stoppages by union members against their employer in order to force their employer to stop dealing with other firms that are involved in labor disputes

activities. Unions must disclose financial information to their members and cannot use union dues for political contributions. Unions cannot charge excessive initiation fees. The president of the United States can ask the courts for an eighty-day suspension of threatened strikes that "imperil the national health and safety." The National Labor Relations Board implements the provisions of the Taft-Hartley Act.

## Landrum-Griffin Act

**Landrum-Griffin Act**

Guarantees all union members the right to vote in union elections, to speak at union meetings, and to see union financial reports

In 1959 Congress passed the **Landrum-Griffin Act,** which is in essence a bill of rights for union members. The act was a response to public pressure to stop the growing corruption and violence of labor unions—a Senate investigation had discovered that some unions were involved in blackmail, embezzlement, arson, and even murder. The act guarantees all union members the right to vote in union elections, the right to speak at union meetings, and the right to see union financial reports. In addition, the Landrum-Griffin Act requires unions to make the following information available to the secretary of labor:

1. union constitutions and bylaws.
2. annual financial reports.
3. financial transactions made by union officials.
4. notice of the calling of union meetings. The act also requires regularly scheduled elections of union officers by secret ballot.

## Impact of Labor Legislation

A look at the early attempts to organize and the current state of labor organization reveals that the impact of labor legislation has been vast. No longer does management consider union members ungrateful or disloyal. Union membership is now seen as a right of employees. The laws acknowledge, however, that employers have a right to run a business and earn a profit. Legal recognition of the right to organize and bargain has led to peaceful and constructive solutions to conflicts between employees and employers.

# ▶ Unionization

Before a union can represent the employees at a Honda plant, a Bethlehem Steel foundry, or any other company, a number of events must take place. A majority of the employees must select a union to represent them. The union must be certified by the National Labor Relations Board. Management must recognize the union as the legal negotiator for all employees. The process of unionization is illustrated in Figure 10-2. The movie *Norma Rae*, which was based on the true story of one woman's effort to unionize employees in the garment factory where she worked, is a realistic portrayal of the process.

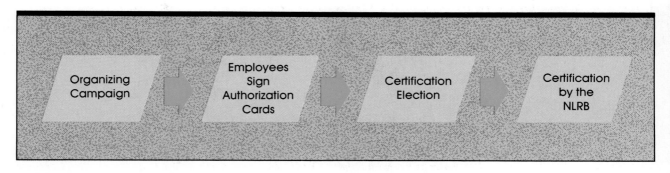

**Figure 10-2**

The Union Organization Process

## The Organizing Campaign

Occasionally, the employees of an organization invite a union to represent them. Most of the time, however, a union initiates the organizational campaign. Union members approach workers and describe what the union can do to improve working conditions. When union organizers feel they have generated enough interest, union officials will ask employees to sign an authorization card to signify their desire for union representation. When at least 30 percent of the employees have signed authorization cards, the union asks the company management to recognize the union as the official representative of all employees. Management seldom agrees to do this, so the union must call for an election.

## The Certification Election

After the company refuses to recognize the union, union officials usually file a request with the National Labor Relations Board for a certification election—a secret-ballot election conducted by the NLRB. If the union does not receive a majority of the votes cast, it is not permitted to hold another formal election among those employees for another year. If the union does receive a majority of votes from employees, it is certified as the legal representative and bargaining agent for all employees (both union and nonunion). Finally, the union must define the **bargaining unit**—that is, the specific group of employees that it will represent. For example, a local unit of the United Auto Workers might define its bargaining unit as all the nonmanagement employees in a Ford manufacturing plant.

The number of certification elections conducted by the NLRB has been declining in recent years, and unions are winning fewer of these elections. By contrast, there has been a sharp rise in the number of decertification elections (held to remove a union as the employees' bargaining agent) and in the number of approved decertifications.

**Bargaining unit**

The specific group of employees that the union will represent

## The Local Union

The backbone of organized labor today is the local union, often referred to as the **local**.

**Local**

The local union

**Local unions offer aid to their members.** The United Mine Workers of America supports strikers by offering free groceries.

Typically, local unions are members of a national union, such as the United Mine Workers, and they follow the national union's constitution, bylaws, and regulations, which specify the number of local officers, election procedures, the frequency of local meetings, financial arrangements with the national organization, and the local's participation in negotiating labor agreements.

Locals vary in size, structure, bargaining arrangements, and officer election procedures. The local has three primary areas of concern: worker relations and membership services, community and political activities, grievance handling and collective bargaining. The functions of the local unions are carried out at periodic (usually monthly) meetings.

# ▶ Collective Bargaining

**Collective bargaining**

The negotiation process through which management and unions reach an agreement

The primary function of labor unions is to negotiate with management for better pay, working hours, and working conditions. **Collective bargaining** is the negotiation process through which management and unions reach an agreement about these issues (Figure 10-3).

## Overview of the Process

Collective bargaining actually begins long before union representatives and management meet face to face at the bargaining table to work out a contract. The union prepares a list of demands—things that it wants from

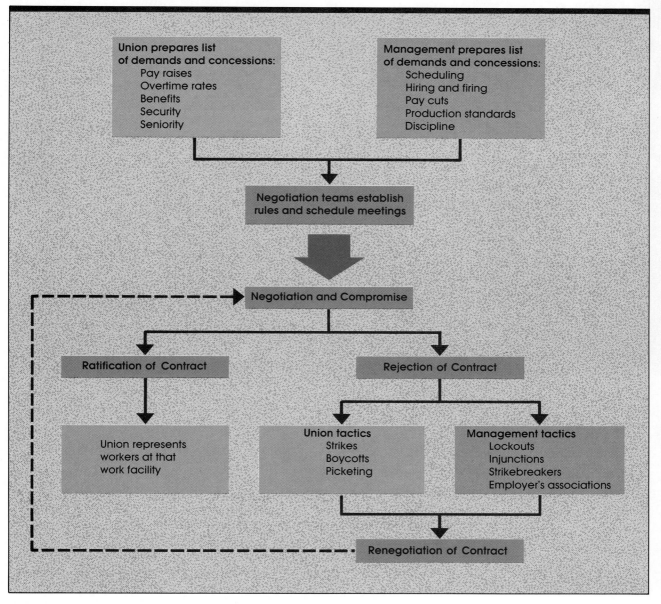

**Figure 10-3**

The Collective-Bargaining Process

management. The list may include pay increases, better health insurance, job rights, and seniority revisions. In the 1987 negotiations between the United Auto Workers and Ford Motor Company and General Motors, the main concern of the union was a guarantee of job security for UAW members.

Management also goes through a preparation stage before going to the bargaining table. Management attempts to define what the company is willing to concede to the union as long as a reasonable level of profitability can be achieved. Management often has demands of its own to make of the union.

**Hotel workers strike in New York City.** Media coverage can help striking union members publicize their greivances against management tactics and can bring the issues to the public's attention.

When Chrysler faced bankruptcy in the early 1980s, Chrysler management asked the UAW to accept wage reductions and layoffs. Had the union not acquiesced, Chrysler might not have survived and many UAW members would have lost their jobs.

When both sides have identified their respective demands and limitations, they are ready to begin negotiations. At the first formal meeting between management and labor representatives, negotiation teams establish rules, policies, and schedules for future meetings. Labor and management submit their lists of demands and limitations. The objective of the negotiations is to reach agreement about a **labor contract,** the formal, written document that spells out the relationship written between the union and management. It guides their relations for a specified period of time, usually two or three years. The contract discusses issues of interest to both sides: These issues are outlined in Table 10-2.

Once labor and management have made their initial positions known, the process of compromise begins, unless labor and management are in agreement at the outset. However, that is rarely the case; and as a result, each party must be willing to give and take a little to obtain a mutually acceptable

**Labor contract**

The formal, written document that spells out the relationship between the union and management

**Table 10-2  Contract Issues**

► Wages
    Form of pay
    Magnitude of pay
    Determinants of pay
    Cost-of-living adjustments
    Shift differential pay
► Hours of work
    Overtime
    Vacation
    Sick time
    Holidays
    Maternity/paternity leave
    Breaks (lunch and coffee)
    Rest periods
► Benefits
    Insurance (health and life)
    Retirement
    Profit sharing (ESOPs)
► Security
    Determination of methods of promotion, transfers
    Job protection
    Protection of the union as bargaining agent
► Other Issues
    Grievance procedures
    Union activities and responsibilities
    Management activities and responsibilities
    Strikes
    Working conditions

contract. For example, in exchange for UAW concessions, Chrysler asked Douglas Fraser, a high-ranking UAW official, to join Chrysler's board of directors. That was a smart move. It gave the union more power in its dealings with Chrysler. It helped union members realize the gravity of Chrysler's situation. Ultimately, it promoted better understanding between labor and management.

In collective bargaining, management tries to maintain control over things like work schedules; the hiring and firing of workers; production standards; promotions, demotions, and transfers; determining the number of supervisors in each department; and discipline. Unions tend to focus on issues like magnitude of wages; better pay rates for overtime, holidays, and undesirable shifts; scheduling of pay increases; and benefit packages (insurance, vacations, holidays, sick days, pension plans, and income-maintenance plans, which are funds established by the employer to supplement state and federal unemployment benefits in the event of a layoff). Many union contracts contain a **cost-of-living escalator clause,** which calls for an automatic increase in wages during periods of inflation to protect the "real" income of the employees. Typically, these clauses call for a 1-cent increase in hourly wages for each 0.3 percent rise in the Consumer Price Index, which is calculated by the Bureau of Labor Statistics. Cost-of-living adjustments (COLAs) have been in the contracts between the UAW and Ford, General Motors, and Chrysler

**Cost-of-living escalator clause**

A clause in a union contract that calls for an automatic increase in wages during periods of inflation

since the 1950s; however, the use of COLAs decreased in the mid-1980s because of periods of recession and fierce foreign competition.

Also in the mid-1980s, unions in the auto, steel, and other industries were forced to provide **givebacks**—wage and benefit concessions made to employers to allow them to remain competitive or, in some cases, to survive and continue to provide jobs for union workers. In 1987, after one of the longest strikes in American history, the United Steel Workers granted wage concessions to USX, LTV, and other steel companies because of shrinking markets. The union's only other choice was to accept layoffs and plant closings.

Other unions have also accepted tradeoffs. The United Auto Workers at General Motors, the Allied Pilots Association at American Airlines, and the Communications Workers of America at AT&T have accepted **two-tier contracts,** which establish a pay scale for newly hired employees that is far less generous than the pay scale of employees with seniority. Two-tier contracts help management reduce labor costs and in the long run may preserve union workers' jobs.

After labor representatives and management negotiate these issues and reach agreement on the terms of a contract, union members vote to accept or reject the contract. If they ratify the contract, it becomes a legally binding agreement between labor and management for the specified period. If union members reject the contract, the bargaining process may continue as before, a third party may be brought in to assist with the negotiations, or the union members may take other action. In the late 1970s, when chemical workers could not reach a mutually acceptable agreement with Fina, they went on strike for several months.

The current trend in labor contracts is for labor and management to spell out every detail in an attempt to avoid disputes later on. Because all parties want highly detailed contracts, negotiations often last for months, and the resulting documents are quite lengthy.

# Types of Collective Bargaining

Collective bargaining may take place locally, throughout an industry, or with a coalition of unions. **Local-market bargaining** involves local contracts between local unions and local businesses; the national unions do not participate in the negotiations. This type of bargaining typically takes place in industries where the firm competes in local areas only. Examples include building construction, retail food stores, and newspapers.

**Industry-wide bargaining** occurs in industries where firms are involved in a nationwide market. In such cases, contracts involve the national unions, and as a result a standard contract is drawn up covering all employees in the industry, though with certain local adjustments. The South-Central United Food & Commercial Workers Union negotiates with Kroger and other chain grocery stores in the South. Other industries in which industry-wide bargaining takes place are women's apparel and furniture manufacturing.

**Coalition bargaining** occurs frequently in industries where unions are small and weak. Several different unions band together to strengthen their bargaining power. In this case, contracts are between several different unions and one employer.

---

**Givebacks**

Wage and benefit concessions made to employers to allow them to remain competitive

**Two-tier contracts**

Contracts which establish a pay scale for newly hired employees that is far less generous than the pay scale of employees with seniority

**Local-market bargaining**

Local contracts between local unions and local business

**Industry-wide bargaining**

Contracts that involve the national unions, and as a result a standard contract is drawn up covering all employees in the industry

**Coalition bargaining**

Occurs in industries where unions are small and weak; several different unions band together to strengthen their bargaining power

**Seeking a satisfying contract.** These Chicago schoolteachers have the support of their union to help them during their strike for better contracts. Unions have successfully organized state and municipal employees such as police officers and teachers.

## ▶ Dispute Resolution

Even though the labor contract is a legal document, management and labor frequently interpret it differently. Management, for example, may believe a seniority clause refers to seniority throughout the plant; but employees believe the clause refers to seniority within a specific job. When an employee or the entire union believes that management is violating some provision of the union contract, the individual or the union files a grievance. A **grievance** is a formal, written complaint.

A typical grievance is handled in the following way: The employee (or the union, if that is the case) files a complaint with the **shop steward**, a union representative. The shop steward submits the grievance to the employee's immediate supervisor, and the shop steward and supervisor try to resolve the problem. If they succeed, the dispute resolution process ends. If they are not able to settle the dispute, the steps shown in Figure 10-4 are taken. If a grievance cannot be resolved by top management and the national union, it is submitted to an outside arbitrator for a final and binding decision.

**Grievance**

A formal, written complaint

**Shop steward**

A union representative

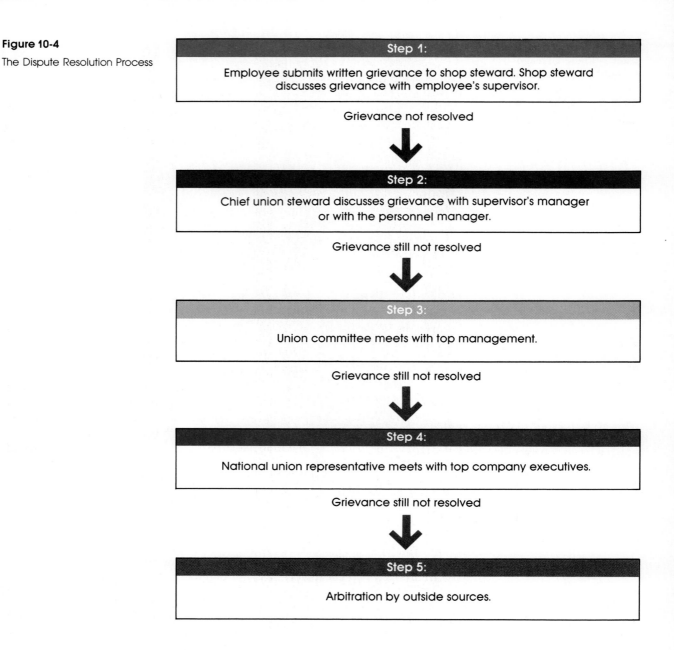

**Figure 10-4**

The Dispute Resolution Process

**Step 1:**

Employee submits written grievance to shop steward. Shop steward discusses grievance with employee's supervisor.

Grievance not resolved

**Step 2:**

Chief union steward discusses grievance with supervisor's manager or with the personnel manager.

Grievance still not resolved

**Step 3:**

Union committee meets with top management.

Grievance still not resolved

**Step 4:**

National union representative meets with top company executives.

Grievance still not resolved

**Step 5:**

Arbitration by outside sources.

## ▶ Reaching a Settlement

Management and union members normally reach mutually agreeable decisions without outside assistance. Sometimes, even after lengthy negotiations, management and labor are not able to agree on a contract issue or the resolution of a grievance. In such cases, they have three choices: conciliation, mediation, and arbitration.

# Conciliation

**Conciliation** involves bringing in a neutral third party, a conciliator, whose role is simply to keep labor and management talking. The conciliator has no formal power over union representatives or over management. The conciliator's goal is to get both parties to focus on the issues and to prevent negotiations from breaking down. The Federal Mediation and Conciliation Service provides conciliators to labor disputes without charge to either party.

# Mediation

**Mediation**, like conciliation, involves bringing in a neutral third party, a mediator, whose role is to suggest or propose a solution to the problem. Mediators have no formal power over either labor or management. Their services can be retained without charge from the Federal Mediation and Conciliation Service.

# Arbitration

**Arbitration**, like conciliation and mediation, involves bringing in a neutral third party, an arbitrator, whose role is to decide how to settle the dispute. An arbitrator's solution is legally binding and enforceable. Generally, arbitration takes place on a voluntary basis—management and labor must agree to it. The Federal Mediation and Conciliation Service supplies a list of arbitrators, and management and labor together select the arbitrator who will settle their case. The cost of arbitration (the arbitrator's fee plus expenses) is usually split equally between the parties. Occasionally, management and labor submit to **compulsory arbitration**, in which an outside party (usually the federal government) requests arbitration as a means of eliminating a prolonged strike that threatens to disrupt the economy.

# ▶ Labor and Management Pressure Tactics

Most labor disputes are handled through collective bargaining or through grievance procedures. Occasionally, however, management or labor may resort to more drastic measures to achieve its objectives. Pressure tactics used by labor include strikes, picketing, and boycotts. Pressure tactics used by management include lockouts, injunctions, and employers' associations.

## Labor Tactics

A strike is a walkout by employees. It is one of the most effective weapons against management that labor unions have. By striking, the union makes carrying out the normal operations of a business difficult at best and impossible at worst. Because members of other unions will usually attempt to honor the picket lines of a striking union, a fairly small union may be able to shut down the operations of a company completely. Striking employees do not receive wages from the firm. As a result, most labor unions maintain strike funds

**Safety in the skies.** Airline pilots are becoming more vocal about safety hazards. Continental Airlines pilots went on strike to protest unsafe planes, and to force management to take corrective action.

from which strikers receive some income while off the job. A strike that does not have the authorization of the union is called a wildcat strike.

Although strikes receive widespread publicity, they are a weapon of last resort. The threat of a strike is often enough to get management to back down. Some of the most famous strikes in American history were against Chrysler and General Motors by the United Auto Workers. In 1988 the Screen Actors Guild went on strike, halting production of many television commercials. A strike during the same year delayed the start of the 1988 fall television series. Nevertheless, the number of worker-days actually lost to striking is less than the amount lost to the common cold.

Although federal and most state and municipal employees are permitted to engage in collective bargaining, they are not permitted to strike. Thus, when the Professional Air Traffic Controllers Organization struck in 1981 to call attention to their contract demands, President Ronald Reagan fired them. Some public workers get around no-strike laws by calling in sick en masse. Newspapers have humorously referred to such sickouts by police officers as the "blue flu."

Picketing is a public protest against management practices and involves workers marching (often waving anti-management signs and placards) at the employer's plant. Picketing workers hope that their signs will arouse sympathy for their demands from the public and from other unions. Picketing is protected by the Constitution as a form of free speech, as long as the picketers do not become violent or intimidating. Picketing may occur as a protest or in conjunction with a strike.

A **boycott** is an attempt to keep people from purchasing the products of a company. In a boycott, union members are asked not to do business with the boycotted organization. Some unions may even impose fines on members who ignore the boycott.

## Management Tactics

A **lockout** is management's version of a strike; management actually closes a work site so that employees cannot go to work. Lockouts are used, as a general rule, only when a union strike has partially shut down a plant and it seems less expensive for the plant to shut down completely.

An injunction is a court order that prohibits some practice. Before the passage of the Norris-LaGuardia Act, management used injunctions to stop all types of strikes. Today, the use of injunctions is limited to stopping violence, picketing, and damage to company property.

**Strikebreakers** are people hired by management to replace striking employees. Striking union members usually refer to them, and anyone else who crosses picket lines, as scabs. Managers hire strikebreakers in order to continue operations and reduce the losses associated with strikes—and to show the unions that they will not bow to their demands. When National Football League players went on strike in 1987, team owners hired nonunion players to play scheduled football games. Strikebreaking is generally a last-resort measure for management because it does great damage to the relationship between management and labor. AT&T resorted to this tactic several times to keep telephone service from breaking down.

**Employers' associations** are organizations formed by employers to present a united front in dealing with labor unions. Employers' associations, like labor unions, may represent individual employers in disputes—especially in industries characterized by many small employers and one large labor union. The National Association of Manufacturers and the United States Chamber of Commerce are employers' associations.

**Boycott**

An attempt to keep people from purchasing the products of a company

**Lockout**

Management's version of a strike; management closes a work site so that employees cannot go to work

**Strikebreakers**

People hired by management to replace striking employees

**Employers' associations**

Organizations formed by employers to present a united front in dealing with labor unions

# ▶ The Future of Organized Labor

In recent years, union growth has slowed and prospects for growth among blue-collar workers do not look good. One reason for this prediction is that most blue-collar workers have already been organized. Another reason is the changing make-up of the American work force. Table 10-3 shows the expected growth rate for various industries. Factories have become more automated and need fewer blue-collar workers. Furthermore, the United States is shifting from a production to a service economy, and this change is also decreasing the demand for blue-collar workers.

| Occupation group | Number (000) | Percent distribution |
|---|---|---|
| Professional and technical workers | 16,900 | 14.8 |
| Managers and administrators, except farm | 12,200 | 10.7 |
| Sales workers | 7,600 | 6.7 |
| Clerical workers | 21,700 | 19.0 |
| Craft and kindred workers | 14,900 | 13.1 |
| Operatives | 16,600 | 14.6 |
| Nonfarm laborers | 5,100 | 4.5 |
| Service workers | 16,700 | 14.6 |
| Farmers and farm laborers | 2,400 | 2.1 |
| Total employment | 114,000 | 100.0 |

Before 1962, government employees were prohibited from joining labor unions. Since that time, more than half of all federal employees have become union members. Although these employees are prohibited by law from striking, they do have the right to bargain collectively. Unions have also been successful at organizing state and municipal employees such as police officers, firefighters, sanitation workers, doctors and hospital employees, zookeepers, and schoolteachers.

The success of labor unions has not been as pronounced in other areas. Although approximately forty thousand agricultural and fishing workers now belong to unions, unionization in those industries is less than 25 percent. White-collar union membership now totals approximately 3.8 million, or one-eleventh of all white-collar workers in the United States. Unionization in service industries is also less than 25 percent.

The economy itself is also reducing the role played by unions. In response to foreign competition, especially from Japan, American companies are scrambling to find ways to make domestic plants more productive and cost-efficient. Job enrichment programs and participative management are blurring the line between management and workers. Because workers' say in the way plants are run is increasing, their need for union protection is decreasing. General Motors hopes to take advantage of this situation at its new Saturn manufacturing plant in Tennessee. Changes in work rules at the Saturn plant will lessen UAW influence over working conditions, and the union is not happy about its diminished role. Many manufacturers are watching the GM Saturn plant to see what happens, feeling that it is a strong indicator of the future direction of labor unions.

Not only must labor unions struggle with declining numbers of blue-collar workers and try to appeal to new segments of the work force, but they must also deal with a new generation of workers. Today's workers are better educated than workers in previous generations. They have grown up during times of economic prosperity, and have no memory of the Great Depression and no experience of economic hardship. They desire challenging work and dislike both union and management bureaucracies. In fact, public approval of labor unions is steadily decreasing. Seventy-six percent of the American people favored labor unions in 1953. In 1981 only 55 percent approved of labor unions. Many people seem to think that American workers are over-privileged and that labor unions only hurt businesses in the long run. The new generation of workers is interested in the environment, flexible working conditions, and shared decision making.

If labor unions are to continue growing, they will need to address the needs of this new generation of workers and seek members in nontraditional groups such as women, white-collar workers, agriculture workers, government employees, and service workers. Management Encounter 10-3 describes the AFL-CIO's efforts to boost its membership.

# Management Encounter 10-3

## AFL-CIO Tries to Boost Membership with New Strategy

Membership in American labor unions has been declining steadily since World War II. In the mid-1950s, one in three U.S. workers belonged to a union; today, only one in five workers belongs. In addition to the decline in labor union membership, the unions have also lost much of their power and influence.

Several factors are behind the decline of union power and membership. Perhaps the most important factor has been the relative ineffectiveness of the unions. Even though union members continue to earn about 30 percent more than nonunion workers (when comparing median weekly income), the gap between them is closing. In 1986, nonunion workers in private industry got average pay hikes of 3.5 percent, while union workers got raises of only 2 percent. Moreover, many union workers covered by collective-bargaining agreements earn the same pay they received before the unionization process, or even less. Thus, workers are finding out that belonging to a union no longer ensures prosperity. In addition, ever since the AFL-CIO expelled the Teamsters in 1957 for corrupt practices, public opinion of unions has been on the decline. Finally, AFL-CIO affiliates often compete among themselves to unionize the same group of workers. Not only is this inefficient, but it is expensive as well.

To combat these factors, the AFL-CIO has implemented a new strategy to increase union membership and power. The AFL-CIO is first trying to concentrate power in its high command. By doing this, it hopes to avoid some of the competition among its affiliates and make organizing efforts more effective in factories and offices.

The AFL-CIO Executive Council is taking more responsibility for its affiliates. Under the new strategy, if two or more unions clash over who gets to organize a particular group of workers, the unions can take their dispute to a mediator picked by the council. If mediation cannot resolve the situation, the dispute goes before an AFL-CIO umpire. The unions must then agree to follow the umpire's ruling or face sanctions. The AFL-CIO hopes that this new policy, which radically reduces the autonomy of member unions, will show that organized labor is more willing to compromise today than in the past. In addition, AFL-CIO unions are now trying to be more responsive to their members' wishes. They are expanding their services and are offering benefits to workers who cannot be represented in collective bargaining, establishing retraining programs for laid-off workers, catering to the needs of women workers, and helping with community economic development projects.

The AFL-CIO's immediate goal in implementing these changes is an increase in affiliate memberships and a better public image for organized labor as a whole. The AFL-CIO hopes that increased membership translates to increased power, which would be good news for all current union members.

These facts are from Jane Connolly, "Why Not Try Union Democracy?" *The Nation*, September 5, 1987, pp. 192–95; "Declining Force, Increasing Power," *The Economist*, February 4, 1987, pp. 23–24, 27; and Joe Rosenbloom III, "Labor Tries to Rebound with New Strategy," *Inc.* (September 1986): 17.

# Summary and Review

▶ A labor union is a group of workers who have joined together to deal with employers and achieve common goals. Craft unions represent workers in a specific craft or trade. Industrial unions represent workers in a particular industry.

▶ Before the Industrial Revolution, most efforts to organize labor were unsuccessful. The Knights of Labor, the first national union, was formed in 1869. The AFL and CIO followed, unionizing trades, skills, and industries. The Norris-LaGuardia Act, the Wagner Act, the Taft-Hartley Act, and the Landrum-Griffin Act affected relations between labor and management.

▶ Management and the unions use collective bargaining to negotiate a labor contract. They list their demands and limitations and then compromise until an agreement is reached. A third party may be brought in to help with negotiations if an agreement cannot be reached.

▶ Grievance procedures begin with an employee's complaint, filed with a union representative. Efforts to resolve a grievance begin at low levels of the organization and progress upward until a solution is reached.

▶ Pressure tactics used by labor unions are strikes, picketing, and boycotts. Pressure tactics used by management are lockouts, injunctions, strikebreakers, and employers' associations.

# Key Terms and Concepts

labor union
Knights of Labor
American Federation of Labor
Congress of Industrial Unions
AFL-CIO
injunctions
Norris-LaGuardia Act
Wagner Act
National Labor Relations Board
Taft-Hartley Act
closed shop
union shop
right-to-work laws
agency shop
featherbedding
secondary boycotts
Landrum-Griffin Act
bargaining unit
local union

collective bargaining
labor contract
cost-of-living-escalator clause
givebacks
two-tier contract
local-market bargaining
industry-wide bargaining
coalition bargaining
grievance
shop steward
conciliation
mediation
arbitration
compulsory arbitration
boycott
lockout
strikebreakers
employers' associations

# Checking Your Understanding

This chapter introduced you to the subject of labor unions and management. To test and reinforce your understanding, fill in the blanks below.

1. _____ involves bringing in a neutral third party to prevent contract negotiations from breaking down.

2. The _____ union is the backbone of organized labor.

3. The work stoppage used by labor to achieve its objectives is called the _____.

4. Workers holding signs and patrolling the entrances to a plant are _____.

5. The negotiation process through which management and unions reach agreement is called _____ _____.

6. A group of workers who have joined together to deal with employers and achieve common goals is a _____ _____.

7. Details of union activities and responsibilities, wages, insurance coverage, employee rights, grievance handling, and arbitration for a specified period of time are spelled out in the _____ _____.

8. A factory in which management could hire only union members was a _____ _____.

9. The first act clearly aimed at protecting the rights of unions was the _____ _____ Act.

10. A _____ occurs when management closes a work site so that employees may not go to work.

11. _____ are sought by management to stop violence, picketing, or damage to company property; they were once used to stop all strikes.

# Topics for Review and Discussion

1. Describe the function of the labor union.
2. Describe the evolution of the labor union in America.
3. Discuss the negotiation process through which management and unions reach an agreement on a contract.
4. Briefly explain the three types of collective bargaining. How do they differ?
5. List all the characteristics of labor contracts.
6. What are the ways in which a settlement may be reached? Briefly describe each.
7. How is a grievance normally handled?
8. Besides collective bargaining and the grievance procedures, what other alternatives are available to labor and management to handle labor disputes?
9. Does the federal government play any role in labor-management relations? Explain.

# Exercises

1. Would you as an employee join a labor union? Why or why not?
2. Under what circumstances would you as an employer use tactics like lockouts and injunctions to handle labor disputes?
3. If collective bargaining and the grievance procedures have not been able to settle a labor dispute, what tactics would you and other employees adopt? Which tactics would be best for which situations? Give examples.

## Case 10-1
### *The Teamsters Union*

The International Brotherhood of Teamsters rejoined the AFL-CIO in 1987 after a 30-year separation. The AFL-CIO expelled the Teamsters in 1957 because the union refused to sign a code of ethics statement and because of the Teamsters' reputed organized crime ties. Labor analysts believe the Teamsters' renewed desire to rejoin the AFL-CIO in 1987 was motivated by the fact that the Justice Department had threatened to use civil racketeering laws as a means to place the entire Teamsters union under court-appointed trusteeship (because of the union's alleged ties to organized crime). Despite this fact, many believe that the merger will make the AFL-CIO stronger because it can present a more unified front to employers.

Others believe the merger is the beginning of a new period of prosperity for the Teamsters. Union membership had fallen from nearly 2 million in the late 1970s to 1.6 million. Teamsters blame most of their troubles on deregulation of the trucking industry in 1980. In fact, most of the Teamsters' membership loss has been in trucking and trucking-related industries.

Deregulation of the trucking industry shook up the entire trucking industry and cost the union more than 100,000 jobs. The Teamsters were forced to make wage and benefit concessions to many weak trucking companies. At the same time, many small, nonunion trucking companies took away some of the big carriers' business, primarily by undercutting Teamsters' wages. In 1985 in an effort to stop job losses, the union established two-tier contracts that allowed companies to pay newly hired truckers only 70 percent of the union wage. The union also agreed to give up its cost-of-living clause and accepted lower pay and fringe benefits for part-time drivers, who had received full pay. These changes helped the Teamsters get labor costs under control (they have risen less than 10 percent since 1985).

However, union negotiators are faced with a dilemma because of the success that large union carriers enjoyed in 1986 and 1987. Union negotiators believe the large companies can afford to pay truckers higher salaries and more benefits now that they are profitable again. Drivers at smaller, weaker carriers, however, fear that their companies will be forced to close if the

Teamsters ask for higher wages. The union hopes that it can avoid this and keep the large carriers happy at the same time. It is permitting drivers from weaker trucking companies to accept profit-sharing and employee stock ownership plans in exchange for wage concessions of up to 15 percent. This plan seems to be working, because many members at financially weak carriers have accepted wage cuts in exchange for stock.

The Teamsters' merger with the AFL-CIO also puts an end to one of the union's most successful recruiting tactics. Union insiders say that the Teamsters union has gained thousands of new members in recent years by persuading workers in other unions to quit and join the Teamsters. These raids are often at the expense of industrial and factory unions affiliated with the AFL-CIO. However, federation rules prohibit such raiding and overlapping efforts to organize employees.

In spite of its raiding tactics, the Teamsters have worked hard in other ways in the past few years to broaden their base. The union has gained many new members from among hospital and health care workers, flight mechanics, and retail store clerks. In addition, the Teamsters do more than one-third of all the labor organizing in the U.S. even though they have just 9 percent of all labor union members.

The Teamsters have also taken several steps to regain their once-powerful political strength. The union has started a congressional lobbying campaign and has enlisted the support of several members of Congress. In addition, the Teamsters have created a political action committee (PAC) which has receipts of close to $10 million. This makes the unions' PAC one of the biggest in existence, as well as one of the fastest growing.

Union analysts believe that the merger with the AFL-CIO will give the Teamsters increased political clout and will add credibility to the union in the future. For the first time in 30 years, most of the nation's unions can present a united front in labor negotiations. Moreover, many believe that this merger will pave the way for a period of union growth and prosperity during the 1990s.

---

These facts are from Aaron Bernstein, "The Teamsters: A Break in Forty Miles of Bad Road," *Business Week,* March 21, 1988, pp. 90, 92; Leo Abruzzese, "Teamsters are Shifting Gears for Long Uphill Grade Ahead," *Truck Commerce,* January 19, 1988, pp. 4–5; Aaron Bernstein and Susan B. Garland, "The AFL-CIO: A Tougher Team with the Teamsters," *Business Week,* November 9, 1987, p. 110; Albert R. Karr and Gregory Stricharchuk, "Teamsters' Proposal to Rejoin AFL-CIO Could Help to Improve Union's Image," *The Wall Street Journal,* October 23, 1987, p. 9.

**Questions**

1. What are some of the opportunities and challenges in bringing the Teamsters back into the AFL-CIO?
2. What impact will the broadened base of employees have on the Teamsters in the long run?
3. Do you believe that the 1990s will be a period of union growth and prosperity? Why?

# Case 10-2
## *Eastern Airlines Versus Its Unions*

When Texas Air Corporation acquired Miami-based Eastern Airlines in February 1986, the stage was set for one of the biggest union versus management battles in recent years. Eastern Airlines had the highest costs of any airline in the United States. Texas Air and its chairman Frank Lorenzo had a reputation for imposing tough cost-cutting measures. Immediately following Texas Air's acquisition of Eastern, Lorenzo vowed he would decrease Eastern's high labor costs. He demanded substantial pay cuts and more stringent work rules and promised that Eastern workers would be laid off if costs were not cut.

Eastern's twelve thousand International Association of Machinists (IAM) members, who were earning some of the highest wages in the airline industry, were particularly unhappy about the pay cuts. Some IAM members (most of whom are machinists, janitors, and baggage handlers) were earning as much as $43,000 a year. Lorenzo, believing these wages were too high, was enraged when the machinists refused to accept the 20 percent wage cut agreed to by Eastern's other unions (flight attendants and pilots).

In 1987, Eastern proposed to cut the pay and benefits of IAM workers by $265 million. These cuts would have the greatest effect on unskilled workers such as janitors and baggage handlers, reducing some employees' wages by as much as 60 percent. Eastern wanted to separate the IAM members into divisions of skilled and unskilled workers. The company also wanted to do away with most work rules, seniority rights, and outside contract work. In response to these demands, the IAM requested pay hikes of $10 an hour, further straining relations between the union and Eastern's management.

Late in 1987, Eastern announced losses of $67 million for the third quarter of 1987. Management immediately announced plans for massive layoffs in an attempt to stem the losses. The company at first planned to lay off nearly ten thousand workers but changed its mind because it believed that such a drastic reduction would hurt the airline. Ultimately, the company decided to lay off thirty-five hundred workers, about 9 percent of its work force. The company publicly stated that the main reason behind the layoffs was the union's resistance to cutting costs.

Union members believed Lorenzo's actions were an attempt to merge Eastern's operations with those of the mostly nonunion, low-cost Continental Airlines, which is also owned by Texas Air. They feared that Lorenzo would further redirect some of Eastern's assets to Continental (Eastern had already sold or leased nineteen planes, six of them to Continental). Moreover, the airline discontinued a number of routes, especially in areas where Continental was strong. Eastern officials have sent a clear message to the union that they will do whatever is necessary to lower costs, even downsizing the airline. Union officials, concerned that more layoffs would be forthcoming, vowed to strike if the need arose. Many pilots and flight attendants, however, said they would not honor an IAM picket line.

Lorenzo took several steps to ensure that a strike by the IAM would not cripple Eastern. He set aside more than $300 million in cash to aid the company. He also threatened to liquidate Eastern's assets (through bankruptcy proceedings) if he did not get what he wanted from the union. In November 1987, Eastern began recruiting and training flight crews (at a cost of $6 million per month) to replace union workers if they went on strike. Lorenzo's strike plan included replacement airplane mechanics, security guards, airport services employees, and flight attendants. As a result, Lorenzo believed that an IAM strike would not affect Eastern's schedule of 1,450 flights a day.

Eastern and the IAM entered federal mediation talks in January 1988 to try to resolve their differences. The battle between management and the IAM at Eastern has been a problem for the airline not only in monetary terms but also in declining employee morale. Regardless of the eventual outcome, the dispute promises to be a long, tough fight. Union members are unwilling to give up their high wages, even to save their jobs, and Lorenzo is determined to cut high labor costs in each of Texas Air's units. As one union official put it, "This is the kind of fight only one man walks away from."

---

These facts are from Jo Ellen Davis and Pete Engardio, "Showdown Time at Eastern," *Business Week*, February 8, 1988, pp. 20–21; Mike Sheridan, "Collision Course at Eastern Airlines," *Houston Chronicle*, November 15, 1987, pp. 5-1, 5–10; Paulette Thomas, "Eastern Air Sets Layoff of 9.2% of Employees," *The Wall Street Journal*, November 12, 1987, pp. 3, 8; Pete Engardio, "Why Eastern Is Backing Off from a Union Showdown," *Business Week*, October 12, 1987, pp. 108–109; and Paulette Thomas, "Texas Air Corp.'s Eastern Unit Seeks Steep Pay Cuts from Machinists' Union," *The Wall Street Journal*, October 6, 1987, p. 5.

### Questions

1. Compare and contrast the pressure tactics being used by labor (IAM) and management (Texas Air).
2. Make some suggestions for the resolution of the dispute between Texas Air and the IAM.
3. If the IAM should strike Eastern Airlines, what should Texas Air do to resolve the strike? Based on existing legislation, what are the limitations on Texas Air's options?

# Answers to Checking Your Understanding

1. conciliation
2. local
3. strike
4. picketing
5. collective bargaining
6. labor union
7. labor contract
8. closed shop
9. Norris-LaGuardia
10. lockout
11. injunctions

## Outline

# Chapter 11

# Production and Operations Management

## Objectives

▶ Define production and operations management and identify the activities associated with it.

▶ Define materials management and explain the activities associated with it.

▶ Define production planning and control.

▶ Describe quality control, and explain what is meant by zero defects and quality circles.

▶ Discuss product design, facility location, and facility layouts.

▶ Discuss recent developments in production and operations technology, such as robotics, computer-assisted design, and computer-assisted manufacturing.

# Business Experience

Although a company can make millions of dollars from the sales of one product, it must continue to develop new products and find new uses for old products in order to survive in today's competitive marketplace. Companies now spend billions of dollars on research and development of new products to meet the needs and wants of their customers and keep their profits growing. Du Pont is committed to research and development to find new products and improve old ones. In 1987, the company spent $1.2 billion on research and development.

Du Pont, which once made gunpowder, opened its first chemistry lab for research and development in 1926. The company hired Charles Carothers from Harvard University soon after. Carothers' experiments with polymers (giant molecules) produced a few "accidents." One of those was neoprene, the first synthetic rubber. One of Carothers' assistants, while trying to create another polymer from air, coal, and water, found that he could draw the substance into fibers. After seven years of experimentation, that substance became nylon.

Although Du Pont obtained a patent for nylon, the company never registered the name as a trademark because it recognized that nylon would become vital to everyday life. Du Pont researchers found many uses for nylon in their laboratory, and today nylon is used in hosiery, parachutes, tires, clothes, fishing line, seat belts, and many other common products. Du Pont's research into nylon led Carothers and others to the development of Teflon, Orlon, Dacron, Lycra, and other materials.

In the 1960s, Du Pont chemists tried to find a way to align molecules of carbon into "strings." After much experimentation, they discovered they could align the molecules by pushing them through a syringe. They then froze the "strings" of carbon. They called the resulting substance Fiber B. Twenty-five years and $700 million later, Fiber B became Kevlar, a fiber that is five times stronger than steel.

Du Pont assigned a team to find practical applications for Kevlar. At one point, the team thought that Kevlar would be used in automobile tires, and the company invested money in a plant to produce tons of Kevlar. Tire makers, however, felt that tire buyers would prefer the sound of "steel-belted radials" rather than "Kevlar-belted radials," and the idea fell through. Eventually, the Kevlar team sold the army on the strengths of the product for military use. Kevlar is also used in bulletproof clothing, race-car tires, airplanes, and sails for racing yachts. Du Pont hopes Kevlar will replace asbestos, which can cause cancer, in car brakes, clutches, and other products. After twenty-five years of research, Kevlar is successful: Annual sales of the fiber reached $300 million in 1987.

Du Pont won't be content to sit back and rake in its profits from nylon and Kevlar, however. The company plans to continue to research and develop other new products, as well as find new uses for Kevlar and nylon.

---

These facts are from Kevin Maney, "Nylon: The Fabric of Everyday Life," *USA Today*, January 12, 1988, pp. 1A, 2A; Laurie Hays, "Du Pont's Difficulties in Selling Kevlar Show Hurdles of Innovation," *The Wall Street Journal*, September 29, 1987, pp. 1, 20; and the 1986 Du Pont Annual Report.

# Introduction

All organizations create products for customers. Thus, a county hospital, General Motors, McDonald's, IBM, the Department of Health and Human Services, a university, and countless other organizations have a number of similarities that relate to the activitites necessary to create goods and services. It is the role of production and operations management to acquire the necessary resources to create that product, to plan the specific steps through which those resources must pass to become a finished product, and to make sure the product conforms to standards of appearance, performance, and reliability. The way in which General Motors performs these tasks differs markedly from the way McDonald's or a county hospital performs them. Nonetheless, certain basic steps are similar in all organizations. Figure 11-1 shows four aspects of production and operations control.

Although all organizations differ to some degree in the way they create products, organizations within an industry perform similar functions in a similar manner. The admission procedures used by most hospitals are similar, as are the food preparation methods used by McDonald's and Wendy's to make hamburgers. General Motors and Chrysler use many of the same techniques for assembling automobiles. Such similarities are to be expected. It is entirely possible, however, for organizations in unrelated industries to take similar steps in creating products. The check-in procedures used by hotels and commercial airlines are similar. The way Burger King assembles a hamburger and the way an automobile manufacturer assembles a vehicle are similar (both use automation and an assembly line). Similarities of this sort are based on something other than the product itself.

Figure 11-2 illustrates the process used to transform a group of **inputs** (labor, materials, energy, and money) into **outputs** (goods and services). The transformation process creates final products by combining the inputs in predetermined ways using different types of equipment, administrative procedures, and technology. The transformation process occurs in all types

**Inputs**

Labor, materials, energy, and money

**Outputs**

Goods and services

**Figure 11-1**

Four Aspects of Production and Operations Control

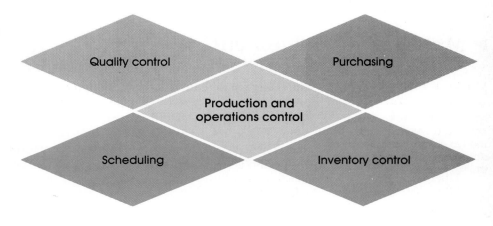

Inputs     Transformation Process     Outputs

**Figure 11-2**
Transforming Inputs into Outputs

of organizations, regardless of the goods or services they offer. The transformation of inputs into outputs is accomplished through the planning of production activities, the accumulation of resources, the scheduling of work, and the controlling of product quality and reliability.

# ▶ The Production and Operations Function

**Production and operations management**

Has primary responsibility for the creation of products to be offered to customers

The organization chart shown in Figure 11-3 is a simplified representation of a typical manufacturing company. The three main functions within a business are finance, marketing, and production and operations. **Production and operations management** has primary responsibility for the creation of products to be offered to customers. The production and operations function is carried out by the departments in Figure 11-3 that are shaded. The manufacturing department and the departments and personnel over which it has jurisdiction, however, have the primary responsibility for the production and operations function. The individual in charge of the manufacturing department, usually a vice president, is responsible for coordinating the activities necessary to create a product. This coordination is achieved with the assistance of departments such as materials management, production planning and control, quality control, and research and development. Research and development will be discussed in Chapter 13.

# ▶ Materials Management

**Materials management**

The development and coordination of the policies, procedures, and systems that are used to obtain, distribute, and store materials needed to create the product

**Materials management** is the development and coordination of the policies, procedures, and systems that are used to obtain, distribute, and store the materials needed to create the product. If the materials management system is inefficient, the organization will not be able to create on time a product that conforms to competitive quality and performance standards.

Specific activities within the materials management department are purchasing, inventory management, traffic management, and shipping and receiving.

**Figure 11-3**

Organization Chart for a Manufacturing Company

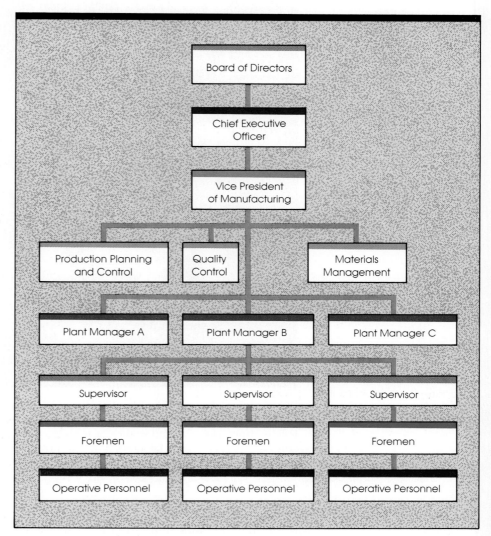

Board of Directors

Chief Executive Officer

Vice President of Manufacturing

Production Planning and Control

Quality Control

Materials Management

Plant Manager A

Plant Manager B

Plant Manager C

Supervisor

Supervisor

Supervisor

Foremen

Foremen

Foremen

Operative Personnel

Operative Personnel

Operative Personnel

# Purchasing

**Purchasing**

The buying of all the materials needed by the organization

**Purchasing**, also known as procurement, is the buying of all the materials needed by the organization. Raw materials, parts, components, manufacturing supplies, office supplies, and equipment are items that must be purchased. People in the purchasing department must locate and evaluate suppliers for the many items the firm uses. They must also be on the lookout for new materials or parts that will do a better job or cost less than those currently being used. The purchasing department aims to obtain items in the right quantities at the lowest cost commensurate with the required quality. There

**Production and operations management in all types of businesses.** Auto assembly plants, airlines, and the food service industry all require operations management. Hilton appreciates the importance of having an individual responsible for the efficient operation of its kitchens. The executive chef (center) is responsible for supervising and performing menu planning, purchasing, and food preparation.

is a public relations dimension to purchasing: The individuals who work in this area must maintain good relations with the companies that are suppliers.

The purchasing function is sometimes very complex. The average automobile, for example, has more than sixteen thousand different parts, each of which is associated with at least one supplier. The magnitude of the task of purchasing is further revealed by the amount of money spent by various organizations. For example, Navistar normally spends around $4 billion in its purchasing activities, and General Motors normally spends around $30 billion.

## Inventory Management

Once the purchasing department has procured the items needed to create a product, some provision has to be made for storing the items until they are required. Every raw material, part, supply, and piece of equipment has to be accounted for, or controlled. **Inventory management** is keeping track of how many of each item are on hand, where each item is, and who has responsibility for each item.

It is impossible and impractical for a company to maintain comprehensive records on every item kept in inventory. A firm does not exercise the same degree of control over paper clips as it does over TV picture tubes because one is more valuable and of greater importance than the other. The **ABC inventory classification system** helps managers control inventory items (see Figure 11-4). This system divides inventory items into three classes. The items that constitute from 60 to 70 percent of the annual dollar expenditure for all inventory items are in Class A. Class A items account for a high percentage of the total dollars spent on inventory each year, but they usually represent a small percentage (up to 20 percent) of the total number of items purchased. Class B items represent from 20 to 30 percent of the total expenditure for inventory but only 20 to 50 percent of the total number of items purchased. Class C items represent a small percentage of the total expenditure for inventory (up to approximately 25 percent) but from 30 to 80 percent of the total number of items purchased.

The ABC system allows inventory managers to determine how much control to exercise over various inventory items. Rubber bands, for example, a Class C item because of their low dollar value, would most likely be controlled by observation. Visual inspection would indicate when the inventory level was getting low and when a replacement order was needed. Computer components, however, might be considered a Class B or a Class A item. They would be given specific inventory numbers, and the number of units in stock would be monitored closely.

**Figure 11-4**

Distribution of Class A, B, and C Inventory Items

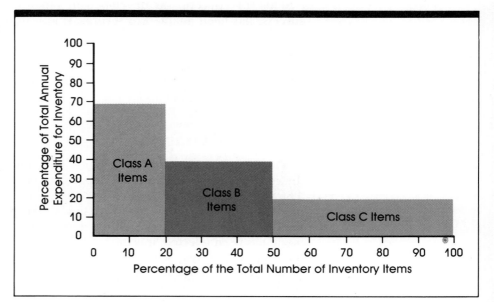

Inventory managers spend a great deal of time trying to determine the proper inventory level for each item. The answer to the question of how many units should be held in inventory depends on variables such as the usage rate of the item, the cost of maintaining the item in inventory, the cost of the paperwork and other procedures associated with ordering or making the item, and the cost of the item itself. Several quantitative approaches may be used to determine how many units of a given item should be procured at one time and when that procurement should take place. Notable among these quantitative approaches is the **economic order quantity (EOQ) method**. The EOQ approach calculates the number of items that should be ordered at one time to minimize the total yearly cost of placing orders and carrying the items in inventory. By considering the number of items needed each year, the cost of preparing and submitting an order, and the cost of keeping items in inventory an efficient order quantity can be determined.

A fairly recent refinement that has its roots in the assembly-line methods of Henry Ford is the **just-in-time (JIT) concept**. JIT tries to minimize the number of units maintained in inventory by providing an almost continuous flow of items from the suppliers to the production facility. For example, if an automobile assembly plant uses five hundred wheel assemblies a day, an inventory manager might order enough for one month at a time. That would be eleven thousand units per order (500 units per day times 22 workdays per month). The carrying costs on such a large inventory could be considerable because of the cost of insurance coverage, recordkeeping, rented or leased storage space, and so on. The just-in-time approach would reduce these costs because wheel assemblies would be purchased in smaller quantities, perhaps in lot sizes of 100, which the supplier would deliver five times a day. For such an approach to be effective, the supplier must be extremely reliable and relatively close to the production facility.

The JIT concept was developed in Japan and, with varying degrees of success, has been adapted to several American companies. Indeed, General Motors, in deciding where to locate its Saturn assembly plant, specifically used proximity to suppliers as one location criterion because the Saturn plant will use the JIT approach and, to allow for frequent deliveries, will have to be close to its sources of supply. Management Encounter 11-1 provides additional information about JIT.

## Traffic Management

**Traffic management** is the selection of a suitable mode of transportation, the coordination of arrivals and departures, and the auditing of freight bills. The traffic manager assesses the reliability, timeliness, and cost of alternative modes of transportation (air, rail, truck, water, pipeline) that can be used for the distribution of products and materials. After a particular transportation mode has been selected, it is the traffic department's responsibility to arrange the shipping terms, schedule arrivals and departures, and attend to the related paperwork. The traffic manager must be well informed about current federal and state regulations pertaining to the transportation of products and other materials, including hazardous waste.

## Management Encounter 11-1

### Just-in-Time Production Improves Efficiency

Although many credit Toyota with developing just-in-time production management (JIT), the concept actually has its origin in the assembly-line methods developed by Henry Ford. Many American companies have been reluctant to use JIT; however, those that have used it are seeing dramatic results in improved efficiency and reduced costs. What is just-in-time production? From a narrow perspective, it is an inventory management system, but in a broader sense, JIT manages the entire production process. In essence, JIT, or *kanban* as the Japanese call it, involves buying parts or supplies and turning them into a finished product in small quantities "just in time" for use.

Traditional manufacturing processes *push* parts through the process, with everyone trying to produce as much and as fast as possible. JIT production *pulls* parts through the process when they are needed for the next stage in production. The entire process is controlled by demand for the product. A company using JIT (Harley-Davidson, General Motors, Hewlett-Packard, and IBM are users of JIT) arranges to have only enough supplies delivered to meet production demand, and suppliers usually deliver components directly to the work station where they are needed. Obviously, this system requires good relations and communications between the supplier and the producer. The company manufactures only enough of the product to meet customer demand and thus does not need to maintain a large inventory of finished or work-in-process products.

Total quality control is vital to the success of JIT. Because the company manufactures products only as needed, workers at each phase of the production process must ensure that products have no defects. To this end, many companies allow workers to halt the production process and correct defects as soon as they are discovered. Not only does JIT cut costs by reducing the defect rate of finished products, it also gives workers a feeling of responsibility and control over their work. Workers are usually responsible for repairing their own defects and maintaining their equipment. Thus, not only does JIT reduce costs through inventory reduction, it also improves the quality of a company's products and increases productivity through improved worker morale and greater worker responsibility.

JIT was in part responsible for the turnaround of Harley-Davidson in the 1980s. The company reduced its inventory by 50 percent, reduced its scrap and rework by 59 percent, and increased overall productivity by 32 percent. The ultimate result of just-in-time production, however, is a dramatic reduction in production costs and an increase in quality. This translates into lower prices for consumers of the company's products and an improved reputation for quality—and that improves profits.

These facts are from W. Christopher Musselwhite, "The Just-in-Time Production Challenge," *Training & Development Journal* (February 1987): 27–29; Sandra Brooks Dornan, "Just-in-Time: The Home-Grown Technique Comes Home," *Production* (August 1987): 60–62; Arjan T. Sadhwani and Mostafa H. Sarhan, "Putting JIT Manufacturing Systems to Work," *Business* (April–June 1987): 30–36; and James B. Byard, "Why Using Just-in-Time Is Getting Back to Basics for American Industry," *Industrial Engineering* (August 1987): 43–44.

## Shipping and Receiving

The role of shipping and receiving is to make sure that the right items are shipped from the facility and received by the facility. After an order is accumulated, it must be properly packaged and labeled and loaded onto the appropriate vehicle. If the business owns the vehicles onto which orders are placed, shipping and receiving may be responsible for managing the fleet of vehicles.

**At Scott Paper, proper packaging is important.** Bales of pulp produced by this Maritime division are shown being loaded onto a freighter in Nova Scotia, Canada. Scott reduces its shipping costs relative to many competitors through the use of wood handling and a barge system.

When materials are received by the organization, shipping and receiving unloads the shipment, identifies the items that are received, prepares the necessary paperwork by completing a receiving report, and then dispatches the items received to the appropriate destination—inspection, storage, or the beginning stages of production.

# ▶ Production Planning and Control

**Production planning**

Determining what products should be produced and by what date they should be completed

Production planning and control are responsible for making certain that the right products are produced in the right quantities at the right time. **Production planning** is determining what products should be produced and by what date they should be completed. **Production control** is scheduling the specific activities necessary to have the products completed by the target date, identifying the tasks that have to be done to complete the product, and following up to make sure things go according to the schedule. The specific activities necessary to achieve this objective may be grouped into three categories: aggregate planning, detailed planning, and dispatching and control.

The planning and control of production must be closely coordinated with the inventory control function. The production of televisions, for example, cannot be planned without some knowledge of the availability of all the necessary components—the chassis, picture tubes, color guns, and so forth. For this reason, managers must keep a careful eye on the inventory of materials and components when they develop a production plan.

# Aggregate Planning

**Aggregate planning** is the first phase of production and inventory planning and control (PIPC). Most organizations produce more than one variety of product. RCA produces both color and black-and-white televisions. They come as table models, consoles, or portables. They have screen sizes of 10 inches, 12 inches, 21 inches, 27 inches, or larger. Aggregate planning develops a demand forecast for a group of products, such as color sets, black-and-white sets, consoles, portables, and so on.

Consider an example involving the production of canoes. A canoe manufacturer produces aluminum canoes—a 15-foot model and an 18-foot model. The following forecast represents the anticipated demand for canoes in June:

June Forecast

| Product | Demand |
|---------|--------|
| 15-foot canoe | 2,000 |
| 18-foot canoe | 2,500 |
| Total | 4,500 |

In this example, the 18-foot canoe requires 1.4 times more labor than the 15-foot canoe; therefore, the aggregate monthly demand for June is 5,500 equivalent units (see Table 11-1). Using this approach, the manufacturer can determine the production needs in equivalent units for each month in a planning period. Aggregate planning is usually done for periods ranging from six months to a year.

The manufacturer must consider the impact of the production requirement on the organization's production capacity. Can the company produce 5,500 equivalent units? To answer this question, management must determine how many hours of labor will be available in June and whether there will be enough to produce 5,500 equivalent units using regular-time labor. If not enough regular-time labor is available, several alternatives may be considered:

▶ *Overtime*: Current employees could be scheduled to work additional hours at an overtime rate of pay. These additional hours, though expensive, might allow the manufacturer to make up the deficit between demand levels and production levels.
▶ *Temporary or part-time employees*: It might be possible to hire workers on a part-time or temporary basis to help produce enough units to meet the requirement.

Table 11-1 Computation of
Aggregate Monthly Demand

| Product | Monthly Demand | Weighting Factor | Equivalent Units |
|---------|----------------|------------------|------------------|
| 15-foot canoe | 2,000 | 1.0 | 2,000 |
| 18-foot canoe | 2,500 | 1.4 | 3,500 |
| Aggregate monthly demand | | | 5,500 |

▶ *Subcontracting*: The manufacturer could enter into a contractual agreement with another canoe manufacturer to produce canoes to specification. Because of the subcontractor's cost and profit requirements, this is probably a very expensive alternative.

▶ *Back-ordering*: Back-ordering means asking customers to wait for their order until the manufacturer has the time and capacity to complete it. Back-ordering usually creates ill will and could cost the company business.

Using one or more of those alternatives, management plays around with the company's production requirement and capacity to meet demand and eventually works out an aggregate production plan that specifies, month by month, how many equivalent units will be produced with regular-time labor, overtime labor, and part-time or temporary employees, how many units will be back-ordered, and how many units will be produced by subcontracting.

Cost is a major factor. Is it cheaper to produce units on overtime or to subcontract them? Should part-time employees be hired, or should units be back-ordered? How much will these approaches cost? In the best of all possible worlds, the company would have the capacity to satisfy the entire production requirement with regular-time labor. Such a high level of capacity, however, would be expensive to maintain, unless management could count on the demand level being nearly the same from one month to the next. If demand varied greatly from month to month, the production capacity needed to satisfy one month's demand would be partly idle during the months when demand was light. For example, one month the capacity to produce 5,500 units might be needed, but next month the capacity to produce only 4,000 would be needed. Maintaining excess capacity is expensive because the company is paying for resources, such as labor, that are not being used to their fullest extent. Excess capacity was one of the problems faced by Volkswagen AG at its American plant; it ultimately closed that plant (Management Encounter 11-2).

After the aggregate production plan is developed, it needs to be broken down into a **master production schedule**, which identifies what products to produce, when they should be produced, and how many are needed. If the aggregate plan indicates that 4,000 equivalent units are needed in September, those 4,000 equivalent units must be translated into a specific number of 18-foot and 15-foot canoes. This process is called disaggregation.

There are several ways to disaggregate equivalent units into actual products. Regardless of which one is used, the result is the master production schedule.

**Master production schedule**

Identifies what products to produce, when they should be produced, and how many are needed

# Management Encounter 11-2

## Volkswagen Gives Up on American Plant

Volkswagen AG, the West German automaker, closed its only U.S. assembly plant in 1988. The plant, which employed twenty-five hundred employees, closed permanently at the end of the 1988 model year. In addition, an unspecified number of white-collar workers were let go from Volkswagen of North America's headquarters in Troy, Michigan. Thus, Volkswagen, the first foreign automaker to build cars in the United States, also became the first to stop manufacturing in the United States.

At one time, Volkswagen was the top seller of foreign cars in the United States. However, because of decreasing demand for its products and increasing Japanese competition, Volkswagen fell on hard times in the United States. Its plant, located in Westmoreland, Pennsylvania, had been running at less than half capacity during its last five years of operation. The plant produced cars on a single eight-hour shift, even though it had been designed to run two shifts. At times, less than one shift was employed, resulting in a utilization rate of less than 40 percent capacity. A plant designed to operate on two shifts that operates on one (or less) does not efficiently use resources—energy, machinery, labor—and probably will not be profitable. Some analysts believed that the Westmoreland plant was losing nearly $120 million annually. Despite Volkswagen's ample resources, the company decided that it could no longer justify those losses.

Many of the plant's problems were blamed on Volkswagen products. The Volkswagen Golfs and Jettas produced at the Westmoreland plant failed to attain the popularity that the Volkswagen Beetle enjoyed with American consumers. Many consumers believed the Volkswagen models did not measure up to Japanese cars in terms of quality and design.

In 1987, the plant made 120 Jettas and 280 Golfs a day. After the plant closed, Volkswagen shifted most of that production back to West Germany. This move fit in with the company's desire to emphasize its German identity and German engineering; Volkswagen wanted to market itself as a low-priced alternative to high-priced German cars.

The Westmoreland plant once supplied about 30 percent of all the Volkswagens sold in America. Today, all Volkswagens sold in the United States are imports. Most come from Volkswagen's low-wage facilities in Brazil and Mexico, which were originally designed to be low-cost suppliers. Volkswagen officials hope that by producing in these low-cost countries, they will ultimately gain an advantage in the market for lower-priced cars.

---

These facts are from John Templeman, "What Ended VW's American Dream," *Business Week*, December 7, 1987, p. 63; Joseph B. White and Thomas F. O'Boyle, "Volkswagen AG to Close or Sell Its U.S. Plant," *The Wall Street Journal*, November 23, 1987, pp. 2, 4; "VW Plans to Halt American Assembly," *Houston Post*, November 21, 1987, p. 3D; and "Volkswagen Bugging Out of U.S. Auto Production," *Bryan–College Station Eagle*, November 21, 1987, p. 8B.

The master production schedule shows the canoe manufacturer how many 18-foot and 15-foot canoes to produce during each month of the planning period and how to meet the production requirement—with regular time, overtime, subcontracting, part-time or temporary employees, or back-ordering. The master production schedule for canoe production from July through December might appear as in Table 11.2.

In July, the company would aim to produce 1,500 15-foot canoes and 1,700 18-foot canoes using regular-time labor. Four hundred 15-foot and 600 18-foot models would be produced on overtime, and 100 15-foot and 200 18-foot canoes would be subcontracted. With the information in the master production schedule, the company could begin making plans for acquiring the resources needed to meet the production requirements in the months ahead.

| Month | 15-Foot Canoes | | | | 18-Foot Canoes | | | |
|---|---|---|---|---|---|---|---|---|
| | Regular-Time Units | Overtime Units | Sub-contracted Units | Total Units | Regular-Time Units | Overtime Units | Sub-contracted Units | Total Units |
| July | 1,500 | 400 | 100 | 2,000 | 1,700 | 600 | 200 | 2,500 |
| August | 1,500 | 200 | 0 | 1,700 | 1,700 | 300 | 100 | 2,100 |
| September | 1,500 | 100 | 0 | 1,600 | 1,700 | 200 | 0 | 1,900 |
| October | 1,500 | 0 | 0 | 1,500 | 1,700 | 0 | 0 | 1,700 |
| November | 1,500 | 0 | 0 | 1,500 | 1,700 | 0 | 0 | 1,700 |
| December | 1,500 | 0 | 0 | 1,500 | 1,700 | 0 | 0 | 1,700 |

**Table 11.2   Master Production Schedule, July Through December**

# Detailed Planning

**Detailed planning**

Planning done one or two months ahead

**Material-needs analysis**

Identifies how many and what kinds of materials will be required to produce the required number of products

**Material-requirements planning**

A process used to determine the net requirements of materials, when they are needed, and when orders should be placed to guarantee on-time delivery

**Detailed planning** is more specific than aggregate planning. Aggregate planning is done on a monthly basis for periods ranging from six months to a year. Detailed planning is done only one or two months ahead.

The first step of detailed planning is to perform a **material-needs analysis**. A material-needs analysis identifies how many and what kinds of materials will be required to produce the 1,900 15-foot and 2,300 18-foot canoes required in July. The materials must be identified so that plans can be made for their procurement. When planning the acquisition of materials, management needs to determine the gross requirement—the total amount of material needed to produce the canoes—and subtract from the gross requirement the quantity of material on hand. The difference between those amounts is the net requirement. If a 15-foot canoe takes 96 square feet of aluminum and an 18-foot canoe takes 114 square feet of aluminum, the gross requirement would be

$$(96 \times 1,900) + (114 \times 2,300) = 444,600 \text{ sq. ft.}$$

If the current inventory of aluminum is 75,000 square feet, the net requirement would be

$$444,600 - 75,000 = 369,600 \text{ sq. ft.}$$

Then, depending on how long it would take to order and receive 369,600 square feet of aluminum, the placement of the order could be timed to ensure the aluminum is present when needed.

Material-needs analysis must be done continuously during the planning period, taking into account not only the net requirements but how long it takes to receive materials after they are ordered. If aluminum is needed in July, the order might have to be placed in May. A technique called **material-requirements planning** is used to determine the net requirements of materials, when they are needed, and when orders should be placed to guarantee on-time delivery. Because of the large number of parts and materials that go into a typical production process, material-requirements planning must be done on a computer.

**Capacity-needs analysis**

Considers the capacity levels of specific departments and machines within each department

After the material-needs analysis has been completed, a **capacity-needs analysis** must be developed to determine capacity requirements. Aggregate planning takes into account the facility's estimated capacity; the capacity-needs analysis considers the capacity levels of specific departments and machines within each department. How many labor hours are available in the cutting department (the department that cuts the aluminum to the desired shape)? How much labor is needed? During this step, management must consider the routing, or the sequence of operations through which the product must pass. The sequence depends on the product specifications developed by the engineering department of the company.

Once management knows through which departments or work stations the product must pass and in what sequence, management can then schedule or assign the work to be done to departments or specific machines. This is the scheduling step. Many approaches have been developed to assist with scheduling, ranging from trial and error to mathematically sophisticated procedures. To be effective, scheduling must take into account the amount of time each product spends at each work station or machine. For example, if the aluminum-cutting process requires .75 hours per unit for 18-foot canoes and .60 hours per unit for 15-foot canoes, the capacity requirement would be

$$(.75 \times 2{,}300) + (.60 \times 1{,}900) = 2{,}865 \text{ hours}$$

If the monthly regular and overtime labor capacity in the cutting department is 3,000 hours, there is deficiency capacity of 75 hours. Subcontracting or back-ordering might be necessary to deal with the overload.

Sequencing (not to be confused with routing) considers the order in which products will be processed. Should the cutting department work on 18-foot or 15-foot canoes first? One way to answer this question is by calculating the run-out time for each product and then sequence the products in terms of which one the company would run out of first. If there are 600 18-foot canoes in inventory and demand averages 100 units per week, then there is a six-week supply in inventory (600 ÷ 100). If there are 800 15-foot models in inventory and an average weekly demand of 80 canoes, the company would run out of 15-foot canoes in ten weeks (800 ÷ 80). The cutting department would work first on the model that would run out first—the 18-foot canoes.

# Dispatching

**Dispatching**

The initiation of action orders to begin work

How does the cutting department know when to begin work on the 18-foot canoes? Something has to trigger the start of work. **Dispatching** is the initiation of action—orders to begin work in this case. In highly automated businesses, work flows from one work station to the next according to a predetermined schedule. In other types of organizations, however, specific orders must be issued to initiate work: work orders or shop orders for work to be done in-house; purchase orders for the materials and components to be supplied by vendors. Once the orders are released, they need to be followed up and possibly expedited to make certain that the necessary items are received in time to satisfy the master production schedule.

# ► Quality Control

Quality, like cost, is a major determinant of success in the marketplace. For the past fifteen years or so, foreign competitors have been challenging American business in the realms of both cost and quality. Nowhere is this more vividly demonstrated than in the automobile industry. Until the mid-1960s, foreign automobiles (with the exception of the Volkswagen Beetle) were a novelty. Now, the prevalence of Japanese-made cars is taken for granted. How did the Japanese car manufacturers make such significant inroads into the American automobile market? This question could be discussed at length, but the answer boils down to the perception of many customers that a Japanese-made car provides higher quality than an American-made car for the same or less money.

This perception that "made in the U.S.A." connotes inferior quality and higher prices is not confined to the automobile industry. It is also common in electronics (televisions, stereo components, and video recorders). A study that evaluated product quality in the room air-conditioner industries in the United States and Japan found that the product made by the Japanese company with the poorest quality level had a failure rate less than half that of the product made by the American company with the best quality.[1] Clearly, if American companies wish to retain their customers, they must be able to compete not only with each other but with competitors from other countries. Management Encounter 11-3 shows that the United States is not the only nation facing challenges from Japan.

## Definition of Quality

It is imperative that an organization develop a philosophy regarding the quality of the product that it creates. Would the philosophy of Rolls Royce PLC, be the same as that of the Ford Motor Company? Probably not. Nor would the quality statement of the Blue Fox restaurant in San Francisco be the same as that of the Squat and Gobble Diner in downtown Podunk. Furthermore, their quality positions should not be the same. A useful, if nebulous, definition of quality is "fitness for use," and use must be defined within the context of the market for which a product is intended. A person in the market for a Rolls Royce would define use differently from a person in the market for a Ford Taurus.

## Management Encounter 11-3

### *The Swiss Army Knife*

The Swiss army knife has become the most celebrated pocketknife in the world. A distinctive red handle with a white cross has made the knife a national symbol of Switzerland. The knife's success is the result of a combination of high quality and a certain mystique.

Carl Elsener started making knives in 1891 for the Swiss government, producing a jackknife called the soldier's knife. Later, he added blades and tools, making the knife more sophisticated. In 1921, after the development of stainless steel, Elsener named his company Victorinox, combining his mother's name and the European name for stainless steel. At about the same time, Wenger, another company in Switzerland, began making knives based on the Victorinox principle. Today, only these two companies have the Swiss government's permission to use the Swiss cross on their knives.

Victorinox uses the finest French and German steel for its blades and springs, which are stamped, hardened, and polished into the final product. The company's production is conducted with a certain amount of secrecy to protect it from Far East imitators. Competitors in Japan, China, and Taiwan make cheap imitations of the Swiss army knife and sell them by mail order. Victorinox does not fight these imitators in court, but company officials stress that a genuine Swiss army knife will have the name of one of the two makers, Victorinox or Wenger, stamped into the shank of the main blade.

Victorinox has spent many years and a great deal of money to perfect its production processes. Some of the machines used are designed and built at the plant in order to keep imitators from copying them. The company produces about twenty thousand knives a day—about 75 percent Swiss army knives and 25 percent regular kitchen knives. It employs about nine hundred workers and is the largest employer in the Swiss state of Schwyz.

Victorinox and Wenger exports about 80 percent of their total output, although the Swiss army still buys forty thousand knives a year. Half of the knives produced are sold in the United States, and about 10 percent of the knives are sold to tourists in Switzerland.

There are about three hundred models of the Swiss army knife, with a wide range of features. The latest top-of-the-line model has blades and tools that do twenty-nine different things. Most models have a corkscrew, a can opener, a screwdriver, a wire stripper, scissors, and a magnifying glass. The knives sell for around $60.

Victorinox officials are optimistic about the future of the Swiss army knife. They believe that the quality of the Swiss army knife will protect it against cheap imitators. Despite its relatively high price, Victorinox believes that the utility of its knife will continue to attract new buyers.

These facts are from William Tuohy, "The Most Celebrated Pocket Knife in the World," *The Hawaiian Star-Bulletin Advertiser*, November 29, 1987, p. 1C; Nathan Cobb, "Best Blade," *The Bryan–College Station Eagle*, April 21, 1988, pp. 1C, 5C.

Fitness for use depends on five general characteristics[2]:

▶ Technological characteristics, such as strength, weight, and hardness
▶ Psychological characteristics, such as taste, beauty, and status
▶ Time-oriented characteristics, such as reliability, durability, and maintainability
▶ Contractual characteristics, such as warranty provisions
▶ Ethical characteristics, such as honesty of sales force and truthful information about the product including defects, if any

Some of these characteristics are more easily measured than others. For example, the fuel economy of an automobile or its reliability defined in terms

**Strong quality control programs create consumer loyalty.**   General Signal Air Brakes' service technicians are shown here inspecting air brakes installed on New York's fleet of subway cars. General Signal is providing satisfaction to their customer, New York City, and also to customers of the subway who are indirect purchasers of General Signal's product.

of frequency of repairs can be measured with some degree of precision. It is more difficult to measure psychological characteristics such as design, color, or status. An organization has to decide exactly which quality characteristics it considers important and then define those characteristics in terms that can be measured.

**Quality control** involves measuring the quality of products and services against established quality standards. Company policies and strategies, as well as perceived marketing opportunities, are inputs into the decision concerning what products or product types should be developed. Once this decision is

**Quality control**

Measuring the quality of products and services against established quality standards

made, product specifications and quality standards must be established so the company can create a product that will compete in the marketplace. Concurrent with product development is process development. Production facilities must be designed that can produce products with the desired specifications. Once the desired quality characteristics, specifications, and standards have been stated in measurable terms, the next step is inspection.

# Inspection

Inspection reveals whether a product meets established quality standards. Some product characteristics may be discerned by fairly simple inspection techniques—weighing the contents of cereal boxes or measuring the tread depth of an automobile tire. Other inspection techniques are more elaborate. Automobile manufacturers use automated machines to open and close car doors to test the durability of latches and hinges. The food-processing and pharmaceutical industries use various chemical tests to determine the quality of their output. Some of the tests used by organizations are "destructive," and others are classified as "performance testing." The repeated opening and closing of car doors to determine the life expectancy of hinges and latches is a destructive test because the test lasts until the product fails. Honda has used a television commercial in which a lawn mower is tested by a pull on the starter rope. The implication is that if the mower starts, it has passed the test. This is an example of a performance test. The test itself does not destroy or damage the product.

Inspection is normally made of purchased items, work-in-process, and finished items. The inspection of purchased items and finished items takes place after the fact; the inspection of work-in-process is preventive. What this means is that purchased items—raw materials, subassemblies, or components purchased from outside suppliers—have been finished and the quality level, whatever it is, is already present in the item. The purpose of inspection is to determine what the quality level is. For items that are being worked on—an automobile moving down the assembly line, a booster rocket at an intermediate stage of completion, or a color monitor that is being assembled—the purpose of the inspection is to find defects before the product is completed so that the corrections can be made.

An important question relating to inspection is how many items should be inspected. If a company produces five thousand television picture tubes a day, should they all be inspected or just some of them? Whether to inspect 100 percent of the output or to sample only part of the output is related to the cost of the inspection process, destructiveness of the inspection process, and the importance of the item to the safety of consumers or others.

Some inspection procedures are very expensive to perform, use elaborate testing equipment, and require a significant number of hours to complete. When the inspection process is expensive, it is usually desirable to take a sample of the output and test that. If the sample passes inspection, the assumption may be made that the items in the lot from which the sample was drawn would also pass inspection. In other words, the quality of all items (the population) is assumed to be the same as the quality of the sample. By using principles of statistical inference, management can structure sampling techniques that assure a relatively high probability of reaching the right conclusion—that is, rejecting a population that does not meet standards and accepting a population that does. Nevertheless, there will always be the chance of making an incorrect decision—accepting a population that *does not* meet standards (because the sample was satisfactory) or rejecting a population that *does* meet standards (because the sample contained too many defective items). That, however, is the risk of sampling.

Sampling is likely to be used when inspection tests are destructive. Determining the life expectancy of light bulbs by turning them on and recording how long they last would be foolish—there is virtually no market for burned-out light bulbs. Instead, a generalization based on the quality of a sample would be applied to the entire population of light bulbs from which the sample was drawn.

Human life or safety depends on the proper functioning of some items, such as the navigational systems installed in commercial airliners. For such items, even though the inspection process is costly, the potential cost in human lives and safety of flawed systems is too great not to inspect 100 percent of the output.

## Zero Defects

Many companies prefer to operate with very small inventories of raw materials and components. To do so, they need to ensure that the materials and components on hand meet the required quality standards, because if they do not meet standards, the inventory will not be large enough to satisfy production requirements when the defective units have been removed. When an inventory is large, defective items can be sent back and replaced with good items from the inventory. The just-in-time system described earlier operates with a very small inventory, and therefore the raw materials and purchased components must be 100 percent acceptable because production would have to stop if defective parts or materials entered the system.

Quality control programs that aim at 100 percent acceptable output are called **zero defect programs.** The goal of zero defects is difficult but not impossible to achieve. It does require exacting inspection techniques and adherence to high quality standards.

## Quality Circles

A quality circle (also called a performance team in some American organizations) is a group of people who usually work in close proximity and whose jobs are somewhat related. The team leader, possibly the foreman of the group, reserves a block of time, maybe an hour per week, during which the group meets to discuss problems that individual members have encountered while performing their jobs. Possible sources of the problem are identified and alternative solutions are evaluated. Once solutions are decided on, they are referred to upper levels of management for implementation. The concept of quality circles was developed in the Japanese automobile industry in an attempt to decrease production costs and increase the operating efficiency of the production system. In spite of the name quality circle, the problems addressed by this approach are not all related to quality. Any problem related to the processes used in creating a product is discussed.

Quality circles are very useful in eliciting workable solutions to operational problems. They draw on the knowledge and expertise of workers who are closest to the firing line and thereby increase the involvement of those operating personnel.

# ▶ Production and Operations Management Effectiveness

Materials management, production planning and control, and quality control are major areas of responsibility for the production and operations manager. Other important areas are product design, facility location, and facility layout. Each of these affects the organization's effectiveness in its efforts to manage materials, plan and control production activities, and control the quality and reliability of products.

## Product Design

The design of the organization's product is dependent on two factors—one external to the organization and one internal. The external factor is what the customers want in the way of a product. Automobile designers, fashion designers, and even fast-food franchises are very sensitive to customers' desires. When medical research began uncovering a relationship between heart disease and cholesterol levels, many restaurants began to add menu items that were low in cholesterol and fat. When fuel costs rose dramatically in the 1970s, American automobile manufacturers changed the design of their cars so that the vehicles would be more fuel-efficient. Clearly, the wants and desires of the customer have an impact on product design.

The internal factor affecting product design has to do with the organization's technical ability to produce a certain product. An organization is restricted by the limitations of its equipment and the skills of its employees. Consequently, an organization may not be able to respond to the needs of the marketplace without changing equipment and upgrading employees' skills, and each of these takes time, planning, and money to accomplish.

**Standardization** Making products according to agreed-to specifiations so that their parts are interchangeable

***Standardization.*** Most firms that produce products in large quantities for many customers have found that they can make products cheaper and faster by standardizing designs. **Standardization** is making products according to agreed-to specifications so that their parts are interchangeable. As a result of standardization, a customer may not get exactly what is wanted, but the product generally costs less than a custom-designed product. Television sets, computers, automobiles, Big Macs, and most medical examinations are standardized products. Standardization speeds up production and quality control and reduces production costs. Even with standardization, some variations are possible. An automobile might come with aluminum alloy wheels or standard wheels, electric windows or manual windows, a sun roof or no sun roof, and so forth. Such variations are actually standard options provided by the manufacturer to give the illusion of personalized service.

*Modular Design.* **Modular design** is building an item in self-contained units, or modules, that can be combined or interchanged to create different products. Personal computers, for example, are generally composed of a number of components that can be installed, removed, or exchanged to give the PC different operating characteristics. Memory can be upgraded by removing one component and adding another. A second disk drive can be added or a disk drive can be replaced by a hard disk drive. Many configurations can be generated by simply changing modular components.

Because many modular components are produced as integrated units, the failure of any portion of a modular component usually necessitates the replacement of the entire component. Modular design allows products to be repaired quickly, thus reducing the cost of labor, but the component itself is expensive, raising the cost of repair materials. Many electronic products use modular design concepts. Examples of such products are televisions, stereo systems, microwave ovens, telephones, and video cassette recorders.

**Modular design**

Building an item in self-contained units, or modules, that can be combined or interchanged to create different products

# Facility Location

Where to locate an organization's facilities is a significant question because once the decision has been made and implemented, the firm must live with the answer. When a firm decides to relocate or open a new facility at a new location, careful attention is paid to the alternatives for such a move. In 1983, General Motors began a location-feasibility study for its Saturn plant. The study considered twenty possible locations, but when plans for the Saturn plant were made public, more and more states and municipalities applied for consideration. These appeals filled eighty legal-size file drawers in GM's headquarters in Detroit. It took GM almost four years to complete the location study and decide to locate the plant in Spring Hill, Tennessee.

To a certain extent, the factors that an organization considers when making a location decision vary from industry to industry. However, certain factors are common to virtually all industries:

▶ *Proximity to the market*: How close a facility is to its customers affects its transportation costs as well as the speed with which it can respond to customers' needs.
▶ *Availability of raw materials*: Some organizations must be close to sources of materials. The steel industry is located in the Midwest, close to iron-ore deposits. The furniture industry is located on the East Coast, close to the hardwood forests that provide lumber for making furniture.
▶ *Availability of transportation*: The availability of various modes of transportation must be considered, as well as the reliability and cost of each mode.

**New approaches to old problems.** Technology has helped Haverfield Aviation find an efficient way to maintain transmission lines—helicopters quickly bring employees to the site where they are needed.

▶ *Availability of power*: The abundance and nature of energy sources, such as natural gas, hydroelectric power, and nuclear power, has to be considered. Consideration must also be given to current and future availability and cost.

▶ *Climatic influences*: The climate affects the construction of the facility and the cost of heating and cooling the facility once it is completed.

▶ *Availability of labor*: The cost and availability of labor are important considerations. Labor rates vary from region to region and from nation to nation. Many organizations have work done abroad, where labor is cheap, and ship components into the United States for final assembly. The type of labor skills needed by the organization must also be taken into account. If required skills are not present in the labor force of a potential location, then that site might be eliminated.

▶ *Community characteristics*: The cultural and entertainment characteristics of a location might be considered. The quality of life afforded by alternative locations might not have a direct impact on the cost of the firm's operations, but it could affect the outlook and morale of the employees who are transferred to the location to work at the new facility.

The facility-location decision is complex because it involves the evaluation of many factors, some of which cannot be measured with precision. Because of the long-term impact of the decision, however, it is one that cannot be taken lightly.

# Facility Layout

Arranging the physical layout of an organization is a complex, highly technical task. Some industrial architects specialize in the design and layout of certain types of businesses. Three basic facility layouts are used in industry: fixed-position layout, process or functional layout, and product or line layout.

Many organizations use a combination of layout designs. For example, an automobile manufacturer may rely on an assembly line but may also use a process or functional layout to manufacture parts. A commercial sign manufacturer may rely on the process layout but also use an assembly line to assemble the components of a sign. No matter which facility layout is used, the cost and efficiency of operations depend on the degree to which the layout works effectively.

***Fixed-Position Layout.*** An organization using a **fixed-position layout** has a central location for the basic product, and all resources required to create the product are brought to that location. The product does not move.

Organizations that use the fixed-position layout are known as project organizations. A **project organization** is one that is involved in large, complex tasks such as construction or exploration. Examples of project organizations include organizations involved in large, complex construction projects such as office buildings, microwave relay stations, or hydroelectric plants. The project organization is typified by an output or product that is unique, reliance on highly skilled labor, production of very few units, and high production costs per unit.

***Process or Functional Layout.*** Firms that use the **process or functional layout** facility organize the transformation process into departments, depending on the type of work to be done. A metal fabrication plant may have a cutting department, a drilling department, and a polishing department. A hospital may have an X-ray unit, an obstetrics unit, and so on. Related processes are grouped within a department.

Organizations that use the process or functional layout are known as intermittent organizations. An **intermittent organization** deals with products of a lesser magnitude than does a project organization; the products created by intermittent organizations are not necessarily unique but possess a significant number of differences. Products such as medical treatment, custom-made kitchen or bathroom cabinets, commercial printing services, and advertising campaigns emanate from intermittent organizations. Intermittent organizations are likely to be able to create a product to customers' specifications and to produce relatively few units of each product. Because of the low level of output, the cost per unit of product is generally high.

***Product or Line Layout.*** An assembly line is the best example of the **product or line layout.** This facility design requires that the work of creating a product be broken down into activities or tasks requiring relatively short

**Advanced automation.** Technological advancement in the area of production and manufacturing has allowed for increased output and long-term cost advantages for many companies. This automated assembly line engages in production with minimum human input.

**Continuous manufacturing organization**

An organization that runs continuously and creates products with many similar characteristics

periods of time and be assigned to workers positioned along the line. The workers remain in one location, and the product moves from one worker to another. Each person in turn performs the required tasks or activities.

A product or line layout is commonly found in an organization known as a continuous manufacturing organization. A **continuous manufacturing organization** is so named because once it is set up, it runs continuously, creating products with many similar characteristics. Examples of products of continuous systems are automobiles, television sets, vacuum cleaners, toothpaste, and meals from a cafeteria. Continuous manufacturing organizations are characterized by the standardized product they produce, the large number of units produced, and the relatively low unit cost of production.

# ► Recent Developments in Production and Operations Management

Every industry has a basic, underlying technology that dictates the nature of its transformation process. The steel industry continually tries to improve steel-making techniques. The health-care industry performs research into medical technologies to improve the quality of health care. Two recent technological developments which have strongly impacted the operations of many organizations are robotics and computer applications.

## Robotics

The industrial robot is less glamorous and considerably less sophisticated than fictional robots such as R2D2 and C3PO in the movie *Star Wars*. An **industrial robot** is a machine "designed to move material, parts, tools, or specialized devices through variable programmed motions, for the performance of a variety of tasks."[3]

The configurations of industrial robots (Figure 11-5) vary considerably because so many robots are created to perform specific functions. A robot designed to transport raw materials from one work station to another looks considerably different from one designed to do spot welding on automobile bodies. Nevertheless, robots have four basic components: the actuator, the manipulator, the end effector, and the sensor.

The actuator provides the power that enables the robot to perform its prescribed movements. Commonly used types of actuators are the hydraulic actuator, which consists of a cylinder driven by hydraulic oil; the pneumatic-drive system, which uses a cylinder driven by air; and the electronic motor. Hydraulic and pneumatic actuators can handle heavy loads and are used when heavy objects must be lifted. The electronic motor cannot handle as much weight as the other two, but it is considerably more accurate in its movements and therefore can be used for operations requiring some degree of precision, such as welding or painting.

The manipulator is the arm and various links (or elongated armatures), joints (points of connection of two links), and the end effector. For purposes of identification, the joints of a robot are numbered, beginning with the joint where the manipulator is attached to the base and increasing as the joints near the end effector.

The end effector is the device at the end of the manipulator that allows the robot to perform its prescribed operations. There are four types of end effectors. The friction gripper places pressure on opposite sides of an object in order to hold it in much the same way that a human hand holds a glass. The physical-constraint gripper places pressure all around an object by filling elastomeric fingers with air or fluid to produce a grip similar to the way a blood-pressure cuff works to place pressure on the upper arm. The attraction gripper holds an object by means of electromagnetism or suction. The support gripper uses a hook or other similar device to support an object.

The sensor provides feedback to the microprocessor concerning the location of the object on which the robot is going to perform its operations.

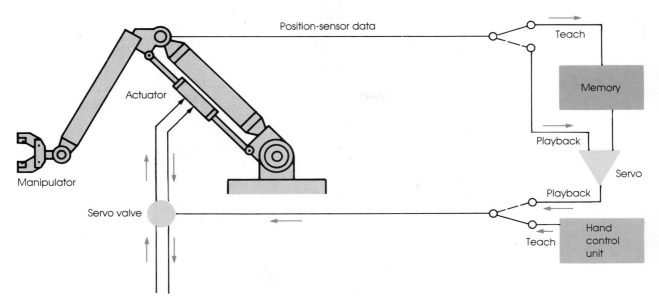

**Figure 11-5**

Components of an Industrial Robot

Robots have been used for years in certain applications. In 1958, Hughes Aircraft built a robot to handle radioactive materials at the Atomic Energy Commission plant in Albuquerque, New Mexico. Recently, the navy, along with others, has been developing unmanned submersibles for both military and civilian purposes. One such submersible was used in the exploration of the wreck of the *Titanic*.

Robots are used in foundry operations. Dependable-Fordath, Inc., located in Sherwood, Oregon, developed a robot that removes molds from the company's molding machines, an application that requires very accurate positioning.

The Klock Company in Manchester, Connecticut, uses robots in its plasma-spraying operation to coat gas turbine blades. This operation is ideally suited for robots because it involves the combination of ceramic or metallic powders with ionized gases that are heated to temperatures in excess of 20,000 degrees Fahrenheit and then sprayed at high velocity. The environment created by this operation is extremely unpleasant, containing noise levels that may exceed 120 decibels, ultraviolet rays that can damage the eyes, and particulate matter that fills the air.

Robots are becoming increasingly important in the automobile industry. They are used to move materials and in assembly operations such as spot welding and painting. As a matter of fact, many assembly operations—not just of cars, but of television sets, telephones, stereo equipment, and many other products—are dependent on industrial robots.

## Computer Applications

Computers have been used in business for several decades and on a relatively large scale since IBM introduced its 650 series in the late 1950s.

**Robotics in business.**
Research Corp. in Danbury, Connecticut is now testing a simple robot designed to deliver meal trays to hospital patients. The robot memorizes the hospital corridors and uses ultrasonic sensors to avoid people. These models sell for approximately $25,000. These robots are desirable because of the labor shortage in the medical field and the fact that hospitals must operate twenty-four hours a day, every day.

**Computer-assisted design (CAD) and computer-assisted manufacturing (CAM)**

A computerized approach that links the design and manufacturing areas, making information readily available

Most of the early applications were of a recordkeeping nature—for example, processing payrolls and maintaining inventory records. More modern business is highly dependent on the computer for a large number of sophisticated functions.

The production and operations area uses computers in the product-design phase as well as in the actual manfacturing of the product. These applications are generally referred to as **computer-assisted design** (**CAD**) and **computer-assisted manufacturing** (**CAM**). As organizational complexity increases—because of varied product lines, complex manufacturing technology, and high volumes of output—the transfer of information becomes increasingly difficult. For example, a design engineer might design a component for a new product without knowing about an engineering drawing for another product that could be adapted to the design.

CAD/CAM is a computerized approach that links the design and manufacturing areas, making information readily available. At G. W. Plastics Company, in Bethel, Vermont, an integrated CAD/CAM system cut design time by 65 percent. Designs generated by a CAD/CAM system at General Electric are teleprocessed from remote locations to Wilmington, North Carolina, where an engineer with a stylus pen electronically creates the manufacturing plan. Cummins Engine Company in Columbus, Indiana, reports that CAD/CAM not only has boosted productivity but has also improved the quality of product designs.[4]

Computers are also used to monitor the transformation process, gathering information about the equipment used to produce the product and about the product itself as it goes from one stage of the transformation process to the next. The computer provides information to an operator who may, if necessary, take corrective action. In the monitoring mode, the computer itself does not take the corrective action.

In some highly automated systems, the computer can be used to control the production process. Data generated by the transformation process concerning the operation of the equipment and certain product characteristics are compared with predetermined standards. If these comparisons are favorable, the process is allowed to continue; if they are unfavorable, the computer is programmed to take corrective action. No direct intervention by human beings is needed.

Computers will continue to make strong inroads into production and operations on two fronts—one dealing with the technology involved in manufacturing and one dealing with the administrative functions and processes used by operations managers. The operations manager must be willing to work with computers and to develop a high degree of computer literacy.

**Computer-assisted design.** Many businesses are highly dependent upon computers as a source of information in their day-to-day operations. A weather radar computer has uses in many areas—air travel, sports, recreation, and news.

# Notes

**1.** David A. Garvin, "Quality on the Line," *Harvard Business Review* 61 (September–October 1983): 65–75.

**2.** J. M. Juran, Frank M. Gryna, Jr., and R. S. Bingham, Jr., *Quality Control Handbook*, 3rd ed. (New York: McGraw-Hill, 1974).

**3.** Joseph P. Ziskowsky, "Robotics—the First Step to CIM and the Factory of the Future," *Robotics and Factories of the Future*, ed. Suren N. Dwivedi (Berlin: Springer-Verlag, 1984), pp. 154–160.

**4.** John Teresko, "CAD/CAM Goes to Work," *Industry Week*, February 7, 1983, pp. 40–42.

# Summary and Review

▶ Production and operations management involves acquiring the necessary resources to create products and services, planning the specific steps through which those resources must pass, and ensuring that products and services conform to standards of quality. Production and operations management includes materials management, production planning and control, quality control, as well as product design, facility location, facility layout, robotics, and computer-assisted design and manufacturing.

▶ Materials management is the development and coordination of the policies, procedures, and systems that are used to obtain, distribute, and store the materials needed to create a product or service. It includes purchasing (the buying of all the materials needed by the organization), inventory management (keeping track of the organization's resources), traffic management (the selection of a suitable mode of transportation, coordination of arrivals and departures, and auditing of freight bills), and shipping and receiving (ensuring that the right items are shipped from the facility and received by the facility).

▶ Production planning and control is determining what products should be produced and by what date they should be completed, and scheduling the specific activities necessary to have the products completed by the target date. Production planning and control includes aggregate planning (developing a demand forecast for a group of products for periods of six months to a year), detailed planning (demand forecasting for only one or two months), and dispatching (the initiation of action).

▶ Quality control involves measuring the quality of products and services against established quality standards. Zero-defect programs aim for 100 percent acceptable output, or no defects in the output of an organization. Quality circles are groups of people who work together to solve problems, often having to do with quality control.

▶ Product design is dependent on what customers want and on the organization's technical abilities. Products may be standardized, modular, or custom-designed. The decision where to locate operations facilities is a crucial one that depends on proximity to the market, availability of raw materials, availability of transportation, availability of power, climatic influences, availability of labor, and community characteristics. Facility layout is the arrangement of the physical layout of an organization. Layouts may be fixed-position layouts (in project organizations), process or functional layouts (in intermittent organizations), or product or line layouts (in continuous manufacturing organizations).

▶ Robots—programmable machines designed to move material, parts, tools, or specialized devices—perform a variety of tasks. They are increasingly used in industry. Computers are also vital to operations, particularly computer-assisted design and computer-assisted manufacturing.

# Key Terms

inputs
outputs
production and operations
materials management
purchasing
inventory management
ABC inventory classification system
economic order quantity method
just-in-time (JIT) concept
traffic management
production planning
production control
aggregate planning
master production schedule
detailed planning
material-needs analysis
material-requirement planning

capacity-needs analysis
dispatching
quality control
zero defect programs
standardization
modular design
fixed-position layout
project organization
process or functional layout
intermittent organization
product or line layout
continuous manufacturing
  organization
industrial robot
computer-assisted design
computer-assisted manufacturing

# Checking Your Understanding

This chapter introduced you to the subject of operations management. To test and reinforce your understanding, fill in the blanks below.

**1.** The _____ _____ creates final products by combining the inputs in predetermined ways using different types of equipment, administrative procedures, and technology.

**2.** _____ is the buying of all the raw materials, parts, components, manufacturing supplies, office supplies, and equipment needed by an organization.

**3.** The _____ _____ _____ _____ tries to minimize the number of units maintained in inventory by providing an almost continuous flow of items from suppliers to the organization.

4. _____ _____ is determining what products should be produced and by what date they should be completed.

5. Developing a demand forecast for a group of products is known as _____ _____.

6. _____ is the sequence of operations through which a product must pass while in production.

7. The order in which products are processed is known as _____.

8. _____ _____ is the measurement of the quality of products and services against some established quality standard.

9. _____ is making products according to agreed-to specifications so that the parts are interchangeable.

10. _____ _____ _____ _____ organize the transformation process into departments according to type of work to be done.

11. _____ _____ are involved in large, complex tasks.

# Topics for Review and Discussion

1. What is the purpose of production and operations management?

2. Classify the following parts (according to the ABC inventory classification system) for use at General Motors:

    rivets
    tires
    screwdrivers
    paint-spraying robot
    steel
    computer-assisted manufacturing system

3. Explain why organizations using the just-in-time concept must have zero defects in their inventory.

4. Assume Ford makes Taurus and Escort models at one of its plants. If consumers want 8,000 Taurus models and 5,000 Escort models, and it takes 1.2 times more labor to make a Taurus model than an Escort, how many equivalent units of each model must Ford make for the month? What is the total aggregate monthly demand?

5. If Ford can make 13,000 cars per month at that same plant, will Ford have excess capacity or will it have to use overtime and temporary workers to meet the demand?

6. Why is quality control so important to success in the marketplace?

7. What are the advantages and disadvantages of standardizing products?

8. In what industry would the fixed-position layout be most efficient? The process or functional layout? The product or line layout? Use real examples.

# Exercises

**1.** Compare and contrast production and operations management at McDonald's with that of Honda of America. Compare and contrast operations management at McDonald's with that of Shearson Lehman Hutton, a brokerage firm.

**2.** Find a real company that uses JIT, either in your local community or in a business journal. Why did the company decide to use JIT? What have been the advantages and disadvantages of using JIT for that particular company? What has been the overall effect on the quality of the company's products or services? What has been the overall effect on the company's bottom line?

**3.** Why has the quality of American products declined in the last two decades? What are businesses doing to improve quality and increase competitiveness with the product quality of other nations? What else can businesses do to improve quality?

## Case 11-1

### *Beech Uses Plastic Technology to Build Airplane of the Future*

Businesspeople frequently need to travel, and many corporations opt to buy their own plane to get their employees where they need to be when they need to be there. Beech Aircraft Company is building a new plane to transport businesspeople for less money. Beech's Starships are different from conventional planes, however. They have no tail and are made of composite plastics. Because the design of the plane is so radical, management of the production process is very important.

In 1987, Jeana Yeager and Dick Rutan made a historic flight around the world without refueling. Their strange-looking plane, *Voyager*, was made of plastic foam, paper honeycomb, and carbon-fiber filaments, all glued together with plastic epoxy. Rutan's brother Burt had designed and built *Voyager* for the historic flight. Burt Rutan also designed Beech's Starship. Like *Voyager*, Starship makes use of advanced plastic-construction technology, carbon fiber, and epoxy resin substitutes.

The Starship is a near-jet turboprop airplane—that is, a high-speed propeller plane that uses jet fuel. Beech made Starship a turboprop rather than a jet because the company has experience in turboprops. Each Starship holds from eight to ten passengers in addition to the pilot and has a top speed of 405 miles per hour. It has a price tag of $3.7 million (most comparably sized business jets cost between $5 million and $7 million). Because of the plastic body, the planes are much more fuel-efficient than traditional planes.

Research and development played a major role in the evolution of the plastic airplane. Beech altered the plane's design many times. To achieve speed, the designers moved the engines as far back as possible. Doing so made the plane noisier because vibrations and wind currents buffeted the tail, so Rutan and his team eliminated the tail, using rear and nose wings to give the Starships the stability normally provided by the tail. However, they couldn't make subtle curves in the wings with steel, so they used composite plastics, but that led to yet another problem: Because composite plastics don't conduct electricity, a bolt of lightning could damage the plane during flight. The designers built a layer of wire mesh into the plane to solve that problem.

According to Beech president James S. Walsh, the development process was expedited because Beech's ample financial resources allowed the company to develop simultaneous alternative solutions to crucial problems. If one solution did not work, engineers applied the next alternative immediately. The company also had to learn about working with carbon-fiber composites, both for the plane itself and for the molds used to make parts for the plane. In fact, nearly half of the research and development costs on the Starship went toward learning how to use the plastic composites. The knowledge will not go to waste: The company plans to incorporate plastic composites into other airplanes and military applications.

Beech had to redesign and expand its manufacturing facilities to accommodate production of the plane. It allocated more than 500,000 square feet of space to building the Starship planes. It also had to design and build nearly every piece of equipment used to manufacture the planes—including the oven used to bake the plastic composites. Beech even adapted a blue-jeans cutting machine to cut patterns out of graphite sheets for the planes. The facility currently has enough space and molds to make four Starships a month.

Beech, which is owned by Raytheon Corporation, has put $300 million into the development of Starship. The first prototype took eight months and $1.8 million to build. Beech had to build the first production models that were tested by the Federal Aviation Administration from the molds used for the actual production of the planes. Thus, Beech had to adapt the factories and build the production equipment, at great expense, before it knew if it would be allowed to build the Starship. The plane was certified by the FAA in 1988.

Although Beech spent a great deal of money on Starship research, development, and production, the company knows the money was well spent. President Walsh says, "We expect to be in this business twenty years from now, and so we must develop new products." Now that Beech has built the first Starships, it must carefully manage inventory and the purchasing and scheduling of resources and maintain quality standards during production. The company must sell five hundred Starships to recoup its research and development expense. It is already on the way to reaching that goal, with orders for fifty planes.

---

These facts are from Thomas G. Donlan, "Poised for Takeoff: Starship Introduces a New Technology," *Barron's*, January 26, 1987, pp. 14, 75; Kevin Maney, "Aircraft Firm Wishes upon Its Starship," *USA Today*, September 29, 1987, pp. 1B, 2B; David

M. North, "Starship 1 Dominates Beech Research Programs," *Aviation Week & Space Technology*, October 22, 1984, pp. 89–91; "Starship Emphasis," *Aviation Week & Space Technology*, October 8, 1984, p. 29; and the 1984 Raytheon Annual Report, p. 14.

**Questions**

1. What are some of the production planning and control concerns in producing Starships?
2. Discuss the importance of quality control in manufacturing the first fifty Starship planes.
3. How did Beech resolve product design issues in developing the Starship?

## Case 11-2
# *Brown & Jenkins Trading Co.*

Brown & Jenkins Trading Co., based in Burlington, Vermont, is a mail-order coffee-bean company. The company procures and roasts its own coffee beans and mails them to customers all over the country. It also offers teas, coffee grinders, coffee makers, and gift packs in its catalog. Owners Ken Brown and Carol Jenkins manage both the production of the coffee beans and the operation of their mail-order service.

Ken Brown and Carol Jenkins got into the mail-order business in 1984 when their employer moved out of state. Brown is a coffee gourmet with years of direct-mail experience. Jenkins, who also appreciates a good cup of coffee, was an experienced accountant. There were few other companies selling coffee by mail at that time, so Brown and Jenkins pooled their savings, obtained a $40,000 loan and went into the coffee-bean mail-order business. They bought some high quality coffee beans and ran some test advertisements for sample packs in magazines read by coffee connoisseurs such as *Gourmet* and *Bon Appetit*. Brown and Jenkins were discouraged when they received only a hundred orders. But then those first customers began to reorder coffee and tell their friends about the company, and the company survived. To keep the initial production costs down, they started the business in their own home. Roasting, grinding, and filling the bags with coffee occurred right in the living room; the orders were packed and shipped from the basement.

The company began to prosper, and soon moved into a renovated brick factory in 1985. Brown and Jenkins also opened a small café in the building that catered to the building's other tenants and businesspeople from the neighborhood. In their first full year of business, Brown & Jenkins sold about $100,000 and in 1986, they doubled that. The business was growing fast, so they closed the café and moved to a larger area in the same building.

Ken Brown handles most of the roasting of the coffee beans and the shipping and packing. Roasting involves a set of production processes similar to that of manufacturing a product from scratch. Carol Jenkins, who has another full-time job, does the bookkeeping and accounting, handles the correspondence, and writes the company's newsletters. The company has two other full-time employees and one part-time employee.

The company buys the best quality green Arabica coffee beans and does not roast them until it receives an order. This practice insures freshness. In addition, since it is difficult to estimate demand for the various flavors of coffee, this avoids the problem of developing excess inventories of slower-selling coffees. Customers can choose from many kinds and flavors of coffee, from the Kenya AA to Jamaican Blue Mountain, the "world's most acclaimed coffee," from the popular Irish Creme to the Viennese Cinnamon. The production process involves precise steps that require careful timing. Brown uses a computer to calculate how many pounds of each variety to roast according to how many orders he must ship that day. He roasts 5,000 to 7,000 pounds of coffee every month on a custom-made Diedrich coffee roaster. The roaster can handle very large batches (forty pounds) of popular coffees or small batches (five pounds) of new flavors that haven't yet become popular. Brown monitors the roasting process constantly because coffee beans go through many changes during the roasting process. Each variety of coffee must be roasted to a specific stage, requiring constant sampling to determine the exact instant when the roasting is complete and ensure the highest-quality coffee.

Most orders are roasted, packed in 12-ounce bags, and shipped on the same day to provide maximum freshness. Customers pay from $5 to $19 for each 12-ounce bag. The coffee is packed in 12-ounce bags instead of pounds to discourage pound-per-pound price comparisons with store-bought coffee and to save money on shipping charges. United Parcel Service then delivers the beans to customers within two or three days.

Carol Jenkins' newsletter serves as a public relations tool to educate old and new customers about the final processing and use of gourmet coffee. The newsletters contain numerous tips on storing, grinding, and brewing coffee, as well as information on new varieties and flavors of coffee. The company currently has 10,000 names on its mailing list and hopes to boost that number to 30,000 by 1989. Brown and Jenkins' 1987 sales were nearly $500,000.

In order to succeed and grow, Ken Brown and Carol Jenkins must manage the production processes involved in roasting quality coffee and maintain good relations with their customers. Their constant attention to production guarantees that their coffee is of the highest quality and freshness.

---

These facts are from Berkeley Rice, "Freshly Ground Success," *Continental Profiles, Inc.*, 1 (March 1988): 13–14; Ken Brown, "All About Coffee," *The Coffee Break* (Fall 1985): 3; "We've Moved," *The Coffee Break* (Fall 1985): 1; The Brown & Jenkins Coffee Catalog.

### Questions

1. Evaluate Brown and Jenkins' initial strategy to work their production out of their home. Would you have recommended a more formal approach to the business and production process? If so why?

2. What changes in the management of the production function would be required if growth continues at its current rapid pace?
3. Are the techniques discussed in this chapter equally useful to General Motors in their automobile assembly lines and Brown and Jenkins in their coffee production? Why?

# Answers to Checking Your Understanding

1. transformation process
2. purchasing
3. just-in-time concept
4. production planning
5. aggregate planning
6. routing

7. sequencing
8. quality control
9. standardization
10. process or functional layouts
11. project organizations

GOVERNMENT AND LEGAL FORCES • ECONOMY • ETHICS AND SOCIAL RESPONSIBILITY • GOVERNMENT AND LEGAL FORCES • ECONOMY • ETHICS AND SOCIAL RESPONSIBILITY • GOVERNMENT AND LEGAL FORCES • ECONOMY • ETHICS AND SOCIAL RESPONSIBILITY • GOVERNMENT AND LEGAL FORCES • ECONOMY • GOVERNMENT FORCES • E AND SOCIA GOVERNM FORCES • AND SOC GOVERNM FORCES • AND SOCIA GOVERNME FORCES • E AND SOCIAL R GOVERNMENT AN FORCES • ECONOMY AND SOCIAL RESPONSIBILI GOVERNMENT AND LEGAL FORCES • ECONOMY • ETHICS AND SOCIAL RESPONSIBILITY • GOVERNMENT AND LEGAL FORCES • ECONOMY • ETHICS AND SOCIAL RESPONSIBILITY • GOVERNMENT AND LEGAL FORCES • ECONOMY • ETHICS AND SOCIAL RESPONSIBILITY •

Finance

Owner

Employee    Customer

Management

Marketing

*Part* III

# MARKETING

- ▶ Marketing Principles
- ▶ Product and Price
- ▶ Distribution
- ▶ Promotion

## Outline

# Chapter 12

# Marketing Principles

## Objectives

After reading this chapter, you will be able to:

▶ Define marketing, and describe its relationship to the exchange process.

▶ Identify the functions of marketing.

▶ Understand the marketing concept and its implications for developing marketing strategies.

▶ Describe marketing decisions such as market segmentation and developing a marketing mix, and explain why these decisions are made.

▶ Describe how marketers conduct marketing research.

get the Product

at a Price willing to pay

at a Place (distribution)

Promotion - and tell people about
- advertising  it.
- publicity (free)
- personel setting
- sales promotion
   ◦ coupons
   ◦ rebates

# Business Experience

Ed Lowe started the cat-litter industry in 1947 when he began selling brown paper bags of dirt with the words "Kitty Litter" scrawled on them. His product met some hostility from retailers at first, but the cat-litter market today exceeds $200 million and is growing. Although Lowe actually invented the cat-litter market, recently he has had to fight for his share of the cat litter market.

Until 1984, Ed Lowe Industries, Inc., sold more cat litter than any other producer; then Clorox introduced Fresh Step cat litter. Clorox had tried to enter the market once before, in 1971. But cats had not liked the smell of Clorox's Litter Green product, and in the end it proved to be no match for Lowe's Kitty Litter Brand and Tidy Cat. The threat from Fresh Step, however, was not so easy for Lowe to overcome. Clorox promoted Fresh Step with the promise that every time the cat scratched at the litter, an herbal fragrance would be released to mask the odors of the litter box. To cat owners, the litter box had never smelled so good.

Lowe, concerned that he would lose his number-one market position, decided to alter his marketing activities, starting with market research to improve his products. His company began with an in-depth survey to find out what cat owners want most from cat litter. The results indicated that owners primarily want odor control, which Lowe's brands, and Fresh Step, offered. The survey also found that cat owners were unhappy with the amount of dust in cat litters. No one had done anything about the dust. Ed Lowe had discovered a hole in the market that no one was filling. He budgeted $4 million to research and develop a dust-free cat litter.

While awaiting the redeveloped product, Lowe introduced a dual odor control for Kitty Litter Brand to prevent Fresh Step from eroding too much of his market share. Then, in January 1986, he introduced his 99 percent dust-free versions of both Kitty Litter Brand and Tidy Cat. He promoted the litters by comparing his products to Fresh Step, even pouring the products out side by side so people could see the difference.

Lowe continued to market his products in 10-pound bags (Fresh Step comes in a 7-pound bag) and to promote his products as a better buy. He also maintained his pricing policy—pricing Kitty Litter Brand a little higher than Fresh Step for a prestige image and pricing Tidy Cat litter 30 cents lower than Fresh Step.

Ed Lowe had to reevaluate his marketing strategy in order to meet the threat posed by Clorox. He utilized product, price, and promotion to ensure that his products met the needs of his consumers—cat owners and their cats. Distribution was also important to ensure that Lowe's products were available where cat owners could purchase them. Lowe continues to promote his cat litters carefully so that they will stay in their number-one positions. Currently, his products hold a 40 percent share, even against private brands of cat litter.

Marketing is very important to the success of an organization. Marketing activities ensure that an organization produces a product (or service or idea) that consumers want to purchase, that consumers know the product is available and how to use it, and that the product is available to consumers when and where they want to buy it and at a price they are willing to pay.

---

These facts are from Joshua Hyatt, "Cat Fight," *INC.* 8 (November 1986): 82–86.

# Introduction

**Marketing**

A group of activities designed to facilitate and expedite exchanges through the creation, distribution, promotion, and pricing of goods, services, and ideas

**Marketing**, a vital part of any business undertaking, is a group of activities designed to facilitate and expedite exchanges through the creation, distribution, promotion and pricing of goods, services, and ideas. Marketing activities ensure that the products consumers want to purchase are available at a price they are willing to pay and that consumers know that the product is available. Marketing activities are carried out by both individuals and organizations in the pursuit of business objectives. They occur in a dynamic environment—that is, an environment of constantly changing laws, regulations, social pressures and opinions, economic conditions, and technological advances.

## ► Nature of Marketing

According to the American Marketing Association, marketing is "the process of planning and executing the conception, pricing, promotion, and distribution of ideas, goods and services to create exchanges that satisfy individual and organizational objectives."[1] Marketing creates value by allowing individuals and organizations to obtain what they need and want. Sellers usually plan and execute activities to make goods, services, and ideas available for buyers. An organization is not going to achieve its objectives unless it provides something that buyers value.

**Exchange**

Giving up one thing in return for something else

An **exchange** is giving up one thing in return for something else. The cash that comes into a company is supplied by buyers who receive benefits in a voluntary *exchange relationship*. The exchange results in the transfer of a good, service, or idea for something of equal value such as money, credit, labor, or goods. The exchange relationship is illustrated in Figure 12-1. The customer must feel good about the purchase or else the exchange will not continue. For example, Cheerios holds the number-one rank in dollar sales among children's cereals because it provides the taste, quality, and value that consumers desire. Satisfied customers providing repeat sales keep Cheerios in the number-one position.

It is important to note what marketing is not: Marketing is not manipulation to get consumers to buy products they don't want. It focuses on many activities such as planning, pricing, promoting, and distributing products. Marketing is not just selling and advertising; it is a systematic approach to satisfying consumers. For an exchange to occur, certain conditions are required. As indicated by the arrows in Figure 12-1, buyers and sellers must be able to communicate about the "something of value" available to each. An exchange does not necessarily take place just because buyers and sellers have something of value to exchange. Each party must be willing to give up its respective "something of value" to receive the "something" held by the other. You are willing to give up your "something of value"—your money or credit—for

**Figure 12-1**

The Exchange Between Buyer and Seller, Resulting in Giving or Taking One Thing in Return for Another.

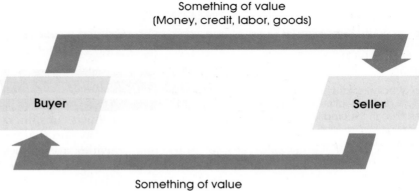

Something of value
(Money, credit, labor, goods)

**Buyer**

**Seller**

Something of value
(Goods, services, ideas)

compact discs, Cokes, football tickets, or a new pair of shoes because you consider those products more valuable or more important to you than holding on to your money or credit potential.

When you think of marketing products, you may think of tangible products—cars, stereo systems, books—as valued products. What most people want, however, is a way to get a job done, solve a problem, gain some enjoyment, or have a good experience. Therefore, the tangible product itself may not be as important to you as the image or the benefits associated with the product. This intangible "something of value" may be competence gained from using a product, or it may be the image evoked by a product such as a designer shirt made by Ralph Lauren.

As indicated in the definition of marketing, a product can be a good, a service, or an idea. A good is physical, concrete, something you can feel and touch. A service is a result of applying human and mechanical efforts to people or objects. Services include dry cleaning, air travel, medical services, and education. Services are just as real as goods, but you can't actually see them and touch them; you have to experience them. Products can also be ideas. Ideas represent philosophies, images, issues, and ways of accomplishing objectives. For a fee, attorneys provide insight about how to solve personal legal problems. Weight Watchers, for a fee, provides ideas to help its members lose weight, develop self-control, and improve their eating habits. Marketing Encounter 12-1 describes how dentists are using marketing to attract new patients.

## Marketing Creates Utility

**Utility**

The power or the ability of a product to satisfy human needs and wants

**Form utility**

Utility created through the production process

The central focus of marketing is to satisfy a human need. **Utility** is the power or the ability of a product to satisfy human needs and wants. A Big Mac at McDonald's, a three-day vacation at Walt Disney World, a new home—all satisfy human needs and wants. Businesses attempt to provide four kinds of utility: form, place, time, and possession. Three of the four kinds (place utility, time utility, and possession utility) are created directly by marketing.

**Form utility** is utility created through the production process. An auto-

# Marketing Encounter 12-1

## *Dentists Attract New Patients with Marketing*

Dentists have traditionally relied on word-of-mouth advertising and patient referrals to attract new patients. Today, however, there are more dentists practicing than ever before. The widespread use of fluoridated water and toothpastes has dramatically decreased the incidence of tooth decay, thereby reducing dentists' primary income source, filling cavities. Moreover, in the 1970s, new federal laws allowed professionals, including dentists, to advertise for the first time. As a result, many dentists have turned to marketing to attract patients in this competitive environment.

The American Dental Association defines marketing as the process designed to "meet the psychological needs of the patient." Dentists are turning to a variety of marketing techniques to accomplish this. Some are simply trying to improve service to existing patients in order to get more patients by referral. They are offering services that were not commonly provided in the past, such as night and weekend services and screenings for oral cancer and gum disease. Many others are using marketing techniques such as advertising, large Yellow Pages advertisements, lectures, and open houses.

Some dentists are using direct mail to solicit new patients. They mail brochures with information about their practices to prospective patients, emphasizing the range of services offered in addition to office hours and staff qualifications. Other dentists have created newsletters or special patient-education brochures. These are sent to newspapers and special groups in order to create or expand the image of an office. Dentists hope these efforts will motivate old and new patients to consider various types of treatment. Creating an image for an office can help a dentist reach people who have never heard of the office, as well as impress current patients with the skills and range of services offered.

Some practices even use promotions such as free gifts to patients, or discounted initial exams. One group of New Jersey dentists occasionally offer a free bike with a set of braces! Other dentists offer coffee and wine while patients are waiting for their turn in the chair. Some even provide stereo headphones to relax patients during the ordeal, and present them with a rose or a hug when it is all over.

Some dentists are taking advantage of the current health craze to bring in new patients. These practices now offer nutritional products for sale in addition to dental services. These dentists hope that the increased emphasis on health will lead the patient to accept treatment and refer other patients.

Nearly half of all dentists now use some marketing techniques. Some practitioners, however, feel that advertising by dental professionals has lowered the overall image of the profession. Nevertheless, marketing by dentists will probably continue to increase as long as there is an excess of dentists and a shortage of patients.

---

These facts are from Cathleen McGuigan, with Bob Cohn and Susan Katz, "A Free Bike with Your Braces," *Newsweek*, May 5, 1986; Paul Duke, Jr. and Albert R. Karr, "Dentists Step Up Services and Marketing as Competition Increases in Crowded Field," *The Wall Street Journal*, November 20, 1987, p. 29; Roger Levin, "Identity Crucial to Successful Marketing of Dental Practices," *Dentist* (November–December 1987): 38; Mark Harley, "Dentists Split on Advertising," *Dentist* (September–October 1987): 31, 38; and Roger Levin, "Specific Marketing Goals Pinpoint Helpful Statistics," *Dentist* (September–October 1987): pp. 36–37.

---

mobile on display in the dealer's showroom possesses form utility. This product would not be available unless it had gone through a series of production steps from the manufacture of sheet steel to the final assembly of finished parts.

**Place utility**

Utility created by making the product available where the buyer wishes to buy it

**Place utility** is utility created by making the product available where the buyer wishes to buy it. Most Americans do not want to travel to West Germany to purchase a Mercedes, and few Americans wish to travel to the Soviet Union

**Time utility**

Utility created by making a product available when customers wish to purchase it

**Possession utility**

Utility created by transferring the ownership of a product to the buyer

to buy Russian vodka. Place utility is created by making the product available at a convenient location.

**Time utility** is utility created by making a product available when customers wish to purchase it. Because some shoppers may wish to shop for a new automobile only on Saturdays, the auto dealers may miss a sale unless the automobiles are available on Saturday. Similarly, due to changes in the seasons, more convertibles may be desired in April, May, and June, and more four-wheel-drive automobiles may be desired in December, January, and February.

**Possession utility** is utility created by transferring the ownership of a product to the buyer. Regardless of whether a product is a good, a service, or an idea, there is a point in time when ownership is transferred by means of a sales receipt or some formal transaction that legally transfers the product from one party to another. The transfer of the possession of the product guarantees the right of the buyer to use that product to satisfy a need.

A key role of marketers is to create place, time, and possession utility to ensure that human needs and wants are served. In order to satisfy customers' needs and wants, certain functions of marketing must be carried out.

**Time utility.** Farmers' markets and roadside stands make fresh produce available to the consumer. It's hard to pass up an opportunity to buy fresh berries or corn on the cob in the summer or pumpkins or cider in the fall when you know they won't be available for long.

# Functions of Marketing

For an exchange to occur, marketing focuses on a very complex set of activities that must be performed to accomplish objectives. There are eight traditional functions of marketing: buying, selling, transporting, storing, grading, financing, marketing research, and risk taking. These functions can be performed by a manufacturer, a wholesaler, retailer, or some other company such as an advertising agency. Each one of these functions provides activities for marketing to accomplish its objectives.

***Buying.*** Industrial buyers, consumers, and retailers who purchase products all make buying decisions. A marketer focuses on buyers' needs and desires in order to determine what products to make available. Understanding consumer buying behavior is of great importance.

**Buying is a marketing function that must be performed in every organization.** Sears, Roebuck buyers find products to purchase in tune with regional lifestyles. Here sportswear buyers review designs with a California manufacturer.

***Selling.*** The exchange process is expedited through selling. Marketers usually view selling as a persuasive activity that is accomplished through promotion (advertising, personal selling, sales promotion, publicity, and packaging).

***Transporting.*** Transporting is physically moving the product from the seller to the buyer. Marketers focus on transportation costs and services.

***Storing.*** Like transporting, storing is an aspect of the physical distribution of products. Storing includes warehousing activities. Warehouses hold products for sometimes lengthy periods in order to create time utility. Frozen orange juice, for example, is desired year-round although the production season for oranges is only a few months out of the year. This means that cold storage for frozen orange juice concentrate must be provided all year.

***Grading.*** Standardizing products and depicting products so that the marketing exchange is facilitated by a clear understanding about the nature and quality of the product—that is the marketer's aim in grading. Products in many industries, such as meat packing, steel, and fruit, are graded according to a set of standards.

***Financing.*** For many products, such as automobiles, refrigerators, and new homes, the purchase and exchange are facilitated because the marketer provides credit that makes the purchasing of the product possible.

***Marketing Research.*** Through research, marketers may ascertain the need for new products and services. By gathering information on a regular basis within the organization they can establish marketing costs and measure performance.

***Risk Taking.*** Risk is the chance of loss associated with marketing decisions that involve the utilization of resources. Developing inventories of products creates a chance of loss if the products don't sell. Spending money to hire a sales force or to conduct marketing research involves risk taking. Most marketing decisions result in either success or failure that is associated with risk.

## The Marketing Concept

The marketing concept is the basic philosophy that guides all marketing activities. The **marketing concept** states that an organization should try to satisfy customers' needs by means of a set of coordinated activities that also allow the organization to achieve its own goals.

According to the marketing concept, a business must find out what consumers need and want and then develop the good, service, or idea that fulfills their need or want. The business must then get the product (or service or idea) to the customer. The process does not stop there. The business must continue to alter, adapt, and develop products to keep pace with the changing needs and wants of consumers. Although customer satisfaction is the goal of the marketing concept, a business must coordinate its marketing activities so that it can achieve its objectives. If it does not achieve its objectives, it will

**Marketing concept**

The concept that states that an organization should try to satisfy customers' needs by means of a set of coordinated activities that also allow the organization to achieve its goals

not stay in business for long. A company, for example, could sell VCRs for $100 and give customers a lifetime guarantee with each one. That would be great for customers but not so great for the organization. Obviously the company must strike a balance between achieving organizational objectives and determining exactly what the customer wants.

Trying to determine the true needs of buyers is increasingly difficult because buying motivation is understood neither by the buyer nor by the organization. Both 7-Eleven and Porsche view psychological satisfaction as an important part of their products:

▶ The president of Porsche states that he does not sell automobiles and knows very little about this market. He sells excitement and self-indulgence to people he calls achievers and risk takers. A Porsche customer must be able to say, "If I were a car, I would want to be a Porsche."[2]

▶ Even 7-Eleven, the nation's leading convenience store, says that it will focus more on on-premise or near-premise pleasure items, rather than concentrating on convenience groceries. It is very interesting to hear the 7-Eleven marketing research director use the term self-indulgence marketing. 7-Eleven sells more beer, cups of coffee, cigarettes, and candy than any other retailer.[3]

The entire organization must adopt a consumer orientation and strive to meet the needs of the customer; otherwise the firm may be awash with products, services, and ideas that consumers do not want or need. Timex, for example, found a very limited market for inexpensive, limited-function home computers and withdrew from the personal computer market. To implement the marketing concept, a firm must have good information about what consumers want, and the organization must coordinate efforts throughout the entire organization.

Orville Wright said that an airplane is "a group of separate parts flying in close formation." The same is true of what most companies are trying to accomplish. They are striving for a team effort to deliver the right product or service to customers. A breakdown at any point in the organization— whether it be in production, purchasing, sales, distribution, or advertising— could result in lost sales, lost revenue, and dissatisfied customers.

Figure 12-2 illustrates what happens when customers' needs are not assessed accurately. Notice how marketing requested the product, how sales ordered it, how engineering designed it, how the plant manufactured it, and how the field service installed it. Everyone in the organization who interacts with customers—down to the shipping department and the truck driver—must know what customers want. They are selling ideas, benefits, philosophies, and experiences, not only products and services.

Someone once said that if you build a better mousetrap, the world will beat a path to your door. Suppose you take the best mousetrap in the world, store it in a warehouse, and air a few television ads stating that you have the best mousetrap in the world. What will happen? Consumers will not beat a path to

As marketing requested it

As sales ordered it

As engineering designed it

As plant manufactured it

As field service installed it

What the customer wanted!!!

**Figure 12-2**
The Breakdown of the Marketing Concept

your warehouse because the market is too competitive. A coordinated effort by everyone involved with the mousetrap is needed to sell the product. The company must reach out to customers and tell them about the mousetrap. The company must also find stores willing to sell the mousetrap to consumers. The company must implement the marketing concept.

# ▶ Developing a Marketing Strategy

**Marketing strategy**

The plan of action for selecting a target market and developing a marketing mix

To satisfy buyers, an organization needs to develop and maintain a **marketing strategy**, which is the core of a successful marketing plan because it provides the plan of action for using the firm's resources and advantages to meet its objectives. A marketing strategy consists of two major steps: selecting a target market and developing, pricing, promoting, and distributing a product to the chosen target market.

# Selecting a Target Market

**Market**

A group of people who have a need along with purchasing power and the desire and authority to spend money on goods, services, and ideas

**Target market**

A group of buyers for whom the organization tailors a marketing strategy that fits their needs and wants

A **market** is a group of people who have a need along with purchasing power and the desire and authority to spend money on goods, services and ideas. Any time a specific market can be delineated, the potential for a target market exists. A **target market** is a group of buyers for whom the organization tailors a marketing strategy that fits their needs and wants; it is a group of consumers on which the organization wishes to focus its efforts.

When choosing a target market, the organization evaluates its own resources and unique abilities. After potential sales, costs, and profits have been analyzed, a target market is identified. Actions taken to satisfy the needs of the target market must be consistent with the organization's overall objectives. Obviously, in selecting a target market, the size of the market and the number of competitors already serving the market are prime considerations.

Marketing managers may define a target market to include a relatively small number of people, or they may define it to encompass the total market. For example, Rolls Royce aims its products at a very exclusive and high-income market—individuals who want the ultimate in prestige in an automobile. General Motors, on the other hand, manufactures cars ranging from

**Volvo has developed an effective marketing strategy.** Its target market desires a durable car that is safe and efficient. Volvo coordinates promotion, such as this ad with the right price and distribution to make sure that its product has the right image.

HOW WELL DOES YOUR CAR STAND UP TO HEAVY TRAFFIC?

VOLVO

Chevrolet Sprints to Cadillacs in an attempt to appeal to many varied tastes, wants, and desires.

Motorcycle manufacturers also appeal to a variety of markets. Kawasaki views its market as men between the ages of 18 and 34 who use a motorcycle for commuting and for weekend entertainment. Honda, with a variety of styles and sizes including street bikes, trail bikes, all-terrain vehicles, and mopeds, attempts to appeal to many different groups of motorcycle enthusiasts. Harley-Davidson has traditionally been the leader in the heavyweight sector of the U.S. motorcycle market. Harley "hogs" have appealed to buyers who want a large, powerful American motorcycle.

Identifying a target market is a very important function of marketing within the organization.

**Market segmentation** is a process of dividing the total market into groups of people who have relatively similar product needs. A **market segment** is a collection of individuals, groups, or organizations that share at least one characteristic or attribute and have relatively similar product needs and desires. Market segmentation is used to zero in on specific target markets so that a satisfactory marketing strategy can be developed.

In a **total-market approach**, the marketer tries to appeal to the total market and assumes that all buyers have similar needs and wants. Crackers are sold by a total-market approach because everyone from six months to 90 years of age is a potential consumer of crackers. There are two common approaches to segmenting markets: the concentration approach, and the multi-segment approach.

In the **concentration approach**, the marketer uses one marketing strategy to direct marketing efforts toward a single market segment. The concentration approach allows a firm to specialize and focus all its efforts on one market segment. A firm can analyze customers' needs carefully and then devote all its efforts to satisfying them. A firm can generate a large sales volume by penetrating a single market segment deeply. Porsche for example, concentrates on the sports segment of the automobile market.

In the **multi-segment approach**, the marketer aims the organization's marketing efforts at two or more segments, developing a marketing strategy for each one. The manufacturer of Raleigh bicycles uses a multi-segment approach and has designed separate marketing strategies for each of several segments—racers, tourers, commuters, and children. Because there are so many different kinds of riders, Raleigh builds many different kinds of bicycles. Many other firms also attempt to use a multi-segment approach to market segmentation. Marketing Encounter 12-2 describes how the Campbell's Soup Company appeals to one of its market segments—the Hispanic population.

When a firm uses either the concentration approach or the multi-segment approach to market segmentation, several requirements must be met:

1. Consumers' needs for the product must be heterogeneous.
2. The segments must be identifiable and divisible.
3. The total market must be divided in a way that allows the segments to be compared with respect to estimated sales potential, cost, and profits.

---

**Market segmentation**

A process of dividing the total market into groups of people who have relatively similar product needs

**Market segment**

A collection of individuals, groups, or organizations that share at least one characteristic or attribute and have relatively similar product needs and desires

**Total-market approach**

Assumes that all buyers have similar needs and wants

**Concentration approach**

Uses one marketing strategy to direct marketing efforts toward a single market segment

**Multi-segment approach**

The marketer aims the organization's marketing efforts at two or more segments, developing a marketing strategy for each one

# Marketing Encounter 12-2
## *Campbell's Markets to the Hispanic Community*

The Campbell's Soup Company is one of a growing number of companies that are targeting products and marketing efforts to different regions of the country and different consumer groups within these regions. One market segment receiving a lot of attention from Campbell's is the Hispanic population.

Although the Hispanic market currently represents only about 7 percent of the total U.S. market, it is growing at a remarkable rate. Since 1980, the country's Hispanic population has grown by 30 percent, five times the growth rate of non-Hispanics. Some experts believe that about 25 million people of Hispanic origin will live in the U.S. by the year 2000. Many marketers, including Campbell's, have dramatically increased marketing efforts targeted at Hispanics.

Despite the size of the Hispanic market, regional differences in the population present some difficulties for marketers. The Mexican population accounts for about 60 percent of the Hispanic population; Central and South American Hispanics, 21 percent; and Caribbean Hispanics, the remaining 19 percent.

When Campbell's launched its major Hispanic marketing campaign in 1987, it had to deal with these regional differences. The company decided to use three different advertisements on Spanish-language television: One commercial was targeted at Mexican-Americans, another was targeted at Hispanics of Caribbean origin, and the third was targeted at mixed Hispanic audiences. The Mexican-American advertisement showed a young woman preparing food in a southwestern-style kitchen with pop music playing in the background. By contrast, the Caribbean ad had a grandmother cooking in a plant-filled kitchen with traditional Caribbean music in the background. By using these subtle differences in advertising, Campbell's avoided lumping all Hispanics together, a mistake frequently made by companies attempting to market to Hispanics for the first time.

In addition to marketing its soups to Hispanics, Campbell's is looking for other ways to tap the lucrative Hispanic market. In 1988, the company introduced a line of Caribbean-style foods under the Casera label. Casera competes head on with Goya Foods, Inc., the market leader. Campbell's also tested some Mexican food items in California under the Casera label to see if there is a demand for these products.

Campbell's management is realizing the importance of the Hispanic market, which is now the second fastest-growing population group in the U.S. The company was one of the first to actively target this market, and it hopes that the Hispanic market will become one of Campbell's most profitable specialty markets in the future.

---

These facts are from Jose de Cordoba, "More Firms Court Hispanic Consumers—But Find Them a Tough Target Market," *The Wall Street Journal*, February 18, 1988, p. 25; Carlos E. Garcia, "Hispanic Market Is Accessible, If Research Is Designed Correctly," *Marketing News*, January 4, 1988, pp. 46–7; Christine Dugas, Mark N. Vamos, Jonathan B. Levine, and Matt Rothman, "Marketing's New Look," *Business Week*, January 26, 1987, pp. 64–9.

4. At least one segment must have enough profit potential to justify developing and maintaining a special marketing strategy.
5. The firm must be able to reach the chosen market segment with a particular market strategy.

Some segments may be difficult if not impossible to reach. For example, it might be difficult to reach a market segment of 30- to 40-year-old males who are introverted and drive subcompact cars. No statistics are available on the market, and thus there is no way to reach it.

**Buyer behavior** is the decision processes and actions of people who buy and use products. Marketers analyze buyer behavior because a firm's mar-

**Buyer behavior**

The decision processes and actions of people who buy and use products

keting strategy should be guided by an understanding of buyers. A major component of the marketing concept is that a firm should create a marketing strategy that satisfies the customers. Carrying out the marketing concept is impossible unless marketers know what, where, when, and how consumers buy; understanding the factors that influence buyer behavior helps marketers develop effective marketing strategies.

Psychological and social variables are important to an understanding of buyer behavior. Psychological factors include perception, motivation, learning, attitudes, and personality. Social factors include social roles, reference groups, social classes, and culture.

**Perception** is the process by which a person selects, organizes, and interprets information received from his or her senses, such as hearing an advertisement or touching a product, in order to understand it. **Motivation** is an internal force that focuses on individuals' behavior to achieve a goal. A buyer's behavior is influenced by a set of motives rather than a single motive. A person buying a home computer may be motivated by several characteristics, such as ease in use, ability to transfer material from the office, price, and other factors. Learning is change in a person's behavior caused by information and experience. If a person's actions bring about a rewarding result, the person is likely to behave in the same way in similar situations. If a person's actions bring about a negative result, however, such as feeling ill after eating a certain product, the person will probably not buy that product again. Attitude is knowledge and positive or negative feelings about something. For example, a person who feels strongly that apartheid in South Africa is wrong may show his or her protest by refusing to buy products made by companies that do business in South Africa. Personality is the organization of the individual's distinguishing character traits, attitudes, or habits. Although market research on the relationship between personality and buying behavior has been inconclusive, some marketers believe that the type of car or clothing a person buys may reflect his or her personality.

**Social roles** are a set of expectations for individuals based on some position they occupy. A person may have many roles: mother, wife, student, and executive. Each of these roles can influence buying behavior. Consider the same woman choosing a breakfast cereal. Her husband wants her to buy a performance cereal, such as Wheaties. Her children hope she will buy a sugary children's cereal such as Captain Crunch. Some of her classmates suggest that she buy a high-fiber cereal such as All-Bran. Some of her colleagues at work think she should buy a nutritious cereal such as Just Right. Thus, a person's buying behavior is affected by opinions of others. **Reference groups** are groups that individuals identify with, adopting the values or attitudes of group members. These can be families, professional groups, civic organizations, or some other group. A person may use a reference group as a point of comparison or a source of information. A person who is new in a community may ask other group members to recommend a family doctor, for example. Social classes are determined by ranking people into higher or lower positions of respect. Criteria vary from one society to another. People within a particular social class may develop common patterns of behavior. People in the upper-middle class, for example, might buy a Mercedes or a

## Perception

The process by which a person selects, organizes, and interprets information received from his or her senses

## Motivation

An internal force that focuses on individuals' behavior to achieve a goal

## Social roles

A set of expectations for individuals based on some position they occupy

## Reference groups

Groups that individuals identify with, adopting the values or attitudes of group members

**A bundle of satisfaction.** Credit cards may provide psychological satisfaction if they provide an identity with one's former school and an easy way of contributing to it.

Porsche as a symbol of their social class. Culture is the integrated, accepted pattern of human behavior, including thought, speech, beliefs, actions, and artifacts. Culture determines what people wear and eat, where they live and travel. The British, for example, buy a great deal of tea, because afternoon tea is a widely-practiced activity in the United Kingdom.

What makes a consumer buy a specific product is hard to determine. A few years ago, Paul Fireman bought the rights to a little-known British running shoe called Reebok. Fireman put together a new, soft-leather version dyed in flashy colors, and suddenly he had a hot-selling consumer product. The whims of teenagers and status-conscious adults determine what is successful in the highly competitive running-shoe market.[4]

Although marketers try to understand buyer behavior, it is extremely difficult to explain exactly why a buyer makes a purchase. The tools and techniques for analyzing consumers are not exact. Marketers may not be able to determine accurately what is highly satisfying to buyers, but they know that trying to understand buyers' wants and needs will put them in a good position to provide consumer satisfaction.

## Developing a Marketing Mix

**Marketing mix**

Four variables that marketers can manipulate to achieve specific goals within a dynamic marketing environment

The second step in developing a marketing strategy is to create and maintain a satisfying marketing mix. The **marketing mix** involves four variables—product, promotion, price, and distribution—that the marketer can manipulate to achieve specific goals within a dynamic marketing environment (Figure 12-3). The buyer or the target market is the central focus of all marketing activities.

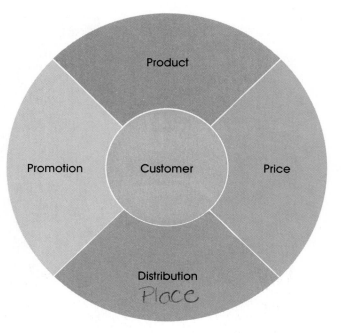

**Product**

A complex of tangible and intangible attributes

***Product.*** A **product**—whether it is a good, a service, an idea, or some combination of those three—is a complex of tangible and intangible attributes. A product has emotional and psychological as well as physical characteristics and includes everything that the buyer receives from an exchange. This definition includes supporting services such as installation, guarantees, product information, and promises of repair. Products usually have both favorable and unfavorable attributes. Therefore, almost every purchase or exchange involves trade-offs as consumers seek to maximize the benefits and satisfaction and minimize the unfavorable attributes. A person who is concerned with quality and style when purchasing an automobile may select Mercedes Benz as the best product to buy. High standards of quality and European styling are the positive attributes that are maximized. The cost of repair and the limited supply of qualified service providers may be unfavorable attributes. In view of the high quality of Mercedes, the consumer may feel that the negative concerns are minimal and thus trade the negative aspects of service and repair for quality and style.

Many products are more valuable because the company that sells them stands for a particular idea or a certain value. IBM is the largest marketer of computers, partially because IBM has maintained a strong commitment to service to make sure that its products run trouble-free and with minimum delays. Caterpillar, one of the largest manufacturers of earth-moving equipment, has been successful because it has done an excellent job of maintaining inventories of spare parts and persuading dealers to provide dependable service to ensure that equipment can be repaired quickly when a mechanical failure occurs.

1936

1955

1965

1968

1972

1980

1986

**Figure 12-4**
The Changing Image of a Product

Sometimes a company creates a character to give its product an image. Many years ago General Mills created the character Betty Crocker to give its baking products a certain image. As Figure 12-4 shows, as styles have changed the company has altered Betty Crocker's appearance to keep her looking like a typical 37-year-old woman engaged in a contemporary lifestyle. The firm portrays Betty Crocker as a serious, orderly, reliable, middle-American woman. Buyers associate those traits with the products that carry the Betty Crocker trademark, and when they purchase a Betty Crocker product they are actually buying all the benefits and satisfaction they think it will provide. Marketing Encounter 12-3 describes how the Pevely Dairy Company tried to improve the image of its products.

***Promotion.*** **Promotion** is a persuasive form of communication that attempts to facilitate a marketing exchange by influencing individuals, groups, or organizations to accept the organizations' products. The promotion variable of the marketing mix involves advertising, personal selling, publicity, and sales promotion.

**Promotion**

A persuasive form of communication that attempts to facilitate a marketing exchange by influencing individuals, groups, or organizations to accept the organizations's products

## Marketing Encounter 12-3
### *Pevely Dairy Co. Changes Its Image*

The Pevely Dairy Co. of St. Louis was founded in 1887. As the company entered its second century of business, it decided it needed a new corporate image and a consumer-oriented marketing strategy. This new strategy coincided with the introduction of several new products, including a line of premium ice cream.

Even though Pevely already had a substantial private-label business, the company wanted to ensure long-term growth by developing brand awareness among consumers. Their main objective was to be the leading marketer, processor, and distributor of Pevely products. The dairy also wanted to emphasize the Pevely brand name, taste, premium quality, healthful attributes, and old-fashioned appeal of Pevely products while maintaining a commitment to goodness and quality. In order to reach these objectives, Pevely had to reposition itself.

After conducting marketing research, the company determined that the main things customers want in dairy products are taste, freshness, and overall quality. Market research also indicated that Pevely's brand name already had high awareness among consumers as well as a high-quality reputation.

Several factors were important in Pevely's change of image. The first was brand loyalty. The company realized it needed to unify all of its products under a common brand to overcome segmentation in consumer brand loyalty. To accomplish this, the company developed a new brand symbol and the campaign, "The Good Taste of Good Health"; both appear on all of its product lines. Although these do not radically depart from Pevely's traditional image, they communicate distinction and emphasize the healthful and good-tasting attributes of the brand.

Pevely also found that price is important to consumers in their purchase decision because many lower-priced store brands held a significant share in Pevely's markets. The company decided to offer products with distinct, value-added difference to differentiate them from the lower-quality, cheaper store brands.

Pevely then tested its repositioned products. The test results showed that consumers clearly preferred a product that emphasized healthful and good-tasting attributes, and that consumers had confidence in the Pevely name. The company then extended its refined image and new positioning strategies to all of its products. The dairy displayed the new brand on Pevely's delivery trucks and trailers as well as its corporate stationery and business forms.

Finally, Pevely's managers and suppliers worked together to establish a set of guidelines to ensure a consistent use of its new brand image. Eventually, the company extended Pevely's new brand image and positioning to the marketing of all existing products. It will also apply to new products the company introduces for its centennial celebration and any future new products. As a result of its repositioning efforts, Pevely now faces the future armed with a new, modern corporate image.

These facts are from "Dairy Adopts Modern Image to Start Its Second Century of Business," *Marketing News*, September 25, 1987, p. 8.

---

**Advertising**

Any paid form of nonpersonal communication transmitted through a mass medium

**Personal selling**

Direct, personal communication with customers and potential customers

**Advertising**, probably the most visible component of promotion, is any paid form of nonpersonal communication transmitted through a mass medium. **Personal selling,** in contrast, is direct, personal communication with customers and potential customers. Advertising may inform potential customers about various products, but by itself it is not sufficient to move many products in today's competitive marketplace. Buyers want to examine the product and any supporting materials; they want information; and they want someone like a salesperson to answer their questions. Of course, personal selling is not the most important promotional variable for all products. The target market for toothpaste, for example, is much too large and inaccessible to rely on personal selling. Establishing personal contact with all users of toothpaste would not be cost-effective; advertising is more appropriate for that type of product.

**Publicity**

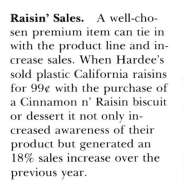

**Publicity**

A nonpersonal communication presented as a news story and transmitted through a mass medium

**Sales promotion**

Activities and materials that persuade customers to make purchases

**Publicity** is a nonpersonal communication presented as a news story and transmitted through a mass medium. The difference between publicity and advertising lies in cost and form. A firm does not pay the media for providing publicity; the firm is not identified as the originator of the story.

**Sales promotion** is activities (such as demonstrations, sweepstakes, and contests) and materials (such as free samples, displays, and coupons) that persuade customers to make purchases. Sales promotion acts as a direct inducement, offering added value or some other incentive to resalers, salespersons, or consumers.

The aim of promotion is to communicate directly or indirectly with individuals, groups, and organizations to facilitate an exchange. When marketers combine advertising, personal selling, publicity, and sales promotion in a promotional mix, they must remember that the firm's promotional objectives are best served by a clear understanding of promotional resources, product

**Raisin' Sales.** A well-chosen premium item can tie in with the product line and increase sales. When Hardee's sold plastic California raisins for 99¢ with the purchase of a Cinnamon n' Raisin biscuit or dessert it not only increased awareness of their product but generated an 18% sales increase over the previous year.

characteristics, target-market characteristics, and the communications program that the firm wishes to implement.

**Price** in the margin
The value placed on what is exchanged

***Price.*** **Price** represents the value placed on what is exchanged. Almost anything of value can be assessed by a price. Because financial price is the measure of value commonly used in an exchange, financial price quantifies value and is the basis of most market exchanges.

Marketers view price as much more than a way of assessing value, however. Price is a key element of the marketing mix because it relates directly to the generation of revenue and is an important factor in determining profits. Additionally, the economic role of price is to allocate products and match them to market opportunities that develop from increases or decreases in demand.

Price can be changed quickly to respond to changes in demand and to the actions of competitors. Price has a psychological impact on customers, and marketers can therefore use it symbolically. If Gucci purses sold for $19.95 and were available in most discount stores, consumers' image of Gucci would be radically different from what it is. This example illustrates the psychological

**Which would you choose?**
Companies often capture market share for their product by matching the competitor's price and increasing quantity.

impact that price can have on consumers. By raising price, an organization can emphasize the quality of a product and try to increase the status associated with owning it. By lowering price, an organization can imply the existence of a bargain and attract customers who go out of their way, spending extra time and effort, to save a small amount. Price plays an important part in efficient marketing.

***Distribution.*** **Distribution** is making products available in the quantities desired to as many customers as possible while holding total inventory, transportation, and storage costs as low as possible. A marketing channel, or channel of distribution, is a group of intermediaries who direct products to customers. These marketing intermediaries, or middlemen, perform many activities designed to move products efficiently from producers to consumers or industrial buyers. The activities involve transporting, warehousing, materials handling, and inventory control, as well as packaging and communication. Each marketing-channel member has different responsibilities within the overall structure of the distribution system.

Critics who suggest that eliminating wholesalers and other intermediaries would lower prices for consumers do not recognize that eliminating wholesalers would not do away with the need for the services they provide. You can eliminate the wholesaler but it is impossible to eliminate the functions they perform. Other institutions would have to perform those services, and consumers would still have to pay for them. In addition, in the absence of wholesalers all producers would have to deal directly with retailers or customers, and all producers would have to keep voluminous records and hire people to deal with customers. Even with direct marketing, consumers might end up paying a great deal more for products as prices rose to reflect the cost of inefficient producers' operations.

# ► The Marketing Environment

The marketing environment influences and structures the development of marketing strategy. Political, legal and regulatory, social, competitive and economic, and technological forces shape the marketing environment:

*Political, legal and regulatory forces*: Laws and regulators' interpretation of laws; law enforcement and regulatory activities; regulatory bodies, legislators and legislation, and political actions of interest groups.

*Social forces*: The public's opinions and attitudes toward issues such as living standards, ethics, lifestyles, and quality of life.

*Competitive and economic forces*: Competitive relationships, employment, purchasing power, and general economic conditions related to prosperity, recession, depression, recovery, shortages, and inflation.

*Technological forces*: Computers, advances in communications and transportation that improve distribution, promotion, and the development of new products.

The forces in the marketing environment are sometimes called uncontrollables; yet they are not totally uncontrollable. A marketing manager has an opportunity to influence environmental variables. Figure 12-5 shows the variables in the marketing environment as they relate to a marketing mix and buyer.

# ▶ Marketing Research

**Marketing research**

A systematic and objective effort to get information about potential customers in order to guide marketing decisions

**Marketing research** is a systematic and objective effort to get information about potential customers in order to guide marketing decisions. (The marketing concept cannot be implemented without information about buyers.) Marketing research gathers information not available to decision makers in any other form. It is conducted on a special-project basis, and research methods vary with

**Figure 12-5**
A Marketing Mix and the Marketing Environment

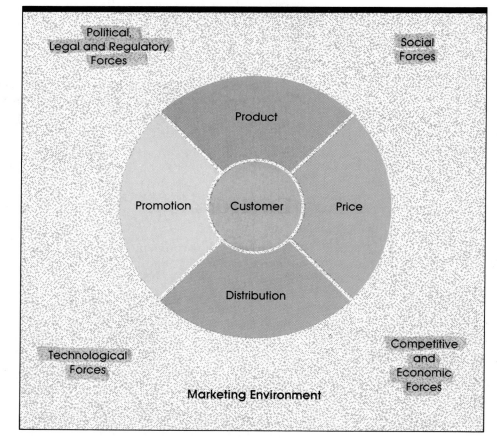

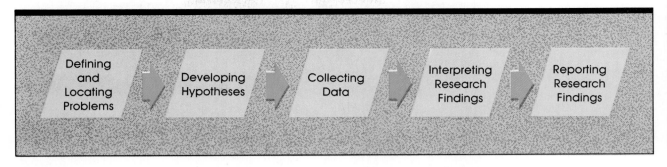

**Figure 12-6**
The Marketing Research Process

the problems studied and with changes in the environment. Marketing research is a five-step process (Figure 12-6):

1. Defining and locating problems
2. Developing assumptions or ideas about the probable causes of events
3. Collecting data
4. Analyzing and interpreting data
5. Reporting research findings in a way that makes them understandable to the decision makers who have to read the reports and attempt to solve problems

**Marketing information system**

Establishes a framework for day-to-day managing and structuring of information gathered regularly from sources both inside and outside of the organization

**Primary data**

Information that is observed and recorded or collected directly from respondents

**Secondary data**

Information compiled inside or outside the organization for some purpose other than changing the current situation

A **marketing information system** establishes a framework for day-to-day managing and structuring of information gathered regularly from sources both inside and outside of the organization. The marketing information system provides a flow of information about costs, sales, profits, and consumer satisfaction.

Two types of data are usually available for decision makers. **Primary data** is information that is observed and recorded or collected directly from respondents. **Secondary data** is information compiled inside or outside the organization for some purpose other than changing the current situation. Examples of secondary data include reports supplied by data services or by the U.S. Bureau of the Census or other government bodies. Secondary data is already available in private or public reports and has been collected or stored within the organization. Primary data must be gathered by researchers, who develop a method to observe phenomena or survey respondents.

Marketing research and information systems are important to an organization's planning and development of strategy. Research and information systems make possible a systematic approach to decision making in marketing. Even though many decisions may be based on experience and intuition, decision making that uses the information generated by marketing research is orderly and logical. Although experienced-based solutions to many minor and recurring problems may be successful, as the number of possible solutions to a problem increases, the value of marketing research and information systems likewise increases.

**Meeting the public.** Focus group interviews are used to learn more about the opinions and views of customers. Usually an interviewer probes a group of people in the firm's target market. In this case a Boston TV station, WBZ-TV, conducts a focus group interview listening to teenage viewers to become more responsive to their interests and needs.

# ▶ Evaluating Marketing Activities

Marketing contributes substantially to the well-being of the economy. Marketing activities affect countless aspects of everyday life. Many marketing activities are required to provide people with satisfying goods, services, and ideas, and these marketing activities do cost money. In fact, about one-half of a buyer's dollar is spent on marketing costs. Thus, a family with a monthly income of $2,000, after allocating about $400 in taxes, would spend approximately $1,600 for goods and services, of which $800 would go directly for marketing activities. How is this money used?

From 25 to 30 percent of all civilian workers in the United States perform marketing activities—personal selling, advertising, packaging, transportation, storage, marketing research, product development, wholesaling, and retailing. In addition, many nonbusiness organizations are involved in marketing activities. For example, a nonprofit theatre, museum, or local mental health foundation uses marketing to raise money for support. Regardless of whether an individual earns a living through performing marketing activities or performs them voluntarily in a nonbusiness organization, most individuals are likely to need marketing skills.

By studying marketing activities, you can evaluate the costs, benefits, and flaws of marketing; then you can evaluate corrective measures such as laws, regulations, and industry guidelines that may be required to stop unfair, misleading, or unethical practices. By understanding more about marketing, you will be able to judge where laws need to be improved and how this improvement should be accomplished. For example, if you have had an unsatisfactory experience with a product warranty, you may have wished that laws were more strictly enforced to make sellers fulfill their promises. If you have bought a product that did not perform properly, you may have wished that you had had more accurate information before making the purchase. By knowing more about marketing, it is possible to improve both your career potential and your ability to make good purchases.

## Notes

**1.** "AMA Board Approves New Marketing Definition," *Marketing News,* March 1, 1985, p. 1.

**2.** Peter Schultz and Jack Cook, "Porsche on Nichemanship," *Harvard Business Review* 64 (March–April 1986): 100.

**3.** Southland Corporation 1986 Annual Report and 1983 Marketing Presentation Handout from Southland Corporation.

**4.** Linda Watkins, "Reebok Keeping a Name Hot Takes More Than Aerobics," *The Wall Street Journal,* August 21, 1986, p. 23.

## Summary and Review

▶ According to the American Marketing Association, marketing is "the process of planning and executing the conception, pricing, promotion, and distribution of ideas, goods, and services to create exchanges that satisfy individual and organizational objectives."

▶ The main focus of marketing is the satisfaction of human needs. The power or ability of a product to satisfy human needs or wants is called utility. Marketing creates three kinds of utility: place utility, time utility, and possession utility.

▶ Marketing is composed of several different and interrelated functions: buying, selling, transporting, storing, grading, financing, marketing research, and risk taking.

▶ The marketing concept is the basic philosophy that guides all marketing activities. In essence, the marketing concept states that an organization should try to satisfy customers' needs through a set of coordinated activities that allow the organization to achieve its goals.

▶ A marketing strategy provides the plan of action for using the firm's resources to meet its objectives. The steps to develop a strategy are selecting a target market and developing and maintaining a marketing mix that satisfies the target market.

▶ The marketing mix is composed of four activities: product, promotion, price, and distribution. Product is a complex of tangible and intangible attributes that a buyer receives from an exchange. Promotion is a persuasive form of communication that attempts to facilitate a marketing exchange by influencing individuals, groups, or organizations. Price is the value placed on what is exchanged. Distribution is making products available in the quantities desired to as many customers as possible.

▶ There are several forces that influence and structure marketing activities: political, legal and regulatory, social, competitive and economic, and technological forces.

▶ Marketing research is a systematic and objective effort to get information about potential customers in order to guide marketing decisions.

# Key Terms and Concepts

marketing
exchange
utility
form utility
place utility
time utility
possession utility
marketing concept
marketing strategy
market
target market
market segmentation
market segment
total-market approach
concentration approach
multi-segment approach
buyer behavior

perception
motivation
social roles
reference groups
marketing mix
product
promotion
advertising
personal selling
publicity
sales promotion
price
distribution
marketing research
marketing information system
primary data
secondary data

# Checking Your Understanding

This chapter introduced you to the subject of marketing. To test and reinforce your understanding, fill in the blanks below.

1. An _exchange_ giving up one thing in return for something else.
2. _____ represents the value placed on what is exchanged.
3. _____ is the power or the ability of a product to satisfy human needs and wants.
4. _____ is a persuasive form of communication.
5. _____ selling is direct, personal communication with customers and potential customers.
6. A market _____ is a collection of individuals, groups, or organizations that share at least one similar characteristic and have relatively similar product needs.
7. _____ is a complex of tangible and intangible attributes and includes everything that the buyer receives from an exchange.
8. _____ is making products available in the quantity desired.
9. _____ is any paid form of nonpersonal communication.
10. _____ data is compiled inside or outside the firm for some purpose other than changing the current situation.
11. Marketing _____ is a systematic and objective effort to get information about potential customers.
12. A _____ is a group of people who have needs for products and who have the ability, willingness, and authority to buy such products.
13. A _____ market is a group of buyers for whom an organization tailors a marketing strategy.
14. Market _____ is the process of dividing the total market into groups that have relatively similar product needs.
15. The marketing _____ involves four variables: product, price, promotion, and distribution.
16. A marketing _____ is the core of a successful marketing plan because it provides the plan of action.
17. _____ data is observed and recorded directly from respondents.

# Topics for Review and Discussion

1. What are the functions of marketing, and how does an organization use marketing activities to achieve its objectives?
2. State the marketing concept.
3. How is market segmentation related to target market?
4. What is the function of the marketing mix? List the variables in the marketing mix.
5. Why are marketing research and information systems important to an organization's planning and development of strategy?
6. List the steps involved in the marketing research process.
7. Briefly describe the factors that influence buying behavior.
8. Why is marketing gaining in importance today? What benefits does it provide to consumers?
9. Discuss the impact of technological forces and political and legal forces on the market.

# Exercises

1. Discuss the decision process and influences involved in purchasing an IBM AT (pc).

2. What is a market? Name a market in which you are a member and one in which you are not.

3. If you are the manager of an ice-cream parlor, how would you define your business? Why?

4. Suggest a way to segment the market for a household detergent.

## Case 12-1
## *Harley-Davidson Shifts Marketing Gears*

Harley-Davidson Motor Co., the Milwaukee-based maker of motorcycles often referred to as "hogs," has traditionally been the leader in the heavyweight (700 cc to 1,340 cc) sector of the U.S. motorcycle market. In the late 1970s, the company's market share began slipping because of competition from Japanese motorcycles (Harley owners call the Japanese bikes "rice burners"). At one point, the company's biggest competitor, Honda, had a 56 percent share of the U.S. market, while Harley-Davidson held on to a paltry 4 percent. Honda was pricing its comparably sized motorcycles about $500 less than Harley-Davidson.

After Harley charged the Japanese with using unfair trade practices, the U.S. International Trade Commission imposed a five-year import tax on heavy motorcycles from Japan to ease competition pressures, but Harley had to solve its other marketing problems on its own. In order to increase its share of the U.S. motorcycle market, the 86-year-old company had to improve its product and attract new buyers. For years, industry experts had said that Harley-Davidson should spend more on developing new products, and had called Harley's flagship twin-cylinder "V" engine an antique. The company had survived largely because of dedicated dealers and loyal, die-hard customers who said they would rather walk than ride a "rice burner." Some of Harley-Davidson's best-known customers are members of the Hell's Angels, the California Highway Patrol, and *Forbes* publisher Malcolm Forbes.

In the past, Harley-Davidson had aimed its bikes at two main target markets: bikers and towers. Bikers are people who fit the popular conception of a motorcycle rider, complete with leather jackets, tattoos, and Harley insignia. Towers are conventional blue-collar workers who tend to take longer trips than do the owners of smaller motorcycles. Now, however, a wider variety of people—including doctors, lawyers, mechanics, executives, and sales clerks—are riding "hogs." In fact, 10 percent of "hog" riders are women. Harley-Davidson is thus expanding its marketing activities to include the new white-collar segment of the motorcycle market. This market segment particularly values the luxury and durability that Harley represents. Company officials hope to widen their target market to include more women, baby boomers, and families with relatively high incomes, although they won't forget the loyal bikers and towers.

To increase its market share, the company is improving old products and developing new ones. Harley-Davidson updated the V engine, eliminating leaks and vibration. It improved the bikes themselves and added new options. It also introduced several mid-size bikes with lower price tags. The new Sportster sells for $3,995. Top-of-the-line road cruisers, however, still fetch as much as $12,000. Harley-Davidson is emphasizing value to consumers while improving its production process to improve quality and cut costs.

Harley-Davidson has promoted itself as an American company fighting against the Japanese. As chairman Vaughn Beals put it, "We're a bunch of Americans who have taken a personal risk on Harley to fend off the Japanese and salvage an American classic." The all-American image increased sales at a time when American patriotism was on the rise. In addition, the company sponsored bike rallies where old Harley lovers and potential customers could try out the improved models. Harley dealers promoted the bikes' improved quality, and the company formed the Harley Owners Group (HOG) to sponsor various activities for Harley owners.

The company's shifting of marketing gears has paid off. Harley's market share has increased to almost 39 percent of the 850cc-and-larger market; Honda's share has declined. Harley has also diversified production: It now builds engines and bomb casings for the government, and it recently purchased a recreational-vehicle manufacturer. The company's situation has improved so much that Vaughn Beals asked the federal government to withdraw the tariff on heavy Japanese bikes one year early. The company says it will not compete with the Japanese for the small-bike market, but it does plan to compete head-on in the heavy and mid-size bike markets, where the hogs have a quality edge.

Harley-Davidson's current success is due in part to the company's dedication to its customers and to its commitment to producing motorcycles that are durable and have a high resale value. Although Harley-Davidson Motor Co. is the last of more than 150 U.S. motorcycle manufacturers, its chance for success is enhanced because it sells more than just motorcycles; it sells a special loyalty and image to its customers.

---

These facts are from Michael Oneal, "Full Cycle," *Continental* 3 (November 1987): 20–24; Rod Willis, "Harley-Davidson Comes Roaring Back," *Management Review* 75 (March 1986): 20–27; Michael Oneal, "Harley-Davidson: Ready to Hit the Road Again," *Business Week,* July 21, 1986, p. 70; and John A. Conway, "Harley Back in Gear," *Forbes,* April 20, 1987, p. 8.

**Questions**

1. How does Harley-Davidson define the marketing segment it tries to capture?
2. How can Harley-Davidson use information about social roles and reference groups to improve its marketing strategy?
3. Suggest how Harley-Davidson should use marketing research to maintain a competitive advantage?

# Case 12-2
## *Indianapolis Markets Itself as a Sports Capital*

Many nonbusiness organizations use marketing to achieve their objectives. Marketing activities may benefit several groups associated with the organization including its clients, members, and the general public. Indianapolis, Indiana, has decided to market itself as the amateur sports capital of the United States.

Indianapolis experienced a 3.2 percent population growth between 1980 and 1985, one of the few cities in the economically plagued Midwest to grow during that period. Nevertheless, city officials realized Indianapolis needed a marketable position to ensure further growth—amateur sports seemed like a real winner.

Of course, Indianapolis is no stranger to the world of sports. The city is the home of the Indianapolis 500, the world's largest auto race, the Indianapolis Colts (NFL) and the Indiana Pacers (NBA). The city seems especially fond of basketball, and Indiana University Hoosier basketball coach Bobby Knight is a household hero. The city already had many sports facilities available from which to market itself as a sports capital.

In addition, the city built the Indianapolis Sports Center in 1979, now the site of the annual U.S. Clay Court Tennis Championships. Market Square Arena, (home of the Indiana Pacers), the Indiana University Natatorium, and the Track and Field Stadium were completed just in time for the 1982 National Sports Festival, the city's first major amateur athletic event. Indianapolis' success in hosting this event boosted its image and gave it the confidence to host future amateur sporting events.

Several organizations in Indianapolis provided grants to help fund these and other sports facilities, but the largest was the Lilly Endowment from Eli Lilly & Co. Its $25 million grant made possible the completion of the $77 million Hoosier Dome in 1984. Actually, the city built the Dome in hopes of attracting a professional football team, and eventually they succeeded in getting the Baltimore Colts to move to Indianapolis. The dome was also the site of the 1984 U.S. Olympic Basketball Exhibition Game, the 1985 NBA All-Star Game, the 1987 World Indoor Track and Field Championship, as well as a number of other sports events.

In 1987, Indianapolis received its biggest honor from the world of sports. It won a bid to host the Tenth Pan American Games, the Western Hemisphere's equivalent of the Olympic Games and the second largest multisport event in the world. The city's numerous modern athletic facilities, and its performance in hosting other events, helped Indianapolis win the honor of hosting the Games in August 1987. The total economic impact on Indianapolis from the Pan American Games was an estimated $175 million.

Sports, which began as a municipal development tool, fueled tremendous growth in Indianapolis. The city's convention business is at an all-time high, and hotel occupancy has increased tremendously. Moreover, the downtown area of the city is in the midst of a revitalization boom because of all the surrounding sports-facility construction. More than twenty-six major downtown developments were opened between 1980 and 1985. Restaurants and bars are opening all over downtown to take advantage of the crowds drawn by sporting events. Retail and residential construction is booming and the city continues to grow.

Perhaps one reason behind the success of the city's marketing strategy is that it encourages its residents to use the various sporting facilities when not in use for scheduled events. For instance, the public can take swimming lessons at the Natatorium and they can jog on the track in Hoosier Dome. Allowing the public to use the sports facilities generated much public support for Indianapolis' objective of being a sports capital, and the campaign might not have succeeded without that support. In fact, Ann Woolman, manager of public relations for the Indianapolis Project, says, "The one thing we've got to keep in mind here is that the city is the people not the buildings." City officials certainly attribute the city's newfound success to the support of its residents.

Indianapolis has used marketing to promote itself as the amateur sports capital of the United States. These activities have greatly benefited the people of Indianapolis, not only in monetary terms, but in the forms of recognition and esteem in the eyes of the sporting world. Residents and natives take a greater pride in being from Indianapolis than ever before. What's next for the city people once called "hick town" and "India-no-place"? In addition to continuing to host various amateur sporting events, city officials hope to be the home of the Olympics at some future date.

These facts are from Richard Kern, "Marketing Indianapolis: Sports and Statistics to Numb the Mind," *Sales and Marketing Management* 138 (May 1987): 45–47; Richard Edel, "Onetime 'Hick Town' Becomes International Star," *Advertising Age*, April 20, 1987, pp. S-7, S-10, S-12; and William Giese, "Hospitable Hoosiers Roll Out the Hype," *USA Today*, July 27, 1987, pp. 1A, 2A.

*[handwritten: take home test due Mon 1st of class]*

**Questions** *[handwritten: 1 page double spaced typed]*

1. When you think of marketing, you may think of tangible products. What is the product that Indianapolis markets?
2. How does a city like Indianapolis implement the marketing concept and its marketing activities?
3. Indianapolis' objective is to be a major sports capital. What is the Indianapolis marketing strategy to achieve this objective?

# Answers to Checking Your Understanding

1. exchange
2. price
3. utility
4. promotion
5. personal
6. segment
7. product
8. distribution
9. publicity
10. secondary
11. research
12. market
13. target
14. segmentation
15. mix
16. strategy
17. primary

## Outline

# Chapter 13

# Product and Price

## Objectives

After reading this chapter, you will be able to:

▶ Define product and understand its importance in the marketing mix.

▶ Describe the research and development process.

▶ Classify products according to their use.

▶ Describe the product life cycle and discuss how it relates to product planning.

▶ Discuss the importance of branding, packaging, and labeling.

▶ Define price and understand its importance in the marketing mix.

▶ Describe various pricing objectives a firm might employ.

▶ Relate the elements of demand, cost, and profit relationships to pricing strategies.

▶ Discuss the various pricing policies a firm might use.

# Business Experience

Wacky Wallwalkers were developed in Japan in 1982 when a manufacturer made a chemical compound that shakes like Jello, feels like a Jujube, and resists lateral movement on flat surfaces. When thrown at a wall, the compound creeps erratically downward, fascinating children (and not a few adults). Though the substance feels a little weird, it leaves no residue on bare fingers or walls, and it is easily cleaned with soap and water. The compound was marketed in the form of an octopus, a symbol of good fortune in the Far East.

Ken Hakuta's parents sent one of the rubbery toys from Japan as a present for Hakuta's young son. Hakuta apparently found them as interesting as his son did. Discovering that no one in North America had rights to the little creatures, he went to Japan and obtained the North American distribution rights and 300,000 Wallwalkers, which he quickly sold. After some initial difficulties, Hakuta bought a factory in South Korea and began manufacturing more toys to meet the demand.

In order to ensure the Wallwalker's success in the United States, Hakuta had to market the product very carefully. The South Korean factory took care of manufacturing, but the Wallwalkers still had to be packaged and priced. Packaging proved to be difficult because of the very properties that make Wallwalkers so attractive. The toys dry out when left in the open air too long and stick to the cellophane wrappers often used to package similar toys. Moreover, Wallwalkers must be displayed in large packaging to make them stand out among other impulse-purchase toys.

Pricing the Wallwalkers was less difficult. The rule of thumb in this industry is a markup of about five times the manufacturing cost plus promotion. This pricing enables the manufacturer to cover the cost of merchandise returns, commissions (sales representatives and distributors), shipping, and miscellaneous costs. Because the Wallwalkers cost only about 30 cents apiece to make, their retail price runs as high as $2.50. (Hakuta gets only about 75 cents per critter.) So far 150 million Wallwalkers have been manufactured.

At one point, Hakuta decided to pull the Wallwalkers completely off the market and offer them only as promotional giveaways through Wendy's hamburger restaurants and in Kellogg's cereals. Hakuta hopes this strategy of unavailability will increase the demand for Wallwalkers and extend their life span.

---

These facts are from Robert A. Mamis, "Gross National Products," *INC.* 9 (April 1987): 43–48.

# Introduction

As the Business Experience illustrates, businesses such as Ken Hakuta's must be effective and creative in marketing products at the right price to satisfy the needs of consumers. Chapter 13 is an examination of both product and price.

# ▶ Nature of Products

**Product**

A complex of tangible and intangible attributes that provide satisfaction and benefits

A **product** is a complex of tangible and intangible attributes that provide satisfaction and benefits. Products should be viewed as more than tangible items. In reality, a product is a psychological bundle of satisfaction. When buyers make a purchase, they are actually buying the benefits and satisfaction they think the product will provide. For example, people are more interested in getting quarter-inch holes than in buying the electric drill to make those holes. The buyer is looking for the benefit, not for the tangible product. No one wants to buy and maintain a washing machine, but consumers do want clean clothes, and a washing machine provides a means to obtain clean clothes.

Products are among a firm's most visible contacts with consumers. If they do not meet the needs and expectations of consumers, sales will be difficult, and the lifespan of the product will be brief. The product is an important variable, often the central focus, of the marketing mix; the other variables (price, promotion, and distribution) must be coordinated with product decisions.

The term *product* refers to goods, services, and ideas. Goods are tangible and have form utility. Most people associate the term product with goods, such as a box of breakfast cereal, a loaf of bread, a book, or some other tangible product.

A service is a product that results when people or machines provide or process something of value to customers. A car wash, a haircut, a checkup by a doctor—these are examples of services.

Services account for about 70 percent of the U.S. gross national product and three-fourths of the nonfarm jobs in the United States. In generating 44 million new jobs in the past thirty years, services have absorbed most of the influx of women and minority workers in the American workforce.[1]

A product can solely be an idea also. For example, one may go to a Weight Watchers seminar to learn how to lose weight. Consultants and attorneys generate ideas for solving problems.

The service component of many products may be more important than the physical characteristics of the product. For example, product information services or warranties may be as important to the buyer of computers, construction equipment, or even automobiles as the hardware of the product itself.

The psychological stimulation provided by a product is an important benefit that the buyer receives. McDonald's, for example, sells more than hamburgers and fries. McDonald's is as much a marketer of services as it is of goods. Consumers purchase not only food but the service of a quick meal that they don't have to prepare themselves. Children, moreover, associate McDonald's with fun, dinner boxes (The Happy Meal), and McDonald's Playland including Ronald McDonald. Marketing Encounter 13-1 describes how the Walt Disney Co. is updating its theme parks to appeal to more sophisticated consumers.

# ▶ Research and Development

**Research and development**

The process of identifying new ideas and technologies that can be developed into new products

For most companies, developing a new product is an important but risky venture. **Research and development** is the process of identifying new ideas and technologies that can be developed into new products. In this context, *new* indicates that a given organization has not marketed the product before, although similar products may be available from other organizations. Each year thousands of products are introduced, but few of them are successes. The RCA video disc was a failure, but the Sony Walkman and Acura Legend have been successful. A firm can take a considerable amount of time to develop a product so that it is ready for the market. It took more than twenty years to get the first photocopier on the market. It took sixteen years to research and introduce the first automatic transmission and thirty-three years for fluorescent lights.

Before introducing a new product, a business must take a number of steps: idea development, screening new ideas, business analysis, product development, test marketing, and commercialization. (Figure 13-1).

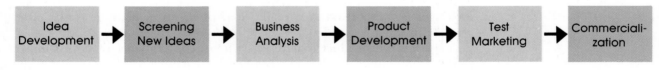

**Figure 13-1**
The Steps in Research and Development

## Idea Development

Most firms that need ideas for new products use a creative but logical approach to develop them. New ideas can come from marketing research, engineers, and sources outside the firm such as advertising agencies and management consultants. Other sources of new ideas are brainstorming and intracompany incentives or rewards for good ideas. The idea for 3M's highly successful Post-it note pads came from a 3M employee who developed the adhesive-backed yellow notes for his personal use.

## Screening New Ideas

In developing a new product, a marketing manager should look at the organization's resources and objectives and make some early projection of economic payoffs. The manager should assess the firm's abilities to produce and market the product. Other factors that the manager should weigh are the desires and wishes of buyers, the competition, changes in technology, social trends, and political and economic considerations. Most new-product ideas are rejected during screening because they seem inappropriate for the organization. For example, 7-Eleven dropped the idea of developing film because consumers did not associate film developing with 7-Eleven stores.

## Marketing Encounter 13-1

### Disney Theme Parks Go High Tech

Although Disneyland and Disney World offer ideas and services instead of goods, Walt Disney Co. still utilizes marketing activities to generate revenue and profits. Disney theme parks have been fairly successful from the beginning, but they have to work to keep customers coming back and to attract new customers. In order to appeal to an increasingly sophisicated public, Disney is introducing new attractions using the latest technology. Because well-educated, computer-literate customers represent a large portion of its business, Disney works hard to keep them entertained so that they can be lured back for a repeat visit.

Disneyland's $32 million Star Tour is a giant aircraft simulator complete with *Star Wars* film footage shown through the windows. The simulator pitches and yaws as if to avoid the meteorites and laser blasts that the passengers see through the window. The pitching ship with stars and meteors whizzing by makes the passengers feel as if they are actually warping through the galaxy.

The interesting thing about Star Tour is that it can be transformed, by changing software and facades, into an entirely different attraction, such as a ride in the LeMans Grand Prix. Disney can create several rides for little more than the price of one. The technology is expensive, but it does give theme parks the ability to add to and upgrade attractions relatively cheaply, and it gives customers a reason to come back to the park another time. Industry analysts believe such flexible rides are the wave of the future at theme parks.

Disney also had *Star Wars* creator George Lucas produce *Captain Eo*, a $17-million music video starring Michael Jackson. Disneyland is currently working on another attraction modeled on the exploits of Indiana Jones, another Lucas creation. Other plans include the longest log-flume ride in the nation, peopled with animated characters from the Disney classic *Song of the South,* and interactive rides that would give passengers some control over the ride experience by means of buttons or levers. The technology for such rides is still a few years away, but when the technology is available, Disney will be ready for it.

Due in part to the increased use of computers, coupled with a demand for space-adventure films, customers expect attractions of increasing technological sophistication. Disney realizes that in order to compete with theme parks such as Universal Studios, Knott's Berry Farm, and Six Flags, it must invest in high-technology attractions now to keep Disney parks fresh in the minds of customers and to keep those customers coming back.

These facts are from Ronald Grover, Mark N. Vamos, and Todd Mason, "Disney's Magic: A Turnaround Proves Wishes Can Come True," *Business Week,* March 9, 1987, pp. 62–69; Nancy Jeffrey, "Joy Rides: Theme Parks Introduce More High-Tech Thrills and Chills," *The Wall Street Journal,* July 2, 1987, p. 21; and Stephen J. Sansweet, "Disney's Imagineers Build Space Attraction Using High-Tech Gear," *The Wall Street Journal,* January 6, 1987, pp. 1, 16.

**Filling a need.** Recognizing a lack of minority-oriented greeting cards in the market in 1983, Taylor Barnes and Wayne Wilson began L'Image Graphics, offering five lines of approximately 140 minority-oriented greeting cards. By 1986, sales were close to $300,000 a year.

## Business Analysis

Business analysis is a basic assessment of a product's compatibility in the marketplace and its potential profitability. Sometimes the business analysis includes **concept testing,** which is research designed to determine potential buyer interest in a new product. Data about the size of the market and competing products is also often studied at this point. The most important question relates to market demand: How will the product affect the firm's sales, costs, and profits?

## Product Development

If a product idea survives the first three steps, it is developed into a prototype that should reveal intangible attributes associated with the product in the consumer's mind. At this stage, design, mechanical, chemical, and other physical aspects of the product must be linked to images of the product or to psychological satisfaction that may be obtained from the product. The product or production process must be shaped to fit buyers' expectations.

Product development is often expensive, and few product ideas make it to this stage. During product development, various elements of the marketing mix must be developed for testing. Copyrights, tentative advertising copy, packaging, labeling, and delineations of a target market are integrated to develop an overall marketing strategy. The company should also determine whether there will be any product liability problems, and if so, take care of them.

**On-site research and development.**   Many companies maintain their own research and development departments. Owens-Corning has several facilities for developing new products, and highly-skilled employees to carry out their scientific investigations, such as these scientists who are studying glass melting.

# Test Marketing

   **Test marketing** is the limited introduction of a product in areas that represent the potential market. Test marketing is not a screening, but it is a trial mini-launch of a product. Test marketing allows a complete test of the marketing strategy in a natural environment, and it gives the organization an opportunity to discover weaknesses in the marketing strategy and eliminate them before the product is fully launched. During test marketing, it is possible to manipulate various factors, such as advertising, price, and packaging, in different market areas and compare and contrast the results.

   Test marketing is not without its risks. Competitors often learn about a potential new product and rush into the marketplace with a similar product if they feel the test marketing is going well. Schick, for example, brought out a double-edge razor less than six months after Gillette test-marketed the Trac II. Also, some companies engage in jamming during test marketing. Jamming is an attempt to distort the results of the test by lowering prices, increasing advertising, or decreasing advertising to make the test marketing look successful. Through jamming, competitors could influence a company to launch a potentially unsuccessful product or keep a company from launching a successful product.

# Commercialization

**Commercialization** is the introduction of a complete marketing strategy and the launch of the product for commercial success. During commercialization, the firm gears up for full-scale production, distribution, and promotion. The firm may introduce the product gradually into markets and expand into adjacent territories after success has been achieved, or it may introduce the product nationally all at one time. Gradual introduction reduces many of the problems incurred in introducing a new product. If there are some early product defects or failures, the firm will experience smaller losses and may be able to correct those weaknesses before going into new geographic areas. On the other hand, the slower the introduction, the more opportunity competitors have to learn about the product's success and rush into territories not yet reached by the gradual introduction.

# ▶ Classifying Products

Products are usually classified as either industrial products or consumer products. **Consumer products** are for household or family use; they are not used for any purpose other than daily living. **Industrial products** are used either directly or indirectly in the operation or manufacturing processes of business organizations. The unique attributes of the product do not determine whether it is an industrial product or a consumer product. What is more important is how the product is used and why the product is purchased. For example, a light bulb purchased to light a living room for a family is a consumer product, but a light bulb purchased to light an assembly line in a factory is an industrial product. Table 13-1 identifies various types of industrial and consumer products.

## Consumer Products

There are many different ways to classify consumer products, but the system used most often distinguishes among convenience products, shopping products, and specialty products. The system is based on consumers' buying behavior and intentions.

*Convenience Products.* Convenience products are bought frequently without a lengthy search and often for immediate consumption. Examples of convenience products include eggs, milk, bread, newspapers, soft drinks, beer, and magazines. Consumers spend virtually no time in planning where to purchase the product and usually take any available brand. The marketing of convenience products usually requires many retail outlets because consumers are not willing to go out of their way for a specific, favorite brand and readily choose a substitute for their preferred brand if it is not available. Businesses spend money to advertise convenience products and to develop attractive packages for them. Retailers move these products frequently, but their profits on these products can be relatively low.

**Table 13-1 Product Classification**

| Consumer Products | Industrial Products |
|---|---|
| Convenience products | Raw materials |
| Shopping products | Major equipment |
| Specialty products | Accessory equipment |
| | Component parts |
| | Processed materials |
| | Supplies |
| | Industrial services |

***Shopping Products.*** Shopping products are purchased after the consumer has compared competitive products with the final purchase. Price, product features, quality, style, service, and image all influence the decision to buy. When purchasing shopping products, buyers allocate a large amount of time for comparing stores and brands. Furniture, audio equipment, bicycles, clothing, and sporting equipment are typical shopping products. Most of these products are expected to have a long life and are purchased less frequently than convenience items. Even though shopping goods last for a

**Comparative shopping can pay off.** Most consumers shop carefully and compare prices, features of the product, and service before they make a major purchase.

longer period of time than convenience goods, most buyers are not highly loyal to a particular brand.

Shopping products require fewer retail outlets than convenience products. Very often shopping products are put in stores that are convenient to each other, in shopping centers or shopping malls, so that consumers may have an opportunity to compare prices, qualities, and styles. Personal selling is important with shopping products.

***Specialty Products.*** Specialty products are products that the consumer makes a special search for and effort to obtain. Consumers know what they want and go out of their way to find it; they are not willing to accept a substitute. Examples of specialty products are ethnic foods, exclusive brands of clothing and shoes, art, and antiques. The purchase of a very expensive product such as an Irwin yacht, a Beechcraft airplane, or an antique Chippendale cabinet would probably be preceded by a special search to find a particular outlet or company that offers the product.

Specialty products are distributed through a limited number of retail outlets. They are purchased infrequently, and usually there is low turnover at the retail level. Advertising and personal selling are used to maintain the appropriate image.

# Industrial Products

Industrial products are usually purchased for the operation of an organization or for the production of other products; thus the major reason for purchasing industrial products relates to specific goals and objectives. Usually the functional aspects of the product are far more important than the image of the product or psychological benefits gained from the purchase.

Industrial products are classified as either capital items or expense items by the purchasing firm. Capital items, such as buildings and equipment, are relatively longer-lived and usually more costly than expense items, which are usually consumed within a year of their purchase. Light bulbs, paper, cleaning materials, and computer diskettes are examples of expense items.

Industrial products can be classified into several other categories: raw materials, major equipment, accessory equipment, component parts, process materials, supplies, and industrial services.

***Raw Materials.*** Raw materials are natural products taken from the earth and oceans and recycled solid waste. Iron ore, bauxite, lumber, and cotton are raw materials. They are usually bought and sold according to grades and specifications, and purchasers usually buy them in large quantities. Processing of some kind is usually required to ready the raw materials for use in production.

***Major Equipment.*** Major equipment is large capital items used for production purposes. Examples include earth-moving equipment, stamping machines, and robotic equipment used on auto assembly lines. Major equipment is usually expensive and is purchased for a specific production process. It is usually used for a long time. Major equipment may be custom-made. Because major equipment is expensive, the decision to purchase it is an important one, sometimes made over a number of years. Financing, repair, and the availability of spare parts are often important considerations.

**Accessory Equipment.**  Accessory equipment is items used for production, office, or management purposes and usually does not become a part of the final product. Examples include computers, typewriters, calculators, hand tools, and compressors. Compared with major equipment, accessory equipment is usually less expensive, purchased routinely, and considered an expense item rather than a capital item. Accessory equipment may be purchased by a central purchasing department of an organization and then distributed and used throughout the organization. Computers and copying equipment, for example, are often purchased by a central purchasing unit and then used by employees throughout the organization.

**Component Parts.**  Component parts are finished items, ready to be assembled into the final product that the company is manufacturing. Tires, wheels, window glass, batteries, and spark plugs are component parts of automobiles. An auto maker typically purchases them from other manufacturers and assembles them into the automobile at the point of final production. Because component parts are viewed not as the final product but only as part of the final product, buyers are most concerned about their quality and suitability relative to the final product.

**Processed Materials.**  Processed materials are materials that are used directly in production or management operations but are not readily identifiable as a component part. A furniture manufacturer, for example, may buy varnish. The varnish is not a component part but is necessary for the completion of the product.

**Supplies.**  Supplies are materials that make production, management, and other operations possible. Paper, pencils, paint, cleaning supplies, and so on are usually considered supplies. Supplies may be divided into three categories—maintenance, repair, and operating—and because of that division they are sometimes called MRO items. Whereas accessory equipment is usually longer-lived capital items, supplies are usually expense items that are used frequently and rapidly and are purchased routinely.

**Industrial Services.**  Industrial services are found in many organizations and include operations such as financial consulting services, legal services, marketing research services, janitorial services, and exterminating services. Purchasers decide whether to provide these services internally or to acquire them from an outside supplier. These services are growing in importance for industrial companies.

# ► Product Line and Product Mix

Product relationships within an organization are of key importance. A product item is a specific version of a product usually designated as a unique offering or unique item among the organization's products. Caffeine-free diet Coke®

**Something for everyone.** Borden offers diverse product lines consisting of snack foods, pasta, ice cream, and even home wallcoverings. The company uses a network of regional companies to get their products to the market-place quickly.

**Product line**

Closely related products that are treated as a unit because of similar marketing strategy and production or end-use considerations

**Product mix**

All the products offered by the organization

is a product item. A **product line** is a group of closely related products that are treated as a unit because of similar marketing strategy and production or end-use considerations. Caffeine-free diet Coke®, Coca-Cola® classic, and new Coca-Cola® are product items in the product line known as Coca-Cola®.

A **product mix** is all the products offered by the organization. Product-mix depth refers to the number of different products in each product line; product mix width refers to the number of product lines in the organization. Table 13-2 shows the relationship between product items, product lines, and the product mix for selected Coca-Cola products. Marketing Encounter 13-2 discusses the product mix at Hasbro, Inc., a toy manufacturer.

# ▶ Product Life Cycle

There are four stages in the life cycle of a product: introduction, growth, maturity, and decline (Figure 13-2). Like people, products are born; they grow; they mature; and eventually they die. Consider black and white televisions. They were introduced after World War II. They took off immediately, enjoyed rapid growth, reached maturity, and then, with the introduction of color television in the mid-1950s started to decline. Most of the televisions sold today are color sets. Black and white sets are available at very low prices for people who want only basic reception.

Some products have very long lives. Ivory Soap was introduced in 1879 and is still popular. In contrast, a new computer is usually outdated within a

**Table 13-2  Product Mix and Product Line for Selected Coca-Cola Company Products**

| Product Mix | | | | |
|---|---|---|---|---|
| Coca-Cola Product Line | Sprite Product Line | Tab Product Line | Fanta Product Line | Mr. Pibb Product Line |
| Coca-Cola® classic<br>Coca-Cola® caffeine-free Coca-Cola<br>diet Coke<br>caffeine-free diet Coke®<br>cherry Coca-Cola<br>diet cherry Coca-Cola | Sprite<br>Diet Sprite | Tab<br>caffeine-free Tab | Grape<br>Orange<br>Strawberry<br>diet Fanta | Mr. Pibb<br>sugar-free Mr. Pibb |

# Marketing Encounter 13-2

## *Hasbro Relies on a Diversified Product Mix*

Hasbro, Inc., is a leading toy manufacturer, with memorable products such as G.I. Joe, Lincoln Logs, Mr. Potato Head, and the games Mousetrap and Operation. In 1987, the company had 34 of the top 100 U.S. toys and sales of $1.3 billion. The keys to Hasbro's success are new products and a diversified product mix.

Hasbro is not dependent on any one product for its success. The company carefully balances its major product categories: infant and preschool products, games and puzzles, girls' toys and dolls, plush products, and boys' action toys. The company has one of the most extensive ranges of products in the toy industry; its product portfolio includes Hasbro itself, Playskool, and Milton Bradley. The introduction of new toys, like My Little Pony and the popular adult game A Question of Scruples, sparks consumers' interest and extends current product lines, making Hasbro a winner with children and their parents.

The company avoids dependence on a single product because that strategy has led to dire consequences for other toy companies. The industry is essentially subject to the whims of children, and what sells this year may sit on the shelves next year when children lose interest. In 1982, 36 percent of the company's revenues

($49 million) came from sales of its revamped G.I. Joe. If children suddenly got bored with the American war hero, the company would be vulnerable. Therefore, instead of pumping the money back into G.I. Joe, Hasbro invested it in new-toy development. Hasbro did not ignore G.I. Joe; indeed, the toy achieved sales of $136 million in 1985, but by then G.I. Joe accounted for only 11 percent of Hasbro's sales.

Hasbro also relies on its reputation for quality, reasonable prices, and extensive advertising to market its many products. Children (and the adults who buy the toys) have traditionally liked Hasbro products because of their durability. Playskool toys are known for their developmental and learning attributes. Hasbro utilizes the resources of three advertising agencies to stimulate the interest of its primary target market: children.

Long ago Hasbro realized that putting all the toys in one toy box is not always a good idea. A diversified product mix and devotion to research and development will ensure that this company continues to make children and their parents smile.

---

These facts are from David Owen, "Where Toys Come From," *The Atlantic Monthly* 58 (October 1986): 64–78; The Hasbro, Inc., 1986 Annual Report; and Sara E. Stern, "Scali, BJK&E Garner Major Toy Business, *Advertising Age*, March 30, 1987, p. 2.

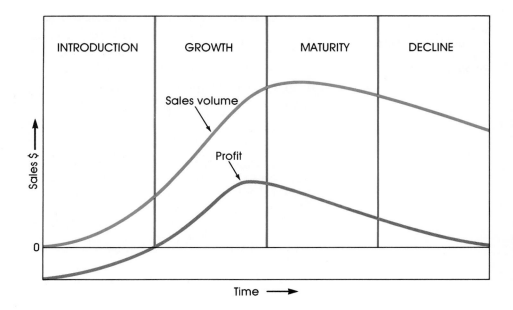

**Figure 13-2**
The Life Cycle of a Product

few years because of technological breakthroughs and rapid changes in the computer industry.

## Introductory Stage

In the introductory stage, consumer awareness and acceptance are limited; sales start at zero; and profits are negative. Profits are negative because the firm has expenditures for research, development, and marketing activities to launch the product. Figure 13-2 shows how sales should move upward from zero, while profits should move from below zero to the point where they break even. Sales accelerate until the growth stage of the life cycle is reached.

During the introductory stage, buyers must be made aware of the fact that the product exists and offers them benefits. Only a few companies may have the expertise to understand the technology or the market needs well enough to launch a new product. Because estimates of the market may vary, it may be difficult to launch products at prices high enough to achieve break-even. Because of these problems, not all new products grow, mature, and go through the entire life cycle. After a short period of time, some products are withdrawn from the market because they are not successful. The IBM Personal Computer Jr. (PC Jr.), for example, was launched and showed some signs of going through the entire product life cycle but was withdrawn shortly after introduction because sales were not high enough to justify ongoing research, development, and commitment to its market.

## Growth Stage

During the growth stage, sales increase at a rapid rate and profits peak and then start to decline (Figure 13-2). The growth stage is critical for a product developing a long life. Competing firms become aware that the product has achieved some success, and their reactions and decisions to enter the market greatly influence the firm's profitability. One reason profits start to decline is that new companies enter the market, driving prices down and increasing marketing expenses, such as for promotion to make the product available. During the growth stage, the firm tries to strengthen its position in the market by emphasizing benefits and identifying market segments that want these benefits.

## Maturity Stage

Industry sales continue to increase at the beginning of the maturity stage; then the sales curve peaks and starts to decline while profits continue to decline. This stage is characterized by severe competition and heavy expenditures for marketing expenses. New competitors emphasize improvements and differentiations of the product. During the maturity stage, weaker competitors start losing interest in the product and move into new products as profits decline.

Procter & Gamble, for example, was losing market share with three of its mature products—Pampers, Tide, and Crest. Competitors such as Huggies (vs. Pampers), Wisk (vs. Tide) and Colgate's Pump toothpaste (vs. Crest) were outpacing Procter and Gamble's traditionally strong brands. As Figure 13-3

**Not better, but different.** Products which become mature in any form may be reintroduced if preserved in a new form or package. Neutrogena, best known for its clear facial soaps, has introduced a new shower & bath gel in liquid form. The pump container provides unique packaging for the product.

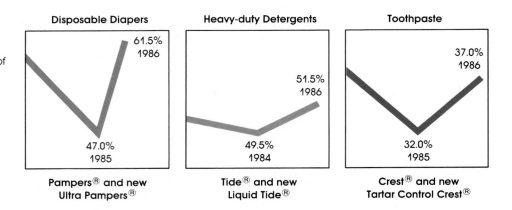

**Figure 13-3**

Procter & Gamble's Market Shares

Source: Faye Rice, "The King of Suds Reigns Again," *Fortune*, August 4, 1986, p. 131; data provided by Drexel Burnham Lambert.

**Disposable Diapers**

61.5%
1986

47.0%
1985

Pampers® and new
Ultra Pampers®

**Heavy-duty Detergents**

51.5%
1986

49.5%
1984

Tide® and new
Liquid Tide®

**Toothpaste**

37.0%
1986

32.0%
1985

Crest® and new
Tartar Control Crest®

Pampers, Ultra Pampers, Tide, Liquid Tide, Crest, and Tartar Control Crest are registered trademarks of the Procter & Gamble Company.

shows, Procter and Gamble successfully introduced new brand extensions, which now maintain a larger market share than the mature product originals. Ultra Pampers (thinner and smaller than competitors' products), Liquid Tide, and Tartar Control Crest are new products developed to offset the decline in sales and profits of their mature predecessors.[2] Procter and Gamble tested the brand extensions for new improvements, and tried to strengthen their position through unique promotion by dealer-oriented activities.

A good example of a mature industry in the United States is the automobile industry. For many years, sales of new automobiles increased. In the last five years, however, sales leveled off after declining significantly from record highs. Overall, profits of automobile companies in the United States have continued to decline as a result of severe competition from foreign manufacturers.

## Decline Stage

During the decline stage, sales continue to fall rapidly. Profits also decline and may become losses as prices are cut and necessary marketing expenditures are made. As profits drop, firms may eliminate certain models or items. In order to cut expenses and squeeze out any remaining profits, marketing expenditures may be cut back, even though such cutbacks accelerate the sales decline. Finally, plans must be made for phasing out the product and introducing new products to take its place.

## Significance of the Product Life Cycle

A company with only one or two products for sale would be unable to remain in existence indefinitely because those products would move through the life cycle and become obsolete. For most companies, evaluating products and the product mix, eliminating older products, and introducing new ones is a continuous process. Ideally, a company has products in various stages of the product life cycle (Figure 13-4). In introducing new products, a company must be willing to take a chance and recognize that its survival and growth are tied to developing new products that consumers want. Consumer goods companies such as Phillip Morris, Inc., Con Agra, and Ralston Purina are continually launching new products to satisfy new consumer desires and identify new market segments.

# Product Positioning in the Product Life Cycle

**Product positioning**

Decisions and activities used to create and maintain a perception of the product in the mind of consumers

As companies introduce new products, they must attempt to position each product so that its unique benefits, attributes, and characteristics can be perceived by the target market. **Product positioning** refers to decisions and activities used to create and maintain a perception of the product in the mind of consumers. Crest, for example, is positioned as a fluoride toothpaste that fights decay for children; Ultra-Brite is positioned as a whitening toothpaste that increases the user's sex appeal. Plaque-fighting toothpastes have recently been introduced. Brands that have this plaque-elimination attribute include Crest and Dentaguard.

Product positioning is related to the concept of market segmentation. Because identifiable groups of consumers usually have unique wants and desires, products with special attributes are created to satisfy these unique desires and wishes. A firm can position a product to compete head-on with existing brands or can attempt to position a product so that it will not compete directly with other brands. Avoiding direct competition is especially important if the firm has one or two competing brands that might be indistinguishable

**Figure 13-4**

Products in Different Stages of the Product Life Cycle

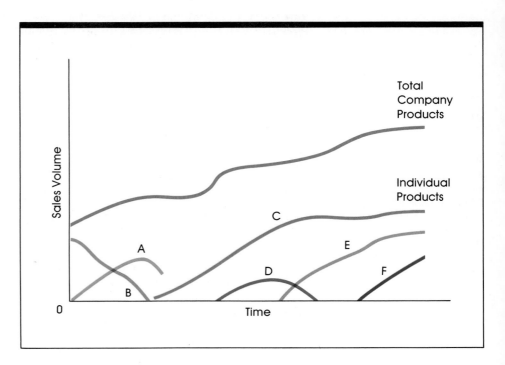

from the new brand that is being launched. For example, by positioning its light beer as a low-calorie beer that is less filling, Miller attempted to minimize the adverse effect on sales of its existing brand, Miller High Life.

If a new product has been developed and the marketing strategy has been planned, the product's attributes and image will give it a distinct appeal. Style, shape, construction, service, color, and any element of the product or the marketing mix could create the right image and appeal. If product positioning is to work, the product's unique image and benefits must be identifiable and clearly understood by the market. The positioning concept is based on the perceptions of consumers, not necessarily on the perceptions of the firm.

# ▶ Branding, Packaging, and Labeling

**Brand**

A name, term, symbol, design, or combination of these that identifies a product and distinguishes it from other products

Branding, packaging, and labeling can be used for identification or distinguishing one product from other products. A **brand** is a name, term, symbol, design, or combination of those that identifies a product and distinguishes it from other products. Packaging involves the development of containers and graphic design for the product. Like branding, packaging influences consumers' attitudes toward the product and their buying decisions. Labeling is related to packaging. Labeling serves not only promotional purposes but also provides important information. The labels of many products, particularly food and drugs, must carry warnings, instructions, certifications, or manufacturers' identifications. Numerous federal laws require disclosure of potential hazards, nutritional information, and fabric content in order to encourage proper use of the product and therefore ensure consumers' satisfaction and protection.

## Branding

**Branding**

Naming and identifying products

**Trademark**

A brand that is registered with the U.S. Patent and Trademark Office and is thus legally protected from use by any firm other than the owner of the trademark

**Branding** is the process of naming and identifying products. The brand name is the part of the brand that can be spoken and consists of letters, words, and numbers, such as WD-40 Lubricant. A brand mark is the part of the brand that is a distinctive design, like the silver star on the hood of a Mercedes or McDonald's golden arches logo. A **trademark** is a brand that is registered with the U.S. Patent and Trademark Office and is thus legally protected from use by any firm other than the owner of the trademark. Registered trademarks include the shape of the Coca-Cola bottle.

Branding provides many benefits to both buyers and sellers. Two major categories of brands are manufacturer brands and private distributor brands. Private distributor brands are middleman or store brands owned and controlled by a wholesaler or retailer. The names of private brands do not usually identify the manufacturer of the product. Retailers and wholesalers use private brands to improve the efficiency of promotion and to generate higher gross margins. Companies such as Sears have been able to develop strong loyalty to a private distributor brand such as Diehard batteries.

Manufacturer brands are brands initiated and owned by the manufacturer to identify products from the point of production to the point of purchase. Green Giant, Sony, and Exxon are examples. The producer usually gets involved in marketing mix decisions about distribution, promotion, pricing, and product development. The producer tries to stimulate demand for the product, which tends to encourage middlemen (both wholesalers and retailers) to make the product available. Competition between manufacturer brands and private distributor brands has been intense over the last few years and is sometimes referred to as the battle of the brands.

Another type of brand that has developed during the last decade is **generic products**—products with no brand name at all. They often come in plain white packages that carry only the generic name of the product—peanut butter, tomato juice, dog food, and so on. Generics have been available in supermarkets for over ten years. Cigarettes, frozen orange juice, and other frequently purchased consumer products are marketed generically. Generic goods appeal to consumers who want to save money and may be willing to sacrifice quality or product consistency in order to get a lower price.

In another approach to branding, each product within the complete product mix of a company has its own brand name. Warner-Lambert, for example, sells many well-known consumer products—Dentyne, Chiclets, Listerine, Halls, Rolaids, Chewels, Dynamint, Trident—each of which is individually branded. As a result of this branding policy, the name of one

**Generic products**

Products with no brand name at all

**No fancy labels.** Most consumers won't sacrifice quality or brand loyalty for the sake of a few cents, but if the saving is substantial some shoppers prefer to buy generic products.

product does not affect the names of other products, and different brands can be directed toward different segments of one market, increasing the company's market share.

Another approach to branding is to develop a family of brands. Each of the firm's products is branded with the same name or with at least part of the name. Gillette, Sara Lee, and IBM use this approach. Sometimes a company uses family branding only for products within a particular product line rather than for all its products. This policy is called line family branding. The same brand is used within a line, but the firm does not use that brand name for a product in a different line. Ralston Purina, for example, has a Chex brand cereal (Wheat Chex, Rice Chex), but on pet-food products the company uses the Purina name (Purina Dog Chow, Purina Cat Chow).

# Packaging

**Packaging** is development of a container and a graphic design in order to enhance the product. A package can perform several functions including protection, economy, convenience, and promotion. Packaging materials are needed first to protect or maintain the product. Milk must be packaged in nonleakable containers so that it can be transported. Potato chips need to be in containers that prevent them from being broken or crushed by the time the consumer is ready to eat them. Proper maintenance of the product through packaging provides economy when the product is packaged in a way that cuts manufacturing costs.

Consumers are often concerned with convenience and safety. California Cooler, the company that introduced the wine cooler, provides its product in containers of four different sizes. The plastic 2-liter bottle provides multiple servings in a reusable container. Other sizes are the 750-milliliter "Big Bro" bottle, the 12-ounce single-server, and the 187 milliliter size for on-premise consumption. This diversity of sizes provides for varying consumer uses and needs.[3] The size or shape of a product, its ease of storage, and safety all relate to convenience.

The promotional aspects of packaging are also important. Choosing the color, texture and design that provide the best image is most important in packaging. A package can perform several promotional roles, including attracting customers' attention and encouraging them to pick up and purchase the product. A firm can create desirable images and associations by designing a package that conveys impressions of richness, luxury, and exclusiveness. Certain colors, patterns, shapes, and textures facilitate the promotional function by stimulating demand. A package that can be reused may also be helpful. Sometimes a package that is appealing, such as the familiar L'eggs pantyhose container, brings a special aura to the product.

# Labeling

**Labeling** is the presentation of information on the package. Labeling can have an important impact on sales. A warranty, for example, is usually a written explanation of the responsibilities of the producer in the event the product fails. This type of information can have a strong impact on sales. A number of federal regulations specify the information that products must

**Multi-purpose packaging.** Packaging can play many roles for a company: functional, innovative, or promotional. Heinz has developed unique and differentiating packaging for its ketchup for both consumer and industrial consumers.

have on them. Clothing, for example, must be labeled with the name of the manufacturer, the country of manufacture, the fabric content, and cleaning instructions. Nutritional labeling is required on many food products. The ingredients of food products must be listed in the order of greatest percentage down to the ingredient that makes up the lowest percentage of the foods total content. Many drugs and cosmetics must carry safety precautions as well as instructions for proper use.

# ▶ Nature of Pricing

**Price**

The value placed on some object involved in an exchange between a buyer and a seller

**Price** is the value placed on some object involved in an exchange between a buyer and a seller. Although the seller usually establishes the price, very often the price is changed or negotiated through interaction between buyer and seller. The buyer usually exchanges purchasing power for satisfaction or for the utility associated with a product. Purchasing power depends on the buyer's income, credit, and wealth.

Price does not always involve money. Barter, the trading of products, is the oldest form of exchange known, and today barter is becoming increasingly popular, especially in trade between nations. It is not unusual for a country that focuses on one agricultural crop, such as sugar cane, to trade it for heavy machinery to use in construction projects.

Because price has become the common denominator to assess value, almost anything in society can be assigned a price related to a financial value. The financial price of the product quantifies the value and is the basis for most exchanges in a market economy.

Price is probably the most flexible variable in the marketing mix. Although it may take years to develop a product, establish channels of distribution, and design and implement promotion, the price of a product may be set and changed in a few minutes. Under certain circumstances, of course, the price may not be so flexible, especially if government regulations prevent dealers from controlling prices.

Probably no industry has experimented more with pricing in the last few years than the airline industry. Passengers who book their flight thirty days in advance, passengers who stay over a weekend, and passengers who fall into certain age categories such as senior citizens or children under the age of 12 are given special rates. Eastern Airlines has developed a new category of passenger service—"Moonlight Flights." Basically cargo flights, these flights run from midnight to 7 A.M. There is no assigned seating; baggage must be carried on or may be checked for a fee; and there are no free snacks or drinks. Passengers can fly for as little as $59 one way. Bookings on these flights have been extremely high.

Most firms have to earn a profit in order to survive, and price is a key variable in the profit formula. Most managers are aware that profit equals revenue minus expenses and that revenue is the product of price times quantity sold:

$$\text{profit} = \text{revenue} - \text{expenses}$$
$$\text{revenue} = \text{price} \times \text{quantity sold}$$

Some firms try to maximize profits by manipulating prices in relation to supply and demand. Profit maximization is more likely an economic theory than it is an attainable goal in the real world. Nevertheless, most firms are aiming at some type of target return on profits, and price plays a key role in obtaining these goals.

# ▶ Pricing Objectives

Pricing objectives are explicit statements about the role of price in an organization's marketing mix. They usually are influenced not only by marketing mix decisions but also by finance, accounting, and production factors. Most companies set a few pricing objectives to reach their goals.

## Survival

The most fundamental pricing objective of a company is survival. Firms will tolerate short-run losses if they believe they are accomplishing something that will lead to long-range profitability. Airlines, for example, sometimes reduce fares in an attempt to build passenger traffic on a particular route.

A new restaurant or supermarket may set prices low for short periods of time in order to attract customers. Automobile companies have been known to discount car prices drastically with rebates or to offer below-market interest rates for short periods of time in order to keep production lines moving and cash flowing into the business. Pricing flexibility allows a company to obtain revenue quickly when profitability is not the most immediate concern. Firms must sometimes adjust prices to meet payrolls and utility bills in order to keep the doors open and stay in business for the long run.

## Maximization of Profits and Sales Volume

Although many firms say that their goal is profit maximization, it is a difficult goal to achieve. In a company with profit maximization goals, management continues to set and increase levels of profitability to optimize its achievement. In contrast, target return goals state a desired level of profitability, such as a 15 percent return on either sales or invested capital.

To maximize sales volume, management sets an acceptable level of profitability and then tries to increase sales by increasing market share. Ford Motor Company has used pricing to increase its share of the European car market. Sales maximization is typical in grocery, gasoline, and appliance businesses. New firms come into the market with low prices in order to gain market share; then they gradually increase prices and their level of service as they mature. One danger is that a firm can increase market share even when sales for the total industry are decreasing. A few years ago, A&P was increasing sales on a monthly basis while sales in the total supermarket industry were declining. Because A&P gained market share in a declining segment of the grocery business, A&P is almost out of business.

## Maintaining the Status Quo

Many firms desire nothing more than to maintain current conditions and current price relationships with customers and competitors. A firm may be very happy with its current market share and may be interested not in beating but in meeting competitors' prices. The industry seems to achieve price stability or maintain a favorable public image toward existing prices. A status quo pricing objective can reduce a firm's risk by helping to stabilize demand for its products and encourage competitors to maintain their prices. Status quo pricing tends to deemphasize price in the marketing mix and can lead to a climate of nonprice competition in an industry. This type of pricing objective seems to be typical in the tobacco industry and in professional services.

# ▶ Demand, Cost, and Profit Relationships

**Demand**

The quantity of a product that consumers are willing to buy at certain prices

In chapter 2 you saw that there is an inverse relationship between price and the demand for products (Figure 13-5). **Demand** is the quantity of a product that consumers are willing to buy at certain prices. The quantity demanded

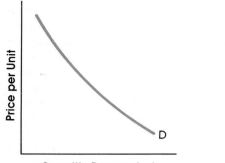

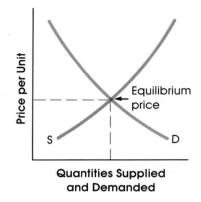

**Figure 13-5**

Relationship between Price and
Quantity Demanded and
Quantity Supplied

**Supply**

The quantity of a product that
producers are willing to sell at
certain prices

**Elasticity of demand**

The relative responsiveness of
changes in quantity demanded
to changes in price

**Break-even point**

Where the cost of making the
product equals the revenue
gained from selling the product

increases as the price decreases; and as the price increases, the quantity demanded decreases. The buyer's needs, ability, willingness, and authority to buy are assumed to be constant, and as long as environmental situations remain stable, this fundamental relationship between price and demand should continue. This economic theory provides an ideal perspective on the relationship between price and quantity demanded.

By contrast, **supply** is the quantity of a product that producers are willing to sell at certain prices. The intersection of supply and demand establishes an equilibrium price, which will exist in the marketplace for a particular product at a certain point in time. Demand can be influenced by many factors, including changes in buyers' attitudes, income levels, and the prices of related goods. Canada Dry Club Soda, for example, outsells all competitors in the U.S. carbonated water market. Price is the fundamental reason for the product's success. Imported waters cost 45 to 200 percent more than their domestic counterparts. The price of a 25-ounce bottle of Ramlosa, a Swedish water, ranges from 99 cents to $1.39, whereas a 34-ounce bottle of Canada Dry Club Soda sells for between 59 and 89 cents.[4]

**Elasticity of demand** is the relative responsiveness of changes in quantity demanded to changes in price. Demand is elastic if a change in price causes an opposite change in total revenue—that is, an increase in price will decrease total revenue, and a decrease in price will increase total revenue. An inelastic demand results in a parallel change in total revenue; an increase in price will increase total revenue; a decrease in price will decrease total revenue. The percentage of change in quantity demanded caused by a percentage change in price is much greater for elastic demand than for inelastic demand. Although marketers cannot base prices strictly on determinations of whether the price seems to be elastic or inelastic, elasticity of demand helps marketers determine what will happen to profit at different price and demand levels. The marketer must also keep in mind the cost associated with different sales volumes and how it affects profits.

In examining a relationship between demand, cost and profits, several terms must be understood. The **break-even point** for marketing a product

**Fixed costs**

Costs that do not vary with the number of units produced or sold

**Variable costs**

Costs that vary directly with changes in the number of units produced or sold

**Total revenue**

Price times quantity

is the point where the cost of making the product equals the revenue gained from selling the product. At the break-even point, fixed and variable costs are important. **Fixed costs** do not vary with the number of units produced or sold. Fixed costs include the cost of buying equipment, renting a building, and paying the company president. Fixed costs do not change as production increases from one shift to two shifts a day; they are costs that do not vary with the level of production. **Variable costs** vary directly with changes in the number of units produced or sold. Variable costs relate directly to the amount of supplies purchased that go directly into the product. Automobile tires, for example, are a direct variable cost for an automobile manufacturer because the number of tires needed and expenses for tires vary directly with the number of automobiles produced.

**Total revenue** equals price times quantity. A simple way to examine the relationship between cost and profits is to determine the break-even point. Knowing how many products a company must sell in order to break even does not assist in predicting the level of profitability but it gives the company a sales goal that it must exceed if it is to earn a profit on a new product. The break-even point is determined by dividing the fixed cost by the contribution of each unit to fixed cost. For example, a product priced at $100 per unit has an average variable cost of $60 per unit; its contribution to fixed cost is $40; the total fixed cost is $120,000; and the break-even point is 120,000 over 40 equals 3,000 units.

$$\text{Break-even point} = \frac{\text{fixed costs}}{\text{per unit contribution to fixed costs}}$$

$$= \frac{120,000}{\$40}$$

$$= 3,000 \text{ units}$$

To use break-even analysis effectively, the marketer should determine the break-even point for various alternative prices. Even then, the analysis may not tell the marketer what price to charge, but it can determine price levels that are probably not desirable. Figure 13-6 shows the break-even analysis chart in a simple and straightforward manner.

# ▶ Pricing Policies

A pricing policy is a rule for taking pricing action. Pricing policies provide guidelines about how the company will achieve its pricing objectives and overall marketing strategy. A pricing policy answers this question: How will price be used as a variable in the marketing mix? Pricing policies may relate to the pricing of new products and to psychological pricing techniques.

## Pricing New Products

Setting the price for a new product is very important. The correct price leads to profitability. The wrong price may mean the instant death of the

**Figure 13-6**
Break-even Analysis

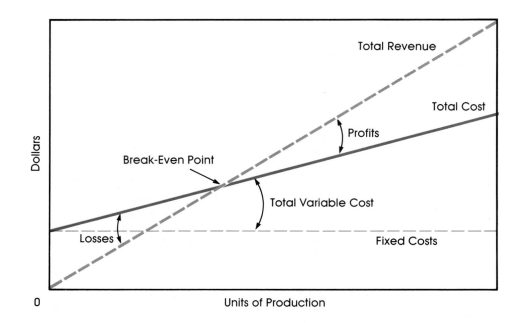

Total Revenue

Total Cost

Profits

Dollars

Break-Even Point

Total Variable Cost

Losses

Fixed Costs

0                                          Units of Production

product. In general, there are two basic approaches to setting the base price for a new product.

**Price skimming**

Charging the highest possible price that buyers who want the product will pay

*Price Skimming.* **Price skimming** is charging the highest possible price that buyers who want the product will pay. Price skimming assumes that demand is inelastic in the introductory stage of the product's life and therefore marketers charge the highest price at which buyers will still buy the product. Skimming allows the company to generate much-needed revenue to help offset the costs of research and development. Also a price that is initially set high guards against setting a low price that does not cover costs. Most firms have found that it is much easier to lower prices when a product has met with success than it is to raise prices. However, if the high price and early profits attract competitors into the market, the price may fall.

**Penetration price**

A low price designed to let a product enter the market and gain market share rapidly

*Penetration Price.* **Penetration price** is a low price designed to let a product enter the market and gain market share rapidly. Penetration pricing is less flexible than price skimming; it is more difficult to raise a penetration price than it is to lower a skimming price. Penetration pricing is used most often when marketers suspect that competitors will enter the market very quickly after the product has been introduced.

There are several advantages to penetration pricing. It may allow the marketer to gain a large market share and discourage competition from entering the market. A penetration price is most appropriate when the demand for products is highly elastic. This means that the market tends to purchase at the penetration price, but many buyers would drop off and fail to buy the product if it were priced above the penetration price. Marketing Encounter 13-3 describes how Parfums de Coeur determined the price for its imitations of designer perfumes.

# Marketing Encounter 13-3
## *Knock-Off Fragrance Pricing*

Pricing is behind the sweet smell of success for fragrance companies like Parfums de Coeur. The company (its name translates to "perfumes of the heart") manufactures copies, or "impostures," of expensive designer perfumes, and markets them to middle- and working-class women who cannot afford the expensive fragrances. For instance, the designer fragrance Opium sells for around $32.50, while Ninja, Parfums de Coeur's knock-off of Opium, sells for $7.50. The company also copies such hot scents as Obsession and Giorgio. Nearly forty companies have joined the knock-off game; some companies are even copying the knock-offs!

Mark Laracy (formerly of Charles of the Ritz) started Parfums de Coeur to fill a hole in the perfume market. Opium was a big seller in the department stores, with a prestige price to match its high-class image. Laracy saw there were no comparable fragrances sold in drug stores for women who could not afford, or who did not want to pay, $30 to $100 for a bottle of perfume. He created his knock-off fragrances just for them. For men, the company markets Lancer, a knock-off of Polo.

Parfums de Coeur uses comparative advertising with slogans such as "If you like Opium (or Giorgio or some other fragrance), you'll love Ninja (or Primo, Turmoil or Confess)." Yet, Parfums de Coeur is not really selling image: It is selling price. The company distributes the scents through drug stores and discount stores like K-mart and Woolworth's and through television advertisements.

Like most companies, Parfums de Coeur followed specific steps in establishing the price of its perfumes. It set its pricing objectives, primarily profit and market share, and assessed its target market's evaluation of price and its ability to purchase the perfumes. Women (and men in the case of the knock-off colognes) who could not afford to purchase the prestige-priced fragrances like Opium and Giorgio might buy economically-priced fragrances that smelled like the expensive ones. They evaluated the prices of the designer fragrances sold in department stores as well as the prices of the mass-market perfumes sold in drug stores. They finally decided that a strategy of penetration pricing would best generate a large market share quickly, while reducing the impact of the designer's prestige pricing policies.

The low-priced knock-offs have not seriously reduced the market share of the designer fragrances they copy; they have instead cut into the sales of the less-expensive mass market brands like Jontue and Revlon. The women who buy the knock-offs want to smell as if they can afford to spend a lot on their appearance. Apparently, Parfums de Coeur's pricing strategy is working; the company sold $60 million of the knock-offs in 1986.

---

These facts are from Pat Sloan, "Knock-offs Deliver Blows to Fragrance Market," *Advertising Age*, March 2, 1987, p. S-14; Amy Dunkin, " 'Obsession' by Any Other Name Name Sells Sweetly," *Business Week*, June 1, 1987, p. 97; and Kevin T. Higgins, "By Any Other Name Would Smell as Sweet—Imposture Line from Parfums de Coeur Striving to Knock Off Designer Brands, Literally and Figuratively," *Marketing News*, January 17, 1986, pp. 1, 12.

# Psychological Pricing

**Psychological pricing**

A policy designed to encourage purchases based on emotional reactions to the price rather than on rational responses to the price

**Psychological pricing** is a policy designed to encourage purchases based on emotional reactions to the price rather than on rational responses to the price. It is used most often at the consumer level when prices are set for final consumers, especially in retailing environments. The assumption behind even/odd pricing is that more of a product will be bought at $9.99 than at $10 because the product seems to be a bargain at the odd price. The assumption behind symbolic/prestige pricing is that high prices connote high quality. The prices of certain fragrances and over-the-counter drugs are set artificially high in order to give the impression of high quality. Consumers associate a drug's price with its potency. It is believed that consumers also associate the quality of clothing with the price they pay.

**Creating a demand.** Many manufacturers of prestige items depend on psychological pricing to maintain demand for their product. If Gucci purses sold for $19.00 they would not have the status or the total sales that the company currently maintains.

# Notes

**1.** James L. Heskeh, "Lessons in the Service Sector," *Harvard Business Review* 65 (March–April 1987): 118.

**2.** Faye Rice, "The King of Suds Reigns Again," *Fortune,* August 4, 1986, pp. 130–31, 134.

**3.** "New Entries Sweeten Wine Cooler Market Share," *Marketing News,* June 20, 1986, p. 16.

**4.** William C. Banks, "The New Age of Aqueons," *Money,* 15 (September 1986): 169–72.

# Summary and Review

▶ A product is a complex of tangible and intangible attributes that provide satisfaction and benefits. A product may be a good, a service, or an idea. Products are among a firm's most important and visible contacts with buyers. If products do not meet the needs and expectations of buyers, sales and survival will be difficult.

▶ The process of research and development includes the steps of idea development, screening new ideas, business analysis, product development, test marketing, and commercialization.

▶ Products are usually classified as either consumer or industrial products. Consumer products can be classified as convenience, shopping, or specialty products. The industrial product classifications are raw materials, major equipment, accessory equipment, component parts, processed materials, supplies, and industrial services.

▶ The life cycle of a product consists of a series of stages that a product goes through from the time it is first put on the market until the time it is withdrawn. These stages are introduction, growth, maturity, and decline. The level of marketing expenses for a product varies according to the maturity of the product.

▶ Branding is the process of naming and identifying products. It includes the brand name, the brand mark, and the trademark. Packaging is the development of containers and graphic designs to enhance products. Packaging is both functional and promotional. Labeling is the presentation of information, such as warranty and content, on the package.

▶ Price is the value placed on an exchange between a buyer and a seller. It is one of the most flexible of the marketing mix, yet one of the most important, because it affects profitability.

▶ Pricing objectives include survival, maximization of profits, maximization of sales volume, and maintaining the status quo. A firm will select a particular objective on the basis of its situation in the industry.

▶ There is an inverse relationship between the price of a product and the quantity of the product demanded. In elastic demand, when the price rises, total revenue falls. In inelastic demand, when the price increases, total revenue increases. The break-even point is the point where the cost of making a product equals the revenue gained from selling the product. These factors can help marketers determine the correct price for a product.

▶ When a firm introduces a new product, it can use one of several pricing policies to compete successfully. These policies include price skimming and penetration pricing.

# Key Terms and Concepts

product
research and development
concept testing
test marketing
commercialization
consumer products
industrial products
product line
product mix
product positioning

brand
branding
trademark
generic products
packaging
labeling
price
demand
supply
elasticity of demand

break-even point
fixed costs
variable costs
total revenue

price skimming
penetration price
psychological pricing

# Checking Your Understanding

This chapter introduced you to the subjects of product and price. To test and reinforce your understanding, fill in the blanks below.

**1.** _____ pricing encourages a purchasing decision based on an emotional reaction to the price.

**2.** The product life _____ is a series of stages through which a product goes from its introduction to and withdrawal from the market.

**3.** A _____ is a brand that is registered with the federal government and is legally protected from use by other companies.

**4.** _____ materials are natural products taken from the earth and oceans.

**5.** The brand _____ is the part of the brand that can be communicated orally.

**6.** _____ is the price times the quantity sold.

**7.** A company reaches its _____ _____ _____ when the cost of making the product equals the revenue from sales of the product.

**8.** _____ of demand is the relative responsiveness of changes in quantity demanded to changes in price.

**9.** A _____ price is designed to let a product enter the market and gain market share quickly.

**10.** A _____ is a complex of tangible and intangible attributes that provide satisfaction and benefits.

**11.** A brand _____ is the distinctive design that identifies a product.

**12.** _____ _____ brands are usually owned by a store or middleman and controlled by a retailer or wholesaler.

**13.** _____ products appeal to customers who desire to save money, even at the expense of consistency and quality.

# Topics for Review and Discussion

**1.** What are the steps to follow to introduce a new product?

**2.** Why would a firm go through test marketing first before introducing a product?

**3.** Use specific products to illustrate the relationship between product item, product line, and product mix.

**4.** In terms of sales and profits, describe each stage of the product life cycle.

**5.** What are three important features used to identify or distinguish a product from other products?

**6.** Use real examples to illustrate individual branding, family branding, and line-family branding.

**7.** What is the significance of knowing elasticity of demand?

**8.** What does a break-even analysis do?

**9.** Distinguish between the two ways to set the base price for a new product.

**10.** Why is there a need to adopt different marketing strategies for different stages in the life cycle of a product?

**11.** Is it possible for a convenience product to become a shopping product or for a shopping product to become a specialty product over time? Why? If so, give some examples.

**12.** Is the decision process involved in buying a consumer product any different from the decision process involved in buying an industrial product?

**13.** Do all products go through all stages of the product life cycle? Can any of the stages be skipped? What kind of product has the characteristics of a long introductory and growth stage, a very short maturity, and a steep decline stage?

**14.** Does a successful test marketing guarantee product success?

# Exercises

**1.** Give an example of each category of consumer products that you have used. Explain why you categorized the products as such.

**2.** The fixed cost for producing Product A is $6 million, regardless of sales volume. Product A can be sold at $15 apiece, and the variable cost is $5 per unit. How many units must be sold in order to break even? How many units must be sold in order to obtain profits of $2 million?

**3.** Classify the following industrial products:

| | |
|---|---|
| tires | steel wheels |
| machinery | factory |
| varnish | microcomputer |
| eraser | stationery |
| water | spark plugs |
| batteries | conveyor belt |
| paint | detergent |
| crane | wrench |
| brake disk | carburetor |
| oil | ball bearings |
| speedometer | timepieces |
| radio | windshield wiper |

## Case 13-1

### *General Mills Launches the Olive Garden Restaurants*

When people hear the name General Mills, they may think of Gorton's seafood, or Betty Crocker cake mixes, or even Cheerios cereal, but probably not Italian restaurants. Nevertheless, General Mills decided to open the Olive Garden restaurants, a chain of Italian restaurants, now the largest chain of Italian cafés in the nation.

Consumers spend $4 out of every $10 of their food bill on dining out, and General Mills wanted more of those dollars. After screening new ideas, the company decided to develop an Italian restaurant. A business analysis highlighted the fact that Italian food was increasing in popularity, yet there were few Italian restaurants in the nation. The company decided this market opportunity was too good to pass up, and invested millions of dollars on developing a prototype Olive Garden restaurant.

General Mills spent months surveying consumers on their restaurant preferences before they test marketed the first restaurant in 1982. Executives from the company's restaurant division sampled as many as thirteen meals a day from other successful restaurants, and they even wined and dined employees from those restaurants to get ideas for their own Olive Garden. They experimented with thousands of recipes and tried at least eighty different spaghetti sauces before finding one that clung to the spaghetti and didn't run to the edge of the plate. They even tested hundreds of Italian recordings before they found the right combination of background music. Their main objective was simply to create a restaurant that people would like.

After carrying out extensive concept testing, General Mills concluded that consumers do not truly like "real" Italian food with its strong taste of garlic and basil, so the Olive Garden serves a cuisine which is only sort-of-Italian. The servers dish up spaghetti and fettucine, but chefs go easy on the herbs and spices. Rather than try to be authentic, the Olive Garden tries to appeal to an unsophisticated general public. The restaurants are thus called the Olive Garden (instead of the Olive Grove), and entrees include "Venetian" chicken cooked in teriyaki sauce, perhaps served with an "Italian Margarita," and a serving of chocolate mousse for dessert. Despite the lack of authenticity, the prices are very good—an average meal runs about $9 with food and wine—and customers began flocking to the restaurant. In 1985, General Mills decided to commercialize and opened up seven more Olive Garden restaurants.

People certainly seem to like the Olive Garden: A typical restaurant has annual sales of more than $2.5 million, earning General Mills some $300,000 before taxes. The company isn't resting on its laurels, though; it's pouring the profits into expansion plans for the chain. Fifty-eight stores are already earning profits, and there are forty more stores on the drawing board for 1988. The company ultimately hopes to operate five hundred stores across the country. General Mills also hopes the Olive Garden will stabilize the unsteady earnings of its restaurant division, which includes 392 Red Lobster restaurants.

It won't be quite so easy for General Mills now, however. The Olive Garden's main competition, the TGI Friday and Bennigans chains, have added Italian items to their menus. Other companies are looking into the market for the first time with an eye at cutting into the Olive Garden's profits.

General Mills has much experience in launching new products, but with billions of dollars at stake, they still must be cautious. The company spent several million dollars alone on testing the idea of an Italian restaurant and developing the first prototype. Only when the first Olive Garden earned a profit did they begin to commercialize and expand. Such extensive research is no guarantee that a new product or service will succeed, but it certainly helps increase the chances for success.

These facts are from Robert Johnson, "Costly Creation: General Mills Risks Millions Starting Chain of Italian Restaurants," *The Wall Street Journal*, September 21, 1987, pp. 1, 8; The General Mills, Inc. 1985, 1986, and 1987 Annual Reports; and the "100 Leading National Advertisers 1987," *Advertising Age*, September 24, 1987, pp. 106–7.

**Questions**

1. Did the Olive Garden develop the right products for its target market? Defend your answer.
2. Did the Olive Garden use price skimming or penetration pricing? Why?
3. How is product and price used to position the Olive Garden against the competition?

## Case 13-2
### *Toys "R" Us Competes Through Price*

Toys "R" Us is the leader of the United States toy market with its chain of 271 supermarket-style toy stores in 31 states. It has long been an innovator, both in its pricing policies and in its toy supermarket format. In 1987 it held nearly 16 percent of the $12.5 billion U.S. toy market. Some analysts have predicted the company may have a 40 percent share of an even bigger U.S. toy market by the 1990s. The company's earnings have increased 35 percent annually since 1978.

Charles Lazarus opened the first Toys "R" Us in 1957 as the Children's Supermart (with the "r's" printed backwards to encourage name recognition), offering name-brand toys and baby goods at discount prices. Today, the chain still offers name-brand toys at 20 to 50 percent below retail cost. Each store stocks over eighteen thousand different items and keeps track of them by a computer system that all but eliminates stock-outs. Managers never place orders, toys just arrive on time, averting the Toys "R" Us definition of a major disaster: not having a certain toy on display and ready for sale.

Toys "R" Us brings customers into the store with baby care products like strollers and disposable diapers discounted below cost. Hopefully, parents will spend the money they save on the discounted baby goods on toys for the baby. Customers come to Toys "R" Us planning to spend a certain amount of money, rather than planning to buy a specific item.

Toys "R" Us stores are usually located along commercial highways, well away from shopping malls. This keeps the company's costs down, and prevents customers from being distracted by other toy sellers. Isolation from shopping malls also means customers will load up their shopping carts because they don't have to lug their purchases through crowded malls.

Toys "R" Us does not base the price for a toy on the manufacturer's price, but instead, bases the price on how much it thinks customers will pay for the toy. Toys "R" Us then decides on the price at which it is willing to purchase the toy from the manufacturer and negotiates with manufacturers to buy the toy at that price. The company has a definite advantage in negotiations because it buys in such large volume. Toy manufacturers are also willing to negotiate with Toys "R" Us because the company often serves as a testing ground for new toys. Price is so important to the Toys "R" Us marketing strategy that even when demand for a toy is high and supplies are short, the company will not raise the price of a toy to make a quick profit. Lower prices here do not mean lower profits.

Market share is the main pricing objective of Toys "R" Us, and the company says it is willing to cut prices even more to remain in its number-one position. Other toy stores are trying to meet the challenge from Toys "R" Us; those that don't change their strategies may wind up out of the toy market altogether. Most stores, like K mart and Macy's expand their toy lines only for the six-week Christmas season and hold sales to attract customers. Although Toys "R" Us never holds sales, it maintains its huge selection, stock, and discount prices all year round. Customers who found good buys at Toys "R" Us at Christmas are likely to return for children's birthdays and other special days, when other retail stores have little to choose from. Even new parents who drop in to Toys "R" Us for discounted baby products often return for toys until their baby outgrows them at age 16 or so. Of course, then there are still sporting goods-type "toys," like basketballs and bicycles, suitable for older teens, young adults, and families of almost any age.

Some competitors have changed to the Toys "R" Us supermarket-style stores and try to meet Toys "R" Us prices all year round. Other stores are using nonprice competition to try to get into the number-one position, by offering educational and baby-sitting services. However, Toys "R" Us intends to rely on its nonprice attributes of convenience, selection and stock, as well as price competition, to hold its position against its imitators.

It has already expanded internationally to Britain, Germany, and Canada with 24 stores. The company has plans for many other stores overseas—200 by 1990—to take advantage of the world toy market, which is nearly double that of the U.S. toy market. Additionally, it opened Kids "R" Us in the U.S., a chain of children's clothing stores similar to its toy stores.

Toys "R" Us has customer loyalty behind it. Customers know they can find "the" toy their child wants, at the best price, at Toys "R" Us. If they can't find it at Toys "R" Us, it doesn't exist. And if the child doesn't like the toy after all, they can return it for a full refund with no questions asked.

---

These facts are from David Owen, "Where Toys Come From," *Atlantic Monthly* 58 (October 1986): 64–78; Anthony Ramirez, "Can Anyone Compete with Toys "R" Us?" *Fortune,* October 28, 1985, pp. 71–72 + ; Mark Maremont, Dori Jones Yang, and Amy Dunkin, "Toys "R" Us Goes Overseas—and Finds that Toys "R" Them, Too," *Business Week,* January 26, 1987, pp. 71–72; Susan Scherreik, "Toys "R" Profitable," *New Jersey Monthly* (October 1986): 45–51; Jesus Sanchez, "Toymakers Make a Play for Market," *USA Today,* Feb. 10, 1987, pp. 1B-2B; and Dan Dorfman, "Toys "R" Us: Mattel Play?" *USA Today,* June 28, 1987, p. 2B.

**Questions**

1. What is the Toys "R" Us pricing objective and how is it implemented?
2. Defend the Toys "R" Us policy of discounting diapers and strollers below cost.
3. How does the Toys "R" Us product mix and price policies work together for profits?

# Answers to Checking Your Understanding

1. psychological
2. cycle
3. trademark
4. raw
5. name
6. revenue
7. break-even point

8. elasticity
9. penetration
10. product
11. mark
12. private distributor
13. generic

## Outline

# Distribution

## Objectives

After reading this chapter, you will be able to:

▶ Define distribution, and explain its role in the marketing mix.

▶ Identify the functions of distribution, and relate them to marketing decisions.

▶ Discuss the concept of marketing channels, and identify the components of various types of channels.

▶ Identify various types of wholesalers, and describe their respective distribution functions.

▶ Explain the role and functions of the retailer in the distribution process.

▶ Describe the activities involved in the physical distribution of goods.

# Business Experience

━━━━━━━━━━━━━━━━━━━━━━━━━━━━━━━━

Wal-Mart Stores, Inc., a chain of over 1200 discount stores, includes Wal-Mart department stores, Sam's Wholesale Clubs, Dot Discount Drugs, and Hypermart USA. These stores are located in twenty-five states predominately in the Midwest and South. The first Wal-Mart store was opened over twenty-five years ago in Rogers, Arkansas.

Wal-Mart is dedicated to a philosophy of continuing, controlled, and profitable growth. The company has been growing at a rate of 30 to 35 percent annually in both sales and profits. Its annual sales exceed $15 billion, producing profits of $628 million (fiscal year 1988). Wal-Mart is the second largest discounter and the fastest growing major retailer in the United States. Throughout Wal-Mart's phenomenal expansion and success, the company has remained true to its goal of providing low prices on quality, name-brand merchandise and guaranteed customer satisfaction. To achieve this goal, inventory and transportation management are necessary.

The Wal-Mart stores range in size from 30,000 square feet to 80,000 square feet. They are located primarily in rural markets, although an increasing number of stores are being located in and around metropolitan areas within the chain's regional trade territory. The trade market for most stores covers large rural areas, and Wal-Mart stores are designed as one-stop shopping centers. Wal-Mart is opening small prototype stores of from 25,000 to 30,000 square feet in communities smaller than typical Wal-Mart towns.

To assure a constant flow of inventory to its stores, Wal-Mart operates fourteen major distribution centers. About 83 percent of the merchandise flows from the manufacturer to the company's distribution centers by means of a trucking network of company-owned trucks, which also carry back unsold merchandise to the distribution centers, eliminating as many miles traveled with empty trailers as possible.

These facts are from Wal-Mart's 1983, 1984, 1985, 1986, and 1987 Annual Reports.

# Introduction

**Distribution**

An orderly process of dividing, dispersing, and delivering products to make them available for customers

Distribution is one of the four major variables of the marketing mix. Products that are promoted and correctly priced will not sell unless they are available for purchase. **Distribution** is an orderly process of dividing, dispersing, and delivering products to make them available for customers. Distribution is facilitated by middlemen—wholesalers and retailers—and their activities involving the transfer of products and ownership. Middlemen create time, place, and possession utility.

This chapter examines marketing channels, retailing, wholesaling, market coverage and the physical distribution of products.

# ▶ Marketing Channels

**Marketing channel**

A group of marketing organizations that direct the flow of products from producers to customers

A **marketing channel**, or channel of distribution, is a group of marketing organizations that direct the flow of products from producers to customers. Marketing channels make products available to buyers when and where they desire to purchase them. Although all organizations distribute their products, marketing channels differ widely in their arrangement. Radio Shack makes its audio and consumer electronic products available through company-owned stores. General Motors and most other auto manufacturers make their products available through franchised dealers who serve as retailers to the public. Even libraries and museums make distribution decisions when they decide where to locate their facilities. Sometimes they make available temporary exhibits to widen the distribution of their products. These examples illustrate the importance of marketing channels in the marketing mix of all organizations.

Vast numbers of marketing channels are used to distribute consumer products and industrial products throughout the United States and all over the world. Marketing channels can be classified according to various arrangements that enable producers and middlemen to move products to consumers.

**Middlemen**

Organizations that bridge the gap between the producer of the product and the ultimate user of the product

**Middlemen,** or intermediaries, are organizations that bridge the gap between the producer of the product and the ultimate user of the product. **Wholesalers** are middlemen who generally buy from producers or from other wholesalers and sell to retailers. They usually do not sell in significant quantities to ultimate consumers. **Retailers** are middlemen who sell products to ultimate consumers for home and household use rather than for resale or for use in producing other products.

**Wholesalers**

Middlemen who generally buy from producers or from other wholesalers and sell to retailers

**Retailers**

Middlemen who sell products to ultimate consumers for home and household use rather than for resale or for use in producing other products

There are two major types of intermediaries determined by how much risk the middleman takes in product ownership: merchant middlemen and agent middlemen. Merchant middlemen actually buy and sell products. Agent middlemen help in the transfer of ownership of products but do not take possession and do not assume the risk associated with ownership. Agent middlemen earn a commission for their service. Both wholesalers and retailers can assume these roles in relation to taking risk in product ownership.

**Weyerhaeuser sells packaging materials directly to Federal Express.** This illustrates a marketing channel where one producer deals directly with another producer. Federal Express purchases in sufficient quantities to make this an effective and efficient relationship.

# Channels for Consumer Products

Typical marketing channels for consumer products are shown in Figure 14-1. In Channel A, the product moves from the producer directly to the consumer. Farmers who sell their fruit and vegetables directly to consumers at roadside stands use a direct-from-producer-to-consumer marketing channel. A firm that sells its products directly at the factory also uses a direct-from-producer-to-consumer marketing channel.

In Channel B, the product goes from producer to retailer to consumer. This type of channel is used for products like college textbooks. Textbook publishers sell to retail bookstores, which make the product available to students. Many of the products sold by Sears, K mart, and J. C. Penney are purchased from manufacturers and then made directly available to consumers.

In Channel C, the product is handled by a wholesaler and retailer before it reaches the hands of the consumer. Producer-to-wholesaler-to-retailer-to-consumer marketing channels distribute a wide range of products including refrigerators, televisions, soda, cigarettes, clocks, watches, and housewares.

In Channel D, the product goes to an agent, a wholesaler, and a retailer before going to the consumer. This long channel of distribution is useful for products that are sold intensively. Candy and some produce are often sold by agents who bring buyers and sellers together. The agents make the products available to wholesalers, who in turn sell to retail stores and outlets that sell to ultimate consumers.

**Figure 14-1**

Marketing Channels for Consumer Products

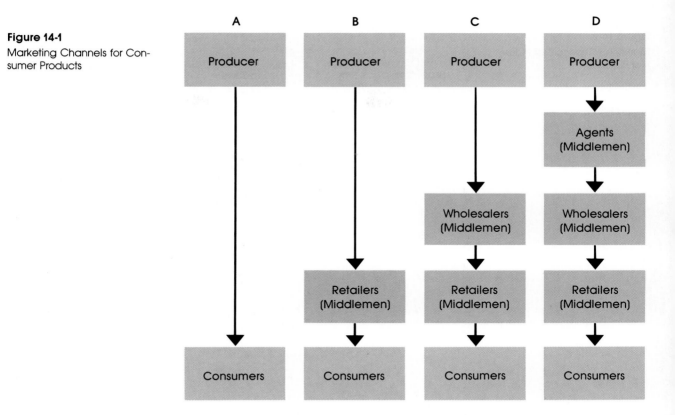

## Channels for Industrial Products

Marketing channels for industrial products tend to be shorter than marketing channels for consumer products. Three marketing channels for industrial products are shown in Figure 14-2. In Channel X, industrial products are sold by the producer to industrial customers. Over half of all industrial products are sold through such channels. Industrial buyers like to deal directly with producers when they are purchasing high priced, complex industrial products and services such as installations, computers, technical equipment, and large bulk shipments or raw materials.

In Channel Y, the product goes from the producer to the manufacturer's agent to the industrial customer. Products such as auto parts may be sold by this distribution method.

In Channel Z, the product moves from producer to industrial distributor to industrial consumer. This type of channel is used by Caterpillar and Kamotsu in the construction industry.

## Importance of Intermediaries

Marketing intermediaries perform marketing functions necessary to expedite exchanges with customers. Although it is possible to eliminate intermediaries or middlemen, the services they provide in moving products from

**Figure 14-2**
Marketing Channels for Industrial Buyers

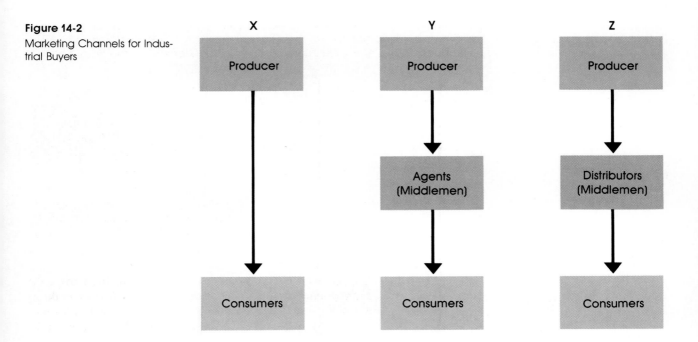

producer to customer cannot be eliminated. There are approximately 1.3 million retailers in the United States.[1] If all wholesalers were eliminated, imagine how difficult it would be for producers to find all the retailers necessary to expose their products to the marketplace.

Widely purchased convenience products like candy and cigarettes are available in millions of outlets. Candy and cigarette producers would have to hire thousands of workers and send out large fleets of trucks to deliver goods directly to retailers, stores, and vending machines. A tobacco wholesaler, for example, usually carries manufacturers' products efficiently to retail locations. Thus, individual producers do not have to maintain fleets of delivery trucks. The use of wholesalers results in a more efficient marketplace in which fewer transactions are needed to make products available to consumers. Without the assistance of intermediaries to organize and assemble product lines efficiently and make products available at the retail level in the quantities and quality that buyers demand, products would probably cost more and be harder to find than they are now.

Critics suggest that the elimination of wholesalers would lower prices for consumers. Wholesalers are sometimes viewed as parasites of no use to consumers. Many consumers believe that wholesalers make high profits and raise prices (Table 14-1). However, without these intermediaries, consumers might end up paying a great deal more for products because of the inefficiencies of producers attempting to reach distant markets. Wholesalers and retailers are actually more efficient and less expensive not only for producers but also for the final users of products.

**Table 14-1 How Consumers Feel about Wholesalers**

Source: © O. C. Ferrell and William M. Pride. National multi-stage area probability sample of 2,045 households, 1985.

| Statement: Wholesalers frequently make high profits which significantly increase prices that consumers pay. | | | |
|---|---|---|---|
| | Total % | Male % | Female % |
| Strongly Agree | 35.5 | 33 | 38 |
| Somewhat Agree | 38 | 40 | 36 |
| Neither Agree nor Disagree | 16 | 14 | 18 |
| Somewhat Disagree | 8 | 9 | 7 |
| Strongly Disagree | 2.5 | 4 | 1 |

# ► Wholesaling

**Wholesaling**

All marketing transactions in which products are sold to industrial, retail, and institutional users for resale or for use in making other products

**Wholesaling** includes all marketing transactions in which products are sold to industrial, retail, and institutional users for resale or for use in making other products. Wholesaling does not include transactions with ultimate household consumers. In 1985, there were over 400,000 wholesaling establishments in the United States.[2]

Wholesalers perform the functions listed in Table 14-2. Wholesaling activities range from planning and negotiating for supplies, promoting, warehousing, and transportation to providing management and merchandising assistance to clients. Wholesalers are extremely important for many products, particularly consumer products, because of the marketing activities they perform. Although it is true that wholesalers themselves can be eliminated, their functions must be passed on to some other organization such as the producer, or another intermediary such as a retailer or the customer. Wholesalers help consumers and retailers by buying in large quantities, then selling to retailers in smaller quantities. By stocking an assortment of products, wholesalers make products available to match demand.

Wholesalers may be divided into three general categories: merchant wholesalers; agents and brokers; and manufacturers' agents, sales branches, and offices. The three categories reflect the activities and functions that wholesalers perform.

## Merchant Wholesalers

**Merchant wholesalers**

Merchants who take title to products, assume the risk of ownership, and are involved in buying, selling, and helping develop inventory assortments for retail customers

**Merchant wholesalers** take title to products, assume the risk of ownership, and are involved in buying, selling, and helping develop inventory assortments for retail customers. Two important types of merchant wholesalers are full-service wholesalers and limited-service wholesalers (Figure 14-3).

*Full-Service Wholesalers.* Full-service wholesalers provide all the services that can be performed by wholesale institutions—taking physical possession of merchandise, providing information about market conditions, offering credit, delivery, and so on—to serve retail customers. General-merchandise wholesalers carry a full product mix, including hardware, drugs, electronics,

| Activity | Description |
| --- | --- |
| Wholesale management | Planning, organizing, staffing, and controlling the institution's operations |
| Planning and negotiating for supplies | Serving as the purchasing agent for customers by negotiating for supplies |
| Promoting | Providing an outside (field) sales force and inside sales, advertising, sales promotion, and publicity |
| Warehousing and product handling | Receiving, storing and stockkeeping, order processing, packaging, shipping outgoingorders, and materials handling |
| Transportation | Arranging local delivery and long-distance shipments |
| Inventory control and data processing | Controlling physical inventory, bookkeeping, recording transactions, keeping records for financial analysis |
| Security | Safeguarding and protecting merchandise |
| Pricing | Developing prices and price quotations on the basis of value added |
| Financing and budgeting | Extending credit, borrowing, making capital investments, and forecasting cash flow |
| Management and merchandising assistance to clients | Supplying information about markets and products and providing advisory services to assist customers in their sales efforts |

plumbing supplies, nonperishable foods, soaps, cosmetics, and other products typically available in neighborhood grocery stores and small department stores. Limited-line wholesalers carry a limited line of products. A limited-line wholesaler might offer oil-drilling equipment, specialty printing services such as raised-letter printing, or chemicals for water conditioning. Specialty-line wholesalers carry a very limited variety of products. These merchant wholesalers generally carry only one product line or a few items within a product line in order to meet their customers' specific needs. A wholesaler that carries only specialty foods such as shellfish is a specialty-line wholesaler.

***Limited-Service Wholesalers.*** Limited-service wholesalers provide only a few functions. Limited-service wholesalers include cash-and-carry wholesalers, truck wholesalers, rack jobbers, drop shippers, and mail-order wholesalers.

Cash-and-carry wholesalers require their retail customers to pay cash, provide their own transportation, and arrange for delivery of their purchases. These middlemen usually carry a limited line of products such as groceries, electrical supplies, or paper products. Truck wholesalers deliver products directly to customers for inspection and selection. A truck wholesaler usually has a regular route, calling on retailers to find out what they need. They

**Figure 14-3**

Types of Merchant Wholesalers
Source: William M. Pride and
O. C. Ferrell, *Marketing: Basic
Concepts and Decisions,* 5th
edition. (Boston: Houghton Mif-
flin Co., 1987) p. 297

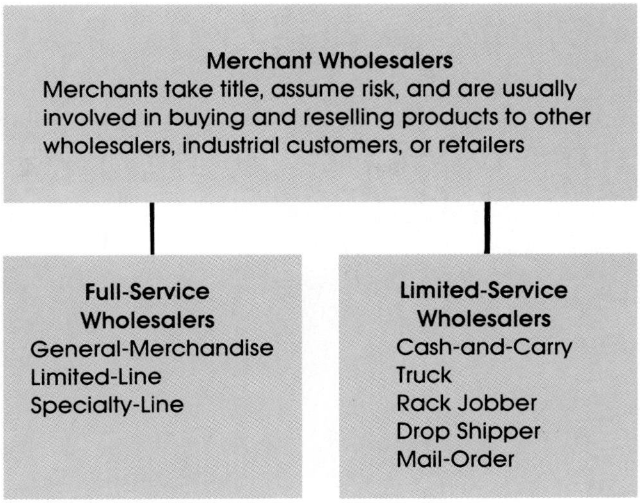

**Merchant Wholesalers**
Merchants take title, assume risk, and are usually involved in buying and reselling products to other wholesalers, industrial customers, or retailers

**Full-Service
Wholesalers**
General-Merchandise
Limited-Line
Specialty-Line

**Limited-Service
Wholesalers**
Cash-and-Carry
Truck
Rack Jobber
Drop Shipper
Mail-Order

supply small grocery stores with perishable goods such as fruits and vegetables, meat, and potato chips. They may also carry supplies for service stations, such as tobacco products. Often, truck wholesalers are small operators who drive their own trucks. Rack jobbers (sometimes called service merchandisers) establish an inventory of products in a section of a retail store and maintain the section for the retailer. Rack jobbers specialize in hardware, housewares, drugs, and cosmetics. They visit the store frequently to refill shelves, set up displays, keep records, and attend to all aspects of product management for the retailer. Drop shippers are limited-service wholesalers who take title to products and negotiate sales but do not take physical possession of products. The product often remains with the producer or in a warehouse. Drop shippers are mainly concerned with arranging the purchase through selling activities. If products are not sold, the drop shipper assumes the loss.

Mail-order wholesalers sell through the mail directly to other retail and industrial intermediaries. Mail-order wholesalers are limited-service wholesalers because their main function is to make available limited product lines such as jewelry, specialty foods, and specialty printing. Small retailers find mail-order wholesalers convenient for products that are small and easy to ship.

## Agents and Brokers

Agents and brokers negotiate purchases and facilitate sales but do not actually take title to products. They are functional middlemen because they perform a number of marketing activities for a commission (Figure 14-4).

***Agents.*** **Agents** represent either a buyer or a seller, usually on a permanent basis. Three types of agents are manufacturers' agents, selling agents, and commission merchants.

**Agents**

People who represent either a buyer or a seller, usually on a permanent basis

**McKesson is a full service wholesaler.** The company provides all the services that can be performed by a wholesaler. Computer-processed documents used to fill customer orders are generated along with price stickers shipped with each order, enabling retailers to restock their store shelves quickly. Computerized conveyor systems help the flow of customers' orders. The retailers' shelves are stocked in record time because McKesson's reordering cycle groups products when they are ordered.

**Figure 14-4**

Types of Agents and Brokers
Source: Adapted from William
M. Pride and O.C. Ferrell, *Marketing: Basic Concepts and Decisions*, 5th edition. (Boston:
Houghton Mifflin Co., 1987) p.
302

**Agents and Brokers**
These functional middlemen do not take title to products and are compensated with commissions for negotiating exchanges between sellers and buyers.

**Agents**
Manufacturers' Agents
Selling Agents
Commission Merchants

**Brokers**
Food Brokers
Real-Estate Brokers
Other Brokers, e.g.,
    Securities, Insurance

Manufacturers' agents usually represent a number of producers who want to sell products or a product line to intermediaries. A manufacturer's agent may enter into an agreement with a producer regarding territories, prices, and products to be sold. The relationship between the agent and the producer is spelled out in a detailed, written agreement that gives the manufacturer's agent sole control over the product in designated areas. A manufacturer's agent will handle product lines and products that are not in competition, but these products make up an assortment of products that may be desired at particular types of retail establishments.

Selling agents, like manufacturers' agents, market products for a manufacturer. Selling agents, however, market all items in a specified product line or the entire output of a manufacturer and have control over the manufacturer's marketing efforts. These agents have full authority over all aspects of the marketing mix and assume the function of a sales department for the manufacturer.

Commission merchants are agents who exercise physical control over products and negotiate sales for producers. These agents are given power to negotiate price in the terms of sale, arrange delivery, and provide transportation. Commission merchants are often used for agricultural products.

**Brokers**

Individuals who bring buyers and sellers together on a temporary basis

***Brokers.*** **Brokers** bring buyers and sellers together on a temporary basis. Food brokers usually specialize in a particular commodity and give customers the benefit of established contacts. Food brokers help buyers and sellers to cope with fluctuating market conditions by making products available, grading, negotiating, and assisting in food inspection.

Real-estate brokers bring buyers and sellers together to exchange real estate. The broker is a go-between and attempts to represent both the buyer and the seller. Real-estate brokers often try to get both parties to compromise and strike an agreement. Other brokers act as go-betweens in the sale of insurance and securities, such as stocks and bonds. The broker represents both buyer and seller in transactions involving an insurance policy (health, life, home, automobile, or a combination of those) or stocks and bonds. Shearson Lehman Hutton, for example, provides brokers who represent both buyer and seller in stock-market transactions. Other brokers may represent buyers and sellers in various industrial transactions, such as chemicals, printing, or containers.

## Manufacturers' Sales Branches and Offices

Sales branches, like merchant wholesalers, provide promotional assistance, office credit, make deliveries, and maintain inventories of products. Sales-branch customers include wholesalers, retailers, and industrial buyers.

Sales offices provide services normally associated with agents. A sales office may have control over prices and promotion and other selling efforts necessary to develop sales. A sales office, like an agent, does not take physical possession of the products. A sales office is essentially an intermediary owned by the manufacturer to provide distribution services. Although a sales office usually does not charge a commission, the expenses associated with operating a sales office can be equated to commissions paid to a selling agent or to a manufacturer's agent.

# ▶ Retailing

**Retailing**

Selling products to ultimate household consumers for personal or family use

**Retailing** focuses on selling products to ultimate household consumers for personal or family use. Retailing usually occurs in a store, but home selling, vending machines, mail-order catalogs, and entertainment such as the annual Corvette show held in Bloomington, Illinois also provide an opportunity for retailing. Retailers are the final link in the marketing channel between producers and consumers. Retailers buy products, develop assortments, and provide additional services to facilitate purchases. By amassing an assortment of products from competing producers and wholesalers, retailers try to create place, time, and possession utilities. Retailers arrange for products to be moved from producers to the retail establishment (place utility). They maintain hours of operation for their retail establishments to make merchandise available when consumers want it (time utility). They also assume the risk of ownership of inventories (possession utility). Marketing Encounter 14-1 provides some guidelines for helping retailers make buying decisions.

An independent retailer is an individual who operates only one retail establishment. Approximately 85 percent of all retailers are independent—that is, they only have one store. Independents account for over half of all retail sales. A chain retailer is an individual or firm that operates more than one retail establishment. By adding outlets, chain retailers reach wide geographic markets. Although chain retailers account for only about 15 percent of total retailers, they represent nearly half of all retail sales.

## Marketing Encounter 14-1
*Guidelines for Effective Buying*

In order for retailers to grow and increase profits, they need to make effective buying decisions. Buying decisions affect the level of control a retailer has over inventory and shape the direction and image of the business. Certain basic principles are important in developing and strengthening a company's buying ability. In addition to getting the best price possible, good buying involves establishing strong business relationships with suppliers and planning promotional schedules.

To obtain the best buys, a retailer should follow several guidelines. One is to order merchandise as frequently as possible, to avoid stockouts, and aim to sell merchandise before payment is due. In any event, the retailer needs to move the merchandise fast enough to avoid accumulating a large inventory. A retailer should consolidate orders as much as possible to take advantage of special offers and trade discounts from suppliers. A retailer needs to keep track of product depth in inventory. Many retailers buy too large a selection of slow-moving products instead of carefully choosing where to have the most product depth in order to get the most out of their buying dollars. A retailer needs to have an efficient system for recording and tracking orders and sales. Such records tell the retailer when the last order was placed, who placed it, and how much is presently in stock.

A retailer should take time to develop a personal relationship with suppliers' representatives. Dealing regularly with one representative from each company ensures consistency and improves service because the representative knows what the retailer needs and wants. In addition, the more a retailer is able to order from one distributor, the larger the discounts that distributor will be able to offer. Long-term relationships with suppliers usually guarantee their help with problems or special requests.

In order to make good buying decisions, a retailer must know what to buy. Factors such as sensitivity to the market and intuition are important, but retailers need to be knowledgeable about the products they want to buy and educate themselves about new products. Things to consider in making buying decisions about new products include checking for duplications and looking at the product's pricing structure to see if it fits in with other products in its category.

Making good buys and deals for special discounts and promotions requires several skills. The first is advance planning. A retailer should contact distributors early to find out about upcoming specials because they are usually planned two or three months before a promotion. Retailers should negotiate aggressively. Negotiation involves being honest as well as not being afraid to ask for discounts on items inot included in the specials. Retailers need to be conservative when buying seasonal or holiday items.

Retailers should consider all these factors because buying decisions affect whether a company winds up in the red or in the black.

These facts are from "A Buyer's Guide: Tips to Sharper Buying," *Natural Foods Merchandiser* (October 1987): 10–16.

---

Retail establishments include department stores, mass merchandisers, and specialty stores, and any of them may be owned independently or by a chain. Retailing may also take place in various nonstore settings.

## Department Stores

**Department stores**

Offer wide assortment of products; usually organized into departments

**Department stores** offer wide assortments of products and usually are organized into departments to assist marketing efforts and internal store management. Department stores usually offer housewares, clothing, home furnishings, appliances, and cosmetics; they may also offer automotive, recreational, and sports equipment. Sears, J. C. Penney, and other department stores sell insurance and income-tax preparation services. Because of competition from other types of stores, department stores have begun to emphasize high-profit items like clothing instead of appliances and slow-moving items that take up a lot of space. Department stores also put excitement in shopping with innovative interiors that eliminate humdrum shopping experiences. These stores offer many services—credit, delivery, personal assistance, liberal return policies. They are shopping stores in that their unique, pleasant environments afford consumers an opportunity to compare price, quality, and service within the store and with competing stores. Marketing Encounter 14-2 describes how department stores are adapting to competition from specialty retailers.

**Mass merchandisers**

Offer few consumer services and focus on keeping prices low, turning over products quickly, and achieving a large sales volume

## Mass Merchandisers

**Mass merchandisers**—discount houses, supermarkets, and super stores—generally offer fewer consumer services than department stores and focus more on keeping prices low, turning over products quickly, and achieving a

---

# Marketing Encounter 14-2
## *The Future of Department Stores*

Department stores have adapted to many changes throughout their history, and they undoubtedly will have to make more in order to compete successfully with specialty retailers and deal with the overstored environment faced by general merchandise retailers. Specialty retailers such as The Limited and Benetton, in particular, have responded to the increasingly diverse attitudes, life styles, and purchase motivations of shoppers. These retailers have undertaken greater risks by creating their own merchandise labels, a role assumed by the brands carried by department stores, as well as new trading vehicles to exploit emerging market segments.

Department stores were the first to offer a large variety of merchandise and one-stop shopping under one roof. Today, department store managers realize that their stores need to make drastic changes if they are to retain their former preeminence. Department stores have resorted to the heavy use of off-price promotions to maintain their sales growth. Some are evolving into limited-line specialty retailers with a more narrowly defined base of customers, a trend that is likely to continue. In the future, department stores will accord more emphasis on those elements of their merchandise assortments that reinforces how many of their image-conscious shoppers seek to express themselves. There will also be greater emphasis on pro-

prietary items designed and preduced to reflect how a particular store seeks to be positioned.

As the markets of many department stores continue to mature, they will spin off well-defined departments into free-standing specialty chains. This method of growth enables the department store to target emerging market segments. Thus, department stores will conceptually become multi-vehicle distribution channels.

Some industry experts believe that in the future department stores will have to emphasize a more proactive marketing stance rather than according merchandising the central role. This new approach will make use of more creative thinking, research and planning—tools that will help department stores find latent demand in underdeveloped market segments. Thus, the organization of these new stores will need to be more flexible than in the past to satisfy the demands of this new marketing orientation.

The future looks bright for department stores, even though major changes are necessary. An entrepreneurial approach by management and an ability to respond quickly to trends will contribute to the revitalization of the department store industry.

These facts are from Walter K. Levy, "Department Stores—The Next Generation: Form and Rationale," *Arthur Andersen and Co. Retailing Issues Letter* 1 (1987).

---

large sales volume. Mass merchandisers appeal to large mass markets and generally pride themselves on their efficiency and economy.

Discount houses are self-service general merchandise stores like K mart, Wal-Mart, Target, and Zayre. They carry a wide assortment of products, have plain, functional environments, and offer low-priced promotional items on a regular basis.

Supermarkets are large self-service stores such as Safeway and Kroger that carry a wide assortment of food products and nonfood products such as small housewares, automotive supplies, and clothing. Supermarkets sell convenience products, concentrate on maintaining low prices, and try to operate efficiently because net profits after taxes are usually less than 1 percent of sales. The supermarket is being challenged by the super store, which is a different type of mass merchandiser.

Super stores carry most of the food and nonfood products found in discount houses and supermarkets. In super stores such as Sam's Wholesale Clubs and Food 4 Less grocery stores, a complete line of food products is combined with housewares, hardware, garden products, automotive services, and appliances. Compared with supermarkets, super stores usually have at least twice as much consumer traffic and from three to four times the sales volume. Super stores are known for their use of advanced technology and operating techniques that cut costs and increase sales. They often use high-profile shelving, display a large assortment of products to reduce handling, and concentrate on providing an efficient and no-frills atmosphere for selling.

## Specialty Stores

Specialty stores

Stores that carry a narrow assortment of products, but their product lines run deep

**Specialty stores** carry a narrow assortment of products, but their product lines run deep. Specialty stores—appliance stores, sporting goods stores, and high-fashion clothing stores, shoe stores, florists, bakery shops—provide a great deal of variety, although they generally carry a single product line. Individual specialty stores usually have a unique image, and the owner tries to provide unique services to a special market segment. Some specialty stores are part of a chain. Radio Shack, for example, is a consumer electronics specialty store that operates hundreds of units throughout the world.

## Nonstore Retailing

Nonstore retailing

Selling to the ultimate consumer in settings outside the regular store environment

**Nonstore retailing** is selling to the ultimate consumer in settings outside the regular store environment. It includes in-home sales, telephone selling, mail order, vending machines, and catalog sales.

In-home retailing is personal selling in the home, usually through prearranged contacts with consumers. In-home retailing can also occur through cold canvassing—direct contact without prearrangement. Fuller Brush, Avon, Electrolux, and Amway are organizations that find prospects in advance, go to the home, and make household products available. Door-to-door selling without prearranged invitation is a very small portion of total retail sales, probably less than 1 percent. Many communities have banned this type of selling because of the use of fraudulent techniques by the salespeople.

Telephone retailing is using the phone to sell products. Real estate, home

**One-stop shopping.** Home Depo is a specialty store for home improvement do-it-yourselfers. The store provides an in-depth selection of over 25,000 items in each of its eighty stores.

repairs, automobiles, investments, and insurance are products often sold over the telephone. The caller may use a list of prospective clients or may make calls to first-time customers, sometimes referred to as cold calls. A variation of telephone retailing involves an advertisement that encourages consumers to call for information or call to purchase a product. Television commercials sometimes show a product demonstration and then give an 800 number for the consumer to call to charge the purchase on a credit card. Telephone retailing is growing very rapidly because of the ease and efficiency it brings to purchasing a wide range of products.

Nonpersonal sales are sales that do not involve salespeople. Examples of nonpersonal selling are automatic vending machines, mail-order retailing, and catalog retailing. Automatic vending machines include coin-operated self-service machines that make a wide assortment of products available including beverages, cigarettes, snack foods, insurance, and laundry soap. Vending machines account for a very small percentage of total consumer sales, but they are used widely, most notably in the form of automatic teller machines (ATMs), which dispense cash.

Mail-order retailing is selling through the mail. Mail-order retailing is an efficient way to contact consumers who are located in remote areas or have limited time to shop. Mail-order houses mail catalogs and brochures containing pictures and product information and order blanks to prospective customers. Catalog retailing is a special type of mail-order retailing that allows the consumer to order from a catalog in the store or by telephone. L. L. Bean and Lillian Vernon are popular catalog retailers; many customers order merchandise from Sears and J. C. Penney, too. Mail orders are usually delivered by the U. S. Postal Service or by United Parcel Service.

**Avon is changing its image.**   Avon is one retailer that has always depended on door-to-door sales to bring its product and customer together. In recent years, however, it has expanded its customer base to people outside the traditional market.

# ▶ Marketing Channel Integration

**Channel integration**

Combining channel members at one level, or the producer can take over the wholesaler role

The various stages in the marketing channel can be combined under one management to provide **channel integration.** Marketing channel integration can involve combining channel members at one level, such as the retailer level, or the producer can take over the wholesaler role as indicated in Figure 14-5. Integration is used to improve coordination, quality, and operational efficiency, as well as to reduce costs. Market channel integration can be either vertical or horizontal.

**Horizontal integration** involves combining stages or units at one level of operation such as retailing. To integrate horizontally, an organization could expand the number of production units or wholesale units. McDonald's illustrates horizontal integration at the retail level in fast food.

**Horizontal integration**

Combining stages or units at one level of operation

Chapter 14   Distribution                                          **465**

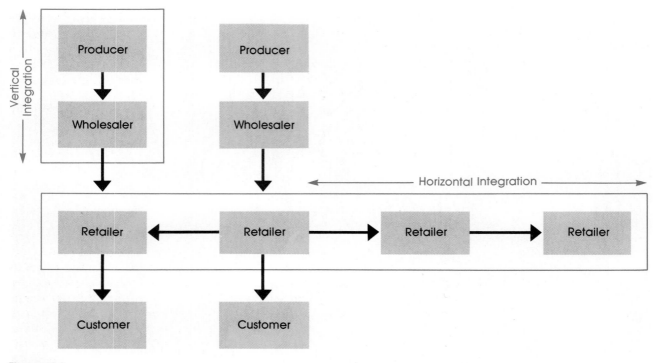

**Figure 14-5**
Marketing Channel Integration

**Vertical integration**

Combining planned distribution systems under one management

**Vertical integration** involves combining planned distribution systems under one management. In this form of marketing channel, different intermediaries may be combined under the management or ownership of a single channel leader to reduce costs, improve service, or improve coordination among channel members. There are many ways in which a vertical marketing channel can be developed. One channel member may purchase operations or institutions that link the channel and eliminate the need for the intermediary as a separate entity, although the marketing functions provided by that intermediary will still have to be performed at some stage of distribution. A large retailer like 7-Eleven, for example, may purchase a regional wholesaler that supplies groceries and nonfood items in order to gain more control over and efficiency in operations. Complete vertical integration involves a business controlling all functions, from production to the final buyer. Major oil companies such as Mobil achieve vertical integration by owning wells, transportation facilities, refineries, and service stations that provide Mobil products to consumers. Manufacturers' sales branches provide a good example of a vertical marketing channel. A sales branch is owned and maintained by a manufacturer, essentially taking over the wholesaling function.

In an administered vertical marketing channel, authority and control remain with one channel member who determines policies and marketing mix decisions for the entire channel. Xerox, IBM, Magnavox, Kellogg, and Sears use administered vertical marketing channels.

In a contractual vertical marketing channel, channel relationships are formalized through contracts or other legal agreements. Franchise organizations such as McDonald's, Kentucky Fried Chicken, and Burger King often use contractual vertical marketing channels. The rights and obligations of each member of the agreement are fully specified, and each channel member plays a particular role in the distribution of the product.

In a corporate vertical marketing channel, all stages of distribution are combined under one ownership. Goodyear and Radio Shack are corporations that maintain total control from production, to sales, to the ultimate customer.

# ► Intensity of Market Coverage

**Market coverage**

The number and variety of outlets that make products available to customers

**Market coverage** relates to the number and variety of outlets that make products available to customers. The intensity of market coverage depends on the behavior of customers and the nature of the market. Cold beverages, candy, and bread can be found within a few minutes of most consumers. Other types of products require distribution of a different kind. Consumers' views of products are based on replacement rate, services, consumption time, and product availability. These considerations also have an impact on the intensity of market coverage.

Market coverage may be intensive, selective, or exclusive. The final decision about how widely to distribute a product depends on the target market and the nature of the competition. Wholesalers and retailers provide various intensities of market coverage and must be selected carefully to ensure success.

## Intensive Distribution

**Intensive distribution**

Makes a product available in as many outlets as possible

**Intensive distribution** makes a product available in as many outlets as possible. Because availability is important to purchasers of convenience products such as bread, milk, gasoline, and chewing gum, a nearby location with a minimum of searching time and waiting in line is most important to the consumer. Convenience products are used rapidly and have to be replaced in a short period of time. To saturate markets on an intensive basis, wholesalers and many varied types of retailers try to make the product available at every location where a consumer might desire to purchase it. Most consumers will not go out of their way to find a specific brand of a convenience product.

## Selective Distribution

**Selective distribution**

Used most often for products for which consumers shop and compare price, quality, and style before purchasing

**Selective distribution** uses only a small proportion of all available outlets to expose products. Selective distribution is used most often for products for which consumers shop and compare price, quality, and style before purchasing. Many products sold on a selective distribution basis are associated with service salesperson assistance and selection, technical advice, warranties, or repair service necessary to maintain consumer satisfaction. Typical products include GE appliances, Fender guitars, Pennsylvania House furniture, and

Liz Claiborne clothes. By selling on a selective basis, firms retain control over the product and can increase the level of quality to and satisfaction of the ultimate buyer. Making a product available on a selective basis increases the retailer's incentive to promote the product aggressively.

## Exclusive Distribution

**Exclusive distribution**
When a manufacturer or middleman has the sole right to sell a product in a defined geographic territory

**Exclusive distribution** exists when a manufacturer gives a middleman the sole right to sell a product in a defined geographic territory. Exclusive distribution rights are an incentive for a dealer to handle a product that has a limited market. Exclusive distribution is the opposite of intensive distribution in that products are purchased and consumed over a long period of time and require service or information to develop a satisfactory sales relationship. Products distributed on an exclusive basis include high-quality musical instruments, sailboats, airplanes, and high-fashion leather goods.

# ▶ Physical Distribution

Physical distribution comprises all the activities necessary to move products from producers to customers—inventory planning and control, transportation, warehousing, and materials handling (Figure 14-6). Physical distribution creates time and place utility by making products available when they are wanted, with adequate service and at minimum cost. Both goods and services require physical distribution. The activities are not always performed in the exact order of Figure 14-6 because activities such as transportation may have to be repeated several times during the physial distribution process.

## Inventory Planning and Control

**Inventory planning and control**
The development of adequate inventories or assortments of products that satisfy particular target markets

**Inventory planning and control** is the development of adequate inventories or assortments of products that satisfy particular target markets. Adequate inventory must be maintained to avoid stockouts—product outages—or excessive inventory that increases holding costs. Inventory systems should ensure product availability and efficient inventory management. Toys "R" Us and many other retailers use electronic data processing to update inventory and sales records instantaneously at the point of purchase. Most companies attempt to avoid stockouts by maintaining an overall safety stock, which is the inventory needed to prevent stockout.

The trade-off between the cost of carrying large inventories with infrequent orders and the cost of filling many small orders points to the desirability of identifying an optimal order quantity. The objective of minimizing inventory cost must be balanced against the need to maintain levels of inventory that ensure adequate customer service. Because high inventory costs are associated with a high level of consumer satisfaction, the optimal order quantity often must strike a balance between minimizing cost and maximizing satisfaction.

Effective inventory planning and control depends on good communication.

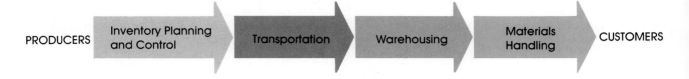

PRODUCERS → Inventory Planning and Control → Transportation → Warehousing → Materials Handling → CUSTOMERS

**Figure 14-6**
Physical Distribution Activities

Inventory decisions have a great impact on consumer service and other aspects of physical distribution.

# Transportation

Transportation, the shipment of products to buyers, is an essential part of distribution. Transportation permits a firm to create time and place utility for its products. Therefore, it is a key element in the flow of goods and services from producer to consumer. Table 14-3 shows the five major modes of transportation used to move products between cities in the United States: railways, motor vehicles, inland waterways, pipelines, and airways.

The movement of many products is made more efficient by the use of physical handling procedures that permit transfers among the different modes. Factors affecting the selection of a mode of transportation include cost, capability (the ability to handle various products), reliability, and availability. Shipping by inland waterway may be inexpensive, but if such a route is not available in a particular area, it cannot be used. Air freight may provide dependable service, but its cost may be so high that the extra speed and dependability may not be worth the expense. Selecting transportation modes requires trade-offs. Unique characteristics of the product and the desires of the market determine the mode selected.

Individual transportation companies, or carriers, usually specialize in one mode of transportation, but moving some products requires the use of more than one mode. **Common carriers** transport goods for the general public for a fee. An airline, for example, may operate on certain established routes to carry certain types of merchandise. Airlines are available to serve all people in an area who have general merchandise that falls within specified categories. An airline may decline to handle items that are dangerous or inappropriate for its particular capabilities.

**Contract carriers** transport products by a contract or agreement. Contract carriers do not operate for the general public and usually work on a contract basis to move specific loads.

**Private carriers** transport their own property in their own vehicles. K mart, for example, has its own fleet of trucks and carries its own merchandise from general warehouses to company-owned stores.

**Freight forwarders** consolidate shipments from several organizations into cost-effective lots. Using a freight forwarder usually increases transit time but lowers shipping costs.

Railroads offer the least expensive transportation for many products. Most railroads are common carriers, and many of the commodities and products

**Common carriers**

A transportation company that transports goods for the general public for a fee

**Contract carriers**

A transportation company that transports products by contract or agreement

**Private carriers**

A transportation company that transports its own property in its own vehicles

**Freight forwarders**

A transportation company that consolidates shipments from several organizations into cost-effective lots

Chapter 14   Distribution          **469**

**Table 14-3  Major Modes of Transportation**
Source: U.S. Bureau of the Census, *Statistical Abstract of the United States 1987,* (Washington, D.C., 1987), p. 579.
ª A ton-mile is the movement of 1 ton (2,000 pounds) of freight for the distance of 1 mile.

| Mode | Ton-Miles Carried (Billions)ª | Percent of total |
|------|-------------------------------|------------------|
| Railways | 898.0 | 37.20 |
| Motor Vehicles | 600.0 | 24.86 |
| Inland waterways | 348.0 | 14.42 |
| Pipelines | 562.0 | 23.28 |
| Airways | 6.4 | .26 |
| Total | 2414.0 | 100.00 |

they carry cannot be easily transported by any other means. Heavy commodities, foodstuffs, raw materials, and coal are examples of products carried by railroads. Dangerous chemicals (carried in tank cars), heavy equipment, and lumber are products that are difficult to transport by any other means.

The use of trucks has increased with the development of the interstate highway system. Trucks have greater flexibility than railroads because they can reach more locations. Trucks handle freight quickly and economically, offer door-to-door service, and are more flexible in their packaging requirements than are ships or airplanes. The trucking industry consists of common carriers, contract carriers, and private carriers.

Air transport offers a high degree of dependability but is the most expensive means of transportation. All airlines are common carriers and provide service for high-value or perishable items such as a small component for a machine that is vital to the production and operation of a factory.

Shipping is the least expensive and slowest form of transportation. Barges are used on rivers, canals, and inland waterways for bulky goods such as iron ore, grain, and heavy equipment. Shipment by inland waterway is limited to cities located on navigable waterways. Cargo ships can be used for international shipments and usually offer the least expensive transportation.

Pipelines are used to transport petroleum, natural gas, semi-liquid coal, wood chips, and certain chemicals. Pipelines are very important for the heavy bulky liquid products that are shipped through them, because they transport these materials quickly and at a relatively low cost. In addition, pipelines can be set up in areas where normal transportation would be difficult, such as the Alaskan oil pipeline.

# Warehousing

Warehousing involves the design and operation of facilities to receive, store, and ship products. A warehouse performs the following functions

1. **Receives goods:** The warehouse receives merchandise delivered by an outside transportation firm or from a factory.
2. **Identifies goods:** The appropriate stock-keeping units are recorded, and a record is made of the quantity of each item received.
3. **Sorts goods:** The warehouse may sort merchandise for placement in appropriate storage areas.

**Toys "R" Us transports its own stock in its own vehicles.** The use of its own trucks allows for some vertical integration performing some wholesale functions.

4. Dispatches goods to storage: The merchandise is put away where it can be found later when needed.
5. Holds goods: The merchandise is kept in storage under proper protection until needed.
6. Recalls, selects, or picks goods: Items ordered are efficiently selected from storage and grouped in a manner useful for the next step.
7. Marshals the shipment: Items making up a single shipment are brought together and checked for completeness or for explainable omissions; order records are prepared or modified as necessary.
8. Dispatches the shipment: The consolidated order is packaged suitably and directed to the right transportation vehicle; necessary shipping and accounting documents are prepared.

Private warehouses are owned and operated by a company for the purpose of facilitating, handling, and moving its own products. Public warehouses are business organizations whose primary purpose is to provide storage and related physical distribution facilities on a rental basis. Regardless of whether a private or a pubic warehouse is used, warehousing is an important function because it makes products available for shipment to match demand at different geographic locations.

# Materials Handling

**Materials handling**

The physical handling and movement of products in warehouse operations and in transportation

**Materials handling** is the physical handling and movement of products in warehouse operations and in transportation. Handling processes may vary significantly due to products' characteristics. Efficient materials-handling procedures increase the useful capacity of a warehouse and improve service to consumers. The coordination of loading and movement systems increases efficiency and reduces costs.

Materials-handling equipment is important in distribution systems. Unit loading is the grouping of boxes on a pallet or skid that is moved by mechanical means such as forklifts, trucks, or conveyor belt systems. Containerization allows a number of unit loads to be shipped in sealed, movable containers that are usually 8 feet wide, 8 feet high, and 10, 20, 25, or 40 feet long. Containerization decreases the need for security measures and cuts down on losses and damage. Marketing Encounter 14-3 discusses theft prevention during physical distribution.

# ▶ Importance of Distribution in a Marketing Strategy

Distribution decisions are among the least flexible marketing mix decisions. Products can be changed over time; prices can be changed overnight; and promotion is usually changed on a regular basis. But distribution decisions often commit resources and establish contractual relationships that are difficult if not impossible to change. To compound the problem, changing competitive relationships or changing target markets sometimes creates the need to restructure the marketing channel. Rapid increases in transportation costs,

---

## Marketing Encounter 14-3
### *Preventing Theft During Physical Distribution*

Theft is inevitable whenever resalable merchandise is distributed. What is surprising is that approximately 85 percent of all cargo thefts are committed by employees during regular working hours.

Most thefts can be prevented if companies give proper attention to packaging, personnel procedures, and warehouse security equipment. In terms of packaging measures, companies can avoid description labeling, consolidate packages into the largest unit possible, construct packages so that tampering can be recognized, and pick up deliveries promptly. Personnel procedures should be designed to minimize access opportunities, screen out dishonest employees, and thoroughly investigate thefts when they occur. The presence of uniformed guards is a psychological deterent to theft and vandalism. Finally, security equipment from simple locks to electronic surveillance devices, can help to secure warehouses. Proper fencing, lighting, and closed-circuit television and alarm systems can also prevent theft.

These facts are from Betsy Haggerty, "To Stop a Thief: A Guide to Cargo Crime Prevention," *Inbound Logistics* (October 1985): 32–34.

---

for example, could create the need for a different distribution strategy. Physical distribution must be altered to take advantage of new technological developments related to different transportation modes. If a firm does not manage its marketing channel to operate in the most efficient manner and provide the best service, then a new competitor will evolve to create a more effective distribution system.

New wholesalers and retailers are constantly evolving. According to the **wheel of retailing concept,** new retailers continually enter the market as low-status, low-margin, low-price operators. As they acquire success, they develop more elaborate facilities, provide more service, and experience higher operating costs. Finally, they become high-price businesses that are vulnerable to newer businesses that go through the same cycle.

Because wholesalers and retailers sometimes fail and do not adjust to new competitive environments, manufacturers must be constantly aware of the role channel members play in distributing their products. Companies that do not properly manage their marketing channels may jeopardize their survival.

**Wheel of retailing concept**

The evolution of wholesalers and retailers from low-status, low-margin, low-price operators to high-price, high service businesses

## Notes

1. *Statistical Abstract of the United States, 1986,* p. 778.
2. *Statistical Abstract of the United States, 1986,* p. 785.

## Summary and Review

▶ Distribution is an orderly process of dividing, dispersing, and delivering products to make them available to consumers.

▶ A marketing channel is a group of marketing organizations that direct the flow of products from producers to consumers.

▶ Different marketing channels are used for consumer products and for industrial products.

▶ Wholesaling includes all marketing transactions in which products are sold for resale or for use in making other products. Wholesaling does not include transactions with ultimate household consumers.

▶ Retailing focuses on selling products to ultimate household consumers for personal or family use.

▶ The intensity of market coverage depends on the behavior of customers and the nature of the market. Consumers view products differently based on replacement rate, services, consumption time, and product availability.

▶ Physical distribution comprises all the activities necessary to move products from producers to customers. It includes inventory planning and control, transportation, warehousing, and materials handling.

# Key Terms and Concepts

distribution
marketing channel
middlemen
wholesalers
retailers
wholesaling
merchant wholesalers
agents
brokers
retailing
department stores
mass merchandisers
specialty stores
nonstore retailing

channel integration
horizontal integration
vertical integration
market coverage
intensive distribution
selective distribution
exclusive distribution
inventory planning and control
materials handling
common carriers
contract carriers
private carriers
freight forwarders
wheel of retailing concept

# Checking Your Understanding

This chapter introduced you to the subject of distribution. To test and reinforce your understanding, fill in the blanks below.

**1.** Marketing _____ perform marketing functions necessary to expedite exchanges with customers.

**2.** _____ merchandisers generally offer fewer customer services than department stores.

**3.** According to the _____ of retailing concept, new types of retailers continually enter the market as low-status, low-margin, low-price operators and evolve into more elaborate facilities.

**4.** Another term for retailer or wholesaler is _____.

**5.** The intermediaries who bring buyers and sellers together on a temporary basis are known as _____.

**6.** Cash-and-carry wholesalers, drop shippers, and mail-order wholesalers are known as _____ -service wholesalers.

**7.** Vending machines and telephone retailing are forms of _____ retailing.

**8.** Complete _____ integration involves control over all marketing functions, from buyer to seller.

**9.** _____ is an orderly process of dividing, dispersing, and delivering products to make them available to customers.

**10.** _____ allows unit loads to be shipped in sealed, movable containers.

**11.** _____ are middlemen who sell products to industrial, retail, and institutional users.

**12.** The intermediaries who represent either buyers or sellers, usually on a permanent basis, are known as _____.

**13.** _____ focuses on selling products to ultimate household consumers for personal or family use.

# Topics for Review and Discussion

1. Why is distribution the least flexible of the marketing mix elements?
2. Describe three industrial marketing channels, and give examples of products distributed by means of each one.
3. What kinds of transactions are excluded from wholesaling?
4. Classify and briefly describe the activities and functions performed by three types of wholesalers.
5. How does a retailer create place, time, and possession utilities?
6. Identify three types of retail stores. How do they differ in width of product mix and depth of product lines?
7. What factors have an impact on the intensity of market coverage?
8. Why is inventory planning and control important?
9. What are the main considerations in selecting a carrier?
10. What functions does a warehouse perform?
11. Why are distribution channels for industrial goods usually shorter than distribution channels for consumer goods?
12. What are the typical marketing channels for consumer products?
13. Under what circumstances would a firm use a selling agent or a manufacturer's agent rather than its own sales force?

# Exercises

1. How have social changes and the economy affected in-home retailing and mail-order retailing?
2. Design a distribution channel for a manufacturer of stuffed toys.
3. Develop a schematic model to illustrate the indispensable role of marketing intermediaries. (Hint: Show the number of contacts that would have to be made with or without a middleman.)

## Case 14-1
## *Distribution of Ralston Purina Products*

St. Louis-based Ralston Purina Company was founded in 1894. Ralston Purina is the world's largest producer of dry dog food and dry and semi-moist cat foods. The company also owns the largest wholesale baker of fresh bakery products in the United States and the largest manufacturer of dry cell battery products. Other consumer products include cereal and canned seafood, and Purina is a major producer of isolated soy protein.

The Grocery Product Group includes pet and consumer foods, and accounts for approximately two-thirds of Ralston Purina sales. Grocery products are marketed primarily in the United States, through manufacturers' sales branches and food brokers, to supermarket chains, wholesalers, industrial buyers, and other retailers. Manufacturers' sales branches use direct sales forces and resemble merchant wholesalers in their operation. The firm may offer credit, give promotional assistance, and provide other services, yet they are part of the manufacturer's operation. Ralston Purina's sales force competes with the sales forces of other national and regional manufacturers for shelf space and consumer acceptance.

Another line within the grocery category is Chicken of the Sea tuna products. These products are sold primarily to supermarkets in the United States through a network of independent food brokers. Food brokers negotiate purchases and expedite sales for a commission but do not own the products. They specialize in a particular commodity and give their customers the benefit of established contacts. Food brokers sell tuna and other grocery products to retailer-owned and merchant wholesalers, supermarket chains, and institutional buyers.

Continental Baking Company, acquired in 1984, is the largest wholesale baker of fresh bakery products in the United States. Through an extensive distribution system, the Continental Baking Company operates fifty-two bakeries nationwide and delivers fresh products to major retailers daily on more than seven-thousand individual routes. These routes are part of the vertically integrated distribution channel of Continental, which owns and controls sales branches or offices.

Ralston Purina acquired the Eveready Battery Company from Union Carbide in 1986. The Eveready Company markets Eveready and Energizer batteries, rechargeable batteries, and battery-powered lighting products and devices in the United States and worldwide. The company has forty-three battery manufacturing facilities in the United States and abroad. It distributes battery products primarily through direct sales forces similar to the products of the Grocery Product Group.

Ralston Purina has been the industry leader in producing widely recognized, high-quality feeds for swine, poultry, cattle, horses, and other animals for almost a hundred years. Although the company sold its domestic agricultural division in 1986, it maintains international operations in agricultural products that include 126 feed-manufacturing and other facilities in twelve countries around the world. Feed products are distributed primarily through a network of more than 3,200 dealers outside the United States. The dealers act as industrial distributors, taking title to products, assuming risk, and directing local marketing efforts aimed at agricultural buyers. The company competes with other large feed manufacturers, with cooperatives and sole proprietorships, and in international markets, with government feed companies.

Ralston Purina's food-protein and industrial polymer products are marketed in the United States primarily through direct sales forces and internationally through brokers and industrial distributors. This dual distribution approach illustrates the necessity to change the marketing channel to match the environment. Ralston Purina has expertise and direct access to the United States market. Thus, a direct vertically integrated marketing channel is most effective. International markets, however, need the expertise and local contacts that brokers and other intermediaries provide.

---

Basic facts are from the Ralston Purina Company 1983, 1984, 1985, and 1986 Annual Reports. Reprinted from Pride/Ferrell, *Marketing: Basic Concepts and Decisions*, 5th ed., 1987, Houghton Mifflin, Boston.

## Questions

1. Ralston Purina produces many products that serve diverse markets. What are the implications for the distribution of its products?
2. Why does Ralston Purina use one method of distribution (sales force) for pet food and another method of distribution (brokers) for its Chicken of the Sea tuna products?
3. What are the similarities and differences between the distribution systems for the Continental Baking Company and the Eveready Battery Company?

---

## Case 14-2
### *The Moo: Stew Leonard's Dairy Store*

In 1967, Stew Leonard learned that the state of Connecticut was going to build a new highway right through his dairy plant. At the time, it seemed like the end of the world for the second-generation dairyman. Leonard asked several customers on his home-delivery milk route what they wanted in the way of dairy services. They advised him to open a retail dairy store with the freshest, lowest-priced products. He built that store—in front of a glass-enclosed dairy plant—and began to sell dairy products at the lowest possible price in 1969. When the store first opened, it carried only eight items.

Today, Stew Leonard's has annual sales of $100 million and serves 100,000 customers per week. The store carries 750 items at any one time, still far less than the 10,000 to 15,000 items stocked by an average supermarket. The store usually carries only one brand of a particular item, but the items Stew Leonard does stock are those that move the fastest. Therefore, he is able to buy by the truckload straight from producers. Taking over some of the functions of the middleman saves both time and money and allows Leonard to pass the savings on to customers. Once the products arrive at the store, they don't stay on the shelves long. Leonard knows that high volume means high turnover, ultimately ensuring freshness.

Many call Stew Leonard's a "Disneyland dairy store" because of its country-fair atmosphere. Leonard believes that shopping at his store should be fun. There are more than a hundred live animals, including goats, cows, chicken, and sheep, in "The Little Farm" in front of the store to entertain children. Several costumed employees wander about the store with product samples and tips on specials. Overhead are singing robots: a farmer, cows, and dogs. Children can enjoy watching milk being pasteurized and processed through the glass walls of the dairy plant. The half-gallons of milk whiz by the windows at a rate of 150 per minute. A store bulletin board displays photographs of customers holding up Stew Leonard shopping bags in unusual places: Stonehenge, the North Pole, the Bermuda Triangle, even underwater. At the entrance to the store is a 3-ton granite rock that carries Stew Leonard's motto: "Rule 1: The customer is always right! Rule 2: If the customer is ever wrong, reread Rule 1."

The store has other unique features. One of these is a suggestion box, which Stew Leonard personally checks every morning. Within twenty-four hours, Leonard implements any of the suggestions he finds worthwhile. Another appealing feature is the twenty-five cash registers, twenty of which are usually open at any one time. If the lines at the registers ever get more than three deep, Leonard instructs a cow- or duck-costumed employee to distribute free snack samples to ease the customers' waiting time. Stew Leonard also provides a bus to pick up elderly shoppers who cannot get to the store on their own. For some of the elderly, the weekly Stew Leonard shopping excursion is their only opportunity to get out of their home, and they regard it as a major social event.

The 10,000-square-foot store has only one large aisle—horseshoe-shaped so that every customer goes past every product. As a result, impulse buying makes up a large proportion of Leonard's business. To increase impulse buying even more, Leonard offers shoppers a variety of free product samples. These activities ensure that many customers who come in only for a carton of milk walk out with a cart full of groceries. Stew Leonard's sells a variety of products, from milk and orange juice to cheese, fruits, and vegetables, from cookies and ice cream to beef, fish, and chicken.

One of the more remarkable aspects of Stew Leonard's store is the high motivation of his employees. More than 450 employees work in the store; 225 of them are under age 21. Leonard encourages his employees to treat customers the way they themselves want to be treated. He refers to his employees as a team and instructs them to pay careful attention to detail. He also encourages them to be independent by giving them responsibility and credit for their actions. The employees are further motivated because Leonard pays them well, and he does most of the hiring from referrals by current employees. In fact, about half of the people who work at Leonard's store work with at least one of their relatives. Leonard's wife, two sons, two daughters, three sisters, two brothers-in-law, and other relatives work at the store, adding to the close family atmosphere.

Many of Stew Leonard's managers worked their way up from after-school jobs. Leonard believes in promoting employees from within the organization because they haven't acquired bad habits working somewhere else. Leonard also keeps up morale by giving employees rewards such as plaques, gift certificates, and profit-sharing opportunities for following Leonard's S.T.E.W. philosophy: Satisfy the customer. Teamwork. Excellence. Wow.

Because of the enormous success of Stew Leonard's "Disneyland dairy store," it is no wonder that Tom Peters, author of *In Search of Excellence*, called the store one of the best-run companies in the country. Stew Leonard has transformed the dull weekly shopping excursion into a social event, gaining loyal customers and employees in the process.

---

These facts are from Joanne Kaufman, "In the Moo: "Shopping at Stew Leonard's," *The Wall Street Journal*, September 17, 1987, p. 26; "Stew Leonard's Fact Sheet," provided by B. L. Ochman Public Relations, New York, New York; and fact sheets provided by the Center for Retailing Studies at Texas A&M University.

### Questions

1. Why is Stew Leonard's dairy store so successful?
2. What could other retailers learn from Stew Leonard to satisfy their customers better?
3. How does Stew Leonard's treatment of his employees impact on his marketing strategy?

## Answers to Checking Your Understanding

1. channels
2. mass
3. wheel
4. middleman
5. brokers
6. limited
7. nonstore
8. vertical
9. distribution
10. containerization
11. wholesalers
12. agents
13. retailing

## Outline

# Chapter 15

# Promotion

## Objectives

After reading this chapter, you will be able to:

▶ Discuss the elements of the promotion mix—advertising, personal selling, sales promotion, and publicity.

▶ Describe the different promotional objectives that firms use to advance their products.

▶ Explain promotional positioning and the role it plays for an advertiser.

▶ Identify various advertising media, and discuss their strengths and weaknesses.

▶ Differentiate publicity from advertising and explore the various forms of publicity.

▶ Describe the different roles of salespersons, and explain how salespersons engage in personal selling.

▶ Identify various types of sales promotion, and explain the reasons for their use.

# Business Experience

In 1987 the 7-Up Company (now combined with Dr Pepper) introduced new Cherry 7-Up and diet Cherry 7-Up. The new products are the first 7-Up soft drinks that do not have a strict lemon-lime formulation; they taste like 7-Up with the addition of a little cherry flavor and have a definite pink color. The new products belong in the "uncola" category made famous by 7-Up in the 1970s, which differentiates them from the many cola and cherry cola products now available. Because people between the ages of 12 and 24 drink nearly half of all soft drinks, the company decided to target promotions for Cherry 7-Up to that market segment.

To capture the attention of its target market, Cherry 7-Up is advertised with the tag "Isn't it cool in pink," and pink is the dominant color in the ads. The television commercials are black and white except for prominent articles such as suspenders, earrings, and of course, Cherry 7-Up itself, which are shown in pink. Pink was chosen as the primary color of the campaign because it is a favorite fashion color of the youth market and because of its eye-appeal.

Advertisements for both regular 7-Up and Cherry 7-Up focus on the life style of the average young person. They show teens in their natural surroundings, experiencing events that teenagers typically experience, such as getting yelled at by parents and being dumped by a girlfriend or boyfriend. The Cherry 7-Up campaign also tries to portray certain qualities that teenagers want to have, such as self-assurance, popularity, and independence. The television spots are backed with light rock music and electronic musical effects known as "pink noise." The ads air on programs such as "Moonlighting," "Miami Vice," "Cheers," and "Family Ties," which appeal to the target market.

Cherry 7-Up's campaign was further supported by a merchandise catalog offering Cherry 7-Up clothes and accessories. The "Cool in Pink" catalog offered items such as Cherry 7-Up T-Shirts and sweatshirts; pink sunglasses, shoelaces, and headbands; gumball machines; radios, neon signs; and Cherry 7-Up watches—items that appeal to most fashion-conscious teenagers. 7-Up hopes it will be "cool" to wear pink sunglasses and jumbo pink shoelaces!

7-Up officials have high hopes for its new promotion campaign. Cherry 7-Up and Diet Cherry 7-Up have already captured 2 percent of the soft-drink market. The company's marketing objective is for Cherry 7-Up to carry at least 25 percent of all 7-Up Sales. Promotion will play a key role in reaching the target market to achieve this objective.

---

These facts are from Jeanette Walls, "Cherry Soda a Fountain of Profits for Seven-Up Co.," *USA Today*, October 27, 1987, p. 1B; "7Up 'in the Pink' with Rollout of Cherry-Flavored Regular, Diet," *Beverage Industry* 78 (January 1987): 53; Michael Weiss, "Seven-Up to Debut New Ad Campaign," *The Dallas Morning News*, February 23, 1987, p. 23; Candace Talmadge, "7Up Campaign Gets Younger Look," *Adweek*, February 23, 1987, p. 6; "Bottlers Hot for Cherry 7Up," *Beverage Industry* 78 (March 1987): 18; and "7UP Targets Youth Market," *Beverage Industry* 78 (April 1987): 23.

# Introduction

**Promotion**

A persuasive form of communication that attempts to facilitate a marketing exchange by influencing individuals, groups, and organizations to accept goods, services, and ideas

**Promotion** is a persuasive form of communication that attempts to facilitate a marketing exchange by influencing individuals, groups, and organizations to accept goods, services, and ideas. Promotion is used not only to sell products but also to influence opinions and attitudes toward a company, its personnel, or its role in society. Most people probably equate promotion with advertising. Promotion, however, also includes personal selling, publicity, and sales promotion. The role that these elements play in a marketing strategy is extremely important.

# ▶ The Promotion Mix

**Advertising**

A paid form of nonpersonal communication transmitted through a mass medium

**Personal selling**

Direct two-way communication with buyers and potential buyers

**Publicity**

A nonpersonal communication transmitted through the mass media but not paid for directly by the firm

**Sales promotion**

A direct inducement offering added value or some other incentive for buyers to enter into an exchange

Advertising, personal selling, publicity, and sales promotion are collectively known as the promotion mix (Figure 15-1). They are called the promotion mix because a strong promotion program results from the careful selection and blending of these elements.

**Advertising** is a paid form of nonpersonal communication transmitted through a mass medium. Advertising is probably the most visible element of promotion and is widely used for products that are consumed in quantities large enough to justify communication through the mass media.

**Personal selling** is direct, two-way communication with buyers and potential buyers. For many products, especially large, expensive products with specialized uses, such as cars, stereos, and houses, personal selling is probably the most important promotional tool variable.

**Publicity** is nonpersonal communication transmitted through the mass media but not paid for directly by the firm. A firm does not pay the media cost for publicity and is not identified as the originator of the message; instead, the message is presented in story form. Obviously, a company can benefit from publicity by releasing to news sources newsworthy messages about the company and its involvement with the public. The action an airline company takes within twenty-four hours after a plane crash, for example, will affect the company's image and the image of the entire air transportation industry for months or even years. Press releases, news articles, and company employees' handling of the families of survivors and victims all shape the long-range image of the carrier that had the accident.

**Sales promotion** involves coupons, contests, and free samples to persuade buyers to purchase products. Sales promotion is a direct inducement offering added value or some other incentive for buyers to enter into an exchange.

Consider the role of a new promotion mix in changing the marketing strategy for TreeSweet orange juice. TreeSweet recognized that its image was mixed. Consumers viewed TreeSweet as being somewhere between a private brand and a premium brand. The company hired a new advertising agency and developed a new promotional effort to clarify its image. The goal

**Figure 15-1**
The Promotion Mix

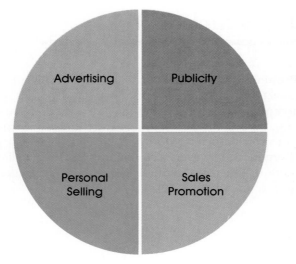

was to associate TreeSweet with premium brands. The company wanted its product to be viewed as the best. The company improved the quality of the product and improved promotional packaging; then it launched an advertising campaign to help change the image of the product. Just changing the product flavor or packaging probably would not have been sufficient. A coordinated effort involving all the elements of the promotion mix was needed.

The role of promotion is to communicate with individuals, groups, and organizations, to facilitate an exchange directly or indirectly. Advertising, personal selling, and sales promotion are especially useful for influencing an exchange directly. Publicity is extremely important when communication focuses on a company's activities and products that are directed at interest groups, current and potential investors, regulatory agencies, and society in general.

# ► Push and Pull Promotional Strategies

**Push strategy**

An attempt to motivate middlemen to push the product down to their customers

Marketers in developing a promotion mix must decide whether to fashion a mix that pushes or pulls the product (Figure 15-2). When a push strategy is used, the marketer attempts to motivate wholesalers and retailers to make the product available to their customers. Sales personnel may be used to persuade middlemen to offer the product, distribute promotional materials, and make promotional allowances for middlemen who agree to carry the product. With promotional allowances the manufacturer shares the cost of local advertising. A **push strategy** attempts to motivate middlemen to push the product down to their customers. A **pull strategy** uses promotion to create

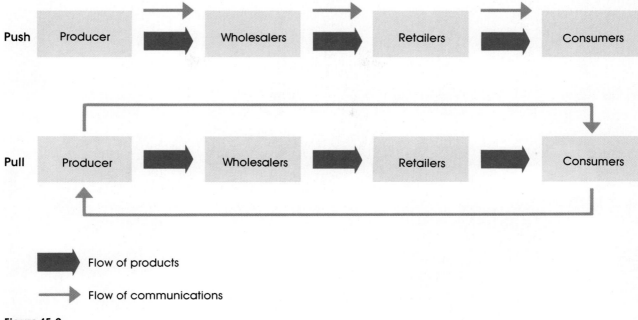

Push    Producer     Wholesalers     Retailers     Consumers

Pull    Producer     Wholesalers     Retailers     Consumers

→ Flow of products

→ Flow of communications

**Figure 15-2**
Push and Pull Strategies

**Pull strategy**

Using promotion to create consumer demand for a product

consumer demand for a product so that consumers exert pressure on marketing channel members to make the product available. For example, when Chiquita introduced its Orange-Banana fruit drink, newspaper inserts were used to promote the product. Since the product was not available in all supermarkets at that time, consumers created a pull for the product by requesting it.

A company can use either strategy, or it can use a variation or combination of the two. The exclusive use of advertising denotes a pull strategy. Personal selling to marketing channel members indicates a push strategy. The allocation of promotional resources to various marketing mix elements probably determines which strategy is used.

# ▶ Objectives of Promotion

The cost and selection of promotional methods reflect the objectives being sought. It is important to recognize that promotion is only one element of the marketing strategy and must be tied very carefully with the goals of the firm, the overall marketing objectives, and the other elements of the marketing strategy being implemented. There may be many reasons for utilizing promotion, but typical objectives for using promotion in the overall marketing effort of a firm are to stimulate demand, to stabilize sales, and to inform, remind, and reinforce customers.

**Effective promotional strategy.** Carteret Savings Bank drew a large crowd to the opening celebration of their retail banking office in Washington, D.C., by making it a festive occasion, complete with balloons and prizes.

## Stimulate Demand

Increasing demand for a product is probably the most typical objective of promotion. Lipton, the number-one marketer of dry-soup mixes, uses promotion aggressively to encourage people to try its soup mixes. In a recent year Lipton doubled its advertising expenditures to attract new customers as well as to increase the frequency of use among existing customers. Lipton's dry soups are designed for those who like the convenience of dry soup but want meat, vegetables, and noodles in the broth. By informing customers about the content of the product, Lipton hopes to stimulate demand. Wendy's implemented a successful regional promotion in Detroit to introduce their baked potatoes. The promotion asked customers to guess how many potatoes were inside a car. The closest guess would win the automobile. The promotion created awareness that Wendy's had baked potatoes and encouraged consumers to come in to Wendy's and register to win prizes.

## Stabilize Sales

Another goal of promotion is to stabilize sales by maintaining the status quo—that is, the current sales level of the product. During periods of slack or decreasing sales, contests, prizes, vacations, and other sales promotions are sometimes offered to customers to maintain sales goals. Advertising is often used to stabilize sales by making customers aware of slack use periods. For example, the most inexpensive time to fly to Hawaii is after Christmas but before the spring-vacation season. At that time, many airlines offer lower cost promotions in conjunction with the use of "Frequent Flyer" miles to encourage travel to Hawaii. A hotel and golf course may offer special rates and special packages and advertise them widely to fill up unoccupied space when sales are declining. Auto manufacturers often provide rebates, free options, or lower-than-market interest rates in order to stabilize sales and production flows during temporary periods of decline. A stable sales pattern allows the firm to run efficiently by maintaining a consistent level of production and storage and utilizing all its functions to maintain a readiness for the time when sales increase.

## Inform, Remind, and Reinforce Customers

An important role of any promotional program is to inform potential buyers about the organization and its products. A major portion of advertising in the United States is informational. Informational advertising is especially prevalent in daily newspapers. Providing information about the availability, price, and technology of a product is very important in encouraging a buyer to move toward a purchase decision. Nearly all forms of promotion entail an attempt to help consumers learn more about a product and company. For example, Diet Rite has used ads to inform consumers that its soft drinks are salt-free. The promotion in conjunction with the salt-free campaign asked consumers to send their salt shakers to the company as part of a "salt-assault" sweepstakes to win a trip to Hollywood.[1] Increased health consciousness has made consumers more concerned about issues such as cholesterol, caffeine, and sodium levels in food products.

Promotion is also used to remind consumers that an established organization is still around and has certain products that have uses and benefits. Often advertising reminds customers that they may need to use a product more frequently or in certain situations. For example, a convenience store may remind potential buyers that shopping there will save them time because it takes only a few moments to make a simple purchase without standing in the long lines found in large supermarkets. Promotion may be used to remind auto owners that routine maintenance, such as oil changes, filters replacements, and minor tune-ups, is necessary at regular intervals to maintain proper performance of their cars. The U.S. Postal Service uses brochures to remind or inform consumers of its lesser-known services such as stamps-by-mail.

Reinforcement promotion attempts to assure current users of the product that they have made the right choice and tells them how to get the most satisfaction from their choice. A company could release publicity statements through the news media about a new use for a product. For example, medical research indicates that taking one aspirin every other day may decrease the likelihood of a heart attack. Therefore, this over-the-counter medicine can be used for other purposes besides its original purpose of relieving pain and headache. In terms of personal selling, a salesperson can congratulate and communicate with a potential customer about previous purchases and offer guidance about the proper use and maintenance of the product—all in the hope of developing a repeat customer.

# ▶ Promotional Positioning

Promotional positioning relates to the use of promotion to create and maintain an image or concept about a product in buyers' minds. Effective promotion influences customers and persuades them to buy. Promotional positioning is a natural result of market segmentation. In both, the firm aims a given product or brand at a portion of the total market. A promotional strategy is used to differentiate the product and make it appeal to a particular market segment. For example, Domino's, the number-two pizza chain in the country, promotes delivery in its advertising. A recent ad campaign emphasized "One Call Does It All." Domino's is number two behind Pizza Hut, which traditionally did not emphasize delivery as a major promotional consideration. Domino's has positioned itself as a quick-delivery pizza chain and therefore has gained a large market share because customers believe that the company provides fast delivery and a quality product.

Lite beer from Miller is positioned as a less filling but highly satisfying low-calorie beer especially suitable for people who want to drink several beers without consuming the calories in regular beer. LA beer from Anheuser-Busch has been positioned as a low-alcohol beer for those who want to drink a lot of beer at a party without feeling the effects of alcohol. Lowenbrau beer, brewed and distributed in the United States by Miller, is positioned as a German beer and is designed to compete head-on with beers imported from Germany and other parts of the world.

Most products have a perceptional image firmly implanted in the minds of consumers. In another example, Puerto Rico was perceived as distant from other vacation spots and not rated favorably, so advertising was designed to position Puerto Rico as "easy to get to," a place offering "fun bars," "great social life," and "beautiful beaches"—"the place to be."[2] Promotion can be used to change or reinforce an image.

# ▶ Advertising

Advertising was defined earlier as nonpersonal communication transmitted through a mass medium. Advertising is paid for by an identified sponsor and

Ray Charles.  Cardmember since 1965.

Membership
has its privileges.℠

Don't leave home without it.
Call 1-800-THE CARD to apply.

**Don't leave home without it.**   The use of white space in advertising often acts to add prestige to a product. American Express has combined this concept with a celebrity endorsement in the print advertisement to promote membership to its credit card service.

is usually directed to a mass market. The fact that advertising is nonpersonal and is paid for by the sponsor distinguishes it as a unique form of promotion over which the seller has total control. Advertising is highly visible as it is transmitted in mass media such as newspapers, television, radio, magazines, outdoor advertising, and direct mail. As Marketing Encounter 15-1 illustrates, some advertising slogans have been quite successful and memorable. Advertising informs, persuades, and entertains, although sometimes it seems to be a nuisance or a clutter. Figure 15-3 shows the growth of expenditures for advertising over the last two decades.

## Uses of Advertising

*Selective Advertising.*  Selective advertising, used to promote a particular brand of a product, such as a Technics Compact Disk player, accounts for the majority of all advertising expenditures. Brand-oriented advertising

# Marketing Encounter 15-1
## *Successful Advertising Slogans*

Can you identify the products and organizations associated with the following slogans and jingles?

"Just for the taste of it."

"Soup is good food."

"Be all that you can be."

"Reach out and touch someone."

"Everything you always wanted in a beer, and less."

"We bring good things to life."

"The friendly skies."

"Don't leave home without it."

"Where's the beef?"

Nearly one out of every four commercials on the best TV commercial lists uses a slogan or jingle, and roughly four out of five magazine advertisements provide a slogan as a key marketing reinforcement. Successful slogans are strong selling ideas that imply or state clear benefits in a few catchy words; jingles are slogans set to music for television and radio. The most powerful slogans and jingles are believable, memorable, and often emotional as well.

Before the U.S. Army started using "Be all that you can be," enlisting in the army was unpopular. The jingle created an awareness of opportunities for individuals to ahieve personal goals, such as higher education, while serving their country. The slogan gave a personal appeal to what many considered a non-personal profession. It has been highly effective in changing the army's image.

AT&T's "Reach out and touch someone" is another successful jingle. It has multiple attributes that increase its persuasive strength. The jingle tells the consumer to act (reach out and touch someone) and to use the product more often, and it contains an emotional appeal that increases consumers' sensitivity to the product. The slogan sells an idea while leaving the consumer with positive, warm feelings.

The use of slogans is much broader today than it was in the past. In the past, slogans were used primarily to instill a brand name into a reader's or listener's consciousness. Today, slogans are used in a more subtle fashion. Now, their goal is image creation rather than brand-name reinforcement. For example, Citibank of New York used the slogan "The Citi never sleeps," an implied reference to New York City, where literally something is happening at all hours of the day and night.

Some companies have grown large and expanded far beyond their original product concept. Slogans and jingles help these companies to maintain a clear image in consumers' minds. For example, General Electric, which is a major defense contractor as well as a household appliance manufacturer, uses the slogan "We bring good things to life" to give it a human touch and a fitting conclusion to its commercials.

Even in a highly visual age, slogans are still widely used to catch consumers' attention and make them remember the product or organization. An effective slogan can help an organization achieve success.

---

These facts are from "Words Still Matter," *Forbes*, May 4, 1987, p. 142; Murray Raphel, "Watch Out for Linguistic Traps," *Bank Marketing* 18 (January 1986): 38–39; and Merle Kingman, "And Now, a Few Words That Sell," *Advertising Age*, October 24, 1983, p. M-28.

---

is used to persuade people to buy a specific product such as a Sony television. Selective advertising often attempts to evoke an immediate response such as a stereo shop offering 25 percent off Bosse speakers for one week only. Most newspaper advertising on a local basis encourages buyers to come in immediately to buy things that they need for daily living such as groceries, clothing, and services such as dry cleaning.

On the other hand, reminder advertising makes buyers aware of a product so that the firm's name and the product are continually in the minds of the public. Auto dealers use this tactic to maintain top-of-mind awareness with potential car buyers. Comparative advertising compares two or more brands.

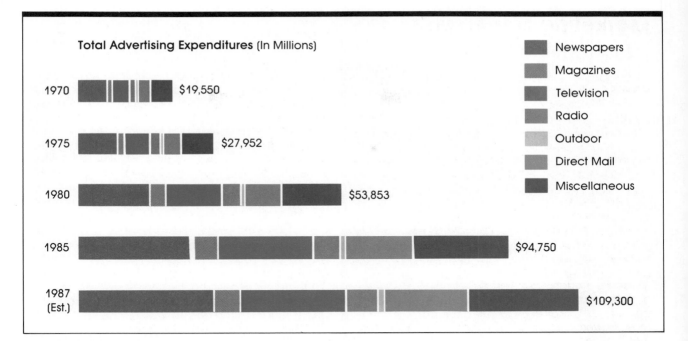

**Figure 15-3**

Total Advertising Expenditures
by Media (dollars)
Source: DDB Needham Worldwide, "Media Trends," 1987.

Most comparisons are based on surveys, technical research studies, or other objective data. Firms that use comparative advertising must make sure that their data is as objective as possible because of stringent requirements that claims be based on scientific and objective assessments. For example, Hanes ran an advertising campaign stating that Fruit-of-the-Loom underwear shrank more than Hanes' brand. Fruit-of-the-Loom reacted with a redesigned product that was priced lower and did not shrink as much.

*Institutional Advertising.* Institutional advertising is designed to enhance a firm's image or reputation. Firms such as AT&T, IBM, and Xerox develop ads to add luster to their overall corporate image. Institutional advertising can also be used to combat a negative image. Union Carbide, for example, has attempted to overcome a negative image resulting from chemical leaks at some of its plants. AT&T promotes long-distance services by emphasizing the quality and dependability offered by a trusted name. Likewise after a plane crash in Detroit, Northwest Airlines used institutional advertising to improve its image and the public's perception of its quality and commitment. Marketing Encounter 15-2 describes how the state of Texas used advertising to get people to stop littering.

*Primary Demand Advertising.* Primary demand advertising aims to increase the demand for all goods, services, or ideas within an industry. The Florida Citrus Commission promotes Florida orange juice. The Washington Apple Growers Association promotes apples from Washington. Recently the

# Marketing Encounter 15-2

## *Don't Mess with Texas*

Companies with profit goals are not the only ones that use promotion activities. Nonprofit organizations like the American Cancer Society and government agencies also use promotion. In the 1980s Texas taxpayers spent $24 million annually to clean up litter along their roads and highways. In 1985, the Texas Department of Highways and Public Transportation was forced to take drastic measures to reduce this hefty trash bill because of budget cuts. However, previous anti-litter promotions had been unsuccessful in persuading Texans to stop littering. Research indicated that the primary Texas litterers were blue-collar men, aged 18 to 35, whom the state called "Bubbas." The state asked ad agency Gurasich, Spence, Darilek and McClure (GSD&McC) to create a promotion campaign to get "Bubba" to stop littering. They were given the tough goal of reducing Texas litter by 25 percent in one year.

The Texas ad agency realized traditional anti-litter slogans that would make other people stop littering don't even slow down a Texan: They had to talk bold and tough to get "Bubba's" attention. Texans in general are quite proud of their state and their frontier heritage. GSD&MC thought "Don't Mess with Texas" would appeal to Texans' state pride, nationalism, and ego; and that Bubba, in particular, would sit up and listen to such a bold appeal.

The agency asked "Bubba's" favorite stars to voice the "Don't Mess with Texas" message on television and radio. Texas musicians Stevie Ray Vaughan, the Fabulous Thunderbirds, Johnny Dee and the Rocket 88's, and Johnny Rodriguez played various "Don't Mess with Texas" themes; Texas sports heroes Ed "Too Tall" Jones, Randy White, and Mike Scott set an example by picking up roadside litter in the ads. Johnny Rodriguez sang his commercials in Spanish to reach Hispanic "Bubbas." The spots were so popular that radio listeners and TV viewers asked stations to run them more often! To increase the impact, more ads (both paid and public service announcements) ran during the spring and summer months when littering reached its peak.

The message appeared on thousands of road signs, and bumper stickers and litter bags with the "Don't Mess with Texas" message were distributed for free.

Texas businesses, civic groups, and individuals sponsored the message on T-shirts, coffee cups, store windows, company trucks, billboards, and even grocery sacks. The state also held "The Great Texas Trash-Off" to encourage Texans to stop littering for one day and pick up trash along the roadsides. It is now an annual event.

In 1986, researchers found that roadside litter had been reduced by 29 percent in less than a year. Deliberate littering dropped by 41 percent, while accidental littering (things blowing out of the back of pick-up trucks, for instance) dropped 18 percent. An awareness survey conducted during the same time found that 60 percent of Texans were familiar with the "Don't Mess with Texas" message. Thus, "Don't Mess with Texas" was quite effective in achieving its objective: To get young, blue-collar Texas men to stop throwing trash on the highway.

The state is expanding the "Don't Mess with Texas" campaign with new spots targeted at a wider public, not just "Bubba." The ads still feature popular Texans, and cartoon figures have been added as well. "Don't Mess with Texas" made Texans feel better about their state, and it gave them a new rallying cry, perhaps one day to replace "Remember the Alamo." The state has spent nearly $2 million on the campaign since it began in 1985, but before the campaign, it spent $24 million a year to pick up the litter. "Don't Mess with Texas" was so successful in reducing litter in Texas that it may have paid for itself.

---

These facts are from "Don't Mess with Texas: A Phenomenal Success," by Gurasich, Spence, Darilek and McClure, Austin, Texas, 1987; "Campaign Gets 'Bubbas' to Quit Messin'," *Marketing News*, June 19, 1987, p. 16; "How to Talk Trash to Texans . . . Plus, the Antidote for Boring Advertising," Gurasich, Spence, Darilek and McClure brochure, Austin, Texas, 1987; personal conversation with Nick Turnham, public affairs officer, Brazos County, Texas Department of Highways and Public Transportation, Bryan, Texas, June 25, 1987; a press release issued by the State Department of Highways and Public Transportation, September 22, 1986; and Michael McCullar, "Trash on Roads Down 29% after Ads," *Austin American-Statesman*, September 22, 1986, pp. A1, A8.

**Drama in print.** An advertisement should focus on key selling points or features and these attributes should be important to the consumer. Sunlight automatic dishwashing detergent focuses on its ability to eliminate spots with this humorous and dramatic print campaign.

International Coffee Association and the National Coffee Association spent millions of dollars to encourage people in the 18-to-34 age group to drink coffee. Leading marketers of coffee contributed to the campaign so that the consumption of coffee would increase or at least remain stable. People between the ages of 20 and 29 average only 1.3 cups of coffee daily compared with 3.4 cups twenty-five years ago. In primary demand advertising, the product, the use of the product, and the benefits of the product are mentioned, but a specific brand is not named. Other organizations that work to stimulate primary demand include the American Pork Producers, the American Dairy Association, and the Beef Council.

## Advertising Media

Advertising media are the vehicles or forms of communication used to reach a desired audience. A **media plan** identifies the media to be used (magazines, television, newspaper, and so on) and the dates and times and cities where the advertisements will appear. Media planning is one of the

**Media plan**

A plan that identifies the media to be used, and the dates and times and cities where the advertisements will appear

services offered by Harris Advertising, described in the profile of Janice Shukle.

Two basic types of media available for advertising are print media and electronic media. Print media, which include newspapers, magazines, direct mail, and billboards, account for one quarter of all advertising expenditures. Electronic media, which include television and radio, account for the other 75 percent of all expenditures. Newspapers, television, and direct mail are the most widely used media in advertising.

*Newspapers.* Newspapers are the leading advertising medium, and over half of all newspaper advertising is purchased by retailers. Newspaper advertising is used so widely by retailers because it is cost-efficient and provides local coverage for retail trade areas. With newspaper advertising, money is not wasted on efforts to reach purchasers who are not within driving distance of the store that is advertised. Newspaper ads can usually be adjusted to react quickly to changing competitive conditions. Audi, in reaction to a *60 Minutes* report on the problem of sudden acceleration in some of its cars, ran newspaper ads in selected markets to address potential concerns with Audis' safety and quality. Because much newspaper advertising is informative, it has high credibility among buyers.

*Television.* Television ranks second to newspapers in total revenue. Because nearly every American home has at least one television set, television

**Providing coverage and coupons.** Although newspaper advertising is able to reach consumers in the target market at a low cost, the number of advertisements and lack of color in many often reduces their impact. Giant Food, Inc. grocery ran a very effective newspaper ad promoting a 15% discount on all LaChoy products.

# Marketing Encounter 15-3

## *Profile: Janice Shukle of Harris Advertising*

In 1987, Harris Advertising was named one of the top 50 woman-owned businesses in Michigan. Under the leadership of Janice Shukle, the agency that began as a small graphics firm in 1978 has evolved into a successful advertising agency with annual billings of $9.5 million. Shukle and her staff combine state-of-the-art graphics with good business sense to meet the promotional needs of Ann Arbor and Detroit businesses, such as the Manufacturers' National Bank of Detroit and the University of Michigan Medical Center. The agency offers research, marketing, media planning and placement, public relations, and promotional services.

Janice Shukle grew up in Ontario, Canada and received her design degree from Seneca College. In 1978 she and her husband founded the Production House in Ann Arbor. The Production House became Harris Graphics in 1982 under a partnership agreement with Richard Buckheim and Richard Rowland. (Harris Graphics took its name from Harris Hall, a historical building that was once part of the University of Michigan, in which the company was housed and which Janice Shukle later bought.) In 1986 and 1987, Janice Shukle bought out Buckheim and Rowland and is now the sole owner of the agency. She began to offer promotional services in addition to graphics and thus changed the name to Harris Advertising. The company now has 23 employees. The agency is currently the second largest in Ann Arbor (in annual billings), but Janice Shukle's personal goal is to make her agency the top agency. In addition to successfully running Harris Advertising, Janice Shukle is also quite active in community affairs, such as the Ann Arbor Area Chamber of Commerce, the Washtenaw United Way, and Catherine McAuley Center.

Janice Shukle recognizes that personal service is the key to her company's success in Ann Arbor and Detroit. Harris employees work directly with more than a hundred clients to determine their needs and tailor an advertising campaign to meet each client's particular promotional objectives. The agency carefully targets its advertising and promotions according to its research. It offers complete in-house production services (graphic design layouts, copywriting, typography) to turn campaigns around quickly and reduce costs to clients, which are mainly business-to-business and other health-care organizations, high technology companies, financial institutions, and others.

In recent years, Harris Advertising has won numerous awards for its work, including three international awards for its advertising campaigns for Holiday Inn West in Ann Arbor and the Michigan Addy Awards for work on the 1986 Ann Arbor: There's No Other City Quite Like It brochure for the Ann Arbor Chamber of Commerce 1987 Michigan State Housing and Development Authority Annual Report.

---

These facts are from a biography provided by Harris Advertising, Inc., 1988; press releases provided by Harris Advertising, Inc., 1988; Marianne Rzepka, "Appreciation: More Than Ever, Businesses Recognize the Need for Savvy Marketing," *The Ann Arbor News*, March 24, 1987, pp. 8–9; Mason Franklin, "Strategic Analysis Report: Harris Advertising, Inc.," April 6, 1988.

---

is a major medium for advertisers. Television advertising is especially useful for large firms whose objective is to reach national or regional markets. A national advertiser such as General Mills can reach national markets through television to promote consumer products such as Wheaties, Total, Lucky Charms, Trix, Gold Medal Flour, Tuna Helper, and Betty Crocker cake mixes because each of these products is widely used and has the potential for being purchased by almost every household. Both local and national firms can buy local time on a single station to cover a particular geographic area. This is especially important if a national firm has a specific image problem or marketing objective in a particular region of the country. Television advertisers can also sponsor a complete show or program or buy time for a 10-, 30-, or 60-second commercial during or between programs.

**Hershey does it again, and again.**   Production of television commercials is costly and time-consuming. Often an agency will have to shoot a commercial spot several times to present the client with the commercial that accomplishes exactly what the sponsor wants.

***Direct Mail.***   Direct-mail advertising is any material that is mailed directly to potential buyers. With direct mail, the advertiser can precisely select the target audience. It is easy to select people who need specific products in a particular target market and to obtain a mailing list so that only those who have that specific need will be contacted. Mailing lists can be obtained for pet owners, owners of sports cars, organic gardeners, golfers, swimmers, and so on. The success of direct-mail advertising depends on the accuracy of the mailing list and the effectiveness of the print material that is sent out. Direct mail is expensive. To be effective it must have high impact and reach buyers who are in the target market.

***Magazines.***   Advertisers can reach very specific markets using magazines. Magazines such as *Car and Driver, Working Woman, Modern Photography,* and *Golf Digest* reach people who have specific interests. General magazines like *Time, U.S. News & World Report,* and *Newsweek* publish regional editions so that advertisers can not only reach mass markets throughout the United States but also zero in on regions where their products and services need promotion or are mainly distributed. The advantage of magazine advertising is that it usually offers higher quality color reproduction than newspapers. Magazines also have a longer life span. For example, issues of *National Geographic* or *Playboy* may be retained for months or years before subscribers finally discard them.

***Outdoor Advertising.***   Outdoor advertising consists of messages on billboards, park benches, taxis, buses, posters, and signs; sky writing; and messages printed on hot-air balloons and blimps. Sign and billboard advertising usually focuses on a specific section of a city or a particular geographic area and is generally inexpensive. The drawback of outdoor advertising is that it is usually seen briefly by individuals in passing and so only a simple message with few words and recognizable graphics should be used. The medium is especially useful for products that can be promoted through graphic images or pictures. Billboards often advertise liquor, cigarettes, and soft drinks and give directions to retail establishments.

***Radio.*** Radio advertising, like magazine advertising, offers a high degree of selectivity in reaching specific target markets. Radio stations usually program for a particular group of listeners. Radio tends to be less expensive than other media, especially if a specific target market can be reached with that station. For example, Hispanic radio stations are excellent vehicles for reaching that market. National advertisers are spending increasing amounts on radio advertising.

Advertisers are using Top 40 record countdown shows and other network programs that offer the advertiser a package of several hundred radio stations.[3] For example, teen rock stations are an excellent medium for advertising acne remedies such as Oxy 10 or Stridex. Country music stations are an obvious medium for promoters of country music albums and records. New Age music stations may reach the 30-to-45-year-old market, and all-news and weather stations may be successful in reaching the over-50 target market. In radio it is important to create a message that can be properly conveyed through the spoken word. Much studio time is spent in trying to perfect a message that will rise above other communication broadcast by the radio station. Even very small businesses can usually afford to use radio. The secret to success with radio advertising is to have a carefully defined target market that is reachable by a particular radio station.

Radio can be highly effective: Several radio stations in Louisiana ran advertisements for the Maison Plummet Mall—an underground shopping mall—with the campaign, "the best deal in town is a hole in the ground." Some five hundred to six hundred listeners called the local Better Business Bureau to find out the location of the mall so they could shop there. There is no Maison Plummet Mall, however. The central Louisiana Area Media Association produced the ads to prove that a modestly priced radio advertisement can heighten public awareness.[4]

There are more than eighty-five hundred commercial radio stations and almost a half billion radios in the United States.[5] The Radio Advertising Bureau projected $6.7 billion expenditures for radio advertising in 1985.

# ▶ Publicity

**Public relations**

A broad set of communication activities designed to maintain favorable relations between an organization and its public

Within an organization, publicity is often viewed as part of public relations. **Public relations** is a broad set of communication activities designed to maintain favorable relations between an organization and its public, which may be government officials, stockholders, buyers, consumer affairs advocates, or other groups.

**Combination pizza.** Although publicity is not paid for directly by an advertiser, an advertiser can almost insure publicity if the event is carefully managed and released to the press. Domino's pizza and Goodyear tire have had great success in drawing publicity through their Indy car sponsorship.

Although publicity and advertising are similar in that both are carried by the mass media, there are several major differences between them. Advertising messages tend to be informative, persuasive, or both; publicity is mainly informative. Advertising is often designed to have an immediate impact or to give specific information to persuade a person to act; publicity usually describes what a firm is doing and the type of products that are being launched, or it offers other newsworthy information that usually is not a call for action. When advertising is used, the organization must pay for media time and must select the type of media it wishes to use to reach target audiences. The mass media willingly carry publicity because they believe it has general public interest. A company may spend money to release information to the press or to call a news conference, but it does not actually buy the media time. It is up to the station to determine the newsworthiness of the message. Therefore, people outside the organization shape the message— either negatively or positively. Advertising can be directed and repeated a number of times; most publicity appears in the mass media once and is not repeated.

In 1988 the Anheuser-Busch Co. and the Adolph Coors Co. received publicity when local newspapers ran stories about their efforts to ship water to communities affected by a fuel spill on the Monongahela River in Pennsylvania. The fuel spill left many Pennsylvania, Ohio, and West Virginia residents without water supplies for a few days. The two major brewers used their production and distribution systems to bottle and transport water to the affected areas in a matter of hours. Both companies said they simply wanted to help out people in need, even at the cost of shutting down beer production lines to bottle the water. (Anheuser-Busch got additional public-relations mileage out of the event by providing its water in beer-size cans with labels indicating the water was donated by the Anheuser-Busch Company.)[6]

There are several forms of publicity. A feature article is usually prepared for a publication and may provide detailed information about a company or its product. A news release is usually a single page of information containing fewer than three hundred words. The news release is made available to the media in the hope that the media will use it and provide information that the company desires to be made public (Figure 15-4).

A captioned photograph is a photograph with a brief description that explains some company event or product. In the fall, it is not unusual for newspapers to run captioned photographs of the new automobile models along with a brief statement: "Here's a picture of the new Chevrolets and Fords that will be available for sale in a couple of weeks."

**Figure 15-4**
A News Release
Courtesy of Procter & Gamble.
Reprinted with permission.

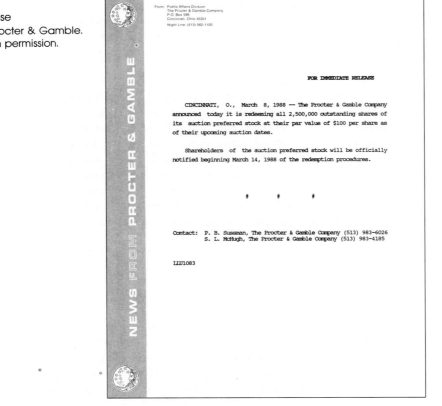

From: Public Affairs Division
The Procter & Gamble Company
P.O. Box 599
Cincinnati, Ohio 45201
Night Line: (513) 562-1100

**NEWS FROM PROCTER & GAMBLE**

FOR IMMEDIATE RELEASE

CINCINNATI, O., March 8, 1988 — The Procter & Gamble Company announced today it is redeeming all 2,500,000 outstanding shares of its auction preferred stock at their par value of $100 per share as of their upcoming auction dates.

Shareholders of the auction preferred stock will be officially notified beginning March 14, 1988 of the redemption procedures.

\#        \#        \#

Contact: P. B. Sussman, The Procter & Gamble Company (513) 983-6026
S. L. McHugh, The Procter & Gamble Company (513) 983-4185

LLU1083

A **press conference** is a meeting with press representatives to announce major events. Companies often hold press conferences when they are about to launch a new product. For example, when Coca-Cola launched diet Coke and announced major changes in its product mix a few years ago, it received national media coverage of its press releases and conferences about those product changes.

Publicity is mainly used to make people aware of the company's products and to enhance the company's public image. Table 15-1 lists some topics for publicity releases that a company might use in order to generate positive awareness.

One of the major roles of publicity management within a company is to manage and control unfavorable publicity. To safeguard the image of the company and foster positive attitudes toward its products, negative information must be countered. The main way to avoid negative publicity is to avoid incidents, statements, and actions that give the company a negative image and that lead to negative public disclosures. It is also necessary to have plans for dealing with unfortunate events so that the negativity of a particular occurrence can be lessened.

Delta Airlines made skillful use of publicity after a major air tragedy in 1985. Delta took decisive action within the first twenty-four hours after the crash to inform the public that the airline had done all it could do to avoid the accident and was doing everything possible to help those affected by the crash. Delta made cooperation with the media a major priority. After one crash, the company decided to allow reporters inside a flight simulator to see for themselves what might have caused the crash. Delta was attempting to demonstrate the extensive training received by its pilots, and that is exactly what the media described.

Delta has a procedures manual for emergency situations and follows it carefully after a major accident. In the case of a fatal crash, Delta's two major tasks are to offer assistance to relatives of those killed and to handle the media. Investigation of the accident is left to the Federal Aviation Administration. One hundred supervisors are called in after a crash to make arrangements for victims' relatives to fly to the crash city. Many Delta staff are assigned to help families cope with the tragedy. Delta also suspends all its advertising for one weekend following a crash because it realizes that publicizing the company name during that time would remind people of the crash and have a negative impact on the company.

# ▶ Personal Selling

Personal selling is a process of informing potential buyers about and persuading them to purchase a product. Personal selling is the most flexible of all promotional methods because it provides marketers with their greatest opportunity to communicate specific information that might trigger a purchase. Of all the promotional elements, only personal selling can zero in on a prospect and attempt to persuade the prospect to make a purchase.

**Table 15-1 Topics for Publicity Releases**
Source: Albert Wesley Frey, ed., *Marketing Handbook,* 2nd ed. (New York: Ronald Press), pp. 19–35. Copyright © 1965. Reprinted by permission of John Wiley & Sons, Inc.

## Marketing Developments

New products
New uses for old products
Research developments
Changes of marketing personnel
Large orders received
Successful bids
Awards of contracts
Special events

## Company Policies

New guarantees
Changes in credit terms
Changes in distribution policies
Changes in service policies
Changes in prices

## News of General Interest

Annual election of officers
Meetings of the board of directors
Anniversaries of the organization
Anniversaries of an invention
Anniversaries of the senior officers
Holidays that can be tied to the
    organization's activities
Annual banquets and picnics
Special weeks, such as Clean-up Week
Founders' Day
Conferences and special meetings
Open house to the community
Athletic events
Awards of merit to employees
Laying of cornerstone
Opening of an exhibition

## Reports on Current Developments

Reports of experiments
Reports on industry conditions
Company progress reports
Employment, production, and sales statistics
Reports on new discoveries
Tax reports
Speeches by principals
Analyses of economic conditions
Employment gains
Financial statements
Organization appointments
Opening of new markets

## Personalities—Names Are News

Visits by famous persons
Accomplishments of individuals
Winners of company contests
Employees' and officers' advancements
Interviews with company officials
Company employees serving as judges for
    contests
Interviews with employees

## Slogans, Symbols, Endorsements

Company's slogan—its history and
    development
A tie-in of company activities with slogans
Creation of a slogan
The company's trademark
The company's name plate
Product endorsements

Although personal selling has a lot of advantages, it is one of the most costly forms of promotion. A sales call on an industrial customer can cost as much as $200 or $300.

Many products require personal selling in order for the company to achieve sales results. A company must have effective salespeople to describe a product's advantages and benefits and to compete with the sales forces of competing firms.

# Types of Salespersons

Many factors affect a marketer's selection of the type of salesperson to employ. The product's complexity, the type of market, and the general nature of distribution in a particular industry are all important considerations. Three distinct categories of salespersons are order takers, creative salespersons, support salespersons.

Order takers are salespeople who execute sales for customers who have already decided to buy the product from a particular organization. Retail

**Wholesale fabric selling.** Because of the face-to-face interaction in personal selling, the message is easily adapted to suit each particular customer's needs. Springs fabrics spends a great deal of time interacting directly with customers, and makes opportunities to brief its customers on new fabric lines.

sales clerks and route salespeople who service retail outlets are examples of order takers. The major role of the order taker is to make sure that supplies are adequate and that there are no problems in the purchase.

Inside order takers are located in sales offices and receive orders by mail or telephone. Outside order takers travel to buyers and take orders directly from them. Order takers may engage in some important sales functions for the organization by encouraging customers to increase the size of their orders or reminding them to purchase certain products. In many organizations, order takers generate the majority of sales.

Creative salespersons are involved in informing and persuading a prospect to buy a product. The creative salesperson tries to increase the firm's sales by finding new customers and encouraging old customers to purchase. A key role of the creative salesperson is to find new prospects and convert them into customers. Products such as automobiles, insurance, furniture, and appliances require the skill of creative salespeople to maintain adequate sales levels.

Support salespersons facilitate and assist in the selling function but usually do not take orders. Support salespersons are used in markets where educating the customer, building good will, and providing service are important for supporting the overall sales volume of the company.

Missionary salespersons are support salespersons usually employed by manufacturers to call on industrial and retail customers to promote products and provide information. If a sales visit is successful, the businessperson may decide at a later date to buy that particular product. Missionary salespersons are especially appropriate for medical supplies, pharmaceutical products, and textbooks. Technical salespersons are support salespersons who provide engineering and other types of technical assistance. They help with product applications, specific system design, and provide technical information about how a product will function best under particular environments or situations. Technical salespersons are often used for computers, machinery and equipment, and steel and chemicals.

## The Personal Selling Process

Probably no two salespeople approach personal selling in exactly the same manner. For most salespeople, however, personal selling is a six-step process: prospecting, approaching, presenting, answering objections, closing, and following up (Figure 15-5).

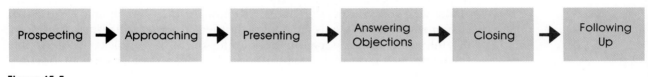

**Figure 15-5**
The Personal Selling Process

***Prospecting.*** The first step in personal selling is to identify potential buyers of the product that is being sold. This can be done by examining directories or trade lists that identify people who use various types of products. The salesperson concentrates his or her efforts on prospects who have needs and wants, financial ability, and authority to purchase the product.

***Approaching.*** The salesperson finds and analyzes information about prospects' needs and desires for products. The information helps the salesperson approach the potential customer. There are different types of approaches. Using a referral, the salesperson explains to the prospect that an acquaintance or some other person has indicated that the prospect might be interested in the product. Using cold canvassing, the salesperson calls on potential customers without any prior notice or referral.

***Presenting.*** After making the approach, the salesperson must make a presentation to get the prospect's attention and to persuade the prospect to buy the product. In making the presentation, it is important for the salesperson to use stimulating methods. Demonstrating the product and using visual aids such as a videotape or slides can assist greatly in the presentation. The salesperson should demonstrate what the product can do and the benefits associated with it.

***Handling Objections.*** Objections are reasons mentioned by the prospect for not buying the product. One of the best ways for a salesperson to handle an objection is to try to anticipate and counter it before it is expressed. Doing this is risky, however, because the salesperson may bring up an objection that the prospect had not thought of. At any rate, objections should be dealt with immediately when they arise. A good salesperson does not dodge objections but finds out what the objections are and tries to deal with them. A successful sale may depend on how well the salesperson handles objections.

***Closing.*** Closing is asking the prospect to buy the product. It is an important step in personal selling because a customer may actually be reluctant to volunteer to purchase a product. Prospects usually need some encouragement or persuasion to make a purchase decision. A trial close involves asking questions that assume the customer is going to buy the product; its purpose is to get answers to identify objections. The trial close indicates what decision is going to be made. Trial closing questions relate to matters such as delivery dates and model colors.

***Following Up.*** A good salesperson follows up on a successful sale to make sure the customer is satisfied with the purchase. The salesperson may check to see whether the product was delivered on time and whether the buyer got exactly what he or she wanted. Waiters and waitresses often ask "How was your dinner?" This is a follow-up question to make sure that customers are leaving satisfied. Only a satisfied customer will return; therefore, the follow-up is necessary for the salesperson to have repeat business. The follow-up helps develop rapport with the buyer and ensure an ongoing relationship.

# ▶ Sales Promotion

Sales promotion provides stimulus for customer purchasing and increases dealer effectiveness in selling products. Sales promotion is used to enhance and supplement other forms of promotion. Sales promotions are generally easier to measure and less expensive than advertising. For example, Sony offered consumers discounts on American Airlines tickets with the purchase of a Sony product. Sony offered this promotion for a limited period of time so that the number of discount certificates was easily measured. In addition, American participation in the program lowered Sony's promotional cost.[7] The major tools of sales promotion are point-of-purchase displays, premiums, trading stamps, sampling and demonstrations, retailer coupons, consumer contests and sweepstakes, refunds, and trade shows.

## Point-of-Purchase Displays

Point-of-purchase displays consist of items such as signs, window banners, display racks, and self-service cartons. These items are used by wholesalers to attract attention, inform, and persuade retailers to carry the particular products. Retailers use them to call attention to specific products within the store. Most point-of-purchase displays are made available to dealers and retailers by manufacturers and wholesalers.

## Premiums and Trading Stamps

A **premium** is a special incentive in the form of a gift that is made available to a customer for buying a product. A box of cereal might contain a free pen or a key chain. Airlines offer free trips after their passengers have logged a certain number of miles traveling with them. For example, after traveling twenty thousand miles, a passenger might get a free trip anywhere in the United States.

Customers save and redeem trading stamps for products. Retailers use trading stamps such as S&H Greenstamps to encourage customers to spend their money at outlets that offer stamps. Although the popularity of trading stamps seems to vary from one decade to another, they have been a very important sales promotion tool for some grocery stores and service stations.

## Sampling and Demonstrations

A **sample** is a free product or service that is offered through coupons or an in-store demonstration. Samples and free demonstrations encourage trial use and purchase of the product and enable the consumer to discover how the product provides its benefits. Although this approach is very costly, it does give the customer a direct involvement with the product that may lead to future purchases. Many food manufacturers set up sampling areas in supermarkets to promote new products, such as frozen pizza or soft drinks.

## Retailer Coupons

When the price of a particular product seems to be a motivation for purchasing, the distribution of cents-off coupons through advertisements or direct mail may be helpful. A detergent manufacturer, for example, might mail out a coupon offering 50 cents off the purchase price of a specific brand such as Tide. The purpose of retailer coupons is to develop brand loyalty and to swell sales volume for a particular brand. Today nearly 80% of all consumers and 2,000 manufacturers use coupons.[8]

## Consumer Contests and Sweepstakes

Consumer contests usually involve solving some type of puzzle. Consumer sweepstakes involve the submission of names, addresses, and phone numbers for the drawing of a prize. Sweepstakes are used to stimulate sales and generate traffic within retail establishments. Sweepstakes are also used to encourage people to buy a product so that they can obtain a coupon or order blank to send off for the sweepstakes entry form.

## Refunds

A **refund** is the return to the consumer of part of the purchase price or the total purchase price of a product. A refund is usually offered by a

**Major industry trade show.** Some trade show are organized for manufactures to show their product line to dealers. Others are designed for the public to create consumer interest. John Deere & Co. holds a trade show with other manufacturers to present its new product line to retailers.

producer who wants to encourage buyers to make a purchase. Refunding is a relatively low-cost promotion tool and is often used for new products. Pepsi has used newspaper advertising to promote a complete refund if you did not enjoy Diet Pepsi or three Diet Pepsi coupons to purchase Pepsi at a discount if you do enjoy the product.

## Trade Shows

A **trade show** is an exhibit, usually an industry-wide exhibition, organized to demonstrate the latest product line to potential customers. Direct purchases may be made at a trade show, or salespeople may get leads to follow up at a later date. Trade shows usually last for a few days, and buyers attend so that they can see the products of competing manufacturers. Trade shows are especially important in fields where new products are developed each year (photography, for example) and where major technological changes occur on a regular basis. Industries such as printing, computers, and publishing have trade shows where competing companies display their products and interact with customers.

# Notes

**1.** "Diet-Rite to Launch 'Salt Assault,'" *Adweek's Marketing Week*, February 22, 1988, p. 3.

**2.** William R. Dillion, Teresa Domzal, and Thomas J. Maden, "Evaluating Alternative Product Positioning Strategies," *Journal of Advertising Research* (August-September 1986): 32.

**3.** Ronald Alsop, "More Firms Tune In to Radio to Stretch Their Ad Budgets," *The Wall Street Journal*, July 17, 1986, p. 25.

**4.** "Underground Mall Exists Only in Ads," *Marketing News*, December 4, 1987, p. 22.

**5.** *Advertising Age*, August 29, 1985, p. 15.

**6.** Joe Agnew, "Positive Image Created by Aiding Crisis Victims," *Marketing News*, February 15, 1988, pp. 1, 2.

**7.** Lisa Phillips and Sara Stern, "Electronic Ad Dollars Down," *Advertising Age*, June 1, 1987, pp. 4, 82.

**8.** Donna Campanella, "Sales Promotion: Couponamania," *Marketing and Media Decisions* 22 (June 1987): 118–22.

# Summary and Review

▶ The promotion mix is made up of advertising, personal selling, publicity, and promotion.

▶ Promotional positioning relates to the use of promotion to create and maintain in the buyer's mind an image of a product. The different elements of the promotion mix work together to create this image.

▶ Advertising has a number of uses as a communication tool for management. It can promote a particular brand or product, enhance a firm's image or reputation, and increase demand for all goods and services in a given industry.

▶ Sales promotion is a direct stimulus to encourage customer purchases and increase the dealer's effectiveness. Sales promotion is used to enhance and supplement other forms of promotion.

▶ Publicity is a nonpersonal form of communication transmitted through mass media. It is not paid for directly by the company. Publicity is usually presented in the form of a news story, without identifying the sponsor.

▶ Personal selling is the most flexible element of the promotion mix because it provides marketers with their greatest opportunity to adjust and communicate specific information to the consumer.

# Key Terms and Concepts

promotion
advertising
personal selling
publicity
sales promotion
push strategy
pull strategy

media plan
public relations
press conference
premium
sample
refund
trade show

# Checking Your Understanding

This chapter introduced you to the subject of promotion. To test and reinforce your understanding, fill in the blanks below.

   **1.** A _____ photograph is a photograph with a brief description that explains some event or product.

   **2.** A person who facilitates and assists in the selling function but is not directly involved in order taking is a _____ salesperson.

   **3.** A free product or service offered through coupons or an in-store demonstration is known as a _____.

   **4.** A _____ is a special incentive in the form of a gift that is made available to consumers for buying a product.

   **5.** _____ salespersons are involved in informing and persuading a prospect to buy a product.

   **6.** _____ is asking the prospect to buy the product.

   **7.** A _____ plan identifies the advertising media to be used and the dates and times and cities where the advertisements will appear.

   **8.** A _____ article is usually prepared for a publication and may provide detailed information about a company or product.

   **9.** Money given back to the consumer to encourage further purchases is known as a _____.

   **10.** Consumer _____ involve submission of names, addresses, and phone numbers for the drawing of a prize.

   **11.** _____ is communication to inform potential buyers about goods, services, and ideas.

   **12.** A person who supports the sales of a company's products with engineering and other types of technical assistance is known as a _____ salesperson.

   **13.** _____ selling is direct, two-way communication with buyers and potential buyers.

   **14.** _____ relations is a broad set of communication activities designed to maintain favorable relations between an organization and its public.

   **15.** A _____ salesperson is usually employed by a manufacturer to call on industrial and retail customers to promote products and provide information.

   **16.** A _____ release is usually a single page of information offered to news services.

# Topics for Review and Discussion

1. Compare and contrast the marketing mix and the promotion mix.
2. List the circumstances in which the push and pull promotional strategies are used.
3. Briefly explain why a firm uses promotion as part of its overall marketing effort.
4. What is the purpose of a promotional strategy?
5. How do publicity and advertising differ? How are they related?
6. Identify and contrast the three uses of advertising.
7. Briefly describe the three leading media used in advertising.
8. Distinguish among the different forms of publicity.
9. What does the personal selling process involve? Briefly discuss the process.
10. How do sales promotion and advertising differ? In your opinion, what are the three most important sales promotion tools?
11. When a sale has been made, is there any need to follow it up? Why or why not?
12. Why is the promotion mix for a consumer goods company different from the promotion mix for an industrial goods company?

# Exercises

1. Procter and Gamble recently mailed sample tubes of Crest toothpaste to all households. Explain the rationale of the action. Do you think P&G will be able to accomplish its objectives?
2. Choose a particular product. How would you as marketing manager allocate your budget among the elements of the promotion mix?
3. Discuss the selling process you would use to sell a microwave oven to your classmates.
4. Design a promotional campaign to combat unfavorable rumors about a company or its products. (Briefly describe the rumor first.)
5. Pick a nearby store, and briefly describe the kinds of sales promotion used and their effectiveness.
6. In what ways is a job interview related to marketing?
7. What steps will you take to sell your old textbooks at the end of the semester?

## Case 15-1
### *People Meters Determine Advertising Rates*

Companies that use television advertising to reach their target markets need to know what programs the target market is watching. Television networks need to know what shows are popular in order to make sales and programming decisions. To obtain that information, for the last thirty years research companies like A. C. Nielsen and Arbitron have used the National Audience Composition (NAC) diary to record information about television viewing choices. In 1987, however, new technology made it possible to access that information more accurately and more quickly through the use of people meters.

The NAC diaries helped networks and advertisers determine what television shows were most popular with certain audiences. The diaries were weekly surveys administered to randomly chosen households. Household members simply filled in the diary, specifying what channels they tuned in during every hour of the day. Information from the diaries was compiled and analyzed to determine how many people watched a particular television show. Researchers rated each show according to its popularity, and the networks used the ratings to determine how much to charge for advertising during each show.

State-of-the-art electronic and computer technology now allows television research companies to utilize people meters. The meter is a small device that attaches to the television. Viewers log on to a remote-control keyboard whenever they enter the television-viewing area, and from minute to minute the meter automatically keeps track of which channel is on. The meters underwent extensive testing and evaluation before their introduction. Researchers believed they would present a more accurate picture of the composition of various program audiences than did the old diaries and would provide the information more quickly.

The four biggest television research companies—A. C. Nielsen, Arbitron, R. D. Percy Co., and London-based AGB Television Research—are investing millions of dollars to install the meters into more households. A. C. Nielsen introduced its people meters into two thousand homes early in 1987, although it continued to obtain data from the NAC diaries. The meter utilized by R. D. Percy is a bit different from meters used by the other companies. It monitors the channels on a *second-by-second* basis and includes a heat sensor that can tell when people enter or leave the room, permitting ratings of commercials for the first time.

People meters have aroused some controversy. The three major American networks expressed doubts about the reliability of the devices; ABC and CBS asked Nielsen to continue to use diary data rather than people-meter data for 1987. Both networks canceled their contracts with Nielsen for that year because they felt that Nielsen was not committing enough of its resources to the diary method of data collection. CBS later signed a contract with AGB Television Research, which also utilizes people meters.

The three networks' concern arises from that fact that the program ratings registered by the people meters seem to be lower than those derived from the diaries. In addition, the 1987 ratings varied dramatically from week to week, even for a single program. It was suggested that the ratings varied so dramatically because viewers simply forgot to log on to the people meter. The networks also had doubts about the small samples on which the research companies based their 1987 ratings. Because the program rating determines how much a network can charge for a commercial during a particular program, the networks feared that lower ratings would mean lost revenues.

To combat the lower ratings, the networks were forced to raise their rates for commercial time in 1987.

Despite the controversy, advertisers like the people meters because they provide more accurate information more quickly than the diaries. The accuracy of a diary depends on the memory and honesty of the person maintaining it. People meters, by contrast, record channel selections automatically once the viewer has logged on to the machine. People meters also provide more information about the viewer—age, sex, income, educational level, ethnic background—to help advertisers reach the appropriate target markets.

Because the networks are reluctant to trust the people meters, the future of the devices is uncertain. The use of people meters over the next few years will establish their reliability and determine whether they will continue to be used to provide demographic data for advertising.

---

These facts are from Marianne Paskowski, "Invasion of the People Meters," *Marketing & Media Decisions* 22 (May 1987): 36–40, 45; "People Meters to Be Sole Tool for '87 Nielsen TV Ratings," *Marketing News*, January 30, 1987, p. 1; Verne Gay, "Networks Zap Debut of Meters," *Advertising Age*, September 7, 1987, pp. 1, 56; Brian Donlon, "TV Rating Rivals Tune In New Device," *USA Today*, September 16, 1987, pp. 1B, 2B; Barry M. Kaplan, "People Meters: What Are the Real Issues?" *Marketing & Media Decisions* 22 (March 1987): 110–16; and Bob Warrens, "People Meters: The Next Logical Step," *Marketing & Media Decisions* 22 (June 1987): 107–08, 112.

**Questions**

1. Why are people meters so controversial?
2. How are people meters impacting on the three networks selling advertising time?
3. Would you use people meter results in purchasing advertising time?

# Case 15-2
## *Delta Makes a Promotion Decision*

One of the roles of promotion is to support a company's image and to maintain a positive relationship between the company and various interest groups within its marketing environment. Nevertheless, unique circumstances sometimes arise where the best promotion is simply no promotion at all. In 1987, Delta Airlines decided not to introduce a promotion program to offset negative publicity surrounding a rash of Delta pilot errors and near-accidents. The public openly wondered what had gone wrong at Delta, the nation's fourth largest airline and one that has always held high safety ratings.

In the period of one month, July 1987, one pilot inadvertently shut off his plane's engines, another pilot landed at the wrong airport, still another pilot landed on the wrong runway (where another jet was taking off), and another pilot narrowly avoided a mid-air collision with another jet. Delta immediately reacted to the accidents by forming an oversight committee of pilots to conduct an internal audit, and a safety review team to study the accidents and determine what caused the errors. As a result of this internal investigation, Delta increased its training activities and monitoring of cockpit training and standards before the Federal Aviation Administration completed its investigation of the accidents.

The FAA investigates all air-traffic accidents and has the power to fine airlines or pilots who violate air safety regulations. The FAA team investigating Delta's accidents examined not only mechanical problems, but also pilot behavior, crew coordination, and cockpit discipline. This team decided that Delta was in general compliance with FAA regulations and did not assess any fines for violations. The FAA report did recommend, however, that Delta increase its emphasis on training and cockpit management guidance, which Delta had already begun to do.

Delta elected at the time of the accidents not to issue any form of apology to the public. The company did send out letters to its frequent flyers, but it emphasized Delta's safety record rather than specifically address the pilot errors. While some people within the industry thought Delta should inform the public about what they were doing about these incidents, Delta management was wary of introducing a new promotion program to combat the negative publicity generated by the incidents. Management felt that such a program would be very difficult to implement because these mistakes were so uncharacteristic of Delta's normally safe performance. Delta also believed it would be very difficult to explain the reasons for these mishaps to the public in an advertising campaign. Moreover, any attempt to reshape the story might be regarded as unethical. The company chose instead to continue to emphasize the airline's outstanding service record and introduced a new advertising campaign, "We Love to Fly and It Shows," with that in mind. In October, the airline announced that Delta had logged the fewest number of consumer complaints (per 100,000 passengers flown) among the leading airlines for the first nine months of 1987. In fact, Delta has received the fewest passenger complaints of the leading airlines every year since 1974.

While promotion usually helps to maintain a positive relationship between a company and its interest groups, special circumstances, such as those encountered by Delta, sometimes call for a decision not to communicate. Delta probably thought an apology would only reinforce the negative publicity, whereas a program focusing on the positive aspects of Delta seemed a more reasonable approach to the situation.

---

These facts are from Clare Ansberry, "Forgive or Forget: Firms Face Decision Whether to Apologize for Their Mistakes," *The Wall Street Journal*, November 24, 1987, p. 29; Candace Talmadge, "Delta Nixes Ads to Help Defuse Image Problem," *Adweek*, July 20, 1987, p. 6; Wayne Beissert, "FAA's Delta Probe to Focus on 'Human Factors,'" *USA Today*, July 17, 1987, p. 3A; "Delta Procedures Met and Exceeded FAA Requirements," Delta press release, September 18, 1987; and "Delta Again Recognized for Passenger Satisfaction," Delta press release, October 12, 1987.

**Questions**

1. Did Delta handle its July negative publicity correctly?
2. Evaluate the combined publicity and new advertising campaign (We love to fly and it shows).
3. Should all firms handle negative publicity the same way Delta handled it?

# Answers to Checking Your Understanding

1. captioned
2. support
3. sample
4. premium
5. creative
6. closing
7. media
8. feature
9. refund
10. sweepstakes
11. promotion
12. technical
13. personal
14. public
15. missionary
16. news

GOVERNMENT AND LEGAL
FORCES ▪ ECONOMY ▪ ETHICS
AND SOCIAL RESPONSIBILITY ▪
GOVERNMENT AND LEGAL
FORCES ▪ ECONOMY ▪ ETHICS
AND SOCIAL RESPONSIBILITY ▪
GOVERNMENT AND LEGAL
FORCES ▪ ECONOMY ▪ ETHICS
AND SOCIAL RESPONSIBILITY ▪
GOVERNMENT AND LEGAL
FORCES ▪ ECONOMY
AND SOCIAL RES
GOVERNMENT
FORCES ▪ E
AND SOCIA
GOVERNM
FORCES ▪
AND SOC
GOVERNM
FORCES ▪
AND SOCIA
GOVERNME
FORCES ▪ E
AND SOCIAL RE
GOVERNMENT AN
FORCES ▪ ECONOMY
AND SOCIAL RESPONSIBILIT
GOVERNMENT AND LEGAL
FORCES ▪ ECONOMY ▪ ETHICS
AND SOCIAL RESPONSIBILITY ▪
GOVERNMENT AND LEGAL
FORCES ▪ ECONOMY ▪ ETHICS
AND SOCIAL RESPONSIBILITY ▪
GOVERNMENT AND LEGAL
FORCES ▪ ECONOMY ▪ ETHICS
AND SOCIAL RESPONSIBILITY ▪

Finance

Owner

Employee     Customer

Management              Marketing

*Part* IV

# FINANCIAL MANAGEMENT

▶ Money and the Financial System

▶ Accounting and Financial Statements

▶ Short-Term Finance: Working Capital Management

▶ Long-Term Finance: Stocks, Bonds, and Securities Markets

▶ Risk Management and Insurance

## Outline

# Chapter 16

# Money and the Financial System

## Objectives

After reading this chapter, you will be able to:

▶ Define money and explain its functions.

▶ Distinguish among commercial banks, savings and loan associations, credit unions, and mutual savings banks, and explain their importance to businesses and individuals.

▶ Distinguish among nonbanking institutions such as insurance companies, pension funds, mutual funds, and finance companies.

▶ Understand the role of the Federal Reserve System in the financial system and describe how the Fed manipulates the money supply to regulate the American economy.

▶ Discuss the future of the banking industry.

# Business Experience

Would you like to make tons of money? Then work for Crane Company. Crane Company is located in Dalton, Massachusetts (population 6,800) and makes currency paper for the United States Treasury Department. The firm employs 730 workers, many of whom are the third or fourth generation to work at Crane.

The business was founded by Zenas Crane in 1801. The company went from one mill with hand production of 125 sheets of paper per day to a company with revenues of more than $100 million in 1987. Seven generations of the Crane family have guided the firm through a civil war, two world wars, and a depression. Crane Company produces the highest quality paper money can buy.

Thomas Crane, president of Crane Company, believes that the so-called new business principles being used today have actually been in use for fifty to sixty years. Mr. Crane feels the secret to running a business is doing the basics well. A firm needs to know their customers, provide a quality product, have good employee relations, and have a good quality work force.

Crane has achieved their management objectives. The firm has great employee relations, an outstanding product, and the company knows the needs of their customers. Crane is considered to be a good employer. Employees receive good wages, a pension, vacations, and life insurance. Crane distributes 25% of profits before taxes to the employee profit-sharing program.

Producing a quality product is second nature to the firm. The firm's 100% rag paper has excellent strength, durability, and texture that is considered the best in the industry. While most firms use wood for their paper products, Crane uses cotton. The company buys raw cotton from Texas and California and leftover cuttings from cotton textile mills. Crane mixes the cotton into thick pulp which is then run through a drying and pressing process. Finally the blank paper is cut into sheets.

The best testimony to how well Crane knows their customer is the fact that they have won the bid for the U.S. Treasury contract for the past 109 years. The U.S. Treasury contract only accounts for 25% of Crane's total business, but Crane is the sole supplier of government currency paper in the U.S. Crane also makes currency paper for many other countries. Crane Company puts silk threads, metallic threads, and fluorescent threads into currency paper and bank notes. These threads make the paper virtually unreproducible and is the primary way of preventing counterfeiting. Crane is also a major supplier of bank note paper to the American Bank Note Company which prints bond and stock certificates for companies traded on the U.S. stock and bond markets.

Another product sold by Crane is stationery, some used in the White House and some used by Tiffany's. Crane also makes tracing paper for engineers and architects, the paper for passports, and high-tech glass fiber paper. It's rather amazing how a small family-owned company like Crane can provide all of the currency paper for the United States of America. One might expect some large multi-billion dollar company to be responsible for producing the currency paper used in U.S. paper money. Crane Company illustrates how a well-managed firm can achieve long-term success and still be a good neighbor.

These facts are from "A Real Tiger in the Paper Trade," *Fortune*, March 28, 1988, p. 52; "Massachusetts Firm Makes Money the Old Fashioned Way: They Churn It," *Chicago Tribune*, October 9, 1986, Section 3, p. 4; Wadsworth R. Pierce, "The First 175 Years of Crane Papermaking," Excelsior Printing Company, North Adams, Massachusetts, 1977.

# Introduction

Finance is the study of how to manage money efficiently. Money is anything generally accepted as a means of paying for goods and services. The flow of money through the economy links consumers to businesses, to employees, and to suppliers of raw materials and finished products.

If you have a checking account, automobile insurance, or a credit card, then you have had experience with several financial institutions. When you enter the working world as a full-time employee, you may become involved with other financial institutions as you make decisions about retirement planning, financing a house, or investing in stocks, bonds, or mutual funds.

This chapter provides an overview of the role of money and the financial system in the economy. It surveys various financial institutions and examines how each participates in the economy. It examines the role of the Federal Reserve Board and explores the future of banking.

# ► Money in the Financial System

Curtis paid Tony four unfiltered Camel cigarettes for a fresh slice of soap weighing less than an ounce. Tony added the four cigarettes to another six he had been saving and paid Morley ten cigarettes for an egg. This could have been a scene in a World War II prison camp, where cigarettes became money among prisoners. If cigarettes can be used in place of dollar bills, then what is money? Anything may be used as money, as long as it is acceptable to everyone as money and everyone regards it as a medium of exchange for goods and services. Throughout history, many things have served as money. American Indians used wampum beads made of polished shells strung together. Other cultures have used salt, cattle, chickens, shells, rocks, coconuts, and precious metals such as gold.

**Fiat money**

Money that the government states is legally acceptable

Americans use **fiat money**—money that is not backed by gold but is instead backed by a government promise that it is legally acceptable as a means of exchange for products. Fiat money usually takes the form of currency—metallic coins and paper money—and is found in all countries that have a central government.

## Functions of Money

No matter what a particular culture uses for money, money itself has three general functions. It serves as a medium of exchange, as a measure of value, and as a store of value.

As a medium of exchange, money facilitates the buying and selling of goods and services and eliminates the need for bartering. Bartering is trading one product or service for another product or service of similar value. For example, someone might trade a dozen eggs for five pounds of potatoes.

**Current currency.** Money is anything that is generally accepted in exchange for goods—most commonly bills and coins but also including checks and credit cards. Shown here are bills from France, England, Germany, the U.S., as well as from other countries.

Bartering is often cumbersome because people must carry around physical goods in order to trade for what they need and want.

As a measure of value, money serves as a common standard or yardstick of the value of all goods and services. For example, $1 will buy a dozen large eggs, $12,000 will buy a good quality automobile, and $90,000 will buy an average-priced home in the United States. At a minimum wage rate of $3.35 per hour, a worker could buy 3.3 dozen eggs for one hour's work. On a teacher's salary of $24,000 per year, a car will cost one-half of a year's wages.

As a store of value, money acts as a way to maintain the value of accumulated wealth until it is needed to purchase goods or services. A person making $600 per week who wants to buy a $500 stereo must save $50 per week for ten weeks to have enough money "stored" up to buy the $500 stereo system.

## Characteristics of Money

In order to be used as a medium of exchange, money must be acceptable, divisible, durable, portable, stable in value, and difficult to counterfeit. All money has these characteristics.

***Acceptability.*** Money must be readily acceptable as payment for goods and services and for the settlement of debts. People must believe in and trust the value of what they use as money. Acceptability is probably the most important characteristic of money: If people do not trust the value of money, businesses will not accept money as payment for goods and services, and people will have to find some other means of purchasing goods and services.

***Divisibility.*** Money must be easily divisible into small units of value in order to facilitate exchanges. If money is to be a measure of value, all items must be valued on a common basis, with a divisible unit of money serving as the medium of exchange. The American dollar meets this requirement because it is divisible into a hundred pennies, twenty nickels, ten dimes, and four quarters. The British pound is divided into twenty shillings or a hundred new pence.

***Portability.*** It must be possible to carry money easily in order for it to function as a medium of exchange. Large, colored rocks could serve as money, but one would need a wheelbarrow to transport them. Paper currency and metal coins are popular throughout the world because they are lightweight and can be carried in large quantities. Paper money was first used in North America in 1685.[1]

***Durability.*** Money must be durable. The same dollar bills are used over and over again. In fact, the average American dollar bill lasts eighteen months and is folded thousands of times. Because of continuous use, money must be able to retain its original qualities over a long period of time and through much handling. Metal coins, then, would seem to be the ideal form of money. Paper currency, however, is far more portable than metal because of its light weight. Coins today are primarily used to provide divisibility.

***Stability.*** Money must be stable and maintain its declared face value. A $10 bill should be worth ten dollars' worth of goods or services from one day to another. Stability allows people who wish to postpone purchases to do so without fear that their money will decline in value. Money declines in value during periods of inflation, when economic conditions cause prices to rise steadily and thereby reduce the purchasing power of a dollar. In some countries with very high inflation, particularly in Latin America, people spend their fiat money as fast as possible before the price of durable goods increases due to rapidly rising prices. Instability destroys confidence in a nation's money, and ultimately the money loses the characteristic of acceptability. Instead of using money that is declining in value, people store their savings in land, gold, or some other physical asset. Table 16-1 shows the inflation rate for many different countries.

***Difficult to Counterfeit.*** Money must be difficult to counterfeit, or duplicate illegally. People will lose confidence in and stop using a currency if it can be counterfeited easily. To make counterfeiting difficult, the U.S. Treasury Department controls the production of American money. The reproduction of money by anyone else in the United States is illegal.

Every country takes some steps to make counterfeiting difficult. Some countries use highly colored money; others use specially watermarked paper

**Table 16-1 Annual Inflation Rates in Selected Countries, 1982–85**

Source: International Monetary Fund, International Financial Statistics Yearbook, 1984 and 1986.

| Country | Consumer Price Indexes | | | | Annual Rate of Inflation |
|---|---|---|---|---|---|
| | 1982 | 1983 | 1984 | 1985 | 1982–85 |
| Japan | 107.7 | 109.6 | 112.1 | 114.4 | 2.0% |
| West Germany | 111.9 | 115.6 | 118.4 | 121.0 | 2.6% |
| Switzerland | 112.5 | 115.9 | 119.3 | 123.4 | 3.1% |
| United States | 117.1 | 120.9 | 126.1 | 130.5 | 3.7% |
| Canada | 124.6 | 131.8 | 137.5 | 143.0 | 4.7% |
| United Kingdom | 121.5 | 127.1 | 133.4 | 141.5 | 5.2% |
| France | 126.8 | 139.0 | 149.3 | 157.9 | 7.9% |
| Venezuela | 127.3 | 135.3 | 151.8 | 169.1 | 9.9% |
| Italy | 137.2 | 157.3 | 174.3 | 190.3 | 11.5% |
| Paraguay | 121.7 | 138.0 | 166.1 | 207.9 | 19.5% |
| Colombia | 158.8 | 190.2 | 220.8 | 273.9 | 19.9% |
| Chile | 131.6 | 167.4 | 200.7 | 262.3 | 25.8% |
| Ecuador | 131.3 | 195.0 | 263.6 | 337.3 | 37.0% |
| Uruguay | 159.5 | 238.0 | 369.6 | 636.5 | 58.6% |
| Mexico | 203.3 | 410.4 | 679.0 | 1,071.2 | 74.0% |
| Peru | 288.4 | 609.0 | 1,280.2 | 3,370.0 | 126.9% |
| Brazil | 407.0 | 984.9 | 2,923.0 | 9,556.0 | 186.3% |
| Israel | 477.8 | 1,173.5 | 5,560.0 | 22,498.0 | 261.1% |
| Argentina | 541.4 | 2,402.9 | 17,462.0 | 134,883.0 | 529.4% |

that is difficult to duplicate. The United States uses special paper containing silk threads. The Bureau of Engraving and Printing will soon begin to use a metallic filament that can be seen with the human eye but cannot currently be reproduced. The Bureau of Engraving and Printing also uses special inks and dyes and highly detailed engraved plates for producing its paper currency.

# The Supply of Money

Today there are widely accepted forms of payment or exchange. All such forms directly accepted in payment for goods and services are considered money. When the federal government measures the supply of money to see whether the economy is growing, it looks at demand deposits and time deposits as well as at currency.

**Demand deposits** are checking accounts—an account at a financial institution into which a person deposits and withdraws funds. A check is a written order authorizing the bank to withdraw a specified amount of money from an established checking account and pay it to an individual or business on demand. Checks are considered to be legal payment for debts, and millions of Americans use checks as a substitute for cash to pay bills.

Checks are more convenient than currency for large payments. Checks also permit people to carry around large sums of money without the risk of loss. If you lose a $5 bill, anyone who finds it can spend it. If you lose a blank check, it is illegal for anyone to forge your signature on it. Your bank has a

**Demand deposits**

Checking accounts at a financial institution into which a person deposits and withdraws funds

**Share draft account**

A demand deposit in a credit union

**M1**

All currency, demand deposits, NOW accounts, Super NOW accounts and share draft accounts

**Time deposits**

Deposit accounts at banks and savings and loan associations that earn money at a specified interest rate

**Money market accounts**

Merge different investors' deposits into one investment fund that buys stocks and bonds

**M2**

Includes time deposits and money market accounts in addition to currency and demand deposits

sample of your signature that it can compare with a suspected forged signature.

There are many types of demand deposits available. Most do not earn interest. Some checking accounts, however, receive interest on the balance of the deposit left in the account. The two most common types of interest-bearing demand deposits are NOW and Super NOW accounts (NOW stands for *negotiable order of withdrawal*). A NOW account pays interest that is usually below other short-term market rates. There are currently no limits on the interest rate banks are allowed to pay on account balances. As market interest rates rise or fall, rates paid on NOW and Super NOW accounts may also change. A Super NOW account requires a minimum balance of from $2,500 to $5,000 and, because of the minimum required balance, pays higher interest rates than does a NOW account. A **share draft account** is a demand deposit in a credit union.

Demand deposits and currency make up one definition of the money supply used by the federal government. $M_1$ refers to all currency, demand deposits, NOW accounts, Super NOW accounts, and share draft accounts.

Some assets are called *near money* because they are very easily turned into cash. For example, **time deposits,** also called savings accounts, are deposit accounts at banks and savings and loan associations that earn money at a specified interest rate. Time deposits are not used for transactions or as a medium of exchange, but the balance in a time deposit can be moved from a savings account to a checking account or turned into cash.

**Money market accounts** are considered near money. The advantage of money market accounts is that they pay interest rates that are more competitive with the rates on other short-term securities such as 30-day U.S. government Treasury bills. Money market accounts compete with Super NOW accounts at financial institutions for deposits. The owner of a money market fund can write a limited number of checks each month in minimum amounts of $500. Because these checks cannot be used for transactions of any size, their usefulness is limited, and they do not qualify as money.

A second definition of the composition of the American money supply, $M_2$, includes time deposits and money market accounts in addition to currency and demand deposits.

Credit cards, or plastic money, as these cards are commonly called, are another form of near money. They have become an increasingly popular substitute for money because of their convenience and acceptance by merchants around the world. Bank-issued credit cards, such as Visa and MasterCard, represent the majority of cards held in the United States. There are currently about 152 million Visa cards and 135 million MasterCards in circulation.[2]

Although many people think of credit cards as money, credit cards are actually a preapproved line of credit granted by the issuing bank or credit company. The organization offering the credit card guarantees payment of a credit charge to merchants and assumes responsibility for collecting the money from the card user. This allows credit cards to function as money for the average consumer. Most bank cards offer the holder an option of paying the monthly balance in full or paying a stated minimum monthly amount with interest charges added to the balance until the full amount has been paid. Bank cards charge an average annual interest rate of 18 percent in 1988, plus an average annual fee of between $15 and $25.

Banks are not the only issuers of credit cards. American Express has long been the dominant card company in the travel and entertainment market. The 25 million American Express cardholders worldwide own green, gold, or platinum cards and pay fees ranging from $45 for a green card to $250 for a platinum card. American Express expects its cardholders to pay their bills in full when they receive the monthly statement as stipulated in the cardmembers' agreement.

Major department stores—Montgomery Ward, Sears, J. C. Penney, Macy's, and others—offer revolving credit-card accounts to encourage consumers to spend money in their stores. **Revolving accounts** are a legal guarantee that a cardholder can purchase goods and services on credit, up to a specified amount, whenever the cardholder wishes. Eighteen million people now use the Sears Discover credit card, which is similar to a bank-issued credit card.[3] Seventy-nine million Americans now carry an average of 2.9 credit cards each from department stores, oil companies, and other retail establishments.[4]

Traveler's checks, money orders, and bank drafts are other common forms of money. Although each is slightly different, they all share a common characteristic: A financial institution, bank, credit company, finance company, or the neighborhood 7-Eleven guarantees that the instrument will be honored and exchanged for cash when it is presented to the institution making the guarantee.

Behind all forms of money other than currency stands people's faith in their ability to exchange checks, traveler's checks, money orders, and other forms of near money into currency. Because people have this faith in the banking system, most do not ask for currency in exchange for checks; they simply deposit these forms of payments to their checking or savings accounts, knowing that they can be exchanged for cash.

**Revolving accounts**

A legal guarantee that a cardholder can purchase goods and services on credit, up to a specified amount

# ▶ The American Banking System

## Commercial Banks

Commercial banks are financial institutions that hold deposits in accounts for individuals and businesses and use some of the deposited funds to make loans to businesses and individuals. They are the oldest and largest of all banking institutions and perform a variety of financial services.

Commercial banks rely mainly on demand deposits and NOW accounts as their major source of funds, and they use only a percentage of those deposits to make loans to businesses and individuals. Because it is unlikely that all the depositors of one bank will want to withdraw their funds at the same time, a bank can safely loan a large percentage of its deposits. However, the federal government requires that all banks keep a certain percentage (3–17%) of their deposits on hand to meet the needs of their depositors.

**Sure it's insured.** All banks that are members of the Federal Reserve System must insure their depositors against loss to a specified limit. The Federal Deposit Insurance Corporation (FDIC) insures customers' deposits up to $100,000 per account.

Federal banks are chartered by the U.S. Comptroller of the Currency. State banks are chartered by the state in which they do business. State banks account for 66 percent of all bank accounts, but federal banks account for about 60 percent of the total deposits.

Until recent years, commercial banks primarily made short-term loans (loans that must be repaid within a year) to help finance business expansion. Today, banks are quite diversified and offer a number of services. Commercial banks provide consumer loans for vacations, for major purchases such as appliances, automobiles, or other durable goods, and even for medical expenses. They issue Visa and MasterCard credit cards. Many banks rent safe-deposit boxes in bank vaults to customers who want to store valuable belongings such as legal documents, jewelry, stamps, and coins. Recently, banks have begun to offer investors the opportunity to buy and sell securities through their discount brokerage services.

Banks also offer saving accounts and certificates of deposit (CDs)—notes issued by a bank guaranteeing a depositor a higher interest rate than a money market account as long as the depositor leaves the funds with the bank for a specified period of time—six months, one year, seven years. The longer the term of the CD, the higher is the interest rate paid by the banking institution. For example, in 1988 a six-month $2,000 CD might pay 6.5 percent interest, and a four-year CD might pay 8 percent. The rates fluctuate according to economic conditions. CDs generally have higher rates of return than savings accounts.

One growing area of service at many commercial banks is trusts. Trusts are legal entities set up to hold and manage assets for a beneficiary. These trusts may include investments in stocks, bonds, real estate, or other types of assets. Husbands and wives may set up a trust so that on the death of one, their joint assets are put in trust and the income from the trust goes to the surviving spouse. When the surviving spouse dies, the trust distributes the remaining assets to the beneficiaries named.

Trust departments of commercial banks have responsibility for managing hundreds of billions of dollars in assets. The Northern Trust Company of Chicago, for example, has over $100 billion under management for pension and retirement plans and trusts. Trust departments are operated separately from the commercial bank. They play a very large role in the indirect flow of financial capital into corporate and government securities. Financial Encounter 16-1 is a profile of Barbara S. Thomas, who is an international banker.

## Other Banking Institutions

***Savings & Loan Associations.*** Savings and loan associations (S&Ls), often called thrifts, are financial institutions that offer savings accounts, checking accounts, and CDs and make long-term loans (for a period of more than a year) for residential mortgages. **Mortgages** are loans made so that a business or individual can purchase real estate, for instance, a home; the real estate itself is pledged as a guarantee that the buyer will repay the loan. If the loan is not repaid, the savings and loan association has the right to repossess the secured property.

**Mortgages**

Loans made so a business or individual can purchase real estate

S&Ls compete directly with commercial banks for deposits, checking accounts, and certain types of loans. At the end of June 1987, S&Ls held $567 billion in residential mortgages, or 32 percent of all residential mortgages.

***Credit Unions.*** A **credit union** is a financial institution owned and controlled by its depositors. Members usually have a common background such as an employer, profession, trade group, or religion. A savings account at a credit union is commonly referred to as a share account; a checking account is called a share draft account. Because the credit union is tied to a common organization, the members (depositors) are allowed to share in the organization and benefits of the credit union. The members can vote for directors and share in the credit union profits in the form of higher interest rates on accounts or lower loan rates because of good earnings.

**Credit union**

A financial institution owned and controlled by its depositors

Credit unions were orginally created to provide depositors with a short-term source of funds for low-interest consumer loans for items such as autos, refrigerators, washing machines, vacations, and education. Credit unions today offer a wide variety of financial services. Credit unions vary in size from very small to very large, and the services provided to their members vary accordingly. Smaller credit unions stick to simple car loans, installment credit, and other basic financial services. Larger credit unions are very competitive with banks and S&Ls and as well as basic services offer money

## Financial Encounter 16-1

### *Profile: Barbara S. Thomas of Bankers Trust*

Barbara S. Thomas, senior vice president in charge of international private banking at Bankers Trust, has had a number of firsts in a long, illustrious career as a corporate lawyer, SEC commissioner, and international banker.

Barbara Thomas graduated from the University of Pennsylvania in 1966 and graduated second in a class of 232 at the prestigious New York University School of Law in 1969. When she first entered the business world, there were few women in high ranking jobs. After law school, she thought she wanted to be a consumer lawyer. When she went to work for Paul, Weiss, Rifkind, Wharton & Garrison, however, she got involved in corporate finance and found that she enjoyed it. Later she moved to the Park Avenue law firm of Kayler, Scholer, Fierman, Hays & Handler, where she specialized in corporate and securities law, and at age 30 became a partner in the firm. In 1980, President Jimmy Carter appointed her a commissioner on the Securities and Exchange Commission, the youngest person and the second woman ever to serve on the commission. As a commissioner, she honed her skills in international securities. She was rather outspoken on many SEC issues, particularly an SEC rule that she believed unfair to small investors.

In 1983 she and her husband, also a lawyer, and their baby son moved to Hong Kong where she went to work for London-based merchant bank Samuel Montagu & Company. Again, she was the first woman member of the board. At Montagu, Thomas was in charge of supervising international security markets and corporate finance. Although women do not play a major role in Asian corporate finance, Thomas quickly made an impression on businessmen in Hong Kong and helped Samuel Montagu get a foothold in Asian markets. In 1986, Thomas and her family moved back to New York when she was appointed senior vice president and head of the international private banking division of Bankers Trust.

In that position, Thomas manages 110 bankers all over the world. She is involved in investment banking and marketing trust services and stocks and bonds. She assists foreigners in investing their money and helps manage the portfolios of both individuals and companies. In essence, Bankers Trust acts as the financial advisor for many foreign investors, and has a discount brokerage for buying and selling stocks. Although Thomas works very long hours, the pay is excellent and she loves her work. She loves the challenge and pressure of international investment banking.

Barbara Thomas has earned the respect of bankers all over the world for her expertise and hard work. Her experiences and success will open doors for other women in the banking industry.

---

These facts are from Cherie Fein, *Getting into Money* (New York: Ballantine Books, 1988), pp. 116–121; "The Unlikely Banker Leading Samuel Montagu's Asian Assault," *International Management* 39 (July 1984): 44, 45; Richard L. Hudson, "At the Staid SEC, Commissioner Thomas Demonstrates Unusual Flair for Publicity," *The Wall Street Journal*, November 10, 1983, p. 24; "A Lady We Like," *The Economist*, March 19, 1983, p. 98.

market accounts, credit cards, and certificates of deposit, discount brokerage, travel services, and more.

***Mutual Savings Banks.*** Mutual savings banks are similar to savings and loan associations except that they are owned by the depositors. They were originally established to provide a safe place for the savings of particular groups of people such as fishermen. They are among the oldest financial institutions in the country and are found mostly in New England. They have not been popular in the rest of the country, and their growth has lagged behind that of commercial banks and S&Ls.

# Insurance for Banking Institutions

The **Federal Deposit Insurance Corporation (FDIC)** was established in 1933 to help stop bank failures throughout the country during the Great Depression. The FDIC insures individual accounts up to a maximum amount of $100,000. When one depositor has several different accounts, each account is protected for the maximum amount of $100,000. All federal banks must be insured by the FDIC; state banks can be insured by the FDIC or be insured privately. Banks pay a fee for this depositor protection.

The **Federal Savings and Loan Insurance Corporation (FSLIC)** was established shortly after the FDIC to provide the same protection to depositors in savings and loan associations. The **National Credit Union Association (NCUA)** insures credit unions.

Congress hoped that the FDIC and FSLIC would make people feel so secure about their savings so that they would not panic and withdraw their money when news of a bank failure was announced. This would keep financially sound banks from experiencing runs that could cause their collapse.

In the 1980s many banks and S&Ls failed, and depositors had to make use of FDIC and FSLIC insurance. The most visible examples of bank failure were Continental Illinois Bank, the sixth largest bank in the country, which was insured by the FDIC, and Home State in Ohio, which carried private insurance. Financial Encounter 16-2 discusses the failure of the Continental Illinois Bank.

# Deregulation of the Banking Industry

**Deregulation** is the repeal of regulations that pertain to a specific industry. Congress passed the Depository Institutions Deregulation and Monetary Control Act of 1980 and the Garn–St. Germain Depository Institution Deregulatory Act of 1982 to deregulate the banking industry. Congress' objective in passing these acts was to strengthen the banking industry and increase the flow of funds to the home-mortgage markets. These acts allowed financial institutions to pay competitive interest rates on accounts, helping banking institutions compete for funds with other financial organizations such as money market funds and retail brokers. The acts allowed banks to pay interest on checking accounts and allowed banks and savings and loans to pay the same interest rates on savings accounts. The many provisions were phased into existence over several years to provide an orderly transition. Tables 16-2 and 16-3 summarize the basic features of these acts.

Before deregulation, savings and loan associations had an advantage because they could offer interest rates on savings accounts that were 0.25 percent higher than the rates offered by commercial banks. Banks can now match S&Ls' interest rate on savings accounts, but S&Ls can now offer credit cards, consumer loans, and discount brokerage services. Although most S&Ls have moved slowly into these unfamiliar areas, deregulation has made the competition between commercial banks and savings and loan associations intense. Since the early 1980s, many savings and loans have gone out of business or merged with other S&Ls, as illustrated in Figure 16-1. Deregulation is likely to have a similar effect on mutual savings banks.

**Table 16-2  Provisions of the Depository Institutions Deregulation and Monetary Control Act of 1980**

▶ Required all commercial banks, mutual savings banks, savings and loan associations, and credit unions to meet reserve requirements imposed by the Federal Reserve Board if they are federally insured or eligible for federal insurance.

▶ Phased out and ultimately eliminated the maximum rates of interest and dividend payments on deposits by 1986.

▶ Allowed:
  a. Banks to provide automatic transfer of funds from savings to checking accounts
  b. Savings and loans to establish remote service units for crediting and debiting savings accounts
  c. Nationwide authorization of NOW accounts
  d. The increase of federal insurance from $40,000 to $100,000
  e. The raising of the loan-rate ceiling from 12 percent to 15 percent for credit unions

▶ Authorized savings and loans to invest up to 20 percent of their assets in consumer loans, corporate loans, and corporate debt securities; removed geographical restrictions for mortgage lending; allowed savings and loans to offer more banking services.

▶ Prohibited states from limiting rates or the amount of interest, financial charges, or other charges with respect to loans, mortgages, or credit sales when residential property is used as collateral.

▶ Simplified the terms of the Truth in Lending Act so that consumers could understand and compare credit terms.

**Table 16-3  Garn–St. Germain Depository Institution Deregulatory Act of 1982**

▶ Increased the flexibility of the Federal Deposit Insurance Corporation and the Federal Savings and Loan Insurance Corporation in the types of financial assistance they can provide to troubled financial institutions and outlined procedures that agencies must follow in order to facilitate the acquisition or merger of failed and failing institutions.

▶ Increased the investment powers of savings and loan associations to improve the range of services they offer to their customers; directed the deregulation committee to create a new deposit instrument that would compete with money market mutual funds; stipulated that the minimum balance for these accounts should not exceed $5,000.

▶ Revised or repealed provisions of banking laws dealing with lending limits, loans to insiders, and banking affiliates.

▶ Authorized alternative mortgage transactions such as variable-rate mortgages for non–federally chartered housing creditors.

▶ Covered miscellaneous subjects such as amendments to the Federal Credit Union Act and truth in lending for student loans; defined a creditor; allowed NOW accounts to be offered to state and local governments; completed a study on optional insurance for large deposits.

# Nonbanking Institutions

Nonbanks are organizations that offer some financial services, such as short- or long-term loans, but do not accept deposits. Nonbanks include insurance companies, pension funds, mutual funds, money market funds, brokerage firms, financial networks, and finance companies.

***Insurance Companies.*** Insurance companies make long-term loans to corporations, make mortgages on commercial real estate, and purchase government bonds. They get the money for these loans from the premiums

**Figure 16-1**

The Decline of the Savings and Loan Association

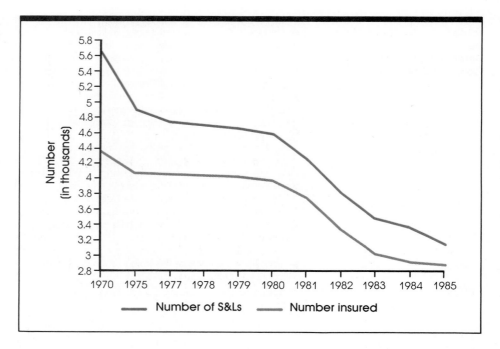

Number (in thousands)

5.8
5.6
5.4
5.2
5
4.8
4.6
4.4
4.2
4
3.8
3.6
3.4
3.2
3
2.8

1970  1975  1977  1978  1979  1980  1981  1982  1983  1984  1985

——— Number of S&Ls      ——— Number insured

paid by individuals and businesses for insurance against the risk of financial loss as a result of death, injury, disability, automobile accident, or some other financial crisis. The function of insurance companies is discussed in detail in Chapter 20.

***Pension Funds.*** Pension funds are pools of money set aside by corporations, unions, and some nonprofit organizations to provide income for members on their retirement. There are private pension funds and public pension funds.

**Individual Retirement Accounts (IRAs)** are one type of private pension fund set aside by individuals to provide for their retirement needs. The IRA can be invested in high risk assets such as commodities or low risk assets like U.S. government securities. The choice is up to the individual. Individuals can defer payment of taxes on the interest from these funds until they retire. Many corporations also provide private pension plans for their employees; these are sometimes established with bank trust departments or life-insurance companies. Funds are deposited under the employee's name in a separate account, and when the employee retires, the money accumulated in the account can be withdrawn in one lump sum or taken as monthly cash payments over some defined time period (usually life).

Social Security, the largest pension fund, is a public fund. (The federal government collects Social Security funds from payroll taxes from employers and deducts them from employees' paychecks. The Social Security Administration makes payments to those eligible to receive Social Security benefits— the retired, the disabled, and young children of deceased parents.) Because the average age of a U.S. citizen is increasing (the median age in 1987 was

**Individual Retirement Accounts**

Private pension fund set aside by individuals to provide for their retirement needs

## Financial Encounter 16-2
### *Federal Insurance: The Continental Illinois Bailout*

In a period of three years, Continental Illinois National Bank and Trust went from being one of the best banks in the United States to one of the worst. The bank reached its peak in 1981. It was the biggest commercial and industrial lender in the nation, earning $255 million for the year. It was ranked as the ninth largest commercial bank, with assets totaling over $41 billion. A series of unexpected events unfolded over the next two and a half years.

In 1982, the First Pennsylvania Bank collapsed, and the Federal Deposit Insurance Corporation (FDIC) refused to insure creditors and accounts exceeding its $100,000 limit. The FDIC would not follow the same path with Continental. It was revealed that in 1980 Continental had purchased a billion dollars worth of energy loans from one of First Pennsylvania's subsidiaries, Penn Square Bank of Oklahoma. The majority of these loans later became uncollectible.

The bank had made sizable loans to less-developed countries such as Brazil, Mexico, and Argentina. It was also a leading lender to several companies that had filed for protection from creditors under Chapter 11 of the Bankruptcy Code. In May 1984, rumors about the bank's financial condition started a massive withdrawal of funds that became the biggest bank run since the Great Depression. Led by large overseas investors, depositors withdrew over $9 billion of the bank's $28 billion deposits within one week. To restore confidence in the bank, the FDIC announced that it would guarantee all of Continental's deposits, even those exceeding the maximum of $100,000. The bank established lending agreements with twenty-eight large money center banks for $5.5 billion. This was supposed to be a safety net for needed funds. To keep Continental from actually collapsing and causing a ripple effect throughout the banking system, the FDIC purchased $4.5 billion of bad loans and injected another $1 billion in cash into the troubled bank. Continental Bank was reorganized with new management and the FDIC owning over 80 percent of its common stock. The Continental rescue was the largest ever by the FDIC. The stock-market crash in October 1987 created another $90 million loss for one of its subsidiaries and reversed some of the progress it had made since 1984.

---

These facts are from Jeff Bailey, Tim Curringham, and Daniel Hertzberg, "Continental Illinois Gets Rescue Package of $4.5 Billion in Record Bailout Attempt," *The Wall Street Journal*, May 15, 1984, p. 3, 25; "Will Megabucks Solve the Problems at Continental Illinois?", *Business Week*, May 28, 1984, p. 31; Jeff Bailey and Jeffrey Zanlow, "Continental Illinois Securities Plummet amid Rumors Firm's Plight Is Worsening," *The Wall Street Journal*, May 11, 1984, p. 3.

---

32 years),[5] the number of people eligible for Social Security benefits is increasing relative to the number of people contributing to the fund. This is increasing the burden on American workers, who currently contribute to Social Security in the expectation that they will receive Social Security benefits when they retire. Inflation of the 1970s and early 1980s further increased the burden on American workers and employers. There is concern that if these trends continue, payroll taxes alone may no longer be able to support this retirement program.

**Mutual fund**

Financial organization that pools investors' funds and invests them in securities

***Mutual Funds.*** A **mutual fund** pools investors' funds and invests them in securities. Individual investors purchase shares in a mutual fund in the hope of earning a high rate of return. A single mutual fund may specialize in managing a common stock fund, bond fund, or even a fund invested in international securities. Thus, mutual funds spread the risk of investing across many securities, minimizing the effects of any one security that does not do well. Mutual funds provide professional financial management for individuals who may not have the skills to invest in particular securities such as government bonds. The managers of the mutual fund try to manage the portfolio to achieve the financial goals and objectives stated in the fund prospectus—a document that spells out the details of the fund's strategy, historical investment record, management costs, and so on.

***Money Market Funds.*** Money market funds are a type of mutual fund that invests in the money market. The money market is the market where short-term debt securities, such as Treasury bills (short-term securities issued by the government), are bought and sold. Treasury bills have a life of between several days and a maximum of one year. They are sold in $10,000 amounts at a discount. For example, you might spend $9,300 to buy a $10,000 Treasury bill. The $700 difference between your purchase price and $10,000 ending value is your return of interest. Money market funds provide services such as check-writing privileges, reinvestment of interest income, diversification of investments, and professional fund management. Large banks, trust departments, corporations, and institutions such as pension funds have turned to money market funds for investing in liquid short-term securities. In 1974, there were only fifteen money market funds with total assets of about $1.7 billion. By 1987, the number of funds had grown to more than 330 with total assets exceeding $296 billion. This rapid growth paralleled an increase in interest rates and made money market funds the fastest-growing financial investment. The increasing popularity of these funds can be attributed to the slightly higher interest rates they earn relative to bank savings and checking accounts.

***Brokerage Firms.*** Brokerage firms buy and sell stocks, bonds, and other assets for their customers and provide other financial services. Merrill Lynch, Shearson Lehman Hutton, Charles Schwab, and A. G. Edwards are brokerage firms. Some brokerage firms offer additional financial services. Merrill Lynch, for example, offers the Merrill Lynch Cash Management Account (CMA), which pays interest on deposits and allows clients to write checks, borrow money, and withdraw cash. Brokers such as Shearson Lehman Hutton/ American Express offer so many services that they have evolved into financial networks.

***Financial Networks.*** **Financial networks** offer consumers a wide variety of financial services that were traditionally offered by banking institutions. Firms such as Sears, K mart, Merrill Lynch, and Shearson Lehman Hutton offer financial services such as interest-earning checking and savings accounts, loans, brokerage services, insurance, and real estate. The marketing strategy behind financial networks is to create a one-stop shopping center for financial services.

With the introduction of the Sears Discover credit card, Sears has emerged as a major competitor in the financial services sector. The Discover card, introduced in 1985, provides a line of revolving credit, access to emergency cash, a check-cashing service, IRAs, use of automated teller machines nationwide, and a package of other financial services. Sears has also developed financial service centers in many retail stores throughout the United States. These centers allow shoppers to purchase insurance from Allstate Insurance;

**Financial networks**

Organizations that offer consumers a wide variety of financial services that were traditionally offered by banking institutions

**An investment opportunity.** Money market mutual funds are a low risk form of savings. Kemper Financial Services offers money management services to its customers. Two of Kemper's money market funds rank among the ten largest in the U.S.

stocks, bonds, and other securities from Dean Witter Reynolds; and real estate from its Coldwell Banker subsidiaries. In California, a Sears customer can bank at Sears-owned Allstate Savings and Loan.

A growing number of nonfinancial firms have been moving into the financial field. These firms include industrial organizations, such as General Motors and General Electric, that in the past confined financial activities to financing customers' purchases. Recently, General Motors decided to move into other financial service areas such as mortgage banking. In 1987, General Electric bought Kidder Peabody, a major brokerage company. General Electric's credit subsidiary now accounts for close to 20 percent of General Electric's revenues and earnings.

Banks and other banking institutions have responded to these competitive threats by adding financial services such as discount brokerage and insurance as well as higher yielding money market accounts. Table 16-4 presents the ten largest diversified financial corporations.

***Finance Companies.*** Finance companies offer short-term loans at higher rates of interest than banks. They are usually a lender of last resort for businesses or individuals whose credit limits at banks have been exhausted. The borrowers are usually high-risk customers who are unable to obtain loans at lower rates. Commercial finance companies make loans to businesses. They require businesses to pledge assets such as equipment, inventories, or

| Corporation | Assets (in Millions) |
|---|---|
| Federal National Mortgage Association | $100,406.0 |
| American Express | 99,476.0 |
| Salomon | 78,164.0 |
| Aetna Life & Casualty | 66,829.9 |
| Merrill Lynch | 53,013.5 |
| Cigna | 50,015.8 |
| First Boston | 48,618.2 |
| Travelers Corp. | 46,299.6 |
| Morgan Stanley Group | 29,190.4 |
| Bear Stearns Co. | 26,939.4 |

accounts receivable as collateral—security against the event the borrower is unable to repay the loan. Consumer finance companies make loans to individuals. Like commercial finance companies, they require some sort of asset as security against the borrower's potential inability to repay the loan. Finance companies obtain their funds by borrowing from corporations and commercial banks.

# ▶ The Federal Reserve System

**Federal Reserve System**

Established by Congress to regulate the nation's banking industry and manage monetary policy

What purpose does money serve in the economy? Who is the guardian of the money supply, and how does money affect economic activity? For answers to these questions, the role of the Federal Reserve System must be examined. Congress established the **Federal Reserve System** in 1913 to regulate the nation's banking industry. Although it is part of the federal government, the Fed, as it is commonly called, remains an independent agency.

## Structure of the Federal Reserve System

The Federal Reserve System is divided into twelve regions. Each region has a Federal Reserve Bank that serves its defined area (Figure 16.2). All the Federal Reserve Banks except those in Boston and Philadelphia have regional branches. The Cleveland Federal Reserve Bank, for example, is responsible for branches in Pittsburgh and Cincinnati.

The Federal Reserve System is divided into a Board of Governors and the Federal Open Market Committee. The Board of Governors is made up of seven members appointed by the president of the United States; each one is subject to the approval of the U.S. Senate. Each member serves for fourteen years, and the terms are staggered so that one expires every two years. One member of the board is appointed by the president to serve a four-year term as the chairman of the Board of Governors. The Federal Open Market Committee is composed of twelve members. Seven members are the members of the Board of Governors; the other positions are filled by the presidents

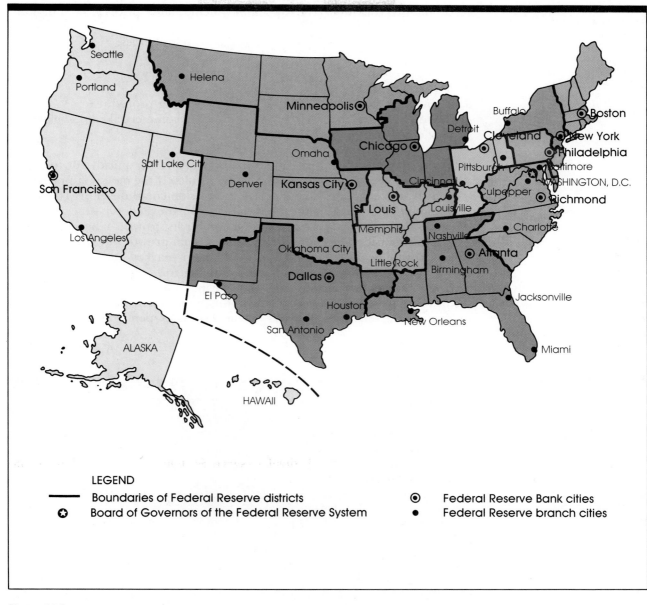

**Figure 16-2**
The Federal Reserve System

of five of the regional reserve banks. The chairman of the Board of Governors also heads the Federal Open Market Committee.

## Functions of the Federal Reserve

The Federal Reserve has control over monetary policy and works with Congress and the president to meet economic goals. The Fed is responsible for creating an economic environment that promotes stable, long-term economic growth, high levels of employment, stable prices (low inflation), and a balance of international payments. To achieve such an environment, the Federal Reserve Board has four major responsibilities:

1. To control the money supply with monetary policy
2. To regulate financial institutions
3. To manage regional and national check-clearing procedures
4. To supervise the federal deposit insurance of commercial banks belonging to the Federal Reserve System

***Monetary Policy.*** If the money supply grows too quickly for too long, the economy gets overheated and inflation results. If the money supply grows too slowly, the economy may stall and a recession could develop. To control the amount of money in the financial system, the Federal Reserve Board monitors the money supply and sets targets for its growth. When the money supply gets outside of the minimum or maximum growth rates, the Fed fine-tunes growth by using four basic tools: open market operations, reserve requirements, the discount rate, and credit controls (Table 16.5).

**Open market operations** are the buying and selling of government securities, usually U.S. Treasury bills, in the public open market. The decision to buy or sell securities is made by the Federal Open Market Committee

**Open market operations**

Buying and selling government securities in the public open market

**Up, up, and away.** Inflation is the condition of rising prices. Usually consumer income does not increase as rapidly as prices. Many foreign countries are victims of double-digit inflation. The prices in this Argentinian meat market reflect the country's high inflation.

Table 16-5  Fed Tools for Regulating the Supply of Money

| Activity | Effect on the Money Supply and the Economy |
|---|---|
| Buy government securities | The money supply increases; economic activity increases |
| Sell government securities | The money supply decreases; economic activity slows down |
| Raise discount rate | Interest rates increase; the money supply decreases; economic activity slows down |
| Lower discount rate | Interest rates decrease; the money supply increases; economic activity increases |
| Increase reserve requirements | Banks make fewer loans; the money supply declines; economic activity slows down |
| Decrease reserve requirements | Banks make more loans; the money supply increases; economic activity increases |
| Relax credit controls | Encourages more people to make major purchases, increasing economic activity |
| Restrict credit controls | Discourages people from making major purchases, decreasing economic activity |

(FOMC) and implemented by the New York Federal Reserve Bank. This monetary tool is the one most commonly used by the Federal Reserve for controlling the money supply. It can be implemented quickly on a daily basis and is very flexible for use in a rapidly changing government securities market.

The Federal Reserve Board manages the money supply within the guidelines set by the FOMC for the variously defined growth targets for $M_1$ and $M_2$. When the Fed buys securities, it writes a check on its own account to the seller of the securities. When the seller of the securities deposits the check, the Fed transfers the balance from the Federal Reserve account into the seller's account, increasing the supply of money in the banking system. The opposite result occurs when the Fed decides to sell securities: the buyer writes a check to the Federal Reserve, and when the funds are transferred out of his or her bank account into the Fed's account, the amount of money in circulation and the overall money supply decline. Remember that checks (demand deposits) are part of the money supply.

**Reserve requirement**

The percentage of deposits that banks must hold in reserve

The Federal Reserve has the authority to set **reserve requirements**—the percentage of deposits that banks must hold in reserve, either in the bank itself or in a Federal Reserve Bank, and not loan to business or individuals. For example, a bank holding $10 million in deposits, with a 10 percent reserve requirement, must have reserves amounting to $1 million:

$$\% \text{ reserve requirements} \times \text{deposits} = \text{required \$ reserves}$$
$$10\% \times \$10,000,000 = \$1,000,000$$

If the reserve requirement were 5 percent, banks would need to keep $500,000 in reserves. Because the reserve requirement is such a powerful tool, the Federal Reserve does not change reserve requirements very often but instead relies on open market operations. In 1980, the Depository Institutions Deregulation and Monetary Control Act gave the Federal Reserve the power to set reserve requirements not only for member commercial banks but for all commercial banks, savings and loan associations, credit unions, and mutual savings banks.

Because checks are money, banks also have a role in creating money. When the Federal Reserve puts new money into the banking system, banks can make loans that end up as checking deposits in the banking system. With a 5 percent reserve requirement, each $1 of new money pumped into the banking system has the potential to increase the money supply by $20:

$$\frac{\text{New infusion of money}}{\text{reserve requirement}} = \text{total potential creation in banking system}$$

$$\frac{\$1}{5\%} \quad \text{or} \quad \frac{\$1}{.05} = \$20$$

**Discount rate**

The rate of interest the Federal Reserve charges for money it lends to any banking institution

The **discount rate** is the rate of interest the Federal Reserve charges for money it lends to any banking institution to meet reserve requirements. The Federal Reserve Bank is lender of last resort to these institutions. When a bank borrows from the Fed, it is said to have borrowed at the "discount window." To discourage those who borrow too frequently from the discount window, the Fed may charge banks a higher interest rate than they could get from other lenders.

The Federal Reserve uses the discount rate to affect bank borrowing and the resultant reserves that can be used to create money through the lending process. When the Fed wants to expand the money supply, it lowers the discount rate to encourage borrowing. When the Fed wants to decrease the money supply, it raises the discount rate. Economists watch changes in this sensitive rate as an indicator of the Fed's monetary policy.

Finally, the Federal Reserve has the authority to set credit controls—that is, it establishes and enforces credit rules for financial insitutions and sets margin requirements on the sale of stocks and bonds. The Fed can determine how much down payment individuals and businesses must make on credit purchases of expensive items such as automobiles and how long a time period individuals or businesses have to pay off the purchases. By raising and lowering minimum down-payment amounts and payment periods, the Fed can stimulate or discourage purchases of expensive items. The Fed also sets the minimum percentage that investors must pay to buy securities with borrowed money. Investors can buy on margin—that is, they do not have to pay the whole purchase price of a stock but can pay a percentage of the price (currently 50 percent) and borrow the rest from the broker who makes the actual sale. By altering the margin requirement, the Fed can encourage or discourage the buying and selling of securities with the borrowed money.

***Regulatory Functions.*** The second responsibility of the Federal Reserve is to regulate commercial banks that are members of the system. The Fed establishes and enforces banking rules that affect monetary policy and competition between banks. The Federal Reserve considers what nonbank activities, such as brokerage services, leasing, and insurance, are appropriate for commercial banks. It also has the authority to approve or disapprove of mergers between banks and the formation of bank holding companies—companies that own several banks.

To ensure that accounting practices and prudent bank behavior are followed, surprise bank examinations are conducted once each year. In 1985 both the Bank of America and First Chicago were audited to determine whether they had set aside the correct amount of reserves to cover losses from potentially bad loans. The Federal Reserve required the banks to set aside several hundred million dollars as additional reserves.

***Check Clearing.*** The Federal Reserve provides national check clearing. The Federal Reserve clearinghouse handles almost all checks drawn on a bank in one city and presented for deposit to a bank in a second city. Any banking institution can present the checks it has received from other banks around the country to its regional Federal Reserve Bank. The Fed clears the check with the appropriate regional Fed, which then sends the check to the bank for payment. Thanks to technological advancements, the whole process takes a maximum of two days and often is accomplished within 24 hours.

The Federal Reserve also clears local checks. It charges a fee for this clearing function, and in big cities like Chicago, New York, and Philadelphia local private clearinghouses compete with the Fed to provide this service more cheaply. Figure 16.3 presents the clearing process by the Federal Reserve Banking System.

***Depository Insurance.*** The Federal Reserve Board is also responsible for supervising the Federal Deposit Insurance Corporation, the Federal Savings and Loan Insurance Corporation, and the National Credit Union Administration.

# ▶ The Future of Banking

There are many ways that money can move through the economy. The choices that the consumer faces are increasing in sophistication and availability. The banking system is expected to undergo some major changes during the next decade as it continues to react to deregulation and begins to institute recent technological developments to speed up the banking process.

## Interstate and Regional Banking

In June 1985, the United States Supreme Court ruled that interstate banking within regions, such as New England or the Southeast, will be allowed. However, states within regions must make mutually acceptable agreements that let banks in each region merge across state lines. Shortly after this ruling, the chairman of the House Banking Committee proposed an interstate

**Figure 16-3**
The Check Clearing Process

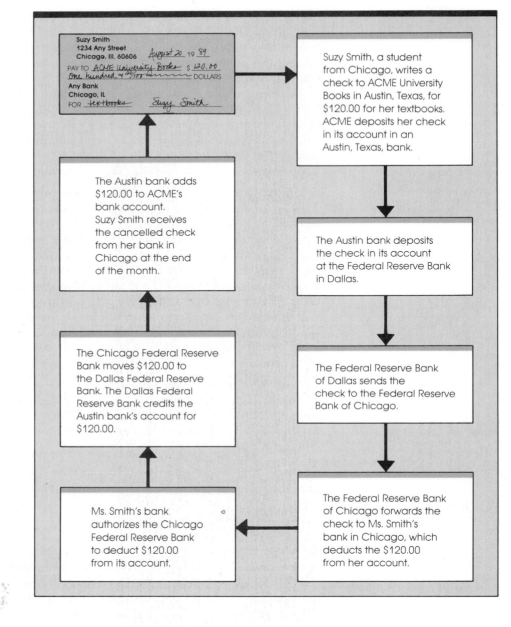

banking bill that would limit interstate banking to geographic regions until 1990. After this date, nationwide interstate banking would allow banks from other states to compete in any region across the country. Other proposals regarding interstate and regional banking have been introduced in Congress. Whatever the final outcome of these bills, they will have a major impact on the banking industry of tomorrow.

**Day & Night, Night & Day.** Banks are becoming more and more consumer oriented, taking current technology and adapting it to clients' needs. Automatic Teller Machines (ATMs) were a major development in consumer service and expanded distribution of banking services. ATMs have made many bank services available to consumers 24 hours a day.

# Electronic Funds Transfer

**Electronic funds transfer**

Transferring funds by means of an electronic terminal, telephone, computer, or magnetic tape that orders a financial institution to debit or credit an account

To reduce costs, banks are turning to technological innovations such as **electronic funds transfer (EFT).** Electronic transfer of funds is the transfer of funds by means of an electronic terminal, telephone, computer, or magnetic tape that orders a financial institution to debit (subtract from) or credit (add to) an account. The most commonly used form of EFT systems are automated teller machines, automated clearinghouses, point-of-sale systems, and home banking systems. Financial Encounter 16-3 describes how EFT may turn America into a checkless society.

**Automated teller machines**

Stand-alone machines that dispense cash, accept deposits, transfer funds from one account to another, and display a customer's account balance

*Automated Teller Machines.* **Automated teller machines (ATMs)** are stand-alone machines that dispense cash, accept deposits, transfer funds from one account to another, and display a customer's account balance. ATMs provide 24-hour service, and ATM users traveling away from home can have access to banking services through ATM networks. To use an ATM, a customer inserts a plastic card (similar to a credit card) that is encoded with the customer's account number. The user types in his or her Personal Identification Number (PIN). The card cannot be used without the PIN code, which only the user knows. The PIN code protects the owner from unauthorized use in the event the card is lost or stolen.

# Financial Encounter 16-3
## *Electronic Funds Transfer*

Electronic funds transfer (EFT) is changing the way Americans pay their bills. Many already use automated teller machines (ATMs) to deposit and withdraw money from bank accounts, but point-of-sale (POS) transactions and home banking are increasing in popularity as well.

Many people believe EFT will eventually lead to a checkless society. In such a society, companies and consumers would pay their bills with a push of a button, not with a check. An increasing number of firms and banks, including General Motors, Sears, Citicorp, the U.S. Treasury, and various supermarket chains, now use EFT to save money and speed up transactions. Some experts feel that by the year 2000, people will make more payments by EFT than by any other method.

Banks have spent more than $100 million to develop computerized home banking. Nevertheless, only about ninety thousand customers are using it. Several factors have contributed to this slow start-up. Home banking usually costs customers $5 to $15 more than a regular checking account does. In addition, merchants and others who receive payments by EFT must have prior authorization to receive funds. Moreover, relatively few homes have a personal computer, and EFT is difficult without one.

People are sometimes reluctant to use EFT. Many businesses and consumers do not want to stop writing checks because inefficiencies in the check-clearing process make it possible to take advantage of the time it takes to process a check. For example, a person can write a check today, even though he or she has no money in the bank, and wait a day or two before depositing money to cover the check. EFT eliminates the float, or lag between the time a person writes a check and the time the payee receives the money for the check. In addition, EFT would eliminate the time credit-card users can wait (often six weeks) before they have to pay for a purchase.

EFT benefits merchants because it ensures that the merchant receives payment when a customer makes a purchase. EFT also allows merchants faster access to the money they receive from purchases, and they can begin to earn interest on this money immediately. EFT saves a merchant the trouble and expense of bundling up checks and credit-card slips at the end of the day and mailing them to the bank.

Although the use of EFT by both businesses and banks is increasing, it is uncertain whether EFT will become as widespread as some analysts are predicting. Increased consumer resistance to EFT may delay the arrival of the checkless society.

These facts are from Eric Gelman, with Doug Tsuruoka, Patricia King, and Christopher Ma, "How America Pays the Tab," *Newsweek*, January, 1985, pp. 40–41; Robert Guenther, "U.S. Treasury Pays Suppliers Electronically," *The Wall Street Journal*, August 24, 1987, p. 15; Michael Totty, "Small Businesses Find Electronic Banking Can Be a Useful Tool in Managing Money," *The Wall Street Journal*, July 22, 1986, p. 11; and John Schoen, "Most Individuals Still Like Their Checkbooks," *The Wall Street Journal*, July 22, 1986, p. 11.

---

Banks introduced ATMs to reduce the cost of teller services. It is estimated that each transaction initiated by a teller costs 52 cents and each ATM transaction costs 21 cents. The rapid growth of ATMs throughout the country has contributed to the reduction of transaction costs. ATMs are everywhere now: shopping malls, student unions, banks, airports, and other public places. Customers can even purchase airline tickets from some ATMs. In 1982, there were an estimated thirty-six thousand ATMs nationwide; by the end of 1986 this figure had increased to sixty-seven thousand.[6]

To make better use of ATMs, some banks have formed ATM networks that allow customers of network banks access to ATMs in any state where a network bank is located. In 1985, New York–based Citicorp announced that it had become a member of an ATM network. This move allowed Citicorp to bypass interstate banking laws and gain access to sixty-five hundred ATMs in 42 states.

**Automated clearinghouses**

Permit payments to be made to and from a bank account by magnetic computer tape

***Automated Clearinghouses.*** **Automated clearinghouses (ACHs)** permit payments such as direct deposits or withdrawals to be made to and from a bank account by magnetic computer tape. Employers can use ACHs to make payroll withdrawals from their bank and transfer money directly to each employee's individual account. Large corporations also use ACHs for dividend and interest payments, and utilities such as telephone companies use ACHs to collect consumers' bills. The federal government is the largest user of automated clearinghouses; over 50 percent of all Social Security payments are made through this system. The high cost of ACH systems limits their use to large-batch processing.

**Point-of-sale systems**

Allow merchants to withdraw money directly from a customer's bank account the moment a purchase is made

***Point-of-Sale Systems.*** **Point-of-sale systems (POS)** allow merchants to withdraw money directly from a customer's bank account the moment a purchase is made. A retailer or grocery store may have a terminal located at the register that allows the cashier to debit a customer's account. Both the store and the customer must belong to the same bank or bank network, and the customer must have a debit card, which requires sufficient cash reserve to cover the cost of purchase. A debit card makes transactions much faster than the traditional check or credit card. Once the card number is entered into the terminal, the sale is complete if sufficient funds are available in the account. Point-of-sale systems reduce check-processing costs and the problems of bad checks. They also increase security because less cash is on hand in the store.

***Home Banking.*** The bank of tomorrow may be in the home. Some major banks are developing home banking systems that will be used in the 30 million households expected to have a personal computer by 1990. In 1983, New York's Chemical Bank initiated the first system, called Pronto. Wells Fargo Bank N.A. of San Francisco is developing a home banking system called Quicken. CBS, IBM, and Sears joined together in 1988 to form a system called Trintex that will offer a whole package of financial services and may include at-home shopping.

The financial system as you know it today will continue to undergo changes. Advances in technology, changing life styles, and consumers' increasing willingness to accept new technology will make personal financial management more timely and responsive to society's need. At the same time, alternative financial services will abound and perhaps confuse some consumers.

# Notes

**1.** Mark Goodman, "Designing the Dollar," *Money* (November 1986): 112–18.

**2.** Jeffrey Kutler, "MasterCard, Visa Hit American Express Co. with Both Barrels," *American Banker*, September 24, 1987, pp. 14, 15.

**3.** Michael Weinstein, "Sears Is 15th Biggest Credit Card Lender; Bankers

Say Discover Grew at Expense of Store Charge," *American Banker,* September 21, 1987, p. 2.

**4.** "Business Bulletin: A Special Background Report on Trends in Industry and Finance," *The Wall Street Journal,* April 7, 1988, p. 1.

**5.** William Dunn, "Baby, the Boom Is Aging," *USA Today,* April 6, 1988. p. 1A.

**6.** Jeffrey Kutler, "US Has Largest Number of ATMs, but Lead Is Slipping; Japan Closes In with Most Machines per Person," *American Banker,* August 18, 1987, p. 24.

# Summary and Review

▶ Money is anything generally accepted as a means of paying for goods and services. Money serves as a medium of exchange, making it easy for people to buy and sell goods and services. Money serves as a measure of the value of goods and services, and it serves as a store of the value of one's wealth. Money must be acceptable, divisible, portable, durable, stable in value, and difficult to counterfeit.

▶ Commercial banks are financial institutions that hold deposits in accounts for businesses and individuals and make loans to individuals and businesses. Savings and loan associations hold deposits (primarily time deposits) for individuals and businesses and make home mortgages. Credit unions are financial institutions owned and controlled by their depositors. Mutual savings banks are similar to savings and loan associations except they are owned by their depositors. These institutions are important because they provide a place to store money, and they help arrange short- and long-term financing for businesses and individuals.

▶ Insurance companies make long-term loans and mortgages and purchase government bonds with money they obtain from insurance premiums. Pension funds are pools of money set aside by organizations or individuals to meet retirement needs. Mutual funds pool investors' money and invest it in securities. Money market funds are mutual funds that invest in the money market. Brokerage firms buy and sell stocks and bonds for investors. Financial networks offer a wide variety of financial services. Consumer and commercial finance companies make short-term loans at higher interest rates than do banks.

▶ The Federal Reserve System regulates the American banking system. It manipulates the money supply by buying and selling government securities, by raising or lowering the discount rate, by raising or lowering bank reserve requirements, and by adjusting down-payment and repayment terms for credit purchases. The Fed also processes checks and oversees federal depository insurance for banking institutions.

▶ In the next few years, banks and other financial institutions will be able to operate across state lines for the first time. Technological innovations such as automated teller machines, automated clearinghouses, point-of-sale systems, and home banking will change the way businesses and individuals conduct their financial affairs.

# Key Terms and Concepts

fiat money
demand deposits
share draft account
$M_1$
time deposits
money market accounts
$M_2$
revolving accounts
mortgages
credit union
Federal Deposit Insurance
    Corporation (FDIC)
Federal Savings and Loan Insurance
    Corporation (FSLIC)

National Credit Union Association
    (NCUA)
deregulation
individual retirement accounts (IRAs)
mutual fund
financial networks
Federal Reserve System
open market operations
reserve requirement
discount rate
electronic funds transfer (EFT)
automated teller machines (ATMs)
automated clearinghouses (ACHs)
point-of-sale systems (POS)

# Checking Your Understanding

This chapter introduced you to the subject of money and banking. To test and reinforce your understanding, fill in the blanks below.

**1.** _____ can be anything generally acceptable as a means of paying for goods and services.

**2.** A _____ _____ is a financial institution owned and controlled by its depositors.

**3.** Money serves as a _____ _____ _____, maintaining the value of one's wealth.

**4.** _____ _____ are a line of credit that can be used to make purchases but must be paid back according to stated terms.

**5.** A _____ _____ _____ allows individuals to participate in the market for short-term securities at market interest rates.

**6.** The _____ _____ is the rate of interest the Fed charges when it lends money to commercial banks for their reserve requirements.

**7.** A _____ _____ is a financial institution that holds deposits for individuals and businesses and makes loans with those funds.

**8.** A _____ _____ offers short-term loans at high rates of interest to high-risk customers.

**9.** An _____ _____ _____ is a free-standing machine that dispenses cash, accepts deposits, and transfers money from one account to another.

**10.** _____ _____ pool investors' money to buy stocks, bonds, and other types of securities.

# Topics for Review and Discussion

1. Differentiate between money and near money. Give examples of each.
2. What are the six characteristics of money? Explain how the American dollar has those six characteristics.
3. Explain how the Federal Reserve uses open market operations to expand the money supply.
4. What are the basic differences between commercial banks and savings and loans?
5. Look at Table 16-1 and discuss how you might behave as a consumer or saver in the various countries. At what rate of inflation would you become more likely to spend than to save?
6. What are some of the advantages of electronic funds transfer systems?
7. Discuss the four economic goals the Federal Reserve must try to achieve with its monetary policy.
8. Why do finance companies charge higher interest rates than commercial banks?
9. Why do credit unions charge lower rates than commercial banks?
10. What is the difference between a credit card and a debit card?

# Exercises

1. Discuss the impact of deregulation on banking today. What changes have taken place since 1980?
2. Pick a country from Table 16-1. Update the consumer price index for the last several years, and compute the rate of inflation from 1986 to now.
3. Survey the banks, savings and loans, and credit unions in your area, and put together a list of interest rates paid on the various types of checking accounts. Find out what, if any, restrictions are in effect for NOW accounts, Super NOW accounts, and regular checking accounts. In which type of account in what institution would you deposit your money? Why?

## Case 16-1
### *Private Insurance: Homestate Savings Bank*

On March 15, 1985, the governor of Ohio closed all seventy-one state-insured thrift institutions. The problems in the Ohio savings and loan industry had begun with the failure of Homestate Savings Bank of Cincinnati. After it was revealed that the thrift could lose as much as $150 million from the collapse of ISM Government Securities Corporation, depositors began to panic and staged an old-fashioned run on the bank. Within one week, $90 million of deposits was withdrawn from Homestate Savings. This forced the thrift to close its doors in order to freeze ninety-two thousand depositors' accounts.

The deposits at Homestate, as well as at the other seventy savings and loans in Ohio, were insured for $100,000 by the Ohio Deposit Guarantee Fund, a private organization with funds totaling $136 million. When depositors learned that Homestate's losses were more than the funds available from the Ohio Deposit Guarantee Fund, they panicked. They also realized that the insurance was not provided by the state of Ohio but by private insurance, and this simply caused a greater loss of confidence in the safety of their money. Heavy withdrawals from the seventy other thrifts insured by the Ohio Deposit Guarantee Fund prompted Ohio bank officials to urge residents to remain calm. But depositors continued to line up to withdraw their money. This forced the governor to take the drastic action of ordering the savings and loans closed until they had applied for federal deposit insurance.

Even though the private insurance offered the same protection as the FDIC or FSLIC, the private insurer did not have the ability to call on the U.S. Treasury for new funds. Federal deposit insurance companies provide peace of mind to depositors that private insurance does not. It seems that federal insurance is enough to prevent most irratonal panics like the run on Homestate Savings.

---

These facts are from "Ohio Urges Depositors to Remain Calm in the Wake of Withdrawals from Thrifts," *The Wall Street Journal*, March 15, 1985; "Closing of Ohio S&Ls After Run on Deposits Is One for the Books," *The Wall Street Journal,* March 18, 1985, p. 1; Martha Brannigan, "Cincinnati Thrift Is Closed After Run on Deposits Due to ESM Unit Collapse," *The Wall Street Journal*, March 11, 1985, p. 3; G. David Wallace, Zachary Schiller, Kathleen Deveny, Dan Cook, and Blanca Riemer, "Tremors from Ohio's Bank Run," *Business Week*, April 1, 1985, pp. 28, 29; Joel Dreyfuss and Philip Mattera, "Ohio Sting," *Fortune*, April 15, 1985, p. 8.

**Questions**

1. Why do you think depositors prefer government insurance over private insurance? FSLIC FDIC
2. What is a run on the bank and why do events like this happen? Fed Res System
3. Explain the possible benefits when the governor of Ohio closed the Ohio savings and loan associations.

## Case 16-2
### *Banking at K mart*

K mart Corp. wants to take the title of number-one retailer away from Sears, Roebuck and Co. To reach this goal, K mart is offering financial services in its stores to increase profits and convenience for K mart customers.

In 1984, First Nationwide Bank (a subsidiary of Ford Motor Company) opened the first branch bank in a K mart store. More than four hundred K mart stores now have bank branches. The K mart banks offer traditional banking services, including checking and savings accounts, home loans, certificates of deposit, IRAs, Visa credit cards, and automated teller machines. Some of the branches make consumer loans and help customers with mortgages. First Nationwide is not the only bank to operate branches in K mart stores. Some banks and S&Ls operate K mart branches, offering real-estate and insurance services in addition to traditional banking functions. Each of the minibanks occupies about 136 square feet of K mart space and is usually open six days a week with some evening hours.

K mart leases space for the minibanks to First Nationwide and other financial institutions, earning immediate rental income as well as a percentage of the bank's profits. And, because a K mart branch costs much less to build and operate than a free-standing bank, the bank can pass the savings along to K mart customers in the form of higher interest rates on money market funds and IRAs. K mart may one day want to take over these financial services operations, but for now it feels that leasing is the best way to learn the banking business without investing a lot of money.

K mart officials want to be sure that its branch banks treat customers fairly while operating under the K mart name. For its part, First Nationwide and other banks want to expand into investments and discount brokerage services while expanding their mortgage and consumer lending activities.

K mart believes that banking activities provide valuable services to its customers, in addition to being profitable. The company stresses, however, that financial services will never be one of its main businesses. K mart simply wants the convenience of banking at the store to stimulate retail sales.

Some industry analysts believe that K mart's venture into convenience banking is a natural expansion for the company because retailers are beginning to recognize that they can offer more than just goods once they have gained consumers' confidence. Others believe that K mart's offering of financial services will reduce Sears' market share because Sears and K mart share a lot of customers. Most Sears stores already offer financial services, including real-estate, investment, and insurance services. There is a hole in the traditional banking market because many Sears and K mart customers are uncomfortable doing business with traditional commercial banks.

Although K mart began offering banking services to increase retail sales and increase customer convenience, some K mart bankers believe that they can challenge Sears' financial services in the future. Only time will tell if K mart can be competitive with Sears in the financial services market.

---

These facts are from Martha T. Moore, "K mart Woos Customers with Bank," *USA Today*, October 2, 1987, pp. 1B, 2B; Joe Agnew, "K mart Celebrates 25 Years with Revitalization of Marketing Strategy and Severing Its Kresge Roots," *Marketing News*, April 24, 1987, pp. 1, 6; and Lebhar-Friedman, Inc., *Inside Retailing*, 12 (July 1987): 1.

**Questions**

1. Why does K mart want to go into the banking business? What are the advantages to K mart?
2. What advantages are there for First Nationwide Bank to be housed in K mart stores? Discuss some reasons for Ford Motor Company buying a bank like First Nationwide and pursuing the strategy of locating in K mart stores?
3. How do you think K mart customers will respond to banking services in a K mart store instead of doing business with a traditional stand-alone bank?

# Answers to Checking Your Understanding

1. money
2. credit union
3. store of value
4. credit cards
5. money market fund

6. discount rate
7. commercial bank
8. finance company
9. automated teller machine
10. mutual funds

## Outline

Financial Statements
(1) Balance Sheet
(2) Income Sheet

# Chapter 17

# Accounting and Financial Statements

## Objectives

After reading this chapter, you will be able to:

▶ Describe general accounting practices, and explain the difference between public and private accounting.

▶ Understand the various components of an income statement, and explain how an income statement measures a firm's profitability.

▶ Describe the standard form of a company's balance sheet, and explain how assets, liabilities, and owners' equity are presented on this financial statement.

▶ Analyze financial statements to ascertain a company's performance.

▶ Read and understand corporate annual reports.

Accounts

Assets = things of value used by businesses in their normal opperation

Liabilities = creditor's claims

(1)

Equity = owner's claim

Revenue

(2)

Expense

# Business Experience

Harsco Corporation's businesses range from industrial services and building products to engineered products and U.S. and foreign government defense contracts. The internal audit team at Harsco is renowned for their outstanding quality and reliability. In the words of Mr. Fazzolari, Harsco's corporate director of auditing, "We're maniacs about excellence. We like to give our customers, corporate management divisions, and our external auditors, the best service and quality of work that you possibly can give someone." Auditing of the company's books is required to make sure that the financial data the company reports are true facts. The auditor's job is to check the financial statements to make sure that no mistakes have been made and that fact equals reality and not fiction.

Mr. Fazzolari's objectives have been realized. His team has earned the respect of his corporation, and of the accounting firm that performs Harsco's external audit. Harsco's computerized audit system not only maximizes the effectiveness of the internal auditing but also makes the job of the external auditor easier. Mr. Fazzolari's success can be attributed to his philosophy and his extensive use of computers. Mr. Fazzolari believes that the internal auditing team should perform both financial and management audits. A financial audit involves reviewing the company's financial statements and providing an opinion and a report; whereas a management audit involves an assessment of the company's performance, an evaluation of opportunities, and the formulation of suggestions. Harsco's internal auditors have successfully combined these two tasks. The ten-member staff uses microcomputers and various software packages when performing audits. Today a firm that does not use computers is at a major disadvantage.

Harsco's internal auditors use standard software such as: word processing, Lotus 1-2-3®, and applications written specifically for the company. These applications include analytical programs, risk analysis, audit schedules, and random number generators. Today computers are used for auditing by large companies such as Harsco and also by small- and medium-sized firms.

In order to perform a complete computer audit it is helpful to have an electronic data processing (EDP) auditor on staff. Harsco's ten-member internal auditing team includes an EDP auditor who is knowledgeable in both auditing and computers. The auditor makes sure the data processing goals coincide with corporate goals, and that internal controls are adequate and being followed. Since EDP auditing is a relatively new profession, there is a need for EDP auditors.

---

These facts are from Salvatore D. Fazzolari, "How Harsco Integrates Financial & Operational Auditing," *Management Accounting*, January 1988, pp. 28–30; Kathy Williams, "Maniacs About Excellence," *Management Accounting*, January 1988, pp. 30–31; Mary M. Lee, "The Challenge of EDP Auditing," *Management Accounting*, March 1988, pp. 52–53; Robert B. Nadel, "Computer Auditing Has Its Time Come," *CPA Journal*, March 1987, pp. 24–29.

# Introduction

### Accounting
The language business uses to record, measure, and interpret financial transactions

**Accounting** is the language business uses to record, measure, and interpret financial transactions ranging from buying new equipment to borrowing money, from paying wages to selling an old building. Accountants carry out the accounting function. All business organizations, no matter how large or small, use the financial information compiled by accountants to make sure the organization is using money efficiently and to make plans for increasing profits. Accounting information is also necessary for groups outside the organization, such as government, creditors, suppliers, employees, and owners.

# ▶ Accountants

An accountant must develop an accounting system that summarizes all transactions into comprehensive financial statements. Accountants are employed either directly or indirectly by a business and are classified as public or private accountants. Figure 17-1 shows who uses accounting information.

### Public accountant
An independent professional who provides accounting services to individuals and businesses for a fee

## Public Accountants

A **public accountant** is an independent professional who provides accounting services to individuals as well as businesses of all sizes for a fee. Most

**Managers are the main users of accounting information.** The information gathered can be related to specific products, stores, sales territories, departments, or even by individual salespersons. Public accountants from Ernst and Whinney visit their client, Sawgrass Pro Shop, and review the revenues with its general manager.

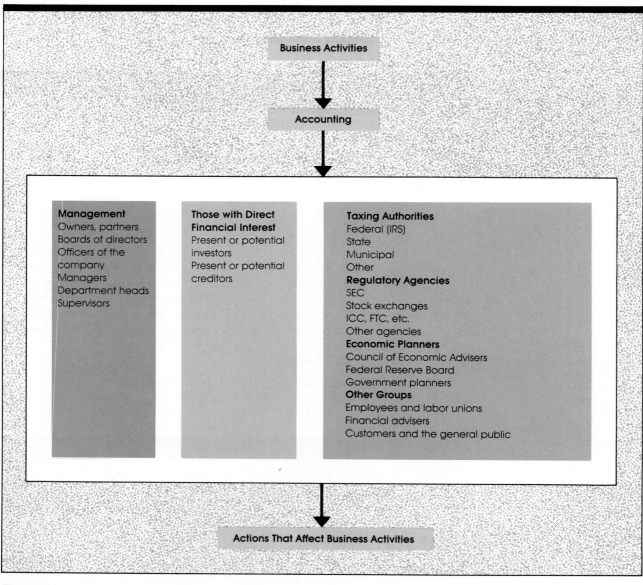

```
                    ┌─────────────────────┐
                    │  Business Activities │
                    └─────────────────────┘
                               │
                               ▼
                    ┌─────────────────────┐
                    │     Accounting      │
                    └─────────────────────┘
                               │
                               ▼
```

**Management**
Owners, partners
Boards of directors
Officers of the
company
Managers
Department heads
Supervisors

**Those with Direct**
**Financial Interest**
Present or potential
investors
Present or potential
creditors

**Taxing Authorities**
Federal (IRS)
State
Municipal
Other
**Regulatory Agencies**
SEC
Stock exchanges
ICC, FTC, etc.
Other agencies
**Economic Planners**
Council of Economic Advisers
Federal Reserve Board
Government planners
**Other Groups**
Employees and labor unions
Financial advisers
Customers and the general public

**Actions That Affect Business Activities**

**Figure 17-1**

The Users of Accounting Information

Source: Needles/Anderson/ Caldwell, *Principles of Accounting,* 2nd ed., © 1984, Houghton Mifflin Co., Boston, p. 484.

public accountants are self-employed or members of large public accounting firms. The services they provide range from the filing of an individual's tax return to a complex audit of a corporation's financial records.

A **certified public accountant (CPA)** is a public accountant who has been certified in the state in which he or she resides. According to *The Encyclopedia of Associations*, there were 242,000 CPAs as of 1987. In order to become a CPA, an accountant must meet certain educational and professional requirements established by the state. The educational requirements include passing a three-part, 2½-day exam covering the full realm of accounting. A certified

| Firm | Annual Revenue (in Billions of Dollars) | |
| --- | --- | --- |
| | Worldwide | U.S. only |
| Peat Marwick | 2.5 | 1.35 |
| Arthur Anderson & Co. | 1.9 | 1.35 |
| Coopers & Lybrand | 1.7 | 0.86 |
| Ernst & Whinney | 1.5 | 0.9 |
| Price Waterhouse | 1.5 | 0.74 |
| Arthur Young & Co. | 1.4 | 0.61 |
| Deloitte, Haskins & Sells | 1.2 | 0.6 |
| Touche Ross & Co. | 1.2 | 0.57 |

**Certified public accountant (CPA)**

A public accountant who has been certified in the state in which he or she resides

public accountant gains the privilege of being able to officially express an unbiased opinion about the accuracy of financial statements reflecting the financial position of a firm. Although a public accountant is not required to become certified, many do so because being a CPA carries a high level of prestige within the accounting profession. The largest public accounting firms are referred to as "the Big Eight." Table 17-1 lists the eight largest public accounting firms. Financial Encounter 17-1 gives tips on how to market a CPA.

## Private Accountants

**Private accountant**

A person who is employed by corporations, government agencies, and other organizations operating on a profit or nonprofit basis

A **private accountant** is employed by corporations, government agencies, and other organizations operating on a profit or nonprofit basis. A private accountant has various titles within a firm—controller, tax accountant, internal auditor. Private accountants prepare and interpret financial statements and in many cases take part in the decision-making process of the firm or organization for which they work. Because private accountants are employed by the organization whose statements they prepare and interpret, their opinions on the financial condition of a firm are usually biased.

**Certified management accountant (CMA)**

Certified private accountants who have some degree of managerial responsibility

A private accountant can become a **certified management accountant (CMA).** The certification is similar to that of the CPA in that a rigorous, multisection exam, developed by the National Association of Accountants, must be passed. The CMA standard was established in 1972 to certify accountants, typically private accountants, who have some degree of managerial responsibility. At the end of 1987, there were 95,000 CMAs.

## ▶ The Use of Accounting Statements

Accounting statements present various types of information. The income statement lists all revenues and expenses of the firm; its primary purpose is to show whether the firm made a profit. The familiar question "What's the

# Financial Encounter 17-1
## *Marketing a CPA Firm*

Prior to 1978, Certified Public Accountants were prohibited from advertising and soliciting. Many CPAs don't know how to advertise their services effectively. Stigge & Stigge, an accounting firm located in Gilroy, California, recently tried to market its services.

Ms. Sherryll L. Stigge, shareholder of Stigge & Stigge, had mixed results from her marketing campaign, but she did learn a few lessons. She placed ads in newspapers, the Yellow Pages, and brochures. She also spoke at engagements, attended community affairs, and hired a consultant. Ms. Stigge first tried advertising at a community festival. Although she had a good time she didn't get any clients, and the cost was $200. Next Ms. Stigge put a $1,000 ad in a local newspaper and produced one client. When Ms. Stigge tried to get a brochure printed, the printer left with the money and Ms. Stigge never got her brochure. Ms. Stigge hired a marketing consultant who conducted a mailing to 1,000 companies; the cost was $2,200 and zero customers responded. Ms. Stigge did have some successful campaigns. An ad in the Yellow Pages cost $720 and accounted for 20% of new customers. Speaking engagements also proved to be an effective way to attract new customers. Ms. Stigge's efforts eventually paid off. Gross billings increased twenty percent each year over the previous year and total billing hours increased from 200 to 6300 hours. The firm now has 300 clients and a staff of four full-time and three part-time professionals. A survey of new clients showed that fifty percent came from personal contact, twenty percent from the yellow pages, ten percent from competitive bids, ten percent from attorney or bank referrals, and ten percent from miscellaneous. Currently the advertising budget is two percent of gross revenue.

Mr. Norman S. Rachlin, CPA, is the founding managing partner of Rachlin & Cohen. He believes that advertising is necessary for a CPA to be successful today. He feels that CPAs should concentrate on retaining good clients, expanding services to existing clients, and then acquiring new clients. Mr. Rachlin believes that a firm could increase its services by fifty percent without adding a new client, simply by expanding service to existing clients. When marketing a CPA firm, Mr. Rachlin suggests stressing the features that make the firm unique. Some of the marketing techniques he cited are: newsletters, brochures, mailing to clients, seminars, financial planning meetings, and a general ledger of referrals. Mr. Rachlin believes marketing is essential for the accounting firm today, and each firm needs to explore various methods to determine which combination is right for it.

Ms. Stigge and Mr. Rachlin mentioned similar methods for marketing a CPA firm. It seems that a marketing strategy depends on the individual firm. Mr. Herbert M. Kaplan offers ten suggestions that all firms can follow to make their marketing more effective. The suggestions are: be market focused, assess your position, establish goals, make your firm stand out, focus your efforts, anticipate market reaction, write it down, monitor and evaluate, make a commitment, and get clients' support. A firm can follow these general guidelines and greatly enhance its marketing efforts.

These facts are from Herbert M. Kaplan, "Specific Strategies To Make Marketing Plans More Effective," *Practical Accountant*, September 1987, pp. 51–59; Norman S. Rachlin, "Marketing For The Local Accounting Firm: Avenues To Pursue," *Practical Accountant*, October 1986, pp. 81–84; Sherryll L. Stigge, "Developing A Marketing Program Without Really Knowing What You Are Doing: One Firm's Experience," *Practical Accountant*, March 1987, pp. 51–54.

**Private, public, or other.**
Accountants provide expertise in the methods and systems of accounting. This rancher knows accounting principles and acts as his own accountant.

bottom line?" comes from the income statement, whose bottom line shows the profit or loss of the company after taxes. The balance sheet, which lists all the assets a company owns from land, buildings, equipment, desks, and material in stock for production of goods, is another important financial statement. It lists all the liabilities—debts that the company owes lenders—and all the equity—the contribution of the owners. The balance sheet, like a snapshot, shows assets, liabilities, and owners' equity at one point in time.

The importance of the income statement and balance sheet should be recognized by the top management of all businesses. The failure of a business can often be linked to owners and managers who ignore the information provided in accounting statements and focus exclusively on the bottom line and making a profit. Although making a profit is what most businesses strive for, failure to use accounting statements to plan the course of an enterprise can lead to bankruptcy. Managers and owners can use accounting statements for internal planning and control and for external purposes such as reporting to the Internal Revenue Service, to stockholders, to creditors, to customers, and to employees. Furthermore, analysis of the firm's current and past financial statements can provide helpful information to both external and internal users of accounting data. Figure 17-2 is an overview of an accounting system.

# Internal Uses

**Managerial accounting** is the use of accounting statements within a business organization. Managerial accounting emphasizes the use of accounting data internally by managers for planning and directing the course of the organization. One of management's greatest concerns should be the flow of cash into the firm. **Cash flow** is a measure of the amount of cash generated by a firm as it operates its business. Cash flow is usually tracked through the use of a cash budget, which forecasts the cash needs of the firm on a weekly or monthly basis. A business can have a highly successful product, with sales doubling or even tripling over the course of a year, yet still be struggling to make payments to suppliers and lenders on a timely basis because of an inadequate cash flow.

Businesses want more cash coming in to the business than is needed to cover the incoming bills that must be paid. A common reason for a so-called cash crunch or cash shortfall is poor planning or a lack of planning.

Managers or owners combine the information provided in accounting statements with ratio analysis, which uses several ratios to measure the financial health of the firm and to anticipate and ward off cash shortfalls before they happen. For example, a manager may find that his or her company is not collecting bills in an efficient manner. The manager may find that although sales have doubled over the year, costs and expenses have tripled. The increase in expenses has reduced the profitability of every dollar of sales. Once the problem has been located, management can use internal accounting to formulate a plan to control expenses or speed up collections.

Managerial accounting is the backbone of forecasting a budget for the coming year. A **budget** is an internal financial statement that forecasts expenditures and revenues for a week, month, quarter, or year. Budgets can present the company as a whole, a division of the company, a department, or some other segment of the organization. Budgets can focus on sales and expenditures or on specific projects such as a new plant or the purchase of new equipment. Regardless of the budget's focus, the major value of a budget is in its analysis of cash inflows to and outflows from the company. A budget forecasts expected monthly sales revenues, which are cash inflows, and forecasts cash outflows, such as operating expenses, and other cash expenses like taxes and dividends. Budgets are expressed in dollar terms and are used by management to assist in reaching goals and controlling expenses. Once complete, the budget forecast can be used as a standard for comparing the actual results achieved by a company with the expected or predicted results.

IBM, like many large companies, starts its budget process in individual departments. Each department submits a budget, and the total of all the department budgets (sub-budgets) comprise the budget for the firm, which is called the **master budget.** The research and development, production,

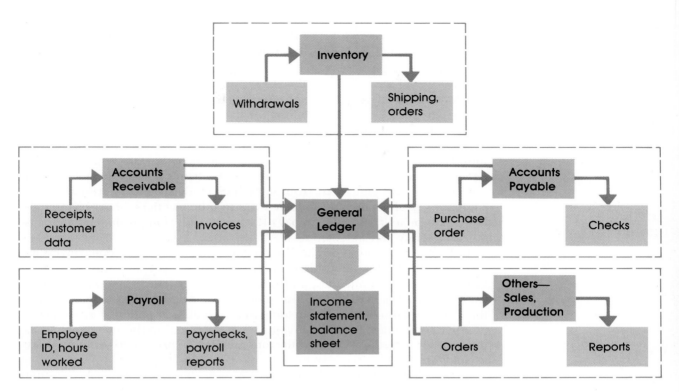

**Figure 17-2**

Overview of an Accounting System. All transactions are posted to the general ledger; from this the income statement and balance sheet are prepared.

Source: Anderson/Sullivan; *World of Computing*, © 1988. Houghton Mifflin Co., Boston, p. 484

sales, advertising, and personnel departments all submit sub-budgets to top management. These departmental budgets are added to other corporate budgets to form the company's master budget. The process of creating the master budget can start at the top with a proposed master budget and filter down to lower levels of the company, or the process can start at the department level and build up to the combined corporate master budget.

## External Uses

Managers and owners use accounting statements to report the financial performance of a business to outside organizations. Income statements and balance sheets are the official records of a company. They are used for filing income taxes, obtaining credit from lenders, and reporting results to stockholders in annual reports. The federal government is interested in the financial statements of the company because the company must pay taxes on its income or profit. Certified public accountants provide the independent opinion that the required financial statements are accurate. The Big Eight accounting firms' audit clients account for over $3.3 trillion in sales.

Corporations in the United States usually keep two sets of books (financial statements), one for the Internal Revenue Service and one for stockholders. There is nothing illegal or unethical about this: Companies generally try to minimize the firm's taxable income by using aggressive accounting conventions. Although it might lower taxes, aggressive accounting conventions also lower a company's reported profits. Stockholders do not always understand that minimizing profits can be in their best interests as long as the firm's total cash flow increases. The cash flow can be increased by minimizing the firm's cash outlay for income taxes. Minimizing profits allows the firm to keep a larger percentage of its cash inflow for investment in new assets, which will benefit the shareholders in future years.

A bank or some other lender is concerned with the ability of a company to meet current and future interest payments if a loan is granted. To determine this ability, a lender examines the firm's ability to repay a loan quickly with cash generated from sales. The lender is also interested in the company's profitability and indebtedness to other lenders. Short-term creditors focus on a firm's ability to pay off loans quickly; long-term lenders focus on profitability and indebtedness.

Individuals or institutions may be potential investors. Institutional investors include college and university endowment funds, pension funds, mutual funds, insurance companies, and other groups. Potential investors want to study a firm's financial statements to determine whether the company meets their investment objectives and compares favorably to potential investments in other companies. Potential investors are interested in the same analysis as the long-term creditor but view the amount of debt relative to owners' equity as a measure of the firm's stability.

Financial Encounter 17-2 explains the role of the Financial Accounting Standards Board.

# ▶ The Income Statement

**Income statement**

Measures the profitability of a firm usually over one year

The **income statement** measures the profitability of a firm over a period of time—a month, a quarter, a year. An example of a typical income statement is presented in Figure 17-3. It covers one year. An income statement has three major categories: revenue, expenses, and net income.

To feel comfortable with financial statements, you must learn some definitions and equivalent terms. For example, *sales* and *revenues* are often interchanged, as are *profit*, *income*, and *earnings*. Table 17-2 lists some commonly used equivalent terms. The terms used in Figure 17-3 are listed first in the table and are followed by widely used synonyms.

All income statements do not have the same format. Different public accounting firms use slightly different terminology in preparing the accounting statements. Different businesses generate income in different ways. Some, like General Motors, are industrial companies manufacturing products; others, like Chemlawn, are service companies; others, like Hertz, rent or lease assets; others are financial companies such as banks, savings and loans, and brokerage firms. Each uses its own accounting principles, which the accounting profession (CPAs) has agreed on. These are sometimes referred to as Generally Accepted Accounting Principles (GAAP).

**Figure 17-3**
Typical Income Statement

```
                        TYPICAL COMPANY
                         Income Statement
                 For The Year Ended December 31, 198X


    Revenues or Sales                               $1,000,000
      Less: Cost of Goods Sold                        -450,000
    Gross Profit                                    $  550,000
      Less: Selling & Administrative Expense          -150,000
            Depreciation                             -100,000
    Operating Income                                $  300,000
      Less: Interest Expense                           80,000
    Income Before Taxes                             $  220,000
      Less: Taxes                                    -100,000
    Net Income                                      $  120,000
      Less: Preferred Dividends                       -20,000
    Income to Common Stockholders                   $  100,000


    Earnings Per Share                                   $1.00
      (100,000 common shares outstanding)
```

Differences in financial statements also arise between statements prepared by accountants for stockholders' annual reports and statements created by financial analysts for investors or loan-credit analysis. Financial analysts often want more detail than that found in the basic income statements presented in the company's annual report, or they want to force the statements into a standard format used for all companies.

**Table 17-2   Equivalent Terms**

| Term | Equivalent Term |
|---|---|
| Revenues | Sales |
| Gross Profit | Gross Income<br>Gross Earnings |
| Operating Income | Operating Profit<br>Earnings Before Interest and Taxes (EBIT)<br>Income Before Interest and Taxes (IBIT) |
| Income Before Taxes (IBT) | Earnings Before Taxes (EBT)<br>Profit Before Taxes (PBT) |
| Net Income (NI) | Earnings After Taxes (EAT)<br>Profit After Taxes (PAT) |
| Income Available to Common Stockholders | Earnings Available to Common Stockholders |

**Figure 17-4**

Income Statement for 3M Company

| STATEMENT OF INCOME | | | 32 |
|---|---|---|---|
| (Amounts in millions, except per share data) | **1987** | 1986 | 1985 |
| **Net Sales** | **$9,429** | $8,602 | $7,846 |
| **Operating Expenses** | | | |
| Cost of goods sold | **5,513** | 5,074 | 4,746 |
| Selling, general and administrative expenses | **2,338** | 2,118 | 1,950 |
| Total | **7,851** | 7,192 | 6,696 |
| **Operating Income** | **1,578** | 1,410 | 1,150 |
| **Other Income and Expense** | | | |
| Interest expense | **95** | 106 | 104 |
| Investment and other income–net | **(82)** | (44) | (51) |
| Total | **13** | 62 | 53 |
| **Income Before Income Taxes** | **1,565** | 1,348 | 1,097 |
| **Provision For Income Taxes** | **647** | 569 | 433 |
| **Net Income** | **$ 918** | $ 779 | $ 664 |
| **Average Number of Shares Outstanding** | **228.6** | 229.3 | 229.9 |
| **Earnings Per Share** | **$ 4.02** | $ 3.40 | $ 2.89 |

Minnesota Mining and Manufacturing Company and Consolidated Subsidiaries for the Years Ended December 31, 1987, 1986 and 1985

The Notes to Financial Statements are an integral part of this statement.

Figures 17-4 and 17-5 present the income statements of two companies for comparison. 3M Company (Minnesota Mining and Manufacturing) is the maker of Scotch® Tape, Post-it™ Notes, 3M Copiers, and thousands of other products. Its income statement more closely follows the generalized income statement shown in Figure 17-3 than does the income statement of the second company, IBM, the world's largest computer company.

# Revenue

**Revenue** is the total amount of dollars generated from sales and related business activities. It may result from the sale of a product, the performance of a service, the rental of property, or any other professional and business activities engaged in for the purpose of generating income. IBM's income statement (Figure 17-5) shows four sources of income: sales from computer products; services from maintenance of computers, software programming; and rentals from other services. These four income categories, when added together, equal gross income (revenues) of $51 billion.

**Revenue**

The total amount of dollars generated from sales and related business activities

**Figure 17-5**
Income Statement for IBM

**Consolidated Statement of Earnings**
for the year ended December 31:

International Business Machines Corporation
and Subsidiary Companies

| (Dollars in millions except per share amounts) | 1986 | | 1985 | | 1984 | |
|---|---|---|---|---|---|---|
| **Gross Income:** | | | | | | |
| Sales | $ 34,276 | | $ 34,404 | | $ 29,753 | |
| Maintenance services | 7,413 | | 6,103 | | 5,266 | |
| Program products | 5,514 | | 4,165 | | 3,197 | |
| Rentals and other services | 4,047 | | 5,384 | | 7,721 | |
| | | $ 51,250 | | $ 50,056 | | $ 45,937 |
| Cost of sales | 16,197 | | 14,911 | | 12,374 | |
| Cost of maintenance services | 3,032 | | 2,561 | | 2,289 | |
| Cost of program products | 1,519 | | 1,194 | | 1,166 | |
| Cost of rentals and other services | 1,958 | | 2,437 | | 3,090 | |
| Selling, general and administrative expenses | 15,464 | | 13,000 | | 11,587 | |
| Research, development and engineering expenses | 5,221 | | 4,723 | | 4,200 | |
| Interest expense | 475 | | 443 | | 408 | |
| | | 43,866 | | 39,269 | | 35,114 |
| | | 7,384 | | 10,787 | | 10,823 |
| Other income, principally interest | | 1,005 | | 832 | | 800 |
| Earnings before income taxes | | 8,389 | | 11,619 | | 11,623 |
| Provision for income taxes | | 3,600 | | 5,064 | | 5,041 |
| **Net Earnings** | | $ 4,789 | | $ 6,555 | | $ 6,582 |
| Per share | | $ 7.81 | | $ 10.67 | | $ 10.77 |

Average number of shares outstanding:
1986—612,838,531
1985—614,084,568
1984—611,426,324

The notes on pages 30 through 40 are an integral part of this statement.

# Expenses

**Expenses**
The costs that are incurred in the daily operation of a business

**Depreciation expense**
One year's charge against the original cost of fixed assets

**Expenses** are the costs incurred in the daily operation of a business. The number and type of expense accounts vary from business to business. In IBM's income statement (Figure 17-5), expenses are consolidated into seven accounts. Each income account has a matching expense account that includes all costs associated with generating revenues in each of IBM's business sectors. The cost of the sales account, for example, contains such expenses as the cost of manufacturing computers, the cost of keeping inventories of computers, and a depreciation expense. **Depreciation expense** is one year's charge against the cost of owning such things as plant and equipment. These assets have a limited number of years of useful life to a company before their value reaches zero and they have to be replaced. For example, when a new piece of equipment is purchased, the cost of the equipment is paid in cash. The depreciation expense is one year's charge against the original cost of the equipment. Although fixed assets have an estimated life, the IRS determines an artificial life over which the total cost of the asset can be expensed. The fact that the equipment equals a zero value on the balance sheet when it is

# Financial Encounter 17-2

## *The Role of the Financial Accounting Standards Board*

The Financial Accounting Standards Board (FASB) is a private organization responsible for establishing standards of financial accounting and reporting. Prior to the establishment of the FASB in 1973, the Accounting Principles Board (APB) had carried out this responsibility. The FASB is independent of all other business and professional organizations. Its official mission is to establish and improve standards of financial accounting and reporting for the guidance and education of the public, including issuers, auditors, and users of financial information.

The FASB has seven full-time members. Although not all members are CPAs, each member must have knowledge of accounting, finance, and business, as well as concern for the public interest in matters of financial accounting and reporting. Board members are appointed to five-year terms and are eligible to serve one additional five-year term. Each member has one vote. When making a decision, each member is expected to consider the views of other board members as well as the results of research and public comment on the issues. FASB members rely on staff to gather and organize information on which board decisions can be based.

To carry out its mission, the FASB does a variety of things. It develops broad accounting concepts as well as standards for financial reporting. It tries to improve the usefulness of financial reporting by stressing relevance, reliability, and consistency in accounting practices. It tries to correct deficiencies in financial reporting promptly. In addition, the board strives to improve the common understanding of, and confidence in, information contained in financial reports. For instance, in 1988 the FASB created a new rule requiring companies to list the stocks their employee pension plans own and how much those plans owe. This rule was designed to insure that investors know exactly how much a company's employee pension plan is worth.

The FASB follows certain guidelines in making its decisions. First, it strives to be objective and to report information in a neutral manner. Second, the board carefully considers the views of its constituents. Final decisions, however, arise from the FASB's own judgment. Third, the board revises standards only when the expected benefits exceed the perceived costs. The board follows the saying, "If it ain't broke, don't fix it," because changes in accounting practices are often resisted by those who use them regularly. Fourth, when the board makes changes it tries to minimize the disruption of current reporting practices by setting reasonable time frames for the changes. Finally, the board reviews the effects of past decisions and changes them as needed.

Standards are adopted by a majority vote of the FASB. Because the board often faces complex and diverse issues, close votes (4–3) are fairly common. In many cases, the board may be unanimous on fundamental issues yet divided on less-significant issues. Board members must frequently compromise to obtain a majority decision.

The FASB performs a useful service for the economy. By establishing accounting standards, the FASB makes it possible for businesspeople to base decisions on understandable financial information.

---

These facts are from Cynthia Crossen, "New Accounting Rule May Affect Pensions of Millions of People," *The Wall Street Journal,* January 18, 1988, pp. 1, 12; Sidney Davidson, "Some Significant Standards," *Journal of Accounting,* (May 1987): 135; "Facts About FASB," provided by the Financial Accounting Standards Board (1987), pp. 1, 2, 5; Robert Van Riper, "Due Process and the Decision-Making Process," *FASB Viewpoints,* a supplement to the newsletter of the Financial Accounting Standards Board, October 31, 1986, pp. 1–2.

---

fully depreciated, does not necessarily mean the asset can no longer be used or is worthless.

The three remaining expense accounts are selling, general and administrative expense; research, development, and engineering expense; and interest expense. The cost of selling includes advertising and the expense of the sales force. General and administrative expense includes the salaries of the executives and their staff and the cost of owning and maintaining office

**Darryl Strawberry.** Salaries are a major budget expense, especially if you are paying salaries to major league baseball players.

buildings. Expenses for research and development cover the cost of the people (engineers and scientists) who develop and test new products and the cost of the material used to build prototypes and samples. For example, General Motors has said it cost half a billion dollars to develop the new Quad-4 engine found in selected 1988 GM cars. Interest expense is the direct cost of borrowing money.

## Net Income

**Net income**

The profit left after all expenses have been deducted from revenue

**Net income** is the profit left after all expenses (including nonoperating expenses such as taxes) have been deducted from revenue. Before accountants arrive at the net income (earnings) figure on an income statement, they may divide profits into sections such as operating income and income before federal and state income taxes. IBM does not break out its income in this fashion, but 3M Company (Figures 17-4 and 17-5) does. Notice that both companies present not only the current year's results but also the previous two years' income statements. This allows a comparison of performance from one period to another.

Both companies report their earnings per share—that is, for each share of stock outstanding. IBM earned $7.81 per share or $4,789 billion in net earnings on 612,838,531 shares outstanding. 3M Company earned $4.02 per share or $918 million in net earnings on 112,000,000 shares outstanding. The per share data allows investors to compare one company with another just in terms of earnings. Earnings-per-share comparisons eliminate differences between the size of a company's earnings and the different amounts of common stock outstanding and put the comparison of earnings on a share versus share basis for competitive companies.

# ▶ The Balance Sheet

**Balance sheet**

A snapshot of a company's financial position at a given moment

The second basic accounting statement is the balance sheet. The **balance sheet** is a snapshot of a company's financial position at a given moment. It indicates what the firm owns and what proportion of the assets are financed with borrowed money or with owners' money. Figure 17-6 shows a balance sheet as of December 31, 198x. It does not try to represent the result of transactions for a specific month, quarter, or year. It is an accumulation of all transactions that have affected the company since its beginning. Generally, balance-sheet items are stated on an original-cost basis rather than at current values. Figure 17-6 presents a balance sheet with dollar figures. The reason this statement is called a balance sheet is that it must show a balance: Assets *must* equal liabilities plus owners' equity.

Balance sheets can be presented in two different formats. In one version, assets, liabilities, and ownership interest are presented in a vertical format, with assets at the top followed by liabilities and the owner's investment. In the second version, assets are presented on the left side and liabilities and owners' investment are on the right side. The vertical format (shown in Figure 17-6) is the one widely used in corporate annual reports.

Balance sheets for both 3M Company and IBM are presented in Figures 17-7 and 17-8, respectively.

## Assets

Asset accounts are listed in their order of liquidity—that is, how easily an asset can be converted into cash at its fair market value. Current assets are items that may be converted into cash within one year (or within the normal operating cycle of the firm). Cash, the first item, is followed by marketable securities, accounts receivable, and inventory. **Marketable securities** are temporary investments of excess cash (they are discussed in Chapter 18). The value shown in the account is the lower of cost or current market value. **Accounts receivable** is money owed the company and includes an allowance for bad debts—those accounts receivable which management does not expect to collect. The bad-debts account is usually based on historical evidence of collections and is deducted from accounts receivable to give a more realistic value of the asset account. Inventory may be in the form of raw material (steel or a natural resource like coal); it can also be goods in process, such as a partially completed automobile, or a finished product ready for delivery.

**Accumulated depreciation** is the sum of all past and current depreciation charges (expenses) on owned assets. (Accumulated depreciation is not to be confused with the depreciation expense listed on the income statement;

**Marketable securities**

Temporary investments of excess cash

**Accounts receivable**

Money owed the company by customers

**Accumulated depreciation**

The sum of all depreciation charges on currently owned assets

**Figure 17-6**
Typical Balance Sheet

TYPICAL COMPANY
Balance Sheet
December 31, 198X

ASSETS

Current Assets
| | | |
|---|---|---|
| Cash | | $  20,000 |
| Marketable Securities | | 50,000 |
| Accounts Receivable | | 100,000 |
| Inventory | | 180,000 |
| Prepaid Expense | | 30,000 |
| Total Current Assets | | $ 380,000 |

Fixed Assets
| | | |
|---|---|---|
| Investments | | 80,000 |
| Gross Property, Plant & Equipment | $600,000 | |
| Less: Accumulated Depreciation | −240,000 | |
| Net Property, Plant & Equipment | | 360,000 |
| Other Assets | | 60,000 |
| TOTAL ASSETS | | $ 880,000 |

LIABILITIES AND OWNERS' EQUITY

Current Liabilities
| | | |
|---|---|---|
| Accounts Payable | | $ 200,000 |
| Wages Payable | | 25,000 |
| Taxes Payable | | 30,000 |
| Notes Payable | | 30,000 |
| Other Current Liabilities | | 15,000 |
| Total Current Liabilities | | $ 300,000 |

Long–Term Liabilities & Equity
| | | |
|---|---|---|
| Long–Term Debt | | 80,000 |
| Deferred Income Taxes | | 100,000 |
| Other Liabilities | | 40,000 |

Owners' Equity
| | | |
|---|---|---|
| Capital Stock (100,000 shares @ $1.00 par value) | 100,000 | |
| Capital In Excess of Par | 50,000 | |
| Retained Earnings | 210,000 | |
| New Owners' Equity | | 360,000 |
| TOTAL LIABILITIES AND OWNERS' EQUITY | | $ 880,000 |

**Figure 17-7**

Balance Sheet for 3M Company

| BALANCE SHEET | | | 34 |
|---|---|---|---|
| (Dollars in millions) | | **1987** | 1986 |
| **ASSETS** | | | |
| **Current Assets** | | | |
| Cash and securities | | **$ 594** | $ 545 |
| Accounts receivable–net | | **1,615** | 1,442 |
| Inventories | | **1,770** | 1,654 |
| Other current assets | | **250** | 320 |
| Total current assets | | **4,229** | 3,961 |
| **Investments** | | **506** | 433 |
| **Property, Plant and Equipment–net** | | **2,931** | 2,754 |
| **Other Assets** | | **365** | 200 |
| Total | | **$8,031** | $7,348 |
| LIABILITIES AND STOCKHOLDERS' EQUITY | | | |
| **Current Liabilities** | | | |
| Accounts payable | | **$ 586** | $ 519 |
| Payrolls | | **284** | 271 |
| Income taxes | | **276** | 254 |
| Other current liabilities | | **521** | 368 |
| Short-term debt | | **264** | 411 |
| Total current liabilities | | **1,931** | 1,823 |
| **Deferred Income Taxes** | | **312** | 386 |
| **Other Liabilities** | | **293** | 240 |
| **Long-Term Debt** | | **435** | 436 |
| **Stockholders' Equity–net** | | **5,060** | 4,463 |
| Shares outstanding–1987: 227,492,769; 1986: 228,532,762 | | | |
| Total | | **$8,031** | $7,348 |

Minnesota Mining and Manufacturing Company and Consolidated Subsidiaries as of December 31, 1987 and 1986

The Notes to Financial Statements are an integral part of this statement.

depreciation expense is the current year's charge against assets.) Net property, plant and equipment indicates the amount of fixed assets at original cost that has not yet been expensed in the form of depreciation.

Investments, unlike marketable securities, represent a commitment of funds for at least one year. They may represent the commitment of funds to long-term securities or investments in other corporations. Frequently, the account contains common stock in companies that the firm has an interest in acquiring.

# Liabilities

Total assets are financed through borrowing (liabilities) or owners' investments (owners' equity). Liabilities represent financial obligations of the firm

**Figure 17-8**

Balance Sheet for IBM

## Consolidated Statement of Financial Position

International Business Machines Corporation and Subsidiary Companies

at December 31:

| (Dollars in millions) | 1986 | | 1985 | |
|---|---|---|---|---|
| *Assets* | | | | |
| **Current Assets:** | | | | |
| Cash | $ 755 | | $ 896 | |
| Marketable securities, at cost, which approximates market | 6,502 | | 4,726 | |
| Notes and accounts receivable – trade, net of allowances | 9,971 | | 9,757 | |
| Other accounts receivable | 854 | | 809 | |
| Inventories | 8,039 | | 8,579 | |
| Prepaid expenses and other current assets | 1,628 | | 1,303 | |
| | | $ 27,749 | | $ 26,070 |
| **Plant, Rental Machines and Other Property** | 38,121 | | 34,483 | |
| Less: Accumulated depreciation | 16,853 | | 14,803 | |
| | | 21,268 | | 19,680 |
| **Investments and Other Assets:** | | | | |
| Program products, less accumulated amortization (1986, $2,226; 1985, $1,765) | 2,199 | | 1,964 | |
| Investments and sundry assets | 6,598 | | 4,920 | |
| | | 8,797 | | 6,884 |
| | | $ 57,814 | | $ 52,634 |
| *Liabilities and Stockholders' Equity* | | | | |
| **Current Liabilities:** | | | | |
| Taxes | $ 2,583 | | $ 3,089 | |
| Loans payable | 1,410 | | 1,293 | |
| Accounts payable | 1,970 | | 1,823 | |
| Compensation and benefits | 3,001 | | 2,460 | |
| Deferred income | 414 | | 391 | |
| Other accrued expenses and liabilities | 3,365 | | 2,377 | |
| | | $ 12,743 | | $ 11,433 |
| **Long-Term Debt** | | 4,169 | | 3,955 |
| **Other Liabilities** | | 2,004 | | 1,606 |
| **Deferred Income Taxes** | | 4,524 | | 3,650 |
| **Stockholders' Equity:** | | | | |
| Capital stock, par value $1.25 per share | 6,321 | | 6,267 | |
| Shares authorized: 750,000,000 | | | | |
| Issued: 1986—606,614,368; 1985—615,741,687 | | | | |
| Retained earnings | 27,834 | | 27,234 | |
| Translation adjustments | 307 | | (1,466) | |
| | 34,462 | | 32,035 | |
| Less: Treasury stock, at cost | 88 | | 45 | |
| Shares: 1986—691,419; 1985—323,425 | | | | |
| | | 34,374 | | 31,990 |
| | | $ 57,814 | | $ 52,634 |

The notes on pages 30 through 40 are an integral part of this statement.

---

to short-term creditors (current liabilities) and long-term creditors. Among the short-term obligations, **accounts payable** represent amounts owed on an open account with a company's suppliers. The balance sheet in Figure 17-6 lists wages payable and taxes payable separately. Sometimes these accounts are consolidated into an accrued expense category. An **accrued expense** is generated when a financial obligation has been incurred by the company but payment has not yet taken place.

# Owners' Equity

The accounts listed in the owners' equity section of a balance sheet may differ from company to company. Some companies may include common stock and preferred stock outstanding. Other companies may have two or

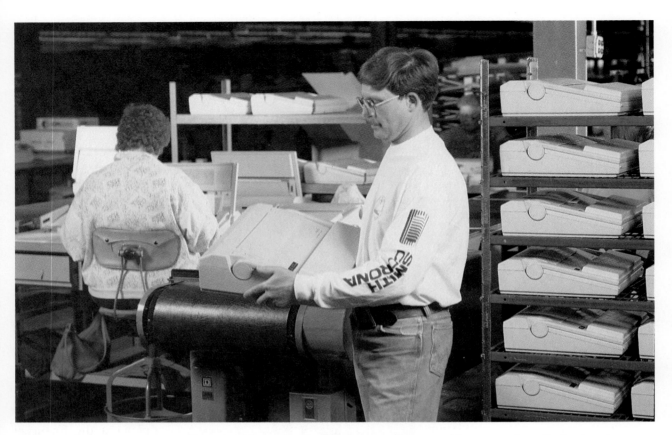

**Inventory is an asset.** The balance sheet provides a snapshot of a business's financial position at a particular point in time. Balance sheets summarize a firm's assets, liabilities, and owners' equity. Smith Corona, a typewriter manufacturer, maintains large inventories of its new PWP6 combination portable typewriter and word processor in its introductory stages.

three different classes of common stock outstanding. Finally, many annual reports consolidate all equity accounts into one equity category, and the detail is presented in footnotes to the annual report.

# ▶ Ratio Analysis

The income statement shows the profit or loss of the firm, and the balance sheet itemizes the firm's holdings of assets, debts, and obligations. Together the income statement and balance sheet answer two questions: (1) How much did the firm make or lose? (2) What is a measure of the firm's worth based on historical values found on the balance sheet? Ratio analysis takes information from these two statements and brings the information into sharper focus so that the banker, manager, stockholder, and others can measure the operating efficiency, profitability, and sources of financial capital of one firm relative to other firms.

A ratio is one number divided by another; the resultant number shows the relationship between the two numbers. The ratio between 375 miles traveled and 15 gallons of gasoline used is 25/1 or 25:1. You might recognize this as 25 miles per gallon and use this ratio to determine which car gets the best gas mileage. Students are familiar with grade-point averages. In a 4.00-system, an A equals 4 points, a B equals 3 points, a C equals 2 points, and a D equals 1 point. A student who completes 45 hours of class and has 135 grade points has attained a 3.00 average (135 grade points divided by 45 credit hours), which translates into a B.

Ratios provide information, but you must know what is being measured in order to construct a ratio and to understand the significance of the resultant number. Financial ratios are used to weigh and evaluate the operating performance of a firm. An absolute value such as earnings of $70,000 or accounts receivable of $200,000 may not provide as much information as a ratio. Whether those dollar amounts are good or bad depends on their relation to other numbers. If a company earned $70,000 on $700,000 of sales (10 percent return on sales), that might be quite satisfactory. However, $70,000 earned on sales of $7 million provides a meager 1 percent return on sales, which is poor.

After a ratio is computed, the results should be compared to those achieved by other companies in the same industry as well as to the company's own past record or performance. Company management, physical facilities, and numerous other factors should be used to supplement the financial findings to rate a company's performance. The ratios discussed in this chapter are a sampling of the major ratios used for financial analysis:

▶ **Profitability ratios**
  Profit margin
  Return on assets
  Return on equity
▶ **Asset utilization ratios**
  Receivable turnover
  Inventory turnover
  Total asset turnover
▶ **Liquidity ratios**
  Current ratio
  Quick ratio
▶ **Debt utilization ratios**
  Debt to total assets
  Times interest earned
▶ **Per share data**
  Earnings per share
  Dividends per share
  Book value per share

The discussion that follows is based on the 1987 financial statements for IBM presented in Figures 17-5 and 17-8; data is expressed in millions of dollars.

# Profitability Ratios

**Profitability ratios**

Measures how much operating income or net income a firm is able to generate relative to the assets, owners' equity, and sales

**Profitability ratios** measure how much operating income or net income a firm is able to generate relative to its assets, owners' equity, and sales. The numerator used in these examples is always net income (earnings after tax). Sometimes analysts want to measure operating income rather than after-tax income, and the denominator reflects that desire.

|  | | **1985** | **1987** |
|---|---|---|---|
| Profit margin $= \dfrac{\text{net income}}{\text{sales}}$ | | $\dfrac{\$\ 6,582}{\$45,937} = 14.3\%$ | $\dfrac{\$\ 5,285}{\$54,217} = 9.7\%$ |
| Return on assets $= \dfrac{\text{net income}}{\text{assets}}$ | | $\dfrac{\$\ 6,582}{\$42,808} = 15.4\%$ | $\dfrac{\$\ 5,285}{\$63,688} = 8.3\%$ |
| Return on equity $= \dfrac{\text{net income}}{\text{equity}}$ | | $\dfrac{\$\ 6,582}{\$26,489} = 24.8\%$ | $\dfrac{\$\ 5,285}{\$38,263} = 13.8\%$ |

**Profit margin**

Ratio based on information in the income statement

The **profit margin** is a ratio based on information in the income statement. The higher the profit margin, the better the cost control within the company and the higher is the return on every dollar of revenue (sales). The ratio of 9.7 percent indicates that for every $1 of sales, IBM generates profits of $.097.

**Return on assets**

Shows how much income the firm produces for every dollar invested in assets

The return on assets is a ratio that uses information from both the income statement and the balance sheet. **Return on assets** shows how much income the firm produces for every dollar invested in assets. In the case of IBM, every $1 of assets generates a 8.3 percent return or profits of $.083. Special attention should be paid to the age of the assets in analyses of returns on assets. In an inflationary economy, plant and equipment purchased many years ago may be carried on the books (balance sheet) at values below their replacement costs. A 20 percent return on assets purchased thirty years ago may be inferior to a 15 percent return on newly purchased assets, because the costs of equipment are now much greater, a fact not revealed by the numbers on the balance sheet.

**Return on equity**

Net income divided by stock holders' equity

Stockholders are often concerned about the returns on their investment, and they use the **return on equity** ratio as their yardstick. Since some of the assets are financed by debt, the equity is much less than total assets and the returns on equity are higher than returns on assets. IBM earned a 13.8 percent return on stockholders' equity.

# Asset Utilization Ratios

**Asset utilization ratio**

Measures how efficiently a firm uses its assets to generate $1 of sales

**Asset utilization ratios** measure how efficiently a firm uses its assets to generate $1 of sales. Asset utilization ratios help explain why one firm is able to generate a higher return on assets than another. The more sales each dollar of assets can generate, the more profitable the firm will be given equal profitability ratios. The ratios in this category all relate balance-sheet assets to sales, which is found on the income statement. IBM's high return on assets can be explained by its high turnover ratios.

**Receivable turnover**

Annual sales divided by receivables

**Inventory turnover**

Annual sales divided by inventory

**Total asset turnover**

Measures the efficiency of the combined total assets in supporting sales

$$\text{Receivable turnover} = \frac{\text{sales}}{\text{receivables}} \quad \frac{\$45{,}937}{\$\ 8{,}111} = 5.7X \quad \frac{\$54{,}217}{\$12{,}757} = 4.2X$$

$$\text{Inventory turnover} = \frac{\text{sales}}{\text{inventory}} \quad \frac{\$45{,}937}{\$\ 6{,}598} = 7.0X \quad \frac{\$54{,}217}{\$\ 8{,}645} = 6.3X$$

$$\text{Total asset turnover} = \frac{\text{sales}}{\text{total assets}} \quad \frac{\$45{,}937}{\$42{,}808} = 1.1X \quad \frac{\$54{,}217}{\$63{,}688} = .85X$$

These ratios all indicate that IBM's asset efficiency has declined between 1985–1987. In 1987 receivables were collected 4.2 times per year or about every 85 days. Inventory does not seem excessive. The inventory turnover of 6.3 times indicates that IBM replaces its inventory 6.3 times per year or about every 57 days. **Total asset turnover** measures the efficiency of the combined total assets in creating sales. IBM generates $.85 in sales for every $1 of total assets.

# Liquidity Ratios

**Liquidity ratios**

Indicates the business's ability to pay off short-term debt and interest expenses

Short-term creditors are most interested in a company's ability to pay off short-term debt by liquidating short-term assets. **Liquidity ratios** compare current assets to current liabilities as an indicator of the speed with which a company can turn these assets into cash in order to pay off its short-term debt. High liquidity ratios may satisfy a creditor's need for a safety cushion, but ratios that are not too high may indicate that the firm is not using its current assets efficiently.

$$\text{Current ratio} = \frac{\text{current assets}}{\text{current liabilities}} \quad \frac{\$20{,}375}{\$\ 9{,}640} = 2.1X \quad \frac{\$31{,}020}{\$13{,}377} = 2.3X$$

$$\text{Quick ratio} = \frac{\text{current assets} - \text{inventories}}{\text{current liabilities}} \quad \frac{\$13{,}777}{\$\ 9{,}640} = 1.4X \quad \frac{\$22{,}375}{\$13{,}377} = 1.7X$$

The 1987 current ratio indicates that for every $1 of current liabilities, IBM has $2.30 of current assets. The quick ratio (also known as the acid test) is an even more stringent measure of liquidity because it eliminates inventory, the least liquid current asset. IBM has $1.70 of current assets (after subtracting inventory) for every $1 of current liabilities. This is a very high liquidity ratio, indicating a great deal of safety for IBM's short-term creditors. Both these ratios have improved between 1985 and 1987.

The liquidity ratios are best examined in conjunction with the receivable turnover and inventory turnover ratios. High turnover ratios for IBM would imply that cash is flowing through the company quickly, and this would also improve the company's liquidity. IBM could probably have much lower current and quick ratios without causing much concern among creditors.

# Financial Encounter 17-3
## *The Future of Accounting*

What took an auditor over one thousand hours in 1986 will be accomplished in one hour in the year 2,000. This increase in productivity is expected to occur and will be fueled by computers. The business world will use computers in every facet of operation. All transactions will be done over computers, thus eliminating the need for invoices and supporting paperwork. Most of the mail will be transmitted over computers via an electronic mail system (EMS). Each user will be assigned a set of security codes to ensure that they receive only their own mail. Computer users will be able to use their monitors to see the person at the other end of the transaction. Accountants will be able to perform their traditional tasks extremely rapidly; therefore they will have more time for other tasks.

Auditors will carry portable computers that hold ten gigabytes (ten billion pieces) of information per square inch. In 1986, a computer with that much memory would have filled a large room. All large firms will have databases of information which the auditor will easily access. For security reasons users of these databases will be identified by their fingerprints. Computers will communicate to one another and share databases. The auditor will simply give the task to the computer and it will communicate with other computers, gather all the needed information, and then process the information into the desired form. These computers will be instructed by human voice commands, therefore the speed of the computer is limited only by the speed of the operator's voice. As a result colleges may offer courses that teach students to speak faster and more clearly.

The basic college accounting sequence would consist of traditional accounting classes along with many information system classes. Classes that teach ethical standards and public responsibility would be required of the CPA. The change in accounting curriculum would be preceded by a change in the exam to become a Certified Public Accountant. The new test will deal more with information technologies, and the ethical considerations of accountants who perform both consulting and auditing for the same client. The American Accounting Association committee report on the future of accounting education (1986) stated: "Accounting should be viewed as a broad economic information development and distribution process, based on the design, implementation, and operation of multiple types of information systems."

The CPA will evolve into an independent information specialist. He will be the foremost authority on information gathering, analysis, and reporting. The large CPA firms' bread and butter business will be financial and information consulting.

These facts are from: John R. Meinert, "The CPA In Business: A Look At Our Past, Present, And Future," *Journal of Accountancy*, May 1987, Vol. 161, No. 5, pp. 262–275; Robert Mednick and Gary John Previts, "The Scope of CPA Services: A View Of The Future From The Perspective Of A Century Of Progress," *Journal Of Accountancy*, May 1987, Vol. 161, No. 5, pp. 220–238; David H. Abramson, "The Future of Accounting: Scenarios For 1996," *Journal Of Accountancy*, October 1986, Vol. 160, No. 10, pp. 120–124; Russell E. Andrews, "An Audit Odyssey 2001," *L&H Perspective*, 1982, Vol. 8, No. 1, pp. 24–27.

# Debt Utilization Ratios

**Debt utilization ratios**

Tells the analyst how much debt the company is using relative to other sources of capital such as owners' equity

**Debt utilization ratios** tell the analyst how much debt the company is using relative to other sources of capital such as owners' equity. The more assets are financed by debt, the more risk a firm may be exposed to. Managers of most corporations find it wise to keep debt-to-asset levels below 50 percent. A general rule is that if sales fluctuate greatly over the years (as they do in the automobile industry), less debt should be used. If sales are very stable (as they are in electric utilities), more debt can be used safely without incurring more risk. The risk of using debt is that it carries an interest charge that must be paid monthly, quarterly, or semiannually. If sales decline and profitability evaporates, the ability to pay interest could be severely diminished. The greater the debt, the higher are the interest payments. Chrysler's near bankruptcy is a good example of why automobile companies ought to have low debt ratios.

|  |  | **1985** | **1987** |
|---|---|---|---|
| Debt to total assets | $= \dfrac{\text{total debt}}{\text{total assets}}$ | $\dfrac{\$16,319}{\$42,808} = 38.1\%$ | $\dfrac{\$25,425}{\$63,688} = 40\%$ |
| Times interest earned | $= \dfrac{\text{income before interest \& taxes}}{\text{interest}}$ | $\dfrac{\$12,301}{\$\ \ \ 408} = 29.5X$ | $\dfrac{\$\ 9,094}{\$\ \ \ 485} = 18.8X$ |

**Debt to total assets**

A ratio that indicates how much of the firm's assets are financed by debt

Debt utilization ratios are based on balance-sheet and income statement data. **Debt to total assets** indicates how much of the firm is financed by debt and how much is financed by equity. This may not be apparent from the ratio, but it is from the balance sheet, where sources of financial capital are either debt from lenders or equity from owners. For example, for every $1 of total assets, IBM has $.40 of total debt. In other words, 40.0 percent of the firm's assets are financed with borrowed money and the rest (60.0 percent) is financed with owners' equity. IBM does not seem to be using too much debt to finance its assets.

The times interest earned ratio is based on data from the income statement. IBM has safely covered its interest expense. For every $1 in interest IBM paid in 1987, the company earned $18.80 of income before interest and taxes, certainly providing some safety for its creditors.

## Per Share Data

**Per share data**

Used by investors to compare the performance of one company to another on an equal per share basis

**Per share data** is used most by investors to compare the performance of one company to another on an equal per share basis. Shareholders (owners) usually want to look at several ratios on a per share basis. The more shares that are outstanding, the less income is available for each share. Companies have different numbers of shares outstanding, and for comparative purposes, analysts, shareholders, and potential investors especially want to be able to compare firms on a share-for-share basis.

|  |  | **1985** | **1987** |
|---|---|---|---|
| Earnings per share | $= \dfrac{\text{earnings available for common stockholders}}{\text{number of shares outstanding}}$ | $\dfrac{\$\ 6,582}{611} = \$10.77$ | $\dfrac{\$\ 5,258}{603} = \$\ 8.72$ |
| Dividends per share | $= \dfrac{\text{dividends paid to common stockholders}}{\text{number of shares outstanding}}$ | $\dfrac{\$\ 2,507}{611} = \$\ 4.10$ | $\dfrac{\$\ 2,654}{603} = \$\ 4.40$ |
| Book value per share | $= \dfrac{\text{stockholders' equity}}{\text{number of shares outstanding}}$ | $\dfrac{\$26,489}{611} = \$43.35$ | $\dfrac{\$38,263}{603} = \$63.45$ |

**Earnings per share**

Earnings available for common stockholders divided by the number of shares outstanding

**Table 17-3  Industry Analysis**
*Note*: The asterisks indicate the best ratio for each category.

| Ratio | Digital Equipment | Unisys | NCR | Hewlett-Packard | IBM |
|---|---|---|---|---|---|
| Profit margin | 12.11%* | 5.95% | 7.43% | 7.96% | 9.7% |
| Return on assets | 17.30% | 8.70% | 17.65%* | 11.94% | 12.02% |
| Return on equity | 18.07% | 12.72% | 38.32%* | 12.82% | 13.74% |
| Receivable turnover | 3.75X | 4.43X | 5.06X* | 4.96X | 3.92X |
| Inventory turnover | 6.09X | 5.23X | 7.40X* | 6.58X | 6.27X |
| Total asset turnover | 1.43X | 1.46X | 2.37X* | 1.50X | 1.24X |
| Current ratio | 3.27* | 1.33 | 1.72 | 2.22 | 2.32 |
| Quick ratio | 2.53* | 0.79 | 1.25 | 1.63 | 1.67 |
| Debt to total assets | 4.26%* | 31.58% | 9.01% | 6.88% | 12.54% |
| Times interest earned | 52.70X | 7.08X | 67.54X | 108.45X* | 27.49X |

Earnings of IBM declined between 1985 and 1987. By comparing denominations we can also tell that IBM must have bought back about 8 million shares of common stock from the stockholders. The combination of these two forces lowered earnings per share by $2.05. Stockholders did not have as much profit in 1987 as in 1985 for each share owned.

**Dividends per share**

The actual cash received for each share owned

**Book value per share**

Indicates what the stockholders' investment has been on a per share basis

**Dividends per share** is the actual cash received for each share owned and is therefore very important to an investor. An investor who has 40 shares would receive a cash payment of 40 × $4.40 or $176 during the year. **Book value per share** indicates what the stockholders' investment has been on a per share basis. Since this book value reflects assets at cost and not market value, it is usually not a good indicator of the actual price of the common stock.

# ▶ Industry Analysis

Numbers in a vacuum are not particularly useful for measuring a firm's performance. A yardstick or a standard against which to measure ratios is needed. Industry ratios are commonly used as a comparative measure.

One way to analyze IBM is to compare it to several other firms in the industry—Digital Equipment, Unisys, NCR, and Hewlett-Packard (Table 17-3).

It is clear why IBM is considered the industry leader. Although Digital Equipment has safer liquidity ratios and a less risky debt to asset ratio, IBM has its interest expense covered more than two times NCR's times interest earned ratio. If IBM is the strongest of the group, then Unisys is the weakest, with the lowest profitability ratios and weak liquidity ratios.

It is also helpful to have a longer time perspective on these ratios, to see whether IBM is improving its performance. This would require analyzing the trends presented by ratios over an appropriate time period such as five or ten years.

# Summary and Review

▶ Accountants gather, record, and interpret financial transactions. Public accountants can be certified public accountants (CPAs) who provide accounting services to individuals or businesses for a fee. Private accountants can be certified management accountants (CMAs) who work for corporations, government agencies, and other organizations.

▶ Accounting statements are used internally by management to judge the performance of the firm. Financial statements are also used to plan and direct future activity and to control corporate activity and measure goal achievement. One widely used accounting statement is the budget—a detailed plan reflecting expected revenues, operating expenses, cash receipts, and outflows for a given time period.

▶ The income statement is the major device for measuring the profitability of a firm over a period of time. This financial statement is a major source of information for managers, investors, creditors, and employees. There are three basic parts to the income statement: revenues, expenses, and net income.

▶ The balance sheet summarizes the firm's assets, liabilities, and owners' equity on an accumulative basis since the beginning of the firm. This statement represents the firm at one point in time. As time passes, the balance sheet changes. On the balance sheet, assets must equal liabilities plus owners' equity. The balance sheet has several major classifications: current assets, fixed assets, current liabilities, long-term liabilities, and owners' equity.

▶ Ratios such as the profitability, asset utilization, liquidity, debt utilization, and per share data help review corporate performance on a standardized basis. Ratios should be used to compare a company's present performance with its past performance and to compare its performance with that of the best companies in its industry.

# Key Terms and Concepts

accounting
public accountant
certified public accountant (CPA)
private accountant
certified management accountant
   (CMA)
managerial accounting
cash flow
budget
master budget
income statement
revenue
expenses
depreciation expense
net income
balance sheet
marketable securities

accounts receivable
accumulated depreciation
accounts payable
accrued expense
profitability ratios
return on assets
asset utilization ratios
total asset turnover
receivable turnover
inventory turnover
liquidity ratios
debt utilization ratios
debt to total assets
per share data
earnings per share
dividends per share
book value per share

# Checking Your Understanding

This chapter introduced you to the subject of accounting and financial statements. To test and reinforce your understanding, fill in the blanks below.

1. Another name for debt is _____.
2. A liquidity ratio that excludes inventory from the ratio is called the _____ ratio.
3. Net property, plant and equipment is the value of the fixed assets after _____ depreciation has been subtracted.
4. Current liabilities owed to a bank are often referred to as _____ payable.
5. _____ expense is the annual amount charged against plant and equipment and shows up on the income statement.
6. _____ minus expenses equals profits.
7. An asset that can be turned into cash quickly is said to have good _____.
8. Assets that are expected to be turned into cash within the next twelve months are called _____ assets.
9. _____ securities are held as temporary investments instead of holding cash.
10. A liquidity ratio that divides current assets by current liabilities is called the _____ ratio.
11. Accounts receivable that are written off as uncollectible are referred to as _____ debts.
12. The higher the _____ to asset ratio, the greater is the risk to a long-term creditor.
13. _____ _____ appear on the upper part of a vertical balance sheet or on the left side of a horizontal balance sheet.
14. Income before interest and taxes is sometimes referred to as _____ income.
15. The net income divided by the total number of common shares outstanding is called earnings _____ share.
16. Income after taxes is sometimes referred to as _____ income.

# Topics for Review and Discussion

1. Why are accountants so important to a corporation? What function do they perform?
2. Why not just take revenues minus all expenses and get the net income after taxes instead of creating so many intermediate income subheadings.
3. The income statements of all corporations are in the same format. True or false? Discuss.
4. Discuss the advantages and disadvantages of having detailed income statements or general income statements.
5. Together the income statement and balance sheet answer two basic questions. What are they?

**6.** Discuss the assets found in the current asset section of the balance sheet. How are they ordered within the group?

**7.** Inventory can take many different forms. What are the most usual categories?

**8.** Which accounts appear under "current liabilities"?

**9.** Discuss the internal uses for financial statements.

**10.** What is a budget?

**11.** Discuss the external uses for financial statements.

**12.** What are the five basic ratio classifications? What ratios are found in each category?

**13.** Discuss the different information provided by the profit margin, return on assets, and return on equity.

**14.** Why are the debt ratios an important part of assessing the risk of the firm?

# Exercises

**1.** Go to the library and pick up the annual report of a company with which you are familiar. Read through the financial statements, and then write up an analysis of the firm's performance using ratio analysis. Look at data for several years, and analyze whether performance is improving, getting worse, or staying the same.

**2.** Form a group of three or four students to do an industry analysis. Each student takes a company in the same industry, and then all compare results. The following companies would make good group projects:

*Automobiles*
Chrysler
Ford
General Motors

*Chemicals*
Du Pont
Dow Chemical
Monsanto

*Petroleum*
Chevron
Exxon
Mobil
Amoco

*Computers*
IBM
Digital Equipment
Data General
Apple Computer

*Retail*
Sears
J C Penney
K mart
The Limited

*Pharmaceuticals*
Merck
Lilly
UpJohn

*Foods/Tobacco*
RJR Nabisco
Phillip Morris
American Brands

*Software Films*
Ashton Tate
Lotus Development
Microsoft

| Airlines | Foods |
|---|---|
| United Air Lines | General Mills |
| American Airlines | Pillsbury |
| Delta Airlines | Kellogg |
| Northwest Airlines | Hershey |

| Hospital Supply | Brewing |
|---|---|
| Baxter Travenol | Anheuser-Busch |
| Johnson & Johnson | Adolph Coors |
| American Home Products | G. Heileman Brewing |

## Case 17-1
### ZZZZ Best

Barry Minkow founded ZZZZ Best Co., a carpet-cleaning firm, when he was 15 years old. He ran the business from his family's garage in Reseda, California. The company became one of the biggest carpet-cleaning firms in California, and Minkow was a millionaire by age 18. Minkow took his company public by selling its stock when he was 21, and his personal worth was estimated at close to $10 million. At that time, ZZZZ Best ("Zeee Best") had thirteen hundred employees and 1986 sales of $4.8 million. Minkow boldly predicted that 1987 revenues would exceed $50 million.

In July 1987, ZZZZ Best management filed for bankruptcy protection and sued Minkow for misappropriating $21 million in company funds. In addition, several customers accused ZZZZ Best of overcharging them in a credit-card scam. Minkow publicly admitted the overcharges but blamed them on subcontractors and employees. He also said that he had fired those who were responsible and that he personally had repaid the charges.

The Securities and Exchange Commission (SEC) and other law enforcement agencies began a series of investigations into Minkow and his company. It became apparent that ZZZZ Best was built on a foundation of lies, dishonesty, and inconsistent accounting practices. The company had submitted phony credit-card charges and had issued press releases claiming millions of dollars in bogus contracts, sending the price of the company's stock ever higher. The SEC is investigating other charges, including the possibility of phony receivables, bogus financial and accounting statements, organized-crime connections, and securities law violations by Minkow and other executives. The SEC wants to place an independent trustee in charge of the company until its accounting records can be sorted out.

The Los Angeles police department investigated charges that ZZZZ Best was a money-laundering operation for organized crime. Their investigation linked Minkow and ZZZZ Best with drug dealings and organized-crime members.

These allegations ultimately led Minkow to resign from ZZZZ Best for "health reasons." But his resignation was not the end of his troubles. ZZZZ Best's new management sued Minkow for embezzling $3 million of the company's funds for his personal use and misappropriating $18 million to perform fictitious insurance restoration work. The suit charged that Minkow actually diverted this money to an associate's refurbishing business, which was part of an elaborate scheme designed to allow Minkow to take corporate funds for his own and others' personal use. According to the suit, these discrepancies in the company's accounting practices are the reasons behind the bankruptcy filing. As a result, ZZZZ Best's accounting firm quit, and the company's new board of directors began taking a long, hard look at the company's books and accounting procedures.

The turn of events at ZZZZ Best caused its stock price to plummet from a high of $18.38 a share to less than $1 a share. Many investors lost a lot of money. One is reported to have lost $7 million. Unhappy investors have filed numerous lawsuits against the company, claiming they were misled by the press releases.

ZZZZ Best suspended all operations at the end of July 1987. It will be many months or even years before the investors of ZZZZ Best, the SEC, and Los Angeles police figure out what happened to Barry Minkow's company and where all the money went.

---

These facts are from Philip Elmer-DeWitt, with Scott Brown, "ZZZZ Best May Be ZZZZ Worst," *Time*, July 20, 1987, p. 56; Jeff B. Copeland, with Michael A. Lerner, "A Whiz Kid Goes Wrong," *Newsweek*, July 20, 1987, p. 40; "ZZZZ Best Co. Suspends Carpet Cleaning Business," *The Wall Street Journal*, July 16, 1987, p. 2; Kevin Kelly, "Wall-to-Wall Trouble for the Carpet-Cleaning King," *Business Week*, July 13, 1987, p. 83; Kathy Rebello, "From Rugs to Riches—to Ruin," *USA Today* July 13, 1987, pp. 1A, 2A; Daniel Akst, "How Whiz-Kid Chief of ZZZZ Best Had, and Lost, It All," *The Wall Street Journal*, July 9, 1987, pp. 1, 12; and Daniel Akst, "ZZZZ Best Co. Suit Accuses Five of Fraud," *The Wall Street Journal*, July 7, 1987, p. 12.

### Questions

1. How can a certified public accountant protect investors from fraud such as occurred in ZZZZ Best?
2. What ethical issues from Chapter 5 apply to this case?
3. Would better internal controls and budgets have saved ZZZZ Best from bankruptcy?

---

## Case 17-2
### *Auditing & Consulting: A Question of Ethics*

Today accounting firms offer both auditing and consulting services. Sometimes they perform these services for the same client. When this occurs a conflict of interest may arise. Auditors are supposed to be independent from the firms they audit and they may lose this independence when they are involved with consulting. In fiscal 1988 five of the top ten consulting firms were accounting firms. Consulting represented anywhere from 31% to 12% of the big eight's U.S. revenues in fiscal 1986 and consulting revenues have been increasing rapidly. The average big eight accounting firm gets 27% of their consulting business from audit clients; this number ranges from 39%–12% with the larger consulting firms at the high end and smaller firms at the low end.

Proponents contend that auditors are in an ideal position to perform consulting and disallowing this would be a disservice to the profession and to the public. Opponents argue that auditors can not possibly perform consulting for their clients and still remain independent and objective during audits. This issue has been debated and studied by accounting firms, the American Institute of CPAs, (AICPA), the SEC, the Public Oversight Board, Congress, and Senate subcommittees.

The first study was conducted by the American Institute of CPAs (AICPA) in 1974. The commission found no cases where auditors sacrificed independence because of their consulting role and recommended no prohibition of management services by auditors. In 1976 and 1977 Congress initiated two investigations of the accounting firm's auditing-consulting function. No legislation resulted from these committees. In the late 1970s the Securities and Exchange Commission Public Oversight Committee (SECPS) was formed to oversee accounting firms. The SECPS felt that some services impaired independence, and required its firms to disclose management advisory services. In addition the SEC issued Accounting Series Release 250 that required public companies to state in proxy statements fees for nonaudit services that totaled three percent or more. The SECPS set up the public oversight board (POB) which concluded that auditors should be allowed to perform consulting services. The SEC was not convinced by the report and in Accounting Series Release 264 said that firms should pause before hiring their auditors for management consulting. This statement had a detrimental effect on the industry's consulting business. In 1981 and 1982 the SEC retracted both releases. In 1985 a House committee began a new investigation that should address accountants' scope of practice. This investigation is still underway— and the debate continues: the advocates call for unrestricted scope of services, and the proponents want some restrictions on accountants' scope of practice.

Opponents argue that auditing and consulting create a conflict of interest. An auditor is a public servant and a consultant is a corporation's servant. When situations arise that create conflict, who will the accountant ultimately serve? Everyone can think of scenarios where conflict could arise. One such situation would occur if an auditor was hired for tax consultant: The consultant would want to tell the firm it could save them loads of money, but perhaps the auditor would have to bend the tax law, regulations, and revenue rulings to meet his promises. Auditors might start making business deals and directing business strategy for audit clients, and this could create problems. When an accounting firm is involved in management decisions they could be tempted to use shaky auditing procedures to make their performance appear superior. This would mislead the public and break the auditor's independence from the firm. Warren E. Burger, as Chief Justice of the United States, delivered the unanimous verdict of the Court in *U.S.* v. *Arthur Young & Co.* 465 U.S.

805 (1984), thus: "Public faith in the reliability of a corporation's financial statements depends on the public perception of the outside auditor as an independent professional. . . . If the investors were to view the auditor as an advocate for the corporate client, the value of the audit function itself may well be lost."

Accounting firms argue that performing auditing and consulting for the same firm creates potential conflict, but firms have chinese walls which prevent any wrongdoings. A chinese wall is an imaginary wall between two departments in a firm that have conflicting interest. The accounting firms add that 60%–90% of their consulting clients get audits done elsewhere. During a lecture at DePaul University's Graduate program, Kenneth Salomon, managing partner of Laventhol & Horwath, acknowledged that there is a potential for a conflict of interest but said his firm has taken safeguards to insure that abuses won't occur.

---

Abraham J. Briloff, "Do Management Services Endanger Independence and Objectivity?" *CPA Journal,* August 1987, pp. 22–27; William D. Hall, "An Acceptable Scope Of Practice," *CPA Journal,* February 1988, pp. 24–33; Ettore Barbatelli, "The Appearance of Conflict When CPA Firms Offer Consulting Services," *Management Accountant,* September 1986, pp. 28–31; The Chicago Tribune, July 8, 1987, p. 16.

### Questions

1. Why shouldn't accountants be allowed to perform both auditing and consulting for clients?
2. Why should accountants be allowed to perform both auditing and consulting for clients?
3. Do you believe accountants should be allowed to perform both auditing and consulting for clients?

# Answers to Checking Your Understanding

1. liabilities
2. quick
3. accumulated
4. wages
5. Depreciation
6. Revenues/sales
7. liquidity
8. current
9. Marketable
10. current
11. bad
12. debt
13. Current assets
14. operating
15. per
16. net

## Outline

# Chapter 18

# Short-Term Finance: Working Capital Management

## Objectives

After reading this chapter, you will be able to:

▶ Define current assets, and explain some methods for managing cash, marketable securities, accounts receivable, and inventory.

▶ Define current liabilities, and identify some of the sources of short-term funds.

▶ Relate the cash-flow process to financial statements. Understand the importance of establishing a sales forecast and a cash budget.

# Business Experience

General Motors Acceptance Corporation (GMAC), formed in 1919, is a wholly owned subsidiary of General Motors. Because GMAC has a good credit rating, it is able to borrow at favorable interest rates. GMAC is then able to offer GM customers auto loans, lower financing, and they are ultimately able to sell more cars. However, GMAC has done more than simply enhance GM's business; it has become a successful financial services company. GMAC accounted for 40% of GM's profits in 1986 and 56% in 1987. In addition to being a profitable corporate subsidiary during peak sales periods, GMAC also able to offers low-cost financing when car sales are slumping. For example, in the mid-1980s, GMAC offered financing as low as 1.9% as an incentive to GM's customers.

GMAC's business is making, servicing, and selling loans. It finances loans by issuing commercial paper, one of the most common forms of short-term debt with normal maturities of 4–6 months. It is a loan backed only by the reputation of the company. Since the European commercial paper market has maturities of 60–90 days, the commercial paper sold by GMAC is appealing to American and foreign investors.

In addition to being one of the largest lenders, GMAC is the largest borrower in the world. It accounts for $30 billion worth of outstanding commercial paper or 10% of all commercial paper that has not matured. While this may be considered a large share of the market, it plays an even more dominant role in the medium-term commercial paper market, accounting for 30% of the outstanding commercial paper. One of GMAC's strongest selling points is its variety and availability of loans. When an investor's note matures, chances are that GMAC is able to offer another one to replace it.

Although GMAC's conservative management believes its future lies in doing what it does best, GMAC's chairman, Robert Murphy, would like to expand the corporation into the insurance business. Currently, GMAC sells insurance only to GM's 800,000 employees. In the future, Mr. Murphy would like to sell insurance to the public. Because of their various financial activities, GMAC and other corporations like them have earned the name of "auto banks."

If compared to banks in the United States, GMAC would be the fifth largest in terms of assets. GMAC is definitely a financial firm that has cut into the bank business, particularly in the $250 billion retail auto loan market. Bank market share of the auto loan market dropped from 47% in 1985 to 41% in 1987 because of the influence of companies like GMAC. GMAC has several advantages over conventional banks including less government regulation. GMAC also has a stronger balance sheet than most commercial banks mainly because of the banks' problems with third world loans. If its current success and continual growth are any indication of what is to come, GMAC may well be on its way to becoming the "bank of the future."

---

These facts are from: Lean Nathans, "And You Thought They Just Sold Cars," *Business Month,* November 1987, pp. 42–48; Michelle Celarier, "Taking On Banks," *United States Banker,* June 1987, pp. 33–39; "Auto Banks?" *The Economist,* September 6, 1987, p. 79; David Sherref, "Borrower Of The Year: GMAC," *Euromoney,* September 1987, pp. 86–89.

# Introduction

**Short-term financial management**

Managing the current assets and liabilities found on the balance sheet

Financial management involves acquiring and managing funds for a business. **Short-term financial management** is managing the current assets and liabilities found on the balance sheet (discussed in Chapter 17): cash, marketable securities, accounts receivable, inventory, accounts payable, wages payable, taxes payable, and notes payable, that is, short-term debt obligations that must be repaid within a year. Financial managers spend much of their time managing current assets and liabilities.

The terms *current* and *short-term*, when referring to assets and liabilities, are used interchangeably throughout this chapter because short-term assets and liabilities are usually replaced by new assets and liabilities within three to four months and always within a year. This chapter focuses on the short-term assets and liabilities and on the management of those assets and liabilities.

# ▶ Short-Term Financial Management

**Working capital management**

Management of current assets and current liabilities

The management of current assets and current liabilities is sometimes called **working capital management** because the current assets and liabilities continually flow through the business and are said to be "working." Business is dynamic: Loans are repaid and more funds borrowed. Accounts receivable are collected and more receivables are generated through the process of selling the firm's products. Wages increase as more workers are hired to meet production increases. Taxes are paid every quarter and increase as the firm becomes more profitable. Thus, current assets and liabilities constantly turn over as they go through the company.

Table 18-1 presents the short-term portion of a balance sheet and the various accounts discussed in Chapter 17. Current assets are the assets that a business expects to turn into cash within a year; they are listed on the balance sheet with the most liquid first (cash) and the least liquid last (inventory). Liquid assets are assets that can be turned into cash quickly at a fair market value. Current liabilities are short-term debts that a business expects to repay within a year and are also listed on the balance sheet in the order in which they are to be paid off.

# ▶ Management of Current Assets

The goal of financial managers who manage current assets is to maximize the return to the business on cash, marketable securities, accounts receivable, and inventory.

**Table 18-1  Short-Term Portion of a Balance Sheet for the Basic Corporation Year Ending December 31, 199X**

| Current Assets | | Current Liabilities | |
|---|---:|---|---:|
| Cash | $ 40,000 | Accounts payable | $ 50,000 |
| Market securities | 25,000 | Wages payable | 15,000 |
| Accounts receivable | 60,000 | Taxes payable | 10,000 |
| Inventory | 100,000 | Notes payable | 30,000 |
| | $225,000 | | $105,000 |

# Managing Cash and Marketable Securities

**Marketable securities**

Temporary investments of extra cash

**Marketable securities** are temporary investments of extra cash and thus are regarded as a substitute for cash. Because they are managed much like cash, the two are discussed together here. Cash ties up business funds just as investments in inventory or plant and equipment do. Unused or idle cash earns no interest; thus financial managers try to minimize the amount of cash kept on hand to pay bills. **Transaction balances** are cash kept on hand by a business to pay normal daily business expenses, such as wages, suppliers, bills, and utilities. Most businesses invest any cash not needed for such transactions in marketable securities or use the funds to reduce debt.

**Transactions balances**

Cash kept on hand by a business to pay normal daily business expenses

Businesses use several techniques to make sure cash flows through the business quickly and efficiently. These techniques include playing the float, using lockboxes and electronic funds transfer, and investing idle cash.

***Playing the Float.*** Many businesses realize that the checks they write to pay suppliers and others are not cashed until the checks have been delivered and deposited in the suppliers' bank accounts. Because of this time lag, the balance shown in the business' checkbook and the amount credited to the business by the bank are not the same; the difference is called a **float**.

**Float**

The difference between the balance in the business' checkbook and the amount credited to the business by the bank

If Pillsbury sends a check to a grain co-op for a wheat purchase, it will probably take two days for the co-op to receive the check by mail. It will probably take another day for the check to be deposited in the co-op's local bank and another day for the check to clear through the banking system. If Pillsbury sent a $10 million check on Tuesday, it may not need to have the $10 million in its bank account until the following Monday. If Pillsbury's financial managers know, through experience and statistical methods, how long the float will be outstanding on a typical transaction, they can invest the difference (the float) in marketable securities during the float period, which in this example is six days (including a weekend). If the company earns 7 percent on $10 million dollars every six days all year long, the company would earn an extra $700,000 profit over the year. Even if Pillsbury played the float only 20 percent of the time, the extra profit would be $140,000.

Huge corporations such as General Motors or Exxon could have billions of dollars in float, and their extra earnings could be quite significant. Playing the float is common and is usually combined with a line of credit, which is an agreement between a business and a bank that the bank will make available a certain amount of short-term funds whenever needed by the business. A credit line ensures that funds are automatically loaned to the firm if a negative balance occurs as a result of a miscalculation of the float time period.

**Managing the mouse's money.** To be successful in business requires strong financial management. Several years ago Disney had high debt and low revenues from its film and theme park divisions. Gary Wilson was hired as Chief Financial Officer (CFO), and immediately started to turn its finances around. All-day ticket prices at the theme park were raised from $18 to $28; fourteen new films were released targeting teen and adult audiences. Several were big box office hits. The result was an all-time high return on assets of 13% in 1987.

**Lockbox**

A post office box used as a mailing address for receiving payments

*Improving Collections Through Lockboxes.* To speed up the collection of payments, some businesses have customers send their payments to a **lockbox**—a post office box used as a mailing address for receiving payments—instead of to the company. The company's bank collects payments directly from the lockbox (post office box) as often as four times each day. The bank can start the check-clearing process immediately and get the money into the company's checking account more quickly than if the checks had been sent directly to the company. The bank then sends the business an accounting of which customers' checks have been received so the company can make the appropriate entries in its accounting journals. This information is often transmitted by computer or delivered to the firm on computer tape.

Companies with many customers that receive hundreds or thousands of checks every day are the biggest users of lockboxes. Large Sears and J. C. Penney retail stores, for example, have hundreds of thousands of retail customers who charge their purchases on a credit card and pay by mail. Because there are hundreds of stores throughout the country, customers mail their checks to regional post offices that are within one day's mail service. All Sears customers in the state of New York, for example, might mail checks to a New York City post office to be picked up by a New York City bank. This cuts down the float time caused by the mail system. After the bank has processed the checks, it can electronically wire the money to the company's major bank at the end of the day.

***Electronic Funds Transfer.*** Large businesses with many customers around the country, such as Greyhound Corporation, use electronic funds transfer for collection practices. Electronic funds transfer is a system that moves money from one financial institution to another by means of computers. Greyhound's local offices deposit checks received each day into local banks, and at the end of the day, Greyhound's financial manager transfers all excess funds by way of computer to its central bank for overnight investment. Although the small amounts deposited at each local bank may not be enough to invest, the accumulation of funds from all over the country could provide several million dollars on a daily basis for investment. This technique is especially useful for international corporations for which physical delivery and check-clearing procedures are slow and cumbersome.

***Investing Idle Cash.*** Cash may be available for investment for one night or for periods ranging from one week to a year. Because cash continually flows through the firm, some idle cash may be available for investment on a continual basis. A financial manager who expects to need unused cash in four days invests it in a four-day marketable security. Marketable securities can be bought and sold by investors at prices determined in securities markets.

Marketable securities are usually very short-term but can have an expected life of up to one year depending on the firm's future need for cash. Marketable securities include U.S. Treasury bills, certificates of deposit, bankers' acceptances, commercial paper, and money market funds.

Many companies invest idle cash in U.S. **Treasury bills** (T-bills), which are short-term debt obligations of the U.S. government. T-bills are considered the safest of all investments. They are issued weekly by the U.S. Treasury and, depending on the day of the week, can have a maturity of from one day to one year.

Another marketable security used by financial managers is **certificates of deposit (CDs)** at commercial banks. These are essentially loans made to the bank on which the bank pays interest. Marketable certificates of deposit are sold by banks in minimum amounts of $100,000. There are secondary markets in which a firm can sell the certificate before it reaches maturity if the business needs the funds. These CDs should not be confused with the ones you buy at your local bank or savings and loan that must be held to maturity.

**A banker's acceptance** is a marketable security arising from international trade. When a foreign company buys American goods, the American seller usually wants a bank to guarantee payment before shipment is made. The foreign buyer gets a bank (usually in the United States) to guarantee the purchase price of the goods with a banker's acceptance. The seller of the goods can sell a banker's acceptance in the financial market, allowing the seller to receive cash before the international customer receives the goods (delivery may take weeks or months if the goods are shipped by sea). This can save valuable time for companies in need of cash.

Businesses with idle cash can also loan money to other companies; these loans are called commercial paper. **Commercial paper** is backed only by the name and reputation of the issuing company. The most common type of commercial paper is financial paper, sold by companies such as General Motors Acceptance Corporation (GMAC), Ford Motor Credit, and General

**Treasury bills**

Short-term debt obligations of the U.S. government

**Certificates of deposit**

Loans made to the bank on which the bank pays interest

**Banker's acceptance**

A marketable security arising from international trade

**Commercial paper**

Short-term loans made to other businesses

Electric Credit, which are the financing subsidiaries of major companies. GMAC, for example, uses the money raised from the sale of commercial paper to loan money to automobile buyers who need financing. GMAC thereby loans money to car buyers rather than having the customer borrow money from a bank or other financial institution.

Excess cash can also be invested in international markets such as the **Eurodollar market**, a market for trading U.S. dollars. U.S. dollars loaned and borrowed from this European money market are called Eurodollars. The U.S. dollar is accepted by all countries in international trade, and thus many dollars end up in international banks. These dollars can be used by international companies to settle their accounts with one another. Countries and companies can also borrow dollars from these banks, most of which are centered in London. The Eurodollar market offers firms with extra dollars a place to earn a higher return at a little more risk than with U.S. Treasury bills.

Large and small firms can always invest excess cash in **money market funds,** which are professionally managed portfolios of marketable securities. These funds invest in Treasury bills, commercial paper, Eurodollars, bankers' acceptances, and other short-term securities. A mutual fund can make large investments through collectively investing funds for thousands of small investors and businesses. The fund buys securities that small investors could not afford to buy or monitor by themselves. Figure 18-1 illustrates money market rates available in several countries.

A small business can also invest in a money market account at a commercial bank or a savings and loan. This is similar to a money market fund except

**Eurodollar market**

A European market for trading U.S. dollars

**Money market funds**

Professionally managed portfolios of marketable securities

**Figure 18-1**

Average Money Market Rates

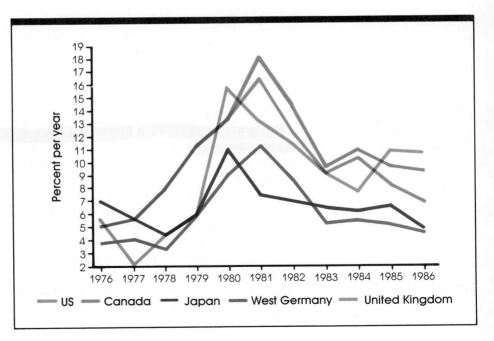

Table 18-2   Short-Term
Investment Possibilities for
Idle Cash
ᵃ The first $100,000 is
guaranteed by federal
depositors' insurance.

| Type of Security | Seller of Security | Interest Rate May 16, 1988 | Safety |
|---|---|---|---|
| T-bills (3 mos.) | U.S. government | 6.31% | Excellent |
| T-bills (6 mos.) | U.S. government | 6.51% | Excellent |
| T-bills (1 yr) | U.S. government | 6.89% | Excellent |
| CDs (3 mos.)ᵃ | U.S. commercial banks | 6.82% | Very good |
| Bankers' acceptances (3 mos.) | U.S. commercial banks | 7.05% | Good |
| Commercial paper (3 mos.) | High-quality companies | 7.10% | Good |
| Eurodollar deposits (3 mos.) | European banks | 7.50% | Good |
| Money market funds | Mutual funds | 5.89% | Very good |
| Money market accountsᵃ | Financial institutions | 5.54% | Very good |

that it is insured by the Federal Deposit Insurance Corporation (FDIC) up to $100,000.

Table 18-2 summarizes the short-term investments available to business firms and presents some sample interest rates for these securities. Interest rates change constantly, and by the time you read this book the rates will be different from those listed in Table 18-2. The safety rankings are relative. All the securities listed in Table 18-2 are low risk, but the U.S. government securities are the safest.

## Managing Accounts Receivable and Inventory

Accounts receivable is the money owed to a business by credit customers. Inventory includes raw materials, goods in process, and finished goods. The relationship between accounts receivable and inventory is usually stable in the long run and both are said to increase automatically along with sales. Accounts receivable and inventory are therefore called spontaneous assets because they increase spontaneously as sales increase. Accounts receivable and inventory, like cash and marketable securities, should be thought of and managed as an investment for maximum profit.

***Accounts Receivable.*** Businesses have accepted terms of trade when they sell on credit. Some businesses may require that customers pay the full amount due in thirty, sixty, or ninety days. Others may offer customers a 1 or 2 percent trade discount to encourage them to pay bills early, and many charge late-paying customers a penalty or financing fee (usually 1 or 1.5 percent). The larger the discount a business offers for early payment, the faster the accounts will be paid. Discounts get cash flowing through the firm faster, but they also reduce profitability. The company must balance the cost of offering discounts against the benefits of receiving cash faster.

One consideration that affects the profitability of accounts receivable is the type of customer to whom a business extends credit. If a business allows only customers with the highest credit rating (those who always pay on time) to purchase goods on credit, the quality of accounts will be high but sales may fall below the optimum production level. On the other hand, if the business

# Financial Encounter 18-1
## *Asset-Based Lenders*

Since 1985 the market for asset-backed securities has grown slowly. About $10 billion of asset-backed receivables were issued in 1986. The slow growth of these receivables can be explained by the negative connotation of asset-backed receivables, the high cost, and the complication of repackaging the securities. In the past, firms that issued asset-backed securities were seen as being short of cash, financially shaky, or in some sort of financial trouble. These securities have a relatively higher cost than some other forms of financing. Some people wonder if the benefits of getting the assets off the balance sheets justify the higher costs. Asset-backed securities are also very complicated to repackage and sell. Despite the drawbacks, asset-backed receivables offer some clear advantages.

Asset-backed securities are marketable securities with assets pledged as collateral. These securities also allow a firm to stay within its target debt-equity ratio, and firms are able to use their funds for more profitable investments.

Successful businesses occasionally need high priced capital. For example, the Los Angeles Lakers Inc. recently borrowed $12 million from Foothill Capital Corp, the largest asset-based lender (ABL) in the country.

ABLs charge high rates to compensate them for the huge risks they incur. In 1983 Foothill loaned $4 million to United Press International (UPI). Foothill was a major creditor of UPI and could have forced the firm to liquidate, but instead allowed UPI to file chapter 11 bankruptcy. Foothill continued to loan to UPI allowing the firm to pay back salaries and benefits to employees. In 1986 Foothill's loan was paid back in full. This shows how an asset based lender can help the economy. Asset-based lenders are earning some respectability in the finance world.

Robert A. Mamis, "Lender Of Last Resort," *INC.*, May 1987, Vol. 9 No. 5., pp. 149–152; Steve Cranford, "Whatever Became of Asset-Backed Receivables?," *Institutional Investor,* April 1987, Vol. XXI No. 4, pp. 231–234; Marci Baker, "Securities Revitalized By Banks," *Pensions & Investment Age,* June 29, 1987, pp. 13–14.

extends credit to risky customers (those who may pay bills late or never), sales could rise but uncollected accounts and bad debts would also rise.

Credit standards are often dictated by industry practices. Industry credit standards may be lower than those of a particular company, but setting standards higher than the industry does could cause a business to lose customers to competitors. To reduce the problem of bad debts, large and small businesses rely on credit ratings provided by local credit bureaus, by national credit-rating agencies such as Dun and Bradstreet, and by industry trade groups.

One way to measure the effectiveness of a firm's account collection procedures is to use the receivable turnover ratio (sales divided by accounts receivable) explained in chapter 17. A receivable turnover ratio of 12 indicates that $1 invested in extending credit through accounts receivable is enough to support $12 of credit sales per year. This assumes that the accounts receivable are paid off every thirty days on average and that the money is continually loaned to customers for new credit sales. Using a 360-day year and assuming that the firm's accounts receivable are paid in an average of thirty days, the receivable turnover is again 12 (360 days divided by 30 days equals 12 times per year).

For example, if Ajax Corporation had annual credit sales of $720,000 and average annual accounts receivable of $60,000, the receivable turnover would be calculated as follows:

$$\text{receivable turnover ratio} = \frac{\text{annual sales}}{\text{average annual accounts receivable}}$$

$$= \frac{\$720,000}{\$60,000}$$

$$\text{receivable turnover ratio} = 12 \times \text{per year}$$

The firm's average collection period (days receivables outstanding) can be calculated by turning around the last calculation and taking the accounts receivable from the annual balance sheet and dividing by the average daily credit sales:

$$\text{average collection period} = \frac{\text{accounts receivable}}{\text{annual credit sales}/360 \text{ days}}$$

$$= \frac{\$60,000}{\$720,000/360 \text{ days}}$$

$$= \frac{\$60,000}{\$2,000}$$

$$\text{average collection period} = 30 \text{ days}$$

If a firm's credit terms specify a thirty-day payment period, any amount over thirty days indicates that on average customers are late with their payments. The bigger the discrepancy, the more trouble the firm is having collecting accounts on time.

Occasionally, when customers do not pay their bills, the business must write off the balance as a bad debt or uncollectible account. A firm may look at the ratio of these bad debts to credit sales to indicate the health of its credit collection policies. Some bad debts are inevitable as customers fail to pay their bills because of bankruptcy or lack of cash. Management should not overreact to bad debts unless the bad debts are out of line with the company's experience or industry norms.

Another way to measure the efficiency of collections is to "age" the accounts receivable by examining the percentage of accounts that are paid within 0 to 30 days, 31 to 60 days, 61 to 90 days, and over 90 days. If the trade terms call for payment in thirty days, most accounts should fall in that category. All others represent late-paying accounts. If the average age of the accounts starts moving into the second two categories, the business is having trouble collecting on accounts, and cash flow is probably slower than it should be.

***Inventory.*** Inventory that the firm makes available for sale is controlled by production in cooperation with the marketing manager (see Chapter 11), but financial managers must coordinate inventory purchases in order to manage cash flows. Most financial managers believe there is an optimum amount to invest in inventory; the amount depends on the level of sales and growth of sales. For accounts receivable, the credit policy, specific terms of trade, and collection practices determine the optimum level. Optimum levels for inventory, however, are affected by the methods of production. If the firm tries to produce goods just in time to meet sales demand, the level of inventory will be relatively low because the firm does not allow a backlog of inventory to build up. If, on the other hand, the firm produces inventory in a constant, level pattern, inventory increases when sales decrease. This occurs because production is greater than sales at certain times, and excess inventory builds up.

The automobile industry is a good example. Because it is inefficient to continually lay off workers in slow times and call them back in better times, Ford, General Motors, and Chrysler try to set output targets each quarter and stick to their plan. Automakers normally like to keep a 60-day supply of inventory. In periods of slow sales, inventories can approach a 100-day supply. With so many cars in inventory, the auto industry often resorts to sales incentive programs to bring supplies back to the 60-day level. Suppliers can affect inventory in the short run by failing to ship goods on time. Strikes by auto workers can also cause inventory problems.

Because there is some risk to not having enough inventory, most businesses maintain an extra amount of inventory to guard against shortages that may result in lost sales. There are inventory models available to determine the optimum level of inventory a firm should have on hand to support a given level of sales. The models also indicate how often the inventory should be ordered so that it is available when needed. Inventory models attempt to minimize the cost of ordering and storing inventory.

# ▶ Managing Current Liabilities

Financial managers who manage current liabilities can obtain short-term funds from suppliers in the form of credit for the purchase of goods, from banks in the form of short-term loans, and from pension funds, insurance companies, and other nonbank financial institutions in the form of loans.

## Managing Accounts Payable

Accounts payable is money owed to suppliers for goods ordered. Just as accounts receivable and inventory are spontaneous assets, accounts payable are spontaneous liabilities. As sales increase and more inventory is purchased to maintain sales levels, higher levels of accounts payable are created by the purchase of more inventory on credit.

**Trade credit**

Credit extended by suppliers for the purchase of their goods and services

The most widely used source of short-term financing is **trade credit**— credit extended by suppliers for the purchase of their goods and services. Trade credit agreements range from the informal (open-book credit) to the formal (promissory notes and trade drafts). Open-book credit is an informal arrangement between a business and a supplier that allows the business to take possession of supplies and pay for them at a later date. A promissory note is a written agreement signed by the borrowing business, which promises it will pay the supplier a specified amount of money on a certain date in exchange for goods. A trade draft is a written agreement signed by the supplier ordering a business to pay a specified amount of money within a certain number of days. In order to take possession of the goods, the business must sign the trade draft, which is then called a trade acceptance. When the agreement is due, the supplier presents it to the borrowing business for payment.

Most suppliers offer a trade discount to businesses that pay their bills early. A supplier, for example, may offer trade terms of "1/10 net 30," meaning that the business may take a 1 percent discount if it makes payment by the tenth day after receiving the bill. Otherwise, the whole amount is due in thirty days. Failure to take the discount can add up to a substantial loss over the year.

The following formula is used to calculate the annual cost of not taking advantage of the trade discount.

$$
\begin{aligned}
\text{annual cost} &= \frac{\text{discount percentage}}{100\% - \text{discount percentage}} \times \frac{360\ \text{days}}{\text{due date} - \text{discount}} \\
&= \frac{1\%}{100\% - 1\%} \times \frac{360\ \text{days}}{30\ \text{days} - 10\ \text{days}} \\
&= \frac{1\%}{99\%} \times \frac{360}{20} \\
&= 1.01\% \times 18 \\
&= 18.18\%
\end{aligned}
$$

In this example, the annual cost would equal 18.18 percent for a 1 percent discount if paid within the first ten days. A firm that places eighteen order per year for $100,000 would save $1,000 for each order (a total savings of $18,000) from taking the discount. If the firm has the $100,000 in cash available, it would be wise to take the discount unless it can earn more than 18.18 percent on marketable securities. If no cash is available for early payment and the firm can borrow money for less than 18.18 percent it should borrow and take the discount.

## Managing Bank Liabilities

Both large and small businesses often obtain short-term funds from banks in the form of a line of credit or a loan. A line of credit is an agreement between a bank and a business in which a bank agrees to lend a specified amount of money to a business whenever the business needs the money, as long as the bank has the funds to lend. Banks also make **secured loans**— loans backed by something of value that the bank can claim if the borrower does not repay the loan—and **unsecured loans**—loans that are backed only by the borrower's good reputation (measured by the borrower's credit rating). Collateral is something of value—real estate, inventory, accounts receivable— that a bank can repossess in the event a borrower defaults, or fails to pay off a secured loan. **Principal** is the amount of money a business borrows; **interest** is a percentage of the principal that the bank charges to use the money for a given length of time.

The **prime rate** is the interest rate charged by banks to their best customers (usually large corporations) for short-term loans. Customers with credit

**Long-term finance for long-term growth.** Long-term financing is used for business expansion, for developing new products, and for equipment improvements. A manager of the Hilo Macaroni factory, maker of popular creme crackers, meets with bank officers from the Bank of Hawaii to discuss financial needs.

**Effective interest rate**

Measures the cost of a loan based on the actual amount of money the borrower has the use of during the period of the loan

**Simple interest loans**

Required a borrower to pay both principal and interest at the maturity date

ratings lower than those of the best customers are generally charged from 1 to 3 percent more than the prime rate. The interest rate on a loan may be fixed for the whole period of the loan, or it may float according to the daily average of the prime rate over the life of the loan. A floating rate can be an advantage when interest rates are falling and a disadvantage when interest rates are rising.

The total interest charge on a loan depends on the length of time the money is borrowed and the interest rate. It is not always easy to judge the real cost of a loan by the dollar interest charged. The **effective interest rate** measures the cost of a loan based on the actual amount of money the borrower has the use of during the period of the loan. It is an annual percentage cost of the loan. Although the *stated* interest rate may be 10 percent, the *effective* interest rate can be quite different. In the following examples exploring the impact of borrowing method on the effective interest rate, we use an example of a one-year loan of $100,000 with a stated annual interest rate of 8 percent.

**Simple-interest loans** require a borrower to pay both principal and interest at the maturity date—when the loan comes due. You may have had such a loan agreement if you borrowed money from your parents to buy a used car. With simple interest, the stated rate and effective rate are the same:

$$\text{effective rate} = \frac{\text{annual interest}}{\text{principal}} = \frac{\$8,000}{\$100,000}$$

$$= 8\%$$

**Discounted loans**

Require a borrower to pay the interest in advance on the day the loan is made

**Discounted loans** require a borrower to pay the interest in advance on the day the loan is made. If a business borrows $100,000 at a stated interest rate of 8 percent, it obtains $92,000 from the bank but pays back the full $100,000. This practice increases the effective interest rate of the loan because the borrower has the use of less money over the life of the loan but yet must still pay the same 8 percent interest rate, or $8,000 interest on $100,000 of principal:

$$\text{effective rate} = \frac{\text{interest}}{\text{principal} - \text{interest}} = \frac{\$8,000}{\$100,000 - 8,000}$$

$$= \$8,000/\$92,000$$

$$= 8.7\%$$

**Compensating-balance loans**

Require a borrower to keep a specified minimum amount of money equal to a percentage of the loan in a checking account at the lending bank.

**Compensating-balance loans** require a borrower to keep a specified minimum amount of money that is equal to a percentage of the loan in a checking account at the lending bank. This minimum balance is called a compensating balance. Again, the borrower does not have the use of the whole loan. This

**Servicing is essential.**
Commercial banks, savings and loan associations, credit unions, and other financial institutions provide short and long-term loans to individuals and businesses. Banks realize the importance of servicing the loan after it is secured. Homestead Financial has improved its technology and modernized its equipment to be able to service loans more efficiently and to foster future growth.

practice helps banks pay for services, such as lockboxes and check clearing, that they offer for "free." A 15 percent compensating balance means that the borrower would get the use of only $85,000 from a $100,000 loan because the other $15,000 had to be left in the company checking account as the compensation balance:

$$\text{effective rate} = \frac{\text{interest}}{\text{principal} - \text{compensating balance}}$$

$$= \frac{\$8,000}{\$100,000 - \$100,000\,(15\%)}$$

$$= \$8,000/\$85,000$$

$$= 9.41\%$$

In the American banking system, the lending bank can loan the $15,000 to someone else and earn enough of a profit to recover the costs of the services provided. Compensating balances increases the cost of the loan for the same reasons that discounted loans do. Some banks have discontinued this practice and now charge a fee for all services provided to the customer.

**Installment loans** require that a borrower repay interest and principal together in periodic payments, usually monthly or quarterly. A new-car loan is a typical example of an installment loan. A thirty-six-month loan requires thirty-six equal monthly payments. On average, the borrower has the use of half of the money over the life of the loan. This causes the effective interest

**Installment loans**

Require that a borrower repay interest and principal together in periodic payments

rate to be almost double the stated interest rate. The following example assumes a $100,000 business loan is repaid in twelve monthly payments:

$$\text{effective rate} = \frac{2 \times \text{annual number of payments} \times \text{interest}}{(\text{total number of payments} + 1) \times \text{principal}}$$

$$= \frac{2 \times 12 \times \$8,000}{(12 + 1) \times \$100,000}$$

$$= \frac{\$192,000}{\$1,300,000}$$

$$= 14.77\%$$

## Managing Nonbank Liabilities

Insurance companies, pension funds, money market funds, and other corporations also make short-term loans to business. Some businesses even obtain loans from foreign organizations. Large companies can borrow Eurodollars in the London market; this source of funds is not usually available for small companies.

Businesses that are in need of short-term funds can borrow money by selling commercial paper—a short-term loan. This form of short-term financing, however, is available only to large borrowers of the highest quality. A very active market exists for commercial paper, which is often a cheaper source of funds than bank loans.

Sometimes businesses find that they can get advantageous rates from nonbank lenders if they pledge some asset as collateral, such as accounts receivable or inventory, to guarantee the loan. Nonbank organizations that make loans prefer collateral when lending to high-risk customers. However, recent innovations in collateralized lending have added some high-quality accounts receivable to the market for secured loans.

In some instances, companies actually sell their accounts receivable to a finance company called a factor. The factor gives the company cash and then assumes the responsibility for collecting the accounts receivable. Because the selling firm's customers send payments to a lockbox, customers may have no idea that a factor has bought the receivables.

# ▶ Coordinating Cash Flows and the Need for Funds

## Cash Flow

**Cash flow**
The movement of money through a business on a daily, weekly, and monthly basis

**Cash flow** is the movement of money through a business on a daily, weekly, and monthly basis. Figure 18-2 shows the relationship between sales, cash, accounts receivables, and inventory. The interaction of these accounts creates cash flow. Until customers purchase goods, there is no sale and therefore no cash flow. The sale of goods generates cash or, if the sale is on credit, creates an account receivable. When the business collects the account receivable, the

**Figure 18-2**
The Cash Flow Cycle

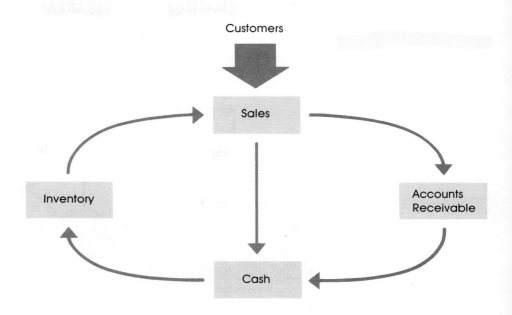

cash received is put into a cash account. The firm uses cash to purchase and manufacture inventory, which is purchased by customers, starting the flow of cash all over again.

Figure 18-3 is an expansion of Figure 18-2. Again, cash moves directly from sales to the cash account or from sales to accounts receivable and, upon collection, to the cash account. The arrow going from the cash account to materials and service signifies payments to suppliers of materials, which are accounts payable. The business also pays employees' wages and other expenses (such as utility expenses) that occur in the production process. Some businesses must pay for both raw materials and labor before the firm has saleable inventory. A department store purchases finished inventory such as suits, carpet, and towels. An automobile manufacturer, for example, purchases steel, glass, rubber, and spark plugs before it can create a saleable product. The sale of inventory completes the cyclical flow of cash through the firm.

To find out how fast inventory is moving through the cash-flow cycle, financial managers use the inventory turnover ratio, which indicates how many dollars of sales will be supported by $1 invested in inventory. An inventory turnover ratio of 6 times means that $1 of inventory supports $6 of annual sales. Another way of using an inventory turnover ratio of 6 times would be to divide 6 into 360 days in a year. This shows that on average, inventory "turns over" or is replaced every 60 days.

The receivable turnover ratio (credit sales to accounts receivable) provides the same type of information for that account. The higher the turnover number, the faster is the cash-flow cycle. Turnover ratios should be examined within the total context of a company's production-sales philosophy and trends in the industry.

**Figure 18-3**
Expanded Cash Flow Cycle

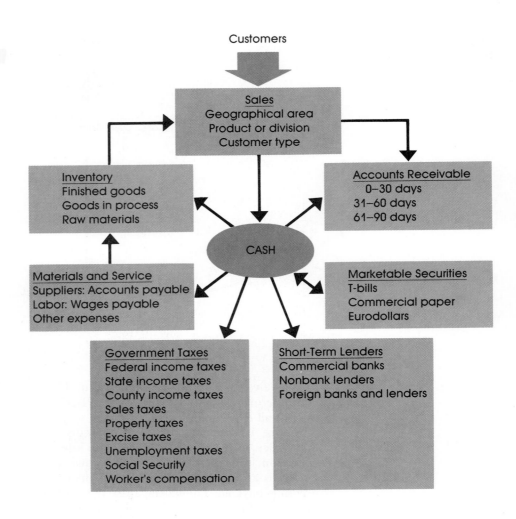

Another arrow in Figure 18-3 goes to the government for taxes, which are another cash outflow. Businesses are responsible for many different types of taxes, including federal, state and sometimes local income taxes. Most local governments levy a sales tax on goods sold. Businesses must also pay property taxes, unemployment taxes, social security, and workers' compensation. Even though the public tends to think that the only relevant taxes are on income and sales, many industries, particularly the alcohol and tobacco industries, must pay excise taxes that are greater than income taxes.

Another source of cash inflow and outflow is loans from bankers and other short-term lenders. Such borrowing creates a cash inflow used to support purchases of inventory or the extension of credit to customers. The firm is obligated to repay loans when they are due, and the repayment becomes a cash outflow. A company occasionally purchases short-term interest-bearing securities if it has temporary amounts of idle cash on hand. When it needs

**Table 18-3  Breakdown of IBM Sales**

| By Geographical Area | By Industry Segments and Classes of Similar Products |
|---|---|
| United States | Information handling |
| Americas and Far East | Processors |
| Europe, Middle East, and Africa | Peripherals |
| | Office systems and work stations |
| | Program products |
| | Maintenance services |
| | Federal systems |
| | Other business |

funds for other business purposes, it sells these securities to create a cash inflow.

Depending on the size and complexity of the business, the cash-flow cycle could be divided into many subsets. IBM, for example, divides its sales by both industry segment and geographical area (Table 18-3). The manager of each geographical area and each industry segment must have knowledge of the cash flow affecting his or her area of sales. Because the financial function is often centralized within a firm, managers in large diversified firms may receive cash-flow data from headquarters in the form of hourly or daily cash-flow updates.

## Planning and Controlling with a Sales Forecast and a Cash Budget

A business can measure whether it is using its short-term assets efficiently and may know where to go to borrow and to invest idle cash, but two crucial points remain unanswered: How much money will the firm need to borrow or invest? When will these needs occur? Cash needs must be anticipated, and borrowing arrangements with commercial banks and other lenders must be made in advance of the day that the firm actually needs the funds. The most widely used planning devices for forecasting and timing cash flow are the sales forecast and the cash budget.

**Sales forecast**

Estimate of the organization's future sales

***The Sales Forecast.*** A financial manager needs a **sales forecast,** or estimate of the organization's future sales, so that he or she can arrange in advance to borrow enough money to buy raw materials to make products and to pay employees' wages. The sales forecast is more difficult to develop in some industries than in others because sales in some industries are cyclical. They vary according to season and economic conditions. Sales of durable goods such as automobiles and large home appliances respond to changes in economic conditions—employment, personal income, interest rates—and may vary from one year to another. During poor economic times, for example, consumers may postpone an automobile purchase until interest rates become more favorable. Businesses must continually adjust production to keep up

**Figuring the finances.** A financial planner's primary responsibility is the organization's financial resources. Because the area of finance crosses over numerous functional areas, financial planners often meet with other executives and managers in the company.

with changing demand in these industries. Sales of necessity goods such as food, however, are relatively constant. A food producer has stable sales because consumers do not put off food purchases, no matter what the economic conditions.

Sales can be forecast in many different ways. Forecasts can be made by statistical methods that use mathematical relationships over time to look into the future. For example, sales may have a historical relationship to the gross national product. A projection of GNP might therefore be helpful in determining the company's sales forecast. Sales forecasts can also be intuitive and rely on feelings from people close to the marketplace, especially the sales force. Most likely the forecast will be a combination of statistical and intuitive forecasts tempered by managerial experience.

*The Cash Budget.* The **cash budget** presents the firm's cash inflow and outflow as an organized schedule. In large companies, the cash budget may be a daily schedule; in smaller companies, weekly or monthly cash budgets are used. Many individuals prepare a monthly cash budget to help them match their income with their expenses. The cash budget includes a collection schedule—a schedule of the firm's inflows for accounts receivable based on a sales forecast and customers' payment patterns. A payment schedule, which presents a schedule of the firm's cash outflow for wages, taxes, accounts payable, utilities, and other cash expenses, is also included. The collection schedule and payment schedule are combined to forecast the ending cash

**Cash budget**

The firm's cash inflow and outflow presented as an organized schedule for each period. Excess cash is usually invested in marketable securities; a forecasted cash deficits indicate that the business must plan to borrow funds to cover the deficit.

Table 18-4 presents a monthly cash budget to demonstrate these concepts. There are several forms that cash budgets can take but the end result provides the same information. One item that is included is a minimum level of cash that the business needs to pay its bills. This figure can be estimated from historical payment patterns or from the average minimum checkbook balance that is needed to pay bills. If the minimum is set too low, the firm will need to borrow money quickly. If the minimum is set too high, the firm may have idle funds available for short-term investment.

The cash budget depends on the sales forecast and an estimate of cash sales and credit sales. This information is important because it indicates when the cash will actually be collected. The collection schedule in Table 18-4 shows the expected cash inflow each month beginning at $28,000 in January and ending at $38,000 in April.

Once a financial manager has forecast the cash inflow, the cash outflow must be created through the payment schedule. The payment schedule includes the major payments such as for materials, salaries, labor, utilities, other production expenses, interest expense, and taxes. January's monthly payment is $33,000.

January's cash inflow of $28,000 and outflow of $33,000 result in a deficit cash flow of $5,000 for the month. The firm had $8,000 at the beginning of the month, and so the cumulative cash after paying the expenses is only

# Financial Encounter 18-3
## *Dun & Bradstreet*

Dun & Bradstreet (D&B) is known for its credit reports on companies. These reports contain various historical information necessary to evaluate the riskiness of companies. The reports help to determine if companies can acquire credit and if so, under what terms. Thus, many firms financing applications depend on Dun & Bradstreet's credit reports. Dun & Bradstreet has one of the largest databases of information in the world. Its database contains information on nine million firms. Dun & Bradstreet uses this database to create credit reports for mailing lists, directories, sales lists, and information about competition. This information can be the key factor that gives a firm the competitive edge.

Dun & Bradstreet has no long-term debt and a cash surplus of $600 million in cash. The company's earnings have been growing at 17 percent over the past five years and return on equity has averaged twenty-six percent. D&B's profits have been increasing for the past twenty-two years. One of the challenges for management is how to maintain its high growth rate. By spending 6 percent of gross revenue on research and development, D&B has been able to sustain its growth. Most of the firm's growth comes from acquisitions. D&B is constantly evaluating potential acquisitions and deciding which direction it wants to go in the future.

Dun & Bradstreet is a key player in the information industry. Its credit reports help to determine if companies acquire financing. D&B is a huge conglomerate involved in over twenty-two businesses. The management at D&B is noted as being one of the best in the world.

Ellen Benoit, "Charles Moritz, Dun & Bradstreet," *Financial World*, April 21, 1987, pp. 48–54; Robert M. Randell, "Dun & Bradstreet Sets Its Own Speed Limit," *Planning Review*, March/April 1987, pp. 8–14, 44; Allison Leigh Cowan, "That Purring You Hear is Dun & Bradstreet's Money Machine," *Business Week*, October 13, 1987, pp. 90–94; Stuart Gannes, "Dun & Bradstreet Redeploys The Riches," *Fortune*, August 19, 1985, pp. 38–47.

**Table 18-4  A Monthly Cash Budget**

|  | December | January | February | March | April |
|---|---|---|---|---|---|
| Sales Forecast | $30,000 | $ 20,000 | $ 30,000 | $ 40,000 | $ 30,000 |
| **Collections schedule** | | | | | |
| Cash sales (20 percent of sales) | | $ 4,000 | $ 6,000 | $ 8,000 | $ 6,000 |
| Credit sales collected 80 percent of prior month's sales | | 24,000 | 16,000 | 24,000 | 32,000 |
| Monthly cash collections | | $ 28,000 | $ 22,000 | $ 32,000 | $ 38,000 |
| **Payments schedule** | | | | | |
| Payment for materials | | $ 15,000 | $ 10,000 | $ 15,000 | $ 20,000 |
| Salaries | | 4,000 | 4,000 | 4,000 | 4,000 |
| Labor expense | | 6,000 | 4,000 | 6,000 | 8,000 |
| Utilities | | 2,000 | 2,000 | 1,500 | 1,000 |
| Other production expenses | | 1,000 | 1,000 | 500 | 500 |
| Interest Expense | | 2,000 | -0- | -0- | -0- |
| Taxes | | 3,000 | -0- | -0- | 3,500 |
| Monthly cash payments | | $ 33,000 | $ 21,000 | $ 27,000 | $ 37,000 |
| **Cash budget** | | | | | |
| Cash flow (collections – payments) | | $ –5,000 | $ 1,000 | $ 5,000 | $ 1,000 |
| Beginning cash balance | | 8,000 | 3,000 | 4,000 | 9,000 |
| Cummulative cash | | 3,000 | 4,000 | 9,000 | 10,000 |
| Less: minimum cash balance | | 7,000 | 7,000 | 7,000 | 7,000 |
| Total loans to maintain minimum cash balance | | –4,000 | –3,000 | | |
| Excess cash (marketable securities) | | | | 2,000 | 3,000 |

$3,000. Management knows from experience that the business needs at least $7,000 in case it does not collect cash according to the forecasts or some unforeseen expenses occur. To play it safe, management wants a minimum of $7,000 in the company's checking account, and therefore borrows $4,000 to bring the minimum cash balance up to $7,000. By April, the company expects to have excess or idle cash of $3,000 that can be invested in marketable securities.

The financial planning aspect of the sales forecast and cash budget is very important, but there is no guarantee that the forecast results will occur. After using the cash budget to forecast cash flow, the financial manager can also use the budget as a controlling device, or a set of goals, to measure the firm's actual performance. The cash budget is an important financial tool in coordinating corporate strategies for sales, production, marketing, and finance. The sales forecast and cash budget are a necessary part of both large and small businesses.

Bankers, moreover, expect companies to provide this information whenever they apply for a loan. Sales forecasts and cash budgets offer the banker some indication that the businessperson knows when the company can repay the loan. The cash budget is often associated with accounting, but it is a necessary tool for the financial manager to manage a series of short-term cash flows. It can be continually updated every month and ties together most of the information discussed in this chapter.

# Summary and Review

▶ Short-term finance is the management of current assets (cash, marketable securities, accounts receivable, and inventory) and current liabilities (accounts payable, wages payable, notes payable, and taxes payable). Financial managers spend much of their time managing current assets and liabilities.

▶ Current assets are those that can be turned into cash within a year. Cash management focuses on increasing the speed of collections through playing the float, the use of lockboxes, electronic funds transfer, and investing in marketable securities.

▶ Management of accounts receivable emphasizes the customer's credit worthiness and the credit terms extended to customers. Inventory management focuses on determing optimum inventory levels that minimize the cost of storing and ordering inventory.

▶ Current liabilities are obligations that must be repaid within a year. These short-term obligations may come from trade credit received from the supplier of inventory, or they may be the result of borrowing from banks or nonbanks.

▶ The effective cost of borrowing from banks varies according to the terms of the loan. Simple interest is the cheapest method of paying interest; discounted loans, compensating-balance loans, and installment loans all raise the effective cost of borrowing.

▶ Cash is used to buy inventory from suppliers; inventory is then produced into finished products and sold. The sale creates either immediate cash or an account receivable for goods sold on credit. When excess cash is available, it is invested in marketable securities or used to pay off liabilities.

▶ The sales forecast is used to determine how much money a business will need to borrow to purchase supplies and pay wages and other expenses. Cash budgets are schedules used to coordinate the flow of funds through the business. The cash budget ties together the collections of accounts receivable and the payments made for inventory, labor, and other cash expenses. The end result is a schedule of cash flow so that the financial manager knows how much money to borrow, when, when a loan can be repaid, and when and for how long excess cash can be invested in marketable securities.

# Key Terms and Concepts

short-term financial management
working capital management
marketable securities
transaction balances
float
lockbox
Treasury bills
certificates of deposit (CDs)
banker's acceptance
commercial paper
Eurodollar market
money market funds
trade credit
secured loans

unsecured loans
collateral
principal
interest
prime rate
effective interest rate
simple-interest loans
discounted loans
compensating-balance loans
installment loans
cash flow
sales forecast
cash budget

# Checking Your Understanding

This chapter introduced you to the subject of short-term finance. To test and reinforce your understanding, fill in the blanks below.

1. A _certificate of deposit_ is a short-term security offered by commercial banks and can be used as an investment for excess cash.

2. One way companies speed up their collection process is to use a _lockbox_ from which the bank collects customers' payments.

3. _Simple Interest_ is computed by taking the interest payment and dividing by the amount borrowed. The rate will be equal to the effective rate of interest.

4. Banks often require borrowers to maintain a _compensating_ balance in their checking accounts as part of a loan agreement.

5. _Trade credit_ refers to the practice of suppliers' extending credit to customers for a specified period of time.

6. The cash budget relies on the _collection schedule_ to determine when cash from sales will be received by the business.

7. A marketable security that arises from foreign trade and can be used as a short-term investment is called a _banker's_ acceptance.

8. A _cash budget_ provides a schedule for planning and controlling the collections, payments, and borrowing and investment of idle cash.

# Topics for Review and Discussion

1. Define working capital management.
2. What are spontaneous assets and liabilities?
3. Describe several ways that a firm may speed up its cash flow.

**4.** What is the float? How does a firm play the float?

**5.** What is the purpose of having a lockbox?

**6.** Efficient cash management techniques invest excess cash in marketable securities. List and describe the marketable securities discussed in this chapter.

**7.** At the end of the year, a business has accounts receivable of $360,000 outstanding. Assume that there are 360 days in the year and that the firm had credit sales of $4,320,000. What is the average collection period?

**8.** Why and how would a financial analyst "age" the accounts receivable?

**9.** If a firm were offering trade credit terms of 2/10 net 30, what would be the cost of not taking the discount?

**10.** What does it mean to have a line of credit at a bank?

**11.** You are able to borrow $10,000 at an interest rate of 10 percent. Compute the effective cost of borrowing if interest is computed based on

a. simple interest

b. a discounted loan

c. a compensating balance of 15 percent

d. a monthly installment loan

**12.** What are some of the sources of short-term funds that would not be available from a U.S. commercial bank?

**13.** If you want to measure the speed of the sales–cash flow relationship, what ratios would you use? What information would they provide?

**14.** How is the minimum cash balance related to the firm's transactions?

**15.** Discuss the purpose of making a sales forecast and a cash budget and ways you might go about making them.

**16.** Explain the major benefits of using a cash budget.

# Exercises

**1.** Using your local newspaper or *The Wall Street Journal,* find the current rates of interest on the following marketable securities:

| Securities | Current Rate |
|---|---|
| T-bills (3 mos.) | _____ |
| T-bills (6 mos.) | _____ |
| Certificates of deposit | _____ |
| Commercial paper (finance paper) | _____ |
| Bankers' acceptance | _____ |
| Eurodollar deposits | _____ |
| Money market deposits | _____ |
| Money market accounts | _____ |

**2.** Diagram the cash-flow process.

a. Explain how cash is related to marketable securities.

b. What is the driving force behind the cash-flow cycle?

c. How do accounts payable tie into the cash-flow cycle?

d. How is the cash-flow process affected by the trade credit terms?

**3.** Create a cash budget for yourself, based on your income from your parents or from your job, that shows all cash inflows and outflows.

## Case 18-1:
## *Buick City: Just-in-Time Illustrated*

Buick City, a General Motors plant located in Flint, Michigan, represents the most extensive use of the just in time concept (JIT) in the United States to date. JIT is noted for its manufacturing benefits which ultimately appear on the balance sheet. This concept makes parts available to the production process just in time to produce the product. By using the JIT approach, Buick City minimized its inventory, thus reducing costs and maximizing profitability. Lower inventory means less inventory financing and less storage space for the inventory.

The JIT system maintains very little inventory, receiving the necessary inventory just in time for production. Inventory levels at Buick City range from one hour to a maximum of sixteen hours worth of parts. This inventory level is extremely low by industry standards. As a result of less inventory, Buick City uses 70% less space than the standard automobile plant.

Buick City could finance its inventory by either borrowing from a bank or by using its own funds; however, both of these methods cost money. If Buick City borrowed from a bank, the cost would be in the form of interest on the loan, whereas using its own funds would entail only their opportunity cost, that is the inability to use the money elsewhere.

It is easy to see how JIT actually saves a company money. For example, if Buick City's average inventory is three-thousand car seats and each car seat costs $500, it would need $1,500,000 to finance its inventory. If Buick City borrows the $1,500,000 from a bank that charges 8% annual interest, the cost of financing the car seats would be $1,500,000 × 8% = $120,000. A standard GM auto plant would have approximately 70% more inventory than Buick City, thus its inventory would be 10,000 car seats. It would need $5,000,000 ($500 × 10,000) to finance its inventory. If it borrowed at the same bank it would cost 400,000 ($5,000,000 × 8%). Comparing Buick City to a standard GM auto plant, we can see that by using the JIT method Buick City saves $280,000. Since Buick City inventories about 4,000 parts, the cost savings by using JIT can be astronomical.

Another benefit of minimizing inventory is reduced inventory storage space, resulting in smaller plants. Buick City is half the size of comparable GM plants, mainly due to less inventory at the plant. Not only does this reduce Buick City's cost for the building, but it also reduces its overhead costs, and actual plant construction costs.

In order to implement a JIT inventory system, suppliers have to be willing to keep inventory on hand and Buick City must be able to communicate with its suppliers quickly. It does this by using electronic data interchange (EDI). EDI enables its computers to communicate with other computers, exchange documents, and perform transactions instantaneously.

The real savings from EDI are realized in the accounting and finance departments. EDI eliminates data rekeying and significantly reduces errors. Computer-to-computer handling of information improves quality and consistency. Auditing of paperwork is virtually eliminated.

There are many ways a JIT system cuts costs and overhead. An EDI methodology helps assure speedy delivery of materials and benefits the accounting and finance divisions by reducing paperwork, errors, clerical and auditing costs. In the future, EDI will also be used a part of a paperless system.

These facts are from Dr. Mehran Sepehri, "Case In Point: Buick City Genuine Just In Time Delivery," *P&IM Review with APICS News,* March 1988, pp. 34–36; Arjan T. Sadhwani, M. H. Sarhan, "Electronic Systems Enhance JIT Operations," *Management Accounting,* December 1987, pp. 25–30; George Foster and Charles T. Horngren, "JIT: Cost Accounting and Cost Management Issues," *Management Accounting,* June 1987, pp. 19–25; Robert D. McIlhatten, "The JIT Philosophy," *Management Accounting,* September 1987, pp. 20–26.

### Questions

1. Explain how just-in-time saves a business money.
2. What is EDI and how does it work?
3. What may be some drawbacks of just-in-time for the manufacturer and supplier?

## Case 18-2
## *Factoring*

Factoring is the sale of receivables to a factoring company. The factoring company is usually paid a service fee that varies in relationship to the riskiness of the accounts receivable, the number of invoices, and the size of the invoices. Invoice discounting is a form of factoring where instead of a service fee, the factor buys the receivables at a discount. The factoring company usually pays 80% cash for approved accounts receivables. The factoring company establishes the company's credit policy, so it is able to control the quality of the accounts receivables.

Factoring can be done under a recourse or non-recourse (full factoring) agreement. When it is done with recourse, the company is ultimately liable for bad credit, and possibly the administrative burden as well. Under a non-recourse agreement, the factor is responsible for credit losses.

There are many variations of factoring. Collection-date factoring is when the factoring company gives the firm credit as soon as it makes a sale. It charges interest on the cash advance until the customer actually pays its bill. Another form of factoring is maturity date factoring. In this case the factor will pay the company its total amount of outstanding invoices on the designated average date of maturity.

Traditionally, factoring was done by large manufacturing firms. Today factoring is being utilized by small and medium-sized firms. These firms use factoring as a source of short-term financing. As a result of this relatively easy cash source they are able to grow more rapidly. Factoring allows a firm to obtain 80% cash immediately for its sales. In addition, some factors provide clients with cash advances. Factoring is a cash advance, not a loan, so it doesn't show up on the balance sheet as debt. Another advantage is that the funds are obtained without the issuance of common stock. The stockholders are still able to maintain the same level of control over the company. By using a factor the firm can eliminate the need for a credit analysis and collection department. The firm also eliminates bad debts and frees management's time for more profitable activities.

A new use of factoring is in the public utilities industry. Public utilities are regulated by the government and are allowed to operate at a designated profitability level. Recently, public utility firms have had numerous rate increases. William F. Malec, president of CSW Credit, a firm that currently factors accounts receivables for a public utility, believes that "nonnotification" factoring (the utility customer pays directly to the utility) is ideal for the industry. The utility company gets its cash virtually the same day the revenue is used. This allows the utility firm to retire more expensive debt, and fund construction and plant improvements. Its need for permanent financing is reduced. Factoring can reduce a utility's revenue requirements. Customer relations won't be hurt by factoring since the utility company deals with the customer and the customer won't even know that factoring is taking place.

However, there are some potential problems with using factoring in the public utilities industry. One problem is the enormous amount of accounts receivable to be processed. Another is the daily and seasonal fluctuations in receivables. The fact that the SEC approved CSW Credit for a public utility firms could pave the road for the future.

---

These facts are from: William F. Malec, "Factoring—An Old Tool Used In A New Setting," *Public Utilities Fortnightly.* July 23, 1987, pp. 29–32; Michael Maberly, "Factoring: A Catalyst For Growth And Profits," *Accountancy,* April 1986, pp. 122–124; Susan E. Bishopric, "Factors Emerge As Financial Management Resource To Small And Medium-Sized Firms," *C&FM,* December 1986, p. 41; Mary Bradenberg, "Why Don't They Use Factoring?" *Accountancy,* January 1987, pp. 100–101; Edward Suarez, "A Guide To Successful Financing Getting Through The Financial Maze," *L&H Perspective,* Spring Summer 1981, p. 17.

### Questions

1. What is the difference between recourse and nonrecourse factoring?
2. What is "nonnotification" factoring?
3. What are some potential problems of using factoring in the public utilities industry?

# Answers to Checking Your Understanding

1. certificate of deposit
2. lockbox
3. simple interest
4. compensating

5. trade credit
6. collection schedule
7. banker's
8. cash budget

## Outline

# Chapter 19

# Long-Term Finance: Stocks, Bonds, and Securities Markets

## Objectives

After reading this chapter, you will be able to:

▶ Understand how decisions about long-term financing affect a business' cash flow and what effects these decisions have on the firm's balance sheet.

▶ Explain how the selection of long-term assets, such as plant and equipment, affect the ability of a business to finance expansion.

▶ Define long-term liabilities, and describe how corporations issue stock and bonds using an investment banker.

▶ Read and evaluate information in stock and bond quotes in financial newspapers.

▶ Discuss the various securities markets in the United States.

# Business Experience

U.S. stock markets are an important source of funds for corporations thinking about selling new shares of stock to the public. There are over 45 million people in the U.S. who own stock, as well as thousands of pension funds that invest for the benefit of employees, and so changes in the value of common stocks affect both business and individuals. During October of 1987 the greatest collapse in stock prices ever seen occurred, sending chills throughout the world.

"From the close of trading Tuesday, October 13, 1987 to the close of trading Monday, October 19, the Dow Jones Industrial Average declined by almost one-third, representing a loss in the value of all outstanding United States stocks of approximately $1.0 trillion.

"What made this market break extraordinary was the speed with which prices fell, the unprecedented volume of trading and the consequent threat to the financial system.

"In response to these events, the President created the Task Force on Market Mechanisms. Its mandate was to determine what happened and why, to do it in sixty days, and to provide guidance in helping to prevent such a break from happening again.

"The precipitous market decline of mid-October was "triggered" by specific events: an unexpectedly high merchandise trade deficit that pushed interest rates to new high levels, and proposed tax legislation that led to the collapse of the stocks of a number of takeover candidates. This initial decline ignited mechanical, price-insensitive selling by a number of institutions . . . and a small number of mutual fund groups reacting to redemptions. The selling by these investors, and the prospect of further selling by them, encouraged a number of aggressive trading-oriented institutions to sell in anticipation of further market declines. These institutions included a small number of pension and endowment funds, money management firms and investment banking houses. This selling, in turn, stimulated further reactive selling . . ."

It becomes clear from reading this much of the report that the collapse was significant in size and scope. This short quote also indicates the interrelationship among economics, taxes, international trade, and the behavior of financial institutions (discussed in chapter 16). Most of what has been presented from chapter 1 to chapter 18 has some effect on stock prices of publicly owned companies which are traded on stock exchanges. The stock market measures the success or failure of management, the impact of the economy, and world economic health. The stock market is where success is rewarded and measured. This is where people like Steve Jobs who founded Apple, Bill Gates of Microsoft, and Ross Perot of Perot Systems were rewarded for building successful companies. This is where "the market" tells stockholders what their companies are worth. Clearly a loss of $1 trillion in less than a week is bad news for everyone associated with the U.S. economy. Why the total value of common stocks could fall so much in such a short time will be debated for many years; it may suffice to say that investors in mass must have thought stocks were overpriced.

---

This information is from the *Report of The Presidential Task Force on Market Mechanisms,* January 1988.

# Introduction

**Long-term financial management**

The managing of the long-term assets and liabilities and owners' equity portion of the balance sheet

Chapter 18 discussed the management of the current assets and current liabilities found on the balance sheet. Chapter 19 discusses **long-term financial management**—the managing of long-term assets and liabilities and the owners' equity portion of the balance sheet. The acquisition of long-term assets is vital to a firm's survival, as is the ability to raise long-term funds to finance the purchase of efficient, modern production facilities.

This chapter deals with long-term assets, liabilities, and owners' equity, such as the company's land, production facilities, equipment, stocks, bonds, and retained earnings. It examines how long-term assets are acquired and how they are involved in the production process and therefore in the generation of cash flow. Next, it discusses sources of long-term financing—corporate bonds, common stock, and retained earnings—and how securities are sold and distributed by an investment banker acting on behalf of a business. Finally, the chapter looks at the securities markets—the place where stocks and bonds are traded by the public and by financial intermediaries such as pension funds and mutual funds.

## ▶ Long-Term Financial Management

**Long-term assets**

Assets that are expected to last for many years

**Long-term liabilities**

Debts that will be repaid over a number of years

**Owners' equity**

The money stockholders have invested in a company

Table 19-1 presents the long-term portions of the balance sheet for Basic Corporation: long-term assets, liabilities, and stockholders' equity. **Long-term assets**, also called fixed assets, are those that are expected to last for many years, such as production facilities (plants), offices, equipment, and contracts to perform services. **Long-term liabilities** are debts that will be repaid over a number of years, such as long-term bank loans and bond issues. **Owners' equity** is the money stockholders have invested in a company and consists of funds from the sale of stock and earnings that have been retained by the firm. These terms were explained in Chapter 17 but are developed more fully in the following sections.

Figure 19-1 brings together short-term and long-term assets and combines them with short-term and long-term sources of financing. The diagram shows how the long-term assets and liabilities interact with the cash-flow cycle as well as with production. Without fixed assets and long-term financing to buy fixed assets, the company cannot generate cash flow. If a business has no production facilities and equipment, it will have no product or service to sell.

## ▶ Long-Term Assets

Businesses need the most technologically advanced, modern equipment they can afford because such equipment produces better goods at a lower cost

## Long-Term Assets

| | | |
|---|---:|---:|
| Fixed Assets | | |
|   Plant & Equipment | $680,000 | |
|     Less: Accumulated Depreciation | −240,000 | |
|   Net Plant & Equipment | | 440,000 |
|   Other Assets | | 60,000 |
| Total Fixed Assets | | $500,000 |
| | | |
| Total Assets | | $725,000 |
|   (current assets from Table 18.1 + fixed assets) | | |

## Long-Term Liabilities & Equity

| | |
|---|---:|
| Long-Term Debt | |
|   8 percent bonds due 2010 | $260,000 |
| Stockholders' Equity | |
| Common Stock ($1 par value; 100,000 shares) | 100,000 |
| Capital In Excess of Par | 200,000 |
| Retained Earnings | 60,000 |
| Total Long-Term Liabilities & Equity | $620,000 |
| | |
| Total Liabilities & Equity | $725,000 |

and at higher volume. In recent years many U.S. businesses have come to realize the cost of having obsolete equipment. Many U.S. steel manufacturers, for example, have inefficient, old production facilities, and as a result American steel production has declined by 50 percent in recent years because foreign competitors with efficient, modern equipment can produce steel less expensively. Similarly, American automakers have had to modernize their production facilities in order to produce cars and trucks that can compete with Japanese and South Korean products.

All businesses need to be able to finance new plants and equipment. Companies can finance new plants and equipment by borrowing money, selling stock, or retaining earnings. Although such financing is easy for profitable businesses, it may be difficult for firms that have experienced years of losses, as many steel companies have. Lack of profits in recent years has kept steel makers from reinvesting profits into new equipment that could enable them to compete with foreign producers. Banks and other lenders do not want to loan money unless the borrower can show that it can pay off loans with earnings. Stockholders do not want to invest in a company that has poor earnings, because of the high risk and low potential for profits. Situations such as these create long-term financing problems for financial managers.

**Figure 19-1**
Long-Term Finance and Cash
Flow

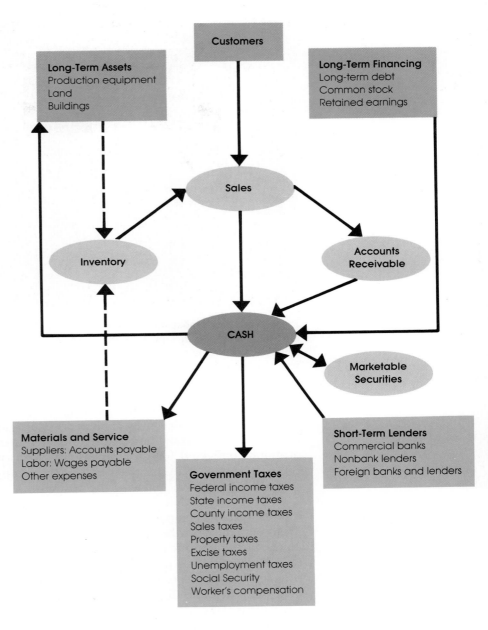

## Capital Budgeting and Project Selection

**Real capital**

Physical assets, such as plant
and equipment, usually referred
to as fixed assets

Table 19-1 shows that the Basic Corporation has total fixed assets of
$500,000. These fixed assets are often called **real capital** or capital assets by
accountants and financial managers. The word *real* indicates that these are
physical assets, such as plant and equipment; the word *capital* indicates that
they are long-term. One job of the financial manager is to select fixed assets,

**Press proof made possible.** Investments are often necessary to maintain growth and remain competitive in the service industry. An executive of Congraf, a New England printing company, meets with a leasing corporation officer to discuss improvements in printing technology.

projects, and investments that will help the company earn a financial return consistent with its objectives. The process of selecting capital assets for the firm is called the capital-budgeting process. The **capital budget** is the amount of money budgeted for the purchase of fixed assets, and capital budgeting is the process of analyzing the needs of the company and selecting the assets that will maximize the value of the business.

Once a business has purchased a new asset, it must continually reevaluate it to measure its compatibility with the firm's needs. If an asset does not live up to expectations, then management must find out why and make adjustments. Sometimes the capital-budgeting process needs to be refined; in other cases, customers and prices may have changed unexpectedly. Occasionally, a company decides to refocus its customer emphasis. In such cases, a business firm will sell whole divisions or subsidiaries that no longer fit into its long-term plans. GE, for example, sold its small appliance division because the unit did not fit into the company's long-term plans.[1]

## Assessment of Risk

Every investment carries a risk. Table 19-2 ranks potential projects according to a qualitative estimate of risk. In the area of foreign investment, risk assessments must include the political climate and the economic stability of the region. An investment in a production facility in England would have much less risk than one in Chile or Panama.

Another factor effecting the riskiness of a new asset is time. The longer the expected life of a project or asset, the greater is its potential risk because

**Table 19-2 Qualitative Assessment of Capital Budgeting Risk**

| Potential Projects | Generalized Levels of Risk |
|---|---|
| Repair old machinery | Lowest risk |
| Buy new equipment for an established market | Moderate risk |
| Add to a product line | Normal risk |
| Introduce a new product in a familiar area | Above normal risk |
| Expand into a new market | High risk |
| Introduce new product in foreign markets | Highest risk |

the ability to predict the future accurately decreases as the length of time covered in the forecast increases.

Risk is also affected by the stability and competitive nature of the marketplace. Dramatic changes that affect markets can happen quickly. This was demonstrated by rapid rises in the price of oil between 1974 and 1975, unexpected increases in inflation and interest rates between 1978 and 1982, the stock market crash of 1987, and the opening of commercial markets in the Soviet Union in 1988 for the first time in seventy years. IBM's latest high-technology computer product may become obsolete in two to three years; a new soft drink from Coca-Cola could be around for decades. Financial managers must consider these issues when making long-term decisions about the purchase of captial assets.

**Large asset, large loan.** The long-term financing needed by large companies can be extraordinary. Unocal Corp. had to raise a large amount of funds to build this offshore California oil platform, but the anticipated production is 20,000 barrels of crude oil per day.

# Cost of Financial Capital

The selection of a project depends not only on accurate projections of the cash flows the new asset will generate, but also on the cost of financing the capital asset. If the cost of financing the project is very high, the return on the asset must be high enough to cover the cost. A business must pay interest on money it borrows and is also expected to provide a return for the owners of the firm. The returns on the company's assets must cover not only the financing costs, but also the operating costs. Otherwise the value of the company may decline, and the company may eventually go out of business.

There is a limited supply of funds available for investment by lenders and potential owners. Interest rates affect the cost of borrowed funds, and dividends and stock prices influence the cost of common stock and retained earnings. The most efficient and profitable companies can attract funds at the lowest cost. Inefficient and high-cost companies must pay a higher cost in order to attract suppliers of funds. This capitalistic system penalizes weak firms and rewards strong firms. Financial Encounter 19-1 profiles Reginald Lewis, who has been quite successful in arranging long-term financing for businesses.

New firms enter high-return industries, eventually driving returns down to normal levels. A good example of this can be found in the personal computer industry in the early 1980s. Apple Computers was earning very high returns on the Apple II. Other computer companies evaluated the personal computer market and concluded that they could manufacture and sell personal computers at lower prices than Apple and still make a return to cover the cost of operations and financing. IBM successfully entered the personal computer market and was soon followed by Compaq, which produced and sold competitive machines at prices even lower than IBM's. As more manufacturers entered the market, the prices of personal computers dropped quickly and sales of personal computers rose. This expanded the market for personal computers but lowered returns on each dollar of new capital assets. Competition forced weak companies out of the industry, leaving the most efficient ones to compete for market share. Some consider this to be "the law of the jungle," but the free enterprise system ensures that it is a way of offering consumers products at the most efficient prices.

# ▶ Long-Term Liabilities

Liabilities take many different forms, but in the end the key word is *debt*. Some corporations are in debt to commercial banks through lines of credit, short-term loans of less than one year, or long-term loans of up to five years. Many corporations are in debt to institutional and individual investors. Institutional investors that make long-term term loans include pension funds, mutual funds, and life-insurance companies.

**Bond**

A long-term debt that is a marketable security

Long-term debt or liabilities most often take the form of bonds. A **bond** is a marketable security that a company sells to raise money. Bonds can be

## Financial Encounter 19-1

### Profile: Reggie Lewis of TLC Group, Inc.

When Reginald Lewis bought all the stock of Beatrice International Food Co. for $950 million in 1987, his company became the largest black-owned business in the United States. Lewis was no stranger to the game of arranging long-term financing. His Lewis & Clarkson law firm helps several large corporations finance minority-owned businesses. Lewis also owns an investment holding company, the TLC Group, Inc.

Reginald Lewis grew up in what he describes as a tough, stimulating neighborhood. He excelled at sports in high school, but he fell in love with economics at Virginia State University. He went on to study securities law at Harvard Law School and joined the law firm of Paul Weiss Rifkind Wharton & Garrison in 1968. In 1973 he formed Lewis & Clarkson, where he specialized in channeling the excess funds of corporations into minority companies in need of money. After a while he became bored; so in 1983, he formed the TLC Group (he won't tell anyone what the TLC stands for), where he could do his own wheeling and dealing.

In 1984 Lewis arranged a leveraged buyout (that is, he bought all the company's outstanding stock with borrowed money) of McCall Pattern Co. for $25 million. He turned the aging sewing company around, doubling its profits to $14 million in just three and a half years. He also left most of the management team at McCall Pattern intact, an unusual action. Lewis sold McCall in 1987 for $95 million.

Because Lewis was so successful in his leveraged buyout of McCall, he had no trouble convincing Mike Milliken of Drexel Burnham Lambert to help him finance the leveraged buyout of Beatrice International Foods.

In addition to the financing from Drexel Burnham Lambert, Lewis obtained a $450 million line of credit and financed the rest of the deal with profit from the sale of McCall Pattern. Drexel Burnham Lambert will own 35 percent of Beatrice International for its clients; Lewis and TLC will own 55 percent; and Beatrice International management will hold the remaining interest in the company, which had sales of $2.5 billion in 1986.

Lewis plans to sell some parts of Beatrice to pay off his debts. As he did at McCall Pattern, Lewis intends to leave Beatrice's management team intact to take care of running the day-to-day operations—no easy feat in itself. Beatrice International currently includes sixty-four separate companies in thirty-one countries and markets everything from juice to potato chips. Lewis will serve as a corporate strategist to scout growth opportunities for his new company.

Minority businesses have traditionally had a hard time obtaining financing, particularly when the ventures were risky, but Lewis' huge success may change that. His good relations with several investment firms and his leveraged-buyout track record may open doors for other minority entrepreneurs.

---

These facts are from Andrew Kupfer, "The Newest Member of the LBO Club," in "Fortune's Business People of the Year," *Fortune*, January 4, 1988, pp. 32–33; Robert H. Bork, Jr., with Cynthia Kyle, "When Wall Street Began to Take Blacks Seriously," *U.S. News & World Report*, August 31, 1987, pp. 44; Nancy J. Perry, "Rags to Riches," *Fortune*, September 14, 1987, pp. 22–23; and Peter Flinch, "Reg Lewis Hits the Big Time—and Takes It in Stride," *Business Week*, August 24, 1987, p. 27.

---

issued by corporations, public utilities, nonprofit corporations, and federal, state, and local governments. Bonds can be transferred from one owner to another in a bond market. Bank debt, in contrast, usually is not transferred but is held by the original lending bank until it is repaid by the borrowing company.

## The Bond Contract

The bond contract sets forth all the terms of agreement between the lender and the bond issuer. It is legally called the indenture. The indenture, which can be over a hundred pages long, specifies the basic items such as par value, maturity date, and coupon rate:

▶ The **par value**, or face value, is the initial value of the bond. The most common par value is $1,000 per bond.
▶ The **maturity date** is the date the bond owner receives the face value of the bond along with the final interest payment.
▶ The **coupon rate** is the guaranteed percentage of face value that the company will pay to the bond owner every year. For example, a bond with a coupon rate of 7 percent on a par value of $1,000 would pay $70 per year in interest. This bond would be said to have a coupon of $70. It is customary to pay interest on bonds every six months; thus, the bond owner would receive $35 semiannually.

Other items covered in the indenture are bond repayment methods, interest payment dates, procedures in case the company fails to make the interest payments, conditions for early repayment of debt, and any conditions requiring the pledging of assets as collateral. The indenture also provides for a financially independent trustee to administer the provisions of the bond contract.

# Types of Bonds

A **secured bond** is one in which the issuing company pledges specific assets to bondholders as a guarantee should the company be unable to make the interest and principal payments. It is not uncommon for airlines, such as Pan American or Piedmont, to use airplanes as collateral for loans. Santa Fe Railways might use railroad cars as collateral. When such equipment is pledged to guarantee bonds, the bonds are called equipment trust certificates because equipment is pledged as collateral. In case of default, the bond trustee can sell the equipment to recover as much of the bondholders' money as possible.

Most bonds are **unsecured bonds**, meaning that no specific assets are pledged to back up the bond. High quality bonds without pledged assets are also called debentures. Debentures are backed by the corporation's reputation and history of earnings. For this reason, only the largest and most respected firms can issue debentures.

Many bonds are paid off at maturity in one lump sum on the maturity date. There are other ways to repay the principal. A company may sell bonds that come due on different maturity dates; these are serial bonds. **Serial bonds** are similar to installment payments, but each bond has its own predetermined maturity date. Some bonds require the company to make semiannual or annual contributions to a fund, called a sinking fund, which is administered by a trustee. The trustee then uses the money to buy back bonds on the market, reducing the total number of the company's bonds outstanding over time. Some sinking funds provide for the elimination of the company's entire bond debt in small portions. Others may retire half of the bond issue before maturity and pay off the other half at maturity in a lump sum. This lump sum is referred to as a balloon payment.

**Zero-coupon bonds**

Bonds sold at less than face value, and no coupon payments over the life of the bond

**Floating rate bonds**

Bonds that do not have fixed coupon payments

**Convertible bonds**

Can be converted into common stock at the request of the bondholder

**Conversion ratio**

Number of shares per bond

**Conversion value**

The conversion ratio times the market price of the stock

**Income bonds**

Bonds that pay interest only if the company earns money

**Bond yield**

Return on investment for a bond

Not all bonds make annual cash coupon payments. **Zero-coupon bonds** are sold by the issuing company at less than the $1,000 face value and have no coupon payments over the life of the bond. The bond owners' return comes from the increase in bond price as the bond reaches face value at maturity.

**Floating-rate bonds** do not have fixed coupon payments; instead, the coupon rate changes with current interest rates. Floating-rate bonds usually have the coupon adjusted every six months based on some six-month average market interest rate. These floating rates are often tied to interest rates on U.S. Treasury securities.

A call feature allows the issuing company to retire the bond before its actual maturity date. Almost all bonds are callable. This call feature can be very beneficial to a company if interest rates drop lower than the coupon rate on the existing bond. For example, assume that Beeline had $100 million of a bond issue outstanding with a coupon rate of 12 percent. This would cost the company $12 million per year in interest. If the company could sell new bonds at a current coupon of 7 percent or $7 million per year interest, the company would save $5 million per year in interest by "calling in" the old bonds with a 12 percent coupon and replacing them with new ones with a 7 percent coupon. The process of selling new, lower, coupon bonds to replace older, higher, coupon bonds is called bond refunding.

**Convertible bonds** can be converted into common stock at the request of the bondholder. They have coupon payments just like debentures and the same general features as most bonds. The unusual aspect of the bonds is that a company may be able to turn debt into equity. For example, suppose that each Beeline bond can be converted to fifty shares of common stock. This fifty shares for one bond would be called the **conversion ratio** (number of shares per bond). After five years of owning a $1,000 Beeline bond and collecting interest, you notice that the common stock of Beeline is selling for $40 per share. If you convert the bond to common stock, you will have fifty shares worth $2,000 (50 shares × $40 per share). This $2,000 is called the **conversion value**. In this case, the price is twice the $1,000 face value of the bond. Given the high conversion value of the Beeline bond, the company will most likely call the bond. When a company calls the bond before maturity, the bond indenture often requires that they pay the bondholder a premium above the face value. Five percent is a common premium. This gives you the choice of fifty shares of stock worth $2,000 or $1,050 of cash for the face value of the bond. Investors should take the $2,000 worth of stock.

Often a company that reorganizes after bankruptcy issues **income bonds**. These bonds pay interest only if the company earns the money. Income bonds are the only bonds that cannot force bankruptcy on a company for failure to pay interest and principal.

## Measuring the Performance of Bonds

The investor in corporate bonds has several different ways of determining rates of return, depending on how long the investor plans to own the bond. The return on investment for a bond is often called the **bond yield**. Each yield calculation means something different, and it is important to know what each means. To do so one must understand a typical bond quote from a daily newspaper such as *The Wall Street Journal.*

**Bond Quotes.** A typical bond quote includes the current market price of the bond, its maturity date, and the coupon rate. A newspaper quote from the New York Bond Exchange might appear as follows:

| Company | Coupon | Maturity | Current Yield | # of Bonds | Daily Price Range | | |
|---------|--------|----------|---------------|------------|------|-----|-------|
| | | | | | High | Low | Close |
| Amoco | 7⅞ | s07 | 8.7 | 75 | 91¾ | 91 | 91 |

From this information a bond investor can determine that the coupon rate is 7.875 percent of $1,000, or $78.75 per year. The s07 means that this bond issue matures in the year 2007. Seventy-five bonds traded on this day. Price quotes can be misleading because they are given as percentages of face value. In this case, 91¾, the highest price on this trading day, was 91.75 percent of $1,000, or $917.50 per bond. When the bond market closed for the day, the price was 91, which translates to $910. From the closing price and coupon rate, you can calculate the **current yield** by dividing the value of the coupon in dollars by the closing price. Thus, the current yield is 8.65 percent. If an investor buys the bond for $910 and receives $78.75 per year, the cash return will be 8.65 percent:

$$\text{Current yield} = \frac{\$\,78.75}{\$910.00} = 8.65 \text{ percent, or } 8.7 \text{ percent rounded}$$

**Bond Yields.** The current yield is a relevant measure if the investor wants to hold the bond for a short period of time and is not concerned about a possible change in price. If an investor plans to hold the bond for a year, however, the annual-rate-of-return calculation will be important. This calculation takes price changes into consideration. In the case of the Amoco bond, assume that the price increased to 95. A price quote of 95 would be an ending price of $950 from a beginning price of $910. What would the investor's annual rate of return be?

$$
\begin{aligned}
\text{Annual rate of return} &= \frac{\text{coupon}}{\text{beginning price}} + \frac{\text{price change}}{\text{beginning price}} \\
&= \text{current yield} \quad + \text{capital gain or loss} \\
&= \frac{\$78.75}{\$910.00} \quad\quad + \frac{\$40.00}{\$910.00} \\
&= 8.65\% \quad\quad\quad + 4.40\%
\end{aligned}
$$

$$\text{Annual rate of return} = 13.05\%$$

Financial Encounter 19-2 describes junk bonds, which are bonds with high rates of return but more risk.

## Financial Encounter 19-2
### *Junk Bonds*

Junk bonds are bonds that offer higher yields than high-quality corporate bonds and are substantially more risky than other corporate bonds because the issuing company has a higher probability of default. Standard & Poor's typically rates junk bonds lower than high-quality corporate bonds to show that they have a significant risk of default.

Junk bonds generally offer yields 2 to 8 percent higher than those of U.S. Treasury securities of comparable maturity range. Junk bonds must be repaid within five to twenty years, but most come to maturity between ten and twelve years. Their interest rate is usually fixed, but it may be changed at certain intervals. Junk bonds may be issued by either public or private companies, and a wide variety of industries now issue them.

Historically, junk bonds were associated with companies in poor financial condition, sometimes called "fallen angels." Investors considered bonds offered by fallen angels poor investments because of declining earnings or too much debt or because economic uncertainty made it doubtful that the company could repay its bond issues. Some financial experts once viewed companies that issued junk bonds as having bad management. Most investors avoided junk bonds, and the market for them was very small. As a result, companies had to offer high yields to attract investors.

Since about 1982, however, junk bonds have dramatically increased in popularity. Entrepreneurs and corporate raiders see them as a tremendous source of capital. Junk bonds are no longer associated only with fallen angels. In 1987 over 20% of new bond issues were issued at junk or high-yield levels.

The junk-bond market has never experienced a major recession or depression. If one were to occur, it could dramatically increase the number of defaults on junk bonds. In fact, the uncertainty of the stock market after October 19, 1987 has dramatically reduced new issues of junk bonds. In addition, rising interest rates have raised doubts among many investors that some corporations may be unable to meet their high coupon payments. Nevertheless, high-class junk bonds issued by established companies are doing quite well. They are increasing in popularity among investors, although they are lowering their yields. Highly rated junk bonds now offer yields only 2 to 3 percent above yields on U.S. Treasury securities.

In 1983, many financial experts predicted that the junk-bond market would collapse following the recession of that year. They were wrong. In 1987, many felt that the stock market crash of October would destroy the junk-bond market. The market was not destroyed but enthusiasm for junk bonds did decline. Nevertheless, junk bonds are still around and continue to be used as a source of financing for many companies.

These facts are from Christopher Farrell, "Junk Bonds Finally Face the Acid Test," *Business Week*, November 16, 1987, p. 64; Daniel Kadlec, "Junk Bonds: Wait and See," *USA Today*, September 28, 1987, p. 3B; and Gordon Massie, "High Yield Bonds: Treasures or Junk," Lecture material 1987.

## ▶ Owners' Equity

Owners' equity represents the owners' investment in a company's assets. The owners purchase shares of the company with the expectation that the company will provide them a return on their investment. Stockholders' equity includes retained earnings, common stock, and preferred stock.

### Retained Earnings

**Retained earnings**

Earnings left after all expenses have been paid

**Retained Earnings** are earnings left after all expenses have been paid; this money belongs to the owners (stockholders). The Basic Corporation's balance sheet in Table 19-1 shows retained earnings of $60,000. When a company has profits left over after paying expenses and taxes, it can pay out some or all the earnings to the stockholders or retain some or all the earnings to invest in new assets for corporate expansion. If the board of directors distributes some of the company's profits to the owners, it issues them cash payments called **dividends**. When the earnings are reinvested in the assets of the firm, they belong to the owners in the form of equity rather than in the form of dividends. Retained earnings are an internal source of funds, or internal equity, because the funds are generated from the operations of the company rather than by selling securities in the market.

## Common Stock

**Common stock** is ownership in a corporation that gives stock owners voting rights. Owners of common stock have the last claim on the company's assets, after creditors and owners of preferred stock. Each stockholder has a stock certificate, which describes how many shares that owner controls. Common stockholders may vote their shares to elect the directors of the company and approve major actions proposed by management and the board of directors—mergers, selection of the firm's CPAs, increasing the total number of shares of common stock outstanding, changes to the corporate charter. When Texas Air bought Eastern Airlines, the stockholders of both Texas Air and Eastern had to vote to approve the merger.

Common stockholders, as the owners of the company, are last in line for profits (in the form of dividends) after all other expenses, including operating expenses, interest expenses, and taxes, are paid. Thus, stockholders are sometimes called residual owners. Figure 19-2 breaks down the ownership of stock in the United States by sex, age, and education.

Common stock is a major source of financial capital for a new company. Basic Corporation sold 100,000 shares of common stock at $3 per share for a total cash inflow of $300,000. Table 19-1 shows that Basic Corporation issued 100,000 shares of stock with a par value of $1. The **par value** of a stock is the dollar amount printed on the stock certificate; the par value of $1 is simply an accounting entry and has no significance with respect to the actual **market value**—the price at which the common stock is currently trading. Because the par value has no real significance, many corporations now issue no-par stock. The $100,000 from the sale of Basic Corporation's (Table 19-1) common stock is allocated to the common stock account on the balance sheet. Because the stock actually sold at $3 per share and had a par value per share of $1, the extra $2 per share is listed in an account called "capital in excess of par." This account shows $200,000 of funds raised.

## Preferred Stock

**Preferred stock** is ownership in a corporation that provides special privileges for preferred stockholders. Preferred stockholders receive dividends before common stockholders. If the company fails and its assets liquidated, preferred stockholders are paid before common stockholders. However, preferred stockholders cannot vote their shares: They cannot elect members of the board of directors, nor do they have any say in the company's

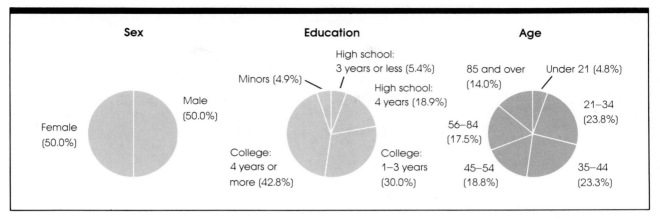

| Sex | Education | Age |

**Sex**

Female (50.0%) | Male (50.0%)

**Education**

Minors (4.9%)
High school: 3 years or less (5.4%)
High school: 4 years (18.9%)
College: 4 years or more (42.8%)
College: 1–3 years (30.0%)

**Age**

85 and over (14.0%)
Under 21 (4.8%)
21–34 (23.8%)
56–84 (17.5%)
35–44 (23.3%)
45–54 (18.8%)

**Figure 19-2**

Stock Ownership in the United States
Source: New York Stock Exchange Inc. Reprinted by permission.

major decisions. The primary advantage of owning preferred stock is that it is a safer investment than common stock in the event the company goes bankrupt.

Cumulative preferred stock is preferred stock that entitles owners to receive dividends accumulated from previous years if the company did not pay dividends in those years. Common stockholders do not receive any dividends until all accumulated dividends have been paid to cumulative preferred stockholders. Noncumulative preferred stock is preferred stock that does not entitle the owners to receive accumulated dividends; owners can receive only the current year's dividend payments, regardless of whether dividends were paid out in previous years or not.

Some corporations may issue convertible preferred stock, which is preferred stock shares that may be converted to common stock if the owner so desires. An investor might choose to convert to common stock if the market price of the common stock rises above the market price of the preferred stock. The same terms that apply to convertible bonds are also true for convertible preferred stock.

## Dividends

The board of directors must declare dividends before they can be paid to the shareholders. All firms do not pay dividends. Many fast-growing firms retain all their earnings because they can earn high returns on the earnings they reinvest. Companies that are growing slowly have less need for large amounts of internal equity and are more likely to pay dividends. Table 19-3 presents a sample of companies and the dividend each paid for a share of its stock. **Earnings per share** (profits divided by the number of shares outstanding) are also provided. The difference between the earnings and dividends represents the earnings retained by the business. The **payout ratio** (dividends per share divided by earnings per share) expresses the percentage of earnings the company paid out in dividends. One hundred percent minus the payout ratio reflects the percentage of earnings the company retained, or the retention ratio. In Table 19-3, Chrysler had the lowest payout ratio (12.12 percent), and Bristol Myers had the highest (52.38 percent).

**Earnings per share**

Profits divided by the number of shares outstanding

**Payout ratio**

Dividends per share divided by earnings per share

Table 19-3  Estimated
Common Stock Earnings and
Dividends for Selected
Companies for 1988
Source: The Value Line
Investment Survey, May 13,
1988. Part 1 Summary Index,
p. 5-19. Used by permission of
Value Line, Inc.

| Company | Earnings per Share | Dividend per Share | Payout Ratio |
|---|---|---|---|
| Bristol Myers | $2.81 | $1.68 | 59.78% |
| Chrysler Corp. | 5.26 | 1.00 | 19.01% |
| Citicorp | 5.19 | 1.48 | 28.51% |
| Honeywell | 6.50 | 2.10 | 32.30% |
| Lilly (Eli) | 4.95 | 2.35 | 47.47% |
| Pfizer Inc. | 4.47 | 2.00 | 44.74% |
| RJR Nabisco | 5.31 | 2.00 | 37.66% |

Three key dates are associated with the declaration of a quarterly dividend. The holder-of-record date is the date the firm examines its books to see who owns its stock. To be listed on the books of the company, an investor must have bought the stock before the ex-dividend date. The ex-dividend date is four days before the holder-of-record date because it takes four days to transfer the shares to a new owner. An investor who buys the stock on the ex-dividend date or later will not own the stock in time to receive a quarterly dividend payment. Thus the investor gets the stock without (ex) the dividend attached. The payment date is the actual date the stockholder receives the dividend check in the mail. Some companies pay dividends in shares of stock instead of or in addition to cash dividends.

## Measuring the Performance of Individual Stocks

Investors in stocks hope to get a return (earn a profit) on their investment. This return comes from the cash dividend and any change in the stock price. Stock prices move up and down based on expectations of a company's performance and the economy in general. If the economy is healthy and Chrysler's profits reflect this healthy economic climate, the price of Chrysler stock will probably increase, creating a gain for the investor. If the stock price declines, the investor will lose money.

It is helpful to understand how to read a stock quote. A newspaper quote for IBM from the New York Stock Exchange might appear as follows:

| 52 Weeks High | Low | Stock | Div. | Yld % | P-E Ratio | Sales 100s | High | Low | Close | Net Chg |
|---|---|---|---|---|---|---|---|---|---|---|
| 175⅞ | 100 | IBM | 4.40 | 3.8 | 13 | 25839 | 116 | 114 | 116 | +2 |

The 52-week high and low columns show that in the last year, the highest price for which a share of IBM stock sold was $175.88 and the lowest price was $100. The stock column indicates that the quote information is for IBM common stock. If the IBM had been followed by the letters "pf," it would indicate that the stock quote was for IBM preferred stock. The dividend column shows that IBM paid a dividend of $4.40 per share of stock outstanding. The dividend gives some indication of the kind of cash return

**Table 19-4  Dividend Yields of Selected Common Stocks**

Source: The Value Line Investment Survey, May 13, 1988. Part 1 Summary Index, p. 5-19. Used by permission of Value Line, Inc.

| Company | Market Price per Share | Dividend per Share | Dividend Yield |
|---|---|---|---|
| Bristol Myers | $40.00 | $1.68 | 4.20% |
| Chrysler Corp. | 23.00 | 1.00 | 4.34% |
| Citicorp | 20.00 | 1.48 | 7.40% |
| Honeywell | 70.00 | 2.10 | 3.00% |
| Lilly (Eli) | 79.00 | 2.35 | 2.97% |
| Pfizer Inc. | 55.00 | 2.00 | 3.63% |
| RJR Nabisco | 49.00 | 2.00 | 4.08% |

**Dividend yield**

The dividend per share divided by the market price per share

**Price-earnings ratio (P-E ratio)**

The ratio of market price per share divided by earnings per share

a company's stock will provide. The **dividend yield** indicates the dividend return on one share of common stock. The dividend yield is calculated by dividing the dividend per share by the market price per share. For IBM the dividend yield is 3.8%, or $4.40 divided by $116 per share. Table 19-4 shows dividend yields of selected common stocks.

Another ratio that is useful in understanding how stock is valued is the price-earnings ratio. The **price-earnings ratio (P-E ratio)** is the ratio of market price per share divided by earnings per share. It tells how much investors are willing to pay for $1 of earnings, allowing investors to compare the relative price of stocks with different earnings per share. In the IBM example, the price-earnings ratio is 13. Using Table 19-5, look at the relationship between price and earnings. Using a price-earnings ratio, investors are willing to pay $14.23 for every dollar of Bristol Myers' earnings but only $4.37 for every dollar of Chrysler's earnings. In fact, if you examine Table 19-5 closely, you will notice that the pharmaceutical stocks are high relative to the other companies. This relationship indicates that investors have expectations of higher growth in earnings and market price. The low P-E companies are not favored and are expected to grow slowly or not at all or even to have declining earnings and market price.

The sales 100s column in the IBM stock quote shows how many shares of IBM stock were traded on this day, listed in hundreds. In this case, 2,583,900 shares of IBM common stock traded hands. The last high and low columns are the highest price and the lowest price, respectively, of that day's trading

**Table 19-5  Common Stock Price-Earnings Ratios for Selected Stocks**

Source: The Value Line Investment Survey, May 13, 1988. Part 1 Summary Index, p. 5-19. Used by permission of Value Line, Inc.

| Company | Market Price per Share | Estimated Earnings per Share | Price-Earnings Ratio |
|---|---|---|---|
| Bristol Myers | $40.00 | $2.81 | 14.23 |
| Chrysler Corp. | 23.00 | 5.26 | 4.37 |
| Citicorp | 20.00 | 5.19 | 3.85 |
| Honeywell | 70.00 | 6.50 | 10.76 |
| Lilly (Eli) | 79.00 | 4.95 | 15.95 |
| Pfizer Inc. | 55.00 | 4.47 | 12.30 |
| RJR Nabisco | 49.00 | 5.31 | 9.22 |

of IBM stock. Finally, the net change shows whether the stock's price rose, fell, or stayed the same. IBM was up $2 per share to close at $116 per share.

The **annual rate of return** describes how much return an investor has earned on common stock held one year. The return includes the cash dividend and any change in price. Using the data from Table 19-4, let us calculate an annual return on Bristol Myers assuming the stock goes from $40 per share to $44 over the next year. If a Bristol Myers investor sells a hundred shares after one year for $44 per share, the annual rate of return would be the dividend yield of 4.20 percent plus a $4 gain on a beginning price of $40. The following example demonstrates the total annual rate of return:

$$\text{Investor's annual rate of return} = \frac{\text{annual dividend}}{\text{beginning price}} + \frac{\text{price change}}{\text{beginning price}}$$

$$\text{Total rate of return} = \text{dividend yield} + \text{capital gain or loss}$$

$$\text{Bristol Myers total return} = \frac{\$1.68}{\$40.00} + \frac{\$4.00}{\$40.00}$$

$$= 4.2\% + 10\%$$

$$\text{Bristol Myers percentage return} = 14.20\%$$

# ▶ Investment Banking

The investment banker, who is the middleman responsible for the process of selling securities for a corporation, is the link between the corporation and the individual or institutional investor. A new issue is the sale to the public of stock or bonds by a corporation. Some new issues are called an initial public offering because they represent the first shares of stock ever issued by a particular company. A company that makes an initial public offering is said to be going public. New issues can also be sold by a company that already has common stock owned by the public. Private placement is a sale of securities directly to an institution and is a private agreement between the company and the financial institution without public examination. The important point is that new issues of stock generate cash for the selling company. New issues of stock and bonds are sold in the **primary market**, the market where firms raise financial capital. It differs from the secondary market, where investors trade stocks and bonds. The company itself is not involved in secondary-market transactions.

Public offerings usually employ an investment banking firm to help sell the securities in the public markets. The investment banking firm establishes an appropriate price for the common stock or the appropriate coupon rate for a bond offering. The investment banker also prepares the prospectus, acts as an underwriter, sets the price, and distributes the securities to other security dealers and to the public.

## The Prospectus

The prospectus is a legal document prepared by the selling company to accompany all offers to sell securities. It is required by the Securities and

**An ice cream empire.** Ben & Jerry's Homemade Inc. started as a small ice cream parlor in 1978 in Vermont. Since then the company has grown steadily. The number of employees has increased and new products have been added. The company went public to finance a new factory that would allow increased production and offered the first shares to Vermonters, at a low minimum buy price. This hasn't hurt Ben & Jerry's profitability, though. In 1987 the company had $31.8 million in sales, and in 1988, sales may surpass $45 million.

Exchange Commission (SEC)—the government agency that regulates both public issues of securities and the financial markets. The prospectus includes detailed information about the proposed use of the corporate funds from the sale and financial data audited by a CPA (certified public accountant). Any information relevant to the value of the stocks being sold must be included in the prospectus; thus this document probably has the most comprehensive information about the company. The company is responsible for the accuracy of the information. The officers and directors of the firm are legally liable if the information is misleading or fraudulent.

## Underwriting

The underwriter guarantees the sales of securities at a set price. The underwriter, usually an investment banking firm, contracts to buy securities from the corporation and resell them to other security dealers and the public. The investment banker takes a risk by guaranteeing the stock price.

## Pricing New Issues

The investment banker determines the price of the stock issue and then, as underwriter, buys the issue from the selling company. If the stock issue is priced too high, few investors will buy the stock from the investment banker. The banker will then have to lower the price and possibly take a loss. If the stock is priced too low, the issuing company will be upset because it did not get the advantage of a fair market price. The pricing process requires a sophisticated understanding of the marketplace and what determines value.

## Distributing New Issues

The distribution of securities to the public buyer requires a selling group of many investment bankers called a syndicate. The syndicate is led by a managing investment banker who is responsible for the prospectus and pricing. Other bankers in the syndicate are responsible for the sale, distribution, and underwriting of their share of the offering. Table 19-6 shows the ten largest underwriters for 1987 based on the sale of securities in which the investment banker was the lead manager of the syndicate.

# ▶ The Securities Markets

**Securities markets**

Provide the mechanism for buying and selling securities for corporations and governments

**Securities markets** provide the mechanism for buying and selling securities for both corporations (stocks and bonds) and governments (T-bills, municipal bonds). Securities markets provide a means for owners (stockholders) and lenders (bondholders) to sell their securities to other investors. Thus, securities markets provide liquidity—the ability to turn security holdings into cash quickly. This is valuable to corporations and investors and helps to keep the cost of financial capital lower than it would be without liquid markets. Without liquid markets, investors would be wary of paying cash for a security without the knowledge that the security could be turned into cash quickly if the need arose.

## Secondary Markets

**Secondary markets**

Exist for the trading of publicly owned securities

**Secondary markets** exist for the trading of publicly owned securities. Secondary trading is the trading (buying and selling) of publicly owned securities between two investors. There are several secondary markets for the trading of stocks and bonds. In a secondary market, the company that issued the stock or bond receives no money from securities transactions, as it does from transactions occurring in the primary markets. For example, if you place an order to buy a hundred shares of Rockwell common stock, you will purchase the stock from another investor who wants to sell a hundred shares of Rockwell common stock.

Secondary trading does indirectly benefit the company that issued the security. Because the price of a company's shares is determined daily on the secondary markets, the company can decide whether to issue new shares of stock and know approximately what price they will bring. Market-determined prices take some of the uncertainty out of setting the price for a new issue.

## Organized Exchanges

Organized exchanges are central locations where investors meet to buy and sell the securities traded on that exchange. Buyers and sellers are not

| Lead Manager | Total Amount | Common Stock | Debt and Other |
|---|---|---|---|
| Salomon Brothers | $40.8 | $1.8 | $39.0 |
| First Boston | 37.6 | 2.2 | 35.4 |
| Morgan Stanley | 31.8 | 2.2 | 29.6 |
| Merrill Lynch | 31.8 | 4.1 | 27.7 |
| Goldman Sachs | 29.2 | 3.3 | 25.9 |
| Drexel Burnham | 21.2 | 2.4 | 18.8 |
| Shearson Lehman | 20.0 | 2.5 | 17.5 |
| Kidder Peabody | 10.0 | 1.4 | 8.6 |
| Prudential-Bache | 5.7 | 1.1 | 4.6 |
| Bear Stearns | 5.6 | 0.3 | 5.3 |

actually present on the "floor" of the exchange. Instead, they are represented by brokers, who act as agents and ensure that orders to buy and sell securities are carried out according to investors' wishes.

Brokers are registered members of an exchange. There are a set number of memberships on all exchanges, and in order to trade on the floor of the exchange, a person must purchase the right to trade from another broker and be admitted by the exchange's membership committee. The membership committee determines eligibility for membership based on the broker's experience, ability to absorb risk (have enough money available to sustain market swings), and other professional characteristics.

There are several different securities markets. They may be regional or national and may sell different types of securities.

***New York Stock Exchange.*** The New York Stock Exchange (NYSE), the largest and most important of all the exchanges in the United States, is located at the corner of Broad and Wall Streets (hence, the media often refer to the financial community as "Wall Street") in New York City and has a fixed membership number of 1,366. Members are said to have a seat on the exchange. These 1,366 seats on the NYSE can be bought and sold by individuals or brokers that meet the requirements of the exchange.

If a company wants its stock to be traded on the New York Stock Exchange, it must apply for a listing and be accepted for trading. Once a company's stock has been listed, it must still meet certain minimum requirements; otherwise the NYSE can delist it—prohibit it from trading on the market. Approximately 1,550 companies trade stock on the NYSE, including some of the world's largest. Table 19-7 is a list of thirty companies that make up the Dow Jones Industrial Average.

Millions of investors follow the activity of the Dow Jones Industrial Average to see whether the stock market has gone up or down. Although these thirty stocks are only a small portion of the ones listed on the NYSE, they make up about 25 percent of the total value of stocks listed on the NYSE. The Dow Jones Industrial Average is not representative of the whole market, but many investors find it a convenient measure of overall market performance.

**New York, New York.** Securities issued by nationwide corporations are traded on the New York Stock Exchange. It is the oldest and most visible stock exchange and handles about 80 percent of all organized stock transactions.

*American Stock Exchange.* The American Stock Exchange (AMEX) is another national stock exchange located on Wall Street in New York City. The AMEX trades smaller companies than the NYSE. For the most part, companies do not choose to be listed on both the NYSE and the AMEX, although dual listing is allowed by the Securities and Exchange Commission. The AMEX has 650 seats and lists more than nine hundred companies.

*Regional Exchanges.* The regional exchanges began their existence trading the securities of local businesses. As those businesses grew, they moved to the national exchanges, but many continued to trade on the regional exchange as well. Chicago, Boston, Baltimore, Cincinnati, and other cities have regional exchanges. The trading on these exchanges today is mostly in the stock of nationally known companies.

More than 90 percent of the companies traded on regional exchanges such as the Midwest Stock Exchange in Chicago (third largest after the NYSE and the AMEX) and the Pacific Coast Exchange in San Francisco and Los Angeles (fourth largest) also trade on the New York Stock Exchange. This is known as dual trading. General Motors and some other companies are traded on as many as five domestic stock exchanges and several foreign stock exchanges, such as the Australian Ordinaries Exchange. Dual trading creates liquidity and, because of the different time zones, allows for longer trading hours

**Table 19-7 Dow Jones Industrial Companies**

| | |
|---|---|
| Allied-Signal | International Paper |
| Alcoa | McDonald's |
| American Express | Merck |
| AT&T | 3M |
| Bethlehem Steel | Navistar International |
| Boeing | Phillip Morris |
| Chevron | Primerica |
| Coca-Cola | Procter & Gamble |
| Du Pont | Sears |
| Eastman Kodak | Texaco |
| Exxon | USX |
| GE | Union Carbide |
| General Motors | United Technologies |
| Goodyear Tire & Rubber | Westinghouse |
| IBM | Woolworth |

during the day. Some exchanges, such as the Midwest Stock Exchange, have very sophisticated computer trading systems, and many large institutional traders transact a sizable portion of their large trades on this exchange. Financial Encounter 19-3 describes investment on foreign stock exchanges.

***Consolidated Tape.*** The Securities Amendments Act of 1975 created a new price quotation system that presents stock price quotations from all exchanges on a moving electronic board called a **ticker tape**. The ticker tape allows brokers at all exchanges to see price quotes for stocks listed on their exchange. You can see the consolidated ticker tape if you visit the local offices of a broker such as Merrill Lynch or A. G. Edwards, or you can watch it on the Financial News Network on cable television.

## Over-the-Counter Markets

The **over-the-counter market (OTC)** has no central location like the other exchanges. Instead, it is a network of dealers all over the country linked by computers, telephones, and teletype machines. Unlike brokers, dealers own the securities they trade, and they buy and sell for their own inventories of securities. Thus dealers must balance their supply of securities by changing the prices they charge to buy and sell. Brokers, on the other hand, act as agents to bring together buyers and sellers and never own the securities they trade.

There are several segments of the over-the-counter markets. The National Association of Securities Dealers divides over five thousand companies into the National Market System (large companies), the national list (smaller companies), and regional and local companies (which are sometimes very small). The OTC is dominated by small companies, but over the last decade, growing companies have chosen to stay on the OTC rather than move to an exchange. Billion dollar companies like Apple Computers, Adolph Coors Co., MCI Communications, and Intel trade "over the counter."

The over-the-counter market trades most corporate bonds and all U.S. government securities. Because of the volume of debt securities traded on the OTC market, it accounts for the largest dollar amount for total securities

**Ticker tape**

A moving electronic board that presents stock price quotations from all exchanges

**Over-the-counter market**

A network of dealers all over the country linked by computers, telephones, and teletype machines

**East, west, and in between.** The securities of regional corporations are traded at small regional exchanges. Some cities, such as Chicago, Los Angeles, and Boston, maintain their own exchanges. Shown here is the Pacific Stock Exchange in Los Angeles after the October 19, 1987 stock market crash.

traded, although it is much smaller in dollar volume than the New York Stock Exchange when it comes to common stock.

With the use of a centralized computer system, OTC dealers have up-to-the-minute information on stock and bond prices. This system is provided by the National Association of Securities Dealers, which oversees the operation of the OTC.

## Measuring Market Performance

Many investors use the Dow Jones Industrial Average as a measure of how the New York Stock Exchange is performing. There are other, broader measures of stock-market performance that are widely followed by the investment community. Investors, especially professional money managers, want to know how their investments performed relative to the market in general. Clients want to know how their professionally managed accounts have performed. Thus, performance measures are very important.

In tracking the performance of a stock market, the numbers listed in the index or average are expressed not as dollars but rather as a number on a fixed scale and are related to some referenced time period. If you know, for example, that the Dow Jones Industrial Average was 860 in August 1982 and 2,600 in September 1987, you recognize that the market more than tripled in that time period (Figure 19-3). The market, as measured by the stock prices of the thirty Dow Jones Industrials, actually went up 302 percent.

# Financial Encounter 19-3

## *International Perspectives: Investing in Foreign Stock Markets*

Investors who have become discouraged with the relatively low rates of return in the American market are turning to foreign markets, which have outperformed the domestic market in recent years. Even in times of extraordinary growth in the U.S. market, its rate of return still lags behind that offered by some foreign markets.

Market practices vary widely among countries, but most are characterized by higher risk as well as the potential for higher returns than are offered by the U.S. market. The Paris Bourse (the French equivalent of the New York Stock Exchange) has done better than any large exchange in Europe in the last few years. In the Asian markets, the Tokyo exchange has been on a large, bullish run throughout most of the 1980s, even after the stock-market crash of 1987, which affected markets around the world. In addition, the markets of Hong Kong, Singapore, and South Korea have done exceptionally well, partly because these countries have experienced a double-digit growth in gross national product. The Australian Stock Exchange All Ordinaries Index (the Australian Ordinaries' equivalent of the Dow Jones Index) has also highlighted healthy gains in the Australian market.

Even though foreign markets have grown at an exceptional rate over the past few years, analysts urge that American investors carefully assess foreign markets before investing in them. Most of the huge gains realized by U.S. investors in the 1980s resulted from a decline in the value of the American dollar. In addition, bullish international markets have increased the prices of foreign stocks so much that it is difficult for investors to spot undervalued foreign stocks.

There are several things investors should look for when investing in international markets. The first is to identify countries with the strongest economic outlook, including expected inflation and projected economic growth. The best time to invest in a particular country's stocks is when the country's annual inflation is low and its annual economic growth is higher than that of the U.S.

Differences in accounting practices make some foreign stocks look overpriced to U.S. investors. Such variations mean that information published in international financial journals is not always accurate because foreign companies may use financial reporting rules that are not as strict as those used in the United States.

Interest rates are another factor to consider. If interest rates are more than about three percentage points above the expected inflation rate, there is a good chance those rates will fall. If interest rates fall, stock prices usually increase. Potential foreign stock investors need to monitor currency exchange rates as well. A declining dollar increases the returns earned on foreign stocks by U.S. investors; a rising dollar decreases returns.

It appears that Americans will continue to pour millions of dollars into foreign stock exchanges as the dollar continues to decline. However, because of the ever-changing nature of these markets, investors must carefully monitor international events to ensure that they continue to receive high rates of return from these markets.

These facts are from Judson Goeding, "Bullish on the Bourse," *Signature* (June 1987): 38–41; Walter L. Updegrave, "Assessing Foreign Markets," *Money* 16 (May 1987): 57–66; and Daniel Burstein, "Trading Places," *United Airlines* 32 (January 1987): 38–43, 73–74.

---

**Bull market**

A period of large increases

**Bear market**

A declining market

A period of large increases, such as the one from 1982 to 1987, is called a **bull market**. The bull is the symbol of an aggressive, charging market and is associated with rising stock prices. The bull market of the 1980s was one of the longest rising markets ever. It was brought to a halt on October 19, 1987, when the Dow Jones Industrial Average fell 508 points, or 23 percent. A declining market is a **bear market**. When the market is falling, the bear is in hibernation. The hibernating bear symbolizes few buyers. The buyers who bid the prices up in bull markets are sleeping in bear markets.

**Figure 19-3**

Dow Jones Industrial Average
(1929–1988)

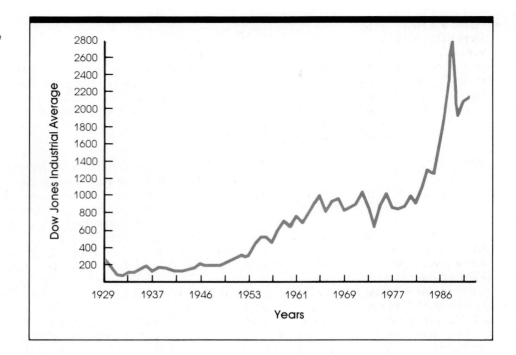

Indexes and averages are used to measure stock prices. An index compares stock prices to a specified base period, such as 1944, 1967, or 1977. An average is an average of certain stock prices. The averages used are usually not simple averages. Some are weighted by value (Standard & Poor's Index); some are weighted by price (the Dow Jones Average); and some are unweighted. Because the market averages of industrial companies' stocks seem to move closely together over time, the major information provided by a stock-market index is the direction of the market and the extent of its change over time.

The Standard & Poor's 500 Index is an average of five hundred industrial companies. The series of index numbers has a base period of 1941–43, which equals 10. The index on June 16, 1988 stood at 269.77.

The New York Stock Exchange Index reflects the prices of all the stocks listed on the New York Stock Exchange. It is a value-weighted index. In other words, a company with a total value (number of shares outstanding times market value per share) of $5 billion would have more impact on the index than would a company with a total value of only $200 million. Because investors measure their increase in wealth on the basis of total value, most analysts agree that a value-weighted index best reflects market performance.

The indexes and averages are broken down by exchanges—AMEX, NYSE, and NASDAQ (the OTC market index). The major indexes are also broken down by industries—a utility index, a financial index, a transportation index, and a composite index that combines the stocks of industrial, financial, transportation, and utility companies into one.

# Securities Laws

Three major laws govern the initial sale and secondary trading of securities. The Securities Act of 1933 covers the sale of new issues of securities. This law was enacted after Congress examined the market fraud existing before and during the stock-market crash of 1929. The primary purpose of this legislation was to compel corporations to disclose all pertinent investment information whenever they were selling a new issue of securities. The law requires that a prospectus be issued with each new public offering.

The Securities Exchange Act of 1934 created the Securities and Exchange Commission to enforce the Securities Act of 1933. The SEC was empowered to regulate trading in the securities markets and the companies listed on the securities markets. The law made the SEC responsible for shareholders' proxy (substitute voting) procedures and the public disclosure of regular reports.

The Securities Amendments Act of 1975 directed the SEC to supervise the development of a national securities market. This market has slowly taken shape by linking markets together with computers and creating more efficient prices. The act also eliminated fixed commissions on public transactions and allowed more competition between securities firms. It provided some of the impetus needed to computerize the stock markets and to create the consolidated ticker tape.

Legislation under consideration involves imposing brief halts in trading in the markets when security prices or the volume of traced securities reaches a predetermined limit.[3] Regardless of what laws Congress chooses to make to prevent another crash, additional legislation will certainly affect long-term financing through stocks and bonds.

# Notes

**1.** Russell Mitchell, with Judith H. Dobizynski, "Jack Welch: How Good a Manager?" *Business Week*, December 14, 1987, pp. 92–103.

**2.** Alan Murray, "Task Force Critique of Wall Street Increases Chances of Stricter Laws," *The Wall Street Journal*, January 11, 1988, p. 12.

**3.** Catherine Young, "Congress Is Taking Its Own Sweet Time on Reform," *Business Week*, April 18, 1988, p. 63.

# Summary and Review

▶ Long-term financial management is managing the long-term assets, liabilities, and owners' equity presented on the balance sheet. Without long-term assets such as plants and equipment, businesses cannot generate cash flow. Long-term financing decisions affect a business' profitability.

▶ Without updating long-term assets, or capital assets, a business cannot maintain profitability. Businesses need the most modern, up-to-date equipment they can afford in order to operate in the most efficient manner possible. Because long-term assets are costly, they must be financed with long-term debt, such as bonds or long-term loans.

▶ Long-term liabilities include long-term loans and bonds. A bond indenture lists the provisions of the bond contract—maturity, coupon rate, repayment methods, call features, sinking-fund provisions, and others. There are many types of bonds: secured and unsecured bonds, zero-coupon bonds, floating-rate bonds, income bonds, and convertible bonds.

▶ Owners' equity represents what owners have contributed to the company and includes retained earnings, common stock, and preferred stock. Investment bankers, acting as underwriters, purchase a stock issue from a corporation, write a prospectus, and price and distribute the stock.

▶ The securities markets consist of primary and secondary markets for stocks and bonds. Primary markets allow companies to sell stock to investors through investment bankers to raise capital. Secondary markets are where investors buy and sell stocks and bonds. The major securities markets are the New York Stock Exchange, American Stock Exchange, Midwest Stock Exchange, Pacific Coast Exchange, and the over-the-counter market.

▶ Investors measure market performance by watching stock-market averages and indexes such as the Dow Jones Industrial Average and the Standard & Poor's Indexes.

▶ The Securities and Exchange Commission currently regulates the primary and secondary markets, as well as the trading of all securities.

# Key Terms and Concepts

| | |
|---|---|
| long-term financial management | current yield |
| long-term assets | retained earnings |
| long-term liabilities | dividends |
| owners' equity | common stock |
| real capital | shares |
| capital budget | par value (stock) |
| bond | market value |
| par value (bond) | preferred stock |
| maturity date | earnings per share |
| coupon rate | payout ratio |
| secured bond | dividend yield |
| unsecured bond | annual rate of return |
| serial bond | price-earnings ratio (P-E ratio) |
| zero-coupon bond | primary market |
| floating rate bond | securities markets |
| convertible bonds | secondary markets |
| conversion ratio | ticker tape |
| conversion value | over-the-counter market |
| income bond | bull market |
| bond yield | bear market |

# Checking Your Understanding

This chapter introduced you to the subject of long-term financing. To test and reinforce your understanding, fill in the blanks below.

1. A _____ is an unsecured corporate bond.
2. The secondary security market where all U.S. government bonds are traded is called the _____ _____ _____ market.
3. An _____ lists details of a bond contract, such as call features, maturity, sinking-fund provisions, and method of repayment.
4. A long-term debt security is a _____.
5. _____ guarantee the price of a new stock issue to the issuing company.
6. In order for a company to force conversion of a convertible bond or to refund an old bond issue, the bond contract must contain a _____ _____.
7. Markets that involve trading between investors are known as _____ markets.
8. The _____ _____ is the cash return provided by one share of a stock.
9. An _____ _____ is responsible for pricing a new stock issue and preparing the prospectus.
10. The _____ _____ is calculated by taking the bond coupon and dividing by the closing market price for the day.
11. Declining stock markets are called _____ markets.
12. Bonds that are sold originally at a discount and pay no cash to the bondholder are _____ _____ _____.

# Topics for Review and Discussion

1. What are fixed assets?
2. List the main sources of funds for financing long-term expansion.
3. What makes up the owners' equity account on a balance sheet?
4. Where are the majority of corporate and government bonds traded?
5. What functions does an investment banker perform?
6. How does a public offering differ from a private placement?
7. Explain the purpose of the prospectus, and list examples of information that could be found in one.
8. What are the functions of the securities markets?
9. Compare the primary and secondary markets.
10. How are the primary and secondary markets related? Could one eixst without the other?

# Exercises

1. The national market system as mandated by the Securities Acts Amendments of 1975 has made slow progress. What changes on the securities markets since 1975 have pushed the U.S. markets closer to a national market system?
2. Select five of the Dow Jones Industrials from Table 19-7. Look up their earnings, dividends, and price for the last five years. Calculate the dividend yields, payout ratios and price-earnings ratios. What kind of picture do you get for each one? How do they compare with forecasts of the next year?

## Case 19-1

### *Microsoft Goes Public*

William Gates founded Microsoft in 1975 to manufacture operating systems and software applications for personal computers. Today, Microsoft is one of the leading makers of computer software. In the 1980s, Microsoft was earning a profit equal to 34 percent of its revenues; the company had no need for additional long-term financing, and Gates was not interested in issuing the company's stock for sale to the public. Over the years, however, Gates had been offering shares of Microsoft to computer programmers and managers to attract them to Microsoft. In 1985, management recognized that by 1987 more than five hundred people would own a piece of Microsoft, and the company would be required to register with the Securities and Exchange Commission (SEC). Because the company would soon have to register anyway, in October 1985 Microsoft mangement began to discuss taking the company public the following year.

Going public with an initial public offering is a long, involved process. Gates and Microsoft's financial managers studied the process for many months before deciding to proceed. Microsoft's first step was to hire an investment bank to serve as underwriter—an agent who guarantees payment of the purchase of a full issue of the company's stock. Microsoft's chief financial officer, Frank Gaudette, was assigned the tough task of choosing an investment bank that would best serve Microsoft's needs and understand its highly technical markets. In December 1985, Microsoft finally chose Goldman Sachs and Alex. Brown to serve as co-underwriters.

The next step was to write the company's prospectus—the legal summary of the proposed stock offering. Many prospective stockholders would base their decision on whether to invest in Microsoft on this document. The writers of the prospectus had to be very careful in their wording to avoid lawsuits from stockholders who might think they had been misled by the prospectus. As a result, the creation of the prospectus involved not only Microsoft's financial team and the underwriters, but attorneys as well.

The prospectus included every detail of the stock offering. Microsoft would issue 2 million shares, raising some $30 million. Current Microsoft shareholders (mostly employees) would receive an additional $10 million for their shares of stock. The underwriters had an option to sell an additional 300,000 shares if they wished. The $40 million deal would place about 12 percent of Microsoft's stock into public hands.

The next step in going public was to set the actual price of Microsoft's stock. The underwriters thought the initial selling price of the stock should be between $17 and $20 a share. Bill Gates, however, thought a range of $16 to $19 would ensure that the underwriters would not have to lower the price to get buyers. He thought any price over $20 would set Microsoft's market value at over half-a-billion dollars, too high for him. Gates won.

The company sent the prospectus to the SEC for review. On February 3, 1986, the company filed for registration with the SEC and sent out thirty-eight thousand copies of the prospectus. Gates and Gaudette then began the "road show"—meeting with prospective stock purchasers and investment bankers in major U.S. cities to convince them that Microsoft's stock was a good buy, without actually touting the stock, which would have gotten them into trouble with the SEC.

At the beginning of March, Microsoft made some minor changes in its prospectus to meet SEC objections. The public-offering process began to move forward rapidly. The stock market had been on a bull run for some months, and the underwriters believed that Microsoft's stock would be hot. They suggested raising the offering price to $25 a share. Gates, Gaudette, and Microsoft president Jon Shirley believed that a range of $21 to $22 was more acceptable. All day on March 7, Microsoft management and the underwriters argued over the price but finally settled on an initial offering price of $21.

They next haggled over the spread—the portion of the price that would go to the underwriters to cover their commissions, underwriting expenses, and fees. They finally agreed that $1.31, or a little over 6 percent of the share, price would go to the underwriters.

At 8 A.M. on March 13, 1986, couriers delivered to the SEC Microsoft's filing package, which included copies of the revised prospectus, the underwriters' agreement to buy the shares, and other items related to the offering. At 9:15, the SEC announced that Microsoft's registration was effective. At 9:35, Microsoft's stock opened for trading for the first time on the over-the-counter market at $25.75 a share. The underwriters quickly exercised their option to sell an additional 300,000 shares. At the end of the day, Microsoft's stock closed at $27.75, with some 2.5 million shares trading hands.

Chariman Bill Gates netted $1.6 million from the sales of some of his own shares when the company went public, and his 45 percent of the company is now worth more than $1 billion. Other Microsoft employees also earned large sums when they sold portions of their Microsoft holdings.

Microsoft's stock quadrupled in value within the next year. As a result, Microsoft split its stock 2-for-1 in 1987. In other words, it doubled the number of shares available for sale to the public, reducing the value of each share by half. Nevertheless, the total value of each stockholder's shares remained the same. A person holding one share of stock worth $100 before the split held two shares of stock worth $50 each, or $100 total, after the split. Microsoft continued to be successful after going public. On March 24, 1988, Microsoft stock traded at $56.50 on the over-the-counter market.

---

These facts are from "NASDAQ National Issues," *The Wall Street Journal*, March 25, 1988, p. 31; Richard Brandt, "The Billion-Dollar Whiz Kid," *Business Week*, April 13, 1987, pp. 68–76; and Bro Uttal, "Inside the Deal That Made Bill Gates $350,000,000," *Fortune*, July 21, 1986, pp. 23–33.

**Questions**

1. Why is the initial selling price of the stock so important on an initial public offering?
2. What process did Bill Gates have to go through to eventually sell shares to the public?
3. How does having the company's shares publicly traded benefit Microsoft and its em-ployees?

# Case 19-2
## *Long-Term Larry Leaves a Legacy*

For 30 years, Lawrence R. Hummel worked as a handyman at Bethany College in West Virginia, which is home to 800 students. In 1953, Hummel took the proceeds from his share of the family dairy farm in West Virginia and became a physical plant employee at Bethany College. For years he lived in an apartment over a garage near the post office in town, collecting discarded lawn mowers and other apparatus under the stairs leading to his apartment.

Hummel was called "Larry" by students and faculty on campus and known for his disheveled appearance and quirky habits. Hummel's clothes were hand-me-downs and he carried most of his daily necessities, along with items he collected during the day, in a yellow bucket.

It seems Hummel was doing more than collecting discarded goods. With the proceeds from the sale of his dairy farm combined with regular investments from his meager salary, he amassed a fortune in securities—worth nearly $1.2 million by the time he died on March 21, 1988 at the age of 82.

Hummel would scavenge copies of *The Wall Street Journal* which Bethany's economics majors had discarded, or read daily copies at the college library, anxious to keep abreast of the daily fluctuations in the stock market. When economics students would throw out *The Wall Street Journal* unread, "he'd grab it and read it from cover to cover," says John Taylor, professor of English at Bethany. He would talk to economics professors about investment ideas. The professors thought Hummel nothing more than an eccentric fixated on the stock market.

Few knew of the extent of Hummel's investments. One who did was Theodore H. Bunnell, director of financial aid and former student at Bethany, who helped Hummel when he ran into some confusion with the Internal Revenue Service. "He was an astute and long-term investor," says Bunnell. "He had an innate intelligence."

At the time of his death, 64.5 percent of Hummel's wealth was invested in common stocks—28 of them in all. The remainder was in a combination of U.S. Treasury notes (15 percent), money market funds (20 percent), and the rest in a variety of small bank accounts. The majority of the stock investments focused on food companies, including H. J. Heinz, Kellogg Co., Kraft, Inc., pharmaceutical companies including A. H. Robins and Schering-Plough, Inc., and home care product companies, including Colgate Palmolive.

"He avoided companies where unions were heavily involved," says Bunnell. "I believe he liked food companies and drug companies because his rationale was those industries go on regardless of the economy," says Bunnell. Hummel's rationale paid off big. Bunnell reports that Hummel continued to own a piece of the family dairy farm until 1976, at which time he sold his remaining share to a nephew for $25,000. "That was his initial investment in Heinz," says Bunnell who was under the impression that Hummel just let the value of that stock grow from there without investing another dime. By the time of his death, H. J. Heinz was Hummel's largest single stock investment—3,600 shares worth $158,850 at the time of his death.

Students at Bethany thought of Hummel as a harmless old codger who hung around the cafeteria when he wasn't mowing lawns or helping with other grounds work at the college. In the evenings he would sometimes sit in "The Barn," the college snackbar, talking to economics majors about his investment philosophy.

At first the economics majors joked with Hummel and thought he was pulling his information from thin air, says Bunnell. "But in doing research, they'd find that he was, if not accurate, awful darn close."

Hummel became something of a legend at Bethany College, not because of his investments or last will and testament which left approximately $600,000 to the college, but more because he was a real character who insisted on working well into his seventies at the college before his lawyer finally convinced him in 1984 to take up residence in a nursing home in Weirton, West Virginia, 20 miles away. At the time of his death, the management of the nursing home was allowing Hummel to perform the same type of grounds work duties he had been doing at Bethany College for more than 30 years.

Diligent research and commitment to a long-term investment in securities paid off big for Hummel and Bethany College. Few at Bethany doubt Hummel's investment wisdom today. "I knew it was true," says Bunnell, "but in 1984, I remember his portfolio being worth around $500,000 or $600,000. It was the degree of his wealth that was a shock."

---

These facts are from Alison E. Juram, "Hummel . . . The Legend and the Legacy," *The Tower*, April 14, 1988, pp. 1,3; "Janitor leaves $1M to College," Associated Press as printed in *The Patriot Ledger*, April 19, 1988, p. 2; "Bequest from the Blue," *Time*, May 2, 1988, p. 57; Joseph A. Gompers, letter to Jeffrey L. Seglin, 13 May 1988.

**Questions**

1. The emphasis on the long term shows that careful principles followed over time will pay handsome returns. Why do you think Larry was so successful as an investor?
2. What characteristics did Larry look for in his common stock investments?
3. How much of Larry's wealth could be attributed to his lack of spending?

# Answers to Checking Your Understanding

1. debenture
2. over-the-counter
3. indenture
4. bond
5. underwriters
6. call feature
7. secondary markets
8. dividend yield
9. investment banker
10. current yield
11. bear market
12. zero coupon bonds

## Outline

# Chapter 20

# Risk Management and Insurance

## Objectives

After reading this chapter, you will be able to:

▶ Define risk, and describe four ways of managing it.

▶ Explain why corporations and individuals purchase insurance to protect them from various risks.

▶ Explain the risks that are insurable and the types of insurance coverage that can be purchased.

▶ Understand the various provisions of automobile insurance and property and liability coverages.

▶ Compare the health insurance offered by providers such as Blue Cross and Blue Shield with the health care provided by health maintenance organizations.

▶ Distinguish between different types of life insurance.

# Business Experience

One of the key fringe benefits firms may offer is lifetime health insurance programs. Everyone knows how expensive doctors' bills can be, not to mention the astronomical costs of hospital visits for emergencies or operations. These bills easily can amount to thousands of dollars. Modern medicine has increased life expectancy steadily over the years. Unfortunately, someone has to pay the bills for this modern medicine.

The larger the firm, the more likely it is they offer postretirement health-care benefits. Firms with over 10,000 employees offer it to 94% of employees, whereas firms with fewer than 100 employees offer it to only 42% of employees. The plans usually cover hospitalization, some doctors' fees, and medicine. Today corporations are taking a hard look at their health care programs.

The average hospital bill for someone who retires at age 65 is $32,000 while the average bill for someone who retires at age 55 is $55,000. The increasing number of retirees to care for adds to these rising costs. The ratio of workers to retirees is currently 3:1 and it will drop to 2:1 by the year 2000.

These increasing costs plus the growing number of retirees translates into huge retiree health-care costs for employers. Some experts say that the present value of future liabilities is 20–40% of company's net worth. At some industrial companies it exceeds their net worth. Some of these future liabilities may show up on balance sheets if the Financial Accounting Standards Board (FASB) has its way. If future retiree health-care costs are considered in corporate planning, corporate profits would be cut in half.

In light of these facts, companies are reevaluating their current health-care programs. According to a 1986 survey, 41% of employers have already made cost-cutting changes in their retiree health plans. Most of these changes were minor; however, future changes could include implementing keep-healthy programs, cutting back benefits, or possibly eliminating retiree health care altogether.

Some companies opt to set up reserves much like pension funds to pay for retiree health costs. A major problem with this is the loss of tax deductions for corporations. Companies get tax breaks for pension fund contributions; those contributions are tax-free. Health care funds do not qualify for these deductions. Another problem is predictability; future pension expenditures are predictable whereas future health-care costs are not.

Some companies are tying the benefits of future retirees to the number of years they worked for the firm. The longer an employee works for the firm, the better the benefits. Other companies are lowering premiums, raising deductibles, and eliminating coverage for employees who take other jobs.

---

These facts are from Amanda Bennett, "Fund Stunned by Retiree Health Costs: Likely Results Include Cuts and Coverage," *The Wall Street Journal*, May 24, 1988, p. 41.

# Introduction

Businesses face risks—loss of market share to a competitor, injury to employees due to accidents on the job, lawsuits filed because of faulty products. One of management's key responsibilities is achieving the organization's objectives. Thus managers must take into account the types of risks the business faces and figure out ways to manage those risks and ensure the survival of the business if losses occur.

This chapter discusses risk and how it can be managed. Because the primary risk-management technique is purchasing insurance, the chapter discusses insurance at length: how it works, what types are available, and how businesses can use it to their best advantage.

# ► Nature of Risk

**Risk**

The possibility of suffering injury or loss

**Risk** is the possibility of suffering injury or loss. A man withdraws his savings to purchase lottery tickets and fails to get a winning ticket. An engineering student in her senior year discovers that the market for engineers has become saturated. The man knew that his chance of winning the lottery was small. The engineering student entered college believing that there would be a demand for engineers four years later when she was entering the job market. Each of these individuals faced risk. For each, one of two outcomes was certain. The man either held a winning ticket, or he did not. The student would either find an engineering job or she would not. Risk results from uncertainty about the future. When the outcome of events is known, there is neither risk nor uncertainty, though there may be loss.

**Speculative risk**

Offers one of three outcomes— no change, a loss, or a gain

Businesses face speculative risk and pure risk. **Speculative risk** offers one of three outcomes—no change, a loss, or a gain. Businesses face speculative risk all the time, for all investments are speculative risks. Most people would not consider investing unless there were some chance of financial gain, but with all investments there is a chance of loss.

Buying new equipment, renting new office space, expanding the number of stores or branch offices—all these activities involve speculative risk. Many businesses expand too soon and too rapidly. They invest their capital in the expansion and then don't generate enough business to keep profits up. J. Bildner & Sons, a Boston-based gourmet food store, made such a mistake, opening new stores in locations that were not right for them. Within a year, Bildner's had to close some of the new stores.

Management tries to reduce speculative risk through careful planning. Businesses that plan well and guess correctly are profitable and endure.

**Pure risk**

Offers the chance of no change at all or the chance of a loss

**Pure risk** offers the chance of no change at all or the chance of a loss. There is no chance for gain or profit. Accidents, fire, and illness are conditions of pure risk. If they happen, there is a loss. If they don't happen, there is neither loss nor gain. Fortunately, many such events are minor and can be readily overcome, or their effects can be absorbed. But occasionally an accident results in death or total loss of property. A fire completely destroys a home or business. An illness is severe enough to require hospitalization and results in the loss of a job.

Thus it is vital that business managers develop ways of managing pure risk. A small firm in particular might be wiped out by a fire, a flood, or other disaster if it is not prepared to deal with the pure risk of such calamities.

# ▶ Risk-Management Techniques

**Risk management**

Ways to deal with the threat of loss posed by events beyond the control of a manager

Risk is an inescapable part of doing business. Managers thus must develop methods of **risk management**—that is, ways to deal with the threat of loss posed by events beyond their control. Once pure risks are identified, the manager can use one of four risk-management techniques: avoiding risk, reducing risk, assuming risk by self-insurance, transferring risk by buying insurance.

In deciding on risk-management techniques, the manager must weigh alternatives. Only one method might work in some cases, but other situations might require a mixture of techniques. The particular combination of risk avoidance, assumption, reduction, and transfer used depends on several factors: what the risk is, how big the loss might be, and what financial resources are available. For example, a business might self-insure or buy insurance to cover losses due to job-related accidents. But it would also probably choose to reduce risk by educating employees about the risks of accidents on the job, posting signs in danger areas, installing safety devices on dangerous machinery, requiring the use of hard hats, and the like.

## Avoiding Risk

Risk avoidance is a means of handling risk in which the source of risk is eliminated. Someone who wishes to avoid the risk of being in an airplane crash may avoid traveling by airplane. Avoidance is an effective way to deal with some risks, but it is not always practical, and it is sometimes impossible. A person may try to avoid car accidents by never getting into a car, cab, or bus, but in most areas of the United States, a car-free existence is not possible. A person afraid of flying may stay out of planes but cannot totally eliminate the risk of being involved in a plane crash because planes sometimes crash into homes, highways, and places of business. Some individuals and firms facing high liability insurance premiums have chosen to avoid the risk of lawsuits by going out of business.

## Reducing Risk

Risk reduction is a common and practical means of handling risk. Under this method, a business takes deliberate steps to lessen the likelihood of a loss. Machinists wear safety glasses, gloves, and safety shoes to reduce the

**McIDAS meteorological system.** Federal Express established its own weather forecast system to ensure up-to-the minute meteorological information for operations. This step lessens the likelihood of a loss. Risk reduction is a common means of handling risk.

risk that they will be injured while operating machinery. Construction workers wear hard hats. Many companies have implemented safety programs designed to educate employees about the causes and prevention of accidents, with good results. Smoke alarms, sprinkler systems, fire extinguishers, and security systems or guards are all means of reducing risk. Risk-reduction techniques do not eliminate the risk of loss; they lessen the likelihood and severity of loss.

## Assuming Risk

Many large companies practice **self-insurance**—that is, they assume risk by making regular payments into a contingency fund to cover losses incurred in the course of business. The payments are usually invested in interest-bearing securities. The fund is set up by determining the dollar amount to which the firm is willing to insure itself. The actual loss experience of the company determines the size of payments into the fund. Self-insurance is usually used in conjunction with other methods.

Even the most liberal self-insurance pool may not be adequate to cover catastrophic losses. For example, a large company may determine that it is willing to self-insure up to $10 million of losses each year. Management puts $10 million of profits into an insurance reserve fund. After one year, the company has losses of $2 million. The $2 million is replaced so that the reserve-fund balance stays constant at $10 million. To supplement this self-insurance of $10 million, the company buys a liability policy from an insurance company to cover all losses above $10 million. Such a policy would protect the company from calamities like the gas leak at a Union Carbide plant at Bhopal, India.

A large and well-diversified company with many branch offices or outlets spread over a large geographic area is most likely to self-insure against certain risks, for two reasons: It may be less expensive to set money aside regularly than to pay insurance premiums on many branches or outlets, and the loss of one branch or outlet will probably not force the company into bankruptcy. A small sole proprietorship, however, might be financially ruined if a serious accident or fire occurred. The small businessperson is least likely to rely on self-insurance as the primary means of handling risk. Some municipalities also rely on self-insurance. The city of Chicago, for example, insures itself against lawsuits and losses. Because of the large tax base, the city builds its loss experience into the budget and hopes that actual losses do not exceed the budgeted amount. If they do, the city would have to increase tax revenues or cut other parts of the budget to find the needed money.

## Transferring Risk to an Insurance Company

By buying insurance, a business (or individual) transfers the risk of financial loss to a company that will pay for that loss. A large number of businesses (or individuals) share in the financial losses of the group. **Insurance** protects each buyer—known as the **insured**—by paying for loss in return for a fee known as a **premium** (usually paid quarterly or annually). The premium varies with the amount of coverage and the size of the potential loss.

For example, a business might buy property insurance for its office building. If the business has just moved into new quarters overlooking the waterfront, it will pay a much higher premium than if it were located in a small building in a run-down warehouse district. If the property is damaged by fire, the insurance company will pay for damages up to the limits agreed on with the business. Neither the insured nor the insurance company has any control over whether an accident will occur, but if one does, the insured will not suffer a large financial loss because it has transferred the risk of that loss to the insurance company.

**Insurance**

Protects a buyer from loss for a fee

**Insured**

The person or business who buys insurance

**Premium**

The fee paid for insurance

# ▶ Insurance Basics

The businesses or individuals who buy insurance from a particular insurance company are policyholders. The insurance policy contains a description of the types of losses or perils that are covered and those that are not covered, the dollar limits of coverage, and other pertinent information. A policyholder who suffers a loss files a claim (a request for payment) with the insurance company. If the loss is covered by the policy, the company will pay the claim— that is, the company will pay the policyholder the cost of the loss up to the limits declared in the policy. The policy limits may include a **deductible**—an amount for which the policyholder is responsible before the insurance company will pay a claim. For example, for homeowners insurance the theft coverage may have a $100 deductible and a $5,000 limit on silver, gold, jewelry, stamp collections, and coins. This would mean that the policyholder

**Deductible**

An amount for which the policyholder is responsible before the insurance company will pay a claim

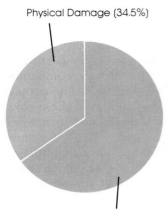

Physical Damage (34.5%)

Bodily Injury Liability (65.5%)

**Figure 20-1**

Premiums Earned on Automobile Insurance

would pay the first $100 of the loss and the insurance company would pay any amount above this up to $5,000. Losses in excess of $5,000 would be uninsured.

Private insurance companies are profit-making businesses that sell financial protection against loss. Figure 20-1 shows premiums earned on automobile insurance. The insurance companies receive premiums from insurance buyers to cover losses, but they have other expenses as well—sales and administrative expenses and taxes. Because premiums alone do not cover all their costs, insurance companies invest the premiums in interest-bearing securities, such as certificates of deposit, stocks, and bonds. Because of the insurance companies' reliance on returns on their investments, their profitability can vary from year to year as the economy and interest rates go up and down. Thus insurance companies need to charge premiums high enough to cover their costs. The law of large numbers helps determine what the premiums should be. Figure 20-2 shows premiums earned and losses paid for automobile insurance.

# The Law of Large Numbers

To help determine how much of their income must come from premiums, insurance companies rely on the law of large numbers, which assumes that while any one policyholder may suffer a loss, out of a total population of policyholders only a few actually will suffer a loss. Therefore, if every policyholder pays a small amount into the insurance company's fund, there

**Figure 20-2**

Premiums Earned and Losses Paid for Automobile Insurance

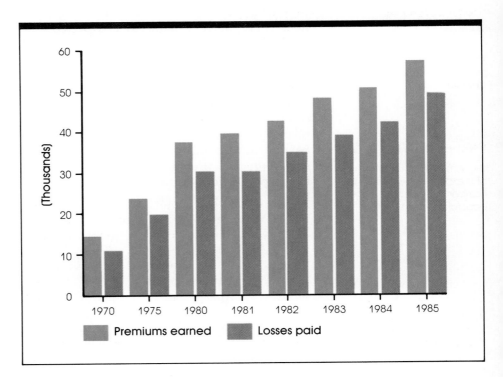

will be enough money in the fund to pay for the damages suffered by the few who actually incur a loss.

The law of large numbers improves insurance companies' ability to make statistical predictions of how many losses there are likely to be in a particular population. Through statistical analysis of past data, insurance companies also estimate the type and severity of the losses that will occur. The people employed by insurance companies to evaluate the probabilities of these risks occurring are **actuaries.** Actuaries are college graduates trained in mathematics and statistics who are required to pass a rigorous series of exams before attaining the position of actuary. Actuaries use data from large numbers of real-world cases to create **actuarial tables**, which list the expected probabilities of each type of risk. The most common actuarial table is one for life expectancy. Once the actuary has created the actuarial tables, an underwriter determines which risks to insure and at what cost (insurance premium).

Insurance is affordable for individuals because the population of insurance buyers is so large. If only one person were insured by a company, then the company would either have to charge the total costs of the potential losses to that one person or absorb the losses itself. If that were the case, there would be no point in buying or selling insurance.

Assume that a company insuring 200,000 households against fire predicts from experience that 2,000 houses will burn each year, causing damages of $30,000 per incident. Assume that each house has a value of $100,000 and that the total insured value of all the houses is $20 billion. The total expected losses would be $60 million, or $3 per $1,000 of insured value. Sixty million dollars would be the total expected loss for all 200,000 policyholders and would be shared on the basis of the insured value of each policyholder's house. The portion of the total expected losses paid by each individual is called the **pure premium**, and in this case the pure premium would amount to an average of $300 per policyholder. The pure premium is determined by dividing the real expected loss by the number of individuals in the population.

To the pure premium is added the cost of maintaining the insurance company's staff, paperwork, claims offices, and other corporate expenses related to servicing the insurance policies. Assume that the total expenses amount to $20 million. The **total premium** paid by each individual is the sum of the pure premium plus expenses divided by the number of individuals in the population. Putting these numbers into equation form demonstrates how an individual premium would be determined on a $100,000 house:

$$\text{Pure premium} = \frac{\text{total expected losses}}{\text{number of policyholders}}$$

$$\$300 = \frac{\$60 \text{ million}}{200,000 \text{ policyholders}}$$

$$\text{Total premium} = \frac{\text{total expected losses} + \text{expenses}}{\text{number of policyholders}}$$

$$\$400 = \frac{\$60 \text{ million} + \$20 \text{ million}}{200,000 \text{ policyholders}}$$

**Actuaries**

College graduates trained in mathematics and statistics who have passed a rigorous series of exams

**Actuarial tables**

Lists of the expected probabilities of each type of risk

**Pure premium**

The portion of the total expected losses paid by each individual

**Total premium**

The sum of the pure premium plus expenses divided by the number of individuals in the population

Because the value of the average houses in the example is $100,000, the $400 total premium is equivalent to $4 per $1,000 of insured value.

## The Law of Adverse Selection

**Law of adverse selection**

Those who are most likely to purchase insurance are those who are most likely to suffer losses

Insurance companies know that the people most likely to purchase insurance are those who are most likely to suffer losses. This is the **law of adverse selection**. People who exhibit adverse selection may have had several accidents in their lifetime or may come from families with a history of health problems. In any case, people seeking insurance who have a higher probability of accident, injury, or health problems than the general population would be said to exhibit adverse selection.

Adverse selection could cause insurance companies to incur extraordinary losses or it could boost insurance premiums to levels that would be unaffordable for many people. For this reason, insurance companies attempt to insure a large, diverse population whose expected losses are independent from each other. They assign different premiums for different degrees of risk. For example, a property insurance premium for a business located in a high-crime area would be higher than that for a business in a well-patrolled, well-lit location. The insurance company usually requires considerable information about policyholders before extending insurance coverage. For auto insurance, this information includes a complete driving history—accidents or tickets—the kind of car, and the purposes for which it is to be used. In most states there are also questions about the age, sex, and marital status of all drivers in the household, and about the percentage of the time each driver is expected to use the car.

A few states—including Montana, Hawaii, Michigan, North Carolina, Massachusetts, and Pennsylvania—have passed legislation prohibiting the use of factors such as age and sex. Insurance companies are strongly opposed to this so-called unisex legislation. They claim that they have definite proof of loss differences reflecting differences in age and sex, and they believe they should be able to charge differential prices based on this information. Equality in insurance premiums is the subject of Financial Encounter 20-1.

For life and health insurance, information about personal and family health history is requested. A statement from the family physician may be required, and discounts may be given to insureds who don't smoke or who are not overweight. For homeowners insurance, questions about the age and construction of the house, about heating and wiring, and about alarms, locks, and smoke detectors are asked.

To counteract the effects of adverse selection, many companies actively pursue as policyholders people considered to be good risks. Agents for these companies search among their existing clients for those with a good health history or driving record in order to sell them other lines of insurance.

## The Rule of Indemnity

**Rule of indemnity**

The policyholder cannot collect more money than was actually lost

To prevent overpaying for policyholders' losses, the insurance industry has established a **rule of indemnity**. According to this rule, the policyholder cannot collect more money than was actually lost. For example, the policy-holder may not buy two property insurance policies and collect from each policy for the same loss due to theft. It is possible to carry two or more policies, but the insurance companies involved would split the reimbursement between them.

# ▶ Requirements for Insurance

**Insurable interest**

An applicant for insurance must be able to show that he or she will actually suffer a personal financial hardship if loss occurs

In order for a company to extend insurance coverage to an applicant, certain requirements must be met. First, the applicant must have an **insurable interest**—that is, the applicant must be able to show that he or she will actually suffer a personal financial hardship if the loss occurs. If the breadwinner of a family dies, the surviving members of the family will definitely suffer a personal financial hardship. If the teen-age son has a car accident that destroys the family car, the family will probably suffer a financial hardship. The family thus has insurable interests in the life of the breadwinner and the family car. The family probably does not have an insurable interest in the life of Michael Jackson and therefore could not logically purchase a life-insurance policy on him.

**Insurable risk**

The loss for which insurance is desired must be fortuitous, measurable, and predictable

Second, the loss for which insurance is desired must be an **insurable risk**. Insurable risks have three key characteristics: They must be fortuitous, measurable, and predictable.

A fortuitous event happens by chance or by accident. Suicide (within the first year or two after the purchase of a life-insurance policy), arson, riot, and war are not considered to be fortuitous events and therefore are not ordinarily insurable risks.

A measurable risk is one that is quantifiable in financial terms—that is, a dollar value can be placed on the loss. The value of a car, house, or building can readily be determined. Although it is impossible to attach a dollar value to the loss of a loved one, it is possible to estimate the value of the family member's lost income over years of regular employment. Estimates of the cost of health and hospital care in any given region are available. On the other hand, it is very difficult to estimate the value of a family pet or Luciano Pavarotti's voice or an art masterpiece, and most insurance companies do not insure such things. A notable exception is Lloyd's of London, which under-writes most risks even if there is no good data about the probabilities of the outcomes.

A predictable risk is one that can be anticipated—that is, its frequency and severity may be estimated from existing statistical data. For example, it is possible to rely on past data to predict the number of fires, traffic accidents, and thefts that will occur each year. Wars, riots, hijackings, and terrorist activities are not generally considered to be insurable risks because their frequency and severity are difficult to predict, and there is no market for insurance against the catastrophic losses they generate. Government programs do insure against some of these types of losses. For example, the U.S.

# Financial Encounter 20-1
## Equality in Insurance Premiums

One of the most controversial topics facing the insurance industry today is whether companies should charge women the same insurance rates as men. Insurance companies say that women should pay higher rates and receive fewer benefits because they live longer than men (on the average). Furthermore, insurance companies believe the two sexes should pay different rates because their claims patterns are different. Many feminists and civil rights groups believe that insurance pricing is discriminatory and that insurance fees should be based on factors over which people have control, not on sex differences.

In 1983, Montana became the first state to pass a comprehensive law prohibiting sex and marital-status discrimination in the insurance industry. Massachusetts passed a similar law in 1988. Although ten other states have rejected an equal-insurance bill, Michigan, New Jersey, New York, and the District of Columbia are considering one. Basically, these laws make it illegal to discriminate on the basis of sex or marital status with regard to insurance premiums, benefits, pension payments, and policies. Although these laws have not had much of an effect on health, disability, or retirement benefits (which are provided by employers on a gender-neutral basis), they have drastically changed the rates that many people pay for individual insurance, particularly auto and life insurance. As a result, many insurance buyers are upset.

For example, women under the age of 25 usually have fewer automobile accidents than do men. Consequently, in the past women paid less for auto insurance than men did. Now, however, women must pay the same rates as men, which are considerably higher. In addition, women's longer life expectancy resulted in life insurance premiums that were lower than those paid by men. Now, women and men must pay the same premium, and in the long run women get less coverage for their money than before.

In spite of the drawbacks of equal-fee laws, there are some advantages for women. The rates that insurers charged women for annuities have traditionally been higher than the rates paid by men. Equal-fee laws guarantee that women will now pay less for annuities. In addition, women now pay less for medical coverage. In the past, they usually paid more for coverage than men because they had more frequent and more expensive claims.

Despite the controversies raised by equal-insurance laws, several things are known for certain. It is impossible to determine the overall cost of gender-neutral insurance. However, many industry experts feel that the overall cost of insurance to all consumers may increase as the result of these laws. In addition, the women most affected by changes in insurance costs are those who live alone or are single heads of households. Only time will determine whether the laws will bring more equality to the sexes or cause undesirable effects on the insurance marketplace.

---

These facts are from John R. Dorfman, "Proposals for Equal Insurance Fees for Men and Women Spark Battle," *The Wall Street Journal*, August 27, 1987, p. 23; "Equal Rates for Both Sexes," *Time*, June 1, 1987, p. 55; Andrea Bennett, "Setting the Unisex Pace," *Best's Review* (January 1986): 22, 24, 106, 108; and Edward J. Zimmerman, "Where the Action Is," *Best's Review* (January 1986): 24, 106.

government has a flood-insurance program that insures buildings located in known flood plains.

Insurance companies maintain the right to establish their own underwriting standards for accepting or rejecting risks. Drivers whose records are below a company's standard are rejected. Some states have mandatory insurance laws. Rejected drivers in such states are insured by the state, which in turn transfers the risk back to the insurance companies writing policies in that state.

Certain kinds of coverage are rejected by some companies. Flood and earthquake damage, for example, cause catastrophic losses that affect the

**Salt Lake City flood.** The National Flood Insurance Association is a government program to insure properties in areas subject to flooding. Many private insurance companies may not want to assume the risk of insuring properties in these flood areas.

total population of an area. Insurance companies may avoid these coverages altogether or offer separate policies or riders on existing policies to cover these risks.

It is essential to the survival of an individual insurance company that coverage be offered for a wide range of risks spread over a very large population. A hypothetical insurer who wrote only property insurance along the Gulf Coast of the United States would very likely have been wiped out in the summer of 1985 because of hurricane damage alone. One who wrote only insurance for racing drivers would also go out of business quickly, unless the premiums were extremely high and low limits were placed on the maximum loss.

# ▶ Sources of Insurance

The importance of insurance in managing risk is underscored by the prominence of the insurance industry in the U.S. economy. It controls assets of more than $1 trillion and receives over $250 billion worth of premiums annually. Table 20-1 lists the ten largest insurance companies in the United States as of 1986. All the firms listed in the table are private insurance companies, yet the single largest insurance source in the United States is the federal government.

## Public Sources

A public insurance company is a federal or state government agency that provides specialized insurance. Policyholders can be businesses or individuals.

| Company | Assets (in billions of dollars) |
|---|---|
| 1. Prudential of America (Newark) | 103,317,115 |
| 2. Metropolitan Life (New York) | 81,581,350 |
| 3. Equitable Life Insurance (New York) | 48,577,698 |
| 4. Aetna Life (Hartford) | 42,957,155 |
| 5. New York Life | 29,793,697 |
| 6. Teachers Insurance & Annuity (New York) | 27,887,103 |
| 7. John Hancock Mutual Life (Boston) | 27,213,497 |
| 8. Travelers (Boston) | 27,210,137 |
| 9. Connecticut General Life (Bloomfield) | 24,806,504 |
| 10. Northwestern Mutual Life (Milwaukee) | 20,187,343 |

Public insurance is available to cover unemployment, pensions, and work-related accidents and injuries. Social Security is perhaps the best-known public insurance program.

**Social Security.** Social Security was initiated by the Social Security Act of 1935. The official title of the program is Old-Age, Survivors, Disability, and Health Insurance (OASDHI). The plan provides retirement income, survivorship and disability benefits, and certain hospital and medical payments. The hospital and medical payments are made under the Medicare and Medicaid programs. Medicare provides limited health care to people over 65 and to other groups of people eligible to receive Social Security. Medicaid pays the medical bills of the poor.

The Social Security program is wide-ranging. Every working person needs a Social Security number, as does everyone who opens a bank account. Funding for Social Security comes from a tax that is paid by employers and employees. Self-employed people pay Social Security taxes based on a percentage of their income. Over 36 million people in the United States receive Social Security benefits, and over nine out of ten employees and their dependents are eligible for the different kinds of benefits. Figure 20-3 shows changes in Social Security from 1940 to 1988.

**Unemployment Insurance.** Unemployment insurance programs are operated at the state level. They provide unemployed workers with money, placement services, and employment counseling. The financial benefits provide only temporary and partial replacement of a person's earnings. They are usually paid for a short period (26 to 39 weeks) and vary according to the person's previous income and state of residence. Unemployment insurance is funded by taxes deducted from employees' paychecks.

**Workers' Compensation.** Every state requires employers to provide their employees with workers' compensation insurance. This insurance guarantees payment of wages and salaries, medical costs, and necessary rehabilitation services to people who are injured in the work place. It also provides benefits to a worker's family in the event the worker dies from work-related

**Figure 20-3**

Changes in Social Security from 1940 to 1986

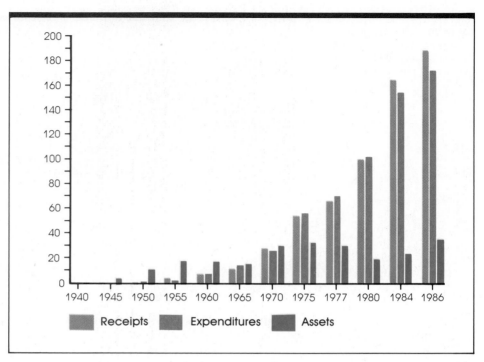

injuries or accidents. The employer alone pays the premiums for workers' compensation insurance.

*Other Public Insurance Programs.* There are many other public sources of insurance. The Federal Deposit Insurance Corporation insures deposits in banks. The Federal Savings and Loan Insurance Corporation insures deposits in savings and loan associations. The National Credit Union Administration insures money held in credit unions. The Federal Housing Administration provides mortgage insurance for lenders, protecting them against default by home buyers. The Pension Benefit Guaranty Corporation provides insurance for pension plans, preventing the loss of retirement benefits if, for example, an employer declares bankruptcy. The National Flood Insurance Association provides insurance against flooding and related problems for properties in areas subject to flooding.

## Private Sources

Private insurance companies can be divided into two categories, stock and mutual, according to type of ownership. A **stock company** is a profit-making company. The stockholders are the owners, and the profits of the company are returned to the stockholders in the form of dividends. A **mutual company** is a nonprofit cooperative; it is owned by its policyholders rather than by stockholders. A mutual company's profits are returned to the policyholders in the form of dividends or reduced insurance premiums. Mutual companies dominate the life-insurance field; stock companies tend to specialize in

**Stock company**
A profit-making company

**Mutual company**
A nonprofit cooperative

**Workers' insurance.** Workers' compensation provides coverage of medical expenses and disability income benefits for those who are injured or become seriously ill from work-related accidents. These mine workers are having a practice rescue so they can be prepared if a real accident happens. These insurance plans are administered by each state and are fully paid by employers.

property and liability insurance. Prudential Insurance Company of America, the largest insurer in the United States (see Table 20-1), is a mutual company.

# ▶ Types of Insurance

Insurance companies offer a multitude of kinds of policies to both businesses and individuals. These policies can be generally divided into three categories: property and liability insurance, life insurance, and health insurance. Managers need to know about all three categories. A business needs to purchase property and liability insurance to protect against losses, and most businesses offer health and life insurance benefits to their employees.

**Property insurance**

Includes fire, homeowners, automobile, and other policies as protection against losses due to physical damage to property

## Property and Liability Insurance

Property and liability insurance provides protection against many perils. **Property insurance** includes fire, homeowners, automobile, and other policies

**Liability insurance**

Covers financial losses to an individual or firm if the insured is held responsible for injuries or other damages

**Coinsurance clause**

Specifies the percentage of the building's value that is protected by insurance

as protection against losses due to physical damage to property. Property insurance would pay for damage to an office that occurred during a burglary. **Liability insurance** covers financial losses to an individual or firm if the insured is held responsible—that is, liable—for injuries or other damages. Table 20-2 lists the kinds of property and liability insurance that are available.

Some policyholders try to save money on insurance premiums by under-insuring property—that is, by insuring a building for much less than it's worth, figuring that no calamity is likely to affect the entire building. To counteract this tendency, insurance companies sometimes require a **coinsurance clause** in the policy specifying the percentage of the building's value (usually 75 or 80 percent) that is protected by insurance. Any claim will be paid only up to the percentage level of insurance coverage. For example, if a building is worth $100,000, a policy might have a coinsurance clause stating that it must be insured for 75 percent of its value, or $75,000. If the building is insured for $75,000, a claim for a $40,000 loss will be paid in full. If the value of the building increases to $125,000 but the policyholder fails to increase coverage, the building is no longer insured at the level specified in the coinsurance clause, and only a portion of a loss will be covered by the insurance company. The portion paid by the insurance company is determined by the following formula:

$$\text{portion paid by insurer} = \text{loss} \times \frac{\text{amount of insurance carried}}{\text{coinsurance \% of value of building}}$$

$$\$32,000 = \$40,000 \times \frac{\$75,000}{75\% (\$125,000)}$$

In this example, $32,000 is the amount of the loss covered by the insurance company. The policyholder is responsible for the other $8,000. Unless the policyholder can afford to absorb a loss of $8,000, it would be wise to increase the insurance coverage.

Businesses that cannot afford to self-insure the entire amount needed may use coinsurance as a means of reducing the cost of insurance. For example, if a business owner determines that he or she can afford to self-insure 20 percent of a total loss, the rest of the loss can be handled through coinsurance.

Property insurance for businesses includes fire insurance, natural disaster insurance, and marine insurance.

***Fire Insurance.*** Many businesses buy fire insurance to cover losses due to fire. Extended fire insurance policies cover damage from windstorms, hail, water, smoke, and riots. As with other kinds of insurance, the premium varies with the degree of risk. Businesses in brick buildings, for example, pay lower premiums than those in wooden buildings. The past record of the location also determines risk. A business in an area with a record of low losses from fire damage pays a lower premium than a building located near an area prone to brush fires.

***Auto Insurance.*** Auto insurance offers three kinds of coverage: liability, physical damages, and medical costs. If a driver is the cause of an accident, he or she is held responsible—that is, liable—for bodily injury, for property damage to the other vehicle, and for medical costs incurred by the passengers

Table 20-2  Property and
Liability Insurance Used by
Business

| Type of Insurance | Coverage |
|---|---|
| Fire insurance | Fire damage. (A comprehensive policy would also cover damage from wind, hail, earthquake, riots, and smoke.) |
| Auto insurance | Bodily injury, collision, fire, theft, and related losses |
| Burglary, robbery, and theft insurance | Unlawful taking of policyholder's property |
| Crime and criminal loss insurance | Employee theft and break-ins |
| Business interruption insurance | Closure of the firm because of serious blizzard, blackout, etc. (to cover loss of earning power) |
| Extra expense insurance | Loss of earning power |
| Marine insurance | Losses suffered by ocean-going ships and their cargoes, oil rigs, and yachts. Inland marine insurance covers goods shipped by air, rail, truck, or inland waterways, as well as damage to bridges, radio and TV towers, and satellite dishes |
| Aviation insurance | Losses to planes, helicopters, and their cargoes |
| Fidelity bond | Misappropriation of funds |
| Surety bond | Failure to perform a job |
| Title insurance | Defective title to property or land |
| Credit insurance | Failure to repay loans |
| Workers' compensation | Injury to workers on the job |
| Professional (malpractice) liability insurance | Malpractice |
| Comprehensive general liability insurance (including product liability) | All kinds of liabilities not excluded from other liability policies |

in both cars. Automobile liability insurance covers these risks to the driver. The limits of liability coverage are expressed as a sequence of three numbers, such as 100/300/50. The first two numbers refer to bodily injury per person and to bodily injury per accident, respectively. In this instance, the driver's insurance company will pay up to $100,000 for each person's injuries in the other vehicle and up to a maximum of $300,000 per accident for all injuries. (Many companies offer only a total limit for bodily injury liability. In this example, the single limit might be $300,000.) The third number, $50,000, is the limit paid under the policy for damage to the other vehicle or to other property damaged in the accident.

The coverages for physical damages are called comprehensive and collision coverage. They cover the insured's vehicle up to its actual book value. Comprehensive coverage is for damage to the insured's car that is caused by theft, fire, vandalism, wind, hail, falling objects, and other perils. Collision coverage is for damage resulting from a collision only. Both coverages are usually subject to a deductible, ranging from $50 to $500 or more, paid by the policyholder when the accident or damage occurs. The deductible prevents policyholders from turning in claims for very minor damage for which the administrative costs could easily exceed the cost of repairs. The deductible also helps to hold down the rates for comprehensive and collision coverage. The policyholder can reduce the cost of his or her insurance significantly by taking a high deductible.

Medical payments coverage pays for injuries sustained by the insured or by the insured's passengers if the insured causes an accident. The limit of this coverage is expressed as a single amount ranging usually from $5,000 to $100,000 per person. The price of all insurance coverages is based on historical information. Drivers who fall into a high-risk category because of previous accidents pay more than those who fall into a low-risk category. The cost of medical coverage also depends on the number of claims in previous periods, the average cost per claim, and the number of people insured.

Several states have adopted what is called no-fault insurance. It is intended to reduce the cost of insurance by restricting the circumstances under which an individual may sue for injuries or damages resulting from an accident. Typically under no-fault insurance, unless injuries are severe or damages extensive, the individual may not sue the other driver. All drivers are required by law to carry insurance, and all payments for claims are received from the policyholder's own insurance company, regardless of who is at fault.

Another important auto coverage is uninsured motorist insurance. It offers protection in the event that the other driver is at fault and either has no insurance or has inadequate liability limits. Many states require drivers to carry minimum limits of uninsured motorist coverage.

***Other Kinds of Property and Liability Insurance.*** Property and automobile insurance covers personal liability for damage or injuries up to the limits in the policy. In the current environment of frequent lawsuits and exceedingly high jury awards, the liability limits under those policies may not be nearly enough to protect the policyholder financially. The insurance company agrees to pay for claims up to the limits of the policy. Once those limits are reached, the remainder of the liability lies with the policyholder.

One kind of liability policy to supplement the liability limits of the auto and property policies is the personal liability umbrella policy. This policy provides usually from $1 million to $5 million of liability coverage in addition to coverage under other policies.

Doctors, lawyers, engineers, and other professionals purchase **malpractice insurance** to protect themselves from financial ruin resulting from malpractice lawsuits. This insurance covers court costs and damage awards up to the specified limits. It is extremely expensive because of the sheer number of lawsuits filed and the size of awards. The cost of this coverage is passed on to clients and patients in the form of higher fees.

Business owners protect themselves by insuring their office buildings, plant and equipment, inventory, and fleets of cars and trucks and against damage, loss and liability, but they also have special insurance needs. If the business

**Malpractice insurance**

Purchased by doctors, lawyers, engineers, and other professionals to protect them from malpractice lawsuits

**Insurance for radio and TV towers.**  Marine insurance protects transporters of goods shipped over water and land and, surprisingly, it protects equipment that transmits TV and radio signals.

has a fire, the loss results not only from the fire itself but also from the loss of business during reconstruction. **Business interruption insurance** may be purchased to offset the temporary loss of business. Insurance is also available to cover losses to a business if one of its suppliers is unable to meet the needs of the business because of a loss of some kind.

Manufacturers purchase **product liability insurance** to cover financial losses resulting from lawsuits over defective parts, food poisoning, negligent maintenance or quality control, and similar occurrences. For example, Jewel Food Stores in Chicago had an outbreak of salmonella poisoning at its Hill Farm Dairy. Salmonella contaminated the milk and caused hundreds of people to be hospitalized; several people died. Product liability insurance covers court costs and damages up to the limits of the policy. It is extremely expensive. The cost of this coverage is passed on to the consumer in the form of higher prices.

Marine insurance protects the transporters of goods, whether the goods are shipped over water or over land. Ocean marine insurance covers ocean-going ships and their cargoes, oil rigs, and yachts. Inland marine insurance covers goods shipped by air, rail, truck, or inland waterway. Inland marine insurance also covers damage to bridges, radio and TV towers, and satellite dishes.

Fidelity bonds offer protection to businesses against dishonest acts perpetrated by employees—embezzlement; theft of inventory, supplies, customer lists, or company secrets; and destruction of records. Surety bonds offer protection to businesses against the nonperformance of a contract. The construction business is the biggest user of surety bonds. If a contractor fails to complete construction work within the defined period of time, the surety bond covers the resulting losses to the business or individual.

Title insurance is available to people or organizations buying real estate; it protects against financial losses due to a problem with the title to the real estate. Credit insurance protects lenders against losses due to unpaid debts.

# Health Insurance

With health care costs rising higher and higher, health insurance is becoming a near necessity. Even minor surgery can run into thousands of dollars. According to recent statistics, one person in six is hospitalized in the United States each year, and annual health care expenditures in the United States are expected to reach $660 billion by 1990.[1]

To protect their employees from financial disaster—and to protect themselves from the potential loss of employees—most businesses provide their employees with some kind of health insurance. Almost 75 percent of the U.S. population is covered by employer-provided health insurance. Some companies pay the full price of the insurance; others require their employees to pay a certain percentage of the premium, which is deducted from their paychecks.

Group health-insurance plans are offered by employers to their employees but are underwritten by a private insurer. The premiums for group plans may be fully paid by the employer or may be partially paid by the employees subscribing to the plans. The loss experience for group plans tends to be better than the averages for private insurance on indivduals, so the rates tend to be lower for groups. Nevertheless, because of rising premiums, some businesses are opting to pay smaller percentages of the group premiums, relying on employees to pick up the rest.

Employers are also trying to cut costs in other ways. Some companies offer wellness programs right at the work place. Their objective is to keep employees healthy and thus cut down on absenteeism. Such programs emphasize nutrition, physical fitness, cessation of smoking, weight loss, and stress reduction.

Health care coverage generally includes hospital expenses, surgical and doctors' fees, major illness, and disability income.

***Hospitalization.*** Hospital expenses such as room fees, emergency-room fees, operating-room charges, and prescription and nonprescription drugs ordered by the doctor or requested by the patient are covered by hospitalization insurance. The insured usually pays a deductible, and the insurance company pays a specified dollar or percentage amount. For example, it is common to have $100 deductibles for each family member and a $25,000 limit for each hospitalization. In this case, the insured pays the first $100, and all fees up to $25,000 are paid by the insurance company. Some policies require the insurance company to pay 80 percent of the amount over $100 and the insured to pay the remaining 20 percent.

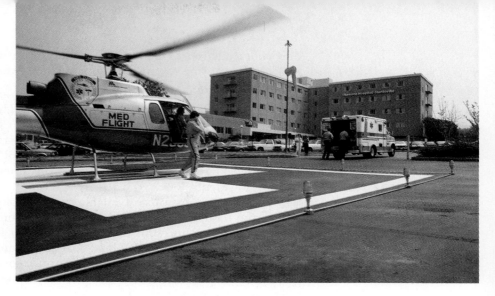

**Health and transportation.** Health insurance is a major benefit most businesses offer their employees. Ancillary services, including transportation of patients, are a part of what health insurance covers.

*Surgical and Medical Payments.* Surgical and medical payments insurance covers the fees of surgeons, anesthesiologists, and other attending physicians, the cost of doctors' visits before and after the surgery, and other related expenses. For each procedure—such as a tonsillectomy, setting a broken leg, or appendectomy—the insurance company will pay a maximum amount. The limit on a tonsillectomy might be $2,000; on a broken leg, $1,500. The better the medical coverage, the higher the limits will be for surgical procedures.

*Major Medical.* Major medical insurance covers expenses associated with serious illnesses such as cancer and serious procedures such as open heart surgery. Major medical insurance covers expenses that exceed the limits of the hospitalization and surgical and medical policies. Because the probability of having a serious medical problem is small, major medical insurance is reasonably priced. Limits of $1 million on a major medical policy are not uncommon.

*Disability Income.* Disability insurance provides steady payments while a worker is sick or disabled and unable to work. Many people who become seriously ill or are hospitalized for an extended period of time lose their jobs. Because the combination of huge medical bills and the loss of wages or salaries can be financially devastating, private insurers offer disability coverage. It is also frequently a significant benefit offered by employers. Usually a disabled worker receives a percentage of lost income—about 60 percent of the total. Social Security supplements this coverage.

*Vision and Dental Insurance.* Vision and dental insurance covers eye exams, glasses, and contact lenses, and regular dental checkups, bridgework, and root-canal work. The policy usually has a deductible or a co-payment provision requiring the insured to pay part of the cost.

*Sources of Health Insurance.* Blue Cross and Blue Shield are probably the best-known sources of health insurance. They offer paid subscription plans in which medical, hospital, and surgical expenses are covered by the pool of funds created from the fees of subscribers. Blue Cross provides hospital insurance and is the largest provider of hospitalization coverage in the United States. Blue Shield provides insurance that covers surgical and medical payments. The two plans are offered in combination to an employer, which makes this insurance available to the employees. The company usually makes the total payment for the employee. Companies often subsidize the cost of Blue Cross and Blue Shield insurance for family members, but usually the employee has to pick up at least part of the family portion of the coverage. Figure 20-4A shows types of health insurance coverage and 20-4B shows that Blue Cross and Blue Shield accounted for nearly 44 percent of health premiums nationwide in 1985.

Subscribers to Blue Cross and Blue Shield have a choice of doctors. They use their family doctor and any specialist that their doctor might send them to for diagnosis or treatment. These doctors are then reimbursed by Blue Cross or Blue Shield for their services, up to the amount specified for the medical procedure.

Aetna, Travelers, Prudential, and many other private insurance companies also offer health insurance. Subscribers can choose any doctor or specialist for treatment. The insurer reimburses the doctors the amounts specified for the procedures used.

Health maintenance organizations are a recent innovation in the health care industry. **Health maintenance organizations (HMOs)** offer comprehensive health services, for a fee, to their members. HMOs employ their own physicians at their own facilities. Members pay a set fee and must choose a physician affiliated with the HMO. HMOs encourage preventive medicine as well as corrective care, with the aim of cutting health care costs. Employers that have more than twenty-five employees and provide health insurance to their employees are required by federal law to offer membership in an HMO as an alternative to traditional health insurance—but only if an HMO has solicited their business. Financial Encounter 20-2 gives more information about HMOs.

Preferred-provider organizations (PPOs) have become an alternative to HMOs. Preferred-provider organizations (PPOs) offer comprehensive health care to a group at a reduced rate. PPOs contract with health insurers or sometimes with businesses. They function like HMOs but offer the employee a larger number of physicians to choose from, and the employee sees the physicians in their own offices. Many businesses are turning to PPOs as a cost-containment measure and sometimes offer incentives to get their employees to join. Some people fear that PPOs, under pressure to cut costs, have no incentive to provide a wide range of services.

As discussed previously, various government programs provide health insurance. Medicare provides limited health care to those over 65, and other groups eligible to receive Social Security. Medicaid provides health care to the poor. Medical payments under these plans are made according to a set

**Health maintenance organizations (HMOs)**

Offer comprehensive health services for a fee, to their members

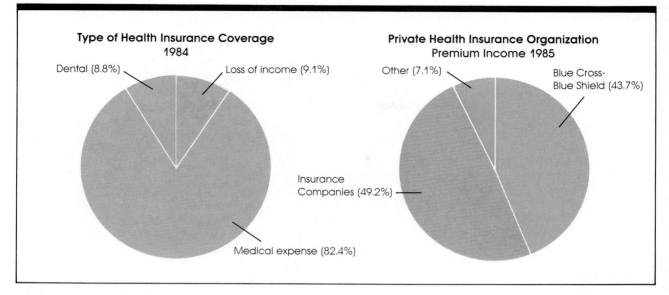

**Type of Health Insurance Coverage 1984**

Dental (8.8%)
Loss of income (9.1%)
Medical expense (82.4%)

**Private Health Insurance Organization Premium Income 1985**

Other (7.1%)
Blue Cross-Blue Shield (43.7%)
Insurance Companies (49.2%)

**Figure 20-4**

Types of Health Insurance Coverage and Percentage of Private Health Insurance Organization

fee schedule determined by the U.S. Department of Health and Human Services.

In recent years there has been much debate over the establishment of a national health-insurance plan. Proponents argue that all medical benefits should be provided, as is done in Great Britain. Others argue for coverage only of catastrophic illnesses. A national health care plan would be very expensive but would provide health care to people who are currently unable to pay for private health insurance.

## Life Insurance

Many businesses offer life insurance as part of their benefits packages. About 96 percent of employees in mid-size and large firms are offered life-insurance plans by their employers.[2] As they do with health insurance, most businesses buy group life-insurance policies and then either pay the full amount or deduct a percentage of the premium from employees' paychecks. Life insurance is also available in individual policies.

Life insurance is different from all other types of insurance because the outcome (death) is certain. It is the timing of the outcome that carries the risk. Life insurance is purchased to aid the survivors of the policyholder. The insurance policy is a written contract between an insurance company and policyholder in which the insurance company agrees to pay a set sum of money upon the death of the policyholder. Those designated by the policy-holder to be paid a sum of money upon the policyholder's death are called beneficiaries.

The policyholder pays a fee to the life-insurance company that is based on the face value of the insurance and the policyholder's age at the time of

# Financial Encounter 20-2
## *Health Maintenance Organizations*

Health maintenance organizations (HMOs) are an alternative to the traditional health-insurance plans offered by many companies and unions. HMOs provide comprehensive health care coverage to individuals for a fixed yearly fee and usually cost less than conventional health insurance. Salaried doctors, nurses, and medical technicians who are affiliated with one or more hospitals provide the health care in a clinic-like atmosphere. HMOs began to gain national attention in the 1970s, and their popularity has been increasing ever since. Today more than 15 percent of the population belongs to HMOs; some predict that number will increase to nearly 50 percent of the population by 1995.

HMOs are popular with consumers and employees for several reasons. Most HMOs emphasize regular checkups, pay for 100 percent of medical care received (including lab and hospital bills), require little paperwork for consumers, and do not have deductibles. Many HMOs offer extras such as full maternity benefits at no additional cost. The average HMO provides 20 percent more benefits than the average conventional health plan for the same premium. Moreover, patients using HMOs generally pay from 25 to 40 percent less per office visit than those who use ordinary health insurance.

HMOs have also been popular with employers and health planners. HMOs allow employers to exercise greater control over how health care is dispensed and paid for than do traditional insurance plans. Patients who use HMOs do not go to the hospital as often and usually use nonphysician care more. In addition, HMOs reduce employers' costs by concentrating on preventive medicine and by ordering fewer laboratory tests. Generally, the cost per person that employers pay for HMOs is less than the premium they pay for group

health-insurance policies covering fee-for-service treatment.

Nevertheless, some people are dissatisfied with HMOs. Many don't want to give up their present doctors and pick doctors from an HMO list of member physicians. In addition, because HMOs aim to keep down costs, many use nurses and medical aides to deal with routine complaints. This practice makes people who prefer to see a physician uncomfortable. At some HMOs, a patient may see a different doctor at each visit, even for the same problem, and this practice too makes many patients unhappy.

Some employers do not like HMOs because the premiums for some are roughly equivalent to those charged for traditional health insurance. Employers have discovered that HMOs are most used by young, healthy workers who have no ties to a regular physician. People with special health needs tend to stay away from HMOs. These factors can increase company costs for regular insurance plans and thus raise overall health care costs for employers.

The increasing cost of health care raises some doubts about the future of HMOs. Moreover, some major insurance companies, such as Cigna and Metropolitan Life, are increasing their traditional health-plan benefits to compete with the HMOs. Only time will tell if HMOs are utilized to the extent that some analysts predict.

---

These facts are from Gene G. Marcial, "HMOs May be Moving into the Recovery Room," *Business Week*, June 8, 1987, p. 124; Charles Schaeffer, with Suzan Richmond, "Second Thoughts on HMOs," *Changing Times* (May 1987): 34–36; Clemens P. Work, with Cynthia Kyle, "Health, Wealth, and Competition," *U.S. News & World Report*, November 10, 1986, pp. 59–60; and Sarah Button White, "New HMOs with Private Doctors," *Money* (September 1986): 179.

purchase. Insurance companies use a mortality table to calculate life-insurance premiums. A mortality table is an actuarial table that predicts how many people in each category are likely to die each year. Table 20-3 is a mortality table for males and females in the U.S.

Life insurance needs vary greatly over the course of a lifetime. A college student with no dependents probably needs only enough coverage for funeral,

**Table 20-3 U.S. Mortality Table for Males and Females**
Source: *Life Insurance Fact Book*, 1986, pp. 112–13.

| Age | Males, Deaths per 1,000 | Expectation of Life (Years) | Females, Deaths per 1,000 | Expectation of Life (Years) |
|---|---|---|---|---|
| 0 | 4.18 | 70.83 | 2.89 | 75.80 |
| 1 | 1.07 | 70.13 | 0.87 | 75.04 |
| 2 | 0.99 | 69.20 | 0.81 | 74.11 |
| 3 | 0.98 | 68.27 | 0.79 | 73.17 |
| 4 | 0.95 | 67.34 | 0.77 | 72.23 |
| 5 | 0.90 | 66.40 | 0.76 | 71.28 |
| 6 | 0.86 | 65.46 | 0.73 | 70.34 |
| 7 | 0.80 | 64.52 | 0.72 | 69.39 |
| 8 | 0.76 | 63.57 | 0.70 | 68.44 |
| 9 | 0.74 | 62.62 | 0.69 | 67.48 |
| 10 | 0.73 | 61.66 | 0.68 | 66.53 |
| 11 | 0.77 | 60.71 | 0.69 | 65.58 |
| 12 | 0.85 | 59.75 | 0.72 | 64.62 |
| 13 | 0.99 | 58.80 | 0.75 | 63.67 |
| 14 | 1.15 | 57.86 | 0.80 | 62.71 |
| 15 | 1.33 | 56.93 | 0.85 | 61.76 |
| 16 | 1.51 | 56.00 | 0.90 | 60.82 |
| 17 | 1.67 | 55.09 | 0.95 | 59.87 |
| 18 | 1.78 | 54.18 | 0.98 | 58.93 |
| 19 | 1.86 | 53.27 | 1.02 | 57.98 |
| 20 | 1.90 | 52.37 | 1.05 | 57.04 |
| 25 | 1.77 | 47.84 | 1.16 | 52.34 |
| 30 | 1.73 | 43.24 | 1.35 | 47.65 |
| 35 | 2.11 | 38.61 | 1.65 | 42.98 |
| 40 | 3.02 | 34.05 | 2.42 | 38.36 |
| 45 | 4.60 | 29.62 | 3.56 | 33.88 |
| 50 | 6.71 | 25.36 | 4.96 | 29.53 |
| 55 | 10.47 | 21.29 | 7.09 | 25.31 |
| 60 | 16.08 | 17.51 | 9.47 | 21.25 |
| 65 | 25.42 | 14.04 | 14.59 | 17.32 |
| 70 | 39.51 | 10.96 | 22.11 | 13.67 |
| 75 | 64.19 | 8.31 | 38.24 | 10.32 |
| 80 | 98.84 | 6.18 | 65.99 | 7.48 |
| 85 | 152.95 | 4.46 | 116.10 | 5.18 |
| 90 | 221.77 | 3.18 | 190.75 | 3.45 |
| 95 | 329.96 | 1.87 | 317.32 | 1.91 |
| 99 | 1,000.00 | 0.50 | 1,000.00 | 0.50 |

burial, and final expenses. The insurance can be taken out (owned) by the parents or by the student. A young breadwinner with a family and a mortgage needs additional coverage for maintenance of the family, education, and protection of the mortgage. When the children are grown and the mortgage is paid off, the breadwinner may need additional coverage for the maintenance of the surviving spouse.

Companies often take out life-insurance policies on key executives. The assumption is that the death of a key executive could cause the company a serious loss until that executive can be replaced. The company is both the beneficiary and the owner of the policy.

**A major benefit.** Many businesses offer life insurance as a part of their benefit packages. Life insurance, purchased to aid the survivors of the policyholder, is also available in individual policies that provide additional benefits such as investment options.

**Term insurance**

Provides a death benefit only and has no cash value

**Decreasing term insurance**

Term insurance for a specified time and at a level premium

**Mortgage protection insurance**

Pays the value of the mortgage if the policyholder dies before paying off the mortgage debt on the family's house

A person who wishes to purchase life insurance must prove to the insurance company that he or she is insurable—that is, healthy at the time the insurance is issued. The insurance company is insuring against the uncertainty of the timing of death. Someone who has a terminal illness or a serious illness that has a high probability of causing an early death will not be able to purchase life insurance. The amount of insurance purchased depends on how much coverage is needed and how much money the policyholder can afford to pay. Most people do not need $1 million of life insurance, but anyone who passes the insurer's physical examination and can afford the payments can buy that much.

Insurance companies have developed a number of life-insurance products over the years to meet the special needs of policyholders at each stage of life. Several different types of life-insurance policies can be used to provide a sum of money upon death. Some even provide money to the policyholder who survives to a certain age. The costs of policies vary widely from one company to another, and the products are sufficiently differentiated that comparing the costs of competitive products is not easy. Term insurance, decreasing term insurance, mortage protection insurance, whole life insurance, endowment insurance, variable life insurance, and universal life insurance are popular kinds of life insurance.

*Term Insurance.* The most common life insurance offered to employees is term insurance. **Term insurance** provides a death benefit only and does not have any cash value that accumulates over the life of the policy. When the term of the policy ends, coverage ends and there is no longer any value to the policy. Term insurance covers the life of the policyholder for a specific amount of money and for a specified period of time. The most common time period is five years, but the term can be between one and twenty years, depending on the age of the insured. After the specified time period, a policyholder who wants to continue his or her life insurance must again prove insurability before taking out a new policy. Renewable term policies do not require proof of insurability but are more expensive than policies that do require proof. Financial Encounter 20-3 profiles Art Williams of the A. L. Williams Co., which offers term life insurance.

*Decreasing Term Insurance.* **Decreasing term insurance** is term insurance for a specified time and at a level premium, but the face value of the policy decreases at a steady rate over the life of the policy. Such a policy is good in situations where the need for protection exists but diminishes with time. For example, a 40-year old father of three children aged 15, 12, and 9 might take out a twenty-year decreasing term policy, figuring that as his children get older and the first one completes college, he will need less coverage. In seven years, the oldest child would complete college, followed by the next two children in ten years and thirteen years. As each child finished college, there would be less need for life insurance to pay for college educations in the event the father died.

*Mortgage Protection Insurance.* **Mortgage protection insurance** pays the value of the mortgage if the policyholder dies before paying off the mortgage debt on the family's house. In the early years of a mortgage, interest

## Financial Encounter 20-3

### Profile: Art Williams of A. L. Williams Co.

In 1967, Art Williams was a high school football coach in Cairo, Georgia. Williams got interested in insurance after the sudden death of his father: Although his father had several whole-life insurance policies, the insurance was not nearly enough to take care of his family. Williams began to sell insurance part time to help his mother and two younger brothers. Before long, his income from insurance commissions exceeded his $10,000-a-year coaching salary.

In 1971, Williams and his family moved to Atlanta, and he began to sell insurance for Waddell & Reed full time. He quickly became one of the company's top agents. However, his use of part-time agents alienated him from the company, and Williams left (with 85 other agents) and formed his own company, the A. L. Williams General Agency (ALW). The agency was based on a radical insurance idea. Instead of offering expensive whole-life insurance (insurance combined with investment features), Williams sold only cheaper term-life insurance (an insurance policy only) and advised clients to invest the savings.

The new company grew rapidly. By 1978, Williams had a sales force of fifteen hundred. In 1987, his army of agents (78 percent part-time) numbered over 180,000, and they sold a staggering $81 billion in face value term-life insurance. That's almost as much protection as was sold by two of ALW's biggest competitors, New York Life and Prudential. Williams sells only term insurance backed by Massachusetts Indemnity and Life Insurance Co. (Milico).

Williams has many critics in the insurance industry. Some competitors believe that his sales methods are misleading. Others say that Williams' company focuses on getting customers to indiscriminately replace their existing whole-life policies with term insurance without regard to the benefits provided. Some believe that Williams rewards his agents more for recruiting other agents than for selling policies. Nevertheless, most critics concede that Williams' products generally offer a better deal than the whole-life policies they replace and provide more insurance coverage for the dollar, especially to young families.

Williams believes that he sells more than just insurance to his employees. He also offers the dream of financial independence. To Williams, every sale is a potential salesperson and vice versa. Therefore, he tells his agents they can build their own successful business by selling insurance and recruiting others.

The success of Art Williams and his insurance company has been phenomenal. Williams is now worth an estimated $200 million. In the next few years, Williams hopes to push the face value of the policies he sells past the $100 billion mark. Despite his success, Williams still retains many of the attributes that made him a good football coach. He sees the insurance game as a war, and he feels that eventually he is going to win.

These facts are from James R. Norman and Dean Foust, "Meet Art Williams, the P. T. Barnum of Life Insurance," *Business Week*, February 15, 1988, pp. 68–72; Mike Macbeth, "Third and Ten," *Canadian Business* 59 (October 1986): 23–34; Gordon S. Findlay, "A. L. Williams Not Yet Home Free," *Best's Review* 87 (August 1986): 78, 80; David Manuel, "All-American Success Story," *The Saturday Evening Post* 258 (April 1986): 62–65, 94.

makes up the bulk of the monthly payments and the principal is reduced slowly. Because mortgage protection insurance is created to pay off the loan, the insurance coverage decreases on the same schedule as the mortgage's loan balance.

**Whole life insurance**

Insurance that has level premiums for life and increasing cash values

***Whole Life Insurance.*** **Whole life insurance** covers the policyholder continually until death or until the policy is canceled. The amount of coverage and the premium remain level throughout the life of the policy. A major advantage of whole life insurance is that as the premiums are paid, the policy builds a cash value, and the policyholder may borrow the money from the insurance company or use it as collateral on a loan. Otherwise, the cash value will be available to the policyholder at the termination of the policy. The continuous coverage and the cash value of the policy make whole life insurance an attractive option for many people.

The total premium on a whole life policy is fixed. It may be paid throughout the life of the insured, or it may be calculated to be paid by the time the insured reaches a certain age. After the insured reaches the paid-up age, the policyholder pays nothing but the insured continues to receive coverage until death. Policy premiums may be paid monthly, quarterly, or annually, or the policy may be purchased at the outset with one lump-sum payment.

**Endowment insurance**

Provides coverage for a set period

*Endowment Insurance.* **Endowment insurance** provides coverage for a set period. If the policyholder dies before the policy matures, the face value of the policy is paid to the beneficiary. If the policy matures and policyholder is still living, the insured receives the face value of the policy. Endowments have level premiums like whole life insurance and are quite expensive, but they provide a method of saving or planning for retirement for many people.

**Variable life insurance**

Builds up an unpredictable cash value because the cash value is usually invested in common stocks

*Variable Life Insurance.* Whole life insurance builds up a predictable cash value over the life of the policy. **Variable life insurance** builds up an unpredictable cash value because the cash value is usually invested in common stocks. The face value of a whole life and a variable life insurance policy may be the same, but the policyholder could use the cash value portion of the variable life policy as a more aggressive investment. The advantage of the variable life policy is that if the policyholder lives past the end of the policy, he or she will have accumulated a large cash value that can be used for retirement.

**Universal life insurance**

Similar to variable life insurance, but the cash value is invested in money market securities

*Universal Life Insurance.* **Universal life insurance** enables the policyholder to adjust the level of coverage or the level of the premium at any time during the life of the policy. The insured may borrow from the policy once the cash value has reached a certain level. This product is similar to whole life insurance, but instead of having a guaranteed cash value built up over the life of the policy, its cash value is invested in money market securities such as U.S. Treasury bills, and the policy's cash value is determined by the rate of return earned on these securities.

# ▶ The Crisis in the Insurance Industry

In April 1988 a Massachusetts man was awarded $15.35 million in damages in an out-of-court settlement—one of the highest cash verdicts or settlements ever for compensatory damages in the United States. The man was paralyzed from the neck down after being struck in the neck by a nail shot through a wall by a high-velocity stud gun. The defendant in the case, Taylor Rental Corp., admitted little if any liability in the accident. (Taylor had rented the stud gun to a carpenter who misjudged the kind of wall material he was shooting nails into.) Nevertheless, Taylor—which is owned by Stanley Works of New Britain, Connecticut—decided to settle because Massachusetts laws regarding such liability cases are such that "a party that might be found to be at fault as little as one percent could be liable for the entire verdict." And, a Stanley Works spokesman said, "We do expect to recover the settlement costs from our insurers." [3]

No one would dispute that the man was severely injured and deserved to receive some sort of damages. Only 40, he lives away from his wife and three children at a rehabilitation hospital. But the settlement of over $15 million points up one of the biggest problems in the insurance industry—skyrocketing damage awards.

In recent years insurance company losses have increased dramatically, partly as a result of covering settlements such as the one involving Taylor Rental. Premium income is not high enough to cover risks from liability suits, and insurance companies are losing money. The losses can be attributed to several factors. The number of liability lawsuits has risen phenomenally. There are now between sixty thousand and seventy thousand per year. At the same time, damage awards have become larger, often running to millions of dollars. Within one decade, in fact, damage awards nearly trebled in size.

Product liability laws are such that people can sue organizations for injuries for which the organization was not really responsible. Suppose a runaway shopping cart at the supermarket strikes your car and dents it. You sue the supermarket for damages. Technically not at fault, the supermarket is likely to settle, mainly to retain the good will of its customers. Courts have tended to uphold the principle of strict liability, which means that even indirect involvement can make a company or indivdual liable. As a result, plaintiffs have tended to sue the organization or individual that has the most money, hoping to get a large cash reward regardless of who was at fault.

People become greedy when they realize how much money they can make in liability suits. Although many lawsuits are warranted—a doctor botches a medical procedure, a child is seriously injured by a defective toy—many are not. Some law firms encourage greedy thinking. They run ads on television giving toll-free numbers for injured people to call to find out whether they are eligible for damages. Liability lawyers often take a percentage of the settlement—usually one-third—and thus it's in their interest to seek big damage awards.

As a result of this crisis, insurance companies are raising premiums to help cover the risk of extraordinary losses. Many have chosen to stop providing liability coverage altogether. The high premiums are having major repercussions. Companies that can't afford the premiums are withdrawing from the risky areas of their business or are ceasing business altogether. For example, many pharmaceutical firms have stopped producing serum for the DTP (diphtheria-pertussis-tetanus) vaccine because of the risk of lawsuits due to side effects of the vaccine. Although the risk of death from pertussis (whooping cough) is 1 in 500 in infants up to age 1, the risk of death from the vaccine is only about 1 in 1.7 million and the risk of permanent neurological damage is 1 in 300,000. But the risk of lawsuits from those who are affected, permanently or not, has caused one manufacturer, Lederle Corp., to stop making the vaccine. Lederle was sued 109 times in 1985 alone.

Because of higher and higher malpractice premiums, many obstetricians have ceased practice. Too many lawsuits were driving up the risks of insuring them. Many day-care centers have had to close because they were unable to pay their rising insurance premiums.

Some courts have held that companies are subject to absolute liability—that is, they are responsible for damages due to hazards that were not known to be hazards at the time. Manville Corp. filed for bankruptcy in 1982. Over sixteen thousand suits had been filed by former workers who had been exposed to asbestos on the job, and Manville had reason to expect thousands more to be filed. Manville contended that it didn't know that asbestos was dangerous at the time its employees were exposed to it.

Will this cycle of suits, high damage awards, and high premiums end? Legislators at both the federal and the state levels have filed bills aiming to limit cash settlements, and a recent federal bill would prevent manufacturers and other firms from being held liable for damages unless they were clearly negligent or their product was unreasonably dangerous.

# Notes

**1.** U.S. Department of Health and Human Services, Health Care Financing Administration, *HCFA Statistics* (Washington, D.C., Government Printing Office, 1986), pp. 3, 4.

**2.** Sal Nuccio, "New Horizons in Insurance" (advertising supplement), *Fortune,* November 12, 1984.

**3.** Ronald Gilrain, quoted in *Boston Globe,* April 7, 1987, p. 50.

# Summary and Review

▶ Risk is the possibility of suffering injury or loss. Risk results from uncertainty about the future. When the outcome of events is known, there is neither risk nor uncertainty, though there may be loss. Businesses face speculative risk and pure risk. Speculative risk may result in no change, a loss, or a gain. Pure risk results either in no change or in a loss. There are four ways of managing pure risk: avoidance, reduction, self-insurance, and transference.

▶ Insurance is the means by which risk is transferred. The insured pays a premium in order to purchase a policy under which the insurance company agrees to pay for injuries or damages up to the limits specified in the policy. When a loss occurs, the insured files a claim for payment with the insurance company.

▶ To help determine how much income premiums must generate, insurance companies rely on the law of large numbers, which assumes that only a few individuals out of a group will suffer a loss. Insurance companies assign different premiums for different degrees of risk to counteract the law of adverse selection, which says that those who purchase insurance are more likely to suffer losses than those who do not.

▶ Before insurance is extended, certain requirements must be met. The policyholder must have an insurable interest. The risk must be an insurable risk. The loss must be fortuitous, measurable, and predictable. Risks must be independent events spread over a wide geographic area.

▶ Sources of insurance include private insurers, which may be either mutual or stock companies, and public insurance programs, such as Social Security and workers' compensation.

▶ There are three major types of insurance: property and liability, health, and life. Property and liability includes auto, fire, homeowners, and many types of business and liability insurance. Health insurance includes hospitalization, medical, surgical, major medical, and disability income benefits. Life insurance provides income to the beneficiary of the policyholder upon the death of the policyholder. Major types of life insurance are whole life, various kinds of term insurance, and endowments.

▶ Recent years have brought a crisis in liability insurance: more lawsuits, higher damage awards, and thus higher insurance premiums. Insurance company profits have declined, and high premiums have forced some businesses and individuals out of business or out of parts of their business.

## Key Terms and Concepts

| | |
|---|---|
| risk | stock company |
| speculative risk | mutual company |
| pure risk | property insurance |
| risk management | liability insurance |
| self-insurance | coinsurance clause |
| insurance | malpractice insurance |
| insured | business interruption insurance |
| premium | product liability insurance |
| deductible | health maintenance organizations |
| actuaries | (HMOs) |
| actuarial tables | term insurance |
| pure premium | decreasing term insurance |
| total premium | mortgage protection insurance |
| law of adverse selection | whole life insurance |
| rule of indemnity | endowment insurance |
| insurable interest | variable life insurance |
| insurable risk | universal life insurance |

## Checking Your Understanding

This chapter introduced you to the subject of risk management and insurance. To test and reinforce your understanding, fill in the blanks below.

**1.** _____ risk is uncertainty that may result in no change, a loss, or a gain.

**2.** Before a company extends insurance coverage, an individual must demonstrate an _____ interest.

**3.** Term insurance that offers the insured the option of additional years of coverage with no proof of insurability is called a _____ term policy.

**4.** An insurance company that is owned by its policyholders and returns profits to the policyholders in the form of dividends or reduced premiums is known as a _____ company.

**5.** _____ _____ life insurance has level premiums over the life of the insured. It includes both a death benefit and a savings plan that builds up cash value.

**6.** No _____ auto insurance is popular in some states. This is because it is supposed to reduce the cost of insurance by restricting the circumstances under which an individual may sue for damages resulting from an accident.

**7.** Alternative health care plans are increasing competition in the health-insurance industry. A popular innovation is the _____ _____ _____, which charges a flat fee for health services and health maintenance as well.

**8.** The policyholder of _____ life insurance has flexibility in determining the level of the annual premium at any time during the life of the policy.

**9.** Accidents, fire, and illness are all examples of _____ risk.

**10.** _____ interruption insurance is used to offset loss of a company's income if a fire causes a firm to cease operations temporarily.

# Topics for Review and Discussion

**1.** Buying insurance transfers risk to an underwriter. There are three other ways of handling risk besides buying insurance. Can these strategies work in concert with insurance, or are they alternatives to insurance? Explain.

**2.** Why do insurance companies use the concept of adverse selection in deciding whom to insure? If this tactic were practiced exclusively, what would be the result for a portion of the total population?

**3.** Several states have mandatory no-fault automobile insurance. Discuss the advantages and disadvantages of no-fault and standard auto coverage.

# Exercises

**1.** In recent years, it has become increasingly difficult for certain segments of the population to get insurance coverage: medical doctors, high school sports programs, and day-care centers. Pick a segment of the economy or population that is currently finding insurance unavailable or very expensive, and examine the implications and ramifications for society in general. *The Reader's Guide to Periodical Literature* in the library is a good place to start.

**2.** As a class project, have groups of three or four students contact several major employers nearby and compare the health care plans offered by each.

**3.** The class chooses five different insurance companies and asks the local agents to provide a computer printout for three separate life-insurance products. Compare whole life, five-year renewable term, and universal life within the same company and from one company to another.

# Case 20-1

## Professors Make Mistakes Too: A St. Louis Restaurant Story

In the spring of 1980, Dr. Gareth S. Gardiner resigned from Southern Illinois University in Edwardsville to launch a career as an entrepreneur and restaurateur in St. Louis, Missouri. He had some experience in rehabilitating a 125-year-old residence, and he was ready for a bigger challenge. One of Gardiner's part-time handymen had purchased a vacant building next to the world headquarters of Anheuser-Busch.

A light bulb went on over Gardiner's head when he saw the building. Anheuser-Busch had recently banned drinking alcoholic beverages on the brewery premises, and Gardiner thought the employees might want to go elsewhere to eat and drink. Gardiner incorporated a restaurant company called Lynch Street Regulars, Inc. (the restaurant was on Lynch Street, and he hoped to have many regular customers). He bought the vacant building from his handyman for $5,000 in stock in the new company and hired him to head the work crew to rehabilitate the building.

Gardiner spent about $45,000 of his own money to get the work started. After several banks turned him down for a commercial loan (most laughed heartily at the thought of a former professor running a restaurant), Gardiner persuaded some investors to buy stock in the new corporation. By early 1981, Gardiner had raised $125,000 from investors, and work on the building was nearly complete. On April 4, 1981, disaster struck.

Early that morning a 7-year-old boy looking for returnable soda bottles walked through a door that had accidentally been left unlocked. He spied a box of matches stored beside paint and other flammables. While playing with the matches, he accidentally set the building on fire, causing $130,000 in damage. Although the restaurant building was worth more than $200,000, Gardiner had purchased a builder's risk insurance policy in the amount of only $75,000 the year before. The insurance policy included a 100 percent coinsurance clause, which required that the insurer insure the building for 100 percent of the replacement cost of the building. Because Gardiner had insured it for only $75,000, he was compensated for only half of the damage. The $75,000 he received from the insurance company was not enough to cover the damages.

Gardiner was angry with himself for not having obtained enough insurance to cover the full loss of the building. Nonetheless, after raising more funds from stockholders and obtaining a $50,000 bank loan (when the prime interest rate was 20 percent), Gardiner opened Lynch Street Regulars in July 1981— but without the meeting and banquet rooms he had planned for the second floor. This led to a second disaster: chronic cash-flow losses.

The restaurant's lively luncheon business, which depended heavily on nearby Anheuser-Busch, was not adequate to offset slow evenings and weekends. Most importantly, Gardiner was not able to tap the lucrative banquet business the brewery and other large companies had to offer. The restaurant lost an additional $60,000 or so on first-year operations, and

Gardiner spent much of that time running about frantically trying to raise enough additional stockholder equity to stave off bankruptcy. Investors became increasingly difficult to find because the restaurant was already losing money. After four years of struggle and continuing financial headaches, Lynch Street Regulars closed its doors, and Gardiner leased the building to a group eager to succeed in the restaurant business.

Gardiner's failure to insure his restaurant adequately was a major factor behind the failure of Lynch Street Regulars. A sound business strategy and an exciting entrepreneurial venture providing jobs for fifteen people ultimately failed because of its founder's mistakes.

---

These facts are from Dr. Gareth S. Gardiner, Professor of Business Administration, Linfield College, McMinnville, Oregon, 1987.

### Questions

1. Under the coinsurance clause, how much insurance should Gardiner have on his building to be reimbursed the whole $130,000 loss?
2. To some extent, because Gardiner did not have adequate insurance, he relied on self-insurance. Why was this not a good strategy for him? Who should use self-insurance?
3. Would business interruption insurance have been helpful in this case?

## Case 20-2
### *Flood Insurance*

In 1987, flooding caused approximately $1 billion in property damage nationally. Because standard homeowner policies do not cover flood damage, most losses were not insured. In order to be insured against floods a homeowner has to take out a special flood policy. Prior to 1968, flood insurance was not available because private insurers would not underwrite flood insurance since they could not cover the cost, let alone make a profit. Flood insurance was unprofitable because claims paid out on flood insurance exceeded premiums. Only people in the high risk category bought flood insurance, and their premiums could not possibly cover the huge losses caused by floods.

In 1968, Congress passed the Federal Flood Insurance Act. This act was motivated by the need for flood insurance and the huge amounts the government was paying out in federal aid after flood disasters. This act made flood insurance practical since the underwriting was done by the government, which paid the difference between premium income and claims paid out. Until 1981 the government lost money on flood insurance.

The National Flood Insurance Agency (NFIA) started the Write Your Own Program (WYO) to tie flood insurance availability to a loss control program. Nationally there are some 18,000 communities that comply with building regulations, thus qualifying for flood insurance under the program. In 1986 there were about 2 million flood insurance policyholders. The Emergency Management Agency, a division of the NFIA establishes the building regulations. If a community doesn't comply with these regulations it will not be eligible for flood insurance or federal disaster assistance. The WYO program has been very successful. In 1985 flood policies increased by 400,000, and coverage increased from $13 billion to $46 billion.

A key advantage of the WYO program is that the consumer deals directly with the insurance agent as opposed to a government agency. This streamlines the claims process and improves the marketing of the program. The insurance agent is better equipped to market the flood insurance than a government agency. Insurance agencies have said that the WYO flood policies are an untapped source for large profits.

Some feel that flood insurance is still inadequate, arguing that according to recent surveys people aren't even aware it exists. They point out that the homeowners in communities that do not comply with federal regulations are not eligible for flood insurance. In addition, the prohibitively high cost of flood insurance makes it impractical for many people. Even the federal disaster program is inadequate. Before receiving these low interest loans the homeowner must get several damage estimates. In addition, they must document all goods lost in the flood at a time when they can barely clean up, let alone fill out paperwork.

---

These facts are from Karen McCombs, "Write Your Own Flood Plan a Success," *Property & Casualty/Employee Benefit National Underwriter,* September 21, 1987, pp. 4–5; *Chicago Tribune,* August 17, 1987, p. 1; *Chicago Sun-Times,* August 15, 1987, p. 6; Douglas Federau, " 'The Federal Flood Program Is Ineffective,' " *Property & Casualty/Employee Benefit National Underwriters,* February 23, 1987, p. 29–30; Sam Friedman, "Flood Insurance Cited as an Untapped Market," *Property & Casualty/Employee Benefit National Underwriter,* October 3, 1986, p. 38; "Flood Insurance to Increase," August 1, 1986, p. 43; "Study Shows Flood Victims Unaware That Insurance Exists," *Risk Management,* p. 112.

### Questions

1. Why is the government underwriting flood insurance?
2. What is a WYO? What are the advantages of the WYO program?
3. What are some complaints about the present flood insurance system?

## Answers to Checking Your Understanding

1. speculative
2. insurable
3. renewable
4. stock
5. Whole
6. fault
7. health maintenance organizations
8. universal
9. insurable
10. Business

## Outline

# Chapter 21

# Computers and Information Systems

## Objectives

After reading this chapter, you will be able to:

▶ Explain why managers need information.

▶ Describe a management information system and explain its role in business.

▶ Explain how computers can facilitate the workings of a management information system by processing data into information.

▶ Differentiate between hardware and software.

▶ Enumerate business capabilities of computers.

▶ List some office applications of computers.

# Business Experience

Although most businesses use computers, people may find it surprising that computers are also used by major league baseball teams. The Major League Baseball Corporation (MLB)—which includes both the American League and the National League—has begun to use computers to centralize player statistics and information on salaries, contracts, scouting reports, and so on. In addition, each of the twenty-six baseball teams uses computers to obtain access to player information quickly. The baseball teams need this information to play more efficiently and to make the game of baseball more profitable.

As part of its corporate sponsorship of major league baseball, International Business Machines agreed to equip the MLB and each of the major league teams with IBM PC XTs. The MLB has an IBM minicomputer, and the teams use IBM PC portable computers and modems to send and receive data on various players while on the road.

The MLB's system combines four different data bases into one source of data on every player who has ever played with a major league team. The first, the Waiver System, lists the status of all active players in the major leagues. This allows teams to obtain information on players who have moved from one team to another or who have been put on waiver and are thus free to be hired by any team. The second data base is the Player Contract Information System, which contains information on all current players' contracts, salaries, and incentives.

The third data base contains baseball statistics. The MLB was using two outside statistical bureaus for statistics, but IBM has developed software to enable MLB to take over this function. Some team managers have learned to use computers to generate ratings and statistics. For example, a manager might use a computer to determine which of the team's batters is best suited to pinch-hit against a left-handed pitcher when the score is tied in the eighth inning and there are two outs.

The fourth data base helps teams monitor players now playing in high school, college, or the minor leagues. Such data helps teams keep up with promising players and lets them know when those players are eligible to play in the big league.

MLB hopes to tie all its information together so that a manager who wants to find out about recruiting or trading for a certain player can obtain biographical data, statistics, experience, salary, and other information on that player before making a decision to trade. Previously, teams had to go to several different sources to obtain such information.

Although the entire system is not yet on-line, the MLB and its teams are already using some of the data. Baseball management has a reputation for being old-fashioned, but most managers recognize that computers can help them do their jobs more quickly and efficiently, ultimately increasing the excitement for fans of one of America's favorite pastimes.

---

These facts are from Don Steinberg, "Networking the National Pastime," *PC Week*, March 31, 1987, pp. C/1, C/7.

# Introduction

Business managers spend a great deal of time making decisions—planning for future operations, implementing current plans, and evaluating past performance. They have a constant need for information to aid in their decision making—information not only about the current situation but also about the past and the future. In an age when computers are helping businesses perform more profitably and efficiently than ever before, it is not surprising that the computer is an enormous aid in managing the flow of information because of its ability to process and store large quantities of data. The computer has transformed all areas of business—from production and marketing to accounting and human resources management. This chapter examines the components of a management information system and discusses computers—what they are, where they came from, and how they are used in business.

# ► The Management Information System

**Information**

Data that is relevant for a specific purpose

**Management information system**

A collection of data that provides information to managers to use in making decisions

Managers need information, not just data. Data are unorganized facts, statistics, opinions, and predictions gathered from various sources inside and outside the company. Confronted with a pile of raw data, a manager would have difficulty making a decision. The data must be sorted and logically organized to produce relevant information. **Information** is data that is relevant for a specific purpose. A sales manager, for example, might want to rank total annual sales by territory over the past five years. Presented with lists of each salesperson's monthly sales reports for those five years, the manager could spend days trying to make sense out of all the names and numbers. To convert such raw data into usable information, many firms use a management information system.

A **management information system (MIS)** is a collection of data that provides information to managers to use in making decisions. The MIS organizes past, present, and projected information from internal and external sources and makes it available to managers in all levels of the organization.

Top management—the president, chief executive officer, and executive vice president—has overall responsibility for the firm. Because they focus on strategic decision making, they need information that will help them decide whether to develop new products, acquire other companies, and implement various plans to use the company's resources to take advantage of opportunities.

Middle managers—plant managers, division managers, and department managers—have a narrower focus than top managers. Concerned with making tactical decisions, they require information that will enable them to develop operating plans for their particular areas and to develop plans that will help them achieve the objectives that top managers have established.

**To make decisions, managers need information.** Computers are important tools that most managers use to develop new plans, implement current plans, and evaluate past performance. Managers need data organized in a useful way and computers assist with this task.

First-line, or supervisory, managers direct the workers. They are concerned with overseeing the firm's day-to-day activities. They require information that will enable them to coordinate the work of their subordinates with the aim of achieving the plans and objectives set by middle management.

Decisions made at the supervisory level are generally routine and well defined; the informational needs of first-line managers can be met by normal data-processing activities such as the preparation of financial statements and routine recordkeeping. Middle managers require a broad range of internal information and rapid processing and retrieval of data. Decision making by top managers is rarely repetitive and is usually complicated by a great deal of uncertainty. The information needed by top management encompasses past data, present data, and future projections and is accumulated over lengthy periods. It often covers a broad range of internal and external business activities and is presented in an extremely summarized form so that many issues can be discussed as conditions warrant.

Because managers—and other users of the MIS—have different needs, the information system must be able to organize data into formats that are usable and accessible.

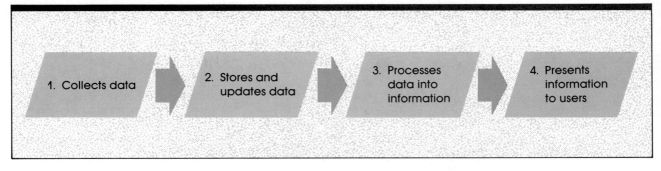

**Figure 21-1**
Four MIS Functions

## How the Management Information System Works

The major task of a management information system is to gather data, store and update it, analyze it, and report it. Data—facts, opinions, statistics, predictions—can be obtained from anyone in any department within the organization and also from external sources (Figure 21-1). Most data comes from within the organization—from company records (such as personnel records), reports (such as sales reports, financial reports, and reports of meetings), and from managers themselves. Typical external sources of data are trade and financial publications, data-gathering firms (such as Dun and Bradstreet), suppliers, customers, consultants, conferences, the U.S. government, and reports of competitors' activity. It is essential that the data be current, complete, and accurate. Out-of-date, incomplete, or inaccurate data can lead to poor or even disastrous decision making. Companies with large management information systems often employ an MIS manager to coordinate the workings of the system and manage the technicians and specialists who actually process the data.

Data is entered into a **data base,** an inventory of related data—past, present, and projected—organized for convenient access. Data is stored in one place, often in a computer, where it is accessible to all users of the system. Although computers are not essential to the storing of data and updating of data bases, they greatly facilitate the task.

Most data must be analyzed, or processed, to be in a form useful to MIS users. The MIS could process stacks of sales data and provide the sales manager with a ranking by sales territory, by year, by sales dollar, by sales representative within each territory, or by some other factor. Figure 21-2 is a diagram of how an MIS works.

**Data base**

A repository of related data organized for convenient access

## The Role of Statistics

Some data coming into a management information system is verbal, such as legal opinions. Most business data, however, is numerical and thus must be processed in some way in order to be meaningful. Statistical methods are particularly helpful, especially when large groups of numbers must be summarized. Statistical methods range from the simple analysis of figures to

**Figure 21-2**
How an MIS Works

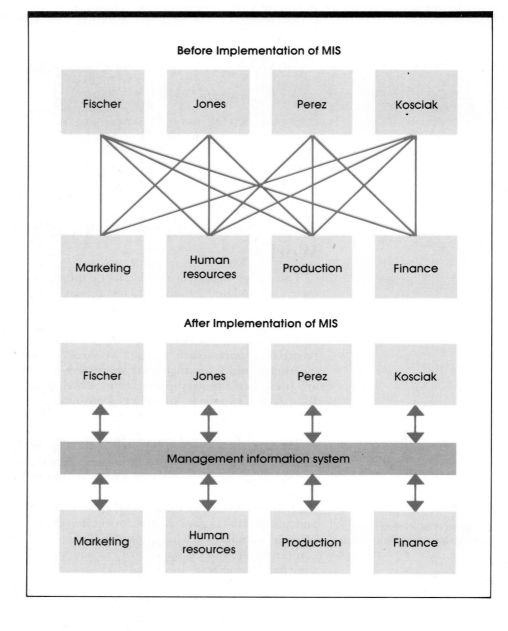

**Before Implementation of MIS**

Fischer   Jones   Perez   Kosciak

Marketing   Human resources   Production   Finance

**After Implementation of MIS**

Fischer   Jones   Perez   Kosciak

Management information system

Marketing   Human resources   Production   Finance

**Statistics**

A collection of numerical data about some event, object, or individual

discover sales or cost trends to computer simulations using hundreds of variables. The basis of nearly all statistical techniques is the use of past experience and data to try to predict the future. **Statistics**—a collection of numerical data about some event, object, or individual—can provide the key that unlocks a wealth of information that a business can depend on.

A statistic measures a certain characteristic of a group of numbers; it is a measure computed from or used to describe a particular group of data. The

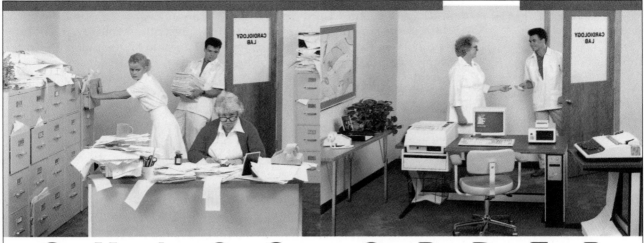

**Marquette Electronics, Inc., promotes a management information system.** Efficiency and productivity should result from an MIS that enables managers to organize information from both internal and external sources. The MIS turns chaos into order.

## Arithmetic mean

The sum of all the items in a group, divided by the number of items in the group

## Median

Represents the middle value in a set of data arranged from the highest to the lowest value

main objective of statistical analysis is to summarize data in a way that presents the main characteristics and relationships of numbers. Statistics are often used in determining employment trends, budgets and cost analysis, investment requirements, quality control, and business trends. Although most managers are not expected to be statistical experts, they must possess a degree of knowledge about basic statistical concepts and terms.

The term *average* is often used to represent a summary of the general behavior of a large number of observations. There are several kinds of averages: the arithmetic mean, the median, and the mode.

The **arithmetic mean,** or simply the mean, refers to the sum of all the items in a group, divided by the number of items in the group. When the term *average* is used, what is usually meant is the arithmetic mean. The **median** represents the middle value in a set of data arranged from the highest to the lowest value. The median is the value that is the halfway point. If there is an even number of items, the median is the mean of the two

**Mode**

The value that occurs most frequently in a set of data

middle values. The **mode** is the value that occurs most frequently in a set of data. If all the values are different, there is no mode.

Both the mean and the median are important and useful measures of the central tendency of a set of data. In some circumstances, the mean is a better measure than the median, and in others the reverse is true. Means, medians, and modes are important statistical tools with distinct definitions and differences. A manager who claims that a figure is an "average" should know the type of average.

# Data-Processing Operations

**Data processing**

The transformation of raw data into a form useful for a particular purpose

**Data processing** is the transformation of raw data into a form useful for a particular purpose. The processing of data for business involves ten basic operations. Whether data is processed manually or by computer, these ten operations must be performed (the following list is in alphabetical order, not in order of occurrence):

1. *Calculating:* The mathematical calculation of data, such as by addition and subtraction.
2. *Classifying:* The separation of one type of data from another. An example is classifying customer orders by check or by credit card.
3. *Communicating:* The transmission of data from one place to another, such as by telephone.
4. *Copying:* The reproduction of data. An example is the copying of a credit-card number from a charge card to a charge slip; this is usually done by an imprinter at the cashier's counter.
5. *Recording:* Putting data into a form that can be used in processing. Optical character recognition is an example of recording information—information is recorded from the product with the use of lasers.
6. *Reporting:* Delivering the desired information or solution, usually in printed form.
7. *Retrieving:* Locating and obtaining the desired data. This is one operation that the computer has speeded up dramatically. It's much quicker to ask the computer to search its memory for certain data than to search through many external files.
8. *Sorting:* Arranging data into desired patterns. This operation is useful for tracking the results of transactions, such as sorting bank checks by branch number.
9. *Storing:* Saving data and information. The ability to store data has been greatly increased through the use of computers. Material that might require several file cabinets can be stored on several disks.
10. *Summarizing:* Condensing large quantities of data into small amounts of meaningful information.

Computers have made giant strides in the field of data processing because of their ready adaptation to these ten data-processing operations. Of the ten, only recording cannot be totally computerized, although the advent of more advanced scanning equipment is beginning to make this possible.

# ▶ Computers: An Overview

**Computer**

An electronic machine that processes data into meaningful information

A management information system does not require computers, but its concepts and practices are closely related to those of computers. An MIS processes data into information relevant to users of the system. A **computer** is an electronic machine that processes data into meaningful information. The large growth in the number of computer installations in both profit and nonprofit organizations reflects significant increases in the amount of available data. Many companies, regardless of size, rely on computer-based information systems to organize, manipulate, and distribute information. Computers are a prime example of the impact of new technology on business practices and capabilities.

## A Brief History of Computers

The history of electronic computers dates only from 1946. A look at five generations of computers shows how rapidly computer technology has advanced in less than fifty years. With each generation, computer size has decreased, storage capacity and speed have increased, and prices have decreased.

The first generation of computers (1946–58) is dated from the invention of the ENIAC (Electronic Numerical Integrator and Calculator). These computers relied on glass vacuum tubes, which were large and produced a great deal of heat. The computers, therefore, were large—the ENIAC covered 15,000 square feet, was 10 feet tall, and weighed 30 tons—and prone to overheating. The tubes tended to burn out frequently, even with air conditioning to cool them. Another first-generation computer was UNIVAC I (Universal Automatic Computer), the first commercial electronic computer. General Electric Company bought a UNIVAC I in 1954, becoming the first business to buy a computer. UNIVAC I was also used by the U.S. Census Bureau.

The invention of the electronic transistor was the next great stride in computer technology; it marks the second generation of computers (1959–64). A transistor is a small electronic switch that controls electrical current. No longer would bulky tubes overheat and inhibit processing; transistors produced little heat, were inexpensive to make, and could process data more rapidly than tubes. Processing speeds began to be measured in microseconds (millionths of seconds).

**Integrated ciruit**

A network of dozens of tiny transistors and connections engraved on small silicon wafers, or memory chips

The invention of the integrated circuit introduced the third generation (1965–71). An **integrated circuit** is a network of dozens of tiny transistors and connections engraved on small silicon wafers, or memory chips. Memory chips further increased the speed of computers and were both smaller and more reliable than transistors wired together. Because of their small size, the size of computers decreased as well, yet storage capacity inceased. The third generation also marked the introduction of the minicomputer and of remote terminals. As technology improved, costs decreased.

The fourth generation of computers (1971–present) arrived with the invention of the large-scale integrated circuit (LSI circuit), which incorporates

**Faster than a speeding bullet.** This Cray supercomputer is an example of a mainframe computer that can serve many users and perform many functions. This supercomputer can process large quantities of data with incredible speed.

even more circuits with different functions on one chip. The microcomputers of today are based on LSI technology, relying on a single integrated circuit known as a **microprocessor**, which is capable of performing large-scale data processing.

Computer scientists are now developing the fifth generation of computers, based on very large-scale integration (VLSI). The aim is for computers to be capable of what is known as **artificial intelligence**—for them to be able to work, to "think," as much like the human mind as possible.

## Types of Computers

Computers can be classified into three categories, based on their size: mainframes, minicomputers, and microcomputers.

*Mainframes.* **Mainframe computers** are the largest and fastest computers available. Because of their large size—they often occupy entire rooms or floors of buildings—and high costs, they are usually used by large corporations, banks, and government organizations. They can process large quantities of data with incredible speed, accomplishing millions of operations per second. Mainframes are usually multi-user, general-purpose computers:

**Microprocessor**

A single integrated circuit capable of performing large-scale data processing

**Artificial intelligence**

For computers to work and to "think," as much like the human mind as possible

**Mainframe computers**

The largest and fastest computers available

**Small and efficient.** This hand-held microcomputer is used by a Federal Express courier to maintain constant tracking of packages shipped by customers. The system is so effective that Federal Express can find out where a package is at any time.

They can serve many users and can perform many functions. A very large mainframe is the supercomputer, which is generally used for scientific applications.

***Minicomputers.*** **Minicomputers** are similar to mainframes but smaller, slower, and less expensive. Minicomputers, which are usually desk-sized, are used in applications too large or too specialized for a microcomputer and too small for a mainframe. Commonly used in middle-size firms or within divisions of large corportions, minicomputers are also popular in research laboratories, colleges, and manufacturing plants.

***Microcomputers.*** **Microcomputers**—also known as personal computers—are the smallest, least powerful, and least expensive of all the computers. They are desktop or lap-top computers whose small size was made possible by the invention of the microprocessor. Widely used for personal use in the home, microcomputers are also popular in small and large businesses that do not require computers with large memory capabilities. Interestingly, microcomputers are much more efficient than most first-generation room-sized computers.

## Computer Hardware

The physical components of a computer—its electronic equipment, cabinet, keyboard, and the like—are known as **hardware**. Regardless of their size, all

**Minicomputers**

Smaller, slower, and less expensive than mainframes

**Microcomputers**

Smallest, least powerful, and least expensive of all the computers

**Hardware**

The physical components of a computer

**Figure 21-3**
How a Computer Works

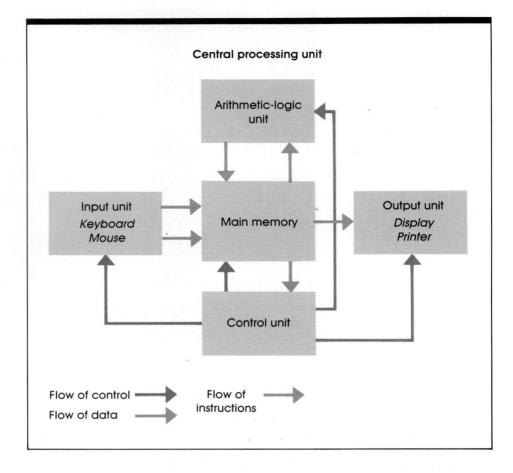

Central processing unit

Arithmetic-logic unit

Input unit
*Keyboard*
*Mouse*

Main memory

Output unit
*Display*
*Printer*

Control unit

Flow of control ➡
Flow of data ➡

Flow of instructions ➡

---

**Central processing unit**

The part of the computer that actually computes

**Primary memory**

A group of chips that store all data entered into the computer

**Control unit**

Controls the computer by gathering data from memory and sending processing instructions to other parts of the computer

**Arithmetic/logic unit**

Performs all mathematical computations and makes comparisons between data

computers contain the same basic hardware (Figure 21-3). Computer hardware can be divided into two categories: the central processing unit and input-output devices—that is, all peripheral equipment used for communication between the user and the computer.

*Central Processing Unit.* The **central processing unit (*CPU*)** is the heart· of the computer. It is the part of the computer that performs computations. The CPU has three components: the primary (or main) memory, the control unit, and the arithmetic/logic unit.

The **primary memory** is a group of chips that store all data entered into the computer. Different computers can store different quantities of data. Memory capacity is measured in bytes. One byte is the capacity to store one character; computers can store thousands, millions, or even billions of bytes. Most computers used in business need at least 64KB (64 kilobytes, or 64,000 bytes) of memory.

The **control unit** does what its name implies: controls the computer by gathering data from memory and sending processing instructions to other parts of the computer. The **arithmetic/logic unit** does the actual computing.

It can perform all mathematical computations and make comparisons between data.

***Input-Output Devices.*** **Input-output devices** are devices that enter data (input) and transmit processed data (output). They permit the user to communicate with the computer. Because they are outside the CPU, input-output devices are known as peripherals.

An input unit is any device used to enter data into the computer. Early computers read data from punched cards or magnetic cards; today data is usually input by means of a keyboard or magnetic tape or disk inserted into a disk drive.

Computer keyboards resemble typewriter keyboards. The lettered keys are arranged in the same way as on typewriters, but computer keyboards also have special function and editing keys. Special keys, for example, move the cursor (a small, blinking symbol that shows the user's location on the computer terminal). A control key gives commands to programs, and other keys can be used to do such things as insert, delete, or move material on the screen.

A disk drive is a device that reads the data stored on disks and feeds that data into the computer. The CPU has a primary storage area; disks provide secondary storage—that is, storage of data to be processed. Small computers usually rely on floppy disks—flexible disks from 3¼ to 8 inches in diameter. Larger computers rely on 8-inch hard disks.

The output unit communicates processed data to the user. The most common output devices are printers and monitors. A monitor is a screen resembling a television screen; in fact, many home computers can hook up to a television screen for output. Monitors can also serve as a means for input. By moving a hand-held device such as a light pen or mouse, the user can make changes in graphics, choose an item from a list of alternatives, or perform other operations. Touch-screen computers are also now available. When the user touches the screen with a finger, body heat allows the finger to act as a light pen.

The modem is yet another output device. Often used with microcomputers, modems allow computers to communicate with each other over telephone lines.

# Computer Software

**Software** is a computer program that gives the computer a set of instructions. A **computer program** is a series of commands written in a particular computer language (such as BASIC, COBOL, or Pascal). A computer programmer usually begins writing a program by preparing a flowchart, which outlines the problem the computer is going to solve. The problem is broken down into a series of questions that can be answered "yes" or "no." Each answer turns one of the computer's circuits on or off.

Some companies employ programmers to create and revise specialized programs or hire outside programmers to do so, but because developing software is both expensive and time-consuming, many businesses now buy ready-made software. The availability of such software has increased markedly in recent years. So many firms now produce software that costs have decreased, making software affordable to many businesses.

# ► Business Capabilities of Computers

Software available for business includes accounting and bookkeeping packages, decision support systems, spreadsheets, word processing, graphics, and desktop publishing.

## Word Processing

Word processing is one of the most popular business applications of computers. The computer keyboard is basically used as a typewriter, but because of the computer's storage capacity, the user can change, add, delete, and move material before printing the final document. The document can be stored for later use. Thus word-processing programs are ideal for standardized letters. With a high-quality printer, a form letter going to hundreds of prospective clients can look as if each copy was typed individually. Only the new name and address need to be input each time.

Most word-processing programs have spelling checks and electronic thesauruses, which suggest synonyms upon request. Some also offer search-and-replace features. If the user wants to change the due date in a standardized collection letter, the program will search for the old date and replace it with the new one. With programs such as Microsoft Word, it is also possible to get on-screen formatting, which permits the user to see on the terminal the exact setup—margins, spacing, page breaks, and so on—that will appear on the final document. Popular word-processing programs are WordPerfect, WordStar, and MacWrite. A profile of Bill Gates, founder of Microsoft Corporation, is given in Information Encounter 21-1.

## Spreadsheets

**Spreadsheet**

An electronic version of a ledger sheet

A **spreadsheet** is an electronic version of a ledger sheet. A spreadsheet program allows the user to organize numerical data into rows and columns. It can store numbers as well as formulas for calculating them. A manager who wants to calculate payroll after giving raises would enter each employee's current salary and percentage salary increase for each. The computer would calculate the rest.

An advantage of spreadsheet programs, such as the popular Lotus 1-2-3, is that they can answer "what-if" questions. For example, a manager might want to estimate profits based on different sales projections. Rather than asking an accountant to calculate each of several different scenarios by hand, the manager has several spreadsheets prepared. Any or all numbers can be changed, and the program will recalculate all the other related numbers.

## Data Management

**File management system**

A collection of programs that will manage data stored in one file

There are two categories of data management software: file management systems (also known as file managers) and data-base management systems. A **file management system** is a collection of programs that will manage data stored in one file. It will keep any large list—such as a list of suppliers—that

# Information Encounter 21-1

## Profile: William Gates of Microsoft

William ("Bill") H. Gates III founded Microsoft Corporation while he was in his teens. Today Microsoft is one of the key companies in the American computer industry and is the number-one manufacturer of software. Microsoft's main product, MS-DOS, is an operating system used on most IBM PCs and IBM PC clones. Gates's company also developed OS/2, an operating system for IBM's Personal System family of computers. These operating systems are vital to the personal computer because they allow users to instruct a computer's hardware to carry out specific tasks.

Bill Gates showed signs of his technical genius from an early age. His father, a Seattle lawyer, and his mother, a director of First Interstate Bank, enrolled him in a private school with high academic standards. It was there that Gates got hooked on computers; he was particularly fascinated by their practical possibilities. In the eighth grade, Gates and two friends wrote a computerized payroll program for their school. They also wrote a program that counted traffic. The traffic-counting program was so successful that they started a company to sell it to city governments; that company grossed $20,000 a year. At Harvard, Gates and his friend Paul Allen developed an operating system for one of the earliest personal computers, based on the BASIC language. Gates (at age 19) and Allen left Harvard and founded Microsoft Corporation in Albuquerque to produce and market their operating system. They moved Microsoft to Seattle in 1979; Paul Allen eventually left the company to do other things.

Microsoft was already prospering when IBM adapted personal computer in 1981. MS-DOS still accounts for 50 percent of Microsoft's sales. The affiliation with IBM led to dramatic growth for Bill Gates's small company. His staff grew to 125, and Microsoft's revenues grew to $16 million. In 1987, Microsoft developed OS/2, an operating system that allows IBM's newest generation of personal computers to take advantage of the power of the new microchip technology. OS/2 allows computers to handle several tasks at once, making them faster and more efficient than ever. Gates's company has developed other computer languages and many other software applications for Apple, IBM, and other manufacturers' computers: spreadsheets, word processing, and Windows, its newest program, which makes IBM computers easier to use by simplifying commands needed to operate them.

In 1986, Bill Gates gave up some of his control of the growing company when he took it public in a deal that netted him more than $350 million. Nevertheless, Gates still retains control of Microsoft as chairman. He serves as Microsoft's chief strategist and oversees product development. Microsoft has grown to fifteen hundred employees and has annual sales of more than $300 million. Despite Microsoft's huge success, Bill Gates has even larger ambitions for his company: He wants to put a personal computer on every desktop.

These facts are from Richard Brandt, "The Billion-Dollar Whiz Kid," *Business Week*, April 13, 1987, pp. 68–72; "The Prodigy with a Program for Success," *U.S. News & World Report*, July 21, 1986, p. 44; Bro Uttal, "Inside the Deal That Made Bill Gates $350,000,000," *Fortune*, July 21, 1986, pp. 23–33.

must be retrieved and displayed quicky. Information from a list of suppliers could be processed and output in different ways: to show which suppliers were given the most work, which met their deadlines, which have certain capacities, and so on. One popular file management program is PFS: FILE.

**Data-base management system**

A file management system for two or more files

A **data-base management system (DBMS)** is a file management system for two or more files. DBMS software, such as dBASE II, is software that will process and update information in multiple files. It also can print reports from those files, make copies of files, and reformat data.

# Decision Support

A **decision support system (DSS)** is software that will aid managers in decision making by helping them anticipate what effect certain decisions will have. Some decision support systems are more broad ranging and offer greater computational and modeling capabilities than spreadsheets; they let managers explore a greater number of alternatives. A DSS, for example, can determine how sales and profits might be affected by higher or lower interest rates, or how sales forecasts, advertising expenditures, production levels, and the like might affect overall profits.

At Brunswick Corp., a diversified billion-dollar corporation, a decision support system from Thorn EMI Computer Software, is used routinely to save time and money in key financial and marketing areas. The software helped Brunswick staff model and analyze scenarios that depicted various corporate reorganizations. These changes were evaluated as measures to prevent an acquisition. The "what-if" analyses indicated that Brunswick's divestiture of its medical group might curtail an unwanted takeover attempt and force the hostile firm to abandon its acquisition bid. Acting on that information, American Home Products was allowed to acquire Brunswick's Sherwood Medical Products Division. Brunswick then remained an independent entity and continued operation.

## Computer Graphics

Graphics programs display data in pictorial form. When numerical data are input, the computer will "draw" a bar graph, pie chart, or other graphic in a matter of seconds. Businesses often use graphics programs to present visual aids in reports or letters or at meetings or conventions.

Some microcomputers allow users to design graphics themselves. With the terminal acting as paper, the user sketches out the artwork with a mouse, a light pen, or even—on some computers—a finger. Information Encounter 21-2 describes the creative use of computers by advertising agencies.

## Desktop Publishing

The birth of desktop publishing in 1985 was due to advances in laser printing and software. In **desktop publishing**, the computer performs the tasks equivalent to those of conventional publishing: writing, editing, typesetting, graphics, page composition (layout), and printing. Thus the user has integrated, creative control at arm's length. Desktop publishing allows a firm to produce high-quality copy on its computer, often for a fraction of the cost of a professionally typeset and printed document. Many firms can now use their computers to produce their own reports, brochures, newsletters, and other publications.

Desktop publishing requires a powerful microcomputer system. It must have a memory capacity large enough to run big programs. It must be fast enough to reformat material instantaneously. Its screen must be able to reflect the final layout of the document—that is, show how the document will look when it is printed. Figure 21-4 is an example of graphics produced by desktop publishing.

**On-the-premises publishing.**   Desktop publishing integrates writing, editing, typesetting, graphics, page composition, and printing. In New York's famous Four Seasons restaurant the manager finalizes the menu with the chef, then uses a personal computer to produce distinctive menus twice a day.

**Figure 21-4**

Example of Graphics Produced by Desktop Publishing

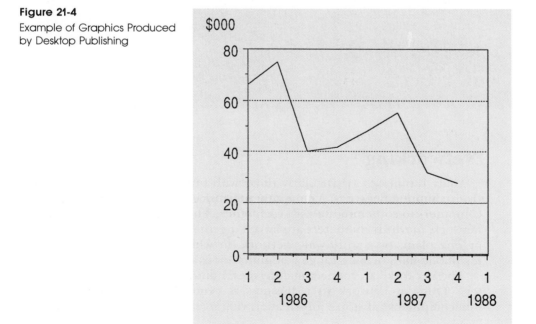

# Information Encounter 21-2
## *The Use of Computers in Advertising*

Although many advertising agencies use computers to cut costs by reducing paperwork and handling administrative tasks, few agencies use computers to create advertisements. That situtation is beginning to change as computers become more sophisticated. Art directors and copywriters are starting to view the computer as a creative tool that can save not only money but time.

The most sophisticated systems availabe to advertisers are the Lightspeed Design 20 and the Design Center, which use images from a variety of sources: photographs, drawings, and three-dimensional objects. The art director can manipulate the images on the screen, changing colors, moving an image to another part of the screen, or superimposing it onto another image. Images can be rotated, squeezed, stretched, or anything else an art director can possibly imagine. The Lightspeed has a color palette of 16.8 million colors and eighteen hundred typefaces. The art director can print the ad and show it to the client for approval, comments, and revisions before sending it to the typesetter.

The main advantage of the Lightspeed and the Design Center is their speed. An agency can create an ad in a matter of hours with these computers, whereas it might take days with pen and paper. Or the agency can create several ads and ask the client which one it likes best. The computers' primary disadvantage is their high cost. Some agencies rent time on a Lightspeed Design 20 at the few design companies that own one.

Several advertising agencies use an Apple Macintosh to create advertisements, including BBDO Los Angeles (which handles the advertising account for Apple Computers), Dally Advertising in Dallas, DDB Needham Los Angeles, and J. Walter Thompson Hispania/West. These agencies use the Macintosh to speed up the creative process in creating advertisements. Dally Advertising carries the process a step further. It creates and typesets newspaper ads on its Macintoshes and then has the print shop call up the ad directly from the disk to print it with typeset quality. Dally says the process costs $12 a page, whereas typesetting an ad from scratch costs $80 a page.

According to an informal *Adweek* poll, 73 percent of the agencies surveyed have computers in the creative department, but most use the machines for writing advertisements rather than for creating graphic designs. Many advertisers do not yet feel comfortable using computers. However, as more advertisers become computer-literate and recognize the time- and money-saving benefits of computers, computers will become one of the main tools for creating advertisements.

---

These facts are from Ron Gales, "Agency Creatives Trip the 'Lightspeed' Fantastic," *Adweek*, March 7, 1988, pp. 24, 26; Betsy Sharkey, "Computer-Age Prophet Spreads the Word," *Adweek*, March 7, 1988, p. 26; Betsy Sharkey, "The Art Department Timidly Turns to Computer Science," *Adweek*, February 29, 1988, pp. 25, 26, 30; Betsy Sharkey, "Macintosh Lets Small Texas Agency Think Big," *Adweek*, Februrary 29, 1988, p. 26; Betsy Sharkey, "Apple's Agency: A State-of-the Art Shop," *Adweek*, February 29, 1988, p. 30.

# Networking

Many businesses—particularly those with branch offices—have benefited from computer networks. A **computer network** is a system that allows different computers to communicate with each other. The network can be a local area network, in which computers are linked together directly within one building or one plant, or a worldwide network, in which computers are linked by telephone lines or long-range communications devices.

The network can connect mainframes, minicomputers, and microcomputers. Often a network in a business is centered on a mainframe or a minicomputer that stores information vital to all parts of the network and is

**Computer network**

A system that allows different computers to communicate with each other

thus the heart of a firm's management information system. Each manager who is a member of the network has a micromputer that stores enough information for the manager's immediate needs and can also communicate with the mainframe or minicomputer. For example, the manager of a sales office might have a microcomputer that stores data about the local representatives' sales for the month. Networking with the home office's mainframe allows that manager to transmit data or to obtain information about inventory levels.

# ► Office Applications of Computers

Many general office functions—accounting, bookkeeping, payroll, even routine typing—can be computerized.

## Order Entry and Fulfillment

All orders can be entered into the computer, which can transmit the information to the warehouse to ensure shipment. The computer can check customers' credit and inventory levels. The computer can print the packing slip to accompany the order, and it can print the invoice. The computer can then keep track of the status of the order and of the account.

## Inventory Control

The computer can update records when merchandise arrives from the manufacturer or factory, when goods are sold, and when merchandise is returned. An inventory control system usually generates reports listing inventory levels and the current dollar volume in sales.

## Accounts Receivable and Payable

Accounts receivable is money owed to the firm. A computer can store information about customers' accounts and print out invoices, statements, and past-due notices. Word-processing programs are often used for printing demands for payment of accounts that are long overdue.

Accounts payable is money owed by the firm. Some firms have completely computerized their accounts payable. The computer keeps track of due dates and prints the checks. It can make automatic payments of regular accounts due, such as rent and insurance premiums.

## Payroll

Payroll can be extremely complex. Some employees are paid fixed salaries; some are paid time wages; some are paid piece wages; and some are paid by commission. Payroll is further complicated by deductions: for health insurance, withholding taxes, and the like. The computer has greatly simplified payroll calculations. Because of the complexity of the software, however, many firms contract with outside payroll service bureaus.

**Order entry and fulfillment made easier.** This telemarketing representative is using minicomputers to respond to customer inquiries and follow up on sales efforts. This reduces product delivery time and increases customer satisfaction.

## Bookkeeping, Accounting, and Auditing

Computers can be of great help in keeping track of the flow of cash and in generating financial reports such as balance sheets, income statements, and profit-and-loss statements. Special software is available to help auditors to analyze and verify a company's financial records. Such software facilitates the cross-checking of inventory with accounts receivable records and the checking of information in financial statements.

## Scheduling

The computer can be used to aid in scheduling—both to print schedules and updates and to formulate schedules, such as for manufacturing processes. A book printer, for example, might computerize its scheduling, inputting data about the length and dimensions of the book, materials to be used (paper, ink, cover cloth), quantity to be printed, and date the raw materials will arrive. The computer develops a schedule for each stage of the printing process so that work schedules for each department can be established.

## Typing, Copying, and Mail

Word processing is often used to produce standardized documents. Word processors are also often used to produce single-copy documents, such as letters, memos, or reports. Many companies use their computer networks to send messages and documents electronically. Such **electronic mail** is sent from someone's keyboard or other input device to another's terminal.

**Electronic mail**
Information is sent from one keyboard to other terminals

**Keeping computers in their place.** Computers must be used as tools to help humans, not as substitutes for them. Computers can be overused, and they can make mistakes. Trained technicians such as this woman, assisted by computers that monitor patients' vital signs, provide 24-hour observation of critical-care patients.

## General Recordkeeping

The computer's storage function makes it ideal for storing information about personnel, equipment, customers, creditors, vendors, mailing lists, and the like.

## ▶ Keeping Computers in Perspective

Computers can be a tremendous advantage to business. They can process data more rapidly and accurately than a human being can, and they can free staff from the drudgery of poring over data and sorting through files. They can store huge quantities of data, thus eliminating the need for file cabinets crammed with records. Their ability to retrieve information is a great time-saver in offices.

# Information Encounter 21-3
## *Coping with Computer Crime*

Although most people think of computer crime as hacking, computer crime today includes embezzlement, theft or alteration of data, illegal copying or use of computer software, and unauthorized use of a computer system. The Computer Task Force of the American Bar Association (ABA) found that more that half of the thousand major corporations and public organizations it surveyed had experienced some computer-crime losses—and the losses averaged between $2 million and $10 million per organization. The financial community is particularly vulnerable to computer crimes because of the widespread use of electronic funds transfer.

The ABA study also found that the computer criminals, in most cases, are employees of the organization affected by the crime. The criminals are usually non-supervisory personnel, such as data-entry clerks, who work on computer terminals every day. Some organizations refer to the criminals as "data diddlers." These clerks alter data while at work, perhaps moving funds from an inactive account into their own account or changing the balance on their charge-card accounts. But no matter who the computer criminals are, the problem of what to do about computer crime still remains.

Many firms are increasingly concerned about who has access to computer systems in an office and how those people are using them. Companies catch the data diddlers much as they do office embezzlers and pilferers: through extensive background checks, close supervision of computer employees, random reviews and audits of the employees' work. Nevertheless, to reduce the opportunity for computer crime, companies must limit access to computers to only those employees who have reason to use them, and they must limit those employees to only the software they need to complete their tasks.

New security technology is helping organizations regulate who has access to a particular system and find out what an employee is doing while on the system. Two basic types of computer security technology are in use or development. Integrated circuit (IC) cards, or "smart cards," are already in use in some organizations. The cards carry computer chips that can be read by a computer. An employee wanting to use the computer system inserts his or her IC card into a reader and types in a Personal Identification Number. If verified and approved, the person is given access to the computer. The security computer then has a record of who is using the computer at what time.

Another computer security measure involves biometric devices, which measure certain aspects of human physiology or behavior. For instance, a scanner might examine a person's fingerprints or eye retinal patterns and compare those patterns to a security clearance list before allowing entrance to restricted systems. Other biometric devices examine signatures and even a person's typing patterns.

Many security companies are developing IC or biometric security devices, and some experts estimate that computer security will be a $500 million industry by 1990. Although these may be drastic measures for preventing computer crimes, they allow management to control who uses the office computer and when and how they use it.

These facts are from Jack Molnar, "Putting Computer-Related Crime in Perspective," *Journal of Policy Analysis & Management* (Summer 1987): 714–16; "Making Security More Secure," *Design News*, August 3, 1987, pp. 24, 25; Barry Render, Richard Coffinberger, Ella P. Gardner, Stephen R. Ruth, and Linda Samuels, "Perspectives on Computer Ethics and Crime," *Business* (January–March 1986): 30–36; and John Naudts, "How Banking Protects Its Technology," *The Bankers Magazine* (September–October 1987): 54–57.

Nevertheless, there are several drawbacks to the use of computers that all potential users should bear in mind. Computers can make mistakes. A computer is only as accurate as the software allows it to be. A programming error can cause both minor mistakes and disasters. A programming error at AT&T eliminated telephone service between the United States and Greece for several months in 1979. A computer's output can be accurate only if its input is accurate. Computer people use the acronym GIGO, which means "garbage in, garbage out." If the user makes a mistake entering a formula in a spreadsheet program, the results will be inaccurate.

Computers are a tool for decision making, not a crutch. Managers must be sure to think for themselves while using a computer. Even when computers are used in decision support systems, they should just support a decision, not make it. The making of the decision is the task of management. A computer can assess quantitative data, but only a human being can contribute gut reactions and intuition.

Computers can be overused. Managers should remember that business associates, clients, and customers appreciate human contact. A computer might shut off all shipments to a long-time customer who is overdue in paying a bill. A phone call from the credit manager might turn up a short-term cash-flow problem and result in a new payment schedule. Without the human element, a good customer might be lost forever.

Computer crime has become a problem and has generated much publicity about computer users who gain access to company files to steal money or just tamper with computer records. Large firms in particular must guard against unauthorized access to computers. Information Encounter 21-3 describes steps business is taking to cope with computer crime.

Wide access to computer files can mean loss of individual privacy. The sharing of data bases increases the possibility of the invasion of privacy. Credit records are sometimes made available to many organizations. Many people object to the widespread dispersal of such information. One reason for their objections is that if a credit record is incorrect, an individual might have trouble obtaining loans or other credit, without knowing why.

A visible sign of the sharing of data bases is junk mail. Many organizations sell their mailing lists. Even hospitals release the names and addresses of women who have given birth recently. The new mothers are then bombarded with mailed (or sometimes telephoned) offers to buy diapers, toys, books, video cassettes, and so on.

In general, computers offer many benefits to business and to society as a whole. But their misuse or overuse can cause misunderstanding, mistakes, or even disaster. The wise user will keep both the advantages and the disadvantages in mind.

# Summary and Review

▶ To make effective decisions, managers need to have access to relevant information.

▶ A management information system gathers raw data—unorganized facts, statistics, opinions, and predictions—from internal and external sources, enters it into a data base, and processes it into relevant information.

▶ Data processing is the transformation of raw data into information that is useful for a specific purpose. There are ten basic data-processing operations:

calculating, classifying, communicating, copying, recording, reporting, retrieving, sorting, storing, and summarizing.

▶ Computers can be classified into three categories: mainframes, the largest and fastest; minicomputers, usually desk-sized; and microcomputers (personal computers), which are desktop or lap-top computers. Mainframes are used by large corporations, banks, and government organizations. Minicomputers are widely used in middle-sized businesses and within divisions of large corporations. Microcomputers are used in the home and are also popular with small businesses. The physical apparatus of a computer is known as its hardware. Computer hardware has two basic components: the central processing unit and input-output (peripheral) devices. The central processing unit has three parts: the control unit, the primary memory, and the arithmetic/logic unit. It is the part of the computer that actually does the computing. Software is the term used for computer programs, the instructional codes recorded magnetically on some medium, such as floppy or hard disks. Although some businesses hire programmers to write software, there are many ready-made software packages available for businesses.

▶ Numerous office tasks can be computerized: order entry and fulfillment; inventory control; accounts receivable and payable; payroll; bookkeeping, accounting, and auditing; scheduling; typing, copying, and mail; and general recordkeeping.

▶ Potential users of computers must keep in mind the shortcomings of computers as well as their benefits. Drawbacks include programming and input errors; overreliance on computers for decision making; overuse of computers, neglecting the human element; computer crime; and invasion of privacy.

# Key Terms and Concepts

information
management information system
  (MIS)
data base
statistics
arithmetic mean
median
mode
data processing
computer
integrated circuit
microprocessor
artificial intelligence
mainframe computers
minicomputers
microcomputers
hardware

central processing unit (CPU)
primary memory
control unit
arithmetic/logic unit
input-output devices
software
computer program
word processing
spreadsheet
file management system
data-base management system
  (DBMS)
decision support system
  (DSS)
desktop publishing
computer network
electronic mail

# Checking Your Understanding

This chapter introduced you to the subject of computers and information systems. To test and reinforce your understanding, fill in the blanks below.

**1.** The _____ _____ is a statistical measure of the sum of all items in a group, divided by the number of items in the group.

**2.** Electronic machines capable of processing large quantities of data are called _____.

**3.** Microcomputers rely on a single integrated circuit known as a _____.

**4.** Of the three types of computers, _____ are most often found in medium-sized businesses and in divisions of large corporations.

**5.** Computer hardware consists of peripheral devices and the _____ _____ _____.

**6.** Peripheral devices are actually _____ _____ devices, used for communication between the user and the computer.

**7.** Computer programs are generally known as _____.

**8.** _____ _____ is a means of producing standardized letters and preparing other printed documents.

**9.** _____ are computerized ledger sheets useful in answering "what-if" questions.

# Topics for Review and Discussion

**1.** What kinds of information do managers need?

**2.** Differentiate between data and information.

**3.** What is a management information system? What is its role in business?

**4.** How do information needs differ among the three levels of management?

**5.** How can computers be used in a management information system?

**6.** What is hardware? What is software? How do they differ?

**7.** What are the components of a computer system?

**8.** What are some business applications of computers? How do you see computers used in your daily life?

**9.** What are the benefits of computers? What are some of their drawbacks?

# Exercises

**1.** In your opinion, who should be responsible for running a management information system—a person with a technical background or a person with a business background?

**2.** In the course of a day you are confronted with information from various sources. How would you establish an information system to help you process and respond to that information?

**3.** What type of information does a marketing manager require? A financial manager? A human resource manager?

# Case 21-1
## *IBM Leads the Computer Market*

In 1952, IBM introduced its first computer, the Model 701, designed for scientists. In 1958, the company revolutionized the computer industry with the introduction of a computer using transistors instead of vacuum tubes. Throughout the years, the company has continued to develop faster and more efficient computers. However, it was the IBM System/360 mainframe computer, introduced in 1964, that propelled IBM's dramatic growth.

Today, IBM has a 70 percent share of the mainframe computer market. Sales of mainframe computers account for 40 percent of IBM's revenues and more than half of its profits. Its current lines, the Sierra and 3090 lines, are some of the fastest, most efficient machines available. IBM's large share of the mainframe market has helped to give it dominance in other markets as well.

One of the markets in which the company has benefited from its mainframe dominance is the personal computer market. IBM introduced its first personal computer (the PC) in 1981; it soon became the industry standard. The PC (and its family members XT and AT) was so successful that businesses all over the world copied it and sold their own versions of the machine. Eventually, the copies or clones, outsold the original 2 to 1. Despite the success of the PC clones, IBM still maintains 32 percent of the personal computer market.

In 1987, partly to reduce the market share of the PC clones, IBM introduced a new line of personal computers, the Personal System/2 family. These machines are faster and have more memory capacity than the old PCs. The new PS/2 models have high-performance microprocessors that permit more sophisticated graphics, expanded data bases, spreadsheets, word processing, and communications programs. In fact, the performance of the PS/2s is close to that of many mainframe computers. The software used by the PS/2s is slightly different from that used on the PCs, making them difficult for competitors to clone. Old PC software, however, will run on the PS/2 machines. Only three months after introduction, PS/2 models accounted for 15 percent of all personal computers sold in U.S. computer stores.

In the last half of the 1980s, IBM moved into supercomputers and software. It hopes to develop software that will enable users to connect PCs, minicomputers, and mainframes and allow customers to set up extensive computer networks. The company is working on Systems Application Architecture (SAA), a framework designed to allow IBM and other companies to develop applications that will work across all IBM systems in the same way. However, because of the complexity of SAA, it may not be available until the mid-1990s.

IBM took a significant step into the software business in 1988 with the introduction of new operating-system software, called MVS/ESA. This software differentiates the company's current line of mainframes from IBM's older mainframes by allowing the former to run faster than before. In fact, MVS/ESA allows programmers to deal with eight thousand times more main memory than was previously possible. The new operating-system software also permits software applications to run as much as 12 percent faster than before, with the biggest increases on larger mainframes. IBM has plans to introduce software that will automate data-storage decision making and increase the speed of information storage.

IBM has also moved into systems integration. For a large fee, IBM analyzes a customer's business and then installs the right mix of hardware and software (not necessarily IBM's) that will make the customer most productive. The company has some experience in this area, and its commercial contracts in 1987 amounted to $1.5 billion. IBM believes the systems integration business will be a lucrative one.

The IBM heritage of outstanding support to buyers of its computers is stronger than ever. The company has urged distributors to offer tips and advice to customers on how to improve the productivity of their machines. IBM works closely with businesses to help them figure out solutions to business problems. In addition, the company developed a special software package, Information Systems Investment Strategies (ISIS), that allows a customer to estimate the costs of a new computer system and calculate its expected benefits.

IBM, like all computer companies, was hurt by the slow growth of the computer industry in the mid-1980s. However, in 1988, the company began a major reorganization designed to strengthen its share of the computer market. The result is a leaner, more efficient IBM, better able to adapt to changes in the volatile computer industry. IBM now appears poised to maintain its leadership in the computer market for years to come.

---

These facts are from Paul B. Carroll, "IBM Introduces Long-Awaited Software to Speed Operation of Its Mainframes," *The Wall Street Journal*, February 16, 1988, p. 4; Geoff Lewis, with Anne R. Field, John J. Keller, and John W. Verity, "Big Changes at Big Blue," *Business Week*, February 15, 1988, pp. 92–98; IBM advertising supplement in *The Wall Street Journal*, January 29, 1988; Geoff Lewis, "Can IBM Continue to Call the Tune?" *Business Week*, June 29, 1987, p. 74; Brenton R. Schlender and David Wessel, "Software Revolution Tied to IBM System," *The Wall Street Journal*, April 3, 1987, p. 6; and Paul B. Carroll and Hank Gilman, "IBM's Next PC Line May Put Industry at Crossroads," *The Wall Street Journal*, March 12, 1987, p. 6.

**Questions**

1. What has led to IBM's dominance of the computer industry?
2. How does customer support fit into IBM's strategy?
3. Explain how software is important to the selection, operation, and market penetration of IBM's computers.

---

## Case 21-2
### *Apple Computers Spins off a Software Company*

Apple Computers, Inc., started Claris Corporation in 1987 to take over most of its personal-computer software business. Apple's management said that the primary goal of the new company is to develop and market innovative software for Apple's Macintosh and Apple II personal computers. Management believed an independent company would be most likely to develop new programs for Apple computers. The spin-off was also designed to appease software developers who had been complaining about having to compete against Apple in developing software applications such as word processing, spreadsheets, and data bases.

Apple's announcement to start Claris came shortly after IBM agreed to establish joint software agreements with Lotus Development Corporation (to design new data base and spreadsheet programs for IBM personal computers) and with Microsoft Corporation. Despite these developments, Claris's management said the company would not emphasize software development for IBM or other competitors' machines.

Apple developed a three-part plan designed eventually to spin off Claris as an independent company. The first step involved moving Claris out of Apple headquarters in Cupertino, California, and into its own building in Mountain View, California. The second step involved giving the company freedom, including the freedom to make any company or product acquisitions that it thought would be beneficial. It also involved discussions with software developers on sharing marketing resources and file formats as well as various development activities and joint ventures. The third step involved marketing Claris-developed products and ultimately, late in 1988, spinning off Claris from Apple into an independent, publicly traded company.

Claris's start-up was actually done in reverse—the company began life with several well-established products and large revenues. Apple software such as MacDraw, MacWrite, MacPaint, Appleworks, and Access II were repackaged and sold under the Claris label. Claris now owns all the rights to these programs, which generate about $35 million in annual sales. In 1988, Claris introduced two new products, MacProject II and MacDraw II, which are totally redesigned versions of existing Apple programs.

Claris hired its management team from a variety of sources, including some of Apple Computers' competitiors, such as Ashton-Tate Co. and Metaphor Computer Systems, Inc. Most of its managers, however, came from Apple, as did many of the company's 107 employees and software engineers. Nevertheless, both Apple and Claris maintain that Claris has to be independent of Apple in the future if it is to be successful.

Claris has taken several steps to establish its own identity. The company adopted a logo that is quite different from Apple's multicolored apple. The Claris label contains white letters on a royal blue background—without an apple. Claris emphasizes customer services and support services for its software in an effort to overcome Apple's poor reputation for customer support.

Spinning off Claris allows Apple to concentrate on computer hardware while Claris concentrates on the software. In the past, Apple was responsible for both. That sometimes created overhead problems and alienated some salespeople and customers. Now, potential customers talk to Apple about computer hardware and to Claris about software.

Claris officials believe their company can be very profitable if it captures a large share of the software market. In 1986, sales of software for Apple computers accounted for about 25 percent of total sales of $575 million, so the needed customer base for Claris products is there. Officials concede that starting a software company from scratch will not be easy, but they are confident that once Claris becomes established, it can become very profitable.

---

These facts are from Brenton R. Schlender, "Claris, Apple's Software Offspring, to Ship Its First Products This Week," *The Wall Street Journal*, January 11, 1988, p. 22; Julie Pitta, "Claris Set to Leave Apple Nest," *Computerworld*, September 14, 1987, pp. 33, 41; Brenton R. Schlender, "Apple to Form Software Unit, Then Spin It Off," *The Wall Street Journal*, April 29, 1987, p. 4.

### Questions

1. Why did Apple spin off its software development division?
2. It seems that customer support is also important to Claris as well as to IBM. Why?
3. What benefits will Apple gain by setting up Claris?

## Answers to Checking Your Understanding

1. arithmetic mean
2. computers
3. microprocessor
4. minicomputers
5. central processing unit
6. input-output
7. software
8. word processing
9. spreadsheets

## Outline

# Chapter 22

# International Business

## Objectives

After reading this chapter, you will be able to:

▶ Understand the basic framework of international trade, including importing, exporting, absolute and comparative trading advantages, balance of trade, and exchange rates.

▶ Describe the basic legal framework of international trade, and discuss how political, social, and cultural considerations affect international trade.

▶ Identify organizations that facilitate trade, and identify barriers to trade.

▶ Explain how a company may enter international trade, and describe situations in which each method of entry is best used.

▶ Distinguish among several international trade organizations.

▶ Discuss the importance of conducting research and developing marketing strategies before entering the international marketplace.

# Business Experience

Pepsi Cola was the first Western consumer product widely sold and consumed in the Soviet Union, so it is fitting that PepsiCo, Inc., should have the honor of signing one of the first joint ventures between an American company and the Soviet Union in many years. In 1974 PepsiCo introduced its soft drinks to the Soviet Union, and in exchange, was allowed to market Russian vodka in the U.S. In 1987 the company's Pizza Hut division signed an agreement with Soviet food service officials to open two Pizza Huts in Moscow in 1988. PepsiCo hopes to open a hundred or more restaurants in the Soviet Union. While there have been other "pizza" restaurants in Moscow, Soviet citizens say they want Western pizza restaurants. Pizza Hut management hopes to translate this into a large market share. PepsiCo is using the two restaurants as an experiment to find out how well a joint venture will work with the Russians.

In 1987 Soviet leader Mikhail Gorbachev relaxed rules on joint ventures with foreign businesses as part of his plan to boost Russia's economy. Many foreign businesses quickly applied for joint ventures there. Western officials believe one of the reasons the Soviets decided to allow joint ventures was because they want first-hand knowledge about the efficient operating systems used in Western fast-food restaurants in order to improve food services in Russia.

Pizza Hut provided the equipment for the two Moscow restaurants; the Soviets built them. Most of the ingredients for pizza are available in Russia, except for a few special flavorings, which Pizza Hut imports. One restaurant sells its pizza for hard currency, which Pizza Hut uses to pay for imported ingredients; the other restaurant sells pizza for rubles—which cannot be converted to foreign currencies. The company pays local bills with the rubles. Pizza Hut trains personnel for the Moscow restaurants at Pizza Huts in London. They are trained to wait on customers courteously and prepare pizza quickly and efficiently, qualities that are relatively unknown in Russian restaurants.

Despite Pizza Hut's enthusiasm for the joint venture, there are some potential problems in dealing with the Russians. Western businesses that have dealt with the Russians in the past have been unhappy with the way profits are returned to them. The Russians often insist that a foreign company receive its profits in the form of product, instead of cash. Pizza Hut management believes it can overcome this problem with the dual currency system.

Another potential problem for the joint venture is quality control. Soviet-produced "pizza" has been a major disappointment to pizza lovers familiar with Western pizza. Pizza Hut hopes that its Russian pizzas will meet company quality standards. Some industry sources believe Pizza Hut will make some modifications in its Russian pizzas, because pizza restaurants often vary their pizza recipe to accommodate geographical differences.

Pizza Hut made history with its joint venture with the Soviets. If the two Moscow restaurants are successful, they could pave the way for other U.S. companies that want to set up operations in the Soviet Union. McDonald's also has plans to open restaurants in Moscow in 1988.

---

These facts are from Mark D'Anastasio, "PepsiCo's Pizza Hut Signs Agreement for Soviet Venture; McDonald's Next," *The Wall Street Journal*, September 18, 1987, p. 11; "You Will Like Fast Food, Comrade," *Fortune*, December 8, 1986, p. 9; Albert Axebank, "Soviet Pizza Lovers Look to PepsiCo," *Journal of Commerce and Commercial*, November 7, 1986, pp. 1, 5A.

# Introduction

International business is the buying, selling, and trading of goods and services across national boundaries. Nations have traded with other nations since the advent of organized government. Before the Industrial Revolution, trade was limited, but today growth and new technology (particularly in transportation and communication) enable many firms to operate on a global basis. Cultural differences are narrowing rapidly, fueling a trend toward globalization. Firms are able to treat the entire world, or large regions of it, as a single market, and as a result of globalization, Americans visiting London, Beijing, and Rome are able to drink Coca-Cola, eat at McDonald's, and see American movies. As globalization continues to narrow cultural and social differences between nations, the importance of international trade will increase.

# ▶ Why Nations Trade

Nations trade with other nations to obtain raw materials and goods that would otherwise be unavailable to them. A nation, or individuals and organizations from a nation, sells surplus materials and goods to acquire funds to buy the goods and materials it needs. Which goods and services a nation sells depends on what resources it has available.

Some nations have a monopoly on the production of a particular item. A nation has an absolute advantage in trade when it is the only source of an item, when it is the only producer of an item, or when it can produce an item more efficiently than any other nation. Because South Africa has the largest deposits of diamonds, one company, De Beers Consolidated Mines, Ltd., virtually controls the world's diamond trade and uses its control to maintain high prices for gem-quality diamonds. The United States, until recently, held an absolute advantage in oil-drilling equipment. But an absolute advantage not based on the availability of natural resources rarely lasts, and Japan and the Soviet Union are now challenging the United States in the production of oil-drilling equipment.

Most international trade is based on comparative advantage, which occurs when a country specializes in products that it can supply more efficiently or at a lower cost than it can produce other items. The United States has a comparative advantage in producing agricultural commodities such as corn and wheat. Colombia has a comparative advantage in the production of coffee.

Until recently, the United States had a comparative advantage in manufacturing automobiles, heavy machinery, airplanes, and weapons. But comparative advantages are not constant. Many Americans drive automobiles made in Japan and West Germany. There are several reasons for this loss of comparative advantage. After World War II, manufacturing facilities in Japan

**International shopping.** Americans often enjoy shopping in foreign countries to take advantage of unique products, low-cost labor (less expensive goods) and non-traditional distribution. These American tourists are shopping on the streets of China for handcrafted artifacts.

and West Germany were rebuilt (with substantial help from the United States); therefore, factories in Japan and West Germany are much more modern than those in the United States. Moreover, there has been a significant difference in the amount spent on research and development and in investments in capital equipment in the United States (Figure 22-1). The U.S. has spent approximately 30 percent less than both Japan and West Germany in recent years on research and development.

Logically, nations should try to specialize in products in which they can develop a comparative advantage. However, some nations prefer to become self-sufficient. Israel, South Africa, and many Communist-bloc countries are striving for self-sufficiency out of fear of economic reprisals by other nations and their perceived need to maintain military preparedness. Some nations want to become self-sufficient in specific commodities. For example, after the energy crisis of the mid-1970s, many Americans believed the United States

**Figure 22-1**

Share of Gross National Product Spent on Nondefense Research Development, 1985
Source: *U.S. News & World Report,* February 2, 1987, p. 21. Data for Japan: *U.S. News & World Report* estimate. Other data: National Science Foundation.

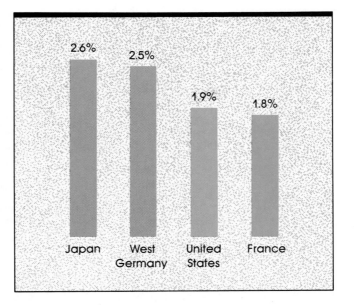

should be self-sufficient in energy resources. The federal government believed the country had become too dependent on other nations, particularly those that were politically volatile, for petroleum products. War between Iran and Iraq in the 1980s did not banish American fears of high gasoline prices and long lines at service stations.

# ▶ Elements of International Business

## Exporting and Importing

**Exporting**

The sale of domestic goods and materials to another nation

**Importing**

The purchase of products and raw materials from another nation

The United States is a leading exporter and importer. **Exporting** is the sale of domestic goods and materials to another nation. **Importing** is the purchase of products and raw materials from another nation. Table 22-1 lists the leading purchasers of U.S. exports and the leading suppliers of U.S. imports. It is interesting to note that 17 out of the top 20 export buyers are also on the import suppliers list.

The United States exports agricultural products and high-tech items such as computers and telecommunications equipment. Colombia exports coffee; it produces more of this product than it can consume domestically. The money received from the export sales of Colombian coffee go back into Colombia's economy, allowing Colombians to purchase imported goods.

The United States imports a variety of raw materials and manufactured goods. It imports nearly all the platinum, industrial diamonds, chrome, and bauxite that it uses. Its largest import is crude and partially refined petroleum.

**Table 22-1  Top Twenty U.S. Export Buyers and Import Suppliers**

Source: U.S. Department of Commerce, *1986 U.S. Foreign Trade Highlights* (Washington, D.C., 1987).

| Export Buyers | Import Suppliers |
|---|---|
| Canada | Japan |
| Japan | Canada |
| Mexico | West Germany |
| Great Britain | Taiwan |
| West Germany | South Korea |
| France | Great Britain |
| Australia | Mexico |
| Netherlands | Italy |
| South Korea | Hong Kong |
| Belgium/Luxembourg | France |
| Taiwan | Switzerland |
| Italy | Brazil |
| Singapore | Singapore |
| Saudi Arabia | Sweden |
| Brazil | China |
| Switzerland | Belgium/Luxembourg |
| China | Netherlands |
| Venezuela | Israel |
| Hong Kong | South Africa |
| Israel | Spain |

Many of these raw-material imports come from politically unstable and occasionally hostile countries. The United States imports very few agricultural products, because it produces most of what it needs; however, coffee, tea, and cocoa must be imported. Figure 22-2 shows the share of the U.S. market held by several types of manufactured goods.

# Balance of Trade

**Balance of trade**

The difference in value between a nation's exports and imports

The **balance of trade** is the difference in value between a nation's exports and imports. When a nation exports more goods than it imports, a favorable balance of trade exists. A favorable balance of trade means that money is flowing into the country. Until about 1970, the United States had a favorable balance of trade due to an abundance of natural resources and the relative efficiency of its manufacturing systems. The balance changed for several reasons:

1. Most American firms focused their attention and capital on domestic markets.
2. The cost of imported oil rose sharply.
3. American economic growth increased, and the increased demand for goods required the importation of foreign goods.
4. Imported goods were of equal or better quality than American-made goods and often were less expensive.
5. Foreign demand for American products was limited because of slow economic growth abroad.

**Figure 22-2**

Share of U.S. Market Held by Foreign Goods, 1981 and 1986
Source: U.S. Department of Commerce, National Association of Manufacturers, and *U.S. News & World Report* estimates.

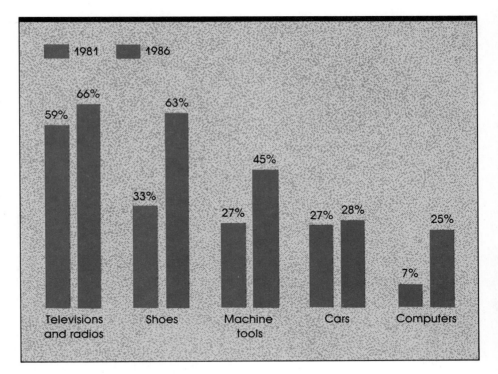

**Trade deficit**

A negative balance of trade; when a nation imports more merchandise than it exports

A nation has a negative balance of trade, or **trade deficit**, when it imports more merchandise than it exports. It must pay for imported products, and money flows out of the country. In 1987 the United States had a trade deficit of $171 billion, because it was importing far more goods than it was exporting.[1] Table 22-2 details the trade deficit of the United States with ten of its leading trading partners. Figure 22-3 illustrates the growth of U.S. trade deficit since 1978.

**Table 22-2  U.S. Trade Deficit with Major Trading Partners (in Billions of Dollars)**
Source: U.S. Department of Commerce, *1986 U.S. Foreign Trade Highlights* (Washington, D.C., 1987).

| Trading Partner | U.S. Imports | U.S. Exports | Trade Deficit |
|---|---|---|---|
| Japan | $85.5 | $26.9 | $58.6 |
| Canada | 68.7 | 45.3 | 23.4 |
| Taiwan | 21.3 | 5.5 | 15.8 |
| West Germany | 26.1 | 10.6 | 15.5 |
| South Korea | 13.5 | 6.4 | 7.1 |
| Hong Kong | 9.5 | 3.0 | 6.5 |
| Italy | 11.3 | 4.8 | 6.5 |
| Mexico | 17.6 | 12.4 | 5.2 |
| Great Britain | 16.0 | 11.4 | 4.6 |
| France | 10.6 | 7.2 | 3.4 |

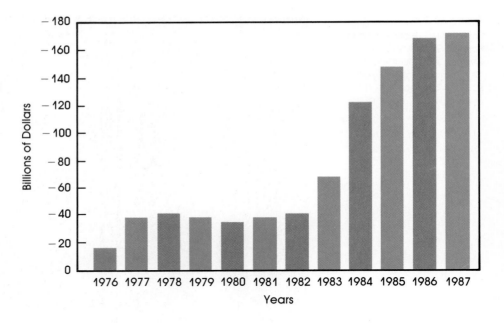

**Balance of payments**

The difference between the flow of money into a country and the flow of money out of the country

**Exchange rate**

The ratio at which one nation's currency can be exchanged for another nation's currency or for gold

The difference between the flow of money into a country and the flow of money out of the country is called the **balance of payments**. A favorable balance of payments means that a country is receiving more money from foreign countries than it is paying to them. The balance of payments includes a country's balance of trade, and it also takes into account foreign investments, foreign aid, military expenditures, and money spent by tourists. International Encounter 22-1 examines the increase in foreign investment in the United States in recent years.

## Exchange Rates

The ratio at which one nation's currency can be exchanged for another nation's currency or for gold is the **exchange rate**. On March 21, 1988, one British pound could be exchanged for $1.83, one Japanese yen for less than one American cent (Figure 22-4). For today's exchange rate, check *The Wall Street Journal* or your local newspaper under the heading "Foreign Exchange Rates."

A government may alter the value of its national currency. Devaluation decreases the value of currency in relation to other currencies. Devaluation of the dollar lowers the cost of American goods abroad and makes trips to the United States less expensive for foreign tourists. Thus, devaluation encourages the sale of domestic goods and tourism. Mexico has repeatedly devalued the peso—from 12 pesos to a dollar in the early 1970s to 2,270 pesos to a dollar in March 1988—in part to encourage other nations to spend their money in Mexico.

**Currency trading.**
Currency values fluctuate based on the stability and economic strength of the country. Currency traders in Frankfurt, Germany, provide the service of exchanging currencies for investors who are trying to anticipate their changing prices.

**Bretton Woods Accord**

Mandated that a nation pay its debts by transferring gold from its reserves to the reserves of the creditor nation

**Floating exchange rate**

Rate which is determined by market conditions and not by a nation's gold reserves

Revaluation increases the value of a currency in relation to other currencies. A revaluation of the dollar would make American goods cost more overseas; it would also mean that one dollar could purchase more foreign goods. Revaluation occurs rarely.

Shortly after World War II, the United States and other industrialized nations signed an international monetary agreement called the **Bretton Woods Accord**, which mandated that a nation pay its debts by transferring gold from its reserves to the reserves of the creditor nation. This process was so complex that in the early 1950s the U.S. dollar, backed by U. S. gold reserves, assumed many of the functions of gold in international trade. By 1971, however, the United States had accumulated trade-payment deficits that exceeded its gold reserves, and President Richard Nixon removed the United States from the gold standard. This action disrupted the international monetary system. Now, most nations, including the United States, use a **floating exchange rate**, which is determined by market conditions and not by a nation's gold reserves.

# FOREIGN EXCHANGE

### Monday, March 21, 1988

The New York foreign exchange selling rates below apply to trading among banks in amounts of $1 million and more, as quoted at 3 p.m. Eastern time by Bankers Trust Co. Retail transactions provide fewer units of foreign currency per dollar.

| Country | U.S. $ equiv. Mon. | U.S. $ equiv. Fri. | Currency per U.S. $ Mon. | Currency per U.S. $ Fri. |
|---|---|---|---|---|
| Argentina (Austral) ... | .2043 | .2043 | 4.895 | 4.895 |
| Australia (Dollar) .... | .7391 | .7390 | 1.3530 | 1.3532 |
| Austria (Schilling) ..... | .08425 | .08389 | 11.87 | 11.92 |
| Belgium (Franc) | | | | |
|   Commercial rate .... | .02831 | .02823 | 35.32 | 35.42 |
|   Financial rate ........ | .02824 | .02820 | 35.41 | 35.46 |
| Brazil (Cruzado) ....... | .009122 | .009182 | 109.62 | 108.91 |
| Britain (Pound) ......... | 1.8295 | 1.8230 | .5466 | .5485 |
|   30-Day Forward .... | 1.8267 | 1.8203 | .5474 | .5494 |
|   90-Day Forward .... | 1.8221 | 1.8149 | .5488 | .5510 |
|   180-Day Forward .... | 1.8152 | 1.8074 | .5509 | .5533 |
|       ⋮ | | | | |
| Japan (Yen) ............. | .007876 | .007816 | 126.96 | 127.95 |
|   30-Day Forward .... | .007893 | .007832 | 126.70 | 127.68 |
|   90-Day Forward .... | .007928 | .007866 | 126.14 | 127.13 |
|   180-Day Forward .... | .007987 | .007923 | 125.21 | 126.22 |
|       ⋮ | | | | |
| SDR ........................ | 1.36696 | 1.36368 | 0.731551 | 0.733313 |
| ECU ........................ | 1.22560 | 1.22422 | .... | .... |

Special Drawing Rights are based on exchange rates for the U.S., West German, British, French and Japanese currencies. Source: International Monetary Fund.

ECU is based on a basket of community currencies. Source: European Community Commission.

z-Not quoted.

# ▶ International Trade Environment

## Legal Framework for International Trade

A firm that decides to enter the international marketplace must contend with the laws of its own nation, international laws, and the laws of the nation with which it will be trading. The United States has a number of laws that affect domestic firms engaged in international trade. The **Webb-Pomerene Export Trade Act**, passed in 1918, exempts American firms from antitrust laws if those firms are acting together to enter international trade. This law allows selected American firms to form a monopoly in order to compete with foreign cartels. These firms are not allowed to limit free trade and competition within the United States or to use unfair methods of competition in international trade. The **Foreign Corrupt Practices Act,** passed in 1978, outlaws direct payoffs to and bribes of foreign governments or business officials by American companies. An American company is allowed to make small gifts where they are customary but may not make large payments or offer bribes to influence the policy decisions of foreign governments. This act specifies penalties for both the company and the individuals involved.

The United States has a variety of friendship, commerce, and navigation treaties with other nations. These treaties allow business to be transacted

**Webb-Pomerene Export Trade Act**

Exempts American firms from antitrust laws if those firms are acting together to enter international trade

**Foreign Corrupt Practices Act**

Outlaws direct payoffs to and bribes of foreign governments or business officials by American companies

## International Encounter 22-1

### *Foreign Investment in the United States*

For the first time since 1914, British and other foreign investors own more of the U.S. economy than Americans own abroad. Ownership in American companies and property by British, Japanese, West German, Korean, Dutch, and other foreign investors reached $1.33 trillion at the end of 1986, a 25 percent increase from 1985. This is a complete reversal of the situation only ten years ago, when U.S. holdings abroad exceeded foreign holdings here. Foreigners now own many familiar American companies, including Carnation, RCA, and Chesebrough Ponds, and some market experts predict that foreign-owned retailing organizations may control 10 percent of the U.S. market by the 1990s.

The wave of foreign investment in the United States has had several effects on the economy. Real-estate values have soared in metropolitan areas where there is a lot of foreign investment. Corporate takeovers are increasing as foreign companies buy out American owners. Many believe this wave of foreign investment is an important factor behind the rise in value of American stocks over the past few years.

A cheap dollar (relative to other currencies) combined with the American trade deficit makes it profitable for foreigners to invest in the United States. Many American properties look like bargains to overseas investors. The U.S. marketplace is especially attractive because of its diversity and opportunity. Foreign investors are further attracted to the United States because of relatively low corporate tax rates. Many foreign investors have huge cash holdings that they

wish to invest. Finally, foreign investors, particularly those who wish to make long-term investments, are attracted by the political stability of the United States.

Some analysts believe that the increase in foreign investment is good for the United States. Foreign investors supply money and ideas needed to improve productivity and decrease the trade gap. Improvements in productivity and a cheaper dollar may even allow the United States to turn its trade deficit into a surplus by the end of the century.

Despite the potential benefits of foreign investment, it has created much controversy. Many feel that foreign investors wield too much power and influence over the American economy. Some U.S. business leaders fear the United States is being "re-colonized" and turned into "a nation of tenants." Others feel that foreign companies do not provide good employment opportunities for Americans.

Many American legislators believe the United States should improve its system for monitoring foreign investment because the trend toward increased foreign investment in the United States, which escalated in the 1980s, is likely to continue into the 1990s. Although no one can predict its long-term effects, foreign investment in the American economy is certain to be a subject of debate for years to come.

These facts are from Stephen Koepp, "For Sale: America," *Time*, September 14, 1987, pp. 52–62; Peter Coy, "The Foreign Connection: Trade Deficit, Cheap Dollar Spurs U.S. Investment from Overseas," *Houston Chronicle*, September 20, 1987, pp. 5-3, 5-4; and "Foreign Retailers Recruit U.S. Talent," *Marketing News*, March 13, 1987, p. 12.

between citizens of the specified countries. A firm engaged in international trade must also be familiar with the tariffs and customs regulations of its own country, of its trading partners, and of any nations acting as middlemen.

The laws of the other nations may be different from those of the United States. Table 22-3 lists some restrictions on advertising in Europe. Many of the legal rights that Americans take for granted do not exist in other countries, and a firm doing business abroad must understand and obey the laws of the host country. Many nations forbid foreign nationals from owning real property outright. They may also have strict laws limiting the amount of local currency

**Table 22-3 European Restrictions on Advertising**
Source: Laurel Wentz, "Local Laws Keep International Marketers Hopping," *Advertising Age*, July 11, 1985, p. 20. Reprinted with permission from *Advertising Age*, July 11, 1985. Copyright © 1985 Crain Communications, Inc.

| Country | Restriction | Justification |
|---------|-------------|---------------|
| France | No tourism advertising | Minimizes the public's spending outside the country |
| | No TV commercials for supermarket chains | Small grocers should not be driven out of business by the larger chains |
| West Germany | Comparative advertising is heavily discouraged and must pass rigorous fairness tests | Comparative advertising is often felt to be misleading and deceptive |
| | Children cannot talk about product benefits or be appealed to in an ad | Children are not to be exploited or taken advantage of |
| Great Britain | Product categories banned from TV advertising: undertakers, the Bible, matrimonial agencies, fortune tellers, private detectives, contraceptives, and pregnancy tests | Whenever the independent Broadcasting Authority receives 10 or more complaints about an ad/product, they ban it |
| Switzerland | People cannot be used in print and TV ads for alcoholic beverages | The consumption of alcohol should not be depicted as glamorous |
| Spain | Tobacco and alcohol (excluding wine and beer) are banned from TV | These products are not viewed as beneficial to the public |

that can be taken out of the country and the amount of foreign currency that can be brought in.

# Political Considerations

The legal framework for international trade is usually quite specific; laws are written down. Although the average businessperson may need help interpreting these laws, the laws apply to everyone and rarely change rapidly. Political considerations, in contrast, are seldom written down and often change rapidly. In the late 1970s, in response to Soviet military activities, the United States placed an embargo on the sale of American wheat to the Soviet Union. In the 1980s, dissatisfaction with apartheid in South Africa led Eastman Kodak, General Motors, and other American firms to sell their holdings there.

Businesses engaged in international trade must consider the relative instability of countries such as Iran, South Africa, and Honduras. A sudden change in power can result in a regime that is hostile to foreign investment. Some businesses have been forced out of a country altogether, as they were when Fidel Castro closed Cuba to American business. Whether they like it or not, companies are often involved directly or indirectly in international politics.

# Social and Cultural Differences

Most people engaged in international trade underestimate the importance of social and cultural differences; yet these differences can derail an important transaction. Culture can be defined as a sort of blueprint of acceptable behavior that is passed from one generation to the next. Unfortunately, cultural norms are rarely written down, and what is written down is usually inaccurate.

Cultural differences include differences in language and body language. To someone who understands English well, the statement "I am going to catch a train" describes an innocuous activity. But translated literally into another language, it may describe a very dangerous one. General Motors has sold the Chevrolet Nova in the United States for many years, but GM had some problems selling the car abroad. In English, *nova* means "bright star" and is an acceptable name for a car. In Spanish, *nova* (*no va*) means "it does not go," which is not an acceptable name for a car. Other companies have had similar difficulties in marketing their products abroad. *Esso* in Japanese means "stalled car," so not surprisingly the Japanese were reluctant to fuel up with Esso gasoline. Americans found a German chocolate confection particularly unappetizing: It was marketed under the name Zit![2]

Differences in body language and personal space also affect international trade. Body language is nonverbal, usually unconscious, communication through gestures, posture, and facial expression. Personal space is the distance at which one person feels comfortable talking to another. Americans tend to stand a moderate distance away from the person with whom they are speaking. Arab businessmen tend to stand face to face with the object of their conversation. This difference in personal space might cause uncomfortable feelings in citizens of these countries when they negotiate with each other.

The people of other nations quite often have a different perception of time as well. Americans value promptness; a business meeting scheduled for a specific time seldom starts more than a few minutes late. In Mexico and Spain, however, it is not unusual for a meeting to be delayed half an hour or more. Such a late start might produce resentment in an American negotiating in Spain for the first time.

Companies engaged in foreign trade must observe the national and religious holidays and local customs of the host country. Most English stop all activities around 4 o'clock every afternoon to have tea, whether they work for the queen or for an American firm. Companies must monitor their advertising to guard against offending customers. In Thailand and many other countries, public displays of affection between the sexes are unacceptable; and in many Middle Eastern nations, it is unacceptable to show the soles of one's feet. Table 22-4 lists additional cultural variations.

Most nations, but not the United States, use the metric system. This lack of uniformity creates problems for both buyers and sellers in the international marketplace. American sellers, for instance, must package goods destined for foreign markets in liters or meters, and Japanese sellers must convert to the English system if they plan to sell a product in the United States. Tools also must be in the correct system if they are to function correctly. Hyundai and

**Table 22-4   A Sampling of Cultural Variations**

| Country/<br>Region | Body Motions | Greetings | Colors | Numbers | Shapes, Sizes,<br>Symbols |
|---|---|---|---|---|---|
| Japan | Pointing to one's own chest with a forefinger indicates that one wants a bath.<br><br>Pointing a forefinger to the nose indicates "me." | Bowing is the traditional form of greeting. | Positive colors are in muted shades.<br><br>Combinations of black, dark gray, and white have negative overtones (black & white are the colors of mourning). | Positive numbers are 1, 3, 5, 8.<br><br>Negative numbers are 4, 9. | Pine, bamboo, and plum patterns are positive.<br><br>Cultural shapes such as Buddha-shaped jars should be avoided. |
| Europe | Raising only the index finger signifies a person wants two items.<br><br>When counting on one's fingers, "1" is often indicated by the thumb, "2" by the thumb and forefinger. | It is acceptable to send flowers in thanks for a dinner invitation, but not roses (associated with sweethearts) or chrysanthemums (associated with funerals). | Generally, white and blue are considered positive.<br><br>Black often has negative overtones. | The numbers 3 and 7 are usually positive.<br><br>13 is a negative number. | Circles are symbols of perfection.<br><br>Hearts are considered favorably at Christmas time. |
| Latin America | General arm gestures are used for emphasis | The traditional form of greeting is a hearty embrace followed by a friendly slap on the back. | Popular colors are generally bright or bold yellow, red, blue, and green | Generally, 7 is a positive number.<br><br>Negative numbers are 13, 14.<br><br>Numerical rating scales are not used. | Religious symbols should be respected.<br><br>Avoid national symbols such as flag colors. |
| Middle East | The raised eyebrow facial expression indicates "yes." | The word "no" must be pronounced three times before it is accepted. | Positive colors are brown, black, dark blues, and reds.<br><br>Pink, violets, and yellows are not favored. | Positive numbers are 3, 7, 5, 9.<br><br>Negative numbers are 13, 15. | Round or square shapes are acceptable.<br><br>The 6-pointed star, raised thumb, and Koranic sayings are to be avoided. |

Source: James C. Simmons, "A Matter of Interpretation," *American Way,* April 1983, pp. 106–11; "Adapting Export Packaging to Cultural Differences," *Business America,* December 3, 1979, pp. 3–7; *Business Week,* December 6, 1976, pp. 91–92; and Carlos E. Garcia, "Hispanic Market Is Accessible, If Research Is Designed Correctly," *Marketing News,* January 4, 1988, p. 46.

**Worldwide support.** It is very important for firms conducting international business to provide service support after the sale. Shown here are two London service representatives from NCR Corporation, part of the international field engineering and customer support network of NCR.

Honda service technicians need metric tools to make repairs on those car models.

The literature dealing with international business is filled with accounts of humorous but generally costly mistakes that occurred because of a lack of understanding of the cultural differences between the buyer and seller. Such problems cannot always be avoided, but they can be minimized by research on the laws, politics, and cultural and social differences of the host country.

# ▶ Trade Barriers

Theoretically, the price and quantity of goods sold is determined by market conditions. However, completely free trade seldom exists. A nation that has a negative balance of trade or payments will try to establish a positive balance through the use of import tariffs, quotas and embargoes, countertrade agreements, and exchange controls.

## Import Tariffs

**Import tariff**

A duty levied by a nation on goods bought outside its borders and imported into the country

An **import tariff** is a duty levied by a nation on goods bought outside its borders and imported into the country. A fixed tariff is a specific amount of money levied on each unit of a product brought into the country. An ad valorem tariff is a duty based on the value of the item. Most countries allow their citizens traveling abroad to bring home a certain amount of merchandise without paying an import tariff. A U.S. citizen may bring $200 worth of merchandise into the United States duty-free. After that, U.S. citizens must pay an ad valorem tariff based on the cost of the item and the country of origin. Thus, identical items purchased in different countries might have different tariffs.

The use of protective tariffs, which raise the price of foreign goods, was a controversial topic in the mid-1980s, as Americans became increasingly concerned over the growing U.S. trade deficit. Protective tariffs allow more expensive domestic goods to compete with foreign ones. Many advocated the imposition of tariffs on products imported from Japan, particularly automobiles, audio components, and computers. However, Congress feared economic reprisals from Japan if the tariffs were levied on Japanese products.

Those who are against protective tariffs argue that their use inhibits free trade and competition. Those who support protective tariffs argue that their use protects domestic industries, particularly new ones, from well-established foreign competitors. Once an industry matures, however, its advocates may be reluctant to let go of the tariff that protected it. Tariffs also help when, because of low labor costs and other advantages, foreign competitors can afford to sell their products at prices lower than those charged by domestic companies. Some Americans argue that tariffs should be used to keep domestic wages high and unemployment low.

## Quotas and Embargoes

**Quota**

The maximum number of units of a particular product that can be imported into a country

A **quota** is the maximum number of units of a particular product that can be imported into a country. A quota may be established by voluntary agreement or by government decree. Recently, the United States imposed an import quota on Japanese economy cars in an effort to reduce the amount of dollars leaving the country.

**Embargo**

The suspension of trade in a particular product by the government

An **embargo** is the suspension of trade in a particular product by the government. Embargoes are generally directed at specific goods or countries and may be established for political, health, or moral reasons. The United States forbids the importing of cigars from Cuba. In 1980 the United States placed an embargo on sales of American wheat and other agriculture products to the Soviet Union to protest that country's invasion of Afghanistan. Health embargoes prevent the importing of various pharmaceuticals, animals, plants, and agricultural products. Some species of parrots may not be imported into the United States because they carry disease. Muslim nations forbid the importing of alcoholic beverages for moral reasons.

**Dumping**

When a country or business firm sells products at less than what it costs to produce them

One common reason for setting quotas is to prohibit dumping. **Dumping** occurs when a country or business firm sells products at less than what it costs to produce them. Japanese firms accused of dumping computer chips in the United States were forced to raise their prices or pay a penalty. The United States requires that a product be sold for not less than its production costs plus 10 percent for overhead and 8 percent for profit.

A firm might dump its products for several reasons. Dumping permits quick entry into a market and allows a company to capture a large market share. Sometimes dumping occurs when the domestic market for a firm's product is too small to support an efficient level of production. In other cases, technologically obsolete products that are no longer salable in the country of origin are dumped overseas. Dumping is relatively difficult to prove, but even the suspicion of dumping can lead to the imposition of quotas.

## Countertrade Agreements

**Countertrade agreements** are bartering agreements between nations. They are fairly common in international trade, especially between Western and Communist-bloc nations. They are most often used when one nation has limited cash resources. That nation pays for its purchases with its own goods. It is estimated that at least 30 percent of all international trade agreements contain countertrade provisions. Pepsi-Cola has arranged with the Soviet Union to trade Pepsi syrup for Stolichnaya vodka. In Rumania Pepsi trades syrup for wine, marketing the wine in the U.S. under its Monsieur Henri label.[3] Ford Motor Company has been offered sheepskins by Peru as partial payment for goods.[4]

## Exchange Controls

**Exchange controls** are restrictions on the amount of a particular currency that can be bought or sold. Some countries control their foreign trade by forcing their businesspeople to buy and sell foreign products through a central agency such as a central bank. If John Deere, for example, receives payments for its tractors in a foreign currency, it may have to sell the currency to that nation's central bank. When foreign currency is in short supply, as it is in many Third World countries, the government uses foreign currency to purchase necessities and capital goods and produces other products locally, thus limiting its need for foreign imports.

# ► Trade Facilitators

## GATT

During the Great Depression of the 1930s, nations enacted so many protective tariffs covering so many products that international trade became virtually impossible. By the end of World War II, there was considerable international momentum to liberalize trade and minimize the effects of tariffs. **GATT,** the **General Agreement on Tariffs and Trade,** signed by twenty-three nations in 1947, provides a forum for tariff negotiations and a place where international trade problems can be discussed and resolved. Currently, over one hundred nations abide by its rules.

GATT has sponsored rounds of negotiations aimed at reducing trade restrictions. Two of the most successful of these sessions were the Kennedy and Tokyo rounds. President John F. Kennedy was granted authority by the Trade Expansion Act of 1962 to call for a round of negotiations to reduce tariffs on more than sixty thousand items. Tariffs were reduced by an average of 40 percent by fifty members of GATT. The Tokyo Round (1973–79) involved one hundred nations. It reduced many tariffs by 30 percent, and the negotiators were able to eliminate or ease nontariff trade restrictions such as import quotas, red tape in customs procedures, and "buy national" agreements. The Tokyo Round also worked to increase the availability of foreign currency.

# Eximbank

**Eximbank**
The export-import bank that provides loans to exporters and extends credit to overseas buyers of American goods and services

**Eximbank**, the Export-Import Bank, is an independent agency of the United States government. It provides loans to exporters who cannot obtain funds from other sources. It also extends or guarantees credit to overseas buyers of American products. **FCIA**, Foreign Credit Insurance Association, was established by Eximbank and private insurance companies. Through FCIA, American exporters can buy insurance to cover political risks (such as loss from nationalization or war) and business risks (such as loss from credit defaults).

**FCIA**
The Foreign Credit Insurance Association

# DISCs

**DISC**
Domestic international sales corporations

In 1971, Congress enacted a law that allows businesses the opportunity to create tax-sheltered subsidiaries known as **DISCs**, domestic international sales corporations. The purpose of the law was to encourage American firms to enter the international marketplace. The law allows American exporters to defer federal income tax on half of their export profits.

# World Bank

**World Bank**
Established and supported by the industrialized nations to loan money to underdeveloped and developing countries

The **World Bank**, formally known as the International Bank for Reconstruction and Development, was established and supported by the industrialized nations including the U.S. in 1946 to loan money to underdeveloped and developing countries. It loans its own funds or borrows funds from member countries to finance a variety of projects ranging from road and factory construction to the construction of medical and educational facilities. The World Bank and other multilateral development banks (banks with international support that help developing countries grow by providing them loans) are the largest source of advice and assistance for developing nations. The International Development Association and the International Finance Corporation are associated with the World Bank and provide loans to private businesses and member countries.

# IMF

**IMF**
International Monetary Fund

**IMF**, the International Monetary Fund, was established in 1947 to promote trade among member nations by eliminating trade barriers and fostering financial cooperation. It makes short-term loans to member countries that have balance-of-payment deficits and provides foreign currencies to member nations. If Peru, for example, wants to purchase machine parts from West Germany but lacks German marks, IMF will loan the marks to Peru. Peru will repay the loan with gold or with various currencies from other transactions.

# Free Trade Zones

**Free trade zones**

Specific areas to which goods can be imported without being subjected to quotas or import tariffs

In 1934, the United States enacted the Foreign Trade Zone Act to set aside specific areas, called **free trade zones**, to which goods can be imported without being subjected to quotas or import tariffs. Within a free trade zone, companies can store, process, assemble, and display foreign products without having to pay import duties, and when the product is re-exported, no duties are collected. Only when the product enters domestic commerce are regular tariffs collected. Companies use free trade zones to reduce their taxes or customs fees. For example, a computer company might have to pay a tariff on each imported component to be assembled into a computer. But if the company ships the parts to a free trade zone and assembles them there, it would save money by paying a single tariff on the whole computer, instead of separate tariffs on each component part. Free trade zones exist in many states, including Florida and California.

# ▶ Organizing International Trade

Most companies proceed slowly once they have decided to enter international trade. Usually, a company needs to obtain specific knowledge about how to deal with tariffs, quotas, and foreign currencies and must research the foreign country's (or countries') economic, political, cultural, and social background as well. Such research will help the company choose the best method for dealing in international trade. International Encounter 22-2 is a discussion of the Latin American market.

There are a number of ways that a firm may enter international trade: exporting, trading companies, licensing, contract manufacturing, direct investment, and joint ventures.

## Exporting

**Exporting**

Selling goods in a foreign market

**Exporting** means that the firm sells its goods in foreign markets. Caterpillar Tractor Company, for example, exports its farm equipment to buyers in other countries. A company can market its wares overseas directly, or it can deal with a middleman commonly called an export agent. Export agents seldom produce goods themselves; they typically handle international transactions for other firms. Export agents either purchase products outright or take them on consignment. If they purchase them outright, they generally mark up the price they paid and attempt to sell the product in the international marketplace. They are also responsible for storage and transportation.

The primary advantage of using an export agent is that the company does not have to deal with foreign currencies or the red tape (tariffs and import quotas) of international marketing. The major disadvantage is that because the export agent must make a profit, the price of the product must be increased or the domestic company must provide a larger discount than it would in a domestic transaction.

## International Encounter 22-2
### *Understanding the Five Nations of Latin America*

Although Latin America is composed of seventeen nations, marketing consultant Marlene L. Rossman believes that it can be divided into five distinct markets: Mexico, Brazil, Caribbean Latin America, European Latin America, and Indian Latin America. The five markets are based on demographical, sociological, and cultural differences. The only inherent similarity between these markets is the language of origin.

Americans have trusted stereotypes that have cost companies millions of dollars in lost sales. For instance, one major U.S. multinational food company successfully test-marketed its products in Mexico and then made a major investment decision to market those products in Brazil based on the Mexican success. After several years of losses, the error was obvious: What sells in Mexico has very little to do with consumer preferences in Brazil. When developing a marketing strategy for Latin America, therefore, it is important to understand the characteristics of Latin America's five markets:

▶ Mexico's proximity and importance to the United States make it a major market. The country's 75 million inhabitants, including 15 million middle-class Mexicans, constitute a major opportunity for American marketers. Two-thirds of all Mexican exports go to the United States, while 6 to 7 percent of U.S. exports go to Mexico. American marketers must keep in mind that Mexicans are very proud of their country's economic progress and feel a strong sense of nationalism.

▶ Brazil is the only Portuguese-speaking country on the South American continent and also the largest Latin American nation. Half of Brazil's population is under twenty years of age, not an uncommon situation in Latin America. Pent-up demand is enormous, particularly in the youth market. U.S. goods are highly valued, and Brazilians admire U.S. economic success.

▶ Caribbean Latin America includes Puerto Rico, the Dominican Republic, Panama, Honduras, Caracas and coastal Venezuela, coastal cities of Colombia, and Cubans in Miami and Tampa, Florida. This market is characterized by a tropical climate, a fairly large black Creole population, and a small upper class that controls most of the industry and politics. The people are warm, open, and friendly and often admire the United States.

▶ European Latin America includes Argentina, Chile, Uruguay, most of Colombia, southern Brazil, Costa Rica, and Lima, Peru. Argentina and Uruguay, especially, have very strong European ties. People are gracious, formal, and receptive to U.S. goods and services.

▶ Indian Latin America includes Bolivia, Paraguay, Ecuador, and Peru (except Lima) in South America and Guatemala and El Salvador in Central America. Spanish is spoken in the capitals and large cities, but people in rural areas speak Indian languages almost exclusively and are steeped in Indian tradition. Poverty and isolation make this a fairly difficult market to penetrate.

These facts are from Marlene L. Rossman, "Understanding the Five Nations of Latin America," *Marketing News*, October 11, 1985, p. 10. Reprinted from *Marketing News*, published by the American Marketing Association.

## Trading Companies

**Trading company**

A link between buyers and sellers in different countries to facilitate trade

A **trading company** acts as a link between buyers and sellers in different countries to facilitate trade. Trading companies are similar to export agencies, but their role in international trade is larger. They buy goods at the best price they can obtain in one country and sell them to buyers in another. They handle all the activities required to move products from one country to another; they even take title to the products. They offer consulting, market research, advertising, insurance, product research and design, warehousing, and foreign exchange services to interested companies.

**Air express.** A firm may manufacture products in its home country for export then for sale in foreign countries. Shown here is the shipment of fresh flowers from Amsterdam en route to the United States.

# Licensing

**Licensing** is a way for a company to enter the international marketplace without spending large amounts of capital abroad and hiring or transferring personnel to handle overseas affairs. It also minimizes problems associated with shipping costs, tariffs, and trade restriction. The licensor agrees to allow the licensee to use its company name, products, patents, brands, and trademarks, as well as its raw materials and production processes. In exchange, the licensee agrees to pay the licensor a flat fee or a royalty. In a **royalty agreement**, the licensee agrees to pay the licensor a fixed fraction of the profits on each unit manufactured or sold. Coca-Cola and PepsiCo frequently use licensing as a means to market their soft drinks in other countries.

Most license agreements run for five or ten years and may be either exclusive or nonexclusive. An **exclusive license** prevents the licensor from selling the license to any other firm in some specific geographic area. The advantage of licensing is that it allows the firm to establish goodwill for its products in a foreign land. This goodwill will help the company if it decides to produce or market its products directly in the foreign country at some future date.

There are two potential disadvantages to licensing. First, if the licensee does not maintain high standards of quality, the product's image may be hurt; therefore, it is important for the licensor to monitor its products overseas and to enforce its quality of standards. The second disadvantage is that licensing does not provide a firm with any overseas sales or marketing experience.

## Contract Manufacturing

**Contract manufacturing**

When a foreign company produces a specified volume of the firm's product to specification and uses the domestic firm's name on the final product

A firm that does not wish to get involved with licensing arrangements may try contract manufacturing. **Contract manufacturing** occurs when a foreign company produces a specified volume of the firm's product to specification and uses the domestic firm's name on the final product. Marketing may be handled by the contract manufacturer or by the original company. Procter & Gamble and Del Monte have used contract manufacturing.

## Direct Investment

**Direct investment**

The purchase of overseas production and marketing facilities

The ultimate step in international marketing is **direct investment**, the purchase of overseas production and marketing facilities. With direct investment, the company may control the facilities outright, or it may be the majority stockholder in the company that controls the facilities. Ford Motor Company owns subsidiaries all over Europe; 3M owns a film-manufacturing facility in Italy.

Direct investment is risky, particularly in politically unstable countries. A major risk is nationalization—that is, the host country assumes ownership of the company's facilities, usually without reimbursing the company for the loss of its property. When Fidel Castro came to power in Cuba, he nationalized many industries and threw all American companies out of the country.

## Joint Ventures

**Joint venture**

When a foreign company finds a local partner to share the costs and operation of the business

Many countries, particularly in the Third World, do not allow foreign nationals to own real property (land, factories, stores) in their country. A foreign company that wants to purchase facilities must set up a **joint venture** by finding a local partner (occasionally, the host nation itself) to share the costs and operation of the business. India, for example, does not allow foreign nationals to own industries, so Union Carbide joined with the Indian government to build a chemical plant at Bhopal. In 1987 Combustion Engineering, Inc., signed a joint venture agreement with the Soviet Union's Ministry of Oil Refining and Petrochemical Industries. Their joint company, Applied Engineered Systems, will make oil and petrochemical controls and help modernize Soviet refineries. It was the first joint venture between an American company and the Soviet Union in almost seventy years.[5]

Until fairly recently, most joint ventures and direct investment occurred when an American firm dealt with a foreign company or government. Investment in American firms by foreign companies is increasing. Nestlé, a Swiss company, bought a controlling interest in the American company Stouffer Food Corporation a few years ago. General Motors and Toyota

**Global cooperation.** A joint venture provides immediate market knowledge and access, reduced risk, and control over product attributes. Ford and Volkswagen collaborated in Brazil to design an engine that both can use.

together manufacture Chevrolet Novas in an American plant (see International Encounter 22-3), and other American automakers are following suit in their own joint ventures with the Japanese.

# ▶ International Trade Organizations

## Multinationals

**Multinational**

A corporation that operates on a worldwide scale, without significant ties to any one nation or region

A **multinational** is a corporation, such as IBM, Exxon, and Citicorp, that operates on a worldwide scale, without significant ties to any one nation or region. Multinationals are more than simple corporations. They often have more assets and larger populations (employees, stockholders, and others) than some of the countries in which they do business.

At first, most multinationals were American firms that had increasing international commitments. Now, a growing number of multinationals have their headquarters in some nation other than the United States. Nestlé, with headquarters in Switzerland, operates more than three hundred plants around

# International Encounter 22-3

## *General Motors and Toyota Learn from Each Other*

In 1984, General Motors and Toyota entered into a joint venture to produce Chevrolet Novas in Fremont, California, at an old GM assembly plant. GM initiated the venture in order to remain cost-competitive in the small-car market. The 50/50 joint venture, which is designed to produce about 150,000 Novas a year, is known as New United Motor Manufacturing, Inc. (NUMMI). Every automaker in the world is watching NUMMI to see what Japan can teach American automakers about making cars.

One of the main lessons learned at NUMMI is managing for quality and efficiency, areas in which the Japanese excel. NUMMI has achieved consistently higher records of quality and productivity than any of GM's thirty-one other car-and-truck assembly plants. Union workers at NUMMI operate under only twenty labor agreements (compared to five thousand when GM ran the same plant alone), and absenteeism at Fremont has decreased from 22 percent to 2.5 percent. That is an odd record, considering that equipment at the plant is old by GM standards and the production techniques are much more labor-intensive than at other GM plants.

The use of the team concept, which makes use of the know-how of workers on the assembly line, in part accounts for the high numbers. This management method uses small, autonomous teams whose members define their own jobs and monitor the quality of their output. These groups conduct their own daily quality assessments. They also have "stop-line" cords that allow them to shut down the assembly line if they encounter a problem. The philosophy at NUMMI is one of absolute attention to detail, teamwork, and integration of practices to transform workers, processes, and suppliers into an effective management system. The workers seem happy, and Chevrolet executives believe that the Nova is the best-built car that GM makes.

NUMMI has become a kind of training ground for GM managers. Since 1984, more than two thousand GM managers have been sent to Fremont to study NUMMI management techniques. These managers then help GM to apply the lessons learned at NUMMI throughout the entire organization. This approach embraces employee involvement, supplier development, quality improvement, and small-lot production in an effort to treat the whole production process as an integrated system.

Performance at the NUMMI plant has shown that General Motors does not need fancy robots and stacks of labor agreements to produce a quality car. Japanese manufacturers have produced quality cars for years without the help of labor unions. The Japanese, however, are learning about labor relations for the first time at NUMMI, and they will apply this knowledge to prevent unions from gaining strength at other plants they operate in the United States.

The NUMMI joint venture has been beneficial to both GM and Toyota. Toyota officials are so happy with the plant that they began to produce fifty thousand of their high-performance Tercels there in 1987—an action they would not have taken unless they believed they would get a quality product. In the future there will undoubtedly be more joint ventures between American and Japanese automakers as they strive for ways to cut costs and improve quality.

These facts are from Andrea Gabor and Jack A. Seamonds, "GM's Bootstrap Battle: The Factory-Floor View," *U.S. News & World Report*, September 21, 1987, pp. 52–53; 1987 General Motors Public Interest Report; William J. Hampton, "Why Image Counts: A Tale of Two Industries," *Business Week*, June 8, 1987, pp. 138–39; and "The Toyota Touch," *The Economist*, December 13, 1986, p. 76.

the world and receives revenues from Europe, North, Central and South America, Africa, and Asia. The Royal Dutch/Shell Group, one of the world's major oil producers, is another multinational. Its main offices are located in The Hague and London.

A problem faced by many multinationals, especially in the Third World, is nationalism. At first, a host country usually welcomes a multinational.

However, as the company's revenues begin to exceed the gross national product of the host country, many citizens start to wonder how much political and economic power the multinational is wielding in their country. As feelings of resentment build, violence may result or the multinational's property may be nationalized.

## Cartels

A **cartel** is a group of firms or nations that agree to act as a monopoly and not compete with each other. Probably the most famous cartel is OPEC, the Organization of Petroleum Exporting Countries, founded in the 1960s to increase the price of petroleum throughout the world and to maintain high prices. Another successful cartel is the De Beers Central Marketing Organization, which markets industrial and gem-quality diamonds for South Africa, the Soviet Union, Zaire, and Botswana.

## Orderly Marketing Agreements

An **orderly marketing agreement** is an agreement between nations to restrict competition between them. Such agreements can vary from highly detailed, written documents to unwritten gentlemen's agreements. During President Gerald Ford's administration, the United States reached agreement with Japan for specialty steel. As part of the agreement, the United States set quotas on steel imports from the Common Market, Canada, Sweden, and other major steel producers.

**Organization of Petroleum Exporting Countries.** Producers of a given commodity may organize to determine issues such as pricing and distribution. OPEC (the oil producing and exporting countries) meets here in Vienna to discuss the pricing of oil on the world market.

# Economic Communities

**Economic communities**

Several nations that band together to promote the movement of resources and products among members

**Economic communities** are formed by several nations that band together to promote the movement of resources and products among members. Member nations usually lower trade barriers among themselves and impose a common external tariff structure on nonmember nations. The European Economic Community, or Common Market, one of the oldest economic communities, was established in 1958. The first six members were Belgium, France, West Germany, Italy, Luxembourg, and the Netherlands. Table 22-5 identifies all the members of the European Economic Community (EEC) and the members of two other economic communities—the European Free Trade Association (EFTA) and the Latin American Free Trade Association (LAFTA). The United States is not a member of any economic community. However, if the current trend toward protectionism continues, the United States may consider the creation of an economic community, probably with Mexico and Canada.

# ▶ International Marketing

## Developing a Marketing Strategy

Because of developments in communication and transportation, international marketing is now possible for even medium- and small-sized firms. The first step of any international marketing program is to determine if there is a potential market for the firm's products. Market research at a distance, particularly when compounded by cultural and social differences, is often difficult. In some nations, literacy rates are quite low, making self-administered questionnaires unsuitable. Because many nations have attitudes about personal privacy that are different from American attitudes, some people may not be willing to participate in marketing research studies. A market researcher should try to detect cultural and social patterns that might relate to marketing the product.

## Product and Promotion

There are five strategies for adapting product and promotion to the international marketplace (Figure 22-5).

**Globalizaton**

A company markets the same products in the same manner everywhere

*Globalization.* **Globalization** means that a company markets the same products in the same manner everywhere. This strategy has worked well for consumer electrical equipment (stereos, TVs, VCRs), although dials and settings might have to be in the local language. It has also worked with American clothing (jeans), movies, soft drinks, rock music, cosmetics, and fast-food restaurants. Pizza Hut, Kentucky Fried Chicken, and Coca-Cola have been fairly successful in such diverse places as Great Britain, Japan, and West Germany. Promotion too can be globalized, although advertising usually must be translated into the language of the host country.

740

| Table 22-5 Major International Economic Communities<br>ᵃ Associate member. | European Economic Community | European Free Trade Association | Latin American Free Trade Association |
|---|---|---|---|
| | France<br>West Germany<br>Italy<br>Belgium<br>Netherlands<br>Luxembourg<br>United Kingdom<br>Ireland<br>Denmark<br>Greece<br>Turkeyᵃ | Austria<br>Iceland<br>Norway<br>Portugal<br>Sweden<br>Switzerland<br>Finlandᵃ | Argentina<br>Brazil<br>Chile<br>Colombia<br>Ecuador<br>Mexico<br>Paraguay<br>Peru<br>Uruguay |

***Promotion Adaptation Only.*** With this strategy, the product remains unchanged and promotion is modified to accommodate legal, language, and cultural differences. McDonald's was not very successful in West Germany until it modified its advertising to promote McDonald's as an alternative to "fine" dining, where the public would find good food, inexpensive prices, and fast service. McDonald's also had to add beer to its menu.

**Michael Douglas in Spain.** Many foreign countries have an intense interest in U.S. products. Shown here is a marquee for the movie *A Chorus Line*, which was exported to Spain. Note the Spanish notations about three Oscar nominations.

***Product Adaptation Only.*** Marketers utilize this strategy when they assume that modified products retain the same function even though they may be used in different ways. With this strategy, an alteration in promotion is not necessary. Product adaptation can be relatively simple—such as changing the electrical plug and voltage on an appliance—or product adaptation can be difficult when a manufacturer runs into resistance to the product based on attitudes and a fundamental lack of knowledge about a new technology. In that case, redeveloping the product may be the only viable option. A soap manufacturer might modify its formulas to take into account local water conditions and methods of washing. Procter & Gamble, for example, produces a laundry soap in bar form for sale in countries where laundry is still done by hand in the nearest stream.

***Product and Promotion Adaptation.*** Sometimes a product takes on a new function in another market. When that happens, both promotion and the product itself must be adapted. European greeting cards, for example, have a space for the sender to write a personal message and are wrapped in cellophane.

***Product Invention.*** This strategy is used when a marketer sees a need for a product in another country, but no product currently meets that need. Colgate-Palmolive developed an inexpensive, plastic, hand-powered washing machine to be marketed for households in underdeveloped countries. This invention gave the company a new market for its laundry soap products.

**Figure 22-5**

International Product and Promotion Strategies.
Source: Adapted from Warren J. Keagan, "Multinational Product Planning Strategic Alternatives," *Journal of Marketing,* January 1969, pp. 58–62. Published by the American Marketing Association.

**Product**

| Promotion | Do not change product | Adapt product | Develop new product |
|---|---|---|---|
| **Do not change promotion** | 1. Globalization | 3. Product adaptation only | 5. Product invention |
| **Change promotion** | 2. Promotion adaptation only | 4. Product and promotion adaptation | |

## Distribution and Pricing

Distribution usually depends on whether a company engages in international trade through licensing, contract manufacturing, or some other strategy. In many developing nations, some distribution channels do not exist; thus, distribution channels even for a single product may vary from country to country. In many countries, one ethnic group occupies a majority position

**International automobile.** The complexity and diversity of international business can best be understood by looking at this Mitsubishi automobile. This car was designed in Japan, assembled in Thailand, and is being driven aboard a ship bound for Canada.

|  | Tokyo | Paris | London | Washington | Pretoria | Brasilia | 16-City Average |
|---|---|---|---|---|---|---|---|
| Steak, per lb. | $24.24 | $5.68 | $5.86 | $4.79 | $2.61 | $1.84 | $5.96 |
| Roast pork, per lb. | $6.10 | $3.16 | $2.82 | $2.59 | $1.31 | $1.42 | $3.06 |
| Whole chicken, per lb. | $2.61 | $2.15 | $1.20 | $0.67 | $0.85 | $0.65 | $1.39 |
| Eggs, doz. | $1.08 | $1.66 | $1.84 | $0.73 | $0.82 | $0.59 | $1.47 |
| Butter, lb. | $4.15 | $2.42 | $1.52 | $1.81 | $0.97 | $2.35 | $2.36 |
| Cheddar cheese, per lb. | $3.96 | $3.20 | $2.07 | $3.12 | $1.67 | $2.56 | $3.35 |
| Milk, per qt. | $1.32 | $0.74 | $0.62 | $0.44 | $0.43 | $0.32 | $0.64 |
| Cooking oil, per qt. | $2.61 | $1.45 | $1.23 | $1.92 | $1.16 | $0.47 | $1.79 |
| Potatoes, per lb. | $1.33 | $0.53 | $0.33 | $0.47 | $0.29 | $0.27 | $0.39 |
| Apples, per lb. | $1.73 | $0.65 | $0.66 | $0.84 | $0.30 | $0.82 | $0.75 |
| Oranges, per lb. | $1.76 | $0.73 | $0.73 | $0.53 | $0.18 | $0.12 | $0.59 |
| Flour, per lb. | $0.73 | $0.44 | $0.21 | $0.21 | $0.22 | $0.08 | $0.33 |
| Rice, per lb. | $1.27 | $0.73 | $0.63 | $0.39 | $0.36 | $0.21 | $0.64 |
| Sugar, per lb. | $0.74 | $0.50 | $0.36 | $0.35 | $0.24 | $0.20 | $0.37 |
| Coffee, per lb. | $11.07 | $3.37 | $5.02 | $3.39 | $4.90 | $1.43 | $4.45 |
| Total | $64.71 | $27.39 | $25.11 | $22.25 | $16.30 | $13.34 | $27.53 |

**Table 22-6  Food Prices in Various World Capitals**
Note: Figures are average retail food prices for May, 1987, in U.S. dollars converted at current exchange rates. "16-city average" is for the 16 capitals surveyed.
Source: U.S. Department of Agriculture.

within a marketing channel; for example, the rice trade in Thailand is controlled by Chinese merchants. Any attempt to move products outside of the regular channels may cause resentment and hostility and make penetrating an already challenging market even more difficult. In addition, if the product requires service or replacement parts, a firm must have a system to provide them, either before marketing or soon after.

The domestic and foreign prices of a product are usually different. Table 22-6 lists prices for some common food items in the various world capitals. Generally, the foreign price is higher because of transportation costs, tariffs, and other expenses. However, in order to keep foreign prices competitive, a firm might decide not to allocate fixed costs to foreign sales. This decision must be made with care to avoid accusations of dumping. Another factor affecting the price of foreign goods is the exchange rate. The devaluation or revaluation of a currency will change the price of goods within a country.

# Notes

**1.** William J. Hampton with Zachary Schiller, Resa King, Rick Melchor, Frank Comes, "Made in the U.S.A.," *Business Week*, February 29, 1988, p. 60.

**2.** David A. Ricks, "How to Avoid Business Blunders Abroad," in *International Marketing*, ed. Subhash C. Jain and Lewis R. Tucker, Jr. (Boston: Kent Publishing Co., 1986), pp. 109–11.

**3.** Philip R. Cateora, *Marketing: An International Perspective* (Homewood, Ill.: Irwin, 1987), p. 84.

**4.** Ibid., p. 85.

**5.** Resa W. King and Peter Galuszka, "The Twain Are Meeting—And Cutting Deals," *Business Week*, December 7, 1987, p. 88; "C-E Establishes First Soviet/American Joint Venture," *World* (C-E's employee publication) 3 (January/February 1988): 6–11.

# Summary and Review

▶ An absolute or comparative advantage in trade may determine what products a company from a particular nation will export.

▶ The elements of international business include importing, or purchasing products and raw materials from another nation, and exporting, selling domestic goods and materials to another nation. Other considerations include the balance of trade and exchange rates.

▶ The legal framework for international trade includes the laws of one's own nation, the laws of the trading nation, and international law. Companies engaged in international trade must also consider the effects of politics and cultural and social differences between nations.

▶ Trade barriers include tariffs, quotas, embargoes, countertrade agreements, and exchange controls. Organizations that facilitate trade include GATT, Eximbank, DISCs, the World Bank, the IMF, and free trade zones.

▶ A company may be involved in international trade through exporting, licensing, contract manufacturing, direct investment, or joint ventures, or as a multinational.

▶ International trade organizations may be in the form of multinationals, cartels, orderly marketing agreements, or economic communities.

▶ A company desiring to enter the international marketplace must do market research, decide how to adapt the product and promotion to the international marketplace, and formulate distribution and pricing policies.

# Key Terms and Concepts

exporting
importing
balance of trade
trade deficit
balance of payments
exchange rate
Bretton Woods Accord

floating exchange rate
Webb-Pomerene Export Trade Act
Foreign Corrupt Practices Act
import tariff
quota
embargo
dumping

countertrade agreements
exchange controls
General Agreement on Tariffs and
    Trade (GATT)
Eximbank
Foreign Credit Insurance Association
    (FCIA)
Domestic International Sales
    Corporations (DISCs)
World Bank
International Monetary Fund (IMF)
free trade zone
exporting

trading company
licensing
royalty agreement
exclusive license
contract manufacturing
direct investment
joint venture
multinational
cartel
orderly marketing agreement
economic communities
globalization

# Checking Your Understanding

This chapter introduced you to the subject of international business. To test and reinforce your understanding, fill in the blanks below.

**1.** A nation that imports more than it exports has a negative _____ _____ _____.

**2.** _____ occurs when a company allows a foreign company to use its name, products, trademarks, materials, and production methods.

**3.** _____ means to sell abroad a country's domestic products and raw materials.

**4.** An _____ is a government-imposed suspension of trade in a particular product.

**5.** An _____ _____ is a duty levied on goods bought outside a nation's borders.

**6.** A group of firms that agree not to compete with each other is a _____.

**7.** The advantage in trade held by a nation that is the only producer of an item is _____ for that item.

**8.** _____ provides a forum for tariff negotiations and discussion of trade problems.

**9.** The rate at which one nation's currency can be exchanged for another nation's currency is the _____ _____.

**10.** _____ are tax-sheltered subsidiaries.

**11.** Increasing the value of a nation's currency is _____.

**12.** A _____ operates on a worldwide scale, without significant ties to one country.

# Topics for Review and Discussion

**1.** Why has the United States lost its favorable balance of trade, and how may it regain a favorable balance of trade?

**2.** Explain why Mexico has repeatedly devalued its peso. What consequences did the Mexican government expect? What benefits?

**3.** If the United States were to impose additional tariffs on automobiles imported from Japan, what would happen to the price of Japanese cars sold in the United States? What would happen to the price of American cars? What action might Japan take to continue to compete in the U.S. automobile market?

# Exercises

**1.** Discuss how you would establish a marketing strategy and how you would implement that strategy to introduce McDonald's to the Soviet Union.

**2.** Why did apartheid in South Africa cause General Motors and Kodak to sell their holdings there?

**3.** Why might the United States be willing to form an economic community with Mexico and Canada? What might be the consequences if such an organization is established? What might be the consequences if such an organization is not established?

## Case 22-1
### *The* Maquiladora *Industries of Mexico*

Because of increased competition from low-cost imports, American businesses have been searching for ways to move production abroad to take advantage of low foreign labor costs. Many American and some Japanese companies have found a low-cost solution in the *maquiladora* industries of Mexico.

The term *maquiladora* comes from the Spanish word *maquila*, which refers to a toll that millers used to collect for grinding other people's grain. Like the millers, the *maquiladora* industries assemble, process, and repair components for foreign companies. They then return the finished or assembled products to the United States where they are sold. The company pays a U.S. tariff only on the value added to the product in Mexico. If part of the product stays behind in Mexico, the company pays a Mexican duty on the product.

The Border Industrialization Plan of 1965 established the *maquiladora* industries to create a coproduction or "twin plant" system between the United States and Mexico. The aim of American companies using the system was to establish a capital-intensive operation on the U.S. side and a labor-intensive operation on the Mexican side. A U.S. plant would supply a Mexican plant with components and the Mexican plant would return the assembled products to the United States for further processing or shipment to customers. Most American companies, however, ship components from *maquiladora* plants that are not near the border and have no need for additional plants, so they have not implemented the twin-plant concept. Instead, they use *maquiladora* plants all over Mexico. However, since 1980 the Japanese have set up twin plants, sending the high-tech work to an American plant and the labor-intensive work to a Mexican plant. The Japanese have thirty *maquiladora* plants in operation and have plans to establish many more.

The *maquiladora* program is attractive to American and Japanese businesses for several reasons. Mexico has one of the lowest labor-cost rates in the world. In fact, Mexico's labor costs are about 39 percent lower than labor costs in Taiwan. Moreover, in recent years, the value of the peso has fallen dramatically relative to the value of the American dollar, making investment in Mexican plants even more profitable. And, because Mexico is so close to the United States, it is less expensive to transport goods and components to and from Mexico than it is to transport them from other countries. American firms also like the *maquiladora* program because it creates jobs in the United States (most of these jobs are white-collar jobs). In addition, because Mexico is so close to the United States, domestic firms do not have to provide the additional compensation usually given to an executive for managing a company in another country.

Mexico too likes the *maquiladora* program. Mexico hopes that *maquiladora* industries will increase economic development by facilitating foreign exchange and providing employment. Mexico especially hopes the plants will help reduce unemployment in the border zone. There were more than fifteen hundred *maquiladora* plants employing nearly 330,000 workers to assemble products for American and Japanese companies at the end of 1988. Mexico intends to eventually link the *maquiladoras* to the rest of the Mexican industries.

Recent legislation in Mexico abolished a law requiring majority Mexican ownership for these companies. As a result, many American and Japanese companies, instead of forming their own subsidiaries, are using Mexican subcontractors to perform assembly operations. Some *maquiladora* plants work for one business, but most work for several. In addition, some enter into "shelter plans" with American or Japanese businesses, whereby the Mexican company provides assembly services until the foreign business is ready to open its own plant or enter into a long-term arrangement with a Mexican company.

The *maquiladora* program is responsible for a large portion of Mexico's foreign exchange. In fact, it accounts for more than one-third of the total exports of Mexican manufactured goods. The program is now responsible for the assembly of labor-intensive product lines such as electronics, auto parts, and textiles. All of these products are labor intensive.

The *maquiladora* program has grown rapidly in recent years. Between 1973 and 1986, new plants grew at a rate of about 10 percent a year. The average number of workers per plant and the average size of the plants have also been increasing.

The future of the *maquiladora* plants looks promising. Mexico's low labor costs and the low value of the peso, combined with savings in transportation costs due to Mexico's nearby location, will continue to make it attractive for foreign firms to locate many of their assembly and manufacturing processes there. In addition, the economic benefits that the American, Japanese, and

Mexican businesses derive from the program make it likely that the *maquiladora* program will continue.

----

These facts are from Benito E. Flores, "Mexico's Maquiladora Industries: An Overview and Perspectives," *Texas A&M Business Forum* (Fall 1987): 27–32; John Hillkirk, "Foreigners Flood Mexico with Plants," *USA Today*, March 11, 1988, pp. 1A, 2A.

**Questions**

1. What impact do *maquiladora* plants have on the balance of trade between the United States and Mexico?
2. Discuss some of the current environmental conditions that are favorable to continued expansion of *maquiladora* plants.
3. How can United States and Japanese companies improve their marketing strategies by producing products in *maquiladora* plants?

## Case 22-2
## *Granada Improves Cattle Worldwide*

Houston-based Granada Embryo Transfer Company is helping ranchers all over the world improve the quality of their cattle. The company extracts cattle embryos from superior animals for implantation in surrogate-mother cows. In addition to engaging in traditional marketing activities, Granada must also concern itself with customs regulations, payments from international ranchers, and interfering governments.

Granada has customers all over the world and recently added two Mexican ranchers to its client list. These Mexican ranchers wanted to improve their herds to increase beef and dairy production as do all of Granada's clients. Importing embryos instead of live animals makes sense because a live animal may not be immune to diseases in a new location, but an implanted embryo obtains immunity from its surrogate mother. Granada's services do not come cheap, however: it charged about $350 per embryo transfer in 1986, and most clients want hundreds of animals to undergo this procedure.

Some clients want Granada to take care of the whole embryo transfer process; others want to purchase only the embryo transfer technology. In the latter case, Granada trains the ranchers in a three-week course at Granada's facilities. For clients who want the whole service, Granada scientists visit the customer's facilities to determine how much support the rancher needs. The team visits the ranch several times during the process to ensure that everything goes well. Nevertheless, it is a little difficult for Granada to evaluate the results of its services because the results are not evident until the calves are born nine months after the implantation.

Granada uses marketing and advertising programs to make American and foreign ranchers aware of its services. The company focuses much of its marketing effort on educating ranchers about embryo transfer technology and its benefits. Its marketing expertise enabled it to bypass overseas sales agents and go directly to the ranchers. Sometimes the ranchers approach Granada first. Granada does have competitors in its business; New York-based Outreach International Ltd. offers similar services in several Asian countries.

Most of the foreign customers who are interested in the high-technology service offered by Granada can afford it and therefore can arrange to pay in American dollars. Many ranchers arrange payment through letters of credit at an American bank. Thus, Granada is somewhat insulated against fluctuating exchange rates and the economic woes of other nations, particularly Mexico. The company does have to worry about customs regulations regarding the transfer of technology and the sale of services across international boundaries. In addition, some foreign governments have tried to obtain the technology for themselves. Like all companies engaged in international trade, Granada must be careful to obey all laws and regulations and yet ensure that it receives all payment that it deserves for its services. That can be especially difficult when dealing with farmers and ranchers in struggling nations.

Several Texas agencies are available to help guide companies like Granada through administrative and official red-tape requirements in Mexico. One of these is the State of Texas Office in Mexico City, which helps Texas companies find customers in Mexico and Mexican businesses find customers and suppliers of goods and services in Texas. The Texas Department of Agriculture specifically locates ranchers in Mexico and matches them with Texans who can assist them with various services. The U.S. Department of Commerce can guide companies through trade relations with other nations.

In spite of the difficulties that are a part of exporting services across national borders, Granada is aware that its service fills an international need. The prospect of international trade intimidates many businesses, but Granada Embryo Transfer Company knows that it is offering farmers and ranchers, regardless of their nationality, an opportunity to improve the quality of their cattle and boost production of beef and dairy products. That technology may ultimately increase the amount of food available to feed a hungry world as well as earn profits for Granada.

---

These facts are from Gary Taylor, "Granada Embryo Transfer Co.," *Texas Business Prospects International*, (August 1986): 60; Michele Kay, "A Willing Texas," *Texas Business Prospects International*, (August 1986): 54, 56; O. C. Ferrell, "Rules of the Exporting Road," *Texas Business Prospects International*, (August 1986): 56, 58; and "Beefing Up China's Cattle," *Business Week*, November 23, 1987, p. 135.

### Questions

1. Why is payment in United States currency so important to Granada in exporting its services to other countries?
2. What are some possible trade barriers that could prevent Granada from exporting to some countries?
3. What can Granada do in its marketing activities to compete with New York-based Outreach International Ltd., which offers similar services?

# Answers to Checking Your Understanding

1. balance of trade
2. licensing
3. exporting
4. embargo
5. import tariff
6. cartel
7. absolute
8. GATT
9. exchange rate
10. DISCs
11. revaluation
12. multinational

## Outline

# Chapter 23

# The Legal Environment of Business

## Objectives

After reading this chapter, you will be able to:

▶ Identify the sources of law that affect business.

▶ Describe the dispute resolution process, and explain how lawsuits are handled in the federal and state court systems.

▶ Identify areas of law that affect the operations of businesses, such as laws concerning contracts, sales, agents, property, bankruptcy, and taxes.

▶ Identify laws that promote competition among businesses.

▶ Recognize the current trend toward deregulation of business, and understand why it is occurring.

# Business Experience

Businesses must ensure that their products and services do not harm consumers as a result of defects, design flaws, or negligence. Consumers who believe they have been injured because of a defective product or negligence can sue the producer for any injuries or damages. American auto makers have been in court many times in recent years because some consumers believe that the lap seat belts used in the back seats of automobiles are unsafe.

Ford Motor Company has been involved in a number of lawsuits which charge that its back-seat lap belts do not provide adequate safety to back-seat passengers; the families of some of the injured and deceased victims say the lap belts are downright dangerous. In December 1987, a jury ordered Ford to pay $3.3 million to a 13-year-old boy who was paralyzed in a 1985 auto accident in which he was wearing a lap belt. The jury said that defects in the design of the seat belt contributed to his injuries, and that Ford was negligent for failing to install safer shoulder belts in the back seat of the car. Ford plans to appeal the judgment. Another passenger in the back seat of the same car died as a result of internal injuries caused by the lap belt he was wearing at the time of the accident. Ford faces another suit in California involving a woman who died wearing a back-seat lap belt. General Motors and American Honda Motor Company have paid huge settlements to victims of similar accidents.

Ford and General Motors insist that the lap belts in back seats are safe, but most auto makers plan to install combination lap-shoulder belts in the back seats of new car models over the next few years. Nevertheless, a study by the National Transportation Safety Board released in 1986 reported that lap belts induced severe and sometimes fatal injuries that might not have occurred had the victim not been wearing a lap belt. The study concluded that lap-shoulder seat belts are the safest. Regulators have not required mandatory lap-shoulder belts in the back seat because of the cost, estimated at $12 per car.

Even if auto makers begin to install lap-shoulder belts now, there are still more than 100 million cars on the road with lap belts in the back seat. The injured boy's father wants Ford to recall almost 2 million Ford Escorts and Mercury Lynxes, which have rear lap belts. He doesn't want other parents to see their children injured because of auto makers' failure to correct flaws in the design of the lap seat belt. The Department of Transportation is investigating the lap-belt problem.

Whatever the outcome of the many pending lawsuits and the Department of Transportation investigation, American auto makers must decide whether the cost of adding lap-shoulder belts outweighs the potential costs from lawsuits resulting from lap-belt injuries. Automobile manufacturers, like all businesses, have an obligation to see that consumers of their products are not harmed because of defects or design flaws. Consumers, however, may settle the issue first: If consumers do not believe the cars are safe, they will stop buying them, and the companies selling unsafe cars will be forced out of business because of their lack of responsiveness to consumers' needs and wants.

These facts are from John R. Emshwiller, "Car Makers Face Lawsuits Alleging Rear Seat Belts Aren't Safe Enough," *The Wall Street Journal*, January 6, 1988, p. 17; "Ordeal of Son's Auto Injury Spurs Father to Seek a Recall," *The New York Times*, January 17, 1988, p. 39; "Ford Must Pay Hurt Boy $3.3 Million, Jury Finds," *The Wall Street Journal*, December 21, 1987, p. 25.

# Introduction

Laws are, in essence, rules developed by society to regulate the conduct of its members. The legal environment of business includes all laws and regulations dealing with the activities of business and the conduct of businesspeople. For instance, Chapter 13 discussed laws that marketers must follow in labeling their products. Many products must have the ingredients listed on the packaging. Such laws protect consumers so consumers know exactly what they are buying.

Laws are categorized as either criminal or civil. Criminal law not only prohibits a specific kind of action, such as murder and bank robbery, but also imposes a fine or imprisonment as punishment for breaking the law. A violation of a criminal law is thus called a *crime*. Ivan Boesky received a three-year prison sentence in late 1987 for violating laws related to the trading of confidential stock-market information.[1] Civil law is all the laws not classified as criminal. Civil law defines the rights and duties of individuals (including business organizations) violations of civil law may result in fines, but not imprisonment.

Every day you read in the newspaper or hear news reports about businesses having legal problems because they violated a government regulation, breached a contract, or acted carelessly. Many of these problems could have been avoided if the business owners had some knowledge of the legal system. This chapter introduces you to some of the legal problems facing business today. An understanding of the laws and government regulations governing business will not only help you avoid legal problems but will also make you aware of your rights in the event that you are wronged in the course of doing business.

# ▶ Sources of Law

Someone who says that an action is "against the law" probably means that the action violates a constitutional principle, a federal or state statute, a federal or state administrative agency's regulation, or a judge's decision.

## Constitutional Law

**Constitutional law**

Specifies how the United States government must behave in its relations with the states and individual citizens

The United States Constitution is the basis of **constitutional law**, which specifies how the United States government must behave in its relations with the states and individual citizens. It also provides a framework for all other areas of law in the United States because it is the supreme law of this country. Laws that violate the Constitution are not enforceable. The Constitution was written in 1787 and has been amended many times to reflect changes in society. Each state also has a constitution that sets forth the organizational framework for that state's laws.

**Court of last resort.** This photo shows the Supreme Court Building in Washington, D.C. The Supreme Court is the highest court in the land. It hears appeals of individuals, organizations, and corporations.

# Common Law

**Common law**

The law established by judges in the process of deciding disputes

**Common law** is the law established by judges in the process of deciding disputes. Their judgments set precedents for deciding similar cases in the future. Recent court rulings in several states, for example, suggest that employers may be punished for "negligent" hiring practices if an employee commits a crime on the job. After a security guard took $200,000 in gold from a Florida mining company, the company sued the guard's employer for failing to check into his criminal record before hiring him.[2] Although there is no statutory law requiring employers to check such details of a prospective employee's history, this case and others may set a precedent that could be used to decide future cases. Legal Encounter 23-1 examines the issue of workers' rights to privacy.

Because judges are bound to follow earlier case decisions, the body of common law is remarkably uniform across the country. Some areas of law that are common law in nature deal with contracts, agencies, and torts; these are defined and discussed later in this chapter.

# Statutory Law

**Statutes**

Laws enacted by a legislature

**Statutes** are laws enacted by a legislature. Most new law being made today is in the form of statutes. The United States Congress passes federal statutory laws; each state legislature enacts state statutes. The laws made by city

# Legal Encounter 23-1
## *Privacy in the Work Place*

Privacy in the work place has become one of the hottest legal topics in the 1980s as businesses delve into the private lives of their workers. Nearly one-third of the *Fortune* 500 corporations screen employees for abuse or casual use of drugs such as marijuana and cocaine and monitor workers' honesty with lie detectors and written tests. Others probe workers with a variety of personality tests. Some businesses have even begun testing employees for diseases, particularly AIDS, and performing genetic tests to determine predispositions to certain costly diseases such as heart disease and cancer. Workers say these measures are a violation of their personal privacy. Employers counter that the tests are necessary to reduce theft and high insurance costs and to increase productivity.

Testing employees and job applicants is not a new idea. In the 1950s, companies gathered huge amounts of information on prospective workers from employment histories, psychological profiles, and personal data. Employees today, however, are upset that companies are able to obtain even more information about their private lives without their consent. Employees are also concerned about electronic and telephone eavesdropping in the work place as well as the potential for employers to unearth very personal information by using electronic data bases. Moreover, workers and unions believe that testing not only identifies drug abusers, thieves, and undesirables, but also weeds out the innocent.

Workers are not striking over the privacy issue; instead, they are filing lawsuits and demanding legislation to protect their privacy rights. They believe their activities outside of work have no bearing on their performance at work and that monitoring activities infringe on their right to privacy. In many cases, the courts have agreed. A Maryland court awarded one worker $1.3 million after her employer fired her for refusing to take a lie-detector test during an investigation of stock thefts. A California court awarded a woman $300,000 in back pay and punitive damages after her employer fired her because she was dating a man who worked for a competitor. Cases involving random drug testing are pending in many state courts.

Not long ago, companies could easily fire workers for what they did off the job. A decade of litigation and legislation involving employee rights has made it more difficult for companies to fire workers for certain activities or behavior outside the office. Therefore, employers believe they are justified in administering more tests and digging deeper into prospective employees' backgrounds in order to find qualified, conscientious employees.

Employers also point out that drug use costs them nearly $50 billion a year in absenteeism and turnover. Employee theft costs another $10 billion annually. In addition, the failure to ensure a safe and drug-free work place can subject a business to large liability claims if someone is injured by an errant employee or faulty product. As a result, employers believe that testing employees is important.

This controversy has pitted employee against employer in a debate to see whose rights are more important: those of companies seeking a productive and safe work force or those of employees trying to protect their privacy. It seems likely that future legislation will bring changes that could be as far-reaching as those that followed the breakthrough of industrial unionism in the 1930s.

These facts are from Larry Reibstein, "Firms Find It Tougher to Dismiss Employees for Off-Duty Conduct," *The Wall Street Journal*, March 29, 1988, p. 29; John Hoerr, with Katherine M. Hafner, Gail DeGeorge, Anne R. Field, and Laura Zinn, "Privacy," *Business Week*, March 28, 1988, pp. 61–68; and Susan Dentzer, with Bob Cohn, George Raine, Ginny Carroll, and Vicki Quade, "Can You Pass the Job Test?" *Newsweek*, May 5, 1986, pp. 46–53.

governments—called ordinances—also fall into this category. Statutory laws include antitrust laws, criminal laws, corporate laws, and tax laws. If you fail to file a federal income tax return, for example, you may be assessed a penalty—a percentage of the amount of money you owe the Internal Revenue Service. If you do not pay the tax and penalty, your assets may be seized by the IRS.

## Administrative Law

**Administrative law** consists of regulations passed by state and federal administrative agencies. Federal administrative agencies, established by Congress, control and influence business by enforcing statutes and regulations to protect consumers and workers, and they promote competition. Federal agencies that regulate business include the Food and Drug Administration (regulates businesses that produce and sell food or medicine), the Federal Trade Commission (regulates many aspects of business including advertising and competition), and the Consumer Product Safety Commission (ensures that products operate as they are intended to, without harming consumers). Table 23-1 describes the major areas of responsibility of several federal regulatory agencies. Administrative law is increasingly important to business.

# ▶ Courts and the Resolution of Disputes

If you borrow money from a bank and do not repay it, the bank may file a lawsuit against you in the proper court, asking the judge of the court to order you to repay the loan and to pay the attorneys' fees the bank incurred in trying to collect the money. The primary method of resolving serious business disputes in the United States is filing a lawsuit. Thus, it is important for all businesspeople to have some familiarity with the American court system.

**Jurisdiction** is the legal power of a court, through a judge, to interpret and apply the law and make a binding decision in a particular case. Federal courts are given this power by the Constitution or by Congress. State legislatures and constitutions determine which state courts hear certain types of cases. Courts of general jurisdiction hear all types of cases; those of limited jurisdiction hear only specific types of cases. The Federal Bankruptcy Court, for example, hears only cases involving bankruptcy. There is some combination of limited and general jurisdiction courts in every state.

The federal government and the state governments have separate and distinct court systems. The two systems coexist; neither is more powerful or more important than the other. It is necessary to discuss both the state and the federal court systems to understand the environment in which business arguments are resolved.

## Federal Courts

In general, federal courts hear cases involving issues of constitutional law, violations of federal laws, disputes between citizens of different states that involve at least $10,000, suits between an American citizen and one of another nation, maritime disputes, bankruptcy laws, postal laws, tax laws, and copyright, patent, and trademark laws. The United States Constitution gives federal judicial power to the United States Supreme Court and to other, lower courts established by Congress. These include a system of trial and appellate (appeals) courts (Figure 23-1).

**Table 23.1 Major Federal Regulatory Agencies**
Source: William M. Pride and O. C. Ferrell, *Marketing: Basic Concepts and Decisions* (Boston: Houghton Mifflin, 1987), p. 45.

| Agency | Major Areas of Responsibility |
|---|---|
| Federal Trade Commission (FTC) | Enforces laws and guidelines regarding business practices; takes action to stop false and deceptive advertising and labeling |
| Food and Drug Administration (FDA) | Enforces laws and regulations to prevent distribution of adulterated or misbranded foods, drugs, medical devices, cosmetics, veterinary products, and particularly hazardous consumer products |
| Consumer Product Safety Commission | Ensures compliance with the Consumer Product Safety Act; protects the public from unreasonable risk of injury from any consumer product not covered by other regulatory agencies |
| Interstate Commerce Commission (ICC) | Regulates franchises, rates, and finances of interstate rail, bus, truck, and water carriers |
| Federal Communications Commission (FCC) | Regulates communication by wire, radio, and television in interstate and foreign commerce |
| Environmental Protection Agency (EPA) | Develops and enforces environmental protection standards and conducts research into the adverse effects of pollution |
| Federal Power Commission (FPC) | Regulates rates and sales of natural gas producers, thereby affecting the supply and price of gas available to consumers; also regulates wholesale rates for electricity and gas, pipeline construction, and U.S. imports and exports of natural gas and electricity |

Trial courts of general jurisdiction in the federal court system are called U.S. District Courts. There is at least one U.S. District Court in every state. If a party to a lawsuit is unhappy with the district judge's decision, the person may appeal the decision to the Court of Appeal for the geographic district in which the district court is located. There are thirteen U.S. Courts of Appeal, which hear all initial appeals from federal trial courts in the United States, as well as appeals from federal administrative agencies.

It is possible to appeal the decision of a U.S. Court of Appeal to the United States Supreme Court. The United States Supreme Court is not required to hear most appeals, so the appealing party must apply to have the Supreme Court hear the case. The Supreme Court grants only a very small percentage of all applications.

## State Courts

Most states have a court system that closely parallels the federal court structure. All states have at least one level of appellate court, or court of

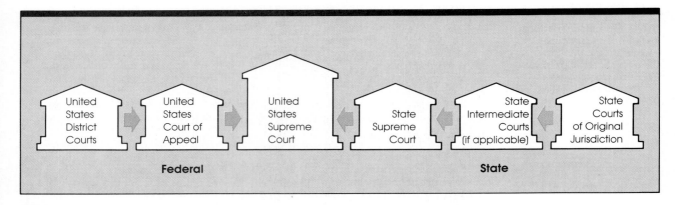

**Figure 23-1**
The Federal Court System

appeal, and most have two levels. A typical state's appellate court system consists of an intermediate appellate and a state supreme court. Usually, a party who feels he or she has not received a fair judgment can appeal to an intermediate appellate court, but a state statute or constitution may limit access to the state supreme court.

It is very common for a state to have a system of general trial courts, which decide a variety of civil and criminal cases, as well as specialized courts that hear cases limited to a particular type—for example, probate court, family court, juvenile court. Many states have small-claims courts that hear cases involving a relatively small amount of money—as little as $500 or as much as several thousand dollars. The televised *People's Court* presided over by Judge Joseph Wapner decides cases taken from California's small-claims courts. Most states also have one or more of the following courts: justice of the peace (JP) courts, municipal courts, traffic courts, county courts.

## Relationship Between State and Federal Courts

Once a case is initiated in either federal or state court, it normally stays within that system until its conclusion. A lawsuit initiated in a state trial court is appealed to the appropriate state appellate court. The judgment of the highest court within a state is usually final, because in most cases further appeal is not possible. If, however, the ruling of the highest state court involves a section of the United States Constitution or the interpretation of federal statutory law, it is possible to apply to have the United States Supreme Court hear the case on appeal.

## Function of the Courts

In a trial court, (whether in a court of general or limited jurisdiction and whether in the state or the federal system), two tasks must be completed. First, the court (acting through the judge in a bench trial or through the jury in a jury trial) must act as the trier of fact. In other words, if there is conflicting evidence, the judge or jury must decide which of the parties to believe. Second, the judge must decide which law or set of laws is pertinent to the case and must then apply those laws to resolve the dispute.

In contrast, an appellate court deals solely with appeals relating to the interpretation of law. Thus, when a case is appealed, it is not retried. Appellate judges do not hear witnesses but instead base their decisions on a written transcript of the original trial. It is not necessary or even desirable for appellate courts to draw factual conclusions. The appellate judge is limited to deciding whether the trial judge made a mistake that probably affected the outcome of the trial. If the trial judge made no mistake (or if mistakes that were made would not have changed the result of the trial), the appellate court will not disturb the trial court's decision. If the appellate court finds a mistake, it usually remands, or sends the case back to the trial court, so that the mistake can be corrected. Corrective action may involve the granting of a new trial. On occasion, appellate courts revise the verdict of the trial court without remanding the case to the trial court.

## Administrative Agencies

Federal and state administrative agencies have some judicial powers. Many administrative agencies, such as the Nuclear Regulatory Commission and the Federal Trade Commission, decide disputes that arise under their regulations. In such disputes, resolution is usually called a hearing rather than a trial. The Federal Trade Commission, along with the U.S. Justice Department, held hearings to decide whether to allow Texas Air Corporation to acquire Eastern Airlines in 1987. In these cases, an administrative law judge decides all issues. The case may be appealed through the appropriate judicial system thereafter.

## Enforcement of Court Orders

A businessperson may win a case at trial and receive a judgment, or court order, requiring the losing party to pay money damages. However, because court orders are not self-enforcing, it may be difficult or even impossible to collect the damages.

Most business lawsuits involve a request for a sum of money, but some business lawsuits request that a court specifically order the other party to do or refrain from doing a certain act. Some losing parties voluntarily make payment according to a court order or judgment, but frequently it is necessary to force the losing party—the judgment debtor—to make payment.

There are several ways to collect on a judgment. The most common method involves seizure of the judgment debtor's property by a sheriff or other legal authority and having that property sold at auction to satisfy the debt. In most states it is possible to garnishee a judgment debtor's wages in order to collect on a judgment. In this case, a judge orders the judgment debtor's employer to withhold a portion of the employee's wages and pay that amount directly to the judgment creditor. Some states place significant restrictions on the use of one or both of these methods of collecting a judgment. Thus, a businessperson deciding whether to bring a lawsuit must

**These dinosaurs are safe.** It is important to protect new products legally—designs and names. Francis Goldwyn developed a set of colorful, velour dinosaurs and was concerned about being copied by competitors so he copyrighted all designs and hired an attorney. His dinosaurs were a big success—and his product was copied. Fortunately for Goldwyn, his careful legal protection helped him win a six-figure settlement from Gerber Products Company.

consider the likelihood of collecting on a judgment. To most people, winning the lawsuit without obtaining damages is a hollow victory.

## Alternative Dispute Resolution Methods

Although the main remedy for business disputes is the lawsuit, other dispute resolution methods are becoming popular. The schedules of state and federal trial courts are often quite crowded; there often are long delays between the filing of a case and the time of trial. Further, complex cases can become quite expensive to pursue through the legal system. As a result, many businesspeople are turning to alternative methods of resolving business arguments: arbitration, mediation, the mini-trial, and litigation in a private court.

**Arbitration**

The submission of a dispute to one or more third-party arbitrators whose decision is final

**Arbitration** involves the submission of a dispute to one or more third-party arbitrators, usually chosen by the disputing parties, whose decision is final. Cases may be submitted to arbitration because a contract requires it or because the parties have agreed to do so. Arbitration can be an attractive alternative to a lawsuit because it is often cheaper and quicker, and the parties can frequently choose arbitrators who are knowledgeable or skilled in the particular area of business at issue. Arbitration results may or may not be binding on the parties.

**Mediation**

The mediator does not make a final binding decision in a case

**Mediation** differs from arbitration in that the mediator does not make a final decision in the case. Instead, a mediator provides suggestions on different ways to resolve a dispute voluntarily between the parties. When the Teamsters Union could not reach an agreement with Pan Am Corporation on wage concessions in 1987, the union and the airline asked the National Mediation Board to help in the negotiations. When talks between the airline and the union remained stalled, the National Mediation Board recommended that the dispute be submitted to arbitration.[3]

# ▶ The Uniform Commercial Code

**Uniform Commercial Code**

A set of statutory laws covering several business law topics

At one time, all states had a variety of laws governing various business practices. Transacting business across state lines was difficult because of the variation in the laws from state to state. To simplify commerce, every state except Louisiana has enacted the Uniform Commercial Code (Louisiana has enacted portions of the code). The **Uniform Commercial Code** is a set of statutory laws covering several business law topics. Articles II and III of the Uniform Commercial Code have the most significant impact on business.

## Sales Law

**Express warranty**

A warranty that can arise from an oral or written statement of fact, a promise, or by simply showing plans, diagrams, or samples in connection with a sale

Article II of the Uniform Commercial Code covers sales agreements for goods but does not cover the sales of stocks and bonds, personal services, or real estate. Article II specifically addresses the rights of buyers and sellers, transfers of ownership, warranties, and the legal placement of risk during manufacture and delivery. Under this article, a sales agreement may be enforced even though it does not specify the selling price or the time or place of delivery. Article II requires that a buyer pay a reasonable price for goods at the time of delivery if the parties have not reached an agreement on price.

**Implied warranty**

Imposed on the producer or seller by law

Article II also deals with express and implied warranties. An **express warranty** can arise from an oral or written statement of fact, a promise, or by simply showing plans, diagrams, or samples in connection with a sale. (The Magnuson-Moss Warranty Act also regulates written warranties voluntarily offered by sellers but is not part of the U.C.C.)

**Warranty of merchantability**

A promise from the manufacturer that the goods are at least of average quality and are safe for their ordinary purpose

An **implied warranty** is imposed on the producer or seller by law, although it may not be a written document provided at the time of sale. Under Article II, a consumer may assume the product for sale has a clear title (in other words, that it is not stolen) and that the product will serve the purpose for which it was made and sold. One of the most important of the implied warranties is the **warranty of merchantability.** A merchant who sells goods implicitly promises that the goods are at least of average quality and are safe for their ordinary purpose.

## Law of Commercial Paper

**Commercial paper**

Written promises or orders to pay a specific sum of money

**Negotiable instruments**

Commercial paper that can be transferred from one person or business to another as long as it meets certain requirements

Article III refers to negotiable **commercial paper,** which are written promises or orders to pay a specific amount of money, such as checks, drafts, certificates of deposit, short-term debt securities, and promissory notes. Article III specifically covers **negotiable instruments,** which are commercial paper that can be transferred from one person or business to another if they meet the following requirements:

- ▶ They must be written and signed
- ▶ They must be an unconditional promise to pay a specified sum of money
- ▶ They must be payable on demand or at some specified date
- ▶ They must be payable to the order of a specified person or business or to the bearer of the paper
- ▶ They may not contain any other promises.

Commercial paper that does not meet all these requirements is legally valid and enforceable, but not negotiable—that is, it cannot be transferred to another person or company. In essence, a negotiable instrument is a substitute for money. A person or company may transfer or sell a negotiable instrument for cash. For example, when you write a check to Sears for automobile tires, Sears essentially "sells" that check to a bank in exchange for cash.

A negotiable instrument must be endorsed before it may be transferred (Figure 23-2). You endorse your paychecks or checks from your parents when you sign the back of the check before depositing it into your bank account. An **endorsement** is the payee's (the one to whom the check is written) signature and instructions on the back of the document. A blank endorsement is the payee's signature only on the back of the instrument. A blank endorsement is dangerous because anyone who finds the check after it has been endorsed can cash it. It is safer to restrict the endorsement.

A restrictive endorsement limits the rights of the party to whom the instrument is endorsed. Many people endorse their checks with their signature and the words "for deposit only," so that the only thing that can be done with the check is to deposit it into the specified account. A special endorsement specifies to whom the instrument is payable. If you endorse a promissory note with the words "pay to Joe Schmoe," Joe Schmoe is the only person who can cash in the note. A qualified endorsement limits the payee's liability if the instrument is not honored. This endorsement, usually in the words "without recourse," means that the person who originally signed the document, not the endorser, is responsible for payment of the instrument.

**Endorsement**

The payee's signature and instructions on the back of a document

# ▶ The Law of Torts

**Tort**

A violation of civil law

**Product liability**

Business' legal responsibility for any negligence in the design, production, sale, and consumption of products

Civil laws define the rights and duties of individuals and businesses. One violation of civil law is a **tort**. A tort may be intentional (for instance, fraud) or result from negligence (as when the driver of a delivery truck loses control of the vehicle and damages a building or injures a pedestrian). In the case of the truck accident, the injured parties might sue the driver and the owner of the truck for damages resulting from the accident.

One important aspect of tort law involves **product liability**—businesses' legal responsibility for any negligence in the design, production, sale, and

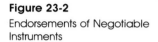

Jane A. Smith

For Deposit Only
Account # 1234-00
Jane A. Smith

Pay to Joe Diaz
Jane A. Smith

Without Recourse
Jane A. Smith

**Blank Endorsement**　　**Restrictive Endorsement**　　**Special Endorsement**　　**Qualified Endorsement**

**Figure 23-2**
Endorsements of Negotiable Instruments

consumption of products. Product liability laws have evolved from both common and statutory law. Some states have expanded the concept of product liability to include injuries by products whether or not the producer is proven negligent. Under strict product liability, a consumer who files suit because of an injury has to prove only that the product was defective, that the defect caused the injury, and that the defect made the product unreasonably dangerous. For example, a carving knife is expected to be sharp and is not considered defective if you cut your finger on it. But an electric knife could be defective and unreasonably dangerous if it continued to operate after you had removed your hand from the switch.

Several automobile manufacturers have paid out millions of dollars to victims of rear seat-belt injuries. The victims and their families felt that the lap belts installed by the car manufacturers did not provide the safety that should have been provided to back-seat passengers. In one Maryland case, a court ruled that the design of the lap belts in the back seat of the Ford Escort was defective.[4]

The significance of tort law has increased over the last few years, and the amount of damages awarded to injured consumers has increased dramatically. Many companies now buy liability insurance to protect themselves against tort liability lawsuits.

# ▶ The Law of Contracts

**Contract**

A mutual agreement between two or more parties that can be enforced in a court

Virtually every business transaction is carried out by means of a contract. A **contract** is a mutual agreement between two or more parties that can be enforced in a court if one party chooses not to comply with the terms of the contract.

**Car corporation chairmen sign a contract.** A contract is a legally enforceable agreement between two or more parties who agree to perform certain activities. The chairmen of two major automobile companies meet here to sign a contract regarding joint production of automobiles.

A "hand-shake deal" is in most cases as fully and completely binding as a written, signed agreement. Individual states require that some contracts be in writing to be enforceable. Most states require that at least some of the following contracts be in writing:

▶ Contracts involving the sale of land or the sale of an interest in land
▶ Contracts to pay somebody else's debt
▶ Contracts that cannot be fulfilled within one year
▶ Contracts for the sale of goods that cost more than $500 (required by the Uniform Commercial Code)

Whether or not a state law requires a particular contract to be written, the best practice is always to put business agreements in writing so that there are no misunderstandings between the parties and either party can easily prove the terms and conditions of the agreement if it is necessary to go to court.

Not all agreements are enforceable. Only those that meet certain requirements—called elements—are enforceable. A person or business seeking to enforce a contract must show that it contains the following elements: voluntary agreement, consideration, contractual capacity of the parties, and legality (Figure 22-3).

## Voluntary Agreement

Most college students have entered into contracts. Borrowing money under a student loan program entails a contractual agreement to repay the money.

**Figure 23-3**

The Elements of a Contract

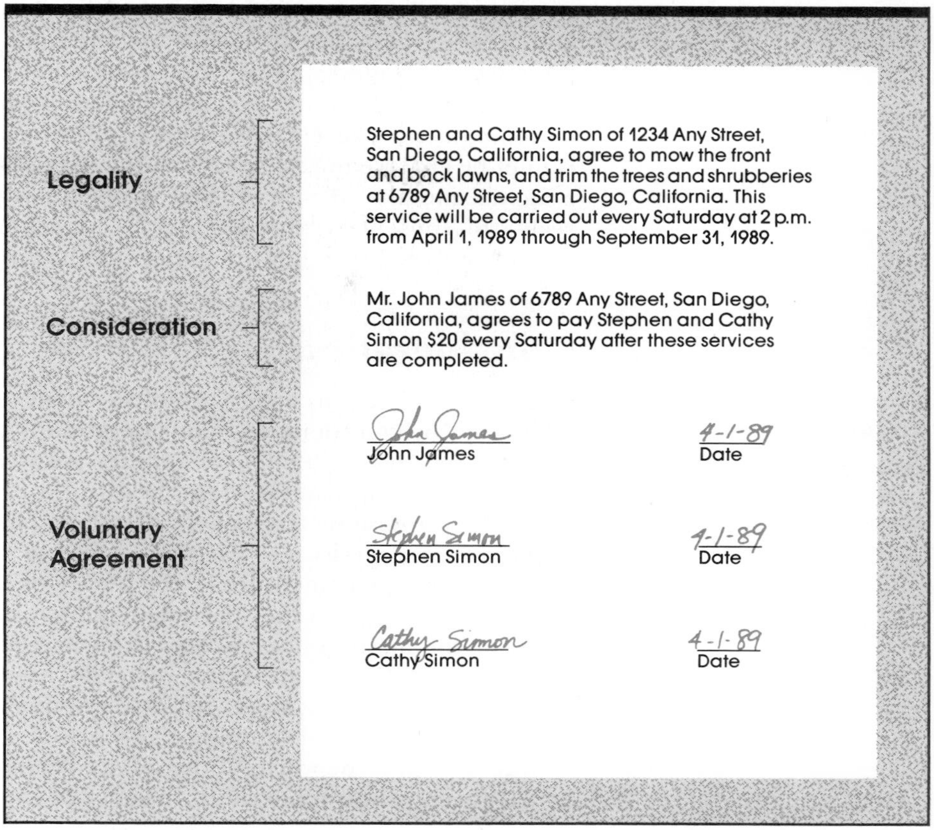

Stephen and Cathy Simon of 1234 Any Street, San Diego, California, agree to mow the front and back lawns, and trim the trees and shrubberies at 6789 Any Street, San Diego, California. This service will be carried out every Saturday at 2 p.m. from April 1, 1989 through September 31, 1989.

Mr. John James of 6789 Any Street, San Diego, California, agrees to pay Stephen and Cathy Simon $20 every Saturday after these services are completed.

*John James*
John James                          4-1-89
                                    Date

*Stephen Simon*
Stephen Simon                       4-1-89
                                    Date

*Cathy Simon*
Cathy Simon                         4-1-89
                                    Date

Legality

Consideration

Voluntary Agreement

**Voluntary agreement**

When one party makes an offer and the other accepts

**Implied contract**

Results from the actions, and sometimes the words, of the parties that indicate an intention to agree without specific agreement

If you rent an apartment or house, your lease is a contract. For such agreements to be considered a contract, both parties must mutually agree to be bound by the terms of the contract. **Voluntary agreement** typically comes about when one party makes an offer and the other accepts. If both the offer and the acceptance are freely, voluntarily, and knowingly made, the acceptance forms the basis for the contract. If, however, either the offer or the acceptance resulted from fraud or force, the party subject to the fraud or force can void, or invalidate, the resulting agreement.

Contracts are usually expressed orally or in writing. However, it is possible to have a contract even though neither party expressed agreement either orally or in writing. An **implied contract** results from the actions, and sometimes the words, of the parties that indicate an intention to agree without specific agreement. For example, one who requests and receives medical services and treatment for an injury understands, and therefore implicitly agrees, that he or she is expected to pay for the services. A court may enforce this implied agreement as a contract even though there was no specific agreement to pay any health care provider. Even in the absence of discussion regarding the price of such services, a court would infer the intention to charge and to pay a reasonable sum under the circumstances. Of course, the best practice is to put all terms and conditions of a contract in writing to minimize misunderstanding. However, unless a state requires a particular contract to be in writing, oral agreements are usually enforceable.

Sometimes an agreement contains all the elements of a contract, yet still cannot be enforced because of fraud, misrepresentation, undue influence, or a factual mistake. If any of these problems is present, the agreement lacks reality of consent because the party's agreement was not given voluntarily but was induced through the use of deceit, force, or mistaken impression.

## Consideration

The second requirement for enforcement of a contract is that it must be supported by consideration. **Consideration** is money or something of value given in return for fulfilling a contract. As a general rule, one cannot force another person to live up to the terms of a promise unless the person who made the promise receives a consideration. The something of value could be money, goods, services, or even a promise to do or not to do something. In the case of an apartment lease, the owner of the apartment agrees to allow the tenant to reside in the apartment and to use the laundry and recreational areas of the apartment complex. In exchange, the tenant gives the owner money—rent. Courts are often reluctant to enforce contracts that are not supported by consideration, because essentially the enforcing party would receive something for nothing. The actual value of the consideration in comparison with the worth of the service rendered is usually immaterial. The courts rarely inquire into the sufficiency of the value exchange.

## Contractual Capacity

**Contractual capacity** is the legal ability to enter into a contract. As a general rule, a court cannot enforce a contract if either party to the agreement lacks contractual capacity. One's contractual capacity may be limited or non-existent.

It is generally accepted that minors (persons under the age of 18) lack full contractual capacity. A minor may enter into a contract but may freely disaffirm, or deny, the agreement at any time before he or she reaches the age of majority. An adult, however, may not disaffirm a contract. In most states, if a minor lies about his or her age to enter into a contract, the minor's right to disaffirm may be limited or even removed. Despite the general rule, minors can usually be held contractually liable for necessary items such as food, clothing, and medical care, to the extent that these items are not available from the minor's family.

Others who have a limited contractual capacity include those who are mentally unstable, retarded, or intoxicated. Still others, such as persons who have been judged insane by a court of law, completely lack the ability to enter into a binding contract. Contracts made with those who are legally insane have no legal standing whatsoever.

# Legality

Legality is the state or condition of being lawful. In order for an otherwise binding contract to be enforceable, both the purpose of the contract and the consideration for the contract must be legal; they cannot be prohibited by law. A contract whereby a bank loans money at a rate of interest prohibited by law, a practice known as *usury*, would be an illegal contract. The fact that one of the parties may commit an illegal act while performing a contract does not render the contract itself illegal, however.

In most cases, the courts maintain a hands-off policy toward illegal agreements and usually do not act to enforce any part of an illegal contract. Thus, if two competing businesses agree to engage in price fixing and one breaks the agreement by discounting, no legal relief is available to the other party. An agreement to sell an illegal drug such as cocaine could not be enforced for the same reason.

# Breach of Contract

**Breach of contract**
The failure or refusal of a party to a contract to live up to his or her promises

**Breach of contract** is the failure or refusal of a party to a contract to live up to his or her promises. In the case of an apartment lease, failure to pay rent would be considered breach of contract. By the same token, an apartment owner or manager who fails to comply with promises specified in the lease, such as failing to repair a broken appliance within a reasonable length of time, has also breached the contract. The breaching party—the one who fails to comply—may be liable for monetary damages that he or she caused to the other party. These damages usually include the actual financial loss suffered by the nonbreaching party.

# ▶ The Law of Agency

**Principal**
The one who wishes to have a specific task accomplished

**Agent**
The one who acts on behalf of the principal to accomplish the task

An agency is a common business relationship created when one person acts on behalf of another and under that person's control. Two parties are involved in an agency relationship: The **principal** is the one who wishes to have a specific task accomplished; the **agent** is the one who acts on behalf of the principal to accomplish the task. Most businesspeople employ agents in many different capacities. For example, a checkout clerk in a Kroger grocery store acts as a sales agent for Kroger. State Farm and other insurance companies generally sell insurance policies through a network of insurance agents. Many homeowners seeking to sell their property do so through the use of a real-estate agent. Corporations must conduct all transactions through agents because the corporation itself has no physical existence and cannot act on its own behalf. In fact, almost any business transaction can be completed through the use of an agent.

The agency relationship is created by the mutual agreement of the principal and the agent. It is usually not necessary that such an agreement be in writing, although putting it in writing is certainly advisable. Third parties may require some written proof that an agency relationship actually exists. In most cases, a principal grants authority to the agent through a formal **power of attorney**, which is a legal document authorizing one to act as someone else's agent. The power of attorney can be used for any agency relationship, and its use is not limited to lawyers. For instance, if you are attending a university far from your home, you can give your parents, through a power of attorney, the authority to withdraw money from your savings account at home and send it to you at school.

Even in the absence of any specific agreement between the principal and the agent, the agent has certain responsibilities or duties with regard to the principal's business.

▶ The *duty of obedience* requires that the agent follow the principal's instructions.

▶ The *duty to use reasonable care* requires the agent to exercise a reasonable degree of care under the circumstances in the completion of the agency purpose. An agent must not be careless or negligent.

▶ The *duty to account for funds and property* entrusted to the agent by the principal prohibits the agent from mixing his or her own funds with funds belonging to the principal.

▶ The agent has the *duty to notify the principal of facts* that are important to the agency purpose.

▶ The agent has the *duty of loyalty to the principal* and may not therefore compete against the principal.

The duty of loyalty would be breached if an employee of a restaurant sold one of the owner's secret recipes to a competitor. Agents are liable for any damages caused by the breach of any one of the agency duties.

An agency relationship can continue as long as both parties so desire. It can be terminated by agreement of the parties, by fulfillment of the purpose of the agency, by mutual agreement, or by the refusal of either party to continue in the relationship. Further, if either the principal or the agent dies, the agency is normally terminated automatically. The bankruptcy of the agent or principal can, but is not required to, terminate the relationship.

When an agent makes a contract or takes other action on the authority of the principal, the resulting action is considered to be that of the principal rather than the agent. Thus, in most cases an agent is not responsible for agreements made on behalf of the principal and under the principal's authority. Not only is a principal liable for authorized contracts made on his or her behalf by an agent, but a principal may also be liable for torts committed by an agent. Thus, if an agent acts within the scope of his or her authority or employment, and in furtherance of the principal's business, the principal is or may be fully and completely liable for any resulting injury. This theory of vicarious liability is known as the doctrine of *respondeat superior* ("let the superior respond"). Thus, if the driver of a department store delivery truck carelessly causes a traffic accident while engaged in his duties, his employer is responsible for the resulting damages.

# ▶ The Law of Property

Property law is extremely broad in scope because it covers the ownership and transfer of all kinds of real and personal property (Figure 23-4). Anything that can be owned falls into the category of property. Property may be subdivided into two major categories: Real property consists of real estate and everything permanently attached to it; personal property basically is everything else. The personal property category can be further subdivided into tangible and intangible personal property. Tangible property is all the items that have a physical existence. Automobiles, business inventory, and clothing are all tangible personal property. Intangible property consists of rights and duties; its existence may be represented by a document or by some other tangible item. For example, accounts receivable, stock in a corporation, goodwill, copyrights, patents, and trademarks are all examples of intangible personal property. Legal Encounter 23-2 discusses some lawsuits involving trademark infringement.

There are various forms of ownership of real property. The rights and duties of the owners are prescribed by the type of ownership.

## Fee-Simple Ownership

Fee-simple ownership is the absolute, unconditional owning of property. The owner has the right to keep, sell, lease, or do whatever he or she wishes to do with the property, subject only to government restrictions.

## Tenancy in Common

Parties can co-own real estate in several ways. The most common method of joint ownership of real estate is tenancy in common, which arises whenever land is transferred to more than one person without restrictions on the type of ownership interest. It is not necessary that ownership interests be equal.

**Figure 23-4**
Types of Property

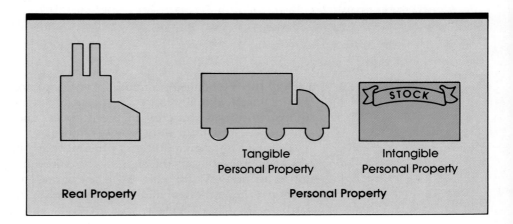

# Legal Encounter 23-2
## *Companies Defend Their Trademarks*

Occasionally, companies find it necessary to take legal action when they feel another company is infringing on their protected trademark or name. The most common trademark infringement situations occur when two products from competing companies have the same name or when one company uses another company's name as part of its own name.

Elizabeth Taylor's Passion perfume, marketed by Parfums International, quickly became one of the best-selling fragrances. The perfume was heavily marketed, and its promotion included personal appearances and television spots by the famous actress. However, Annick Goutal, Inc., of Paris had already marketed a perfume under the name Passion. Annick Goutal sued Parfums International for trademark infringement and won. As a result, Ms. Taylor's fragrance was banned from first-tier department stores such as Neiman-Marcus and Bergdorf-Goodman. The court left it up to Goutal and Parfums International to decide where Ms. Taylor's Passion may be sold. Ms. Taylor's Passion is now sold only in mass-market stores such as Macy's.

The ban was particularly significant to Parfums International because it sold Elizabeth Taylor's Passion in about eleven hundred stores while Goutal's scent had been sold in only sixteen or seventeen. Ms. Taylor's publicists placed part of the blame for the problem on the media. They said that although Parfums International marketed the fragrance as "Elizabeth Taylor's Passion," the media referred to it as "Passion."

McDonald's has also been in court several times in trademark infringement suits. In 1987, the company sued McTravel Travel Services of Chicage because it felt the "Mc" in McTravel was too closely associated with its own trademark name. McDonald's management was concerned that McTravel's name would give consumers the impression they were going to McDonald's or to a place run by McDonald's, when that wasn't the case. As a result of the still-unsettled lawsuit, McTravel toned down the use of its name in advertisements. Instead, it uses the name of its parent company, Private Label Travel.

McSleep Hotels, a divison of Maryland-based Quality International, is also fighting McDonald's. The company filed suit after receiving a letter from McDonald's asking it to use a different name. McDonald's usually sends such a letter to a company before it begins any legal action. McSleep says its name has a Scottish connotation of savings and has nothing to do with McDonald's. Nevertheless, McDonald's believes its name is infringed upon.

McDonald's and Parfums International are two companies that have been in court to protect their right to use their chosen name. A company often spends years and millions of dollars to establish a name and a reputation. If another company uses that name or part of it, the public may become confused. Further, if the infringing company engages in unethical business practices, they may permanently damage the original company's name. Thus, most companies are zealous about defending their trademarks and names.

---

These facts are from Kathleen A. Hughes, "Perfume Firms Go All Out in Effort to Lure Buyers," *The Wall Street Journal*, December 10, 1987, p. 25; Elizabeth Sporkin, "A Legal Stink over Taylor's Passion," *USA Today*, November 23, 1987, p. D1; and Diane Schneidman, "Use of 'Mc' in Front of Travel Firms' Names Leads to Lawsuits," *Marketing News*, November 20, 1987, p. 17.

Each of three tenants in common, for example, could own an undivided one-third interest, but it would also be possible for one co-tenant to own an undivided one-half interest in the property and each of the other two co-tenants one-fourth (or some other) interest.

A tenancy in common occurs when people jointly inherit real estate. Each tenant in common has the right to the undivided use and enjoyment of the entire property. If the parties cannot agree on how to manage or use the property, the real estate may be partitioned by agreement or by court order, so that each party then owns a parcel of land in fee simple. If partition is

**The Pink Panther remains.** The fact that 85% of all U.S. consumers recall the Pink Panther as Owens-Corning spokesman reinforces their decision to keep him as part of their advertising. In addition, they have become the only company to win a trademark for product color—pink, of course.

not feasible under the circumstances, and the parties cannot agree on disposition of the property, a court may order that the property be sold and the proceeds divided proportionally among the tenants in common.

## Joint Tenancy

Joint tenancy occurs when joint tenants receive the real estate in a single transaction and receive equal property interests. Upon the deaths of tenants in common, their interest in the property passes to their heirs. The death of a joint tenant, however, results in the deceased joint tenant's share passing through a right of survivorship to the other joint tenants. For this reason, joint tenancy is sometimes used to simplify the passing of ownership of the property upon the death of the owner.

## Condominium and Cooperative Ownership

A condominium is a building in which units are owned individually and common areas are owned as tenancies in common. A condominium is frequently used in conjunction with the purchase of multi-family living units or multi-unit office buildings. Each condominium owner holds title in fee simple to a particular unit of the building or development, but all condominium owners hold common-use areas such as land, parking areas, and recreation areas as tenants in common. In contrast, owners in a cooperative do not own real estate at all. Instead, a cooperative corporation owns all real estate, which is then rented to shareholders in the corporation. Both of these forms of ownership have become increasingly popular in recent years.

# ► The Law of Bankruptcy

Although few businesses and individuals intentionally default on their debts, it sometimes happens that they cannot fulfill their financial obligations. Businesses may take on too much debt to finance growth. Individuals may charge goods and services way beyond their ability to pay for them. An option of last resort in these cases is bankruptcy, or legal insolvency. Individuals or companies may ask a court of law to declare them unable to pay their debts and to release them from the obligation of repaying those debts. The debtor's assets may then be sold to pay off as much of the debt as possible. In the case of a personal bankruptcy, although the individual is released from repaying debts and can start over with a clean slate, obtaining credit after bankruptcy proceedings is very difficult.

Although the person or company in debt usually initiates bankruptcy proceedings, creditors may also initiate them. There are three basic types of bankruptcy: Chapter 7, Chapter 11, and Chapter 13.

**Chapter 7 bankruptcy** requires that the business be dissolved and its assets liquidated, or sold, to pay off the debts. Individuals declaring Chapter 7 retain a limited amount of exempt assets, the amount of which may be determined by state or federal law, at the debtor's option. Although the type and value of exempt assets varies from state to state, most states' laws allow a bankrupt individual to keep an automobile, some household goods, clothing, and furnishings and at least some of the value of the debtor's residence. All nonexempt assets must be sold to pay debts.

**Chapter 11 bankruptcy** temporarily frees a business from its financial obligations while it reorganizes and works out a payment plan with its creditors. The indebted company continues to operate its business during bankruptcy proceedings. Often, the business sells off assets and less-profitable subsidiaries to raise cash to pay off its immediate obligations. Texaco, Continental Airlines, and AM International have used Chapter 11 bankruptcy to regain control of their finances.

**Chapter 13 bankruptcy** is similar to Chapter 11 but is limited to individuals. This proceeding allows an individual to establish a three-to-five-year plan for repaying his or her debt. Under this plan, an individual ultimately may repay as little as 10 percent of his or her debt.

**Chapter 7 bankruptcy**

Requires the business to be dissolved and its assets liquidated to pay off the debts

**Chapter 11 bankruptcy**

Temporarily frees a business from its financial obligations while it reorganizes and works out a payment plan with its creditors

**Chapter 13 bankruptcy**

Allows an individual to establish a three-year plan for repaying his or her debt

# ► Laws Regulating Competition

Among the many roles filled by the government is that of a watchdog to ensure that businesses behave in accordance with the wishes of society. Congress has enacted a number of laws to regulate trade and encourage competition. Many state legislatures have enacted similar laws governing business competition within specific states.

In spite of numerous laws regulating competition among American businesses, there are still many questions about the regulation of competition.

For instance, it is difficult to decide what is an acceptable degree of competition and whether a monopoly is harmful to a particular market. In some markets, such as utilities, it is not cost-effective to have more than one competitor. For this reason, the government allows utility monoplies, although it heavily regulates them. Furthermore, the antitrust laws are often rather vague and require interpretation, which may vary from judge to judge and court to court. Thus, what one judge defines as a monopoly or trust today may be permitted by another judge a few years from now. Businesspeople need to understand what the law says on these issues and try to conduct their affairs within the bounds of these laws.

# Sherman Antitrust Act

**Sherman Antitrust Act**

A federal statute intended to break up trusts and prevent monopolies by making certain business practices illegal

The **Sherman Antitrust Act** (1890) was one of the first statutes to regulate American competition directly. At that time, a monopoly was known as a trust, and this federal statute was intended to break up trusts and prevent monopolies by making certain business practices illegal. The act declared the following practices illegal:

▶ Price fixing: Two or more businesses agree to charge a specific price for goods.
▶ Market allocation: Businesses agree to divide a market among themselves.
▶ Boycotts in restraint of trade: Businesses agree not to sell or buy from a particular business or individual

The act also gave the Department of Justice power to enforce the provisions of the act. In 1911, the Sherman Antitrust Act was used to break John D. Rockefeller's Standard Oil Trust into many smaller companies to restore competition in the oil industry. In the 1970s, it was cited by the Justice Department as a basis for breaking up AT&T.

# Clayton Act

**Clayton Act**

Outlawed price discrimination, tying agreements, binding contracts, interlocking directorates

Because the Sherman Antitrust Act was somewhat vague, the federal government was unable to use it to halt some specific monopolistic activities. Congress changed that with the **Clayton Act** (1914), which outlawed:

▶ Price discrimination: Discrimination that occurs when a producer or wholesaler charges a large business a lower price for goods than it charges smaller businesses (the Clayton Act does not cover discounts for ordering in large quantities).
▶ Tying agreements: Contracts that require buyers to buy products they do not want along with desirable products.
▶ Binding contracts: Contracts that require a buyer to purchase a product only from a specific supplier.
▶ Interlocking directorates: Directorates in which members of the board of directors of one business also serve as directors for a competing business.
▶ Community of interest: A situation that occurs when one business buys stock in a competing firm to reduce the competition between them.

# Federal Trade Commission Act

The **Federal Trade Commission Act** (1914) declared all unfair methods of competition to be illegal. The act also created the Federal Trade Commission (FTC), a five-member committee empowered to investigate illegal trade practices. The FTC enforces the Sherman Act, the Clayton Act, and the Federal Trade Commission Act. With the passage of the Wheeler-Lea Amendment (1938), the FTC also assumed the responsibility for eliminating all deceptive business practices, whether or not they restrict free trade. Under this part of the act, a seller cannot engage in any practice that is intended to fool or deceive the consumer. The Wheeler-Lea Act also covers truth in advertising.

# Robinson-Patman Act

The Clayton Act outlawed price discrimination but not quantity discounts. Many large retailers used this loophole to gain a competitive advantage over smaller stores. The **Robinson-Patman Act** (1936) outlawed price differentials that substantially weaken competition, unless the seller can justify them by showing that the actual selling costs associated with larger orders are lower. The act also outlawed promotional allowances, unless the seller offers them to both large and small retailers.

In recent years, retailers have charged manufacturers fees to make their products available in retail outlets. For example, stores imposed fees on frozen-food manufacturers who wished to get their new products on freezer shelves. The Robinson-Patman Act may be used to stop this practice. Many manufacturers are contemplating lawsuits against retailers, and if they can prove that they have been blocked from entering the market because of the fees, they may win.[5]

# Other Antitrust Legislation

The **Celler-Kefauver Act** (1950) outlawed mergers through the purchase of assets if those mergers reduced competition. Thus, when Texas Air tried to buy the assets of the bankrupt People Express Airlines in the 1980s, the Federal Trade Commission and the Justice Department did not initially approve the sale because it threatened to reduce competition. Not until Texas Air sold some of its own assets was the sale permitted.

The **Antitrust Improvements Act** (1976) strengthened earlier antitrust laws and gave the Justice Department more investigative authority. The act further allowed the FTC and the Justice Department more time to evaluate proposed mergers and allowed state attorneys general to prosecute businesses found guilty of price fixing.

# ▶ Tax Law

Although many people grumble about the amount of taxes they have to pay and the complexity of the tax forms to be filled out, virtually everyone is required to pay taxes. Tax revenues pay for national defense, social programs, and government itself. Depending on where you live, you may pay city, county, and state taxes in addition to federal taxes. The amount of taxes you pay is based on how much you earn (income tax), how much you own (property tax), and how much you buy (sales tax). The Sixteenth Amendment to the Constitution (1913) gave the federal government the authority to levy a federal income tax to raise revenue. The Tax Reform Act of 1986 greatly simplified the tax-rate structure for individuals.

The U.S. government obtains almost 95 percent of its revenue from taxes, but in the 1980s that was not enough to reduce the federal budget deficit. In fact, during 1987, the government had to borrow about $180 billion to finance the part of the budget not met by taxes.

## Corporate Income Taxes

Corporations must pay federal income tax on all their income, less allowable business expenses. This is a progressive tax, meaning that the company pays an increasing percentage of its income for taxes as its income increases. Corporations pay a federal income tax of 15 percent on the first $50,000 of pre-tax net earnings, 25 percent on the next $25,000, and 34 percent on net earnings over $75,000. There is a 39 percent tax on corporate income taxable between $100,000 and $335,000. If a corporation earns more than $335,000, it will pay federal income taxes at a flat rate of 34 percent. In addition, the stockholders in a corporation also pay a personal income tax on any dividends they receive from the corporation. Thus some corporate profits are taxed twice. Corporations are also subject to state taxes.

Some corporations, known as subchapter S corporations, pay no federal income tax at all. Instead, net earnings flow through the corporation and are taxed directly to the shareholders. Subchapter S status is chosen by the corporation and approved by the Internal Revenue Service (IRS). Usually, only corporations with relatively few shareholders may elect this tax status.

## Individual Income Taxes

As an individual, you pay a personal income tax. The personal income tax is also a progressive one. As a result of the 1986 Tax Reform Act, there are two tax rates for individuals. An unmarried individual with an income of less than $17,850 a year is taxed at a rate of 15 percent; one with an income greater than that amount is taxed at a rate of 28 percent.

Most federal income tax is withheld from your paycheck in proportion to the amount of your salary. Your employer sends the deducted amount directly to the IRS. In April of every year, you are required to fill out a tax return giving information on all your income, whether earned at work, from investments, or received as dividends from stock ownership. If you did not have enough money deducted from your paycheck, you may owe additional taxes. If you own a sole proprietorship or are a partner in a partnership, you have to withhold your own taxes and make four quarterly estimated tax payments to the IRS. Individuals also pay income taxes to the state in which they reside, if taxes are required in that state, in addition to federal income taxes.

## Other Taxes

Most states and some local governments levy a sales tax on consumer products. Thus, each time you purchase a taxable product, you pay a proportion, perhaps 5 percent, of the price in tax. The tax varies from state to state. A person buying a blouse in Macy's in New York City would pay a sales tax of 8.25 percent; a person buying the same blouse at Lord & Taylor's in Ann Arbor, Michigan, would pay 4 percent.

Sales taxes are collected by retailers, who pay the collected taxes to the appropriate government. A sales tax is a regressive tax because it assumes a greater percentage of a lower income than it does of a higher income. Although sales taxes are traditionally a revenue-raising method employed by state governments, many city and county governments are turning to small sales taxes to increase their incomes. In Texas, the state sales tax is 6 percent, and many Texas cities levy an additional 1 or 2 percent sales tax on the same items.

Local governments have traditionally raised money by means of a property tax. This tax is a percentage of the appraised value of real property, usually a home or land. Cities, counties, and special districts (such as a water conservation district, a school district, a fire district) typically state property tax in terms of so many cents per $100 of appraised value. Thus, a homeowner with a house appraised at $100,000 paying 7 cents per $100 would pay $70.00 in property tax to the appropriate government. Accordingly, a property tax is a proportional tax, meaning that the taxpayer pays a fixed percentage of the tax base (property value in this case). Legal Encounter 23-3 describes efforts in Florida to tax advertising.

## ► Regulation Versus Deregulation

The federal, state, and local governments regulate every aspect of the business world through laws and administrative regulations. Since the beginning of the twentieth century there has been a trend toward increasing regulation of more and more aspects of business, from taxes to pollution of the environment, from hiring and firing of employees to the health and safety of workers. In the 1980s, however, many people began to question the amount and cost of regulating business. Regulating business and industry costs billions of dollars (in paperwork, legal fees, employees' salaries, and so on), and because of the dramatically growing federal budget deficit, Congress wanted to reduce government expenditures.

Corporations want a reduction in regulation to eliminate the red tape and the expense of complying with regulations. Whirlpool spent $20 million in one year complying with government regulations.[6] Those in favor of deregulation point out that businesses seldom engage in the abuses that brought about regulation in the first place, such as the formation of monopolies and market allocation. Like Adam Smith in *The Wealth of Nations*, proponents of

# Legal Encounter 23-3
## *The Florida Advertising Tax*

Government laws and regulations have a significant impact on the business environment. However, businesses are not completely powerless, and they may utilize their resources to protest laws and taxes they believe unfair. In July 1987, when Florida levied a service tax that included a 5 percent tax on all advertising in the state, businesses and advertisers joined together to get the controversial tax repealed.

State officials desperately needed to raise money to meet the needs of the fastest-growing population in the nation. However, Florida's constitution prohibits a state income tax and limits property taxes, so state legislators expanded the state's 5 percent sales tax to include a wide variety of services, including pet care and advertising. State officials expected to raise about $100 million in 1988 from the advertising tax alone. Other states, including Hawaii, Iowa, New Mexico, and South Dakota, have a broad tax on services, but Florida was the first state to tax advertising.

The advertising tax covered not only Florida newspapers, magazines, billboards, direct-mail advertising, television and radio stations, and cable systems, but also national advertisers, based on the number of viewers or readers in Florida who were exposed to a national ad. The tax even covered production costs for advertising.

A study by Wharton Econometric Forecasting Advocates at the University of Pennsylvania predicted dire consequences for the state's economy if it went ahead with the tax. The study forecast that many businesses, advertisers, and media would leave Florida. The study also predicted that organizations would reduce or stop advertising and that a decrease in the production and consumption of products would result, employment and earnings would suffer, and many businesses would raise prices and fees to continue operations, passing the cost of the tax to the consumer, not to the service provider as the tax was intended to do.

Many of the Wharton study's predictions were validated. Corporations, media organizations, and advertising agencies were outraged when the tax went into effect. Several national corporations, including Procter & Gamble and Kellogg, dropped millions of dollars of Florida advertising, and many others threatened to follow suit. Others threatened to raise prices. To protest the tax, many companies and associations canceled conventions that they had scheduled in Florida. Because conventions pump billions of dollars into Florida's economy every year, the effect of the cancellations was devastating.

Although the Florida Supreme Court upheld the constitutionality of the controversial tax, major advertisers and corporations continued to campaign for its repeal. Anti-tax advertising and the complexity and confusion of administering the tax itself gradually turned public opinion against the tax. The Florida legislature repealed the tax on December 10, 1987, and voted to replace its revenue with a 1 percent increase in the state sales tax.

Florida's unhappy experience will serve as a lesson to other states considering a tax on services. Florida businesses and national advertisers used their power and marketing skills to sway public opinion against what they felt was an unfair tax. As a result, it will probably be a while before any state tries to tax advertising. However, as federal and state governments become desperate for additional revenue to meet the needs of their residents, more of them will be looking at the largely untaxed service sector as a source of money.

---

These facts are from Martha Brannigan, "Repeal of Florida 5% Service Tax Caps Controversy Other States Viewed Warily," *The Wall Street Journal*, December 11, 1987, p. 7; Jeanne DeQuine and Stephan Stern, "Fla. High Court Upholds Service Tax," *USA Today*, July 15, 1987, p. 3A; Alex Taylor III, "Why Florida Faces Tax Rebellion," *Fortune*, July 6, 1987, pp. 82–83. Joe Agnew, "Advertisers and Media Gird Against Advertising Tax," *Marketing News*, June 19, 1987, pp. 1, 20; James Cox, "State Sees Advertisers Paying $100M," *USA Today*, June 23, 1987, pp. 1B, 2B; and Sydney P. Freedberg, "Fate of Florida's Tax on Services May Make Others Go Slow," *The Wall Street Journal*, September 21, 1987, pp. 1, 8.

| Table 23.2 Laws Deregulating Various Industries | Act | Industry Deregulated |
| --- | --- | --- |
| | Staggers Rail Act (1980) | Railroads |
| | Depository Institutions Deregulation and Monetary Control Act (1980) | Banking |
| | Airline Deregulation Act | Airlines |

deregulation argue that the market will adequately regulate itself without policing from the government.

Thus, the trend toward deregulation began (Table 23-2). During the administrations of Presidents Ford, Carter, and Reagan, the federal government tried to reduce the activities of federal agencies, although with limited success. During Ronald Reagan's administration, the government revised and even revoked many regulations to reduce paperwork and the delays associated with regulations. In some cases, administrative agencies simply stopped enforcing laws that they thought should be revoked. Some industries, such as the railroad industry, are in a state of decline and may no longer require regulation. The Staggers Rail Act (1980) accordingly reduced the power of the Interstate Commerce Commission to regulate the rail industry. An increase in corporations' acceptance of their social responsibility has prompted business to continue to act in good faith even after deregulation.

Although the deregulation trend has begun, reaction to deregulation is still mixed. The public has always been wary of business and is concerned that deregulation will allow business to take advantage of consumers. Nevertheless, deregulation has saved many businesses a great deal of money, and the savings are often passed onto consumers. Deregulation of the airline industry led to price wars among the major airlines, and accordingly airline fares in the 1980s were the lowest in many years.

The future of deregulation depends on the behavior of business. If businesses behave in a socially responsible manner and continue to work to meet the needs and wants of consumers, the deregulation trend is likely to continue. However, if product safety, working conditions, and the state of the environment decline, the government may decide to reinstate regulation.

## Notes

1. "Boesky Sentenced to 3 Years," *Orlando Sentinel*, December 19, 1987, p. A-1.
2. Larry Reibstein, "Firms Face Lawsuits for Hiring People Who Then Commit Crimes," *The Wall Street Journal*, April 30, 1987.

**3.** Teri Agins, "Federal Mediators Expected to Release Pan Am, Teamsters from Contract Talks," *The Wall Street Journal*, January 11, 1988, p. 4.

**4.** John R. Emshwiller, "Car Makers Face Lawsuits Alleging Rear Seat Belts Aren't Safe Enough," *The Wall Street Journal*, January 6, 1988, p. 17.

**5.** Christin Donahue, "Pay-Offs to Supermarkets," *Adweek's Marketing Week*, January 4, 1988, p. 5.

**6.** *CORS Report: A Closer Look at the Cost of Government Regulation* (Benton Harbor, Mich.: Whirlpool Corporation, 1979).

# Summary and Review

▶ Criminal law prohibits certain activities and imposes a punishment when the law is violated. Civil law defines the rights and duties of individuals and businesses. The legal environment of business includes all laws and regulations dealing with the activities of business and the conduct of businesspeople.

▶ Business law comes from a variety of sources: the United States Constitution and state constitutions; common law; federal, state and local statutes: regulations established by administrative agencies.

▶ Businesses or individuals that believe they have been wronged may file a lawsuit in the proper court to obtain redress. Many suits are heard in a general trial court; specific types of cases may be heard in a court of limited jurisdiction. A judge or jury examines the facts of the dispute and decides which party is at fault. If one of the parties is not happy with the decision, that party may appeal the decision to a higher court, usually a court of appeal. Some cases may be appealed to the United States Supreme Court. Whether a case is heard in a state or federal court depends on how much money is involved, what laws have been violated, who is involved, and where the dispute occurred. If a dispute involves a federal constitutional issue, it should be heard in a federal court.

▶ Areas of law with which businesspeople must be familiar include sales law and the law of commercial paper, tort law, contract law, the law of agency, property law, bankruptcy law, and tax law.

▶ Businesspeople should be aware of laws promoting competition among businesses and prohibiting specific practices that are unfair or deceptive: the Sherman Antitrust Act, the Clayton Act, the Federal Trade Commission Act, the Robinson-Patman Act, and the Celler-Kefauver Act.

▶ There is a trend toward reducing the regulations businesses must follow. Businesspeople tend to believe that the forces of supply and demand adequately regulate most markets without government interference. Some industries may no longer require regulation. Furthermore, the government can no longer afford the expense of enforcing regulations, and businesses do not want to assume the expense of self-regulation. Although consumers are somewhat wary of deregulation, deregulation of certain industries, particularly the airline and banking industries, has made businesses more responsive to the needs of consumers.

# Key Terms and Concepts

| | |
|---|---|
| constitutional law | voluntary agreement |
| common law | implied contract |
| statutes | consideration |
| administrative law | contractual capacity |
| jurisdiction | breach of contract |
| tort | principal |
| product liability | agent |
| arbitration | power of attorney |
| mediation | Chapter 7 bankruptcy |
| Uniform Commercial Code | Chapter 11 bankruptcy |
| express warranty | Chapter 13 bankruptcy |
| implied warranty | Sherman Antitrust Act |
| warranty of merchantability | Clayton Act |
| commercial paper | Federal Trade Commission Act |
| negotiable instruments | Robinson-Patman Act |
| endorsement | Celler-Kefauver Act |
| contract | Antitrust Improvements Act |

# Checking Your Understanding

This chapter introduced you to the subject of the legal environment of business. To test and reinforce your understanding, fill in the blanks below.

**1.** _____ _____ is derived from judges' decisions in deciding disputes.

**2.** The legal power of a court to interpret and apply the law and to render a binding decision in a particular case is called _____ .

**3.** One _____ _____, which acts as a substitute for money, is a check.

**4.** A _____ _____ specifies who may exchange a check for cash.

**5.** A _____ is a mutual agreement between two or more people.

**6.** A _____ _____ _____ occurs when one party to a contract fails to comply with the terms of the contract.

**7.** An _____ acts on behalf of an individual or corporation to accomplish a specified task.

**8.** A _____ _____ _____ occurs when two or more people own an undivided interest, although not necessarily an equal interest, in a property.

**9.** In _____ _____ bankruptcy, a business sells all its assets to pay its debts.

**10.** A _____ _____ takes an increasing percentage of an individual's or a business' income as that income increases.

# Topics for Review and Discussion

**1.** You, a resident of Hawaii, purchased a coffee maker from Acme Coffee Makers, Inc., of Nevada. Several months later the machine catches on fire even though it was not turned on. Because you sustained several thousand dollars in damages from the fire, you decide to sue Acme for negligence in the design of the coffee maker. In what type of court will you file your suit? If you lose your suit, to what court will you appeal your case?

**2.** Explain the difference between a progressive tax and a regressive one. Explain, using examples, why a regressive tax takes a greater proportion of the income of low-income families than of high-income families.

# Exercises

**1.** Discuss the pros and cons of deregulation. Use specific industries to defend your viewpoint.

**2.** If you rent an apartment, bring your lease to class. What does the owner/manager of the apartment promise to do? What is the consideration? Where do both parties show voluntary agreement? Is the lease legal? On what legal grounds might one or both of the parties terminate the agreement? Discuss what happens if one of the parties breaks the lease.

---

## Case 23-1
### *Texaco Declares Chapter 11 Bankruptcy*

Texaco, Inc., and two of its subsidiaries filed Chapter 11 bankruptcy proceedings on April 12, 1987. Chapter 11 bankruptcy does not involve liquidation of a company's assets but instead allows a company time to develop a plan to repay its creditors. A Texas court ordered Texaco to pay $10.53 billion to Pennzoil Corporation for interfering with Pennzoil's purchase of Getty Oil. Texaco was forced to file for bankruptcy protection to prevent Pennzoil from seizing its assets while Texaco's management devised a plan for paying the judgment.

In the 1980s, Texaco was running out of oil reserves. Getty Oil had abundant oil and natural gas reserves, and ownership of Getty would have allowed Texaco to assume Getty's oil and natural gas reserves and to lower its research and development costs. In 1984, Texaco offered to buy Getty Oil's outstanding stock at $125 per share. However, Pennzoil had already made an offer of $112 a share for Getty Oil, and Getty's management had agreed "in principle" to accept Pennzoil's offer. Getty's management, however, decided Texaco's offer was better and reneged on the deal with Pennzoil. Pennzoil chairman J. Hugh Liedtke was furious and sued Texaco for interfering with its purchase of Getty Oil.

In December 1985, a Texas court ruled that Texaco had to pay Pennzoil $7.53 billion in compensatory damages and $3 billion in punitive damages for improperly interfering with Pennzoil's purchase of Getty Oil. In January 1986, Texaco got a federal injunction that ruled that Texaco did not have to obtain a $12 billion bond while it appealed the judgment to the Texas Court of Appeals. That court upheld the judgment in February 1987. In April 1987, the U.S. Supreme Court overturned the federal injunction and required that Texaco post a $12 billion bond or else Pennzoil would have the right to begin seizure of Texaco's assets. Texaco chairman James W. Kinnear feared that Texaco could not afford to pay that amount without jeopardizing its operations and filed for bankruptcy on April 12.

Under Chapter 11 bankruptcy proceedings, Texaco was required to file a reorganization plan that provided for paying off its creditors, including Pennzoil. That reorganization plan had to be approved by at least two-thirds of the company's stockholders and by the federal bankruptcy court judge. While Texaco's financial executives were devising the reorganization plan, Chairman Kinnear spent the rest of 1987 trying to negotiate a reduced settlement with Pennzoil's Liedtke. The companies were unable to compromise until financier Carl Icahn (who had acquired 12 percent of Texaco's stock in November 1987) stepped in to facilitate negotiations between Kinnear and Liedtke. In December, through Icahn's cajoling, Pennzoil agreed to settle its claim to Texaco's assets for $3 billion instead of the $11 billion (the original settlement plus interest) required by the court.

Texaco then filed its reorganization plan, which included provisions for payment of the $3 billion to Pennzoil. In March 1988, 96 percent of Texaco's stockholders approved the reorganization plan. The plan was then filed with the bankurptcy court for approval by the presiding judge. Judge Howard Schwartzberg approved the reorganization plan on March 24, 1988, permitting Texaco to emerge from Chapter 11 bankruptcy on April 7, 1988.

Texaco obtained a $3 billion line of credit so that it could make the payment to Pennzoil's bank by April 7, 1988. The company will probably sell some of its assets to repay the $3 billion loan. Chairman Kinnear says the company will be restructured to become a leaner, more efficient organization able to be more responsive to the volatility of the oil and gas industry. Texaco has also boosted its exploration and production efforts. The company may sell some of its refining and marketing divisions to finance its payments to its creditors and its increased oil exploration efforts. It may also engage in more joint ventures with other oil companies and other nations. There is also some speculation that Texaco may be sold, although Chairman Kinnear says the company is not for sale.

Texaco was not "broke" when it filed Chapter 11 bankruptcy proceedings, but payment of the $11 billion judgment to Pennzoil would have jeopardized the company's ability to conduct business. Texaco's management saw bankruptcy proceedings as a way to buy their company some breathing room while they devised a plan for settling the company's debts. Other companies—Continental Airlines, Manville Corporation, and Wilson Foods, for example—filed for Chapter 11 protection for similar reasons in the 1980s.

---

These facts are from Allanna Sullivan, "Texaco's War with Pennzoil Ends Officially," *The Wall Street Journal*, March 24, 1988, pp. 3, 6; Allanna Sullivan and Thomas Petzinger, Jr., "Giant Steps: Settlement Achieved, Texaco and Pennzoil Face New Challenges," *The Wall Street Journal*, December 21, 1987, pp. 1, 10; David Landis, "Finale for Dispute Still Long Way Off," *USA Today*, December 14, 1987, pp. 1, 2B.

### Questions

1. How many different types of laws can you identify that apply to the Texaco case?
2. How did Texaco use the bankruptcy laws to its advantage and which bankruptcy law did it use?
3. What might have happened if Texaco did not declare bankruptcy?

## Case 23-2

# *R. Foster Winans Goes to Prison for Insider Trading*

In the 1980s, insider trading—investing in publicly traded stocks on the basis of illegally obtained, or "inside," information—greatly undermined public confidence in the American financial community. Many scandals received publicity in the business press, and the reputations of many respected investment firms were tarnished as the Securities and Exchange Commission (SEC) investigated incident after incident. One such case helped the SEC define more broadly what constitutes insider trading, although many are still unclear about what insider trading is and who may be an inside trader.

In 1981, R. Foster Winans joined *The Wall Street Journal* as a reporter. In 1982, he became one of two writers of the daily "Heard on the Street" column, which provides information, including opportunities and warnings, about the fate of specific industries or companies. A reporter like Winans could write that a certain company may not have a profitable year, and that prediction could result in a reduction of the company's stock price the next day.

In 1983, Winans and David Carpenter gave Kidder Peabody brokers Peter Brant and Kenneth B. Felis advance information about "Heard on the Street" topics. The brokers used this information to buy or sell stocks in advance of the column's appearance in the *Journal*. In late 1983 and early 1984, the brokers made pre-publication trades based on twenty-seven columns, earning approximately $690,000 in profits. In November 1983, Kidder Peabody management noted a correlation between "Heard on the Street" columns and trading in the Brant and Felis accounts. A Securities and Exchange Commission investigation began shortly afterward.

At first, Brant, Felis, and Winans denied any wrongdoing. In March 1984, Winans and Carpenter went to the Securities and Exchange Commission and admitted their part of the scheme to use "Heard on the Street" insider information for a profit. Because the Securities and Exchange laws on insider trading are somewhat vague, the federal government used mail- and wire-fraud laws to convict Winans, Carpenter, and Felis.

The Securities and Exchange Commission has argued that anyone who uses private corporate information with a goal of profiting in stock transactions before the public hears the news should be guilty of inside trading. The Winans case raises questions about insider-trading laws because the information Winans passed on was not corporate inside information, and he was not a true insider. Winans maintained that he did not defraud *The Wall Street Journal*. He believed that he violated only work-place rules. The court, however, ruled that Winans violated his obligation to protect his employers' confidential information and exploited that information for his own personal benefit. In short, he conspired to make stock trades based on *The Wall Street Journal's* confidential information.

The court sentenced Winans to eighteen months in jail on the grounds that he violated securities laws by trading on information misappropriated from the *Journal*, in violation of the business journal's conflict-of-interest policy. In November 1987, Winans appealed the case in the United States Supreme Court; the judges ruled unanimously that Winans, Carpenter, and Felis violated wire- and mail-fraud laws when they profited from trading based on the advance knowledge of Winans' "Heard on the Street" column. The mail- and wire-fraud charges were the key to the criminal proceedings that resulted in the jail term.

On the other hand, the Supreme Court split 4 to 4 (one Supreme Court seat was vacant at the time) on whether Winans and the others violated securities laws based on misappropriation of confidential "corporate" information. This left a key issue unsettled: the validity of the Securities and Exchange Commission's so-called misappropriation theory, which defines what constitutes insider trading. Thus, the definition of insider trading is still vague. Many members of the financial community hope Congress will write a specific definition of insider trading. Until Congress does that, mail and wire fraud will be the keys to criminal prosecution in insider-trading cases.

---

These facts are from Ann Kates and Daniel Kadlec, "Decision Emboldens Prosecutors," *USA Today*, November 17, 1987, p. 1; Catherine Yang, "Commentary: Insider Trading: The High Court Hasn't Ended the Confusion," *Business Week*, November 30, 1987, p. 34; Gary Weiss, "Commentary: The SEC Isn't Clearing Up Anything," *Business Week*, August 24, 1987, p. 22; and William Schreyer, "Ethics in Wall Street," *American Way*, September 1, 1987, p. 12.

**Questions**

1. How did the Winans case increase the understanding of the legal definition of inside trading?
2. What set of laws covers the concept of insider trading?
3. Which laws were actually used to convict Foster Winans?

# Answers to Checking Your Understanding

1. common law
2. jurisdiction
3. negotiable instrument
4. special endorsement
5. contract
6. breach of contract
7. agent
8. tenancy in common
9. chapter 7
10. progressive tax

# Careers in Management

All organizations need managers to plan, organize, staff, direct, and control organizational resources so that the organization can achieve its objectives. All managers must possess certain skills—leadership, technical skills, conceptual skills, human relations skills, and inferential skills—so that they can lead the organization toward those objectives. Some organizations need only one manager (perhaps the owner), but large corporations may need hundreds of upper, middle, and first-line managers. As a result, there are many possible careers in the field of management.

Managerial jobs will open up faster than other jobs through the year 1995. In fact, the U.S. Department of Labor predicts there will be 1.3 million managerial job openings in the 1990s. Some industries will need more managers than others. Health care managers and administrators, in particular, will be in demand well into the twenty-first century as the world's population ages. Managers in service-related industries (information, finance, and food services) will also be in great demand; these are the fastest-growing jobs in the economy. Managers in education (principals and assistants), however, will be in less demand because the rate of population growth is slowing.

Despite the fact that the outlook for managerial jobs is very good, competition for middle-management jobs in the next decade will be intense after the wave of company restructurings in the last half of the 1980s. Many companies eliminated several layers of middle management to save costs; those jobs will never be replaced. The middle managers who lost those jobs are now competing with recent college graduates for management positions. The merging of many large companies in the 1980s is also responsible for the loss of many middle-management jobs. Nevertheless, managers with exceptional human relations and technical skills will be in great demand at all three levels of management.

Managers in all industries in the 1990s need to develop expertise in several new areas as the nature of the marketplace changes. In the past, technological developments occurred slowly, but in the 1990s, technological changes will be evolving constantly. As a result, managers need to be masters of technology. Computer skills are a must for those seeking careers in management. Computers now give managers access to a tremendous amount of information, information that is necessary for an organization to be competitive. Managers can use computers to reduce paperwork, process information, develop products and services, and design production facilities. Managers must learn how to harness technology, particularly the power of computers, to stay ahead of competitors.

Managers in the 1990s need to be global strategists, too. International trade increased dramatically in the last decade, and as a result, the most successful businesses of the 1990s will be those that can develop products and services for the global marketplace, not just the United States. Managers who can develop, adapt, and manage products for international markets will be the most successful and in greatest demand. Managers, therefore, need to have an understanding of not only foreign languages, but also foreign cultures.

The globalization of the marketplace means that managers must also be politicians. Managers must learn to deal with complex international trade laws and regulations and the social aspects of different cultures. Managers must learn to deal diplomatically with managers and officials from other nations as well as communicate their objectives to other managers and employees in the United States.

Finally, managers in the 1990s must hone old-fashioned leadership skills to guide their companies through times of change. Some experts suggest that the manager of the 1990s will be more of a coach than a commander of the company's employees. Managers need to motivate employees to increase productivity and encourage employees' input and ideas. Employee involvement in an organization not only boosts morale, but also generates ideas for new products and services and ultimately increases profits. Effective management of people may be one area in which a company can make dramatic productivity increases and cost decreases.

Career opportunities in management can be broken down into five distinct areas: administration, human resources, production and operations, marketing, and finance. Here is a sampling of management careers in the areas of administration, human resources, and production and operations management.

/ / / / / / / / / / / /

## Human Resources Management

Human resources managers are involved in activities designed to ensure that an organization has employees in sufficient quantity and of sufficient quality so that the organization may achieve its objectives. Human resources managers develop systems for recruiting, selecting, and hiring employees; develop and implement employee benefit programs; develop and maintain training programs; develop and maintain performance appraisal programs; and ensure that an organization abides by legal regulations concerning employment practices. Personnel manager, compensation analyst, affirmative action officer, and labor-relations specialist are possible careers in human resources management.

| Position Title | Job Description | Educational Requirements | Salary Range |
|---|---|---|---|
| Personnel manager | Develops job descriptions. Develops recruiting campaigns. Interviews applicants and assesses their qualifications. Hires employees who meet the needs of the organization | Bachelor's degree required; degree in human resources preferred | $25,000–$50,000 |
| Compensation analyst | Assesses job descriptions. Designs organization chart. Studies salary and wage levels for the industry and for specific jobs. Sets dollar salary and wage levels for jobs within the organization | Bachelor's degree required; background in finance helpful | $20,000–$50,000 |
| Affirmative action officer | Studies federal and state regulations affecting hiring and compensating employees. Ensures that the organization's policies are in compliance with these laws. Handles complaints regarding discriminatory practices | Bachelor's degree required; background in law helpful | $20,000–$40,000 |
| Labor-relations specialist | Studies labor law, collective bargaining, and contract negotiations. Conducts contract negotiations. Administers labor contracts. Handles grievances | Bachelor's degree required, usually in human resources management or labor law | $25,000–$50,000 |

/ / / / / / / / / / / /

## Administrative Management

Administrative managers are also called administrators and general managers. Administrative managers may manage an entire business or a single department. They do not specialize in a particular area but instead provide overall direction for an organization or department. They coordinate and direct the activities of specialized managers to ensure that the organization reaches its objectives. Health-services administrators, school principals, and office managers are a few of the careers possible in administrative management.

| Position Title | Job Description | Educational Requirements | Salary Range |
|---|---|---|---|
| Health-services administrator | Plans, organizes, staffs, directs, and controls hospitals, HMOs, nursing homes, and clinics | Master's degree usually required, such as a master's in health administration | $50,000–$125,000 |
| School principal | Plans, organizes, staffs, directs, and controls educational institutions | Master's degree usually required; must have certificate of school administration | $25,000–$60,000 |
| Office manager | Organizes, directs, and controls secretarial staff. Facilitates communications among office workers and others in the organization | Secretarial experience; some jobs may require a two-year college or a bachelor's degree | $20,000–$40,000 |

/  /  /  /  /  /  /  /  /  /  /  /

## Production and Operations Management

Production and operations managers are involved in the actual transformation of an organization's resources into goods and services. These managers plan and design production facilities, plan the capacity of those facilities, plan the degree of automation in the production process, plan the output of production to meet anticipated demand, purchase raw materials and supplies, control inventory, schedule, and control quality. Foreman, inventory manager, and quality inspector are a few of the possibilities for careers in production and operations management.

| Position Title | Job Description | Educational Requirements | Salary Range |
|---|---|---|---|
| Foreman | Motivates blue-collar workers. Meets production goals and schedules. Ensures that safety rules are observed | On-the-job experience; junior-college or bachelor's degree helpful | $15,000–$30,000 |
| Inventory manager | Maintains an adequate supply of raw materials, supplies, and equipment to produce goods. Minimizes inventory storage costs. Minimizes lead time | Bachelor's degree required; some jobs require an M.B.A.; production experience helpful | $20,000–$50,000 |
| Quality inspector | Inspects finished goods for compliance with quality standards. Directs flawed products to proper service area | On-the-job training; bachelor's degree in engineering helpful | $20,000–$50,000 |

Source: U.S. Department of Labor, Bureau of Labor Statistics, *Occupational Outlook Handbook, 1986–1987*, pp. 23; Clemens P. Work, with Beth Brophy, Andrea Gabor, Mike Tharp, Alice Z. Cuneo, "The 21st Century Executive," *U.S. News & World Report*, March 7, 1988, pp. 48–51; Tom Jackson, "Living & Working in the 1990s," *Business Week's Guide to Careers* 5 (September 1987): 94, 96, 98; Bob Weinstein, "What I Do on the Job: Human Resource Manager," *Business Week's Guide to Careers* 4 (March 1986): 32–33; and Nicholas Basta, "Inventory and Distribution," *Business Week's Guide to Careers* 3 (Spring–Summer 1985): 23.

# Careers in Marketing

All organizations need people to perform marketing activities. Businesses need people with marketing skills, but so do nonbusiness organizations such as hospitals, the U.S. Postal Service, and religious organizations. All marketers must possess certain skills—the ability to do their part in implementing marketing plans and technical competency to recognize customer's needs and satisfy them with their firm's products. Most marketers also need the management skills discussed in the Careers in Management appendix.

For the 1990s, marketing provides one of the brightest career paths for rapid advancement in business. Whether in manufacturing industries, financial services, health care, or professional services, companies will pay high salaries to people who can work to develop new products, use marketing research to stay on the top of emerging trends, and in general create sales. The 1988 College Placement Council Salary Survey estimates the average starting salary in marketing for a Bachelor's-level degree is $20,844. Entry-level marketing position salaries have increased about 6 percent annually over the past ten years.

Marketers in the 1990s will have many opportunities for jobs in the service industries as well as for marketing advanced-technology products. The Bureau of Labor Statistics estimates that only about 6 percent of the jobs the economy creates between now and the year 2000 will be in high-tech industries. On the other hand, the application of advanced-technology products will have a major impact on the rest of the economy. John Stodden, in the 1988 edition of *Business Week Careers' How to Get a Job Guide*, rated technical sales as the best career opportunity for the 1990s. Other experts rank retailing as one of the top ten industries for the future.

Broad areas of career opportunity in marketing include marketing research, sales, purchasing, advertising, retailing, and direct marketing. With between one-fourth and one-third of the civilian work force in the United States employed in marketing-related jobs, it is clear that marketing offers many diverse career opportunities.

## Marketing Research

Marketing researchers gather and analyze data relating to specific problems. Marketing research firms are usually employed by a client organization that is contracting to purchase marketing research services. The services include product testing, package testing, advertising testing, test-market research, and new-product research.

A researcher may be involved in one or several stages of research, depending on the size of the project, the organization of the research unit, and the researcher's experience. Marketing research trainees in large organizations usually perform a considerable amount of clerical work, such as compiling secondary data from a firms' accounting and sales records and from periodicals, government publications, syndicated data services, and unpublished sources. A junior analyst may edit and code questionnaires or tabulate survey results. Trainees also may participate in the gathering of primary data by learning to conduct mail and telephone surveys, conducting personal interviews, and employing observational methods of primary data collection. As a marketing researcher gains experience, he or she may become involved in defining problems and developing hypotheses; designing research procedures; and analyzing, interpreting, and reporting findings. Exceptional personnel may assume responsibility for entire research projects.

The three major career paths in marketing research are with independent marketing research agencies and data suppliers, the marketing research departments of advertising agencies, and marketing research departments in businesses. In a company where marketing research plays a key role, the researcher is often a member of the marketing strategy team. In marketing research agencies, one deals with many clients, products, and problems. Advertising agencies use research as an ingredient in developing and refining campaigns for existing or potential clients.

| Position Title | Job Description | Educational Requirements | Salary Range |
|---|---|---|---|
| Marketing research trainee | Compiles secondary data from a firm's accounting and sales records, periodicals, syndicated data services, and unpublished sources. Involvement in editing and coding questionnaires or tabulating survey results. Primary data collection and interviewing | Bachelor's degree in general business administration or social science | $20,000–$25,000 |
| Marketing research director | Defines marketing problems, develops hypothesis, and designs research procedures. Analyzes, interprets, and reports research findings | M.B.A. or a bachelor's degree plus experience | $35,000–$60,000 |
| Survey coordinator | Implements survey sampling design. Hires interviewers or manages subcontractors that conduct interviews. | Bachelor's degree in business administration or social science or a two-year degree plus experience | $15,000–$25,000 |

## Sales

Personal selling offers more employment opportunities than any other area of marketing. Personal selling usually involves informing customers and persuading them to purchase products through personal communication. Individual selling jobs vary enormously with respect to the type of businesses and products involved and the educational background and skills required. The specific activities performed by sales personnel are very diverse. Some sales jobs focus more on communication and education than on closing the sale. Other sales positions focus on persuading the customer to purchase and on closing the sale. Because the work is so varied, sales occupations offer many career opportunities for people with a wide range of qualifications, interests, and goals. Some of the highest-paying jobs in marketing are in sales.

Several personal characteristics are important to a successful career in sales. Empathy, the ability to understand what someone else is thinking and feeling, is a necessity, as is the ability to accept rejection and to develop personal coping strategies. Perseverance—the ability to see "no" as a rejection of your product and not of yourself—is also necessary. A successful salesperson is not tortured by self-doubt every time his or her product is rejected.

A salesperson often must educate the buyer about various options and technologies. Thus salespeople are most likely to be successful if they are selling a product they are interested in or believe in. People interested in a career in sales need to determine the type of activities that they most like. Some people enjoy using computers and crunching numbers; others are at their best interacting with other people. The point is that individuals considering a career in sales need to select a product that suits their interests, style, and personality.

| Position Title | Job Description | Educational Requirements | Salary Range |
|---|---|---|---|
| Sales trainee | Entry-level sales position that normally involves direct selling to customers | Bachelor's degree in liberal arts or business or two-year degree in sales | $16,000–$30,000 |
| Wholesale sales representative | Plans and negotiates transactions with retailers and producers. Assists customers with sales, advertising, sales promotion and publicity. Handles transportation and storage activities. Provides customers with inventory control and technical, management, and merchandising assistance | Bachelor's degree in business administration or in a field related to the industry or a two-year degree plus sales experience | Commission oriented; $35,000–$50,000 |
| Manufacturer's sales representative | Sells the firm's products to wholesalers, retailers, and industrial buyers; performs the same activities as the wholesale sales representative | Bachelor's degree in business or liberal arts or a two-year degree plus sales experience | $30,000–$50,000 |

/ / / / / / / / / / / /

# Purchasing

Buyers, or purchasing agents, are responsible for maintaining an adequate supply of the goods and services that an organization needs. Industrial buyers purchase all items needed for the production of other products and for day-to-day operations. Industrial buyers in large firms often specialize in a single, specific class of products such as computers and communication equipment. Purchasing career opportunities also exist in service companies and in nonprofit organizations such as schools and hospitals as well as in government.

Purchasing agents try to make objective and rational decisions. If products are standardized, price is a key consideration. Suppliers may bid on large orders. At other times, the need for specialized equipment may require the purchasing agent to work with manufacturers to obtain items made to specifications.

| Position Title | Job Description | Educational Requirements | Salary Range |
|---|---|---|---|
| Purchasing agent for a manufacturing firm | Secures materials necessary to produce or assist in the production of the company's products. Selects suppliers who offer the best value in quality, service, and price | Bachelor's degree in business administration, engineering, science, or technical areas | $35,000–$60,000 |
| Purchasing agent for a service company | Secures products necessary for the firm to provide its services | Bachelor's degree in liberal arts, business administration, or technical area | $20,000–$50,000 |
| Procurement administrator | Secures products for nonprofit organizations such as schools, hospitals, and government agencies | Bachelor's degree in liberal arts, business administration, or technical area | $20,000–$50,000 |

/ / / / / / / / / / / /

# Advertising

Advertising needs individuals with diverse skills to fill a variety of jobs. Creative imagination, artistic talent, and expertise in expression and persuasion are important to copywriters, artists, and account executives. Interpersonal skills and managerial ability are vital to the success of advertising account managers, media buyers, and production managers. Research directors must have a solid understanding of research techniques and consumer behavior.

Advertising agencies often perform advertising activities for companies. Account executives are the link between the client and the ad agency. The account executive explains the client's needs to the agency's creative group, which produces the final advertising. The account executive coordinates the activities of the agency staff to develop an effective advertising campaign.

A variety of organizations employ advertising personnel. Although advertising agencies are perhaps the most visible and glamorous of employers, many manufacturing firms, retail stores, banks, utility companies, and professional and trade associations maintain advertising departments. Advertising jobs also can be found with television and radio stations, newspapers, and magazines. Other businesses that employ advertising personnel include printers, art studios, letter shops, and package-design firms.

| Position Title | Job Description | Educational Requirements | Salary Range |
|---|---|---|---|
| Account coordinator | Assists the account executive in handling promotional activities, product/competitor research, and other projects as needed | Bachelor's degree in liberal arts, communications, journalism, marketing, advertising, or business administration; some two-year-degree opportunities exist | $12,000–$20,000 |
| Account executive | Handles day-to-day activities on accounts: promotions, sales analysis, client interaction. Responsible for long-term planning activities. | Bachelor's degree in liberal arts, marketing, or business administration; M.B.A. desired in largest agencies | $20,000–$40,000 |
| Account supervisor | Manages all aspects of handling a particular account: media, accounting, creative development, account executives, suppliers, and the client | Bachelor's degree in liberal arts, marketing, advertising; master's degree helpful | $35,000–$65,000 |

# Direct Marketing

Direct marketing involves activities in which the seller uses telephone, mail, print, or television to solicit a response. For example, Shell Oil uses its credit-card billings (direct mail) to sell a variety of consumer products; L. L. Bean sells products through its catalog.

The telephone is a major vehicle for selling many consumer products, such as magazines and newspapers. Telemarketing involves direct selling to customers using a variety of technological improvements in telephone services and is estimated to be a hundred-billion-dollars-a-year industry. Most telemarketing sales come from businesses selling to other businesses, not from telephone calls to consumers at home.

The most important asset to develop in direct marketing is experience. An entry-level position in direct marketing is a steppingstone toward career advancement.

| Position Title | Job Description | Educational Requirements | Salary Range |
|---|---|---|---|
| Telemarketing co-ordinator | Manages the solicitation of sales through the telephone | Bachelor's degree in communication, business administration, or liberal arts; experience most important | $15,000–$30,000 |
| Catalog manager | Develops marketing strategies and selects and acquires products for mail-order catalogs | Bachelor's degree in liberal arts or business administration; experience most important | $20,000–$40,000 |
| Fund-raising manager | Directs marketing efforts to obtain financial support for nonprofit organizations | Bachelor's degree in liberal arts or business administration; experience most important | $20,000–$50,000 |

/ / / / / / / / / / / /

## Retailing

There are career opportunities in retailing that are typical of jobs found in any service organization. There are ample opportunities for management positions. Besides managing salespeople, retailers select and order merchandise and focus on promotional activities, inventory control, customer credit operations, accounting, personnel, and store security.

In large department stores, retail management personnel rarely get involved with actually selling to customers; these duties are performed by retail sales people. Large retail stores offer a variety of management positions: assistant buyers, buyers, department managers, section managers, store managers, division managers, regional managers,

and vice president of merchandising. Small retail organizations may require management personnel to perform selling activities as well as most of the other activities in marketing.

In the past, retail managers began their careers as salesclerks, and there are still opportunities for advancement from the salesclerk position, especially in small stores. Today, many large retailers hire college-educated people, put them through management training programs, and then move them directly into management positions. Salaries have increased as retailers have recognized the importance of developing well-trained, competent managers.

| Position Title | Job Description | Educational Requirements | Salary Range |
|---|---|---|---|
| Department manager | Responsible for running a specific sales area: customer service, supervision of salespeople, merchandising, and inventory control. Responsible for achieving departmental sales and profit goals | Bachelor's degree in liberal arts, business administration, marketing, fashion merchandising, or home economics | $20,000–$40,000 |

| | | | |
|---|---|---|---|
| Buyer | Responsible for sales and profits of a specific merchandise category: planning, pricing, and promotion. Extensive travel to select merchandise in the United States and abroad | Bachelor's degree in liberal arts, business administration, marketing, fashion merchandising, or home economics | $20,000–$40,000 |
| Store manager | Total responsibility for sales management, profitability, merchandise presentation, sales promotion, and personnel. The company's direct representative with customers | Bachelor's degree in liberal arts, business administration, or marketing; M.B.A. helpful | $20,000–$60,000 or more |

Source: William M. Pride and O. C. Ferrell, *Marketing: Basic Concepts and Decisions* (Boston: Houghton Mifflin, 1989); *CPC Annual, 1987–1988*, p. 44; John Stodden, "The Best Careers for the 90s," *Business Week Careers' How to Get a Job Guide*, 1988 ed., pp. 4–7; Steven S. Ross, "10 Top Industries for the Future," *Business Week Careers* (Spring–Summer 1987), pp. 21–24; Judith D. Schwartz, "Are You Psyched for Sales?" *Business Week Careers* (Spring–Summer 1988), pp. 30–33.

# Careers in Finance

Knowledge, experience, and judgment can be applied to a wide variety of positions involving finance. Even nonprofit private and government agencies have positions that involve money management, and these organizations also require the skills and abilities of finance people.

A knowledge of computers is becoming increasingly important in finance. And, because computers enable people to store, manage, and understand large amounts of financial and statistical information, computer skills and the ability to work with computer applications such as spreadsheet programs and statistical analysis packages are becoming vital elements of an education in finance. Professional workers are almost always managers of information, and the ability to utilize the most important tool of information management—the computer—will be an essential skill in the field of finance.

In addition, because virtually all finance careers will require some interaction with other areas of business, an understanding of those areas is important for the development of an effective working relationship. For example, a stock brokerage firm must market its services to potential customers; thus both marketing and finance will be important in the brokerage field.

An appreciation of the human skills of management is also an essential element of success in the field of finance (and in fact, in any other business field as well). Businesspeople need to understand the concepts of motivation, communication, persuasion, and negotiation—that understanding is not limited to any particular field but is applicable to all. The social sciences and the liberal arts have many valuable insights to contribute to the understanding of human behavior, and increasingly the emphasis in business is shifting from a concentration on quantitative information to a more broadly based view that emphasizes the human relationships that make up a business organization.

Careers in finance can be broken down into three distinct areas: financial management, accounting, and economics.

## Financial Management

Financial management involves efficiently managing funds for individuals, businesses, and other organizations. Although all areas of financial management require basic financial and management skills, there are many diverse areas of financial management in which one can find employment opportunities. Following is a small sampling of the many career opportunities available in the areas of corporate finance, insurance and risk management, investments, and financial institution management.

| Position Title | Job Description | Educational Requirements | Salary Range |
| --- | --- | --- | --- |
| Corporate financial analyst | Monitors a firm's financial position, its future funding needs, and its financial performance. | Bachelor's degree required. M.B.A. often required, may be helpful. Accounting skills a must | $17,000–$25,000 |
| Credit analyst/ credit officer | Analyzes customer requests of credit; approves or disapproves request according to internal guidelines. | Two-year college or bachelor's degree required; accounting skills necessary | $17,000–$25,000 |
| Insurance sales agent | Sells insurance policies to individuals, businesses and other organizations as an agent for one or more companies. May also provide consulting or planning services to clients. | Two-year college or bachelor's degree often required. Training programs often required | $15,000–$30,000 |

| | | | |
|---|---|---|---|
| Actuary | Collects and analyzes statistics about the probability of insured risks actually occurring. Uses actuarial analysis and conclusions to determine the cost of insurance premiums. | Bachelor's degree in mathematics with strong emphasis on statistics required | $25,000–$50,000 |
| Retail stockbroker/ securities sales | Handles orders to buy and sell securities. Advises customers on securities sales and purchases. May provide financial planning services to individuals. May specialize in selling to a particular group of customers. | Two-year college degree required. Bachelor's degree often required. Additional training programs and licensing may be required by employers or federal regulations | $25,000–$40,000 |
| Financial planner | Assists individuals in planning and managing incomes, taxes, investments, real estate, and estate-planning needs. May be self-employed or work for large financial planning firms, accounting firms, or financial institutions. | Vary widely. Most positions require at least a two-year college degree. A bachelor's degree and additional training and certification are helpful. | $17,000–$22,000 |
| Bank teller | Processes customer withdrawals, deposits, and other transactions. Some specialized positions available—such as note tellers. | High-school diploma required. Some two-year colleges offer training programs and certification | $14,000–$18,000 |
| Loan officer | Analyzes applications for commercial, mortgage, and personal loans, and analyzes applicant characteristics. Determines eligibility for loans up to limits allowed by organization's policy. May also examine the collateral offered for a loan. | Bachelor's degree required. Strong accounting skills usually required for commercial and some mortgage loan jobs. M.B.A. may be required. | $22,000–$30,000 |

## Accounting

The field of accounting has become more challenging as government regulations have required accountants to provide more and more information and to interpret this information in order to make it understandable to users. In addition, many users of accounting information are demanding that accountants make their information clearer and easier to understand and use.

There are three broadly defined subfields of accounting: public accounting, managerial accounting, and government accounting. Each requires a reasonable degree of mathematical ability, and computer literacy is frequently a professional requirement for a career in accounting. Accountants may receive certification as a Certified Public Accountant (CPA) or Certified Management Accountant (CMA). Here is a sampling of some of the careers possible in all three areas of accounting.

| Position Title | Job Description | Educational Requirements | Salary Range |
|---|---|---|---|
| Junior public accountant | Reviews and examines clients' financial records. Performs transactions tests to check the accuracy of information. Studies tax and reporting laws applicable to clients. Conducts auditing procedures under the direction of an audit manager. Does background research. | Bachelor's degree in accounting required | $25,000–$35,000 |

| Junior public auditor | Analyzes and verifies the accuracy of accounting records. Prepares reports of accuracy and compliance with accounting standards. Conducts auditing procedures. | Requires a bachelor's degree in accounting, with knowledge of law and statistics | $25,000–$35,000 |
| Budget clerk/ analyst | Prepares budgets for departments, divisions, or a company. Analyzes budgets over time to verify that they are being followed. Initiates reports when variations exist. | Two-year college or bachelor's degree required | $22,000–$28,000 |
| Internal tax accountant | Assists financial managers and senior tax accountants in preparing tax returns and weekly or monthly tax reports. | Requires bachelor's degree in accounting | $25,000–$40,000 |
| Government financial analyst | Examines and analyzes budget requests, expenditure and revenue forecasts, and cost data submitted by government agencies and departments. | Requires bachelor's degree in accounting | $18,000–$28,000 |
| Tax return examiner | Examines the tax returns filed by firms and individuals for compliance with tax laws and regulations. Prepares reports of noncompliance as needed. | Requires bachelor's degree in accounting plus computer and statistics skills | $25,000–$35,000 |

✒ ✒ ✒ ✒ ✒ ✒ ✒ ✒ ✒ ✒ ✒ ✒

## Economics

Economics is a fascinating and challenging field, but the job prospects for a student with a degree in economics depend strongly on the student's choice of a minor field and on the types of courses taken within the student's economics major. A bachelor's degree in economics can also provide an excellent foundation for continuing one's education as career interests are altered or sharpened with the passage of time. The study of economics can make the study of advanced fields a great deal more understandable.

Career opportunities for economists are divided into two areas: business and government. Following is a selection of possible career choices from both areas.

| Position Title | Job Description | Educational Requirements | Salary Range |
|---|---|---|---|
| Economic analyst | Varies by type of firm. Many analysts keep track of relationships between two or more series of data to develop predictive models. Others assist senior analysts in the preparation of reports on the impact of economic changes on a firm's operations. Others examine price and cost data to enable a firm to price its products appropriately and to react to changes in competitors' prices | Requires bachelor's degree in economics | $15,000–$25,000 |
| Forecasting staff | Prepares forecasts of costs, sales, revenues, and any other macro-economic or microeconomic variables requested by management. Keeps track of current economic activity to predict affects on the firm's operations. Maintains statistical files and data bases. Assists senior staff in developing and testing new and more accurate forecasting methods. | Requires bachelor's degree in economics, plus computer and statistical analysis skills | $20,000–$30,000 |

| | | | |
|---|---|---|---|
| Government economic forecaster | Predicts future values of economic variables. Develops and maintains files of data. Assists senior economists in developing and testing models for prediction and analysis purposes. Assists in preparing regular and occasional reports of economic events. | Requires bachelor's degree in economics, plus strong math and computer skills | $20,000–$30,000 |
| Economic development staff | Primarily at the state or local level. Assists policy makers and political leaders in creating or modifying economic conditions so that economic growth is encouraged. Analyzes the effects of specific policy recommendations on the rate of local or state economic growth. | Requires bachelor's degree in economics | $18,000–$28,000 |

Students interested in more detailed information, additional career opportunities, and salary information can refer to *The Occupational Outlook Handbook*, published annually by the U.S. Department of Labor, and various financial journals and career-information magazines.

# Glossary

## A

**ABC inventory classification system** A system that helps managers control inventory items by dividing them into three classes. (Ch. 11)

**Accommodation strategy** When a business assumes responsibility for its actions. (Ch. 3)

**Accountability** Employers are answerable to a superior for the outcome of a project. (Ch. 7)

**Accounting** The language business uses to record, measure, and interpret financial transactions. (Ch. 17)

**Accounts payable** Amounts owed on an open account with a company's suppliers. (Ch. 17)

**Accounts receivable** Money owed the company by customers. (Ch. 17)

**Accrued expense** Generated when a financial service has been provided or an obligation incurred by the company but payment has not yet taken place. (Ch. 17)

**Accumulated depreciation** The sum of all depreciation charges on currently owned assets. (Ch. 17)

**Active Corps of Executives (ACE)** A volunteer agency funded by the SBA to provide advice for small firms.

**Actuarial tables** A list of the expected probabilities of each type of risk. (Ch. 20)

**Actuaries** College graduates trained in mathematics and statistics and who have passed a rigorous set of exams. (Ch. 20)

**Administrative law** Consists of regulations passed by state and federal administrative agencies. (Ch. 23)

**Administrative managers.** Managers who are not specialists but who manage an entire business or a segment of a business. (Ch. 6)

**Advertising** A paid form of nonpersonal communication transmitted through a mass medium. (Chs. 12 and 15)

**Affirmative action program** Programs designed to increase job opportunities for women and minorities. (Ch. 9)

**AFL-CIO** A federation of craft and industrial unions. (Ch. 10)

**Age Discrimination in Employment Act** Outlaws discrimination based on age. (Ch. 9)

**Agents** People who represent either a buyer or a seller, usually on a permanent basis (Ch. 14); those who act on behalf of the principal to accomplish the task. (Ch. 23)

**Agency shop** A factory or other business establishment in which union membership is not required. (Ch. 10)

**Agenda** Contains both specific and vague items, covering short-term goals and long-term objectives. (Ch. 6)

**Aggregate planning** The first phase of production and inventory planning and control. (Ch. 11)

**American Federation of Labor (AFL)** Formed by the merger of one faction of the Knights of Labor with a group of unaffiliated craft unions. (Ch. 10)

**Annual rate of return** Describe how much of a return an investor has earned on one share of a particular stock. (Ch. 19)

**Antitrust Improvements Act** Strengthened earlier antitrust laws and gave the Justice Department more investigative authority. (Ch. 23)

**Arbitration** The submission of a dispute to one or more third-party arbitrators whose decision is final. (Ch. 23)

**Arithmetic/logic unit** Performs all mathematical computations and makes comparisons between data. (Ch. 21)

**Arithmetic mean** The sum of all items in a group, divided by the number of items in the group. (Ch. 21)

**Artificial intelligence** The ability of computers to work and to think as much like the human mind as possible. (Ch. 21)

**Assessment centers** Used to identify employees who have managerial potential and to provide them with specialized training. (Ch. 9)

**Asset utilization ratio** Measures how efficiently a firm uses its assets to generate $1 of sales. (Ch. 17)

**Autocratic leaders** People who make all the decisions and then tell employees what must be done and how to do it. (Ch. 6)

**Automated clearinghouses (ACHs)** Permit payments to be made to and from a bank account by magnetic computer tape. (Ch. 16)

**Automated teller machines** Stand-alone machines that dispense cash, accept deposits, transfer funds from one account to another, and display a customer's account balance. (Ch. 16)

---

**B**

**Balance of payments** The difference between the flow of money into a country and the flow of money out of the country. (Ch. 22)

**Balance of trade** The difference in value between a nation's exports and imports. (Ch. 22)

**Balance sheet** A snapshot of a company's financial position at a given moment. (Ch. 17)

**Bargaining unit** The specific group of employees that the union will represent. (Ch. 10)

**Bear market** A period of decreases in the stock market. (Ch. 19)

**Behavior modification** Involves changing behavior and encouraging appropriate behavior by relating the consequences of behavior to the behavior itself. (Ch. 8)

**Benefits** Nonwage and salary forms of compensation. (Ch. 9)

**Better Business Bureau** A self regulatory agency supported by local businesses. (Ch. 13)

**Board of directors** Elected by the stockholders to oversee the general operation of the corporation. (Ch. 4)

**Bond** A long-term debt that is a marketable security. (Ch. 19)

**Bond yield** Return on investment for a bond. (Ch. 19)

**Bonuses** An addition to regular compensation for exceptional performance. (Ch. 17)

**Book value per share** Indicates what the stockholders' investment has been on a per share basis. (Ch. 17)

**Boycott** An attempt to keep people from purchasing the product of a company. (Ch. 10)

**Brand** A name, term, symbol, design, or combination of these that identifies a product and distinguishes it from other products. (Ch. 13)

**Breach of contract** The failure or refusal of a party to a contract to live up to his or her promises. (Ch. 23)

**Break-even point** Where the cost of making the product equals the revenue gained from selling the product. (Ch. 3)

**Bribes** Personal payments, gifts, or special favors granted improperly to influence the outcome of a decision. (Ch. 13)

**Brokers** Individuals who bring buyers and sellers together on a temporary basis. (Ch. 14)

**Bretton Woods Accord** Mandated that a nation pay its debts by transferring gold from its reserves to the reserves of the creditor nation. (Ch. 22)

**Budget** An internal financial statement that presents expenditures and revenues for a week, month, quarter, or year. (Ch. 17)

**Bull market** A period of large increases in the stock market. (Ch. 19)

**Business interruption insurance** Offsets the temporary loss of business resulting from disaster. (Ch. 20)

**Business plan** A meticulous statement of the rationale for the business and a step-by-step explanation of how it will achieve its goals. (Ch. 5)

**Buyer behavior** The decision processes and actions of people who buy and use products. (Ch. 12)

## C

**Capacity-needs analysis** Considers the capacity levels of specific departments and machines within each department. (Ch. 11)

**Capital** Long-term funds provided to finance the purchase of assets. (Ch. 5)

**Capital budget** The amount of money budgeted for the purchase of fixed assets. (Ch. 19)

**Capitalism** An economic system in which individuals own and operate the majority of businesses that provide goods and services. (Ch. 2)

**Cartel** A group of firms or nations that agree to act as a monopoly and not compete with each other. (Ch. 22)

**Cash budget** The firm's cash inflow and outflow presented as an organized schedule. (Ch. 18)

**Cash flow** The movement of money through a business on a daily, weekly, and monthly basis. (Chs. 17 and 18)

**Celler-Kefauver Act** Outlawed mergers through the purchase of assets if those mergers reduced assets. (Ch. 23)

**Central processing unit (CPU)** The part of the computer that actually computes. (Ch. 21)

**Certificates of deposit (CDs)** Loans made to a bank on which the bank pays interest. (Ch. 18)

**Certified management accountant (CMA)** Certified accountants who have some degree of managerial responsibility. (Ch. 17)

**Certified public accountant (CPA)** A public accountant who has been certified in the state in which he or she resides. (Ch. 17)

**Channel integration** Combining channel members at one level, or the producer can take over the wholesaler role. (Ch. 14)

**Chapter 7 bankruptcy** Requires the business to be dissolved and its assets liquidated to pay off the debts. (Ch. 23)

**Chapter 11 bankruptcy** Temporarily frees a business from its financial obligations while it reorganizes and works out a payment plan with its creditors. (Ch. 23)

**Chapter 13 bankruptcy** Allows an individual to es-

tablish a three- to five-year plan for repaying his or her debt. (Ch. 23)

**Classroom training** Lectures, conferences, films, case studies, and other techniques used in a classroom to teach employees about the job and its requirements. (Ch. 9)

**Clayton Act** Outlawed price discrimination, tying agreements, binding contracts, and interlocking directorates. (Ch. 23)

**Closed shop** A factory or other business establishment in which management could hire only union members. (Ch. 10)

**Coalition bargaining** Occurs in industries where unions are small and weak; several different unions band together to strengthen their bargaining power. (Ch. 10)

**Code of ethics** Statements of ethics-related policy. (Ch. 3)

**Coinsurance clause** Specifies the percentage of the building's value that is protected by insurance. (Ch. 20)

**Collateral** Something of value that a bank can repossess in the event that a borrower defaults or fails to pay off a secured loan. (Chs. 5 and 18)

**Collective bargaining** The negotiation process through which management and unions reach an agreement. (Ch. 10)

**Commercial paper** Written promises or orders to pay a specific amount of money. (Ch. 23)

**Commercialization** The introduction of a complete marketing strategy and the launch of the product for commercial success. (Ch. 13)

**Commission** The payment to the employee of a fixed amount or a percentage of the employee's sales. (Ch. 9)

**Common carrier** A transportation company that transports goods for the general public for a fee. (Ch. 14)

**Common law** The law established by judges in the process of deciding disputes. (Ch. 23)

**Common stock** Ownership in a corporation that gives stock owners voting rights. (Ch. 4 and 19)

**Communism** A society in which the people, without regard to class, own all the nation's resources. (Ch. 2)

**Comparable worth** The idea that a woman's and a

man's pay should be equal when their jobs require equal levels of education, training, skills, responsibility, and effort. (Ch. 9)

**Compensating-balance loans** Require a borrower to keep a specified minimum amount of money equal to a percentage of the loan in a checking account at the lending bank. (Ch. 18)

**Competition** The rivalry among businesses to gain sales. (Ch. 2)

**Compressed work week** A four day (or shorter) period in which an employee works forty hours. (Ch. 8)

**Compulsory arbitration** When an outside party requests arbitration as a means of eliminating a prolonged strike that threatens to disrupt the economy. (Ch. 10)

**Computer** An electronic machine that processes data into meaningful information. (Ch. 21)

**Computer-assisted design (CAD)** A computerized approach that links the design and manufacturing areas, making information readily available. (Ch. 11)

**Computer-assisted manufacturing (CAM)** A computerized approach that links the design and manufacturing areas, making information readily available. (Ch. 11)

**Computer network** A system that allows different computers to communicate with each other. (Ch. 21)

**Computer program** A series of demands written in a particular computer language. (Ch. 21)

**Concentration approach** Uses one marketing strategy to direct marketing efforts toward a single market segment. (Ch. 12)

**Concept testing** Research designed to determine potential buyer interest in a new product. (Ch. 13)

**Conceptual skills** The ability to think in abstract terms; the ability to see how parts fit together to form the whole. (Ch. 6)

**Conciliation** Bringing in a neutral third party, a conciliator, to keep labor and management talking. (Ch. 10)

**Congress of Industrial Organizations (CIO)** A national labor union which focused on the affiliation of individual industrial unions. (Ch. 10)

**Consideration** Money or something of value given in return for fulfilling a contract. (Ch. 23)

**Constitutional law** Specifies how the United States government must behave in its relations with the states and individual citizens. (Ch. 23)

**Consumer products** Products for household or family use. (Ch. 13)

**Consumerism** The activities undertaken by independent individuals, groups, and organizations to protect their rights as consumers. (Ch. 3)

**Continuous manufacturing organization** An organization that runs continuously and creates products with many similar characteristics. (Ch. 11)

**Contract** A mutual agreement between two or more parties that can be enforced in court. (Ch. 23)

**Contract carrier** A transportation company that transports products by contract or agreement. (Ch. 14)

**Contractual capacity** The legal ability to enter into a contract. (Ch. 23)

**Control unit** Controls the computer by gathering data from memory and sending processing instructions to other parts of the computer. (Ch. 21)

**Controlling** The process of evaluating and correcting activities to keep the organization on course. (Ch. 6)

**Conventional stage of moral development** The individual believes that right is that which society or a significant reference group defines as proper. (Ch. 3)

**Conversion ratio** Number of shares per bond. (Ch. 19)

**Conversion value** The conversion ratio times the market price of the stock. (Ch. 19)

**Convertible bonds** Can be converted into common stock at the request of the bondholder. (Ch. 19)

**Cooperative (co-op)** An organization composed of individuals or small businesses that have banded together to reap the benefits of belonging to a larger organization. (Ch. 4)

**Corporate charter** Issued to the company by the state in which the business incorporates. (Ch. 4)

**Corporation** A separate legal entity created by the state. (Ch. 4)

**Cost-of-living escalator clause** A clause in a union contract that calls for an automatic increase in wages during periods of inflation. (Ch. 10)

**Countertrade agreements** Bartering agreements between nations. (Ch. 22)

**Coupon rate** The guaranteed percentage of face value that the company will pay to the bond owner every year. (Ch. 19)

**Credit union** A financial institution owned and controlled by its depositors. (Ch. 16)

**Culture** The integrated, accepted pattern of human behavior. (Ch. 12)

**Cumulative voting system** Allows stockholders owning less than 50 percent of the total shares of a corporation to elect a minority of directors. (Ch. 4)

**Current yield** The coupon in dollars divided by the market price of the bond. (Ch. 19)

**Customer departmentalization** Grouping jobs around the needs of various types of customers. (Ch. 7)

---

**D**

**Data base** A repository of related data organized for convenient access. (Ch. 21)

**Data-base management system (DBMS)** A file management system for two or more files. (Ch. 21)

**Data processing** The transformation of raw data into a form useful for a particular purpose. (Ch. 21)

**Debt to total assets** A ratio that indicates how much of the firm's assets are financed by equity. (Ch. 17)

**Debt utilization ratios** Tells the analyst how much debt the company is using relative to other sources of capital such as owners' equity. (Ch. 17)

**Decision making** The process of making logical choices among options. (Ch. 6)

**Decision support system (DSS)** Software that will aid managers in decision making by helping them anticipate what effect certain decisions will have. (Ch. 21)

**Decreasing term insurance** Term insurance for a specified time and at a level premium. (Ch. 20)

**Deductible** An amount for which the policyholder is responsible before the insurance company will pay a claim. (Ch. 20)

**Defense strategy** When a business tries to minimize or avoid additional obligations. (Ch. 3)

**Delegation of authority** Assigning tasks to employees and at the same time giving the employees the power to make the commitments, use the resources, and take the actions that are necessary to accomplish the tasks. (Ch. 7)

**Demand** The quantity of a product that consumers are willing to buy at certain prices. (Chs. 2 and 13)

**Demand deposits** Checking accounts at a financial institution into which a person deposits and withdraws funds. (Ch. 16)

**Democratic leaders** People who allow their employees to get involved in decisions. (Ch. 6)

**Departmentalization** Grouping jobs into working units that are usually called departments but may also be called units, groups, or divisions. (Ch. 7)

**Depreciation expense** One year's charge against the original cost of fixed assets. (Ch. 17)

**Deregulation** The repeal of regulations that pertain to a specific industry. (Ch. 16)

**Desktop publishing** The computer performs the tasks equivalent to those of conventional publishing. (Ch. 21)

**Detailed planning** Planning done one or two months ahead. (Ch. 11)

**Development** Teaching managers and professionals how to perform their jobs. (Ch. 9)

**Direct investment** The purchase of overseas production and marketing facilities. (Ch. 22)

**Directing** Motivating and leading employees to achieve organizational objectives. (Ch. 6)

**Disaggregation** Translating equivalent units into specific numbers. (Ch. 11)

**Discount houses** Self-service general merchandise stores operating on high turnover and low margin. (Ch. 14)

**Discount rate** The rate of interest the Federal Reserve charges for money it lends to any banking institution. (Ch. 16)

**Discounted loans** Require a borrower to pay the interest in advance on the day the loan is made. (Ch. 18)

**Dispatching** The initiation of action—orders to begin work. (Ch. 11)

**Distribution** Making products available in the quantities desired to as many customers as possible (Ch. 12); an orderly process of dividing, dispersing, and delivering products to make them available for customers. (Ch. 14)

**Dividend yield** The dividend per share divided by the market price per share. (Ch. 19)

**Dividends per share** The actual cash received for each share owned. (Ch. 17)

**Domestic international sales corporations (DISCs)** Allows businesses the opportunity to create tax-sheltered subsidiaries. (Ch. 22)

**Dumping** Occurs when a country or business firm sells products at less than what it costs to produce them. (Ch. 22)

---

**E**

**Earnings per share** Profits divided by the number of shares outstanding. (Ch. 19)

**Economics** The study of how resources are distributed for the production of goods and services within a social system (Ch. 2)

**Economic communities** Several nations that bond together to promote the movement of resources and products among members. (Ch. 22)

**Effective interest rate** Measures the cost of a loan based on the actual amount of money the borrower has the use of during the period of the loan. (Ch. 18)

**Economic order quantity method (EOQ)** Calculates the number of items that should be ordered at one time to minimize the total yearly cost of placing orders and carrying the items in inventory. (Ch. 11)

**Economic system** Determines how a society distributes its resources to produce goods and services that satisfy the needs of its people. (Ch. 2)

**Elasticity of demand** The relative responsiveness of changes in quantity demanded to changes in price. (Ch. 13)

**Electronic funds transfer (EFT)** Transferring funds by means of an electronic terminal, telephone, computer, or magnetic tape that orders a financial institution to debit or credit an account. (Ch. 16)

**Electronic mail** Information is sent from one keyboard to other terminals. (Ch. 21)

**Embargo** The suspension of trade in a particular product by the government. (Ch. 22)

**Employee Retirement Income Security (ERISA)** An act which specifies when and how employees are entitled to receive pensions. (Ch. 9)

**Employer's associations** Organizations formed by employers to present a united front in dealing with labor unions. (Ch. 10)

**Employment Act of 1946** Gave the government the right to take certain actions to minimize the disruptive effects of economic fluctuations and reduce unemployment. (Ch. 2)

**Endorsement** The payee's signature and instructions on the back of a document. (Ch. 23)

**Endowment insurance** Provides coverage for a set period. (Ch. 20)

**Entrepreneur** A person who risks his or her wealth, time, and effort to develop, for profit, an innovative product or way of doing something. (Ch. 2)

**Equal Employment Opportunity Commission (EEOC)** A federal agency created by the Civil Rights Act of 1964 to enforce Title VII. (Ch. 9)

**Equal Pay Act** Mandates that men and women who do equal work must receive the same wage. (Ch. 9)

**Equilibrium price** The price where the quantity of products that businesses are willing to supply equals the quantity of products that consumers are willing to buy at a specific point in time. (Ch. 2)

**Equity** The ownership position in assets which does not include assets financed through borrowing. (Ch. 5)

**Equity theory** How much people are willing to contribute to an organization depends on their assessment of the fairness or equity of the rewards they will receive in exchange. (Ch. 8)

**Esteem needs** The need for self-respect and respect from others. (Ch. 8)

**Ethics** The study of morals and moral choices. (Ch. 3)

**Eurodollar market** A European market for trading U.S. dollars. (Ch. 18)

**Exchange** Giving up one thing in return for something else. (Ch. 12)

**Exchange controls** Restrictions on the amount of a particular currency which can be bought or sold. (Ch. 22)

**Exchange rate** The ratio at which one nation's currency or gold can be exchanged for another nation's currency or gold. (Ch. 22)

**Exclusive distribution** When a manufacturer or middleman has the sole right to sell a product in a defined geographic territory. (Ch. 14)

**Exclusive license** Prevents the licensor from selling the license to any other firm in some specific geographic area. (Ch. 22)

**Eximbank** The export-import bank that provides loans to exporters and extends credit to overseas buyers of American goods and services. (Ch. 22)

**Expectancy theory** A theory that proposed that motivation depends not only on how much a person wants something but on the person's perception of how likely he or she is to get it. (Ch. 8)

**Expenses** The costs that are incurred in the daily operation of a business. (Ch. 17)

**Exporting** The sale of domestic goods and material to another nation. (Ch. 22)

**Express warranty** A warranty that can arise from an oral or written statement of fact, a promise, or by simply showing plans, diagrams, or samples in connection with a sale. (Ch. 23)

**External sources** Those sources for recruiting outside of the firm. (Ch. 9)

---

**F**

**Feasibility** The practicality of an option. (Ch. 6)

**Featherbedding** The practice of requiring an employer to hire unnecessary workers or assign unnecessary work. (Ch. 10)

**Federal deficit** The difference between government revenue (taxes) and government expenditures. (Ch. 2)

**Federal Depository Insurance Corporations (FDIC)** Insures individual accounts up to a maximum amount of $100,000. (Ch. 16)

**Federal Reserve System** Established by Congress to regulate the nation's banking industry and manage monetary policy. (Ch. 16)

**Federal Savings and Loan Insurance Corporation (FSLIC)** Established to provide protection to depositors in savings and loan associations. (Ch. 16)

**Federal Trade Commission Act** Declared all unfair methods of competition to be illegal. (Ch. 23)

**Fiat money** Money that the government states is legally acceptable. (Ch. 16)

**File management system** A collection of programs that will manage data stored in one file. (Ch. 21)

**Financial managers** Managers who deal primarily with the organization's financial resources. (Ch. 6)

**Financial networks** Organizations that offer consumers a wide variety of financial services that were traditionally offered by banking institutions. (Ch. 16)

**Financial resources** The organization's supply of money and other variable assets. (Ch. 6)

**First-line management** Managers who supervise workers. (Ch. 6)

**Fiscal policy** Changing the levels of government spending and government income. (Ch. 2)

**Fixed costs** Costs that do not vary with the number of units produced or sold. (Ch. 13)

**Fixed-position layout** Requires an organization to have a central location for the basic product, and all resources required to create the product are brought to that location. (Ch. 11)

**Flextime** A system of working that allows employees to choose their starting and ending times as long as they work for a specified core period. (Ch. 8)

**Float** The difference between the balance in the checkbook and the amount credited to the business by the bank. (Ch. 18)

**Floating exchange rate** Rate which is determined by market conditions and not by a nation's gold reserves. (Ch. 22)

**Foreign Corrupt Practices Act** Outlaws direct payoffs to and bribes of foreign governments or business officials by American companies. (Ch. 22)

**Foreign Credit Insurance Association (FCIA)** Established by Eximbank and private insurance companies allowing Americn exporters to buy insurance to cover political and business risks. (Ch. 22)

**Form utility** Utility created through the production process. (Ch. 12)

**Franchise** A license to sell another's products or to use another's name in business, or both. (Ch. 5)

**Franchisee** The purchaser of the franchise. (Ch. 5)

**Franchiser** The company that sells the franchise. (Ch. 5)

**Free-market communism** A modified form of communism. (Ch. 2)

**Free-rein leaders** People who let their employees work without much interference. (Ch. 6)

**Free trade zones** Specific areas to which goods can be imported without being subjected to quotas or import tariffs. (Ch. 22)

**Freight forwarder** A transportation company that consolidates shipments from several organizations into cost-effective lots. (Ch. 14)

**Functional departmentalization** Grouping jobs according to business function. (Ch. 7)

**Functional structure** Divides general managing duties into functional areas and a separate supervisor manages each functional task. (Ch. 7)

## G

**The General Agreement on Tariffs and Trade (GATT)** Provides a forum for tariff negotiations and a place where international trade problems can be discussed and resolved. (Ch. 22)

**General partnership** A complete sharing in the management of a business. (Ch. 4)

**Generic products** Products without any brand name. (Ch. 13)

**Givebacks** Wage and benefit concessions made to employers to allow them to remain competitive. (Ch. 10)

**Globalization** A company markets the same products in the same manner everywhere. (Ch. 22)

**Goal** The satisfaction of some need. (Ch. 8)

**Grapevine** An informal channel of communication separate from management's formal, official communication channels. (Ch. 7)

**Grievance** A formal, written complaint. (Ch. 10)

**Gross national product** The sum of all goods and services produced in a nation during a year. (Ch. 2)

## H

**Hardware** The physical components of a computer. (Ch. 21)

**Health maintenance organizations (HMOs)** Offers comprehensive health services for a fee to their members. (Ch. 20)

**Hierarchy of objectives** Ordering objectives so that the achievement of all low-level objectives result in the achievement of higher organizational objectives. (Ch. 7)

**Holding company** A corporation that has control over one or more other corporations through ownership of its common stock. (Ch. 4)

**Horizontal integration** Combining stages or units at one level of operation. (Ch. 14)

**Human relations** The study of the behavior of individuals and groups in organizational settings. (Ch. 8)

**Human relations skills** The ability to deal with people, both inside and outside the organization. (Ch. 6)

**Human resources** All the people who work in an organization. (Chs. 6 and 9)

**Humanistic philosophy** Focuses on human rights and values and asserts the dignity and worth of the individual. (Ch. 3)

## I

**Implied contract** Results from the actions, and sometimes the words, of the parties that indicate an intention to agree without specific agreement. (Ch. 23)

**Implied warranty** Imposed on the producer or seller by law. (Ch. 23)

**Import tariff** A duty levied by a nation on goods bought outside its borders and imported into the country. (Ch. 22)

**Importing** The purchase of products and raw materials from another nation. (Ch. 22)

**Income statement** Measures the profitability of a firm over a period of time—a month, a quarter, or a year. (Ch. 17)

**Individual Retirement Accounts (IRAs)** Private pension fund set aside by individuals to provide for their retirement needs. (Ch. 16)

**Industrial products** Products used either directly or indirectly in the operation of manufacturing processes of business organizations. (Ch. 13)

**Industrial robot** A machine designed to move materials, parts, tools, or specialized devices through programmed motions, for the performance of a variety of tasks. (Ch. 11)

**Industry-wide bargaining** Contracts that involve the national unions and as a result a standard contract is drawn up covering all employees in the industry. (Ch. 10)

**Inflation** A continuing rise in prices. (Ch. 2)

**Inferential skills** The ability to identify relevant issues and recognize the degree of their importance, understand the relationships between issues, and perceive the underlying causes of a situation. (Ch. 6)

**Informal leaders** Individuals who have no formal authority over others yet can influence the behavior of others. (Ch. 7)

**Informal organization** The personal and social relationships that evolve in the work environment. (Ch. 7)

**Information** Data that is relevant for a specific purpose. (Ch. 21)

**Injunction** A court order that prohibits employees from participating in union activities. (Ch. 10)

**Inputs** Labor, materials, energy, and money. (Ch. 11)

**Input-output devices** Devices that enter data and transmit processed data. (Ch. 21)

**Installment loans** Require that a borrower repay interest in periodic payments, usually monthly or quarterly. (Ch. 18)

**Insurable interest** An applicant for insurance must be able to show that he or she will actually suffer a personal financial hardship if loss occurs. (Ch. 20)

**Insurable risk** The loss for which insurance is desired must be fortuitous, measurable, and predictable. (Ch. 20)

**Insurance** Protects a buyer from loss for a fee. (Ch. 20)

**Insured** The person or business who buys insurance. (Ch. 20)

**Integrated circuit** A network of dozens of tiny transistors and connections engraved on small silicon wafers, or memory chips. (Ch. 21)

**Intensive distribution** Makes a product available in as many outlets as possible. (Ch. 14)

**Interest** A percentage of the principal that the bank charges to use the money for a given length of time. (Ch. 18)

**Intermittent organization** Organizations that use the process or functional layout. (Ch. 11)

**Internal sources** The organization's current employees. (Ch. 9)

**The International Monetary Fund (IMF)** Established to promote trade among member nations by eliminating trade barriers and fostering financial cooperation. (Ch. 22)

**Inventory management** Keeping track of items. (Ch. 11)

**Inventory planning and control** The development of adequate inventories or assortments of products that satisfy particular target markets. (Ch. 14)

**J**

**Job analysis** The determination, through observation and study, of pertinent information about a job. (Ch. 9)

**Job description** A formal, written description of a specific job. (Ch. 9)

**Job enlargement** Adding tasks to a job instead of treating each task as a separate job. (Ch. 8)

**Job evaluation** A systematic procedure to determine the relative worth of various jobs. (Ch. 9)

**Job rotation** A process that allows employees to move from one job to another in an effort to relieve the boredom that is often associated with job specialization. (Ch. 8)

**Job sharing** When two people do one job. (Ch. 8)

**Job specification** A written description of the qualifications necessary for a specific job. (Ch. 9)

**Joint partner** A partnership established for a specific project or for a limited time. (Ch. 4)

**Joint venture** When a foreign company finds a local partner to share the costs and operation of the business. (Ch. 22)

**Jurisdiction** The legal power of a court, through a judge, to interpret and apply the law and make a binding decision in a particular case. (Ch. 23)

**Just-in-time concept (JIT)** Minimizing the number of units maintained in inventory by providing an almost continuous flow of items from the supplies to the production facility. (Ch. 11)

## K

**Knights of Labor** The first national labor union, founded in 1869. (Ch. 10)

## L

**Labeling** The presentation of information on the package. (Ch. 13)

**Labor contract** The formal, written document that spells out the relationship between the union and management. (Ch. 10)

**Labor union** A group of workers who have joined together to deal with employers and to achieve objectives. (Ch. 10)

**Landrum-Griffin Act** Guarantees all union members the right to vote in union elections, to speak at union meetings, and to see union financial reports. (Ch. 10)

**Law of adverse selection** Those who are most likely to purchase insurance are those who are most likely to suffer losses. (Ch. 20)

**Leadership** The ability to influence employees to work towards achieving organizational goals. (Ch. 6)

**Liability insurance** Covers financial losses to an individual or firm if the firm is held responsible for injuries or other damages. (Ch. 20)

**Licensing** A way for a company to enter the international marketplace without spending large amounts of capital abroad and hiring or transferring personnel to handle overseas affairs. (Ch. 22)

**Limited partnership** Has at least one general partner and at least one limited partner. (Ch. 4)

**Line-and-staff structure** An attempt to combine the strengths of the line structure and functional structure. (Ch. 7)

**Line of credit** An agreement by which a financial institution promises to lend a business a predetermined sum on demand. (Ch. 5)

**Line structure** Direct lines of authority that extend from the top executive to the employees of the lowest level of the organization. (Ch. 7)

**Liquidity ratios** Indicate the business's ability to pay off short-term debt and interest expenses. (Ch. 17)

**Local** The local union. (Ch. 10)

**Local-market bargaining** Local contracts between local unions and local businesses. (Ch. 10)

**Lockout** Management's version of a strike; management closes a worksite so that employees cannot go to work. (Ch. 10)

**Long-term assets** Assets that are expected to last for many years. (Ch. 19)

**Long-term financial management** The managing of the long-term assets and liabilities and owners' equity portion of the balance sheet. (Ch. 19)

**Long-term liabilities** Debts that will be repaid over a number of years. (Ch. 19)

## M

**M1** All currency, demand deposits, NOW accounts, Super NOW accounts, and share draft accounts. (Ch. 16)

**M2** Includes time deposits and money market accounts in addition to currency and demand deposits. (Ch. 16)

**Mainframe computers** The largest and fastest computers available. (Ch. 21)

**Maintenance factors** Relate to the work setting, not to the content of the work. (Ch. 8)

**Majority voting system** Allows stockholders owning over fifty percent of the common stock of a corporation to elect all the directors. (Ch. 4)

**Malpractice insurance** Purchased by doctors, lawyers, engineers, and other professionals to protect them from malpractice lawsuits. (Ch. 20)

**Management** The process of coordinating human, physical, and financial resources to achieve an organization's objectives. (Ch. 6)

**Management information system (MIS)** A collection of data that provides information to managers to use in making decisions. (Ch. 21)

**Managerial accounting** The use of accounting statements within a business organization. (Ch. 17)

**Market** A group of people who have a need along with purchasing power and the desire and authority to spend money on goods, services, and ideas. (Ch. 12)

**Market coverage** The number and variety of outlets that make products available to customers. (Ch. 14)

**Market segment** A collection of individuals, groups, or organizations that share at least one characteristic or attribute and have relatively similar product needs and desires. (Ch. 12)

**Market segmentation** A process of dividing the total market into groups of people who have relatively similar product needs. (Ch. 12)

**Market value** The price at which the common stock is currently trading. (Ch. 19)

**Marketable securities** Temporary investments of excess cash. (Chs. 17 and 18)

**Marketing** A group of activities designed to facilitate and expedite exchanges through the creation, distribution, promotion, and pricing of goods, services, and ideas. (Ch. 12)

**Marketing channel** A group of marketing organizations that direct the flow of products from producers to customers. (Ch. 14)

**Marketing concept** The concept that states that an organization should try to satisfy customers' needs by means of a set of coordinated activities that also allow the organization to achieve its goals. (Ch. 12)

**Marketing information system** Establishes a framework for day-to-day managing and structuring of information gathered regularly from sources both inside and outside of the organization. (Ch. 12)

**Marketing manager** A manager who is responsible for planning, pricing, promoting products, and making them available to customers. (Ch. 6)

**Marketing mix** Four variables that marketers can ma-

nipulate to achieve specific goals within a dynamic marketing environment. (Ch. 12)

**Marketing research** A systematic and objective effort to get information about potential customers in order to guide marketing decisions. (Ch. 12)

**Marketing strategy** The plan of action for using the firm's resources and advantages to meet its objectives. (Ch. 12)

**Maslow's Hierarchy** The order in which people strive to satisfy their needs. (Ch. 8)

**Mass merchandisers** Offer few consumer services and focus on keeping prices low, turning over products quickly, and achieving a large sales volume. (Ch. 14)

**Master budget** The total of all department budgets which composes the budgets for the firm. (Ch. 17)

**Master production schedule** Identifies what products to produce, when they should be produced, and how many are needed. (Ch. 11)

**Material-requirements planning** A process used to determine the net requirements of materials, when they are needed, and when orders should be placed to guarantee on-time delivery. (Ch. 11)

**Materials handling** The physical handling and movement of products in warehouse operations and in transportation. (Ch. 14)

**Materials management** The development and coordination of the policies, procedures, and systems that are used to obtain, distribute, and store materials needed to create the product. (Ch. 11)

**Materials needs analysis** Identifies how many and what kinds of materials will be required to produce the required number of products. (Ch. 11)

**Matrix structure** Involves setting up teams from different departments thereby creating two or more intersecting lines of authority. (Ch. 7)

**Maturity date** The date the bond owner receives the face value of the bond along with the final interest payment. (Ch. 19)

**Media plan** A plan that identifies the media to be used, and the dates, times, and cities where the advertisements will appear. (Ch. 15)

**Median** Represents the middle value in a set of data arranged from the highest to the lowest value. (Ch. 21)

**Mediation** The submission of a dispute to one or more third-party mediators whose decision is not necessarily final. (Chs. 10 and 23)

**Merchant wholesalers** Merchants who take title to products, assume the risk of ownership, and are involved in buying, selling, and helping develop inventory assortments for retail customers. (Ch. 14)

**Microcomputers** The smallest, least powerful, and least expensive of all the computers. (Ch. 21)

**Microprocessor** A single integrated circuit capable of performing large-scale data processing. (Ch. 21)

**Middle management** Plant managers, division managers, and department managers. (Ch. 6)

**Middlemen** Organizations that bridge the gap between the producer of the product and the ultimate user of the product. (Ch. 14)

**Minicomputers** Smaller, slower, and less expensive than microcomputers. (Ch. 21)

**Mission** The broad task the organization wants to achieve. (Ch. 6)

**Mixed economy** An economy that has elements from more than one economic system. (Ch. 2)

**Modular design** Building an item in self-contained units, or modules, that can be combined or interchanged to create different products. (Ch. 11)

**Money market accounts** Merge different investors' deposits into one investment fund that buys stocks and bonds. (Ch. 16)

**Money market funds** Professionally managed portfolios of marketable securities. (Ch. 18)

**Monopolistic competition** When there are fewer businesses than in pure-competition systems and businesses focus on creating differences between their products. (Ch. 2)

**Monopoly** When there is only one producer of a product in a given market. (Ch. 2)

**Moral philosophy** A set of principles setting forth what is believed to be the right way to behave. (Ch. 13)

**Mortgage** A loan made so a business or individual can purchase real estate. (Chs. 5 and 16)

**Mortgage Protection insurance** Pays the value of the mortgage if the policyholder dies before paying off the mortgage debt on the family's house. (Ch. 20)

**Motivating** Giving employees reasons or incentives to work to achieve organizational objectives. (Ch. 6)

**Motivation.** An internal force that focuses an individuals' behavior to achieve a goal. (Chs. 8 and 12)

**Motivational factors** Relate to the content of the work. (Ch. 8)

**Multi-segment approach** The marketer aims the organization's marketing efforts at two or more segments, developing a marketing strategy for each one. (Ch. 12)

**Multinational** A corporation that operates on a worldwide scale, without significant ties to any one nation or region. (Ch. 16)

**Mutual company** A nonprofit cooperative owned by its policyholders rather than its stockholders. (Ch. 20)

**Mutual fund** Financial organization that pools investors' funds and invests them in securities. (Ch. 16)

## N

**Narrow span of management** A manager directly supervises only a few subordinates. (Ch. 7)

**National Advertising Review Board (NARB)** A self-regulatory unit created by the Council of Better Business Bureaus, a national organization, and three advertising trade organizations. (Ch. 3)

**National Credit Union Association (NCUA)** Insures credit unions. (Ch. 16)

**National debt** The total amount of money the federal government has borrowed. (Ch. 2)

**National Labor Relations Board (NLRB)** A board that supervises union elections and polices management policies regarding unions. (Ch. 10)

**Need** The difference between a desired state and an actual state. (Ch. 8)

**Negotiable instruments** Commercial paper that can be transferred from one person or business to another as long as it meets certain requirements. (Ch. 23)

**Net income** The profit left after all expenses have been deducted from revenue. (Ch. 17)

**Nonstore retailing** Selling to the ultimate consumer in settings outside the regular store environment. (Ch. 14)

**Norris-LaGuardia Act** Outlawed yellow-dog contracts

and blacklists and made it more difficult for management to obtain injunctions. (Ch. 10)

## O

**Occupational Safety and Health Administration (OSHA)** An organization that enforces the condition of the Occupational Safety and Health Act of 1970 requiring employers to inspect work facilities and remove all hazards. (Ch. 9)

**Oligopoly** When very few businesses sell a product. (Ch. 2)

**On-the-job training** Workers learn by actually performing the tasks of the job. (Ch. 9)

**Open market operations** Buying and selling government securities in the public open market. (Ch. 16)

**Order takers** Salespeople who execute sales for customers who have already decided to buy the product from a particular organization. (Ch. 15)

**Orderly marketing agreement** An agreement between nations to restrict competition between them. (Ch. 22)

**Organization** Any group of individuals who work together for the achievement of some stated or implied objective. (Chs. 6 and 7)

**Organizational manual** A written description of authority relationships which details the functions of major organizational units and describes job procedures. (Ch. 7)

**Organizational layers** The levels of management in an organization. (Ch. 7)

**Organizing** The structuring of resources and activities to accomplish objectives in an efficient and effective manner. (Chs. 6 and 7)

**Orientation** A new employee's introduction to the organization. (Ch. 9)

**Outputs** Goods and services. (Ch. 11)

**Over-the-counter market (OTC)** A network of dealers all over the country linked by computers, telephones, and teletype machines. (Ch. 19)

## P

**Packaging** The development of a container and a graphic design in order to enhance the product. (Ch. 13)

**Par value** The dollar amount printed on the stock certificate or the value of the bond. (Ch. 19)

**Partnership** An association of two or more persons who carry on as owners of a business for profit. (Ch. 4)

**Payout ratio** Dividends per share divided by earnings per share. (Ch. 19)

**Penetration price** A low price designed to let a product enter the market and gain market share rapidly. (Ch. 13)

**Per share data** Used by investors to compare the performance of one company to another on an equal per share basis. (Ch. 17)

**Perception** The process by which a person selects, organizes, and interprets information received from his or her senses. (Ch. 12)

**Performance appraisal** Identifying an employee's strengths and weaknesses on the job. (Ch. 9)

**Personal selling** Direct, personal communication with customers and potential customers. (Chs. 12 and 15)

**Personnel managers** Managers who deal with employees in a formalized manner. (Ch. 6)

**Physical resources** The raw materials, supplies, machinery, and equipment used by the organization. (Ch. 6)

**Physiological needs** The essentials for living—water, food, shelter, and clothing. (Ch. 8)

**Power of attorney** A legal document authorizing one to act as someone else's agent. (Ch. 23)

**Preconventional stage of moral development** The individual is concerned with his or her immediate interests and external rewards and punishments. (Ch. 3)

**Preemptive right** The right of common stockholders to purchase shares of the stock from the corporation. (Ch. 4)

**Preferred stock** Ownership in a corporation that provides special privileges for preferred stockholders. (Chs. 4 and 19)

**Premium** Special incentive in the form of a gift that is made available to a customer for buying a product (Ch. 15); the fee paid for insurance (Ch. 20).

**Press conference** A meeting with press representatives to announce major events. (Ch. 15)

**Price** The value placed on some object involved in an exchange between a buyer and a seller. (Chs. 12 and 13)

**Price-earning ratio (P-E ratio)** The ratio of market price per share divided by earnings per share. (Ch. 19)

**Price skimming** Charging the highest possible price that buyers who want the product will pay. (Ch. 13)

**Primary data** Information that is observed and recorded or collected directly from respondents. (Ch. 12)

**Primary market** The market where firms raise financial capital. (Ch. 19)

**Primary memory** A group of chips that store all data entered into the computer. (Ch. 21)

**Prime rate** The interest rate charged by banks to their best customers (usually large corporations) for short-term loans. (Ch. 18)

**Principal** The amount of money a business borrows (Ch. 18); one who wishes to have a specific task accomplished (Ch. 23).

**Principled stage of moral development** The individual sees beyond norms, law, or authority to determine what is right or ethical. (Ch. 3)

**Private accountant** A person who is employed by corporations, government agencies, and other organizations operating on a profit or nonprofit basis. (Ch. 17)

**Private carrier** A transportation company that transports its own property in its own vehicles. (Ch. 14)

**Private corporation** Has only a few shareholders, closely involved in managing the business. (Ch. 4)

**Proactive strategy** A business assumes responsibility for its actions and responds to accusations made against it without outside pressure or the threat of government intervention. (Ch. 3)

**Process or functional layout** Facility design that organizes the transformation process into departments, depending on the type of work to be done. (Ch. 11)

**Product** A complex of tangible and intangible attributes that provide satisfaction and benefits. (Chs. 12 and 13)

**Product departmentalization** Grouping jobs around the products of the firm. (Ch. 7)

**Product liability** Business' legal responsibility for any negligence in the design, production, sale, and consumption of products. (Ch. 23)

**Product liability insurance** Covers financial losses resulting from lawsuits over defective parts, food poisoning, negligent maintenance, or quality control. (Ch. 20)

**Product line** Closely related products that are treated as a unit because of similar marketing strategy and production or end-use considerations. (Ch. 13)

**Product mix** All the products offered by the organization. (Ch. 13)

**Product positioning** Decisions and activities used to create and maintain a perception of the product in the mind of the consumers. (Ch. 13)

**Production and operations management** The part of an organization that has primary responsibility for the creation of products to be offered for customers. (Ch. 11)

**Production and operations managers** Managers who are concerned with the actual transformation of the firm's resources into goods and services ready for the marketplace. (Ch. 6)

**Product or line layouts** Facility design that requires the work of creating a product to be broken down into activities or tasks requiring relatively short periods of time and to be assigned to workers positioned along the line. (Ch. 11)

**Production control** Scheduling the specific activities necessary to have the products completed by the target data, identifying the tasks that have to be done to complete the product, and following up to make sure things go according to schedule. (Ch. 11)

**Production planning** Determining what products should be produced and by what date they should be completed. (Ch. 11)

**Profit sharing** Distributing a percentage of company profits to the employees whose work helped to generate those profits. (Ch. 9)

**Profitability ratios** Measures how much operating income or net income a firm is able to generate relative to the assets, owners' equity, and sales. (Ch. 17)

**Project organization** An organization that is involved in large, complex tasks. (Ch. 11)

**Promotion** A persuasive form of communication that

attempts to facilitate a marketing exchange by influencing individuals, groups, and organizations to accept goods, services, and ideas (Chs. 12 and 15); an advancement, or vertical movement, within an organization to a position with increased authority, responsibility and salary (Ch. 9).

**Property insurance** Includes fire, homeowners', automobile, and other policies as protection against losses due to physical damage to property. (Ch. 20)

**Proxy** A written authorization by which stockholders assign their voting privilege to another individual. (Ch. 4)

**Psychological pricing** A policy designed to encourage purchases based on emotional reaction to the price rather than on rational responses to the price. (Ch. 13)

**Public accountant** An independent professional who provides accounting services to individuals and businesses for a fee. (Ch. 17)

**Public corporation** Issues certificates of ownership that may be traded on stock exchanges. (Ch. 4)

**Public relations** A broad set of communication activities designed to maintain favorable relations between an organization and its public. (Ch. 15)

**Publicity** A nonpersonal communication presented as a news story and transmitted through a mass medium. (Chs. 12 and 15)

**Purchasing** The buying of all the materials needed by the organization. (Ch. 11)

**Pure premium** The portion of the total expected losses paid by each individual. (Ch. 20)

**Pure risk** Offers the chance of no change at all or the chance of a loss. (Ch. 20)

---

**Q**

**Quality control** Measuring the quality of products and services against established quality standards. (Ch. 11)

**Quota** The maximum number of units of a particular product that can be imported into a country. (Ch. 22)

---

**R**

**Reaction strategy** When a business allows a condition or problem to go unresolved until the public finds out about it. (Ch. 3)

**Real capital** Physical assets, such as a plant and equipment, usually referred to as fixed assets. (Ch. 19)

**Real gross national product** Measures economic output in constant dollars. (Ch. 2)

**Recession** Six continuous months of negative growth in the real gross national product. (Ch. 2)

**Recruiting** The process of attracting qualified applicants for a job. (Ch. 6)

**Reference groups** Groups that individuals identify with, adopting the values or attitudes of group members. (Ch. 12)

**Refund** The return to the consumer of part of the purchase price or the total purchase price of a product. (Ch. 15)

**Research and development** The process of identifying new ideas and technologies that can be developed into new products. (Ch. 13)

**Responsibility** The obligation of the employer to carry out the assigned task satisfactorily. (Ch. 7)

**Retailers** Middlemen who sell products to ultimate consumers for home and household use rather than for resale or for use in producing other products. (Ch. 14)

**Retailing** Selling products to ultimate household consumers for personal or family use. (Ch. 14)

**Retained earning** Earnings left after all expenses have been paid. (Ch. 19)

**Return on assets** Shows how much income the firm produces for every dollar invested in assets. (Ch. 17)

**Revenue** The total amount of dollars generated from sales and related business activities. (Ch. 17)

**Reserve requirement** The percentage of deposits that banks must hold in reserve. (Ch. 16)

**Revolving accounts** A legal guarantee that a cardholder can purchase goods and services on credit, up to a specified amount. (Ch. 16)

**Right-to-work laws** Laws that ensure that all employees have the right to work without being forced to join a union. (Ch. 10)

**Risk** The possibility of suffering injury or loss. (Ch. 20)

**Risk management** Ways to deal with the threat of loss posed by events beyond the control of a manager. (Ch. 20)

**Robinson-Patman Act** Outlawed price differentials that substantially weaken competition. (Ch. 23)

**Routing** The sequence of operations through which the product must pass. (Ch. 11)

**Royalty agreements** The licensee agrees to pay the licensor a fixed fraction of the profits on each unit manufactured or sold. (Ch. 22)

**Rule of indemnity** The policyholder cannot collect more money than was actually lost. (Ch. 20)

---

**S**

**Salary** A financial reward calculated weekly, monthly, or on an annual basis. (Ch. 9)

**Sales forecast** Estimate of the organization's future sales. (Ch. 18)

**Sales promotion** A direct inducement offering added value or some other incentive for buyers to enter into an exchange. (Chs. 12 and 15)

**Sample** A free product or service that is offered through coupons or in-store demonstration. (Ch. 15)

**Secondary boycotts** Boycotts or work stoppages by union members against their employer in order to force their employer to stop dealing with other firms that are involved in labor disputes. (Ch. 10)

**Secondary data** Information compiled inside or outside the organization for some purpose other than changing the current situation. (Ch. 12)

**Secondary markets** Exist for the trading of publicly owned securities. (Ch. 19)

**Secured bond** One in which the issuing company pledges specific assets to bondholders as a guarantee. (Ch. 19)

**Secured loan** Loans backed by something of value that the bank can claim if the borrower does not repay the loan. (Ch. 18)

**Securities and Exchange Commission (SEC)** Government regulatory agency. (Ch. 4)

**Securities markets** Provides the mechanism for buying and selling securities for both corporations (stocks and bonds) and governments (T-bills, principal bonds). (Ch. 19)

**Security interest** A financial interest in personal property or fixtures that secures the payment of a debt or obligation. (Ch. 5)

**Selection** A series of steps through which the best applicants are offered jobs. (Chs. 6 and 9)

**Selective distribution** Used most often for products for which consumers shop and compare price, quality, and style before purchasing. (Ch. 14)

**Self-actualization needs** Maximizing one's potential. (Ch. 8)

**Self-insurance** Companies assume risk by making regular payments into a contingency fund. (Ch. 20)

**Separation** The departure of the employee from the organization. (Ch. 9)

**Service Corps of Retired Executives (SCORE)** A volunteer agency funded by the SBA to provide advice for small firms. (Ch. 5)

**Share draft account** A demand deposit in a credit union. (Ch. 16)

**Sherman Antitrust Act** A federal statute intended to break up trusts and prevent monopolies by making certain business practices illegal. (Ch. 23)

**Shop steward** A union representative. (Ch. 10)

**Simple-interest loans** Require a borrower to pay both principal and interest at the maturity date. (Ch. 18)

**Small business** Any business that is independently owned and operated, is not dominant in its field and does not employ more than five-hundred people. (Ch. 5)

**Small Business Administration (SBA)** An independent agency of the federal government that offers managerial and financial assistance to small businesses. (Ch. 5)

**Social audit** The systematic examination of the objectives, strategies, organization, and performance of the social responsibility function. (Ch. 3)

**Social needs** The need for love, companionship, and friendship; the desire of acceptance by others. (Ch. 8)

**Social responsibility** The obligation a business assumes to maximize its positive impact and minimize its negative impact on society. (Ch. 3)

**Social roles** A set of expectations for individuals based on some position they occupy. (Ch. 12)

**Socialism** An economic system in which the government owns and operates basic industries. (Ch. 2)

**Software**   Computer programs that give the computer a set of instructions. (Ch. 21)

**Sole proprietorship**   A business owned and operated by one individual. (Ch. 4)

**Span of management**   The number of subordinates who report to a particular manager. (Ch. 7)

**Specialization**   A division of labor that involves dividing work into small, specialized tasks and assigning employees to do a single task. (Ch. 7)

**Specialty stores**   Stores that carry a narrow assortment of products, but their product line runs deep. (Ch. 14)

**Speculative risk**   Offers one of three outcomes—no change, a loss, or a gain. (Ch. 20)

**Spreadsheet**   An electronic version of a ledger sheet. (Ch. 21)

**Staffing**   Hiring people to carry out the work of the organization. (Ch. 6)

**Stagflation**   The situation of high levels of unemployment combined with high rates of inflation. (Ch. 2)

**Standardization**   Making products according to agreed-to specifications so that their parts are interchangeable. (Ch. 11)

**Strategic plans**   The long-range plans developed by top-level managers, used to assess opportunities and determine the use of resources. (Ch. 6)

**Statistics**   A collection of numerical data about some event, object, or individual. (Ch. 21)

**Statutes**   Laws enacted by a legislature. (Ch. 23)

**Strikebreakers**   People hired by management to replace striking employees. (Ch. 10)

**Stock company**   A profit-making insurance company owned by the stockholders. (Ch. 20)

**Structure**   The arrangement or relationship of positions within an organization. (Ch. 7)

**Subsidiary corporation**   A corporation that has the majority of its stock owned by another corporation. (Ch. 4)

**Supply**   The quantity of a product that producers are willing to sell at certain prices at a specific time. (Chs. 2 and 13)

**Supply-side economics**   A policy that advocated reducing taxes and balancing the federal budget. (Ch. 2)

## T

**Tactical plans**   Short-range plans that enable the organization to make quick changes when situations unforeseen by the strategic plan arise. (Ch. 6)

**Taft-Hartley Act**   An act designed to balance the power between unions and management. (Ch. 10)

**Target market**   A group of buyers for whom the organization tailors a marketing strategy that fits their needs and wants. (Ch. 12)

**Technical expertise**   The specialized knowledge needed to perform a job. (Ch. 6)

**Term insurance**   Provides a death benefit only and no cash value. (Ch. 20)

**Territorial departmentalization**   Grouping jobs by geographic location. (Ch. 7)

**Test marketing**   The limited introduction of a product in areas that represent the potential market. (Ch. 13)

**Theory X**   A theory that assumes that workers generally dislike work and must be forced to do their jobs. (Ch. 8)

**Theory Y**   A theory that assumes that workers like to work and that under proper conditions employees will seek out responsibility. (Ch. 8)

**Theory Z**   A management philosophy that stresses employee participation in all aspects of company decision making. (Ch. 8)

**Ticker tape**   A moving electronic board that presents stock price quotations from all exchanges. (Ch. 19)

**Time deposits**   Deposit accounts at banks and savings and loan associations that earn money at a specified interest rate. (Ch. 16)

**Time utility**   Utility created by making a product available when customers wish to purchase it. (Ch. 12)

**Top management**   The president and other top executives who have overall responsibility for the organization. (Ch. 6)

**Tort**   A violation of civil law. (Ch. 23)

**Total assets turnover**   Measures the efficiency of the combined total assets in supporting sales. (Ch. 17)

**Total-market approach**   The marketer tries to appeal to the total market and assumes that all buyers have similar needs and wants. (Ch. 12)

**Total premium** The sum of the pure premium plus expenses divided by the number of individuals in the population. (Ch. 20)

**Total revenue** Price times quantity. (Ch. 13)

**Trade credit** Credit extended by suppliers for the purchase of their goods and services. (Ch. 18)

**Trade deficit** The difference between the amount of products exported to other nations and the amount of foreign products imported into a nation. (Chs. 2 and 22)

**Trade show** An exhibit organized to demonstrate the latest product line to potential customers. (Ch. 15)

**Trademark** A brand that is registered with the U.S. Patent and Trademark Office and is thus legally protected from use by any firm other than the owner of the trademark. (Ch. 13)

**Trading company** A link between buyers and sellers in different countries to facilitate trade. (Ch. 22)

**Traffic management** The selection of a suitable mode of transportation, coordinating arrivals and departures, and auditing freight bills. (Ch. 11)

**Training** Teaching employees at the production level how to do their jobs. (Ch. 9)

**Transactions balances** Cash kept on hand by a business to pay normal daily business expenses. (Ch. 18)

**Transfer** A horizontal move from one job to another within a company. (Ch. 9)

**Two-tier contracts** Contracts which establish a pay scale for newly hired employees that is far less generous than the pay scale of employees with seniority. (Ch. 10)

## U

**Undercapitalization** The lack of funds to operate a business normally. (Ch. 5)

**Uniform Commercial Code** A set of statutory laws covering several business law topics. (Ch. 23)

**Union shop** A factory or other business establishment in which management may hire any qualified employee, but after a specified period of time, the employee must join the union. (Ch. 10)

**Universal life insurance** Similar to variable life insurance, but the cash value is invested in money market securities. (Ch. 20)

**Unsecured bond** No specific assets are pledged to back up the bond. (Ch. 19)

**Unsecured loan** A loan that is backed only by the borrower's good reputation (measured by the borrower's credit rating). (Ch. 18)

**Utility** The power or the ability of a product to satisfy human needs and wants. (Ch. 12)

**Utilitarian philosophy** Seeking the greatest satisfaction for the largest number of individuals. (Ch. 13)

## V

**Variable costs** Costs that vary directly with changes in the number of units produced or sold. (Ch. 13)

**Variable life insurance** Builds up predictable cash value because the cash value is usually invested in common stocks. (Ch. 20)

**Vertical integration** Involves combining planned distribution systems under one management. (Ch. 14)

**Voluntary agreement** When one party makes an offer and the other accepts. (Ch. 23)

## W

**Wages** Financial rewards based on the number of hours the employee works or the level of output achieved. (Ch. 9)

**Wage/salary survey** An overview of job evaluations, rates paid by competitors, the cost of living, government legislation, and the organization's ability to pay. (Ch. 9)

**Wagner Act** Reorganized employees' rights to negotiate with employers. (Ch. 10)

**Warrant of merchantibility** A promise from the manufacturer that the goods are at least of average quality and are safe for their ordinary purpose. (Ch. 23)

**Webb-Pomerene Export Trade Act** Exempts American firms from antitrust laws if those firms are acting together to enter international trade. (Ch. 22)

**Wheel-of-retailing concept** The evolution of wholesalers and retailers from low-status, low-margin, low-price operators to high-price, high-service businesses. (Ch. 14)

**Whole life insurance** Insurance that has level premiums for life and increasing cash values. (Ch. 20)

**Wholesalers** Middlemen who generally buy from producers or from other wholesalers and sell to retailers. (Ch. 14)

**Wholesaling** A marketing transaction in which products are sold to industrial, retail, and institutional users for resale or for use in making other products. (Ch. 14)

**Wide span of management** A manager directly supervises a very large number of employees. (Ch. 7)

**Work sharing** A job-saving move in which a company faced by hard financial times shortens the work week of all employees by a few hours. (Ch. 8)

**Working capital** Short-term funds necessary to fund the regular operations of the business. (Ch. 5)

**Working capital management** Management of current assets and current liabilities. (Ch. 18)

**World Bank** Established and supported by the industrialized nations to loan money to underdeveloped and developing countries. (Ch. 22)

---

**Z**

**Zero defect programs** Quality control programs that aim at 100 percent acceptable output. (Ch. 11)

# Name Index

Beretta automobiles, 44
Bergdorf-Goodman, 772
Bethany College, 646–647
Bethlehem Steel, 252, 260, 637(table)
Betty Crocker, 396
Bic Corporation, 72
Bic lighters, 71–72
Bing, Dave, 149
Bing Steel, Inc., 149
Bingham, R.S., Jr., 370n
Birch, David L., 164n
Bloch, Henry W., 145
Bloch, Richard, 145
Blue Cross, 670
Blue Shield, 670
Board of Governors (Federal Reserve System), 534
Boeing, 637(table)
Boesky, Ivan F., 99–100, 755
Borden, Inc., 236–237
Brant, Peter, 785–786
Brimberg, Bud, 146
Bristol Myers, 629, 630(table), 631 and *table*
British Petroleum, 121(table)
Brophy, Beth, 264n, 300n
Brown, Alex., 644
Brown, Ken, 375–376
Brown & Jenkins Trading Co., 375–376
Brown & Williamson Tobacco Corporation, 94
Brunswick Corp., 700
Brynner, Yul, 170
Buckheim, Richard, 495
Buick automobiles, 218
Buick City, 610
Burger, Warren E., 582–583
Burger King, 285, 467
Burpee, W. Atlee & Co., 152
Business Cards Tomorrow, 168

Cadbury, Adrian, 96n
Caffeine-free Coca-Cola, 19, 425(table)
Caffeine-free Diet Coke, 19, 423–424, 425(table)

Caffeine-free Tab, 19, 425(table)
Cahan, Vicky, 59n
California Asiatic Oil Co., 128(table)
California Cooler, 432
Campanella, Donna, 507n
Campbell's Soup Company, 228, 255, 393
Canada Dry Club Soda, 436
*Captain Eo*, 417
*Car and Driver*, 496
Carnation, 99, 725
Carnegie, Andrew, 48
Carothers, Charles, 342
Carpenter, David, 785–786
Carter, Jimmy, 527
Casera foods, 393
Castro, Fidel, 19, 726, 736
Cateora, Philip R., 745n
Caterpillar Tractor Company, 189, 396, 453, 733
CBS (Columbia Broadcasting System), 510, 543
CB Sports, 156
Celis, William, III, 96n
Chandeleur Pipe Line Co., 128(table)
Chaparral Steel Co., 268–269
Charles Schwab, 532, 637
Cheerios cereals, 383
Chemical Bank, 543
Chemlawn, 560
Cherry Coca-Cola, 425(table)
Cherry 7-Up, 482
Chesebrough Ponds, 725
Chevrolet automobiles, 44, 218, 254, 727, 737, 738
Chevron Canada Limited, 128(table)
Chevron Capital U.S.A., Inc., 128(table)
Chevron Chemical Company, 128(table)
Chevron Corporation, 127, 128(table), 637(table)
Chevron do Brasil Ltda., 128(table)
Chex brand cereal, 432
Children's Supermart, 445

Chin, Leeann, 157
China Kwik stores, 5
Chiquita, 485
Chrysler Corporation, 11–12, 17–18, 51, 112, 115, 178, 190, 192, 231, 264, 293, 311, 324, 325, 330(illus.), 575, 595, 629, 630(table), 631 and *table*
Chun King Corp., 5
CIB (Continental Illinois National Bank and Trust), 77, 528, 531
Cigna, 534(table), 672
CIO (Congress of Industrial Organizations), 314
Citibank, 490
Citicorp, 542–543, 630(table), 631(table)
Claris Corporation, 711–713
Cleveland Federal Reserve Bank, 534
Clorox, 382
Coca-Cola Classic, 19, 186, 424, 425(table)
Coca-Cola Company, 19, 21, 424, 425(table), 500, 637(table), 717, 735, 740
Coldwell Banker, 533
Colgate-Palmolive, 742
Colletti, Deborah, 164n
Columbia Broadcasting System (CBS), 510, 543
Columbia Pictures, 19
Combustion Engineering, Inc., 736
Common Market (EEC; European Economic Community), 740
Communications Workers of America, 326
Compaq Computer, 622
Congress of Industrial Organizations (CIO), 314
Connecticut General Life, 661(table)
Consumer Product Safety Commission, 85, 758, 759(table)

Continental Airlines, 338, 774, 785
Continental Illinois National Bank and Trust (CIB), 77, 528, 531
Cook, Jack, 405n
Copeland, Jeff B., 581n
Corsica automobiles, 44
Co-Steel International of Canada, 268
Costello, Erdlen & Co., 146
Costello, J. Paul, 146
Council of the Better Business Bureaus, 94
Cracker Jack snacks, 237
Crane, Thomas, 518
Crane, Zenas, 518
Crane Company, 518
Creamette pasta makers, 236–237
Creech, Bill, 210
Creel, Wes, 176
Creel Morrell Inc., 176
Cremora coffee creamer, 237
Crest toothpaste, 64, 427, 429
CSW Credit, 612
Cummins Engine Company, 368

Daily Advertising, 702
Daimler-Benz, 121(table)
Danbury Plumbing Supply, 250
Davis, Keith, 264n
Dawson, Andre, 34
dBase II, 699
DDB Needham, 702
Dean Witter Reynolds, 533
De Beers Central Marketing Organization, 739
De Beers Consolidated Mines Ltd., 717
Decyk, Roxanne, 190
Deere, John, 47
Dell, Michael, 50
Dell Computers, 48
Del Monte, 736
DeLorean, John, 218
Delta Airlines, 500, 511–512

Dentaguard, 429
Dependable-Fordath, Inc., 367
Deschaine, Dennis, 134
Deschaine, Monique, 134–135
Design Center, 702
Detroit Automobile Company, 130
Diamond-Star, 11–12
Diehard batteries, 430
Diet Cherry Coca-Cola, 425(table)
Diet Cherry 7-Up, 482
Diet Coke, 19, 425(table), 500
Diet Fanta, 425(table)
Diet Pepsi, 506
Diet Rite, 487
Diet Sprite, 425(table)
Digital Equipment Corp., 65, 576 and *table*
Dillion, William R., 507n
Discover card, 532
Disneyland, 417
Dobrzynski, Judith H., 641n
Doctor's Associates Inc., 142
Domino's Pizza, 9, 161–162, 303–304, 488
Domzal, Teresa, 507n
Donahue, Christin, 781n
Doniger, Joanna, 143–144
Donnelly, Robert M., 176
Dot Discount Drugs, 450
Dow Jones, 64
Dow Jones Industrial Average, 120, 616, 635, 638–640
Dow Jones Industrials, 119, 121(table)
Doxsee Food Corporation, 237
Dressang, Joel, 96n
Drexel Burnham Lambert, Inc., 99, 623, 635(table)
Dr. Pepper, 48, 482
Dryden, Steven J., 59n
Dun and Bradstreet, 593
Dunkin' Donuts, 158, 161
Dunn, William, 544n
du Pont de Nemours, E.I., 90, 342, 637(table)

Eagle brand ice cream, 236
Eastern Airlines, 71, 72, 338–339, 434, 628, 761
Eastman Kodak, 292, 637(table), 726
Edison, Thomas, 48
Ed Lowe Industries Inc., 382
Edwards, A.G. Company, 532, 637
EEC (European Economic Community; Common Market), 740
EEOC (Equal Employment Opportunity Commission), 282
E.F. Hutton, 78
EFTA (European Free Trade Association), 740
E.I. du Pont de Nemours, 90, 342, 637(table)
Electrolux, 463
Electronic Data Systems, 48–49
Electronic Numerical Integrator and Calculator (ENIAC), 693
Eli Lilly & Co., 410, 630(table), 631(table)
Elizabeth Taylor's Passion perfume, 772
Elmer's glues, 237
Elsener, Carl, 357
Embassy/Tandem Productions, 19
Emergency Management Agency, 683
Emshwiller, John R., 781n
Engardio, Pete, 27n
ENI, 121(table)
ENIAC (Electronic Numerical Integrator and Calculator), 693
Environmental Protection Agency (EPA), 90, 759(table)
Equal Employment Opportunity Commission (EEOC), 282
Equitable Life Insurance, 661(table)
Esprit, 150

Esprit de Corp., 149
Esso gasoline, 727
Ettridge, Steve, 259
European Economic Community (Common Market; EEC), 740
European Free Trade Association (EFTA), 740
Eximbank (Export-Import Bank), 732
Extra-Strength Tylenol capsules, 93
Exxon, 119, 189, 431, 637(table)
FAA (Federal Aviation Administration), 86, 374, 500
Family Casserole frozen foods, 153
FASB (Financial Accounting Standards Board), 564
Fazzolari, Salvatore D., 552
FCC (Federal Communications Commission), 759(table)
FCIA (Foreign Credit Insurance Association), 732
FDA (Food and Drug Administration), 85, 92, 758, 759(table)
FDIC (Federal Deposit Insurance Corporation), 528, 531, 539, 592, 662
Federal Aviation Administration (FAA), 86, 374, 500
Federal Bankruptcy Court, 758
Federal Communications Commission (FCC), 759(table)
Federal Deposit Insurance Corporation (FDIC), 528, 531, 539, 592, 662
Federal Express, 140, 452(illus.), 653(illus.)
Federal Housing Administration, 662
Federal Mediation and

Conciliation Service, 329
Federal National Mortgage Association, 534(table)
Federal Open Market Committee (FOMC), 534, 535, 536–537
Federal Power Commission (FPC), 759(table)
Federal Reserve Bank, 534
Federal Reserve Board, 22, 53, 536, 539
Federal Reserve System, 534–539
Federal Savings and Loan Insurance Corporation (FSLIC), 528, 539, 662
Federal Trade Commission (FTC), 22, 94, 163, 758, 759(table), 761, 775
Felis, Kenneth B., 785–786
Felly, Al, 145
Ferrell, O.C., 96n, 200n
Fiber B, 342
Fields, Debbi, 4
Fields, Randy, 4
Fina, 326
Financial Accounting Standards Board (FASB), 564
Financial News Network, 637
Fireman, Paul, 395
First Boston, 534(table), 635(table)
First Chicago Bank, 539
First Nationwide Bank, 547–548
First Pennsylvania Bank, 531
Fisher Cheese, 237
Flood, Curt, 34
Florida Citrus Commission, 491
Florida Supreme Court, 779
FOMC (Federal Open Market Committee), 534, 535, 536–537

Mayo, Elton, 245
Maytag, 260
Mazda, 112
MCI Communications, 637
Meadow Gold Dairies, 236
Medicaid, 661, 670
Medicare, 661, 670
Mellon, Andrew, 48
Merck & Co., 64, 135–136, 637(table)
Mercury Business Services, 140, 141
Mercury Lynx automobiles, 754
Merle Harmon's Fan Fair, 159
Merrill Lynch, 532, 534 (table), 635(table)
Merrill Lynch Capital Management Account (CMA), 532
Merv Griffin Enterprises, 19
MESBICs (Minority Enterprise Small Business Investment Companies), 157
Metaphor Computer Systems, Inc., 712
Metropolitan Life, 661 (table), 672
Mevacor, 135, 136
Microsoft Corporation, 48, 146, 644–645, 699, 712
Midwest Stock Exchange (Chicago), 636, 637
Milico (Massachusetts Indemnity and Life Insurance Co.), 675
Miller Brewing Company, 430, 488
Milliken, Mike, 623
Milton Bradley, 425
Ministry of Oil Refining and Petrochemical Industries, 736
Minkow, Barry, 580–581
Minnesota Mining and Manufacturing, 562. See also 3M Company
Minority Enterprise Small Business Investment Companies (MESBICs), 157

Mister Donut, 161
Mitchell, Russell, 641n
Mitsubishi, 11–12, 112, 115
Mobil, 466
Model T, 83, 130
*Modern Photography*, 496
Monaghan, Thomas, 9, 50
Monahan, Ellen, 193
Monsieur Henri wine, 731
Montgomery Ward, 524
Moore, Rob, 164n
Morgan, J.P., 48
Morgan, J.P. Company, 65
Morgan Stanley Group, 534(table), 635(table)
Morton, Peter, 169, 170
Moskowitz, Daniel B., 96n
Moss, Phil, 200n
Mrs. Fields' Cookies, 4, 48
Murphy, Robert, 586
Murray, Alan, 641n
MVS/ESA, 710–711

Nabisco, 141
NAC (National Audience Composition) diary, 510–511
Nader, Ralph, 86
NARB (National Advertising Review Board), 94
NASA (National Aeronautics and Space Administration), 227
National Advertising Review Board (NARB), 94
National Aeronautics and Space Administration (NASA), 227
National Alliance of Businessmen, 88
National Association of Accountants, 555
National Association of Manufacturers, 331
National Association of Securities Dealers, 637, 638
National Audience Com-

position (NAC) diary, 510–511
National Broadcasting Company (NBC), 225
National Coffee Association, 493
National Credit Union Administration, 539, 662
National Credit Union Association (NCUA), 528
National Flood Insurance Agency (NFIA), 683
National Flood Insurance Association, 662
National Football League (NFL), 18, 310, 331
National Football League Players' Association (NFLPA), 310
*National Geographic*, 496
National Labor Relations Board (NLRB), 317, 320, 321
National League, 686
National Market System, 637
National Mediation Board, 763
National Sports Festival, 410
National Transportation Safety Board, 754
NATO (North Atlantic Treaty Organization), 199
Navistar International Corporation, 190, 242, 346, 637(table)
NBA All-Star Game, 410
NBC (National Broadcasting Company), 225
NCR Corporation, 576 and *table*
NCUA (National Credit Union Association), 528
Near East Food Products, Inc., 151
Nielsen, A.C. Company, 510
Neiman-Marcus, 772
Nestlé Foods Corporation, 736, 737–738
Nestlé S.A., 70

New Coke, 19, 21, 186
*Newsweek*, 496
New United Motor Manufacturing, Inc. (NUMMI), 254, 738
New York Federal Reserve Bank, 537
New York Life, 661(table)
New York Stock Exchange (NYSE), 635, 638, 640
*New York Stock Exchange Index, the*, 640
NFIA (National Flood Insurance Agency), 683
NFL (National Football League), 18, 310, 331
NFLPA (National Football League Players' Association), 310
Ninja fragrance, 439
Nissan, 112
Nixon, Richard, 723
NLRB (National Labor Relations Board), 317, 320, 321
NoneSuch mincemeat, 237
North Atlantic Treaty Organization (NATO), 199
Northern Trust Company (Chicago), 526
Northwest Airlines, 86, 491
Northwestern Mutual Life, 661(table)
Novak, William, 264n
Novus Windshield Repair, 158
Nuccio, Sal, 678n
Nuclear Regulatory Commission, 761
NUMMI (New United Motor Manufacturing, Inc.), 254, 738
NYSE (New York Stock Exchange), 635, 638, 640

OCAW (Oil, Chemical, and Atomic Workers), 317
Occupational Safety and Health Administration (OSHA), 87

Office of Strategic Services, 291
Ohio Deposit Guarantee Fund, 547
Oil, Chemical, and Atomic Workers (OCAW), 317
Oldenburg, Don, 300n
Oldsmobile, 83
Oldsmobile automobiles, 218
Olestra cholesterol-free fat substitute, 64
Olive Garden restaurants, 443–445
One Night Stand, 143–144
OPEC (Organization of Petroleum Exporting Countries), 739
Opium fragrance, 439
Ouchi, William, 253
Outreach International Ltd., 750
Owens-Corning, 419(illus.), 773(illus.)
Oxy 10, 497

Pacific Coast Exchange (San Francisco), 636
Packard, David, 266–267
Pampers, 427
Pan Am Corporation, 763
Pan American Games, 410
Paragon Steel Company, 149
Parfums de Coeur, 439
Paris Bourse, the, 639
Parkinson, C. Northcote, 224, 234n
Passion perfume, 772
Paulucci, Jeno F., 5, 50
Payson, Martin F., 300n
Penney, J.C., 195, 452, 461–462, 464, 524, 589
Pennzoil Corporation, 783–784
Pension Benefit Guaranty Corporation, 299, 662
People Express Airlines, 775
PepsiCo Inc., 186, 506, 731, 735

Pepsi Cola soft drink, 716
Percy, R.D. Co., 510
Perot, Ross, 48–49
Peters, Thomas J., 64
Petzinger, Thomas, Jr., 96n
Pevely Dairy Co., 398
Pfizer Inc., 630(table), 631(table)
PFS: FILE, 699
Phillip Morris, 65, 637(table)
Phillips, Lisa, 507n
Phillips Petroleum Company, 297
Pillsbury Corporation, 5
Pizza Hut, 80, 488, 716, 740
Plan-A-Flex Home Designer kits, 146
Playskool, 425
POB (Public Oversight Board), 582
Polaroid, 45, 48, 254
Polo fragrance, 439
Pontiac, 218
Pontiac automobiles, 218
Porsche, 389, 392
Prell shampoo, 63
Primerica, 637(table)
Private Label Travel, 772
ProCreations, 146
Procter, William, 62
Procter, William Cooper, 63
Procter & Gamble Co., 9, 62–64, 65, 66, 87, 194, 221, 227, 254, 288, 427–428, 637(table), 736, 742, 779
Production House, 495
Project Access to Computer Training (PACT), 101–102
Pronto, 543
Prudential-Bache, 635(table)
Prudential Insurance Company of America, 661(table), 663, 670
Public Oversight Board (POB), 582
Puerto Rico, 468
Purina Cat Chow, 432
Purina Dog Chow, 432

Purina Puppy Chow, 195, 196–198

Quad-4 engine, 565
Quad/Graphics, 151
Quadracci, Henry, 151
Quality International, 772
Question of Scruples, A, 425
Quicken, 543

Rachlin, Norman S., CPA, 556
Radio Shack, 451, 463, 467
Raines, Tim, 34
Raleigh bicycles, 392
Ralston Purina Company, 195, 196, 197, 198, 432, 475–476
Ramlosa, 436
Raytheon Corporation, 374
RCA Corp., 225, 351, 725
RCA video disc, 416
R.D. Percy Co., 510
RealLemon lemon juice, 237
Red Lobster restaurants, 444
Reebok, 395
Reibstein, Larry, 780n
Reidenbach, R. Eric, 96n
ResTrac software system, 146
Reynolds, R.J. Company, 5
Rice, Faye, 440n
Richland 25's cigarettes, 94
Ricks, David A., 744n
R.J. Reynolds Company, 5
RJR Nabisco, 65, 630(table), 631(table)
Robin, Donald P., 96n
Rockefeller, John D., 48, 252
Rolls Royce, 391
Ross, Irwin, 300n
Rossman, Marlene L., 734
Rother, Dennis, 28–29
Rother's Bookstore, 28–29
Rowland, Richard, 495
Royal Dutch Shell Group, 121(table), 738

Rubbermaid, 64
Rutan, Dick, 373, 374

Saab (Svenska Aeroplan Aktiebolaget), 16
Saab 900 automobiles, 16
Saab-Scania, 16
Safeway, 463
Salisbury, Peter, 140
Salisbury, Wendy, 140
Salomon, Kenneth, 583
Salomon Brothers, 534(table), 635(table)
Samsung International, 255
Sam's Wholesale Clubs, 450, 463
Samuel Montagu & Company, 527
Sapit, Donald, 205, 206
Sapit, Mike, 206
Sara Lee, 432
SBA (Small Business Administration), 110, 157, 158
SBDCs (Small-Business Development Centers), 158
Scania-Vabis, 16
Schares, Gail, 59n
Schick, 419
Schlesinger, Len, 272
Schreyer, William A., 100
Schuchman, Abe, 96n
Schultz, Peter, 405n
Schwab, Charles, 252
Schwartzberg, Howard, 784
SCORE (Service Corps of Retired Executives), 158
Scredon, Scott, 200n
Screen Actors Guild, 311
Sears, Roebuck and Co., 119, 222–223, 430, 452, 461–462, 464, 466, 524, 532–533, 542, 543, 547, 548, 589, 637(table)
Sears Discover credit card, 524, 532
Securities and Exchange Commission (SEC), 99, 100, 126, 527, 580, 582, 612, 632–633, 641, 644–645, 785, 786

U.S. Postal Service, 92
United States Steel Corporation, 48
U.S. Supreme Court, 539, 758, 759, 760, 784
U.S. Surgeon General, 73
U.S. Treasury Department, 518, 521, 542, 590
U.S. Treasury securities, 627
United Steel Workers, 311, 326
United Technologies, 637 (table)
United Way, 102
UNIVAC I (Universal Automatic Computer), 693
University of Texas, 29
UPI (United Press International), 593
USX, 326, 637(table)

Vagelos, Roy, 135, 136
Vaughan, C.B., 156
Velde, Marjolijn van der, 164n
Ventres, Romeo, 237
Victorinox, 357

Visa, 523, 525
Visa credit cards, 548
Volkswagen, 121(table)
Volkswagen automobiles, 353
Volkswagen of North America, 353
Vroom, Victor, 257

Wacky Wallwalkers, 414
Waldman, Peter, 164n
*Wall Street Journal*, 275–276, 626, 635, 785–786
Wal-Mart Stores, Inc., 65, 450, 463
Walsh, James S., 374
Walt Disney Co., 417
Wapner, Joseph, 760
Warner-Lambert, 431
Warrens, Bob, 511n
Washington Apple Growers Association, 491
Waterman, Robert, 64
Waterman, Robert H., Jr., 164n
Watkins, Linda, 405n
W. Atlee Burpee & Co., 152
Weight Watchers, 384

Weinstein, Michael, 543n
Welch, John Francis "Jack," 225
Welles, Chris, 27n
Wells Fargo Bank N.A., 543
Wendy's, 285, 486
Wendy's Old Fashioned Hamburgers, 158–159
Wenger, 357
Werther, William B., Jr., 264n
Western Electric Company, 245
Westinghouse, 254, 291, 637(table)
Whirlpool, 778
Whitney, Eli, 47
Williams, Art, 675
Williams, A.L. General Agency, 675
Williams, Greg, 164n
Wilson Foods, 785
Winans, R. Foster, 785–786
Winer, Deborah Grace, 164n
Winn Dixie, 297
Wise brand snacks, 236

Wisk, 427
Woolman, Ann, 411
Woolworth, 637(table)
WordPerfect, 698
WordStar, 698
*Working Woman*, 496
World Bank (International Bank for Reconstruction and Development), 732
World Indoor Track and Field Championship, 410
Wozniak, Steve, 48, 146
Writer's Guild, 18
Write Your Own Program (WYO), 683

Xerox, 45, 466

Yeager, Jeana, 373
Young, Catherine, 641n

Zayre, 463
Zimmer, Janice, 167–168
Zimmer, Mark, 167–168
Ziskowsky, Joseph P., 370n
ZZZZ Best Co., 580–581

# Subject Index

American Stock Exchange (AMEX), 636
Annual rate of return, 626
  on stock, 632
Annual report, of corporations, 126, 127
Antitrust Improvements Act, 776
Antitrust laws, 774–776
Appellate judges, 761
Application, 277–280, 278–279(illus.)
Apprenticeships, 290
Approaching, in personal selling, 503
Arbitration, 329, 762
  compulsory, 329
Arithmetic/logic unit, 696–697
Arithmetic mean, 691
Articles of partnership, 112–113
Assembly line
  Industrial Revolution and, 47
  just-in-time concept and, 348, 349
Assessment centers, 291
Asset(s)
  on balance sheet, 566, 568
  current, 566, 587–595
  fixed, 617–622
  long-term, 617–622
  ratio of debt to, 575
  return on, 572
  spontaneous, 592
Asset turnover, 573
Asset utilization ratios, 572–573
ATMs, see Automatic teller machines
Attitude, buyers' behavior and, 394
Auditing
  computers and, 704
  social, 95
Australian Ordinaries Exchange, 636
Authority, delegation of, 216–219
Autocratic leaders, 192
Auto insurance, 664–666
  liability, 664–665
  premiums earned and losses paid for, 655 and *table*

Automated clearinghouses (ACHs), 543
Automated teller machines (ATMs), 464, 541–543
Automatic vending machines, 464
Average(s)
  statistical, 691
  stock prices and, 640

Back-ordering, production planning and, 352
Bad debts
  allowance for, 566
  reducing problem of, 593
  writing off, 594
Balance of payments, 722, 725
Balance of trade, 720–722
Balance sheet, 557, 566–570, 567(illus.), 568(illus.), 569(illus.)
  external uses of, 559
  short-term portion of, 587, 588(table)
Balloon payment, 624
Bank(s). *See also* Banking industry; Federal Reserve Banks; Investment banking
  commercial, 524–526
  discount rate and, 538
  federal, 525
  interstate and regional, 539–540
  reserve requirements of, 537–538
  savings, mutual, 527
Banker's acceptance, 590
Bank examinations, 539
Banking industry, 524–534. *See also* Bank(s); Federal Reserve Banks; Federal Reserve Board; Federal Reserve System; Investment banking
  commercial banks in, 524–526
  credit unions in, 526–527

deregulation of, 528, 529(table)
electronic funds transfer and, 464, 541–543, 590
future of, 539–543
holding companies in, 127
insurance and, 528
interstate and regional banking and, 539–540
mutual savings banks in, 527
nonbanking institutions in, 529–534
savings and loan associations in, 526
supply of money and, 522–524
Bank liabilities, managing, 596–600
Bankruptcy, 124, 126(illus.), 774
  of agent, 770
  chapter 7, 774
  chapter 11, 774
  chapter 13, 774
Bargaining unit, 321
Bartering, 519–520
Bear market, 639
Behavior
  of buyers, 393–394
  ethical, 75–79
  factors influencing, 75 and *illus*.
Behavior modification, 259
Benefits, 297–299, 299(table), 650
Better Business Bureau, 94
Big Eight accounting firms, 559
Binding contracts, 775
Biometric devices, computer security and, 706
Blacklist, 316
Black market, in communist economy, 40
"Blue-chip" stocks, 120
"Blue flu," 330
Board of directors, 118–119
Board of Governors, 534, 535

Body language, international trade and, 727
Bond(s), 622–627. *See also* Investment banking
  convertible, 625
  coupon rate and, 624
  fidelity, 667
  floating-rate, 625
  junk, 627
  maturity date of, 624
  par value of, 624
  secured and unsecured, 624
  serial, 624
  surety, 667–668
  zero-coupon, 625
Bond contract, 623–624
Bond sinking fund, 624
Bond yield, 625–626
Bonuses, 297
Bookkeeping, computers and, 704
Book value per share, 576
Boycott(s), 331, 775
  secondary, 319
Brand, 430
Branding, 430–432
Brand mark, 430
Brand-oriented advertising, 489–490
Brazil, as market, 734
Breach of contract, 769
Break-even analysis, 436–437, 438(illus.)
Break-even point, 436–437
Bretton Woods Accord, 723
Bribes, 72
British pound, divisibility of, 521
Brokerage firms, 532
Brokers, 459(illus.), 459–460
  in organized exchanges, 635, 637
  real-estate, 459
Budget, 558
  capital, 619–620
  cash, 604–607, 608(table)
  master, 558–559
Buffers, organizational, 232, 233(illus.)
Bull market, 639

Business, 4–26. *See also* Business organization(s)
customers and, 20
economy and, 22
employees and, 18
ethics and social responsibility and, 23–24
everyday importance of, 9–14
finance and, 17–18
government and legal forces and, 22–23
international, understanding, 13–14
management and, 18–19
marketing and, 20
owners and, 16–17
trends, in, 24–25
Business analysis, for new products, 418
Business decisions, right to, 41
Business ethics, 71. *See also* Ethics
Business interruption insurance, 667
Business organization(s). *See also* Organization(s); *specific types of organizations*
forms of, 106–131
Business owners, 16–17. *See also* Entrepreneurs
insurance carried by, 666–668
relationship with employees and customers and, 7–8, 8(illus.)
Business plan, 155
Business relationships, ethics and, 74
Business responsibility, of partnership, 115
Buyer behavior, 393–394
Buying, as function of marketing, 387
Buying decisions, retailing and, 461

CAD, *see* Computer assisted design
Cafeteria-style benefits programs, 298

Call feature, 625
CAM, *see* Computer assisted manufacturing
Capacity-needs analysis, 355
Capital, 156, 178
coordinating cash flows and the need for funds and, 600–607
for corporations, 124–125
current assets and, 587–595
current liabilities and, 595–600
financial, 622
physical, 35
real, 619
working, 155. *See also* Working capital management
Capital budgeting, 619–620
Capitalism, 40–45
communism and socialism compared with, 37(table)
competition in, 40, 42–45
laissez-faire, 40
modified, 41
pure, 40
rights of, 41
in United States, 46–49
Capital items, 422
Captioned photograph, 499
Caribbean Latin America, as market, 734
Cartels, 739
Cash
idle, investing, 590–592
managing, 588–592
Cash-and-carry wholesalers, 456–457
Cash budget, planning and controlling with, 604–607, 606(table)
Cash flow, 558, 560, 600
coordinating with need for funds, 600–607
Cash flow cycle, 600–603, 601(illus.), 602(illus.)

Catalog retailing, 464
CDs, *see* Certificates of deposit
Celler-Kefauver Act, 776
Centralization, 222
degree of, 222–223
Centralized organization, 222
Central processing unit (CPU), 696–697
Central purchasing, franchises and, 162
CEO, *see* Chief executive officer; Top management
Certificate of incorporation, 125
Certificates of deposit (CDs), 525–526, 590
Certified management accountant (CMA), 555
Certified Public Accountants (CPAs), 554–555, 574
opinion section and, 559
Chain retailer, 460
Channel integration, *see* Marketing channel integration
Chapter 7 bankruptcy, 774
Chapter 11 bankruptcy, 774
Chapter 13 bankruptcy, 774
Check clearing, 539
Checking accounts, 522–523
at credit unions, 526
Chief executive officer (CEO), 18–19. *See also* Top management
Choice, right to, 41, 86
CIO, *see* Congress of Industrial Organizations
Civil Rights Act of 1964, 87, 283
Classroom training, 290–291
Clayton Act, 775
Climate, facility location and, 363
Closed shop, 318

Closing
in personal selling, 504
of sole proprietorship, 110
CMA, *see* Certified management accountant
Coalition bargaining, 326
Codes of ethics, 77
Coinsurance clause, 664
COLAs, *see* Cost-of-living adjustments
Collateral, 156, 596
Collateralized loans, 600
Collections, lockboxes and, 589
Collection schedule, 604
Collective bargaining, 322–326, 323(illus.)
Colleges
accounting curriculum in, 574
as source of managers, 195
Collision insurance coverage, 665, 666
Colombia, exports of, 719
Commercial banks, 524–526
Commercialization, 420
Commercial paper, 590–591, 600
law of, 763–764
Commission, 296
Commission merchants, 459
Committees, 227–228
ad hoc, 227–228
standing, 228
Common carriers, 469
Common law, 756
Common Market, 740
Common stock, 119, 130, 628
class B, 130
convertible bonds and, 625
dividends on, 119, 631 and *table*
rights of stockholders and, 120–123
Communication
advertising as, 483
downward and upward, 229
ethical, 73–74
grapevine and, 231
publicity as, 483
Communism, 36–40

Dollar
    divisibility of, 521
    Eurodollar market
        and, 591
    gold standard and, 723
    as international cur-
        rency, 58
Domestic international
    sales corporations
    (DISCs), 732
Door-to-door selling, 463
Dow Jones Industrial Av-
    erage, 120, 635,
    638, 639, 640
Dow Jones Industrials,
    119, 121(table)
Downward communica-
    tion, 229
Drop shippers, 457
Drug testing, employment
    and, 757
DSS, *see* Decision support
    system
Dumping, 730–731
Durability, of money, 521

Early-retirement pack-
    ages, 284
Earnings, 560, 565–566.
    *See also* Wage(s)
    retained, 627–628
Earnings per share, 565–
    566
Economic communities,
    740
Economic contraction, 53
Economic cycles, govern-
    ment intervention
    in, 53–55
Economic expansion, 53
Economic forces, in mar-
    keting environment,
    401
Economic order quantity
    (EOQ) method, 348
Economics, 35
    supply-side, 55
Economic systems, 34–46
    American, 46–59
    capitalist, 40–45
    communist, 36–40
    mixed, 46
    nature of, 35–36
    questions to be an-
        swered by, 35
    socialist, 40
Economy, 22. *See also*
    American economy;

Economic systems
    manufacturing, 47
    service, 47
    union membership
        and, 332
EEC, *see* European Eco-
    nomic Community
EEOC, *see* Equal Employ-
    ment Opportunity
    Commission
Effective interest rate,
    597
Effectiveness
    managerial, 185–186
    of production and op-
        erations manage-
        ment, 361–365
Efficiency, managerial,
    186
EFT, *see* Electronic funds
    transfer
EFTA, *see* European Free
    Trade Association
Elasticity of demand, 436
Electronic funds transfer
    (EFT), 464, 541–
    543
    cash management and,
        590
Electronic mail system
    (EMS), 574, 704
Electronic media, for ad-
    vertising, 494–495,
    497
Elements, contract law
    and, 766–769
Embargo, 730
Employee(s), 18. *See also*
    Human resources
    management
    of corporations, 127
    government, in unions,
        332
    motivating, 184–185.
        *See also* Human re-
        lations
    orientation of, 281
    recruiting, 183–184,
        275–276
    selection of, 276–281,
        278–279(illus.)
    of sole proprietorship,
        111
    temporary or part-
        time, 351
Employee participation,
    253–254, 332
Employee Retirement In-

come Security Act
    (ERISA), 299
Employee stock owner-
    ship plans (ESOPs),
    297
Employer Indentification
    Number, 125
Employer's associations,
    331
Employment. *See also* Un-
    employment
    company size and,
        145(table)
    discrimination in, 87–
        88, 285–288,
        286(illus.),
        287(illus.)
    drug testing and, 757
    number of companies
        by size of,
        143(table)
Employment Act of 1946,
    53
Employment agencies,
    194, 276, 277
Employment needs, ana-
    lyzing, 273–274
Employment practices,
    86–88. *See also* Hu-
    man relations man-
    agement
    equality issues and,
        87–88
    safety and manage-
        ment issues and, 87
    training for hard-core
        unemployed and,
        88
EMS, *see* Electronic mail
    system
End effector, of industrial
    robot, 366
Endorsement, 764,
    765(illus.)
Endowment life insur-
    ance, 676
ENIAC (Electronic Nu-
    meral Integrator
    and Calculator), 693
Entrepreneurs, 146–155.
    *See also* Small busi-
    ness
    early, 48
    keys to success of,
        150–152
    modern, 48–49, 50
    paths to failure of,
        152–155

rewards of, 147–148
    risks of, 148–150
    role in American econ-
        omy, 47–49
    training programs for,
        157–158
Environment
    impact on organiza-
        tions, 231–232,
        232(illus.)
    of international trade,
        724–729
    legal, *see* Law(s); Legal
        environment
    marketing, 401–402
    pollution and, 88–90
EOQ, *see* Economic order
    quantity method
Equal Employment Op-
    portunity Commis-
    sion (EEOC), 282–
    283
Equality, in employment,
    87–88, 285–288,
    286(illus.),
    287(illus.)
Equal opportunity, in em-
    ployment, 87–88
Equal Opportunity Em-
    ployer, 283
Equal Pay Act, 284
Equilibrium price, 42,
    43(illus.)
Equipment
    accessory, 423
    major, 422–423
Equity theory, 255–257
ERISA, *see* Employee Re-
    tirement Income
    Securty Act
ESOPs, *see* Employee
    stock ownership
    plans
Esteem needs, 427–248
Ethics, 23–24, 71–79, 81
    business, 71
    codes of, 77, 78–79
    communications and,
        73–74
    conflict of interest and,
        72
    in decision making,
        75–79
    defined, 71–72
    fairness and honesty
        and, 73
    relationships within a
        business and, 74

Franchise, 158
Franchisee, 158
Franchiser, 158
Franchising, 158–163
  advantages of, 160–162
  disadvantages of, 163
  failures and, 160
  growth in, 158–159, 160(illus.)
  legal protections for franchisees and, 163
Free-market communism, 38–39
Free-rein leaders, 192
Free trade zones, 733
Freight forwarders, 469
Friends, as source of capital, 156
Fringe benefits, 297–299, 299(table), 650
FSLIC, *see* Federal Savings and Loan Insurance Corporation
FTC, *see* Federal Trade Commission
Full-service wholesalers, 455–456
Functional departmentalization, 214
Functional layout, 364
Functional managers, 227
Functional structure, 226 and *illus.*
Fund(s)
  coordinating cash flow and need for, 600–607
  for corporations, 124–125
  flow of, 51–52, 52(illus.)
  money market, 352, 591–592
  mutual, 531–532
  for partnerships, 116
  pension, 530–531
  for sole proprietorships, 110
Funding, 178
  for small businesses, 155(illus.), 155–157

Garn-St. Germain Depository Institution De

regulatory Act of 1982, 528, 529(table)
GATT, *see* General Agreement on Tariffs and Trade
General Agreement on Tariffs and Trade (GATT), 731–732
General and administrative expense, 564–565
Generalist, sole proprietor as, 110
General-merchandise wholesalers, 455–456
General partnership, 111
Generic products, 431
GIGO (garbage in, garbage out), 707
Givebacks, 326
Globalization, international marketing and, 740
GNP, *see* Gross national product
Goal, 243
Going public, 119, 632
Gold standard, 723
Good, 384
Government, 22–23
  in American economy, 49–55
  avoidance of intervention by, 92–95
  in capitalist economy, 40
  in communist economy, 37
  as consumer, 22–23
  insurance provided by, 660–662, 670–671
  in socialist economy, 40
  as user of financial statements, 559
Government employees, in unions, 332
Government regulation, *see* Regulation
Grading, as function of marketing, 388
Grapevine, 231
Grievance, 327
  resolution of, 327, 328(illus.)

Gross national product (GNP), 51–53, 53(illus.), 54(illus.)
  real, 52–53
Growth, of small businesses, 153–154
Growth stage, 426–427
Guaranteed loans, for small businesses, 157

"Hand-shake deal," 766
Hard disks, 697
Hardware, 695–697
Hawthorne effect, 245
Hawthorne studies, 245
Headhunters, 194, 276, 277
Health care industry, unionization of, 312
Health insurance, 668–671
  as benefit, 650
  group, 668
  national, 671
  sources of, 670–671
Health maintenance organizations (HMOs), 670, 672
High technology, small businesses in, 146
HMOs, *see* Health maintenance organizations
Holder-of-record date, 630
Holding companies, 127–128
Holidays, international trade and, 727
Home banking, 543
Honesty, 73
Horizontal integration, 465
Hospital(s), unionization of, 312
Hospitalization insurance, 668
Humanistic philosophy, 76
Human relations, 242–264
  behavior modification and, 259
  early studies of employee motivation and, 243–245

equity theory and, 255–257
  expectancy theory and, 257–258
  Herzberg's motivational and maintenance factors and, 249–251
  job design and, 259–264, 260(table)
  McGregor's Theory X and Theory Y and, 251–253, 254(table)
  Maslow's hierarchy of needs and, 246–249
  modified participative management and, 254
  nature of, 243
  quality circles and, 254–255
  Therory Z and, 253–254
Human relations skills, of managers, 194
Human resources, 35, 177, 273
Human resources management, 189, 272–300
  benefits and, 297–299, 299(table)
  discrimination and, 285–288
  financial compensation and, 293–297, 294–295(table)
  industrial safety and, 300
  legal considerations in, 281–285, 282(table)
  nature of, 273
  orientation and, 281
  performance appraisal and, 291–292
  planning and, 273–275
  promotions, transfers, and separations and, 292–293
  recruiting and, 275–276
  selection and, 276–281
  training and development and, 289–291

IC, *see* Integrated circuit cards
Ideas, *see* Product ideas

Image, of product, 397 and *illus.*, 398

IMF, *see* International Monetary Fund

Implied contract, 767–768

Implied warranty, 763

Import(s), of United States, 58(illus.), 58–59

Importing, 719–720, 720(table)

Import tariffs, 729–730

In-basket simulation, 291

Income, 560. *See also* Wage(s)
disability, 669
net, 565–566

Income statement, 555, 557, 560–566, 561(illus.), 562(illus.), 563(illus.)
expenses on, 563–565
external uses of, 559
net income on, 565–566
revenue on, 562

Income taxes. *See also* Tax(es) corporate and individual, 777

Incorporation, 125. *See also* Corporations

Indemnity, rule of, 657–658

Indenture, 623–624

Independent retailer, 460

Index(es), stock prices and, 640

Indian Latin America, as market, 734

Individual Retirement Accounts (IRAs), 530

Industrial products, 420, 421(table), 422–423
marketing channels for, 453, 454(illus.)

Industrial Revolution, 46–47
labor unions and, 311–313
recognition of social responsibility and, 83

Industrial robots, 366–367, 367(illus.)

Industrial safety, 50, 300

Industrial services, 423

Industrial unions, 311

Industry(ies)
cottage, 46
expected growth of, 331, 332(table)

Industry analysis, 576

Industry-wide bargaining, 326

Inferential skills, of managers, 194

Inflation, 52–53
monetary policy and, 54–55
stagflation and, 55

Inflation rate, 521, 522(table)

Informal leaders, 230

Informal organization, 230–231

Information, 687. *See also* Data accounting, 553, 554(illus.)
management levels and, 687–688

Informational advertising, 487

In-home retailing, 463

Initial public offering, 632

Injunction, 316

Inland marine insurance, 667

Input(s), 343
transforming into outputs, 343–344(illus.)

Input-output devices, 697

Input-output ratio, equity theory and, 255–257

Inside directors, 119

Inside order takers, 502

Inspection, 359–360

Installment loans, 599–600

Institutional advertising, 491

Insurable interest, 658

Insurance, 654–678. *See also* Risk management automobile, 655 and *table*, 664–666
for banking institutions, 528, 531
business interruption, 667

depository, 528, 531, 539, 662
disability income, 669
fidelity bonds and, 667
fire, 664
health, 650, 668–671, 672
inland marine, 667
insurance industry crisis and, 676–678
law of adverse selection and, 657
law of large numbers and, 655–657
liability, 664–668, 665(table), 676–678
life, 671–676
malpractice, 666
marine, 667
ocean marine, 667
private sources of, 662–663
product liability, 667
property, 663–664, 665(table)
public sources of, 660–662
requirements for, 658–660
rule of indemnity and, 657–658
self-insurance and, 653–654
surety bonds and, 667–668
title, 668
unemployment, 298, 661–662
workers' compensation, 661–662

Insurance companies
financial services offered by, 529–530
largest, 660, 661(table)

Insured, 654

Intangible products, 177

Intangible property, 771

Integrated circuit, computer development and, 693

Integrated circuit (IC) cards, 706

Intensive distribution, 467

Interest, 596
conflict of, 72
insurable, 658

in partnership, sale of, 115
security, 156

Interest expense, 565

Interest rate(s)
deregulation of banking industry and, 528
effective, 597
floating, 597
foreign investments and, 639
for money market, 591(illus.)
prime, 596–597
stated, 597

Interlocking directorates, 775

Intermediaries, *see* Middlemen

Intermittent organization, 364

Internal sources, recruiting from, 275

International Bank for Reconstruction and Development (World Bank), 732

International business, 716–744
balance of trade and, 720–722
environment of, 724–729
exchange rates and, 722–723
exporting and importing and, 719–720, 720(table)
marketing and, 740–744
organizing, 733–737
trade and, 717–719
trade barriers and, 729–731
trade facilitators and, 731–733
trade organizations and, 737–740
understanding, 13–14

International Monetary Fund (IMF), 732

Interview, selection and, 281

Introductory stage, 426

Inventory management, 346–348, 349, 594–595

ABC inventory classification system and, 347 and *illus.*
economic order quantity method and, 348
just-in-time concept and, 348, 349
Inventory planning and control
computers and, 703
physical distribution and, 468–469
Inventory turnover ratio, 573, 601
Investment(s)
direct, 736
foreign, 639, 725
of idle cash, 590–592
short-term, 592 and *table*
Investment banking, 632–634
distributing new issues and, 634
pricing new issues and, 633–634
prospectus and, 632–633
underwriting and, 633
Investors, as users of accounting information, 560
IRAs, *see* Individual Retirement Accounts

Jamming, 419
Japanese management, 254–255
American management and Theory Z management compared with, 253–254, 255(table)
JIT, *see* Just-in-time concept
Job analysis, 274–275
Job description, 274
Job design, 259–264, 260(table)
scheduling stategies and, 261–262
Job enlargement, 260
Job enrichment, 261
unions and, 332
Job evaluation, 274
Job rotation, 260
Job seeking, 12–13

Job sharing, 262
Job specification, 274
Job stress, 258
Joint tenancy, 773
Joint ventures, 112
international, 736–737
Judges, appellate, 761
Junk bonds, 627
Junk mail, computers and, 707
Jurisdiction, 758
Just-in-time (JIT) concept, 348, 349
zero defects and, 360

Knights of Labor, 314
Korean management, 255

Labeling, 430, 432–433
Labor
availability of, 363
hours of, 351–352
Labor contract, 324–326
labor and management pressure tactics and, 329–331
reaching settlement on, 328–329
two-tier, 326
Labor-management legislation, 315–320
Labor unions, 311–333
collective bargaining and, 322–326
craft, 311
declining membership of, 333
dispute resolution and, 327, 328(illus.)
future of, 331–333
history of, 311–315
impact on organizations, 231
industrial, 311
labor-management legislation and, 315–320
mediation and, 763
pressure tactics of, 329–331
rationale for, 311
reaching settlement and, 328–329
right-to-work laws and, 284, 318, 319(illus.)
types of, 311
unionization and, 320–322, 321(illus.)

LAFTA, *see* Latin American Free Trade Association
Laissez-faire capitalism, 40
Land pollution, 90
Landrum-Griffin Act, 320
Language
computer, 697
international trade and, 727
Large numbers, law of, 655–657
Large-scale integrated circuit (LSI circuit), computer development and, 693–694
Latin America, markets in, 734
Latin American Free Trade Association (LAFTA), 740
Law(s). *See also* Legal environment
administrative, 758
of adverse selection, 657
of agency, 769–770
antitrust, 774–776
of bankruptcy, 774
benefits required by, 298
of commercial paper, 763–764
common, 756
constitutional, 755
of contracts, 765–769
deregulating banking industry, 528, 529(table)
employment discrimination and, 285
governing employee recruitment and selection, 281–285, 282(table)
governing insurance industry, 657, 659
governing international trade, 724–726, 726(table), 731, 733
labor-management, 315–320
of large numbers, 655–657
patent, 45
of property, 771–773

protecting franchisees, 163
right-to-work, 284, 318, 319(illus.)
role in American economy, 49–50
sales, 763
securities and, 641
sources of, 755–758
statutory, 756–757
tax, 776–778
of torts, 764–765
uniform commercial code and, 763–764
Layoff, 293
Leader(s)
autocratic, 192
democratic, 192
free-rein, 192
informal, 230
Leadership, 192
Learning, buyers' behavior and, 394
Legal environment, 22–23, 754–780. *See also* Law(s); Regulation
competition and, 774–776
courts and dispute resolution and, 758–763
marketing and, 401
regulation versus deregulation and, 778, 780
sources of law and, 755–758
Legality, contract law and, 769
Liability(ies)
on balance sheet, 568–569
bank, 596–600
current, 569, 595–600
limited, of corporations, 124
long-term, 617, 622–626
nonbank, 600
product, 667, 764–765
unlimited, of sole proprietorship, 110
Liability insurance, 664–668, 665(table)
automobile, 664–665
insurance industry crisis and, 676–678

international market-
ing and, 740–742
in marketing mix,
397–400
objectives of, 485–488
packaging and, 432
personal selling and,
500–504
positioning and, 488
promotion mix and,
483–484
publicity and, 497–500
push and pull strate-
gies for, 484–485,
485(illus.)
reinforcement, 487–
488
sales, 399, 483–484,
504–506
Promotional positioning,
488
Property
condominium and co-
operative ownership
of, 773
fee-simple ownership
of, 771
intangible, 771
joint tenancy of, 773
personal, 771
private, right to, 41
real, 771
tangible, 771
tenancy in common
and, 771–773
underinsuring, 664
Property insurance, 663–
664, 665(table)
Property, plant, and
equipment, 617–
622
Property tax, 778
Prospecting, in personal
selling, 503
Prospectus, 632–633
Protective tariffs,730
Proxy, 122
Psychological pricing, 439
Public accountants, 553–
555
Public accounting firms,
555 and *table*
Big Eight, 559
marketing, 556
Public corporation, 119–
120
Public insurance com-
pany, 660–661

Publicity, 399, 483, 497–
500
negative, 501(table)
Publicity release, topics
for, 501(table)
Public offerings, 632
initial, 632
Public relations, 497
Public warehouses, 471
Pull strategy, 484–485,
485(illus.)
Purchase decision, 10–12
Purchasing, 345–346
franchises and, 162
Pure capitalism, 40
Pure competition, 42
Pure premium, 656
Pure risk, 651–652
Push strategy, 484–485,
485(illus.)

Qualifications, job specification and, 274
Quality, definition of,
356–359
Quality circles, 228, 254–
255, 360–361
Quality control, 356–361
definition of quality
and, 356–359
inspection and, 359–
360
quality circles and,
360–361
zero defects and, 360
Quick ratio, 573
Quotas, 730–731

Rack jobbers, 457
Radio advertising, 497
Railroads
deregulation of, 780
Industrial Revolution
and, 47
physical distribution
and, 469–470
Ratio
asset utilization, 572–
573
conversion, 625
of debt to assets, 575
debt utilization, 574–
575
input-output, 255–257
inventory turnover,
573, 601
liquidity, 573
payout, 629

price-earnings, 631
profitability, 572
quick, 573
receivable turnover,
573, 593–594, 601
Ratio analysis, 570–576
Raw materials, 422
availability of, 362
Reaction strategy, 91
Real capital, 619
Real estate brokers, 459
Real gross national prod-
uct, 52–53
Real property, 771
Receivable turnover ratio,
573, 593–594, 601
Recordkeeping, com-
puters and, 705
Recruiting, 183–184,
275–276
from external sources,
275–276
from internal sources,
275
laws governing, 281–
285, 282(table)
Reference checking, 281
Reference groups, buyers'
behavior and, 394–
395
Refunds, 505–506
Regressive tax, 778
Regulation
deregulation versus,
778–780
by Federal Reserve
System 538–539
in marketing environ-
ment, 401
of partnership, 114
self-regulation and,
92–95
of sole proprietorship,
109
Regulatory agencies, 22,
758, 759(table)
Reinforcement promo-
tion, 487–488
Reminder advertising,
490
Renewable term insur-
ance, 674
Reputation, of small businesses, 151–152
Research, marketing,
402–403, 403(illus.)
Research and develop-
ment, 416. *See also*

New product devel-
opment expense
for, 565
Reserve requirements,
537–538
Resources. *See also* Capital; Funding
financial, 178
human, 35, 177, 273.
*See also* Human re-
sources manage-
ment
natural, 35
personal, as source of
capital, 155–156
physical, 177–178
*Respondeat superior* doctrine, 770
Responsibility, 217
Retailer(s), 145, 451
chain, 460
independent, 460
Retailer coupons, 505
Retailing, 460–464
catalog, 464
department stores and,
524, 461–462
in-home, 463
mail-order, 464
mass merchandisers
and, 462–463
nonstore, 463–464
small businesses in,
145
specialty stores and,
463
telephone, 463–464
wheel of, 473
Retained earnings, 627–
628
Retirement, 293
early, 284
health-care benefits
following, 650
Return on assets, 572
Revaluation, 723
Revenues, 560
on income statement,
562
total, 437
Revolving credit, 524
financial networks and,
532
Right
to be heard, 86
to be informed, 86
of capitalism, 41
to choose, 86

Subject Index

**I-25**

Right *(Cont.)*
of common stockholders, 120–123
preemptive, of common stockholders, 122–123
of preferred stockholders, 123–124
to safety, 85
Right-to-work laws, 284, 318, 319(illus.)
Risk, 651–652
assessment of, 620–621, 621(table)
assuming, 653–654
avoidance of, 652
insurable, 658–659
junk bonds and, 627
measurable, 658
predictable, 658–659
pure, 651–652
reduction of, 652–653
speculative, 651
transferring to insurance company, 654
Risk management, 651–654. *See also* Insurance
nature of risk and, 651–652
techniques for, 652–654
Risk taking, as function of marketing, 388
Robinson-Patman Act, 776
Robotics, 366–367, 367(illus.)
Routing, 355
Royalty agreement, 735
Rule of indemnity, 657–658

Safety
employment and, 87
industrial, 50, 300
products and, 85
Salary, 296
as maintenance factor, 250
Sales, 560. *See also* Selling
of accounts receivable, 600
promotion to stabilize, 487
Sales branches, 460, 466
Sales forecast, 603–604
Sales law, 763

Sales offices, 460
Salespersons, 501–503
creative, 502
missionary, 503
support, 502–503
technical, 503
Sales promotion, 399, 483–484, 504–506
consumer contests and sweepstakes in, 505
point-of-purchase displays and, 504–505
premiums and trading stamps in, 505
refunds in, 505–506
retailer coupons in, 505
sampling and demonstrations, in, 505
trade shows and, 506
Sales tax, 778
Sales volume maximization, as pricing objective, 435
Sampling, 359–360, 505
Savings accounts, 526–527
at credit unions, 526
Savings and loan associations (S&Ls), 526
decline of, 528, 530(illus.)
SBA, *see* Small Business Administration
SBDCs, *see* Small-business Development Centers
SBIs, *see* Small Business Institutes
Scheduling, computers and, 704
Schools, as source of managers, 195
Scientific management, 244
SCORE, *see* Service Corps of Retired Executives
Screening, of new-product ideas, 417
Secondary boycotts, 319
Secondary data, 403
Secondary markets, 634
Secondary trading, 634
Secrecy, as advantage of sole proprietorship, 108
Secured bond, 624

Secured loans, 596
Securities Act of 1933, 641
Securities Amendments Act of 1975, 637, 641
Securities and Exchange Commission (SEC), 126
creation of, 641
prospectus and, 632–633
Securities Exchange Act of 1934, 641
Securities markets, 634–641
measuring market performance and, 638–640
organized exchanges and, 634–637
over-the-counter market and, 637–638
secondary, 634
securities laws and, 641
Security, as maintenance factor, 250
Security interest, 156
Security needs, 247
Selection, 184, 276–281
application and, 277–280, 278–279(illus.)
interviewing and, 281
laws governing, 281–285, 282(table)
reference checking and, 281
testing and, 280–281
Selective advertising, 489–491
Selective distribution, 467–468
Self-actualization needs, 248
Self-insurance, 653–654
Self-regulation, social responsibility and, 92–95
Self-sufficiency, of nations, 718–719
Selling. *See also* Sales
door-to-door, 463
as function of marketing, 388
nonpersonal, 464
personal, 398–399,

463, 483, 488, 500–504
Selling agents, 459
Sensor, of industrial robot, 366
Separations, 293
Serial bonds, 624
Service(s), 384
industrial, 423
small businesses in, 145–146
Service Corps of Retired Executives (SCORE), 158
Service economy, 47
Service merchandisers, 457
Share account, 526
Share draft account, 523, 526
Shareholders, *see* Stockholders
Sherman Antitrust Act, 41, 49–50, 316, 775
Shipping and receiving, 349–350
physical distribution and, 470
Shopping products, 421–422
Shop steward, 327
Short-term financial management, 586–607
Short-term financing, 17
Sickouts, 330
Simple-interest loans, 598
Sinking fund, 624
S&Ls, *see* Savings and loan associations
Slogans, 490
Small business, 141–158. *See also* Entrepreneurs
defined, 141–143
failure rate of, 148–150
financial resources available to, 155–157
financial risks of running, 148–150
importance to American economy, 143–144
management help for, 157–158
nature of, 141–146
owning, 146–155

proportion by industry, 143(table)
SBA standards for size of, 142(table)
Small Business Administration (SBA), 141
as source of management help, 158
standards for business size and, 142(table)
Small-Business Development Centers (SBDCs), 158
Small Business Institutes (SBIs), 158
Smoking, restrictions on, 86
Social audits, 95
Social factors
international trade and, 727–729
in marketing environment, 401
Socialism, communism and capitalism compared with, 37(table)
Social needs, 247
Social responsibility, 23–24, 79–95
accommodation stategy for, 92
consumerism and, 85–86
defense strategy for, 91–92
early developments in, 83–84
employment practices and, 86–88
evolution of concept of, 82–84
groups evaluating, 81–82
Industrial Revolution and recognition of, 83
nature of, 80
proactive stategy for, 92, 93
reaction strategy for, 91
self-regulation and, 92–95
today, 84
Social roles, buyers' behavior and, 394

Social Security, 298, 530–531, 661
automated clearinghouses and, 543
Social Security Act, 661
Software, 697
Sole proprietorships, 107–111
advantages of, 108–110
disadvantages of, 110–111
partnerships and corporations compared with, 108(illus.)
Soviet Union
foreign joint ventures in, 716
free-market communism in, 38, 39
Span of management, 219–221, 220(illus.)
organizational layers and, 220–221
wide and narrow, 219–220
Specialization, 212–214, 214(table)
within partnership, 113
Specialty-line wholesalers, 456
Specialty stores, 463
Speculative risk, 651
Spontaneous assets, 592
Spreadsheets, 698
Stability, of money, 521
Staffing, as function of management, 183–184
Stagflation, 55
Staggers rail Act, 780
Standardization, product design and, 361–362
Standard of living, in communist economy, 37–38
*Standard & Poor's 500 Index*, 640
Standing committee, 228
State courts, 759–760
relationship between federal courts and, 760
Stated interest rate, 597
Statistics, management in-

formation systems and, 689–692
Status quo, as pricing objective, 435
Statutory law, 756–757
Stock(s), 119–120. *See also* Common stock; Investment banking
"blue-chip," 120
dividends on, 119, 628, 631(table)
earnings per share and, 565–566
individual, measuring performance of, 630–632
no-par value, 125
owner's equity and, 569–570
par value, 125, 628, 629(illus.)
per share data and, 575–576
preferred, 119–120, 123–124, 628–629
transfer of ownership and, 124
Stock brokers, 635, 637
Stock certificate, 628
Stock company, 662
Stock exchanges, 634–637
foreign, 639
regional, 636–637
Stockholders, 617, 628
of common stock, 120–123
of preferred stock, 123–124
Storage, as function of marketing, 388
Store(s)
department, 461–462, 524
specialty, 463
super, 463
Strategic plans, 182–183
Strategy, marketing, *see* Marketing strategy
Stress, job, 258
Strike(s), 329–331
injunction and, 316
Taft-Hartley Act and, 318
wildcat, 330
Strikebreakers, 331
Strike funds, 329–330
Structure, 211. *See also*

Organizational structure
Subcontracting, production planning and, 352
Subsidary corporations, 127
Supermarkets, 463
Super NOW accounts, 523
Super stores, 463
Supervisory managers, *see* First-line management
Supplies, 423
Supply, 42, 436
of money, 522–524
relationship to demand and price, 436(illus.), 436–437
Supply-side economics, 55
Support salespersons, 502–503
Surety bonds, 667–668
Surgical insurance, 669
Survival, as pricing objective, 434–435
Sweepstakes, 505
Symbolic/prestige pricing, 439
Syndicate, 634

Tactical plans, 183
Taft-Hartley Act, 318–320
Tangible products, 177
Tangible property, 771
Target market, 391–395
Tariffs, 729–730
ad valorem, 729
fixed, 729
protective, 730
Task force, 228
Tax(es)
on advertising, 779
in cash flow cycle, 602
on corporations, 109, 125, 126, 128, 177
on holding companies, 128
income, 777
on partnerships, 116
property, 778
regressive, 778
sales, 778
on sole proprietorship,

Variable costs, 437
Variable life insurance, 676
Vending machines, 464
Vertical integration, 466–467
Vertical marketing channel, 466–467
  administered, 466
  contractual, 467
  corporate, 467
Very large-scale-integration (VLSI), computer development and, 694
Vision insurance, 669–670
VLSI, *see* Very large-scale-integration
Voluntary agreement, contract law and, 766–768
Voting
  of common stock, 121–122
  preferred stock and, 123

Wage(s), 293–297, 294–295(table)

minimum, 284–285, 285(table), 313
  piece, 244, 296
  time, 296
Wage gap, 285–286, 286(illus.)
Wage/salary survey, 296
Wagner Act, 316–317
Wall Street, 635
Warehouse
  functions of, 470–471
  private and public, 471
Warehousing, physical distribution and, 470–471
Warranty
  express, 763
  implied, 763
  labeling and, 432
  of merchantability, 763
Water pollution, 88–89
Webb-Pomerone Export Trade Act, 724
Wellness programs, 668
Wheel of retailing concept, 473
White-collar employees, in unions, 332
Whole life insurance, 675–676

Wholesalers, 451
  cash-and-carry, 456–457
  full-service, 455–456
  general-merchandise, 455–456
  importance of, 454, 455(table)
  limited-line, 456
  limited-service, 456–457
  mail-order, 457
  merchant, 455–457, 457(illus.)
  specialty-line, 456
  truck, 456–457
Wholesaling, 455–464
  agents and brokers in, 457–460, 459(illus.)
  manufacturers' sales branches and offices in, 460
Wide span of management, 219, 220
Wildcat strike, 330
Women
  employment discrimination and, 285–288, 286(illus.), 287(illus.)

equality in employment and, 87–88
Word processing, 698
Workers' compensation, 298, 661–662
Working capital, 155
Working capital management, 586–607
  coordinating cash flows and the need for funds and, 600–607
  current liabilities and, 595–600
  current liabilities and, 595–600
Work sharing, 262
Work week, compressed, 262
World Bank, 732
Writing off, of bad debts, 594

Yield
  on bonds, 625–626
  current, 626
  dividend, 631 and *table*
Yugoslavia, free-market communism in, 38

Zero-coupon bonds, 625
Zero defects, 360

## Credit *(continued from p. iv)*

Touchton; **p. 154,** Rod Hanson; **p. 159,** © 1985 Bob O'Shaughnessy/The Stock Market; **p. 162,** © 1987 Todd Gray. ***Chapter 6*** **P. 179,** © 1988 Lou Jones; **p. 181,** Scott Paper Company; **p. 182,** photo by Gary Krueger; courtesy of Walt Disney; **p. 184,** © 1986 Jon Feingersh/Stock, Boston; **p. 188,** courtesy of Bayer AG; **p. 193,** © 1987 Jim Caccavo/Picture Group; **p. 196,** courtesy of American Airlines; **p. 200,** Randy Matusow. ***Chapter 7*** **P. 215,** photo by Chris Maynard; courtesy of The Dunn & Bradstreet Corp.; **p. 221,** courtesy of Household International; **p. 229,** Steve Hockstein; **p. 230,** © Berle Cherney/Uniphoto; **p. 233,** Charles Cherney, Chicago Tribune; **p. 233,** photo by Bryan Smothers, Houston, Texas; courtesy of Sysco Corporation. ***Chapter 8*** **P. 245,** © 1983 Jeffry W. Myers/Stock, Boston; **p. 246,** © 1989 Bob Sacha; **p. 248,** courtesy of Marriott Corporation; **p. 249,** © 1988 John Barr/Gamma-Liaison; **p. 251,** courtesy of Public Service Enterprise Group, Inc.; **p. 257,** photo by Warren Faubel Photography; courtesy of Union Bank; **p. 261,** C. Bruce Forster; **p. 263,** courtesy of USX Corporation. ***Chapter 9*** **P. 276,** photo by Michael Mauney, Chicago, Illinois; courtesy of Walgreen Co.; **p. 280,** © 1988 Andy Freeberg; **p. 282,** © 1984 Charles Gupton/Uniphoto; **p. 283,** © John Coletti/The Picture Cube; **p. 289,** courtesy of ITT Corporation; **p. 290,** courtesy of Marine Midland Bank; **p. 297,** photo by Scott Maclay; courtesy of Gannett Co., Inc.; **p. 299,** Robb Kendrick. ***Chapter 10*** **P. 313,** Jocelyn Boutin/The Picture Cube; **p. 315,** © 1987 Cindy Charles; **p. 322,** © Owen Franken/Stock, Boston; **p. 324,** © 1985 A. Tannenbaum/Sygma; **p. 327,** © 1987 Richard Faverty/Gamma-Liaison; **p. 330,** © Ellis Herwig/Stock, Boston. ***Chapter 11*** **P. 346,** design & photo direction: H. A. Boelter; photography: NTA, Inc.; **p. 350,** Scott Paper Company; **p. 358,** courtesy of General Signal Corporation; **p. 363,** photo by Haverfield Helicopters; courtesy of American Electric Power Service Corporation; **p. 365,** © 1987 Ted Horowitz/The Stock Market; **p. 368,** Hank Morgan; **p. 369,** © Brownie Harris/The Stock Market. ***Chapter 12*** **P. 386,** © Philip Jon Bailey/The Picture Cube; **p. 387,** Sears, Roebuck and Co. 1986 Annual Report; photo by Jay Silverman; **p. 391,** Volvo North America Corp.; **p. 395,** Barnett Banks, Inc. 1986 Annual Report; **p. 399,** courtesy of Hardee's Food Systems, Inc., **p. 400,** courtesy of Tyco Toys, Inc.; **p. 404,** Westinghouse Electric Corporation. ***Chapter 13*** **P. 418,** Rene Sheret/Folio; **p. 419,** Mark Ferri; **p. 421,** © Rob Nelson/Stock, Boston; **p. 424,** Dana Fineman/Sygma; **p. 427,** © Neutrogena; **p. 431,** © 1987 Charles Gupton/Uniphoto; **p. 433,** Brad Trent/DOT; **p. 440,** © Miro Vintoniv/Stock, Boston. ***Chapter 14*** **P. 452,** courtesy of Weyerhaeuser Company; p. 458 (all four photos), © 1986 John Blaustein; **p. 464,** © 1987 Nina Barnett; **p. 465,** Katherine Lambert; **p. 471,** courtesy of Toys "R" Us, Inc. ***Chapter 15*** **P. 486,** photo by Ken Haas; courtesy of Carteret Bancorp, Inc.; **p. 489,** permission granted by American Express and Mr. Ray Charles; **p. 493,** Lever Brothers Company; **p. 494,** courtesy of Giant Food, Inc.; **p. 496,** reprinted by permission by Hershey Foods Corporation; HERSHEY'S is a registered trademark of Hershey Foods Corporation; **p. 498,** The Goodyear Tire and Rubber Company; **p. 502,** Deere & Company; **p. 506,** Springs Industries, Inc. ***Chapter 16*** **P. 520,** A. Nogues/Sygma; **p. 525,** © 1981 Lou Jones; **p. 533,** courtesy of Kemper Corporation; **p. 536,** Eddie Adams/Gamma-Liaison; **p. 541,** courtesy of First Interstate Bancorp. ***Chapter·17*** **P. 553,** Black Star/courtesy of Ernst & Whinney; printed with permission of PGA Tour, Inc.; **p. 557,** Bruce McAllister/Uniphoto; **p. 565,** Gina Minielli, New York Mets; **p. 570,** courtesy of Smith Corona. ***Chapter 18*** **P.**

**589,** Michael Tamborrino; **p. 597,** courtesy of Bank of Hawaii; **p. 599,** Marvin Silver; **p. 604,** photo by John Rae; courtesy of Perini Corporation. *Chapter 19* **P. 620,** 1987 Old Stone Corporation Annual Report; photographer, Ric Murray; **p. 621,** photo by Lon Harding, courtesy of Unocal Corporation; **p. 633,** © 1988 Seth Resnick/Picture Group; **p. 636,** © 1987 John Chiasson/Gamma Liaison; **p. 638,** Ben Martin/Time Magazine. *Chapter 20* **P. 653,** courtesy of William Taufic and Federal Express; **p. 660,** Ravell Call/Picture Group; **p. 663,** courtesy of Quaker State Corporation; **p. 667,** courtesy of General Signal Corporation; **p. 669,** photo by John F. Johnston; courtesy of Humana, Inc.; **p. 674,** © 1988 Metropolitan Life Insurance Co., NY, NY; Peanuts characters © 1952, 1958 United Feature Syndicate, Inc.; reprinted courtesy of Metropolitan Life Insurance Co., and United Feature Syndicate. *Chapter 21* **P. 688,** Sean Kernan/Stock Option; **p. 691,** courtesy of Marquette Electronics, Inc.; **p. 694,** © Michael L. Abramson/Woodfin Camp; **p. 695,** © 1986 Angel Franco/Woodfin Camp; **p. 701,** © Tom Hollyman/Hewlett Packard; **p. 704,** © Tom Hollyman/Hewlett Packard; **p. 705,** © Tom Hollyman/Hewlett Packard. *Chapter 22* **P. 718,** © Paul Conklin; **p. 723,** © 1983 Régis Bossu/Sygma; **p. 729,** courtesy of NCR Corporation; **p. 735,** © 1985 P. Vauthey/Sygma; **p. 737,** Paulo Fridman/Sygma; **p. 739,** © N. Noe/Gamma-Liaison; **p. 741,** © 1987 Cindy Charles; **p. 742,** Eric Meyer; **p. 743,** © Peter Charlesworth/JB Pictures. *Chapter 23* **P. 756,** © Owen Franken/Stock, Boston; **p. 762,** Theo Westenberger; **p. 766,** © Cindy Charles; **p. 773,** Mark Ferri.

The authors are grateful for permission to include:

"Rother Brothers Are Booked into a Growth Path" by Darla-Jean Weat Vol. 1, No. 6, September, 1987. Reprinted by permission of the author. "Chevrolet Faces Rough Ride in Bid to Regain Sales Lead from Ford" by Melinda Grenier Guiles from *The Wall Street Journal* October 6, 1987. Reprinted by permission of *The Wall Street Journal,* © Dow Jones & Company, Inc. 1987. All rights reserved. Adapted "Eight Attributes" from *In Search of Excellence* by Thomas J. Peters and Robert H. Waterman, Jr. Copyright © 1982 by Thomas J. Peters and Robert H. Waterman, Jr. Reprinted by permission of Harper & Row, Publishers, Inc. "Spokeswoman" by Paul B. Brown reprinted with permission, *Inc.* magazine, June, 1987. Copyright © 1987 by *Inc.* Publishing Company, 38 Commercial Wharf, Boston, MA 02110 "Mercury Business Services" by Jeffrey L. Seglin from *America's New Breed of Entrepreneurs,* Washington, D.C.: Acropolis Books, 1985. Reprinted by permission. "It's Mac Tonight for Phil Springer's Crews" by Darla-Jean Weatherford. *The Courier,* Vol. 1, No. 7, October, 1987. Reprinted by permission of the author. "Ballad of a Mad Cafe" by Jeffrey Trachtenberg. *Forbes,* November 19, 1984, pp. 288–294. Reprinted by permission. "Stop the Treadmill, I Want to Get Off," by Paul B. Brown reprinted with permission, *Inc.* magazine, May, 1987. Copyright © 1987 by *Inc.* Publishing Company, 38 Commercial Wharf, Boston, MA 02110. "Four-Star Management" by Jay Finegan reprinted with permission, *Inc.* magazine, January, 1987. Copyright © 1987 by *Inc.* Publishing Company, 38 Commercial Wharf, Boston, MA 02110. "The Turnaround" by Lucien Rhodes, with Patricia Amend reprinted with permission, *Inc.* Magazine, August, 1986. Copyright © 1986 by *Inc.* Publishing Company, 38 Commercial Wharf, Boston, MA 02110. "Rockefeller, Schwab & How to Run a Business" by Burt Folsom is reprinted with permission of Administrative Radiology Journal, a Glendale Publishing Corp. publication, Glendale, California. "May the Force Be With You" by Bruce G. Posner reprinted with permission, *Inc.* magazine, July, 1987. Copyright © 1987 by *Inc.* Publishing Company, 38 Com-